The Encyclopedia of Religion

The Encyclopedia of Religion

Mircea Eliade

EDITOR IN CHIEF

Volume 3

MACMILLAN PUBLISHING COMPANY
New York
Collier Macmillan Publishers
London

MACMILLAN PUBLISHING COMPANY
866 Third Avenue, New York, NY 10022

Collier Macmillan Canada, Inc.

Library of Congress Catalog Card Number: 86-5432

PRINTED IN THE UNITED STATES OF AMERICA

printing number
1 2 3 4 5 6 7 8 9 10

Library of Congress Cataloging-in-Publication Data

The Encyclopedia of religion.

Includes bibliographies and index.
1. Religion—Dictionaries. I. Eliade, Mircea, 1907–1986. II. Adams, Charles J.
BL31.#46 1986 200'.3'21 86-5432
ISBN 0-02-909480-1 (set)
ISBN 0-02-909720-7 (v. 3)

Acknowledgments of sources, copyrights, and permissions to use previously published materials are gratefully made in a special listing in volume 16.

Abbreviations and Symbols Used in This Work

abbr. abbreviated; abbreviation
abr. abridged; abridgment
AD *anno Domini,* in the year of the (our) Lord
Afrik. Afrikaans
AH *anno Hegirae,* in the year of the Hijrah
Akk. Akkadian
Ala. Alabama
Alb. Albanian
Am. *Amos*
AM *ante meridiem,* before noon
amend. amended; amendment
annot. annotated; annotation
Ap. *Apocalypse*
Apn. *Apocryphon*
app. appendix
Arab. Arabic
'Arakh. *'Arakhin*
Aram. Aramaic
Ariz. Arizona
Ark. Arkansas
Arm. Armenian
art. article (pl., arts.)
AS Anglo-Saxon
Asm. Mos. *Assumption of Moses*
Assyr. Assyrian
A.S.S.R. Autonomous Soviet Socialist Republic
Av. Avestan
'A.Z. *'Avodah zarah*
b. born
Bab. Babylonian
Ban. Bantu
1 Bar. *1 Baruch*
2 Bar. *2 Baruch*
3 Bar. *3 Baruch*
4 Bar. *4 Baruch*
B.B. *Bava' batra'*
BBC British Broadcasting Corporation
BC before Christ
BCE before the common era
B.D. Bachelor of Divinity
Beits. *Beitsah*
Bekh. *Bekhorot*
Beng. Bengali
Ber. *Berakhot*
Berb. Berber
Bik. *Bikkurim*
bk. book (pl., bks.)
B.M. *Bava' metsi'a'*
BP before the present
B.Q. *Bava' qamma'*
Brāh. *Brāhmaṇa*
Bret. Breton
B.T. Babylonian Talmud
Bulg. Bulgarian
Burm. Burmese
c. *circa,* about, approximately
Calif. California
Can. Canaanite
Catal. Catalan
CE of the common era
Celt. Celtic
cf. *confer,* compare
Chald. Chaldean
chap. chapter (pl., chaps.)
Chin. Chinese
C.H.M. Community of the Holy Myrrhbearers
1 Chr. *1 Chronicles*
2 Chr. *2 Chronicles*
Ch. Slav. Church Slavic
cm centimeters
col. column (pl., cols.)
Col. *Colossians*
Colo. Colorado
comp. compiler (pl., comps.)
Conn. Connecticut
cont. continued
Copt. Coptic
1 Cor. *1 Corinthians*
2 Cor. *2 Corinthians*
corr. corrected
C.S.P. Congregatio Sancti Pauli, Congregation of Saint Paul (Paulists)
d. died
D Deuteronomic (source of the Pentateuch)
Dan. Danish
D.B. Divinitatis Baccalaureus, Bachelor of Divinity
D.C. District of Columbia
D.D. Divinitatis Doctor, Doctor of Divinity
Del. Delaware
Dem. *Dema'i*
dim. diminutive
diss. dissertation
Dn. *Daniel*
D.Phil. Doctor of Philosophy
Dt. *Deuteronomy*
Du. Dutch
E Elohist (source of the Pentateuch)
Eccl. *Ecclesiastes*
ed. editor (pl., eds.); edition; edited by
'Eduy. *'Eduyyot*
e.g. *exempli gratia,* for example
Egyp. Egyptian
1 En. *1 Enoch*
2 En. *2 Enoch*
3 En. *3 Enoch*
Eng. English
enl. enlarged
Eph. *Ephesians*
'Eruv. *'Eruvin*
1 Esd. *1 Esdras*
2 Esd. *2 Esdras*
3 Esd. *3 Esdras*
4 Esd. *4 Esdras*
esp. especially
Est. Estonian
Est. *Esther*
et al. *et alii,* and others
etc. *et cetera,* and so forth
Eth. Ethiopic
EV English version
Ex. *Exodus*
exp. expanded
Ez. *Ezekiel*
Ezr. *Ezra*
2 Ezr. *2 Ezra*
4 Ezr. *4 Ezra*
f. feminine; and following (pl., ff.)
fasc. fascicle (pl., fascs.)
fig. figure (pl., figs.)
Finn. Finnish
fl. *floruit,* flourished
Fla. Florida
Fr. French
frag. fragment
ft. feet
Ga. Georgia
Gal. *Galatians*
Gaul. Gaulish
Ger. German
Giṭ. *Giṭṭin*
Gn. *Genesis*
Gr. Greek
Ḥag. *Ḥagigah*
Ḥal. *Ḥallah*
Hau. Hausa
Hb. *Habakkuk*
Heb. Hebrew
Heb. *Hebrews*
Hg. *Haggai*
Hitt. Hittite
Hor. *Horayot*
Hos. *Hosea*
Ḥul. *Ḥullin*
Hung. Hungarian
ibid. *ibidem,* in the same place (as the one immediately preceding)
Icel. Icelandic
i.e. *id est,* that is
IE Indo-European
Ill. Illinois
Ind. Indiana
intro. introduction
Ir. Gael. Irish Gaelic
Iran. Iranian
Is. *Isaiah*
Ital. Italian
J Yahvist (source of the Pentateuch)
Jas. *James*
Jav. Javanese
Jb. *Job*
Jdt. *Judith*
Jer. *Jeremiah*
Jgs. *Judges*
Jl. *Joel*
Jn. *John*
1 Jn. *1 John*
2 Jn. *2 John*
3 Jn. *3 John*
Jon. *Jonah*
Jos. *Joshua*
Jpn. Japanese
JPS Jewish Publication Society translation (1985) of the Hebrew Bible
J.T. Jerusalem Talmud
Jub. *Jubilees*
Kans. Kansas
Kel. *Kelim*

Ker. *Keritot*
Ket. *Ketubbot*
1 Kgs. *1 Kings*
2 Kgs. *2 Kings*
Khois. Khoisan
Kil. *Kil'ayim*
km kilometers
Kor. Korean
Ky. Kentucky
l. line (pl., ll.)
La. Louisiana
Lam. *Lamentations*
Lat. Latin
Latv. Latvian
L. en Th. Licencié en Théologie, Licentiate in Theology
L. ès L. Licencié ès Lettres, Licentiate in Literature
Let. Jer. *Letter of Jeremiah*
lit. literally
Lith. Lithuanian
Lk. *Luke*
LL Late Latin
LL.D. Legum Doctor, Doctor of Laws
Lv. *Leviticus*
m meters
m. masculine
M.A. Master of Arts
Ma'as. *Ma'aserot*
Ma'as. Sh. *Ma'aser sheni*
Mak. *Makkot*
Makh. *Makhshirin*
Mal. *Malachi*
Mar. Marathi
Mass. Massachusetts
1 Mc. *1 Maccabees*
2 Mc. *2 Maccabees*
3 Mc. *3 Maccabees*
4 Mc. *4 Maccabees*
Md. Maryland
M.D. Medicinae Doctor, Doctor of Medicine
ME Middle English
Meg. *Megillah*
Me'il. *Me'ilah*
Men. *Menaḥot*
MHG Middle High German
mi. miles
Mi. *Micah*
Mich. Michigan
Mid. *Middot*
Minn. Minnesota
Miq. *Miqva'ot*
MIran. Middle Iranian
Miss. Mississippi
Mk. *Mark*
Mo. Missouri
Mo'ed Q. *Mo'ed qaṭan*
Mont. Montana
MPers. Middle Persian
MS. *manuscriptum*, manuscript (pl., MSS)
Mt. *Matthew*
MT Masoretic text
n. note
Na. *Nahum*
Nah. Nahuatl
Naz. *Nazir*
N.B. *nota bene*, take careful note
N.C. North Carolina
n.d. no date
N.Dak. North Dakota
NEB New English Bible
Nebr. Nebraska
Ned. *Nedarim*
Neg. *Nega'im*
Neh. *Nehemiah*
Nev. Nevada
N.H. New Hampshire
Nid. *Niddah*
N.J. New Jersey
Nm. *Numbers*
N.Mex. New Mexico
no. number (pl., nos.)
Nor. Norwegian
n.p. no place
n.s. new series
N.Y. New York
Ob. *Obadiah*
O.Cist. Ordo Cisterciencium, Order of Cîteaux (Cistercians)
OCS Old Church Slavonic
OE Old English
O.F.M. Ordo Fratrum Minorum, Order of Friars Minor (Franciscans)
OFr. Old French
Ohal. *Ohalot*
OHG Old High German
OIr. Old Irish
OIran. Old Iranian
Okla. Oklahoma
ON Old Norse
O.P. Ordo Praedicatorum, Order of Preachers (Dominicans)
OPers. Old Persian
op. cit. *opere citato*, in the work cited
OPrus. Old Prussian
Oreg. Oregon
'Orl. *'Orlah*
O.S.B. Ordo Sancti Benedicti, Order of Saint Benedict (Benedictines)
p. page (pl., pp.)
P Priestly (source of the Pentateuch)
Pa. Pennsylvania
Pahl. Pahlavi
Par. *Parah*
para. paragraph (pl., paras.)
Pers. Persian
Pes. *Pesaḥim*
Ph.D. Philosophiae Doctor, Doctor of Philosophy
Phil. *Philippians*
Phlm. *Philemon*
Phoen. Phoenician
pl. plural; plate (pl., pls.)
PM *post meridiem*, after noon
Pol. Polish
pop. population
Port. Portuguese
Prv. *Proverbs*
Ps. *Psalms*
Ps. 151 *Psalm 151*
Ps. Sol. *Psalms of Solomon*
pt. part (pl., pts.)
1 Pt. *1 Peter*
2 Pt. *2 Peter*
Pth. Parthian
Q hypothetical source of the synoptic Gospels
Qid. *Qiddushin*
Qin. *Qinnim*
r. reigned; ruled
Rab. *Rabbah*
rev. revised
R. ha-Sh. *Ro'sh ha-shanah*
R.I. Rhode Island
Rom. Romanian
Rom. *Romans*
R.S.C.J. Societas Sacratissimi Cordis Jesu, Religious of the Sacred Heart
RSV Revised Standard Version of the Bible
Ru. *Ruth*
Rus. Russian
Rv. *Revelation*
Rv. Ezr. *Revelation of Ezra*
San. *Sanhedrin*
S.C. South Carolina
Scot. Gael. Scottish Gaelic
S.Dak. South Dakota
sec. section (pl., secs.)
Sem. Semitic
ser. series
sg. singular
Sg. *Song of Songs*
Sg. of 3 *Prayer of Azariah and the Song of the Three Young Men*
Shab. *Shabbat*
Shav. *Shavu'ot*
Sheq. *Sheqalim*
Sib. Or. *Sibylline Oracles*
Sind. Sindhi
Sinh. Sinhala
Sir. *Ben Sira*
S.J. Societas Jesu, Society of Jesus (Jesuits)
Skt. Sanskrit
1 Sm. *1 Samuel*
2 Sm. *2 Samuel*
Sogd. Sogdian
Soṭ *Soṭah*
sp. species (pl., spp.)
Span. Spanish
sq. square
S.S.R. Soviet Socialist Republic
st. stanza (pl., ss.)
S.T.M. Sacrae Theologiae Magister, Master of Sacred Theology
Suk. *Sukkah*
Sum. Sumerian
supp. supplement; supplementary
Sus. *Susanna*
s.v. *sub verbo*, under the word (pl., s.v.v.)
Swed. Swedish
Syr. Syriac
Syr. Men. *Syriac Menander*
Ta'an. *Ta'anit*
Tam. Tamil
Tam. *Tamid*
Tb. *Tobit*
T.D. *Taishō shinshū daizōkyō*, edited by Takakusu Junjirō et al. (Tokyo, 1922–1934)
Tem. *Temurah*
Tenn. Tennessee
Ter. *Terumot*
Ṭev. Y. *Ṭevul yom*
Tex. Texas
Th.D. Theologicae Doctor, Doctor of Theology
1 Thes. *1 Thessalonians*
2 Thes. *2 Thessalonians*
Thrac. Thracian
Ti. *Titus*
Tib. Tibetan
1 Tm. *1 Timothy*
2 Tm. *2 Timothy*
T. of 12 *Testaments of the Twelve Patriarchs*
Ṭoh. *Ṭohorot*
Tong. Tongan
trans. translator, translators; translated by; translation
Turk. Turkish
Ukr. Ukrainian
Upan. *Upaniṣad*
U.S. United States
U.S.S.R. Union of Soviet Socialist Republics
Uqts. *Uqtsin*
v. verse (pl., vv.)
Va. Virginia
var. variant; variation
Viet. Vietnamese
viz. *videlicet*, namely
vol. volume (pl., vols.)
Vt. Vermont
Wash. Washington
Wel. Welsh
Wis. Wisconsin
Wis. *Wisdom of Solomon*
W.Va. West Virginia
Wyo. Wyoming
Yad. *Yadayim*
Yev. *Yevamot*
Yi. Yiddish
Yor. Yoruba
Zav. *Zavim*
Zec. *Zechariah*
Zep. *Zephaniah*
Zev. *Zevaḥim*

* hypothetical
? uncertain; possibly; perhaps
° degrees
\+ plus
− minus
= equals; is equivalent to
× by; multiplied by
→ yields

C

CABALA. *See* Qabbalah.

CABASILAS, NICHOLAS (c. 1322–1395), born Nicolaos Chamaetos Cabasilas; Greek Orthodox theologian and saint. A native of Thessalonica, Cabasilas studied there and in Constantinople. One of his teachers was his uncle Nilos Cabasilas, an adherent and successor of Gregory Palamas in the see of Thessalonica. Cabasilas served for ten years as counselor to the emperor John VI Cantacuzenos (1341–1354). In 1353 his name was put forward as a candidate for the patriarchal chair, although he was a layman. During the second half of his life, he resided in Constantinople, mostly in the monastery of Mangana, as a layman or as a monk, devoting himself to theological studies.

Gennadios Scholarios, the first patriarch after the fall of Constantinople, characterized Cabasilas's writings as "an ornament to the church of Christ." With an imposing style, apophthegmatic, prophetic, and poetical, he expresses genuine religious feeling and deep faith.

One of Cabasilas's most important works is *Interpretation of the Holy Liturgy,* a spiritual explanation of what is said and done during the Divine Liturgy, which he considers a real image of divine worship in heaven as well as of the earthly life of the incarnated God. In his thought the participation of the church in the sacraments *(mustēria)* is not symbolic, but real, as is the participation of the members of the body in the heart. By participating in the mysteries (i.e., the Body and Blood of Christ), the faithful do not incorporate these elements into the human body as they do other food; rather, the faithful themselves are incorporated into these elements. Man's union with Christ, soul with soul and body with body, brings complete peace, which makes the many one; disturbance makes the one many.

Cabasilas's second great work, *On the Life in Christ,* presents an anatomy of the spiritual life in the framework of the incarnation, repeated and continued in the sacraments of the church. Cabasilas's thought revolves around the fact of salvation through union with God. The destination of humankind from the moment of its creation to the end of its history is this: union with God.

For Cabasilas, the distinguishing property of God is goodness. God is good in an excelling way, and the nature of good is to pour itself out and be distributed. Thus humankind is created good from the beginning, both God-like and Christ-like, with the purpose of being united with God in the future. The incarnate Word of God encounters a God-like kernel in each human being and from this encounter a new life springs, which leads to perfection in life in Christ. Perfection is the supreme and complete gift of God. All things have been made for perfection.

The present world is in the process of giving birth to the inner person, who is molded and formed in the present life, but who is born only in the future world. The moment of transition is the most delightful of visions. "Christ descends from heaven to earth brilliantly, the earth raises up other suns toward the sun of justice. All is full of light" (*Life in Christ* 6.16).

In 1983 Cabasilas was canonized a saint of the Greek Orthodox church and his feast fixed on 20 June. His writings are widely read in many languages.

BIBLIOGRAPHY

Works by Cabasilas. An unsatisfactory edition of the main texts, by Fronto Ducaeus, is reprinted in *Patrologia Graeca,* edited by J.-P. Migne, vol. 150 (Paris, 1865). All modern translations of Cabasilas's two great treatises, based on this text, are necessarily unsatisfactory too. *Explication de la divine liturgie,* edited and translated by Sévérien Salaville, in *Sources Chrétiennes,* vol. 4 (Paris, 1967), follows the same text collated with one Parisian manuscript. An English translation by Joan M. Hussey and P. A. McNulty is also available as *Interpretation of the Divine Liturgy* (London, 1960). While working on my own translation into modern Greek, I prepared another, more correct original text, based on four manuscripts; see *Nikolaos Cabasilas,* no. 22 in the series "Philokalia" (Thessaloniki, 1979–).

Works about Cabasilas. *Die Mystik des Nikolaus Cabasilas vom Leben in Christo,* edited by Wilhelm Gass (1849; 2d ed., Leiden, 1899), was excellent in its time. The work of Myrna Lot-Borodine, *Un maître de la spiritualité byzantine au quatorzième siècle, Nicolas Cabasilas* (Paris, 1958), in spite of its oratorical style, is very interesting. Special aspects of Cabasilas's thought are treated in Ermanno M. Toniolo's *La mariologia di Nicola Cabasila* (Vicenze, 1955); Ihor Ševčenko's "Nicolas Cabasilas' 'Anti-zealot' Discourse: A Reinterpretation," *Dumbarton Oaks Papers* 11 (1957): 79–171; and Jean Vafiadis's *L'humanisme chrétien de Nicolas Cabasilas: L'épanouissement de la personne humaine dans le Christ* (Strasbourg, 1963). For readers of modern Greek, two important works are Athanasios Angelopoulos's *Nikolaos Kabasilas Chamaetos, Hē zōe kai to ergon autou* (Thessaloniki, 1970) and Panagiotes Nellas's *Hē peri dikaiōseōs didaskalia Nikolaou tou Kabasila* (Piraeus, 1975).

PANAGIOTIS C. CHRISTOU
Translated from Greek by Philip M. McGhee

CAIN AND ABEL, the first two sons of Adam and Eve, the progenitors of the race according to the Bible, after their banishment from the garden of Eden (*Gn.* 4). Cain (Heb., Qayin), the elder, was a farmer; Abel (Heb., Hevel) was a shepherd. The biblical text jumps from their birth to a later episode when both made (apparently votary) offerings to the Lord: Cain presented a meal offering of his fruits and grains, while Abel offered up the firstlings of his sheep. The offering of Cain was rejected by the Lord, and that of Abel was accepted. No reason for this is given, and generations of pious attempts to justify this event have been made by contrasting the intentions of the donors and the nature and quality of their donations. Cain's despondency led to a divine caution to resist the temptation to sin (*Gn.* 4:6–7); presumably this refers to the jealous urges and hostile resentments Cain felt. But the elder brother was overwrought and killed his brother in the field. This led to the punishment of Cain: like his father, he would not farm a fertile earth; and, like him, he would be banished "eastward of Eden." Fearing further retribution, Cain was given a protective "sign," whose aspect delighted the fancy in later legends and art. There is a deliberate reuse of the language of the temptation and punishment of Adam and Eve (*Gn.* 3) in the ensuing account of the temptation and punishment of Cain (*Gn.* 4:1–17).

The murder of Abel by Cain in *Genesis* 4:1–17 is the first social crime recorded in the Bible, and it complements on the external level the inner temptation and misuse of will depicted in similar language in *Genesis* 3. The tradition of Cain's act of murder and his subsequent punishment is followed by a genealogical list that presents him as the progenitor of several culture heroes. His son, Enoch, founded the first city (*Gn.* 4:18); and two other descendants, Jubal and Tubal-cain, were respectively named the cultural ancestors of "all who play the lyre and the pipe" (*Gn.* 4:21) and those "who forged all implements of copper and iron" (*Gn.* 4:22). There is thus an anachronistic blending of Cain, whose name means "smith," with an ancient agricultural forebear. In so presenting Cain as the ancestor of technology and culture, the tradition displays a pessimistic attitude toward such achievements (complementing the attitude taken in the tower of Babel episode, in *Genesis* 10:1–9) and shows a profound psychological insight into the energies and drives that underlie civilization. The episode of *Genesis* 4:1–17 may reflect an old literary motif of debates between farmers and herdsmen as well as the fairly universal theme of fraternal pairs who represent contrasting psychological and cultural types.

Early rabbinic interpretation drew forth various elements of the story for moral and theological emphasis. The Midrash elaborates the psychology of fraternal strife (*Genesis Rabbah* 22.7), depicts Cain's impious rejection of divine justice when his offering is rejected but also notes his act of repentance in the end (*Gn. Rab.* 11.13), and shows the cycle of violence that was unleashed by Cain's act, since this deed led to his accidental death at the hands of his descendant Lamech who, in grief, accidentally killed his own son as well (*Gn.* 4:23–24). Early Christian tradition focused on Abel as the head of a line of prophets who were killed (*Mt.* 23:25) and emphasized his innocent blood (cf. *Heb.* 12:24); thus they set the framework for the typology that related Abel's innocent death to that of Jesus and saw Cain as representing the children of the devil (*1 Jn.* 3:12). For Augustine, Cain was furthermore identified with the Jews. The topos of Cain and Abel recurs in the medieval mystery plays, and the murder of Abel was a common iconographic motif in Christian and Jewish art.

BIBLIOGRAPHY

Aptowitzer, Vigdor. *Kain und Abel in der Agada den Apokryphen, der hellenistischen, christlichen und muhammedanischen Literatur*. Vienna, 1922.

Fishbane, Michael. *Text and Texture*. New York, 1979. See pages 23–27.

Ginzberg, Louis. *The Legends of the Jews* (1909–1938). 7 vols. Translated by Henrietta Szold et al. Reprint, Philadelphia, 1937–1966. See volume 1, pages 55–59.

Réau, Louis. *Iconographie de l'art chrétien*, vol. 2. Paris, 1956. See pages 93–100.

Speiser, E. A. *Genesis*. Anchor Bible, vol. 1. Garden City, N.Y., 1964. See pages 29–38.

MICHAEL FISHBANE

CAITANYA, religious name of Viśvambhara Miśra (1486–1533), Indian Vaiṣṇava revivalist and mystic, revered by many Hindus as an embodiment of the divine Kṛṣṇa and Rādhā. Born at the onset of a lunar eclipse (27 February 1486) at Nadia (Nabadwip), center of Sanskrit learning in Muslim-ruled Bengal, Viśvambhara ("world sustainer," i.e., Viṣṇu) was the second son of a Vaiṣṇava brahman family. He became a teacher of Sanskrit and married Lakṣmīpriyā and, at her death, Viṣṇupriyā. At the age of twenty-two he journeyed to Gaya to perform Śrāddha (observances for the dead) for his late father and his first wife, but was suddenly overwhelmed by devotion *(bhakti)* to Kṛṣṇa. He subsequently took Vaiṣṇava initiation from Īśvara Purī and was soon hailed by the Vaiṣṇavas of Nadia as their charismatic leader. For over a year Viśvambhara manifested aspects of divine *avatāras,* proclaimed the praises of Lord Kṛṣṇa, and challenged the Muslim authorities by leading *kīrtana* (religious chanting) parties throughout Nadia. These activities culminated in Viśvambhara's renunciation of worldly ties and the change of his name to Kṛṣṇa-Caitanya ("he whose consciousness is Kṛṣṇa"), at the feet of the ascetic Keśava Bhāratī (February 1510).

For several years Caitanya traveled throughout India calling for devotion to Kṛṣṇa and chanting Kṛṣṇa's names. In 1516 he settled permanently at Puri, Orissa. There he worshiped the temple deity, Jagannātha (i.e., Kṛṣṇa), counseled disciples, and experienced turbulent ecstasies of devotion, often tormented by the sense of separation *(viraha)* from Kṛṣṇa. There is no confirmed report of the circumstances of his death at Puri in the month of Āṣāṛh (possibly 9 July), 1533. The most reliable and informative of several traditional accounts of Caitanya's life are Vṛndāvanadāsa's *Caitanya-bhāgavata* (c. 1545; in Bengali) and Kṛṣṇadāsa Kavirāja's *Caitanya-caritāmṛta* (probably 1612, but arguably a few decades earlier; in Bengali).

Caitanya's teachings are grounded in the *Śrīmad bhāgavatam.* Transcendent reality *(brahman)* is understood to be fully personal *(bhagavān),* and Kṛṣṇa is seen as the quintessence of divine personhood. Human beings are minute emanations, paradoxically different and yet not different *(acintya-bhedābheda)* from their divine source. A soul undergoes rebirth until by divine mercy *(kṛpā)* it realizes its true nature as the devoted servant of Kṛṣṇa. In the present, degenerate age *(kaliyuga),* people cannot fulfill all religious duties, but Kṛṣṇa, in the merciful guise of Caitanya, promulgates a simple, universally accessible religious norm *(yugadharma)* to deliver souls from bondage to spiritual ignorance *(avidyā)* and other ills. Devout souls may imitate the roles and sentiments displayed by Kṛṣṇa's eternal companions: servants, parents, friends, or lovers. Caitanya himself was so immersed in the passionate love for Kṛṣṇa epitomized by Kṛṣṇa's divine mistress Rādhā that his companions at Puri, and eventually most Gauḍīya (Bengali) Vaiṣṇavas, came to discern in him the dual presence of Kṛṣṇa and Rādhā.

Caitanya himself left at most eight Sanskrit stanzas, but he inspired and guided men of great learning and ability, notably the Gosvāmins ("pastors") of Vṛndāvana. [*See* Vṛndāvana.] Their theological works in Sanskrit include commentaries by Sanātana (on the tenth canto only) and Jīva on the *Śrīmad bhāgavatam;* an aesthetic theology of *bhakti* in two works by Rūpa, *Bhaktirasāmṛtasindhu* and *Ujjvalanīlamaṇi;* inspirational plays and poems by Rūpa, Raghunāthadasa, and others; *Haribhaktivilāsa,* a liturgical and disciplinary compendium by Gopāla Bhaṭṭa and Sanātana; *Bṛhadbhāgavatāmṛtam,* an allegory by Sanātana of the soul's pilgrimage; and *Ṣaṭsandarbha,* a summary of Vaiṣṇava theology by Gopāla Bhaṭṭa and Jīva.

Caitanya and the movement he inspired enthusiastically propagated devotion toward Kṛṣṇa in Bengal, Orissa, and, to a lesser extent (through the Dāmodariyā sect), Assam. Restoration of sites sacred to Kṛṣṇa in the Mathurā-Vṛndāvana (Brindavan) region owed much to the zeal of Caitanya. Vernaculars of eastern India, especially the Bengali, are much the richer for a host of original biographies, songs, and poems, and for varied translations and adaptations from Sanskrit works on Kṛṣṇa and Caitanya. Bengali culture as a whole, even in its Muslim and non-Vaiṣṇava Hindu sectors and as refracted through modern exponents such as Rabindranath Tagore, has been influenced profoundly by the symbolism and values of Caitanya's humane and sensitive devotion to God as Kṛṣṇa.

Through the ministries of certain of Caitanya's married associates (e.g., Advaita Ācārya and Nityānanda) and their descendants (also called Gosvāmins), and Vaiṣṇava mendicants (Bairāgis), the majority of Bengali Hindus in the middle castes and considerable minorities in the upper and lower castes came to profess faith in Kṛṣṇa-Caitanya. Yet Caitanya Vaiṣṇava prestige was on the wane in British-influenced Bengal of the late nineteenth century when Kedarnath Datta (Bhaktivinode Thakur, 1838–1914), a government official of *kāyastha* caste, launched a vigorous revitalization movement. His son, Bimalprasad Datta (Bhaktisiddhanta Sarasvati, 1874–1937), organized the Gauḍīya Maṭh, a network of monastic houses and temples centered in Calcutta and Mayapur (Nadia) and dedicated to preaching and publishing. One of Bhaktisiddhanta's disciples, Abhaycaran De (A. C. Bhaktivedanta, 1896–1977), inaugurated the International Society for Krishna Consciousness in New York in 1966. Its several thousand devotees, mostly non-Indian, currently propagate faith in Kṛṣṇa-Caitanya worldwide.

[*For further discussion of theistic systems centering on Kṛṣṇa, see* Kṛṣṇaism. *See also* Rādhā; Kṛṣṇa; *and* Bengali Religions.]

BIBLIOGRAPHY

An invaluable guide both to biographies of Caitanya and to theological works by the Gosvāmins of Vṛndāvana is Sushil Kumar De's *Early History of the Vaiṣṇava Faith and Movement in Bengal*, 2d ed. (Calcutta, 1961). The foremost critical assessment of materials for the life of Caitanya is in Bengali, Bimanbehari Majumdar's *Śrī Caitanya cariter upādān*, 2d ed. (Calcutta, 1959). Kṛṣṇadāsa Kavirāja's traditional account of Caitanya's life is available in English translation by A. C. Bhaktivedanta, with Bengali text and didactic commentary, *Śrī Caitanya-caritāmṛta*, 17 vols. (Los Angeles, 1974–1975). A more scholarly translation by Edward C. Dimock, Jr. will be forthcoming from Harvard University Press. For modern biographies drawing upon traditional sources see Walter Eidlitz's *Kṛṣṇa-Caitanya: Sein Leben und seine Lehre* (Stockholm, 1968) and A. K. Majumdar's *Caitanya: His Life and Doctrine* (Bombay, 1969). Edward C. Dimock, Jr.'s *The Place of the Hidden Moon: Erotic Mysticism in the Cult of the Vaiṣṇava-Sahajiyā Cult of Bengali* (Chicago, 1966) finely distinguishes orthodox (theistic) from *sahajiyā* (Tantric) piety, but may err in identifying certain of Caitanya's associates as *sahajiyā*.

JOSEPH T. O'CONNELL

CAKRAS. The Sanskrit term *cakra* ("wheel, discus, circle") is sometimes used as a name for ritual diagrams employed in Hindu religious practice (*pūjā*) or in meditation, as symbols of the deity, and sometimes as a name for sacred enclosures where rites are performed. A well-known instance of the former usage is the Śrīcakra of the goddess Tripurasundarī. In such cases, *cakra* may be taken to be synonymous with *maṇḍala* or *yantra*.

Cakra is also a name for the "centers"—also called "lotuses" (*padma* or *kamala*)—of the subtle body of the Hindu and Buddhist traditions. Simply stated, for the Hindu tradition a living being is made up of three elements: the gross or physical body, the subtle body, and the self, or spirit. This spirit is a fragment or an aspect of the godhead, supreme consciousness. It is deemed to be enclosed within the two other elements, which form around it several "sheaths" (*kośa*s) of diminishing subtlety. In this Hindu conception, the subtle body is an essential part of human individuality. It is considered to be made up of a varying number of factors, from eight to thirty-one, which, however, always include *manas* (mind organ), *buddhi* (intellect), and *ahaṃkāra* (individuating factor). These psychic components of the individual are the part of the subtle body that perceives, thinks, and decides, whereas the self is the "inner witness" *(sākṣin)*, the pure awareness that transcends all psychological states.

The notion of the subtle body goes back to the ancient doctrine presented by the Sāṃkhya philosophies. [*See* Sāṃkhya.] It was further elaborated in Puranic and still more in Tantric Hinduism, where it plays a very important role, especially in Yoga. There, the subtle body appears as an imaginative construct superimposed on (although not limited to) the physical body. It is neither purely psychic nor purely somatic but partakes of both aspects. It both lies at the root of and links together physiological and psychological processes. It is believed to be made up of a web of seventy-two thousand arteries or channels (*nāḍī*s) through which the cosmic and vital energy *(prāṇa)* circulates, and of a few centers, usually called wheels (*cakra*s), receptacles (*ādhāra*s), or knots (*granthi*s), where these arteries converge and supposedly meet the nerves of the physical body.

Three of the *nāḍī*s, called by the Hindus *iḍā*, *piṅgalā*, and *suṣumnā*, are the principal ones. They extend along the spinal column from a spot between the genital organs and the anus, the *mūlādhāra*, the lowest *cakra*, to another spot on the top of the skull, called *brahmarandhra* ("the opening of Brahmā"), where there is said to be a thousand-petaled white lotus *(sahasrārapadma)*, often considered the highest *cakra*. The main aim of Tantric yogic practices is to cause the cosmic energy in man *(kuṇḍalinī)* to flow upward in the central channel, *suṣumnā*, from the *mūlādhāra*, through the *cakra*s that are tiered along that channel, to the uppermost center. [*See* Kuṇḍalinī.]

Although some of the *cakra*s coincide with neural

plexuses, they have no physical existence. They may correspond however to psychosomatic sites experienced during yoga. During the practice of yoga, they are to be visualized in the minutest detail: shape, number of spokes or petals (they are likened to lotuses), colors, diagrams, various symbols and Sanskrit letters or *mantras*, and also deities, which are supposed to reside in each of them as in a *maṇḍala*. These mental images are vividly conjured up in meditation, each in its proper place in the body or outside it. Since each *cakra* corresponds to a particular level of cosmic energy and is supposedly related to certain cosmic phenomena or divisions, and to specific mental and physiological functions or processes, each, when "awakened," produces in the adept particular physical or spiritual effects, all of which result from the creative power of the intense meditation *(bhāvanā)* that conjures them up. The *cakras* are thus both symbols and stages of an inner experience that is at the same time corporeal, mental, spiritual or religious, and cosmic.

The usual listing of the *cakras* is that of the so-called *ṣaṭcakra* ("six-*cakra*") system. It begins with the *mūlādhāra*, in the sacrococcygeal plexus, with four petals. Slightly above is the *svādhisthāna*, usually visualized as just above the root of the penis, with six petals. Then the *maṇipūra*, with ten petals, near the solar plexus; the *anāhata*, near the heart, with twelve petals; the *viśuddha*, in the region of the throat, with sixteen petals, and the *ājñā*, between or just above the eyebrows, with two petals. Above these six, at the crown of the head, is the *sahasrāra*, the inverted white lotus with a thousand petals. In Buddhist Tantric yoga, there are usually only four *cakras*, situated in the regions of the navel, heart, throat, and head; associated with gods, elements, and so forth, they thus are parts of a micro- and macrocosmic symbolic pattern.

The number of *cakras* varies. Two or three are sometimes added in between the usual six (or seven). Some Tantric traditions add another one, situated twelve fingersbreadths above the head, the *dvādaśānta* (there are sometimes two *dvādaśānta*, "inner" and "outer"). A thousand-petaled lotus may also be added near the *mūlādhāra*, whereas the "bulb" *(kanda)*, egg-shaped, just above the genitals, where many *nāḍīs* meet, is also sometimes counted as a *cakra*.

Cakras may be added to or subtracted from the usual list whenever needed. Some traditions add intermediate centers between the *cakras*, usually called *granthis*, numbering five or more. The Kula tradition has a fourfold pattern of *cakras*: *piṇḍa*, *pada*, *rūpa*, and *rūpātīta* or *granthi*. The Nāthas and several other Śaiva groups have a ninefold system to which they add other centers. The *Netra Tantra* (chap. 7), for instance, describes two types of yogic practices: one type has six *cakras*, supplemented with twelve *granthis*, sixteen *ādhāras*, five "voids" (*śūnyas*), three "objects" (*lakṣyas*), and so forth; the other type adds only seven "places" (*sthānas*), twelve *granthis*, and five *śūnyas* to the usual six *cakras*.

Thus, there is not one *cakra* pattern only, but several, answering the needs of different ritual yogic practices, which themselves reflect different cosmological, theological, or liturgical systems. Since there are various cults and practices within the same tradition, the same text (e.g., the *Netra Tantra* cited above) may describe different systems. There seems to be no systematized *ṣaṭcakra* pattern in the older Tantras; it was probably not fixed until later, when it was to become the most common of all the patterns.

[*See also* Tantrism; Yantra; *and* Maṇḍalas, *article on* Hindu Maṇḍalas.]

BIBLIOGRAPHY

Avalon, Arthur (John Woodroffe), trans. and ed. *Kāmakalāvilāsa by Puṇyānandanātha*. 2d rev. ed. Madras, 1953.

Avalon, Arthur, trans. and comp. *The Serpent Power, Being the Shat-Chakra-Nirūpaṇa and Pādukā-Pañchakā, Two Works on Laya Yoga*. 7th ed. Madras, 1964. Still the basic work on *cakra* and *kuṇḍalini*.

Dasgupta, Shashibusan. *An Introduction to Tantric Buddhism*. Calcutta, 1950.

Eliade, Mircea. *Yoga: Immortality and Freedom*. 2d ed. Princeton, 1969.

André Padoux

CAKRAVARTIN is a Sanskrit noun referring to an ideal universal king who rules ethically and benevolently over the entire world. Derived from the Sanskrit *cakra*, "wheel," and *vartin*, "one who turns," the term *cakravartin* (Pali, *cakkavatti*) in classical Hindu texts signifies that all-powerful monarch "whose chariot wheels turn freely" or "whose travels are unobstructed." Such a ruler's unsurpassed and virtuous rule is described as *sarvabhauma;* it pertains to all creatures everywhere. Buddhist and Jain literatures describe their enlightened founders (the Buddha or Buddhas and the *tīrthaṅkaras*, respectively) in similar terms, the notion being that religious truth transcends local or national limitations and applies to all people everywhere. This idea is particularly evident in Buddhist oral and scriptural traditions, which frequently refer to Gautama as a *cakravāla cakravartin*, an illuminator of *dharma* (life in adherence to compassionate truth) in all regions of the world. From the symbol of the turning wheel, a sign of universal sovereignty, comes the description of the Buddha as *dharmacakrapravartayati*, "he who sets the wheel of law in motion," and thus the name of his first sermon, *Dharmacakrapravartana Sūtra* (Pali, *Dhammacakkappavattana Sutta;* the Sūtra on the Turning Forth of the Wheel of Dharma), in which the Buddha presents his insights into the Four Noble Truths. After his death in 480 BCE, Gautama's followers cremated his body and enshrined his relics in a stupa, just as they would have done with a universal monarch.

History of the Cakravartin as an Imperial Ideal. The general South Asian notion that the king was to have extensive rule dates at least as far back as the high Vedic era (1200–800 BCE) and possibly to the centuries preceding. The Vedic ritual coronation of the king (Rājasūya), for example, was preceded by a ceremony in which a wild stallion was left to wander at will throughout the land for an entire year, at which time it was sacrificed in the important rite known as the Aśvamedha, and all of the territory it had covered in that year was held to be the king's domain. The actual term *cakravartin* was known in the late fifth and early fourth centuries BCE by the compilers of the *Maitri Upaniṣad,* who used the noun when listing the names of several kings who had renounced their royal prerogatives in favor of the life of ascetic contemplation (*Maitri Upaniṣad* 1.4).

Direct discussions of the *cakravartin* as an imperial ideal appear as early as Kauṭilya's *Artha Śāstra* (c. 300 BCE), a court manual of polity, diplomacy, economy, and social behavior. In his descriptions of the range of an emperor's influence *(cakravarti-kṣetra),* Kauṭilya notes that the king should undertake any task he feels will bring him and his people prosperity and that he should have power "from the Himalayas to the ocean." Kauṭilya may have had in mind the prestige and hopes of the first Mauryan king, Candragupta, who reigned from about 321 to 297 and whom Kauṭilya reportedly served as chief minister. Candragupta was perhaps the first ruler to unify all of the lands from the shores of the southern tip of India to the Himalayas in the north and the Kabul Valley in the northwest. Edicts and other lessons inscribed on pillars and cliffs describe the last Mauryan king, Aśoka (d. 238 BCE?) as a *cakravartin* under whose patronage the Buddhist Dharma spread throughout South and Southeast Asia. Chroniclers in the courts of the Śātavāhana emperors (first to second centuries CE) similarly defined their kingdoms as that world extending from the eastern, southern, and western oceans to the mountains. The Guptas, too, viewed themselves as the rulers of empires. Skandha Gupta I, who reigned from 455 to 467 CE, for example, is depicted in the Janagadh inscriptions (dated mid-fifth century CE) as a leader whose rule was the entire earth bounded by the four oceans and within which thrive several smaller countries. The Western Cāḷukyas (sixth to eighth and tenth to twelfth centuries) described themselves as the emperors of the lands between the three seas, while the Vijayanagara rulers (fourteenth to seventeenth centuries) labeled themselves the masters of the eastern, western, southern, and northern seas.

Thus the South Asian political imagination up to the seventeenth century generally included the ideal of a unified rule, and various kings have identified themselves as universal monarchs: hence the common royal titles *samrāj* ("supreme monarch," i.e., the one who rules over all princes and principalities), *rājādhirāja* ("king above kings"), *ekarāja* ("the only king"), *paramabhaṭṭārka* ("most venerable lord"), *diśampati* ("lord of the lands"), and *digvijayin* ("conqueror of the regions").

Buddhist and Jain literatures have distinguished three types of *cakravartin.* A *pradeśa cakravartin* is a monarch who leads the people of a specific region and may be thought of as a local king. A *dvīpa cakravartin* governs all of the people of any one of the four continents (*dvīpas*, literally "islands") posited by ancient Indian cosmologies and is, accordingly, more powerful in the secular realm than the *pradeśa cakravartin.* Superior even to a *dvīpa cakravartin,* however, is the *cakravāla cakravartin,* the monarch who rules over all of the continents of the world. It is the political paramouncy of the *cakravāla cakravartin* with which the Buddha's religious supremacy is compared.

Religious Dimensions of the Cakravartin Ideal. The source of the image of the king as a *cakravartin* is not to be found, however, in its political history. Rather, it is the powerful and evocative South Asian mythic and religious themes regarding the *cakravartin* with which various kings identified. According to South Asian sovereign myths (many of which suggest a solar origin), the *cakravartin*—here, a paradigmatic figure—while deep in meditation sees a peaceful and pleasantly glowing wheel *(cakra)* turning slowly in the sky above him. Knowing this wheel to be a call to unify all peoples, the king leads his armies out in all directions to the farthest horizons, all the way to the universal ring of mountains *(cakravāla)* that lie beyond the oceans and that mark the final edge of the concentric world. Guided by the celestial wheel, and borne upon the atmosphere by flying white elephants and horses, he ends all strife and suffering as he brings all people everywhere under his virtuous rule. Thus, *cakravālacakravartī cakram vartayati:* the universal monarch turns the wheel of righteousness throughout the whole world.

The mythic *cakravartin,* therefore, was a ruler in whose virtue and strength all people, regardless of their homeland, could find guidance. He was a pacifying leader whose power was embodied in his unifying skills.

Hence it may be no coincidence that the religious traditions in which the *cakravartin* is given the most prestige revolve around the ideologies and aspirations of the *kṣatriya* class of Indian society, that group who were to protect society, serve as its soldiers, rule its courts, and sit on its thrones. For some *kṣatriya* communities, as, for example, those represented by the epics *Mahābhārata* and *Rāmāyāṇa* (c. 300 CE), the most appropriate person to become a universal monarch was somebody who already was a king, someone who could extend his rule through martial and diplomatic skill.

Even for some *kṣatriya* traditions, however, the true *cakravartin* renounces the political life of the secular king and guides the people through the power of his spiritual virtue. Such is the case for the early Jain and, particularly, Buddhist communities, whose histories of their founders suggest the notion that to them religious truth is more powerful and universal than political prestige. According to both Jain and Buddhist literatures, both Vardhamāna Mahāvīra (the most recent of the twenty-four Jain *tīrthaṃkaras*) and Siddhārtha Gautama (the Buddha) were born into powerful royal families, both displayed the characteristic physical signs of a *mahāpuruṣa* ("great man"), and thus were certain to become secular *cakravartins*. Both traditions further maintain that their founders, however, chose not to enjoy the political power and privileges incumbent on the universal monarch but, rather, to seek understanding of the deepest dimensions of existence itself and—especially in the case of the Buddha—to teach that understanding to all.

[*See also* Kingship, *article on* Kingship in Southeast Asia.]

BIBLIOGRAPHY

Readers interested in the history of imperial rule in India may consult any of a number of good works on the history of India. A good, if relatively short, reference is *An Advanced History of India* (London, 1948), by Ramesh Chandra Majumdar and others. For more thorough studies by various respected historians, see *The History and Culture of the Indian People*, 11 vols., under the general editorship of Ramesh Chandra Majumdar (Bombay, 1951–1969): see especially volume 2, *The Age of Imperial Unity;* volume 3, *The Classical Age*, pp. 1–360; volume 4, *The Age of the Imperial Kanauj;* and volume 5, *The Struggle for Empire.* A more impressionistic depiction of the *cakravartin* ideal is found in Heinrich Zimmer's *Philosophies of India*, edited by Joseph Campbell, "Bollingen Foundation Series," no. 26 (1951; reprint, Princeton, 1969), pp. 127–139. Finally, for an example of the *cakravartin* ideal as expressed in religious myth, see Frank E. Reynolds and Mani Reynolds's translation of a Thai Buddhist text, *Three Worlds According to King Ruang* (Berkeley, 1982), pp. 135–172.

WILLIAM K. MAHONY

CALENDARS. [*This entry consists of three articles: an overview of the magico-religious origins and functions of calendars and two companion pieces on calendars in the native religions of Mesoamerica and South America. See also the entries on the religious calendars of various traditions:* Buddhist Religious Year; Chinese Religious Year; Christian Liturgical Year; Fasti; Hindu Religious Year; Islamic Religious Year; *and* Jewish Religious Year.]

An Overview

The absence of a historical dimension and the scant attention paid to the religious aspect of the question are the most notable limitations of the specialized literature on calendars during the last century and into the first decade of the present century. Thus, such monumental works as L. Ideler's *Handbuch der mathematischen und technischen Chronologie* (Berlin, 1825–1826), F. Ginzel's work of the same title (Leipzig, 1906–1911), and even the entry "Calendars" in James Hastings's *Encyclopaedia of Religion and Ethics*, vol. 3 (Edinburgh, 1910), although they provide indispensable information, amount to little more than unconnected descriptions of various calendars. These descriptions are not satisfactorily situated against the background of the cultures in question, but are treated as if they are solely concerned with chronology and astronomy.

The sacral aspect of the question has, however, been discussed in the subsequent scientific literature, in which the specialists are divided into two opposing camps: those who believe the calendar originated as a secular phenomenon purely utilitarian in its purposes (a view accepted by the majority of scholars), and those who believe it was originally a religious institution (Ernst Cassirer, Martin P. Nilsson, Henri Hubert and Marcel Mauss, Gerardus van der Leeuw, Mircea Eliade, and others). Less common are harmonizing positions such as that of Bronislaw Malinowski, who in an article on the calendar of the Trobriand Islanders (*Journal of the Anthropological Institute* 57, 1927, pp. 203ff.), viewed systems for computing time as meeting both practical and sacral demands.

Disagreement on the subject has been largely overcome since the publication of such works as Mircea Eliade's *Cosmos and History: The Myth of the Eternal Return* (New York, 1954) and Angelo Brelich's *Introduzione allo studio dei calendari festivi* (Rome, 1955). The reality of periodicity in the world; the religious importance of this periodicity in helping to overcome the crisis that is coextensive with human existence (the duration of which is irreversible) by establishing frequent contact with the sacred time proper to the feast or festival (which is outside of ongoing duration); the parallelism between natural and sacral periodicity, both of which have as a constant a continual renewal in the same forms, so that in even the most diverse civilizations the sacral periodicity provides an effective means of keeping a timely eye on the natural periodicity—all these ideas are now well established in our discipline. As a result, any modern work on any aspect of the vast complex of problems raised by calendars must nowadays start with the acceptance of a concept that proves to be constant across the most varied cultural contexts and the most diverse calendrical forms and manifestations, namely, that time is of interest not in and of itself and as a simple fact of nature, but only as a dimension of life that can be submitted to cultural control.

Such control is very difficult to exercise over something abstract, especially in social contexts still far from possessing even rudimentary astronomical knowledge. Nevertheless, by making use of a procedure now familiar to historians of religion, the various civilizations managed to gain this kind of control. They did so especially by *concretizing* time, whether this be understood in absolute terms or in relation to the various measurements (hours, days, months, years, etc.) that were gradually imposed on time, depending on the culture in question.

Mythology makes clear how the chronological dimension (especially if limited to the distinction and alternation of the light and dark times of the day, or to the lunar phases, which are harmoniously ordered within the arc of the month) can acquire such a material form in the minds of the peoples under study that it becomes the subject of stories without causing the least disturbance in the civilizations involved. It is told, for instance, that time was wrapped in leaves (the Sulka of New Britain); enclosed in a bag (the Micmac of Nova Scotia); kept in a box (the Tlingit of the U.S. Northwest Coast) or a trunk (the Hausa of the Sudan) and later taken out; extracted from the wattles of a fowl (the Nandi of northeastern Africa); hidden and found (the Pomo of California); hung up (the northern Paiute of Nevada); hoisted up to heaven (the Pomo; the Aleut of Alaska); pierced by arrows (the Caddo of eastern Texas); or cut up with an obsidian knife (natives of Mota in Melanesia). In each case, time is looked upon not only as something very concrete but also and especially as something capable of being handled at will.

Meanwhile the concrete treatment of time was strengthening this tendency toward materialization of the chronological sphere, for the latter was being treated in such a way as to acquire an ideal spatial coherence. As a macroscopic example, one can cite the persistent attempts to identify time with space, both in language and in the calendar, by the primitive cultures of North America—a tendency also found at a higher cultural level in the Aztec calendar, and in the Indo-European area as well (Müller, 1967). In addition, a real spatiotemporal dimension is found in Roman religion, where close, complex, and functional relations are discernible in the mythological tradition and in cult, as well as in the calendrical linking of the two, between time and Terminus (the symbol of boundaries and, at the same time, a divinity in charge of the juridical, political, and sacral aspect of territory). Moreover, the projection of a cosmic framework on the layout of the circus, and this in such a detailed form (with the aid of a rich set of symbols) as to make the circus a universe in miniature, automatically transformed the chariot races in the arena into the course of the sun through the arc of the year.

Thus, it can be a rather short step from the concretization of time to its material embodiment. The example just given shows how, while the spectator at the circus (which is assimilated to the vault of heaven) feels himself to be witnessing the calendrical rotation of the sun, the charioteer is a direct protagonist in this drama as he drives his chariot.

Yet the title "protagonist of time" belongs with greater justice to those who, through actions in which it is not easy to distinguish the sacred and profane dimensions, do not limit themselves to concretizing and materializing time but also embody it in a true calendrical system. Thus the native who in certain cultures uses knotted cords for computing time does not simply concretize this dimension by pinning it down to so many firmly fixed points of its otherwise limitless and therefore uncontrollable extension but also defines it in a calendrical manner that, though rudimentary, proves functional in relation to the needs of his society. The astronomer in ancient Peru, who used stone columns called "tools for knotting the sun" *(inti-huatana)* as a position for observing the stars, did not merely give material form to that which in and of itself would be simply the calculation of solstices and equinoxes; he also carried this materialization to a higher level by developing a calendar that was primarily a means of binding the heavenly corps in its otherwise incoherent and unusable movements. (But note, too, among the Aztecs, the "knot of years," or *xiuhmolpilli*, a great cycle of fifty-two solar revolutions subdivided into four periods of thirteen years that were described as "knotted together," *thalpilli*.) The magistrate in ancient Rome who was in charge of the ritual hammering in of the *clavus annalis* ("nail of the year") on the Ides of September (which was New Year's Day in one of the many Roman calendrical systems) thereby not only turned time from an abstraction into something that could be pinned down but also compelled it to remain, from one September to the next, within the limits of the solar year.

It is possible to view in a similar perspective those who, in civilizations already familiar with writing, either ideally or in actual fact superintended the compilation of calendars, and this specifically in the form of inscriptions. In this case the concretization of time was accomplished either by binding the dimension of time to stones and/or metals, which were moved about or incised to this end, or by imprisoning it in the no less constraining nets of the various graphic forms. Evidence here is the widespread use in the ancient Near East of the alphabet as a calendrical memorandum as early as the second millennium BCE (Bausani, 1978), as well as the example, cited above, of the *clavus annalis,* which in early Rome was regarded both as a palpable sign of the year and as a functional "writing" of a chronologico-juridical kind at a time when few people could read the symbols of the alphabet.

The key role played by human beings in these operations whereby time is concretized and straitjacketed (especially within the compass of, and for the purposes of drafting, calendrical systems that are more or less developed according to cultural level and social demands) is such that, in case of need, the materialization of time can be further specified by giving it human traits in the true and proper sense. This specification may be limited to introducing into the calendar the physiological rhythms of those who are the protagonists of time. This is seen in the assimilation, widespread and found in the most diverse cultures, of the lunar month of twenty-eight days to the menstrual cycle of the same duration; or in the projection of the period of human gestation (260 days) onto the identical time period of nine lunar revolutions, as in the Aztec *tonalamatl* or the Numan calendar at Rome.

But this process of specification can also lead to a more or less concealed identification of a segment of time (located within the calendar and thus describable in precise terms) with a part or belonging of a person who usually enjoyed an important sociocultural and, in particular, religious status. Thus, as a result of Islamic influence on the Cham of Cambodia, to give but one example, the first three days of every lunar cycle are assimilated to the three favorite wives of Muḥammad, and every year of the twelve-year cycle is equated with one of the Prophet's members.

Finally, this process can even find expression in a personification of time in its various parts. Thus in Achaemenid Iran the retinue of the magi seems to have usually comprised 365 young men dressed in red, one for each day of the year, with the color symbolizing the lighted period of the day. At Rome, on the ides of March (New Year's Day, according to one of the many Roman calendrical systems), all the negative aspects of the old year were eliminated through the ritual expulsion from the city of the mythical carpenter Mamurius Veturius.

This kind of progressive, and in some cases even paroxysmic, personification of time seems on closer examination to be simply an expression of the persistent tendency to *re-create,* on several distinct but complementary levels, the temporal dimension that is so important at the human level, thus asserting the priority of the unqualifiedly cultural essence of time over the mere natural fact of time.

If, on the one hand, this cultural point of reference is indispensable because it is linked to any latent or open calendrical system, on the other hand such a system, whatever its character (heliacal rising of a constellation; blooming of a species of plant; period of sowing and/or harvesting; migration of animals; etc.), becomes by this very fact a field of action for the cultural process, which immediately begins to act therein in the form of well-defined and often massive interventions. In the case, widespread in both higher and primitive civilizations, of a discrepancy between the lunar and solar years, for example, the intervention takes the form of an intercalation that makes up for the difference; in other words, a portion of human, cultural time is inserted into the living body of natural time, which is computed on the basis of the revolution of the heavenly bodies.

The awareness that the intercalated period is the work of man, and the conviction that, as such, it merits a privileged position are made manifest at various levels. This is seen in the view that the year, having been thus manipulated, is now complete as compared with nature's presumably defective version of it, whence the designation—prevalent among various primitive peoples, but also found in Mesopotamia, Rome, and China—of the year or month as "full" or "empty." It is seen too in the systematic insertion of such intercalated periods immediately after moments in the calendar that sanctioned human control over the world of nature: at Rome, for example, the intercalation came immediately after the celebration of Terminalia, a festival that appealed to mythical time in order to give sacral confirmation to the cultural definition of space. Further evidence is found in the tendency to locate during the intercalated period those events that were of capital importance for the particular civilization and that evidently could not be left to the blind and irrational course of nature's time, precisely because these events were due in the maximum degree to the human will and creativity. A prime example: the definitive liquidation of monarchic rule, which was constantly assimilated to the negativity of the period of origins, in order to make way for a republic was traditionally dated by the Romans on the very day, 24 February, on which the intercalation usually began.

A negative proof pointing in the same direction is the resistance to and even rejection of intercalation in those civilizations that most clearly show the assimilation of natural time to sacred time. Such rejection was preferred despite the inevitable practical nuisances it entailed—above all, discrepancy with the rhythm of the seasons. Two examples among many can be cited. First, in ancient Egypt (which adopted the practice of intercalation only in the Alexandrian period, and then not without hindrances) an oath not to intercalate was taken by the pharaoh, who, in his capacity as the future Osiris and, therefore, an important participant in the field of action proper to the sun god Re, was probably reluctant to intervene in a dimension of reality that was projected in its ideal form onto the sacral level. Second, Muḥammad categorically prohibited changing the number of the months, which "Allāh ordained . . . when he created the heavens and the earth" (surah 9:36 of the Qur'ān), and which "Allāh has sanctified" (surah 9:37). Thus the Islamic lunar year, though without any correspondence to the seasons, has proved surprisingly functional for a religion now practiced in varying latitudes. Such interventions in the course of time became even more drastic in the great calendrical reforms of Julius Caesar (46 BCE) and Pope Gregory XIII (1582 CE).

This kind of attempt to reduce time to a cultural creation is even more pronounced in those widespread cases in which the most varied means are used to emancipate time from natural phenomena on which calendrical computation is usually based and to replace these phenomena with others. Thus, the Aztecs chose the duration of human gestation, and not the Venusian year to which astronomy bears witness, as the basis of the *tonalamatl;* the Egyptians based their calendar on the rising of Sirius (Sothis), "the second sun in the heavens," and not on the true sun; while, in the most diverse primitive cultures, it is the periodic return of the ancestors, regarded as dispensers of foodstuffs, and not the particular seasonal moment that gives a specific economic meaning to the great New Year festival. Comparable motivations probably explain the otherwise incomprehensible perseverance, on the part of the most varied types of civilization, in adopting lunisolar calendars and continuing to use them right down to the present day, despite such problems as the discrepancy between festive complex and seasonal moment, the consequent necessity of intercalating, and so on. It is as though this very difference of a few days or parts of a day represents a kind of margin of security for man, who thus has leeway to act on natural time instead of passively enduring it.

This desire to be actors rather than spectators in the development of calendrical time is even more evident in those systems in which, by highly artificial means, months are established whose duration is identical with or superior to the lunar month, and in which a short period is set apart and defined in a special way, independent of the features this period may assume from time to time in any other culture. By way of example, we may think of the five "supernumerary" *(nemontemi)* days that the Aztecs set apart at the end of the 360-day year, considering them to be *nefasti* (taboo) and unsuited for work of any kind; or, in the Egyptian calendar, of the *epagomenai* ("superadded") days that did not conclude the old year, as might have been expected, but were a prelude to the new year, a kind of "little month" directly linked to the mythical time in which the gods were born. Similarly, in the Zoroastrian religion the "days of the *Gathas*" were added to the end of the year; on these days, the celebrants, assuming the title of Saoshyant ("rescuers"), participated ritually as protagonists in the renewal of the world. Along the same line, but at a more advanced level, is the creation of units of time comprising several or more days, months, years, centuries, or even millennia, which apparently, at least, are independent of the rhythms of nature. Examples include the very widespread seven-day week (already used in Mesopotamia); the cycles of three days and three, seven, and thirty years among the Celts; the seven-year period, the jubilee, and the groups of seven-year periods among the Hebrews; the *octaetēris* or eight-year period of the Greeks; the Aztec *xiuhmolpilli;* and the Indian *kalpa.*

But perhaps the most radical humanization of the chronological dimension (the one in which the cultural intervention into nature is the most extensive, and the dependence on nature for the computation of time is reduced to a minimum that is obscured and even deliberately ignored) is found in cases in which the historical situation determines and defines the calendar. We may pass over those restructurings that are promoted or imposed on time by important politicians (i.e., the aforementioned Julian reform). In some civilizations, the personal name of the ruler was given to the current year (eponymy among the Assyrians and in the classical world, the "regnal name" in prerevolutionary China), or events of capital importance led to a complete resystematization of the calendrical pattern, the beginning, rhythm, and shape of which, though in substance inevitably following traditional lines, had to be at least formally determined by the new order of things. The prime example here is the French revolutionary calendar, which, though it started at a particular equinox, numbered 365 days, needed periodic intercalation, and linked the new names of the months with seasonal motifs, nonetheless presented new features: a beginning (22 September) that officially coincided not with the autumn equinox but with the inauguration of the republic (22 September 1792); the abolition of the seven-day week in favor of the decade or ten-day week; the elimination of feasts; and the nonetheless festive solemnization of five or six days (significantly called *sansculottides*) added at the end of the year as a definitive break with Christian worship.

In connection with the historicization of time, one may also consider such phenomena as the adoption of calendrical systems belonging to other civilizations, as, for instance, the entrusting of calendar reform in China in 1629 to the Jesuits, and the adoption of the Gregorian calendar as the only valid one for civil purposes by the republican government of China in 1930; the acceptance by Japan in 1684 of the Chinese calendar as reformed by the Jesuits and then in 1873 of the Gregorian calendar; and the adoption of the Gregorian calendar by Russia after the October Revolution in 1917 and by various primitive peoples as they gradually accepted the lifestyles of the Western civilizations. Finally, there is the tendency, which practical considerations and economic reasons have made stronger than ever in our day, to create a universal and perpetual calendar that is binding on all. Such a calendar would be supremely artificial, since it seeks to be as independent as possible of natural rhythms, but for that very reason would transcend the various cultures.

[*See also* Chronology *and* Sacred Time.]

BIBLIOGRAPHY

The extensive bibliography of scientific writing on the subject has been brought together and discussed splendidly by Angelo Brelich in his *Introduzione allo studio dei calendari festivi*, 2 vols. in 1 (Rome, 1955). The reader is also referred to this work for the historico-religious approach to calendrical problems. Festive time in relation to the New Year is extensively discussed and documented in Vittorio Lanternari's *La grande festa*, 2d ed. (Bari, 1976). On the concretization of time at various levels, compare the following works: Werner Müller's "Raum und Zeit in Sprachen und Kalendern Nordamerikas und Alteuropas," *Anthropos* 57 (1962): 568–590, 68 (1973): 156–180, 74 (1979): 443–464, 77 (1982): 533–558; Hugh A. Moran and David H. Kelly's *The Alphabet and the Ancient Calendar Signs*, 2d ed. (Palo Alto, Calif., 1969); Alessandro Bausani's "L'alfabeto come calendario arcaico," *Oriens Antiquus* (Rome) 17 (1978): 131–146; J. H. Scharf's "Time and Language," *Gegenbaurs morphologisches Jahrbuch* 128 (1982): 257–289; and Ulrich Köhler's "Räumliche und zeitliche Bezugspunkte in mesoamerikanischen Konzepten vom Mondzyklus," *Indiana* 7 (1982): 23–42. Also compare my *Elementi spettacolari nei rituali festivi romani* (Rome, 1965); *Terminus: I segni di confine nella religione romana* (Rome, 1974); and "La scrittura coercitiva," *Cultura e scuola* 85 (1983): 117–124. Raffaele Pettazzoni treats the primitive myths on the origin of time and provides a bibliography in his *Miti e leggende*, 4 vols. (Turin, 1948–1963). Alexander Marshak discusses Paleolithic systems of noting time in *The Roots of Civilization: The Cognitive Beginnings of Man's First Art, Symbol, and Notation* (New York, 1972). While Marshak's views are somewhat controversial, they have been widely discussed.

GIULIA PICCALUGA
Translated from Italian by Matthew J. O'Connell

Mesoamerican Calendars

[*This article examines how the cosmological mythology of Mesoamerican peoples, particularly the Aztec, was encoded in their calendrical system. For further, descriptive treatment of Mesoamerican calendars, see* Mesoamerican Religions, *overview article, and* Maya Religion.]

According to stratigraphic probes, Mesoamerica (Mexico and Central America) had been the depository of an uninterrupted civilization for more than five thousand years by the time of the Spanish conquest in the early sixteenth century (Séjourné, 1983). This civilization and its inhabitants were physically destroyed, morally maligned, and intellectually misunderstood by the European invaders. It is difficult to investigate Mesoamerican civilization because there is so little left of it, with the exception of artifacts cut off from context and, therefore, from the better part of their significance. Nevertheless, once one encounters the fascinating multitude of pre-Hispanic buildings, sculptures, ceramics, murals, and other works that have been revealed by excavations in this region, the quest for the body of thought that held Mesoamerican culture together becomes imperative. Surviving historical texts, signs, myths, and cosmological concepts, when studied together with archaeological discoveries, indicate that Mesoamerican thought and the system of symbols that informed it were focused in the mythological figure Quetzalcoatl, the hero revered as the creator of this extraordinary cultural universe and of its most significant expression, the calendar.

Quetzalcoatl, the Culture Hero. The Nahuatl word *Quetzalcoatl* combines the words *quetzal*, a fragile, royal-plumed Central American jungle bird, and *coatl* ("serpent"). The attributes of the god Quetzalcoatl, who is represented by a feathered serpent, are innumerable, complex, and contradictory: he is at once the son and the father of men and the creator of himself; a chaste priest and a licentious sinner; the spiritual guide of youth (as the patron of boarding schools) and an example of excess and transgression. At home in obscure and solitary retreats, he is the patron of itinerants who travel through Mesoamerica exchanging knowledge and precious materials. He is a citizen of the ground, of the skies, and of the depths. He is the discoverer of earthly food, underground gems, and the celestial laws, and he is the creator of all the arts.

Perhaps most importantly, Quetzalcoatl is the framer of the philosophical and cosmological concepts that are essential to the worldview of Mesoamerican civilization. In one myth, described below, he conceives the point uniting the duality of the "heaviness" and the spirituality that constitute the human phenomenon. He is the author of an artificial calendar that, by joining its cycle to the cycles of natural bodies, which have durations different from its own, forms a fifty-two year cycle which names and enciphers all that exists in the world. The mechanism of Quetzalcoatl's calendar, also described below, parallels the myths of his life and death so closely that both seem cast in a common cultural mold.

Quetzalcoatl's attributes and his contributions to Mesoamerican culture are presented in the myth celebrating his passage on earth, which is recounted in fragments in various texts. He begins this passage as the sovereign of a rich and powerful kingdom, the capital of which is the legendary city Tollan-Teotihuacán (see Codex Vaticanus and *Leyenda de los isles*). He is an incorruptible ascetic, whom demons one day decide to subvert; they attempt a subterfuge to "give him his body" by approaching him with a mirror. The transformation takes place, first by means of the reflection of his face and then by means of the intoxication caused by his ingestion of five glasses of wine.

Here the versions of the myth bifurcate: in one tradition, Quetzalcoatl is horrified by the sight of his own face and swears never to appear before his people again; in another, he gives himself over to the pleasures of the flesh while under the influence of the drink. These two variants, and also a third in which Quetzalcoatl is forced by the demons to initiate the practice of human sacrifice, lead to a common turn: he leaves his wealthy native land of Tollan and embarks on a long pilgrimage punctuated by marvelous and prodigious deeds.

This pilgrimage, on which Quetzalcoatl follows the calling of the sun god, ends when he disappears into the vast sea on a raft of braided serpents, according to the informants of the Spanish compiler of Mesoamerican lore Fray Bernardino de Sahagún (1499-1590). The *Anales de Cuahtitlan*, from the anonymously written collection of Nahuatl myths called the Codice Chimalpopoca (c. 1570), relates the following story:

> It is said that having reached the celestial shore of the divine water [the seacoast], he [Quetzalcoatl] stopped, cried, seized his garments, and put on his insignia of feathers and his green mask. Then, when he was adorned, he set fire to himself and burned. It is said that when he burned, his ashes were at once raised up and that all the precious birds that rise to the skies came to see them. When the ashes disappeared, they saw the heart of Quetzalcoatl rise. They knew that it rose to the skies and entered the skies. The old men say that the heart became the star that rises at dawn; they also say that it appeared when Quetzalcoatl died, and therefore they named him Lord of the Dawn.
>
> (trans. from Velázquez, 1945, p. 11)

Thus Quetzalcoatl is identified with the Morning Star (i.e., the planet Venus) by virtue of his transfiguration into light as recounted in this myth. Such an identification is strengthened by evidence implicit in the Mesoamerican calendar. Quetzalcoatl's birthdate and that of the Morning Star are the same—Ce Acatl, or 1 Reed. It is by the name Ce Acatl that Quetzalcoatl was known in his role as patron of boarding schools.

But the central episode in the life of Quetzalcoatl—the episode that leads to the creation of the world—is his descent to hell to rescuscitate the bones of his ancestors (or of his own father). Strangely neglected by many chroniclers, including Sahagún, this episode is briefly recorded in the *Anales de Cuahtitlan*:

> They say that when he died, he did not appear for four days because he had gone to dwell among the dead, and that in four days he provided himself with great arrows, and that therefore in eight days there appeared a great star called Quetzalcoatl. And they add that at that time he was enthroned as Lord. (trans. from Velázquez, 1945, p. 11)

A more complete version of this myth, of inestimable value in the reading of hieroglyphs, is told in the *Leyenda de los soles* (Legend of the Suns), which also forms part of the Codice Chimalpopoca. This version places Quetzalcoatl's underworld journey, and his subsequent transformation into the Morning Star, at the end of the era during which the gods had labored to bring humanity, the race that would release the world from darkness, to birth. The salvage of the bones succeeds despite the fall of the Feathered Serpent caused by his panic. It is this doublet, which appeared in the moment of supreme danger, that later became the Fifth Sun, the star of the era of Movement awarded to Quetzalcoatl.

Apart from its deep spiritual significance and the beauty of its metaphors, this myth is distinguished by the severity with which it imposes the duty of participation in accomplishing the moral that it conveys. For the culture hero is not limited to showing the path for attaining his individual fulfillment; he also produces the means by which each member of the community is attached to the same destiny as his own. This instrument is Quetzalcoatl's calendar, undoubtedly the most important among his many creations, constituting the foundation of Mesoamerican civilization. An "artificial" calendar of 260 days infuses life and time with significance through an interplay of symbols, numbers, and rituals that are derived from the events and themes of the myth of Tollan's king. In fact, the myth and the calendar run so closely parallel that it is likely they were created simultaneously. Features of the calendar are analogous to Quetzalcoatl's "assumption of body," to his transfigurations, in increasingly brilliant light, first as Venus, then the Sun, and to his descents to the land of the dead with their respective redoublings.

The Calendar. The Mesoamerican calendar represents a technique for reckoning time extending all the way back to the cosmogony. Composed of 260 days (approximately the time of human gestation), the "artificial" calendar is generated from a series of twenty hieroglyphs that represent plants, animals, natural forces, abstract ideas, and human artifacts. Thus the calendar symbolically intermingles disparate realms of experience with the symbolic value of numbers in a way characteristic of Mesoamerican thought. To form this 260-day year, the invariable sequence of twenty hieroglyphs, or day names (see table 1), is broken up into thirteen-day "weeks": that is, the hieroglyphs advance daily in their unvarying sequence of twenty, while the numbers that precede them and that designate each as a date advance only to 13 and then recommence at 1 after each "week" is completed. Thus the fourteenth hieroglyph, Jaguar, is in fact the first day of the second week, and so it is there designated 1 Jaguar. In the third week it appears as 8 Jaguar, in the fifth as 2 Jaguar, in the sixth as 9 Jaguar, and so on. In order to produce 260, which determines the mathematical encounter of various celestial bodies every 104 years, this unit of 20 explodes by the intromission of the number 13, which alters its numerical continuity. If one realizes that the number is the element that transmits the significative adhesion of the image to the time that it indicates, one can deduce the complexity and the thickness of the symbolic fabric that keeps encircling the universe through the centuries (Séjourné, 1982).

The 260-day calendar is fused with the solar calendar, thus losing its integrity within a greater whole than it alone comprises. The 365-day year was composed of eighteen "months" of twenty days each; the remaining five days at the end of this vague solar year were considered a separate unity because of the symbolic mobilizing of residue that this number effects in all computations. Before again reaching its numerical wholeness, the 260-day calendar would have to wait for the conjunction that occurs between the 260- and 365-day calendars only once every fifty-two years. The unity of the two revolutions is so complete that, after 18,890 days of

TABLE 1. *Sequences of Day Names and Numbers in the Aztec Calendar*[1]

Day Name		Day Number		
Nahuatl	English Equivalent	First Sequence of 20 Days	Second Sequence of 20 Days	Third Sequence of 20 Days
Cipactli	Alligator	1 (week 1)	8	2
Ehécatl	Wind	2	9	3
Calli	House	3	10	4
Cuatzpallin	Lizard	4	11	5
Coatl	Serpent	5	12	6
Miquiztli	Death	6	13	7
Mazatl	Deer	7	1 (week 3)	8
Tochtli	Rabbit	8	2	9
Atl	Water	9	3	10
Itzcuintli	Dog	10	4	11
Ozomatl	Monkey	11	5	12
Malinalli	Grass of Penance	12	6	13
Acatl	Reed	13	7	1 (week 5)
Ocelotl	Jaguar	1 (week 2)	8	2
Cuauhtli	Eagle	2	9	3
Cozacuauhtli	Vulture	3	10	4
Ollin	Movement	4	11	5
Tecpatl	Stone Knife	5	12	6
Quaihuitl	Rain	6	13	7
Xochitl	Flower	7	1 (week 4)	8

[1]This table shows only the first 60 days of the 260-day cycle.

traveling together, the difference between their respective quantities disappears: the last day of the month coincides at that point with the last of the twenty hieroglyphs, and the beginning of the next cycle of fifty-two years starts on the first day of the first month and of the first series of thirteen days.

In the ancient Mesoamerican painted books, these series of thirteen-day weeks are accompanied by guardians who carry their meanings as well as by illustrations that expand and deepen these meanings. The twenty illustrations allow the identification of the iconographical ensemble of 260 days with the mythical stages of Quetzalcoatl's life. Once this identity between myth and computation is established, one discovers that the multiplicity of characters who intervene not only in the series but also in the months—characters whom the chroniclers called "gods"—are in fact the representations of the culture hero at every point of time and space through which he travels.

Each of the eighteen months of the solar year was celebrated by a festival that derived its meaning from the particular characteristics assigned to that part of the year; these characteristics seem to have been determined by the seasonal variations of the sun's light. The variations, which play a major role in the symbolics, were noted with such precision that they were seen to dictate the daily procession of the day-hieroglyphs. The ritual importance of equinoxes, solstices, the passages of the sun through the zenith, the changes of the season, and so on, also undoubtedly originated in the meaning seen in these variations. The monthly festivals included realistically presented dramas. These were long theatrical representations, in several acts, that were at times performed secretly for a few people and at others lavishly staged and involving the participation of the entire community. The staging was always impressive. Arduous work of comparison discovers an exact correspondence between the significance of these dramas and of their protagonists on the one hand and the iconographical context of the guardians of the twenty series on the other hand; this correspondence makes any day from the artificial calendar (during the course of the year) indivisible from the space that it occupies in time (i.e., the month). It follows that the same hieroglyph carrying the same number in the same month can recur only once in fifty-two years. Obviously then, a "birthday" anniversary can occur, at best, only once in a person's lifetime. Birthdays are therefore given great attention in Mesoamerican society, and are associated, through monthly representations, with the initiation dates of a person's spiritual life, such as the place of his fusion with the world and his passage into the next.

Mesoamerican Cosmology. The meanings of the Quetzalcoatl myth, embodied in his calendrical system, also inform various aspects of Mesoamerican cosmology. This cosmology, including myths of origin, descriptions of past eras, and a sense of how and why the universe develops, is ordered in terms of Quetzalcoatl's calendar and so is filled with dates and the symbolic significance that these dates carry. The calendar thus lends meaning not only to the present but also to the past and the future; Mesoamerican cosmology in this sense is built around Quetzalcoatl, whose achievements as the founder of human culture represent the crown of creation.

In the *Leyenda de los soles* is one of the rare surviving descriptions of the Aztec's picture of the world's laborious development toward the era of humankind. According to the story related here, the world had passed through four previous stages (known as "Suns") before reaching the present era, which is characterized by the coming of human beings. Each of the previous stages is identified with a particular day name, and the catastrophe that, in each case, brings the era to its close is associated with the destructive power of the creature or natural force after which the era is named.

The First Sun is called Nahui Ocelotl, or 4 Jaguar; it ends when those who live during this time are devoured by wild beasts. The Second Sun, named Nahuecatl, or 4 Wind, ends when everything is carried away by a wind. The Third Sun, Nahui Quiyahuitl (4 Rain), is brought to its close by a devastating rain of fire, and the Fourth Sun, called Nahui Atl (4 Water), is terminated by a flood that ends the world.

An examination of the various versions of these creations reveals that the quest anxiously undertaken by the gods has as its aim the advent of man, for the gods declare, "There will be neither glory nor greatness in our creation until the human creature is created, the Formed man" (trans. from Recinos, 1947, p. 87). But if the conceptual reflection and the consciousness (which the calculations underline so well) that the symbolics and the myth of the culture hero do not demonstrate that the creation of the human phenomenon had already taken place, then to what kind of creature is reference being made? Nevertheless, the lamentations increase with each failure: "The gods consulted with one another and cried, 'Who shall live in this place, now that the sky has been bound and the Lord of the Earth has stopped? Who will live in this place, o gods?' " (trans. from Velázquez, 1945, p. 121). Among the gods who display this cosmic impotence, as well as the hope put in a creature that will busy itself with the fate of the sky and of the earth, is Quetzalcoatl. That is, there is an essential want in the march of the universe that the culture hero has not yet succeeded in overcoming. The *Popol Vuh* refers to the nature of this want:

> Thereupon, they spoke to those gods, the Grandmother of the Day, the Grandmother of the Dawn, who were so named by the Diviners, the Creator and Maker. . . . And thus said Huracán, Tepeu, and Gucumatz [the Quiché name for Quetzalcoatl] when they were called to the Soothsayer and Maker, who are the Diviners: we must gather and find the means so that the man we form, the man whom we are going to create, sustains and nourishes us, invokes and remembers us. So they confer, Grandfather, Grandmother, Our Grandfather, Our Grandfather, Ixpiyacoc, Ixmucane, so that they vow that we will rise, that we are invoked, that we are adored, so that we are remembered by created man, by made man, by mortal man. That is how it was done.
>
> (trans. from Recinos, 1947, pp. 91–92)

Thus the element that will set the universe in order is the mortality of man, which carries with it the consciousness of the finitude of individual life. For this reason, Quetzalcoatl's death and his subsequent transfiguration into the light of the Morning Star occupy a central place in the culture hero's myth and in his principal creation, the human Sun. The *Leyenda de los soles* tells how Quetzalcoatl descends to the land of the dead to revive his ancestors' bones, and how through this confrontation with death he initiates the era of mankind. While Quetzalcoatl himself perishes, his ascension into the heavens as the Morning Star heralds the dawn of the mortal age. The following passage comes from the Codex Telleriano Remensis:

> This Tlahuizcalpantecuhtli [the planet of Venus] is Quetzalcoatl. They say that he is that star that we call the Morning Star. This Tlahuizcalpantecuhtli means "lord of the morning" when the day dawns, and at the same time it is lord of that clarity when the night is falling. Veritably it is the light on things or on the face of the earth.
>
> (trans. from Nuñez, 1964, pl. 14)

Furthermore, the Sun of the age of mortals, called the Fifth Sun, rises after the Morning Star from the body of Xolotl, the double of Quetzalcoatl who helped the culture hero when he confronted death in the underworld.

The philosophical significance of this redoubling, in which Quetzalcoatl's personality is magnified and enriched, and by which he initiates the era of humanity, leads to a number of interesting questions. Apparently the action of doubling is essential to the processes of human destiny implicitly expressed in the calendar. Does this perhaps imply that a spiritual idea, like Quetzalcoatl's hope for the advent of man in the void before the Fifth Sun, must be translated into an act to acquire its real meaning, and that the fruit of imagination can be born only through an existential experience? And since the agency through which Quetzalcoatl's experience in the underworld ends in success is none other than his own double, in what philosophical sense can successful experience be said to depend upon such aid? Though Xolotl appears as Quetzalcoatl's double, he is nevertheless a creature from beyond Quetzalcoatl's experience, and it is as a guide to the Beyond that Xolotl offers his assistance. The actions of Quetzalcoatl succeed, it seems, because he receives help from a being that is at once the double of himself and beyond himself.

The poetic eloquence of the *Popol Vuh* describes Quetzalcoatl's retreat, prior to the beginning of the Fifth Sun and of Quetzalcoatl's experiences on earth, as the starting point of his quest for the new race to populate the universe.

> There was only immobility and silence in the darkness, in the night. Only the Creator, the Maker, Tepeu, Gucumatz [Quetzalcoatl], and the forefathers were in the water, surrounded with light. They were hidden under green and blue feathers and were therefore called Gucumatz. By nature they were great sages and great thinkers. In this manner the sky existed, and also the Heart of Heaven, which is the name of God. . . .
>
> Then came the word. Tepeu and Gucumatz came together in the darkness, in the night, and Tepeu and Gucumatz talked together. They talked then, discussing and deliberating; they agreed, they united their words and their thoughts.
>
> Then while they meditated it became clear to them that when dawn would break man must appear.
>
> (trans. from Recinos, 1947, pp. 81–82)

Everything that helps form our understanding of Mesoamerican thought—the calendars, the monthly dramas, archaeological discoveries, and the Spanish texts of the sixteenth century—clearly indicate that in this cosmology the only man able to assure the progress of the universe is a man of action who continually strives through his works to benefit society at large. Thus up to the European invasion the disciples and descendants of Quetzalcoatl called themselves the Great Artisans and placed the highest value on works of cultural significance.

From this idea it follows that these peoples, sometimes considered by scholars to be without history, were in fact conscious not only of their future but also of their responsibility as agents of their own history. This consciousness manifested itself in their concern for their social environment and nourished a vigorous ethical code through various institutions, beliefs, laws and duties, economic activities, and so on.

Thus Mesoamerican cosmology accounts for the creation of the universe in terms of individuals and societies that continually try to surpass themselves in fulfillment of the task that history has set for them. This drive toward greater and greater achievement becomes clear in the following example (Séjourné, 1983). According to this myth, the birth of the Fifth Sun occurs in the city of Teotihuacán, that is, in a purely man-made milieu. This metropolis, which was the greatest of pre-Columbian America, is surrounded by an area that contains the vestiges of numerous ancient cities that had preceded it, dating back at least two millennia. It has been proved by archaeological discoveries that these earlier cities participated in the construction of a sophisticated hydraulic system, which served as the foundation for the great city Teotihuacán that was to follow. Once the people of the earlier cities had refined the sciences and arts considered necessary for this undertaking, they together constructed their common capital, which came to evince an artistic magnificence that reflected the splendor of the Fifth Sun that rose in myth from the city's womb.

[*See also* Aztec Religion *and* Quetzalcoatl.]

BIBLIOGRAPHY

Durán, Diego. *Historia de las Indias de Nueva España y Tierra Firme* (c. 1581). 2 vols. Mexico City, 1951. Reprint of 1867–1880 edition.

Nuñez, José Corona, ed. *Códice Telleriano Remensis*. 4 vols. Mexico City, 1964. Based on the compilation of Lord Kingsborough.

Recinos, Adrian, ed. *Popol Vuh: Las antiguas historias del Quiché*. Mexico City, 1947.

Sahagún, Bernardino de. *Historia general de las cosas de Nueva España* (compiled 1569–1582; first published 1820). Translated by Arthur J. O. Anderson and Charles E. Dibble as *Florentine Codex: General History of the Things of New Spain*. 13 vols. (Santa Fe, N.Mex., 1950–1982).

Séjourné, Laurette. *La pensée nahuatl chiffrée par les calendriers*. Mexico City, 1982.

Séjourné, Laurette. *La arqueología en el Valle de México*. Mexico City, 1983.

Velázquez, Primo Feliciano, trans. and ed. *Códice Chimalpópoca: Anales de Cuauhtitlan y Leyenda de los soles*. Mexico City, 1945. Translated from Nahuatl.

LAURETTE SÉJOURNÉ
Translated from French by Irina Rybacek

South American Calendars

At the time of the Spanish conquest of the New World in the early sixteenth century, the peoples of Mesoamerica and the Andes were living in highly developed civilizations supported by well-integrated political and religious organizations. The Aztec, Mixtec, and Maya of Mesoamerica produced codices in which are described their gods, priests, religious paraphernalia, and so on. Their knowledge was organized by way of an elaborate calendar that bore no relationship to any kind of calendrical system known to the Spanish. The chroniclers soon realized, however, that an important aspect of these Mesoamerican calendars was the repeating succession of 260 days. The 260-day "year" was divided into thirteen "months," each comprising twenty days irrespective of observations of the sun, moon, and other celestial bodies.

Unlike the Mesoamericans, the Andean peoples did not leave codices or a hieroglyphic script (as was used, for instance, by the Maya from their early history onward). They apparently had no tradition of a historical chronology and left no dated monuments. However, a recent analysis of Peruvian *quipus*—knotted strings that were used for various administrative purposes—demonstrates that Andean peoples were capable of highly abstract, mathematical thought. Accordingly, we may assume that the conclusion reached by certain Spanish chroniclers that the *quipus* were used for calendrical purposes is valid. Indeed, José de Acosta, an early chronicler who thoroughly studied the cultures in both parts of what we now call nuclear America and who compared the Andean and Mesoamerican calendars, favored the Andean system because of its technical accomplishments. Thus it may be reasonable to assume that the political and religious needs of the Andean states crystallized into a common calendrical tradition of a complexity comparable with that of Mesoamerica; but its organizing principles may have been as different from those of the Mesoamerican tradition as these differed from the European.

Accounts by Early Chroniclers. When the Spanish conquistadors entered Cuzco, the capital of the Inca empire, the Inca territory stretched from what is now northern Ecuador south to Chile and Argentina. Spanish chroniclers have left us some data on the astronomical and calendrical ideas of the people living on the north coast of Peru, a rich description of myths and rituals of Quechua-speaking peoples in central and southern Peru, and some bits and pieces of astronomical and calendrical lore from the Aymara-speaking peoples living around Lake Titicaca. But it was only in Cuzco that the chroniclers became aware of the rich tradition of the Inca's history, myths, and rituals, as well as of their seasonal activities (e.g., agriculture and llama husbandry) and astronomical observations and beliefs about the sun, moon, and stars. Many scattered data of critical importance in the reconstruction of the Inca calendar have survived. Nonetheless, although some chroniclers may have been aware of the importance of some of these data for the reconstruction of the calendar, they themselves recorded little more than the names of the months. They assumed that the Inca calendar comprised twelve months but barely analyzed what kinds of "months" they were in fact dealing with. The actual reconstruction of the Inca calendar—going well beyond the chroniclers' list of twelve names—enables us to realize the magnitude of the debt owed by the Inca to the states and cultures that preceded them: those of Huari, Tiahuanaco, and Chavín in the Andean highlands and those of Nazca, Mochica, and Paracas on the coast. The Spaniards' interpretations of the Inca data provide only a faint idea of what a pre-Conquest calendar might have looked like.

Some seventeen years after the Conquest, Juan de Betanzos became the first chronicler in Cuzco to attempt an account of the months. His description, however, is inextricably interwoven with a recording of Inca history, especially with those events that concern the legendary reorganization of Cuzco after the city had successfully rejected a foreign attack. He intimates the close relationship between Cuzco's calendar and its political organization, an aspect with which he was probably more familiar than any later chronicler. But he leaves the technical problem of the calendrical count unresolved. In 1574, the priest Cristóbal de Molina wrote the first detailed account of calendrical rituals in Cuzco. Juan de Polo de Ondegardo, a lawyer, had probably written a similar report some years earlier, but it was lost. In 1584, the third Council of the Peruvian Church published a shorter version of Polo's calendar; it is this version, or the knowledge of the existence of a longer report, that heavily influenced all later accounts given by the major chroniclers (e.g., Cavello de Balboa, Murua). Only the later indigenous chronicler Felipe Poma de Ayala provides substantial new information on the economic use of the calendar; and yet another indigenous chronicler, Juan de Santa Cruz, refers to the mythological data pertaining to it. The description given in 1653 by Bernabé Cobo, the last chronicler, is probably the most faithful to those of Polo and Molina.

Polo and Molina's Interpretations. Although they themselves do not seem to have grasped the calendrical problem completely, Polo and Molina give us the best evidence with which to evaluate the character of the months. Polo, for example, tells us, "[The Inca] divided the year into twelve months by the moons, and the other days that remained were added to the [different] moons themselves." Polo claims to be speaking of synodical months, that is, those that mark the period between new moons in a sequence independent from the solar year; nonetheless, he says that the eleven days that these twelve months are short of a year were added to the individual months. If he is right on this last point, we can assume that the Inca calendar had solar months, each thirty or thirty-one days long, bearing no connection to the phases of the moon. Polo refers to certain monthly observations of sunrises and sunsets that reinforce this claim. When considered together with important information from Molina, Polo's critical data underscores the fact that the Inca calendar included synodical, as well as solar, months.

According to Molina (1574), the Inca year began with the lunar month marked by the June solstice; this month started with the first new moon after the middle of May. Molina, however, was still using the Julian calendar; his "middle of May" is thus equivalent to 25 May in the Gregorian calendar, which was not introduced to Cuzco until ten years after Molina wrote his account. Accordingly, any month beginning with a new moon after 25 may would include the date of the June solstice, 21 June (Zuidema, 1982a).

Molina then describes the subsequent lunar months, stressing in particular the observations of a new moon and full moon in the fourth month. This was the month in which crops were planted and all women, including the queen, celebrated the moon. Molina then comes to the seventh month, Capac Raymi ("royal feast"), during which noble boys were initiated into manhood. During the eighth month, Capac Raymi Camay Quilla ("royal feast, moon of Camay"), rituals were dedicated to the rains, which would subside in the months to come. Molina's section on the seventh month has a day-to-day account of its ritual events but makes no reference to the moon; the eighth month, however, is described solely in terms of the lunar cycle.

Polo says that Capac Raymi originally began in January but was later moved back to December, the month "when the Sun reaches the last point on its road towards the South pole." Whatever historical information he thought could be derived from this statement, the most satisfactory reading in calendrical terms would be that Capac Raymi ended on the December solstice itself and that Camay Quilla began thereafter. Molina's description of ritual held at the end of Capac Raymi also seems to imply the same conclusion. But if both Polo and Molina were right about the lunar character of the months, then it is possible that a given Capac Raymi may not have included the December solstice at all, for the month of Inti Raymi could have begun just after 25 May (there are 211 days from 25 May to 22 December;

seven synodical months have only 206). From these data alone we cannot determine exactly how the Inca solved this calendrical discrepancy but we can conclude that they were aware of it and had probably devised a solution.

Later chroniclers, including modern writers, did not take into account Molina and Polo's critical data, although they sometimes opted for either lunar or solar months. Thus Clements R. Markharm (1910) interprets the calendar as consisting of solar months; the first month, he says, starts on the June solstice. John Howland Rowe, on the other hand, in his influential article "Inca Culture at the Time of the Spanish Conquest" (1944) chooses—on the authority of Polo, he claims—lunar months. Later studies on Inca culture generally follow Rowe's example. These accounts differ by as much as two months in their assessment of the location in the calendar of a particular month, making the relationship between specific ritual and seasonal activities difficult to understand.

Archaeoastronomy at Coricancha. The calendrical problem cannot be resolved on the basis of Molina and Polo's data alone. Fortunately, research on the alignment of certain Inca buildings (Zuidema, 1982a; Aveni, 1981; Urton and Aveni, 1983; Urton, 1981; Ziolkowski and Sadowski, 1984) enables us to evaluate additional types of calendrical and astronomical data. I will mention here the data based on the architecture of the Coricancha ("golden enclosure")—properly known as the Temple of the Sun—and on the rituals and myths associated with it. Located in the center of Cuzco, the Coricancha included four one-room buildings that served as temples, each facing the other two by two. The more important buildings were said to face the rising sun during the June solstice. But exact measurements by Anthony F. Aveni and myself revealed that the temples face the point on the horizon at which the sun rises on 25 May. This alignment not only supports the validity of Molina's data regarding when the Inca year began but also helps us interpret other significant information. For example, in exactly the same direction of the sunrise, but just beyond the horizon, is a legendary place called Susurpuquio, well known for its important role in Inca mythology. It was here that Pachacuti Inca, the king who set the Inca on the road to conquest, had met his father, the sun god, who predicted that he and his people would share a future filled with military success. The direction toward Susurpuquio coincides closely with that of the rise of the Pleiades, the "mother" of all stars. The reappearance of the Pleiades in early June, after they had disappeared from the southern sky for some fifty days, generally marked the beginning of the year for people in central and northern Peru. In Cuzco, the full moon of the month that included the June solstice would have occurred after the Pleiades first rose in the morning sky. The Inca data on the Pleiades, the sun, and the moon replicate in detail the more general Andean concepts of celestial, calendrical, and social order established in relation to the Pleiades; we see here the Inca debt to the Andean cultures that preceded them.

Calendrical Social Division. Another way to further our understanding of the Inca calendar is to analyze the integration that obtained between the calendar and the empire's political hierarchy and its territorial organization. Betanzos cites this integration but gives no technical details on it. An anonymous, but rather early and well-informed, chronicler mentions how Pachacuti Inca, the king who reorganized Cuzco, divided the population of the Cuzco Valley into twelve groups. His purpose was to make each group take "account of its own month, adopting the name and surname of that lunar month, and of what it had to carry out in its month; and it was obliged to come out to the plaza on the first day of its month by playing trumpets and by shouting, so that it was known to everybody" (my translation, from Maúrtua, vol. 8, 1908). Whereas his father had brought order to the observance of lunar months, Pachacuti Inca erected pillars on the horizon from which the sun could be observed. This was an attempt to integrate the months into an account of the solar year.

The Ceque Calendar. Based on original information from Polo, Cobo describes a similar problem with the calendar and establishes the close link between customs of each Cuzco group and astronomical observations. His description is based on an important Andean political concept, which expresses the visual and directional relationship between the political divisions and their political and ritual center. For this purpose the Inca employed a system of forty-two "directions" called *ceques* ("lines").

The *ceques* were imaginary lines that radiated from Coricancha to points on the horizon. They were distributed in groups of three over four quarters of the territory; in one quarter, however, fifteen directions, that is, fourteen *ceques* (in this case, two *ceques* were taken together as one), were used. The twelve political divisions of Cuzco were individually associated not only with a different group of three *ceques* but also with one particular *ceque* in each group. Each *ceque* linked the division with the location of the land in the valley that it had been given by Pachacuti Inca. Lands in the fourth quarter were also divided between only three divisions; we notice that in this quarter the fourteen *ceques* were also rebundled into three groups of *ceques* (which had four, four, and six ceques, respectively).

Each of the twelve political divisions had an important ritual obligation to bring offerings to a cultic place on the horizon. The sun would then arrive at this place, either at sunset or sunrise, sometime during its annual journey. These twelve places on the horizon were called *sayhuas*; two extra ones, called *sucancas*, were necessary to comply with astronomical observations. The *ceque* system used the whole horizon, although the sun rises and sets in only part of it. Therefore a *sayhua* or *sucanca* was not necessarily located along a *ceque* that stretched between the horizon and the land of the political division that was in charge of its cult. People first worshiped a series of cultic places, called *huacas*, that were located along the three *ceques* associated with their division. They would then turn to the corresponding *sayhuas*, located in another direction, and offer the remains of whatever had been served to the *huacas*.

Cobo lists the *huacas* that were served before the *sayhuas* and *sucancas*. If this list is complete (328 *huacas*), as it indeed appears to be, then it allows us to suggest various calendrical consequences. Although it would not be appropriate here to carry out a technical analysis of Cobo's list, certain general characteristics of such a *ceque* calendar can be proposed.

One observation of the sun was made along a *ceque* radiating from the Temple of the Sun: the one toward sunrise on 25 May. Perhaps one other solar observation was made along a *ceque* in the opposite direction. But all other solar observations were done from higher places just outside town. Based on our data on stars and certain *huacas* in the *ceque* system, we believe that all risings and settings of stars were observed from the Temple of the Sun. In contrast to the *sayhuas*—upright, man-made stone pillars that were used for observing the sun—the *huacas* were mostly natural topographical features whose worship was part of a cult to the earth. The rather irregular numerical distribution of the *huacas* over the *ceques* and groups of three *ceques* seems to be conditioned by their calendrical use. The number of *huacas*—on *ceques*, on groups of *ceques*, and in each of the quarters—reveals that the Inca were concerned with bringing in line the worship of the moon during its full and new phases (these phases occur every twenty-nine and one-half days) with a cult of the sun (the sun is the cause of the moon's phases), as well as with a cult of the stars (against which the moon shifts its position every night). The year can thus be divided into twelve solar months of thirty or thirty-one days each, while the moon will reach the same position among the stars every twenty-seven and one-third nights. Rituals during full and new moons carried out a balancing act between these two cycles related to the sun and the stars; one cycle occurred during the day and the other at night, while the moon can be observed both day and night.

Myths and Legends. Irrespective, however, of where a technical analysis of the *ceque* calendar leads us, the data given by the anonymous chronicler and by Polo and Cobo allow us to integrate Inca ideas of time and space with their calendrical rituals, legendary history, and myths. Each political division carried out rituals during the particular month after which it was named; we can assume, therefore, that each group's ideas about its function in society, its past, and its origin myths are relevant for an understanding of its rituals. Each group worshiped its own mythical ancestor (in the form of a mummy). Influenced by certain ideas of hierarchical order, the Inca integrated these ancestors into the legendary history of their royal dynasty. This line of thought explains why ten of the twelve political divisions were linked genealogically to the dynasty and were called *panacas* (collateral lines of descent from the royal family). The remaining two divisions represented the autochthonous population of the valley of Cuzco, which had been conquered by the Inca.

Specific myths about *panacas* and former kings should help us interpret calendrical rituals. The anonymous chronicler gives us one clue on how to proceed. He claims that each division—that is, each *panaca*—took its name from its particular month. Thus we can argue that the highest-ranked *panaca*, called *capac ayllu*, was in charge of the initiation rituals of noble youths, who were also called *capac churi* ("royal sons"). These rituals occurred during the month of Capac Raymi, which ended on the December solstice. Another *panaca*, called *aucailli* (the "victory song" that was chanted at harvest time), implying that its rituals were conducted in April. But these examples seem to be more exceptions to than confirmations of the rule, and only one chronicler (Murua) relates a myth explicitly linking two political divisions to certain months of the year and their rituals (Zuidema, 1982b).

What makes the following myth interesting is the relationship it establishes between dynastic legends and myths in Inca culture. Pachacuti Inca—who appears in the myth as the son of the first mythical founder of the royal dynasty—establishes a pact with a giant. During a month of heavy rains, the giant comes down on the rushing waters of a river some thirty kilometers from Cuzco. As the rains threaten to destroy the city, Pachacuti, who is characterized in this myth as a brash young warrior, persuades the giant to retreat, and he himself turns to stone. According to the myth, it is because of this pact with the giant that the Inca celebrated Capac Raymi in December. A sequel to the myth deals with the heroic feats of a son of Pachacuti Inca, whose conquests and marriage explain why the Inca celebrated their feast of planting (normally assigned to the month of September, but here to 1 October).

Other, more legendary versions of the first myth convert Pachacuti Inca into the ninth king of the dynasty and the giant into his father, Viracocha Inca; it is these conversions that allow us to relate their *panacas* to specific months. These versions present Pachacuti Inca as the reorganizer of the city, its political system, and its calendar. Both kings are seen as historical persons, but their mythical aspects crystallize them into deities in their own right: they become the thunder god, worshiped by Pachacuti Inca as his personal god, and Viracocha, the god whom the Spanish misinterpreted as the Inca creator god. Viracocha Inca, the king, was thought to be the ancestor of the high priests of Cuzco. It may be suggested here that the giant in the myth should be associated with the society's concerns during the month of March. This was the month in which the priests of the Sun carried out rituals intended to curtail the rains and to prepare for the forthcoming dry season and harvest; they also directed the building of dams in mountain lakes to store irrigation water for use during the dry season.

No dynastic legends like those found at Cuzco were recorded for central Peru by the Spanish chroniclers, who do, however, relate stories of battles, similar to that between Pachacuti and the giant, that were fought between the thunder god and a primordial deity in the times before a great flood.

The story of Pachacuti Inca functioned on two different temporal levels in Cuzco: as a myth that was related to the yearly calendar and as a dynastic legend. It should be observed, therefore, that the temporal sequence was not the same in both cases. In the myth, the giant is associated with a calendrical concern (in March) that followed the one associated with Pachacuti Inca (in December). In the dynasty, Viracocha Inca is the father of Pachacuti Inca. Dynastic interest established a kind of causal link between the legendary versions of the stories told about succeeding kings. But the myths, as seasonal versions of the same stories, did not follow the same temporal sequence.

Here it is probably more the calendrical rituals that, in terms of a closed annual cycle, can bring unity into Inca thought, integrating the cosmological and political aspects of their society. On the basis of the data on Inca months in the chronicles, Henrique Urbano has evaluated the dialectical relationships between the gods Viracocha and Inti (Sun), who symbolize the opposing values of water and fire, respectively. Both are associated with animal symbols: Viracocha with the *amaru* ("serpent"), which is related to farming and the fertility of the earth, and Inti with the *guaman* ("falcon") and *puma* ("mountain lion"), which both represent warfare. In this occurrence, Inti is emblematic of society and of the inside, while Viracocha symbolizes nature and the outside.

Ritual and the Inca Calendar. The analytical value of the data available allows us to study various other aspects of the Andean calendar. One aspect, that of human sacrifice, was of capital importance in the Inca state, establishing political alliances and hierarchical relationships between peoples brought under imperial rule. Victims from all parts of the empire were brought to Cuzco, either to be sacrificed there or to be sent elsewhere to be sacrificed. In journeying to and from Cuzco, they traveled along routes that were as straight as possible and that, like the lines radiating from Cuzco, were called *ceques*. The data suggest that the system of human sacrifices was integrated into the calendar. Various kinds of animals were sacrificed according to the particular occasion; they were eaten or burned, and their blood was also used. Furthermore, ashes, including those of textiles and other products, were saved so that they could be thrown into rivers at appropriate times of the year.

The most important sacrifices of all, however, were those of llamas. These animals were used for various ritual purposes according to their variety (alpaca, llama, guanaco, vicuña), color, age, and sex. The system of llama sacrifice can be reconstructed (Zuidema and Urton, 1976). Iconographic evidence from the Huari and Tiahuanaco (1–1000 CE) cultures demonstrates how deeply rooted llama sacrifices were in Andean society.

Another important aspect of Andean culture is that of divination, studied by E.-J. de Durand (1968). However, the numerous data relating to its importance for the calendar have yet to be coordinated.

Conclusion. The Andean calendar as an exact numerical system for computing days in the year did not survive the onslaught of Western civilization. Many rituals and calendrical customs were integrated, however, into the Catholic calendar; many scholars have reported on this syncretism (Urbano, 1974; Poole, 1984). Their studies, as well as the data from numerous monographs on present-day Andean societies, are extremely valuable in helping us to understand the symbolic values of pre-Conquest rituals. Also, the knowledge of astronomy found among present-day Andean peoples has its principal roots in pre-Conquest culture, notwithstanding the fact that their ancestors were able to integrate Spanish learned and popular notions about the sky and weather into their own systems (Urton, 1981).

The amount of ethnohistorical data that is available for reconstruction of the Inca and other Andean calendars is broader and deeper than had previously been assumed. In Peru, indigenous calendrical notions did not have the overwhelming impact on the Spaniards as they had in Mexico. Interestingly, it is those data that did not seem important to the Spaniards—that did not threaten their missionary and political interests and that lost their significance in colonial society, although they nevertheless happened to be reported—that are the most helpful in understanding pre-Conquest Andean culture and its calendar.

[*See also* Ethnoastronomy.]

BIBLIOGRAPHY

Aveni, Anthony F. "Horizon Astronomy in Incaic Cuzco." In *Archaeoastronomy in the Americas,* edited by Ray A. Williamson, pp. 305–318. Los Altos, Calif., 1981.

Durand, E.-J. de. "Aperçu sur les présages et la divination de l'ancien Pérou." In *La divination,* edited by André Caquot and Marcel Leibovici, pp. 1–67. Paris, 1968.

Maúrtua, Victor M. *Juicio de límites entre el Perú y Bolivia.* Lima, 1908. Volume 8 contains the anonymous "Discurso de la sucesión y gobierno de los Yngas."

Molina, Cristóbal de. *Ritos y fábulas de los Incas* (1574). Buenos Aires, 1947.

Poole, Deborah A. "Ritual-Economic Calendars in Paruro: The Structure of Representation in Andean Ethnography." Ph.D. diss., University of Illinois, Urbana, 1984.

Rowe, John Howland. "Inca Culture at the Time of the Spanish Conquest." In *Handbook of South American Indians,* edited by Julian H. Steward, vol. 2, pp. 183–330. Washington, D.C., 1946.

Urbano, Henrique. "La representación andina del tiempo y del espacio en la fiesta." *Allpanchis Phuturinqua* (Cuzco) 7 (1974): 9–10.

Urton, Gary. *At the Crossroads of the Earth and Sky: An Andean Cosmology.* Austin, 1981.

Urton, Gary, and Anthony F. Aveni. "Archaeoastronomical Fieldwork on the Coast of Peru." In *Calendars in Mesoamerica and Peru,* edited by Anthony F. Aveni and Gordon Brotherston. Oxford, 1983.

Ziolkowski, M. S., and R. M. Sadowski. "Informe acerca de las investigaciones arqueo-astronómicas en el area central de Ingapirca (Ecuador)." *Revista española de antropología americana* 15 (1984): 103–125.

Zuidema, R. Tom. "Inca Observations of the Solar and Lunar Passages through Zenith and Anti-Zenith at Cuzco." In *Archaeoastronomy in the Americas,* edited by Ray A. Williamson, pp. 319–342. Los Altos, Calif., 1981.

Zuidema, R. Tom. "Catachillay: The Role of the Pleiades and of the Southern Cross and α and β Centauri in the Calendar of the Incas." In *Ethnoastronomy and Archaeoastronomy in the American Tropics,* edited by Anthony F. Aveni and Gary Urton, pp. 203–220. New York, 1982 (cited as 1982a in the text).

Zuidema, R. Tom. "The Sidereal Lunar Calendar of the Incas." In *Archaeoastronomy in the New World,* edited by Anthony F. Aveni, pp. 59–107. Cambridge, 1982 (cited as 1982b in the text).

Zuidema, R. Tom, and Gary Urton. "La Constelación de la Llama en los Andes Peruanos." *Allpanchis Phuturinqua* (Cuzco) 9 (1976): 59–119.

R. Tom Zuidema

CALIPHATE. The office of "successor" to the prophet Muḥammad as the leader of the Muslim community is a uniquely Islamic institution. Hence the anglicization *caliphate* is preferable to inadequate translations of the term *khilāfah.* (This article will not address the concept of *khilāfah* in Islamic mysticism.)

Upon Muḥammad's death in AH 11/632 CE there was in existence a self-governing, powerful Islamic community, or *ummah.* It had been shaped by the Prophet in conformity with the revelations he had received, and by the end of his life, his temporal as well as his spiritual authority was unassailable: he was the governor of the *ummah,* an arbitrator of disputes within it, the commander of its military forces, and its principal strategist. He had deputized others as his representatives to distant tribes and regions. The term *khalīfah* in the pre-Islamic sense of "deputy" was apparently used in reference to these assignees.

To the *ummah* the Prophet's death was a shocking, even inconceivable event. The Muslims were suddenly bereft of divine guidance, the source of Muḥammad's charismatic authority. Yet they were sufficiently imbued with the Islamic vision to persevere in efforts to shape the ideal society embodied in that moral imperative.

But who was to lead this society? What was to be his authority? The caliphate, the expression of the temporal leadership of all Muslims conceived as a single community, was the institutional answer. It had emerged *ad hoc,* however, in response to a crisis. Evolving practice framed theoretical constructions, especially in the absence of any agreed Qur'anic foundation. Hence the conduct of those holding the office, the caliphs, elicited sharp and continuing controversy over not only individual moral qualitites but also the character of the institution itself.

The forces at work in this controversy may be divided for the purposes of analysis into Islamic theories of the caliphate and historical influences on the institution.

Classical Theories of the Caliphate. The majoritarian, Sunnī view of the origins of the caliphate is that Muḥammad left no instructions for the future leadership of the *ummah.* Yet on his death the community desperately required an acknowledged leader, since all the latent rivalries that the prophetic message had overwhelmed reemerged in tribal factionalism. The innermost core of the Muslims responded by acclaiming as their leader one of the earliest of their number and certainly among the most prestigious, Abū Bakr (r. 632–634). Whether he was actually proclaimed *khalīfat rasūl Allāh* ("caliph of the messenger of God") is unclear, but all Sunnīs regard him as the first caliph. His role was to lead the *ummah* in peace and in war as the Prophet had done, and to lead the ritual prayers and conduct the pilgrimage, both of which duties he had previously performed on Muḥammad's behalf. Absent from this formulation was the prophetic role that had clothed Muḥammad's acts with nigh impeccable authority. Theoretically, a divinely guided community of Muslims selected the early Sunnī caliphs, while its act of acclamation, the *bay'ah,* constituted an elective ideal that deprecated all subsequent dynasticism.

Evolved Sunnī theory required that a caliph be an adult male from the Quraysh, the leading tribe of Mecca. Soundness of mind and body, knowledge of the religion, piety, and probity are frequently listed among Sunnī criteria. Caliphal preogatives were to lead the prayer, to be recognized in the Friday sermon as the leader of all Muslims, to coin money, to command the army, and to receive on behalf of the *ummah* a fifth of all booty. Later, the Abbasid caliphs (750–1258) arrogated to themselves the right to wear the presumed mantle of the Prophet, a sacred relic in their possession.

Sunnīs generally describe the caliph's duties as follows: to defend the domain of Islam and to extend it if possible, to uphold the *sharī'ah,* the prescribed conduct for a Muslim, to ensure law and order so that Muslims might observe the *sharī'ah* in peace and security, to collect canonical taxes, and generally to administer the *ummah* in consultation with selected counselors.

The Shī'ī conception of the caliphate differs from the Sunnī in the manner of origination and the consequences flowing therefrom. Out of certain verses of the Qur'ān and from selected *ḥadīth* (reports of the Prophet's words or deeds), the Shī'ah adduce that Muḥammad had indeed chosen a successor: his first cousin, son-in-law, and early convert, 'Ali ibn Abī Ṭālib. According to the Shī'ah, a conspiracy among the companions of the Prophet denied 'Alī his rightful position, plunging the community into error the instant Muḥammad died. That the prophet had himself selected 'Alī establishes to Shī'ī satisfaction a leadership of far greater charismatic authority than the Sunnī version, a leadership that for most of the Shī'ah grew to incorporate impeccability and infallible interpretation of scripture.

'Alī did become the fourth caliph, the last of the so-called Rāshidūn or "rightly guided" caliphs, but his designation by the assassins of his predecessor, 'Uthmān ibn 'Affān (644–656) of the clan of Umayyah, precipitated a civil war that rent forever the fabric of the community. When 'Alī was killed in 661, the caliphate passed to the Umayyads (661–750). The Shī'ah would thereafter cleave to the view that only the 'Alids, 'Alī's progeny, could claim the caliphate; their claim alone was divinely sanctioned. Yet the inability of the Shī'ah ever to agree on a particular candidate among 'Alī's descendants condemned their movement to martyrdom, factionalism, and futility.

The conflict between 'Alī and the Umayyads spawned a third interpretation of the caliphate, that of the Khārijīs. In the view of these numerically few but very active dissidents, hostile to both parties following the civil war, the caliph was liable for deposition should he deviate an iota from Muḥammad's practice. The Khārijīs thus depreciated the office to no better than a tribal chieftainship. Arab nomadic groups were, in fact, the milieu from which they drew their support.

Historical Influences on the Caliphate. The evolution of the caliphate reflects in microcosm the forces molding Islamic civilization. Foremost of these was the Islamic moral imperative, expressed in the Qur'ān and the *sunnah,* or custom, of the Prophet. However visionary and inspirational these Islamic teachings were, they offered little specific guidance on the shape of Islamic leadership, principally the prophetic model and a framework of moral principles. But various non-Islamic influences heavily warped these Islamic precepts.

In the first Islamic century Arab tribalism was a continuing challenge to the developing caliphate. Inherited and/or acquired prestige, directly linked to lineage, constituted the basis of Arab leadership concepts. Traditionally power was closely associated with the numerical strength and past reputation of the lineage. Early Muslim caliphs lacked such esteem; only 'Uthmān had both tribal and Islamic prestige. His well-intentioned effort to use tribalism as well as Islamic prestige to enhance the caliph's authority was a major cause of his downfall. Mutual hostilities among the tribes plagued the early Muslim community: the Umayyads were constrained to form tribal marriage alliances to solidify their authority, but rising criticism of their reliance on Arab social custom was a crucial element in the dynasty's overthrow.

The later Umayyads and the early Abbasid dynasty were deeply affected by the tradition of imperial authority in the lands they had conquered. Its advocates, usually newly converted scribes, envisaged a rigidly hierarchical society of privileged rulers and taxpaying ruled, with the caliph as supreme arbiter in all matters. The Abbasid caliphs, therefore, withdrew within a royal city, appeared in public only on ceremonial occasions, ruled despotically and pursued a lifestyle greatly at variance with the Islamic values expressed in the Qur'ān and *sunnah*.

The Abbasids never exclusively adopted their imperial tradition inherited largely from the Sasanid Persians. They were acutely conscious of having acquired power by criticizing the alleged impiety of the Umayyads, so they patronized the *'ulamā'* (religious scholars) as well as poets, musicians, and wine merchants. Even the Islamic aspects of the caliphate, however, succumbed to imperial majesty. Assuming charismatic throne-names, the Abbasids, following the later Umayyads, asserted that their authority derived directly from God, not from Muḥammad and certainly not from the *ummah*. If most of the pious shunned their patronage, still it was during the early Abbasid caliphate that Islamic civilization attained its full grandeur.

By the middle of the tenth century, however, the caliph was a virtual prisoner in his palace, his authority and his majesty evaporated. Between 945 and 1055 the Buyids, tribesmen from Iran professing Shiism, ruled the caliphal capital of Baghdad yet retained the Sunnī caliphate, perhaps recognizing that a pliant puppet symbolizing the unity of Islam was politically more useful to them than a Shī'ī caliph demanding at least their respect. Furthermore, the Buyids refused to recognize the Shī'ī Fatimid caliphate that had emerged in North Africa in 909 and was preparing to advance eastward to establish itself in Cairo (969) with the hegemony of the Muslim world as its manifest goal. As an extremist Shī'ī dynasty, the Fatimids were a menace to both Sunnī and moderate Shī'ī Muslims.

Such a threatening Shī'ī presence in North Africa evoked a response from the remnant of the Umayyad dynasty in Spain (755–1031). Heretofore content with lesser titles despite nonrecognition of their Abbasid successors, the Spanish Umayyads now claimed the caliphate in 929 as a rallying point for nearby Sunnīs. The simultaneous existence of two Sunnī caliphs presented a challenge to those religious scholars bent on accommodating their political theory to the actual historical process. Abū Manṣūr 'Abd al-Qāhir al-Baghdādī (d. 1027), for example, argued that if an ocean should separate the *ummah* into two distant parts, a second caliph was unfortunately justifiable. This view was firmly rejected, however, by the jurist Abū al-Ḥasan al-Māwardī (d. 1058), who would condone no attenuation of the caliphal prerogatives.

Rescue, if it can be so characterized, came in the form of the Seljuk Turks, tribesmen from Central Asia who styled themselves champions of Sunnism while continuing to dominate the caliph. In the eleventh century they reversed the tide of political Shiism, yet in their train came a new influence damaging to the concept of the caliphate: visions of world domination nurtured among pastoralists of the broad Asian steppes. Incipient with the Seljuks, the view reached full force among the pagan Mongols, who would suffer no rival, however moribund, to a Mongol khanate destined to rule the earth. Their assault on Baghdad in 1258 extinguished the classical caliphate.

Although they soon became Muslim, those Mongols who ruled in Islamic lands and the Turco-Mongol dynasties that succeeded them gave little heed to the caliphate. They claimed to rule by divine right and garnished their own tradition with the Persian concepts of a functionally hierarchical society. Islamic scholarship adjusted, however reluctantly, to this new reality: henceforth the *'ulamā'*, claiming to be the guardians of the *sharī'ah*, conferred the title of *khalīfat Allāh* ("deputy of God") upon any ruler who upheld that body of sacred law and ruled righteously. The once-exalted title became one of many with which Muslim rulers of succeeding centuries adorned their chancery documents.

The Mamluk sultans of Egypt, however, adopted an alleged scion of the Abbasid house as legitimator of their oligarchic rule, seemingly a residual authority during the tension-laden interlude between the death of one ruler and the consolidation of his successor. Until 1500, Indian kings used to seek investiture documents from this "shadow caliph" to bolster their tenuous legitimacy. The Ottoman conqueror of Egypt, Yavuz Sultan Selim, then took this putative Abbasid caliph to Istanbul in 1517, an event subsequently exploited by Ottoman sultans of the nineteenth century to substantiate their own caliphal claims.

By the late nineteenth century the force of European imperialism had sparked a revival of the caliphate in a new form that engendered as much controversy among Muslims as had the classical version. The Ottoman sultan, ruling a sprawling empire threatened by European powers, sought to elevate his prestige and retain a link to his lost Muslim subjects by recasting the caliphate into a spiritual office. This device appealed to Muslims under colonial rule, such as in India, tsarist Russia, the Malay Peninsula, and the Indonesian archipelago. Even in British-occupied Egypt it elicited a favorable response. But within the Ottoman empire, non-Muslim nationalists struggling for independence regarded the revived concept of the caliphate as an instrument to marshal Muslim support for their suppression. By the eve of the First World War this view was shared even by some Muslim Arabs who decried the Ottoman caliphate as a sham lacking the slightest trace of a Quraysh pedigree. Both Islamic reformers and Muslim nationalists reviled the Ottoman sultan/caliph and, citing classical scholars to support their contention, characterized the Rāshidūn as the only true caliphs.

In retrospect, it is not surprising that the most secular of the nationalist movements in Muslim countries, the Turkish, should have abolished the Ottoman caliphate in 1924; at the time it came as a shock to the entire Muslim world. The Indian Khilafat Conference (1919–1933), advocating self-rule for Indian Muslims because they owed spiritual allegiance to the caliph, found its cause hopelessly undercut. Muslims elsewhere demanding independence from colonialism had to revise their strategy once they overcame their disappointment.

In the newly independent Arab world a contest for the caliphate emerged, but the effort to revive the "true" caliphate was short-lived. Three conferences over a brief span (1926–1931) broke up in disarray. It was soon apparent that new nation-states opposed the restoration of such a vaguely defined but potentially influential institution unless their own governments could control it.

The quickened religious pulse in the Islamic world today has evoked no noticeable inclination to revive the concept of the caliphate. It would seem that however much Muslims may desire a greater sense of unity, any expression of such sentiment is unlikely to assume the caliphal form. [*See also* Imamate; Ummah; *and* Modernism, *article on* Islamic Modernism.]

BIBLIOGRAPHY

Historical Surveys. In addition to Dominique Sourdel's comprehensive article "Khalīfa" (and its references) in *The Encyclopaedia of Islam,* new ed. (Leiden, 1960–), the only full treatment of the concept of the caliphate and its role in Islamic history is the book by Thomas W. Arnold, *The Caliphate,* the second edition of which, with an additional chapter by Sylvia G. Haim, is to be preferred (Oxford, 1965). Its heavy emphasis on classical Sunnī texts may be leavened by the insights and balance of Marshall G. S. Hodgson throughout the three volumes of his *The Venture of Islam* (Chicago, 1974). Al-Māwardī's exposition of the Sunnī caliphate is ably assessed by H. A. R. Gibb in an article, "Al-Mawardi's Theory of the Caliphate," in his *Studies on the Civilization of Islam,* edited by Stanford J. Shaw and William R. Polk (Boston, 1962). The chapter "Caliphate and Sultanate," in the pioneering *Islamic Society and the West,* vol. 1, part 1, by Gibb with Harold Bowen (Oxford, 1950), unduly reflects the views of Sunnī theoreticians of the caliphate.

Interpretive Works. Most valuable for its able exposition of the early caliphate against the background of Arab culture is H. M. T. Nagel's article, "Some Considerations concerning the Pre-Islamic and the Islamic Foundations of the Authority of the Caliphate," in *Studies on the First Century of Islamic Society,* edited by G. H. A. Juynboll (Carbondale, Ill., 1982), pp. 177–197.

The growth of Persian influences on Islamic ruling institutions is best found in the two-part article by Ann K. S. Lambton, "Quis custodiet custodes? Some Reflections on the Persian Theory of Government," *Studia Islamica* 5 (1956): 125–148; 6 (1956): 125–146. She continues her analysis into the Turko-Iranian period, but her work should be supplemented by Osman Turan's article "The Ideal of World Domination among the Medieval Turks," *Studia Islamica* 4 (1955): 77–90. The chapter "The Mongols, the Turks and the Muslim Polity" in Bernard Lewis's *Islam in History: Ideas, Men and Events in the Middle East* (London, 1973) puts Turan's thesis in a broader perspective.

Intellectual aspects of the recent phase of the history of the caliphate are perhaps best dealt with in Albert Hourani's *Arabic Thought in the Liberal Age, 1789–1939,* 2d ed. (Cambridge, 1983). The Turkish perspective is outlined in the analytical chapters of Bernard Lewis's *The Emergence of Modern Turkey,* 2d ed. (Oxford, 1968), while the abolition of the caliphate and the reaction to it in the Arab world is covered in detail in Arnold Toynbee's "The Islamic World since the Peace Settlement," in the *Royal Institute of International Affairs, Survey of International Affairs, 1925,* vol. 1 (Oxford, 1927).

HERBERT L. BODMAN, JR.

CALLIGRAPHY.

[*This entry comprises four articles that survey important examples of the religious functions of handwriting:*

An Overview
Chinese and Japanese Calligraphy
Hebrew Micrography
Islamic Calligraphy

For related discussion, see Alphabets.]

An Overview

On cave walls and rocks, Paleolithic peoples scratched and scrawled signs in the shape of clubs, shields, rays, and the like, the meaning of which we do not know. Presumably they were some kind of shorthand information necessary to mystical, spiritual secrets. Clearly they express an impulse toward the permanence of writing.

Six thousand years ago Egyptians invented hieroglyphics (lit., "sacred carvings"), pictures of things and thoughts so artistic in themselves that they can be enjoyed for how they look aside from any meaning; in short, these can be considered calligraphy, or "beautiful drawing." Hieroglyphics advanced to the point where they conveyed complicated abstractions—*ankh* (life), *onze* (health), *senb* (power), even *ka*, a totem said to be born with humans and to guide them in heaven after death. Secret books of Pyramid Texts, Coffin Texts, and the like, which reported the history of kings and predicted afterlife voyages, were painted on the walls and carved on the sarcophagi of monumental tomb-temples.

Hieroglyphics were recalcitrant to alphabetical reduction, but already by the second millennium BCE Semitic peoples on the eastern edge of the Mediterranean used sign and symbol abbreviations, first for consonants and later for vowels. They inscribed these with reed, metal, or bone styli on papyrus or palm leaves as well as clay or wax tablets. The cuneiform of Assyria, Babylonia, and Persia recorded not only transcendental matters but events of interest to the state. One Hittite clay tablet describes a chariot race; another, the treaty between a king and his Mitanni enemy. Meanwhile the Phoenician traders passed their alphabet to the Greeks. The earliest example of Greek handwriting dates back nearly three thousand years. It is a scrawl on a pottery shard from a vase awarded as a prize in a music or athletic contest in Athens.

As writing became more worldly, alphabetical rather than pictorial, and therefore more cursive and quick, scribes and government clerks appeared with a clear and impersonal handwriting. With the crumbling of authority from imperial Rome that coincided with the rise of the Christian church, native cultures flourished. Writers were mostly monks whose central occupation was to preserve biblical texts, to copy and recopy psalters and missals as an act of devotion. It is here that calligraphy in the West developed as a fine art. When the differentiation between what we know as uppercase and lowercase letters entered the script, monk-artists illumined each capital letter with pictures literally "illustrating" the meaning of the words they transcribed. The first works of writing as art appeared in Merovingian France and in Hiberno-Saxon Ireland and associated continental centers. During the reign of Charlemagne, luxury manuscripts known as the Golden Gospels adorned the words of the evangelists in letters of gold, silver, and royal purple.

The Hebrew script is found on papyri dating from the eighth century BCE, and throughout Jewish history biblical scribes were admired for diligence and accuracy, but the written word was respected more for what it said than for what it looked like. This is also true in India, where Sanskrit literature has had four thousand years of unbroken religious history. There the paramountcy of *gurus* and "sitting near" as a way to receive enlightenment from the voice of the master rather than by individual study or pouring over books prevented calligraphy from developing independently, even though the *devanāgarī* script was poetically called "the writing of the gods."

FIGURE 1. *Japanese Calligraphy*. Name of the First Patriarch, founder of Ch'an Buddhism in China. Written by the Japanese monk Ikkyū (1394–1481).

Today, only in Muslim countries, China, and especially Japan (see figure 1) can calligraphy per se claim a major position in national culture. It is also in those countries that calligraphy's original values as spiritual and moral discipline continue to be venerated even now.

BIBLIOGRAPHY

Johnston, Edward. *Writing and Illuminating and Lettering*. 14th ed. New York, 1925.

Kapr, Albert. *The Art of Lettering: History, Anatomy, and Aesthetics of Roman Letter Forms*. New York, 1983.

Miner, Dorothy et al. *Two Thousand Years of Calligraphy*. New York, 1965.

FAUBION BOWERS

Chinese and Japanese Calligraphy

Four thousand years ago, it is alleged, the Chinese sage Ts'ang Chieh, whose pastime was to observe birds' footprints in the sand and trace their patterns, conceived China's first writing. These were pictographs or stenographic sketches of familiar objects, animals, or birds, still more or less easily recognized. They formed no sentences or concepts, merely incomplete ideas and phrases. In the pre-Confucian, pre-Buddhist China of the Shang dynasty (1766–1122 BCE) such scripts were used to inscribe the shells and bones used for divination. Early writing is next encountered in China during the Chou dynasty (1122–221 BCE) in the stiff, cold, classic, formal ideograms of the "great seal" style *(ta chuan)* that covered ceremonial bronzes with messages of felicity in the afterlife. These vessels, suitable for cooking or wine, were entombed with their masters, who might need such comforts as they journeyed to join their ancestors. "Great seal" was the writing Confucius read and wrote, and it is still used in China and Japan for signature seals (chops) or ornamental inscriptions of a particularly exalted sort.

Following the unification of China in 221 BCE, the first emperor of the Ch'in dynasty simplified and regularized the written language into the "small seal" style *(hsiao chuan)*. Writing continued in use as ceremony and religious observances, but its importance increased enormously in response to the central authority's demand for records, accounts, and the issuance of edicts and orders throughout the provinces. Within a century the "regular" style *(chen shu)* developed and became the standard form still employed today.

Wang Hsi-chih (321–379 CE), China's greatest calligrapher, created a cursive or "running" script *(hsing shu)*. He arrived at this elegant form of speed writing, which reduces the rigid formality and clarity of "regular" style to impressionistic essentials instantly comprehensible to the expert, after studying geese. He saw in their graceful, turning, supple necks precisely the strength and flexibility required of the calligrapher's brush strokes. The result was that another convenience, and yet another level of artful beauty entered writing.

Many Chinese characters are in a sense pictures (pictographs) representing "things" such as sun, moon, tree, or house; others (ideographs) represent "ideas." But by far the majority of all Chinese characters are now recognized as "logographs," that is, as graphs that represent, strictly, neither pictorial image nor brute idea but words, through a complex system of semantic and phonemic constituents that long ago escaped from a purely visual medium of representation. By combining these graphs in an endless variety of ways to make new words and then compounding them with still others, any word or idea can be expressed. For *thunder and lightning*, for example, combine *rain* and *paddy field*. For *cash money*, put the word for *gold* next to that for a guardian *spear*. Modern notions can be incorporated into the language by the same process. For *electricity*, write *thunder and lightning*, add a tail, and make a compound with the word for *feeling*. The system suits China's monosyllabic language perfectly and adapts into Japanese most conveniently. When the Chinese or Japanese regard a character, they at once see a picture, hear a sound, and perceive a meaning.

Unabridged Chinese and Japanese dictionaries list upward of forty thousand characters today. A knowledge of five thousand is sufficient for reading a newspaper. The number of strokes within a single character ranges from one (meaning "one") to thirty-three (composed of three deer, meaning "rough," "rude," or "wild"). Each stroke is either thick or thin, strong or soft, curved or straight, heavy with ink or dry and faint, pushed against the paper or lightly withdrawn from it. A character, regardless of its number of strokes, must occupy the same amount of space within an invisible square, and must be equidistant from all others on the page. Each stroke composing the ideogram must be written in correct order—from top to bottom, left to right, vertical strokes before horizontal ones.

In 405 CE, Wani, a Korean scribe well versed in Chinese classics, was hired by the imperial court of Japan as tutor to the crown prince. Japan had no written language of its own, and it had become increasingly necessary to communicate with its powerful neighbor, the "center of the universe." Within a century China began sending presents to Japan's emperor—images of Lord Buddha, *sūtras* translated into Chinese from the Sanskrit and Pali, and the teachings of Confucius. Scholars arrived from China bringing with them books, music, medicines (tea among them), the craft of calendar making, and the art of divination. And with them also came the "four perfections of calligraphy"—the brush, paper, ink stick, and ink stone.

Calligraphy in Japan is called *shodō*, "way of writing," and is a way of life, a path or pursuit, like *bushidō*, the path of the warrior, *sadō*, the cult of tea, or Shintō, the way of the gods. In the Nara period (710–784 CE) priests began the practice of *shakyō*, the copying over and over of *sūtras*, the Buddha's teachings and commentaries thereon, a custom that continues to this day. A Chinese priest had said, "If you do not understand, write the *sūtra*. Then you will see its inner meaning." Obediently, priests spent lifetimes at this labor in search of enlightenment (which sometimes came in the middle of an ideographic stroke), as penance, and as a

FIGURE 1. *Chinese Calligraphy.* The large characters read "retirement hut" and illustrate the meaning of the accompanying poem, namely, that the path of spiritual enlightenment lies in withdrawal from the world. Written by Ta-hsiu Cheng-nien, 1928.

means of raising temple funds. Spiritual merit accrued not only to the writer but to the beholder and to anyone who purchased the manuscript.

Japan's earliest poems were in Chinese, but gradually the Japanese broke free and began adapting monosyllabic, short, concise, and tonal Chinese to their own spoken language, which is polysyllabic, highly inflected, and periphrastic with affixes for adjectives and prefixes for nouns. In the ninth century the women of the Heian court devised brief cursive signs called *hiragana*, a syllabary that derived from Chinese and, remotely, was probably inspired by the Sanskrit alphabet known in Chinese translation.

At present, calligraphy is held in highest esteem in Japan. Scholars practice *hitsudan*, or communicating with each other by exchanging notes across a table. (They can also communicate with modern Chinese this way without knowing the pronunciation of a single spoken word.) Great calligraphers are paid as much as fifty thousand dollars a word, and specimens of fine writing adorn shopping bags, cigarette boxes, or signs outside a shop window. *Kabuki* actors are applauded for their calligraphy, and an *onnagata* (a player of female roles) will mix a touch of lipstick in his ink to add eroticism to an autograph. *Kakizome*, the first brush writing of the new year, occurs annually on 2 January, and at "calligraphy meets" more than a thousand participants ranging in age from five to sixty gather in the Great Martial Arts Hall of Tokyo to compete for prizes.

Although the typewriter and the fountain pen have removed calligraphy from the daily life of the average Japanese, many men and women practice it as a form of spiritual discipline. As Aoyama San'u, one of the greatest living calligraphers, expresses it, "In calligraphy you see the reality of the person. When you write you cannot lie, retouch, ornament. You are naked before God."

[*See also the biography of Ikkyū Sōjun.*]

BIBLIOGRAPHY

Ch'en Chih-mai. *Chinese Calligraphers and Their Art.* New York, 1966.

Ecke Tsung Yu-ho. *Chinese Calligraphy.* Philadelphia, 1971.

Hisamatsu, Shin'ichi. *Zen and the Fine Arts.* Tokyo, 1971.

Sansom, George B. *Japan: A Short Cultural History* (1931). Rev. ed. New York, 1962.

Sullivan, Michael. *The Three Perfections.* New York, 1980.

Tazawa Yutaka, ed. *Biographical Dictionary of Japanese Art.* Tokyo, 1984.

FAUBION BOWERS

Hebrew Micrography

The patterning of Hebrew texts into ornamental motifs is a medieval art form that bears the modern name of micrography, "minute writing." Within an artistic tradition almost universally consigned to dependency on one dominant culture or another because of its minority status, this distinctive calligraphic device represents one of the most original aspects of Jewish art.

Emergence of the Art. Micrographic decoration can be found on manuscripts from Yemen to Germany, but its historical origins lie in the eastern Mediterranean, during the first few centuries of Muslim rule. The earliest dated example is the Cairo Codex of the Prophets written in Tiberius in 894/5 CE by the renowned scholar Moshe ben Asher. In the manner of near-contemporary Qur'āns, the manuscript contains five "carpet pages" of geometric and floral motifs, but six other full-page compositions are made up of elaborate micrographic patterns; simpler lettered designs are scattered throughout the margins of the text itself, and at the end, the patron's colophon is similarly framed with writing.

In addition to the Cairo Codex of the Prophets, patterned texts appear on at least fifteen other manuscripts and fragments dating from the tenth or eleventh century, all of which are associated with Egypt, although the scribes frequently come from elsewhere in the Muslim empire. Taken together, these early examples reflect quite clearly the dual Judeo-Muslim context that literally shaped the micrographic art. The meeting ground of the two, of course, was the veneration of the word of God, but while the Muslim scribes gave visual expression to this religious stance through the refinement of the letters that made up the divine words, their Jewish counterparts opted instead to fashion words into patterns. And here, the basic conservatism of the micrographic script, which is never regularized or embellished like the Arabic letters of the Qur'ān, may well reflect a reluctance to alter the alphabet that had been used for centuries in the writing of the Torah scroll (a practice carefully regulated in the Talmud).

The words chosen for patterning were drawn from the Bible itself and the *masorah*, the critical apparatus aimed at keeping the biblical text intact through an elaborate system of word counts. Significantly, the Cairo Codex of the Prophets is also the earliest dated Bible with *masorah*—the activities of Masoretes and scribes alike (and Moshe ben Asher was both) were devoted in their respective ways to the preservation of the sacred scripture. On the popular level, these efforts were endowed with mystical and magical significance as well, through deeply rooted notions of letter symbolism and the power of the word (see figure 1).

In fact, it is this last dimension that suggests a concrete source for the convention of micrographic decoration, namely the amulets and charms that were commonly inscribed, in minuscule letters, with the names of God and biblical verses often patterned around magical figures. In the early micrographic Bibles, this amuletic inspiration—and intent—is apparent throughout, from arcane marginal decorations made up of in-text *masorah* to elaborate geometric carpet pages incorporating propitious biblical verses.

Later Developments. Within the Muslim world, micrography spread from the eastern Mediterranean to

FIGURE 1. *Hebrew Micrography.* Introductory page from a Hebrew Bible with Masoretic notes, Spain, dated 1232 (4992 of the Creation). Biblical verses and notes are in the interlacing surrounding the opening prayer. Written by Yisra'el (ben Mosheh?) ben Qisares for Master Elisha'.
SOURCE: Bibliothèque Nationale, Paris, MS Hébreu 25.

Yemen, where it became a highly developed art in the fifteenth century and continued into the seventeenth. The most striking example is a 1469 Pentateuch (British Museum, MS Or. 2348), with a double-page design that fashions Psalm 119 into a Mamluk metalwork pattern of mountains and fish.

Through the Iberian Peninsula the technique reached Europe by the the thirteenth century. Spanish variants on the Near Eastern repertoire include the addition of a framing text in large letters around carpet pages and the outlining of solid decorations with micrographic borders, as well as a few representational images in micrography illustrating the adjacent Bible text. The most elaborate Spanish Bible (Bibliothèque Nationale, Paris, MS Hébreu 1314–1315) opens with eight carpet pages containing the entire biblical text in micrographic interlace.

In Germany and France, Gothic marginalia—grotesques and heraldic motifs—make their way into the micrographic tradition alongside the Near Eastern interlace, while the carpet pages at the beginning and end of the manuscript give way to full-page designs inserted between individual books of the Bible, including floral and animal motifs around the initial word of the biblical text. Full-page illustrations are also formed from micrographic text, as in the representations of Aaron found at the end of the *Book of Exodus* in a 1294/5 Pentateuch (Bibliothèque Nationale, Paris, MS Hébreu 5).

Apart from a revival of decorated marriage contracts *(ketubot)* in seventeenth-century Italy, micrography, like other manuscript arts, declined in the wake of the printed book. But the technique soon reemerged throughout eastern and western Europe in popular engravings and then lithographs, with subjects ranging from *mizraḥ* and *shiviti* designs to indicate the direction of prayer toward Jerusalem to Bible illustrations, rabbi portraits, and postcard views from Palestine, all of which were often executed in an incongruously realistic style. In the late twentieth century, renewed interest in Jewish art has drawn some modern artists back to traditional micrography techniques.

BIBLIOGRAPHY

The most extensive work on Hebrew micrography has been done by Leila Avrin, whose essay "Micrography as Art," published along with Colette Sirat's "La lettre hébraïque et sa signification" as *Études de paléographie hébraïque* (Paris, 1981), contains many illustrations and relevant bibliography. See also Avrin's "The Illustrations of the Moshe ben Asher Codex of 985 C.E." (Ph.D. diss., University of Michigan, Ann Arbor, 1974).

MIRIAM ROSEN

Islamic Calligraphy

Calligraphy occupies the highest rank among the arts of Islam: according to the tradition of the Prophet, the calligrapher, who knows how to pen in beautiful letters the word of God or even a fragment of the Qur'ān, will certainly go to Paradise. The art of calligraphy developed at an early stage of Islamic history, and soon the ungainly characters of the Semitic alphabet were transformed into decorative letters. An angular, hieratic script developed for the preservation of the Qur'ān; although several early styles existed, it is generally called Kūfī or Kufic (from the city of Kufa in Iraq), and in pious tradition certain features of it are ascribed to ʿAlī ibn Abī Ṭālib, considered the patron of calligraphers. Early Kufic lacks the diacritical marks that were added after 685, as were the signs for vocalization (both in color). A cursive hand was also used, as numerous papyri show. This was developed into several styles for chancelery and copying purposes when the use of paper (introduced from China) became common in the Islamic world after 751. Early Kufic Qur'āns are written on vellum with a reed pen; the format of the books is oblong, and only from about the tenth century was the normal book format adapted for Qur'āns, apparently first in the eastern Islamic world. With this change of format, the lettering too changed: the broad, very impressive early Kufic assumed a taller, more graceful stature, and its developed forms are still used for decorative purposes.

The cursive hand was transformed into true calligraphy by the Abbasid vizier Ibn Muqlah (d. 940), who invented the system of measuring the letters by circles and semicircles, with the first letter, alif, becoming the measure for the other twenty-seven letters. As alif is basically a straight vertical line with the numerical value 1 and is used in mystical speculation as a symbol for Allāh (God), the formation of the letters "in the shape of alif" corresponds in a mystical way to the shaping of Adam "in his, God's, form." The rules of Ibn Muqlah were refined by Ibn al-Bawwāb (d. 1032). Along with the circles, the square dots produced by the tip of the reed pen served as measuring units: an alif could be five, seven, or nine points high, and all the other letters had to be formed accordingly. Ṣūfī interpretation saw here the primordial dot from which everything created developed. Cursive writing replaced Kufic first in books and documents (in early days usually written as scroll), then, in the thirteenth century, also in epigraphy, where the angular letters had grown, between 800 and 1250, into multiple forms of floriated, foliated, and plaited Kufic, which became barely legible but formed exquisite geometrical ornaments (see figure 1). In Iran, a "hanging," slanted cursive developed from grammatical

FIGURE 1. *Islamic Calligraphy.* Plaited Kufic inscription reads "Al'aẓmat lillāh" ("Majesty belongs to God"), formed from turquoise-colored bricks inlaid in unglazed bricks. Sırçalı Medresse (1236), Konya, Turkey.

SOURCE: Schimmel (1970), pl. 19c.

exigencies; it was refined according to Ibn Muqlah's rules to become the "bride of Islamic writings," *nasta'līq*, the ideal vehicle for copying Persian, Turkish, and Urdu poetry.

Calligraphy can be exercised on every material: vellum, papyrus, and paper (paper mills are found from Spain to India); it is woven into silk and linen, embroidered on velvet, used in metalwork and wood, on glass and ceramics, on stones and tiles. Brick and tile compositions result in "square" Kufic, where the names of God and the Prophet (and in Iran, ʿAlī) or religious formulas can cover whole walls in geometrical design. Calligraphy on paper (which includes the patterns for the other types of writing) is written with a reed pen; only very rarely—in early days in Central Asia and India—a brush may have been used. The trimming of the pen in distinct angles and the preparation of the various types of ink belong to the arts the calligrapher has to learn, as he has to study the shape of each and every letter for years before becoming a master who is allowed to sign works with his *katabahu*, "has written." Only in North Africa did pupils write whole words immediately, which accounts for the less "calligraphic" quality of the so-called Maghribi style.

Later calligraphers liked to form *tughrās*—originally the elaborate signature or handsign of a ruler at the beginning of a document. Subsequently the word is applied to all kinds of artistic shapes: mirrored sentences, pious formulas in the shape of birds, lions, or other creatures, faces made of sacred names, or harmonically elaborated calligrams of invocations, prayers, or divine names. The imagery of calligraphy permeates Islamic poetry, and the interpretation of letters according to their numerical value and their "mystical" qualities was, and still is, widespread.

BIBLIOGRAPHY

Numerous publications on calligraphy have been issued recently, most of which are devoted to aesthetic rather than historical purposes. A good brief introduction is Yasin H. Safadi's *Islamic Calligraphy* (Boulder, 1979). Martin Lings's *The Qur'anic Art of Calligraphy and Illumination* (London, 1976) is excellent because it dwells upon the religious character of writing. Ernst Kühnel's small but weighty book *Islamische Schriftkunst* (1942; reprint, Graz, 1972) is still very valuable for its all-around approach and interesting examples. I have provided a brief introduction to the subject in *Islamic Calligraphy* (Leiden, 1970) and delved at greater length into the history, the social situation of the calligraphers, and the uses of calligraphy in Sufism and in poetical parlance in *Calligraphy and Islamic Culture* (New York, 1984).

ANNEMARIE SCHIMMEL

CALVERT, GEORGE

CALVERT, GEORGE (1580?–1632), secretary of state and privy councillor under King James I of England; the first Lord Baltimore, principally known for his efforts in advancing religious toleration in an age that regarded pluralism as dangerous.

Calvert's commitment to religious toleration was a reflection of his unsettled religious life. Born into a Roman Catholic family that was troubled periodically for its allegiance to a proscribed church, he lived as a Catholic during the first twelve years of his life. In 1592 his father succumbed to the harassment of the Yorkshire High Commission and certified his conformity to the rites of the Church of England. George Calvert soon conformed and for the next thirty-two years lived as a Protestant.

At about the age of fourteen Calvert matriculated at Trinity College, Oxford, where he studied foreign languages. After earning his bachelor's degree, he spent three years studying municipal law at the Inns of Court. In 1603, while on a continental tour, he came to the attention of secretary of state Robert Cecil, who was in Paris. Employed as one of his many secretaries, Calvert used Cecil's influence to begin a slow but steady climb in the government of James I. He traveled overseas on a number of diplomatic missions. In Ireland he served as a member of a commission investigating the complaints of Irish Roman Catholics. In 1610 Calvert was named one of the clerks of the Privy Council. Later he assisted James in writing a tract refuting the Dutch theologian Conrad Vorstius. Two years after knighting him in 1617, James appointed Calvert as one of the secretaries of state and made him a member of the Privy Council.

During the negotiations to marry heir apparent Prince Charles to the Spanish Infanta, and to cement an alliance between Spain and England, Calvert, as secretary of state, became closely identified with both the Spanish and Roman Catholic causes. Laboring diligently to achieve the king's goal, Calvert reached the pinnacle of his power in 1621 and 1622. However, when the government scuttled the marriage treaties in 1624, Calvert lost favor at court and came under intense pressure to resign his office. During this crisis, he resolved his religious commitments, declaring his intention to live and die a Catholic. He resigned his office, selling it for three thousand pounds. James elevated him to the Irish peerage by creating him baron of Baltimore.

Out of office, Lord Baltimore turned his attention to his Irish estates and to the supervision of his Newfoundland colony, for which he had received a charter in 1621. In 1628 he returned to Newfoundland intending to colonize the region with a religiously diverse population. However, the forbidding climate and the hostility of the French convinced him to abandon his plans of permanent residency in Newfoundland. Baltimore subsequently journeyed to Virginia and, impressed by what he saw there, returned to England in 1630 to secure a charter for a colony along Chesapeake Bay.

Despite the opposition encountered from some of the Protestant settlers in Newfoundland to his policy of religious toleration, the Catholic Baltimore drew upon his own experiences in government and rejected the dominant concept of *cuius regio eius religio*, namely that the local ruler's religion must be the religion of the region. Rather, he sought to found a colony where Catholics and Protestants could work together to achieve an economically viable enterprise. He died in April 1632, shortly before the Maryland Charter passed its final seals. The founding of the colony in 1634 was left to his son Cecil, the second Lord Baltimore.

BIBLIOGRAPHY

There is to date no modern biography of George Calvert. The most thorough biography is Lewis W. Wilhelm's *Sir George Calvert, Baron of Baltimore* (Baltimore, 1884). It must be used cautiously, however, as it contains many errors. The Maryland Historical Society published the first four chapters of James W. Foster's uncompleted biography under the title *George Calvert: The Early Years* (Baltimore, 1983). Calvert's letters, mostly official, are scattered throughout the State Papers in the Public Record Office (London) and in *The Calvert Papers* in the Maryland Historical Society (Baltimore).

For Calvert's conversion to Roman Catholicism, see my short study " 'The Face of a Protestant, and the Heart of a Papist': A Reexamination of Sir George Calvert's Conversion to Roman Catholicism," *Journal of Church and State* 20 (Autumn 1978): 507–531. For his religious problems in his Newfoundland colony, see R. J. Lahey's "The Role of Religion in Lord Baltimore's Colonial Enterprise," *Maryland Historical Magazine* 72 (Winter 1977): 492–511. For the role of religion in the colony founded by his heir, Cecil Calvert, see my articles "Lord Baltimore, Roman Catholics, and Toleration: Religious Policy in Maryland during the Early Catholic Years, 1634–1649," *Catholic Historical Review* 45 (January 1979): 49–75, and " 'With promise of Liberty in Religion': The Catholic Lords Baltimore and Toleration in Seventeenth-Century Maryland, 1634–1692," *Maryland Historical Magazine* 79 (Spring 1984): 21–43.

JOHN D. KRUGLER

CALVIN, JOHN (1509–1564), primary Protestant reformer, biblical scholar, church organizer, and theologian. Also a humanist and linguist, Calvin helped to shape and standardize French language and literary style.

Calvin was reclusive and reticent; hence the only Calvin we know is the public figure. Of his first twenty-five years we know comparatively little. He was born at Noyon (province of Picardy), France, on 10 July 1509, the fourth of six children born to Gérard Cauvin and Jeanne Lefranc. Christened Jean Cauvin, from his university days he used the name Calvin, the latinized form of Cauvin. He spent his first thirteen years in Noyon, benefiting from the rich traditions of this historic episcopal city where his father served as attorney for the cathedral and secretary to the bishop, Charles de Hangest.

Intimately associated as a youth with the de Hangest household, Calvin developed aristocratic tastes and demeanor. Church benefices permitted him to further his education at the University of Paris; he spent nearly eleven years in Paris, participating in the intellectual life both of the university and the large circle of humanist scholars at the court of the king, Francis I.

At the university, preparing for a career in theology, Calvin had completed the master of arts degree when his father had a falling-out with the bishop. The father ordered his son to change to a career in law. Obediently Calvin moved to Orléans, where the best law faculty in France, under the leadership of Pierre de l'Étoile, was located. Though more interested in humanist studies, he completely immersed himself in the law (at Orléans, Bourges, and Paris) and took his doctorate and his licentiate in three years.

In 1531 Calvin's father died excommunicate. The struggle to secure a Christian burial for his father doubtless soured Calvin's relations with the Roman church. But for the moment the effect of his father's death was to permit him to commit himself to the uninterrupted pursuit of humanist studies.

In 1532 Calvin published his first book, a commentary on Seneca's *On Clemency*. Though distinguished for its learning, the book did not win him any acclaim. His days of humanist study in Paris were cut short when, in 1533, his close friend Nicholas Cop, rector of the University of Paris, delivered an address that incorporated ideas of the Lutheran Reformation. Reaction by the theologians at the Sorbonne was strong, and because Calvin had a hand in the composition of the address, he, along with Cop, was forced to flee for his life. Although scholarly opinion differs, it appears that shortly thereafter he underwent the "sudden conversion" he speaks about later. A marked man in France, Calvin spent the rest of his life in exile.

Having turned his considerable talents to the support of the Reformation, in early 1536 Calvin published at Basel the first edition of his epochal *Institutes of the Christian Religion*. Intended as a defense of the French

Protestants to the king of France, it marked Calvin as the foremost mind of Protestantism. The desired life of solitude and study that permitted its composition could never again be Calvin's. In late July of 1536, he happened to stop in the small city of Geneva; there God "thrust him into the fray," as he was to say. Geneva had recently declared for the Protestant faith under the urging of the fiery evangelist Guillaume Farel, one of Calvin's colleagues from his Paris days. Farel, learning of Calvin's presence in the city, sought him out and urged him to join in the work of reform at Geneva. When Calvin refused, Farel thundered that God would punish him for turning his back on that work. The shaken Calvin heard it as the summons of God and agreed to stay. Except for a three-year period of peaceful study and ministry in Strasbourg (1538–1541), Calvin was henceforth associated with the city and republic of Geneva in a stormy ministry designed to bring the city into conformity with the biblical model as he understood it.

Calvin's ideal for Geneva was that church and state work hand in hand to create and govern a utopian society in which the biblical worldview was enforced. But the Genevan state was determined to keep the church under its control. A man of courage and indomitable will, Calvin took up the battle. Armed only with the power of the pulpit and of the church institutions, through persistence, adherence to biblical principles, organizational talents, and moral conviction, he managed to overcome massive resistance and to see most of his ideals realized. Geneva was transformed from a city of ill repute to one in which a strict moral code regulated the lives of all, regardless of rank or class. In spite of the radical harshness of his policies, by the end of his life Calvin was widely respected, even admired, by the Genevans. From an international perspective, Geneva became the model for the emerging Protestant states, a city of refuge for persecuted Protestants, and the so-called "Rome" of Protestantism. Of perhaps capital importance, Calvin's program—alone among the Protestant groups—included both a training center (in the University of Geneva, which he established) and an acceptance of a missionary mandate to export Calvinism throughout the world. Hence Calvinism, or Reformed Protestantism, was the only Protestant group with universalistic designs.

Unquestionably, Calvin was first and foremost a man of ideas, although he effectively blended thought and action. True to his Renaissance humanist orientation, he was interested only in what was useful. All of his ideas are designed for practical application, whether to an individual religious experience or to a specific activity of the church. Further, the rhetorical and pedagogical program of the humanists formed the basis of his thought, and their devotion to original sources determined his methodology. As a theologian he intended only to set forth scriptural teaching. He accommodated ambiguity and contradiction in his theology, for people are both limited in mental capacity and debilitated by sin, hence totally reliant upon the revelation of God in scripture.

For Calvin, the word of God in scripture is generated by the Holy Spirit and, therefore, properly interpreted only by the Holy Spirit. It is, thus, a spiritual message. Hence Calvin should not be viewed as an academic theologian, or as a theologian writing for intellectual purposes. He wrote for the church, for believers; his purpose was to edify, to form the pious mind that would emerge in reverential, grateful worship and adoration of God. He constantly warned his readers not to indulge in idle speculation, not to seek to know anything except what is revealed in the scripture, not to forget that theology is more of the heart than of the head. Consequently, being biblical, practical, and spiritual, his theology was of a different type from that of most of the later Calvinists who wrote for the university audience, for those who regarded theology as the "queen of the sciences" in the world of ideas.

The principal source for Calvin's thought is, of course, the *Institutes*. This book is best understood as a manual on spirituality. And, although the corpus of his writings is great, Calvin's ideas, whether found in sermons, biblical commentaries, or polemical literature, are consistent with what is presented in the *Institutes*.

In general Calvin had fully accepted Luther's idea that salvation is by grace alone through faith. Beyond this, scholars have been unable to establish that any one specific doctrine is central to his thought. The basic and fundamental development of his thought was not according to the traditional topics of theology, sequentially and logically developed. Formally he organized his material according to the topical format, suggesting that the key to its analysis be sought from the perspective of one or several discrete topics. Yet this approach has only led to an impasse—even to the conclusion that he was in logic and purpose inexact and ambiguous. The often-discussed doctrines of providence and predestination, for example, are presented by Calvin as the response or affirmation of a man of faith, affirming the control of God in his life, not as an epistemological program. To approach his theology from specific topics such as these has not been fruitful. There are, however, larger, general ideas or themes that run through the *Institutes* from the first page to the last like so many threads in an intricate tapestry and that point to what is essential in his thought. He understood the redemptive message to be the same in both the Old and the New Testament; hence his theology can be seen as all of a piece, permitting the dominance of the thematic approach rather than the topical.

Calvin's theological program is based on the dictum of Augustine that man is created for communion with God and that he will be unfulfilled until he rests in God. Calvin usually expresses this idea in terms of a union with the Maker and Redeemer, which is presented as essential to man's spiritual life. Thus the relationship between God and man is made the basis of all theological discourse, and this union or communion is established and maintained through what Calvin calls knowledge, a theme or idea that becomes an ordering principle of his theology. Knowledge of God the creator and knowledge of God the redeemer are the two divisions of his thought. He uses the term *knowledge* practically synonymously with the term *faith*. It comprises both the elements of objective information and its subjective appropriation, but essentially it consists of a reverential and worshipful trust in the goodness and bounty of God. As with all of his theological ideas, two poles or foci must be kept in balance: the knowledge of God and the knowledge of self. God is always—in the context of every theological discussion—at once the great, infinite, and incomprehensible being who calls all things out of nothing, as well as the loving, condescending, and revealing being who calls men and women to commune with him. God is always hidden and revealed, both beyond our comprehension and revealed to us at our level. Humans, albeit the greatest of God's creations, are always dependent creatures, both because we are created to be so and because our sin renders us totally helpless in spiritual things. Consequently God must always be the initiator of any communication with us. And hence humility, sobriety, and teachableness are our principal virtues.

Although he always keeps in mind the perfect condition in which all things were created, because of the cataclysmic event of the Fall, all of Calvin's theology is concerned with redemption, with the restoration of the state that God originally created. Christ alone is the mediator who both reveals and effects this redemption, or restoration. Human beings are in bondage to sinful nature, so anything relating to this restoration must be initiated by God through Christ. Restoration occurs when the person is united to Christ by responding in faith to the provision made through Christ's death and resurrection, but this mystical union occurs only if and when the hidden or secret work of the Holy Spirit engenders that faith. The faithful person is called to obedience, to be a servant of righteousness, to model his or her life after the incarnate Christ. In this sense Calvin's theology is Christocentric. But he did not focus attention only in the area of Christology, for all that Christ does and is, is made real to man only through the work of the Holy Spirit. Indeed, all of his soteriology is presented in the context of the work of the Holy Spirit, "the bond by which Christ effectually unites us to himself." The work of restoration, by the power of the Holy Spirit, is done in the context of the church, God's gracious provision for the activity of preaching and teaching, for the administration of the sacraments, and for the communion (and reproof) of the saints.

Calvinists were the most vital of the Protestant groups, spreading throughout Europe and the New World, triumphing in Switzerland, the Netherlands, and Scotland, and for a time in England and America. Scholarly opinion is divided over whether this success is due mainly to Calvin's theological teaching, to his training and educational program (the complete revamping of the elementary schools and the creation of the University of Geneva), or to his organizational talent. Probably all of these are contributory factors, and perhaps others, but it does seem that the vitality of the Reformed or Calvinist movement, and therefore Calvin's most enduring legacy, is due principally to the nature of his church, to its unique, adaptable, and efficient organization. Although its unique blend of theory and practicality meant that Calvin's theology could be drawn upon by a variety of different interests, it can also be shown that his theology was revised almost beyond recognition very shortly after his death and that the *Institutes* were not widely read in the late sixteenth and early seventeenth centuries. Moreover, while the educational system produced an informed and well-trained church membership that was designed to be educationally self-perpetuating, it seems undeniable that the unique organizational structure of the Calvinist church was required for the growth and development of the educational program. Calvin appears to have recognized as much, for on his return to Geneva in 1541, his first major undertaking was to secure approval of his *Ecclesiastical Ordinances*, which set forth the organization of the church.

Calvin developed a representative form of church government with the fundamental activity based in the local church. The leadership was elected from the local membership, and the power, which ultimately resided in the local membership as a whole, was vested in these elected officials, not in the clergy. While there are three higher levels of authority above the local church, established in ascending representative bodies and culminating in the national or general assembly, part of the genius of this organization lies in the ability of the local church, in times of emergency, to function without the meeting of the upper-level bodies. As a result these Calvinist churches were nearly impossible to eradicate. Silencing the minister and arresting the leadership only temporarily disrupted the church, for the minister was not an essential element in the church's continuance, and in a short time new leaders would be elected. So the church could survive, even flourish, under conditions of severe persecution. Beyond the necessary capacity to continue to exist in times when religious persecution and wars were the order of the day, the representative nature of the church responded to the psychological and political reality that humankind is more likely to be committed to a cause when participation in the decision-making process is involved. The impact of the representative nature of the Calvinist church has been significant in the development of the democratic political structures of the Western world.

BIBLIOGRAPHY

Primary Sources. The numerous works of Calvin are available, in the original texts, in the fifty-nine volumes of the magisterial *Ioannis Calvini opera quae supersunt omnia,* edited by J. W. Baum and others (Braunschweig, 1863–1900), and in its continuation, the *Supplementa Calviniana,* a collection of subsequently discovered sermons edited by Erwin Mülhaupt and others (Neukirchen, 1961–), seven volumes to date with more to come. In English, the best edition of the *Institutes of the Christian Religion* is that of J. T. McNeill, translated by Ford Lewis Battles (Philadelphia, 1960) in two volumes. Many other works are available in English translation, including the important edition of *The New Testament Commentaries* edited by Thomas F. Torrance and David W. Torrance (Edinburgh, 1959–).

Secondary Sources. An excellent guide to the secondary literature is J. T. McNeill's "Fifty Years of Calvin Study: 1918–1968," which is prefaced to Williston Walker's *John Calvin, the Organiser of Reformed Protestantism, 1509–1564* (reprint, New York, 1969). T. H. L. Parker's *John Calvin* (Philadelphia, 1975), is fully informed and reliable, but the fullest and best biography, in spite of its hagiographic character, is Émile Doumergue's seven-volume *Jean Calvin, les hommes et les choses de son temps* (Lausanne, 1899–1927).

On Calvin's thought and influence, current scholarly opinion can be found in the proceedings of the International Congress on Calvin Research edited by W. H. Neuser in three volumes (vols. 1–2, Kampen, Netherlands, 1975, 1979; vol. 3, Bern, 1983). Benoît Giradin's *Rhétorique et théologique . . .* (Paris, 1979) is indispensable for the explication of the nature and structure of his thought, and E. A. Dowey's *The Knowledge of God in Calvin's Theology* (New York, 1952) is one of the better introductions. Richard Stauffer's *Dieu, la création et al providence dans la prédication de Calvin* (Bern, 1978) is an excellent corrective to the exclusively Christocentric interpretation of many recent scholars. On Calvin's influence, Robert M. Kingdom's *Geneva and the Coming of the Wars of Religion in France, 1555–1563* (Geneva, 1956) and *Geneva and the Consolidation of the French Protestant Movement, 1564–1572* (Geneva and Madison, Wis., 1967) are representative and excellent studies.

BRIAN G. ARMSTRONG

CAMPBELL, ALEXANDER (1788–1866), one of the founders and the foremost early leader of the Disciples of Christ. Campbell was born in County Antrim, Northern Ireland, the son of a Presbyterian minister, Thomas Campbell. He immigrated to America in 1809, joining his father, who had come two years earlier. When he arrived, Campbell discovered that his father had broken with the Presbyterian church and had begun a small, nonsectarian "Christian association." Having been exposed to similar New Testament primitivist ideas in Scotland, young Campbell embraced his father's reform and quickly became the most prominent leader of the new movement. For a time the Campbells were Baptists, and from 1823 to 1830 Alexander edited the *Christian Baptist,* a periodical that attracted many supporters in the West and South. Beginning in the 1830s Campbell and his "Reforming Baptist" supporters separated into independent churches. Campbell preferred the name Disciples of Christ, but local churches frequently were called Christian Church or Church of Christ. In 1832 the church nearly doubled in size through a union with the Christian movement led by Barton Stone of Kentucky; Campbell quickly became the dominant figure in the united denomination.

From 1830 until 1864 Campbell edited a journal called the *Millennial Harbinger,* which became a mirror of his maturing thought. The heart of Campbell's plea was an appeal for Christian union through the "restoration of the ancient order of things," that is, by restoring New Testament Christianity. Prior to 1830 Campbell was extremely iconoclastic in his attacks on the popular churches, ridiculing the clergy and seeming to attack all cooperative societies. After 1830 he became a more constructive builder and seemed confident that the millennium was about to begin, initiated by the restoration movement. In 1849 a group of Disciples leaders established the young church's first national organization, the American Christian Missionary Society, and, although he was not present at the meeting, Campbell accepted the presidency of the society.

Campbell's formal college training consisted of less than one year at Glasgow University, but he was a man of considerable erudition. He established a national reputation as a debater, especially as a result of widely publicized debates with the renowned Scottish socialist and atheist Robert Owen, in 1829, and with the Roman Catholic archbishop of Cincinnati, John B. Purcell, in

1837. Campbell became financially independent as a result of his marriage to Margaret Brown in 1811, and he spent the remainder of his life living near his wife's home in Brooke County in western Virginia. He became a moderately wealthy man, and in 1829, in his only venture into politics, he was elected a delegate to the Virginia Constitutional Convention. In 1841, Campbell established Bethany College near his home. Until his death he served as president and professor of moral sciences at the college and trained a generation of leaders for Disciples churches. Campbell traveled and preached widely throughout the United States, as well as in England and Scotland. The aging reformer was discouraged by the sectional tension caused by the slavery debate and the Civil War. He counseled moderation and believed that the restoration movement could survive the tragedy, but by the time of his death his millennial hopes had given way to pessimism.

[*See also* Disciples of Christ.]

BIBLIOGRAPHY

No satisfactory biography of Alexander Campbell has yet been written. Probably the best source of information about the reformer is still the classic study written by his friend Robert Richardson, *Memoirs of Alexander Campbell,* 2 vols. (Philadelphia, 1868–1870). A novel based on Campbell's life is Louis Cochran's *The Fool of God* (New York, 1958). Useful specialized studies include Harold L. Lunger's *The Political Ethics of Alexander Campbell* (Saint Louis, 1954); R. Frederick West's *Alexander Campbell and Natural Religion* (New Haven, 1948); and D. Ray Lindley's *Apostle of Freedom* (Saint Louis, 1957). The most comprehensive statement of Campbell's ideas can be found in his own *The Christian System,* 4th ed. (1866; reprint, New York, 1969).

DAVID EDWIN HARRELL, JR.

CANAANITE RELIGION. [*This entry consists of two articles,* An Overview *and* The Literature. *The first is concerned with Canaanite religious phenomenology from a historical and social perspective; the second focuses on Canaanite mythological and epic texts.*]

An Overview

The term *Canaanite* is variously used in both ancient and modern sources. Most popularly, it refers to the indigenous population of the southwestern Levant, which, according to biblical traditions, was displaced by Israelite conquerors late in the second millennium before the common era. This popular usage is, however, both too narrow geographically and fraught with sociohistorical difficulties. In this article, the term *Canaanite religion* will refer mainly to the one Northwest Semitic religion of the second millennium that is presently well attested, the Ugaritic. It should be borne in mind, however, that ancient sources do not necessarily support the often-asserted equation of "Ugaritic" with "Canaanite," if the terms of the equation are linguistic, ethnic, or political. And in any case, the undoubtedly idiosyncratic Ugaritic data do not facilitate a generally applicable description of "Canaanite" (or, more accurately, "Northwest Semitic") religion.

Before the late nineteenth century, there were only two sources for the study of the Canaanite religion. The first, the Hebrew scriptures, contains numerous references to the Canaanites and their practices, which are generally condemned as abominable (e.g., *Lv.* 18:3, 27–28). As early as the first century BCE, the biblical commentator Philo of Alexandria recognized that Canaan was the biblical symbol of "vice," which the Israelites were naturally bidden to despise (*De cong.* 83–85). It is generally agreed that the biblical witness to Canaanite religion is highly polemical and, therefore, unreliable; biblical evidence must at the least be used with extreme caution, and in conjunction with extrabiblical sources.

The second source for knowledge of Canaanite religion was those classical texts that preserve descriptions of aspects of it. The best known of these are the *Phoenician History* of Philo Byblius, of which portions are preserved in Eusebius's *Praeparatio evangelica,* and *The Syrian Goddess,* attributed (perhaps falsely) to Lucian of Samothrace. The reliability of Philo Byblius, however, has been the subject of scholarly debate, and the present consensus is that the comparability of the *Phoenician History* with authentic Canaanite data should not be overstressed. At best, Philo's information probably sheds light on the religion of late hellenized Phoenicians, and offers no direct evidence for second-millennium Canaanite religion. The same generalization applies to (Pseudo-) Lucian, despite a few scholarly claims to the contrary.

Firsthand evidence for Canaanite culture in the second millennium BCE (or, in archaeological terms, the Middle Bronze and Late Bronze periods) comes from artifactual evidence found at many archaeological sites (more than sixty for the first part of the Middle Bronze period alone—mostly tombs) and from textual evidence stemming mainly from three great discoveries: (1) the eighteenth-century royal archives of "Amorite" Mari (Tell Hariri, on the Euphrates River near the present border between Syria and Iraq); (2) the diplomatic correspondence between several Levantine vassal princes and the pharoahs Amenophis III and IV (first half of the fourteenth century), found at Tell al-ʿAmarna (about 330 km south of Cairo on the east bank of the Nile); and (3) the mainly fourteenth- and thirteenth-century texts found at Ras Shamra (ancient Ugarit) and nearby Ras Ibn Hani, both within the present-day administrative district of Latakia, on the Mediterranean coast of Syria. The artifactual evidence is crucial for understanding material culture, socioeconomic developments, population movements, and the like, and provides considerable data about funerary practices. Most significant for the study of religion are the figurines, thought to represent gods and goddesses, that have been recovered in virtually every archaeological context. These will be discussed below with other manifestations of popular religion.

The ancient city of Mari was peripheral to both the Mesopotamian and the Levantine spheres of influence. Culturally and linguistically, it was clearly West Semitic, but to label it "Canaanite" goes beyond the evidence (the designation "Amorite" represents, to some extent, a scholarly compromise). The Mari texts are virtually all concerned with economic, juridical, and administrative matters. One text in particular testifies to the eclecticism and heterogeneity of Mari's religious cult in the eighteenth century. It lists the sacrificial sheep distributed among the various gods and temples of Mari, and the list of gods is a mixture of Semitic and non-Semitic deities from east and west, along with some gods perhaps unique to Mari. This list of diverse gods may be supplemented by the more than one hundred forty divine names (at least two dozen of which are West Semitic) attested as components of personal names in the Mari archives.

The most striking group of Mari texts is the small collection of so-called prophetic texts. These twenty-odd letters attest to a type of oracular speaking that shows significant affinities with biblical prophecies of a millennium later. Some of this oracular speaking seems to have been done by cultic personnel, and some apparently consisted of messages transmitted by the gods through ordinary people. In either case, it clearly deviated from the normal (and presumably normative) mode of divine intermediation, which was, as generally in the ancient Near East, divination in its various forms. Local temple officials probably felt that the extraordinary behavior, and the messages transmitted by it, had to be reported to higher authorities. It may be suggested, on the basis of these Mari texts and related evidence, that the phenomenon broadly termed *"prophecy"* represented a peculiar and peripheral kind of divine intermediation among the West Semites generally.

Most of the Amarna letters report on Levantine military, economic, and political matters to the Egyptian court. The letters were written in Babylonian, the diplomatic language of the period, but they regularly reveal the Canaanite character of their authors—in personal names, peculiar scribal practices, and, especially, the use of characteristic Canaanite vocabulary and turns of phrase. While none of the Amarna letters is directly concerned with religion, important information can be derived from the divine names and epithets mentioned in passing (and as components of personal names), and from Canaanite religious and liturgical clichés that have been incorporated into the epistolary style. For example, the son of Aziru, prince of Amurru, writes as follows to the Egyptian court: "You give me life, and you give me death. I look upon your face; you are indeed my lord. So let my lord hearken to his servant." Such expressions, which are frequent in the correspondence, are probably borrowed liturgical formulas, perhaps from lost Canaanite prayers that were probably comparable to the biblical psalms. A systematic study of all such formulas might shed considerable light on Canaanite religious conceptions of the mid-second millennium.

Without slighting the importance of the Mari and Amarna material, by far the most significant evidence for Canaanite religion in the second millennium is found at Ugarit. From the beginning of the millennium until the city's destruction at the hands of the Sea Peoples (c. 1180–1175 BCE), Ugarit was a thriving cosmopolitan trading center. In the Middle Bronze period (2000–1600; Level II of the Ras Shamra excavations), Ugarit underwent considerable expansion. During this period, two large temples (dedicated to the gods Baal and Dagan respectively; see below) were erected on top of older ruins, forming, in effect, an acropolis in the city. The pottery of the period is predominantly Canaanite, and other material evidence demonstrates that Ugarit was in contact with Egypt, the Aegean, and Mesopotamia. At the same time, Ugarit's population was augmented by an influx of Indo-European-speaking Hurrians from the northeast.

The best-attested period at Ugarit is the last two centuries of its existence (Late Bronze III, c. 1365–1180; Level I.3 of the Ras Shamra excavations). The Ugaritic texts date from this period, although some of the religious texts are undoubtedly older, and were merely written down at this time. One of the most important developments in human history was the invention, during the reign of Niqmad II (c. 1360–1330), of a cuneiform alphabetic script (the world's oldest alphabet) adapted to the Ugaritic language. It seems likely that this invention was specifically for the purpose of setting ancient religious documents in writing, since diplomatic and administrative texts could be, and often were, written in Akkadian. At the instigation of Niqmad II, the great mythological texts that are at the heart of the Ugaritic religion were incised on clay tablets. They were preserved in the library of the high priest, which was located on the acropolis near the two temples.

In addition to the mythological texts from the high priest's library, the excavations of this and several other archives of Ugarit and Ras Ibn Hani have turned up related mythological material, descriptive ritual texts, lists of sacrificial offerings, god-lists, prayers and liturgies, incantations, divinatory texts, and dedicatory inscriptions. These may be used, with due caution, as the basis of a description of Ugaritic religion.

Deities. The essential information about Ugarit's deities comes from what appears to be a canonical god-list. Two nearly identical copies of the basic list have been published, along with an Akkadian "translation." In addition, the list is incorporated, with minor variations, into a list of sacrificial offerings. This list shows that the basic cultic pantheon of Ugarit numbered thirty-three or thirty-four gods. One of the most controversial problems confronting Ugaritic scholarship is the imperfect correspondence between the god-list and the gods who are prominent in the mythological texts. The myths probably represent an older stratum of Ugaritic religion, and were undoubtedly "reinterpreted" in the light of subsequent developments in the cult.

Two reasons are generally given for the order of the gods in the list: either it reflects their relative importance, or else it gives the order in which their symbols were paraded in a cultic procession. The list begins with two or three Ils (El)—the sources are evenly split on the number. *Il* is the common Semitic word for "god"; it is the proper name of the head of the Ugaritic pantheon in the mythological texts. The first Il in the god-list is associated with Mount Sapan (Tsafon), the Canaanite Olympus, which was traditionally identified with Jebel al-Aqra, about fifty kilometers north of Ugarit at the mouth of the Orontes River. (The mountain was itself deified, and appears in the god-list in place 14/15.) In all likelihood, the term *sapan,* which means "north," was taken to be a metaphor for the god's temple (as in the Bible, Psalm 48:3), and not as a simple geographical designation. Thus the *Il* of *sapan* is the numen manifest in the sanctuary, which is the earthly representation of the divine abode. Sapan, it should be noted, is not the abode of Il in the mythological texts, but of Baal (see below).

The second Il is called *Ilib.* The Akkadian and Hurrian parallels show that this name is a portmanteau composed of the elements *il* ("god") and *ab* ("father"), but the precise significance of the combination is uncertain. Most likely the name denotes an ancestral spirit, the numen manifest in the Ugaritic cult of the dead. In the Ugaritic epic of Aqhat, the ancient worthy Danil, whose epithets mark him as one of the deified dead, seeks a son who will "erect a stela for his *ilib*"—that is, for the divine spirit of his dead father. The affinity of Il with the Ugaritic cult of the dead is shown in a mythological fragment in which the god participates in a *marzih* feast (an orgiastic revel comparable to the Greek *thiasos*), the ritual banquet of the funerary cult. Il drinks himself into a stupor (as is customary at such affairs), and has to be carried off by his faithful son. (This, too, is one of the duties of the son enumerated in the epic of Aqhat.)

The third Il is presumably to be identified with the head of the pantheon in the mythological texts. His epithets and activities in those, and in the cultic texts, provide a fair picture of his character. He is the father of the gods, who are called his "family" or "sons," and he is styled "father of humankind" and "builder of built ones." He may have been regarded as the creator of the world, but the Ugaritic evidence is inconclusive on this point. He bears the epithet "bull," a symbol of virility and power (although one mythological text casts some doubt on his sexual prowess). He is serene in his supremacy, a source of "eternal wisdom," "beneficent and benign"; a unique and problematic text that may be a prayer to Il seems even to hypostatize his "graciousness."

The three Ils comprise the three principal aspects of Ugaritic "godship," or numinous power, that are denoted by the term *il:* (1) it is the wise and sovereign power that brought gods and humans into being; (2) it abides in any sacred place; and (3) it is the tangible presence of the spirits of the dead.

The next deity on the list is Dagan. The Mari texts attest to his great importance in the Middle Euphrates region (especially Terqa). The most common explanation of his name relates it to the West Semitic word for "grain," but this is by no means certain; other (even non-Semitic) etymologies are possible. One of the two temples on the acropolis of Ugarit was evidently consecrated to Dagan. During excavations carried out in 1934, two inscribed stone slabs were found just outside the temple. The inscriptions, the only known examples of Ugaritic carved in stone, commemorate *pgr* sacrifices of a sheep and an ox offered to Dagan. Since so little is known of Dagan's character at Ugarit, and since the term *pgr* is controversial (perhaps "mortuary offering" is the best interpretation), it is not possible to say anything definitive about these stelae.

Despite his obvious prominence in the cult, Dagan plays no role in Ugaritic mythology. The god Baal bears the epithet "son of Dagan," but that is itself problematic, since Il was supposedly the father of the gods. Three explanations are possible: (1) Dagan was in some sense identified with or assimilated to Il; (2) the epithet represents a variant tradition of Baal's paternity; or

(3) the epithet "son" is not to be taken literally but as an indication that Baal belongs to some class of gods exemplified by Dagan.

Following Dagan come seven Baals. The first is the Baal of Mount Sapan, who dwells in the same place as the Baal in the mythological texts (the "heights" or "recesses" of Sapan); the term *sapan* surely refers to the Baal temple of Ugarit as well. The Akkadian rendition of *Baal* is *Adad,* which is the name of the most prominent West Semitic mountain and weather god. The same Ugaritic "prayer" that mentions the graciousness of El also establishes the threefold identification of Adad (the variant Hadd occurs in the mythological texts) with Baal of Mount Sapan and Baal of Ugarit.

The significance of the other six Baals (none qualified by epithets and all identified with Adad) is uncertain, although sevenfold lists of all sorts, including divine heptads, are common throughout the ancient Near East: the number seven evidently denotes completeness or perfection. If the extra six Baals have some specific function, they might represent local manifestations or sanctuaries of Baal, separate cult symbols, or hypostatized attributes.

The name *Baal* is derived from the common Semitic noun meaning "lord, master, husband." The god's full title in the mythological texts is "prince, lord *(baal)* of the earth," and his principal epithet is "most powerful one" *(aliyan).* He is also called "high one" *(aliy)* and "rider of the clouds," both names clearly illustrating his character as a weather god.

In contrast to the numinous Il, Baal represents the divine power that is immanent in the world, activating and effectuating things or phenomena. Given the paucity of rainfall in most of the Levant, it is not surprising that the lord of the storm is the most prominent god of this type (cf. the ubiquitous Phoenician Baal Shamem, "lord of the heavens," and his famous encounter with the Israelite god in *1 Kings* 18). On his shoulders rests the burden of bringing fertility and fecundity to the land, and as such he is venerated by the rest of the gods and declared their "king."

But the kind of god who is immanent in the natural world is also subject to its flux. Thus, in the mythological texts, Baal has three enemies. The first two, Yamm ("sea") and the desert gods who are called "devourers," represent the destructive potential inherent in nature. Baal succeeds in subduing Yamm (and undoubtedly also the "devourers"), but he is in turn defeated by his third and greatest adversary, Mot ("death"; never mentioned by this name in the cultic texts). Nothing that is in the world, gods included, can escape death.

Following the seven Baals, the god-list continues with Ars wa-Shamem ("earth and heaven"). Binomial deities are common in Ugaritic; they represent either a hendiadys (as in this case) or a composite of two related gods who have been assimilated to one another. This god's function is unknown; perhaps the domain over which Baal holds sway is deified. There are also two other geographical deities: Sapan (discussed above) and "Mountain and Valley" (significance unknown, unless it defines the domain of Athtar, the god occupying the preceding place on the god-list).

The remaining divine names on the list may be grouped in four categories: individual goddesses and gods who are known or at least mentioned in the mythological texts; collective terms that designate groups of lesser deities; Hurrian deities; and otherwise unknown or poorly attested gods.

The two most prominent goddesses in the mythological texts are Athirat (Asherah) and Anat. Athirat is the consort of Il, and as such she is the highest-ranking goddess in the pantheon. Her full title is "Lady Athirat of the sea" (or perhaps "the lady who treads the sea"). She is the mother of the gods, bearing the epithet "progenitress of the gods." She is also called Ilat ("goddess"), the feminine form of Il. Athirat's activities in the mythological texts are not always clear, but she seems to specialize in zealous intervention on behalf of her divine offspring.

In contrast to the maternal goddess Athirat, Anat is a violent goddess of sexual love and war, "sister" (perhaps consort) of Baal and vanquisher of Baal's enemy Mot. Her principal epithet is "maiden," a tribute to her youth, beauty, and desirability, but pugnacity is her primary trait in the mythological texts, as well as in the epic of Aqhat; there, she secures the magic bow of the title character by arranging his death.

Iconographic evidence from Ugarit and elsewhere may be associated with both of the principal divine pairs, Il/Athirat and Baal/Anat. The first two are represented as a royal pair, either standing or enthroned. Baal is typically depicted with his arm upraised in smiting position, and Anat is naked and voluptuous, sometimes standing on a lion's back, an Egyptian Hathor wig on her head, with arms upraised and plants or animals grasped in her hands. Only the Anat figures can be identified with any certainty, because of an Egyptian exemplar that bears the inscription "Qudshu-Ashtart-Anat."

Although the precise significance of Qudshu is uncertain (perhaps she is the same as Athirat?), the Egyptian inscription seems to demonstrate the fusion of the West Semitic Anat with the great Mesopotamian goddess Ishtar (Ugaritic Athtart; the biblical Ashtoret). This fusion is apparent in the binomial Athtart wa-Anat, which occurs in two Ugaritic incantation texts and is the ultimate source of the name of the first-millennium "Syrian goddess" Atargatis. In some mythological and cultic texts, as in the god-list, Athtart still has some independent status. (Paradoxically, in Israel it is Anat who has disappeared, evidently assimilated to Ashtoret.) Her beauty is proverbial, but her principal trait is pugnacity; like Anat, she is a divine huntress.

The textual and iconographic evidence suggests that a central feature of Ugaritic religion was the veneration of two divine pairs. One pair apparently symbolized kingly and queenly sovereignty over the world—Il and Athirat; the other represented brother and sister, caught in the flux and turmoil of the world, engaged in constant struggle for survival and supremacy—Baal and Anat.

There are three other Canaanite goddesses on the god-list. Shapash is the all-seeing sun (male in Mesopotamia, but female at Ugarit), "luminary of the gods." Pidray ("fat"?) and Arsay ("earth," perhaps, on the basis of the Akkadian parallel, having some connection with the netherworld) are two of the daughters of Baal; the third, Talay ("dew"), does not appear on the god-list. Two other non-Canaanite goddesses are on the list, undoubtedly via the Hurrians, although the deities themselves are not necessarily Hurrian in origin: Ushharay (Ishhara), the scorpion goddess, who appears in several cultic texts but never in the myths, and Dadmish, probably a warrior goddess but very poorly attested. The one remaining goddess on the list is Uthht (pronunciation uncertain; the sex of the deity is, in fact, only surmised from the feminine ending); possibly Mesopotamian in origin, and most likely signifying a deified incense burner.

Seven male deities remain on the god-list, all but one of whom are at least mentioned in the mythological texts. Yarih is the moon god, and he figures prominently in a poem that describes his marriage to the moon goddess, Nikkal. This text is undoubtedly a Hurrian myth in Ugaritic guise. The other clearly astral god is Shalim (the divine element in the name of the city Jeru*salem* and of King *Solom*on), who represents the evening twilight or Venus as evening star. Since the root *sh-l-m* can signify "conclusion, completion," it is appropriate that Shalim is the last name on the list. Elsewhere, he is often paired with his sibling Shahr, who is the dawn or the planet Venus as morning star. The birth of the pair is described and celebrated in a Ugaritic poem.

Three of the gods play important roles in the mythological texts about Baal. Yamm is one of Baal's principal adversaries; he is identified with or accompanied by two fearsome sea monsters, Litan (the biblical Leviathan) and Tunnan (the biblical Tannin). The god Athtar (the masculine form of Athtart) is often associated with a prominent South Arabian astral deity, but the Akkadian translation of his name identifies him with the Hurrian warrior god Ashtabi. When Baal is killed by Mot, Athtar, styled "tyrant," is appointed king in his stead.

The god Kothar ("skilled one"; also known as Kothar wa-Hasis, "skilled and wise one") is the divine craftsman. In various sources he is a master builder, weapon maker, seaman, and magician. It has been suggested that he is the genius of technology.

The god Rashap (the biblical *Reshef*, which means both "pestilence" and "flame") is blamed in the epic of Kirta for the demise of part of the title character's family. But Rashap's real importance at Ugarit and Ras Ibn Hani emerges from the cultic texts, where he is the recipient of numerous offerings. In the late third millennium, he was one of the patron gods of the kings of Ebla. He also found his way to Egypt, where he was patron god of Amenophis II and one of the most popular gods in the cults of the nineteenth dynasty.

The Akkadian version of the Ugaritic god-list identifies Rashap with Nergal, the Mesopotamian king of the netherworld. That identification, along with other Canaanite and Egyptian evidence, leads me to suggest that Rashap is the god who, in one mythological text, is called Rapiu, the "healer," the eponymous patron of the deified dead, the *rapium* (the biblical *refa'im*). Most scholars, however, consider "Rapiu" to be an epithet of Il.

The remaining god on the list is Kinar, who is perhaps the deified lyre. Nothing is known about him, but he has been identified with the Cypriot hero Kinyras, father of Adonis.

Finally, the god-list includes four collective terms. The first, *kotharat*, designates a band of female divine singers and wet-nurses who appear on sad and joyful occasions in the Aqhat epic and the Nikkal poem, respectively (also, perhaps, in Psalm 68:7). Although their name suggests an affinity with the god Kothar, nothing further can be said about this. They bear an epithet that is problematic: the two most plausible translations are "daughters of joyous song, the swallows" and "shining daughters of the morning star [or the new moon]."

The next collective term apparently designates the "two allies of Baal," perhaps his messengers, Gapn ("vine") and Ugar ("field"). The third collective term is *puhr ilim*, the "assembly of the gods," which designates the host of lesser deities—unmentioned by name in the god-list—who constitute the progeny of Il and Athirat. In other texts, this assemblage bears other epithets, including "sons of Il" and "the family of the sons of Il"; the precise significance of these terms is much debated, but they all seem to pertain to the general Near Eastern notion of a "divine assembly" over which one god reigned supreme.

The last collective term is *malikum*, which literally means "kings." It designates the deified dead kings of Ugarit, the most important members of the larger assemblage of deified dead ancestors (*rapium*, mentioned above). The *malikum* are invoked by name in an extraordinary Ugaritic liturgy entitled the *Document of the Feast of the Protective Ancestral Spirits*. It may be inferred that the patron of the *malikum* was the ubiquitous Malik (biblical Molech), who is almost certainly to be equated with Death himself.

Many other deities who do not figure in the standard god-list are mentioned in various texts and as components of personal names. Huge, malleable pantheons characterized every major urban center of the ancient Near East, and Ugarit was no exception (see Johannes C. de Moor, "The Semitic Pantheon of Ugarit," *Ugarit-Forschungen* 2, 1970, pp. 185–228).

Rituals and Cultic Personnel. Most older descriptions of Canaanite religion explain it in terms of the seasonal cycle and concomitant fertility rites. The evidence for this characterization comes from first-millennium sources, especially the anti-"Canaanite" polemics of the Hebrew scriptures, and from the *a priori* claims of the "myth-and-ritual" approach to religion. When the mythic texts about the Ugaritic Baal were deciphered and pieced together, the tendency was naturally to make them conform to the older theories about Canaanite religion. Those texts were thus described as a mythic representation of the seasonal cycle, which was either recited as the accompaniment to fertility rites or served as the libretto of a fertility-cult drama.

Assuming that the biblical and related data are reliable, they evidently refer to local manifestations of first-millennium Phoenician cults (such as that of northern Israel). The simple assumption of continuity between second-millennium Canaan and first-millennium Phoenicia is unjustified—as is, more generally, the facile identification of "Canaanites" with "Phoenicians."

As for the myth-and-ritual claim, the seasonal interpretation of the Baal texts is by no means certain. There is no evidence that the Baal texts were ever used in conjunction with cultic activity. In fact, there is only one Ugaritic mythological text containing rubrics for ritual performance (discussed below); it apparently entails some sort of fertility rite, but one not necessarily connected with the seasonal cycle. Knowledge of the Ugaritic calendar and its fixed festivals is too scanty to permit the claim that Ugaritic religion was organized with respect to the agricultural year.

The Ugaritic ritual texts describe a highly organized sacrificial cult under the patronage of the king. The sacrifices seem to be of the gift or tribute type; that is, they were performed to curry favor with the gods, to secure their aid and protection. It is undeniable that offerings might have been made to deities (particularly chthonic ones) to promote the fertility of the land and the fecundity of the flocks. But the one mass public ritual that has survived, and the one attested prayer to Baal as well, both seem more concerned with protection from Ugarit's potential military opponents. In view of the shifting alliances and political instability that marked Ugarit's last two centuries, this concern seems only natural.

Most of the known Ugaritic rituals were performed by or on behalf of the king. The best-attested type of ritual is found in seven different texts. In it the king of Ugarit performs, at specified times, a ritual lustration to purify himself, and then offers a series of sacrifices to various deities. At sundown, the king "desacralizes" himself in a way that is not clear. The most interesting of these texts is evidently a prescriptive ritual to which is appended a prayer to Baal, perhaps recited by the queen, that seems to specify the occasion on which the rites were to be performed.

This text begins with a date formula and a list of offerings: "On the seventh day of the month of Ibalat [otherwise unknown]" sheep are offered to several gods, notable Baal and "the house of Baal of Ugarit." Then "the sun sets and the king performs the rite of desacralization." On the seventeenth day of the month, the king (re)purifies himself and makes another series of sacrifices, perhaps accompanied by a festal banquet (if this is the correct sense of the technical term *dbh*). (Another of the main sacrificial terms, *th*, which seems to denote "gift offering," also occurs here.) The king remains in his purified state and continues the series of offerings on the eighteenth day. Then the text breaks off. The reverse of the tablet begins with broken references to rites performed on the second day (of what, is unspecified). On the fourth, birds are offered; on the fifth the king offers a *shlmm* sacrifice to Baal of Ugarit in the temple, along with the liver of an unspecified animal (which has presumably been used for divination) and an offering of precious metal. The *shlmm* offering, well attested in biblical Hebrew and Punic cultic texts, was probably the most common type of sacrifice at Ugarit. The term is traditionally translated "peace offering," but it seems actually to have been a "gift" or "tribute" to the god. In some texts (but not this one), the *shlmm* is described as a *shrp*, which probably signifies that it was wholly consumed by fire.

On the seventh day, at sundown, the king performs the ritual desacralization, evidently aided in this case by cultic functionaries called "desacralizers." Then the queen is anointed with a libation of "a *hin* [liquid measure] of oil of pacification for Baal"; the text concludes with the following prayer, perhaps recited by the queen:

> When a strong enemy assails your gates,
> A mighty foe attacks your walls,
> Raise your eyes unto Baal:
> "O Baal, chase the strong enemy from our gates,
> The mighty foe from our walls.
> A bull, O Baal, we consecrate;
> A vow, O Baal, we dedicate;
> A firstborn [?], O Baal, we consecrate;
> A *htp* sacrifice, O Baal, we dedicate;
> A tithe, O Baal, we tithe.
> To the sanctuary of Baal let us ascend,
> On the paths to the House of Baal let us walk."
> Then Baal will hear your prayer,
> He will chase the strong enemy from your gates,
> The mighty foe from your walls.

None of the other royal rituals offers such specific information about its occasion as the one just described, but they all have the same basic character. Another group of texts merely lists the sacrificial offerings and the gods to whom they were offered. These texts sometimes begin with the rubric "when the king makes an offering," but they do not describe any accompanying rituals.

A second type of ritual is preserved in three texts that describe the transfer of cult statues from one place to another. The clearest of these begins "When Athtart of *hr* [meaning uncertain] enters into the sanctuary [?] of the king's house. . . ." It is not clear whether the term *king* refers to Ugarit's king or to a god (perhaps both?); the "house" could be a royal palace or temple. A group of offerings is then made in the "house of the stellar gods" (meaning uncertain), including oblations, vestments, gold, and sacrificial animals. The rites are repeated seven times. The remainder of the text describes essentially the same rituals as those performed for a different collection of gods (on a different occasion?), the poorly attested *gthrm*.

One substantial ritual text is unique in the corpus, and has been the subject of many studies. It is unique in its poetic/hymnic quality and in the acts it describes. It seems to depict a great public assembly in which the entire population of Ugarit, male and female, king and commoner alike, participated. The ritual appears to have been a mass expiation or purgation of sins, or some sort of mass purification rite, designed to protect Ugarit against its threatening neighbors. A parallel has been drawn between it and the Jewish Yom Kippur, the "day of purgation [of sin]." In the Ugaritic text, the men and women of the community are alternately summoned to offer sacrifices, which they do. While the sacrifices are performed the people sing, praying that their offerings will ascend to "the father of the sons of Il" (that is, to Il himself), to the "family of the sons of Il," to the "assembly of the sons of Il," and to *Thkmn wa-Shnm,* Il's son and attendant (the one who cares for him when he is drunk; in one of his epithets, Il is called "father of *Shnm*").

Only one mythological text, the poem about the birth of Shahr and Shalim (the *ilima naimima,* "gracious gods"), includes rubrics for ritual performance. These rubrics, interspersed throughout the poem, describe the activities of the king and queen, and of cultic functionaries called *aribuma* (some kind of priests?) and *thananuma* (members of the king's guard?). They offer sacrifices, participate in a banquet, and sing responsively to musical accompaniment. It seems almost certain that the poem itself was acted out as a type of ritual drama. It describes the subjugation of Death by some sort of pruning rite, followed by Il's sexual relations with Athirat and Rahmay ("womb" = Anat?). The poem concludes with the birth of Shahr and Shalim, and their youthful activities. The text and its accompanying ritual may commemorate (or attempt to foster) the birth of a royal heir to the reigning king and queen of Ugarit; they bear some relation to Mesopotamian sacred marriage rites and to Hittite rituals designed to protect the life and vigor of the king and queen.

Most difficult to reconstruct, but obviously of great importance, was the Ugaritic cult of the dead. The dead were summoned, by a liturgy accompanied by offerings, to participate in a banquet. The banquet, which was apparently a drunken orgy, was intended to propitiate the dead and to solicit the aid and protection provided by their numinous power. The most important group of the deified dead was comprised of Ugarit's kings *(malikum).* The larger assemblage, variously called "healers" *(rpim),* "healers of the netherworld" *(rpi ars),* "ancient healers" *(rpim qdmyn),* "divine spirits" *(ilnym),* and "assembly of Ditan/Didan" *(qbs dtn/ddn),* included two men who are prominent in the epic texts, Danil and Kirta, as well as several other spirits who are identified by name in a liturgical invocation of the dead.

The funerary feast itself was called a *marzih* (or *marzi*), a feast. It was held at a special location: one text describes problems concerning the rental of a *marzih* hall; a poorly preserved fragment of the Aqhat epic suggests that the *marzih* was held at a sacred "threshing floor" or "plantation," perhaps within the royal palace.

Another important text invokes the god Rapiu, "king of eternity" (that is, of the netherworld). Rapiu is clearly the patron of the deified dead; at first he is invited to drink, and at the end of the text he is asked to exert his "strength, power, might, rule, and goodness" for the benefit of Ugarit. If Rapiu is indeed to be identified with Il, this text comports well with the mythological fragment that depicts Il getting drunk at a *marzih*.

Alongside the cult of the dead must be placed the texts that apparently describe the ritual offerings to the gods of the netherworld *(ilm ars)*. The clearest of these begins with an offering to Rashap and mentions several other chthonic deities. There is also a strange god-list that appears to include a collection of netherworld demons. Finally, an inscribed clay model of a liver may record a sacrifice offered to a person (or deity?) who is "in the tomb."

The considerable activity that took place in the Ugaritic cult demanded an extensive array of cultic personnel. Unfortunately, while the names of many cultic officials are known, their precise function is not. It can be assumed, of course, that "priests" participated in the royal rituals described above, but the ritual texts do not specify how. Apart from the "desacralizers," the *thananuma* and *aribuma* already mentioned, several other kinds of personnel figure prominently. Except for the queen, who participated in some rituals (one broken text from Ras Ibn Hani describes a "*dbh* [sacrificial rite] of the queen"), all the important cultic functionaries attested by name or title are male.

After the king, the highest-ranking religious official was probably the *rb khnm*, the "chief of the priests." Under him were orders or guilds of *khnm* ("priests"); the term corresponds to the Hebrew *kohanim*, but there is no necessary similarity of function. The priests either were connected with the palace or they earned their living at the many shrines in Ugarit and its environs. They appear on administrative lists of personnel and on a military payroll. Other administrative texts detail allotments of oil and wine to various shrines. One of the high priests is also designated *rb nqdm*, "chief of herdsmen." In all likelihood, there was a consecrated group of herdsmen whose task was to maintain the royal flocks to be used in the cult.

The second major category of priests is called *qdshm*, "devotees" (comparison with Hebrew *qedeshim*, "cult prostitutes," is almost certainly misleading). They appear only on administrative lists, in all but one case in conjunction with *khnm*. Nothing can be said about their function at Ugarit.

Two categories of cult functionaries are attested in Akkadian texts from Ugarit, but they have no certain Ugaritic equivalents. One is the *awilu baru*, which is either an omen priest or some sort of oracular seer; one of these men is also called "priest of Adad [i.e., of Baal]". The other, aptly characterized by Anson F. Rainey (1967) as "a sort of religious brotherhood" (p. 71), is "men of the *marzi/marzih*." Their activity was almost certainly related to the ritual feasts of the Ugaritic cult of the dead. Several other terms probably designated groups associated with the cult. There were singers, instrumentalists, and libation pourers who served as temple attendants, along with a group of uncertain function called *ytnm*, who may be compared with the problematic biblical *netinim*.

Finally, there is the well-attested and much-debated term *insh ilm*. Some scholars think that it is a divine name; others argue that it denotes cultic personnel. If the latter, then these people performed some function in the sacrificial rites, and seem to have been rewarded for their labor with "birds."

Popular Religion. As is generally the case in the ancient Near East, little can be said with any certainty about popular religion at Ugarit, since only kings, priests, and members of the elite are represented in the texts. The Ugaritic texts were apparently only a part of the larger cosmopolitan scribal tradition of Ugarit, which was modeled on the Babylonian scribal schools. The same scribes who produced the *Baal* texts were also trained to write in Babylonian cuneiform, and they copied Sumerian and Akkadian texts in almost every genre. Surviving evidence demonstrates that Ugarit's educated elite was conversant with the Mesopotamian Gilgamesh traditions, wisdom and proverbial literature, and legal formulas, although little of this material is reflected in texts in the Ugaritic language.

It is not at all certain, then, how much of the literary tradition might have filtered down to the commoners of Ugarit. Still, speculation about popular religion may be made in four areas: conceptions of gods reflected in personal names; the evidence of votive figurines; evidence for magic and divination; and possible religious, ethical, or "wisdom" teachings derived from the texts.

Popular conceptions of the gods may emerge from a consideration of personal names, since a great number of names are composites of divine names (or surrogates) and nominal or verbal elements. The standard collection of Ugaritic personal names, Frauke Gröndahl's *Die Personennamen der Texte aus Ugarit* (Rome, 1967), lists over fifty divine elements that appear in them. The most popular are Il, Baal, Ammu ("uncle," a surrogate for a divine name), Anat and her "masculine" equivalent Anu, Athtar, Yamm, Kothar, Malik, Pidr (masculine equivalent of Pidray?), Rapiu, Rashap, and Shapash. In some names, a god is described as father, mother, brother, sister, or uncle (e.g., *Rashapabi*, "Rashap is my father"). In others, the bearer of the name is the god's son, daughter, servant, or devotee (e.g., *Abdi-Rashap*, "servant of Rashap"). A large class of names describes characteristics of the gods; those composed with Il, for example, emphasize his kingship (*Ilimilku,* "Il is king") and justice (*Danil,* "Il judges"; *Ilsdq,* "Il is just"), his creativity (*Yakunilu,* "Il establishes"; *Yabniilu,* "Il builds") and his love (*Hnnil,* "Il is gracious").

The second class of evidence for popular religion comes from metal figurines that are generally thought to represent gods and goddesses. A comprehensive catalog of these figurines, compiled by Ora Negbi (1976), describes over seventeen hundred of them. They are considered to have been miniature copies of now-lost wooden cult statues, and were probably used as votive idols. The fact that so many have been found at cultic sites suggests that they had some ceremonial function. Negbi notes that these idols "may have been used as amulets for magic purposes in domestic and funerary cults as well" (p. 2).

As mentioned above, the figurines at Ugarit attest to the popularity of two distinct types of divine pairs, a kingly and queenly figure (Il and Athirat) and a smiting god and voluptuous goddess (Baal and Anat, with Anat occasionally portrayed as a war goddess). The latter pair is the better attested in Late Bronze Ugarit; figurines have been found in deposits from this period in and around both of the temples on the acropolis.

Some textual evidence has been recovered for magic and divination at Ugarit. There are two versions of a long and impressive incantation against the bite of a venomous serpent; several important deities are summoned from their mythical abodes during the course of the incantations.

Inscribed clay models of lungs and livers show that extispicy (divination by the examination of animal viscera) was practiced at Ugarit. The practice was undoubtedly borrowed from Babylonia, but it was given a distinctive Canaanite cast by the incorporation of West Semitic sacrificial rites. Another borrowing from the Babylonians is attested in three omen texts that describe the predictive value of unusual human and animal births. These texts clearly parallel the famous Babylonian *shumma izbu* omen series; unfortunately, they are all quite fragmentary.

Finally, one very difficult text reports a divine oracle. It begins: "When the lord of the great/many gods [Il?] approached Ditan, the latter sought an oracle concerning the child." Some individual presumably wishes to inquire of Il about his (sick?) child. (A comparable episode occurs in the Kirta epic.) Il can be reached through an intermediary, Ditan, the eponymous patron of those deified dead known as the "assembly of Ditan." The text continues with a series of instructions (broken and unclear) that will enable the inquirer to obtain the desired oracular response. The text seems to conclude with several instructions, "and afterward there will be no suffering [?]".

Taken together, these texts indicate a lively interest in the mantic arts at Ugarit. There is practically no evidence, however, about the specialists who practiced those arts; perhaps that is because they operated on the periphery of the official cultic institutions.

The most problematic aspect of popular religion is the interpretation of the Ugaritic religious texts. Assuming that they were in some way normative and that they were diffused orally, they would embody the religious "teachings" of Ugarit. There are, however, no surviving interpretations of the texts or expositions of religious doctrine that explain what those teachings might have been or what impact they had on the life of a community of believers. The Ugaritic mythic and epic texts (as opposed to the descriptive ritual texts) can be read as homilies on the nature of the world in which people live. Ancient readers or hearers of these texts would have sought their own place in the "cosmos" they describe. Ugaritic believers, like modern believers, would presumably have formulated a special application of sacred texts to their own lives.

The *Baal* texts punctualize eternal truths in a symbolic realm that is only superficially remote from human experience. The gods experience joy and mourning, battle and tranquillity, life and death, power and impotence. The mightiest of the gods confronts the world's challenges and surmounts them all, until he encounters Death, the one enemy to whom gods and humans alike succumb. Baal's triumphs and trials, furthermore, illustrate the contiguity and interrelationship of everything in the world: the gods, nature, the political order, and human life are all part of the same order. When Baal is vanquished, political order collapses and the earth turns infertile—not because Baal "symbolizes" order and fertility in some simplistic way, but because the intricate balance of the world has been subverted. The same upset of the natural order occurs when Kirta, a human king, becomes mortally ill.

Overarching the flux of the world, and apparently not subject to it, is the wise and beneficent Il. At critical moments in the *Baal* texts, the gods journey (or send emissaries) to him in order to obtain his favor and advice. After Kirta's family is annihilated by malevolent forces, Il comforts the king in a dream; later on, Il provides the cure for Kirta's terrible illness. And in the Aqhat epic, Baal implores Il to grant a son to the childless Danil. Il consents, and appears to Danil in a dream with the good news. In every case, Il manifests transcendent power that is wielded justly, in response to urgent pleas.

The epic texts (perhaps "historico-mythic" would be

a better designation for them) *Aqhat* and *Kirta* parallel and supplement the mythic texts. They narrate the existential encounter of humans with the gods. Historical (or pseudohistorical) figures become exemplary or admonitory paradigms of human behavior.

The crises that move the plot of the *Aqhat* text demonstrate the conjunction and contiguity of the human and divine realms. Danil, who is, like Kirta, a man become god (one of the deified *rapium*—from the point of view of the reader, that is), is an embodiment of that contiguity. Danil is clearly an ideal type, pious and just; he brings his plea for a son before the gods in humble obeisance, and he is rewarded. The incubation rite performed by Danil at the beginning of the story seems to be a model of personal piety.

Other aspects of the *Aqhat* text suggest ethical teachings as well. The long-sought son, Aqhat, is presented as the archetypical huntsman, recipient of a magic bow fashioned by the craftsman god Kothar. But the bow is not an unequivocal blessing: it arouses the envy of Anat, and makes Aqhat so secure in his own power that he rudely dismisses the goddess. Aqhat's folly parallels Baal's when, secure in his new palace (also the work of Kothar), he presumptuously challenges Death. Even the cleverest invention affords no protection for one who oversteps his bounds and incurs divine wrath. Aqhat's death is avenged by his sister Pughat, a model of love and devotion, just as Baal's sister Anat acts on the god's behalf in the mythic texts.

The Kirta epic, like that of Aqhat, begins with its hero childless, this time because of catastrophe instead of impotence. Dramatic tension arises from the situation of a king without an heir, which could result in disruption of both the political and the natural order. The story conveys the fragility of power and the delicate relationship between humans and deities.

Kirta enjoys the favor of Il, "father of humankind," who calls the king "gracious one, lad of Il." Kirta is instructed to perform a series of rituals in order to secure victory in battle and a new wife. He does so faithfully, but he also stops to make a vow in the sanctuary of "Athirat of Tyre, goddess of the Sidonians." This act of personal piety leads to disaster: Kirta achieves his victory and builds a new family, but he is stricken with a mortal illness for his failure to fulfill the vow. His beneficent "father" Il intervenes once again in his behalf, but the story concludes with Kirta's son attempting to usurp the throne, accusing Kirta of unrighteousness (reason enough, evidently, to depose a king). The vicissitudes of kingship continue.

The texts are all firmly on the side of reward for virtue and piety, and punishment for wickedness, blasphemy, and folly. Yet even someone who is justly suffering the wrath of the gods may appeal to the gracious Il and be heard.

Survivals. Survivals of Canaanite religion are observable in two first-millennium cultural spheres, the Levant and the Aegean. Phoenician religion, both in the Levant and in its wider Mediterranean sphere of influence, represents, to some extent, a continuation of Canaanite traditions. Northern Israel's official cult was among the Levantine successors of Canaanite religion. It has often been noted that biblical polemics against that cult (for example, in the *Book of Hosea*) are directed against a characteristically Canaanite feature—the idea that the god (in this case Yahveh = Baal) was immanent in nature and subject to its flux. The Israelite god was, on the other hand, comfortably assimilated to the transcendent Il.

In the Aegean area, the nature of Canaanite influence is more controversial. But there is compelling evidence for the existence of direct West Semitic contact with Mycenaean Greece, creating a legacy of Semitic names, literary motifs, and religious practices that became part of the Hellenic cultural heritage.

BIBLIOGRAPHY

There are excellent, comprehensive articles on Amarna, Mari, and Ras Shamra in the *Dictionnaire de la Bible, Supplément*, vol. 1, cols. 207–225 (by Édouard Dhorme); vol. 5, cols. 883–905 (by Charles F. Jean); and vol. 9, cols. 1124–1466, respectively (Paris, 1928–). The Ras Shamra article, by several distinguished experts, is magisterial—the best survey to be found anywhere. In English, the journal *Biblical Archaeologist* has published a number of good survey articles: on Mari by George E. Mendenhall, vol. 11 (February 1948), pp. 1–19, and by Herbert B. Huffmon, vol. 31 (December 1968), pp. 101–124 (on the "prophetic texts"); on Amarna by Edward F. Campbell, vol. 23 (February 1960), pp. 2–22; on Ugarit by H. L. Ginsberg, vol. 8 (May 1945), pp. 41–58, and by Anson F. Rainey, vol. 28 (December 1965), pp. 102–125. All of these articles have been reprinted in *The Biblical Archaeologist Reader*, edited by David Noel Freedman and G. Ernest Wright, vols. 2 and 3 (Garden City, N.Y., 1961–1970). More recently, *Biblical Archaeologist* 47 (June 1984) is a special issue devoted to Mari.

Turning specifically to Ugarit, an excellent popular introduction is Gabriel Saadé's *Ougarit: Métropole cananéenne* (Beirut, 1979). Saadé gives a thorough account of the excavations, with complete bibliographical information and many illustrations. Most of the technical information is derived from articles in the journal *Syria*, beginning with volume 10 (1929), and from the volumes in the series "Mission de Ras-Shamra," 9 vols., edited by Claude F.-A. Schaeffer (Paris, 1936–1968). Two other useful works on the archaeological data are Patty Gerstenblith's *The Levant at the Beginning of the Middle Bronze Age* (Winona Lake, Ind., 1983) and Ora Negbi's *Canaanite Gods in Metal* (Tel Aviv, 1976).

A good detailed account of Ugarit's history is Mario Liverani's *Storia di Ugarit* (Rome, 1962), and an unsurpassed description of Ugaritic society is Anson F. Rainey's *The Social Structure of Ugarit* (in Hebrew; Jerusalem, 1967). Readers of English can consult Rainey's Ph.D. dissertation, "The Social Stratification of Ugarit" (Brandeis University, 1962).

On the study of Canaanite religion before the discovery of Ugarit, there is a fine survey by M. J. Mulder, "Von Seldon bis Schaeffer: Die Erforschung der kanaanäischen Götterwelt," in the leading scholarly journal devoted to Ugaritic studies, *Ugarit-Forschungen* 11 (1979): 655–671. The best general introduction to Canaanite religion is Hartmut Gese's "Die Religionen Altsyriens," in *Die Religionen Altsyriens, Altarabiens und der Mandäer* (Stuttgart, 1970), pp. 3–181. On the Canaanite gods, the standard work is still Marvin H. Pope and Wolfgang Röllig's "Syrien," in *Wörterbuch der Mythologie*, edited by H. W. Haussig, vol. 1 (Stuttgart, 1965), pp. 219–312. On the rituals and cultic personnel, an excellent presentation of the data is Jean-Michel de Tarragon's *Le culte à Ugarit* (Paris, 1980), which should be consulted alongside Paolo Xella's *I testi rituali di Ugarit* (Rome, 1981). There is an exceptionally interesting theoretical discussion of Canaanite religion by David L. Petersen and Mark Woodward in "Northwest Semitic Religion: A Study of Relational Structures," *Ugarit-Forschungen* 9 (1977): 232–248. The outstanding representative of the myth-and-ritual approach is Theodor H. Gaster's *Thespis*, 2d ed. (1961; New York, 1977).

There is not yet an adequately introduced and annotated English translation of the Ugaritic texts. The best English translations are those of H. L. Ginsberg, in J. B. Pritchard's *Ancient Near Eastern Texts relating to the Old Testament*, 3d ed. (Princeton, 1969), pp. 129–155, and those in J. C. L. Gibson's revision of G. R. Driver's *Canaanite Myths and Legends*, 2d ed. (Edinburgh, 1978). The serious student should consult *Textes ougaritiques*, translated and edited by André Caquot and others (Paris, 1974), and the even more comprehensive Spanish work by Gregorio del Olmo Lete, *Mitos y leyendas de Canaán según la tradición de Ugarit* (Madrid, 1981), complemented by the same author's *Interpretación de la mitología cananea* (Valencia, 1984). A more popular introduction and translation that is both readable and of high quality is Paolo Xella's *Gli antenati di Dio* (Verona, 1982). A comparable but inferior volume in English is *Stories from Ancient Canaan*, edited and translated by Michael D. Coogan (Philadelphia, 1978).

Works on Ugarit and the Bible are legion. The serious student is directed to *Ras Shamra Parallels*, edited by Loren R. Fischer, 2 vols. (Rome, 1972–1975). The contributions are uneven in quality, but the many proposed parallels are presented with full bibliographic information. A convenient survey of comparative studies is Peter C. Craigie's "Ugarit and the Bible," in *Ugarit in Retrospect*, edited by Gordon Douglas Young (Winona Lake, Ind., 1981), pp. 99–111. John Gray's *The Legacy of Canaan*, 2d ed. (Leiden, 1965), has become a standard work in this area; its great learning and originality are marred by eccentricity, especially in the translation of the Ugaritic texts. On the most important classical account of "Canaanite" religion, see the definitive work by Albert I. Baumgarten, *The Phoenician History of Philo of Byblos* (Leiden, 1981). Semitic influence on the Aegean world is one of the main topics of Cyrus H. Gordon's stimulating book *Before the Bible: The Common Background of Greek and Hebrew Civilizations* (London, 1962); a more technical work on the subject is Michael C. Astour's brilliant *Hellenosemitica* (Leiden, 1967).

Alan M. Cooper

The Literature

The scope of this article needs definition. *Canaanite* designates the culture of the region often known as the Levant, roughly comprising the modern countries of Syria, Lebanon, Israel, and Jordan, beginning with the earliest extensive written records in the third millennium BCE and ending with the start of the Hellenistic period in the fourth century BCE. The term *Canaanite* did not have such a broad definition in antiquity; generally, and especially in the Bible, Canaan is the southwestern part of this region. The sources are not consistent in this usage, however, and many modern scholars apply it to the regions that in the first half of the first millennium BCE were divided into the political units of Phoenicia, Israel (later Israel and Judah), Ammon, Moab, Edom, and, not infrequently, Aram, especially Aram-Damascus.

The term *literature* is used here to mean extended works composed in poetic style, specifically several dozen clay tablets, inscribed with an alphabetic cuneiform script, that have been found at ancient Ugarit (modern Ras Shamra) on the Syrian coast in excavations since 1929. The much larger body of material found there includes a variety of documents not germane to our topic, such as diplomatic correspondence, lists of ritual offerings, economic texts, and notes for the care and treatment of horses. But even these contain valuable evidence for religious practice, especially in the names of the gods listed as recipients of offerings, names that were used as components of personal names.

Most of the literary texts were found in the temple precinct of ancient Ugarit, on the city's acropolis. This is not merely a result of scribal activity in the sacred quarter, since the secular archives were found in the royal palace area and other libraries existed elsewhere in the city; rather, the presence of our texts in a religious context indicates that they had some specifically religious function. Unhappily, few of them have any rubrics, and other, specifically ritual texts, such as the lists of offerings and the inscriptions on clay models of livers and lungs used for divination, provide no clue to the cultic setting in which the literary texts were used. Presumably at least some of them were read or recited periodically at festivals, as were the Homeric poems in ancient Greece; others may have been actual librettos for ritual activities.

The major mythological and epic texts were written on clay tablets that were fired after being inscribed on both sides in one to four columns. The lines are written continuously, with divisions between the words but without other spacing except for occasional dividing lines between sense units and episodes; these, however, are not used systematically. Not infrequently the tablets have a title at the beginning; thus, two of the three parts of the Kirta cycle are marked "Concerning Kirta," and one tablet of each of the Baal and Aqhat cycles has a corresponding heading. Such a cataloging device may have been used more regularly, but since a significant number of the tablets are broken at the edges we cannot be sure. The incomplete preservation of many of the tablets also makes it more difficult to follow the sequence of the narratives and hence to interpret them; this explains the conjectural analyses below.

Four tablets have concluding notations; the most complete reads: "The scribe was Ilimilku from Shubanu, the apprentice of Attanu-Purlianni, the chief priest, the chief herdsman; the sponsor was Niqmaddu, king of Ugarit, master of Yargub, lord of Tharumani." As this colophon indicates, the texts were written down under royal patronage, illustrating the close connection between palace and temple. More significantly, they may indicate that the tablets were dictated to the scribe; in any case, we are dealing with an originally oral literature, perhaps at the precise moment of transition to a written medium.

Among the characteristics that Canaanite literature shares with other oral literatures is the use of stock epithets for human and divine characters, a technique most familiar from the *Iliad* and the *Odyssey*. Thus, El, the head of the pantheon, is variously called "the bull," "the creator of all," "the father of years," "the kind, the compassionate," and "the king"; Baal is "the prince," "the conqueror (of warriors)," and "the lord of the earth"; Kirta, the hero of the epic called by his name, is "the gracious one," "the noble," "the servant of El"; and Danel, the father of the title character of *Aqhat*, is "the hero" and "the Healer's man." The poets apparently chose the epithet that was most appropriate for the context and that best fit the meter.

Another device familiar from the Homeric poems is the use of formulaic units to narrate standard scenes: the offering of a sacrifice, the saddling of an ass, the preparation of a banquet, the journey of a god or goddess to El's abode. Thus, with appropriate changes of number and gender, the following lines occur some six times in the extant corpus:

> Then she headed toward El,
> at the source of the two rivers,
> in the midst of the two seas' pools;
> she opened El's tent and entered
> the shrine of the King, the Father of Years.
> At El's feet she bowed down and adored;
> she prostrated herself and worshiped him.

Also characteristic of Ugaritic literature is the almost verbatim repetition of large blocks of lines; this is found in the giving of a command and its execution, the occurrence of a dream and its telling, and in various specific narratives.

Finally, like other ancient eastern Mediterranean literatures, this originally oral Canaanite literature was poetic. Since the texts were written almost entirely without vowels, it has so far not been possible to establish the metrical principles underlying the poetry, and rhyme was not used. But one formal characteristic can be identified, traditionally called parallelism and fortunately not obscured by translation. In Canaanite poetry the basic element is a unit of two or three lines in which one thought is extended by repetition, paraphrase, or contrast. Thus, the lines

> "Let me tell you, Prince Baal,
> let me repeat, Rider on the Clouds:
> behold, your enemy, Baal,
> behold, you will kill your enemy,
> behold, you will annihilate your foes;
> you will take your eternal kingdom,
> your dominion forever and ever"

consist of three units, each of which expresses a complete thought. This stylistic feature is familiar from the other major source of Canaanite literature, the Hebrew scriptures, for the same building blocks of Canaanite verse—parallel pairs—are used there as well:

> Behold, your enemies, Yahveh,
> behold, your enemies have perished,
> all evildoers have been scattered. (*Ps.* 92:9)

> Your kingdom is an eternal kingdom,
> your rule is forever and ever. (*Ps.* 145:13)

The reason for this similarity of form and content is cultural: notwithstanding the significant geographical and temporal differences between Ugarit and Israel, they were part of a larger cultural entity that shared a common poetic and religious vocabulary.

This commonality is significant, for the literature of ancient Israel preserved in the Bible is able to shed much light on obscurities and gaps in the Canaanite literature from Ugarit. Conversely, the Ugaritic texts enable us to understand the Canaanites better on their own terms instead of through the often virulent polemics of the biblical writers. Each body of literature thus illumines the other, as will be seen below.

Mythological Texts

Here we will consider texts in which the protagonists are divine and no reference is made to human persons or a historical time frame.

The Baal Cycle. The major cycle of preserved Canaanite literature from Ugarit has to do with the deity Baal, the central god in the Ugaritic pantheon. Although the high god El was worshiped at Ugarit, as throughout the Semitic world, and figures in a number of texts, Baal seems to have supplanted him as the major deity by the late second millennium BCE; this is confirmed both by nonliterary sources, such as ritual lists and personal names, and by the Baal cycle, whose theme in brief is the affirmation "Baal the Conqueror is our king!"

More than a dozen tablets contain various episodes or variants of the Baal cycle, indicating the god's importance at Ugarit, but many of them are fragmentary. Furthermore, scholars have reached no consensus on the order of the texts, and so any sustained development of the plot of the cycle is difficult to arrive at. What is clear is the main thrust of three episodes: Baal's battle with Sea, the construction and dedication of Baal's house, and Baal's encounter with Death.

Baal and Sea. El, the head of the pantheon, had apparently encouraged a rivalry between two deities of a younger generation: Sea (Yamm), called "El's darling" and also by the parallel titles Prince Sea and Judge River, and Baal, the son of Dagan (whose name means "grain"). Initially Sea seems to have gained the upper hand. He sends the council of the gods over which El presides an ultimatum:

> "Message of Sea, your master,
> your Lord, Judge River:
> 'El, give up the one you are hiding,
> the one the masses are hiding,
> give up Baal and his powers,
> the son of Dagan: I will assume his inheritance.' "

Although El and the divine assembly are willing to capitulate to Sea's demand, Baal is not, and he proceeds to engage Sea in battle. With the help of magical clubs fashioned for him by Kothar wa-Hasis ("skillful and wise"; the divine craftsman, the Canaanite equivalent of the Greek Hephaistos), Baal defeats his adversary:

> The club danced in Baal's hands,
> like a vulture from his fingers;
> it struck Prince Sea on the skull,
> Judge River between the eyes;
> Sea stumbled;
> he fell to the ground;
> his joints shook;
> his frame collapsed.
> Baal captured and drank Sea;
> he finished Judge River.

This brief episode cannot be fully understood without reference to similar and more detailed Near Eastern myths, especially that preserved in the Babylonian *Enuma elish.* There the council of the gods is threatened by the primeval goddess Tiamat ("sea"). The only deity able to rescue the gods is the young storm god, Marduk, who agrees to do so only if he is given complete authority over gods and human beings. Following their battle, described in lavish detail, Marduk forms the elements of the cosmos from the corpses of his defeated adversaries, and is proclaimed supreme ruler. Despite differences of detail, we seem to have here two versions of a single story that tells how a younger god comes to assume leadership over his fellows; similar stories of origins are found in ancient Anatolia, Greece, and India. Like Marduk, Baal is a storm god: he is called the "rider on the clouds" (compare the Homeric epithet of Zeus, "the cloud-gatherer"); his weapon is the lightning bolt; he is responsible for the rains in their season.

Many of these aspects of Baal are also attributed to the Israelite Yahveh. Thus, he too is the "rider on the clouds" (*Ps.* 68:4); he

> makes the clouds his chariot,
> walks on the wings of the wind,
> makes the winds his messengers,
> fire [and] flame his ministers. (*Ps.* 104:3–4)

There are also allusions in various biblical passages to a primeval conflict between Yahveh and the sea; especially noteworthy is *Job* 26:12–13:

> With his power he stilled the sea,
> with his skill he smote Rahab,
> with his wind he bagged Sea,
> his hand pierced the fleeing serpent.

(Compare *Psalms* 89:9–10 and *Isaiah* 27:1.)

The Bible does not, however, present a completely developed version of this primeval struggle, for in ancient Israelite tradition the normative event was not mythical but historical: the defeat of the Egyptian army at the Red Sea. But frequently the language used to celebrate this event was derived from Canaanite myth. Thus, *Psalms* 77:15–20 incorporates into a remembrance of God's ancient deeds the following:

With your arm you redeemed your people,
the sons of Jacob and Joseph.
The waters saw you, God,
the waters saw you and writhed,
indeed, the deeps trembled;
the clouds poured out water,
the thunderheads sounded their voice,
your arrows were in constant motion. . . .
Through the sea was your way,
and your path through the mighty
waters. . . .
You led your people like a flock,
by the hand of Moses and Aaron.

(Compare *Isaiah* 51:9–10.)

Furthermore, the very parallel terms used of Baal's adversary are put into service by biblical poets, as in *Habakkuk* 3:8:

Were you not angry at the river, Yahveh,
was your rage not against the river,
was your wrath not against the sea?

And in *Psalms* 114:1–3 the formulaic pair "sea/river" is partially historicized:

When Israel came out of Egypt,
the house of Jacob from people of a different language . . .
the sea saw and fled,
the Jordan turned back.

In the more fully elaborated prose accounts of the story of Israel's deliverance, the splitting of the Red Sea is repeated at the crossing of the Jordan, again reflecting the ancient parallelism.

Baal's house. After a considerable gap, the Baal cycle continues with a description of Baal's victory banquet. One of Baal's servants prepares an appropriate spread for "Baal the Conqueror, the Prince, the Lord of the Earth":

He put a cup in his hand,
a goblet in both his hands,
a large beaker, manifestly great,
a jar to astound a mortal,
a holy cup that women should not see,
a goblet that Asherah must not set her eye on;
he took a thousand jugs of wine,
he mixed ten thousand in his mixing bowl.

Another break in the text occurs here, and then we have a lengthy account of a battle waged by Anat, the most vividly described of the three major goddesses in the Ugaritic texts. The other two, Asherah (Athiratu in Ugaritic) and Astarte (Athtartu), appear only infrequently and generally in formulaic passages that shed little light on their characters. Anat, on the other hand, is a major figure in the Baal cycle, a position that is appropriate in view of her relationship to Baal: she is his sister and his wife. As this description of her martial style indicates, Anat is a violent deity:

Heads rolled under her like balls,
hands flew over her like locusts,
the warriors' hands like swarms of grasshoppers.
She fastened the heads to her back,
she tied the hands to her belt.
She plunged knee-deep in the soldiers' blood,
up to her hands in the warriors' gore;
with a staff she drove off her enemies,
with the string of her bow, her opponents.

After this gory battle Anat purifies herself:

She drew water and washed,
the heavens' dew, the earth's oil,
the rain of the Rider on the Clouds,
dew that the heavens pour,
rain that is poured from the stars.

In the next scene, Baal sends messengers to summon Anat; his invitation is lyrical in tone:

"Message of Baal the Conqueror,
the word of the Conqueror of Warriors:
'Remove war from the earth,
set love in the ground,
pour peace into the heart of the earth,
rain down love on the heart of the fields.
Hasten! hurry! rush!
Run to me with your feet,
race to me with your legs;
for I have a word to tell you,
a story to recount to you:
the word of the tree and the charm of the stone,
the whisper of the heavens to the earth,
of the seas to the stars.
I understand the lightning that the heavens do not know,
the word that human beings do not know,
and earth's masses cannot understand.
Come, and I will reveal it:
in the midst of my mountain, the divine Tsafon,
in the sanctuary, in the mountain of my inheritance,
in the pleasant place, in the hill I have conquered.' "

When Anat sees Baal's messengers approaching she is overcome with fear that Baal is threatened by another enemy. She lists the various enemies of Baal who have been defeated; first among them is Sea, who is given a full range of epithets, including "the dragon," "the twisting serpent," and "the seven-headed monster." Curiously, Anat herself claims credit for Sea's defeat, as for that of the other enemies named. Clearly there was more than one version of Baal's defeat of Sea, for the one preserved does not depict Anat as a participant in the battle; similarly, we have no account of combat between Baal and such adversaries as "the divine calf, the Rebel," "El's bitch, Fire," or "El's daughter, Zebub." These gaps in our knowledge are salutary reminders of the limited nature of our sample of Ugaritic literature, and of the difficulty of combining the several tablets of the Baal cycle into a continuous narrative.

When Baal's messengers assure Anat that there is no danger and issue Baal's invitation, Anat proceeds to visit Baal. Again a section is missing, and as the text resumes we finally come to the point of this tablet: the construction of a permanent abode for Baal. In the gap he apparently complains to Anat that despite his victory over Sea, he has no house like the other gods. The word *house* in Ugaritic, as in Hebrew, has several senses; here it means not just a dwelling but a permanent abode for the god, hence a temple. The construction of a temple for the god who has been victorious over the forces of chaos is a typical motif; in *Enuma elish* in particular, after Marduk establishes cosmic order and creates human beings from the blood of Tiamat's spouse, the gods themselves build a temple for Marduk, and after its completion are his guests at an inaugural banquet. Baal's elevation to kingship over the gods and human beings is therefore incomplete as long as he has no house like the other gods.

Anat goes to El to obtain his approval for the erection of a temple for Baal; her request includes a characteristic threat of violence if she is refused:

"I'll smash your head;
 I'll make your gray hair run with blood,
 your gray beard with gore."

Before El can give his assent, however, his consort, Asherah, has to agree; mollified by a bribe of marvelous gifts specially fashioned by Kothar, the divine craftsman, she intercedes for Baal:

"You are great El, you are truly wise;
 your gray beard truly instructs you. . . .
Now Baal will begin the rainy season,
 the season of wadis in flood;
and he will sound his voice in the clouds,
 flash his lightning to the earth.
Let him complete his house of cedar!
 let him construct his house of bricks!"

Anat brings the news of El's approval to her brother; Baal then gathers appropriate building materials—silver, gold, lapis lazuli—and commissions Kothar to begin work. As they discuss the plans, Kothar recommends that a window be included; despite his repeated urgings, Baal refuses. The house is built, and with the other gods Baal celebrates its completion at a banquet, after which he goes on a triumphal tour of his domain. When he returns, he has apparently changed his mind about the window, and at his request Kothar makes one; from this window, appropriately described as a slit in the clouds, Baal thunders, the earth quakes, and his enemies flee; the enthronement of Baal as king is complete.

Baal and Death. The above episode concludes with this proclamation by Baal:

"No other king or non-king
 shall set his power over the earth.
I will send no tribute to El's son Death,
 no homage to El's Darling, the Hero.
Let Death cry to himself,
 let the Darling grumble in his heart;
for I alone will rule over the gods;
 I alone will fatten gods and human beings;
 I alone will satisfy earth's masses."

This challenge to Death is best explained by the incomplete nature of Baal's triumph: while he has defeated Sea and has been proclaimed king by the divine assembly, the major force of Death is still unsubdued.

Like Sea, Death is El's son; apparently Baal's accession to kingship over the gods requires the elimination of this rival as well. The enigmatic dispute between Baal and Kothar about whether Baal's house is to have a window may be an indication of Baal's awareness of this requirement. Baal's initial reluctance can be better understood by reference to *Jeremiah* 9:21:

Death has come up through our windows,
 he has entered our fortresses,
cutting down the children in the street
 and the young men in the squares.

Since the decipherment of Ugaritic it has become clear that in many biblical passages that mention death there is at least indirect reference to the Canaanite deity representing death (Hebrew and Ugaritic, *mot*) and not merely a designation of the cessation of life. The verse in *Jeremiah* is one such passage, and may reflect a popular belief that the god Death entered a house through the window. Seen in this light, Baal is at first unwilling to include a window in his house because he fears giving Death access; later, after his inaugural banquet and triumphal march, his grasp of power is, he thinks, more secure.

In any event, having proclaimed his supremacy, Baal sends messengers to Death; their names are Gapn and Ugar ("vine" and "field," appropriately reflecting Baal's aspect as god of the storm that brings fertility and thus anticipating the coming contest with its antithesis). Baal directs them:

"Head toward the midst of his city, the Swamp,
 Muck, his royal house,
 Phlegm, the land of his inheritance."

Death's underworld domain is, like the grave, a damp, dark, unpleasant place; it is reached from his earthly territory, the barren, hot desert, where (Baal continues)

> "Sun, the gods' torch, burns,
> the heavens shimmer under the sway of El's
> Darling, Death."

Suitably warned and instructed, Baal's two messengers leave. Because the text is broken here and we may even be missing an entire tablet, it is not wholly clear what the gist of Baal's message is; a plausible guess is that Baal wishes to invite Death to his new palace. But Death will have none of such niceties; Baal is condemned for his destruction of Sea and its cosmic consequences, and the sentence is death at Death's hands. Gapn and Ugar return with Death's reply:

> "One lip to the earth, one lip to the heavens;
> he stretches his tongue to the stars.
> Baal must enter inside him;
> he must go down into his mouth,
> like an olive cake,
> the earth's produce,
> the fruit of the trees."

Without any sign of resistance, Baal agrees:

> "Hail, El's son Death!
> I am your servant; I am yours forever."

The tablet is very fragmentary here, leaving only the skeleton of a plot. Baal is to take with him all his accoutrements—cloud, winds, lightning bolts, rain—and companions, and to proceed to the underworld; then, we are told, "the gods will know that you have died." Apparently he does so, for when a readable text resumes two messengers are reporting to El:

> "We arrived at the pleasant place, the desert pasture,
> at the lovely fields on Death's shore.
> We came upon Baal:
> he had fallen to the ground.
> Baal the Conqueror has died;
> the Prince, the Lord of the Earth, has perished."

El's reaction is, initially, one of grief:

> He poured earth on his head as a sign of mourning,
> on his skull the dust in which he rolled;
> he covered his loins with a sackcloth.
> He cut his skin with a knife,
> he made incisions with a razor;
> he cut his cheeks and chin,
> he raked his arms with a reed,
> he plowed his chest like a garden,
> he raked his back like a valley.
> He raised his voice and shouted:
> "Baal is dead: what will happen to the peoples?
> Dagan's son: what will happen to the masses?"

Meanwhile, Anat independently discovers Baal's corpse, and she too mourns in the same typical fashion. Afterward, with the help of Sun, she brings Baal's body back to Mount Tsafon, where she buries him and offers the appropriate funerary sacrifice. Then she heads toward El's abode, where her announcement of Baal's death occasions El's suggestion to Asherah that one of her sons replace Baal as king; at least two try and are found wanting.

After a considerable gap in the text, Anat is described as she is about to encounter Death:

> Like the heart of a cow for her calf,
> like the heart of a ewe for her lamb,
> so was Anat's heart for Baal.

Anat grabs Death's clothes and insists that he give up her brother; Death refuses, or at least is unable to grant her request. Time passes; in Baal's absence the forces of drought and sterility are dominant; "the heavens shimmered under the sway of El's son, Death." Again Anat approaches Death; no words are exchanged, but this time Baal's sister is as violent in grief as she is in battle:

> She seized El's son, Death:
> with a sword she split him;
> with a sieve she winnowed him;
> with a fire she burned him;
> with a hand mill she ground him;
> in the fields she sowed him.

This agricultural imagery is striking: for Baal, the dead god of fertility, to be restored to life, for Death, the living god of sterility, to be destroyed, the mysterious processes of the natural cycle have to be ritually repeated. It is important to note that we are dealing here not with an annual cycle but rather with the periodic disaster that a prolonged drought can cause; if the life-giving winter rains are to fail, there will be no crops, no food for animals or humans. In myth this is represented by the struggle between Baal and Death; with Baal dead, the forces of sterility prevail, and Baal can be revivified only by Death's death. Only if Death, whose appetite is insatiable, whose gaping jaws have swallowed up Baal like a lamb or a kid, is himself swallowed up, can Baal's power return.

In the next scene, El has a prophetic dream in which he foresees Baal's restoration and its effects:

> In a dream of El, the Kind, the Compassionate,
> in a vision of the Creator of All,
> the heavens rained down oil,
> the wadis ran with honey.

Baal is restored to power, and, as a later heir of Canaanite tradition would put it (*1 Cor.* 15:54–55):

> Death is swallowed up in victory.
> Where, O Death, is your victory?
> Where, O Death, is your sting?

(Compare *Isaiah* 25:8 and *Hosea* 13:14.)

The Baal cycle does not quite end here; there remain his revenge on his rivals and yet another successful struggle with Death after a seven-year interval; the latter confirms the analysis of this last episode as the mythical representation of an occasional rather than an annual event.

The relationship between El and Baal is complex. On a narrative level, it is difficult not to sense El's less than enthusiastic acceptance of Baal's dominion. In the first episode he is willing to hand Baal over to Sea, "El's darling"; in the second, both he and Asherah are scornful of Baal's position, for "he has no house like the other gods"; and in the third, despite his real (although stylized) grief at Baal's death, he is quick to suggest replacements from his own family. Furthermore, throughout the cycle, El remains the head of the pantheon and presides over the council of the gods. Yet this very cycle, the most extensive among the surviving texts from Ugarit, tells of Baal's rise to some kind of preeminence. At the very least it can be suggested that Canaanite ideology was not static; and the mythological literature reflects this lack of rigidity. While Baal had become the patron god of Ugarit, this did not mean that its citizens rejected either the worship of El or the traditional understanding of his role in the world of the gods.

Other Mythological Texts. In other texts from the same archaeological context as the Baal cycle, El has a dominant, sometimes even an exclusive, role. I shall deal briefly here with a few of the better-preserved texts that also have to do with the Canaanite gods.

Birth of the beautiful and gracious gods. Unlike the other texts treated here, this tablet (of which some seventy-six lines survive) combines mythological material with ritual rubrics; the former is apparently the accompanying libretto for the action prescribed by the latter.

The central portion of the tablet describes the conception and birth of the deities Dawn (Shahr) and Dusk (Shalim). As it opens, El is at the seashore, where two women became aroused as they observe his virility:

> El's hand [a euphemism] grew as long as the Sea's,
> El's hand as long as the Ocean's.

In language full of *double entendre* we are told how El shoots and cooks a bird, and then seduces the women:

> The two women became El's wives,
> El's wives forever and ever.
> He bowed low, he kissed their lips;
> behold, their lips were sweet,
> as sweet as pomegranates.
> When they kissed, they conceived,
> when they embraced, they became pregnant;
> they began labor and gave birth to Dawn and Dusk.

Two divine sons are thus sired by El, who is in full possession of his vigor and virility. As his offspring, they "suck the breasts of the Lady," El's principal consort, the goddess Asherah. But the two young gods have insatiable appetites, comparable (since the same formula is used) to that of Death himself:

> One lip to the earth,
> one lip to the heavens:
> into their mouths entered
> the birds of the heavens and the fish in the sea.

So, at El's command, they are banished to the desert; after seven years they are finally allowed to reenter the land by "the guard of the sown"; here the text breaks off.

This summary does not begin to deal with the many problems of interpretation posed by the laconic text, nor is it clear how the first portion of the tablet is related to the material just recounted. The tablet begins with a first-person invocation to "the beautiful and gracious gods," almost certainly Dawn and Dusk, who are minor but established figures in the Ugaritic pantheon; Dawn also occurs in biblical tradition (*Is.* 14:12). Their exile in the desert may be a mythical explanation of their perceived origin: in the ancient view both day and night rose in the east, and from the Canaanites' perspective the eastern limit of their territory was the great Syrian desert.

The details of the ritual, in which particular words and actions are to be repeated seven times and performed in the presence of the king, queen, and royal court, are highly obscure. Various deities are mentioned, various sacrifices are to be offered, and while there are some verbal connections with the mythic section, it is difficult to interpret the whole with coherence; yet it is improbable that the two parts are not somehow related. What is clear is that the myth depicts El with full enjoyment of his generative powers, and it is likely that the concern underlying both the ritual and the narrative parts is the maintenance of fertility.

Marriage of Nikkal and the moon god. This relatively brief text is a kind of epithalamium celebrating the marriage of the moon god (Yarikh), "the heavens' lamp," to Nikkal wa-Ib. The first part of the latter's composite name is ultimately derived from the Sumerian title of the moon goddess Ningal, "great lady," and its second half is connected with the word for "fruit." The tablet opens with an invocation of Nikkal and Khirkhib, an otherwise unknown deity called "the king of summer," and then tells of the Moon's passion for Nikkal. To obtain his intended bride he uses the services of Khirkhib, the divine marriage broker, offering to pay her father as bride-price a thousand silver pieces, ten thousand gold pieces, lapis lazuli gems, and real estate as well.

Khirkhib suggests that Moon marry instead Baal's daughter Pidray ("misty"), or someone else, but Moon is adamant; the marriage with Nikkal is arranged, and the bride-price is paid:

> Her father set the beam of the scales;
> her mother the trays of the scales;
> her brothers arranged the standards;
> her sisters took care of the weights.

This portion of the tablet ends with another invocation: "Let me sing of Nikkal wa-Ib, the light of Moon; may Moon give you light."

The brief second part of the tablet consists of another hymnic invocation of the goddesses of childbirth, the Wise Women (Kotharatu), also called "the Singers, the Swallows." Their presence, as in the account of the birth of Aqhat (see below), guarantees the conception and safe delivery of babies.

El's banquet. This short tablet provides a candid glimpse of the gods, and especially El, as they participate in a ritual symposium. El invites the gods to his house, where he has prepared a feast; among those present are Moon, Astarte, and Anat.

> The gods ate and drank;
> they drank wine until they were full,
> new wine until they were drunk.

At this point the party becomes rowdy, and the guests are rebuked by El's gatekeeper; El too is chided, apparently for allowing the unruly behavior. Then, however, El himself becomes intoxicated, and decides to retire; en route he has an alcoholic hallucination of a figure with two horns and a tail (a possible satanic prototype). Despite the support of two attendants,

> El fell in his excrement and urine,
> El [became] like those who go down into the earth.

In other words, he is dead drunk. The reverse side of the tablet is extremely fragmentary, but appropriately, it seems to contain a remedy for hangover.

In the middle of the text, El is described as seated, or enthroned, in his *mrzh* ("symposium"). The *mrzh* was a chronologically and geographically widespread ritual institution, mentioned several times in texts from Ugarit (including once in the fragmentary Refaim texts, discussed below), twice in the Bible (*Jer.* 16:5, *Am.* 6:7), and in Phoenician/Punic texts from Sidon and Marseilles. In Aramaic it is referred to in a text from Elephantine in Egypt; in Nabatean, from Petra, and frequently at Palmyra. Scholars disagree as to the precise character of this institution, especially its possible connection with funereal practices and memorials; there is no doubt that in this text we have at least part of its mythological background.

Epic Texts

The two major Canaanite literary cycles with human protagonists are *Aqhat* and *Kirta*. As in more familiar classical epics, however, and as in other ancient Near Eastern sources, such as the Mesopotamian Gilgamesh epic, the gods play a significant role in the narrative; from a temporal point of view, actions in both the divine and human realms occur on a single continuum. Thus, while a specific time is not indicated in either of these two texts, we are dealing with a period that is historical at least in the sense that the cosmic order has been established.

Aqhat. This title is an ancient one, appearing as a cataloging device at the beginning of the third major tablet of the cycle that is preserved. Nevertheless, the story is part of a larger one about Aqhat's father, Danel, a royal figure whose righteousness and wisdom were legendary (see *Ez.* 14:14, 14:20, 28:2). The surviving remnants of the cycle deal with the relationship of Danel and his son, and as the extant story begins, Danel is described performing a seven-day incubation ritual, occasioned by his lack of progeny.

A period of seven days or seven years occurs some five times in *Aqhat*, and elsewhere in the Ugaritic corpus as well: Baal's initial defeat of Death lasted seven years, and as we shall see, Danel will curse the land by calling for an absence of Baal's generative powers:

> "For seven years let Baal fail,
> eight, the Rider on the Clouds:
> no dew, no showers,
> no surging of the two seas,
> no benefit of Baal's voice."

We are reminded of the alternation of seven years of plenty and seven of famine in the biblical story of Joseph. This frequent use of the number seven applies to days as well; in both the Ugaritic texts and the Bible, seven days is the conventional length of a journey, and the revelation about to be made to Danel recalls God's call to Moses on the seventh day (*Ex.* 24:16). Other biblical examples include the seven days of creation at the beginning of *Genesis*, and the literal *tour de force* of the collapse of Jericho, which occurred on the seventh day after seven priests blowing on seven trumpets had marched seven times around the city. It is unlikely that this repeated use of seven is much more than literary convention, but its frequent occurrence in Ugaritic and biblical literatures underlines the close relationship between them.

On the seventh and final day of Danel's ritual, Baal, Danel's patron, addresses the assembly of the gods on Danel's behalf:

"Unlike his brothers, he has no son;
no heir, like his cousins;
yet he has made an offering for the gods to eat,
an offering for the holy ones to drink."

In response, El blesses Danel and then catalogs the benefits which a son will provide:

"When he kisses his wife she will become pregnant;
when he embraces her she will conceive:
she will become pregnant, she will give birth, she will conceive;
and there will be a son in his house,
an heir inside his palace,
to set up a stela for his divine ancestor,
a family shrine in the sanctuary;
to free his spirit from the earth,
guard his footsteps from the Slime;
to crush those who rebel against him,
drive off his oppressors;
to eat his offering in the temple of Baal,
his portion in the temple of El;
to hold his hand when he is drunk,
support him when he is full of wine;
to patch his roof when it leaks,
wash his clothes when they are dirty."

Heartened by the divine promise, Danel returns to his palace, where with the assistance of the Wise Women, the goddesses of marriage and childbirth, conception occurs after seven days.

This list of ritual and personal filial duties suggests that one of the epic's purposes was didactic: to school its audience in proper social behavior, which included not only the responsibilities of a son to his father but the model conduct of kings, of daughters and sisters, and, in fact, of all humans in their complex relationships with one another and with the gods.

The picture of the childless patriarch is a commonplace in Canaanite literature; as we shall see, the opening of *Kirta* is remarkably similar to that of the Danel cycle. Furthermore, in *Genesis*, Abraham, Isaac, and Jacob each are initially either childless or lacking descendants from their favorite or principal wives. In each case, offspring are promised by their patron deity: in Abraham's case, in the context of a nocturnal revelation, like Danel's (*Gn.* 15); and in Isaac's, in response to a prayer by the patriarch (*Gn.* 25:21). In the more extensive Jacob cycle the promise of numerous descendants is made at night (*Gn.* 28:11–17) and is granted in response to Jacob's favorite wife Rachel's specific prayer (*Gn.* 30:22). The stories of Hannah (Samuel's mother), of Samson's parents, and to some extent of Job are further variations of this motif. In the biblical narratives of Israel's ancestors as preserved in *Genesis* it is further significant that the patron deity who pronounces the blessing on each patriarch, although called Yahveh in the present sources, is elsewhere unequivocally identified as El (see *Ex.* 6:3; cf. *Gn.* 14:19–20, 49:25). As his epithets in biblical literature and especially in *Genesis* make clear, this is none other than the head of the Canaanite pantheon. It is noteworthy that in *Aqhat*, even though Baal is Danel's patron (as his epithet, "the Healer's man," indicates), the blessing is given by El; Baal acts only as mediator between the childless king and "El, the Bull, the Creator of All."

The middle third of this first of the cycle's three tablets is missing; in this section the birth of Danel's son Aqhat must have been related. The story then resumes. As Danel is engaged in typical royal judicial activity at the city gate, judging the cases of widows and orphans, he sees Kothar approaching with a bow and arrows. The divine craftsman gives this weapon to Danel as a gift for his son; after a suitable feast, prepared by Danel's wife for their divine guest, the god departs.

In the next episode Anat, having seen the wonderfully crafted weapon, offers to buy it from Aqhat; the latter refuses, proposing instead that he will supply the raw materials necessary for the construction of another one by Kothar. Anat goes further:

"If you want eternal life, Aqhat the Hero,
even if you want eternal life, I'll give it to you,
immortality—I'll make it yours.
You'll be able to match years with Baal,
months with the sons of El."

Again Aqhat refuses, and this time his response goes beyond the proper limits:

"Don't lie to me, Virgin,
for with a hero your lies are wasted.
A mortal—what does he get in the end?
what does a mortal finally get?
Plaster poured on his head,
lime on top of his skull.
As every man dies, I will die;
yes, I too will surely die.

And I have something else to tell you:
bows are for men!
Do women ever hunt?"

The first part of Aqhat's response, while realistic, is bad enough: he implicitly denies Anat's ability to provide what she had promised, since from his perspective old age and death are inescapable. But in insulting her prowess with such weapons, Aqhat is challenging the goddess's very essence. Anat replies with a characteristically furious threat, and goes to report the matter to El.

The second and shortest tablet of the cycle retains only two of its original four columns. In the first El accedes, apparently with reluctance, to Anat's insistence on revenge, and in the last Anat carries out her threat:

When Aqhat sat down to eat,
the son of Danel to his meal,
vultures swooped over him,
a flock of birds soared above.
Among the vultures swooped Anat;
she set him [Yatpan, Anat's henchman] over Aqhat.
He struck him twice on the skull,
three times over the ear;
like a slaughterer he made his blood run,
like a butcher, run to his knees.
His breath left him like wind,
his spirit like a breeze,
like smoke from his nostrils.

The end of this tablet and the beginning of the next are badly broken; apparently Anat regrets her action, at least in part because while Aqhat was being killed his bow dropped into the sea.

When the text becomes legible, Danel is again sitting at the gate presiding over legal matters. His daughter Pughat notices that the vegetation has withered, and that vultures are swooping over her father's house; both are clear signs of violent, unnatural death. With his clothes torn in mourning, Danel

cursed the clouds in the still heat,
the rain of the clouds which falls in summer,
the dew which drops on the grapes.

Thus Danel invokes a seven-year drought, the absence of Baal's pluvial benefits. Then, at her father's instructions, Pughat,

who got up early to draw water,
who brushed the dew from the barley,
who knew the course of the stars,
in tears she saddled the ass,
in tears she harnessed the donkey,
in tears she lifted her father,
she put him on the ass's back,
on the splendid back of the donkey.

At this point neither Danel nor Pughat is aware of Aqhat's death; together they set out on a tour of the blasted fields. There Danel poignantly wishes that they could be restored, so that

"the hand of Aqhat the Hero would harvest you,
place you in the granary."

While they are still in the fields, messengers appear and relate the facts of Aqhat's death. Danel is stricken:

His feet shook,
his face broke out in sweat,
his back was as though shattered,
his joints trembled,
his vertebrae weakened.

Finally, Danel lifts up his eyes, sees the vultures overhead, and curses them:

"May Baal shatter the vultures' wings,
may Baal shatter their pinions;
let them fall at my feet.
I will split their gizzards and look:
if there is fat, if there is bone,
I will weep and I will bury him,
I will put him into the hole of the gods of the earth."

Three times Danel examines the innards of various vultures for remains of Aqhat; they are found at last inside Samal, the mother of vultures, and presumably are given proper burial. Danel then curses the three cities near the scene of the crime, and returns to his palace to begin the mourning period. For seven years the mourning goes on, and at its conclusion Danel dismisses the mourners and offers the appropriate sacrifice.

In the last brief episode, Pughat asks her father's benediction:

"Bless me, that I may go with your blessing;
favor me, that I may go with your favor:
I will kill my brother's killer,
put an end to whoever put an end to my mother's son."

The blessing having been given, Pughat, like the Jewish heroine Judith, applies cosmetics and puts on her finery; but under it she hides a sword. She reaches Yatpan's tent at sundown, and he welcomes her, boasting:

"The hand that killed Aqhat the Hero
can kill a thousand enemies."

Our text ends tantalizingly:

Twice she gave him wine to drink,
she gave him wine to drink.

Interpretation of this epic is difficult because of the gaps in the narrative and the abrupt break at the end of the preserved portion, but some light is shed on the main lines of the story by other ancient sources. The encounter between Anat and Aqhat is reminiscent of similar episodes in classical literatures, and especially of a portion of the Gilgamesh epic. There, the goddess Ishtar (Inanna) tries to seduce Gilgamesh; he repudiates her advances and reminds her in arrogant, insulting detail how she had behaved toward other mortals she had loved after she had finished with them. Ishtar is naturally furious, and complains bitterly to her father, Anu, the head of the pantheon. At first he resists her desire to take revenge on Gilgamesh by setting against him a powerful animal adversary, the Bull of Heaven, telling her that if her request is granted there will be seven years of drought. Finally, however, Anu relents, when Ishtar tells him that she has stored up sufficient grain and fodder.

The parallels between this episode and *Aqhat* are numerous and striking, but there are also significant differences. While Ishtar is the Mesopotamian counterpart of Anat, a goddess of love and of war, Gilgamesh and Aqhat are not simply literary cultural variants. In particular, it seems unlikely that the bow in the Ugaritic epic is a symbolic substitute for Aqhat's sexual organ: since it had been manufactured by Kothar, a substitute could be made for it, and after Aqhat's death it dropped into the sea.

The Egyptian myth of Osiris offers another avenue of comparison. In that tale Isis, the sister (and wife) of the dead Osiris, retrieves the murdered corpse of her brother, gives it a proper burial, and then encourages their son Horus to avenge his father's death; Osiris is, significantly, the god of the regenerating vegetation.

It seems, then, that we have a complex set of themes in the Gilgamesh, Osiris, and Aqhat cycles, with one common thread, the threat to continued fertility. Extrapolating from these links, we may suppose first that Pughat does avenge her brother's death, probably by destroying Anat's henchman Yatpan. Second, given the importance assigned to Danel's lack of an heir and the positive recollection of him in *Ezekiel,* it is difficult not to assume that he, like Job, is granted rehabilitation, that the land is restored to production, and that a substitute son is born, all in other episodes of the Danel cycle not yet discovered.

Three other tablets, extremely fragmentary ones, give some hint of the outcome of the story. Like most of the texts treated in this article, they were written down by Ilimilku, and since one of them mentions Danel by name they are part of the larger Danel tradition. Most scholars refer to them as the Refaim texts, after the Hebrew pronunciation of the name of their principal figures, the Refaim; this title is probably to be translated (despite the Hebrew vocalization) as "the Healers," although some prefer "the Healthy [or Healed] Ones." These "Healers" seem to have been minor deities of the underworld (cf. *Job* 26:5; in other biblical passages the term *refa'im* is used for the legendary pre-Israelite inhabitants of the land of Canaan, probably by extension from the sense of the deified dead). They also seem to have been connected with Baal; recall Danel's epithet, "the Healer's man."

In these texts the Healers visit Danel's threshing floor and plantation, presumably to restore them. Four broken lines read as follows:

> "Behold your son,
> behold . . . your grandson . . .
> the small one will kiss your lips."

It is tempting to see here the promise, if not the fact, of a new heir for Danel. It has even been conjectured that Aqhat himself was restored to life, somewhat analogously to Baal's resurrection, but this is unlikely since Aqhat was human, not divine, and he himself had stated the Canaanite view of mortality: "As every man dies, I will die."

Kirta. This epic, consisting of three tablets, is incomplete: at least one additional tablet is missing, since the third ends abruptly in mid-sentence. Its eponymous hero, Kirta (a name also vocalized as Keret), was, like Danel, a king, and as the story begins we learn that he too had no heir. As he laments his lot, he has a revelatory dream in which El appears to him; parallels in *Aqhat* and in the ancestral stories of *Genesis* indicate that his sleep may have been part of a formal incubation ritual. El's instructions to Kirta amount to more than ninety lines of text, and they are immediately repeated, with only minor variations, as the childless ruler carries out the divine commands.

First Kirta offers a sacrifice to the gods, and then he prepares an army for his campaign against King Pabil of Udm, whose daughter, the Lady Hurriya, is to be given to Kirta as his wife. There is almost universal conscription:

> The bachelor closed his house;
> the widow hired a substitute;
> the sick man carried his bed;
> the blind man was assigned a station;
> even the new husband came out:
> he entrusted his wife to another,
> his love to a stranger.

This army proceeds like a swarm of locusts for three days, after which they arrive at the sanctuary of Asherah of Tyre. There Kirta vows that if his suit is successful, he will donate double the bride-price to the goddess. On the evening of the seventh day he reaches Udm and lays siege to the city:

They attacked the cities,
 they raided the towns;
they drove the woodcutters from the fields,
 and the gatherers of straw from the threshing floors;
they drove the water carriers from the well,
 and the women filling their jars from the spring.

After seven days of siege Pabil begins to negotiate, offering Kirta silver, gold, slaves, and chariots. But Kirta rejects these, insisting that there is only one thing he wants:

"Give me rather what is not in my house:
 give me the Lady Hurriya,
 the fairest of your firstborn:
her fairness is like Anat's,
 her beauty is like Astarte's,
her eyebrows are lapis lazuli,
 her eyes are jeweled bowls."

This is the end of the narrative of Kirta's fulfillment of El's command, and also the conclusion of the first tablet. The beginning of the second tablet is damaged; as the text resumes Pabil accedes to Kirta's suit, with regret:

"As a cow lows for her calf,
 as recruits long for their mothers,
 so will Udm sigh."

After some missing lines, the council of the gods assembles in procession. Some of their number are listed: the Bull (El), Baal the Conqueror, Prince Moon, Kothar-wa-Hasis, the Maiden (Anat), Prince Reshef. This assembly gathers to witness El's blessing, at Baal's behest, of Kirta's marriage:

"Kirta, you have taken a wife,
 you have taken a wife into your house,
 you have brought a maiden into your court.
She will bear seven sons for you,
 she will produce eight for you;
she will bear Yassib the Lad,
 who will drink the milk of Asherah,
 suck the breasts of the Virgin Anat,
 the two wet nurses of the gods."

The close association of the offspring of royal but human parents with the gods is a feature of the Canaanite ideology of kingship.

Seven years passed, and El's blessing proves effective, but Asherah is angry because Kirta has forgotten his vow. Meanwhile, Kirta plans a feast for his nobles, but during its preparation he is stricken with a mortal disease, apparently as a punishment from Asherah.

As the third tablet opens, Kirta's son Ilihu is expressing consternation at his father's illness:

"How can it be said that Kirta is El's son,
 an offspring of the Kind and Holy One?
Or do the gods die?
 Will the Kind One's offspring not live on?"

Ilihu shares his dismay with his sister Thimanit ("the eighth," or Octavia), who repeats her brother's words of confusion. After another gap we learn of the disastrous consequences of Kirta's illness:

The plowmen lifted their heads,
 the sowers of grain their backs:
gone was the food from their bins,
 gone was the wine from their skins,
gone was the oil from their vats.

Again there is a break, and then El intervenes personally; he asks the divine council seven times if any of their number can cure Kirta, "but none of the gods answered him." Finally he takes the task upon himself:

"I will work magic,
 I will bring relief;
I will expel the sickness,
 I will drive out the disease."

To do so he creates the goddess Shataqat ("she causes [disease] to pass away"), and sends her to Kirta. She succeeds; "death was broken," and Kirta's appetite returns.

In the final scene, after Kirta has been restored to his throne, his rule is challenged by one of his sons, on the ground that because of his weakness he has ceased to perform the expected functions of a king:

"You do not judge the cases of widows;
 you do not preside over the hearings of the oppressed;
you do not drive out those who plunder the poor;
 you do not feed the orphan before you,
 the widow behind your back."

Kirta's response is to curse his son, praying that Horon, an underworld deity, and Astarte, "the name of Baal," will smash his son's skull.

While the plot of this cycle is relatively straightforward (at least where the text is continuous), *Kirta* is most informative about the Canaanite ideology of kingship. Among the duties of the king was to maintain the social order; he did so by his effective support of the powerless in society—the poor, widows, orphans—all groups who are mentioned in innumerable ancient Near Eastern sources as the special responsibility of kings, both divine and human. Thus his son's attempted coup to seize Kirta's throne was motivated by the alleged lack of justice for the powerless; Absalom's revolt against his father, King David, in *2 Samuel* 15 was initially successful because Absalom was able to appeal to a similar failure in the royal administration of justice. Another aspect of the maintenance of the social order was the provision for an orderly succession; Kirta's (and Danel's) desire for male descendants was prompted by the recognition of this royal responsibility.

The most complex feature of Canaanite royal ideology, however, was the quasi-divine status of the king; as the repeated question of Kirta's children shows, it was puzzling to the Canaanites as well: "Will the Kind One's offspring not live on?" The Kirta cycle probably recounts the legendary tale of the founder of a Canaanite dynasty. While there is evidence suggesting that the kings of Ugarit, like those of the Hittites, were deified after their death, there is no suggestion of actual divine parentage for them. Kirta's epithet "El's son" must therefore have a nonbiological sense, expressing in mythological language the close connection between human and divine rule. Thus, just as Baal was responsible for the continuing fertility of the earth, which failed during the period of his subjugation to Death, so the king shared in this responsibility; when Kirta was ill, the natural order was upset. (Psalm 72, one of the Israelite royal hymns, is an extended elaboration of the positive connection of natural prosperity with the king.)

The evidence of a number of biblical passages that speak of the king as the son of Yahveh is instructive here. The language of divine sonship is not just a literary device but seems to have been part of the actual coronation ceremony, in which the newly anointed king would proclaim:

"I will tell of Yahveh's decree.
He said to me, 'You are my son;
this day I have given birth to you.'"
(*Ps.* 2:7)

Similar language occurs in *2 Samuel* 7:14; and in *Isaiah* 9:2–7, a prophetic coronation oracle, the divine council itself proclaims:

"To us a child has been born,
to us a son has been given."

The language of sonship also occurs in *Psalms* 89:26, immediately after a passage that expresses in the clearest way the close relationship between deity and king. Earlier in the psalm Yahveh is praised as the one who (like Baal) rules the raging of the sea, scattering his enemies with his mighty arms (vv. 9–10); in verse 23 the deity states, using the traditional parallel formula for the storm god's enemy, that he will share his cosmic powers with the Davidic king:

"I will set his hand on the sea,
and on the rivers his right hand."

Conclusion

This article has dealt primarily with the corpus of Canaanite literature from Ugarit, and has not discussed in detail the many other Canaanite sources extant. Most prominent among these are the hundreds of inscriptions from the first millennium BCE in Phoenician, Aramaic, Hebrew, Moabite, Ammonite, and Edomite, and the recently discovered texts from Tell Mardikh (ancient Ebla) in Syria, which are still in the process of publication and are not sufficiently understood. It should be realized, however, that with rare exceptions this material is not literature in the sense in which the term has been interpreted above.

I have attempted at least to adumbrate the significance of the Ugaritic texts for the interpretation of the other great corpus of literature that may be subsumed in the designation *Canaanite*—the Bible. Much more could be added on this topic, including discussion of the council of the gods, the enthronement festival of the deity as represented in *Psalms*, and in general the pervasive use of Canaanite imagery, formulas, and ideology by biblical writers, especially when describing the character and activity of Yahveh. The writers were themselves aware of this relationship and the problems it raised; this partially explains the consistent portrayal of ancient Israel as—at least in the ideal—a people set apart from their historical context, their hostility toward their non-Yahvistic neighbors, and the insistence on the uniqueness of Yahveh. Yet biblical tradition can, on occasion, be remarkably candid about the origins of Israel and its culture. In the light of Canaanite religious and mythological literature, the declaration of the prophet Ezekiel to Jerusalem is strikingly apposite: "Your origin and your birth are of the land of the Canaanites" (*Ez.* 16:3).

BIBLIOGRAPHY

The official publication of the major Ugaritic texts is Andrée Herdner's *Corpus des tablettes en cunéiformes alphabétiques découvertes à Ras Shamra–Ugarit de 1929 à 1939* (Paris, 1963); the first volume contains the texts, preceded by extensive bibliographies and copiously annotated, and the second contains photographs and hand copies. A fuller edition, based on reexamination of the actual tablets, is Manfred Dietrich, Oswald Loretz, and Joaquin Sanmartín's *Die keilalphabetischen Texte aus Ugarit, einschliesslich der keilalphabetischen Texte ausserhalb Ugarits*, vol. 1, *Transkription* (Neukirchen-Vluyn, West Germany, 1976).

Several accessible translations for the general reader exist. The translations in this article are, for the most part, taken from *Stories from Ancient Canaan*, edited and translated by me (Philadelphia, 1978). The work also includes helpful introductions to each of the four cycles translated, as well as to the Canaanite material from Ugarit in general. A standard translation by one of the pioneers of Ugaritic scholarship is Harold Louis Ginsberg's "Ugaritic Myths, Epics, and Legends," in *Ancient Near Eastern Texts relating to the Old Testament*, 3d ed., edited by J. B. Pritchard (Princeton, 1969), pp. 129–155. It still remains useful despite its archaic biblicizing style. Cyrus Herzl Gordon's *Ugaritic Literature: A Comprehensive Translation of the Poetic and Prose Texts* (Rome, 1949) contains a number of nonliterary texts in addition to the myths and epics.

Two relatively recent and extensively annotated versions will be especially useful to readers with knowledge of Ugaritic, Hebrew, and other ancient Semitic languages: *Textes ougaritiques*, vol. 1 of *Mythes et légendes*, translated and edited by André Caquot, Maurice Sznycer, and Andrée Herdner (Paris, 1974), and *Canaanite Myths and Legends*, 2d ed., edited by John C. L. Gibson (Edinburgh, 1978).

The above translations and interpretations are based on systematic study of the entire corpus of texts from Ugarit. Two major treatments of the language of the Ugaritic texts are Cyrus Herzl Gordon's *Ugaritic Textbook*, 3 vols. (Rome, 1965), and Stanislav Segert's *A Basic Grammar of the Ugaritic Language* (Berkeley, 1984).

Since their discovery and decipherment the texts have been the focus of a steady stream of investigation. Among the most important treatments are Umberto Cassuto's *The Goddess Anath: Canaanite Epics of the Patriarchal Age*, translated by Israel Abrahams (Jerusalem, 1971), Theodor H. Gaster's *Thespis: Ritual, Myth, and Drama in the Ancient Near East* (New York, 1950), John Gray's *The Legacy of Canaan: The Ras Shamra Texts and Their Relevance to the Old Testament*, 2d ed. (Leiden, 1965), and Marvin H. Pope's *El in the Ugaritic Texts* (Leiden, 1955).

A number of studies have dealt specifically with the relationships between the Ugaritic corpus and the Bible. One of the most influential is Frank Moore Cross's *Canaanite Myth and Hebrew Epic: Essays in the History of the Religion of Israel* (Cambridge, Mass., 1973). A number of Cross's students have written more detailed treatments of individual topics; among these are Richard J. Clifford's *The Cosmic Mountain in Canaan and the Old Testament* (Cambridge, Mass., 1972), Patrick D. Miller's *The Divine Warrior in Early Israel* (Cambridge, Mass., 1973), and E. Theodore Mullen, Jr.'s *The Divine Council in Canaanite and Early Hebrew Literature* (Cambridge, Mass., 1980).

Finally, a recent popular introduction to the discoveries from Ugarit, with a valuable annotated bibliography, is Peter C. Craigie's *Ugarit and the Old Testament* (Grand Rapids, Mich., 1983).

MICHAEL DAVID COOGAN

CANDOMBLÉ. *See* Afro-Brazilian Cults.

CANDRAKĪRTI (Tib., Zla-ba-grags-pa; Chin., Yüeh-ch'eng; Jpn., Gesshō), Indian Buddhist dialectician. Scholars have identified at least three Candrakīrtis. The first, who will be referred to as "Candrakīrti I," was a renowned Madhaymaka (Mādhyamika) philosopher who lived around 600–650 CE; the second, "Candrakīrti II," was a Tantric master assumed to have lived slightly later than the former; and the third, "Candrakīrti III," was a Buddhist thinker of the eleventh century. Biographies are available only in Tibetan sources such as the histories of Bu-ston, Tāranātha, and Sum-pa-mkhan-po. These sources are not particularly helpful to the historian, for they tend to confuse history and legend and freely interchange the lives of the three Candrakīrtis. This did not pose a great problem in Tibet, however, for the Tibetan tradition acknowledges only one Candrakīrti, who lived for three or four hundred years.

Candrakīrti I wrote several important commentaries on the works of Nāgārjuna and Āryadeva: (1) the *Prasannapadā* (available in Sanskrit in Bibliotheca Buddhica 4, hereafter cited as Bibl. Bud.), a commentary on Nāgārjuna's *Mūlamadhyamakakārikā;* (2) the *Yuktiṣaṣṭikāvṛtti* (Derge edition of the Tibetan Tripiṭaka 3864, hereafter cited as D.; Peking edition of the Tibetan Tripiṭaka 5265, hereafter cited as P.); (3) the *Śūnyatāsaptativṛtti* (D. 3867, P. 5268); and (4) the *Catuḥśatakaṭīkā* (D. 3865, P. 5266, partially available in Sanskrit), a commentary on Āryadeva's *Catuḥśataka.* He also composed works of his own inspiration: (1) the *Madhyamakāvatāra*, with its autocommentary, the *Madhyamakāvatārabhāṣya* (Tib. edition in Bibl. Bud. 9), an introduction to the basic Madhyamaka treatise of Nāgārjuna; and (2) the *Pañcaskandhaprakaraṇa* (Tib. edition, Lindtner, 1979), a treatise on Abhidharma topics (five aggregates, twelve bases, and eighteen elements) from the Madhaymaka point of view. Opinions differ concerning the authorship of the work entitled *Triśaraṇa[gamana]saptati* (D. 3971, 4564; P. 5366, 5478). According to Lindtner it was composed by Candrakīrti I, but according to Ruegg (1981), by Candrakīrti II. As to the chronological order of these treatises, one can only state with certainty that the *Madhyamakāvatāra* (probably with the autocommentary) was composed before the two large commentaries, the *Prasannapadā* and the *Catuḥśatakaṭīkā*, since both of the latter refer to the former.

Candrakīrti I expounded the Madhyamaka philosophy of Nāgārjuna and defended the position of Buddhapālita (c. 470–540) against the criticism of Bhāvaviveka (c. 500–570), who had wanted to adopt independent inferences. Candrakīrti I thus tried to reestablish the *prasaṅga* method of reasoning. Tibetan doxographers accordingly classified him with Buddhapālita as representative of the Prāsaṅgika school. He also lodged criticism against the doctrines of the Buddhist logico-epistemological school and the metaphysical and gnoseological theories of the Yogācāra-Vijñānavādins.

Candrakīrti II composed a few Tantric works, the most important of which is the *Pradīpoddyotana* (D. 1785, P. 2650), a commentary on the *Guhyasamāja Tantra*. Candrakīrti III composed the *Madhyamakāvatāra-prajñā* or *Madhyamakaprajñāvatāra* (D. 3865, P. 5264) and together with the translator 'Gos-khug-pa-lhas-btsas translated it into Tibetan. If the identification of Dpal-ldan-zla-ba with Candrakīrti III is correct, this same pair of translators also translated Kṛṣṇapāda's commentray on the *Hevajra Tantra* (D. 1187, P. 2317). 'Gos-khug-pa-lhas-btsas also translated the *Pradīpoddyotana* with Rin-chen-bzaṅ-po (958–1055) and others. We can thus fix the date of Candrakīrti III within the eleventh century.

Although Candrakīrti I and III are certainly two different people, it may be possible that Candrakīrti II is identical with either Candrakīrti I or III. Research on this point remains open.

[*See also* Mādhyamika.]

BIBLIOGRAPHY

Lindtner, Christian. "Candrakīrti's *Pañcaskandhaprakaraṇa.*" *Acta Orientalia* 40 (1979): 87–145.

May, Jacques, trans. *Candrakīrti, Prasannapadā Madhyamakavṛtti: Commentaire limpide au traité du milieu.* Paris, 1959.

Ruegg, David S. *The Literature of the Mādhyamaka School of Philosophy in India.* Wiesbaden, 1981.

Mimaki Katsumi

CANISIUS, PETER (1521–1597), doctor of the church, Jesuit priest, educator, theologian, and saint. Born at Nijmegen, Peter Canisius was educated at the University of Cologne. Sent by his father, Jakob Kanijs, to study law at Louvain in 1539, Peter, determined to be a priest, returned to Cologne and in 1541 became the first German Jesuit. He helped to found the first German Jesuit house at Cologne and in 1546 was ordained a priest. In 1547, Cardinal Truchsess of Augsburg appointed Canisius as his theologian at the Council of Trent. Between the first and second sessions of the council, Canisius went to Rome for further spiritual training with Ignatius Loyola, founder of the Society of Jesus. From 1548 to 1580 Canisius worked out of Germany, traveling to Austria and Poland as Jesuit provincial, counselor to princes, and founder of Jesuit schools. Three times Emperor Ferdinand I (1556–1564) asked Canisius to become bishop of Vienna, but each time he refused. From 1556 to 1569 Canisius served as the first Jesuit provincial of upper Germany. In 1580 he was sent to Fribourg in Switzerland to help found a Jesuit college; it was his last assignment.

Canisius's primary work was reestablishing Roman Catholicism or strengthening it where it was threatened by Protestantism, especially in Germany, Austria, and Poland. His means were manifold, but chief among them was education through the establishment of twenty Jesuit colleges between 1549 and 1580. From these colleges came staunchly Roman Catholic political and spiritual leaders.

Frequently, Canisius had to deal directly with Protestants, as at Worms in 1557 and at Augsburg in 1566, or indirectly through his advice to Catholic princes to whom he was appointed secret nuncio by the pope. While he dealt severely with heretical books and what he deemed overly lenient policies on the part of princes, he distinguished between obdurate heresy and that of people who had been led astray. These latter should not be coerced, he argued, but persuaded. To prepare Catholics to meet Protestant arguments, Canisius drew up catechisms that, while not attacking Protestants frontally, gave Catholics a thorough grounding in the Catholic side of controversial issues such as justification and the Lord's Supper. Canisius also answered Protestant controversialists, especially the Centuriators, Flacius Illyricus and Johann Wigand, who had prepared the *Magdeburg Centuries*, a century-by-century history interpreted from a Lutheran perspective.

Toward his flock, Canisius was a kindly and practical superior and pastor. He served as cathedral preacher at Augsburg, Innsbruck, and Fribourg, and through his direct and pious sermons won back thousands to the Roman Catholic sacraments. Pope Leo XIII (1898–1903) dubbed Canisius "the second apostle of Germany after Boniface." He was canonized on 21 May 1925 and declared a doctor of the Catholic church by Pope Pius XI.

BIBLIOGRAPHY

The best source for Canisius's life is a multivolume edition edited by Otto Braunsberger, *Beati Petri Canisii Societatas Iesu epistulae et acta*, 8 vols. (Freiburg, 1896–1923). Friedrich Streicher has edited a critical edition of Canisius's catechisms: *S. Petri Canisii doctoris ecclesiae catechismi Latini et Germanici*, 2 vols. (Munich, 1933–1936). The *Bibliothèque de la Compagnie de Jésus*, compiled by Carlos Sommervogel (1891; reprint, Paris, 1960), contains a bibliography of Canisius's publications in volume 2, pages 617–688. The standard life of Canisius is by James Brodrick, *St. Peter Canisius, S.J., 1521–1597* (1935; reprint, Baltimore, 1950).

Jill Raitt

CANNIBALISM is both a concept and a practice that involves death, food, sacrifice, revenge, aggression, love, and destruction of one's own kind. The many and varied examples of cannibalism are difficult to summarize, except in terms of the widespread association between ideas of death, power, unity of body and spirit, and the efficacy of consumption to acquire the body and spirit of the object consumed. Thus sacrifice, the aggressive destruction of enemies, and the devoted incorporation of a loved one may be facets of cannibalism in different cultural contexts. Anthropologists distinguish between endocannibalism, eating a member of the same group, and exocannibalism, eating a member of some other group, frequently an enemy. The first is most often associated with sacrifice, familial devotion, reincarnation, and other sentiments of group welfare and continuity, the latter with revenge upon or destruction of enemies.

The symbolism of the sacrifice and consumption of human offerings pervades religious thought in European and Middle Eastern tradition; this symbolism is explored by Burkert (1983). Cannibalism is a very common theme in mythology and folk tales (Lévi-Strauss, 1969). As a practice, it has been reported in Polynesia, Melanesia, North and South America, and Africa (Volhard, 1939; Tannahill, 1975). The occurrences have no simple correlation with patterns of subsistence, ecology, food supply, or other cultural conditions.

Cannibalism is said by Sagan (1974), in a psychoanalytic explanation, to be characteristic of primitive communities and to be connected with magic rather than with civilization and religion. His study omits discussion of Aztec religion, human sacrifice, and cannibalism. Exaggerated or unfounded reports of cannibalism are, as has been noted by Arens (1979), very widespread. Here I can only summarize a few of the better described cases, to examine connections between cannibalism and the beliefs, including religious beliefs, of the peoples concerned. It is not my intention to consider cannibalism a religion, or even a ritual act in all of its occurrences. Cannibalism as a practice employed by those in extreme need of food, or survival cannibalism, while well documented (Simpson, 1984), will not be treated.

Perhaps the most celebrated large-scale human sacrifice and cannibalism was that of the Aztec, as recorded by many early reports. Aztec religion involved many kinds of offerings. The Sun, patron of warriors, required human hearts and human blood for nourishment: human sacrifice was essential. The victims were usually prisoners or purchased slaves; in the ritual their hearts were removed and placed in a vessel, and their heads were placed in a skull rack. The limbs and sometimes other portions of the victims' bodies might be cooked and eaten by the rulers, nobles, and wealthy persons. Aztec priests also practiced autosacrifice, drawing their own blood as an offering.

It has been argued that cannibalism had a nutritional purpose, since the Aztec of the late prehistoric and early historic period had depleted their game supply and lacked domestic herbivores. Very large numbers of human victims are said by Harner (1977) and Harris (1977) to have been consumed by the Aztec upper classes. The argument claims that cannibalism is a response to the pressure of overpopulation and meat shortage, disguised as propitiation of the gods. However, this reasoning and the extent of cannibalism are disputed by others, who make it clear that the public ritual of blood sacrifice was vital in Aztec religion.

Among the Kwakiutl of the Northwest Coast of North America a major feature of the winter ceremonies is the Hamatsa dancer, who symbolizes hunger, craving for human flesh, the fire that transforms, regurgitation, or rebirth, and is later tamed so as to become a member of society. Here the cannibal image is the key to the relation between man and supernatural forces. The idea of a cannibal spirit is also found in the Northeast Woodlands of North America, where winter isolation and fear of starvation may contribute to the fantasy of a man possessed or turned wild to devour his neighbors: the "Windigo psychosis."

The idiom of cannibalism in myth is worldwide and has an extensive range of context and meaning. Lévi-Strauss (1969) points to the universe of oppositions, associations, and transformations of humans and animals: death and rebirth, cooked and raw food, death and rotting, cannibal and ogre. South America is only one of the areas where these themes are mythically elaborated and cannibalism practiced. There, the two forms of endocannibalism and exocannibalism are strikingly contrasted.

Endocannibalism is interpreted as a ritual act that protects the living against the negative effects of death and the danger of attack by the soul of the deceased. This takes several forms, from eating the flesh (among the Guayaquí) to burning the flesh and pounding the bones to a powder to be dissolved and drunk (among the Amahuaca; see Clastres, 1974; Dole, 1962; and Zerries, 1960). A very common related concept is that the powers of the deceased are ingested along with the remains.

The exocannibalism of the Tupinamba and other tribes of South America (Métraux, 1949; Forsyth, 1983) was traditionally associated with intertribal and intercommunity warfare. War was highly ritualized, being preceded by dreams and magical rites, and victory was celebrated with further rites, cannibal feasts, and a display of head trophies by the victors. Prisoners taken might be kept for a long time and then tortured before they were killed and eaten. It is said that among some of these peoples, war was waged for revenge and to obtain victims for ritual sacrifice and cannibal feasting.

The raiding of enemy villages and consumption of enemy dead or the taking of captives who are later killed and eaten is also described in Melanesia and Polynesia. Some of these peoples buried human bodies for a period before exhuming them and consuming them for ritual purposes or as food.

In West Africa among, for example, the Sherbro, certain secret societies, such as the Human Leopard and Alligator, are said to require head-hunting and cannibalism as a qualification for membership (MacCormack, in Brown and Tuzin, 1983). Witches and sorcerers acquire and renew their power by the consumption of human flesh. In this way the powers of the deceased are acquired. Accusations of cannibalism are a political weapon still powerful among the contemporary Sherbro of Sierra Leone.

Cannibalism and witchcraft beliefs are commonly associated (Strathern, 1982). Thus a witch may obtain personal *mana* or power by consuming a victim. The notion that witches feed upon the blood and body of their victim and that death results from this loss of body substance is noted in many areas among unrelated peoples. In some, a cult group of witches is believed to teach and share the techniques and the cannibalistic acts, real or symbolic; but there is also a belief in a solitary cannibal witch.

The discovery and control of Pacific islanders in the eighteenth, nineteenth, and twentieth centuries is well documented in the accounts of recorders for exploratory expeditions, missionaries, administrators, and magistrates, and latterly anthropologists whose local informants described and explained their cannibal beliefs and practices. In New Zealand, Maori cannibalism in warfare not only provided contributions to the warriors' diet but also had a profound symbolic significance: to degrade the loser. The slain enemy was converted into food and the bones into objects of common use. The desecration of the corpse of a chief was especially relished by the victors (Bowden, 1984). Myth and historical practices of Fijian cannibalism together provide an understanding of the interconnections between the Fijians' surrender of their sisters to foreign husbands for marriage payment of valuable whale teeth, and their capture of foreign war prisoners for cannibalism. Human sacrifice accompanied the building of sacred houses and canoes and the ceremonial visits of allied chiefs. A Fijian chief oversaw an exchange cycle that included the symbolic transformation of valued objects—raw women (as wives) and cooked men (the foreign cannibal victims); by this process, political alliances were confirmed. The cannibal victims were consecrated to the major war god, who was represented by the chief.

Fijian cannibalism, first described in the nineteenth century, was explained in the following century by Sahlins (in Brown and Tuzin, 1983). In some parts of Melanesia, cannibalism is explained by contemporary anthropologists citing recent practitioners. There are a number of peoples in the Highlands of New Guinea who are known to be cannibals, as well as many others who are not. The Fore (Lindenbaum, 1979) and some neighboring peoples were cannibals: in the northern Fore region, dead enemies were eaten by men and women, while in the southern region women and children ate kin and members of the residential group who had died. Similarly, Gimi women cooked and ate the dead of the local group (Gillison, in Brown and Tuzin, 1983). The dietary value of New Guinea cannibalism has been provided as an explanation, since many of the cannibal groups had limited access to other forms of meat, whether game or domestic pigs. However, some of the noncannibals who regarded the practice as disgusting or barbarous had no more meat than did the cannibals. While the Fore are described as valuing the meat as food, cannibal practice most often carries ritual values, too. When Gimi women ate human flesh they prevented the ravages of decomposition and were fertilized so as to begin the process of reincarnation. The symbolism of the flute, which in an important Gimi myth was stolen from women by men, associates bamboo with the phallus. Bamboo is used for cooking and in sacred flutes that represent the penis. Men were not permitted to be secluded with women or to partake in a cannibal feast. Gimi men had to present pork to women after their cannibal feast so as to reward and repay them for their role in reproduction.

Elsewhere in the Papua New Guinea mountain area until the middle of the twentieth century the Bimin-Kuskusmin (Poole, in Brown and Tuzin, 1983) and the neighboring Miyanmin ate enemy dead: while the latter ate all of a human body, the former dismembered bodies, buried heads, and ate to defile the enemy. In the same area, the Oksapmin were not cannibals. The Bimin-Kuskusmin distinguished between hard body parts that were considered male and were eaten by men and those parts, flesh and fat, that were considered female and were eaten by women. The Great Pandanus Tree rite was an occasion for feasting upon game and human victims obtained by raiding a nearby group. Poole's interpretation of this ritual includes the cultural meaning of male and female substances, ritual expression of myth, relations between the sexes, fertility, and death.

While Sagan (1974) and other psychological theorists see in aggression and interpersonal conflict the source and meaning of cannibalism, this Cook's tour of practice and belief would rather demonstrate the diversity of cultural meanings. Cannibalism is clearly an emotionally charged and culturally significant act, real and symbolic, but it has no single meaning. The anthropological distinction between endocannibalism and exocannibalism is of limited value; cannibalism's multiple symbolism and its connections with mythic themes of sacrifice and destruction are understood best within a specific cultural context.

[*See also* Human Sacrifice *and* Aztec Religion.]

BIBLIOGRAPHY

Books and articles on cannibalism may be general, theoretical, or interpretive, or they may present descriptive case studies that analyze cannibalism in particular cultural settings. In fact, many works combine both features, applying a theoretical approach to particular case studies.

General Works

Arens, William. *The Man-Eating Myth.* Oxford, 1979. Finds the evidence for cannibalism unconvincing.

Harris, Marvin. *Cannibals and Kings.* New York, 1977. Presents a materialist-ecological explanation of cannibalism.

Sagan, Eli. *Cannibalism.* New York, 1974. A popular psychoanalytic study of cannibalism in general, relating it to aggression and sublimation of aggression.

Tannahill, Reay. *Flesh and Blood.* New York, 1975. A popular work that surveys the prehistoric data and historical literature concerning cannibalism.

Volhard, Ewald. *Kannibalismus* (1939). New York, 1968. Encyclopedic review of distribution and forms of cannibalism within the framework of the cultural theory of Leo Frobenius.

Studies of Areas and Cases

Bowden, Ross. "Maori Cannibalism: An Interpretation." *Oceania* 55 (1984): 81–99.

Brown, Paula, and Donald Tuzin, eds. *The Ethnography of Cannibalism.* Washington, D.C., 1983. Presents a group of case studies, some cited in the text of the article: Poole on the Bimin-Kuskusmin, Gillison on the Gimi, MacCormack on the Sherbro, and Sahlins on the Fijians, with a commentary by Shirley Lindenbaum.

Burkert, Walter. *Homo Necans.* Berkeley, 1983. Essentially a study of the ritualization of sacrifice. Cannibalism as imagery rather than practice.

Clastres, Pierre. "Guayaki Cannibalism." In *Native South Americans,* edited by Patricia J. Lyon. Boston, 1974.

Dole, Gertrude. "Endocannibalism among the Amahuaca Indians." *Transactions of the New York Academy of Sciences* 24 (1962): 567–573.

Forsyth, Donald W. "The Beginnings of Brazilian Anthropology: Jesuits and Tupinamba Cannibalism." *Journal of Anthropological Research* 39 (1983): 147–178.

Harner, Michael J. "The Ecological Basis for Aztec Sacrifice." *American Ethnologist* 4 (1977): 117–135.

Lévi-Strauss, Claude. *The Raw and the Cooked.* New York, 1969. Discusses myths of cannibalism and the symbolism of raw, cooked, and rotten food, especially among South American tribes.

Lindenbaum, Shirley. *Kuru Sorcery.* Palo Alto, Calif., 1979. A discussion of the importance of sorcery belief in the reactions of the Fore to the kuru disease, which was spread by contact with victims of the disease, mainly through cannibalism.

Métraux, Alfred. "The Tupinamba." In *Handbook of the South American Indians,* edited by Julian H. Steward, vol. 3. Washington, D.C., 1949.

Métraux, Alfred. "Warfare, Cannibalism and Human Trophies." In *Handbook of the South American Indians,* edited by Julian H. Steward, vol. 5. Washington, D.C., 1949.

Simpson, A. W. *Cannibalism and the Common Law.* Chicago, 1984. An extended analysis of a case of survival cannibalism and the legal proceedings that followed.

Strathern, Andrew. "Witchcraft, Greed, Cannibalism and Death: Some Related Themes from the New Guinea Highlands." In *Death and the Regeneration of Life,* edited by Maurice Bloch and Jonathan Parry. Cambridge, 1982. Compares and discusses the themes of cannibalism, witchcraft, sacrifice, exchange, recreation, and the enemy.

Walens, Stanley. *Feasting with Cannibals.* Princeton, 1981. A symbolic analysis of Kwakiutl cannibal spirits and dances.

PAULA BROWN

CANON. Because employment of the term *canon* (usually as a synonym for *scripture*) in comparative religious studies is both commonplace and subject to a growing scholarly debate, the classic usage will be considered at the outset. Subsequently, a consideration of contemporary applications of the term within the study of world religions will follow in order to illustrate its usefulness and to show some of the hermeneutical issues implicit in such usage. Since the use of *canon* to mean both a norm and an attribute of scripture arose first within Christianity, some special attention must necessarily be given to present debates in the study of that religion. However, the focus of this treatment is on the wider implications concerning the value of this term in a comparativist description of world religions.

Etymology and Earliest Historical Usages. The Greek word *kanōn,* which gave rise to its later European and English equivalents, is a Semitic loanword basically signifying a reed, as seen in biblical passages such as *1 Kings* 14:15 and *Job* 40:21. The semantic usage that occurs in Hebrew *(qaneh)*, Assyrian *(qanu)*, Ugaritic *(qn)*, and similarly in Aramaic, Syriac, Arabic, and modern Hebrew, derives in turn from the even more ancient non-Semitic Sumerian *(gi, gi-na)*, with the same import. In the above Semitic languages, the basic conception of a reed generated a semantic field that included in Hebrew, for example, the description of either a standard of length or a straight or upright object. Images of a standard of length that occur in biblical passages are the measuring rod *(qeneh ha-middah)* in *Ezekiel* 40:3 and 40:5 and a full reed of similar length in *Ezekiel* 41:8. The straight or upright object is exemplified as the shaft of a lampstand in *Exodus* 25:31, the branches of a lampstand in *Exodus* 25:32, and a shoulder blade in *Job* 31:22.

The Greek usage of this common Semitic term extended these derivations to include a great variety of figurative applications. Besides associating this term with various instruments of measure and design, Greeks came to regard lists, catalogs, or tables in the sciences as "canons." Likewise, the humanities and anthropology sought to describe "the norm" *(ho kanōn)*, for example, in grammar, aesthetics, music, physical beauty, ethics, the perfection of form in sculpture, and so forth. Epicurus wrote a book, now lost, entitled *Peri kritēriou hē kanōn*, focused on the "canonics" of logic and method. Epictetus, and the Epicurians similarly, sought to find a formal basis *(kanōn)* for distinguishing truth from falsehood, the desirable from the undesirable.

In the area of religion, Christianity drew heavily from this Hellenistic milieu and came to assign a new and unique role to the term *canon*. In the New Testament itself, the Greek term is used only by the apostle Paul as a standard of true Christianity in *Philippians* 3:16 and in a late text, *Galatians* 6:16, and as a divinely delimited mandate or authorization in *2 Corinthians* 10:13–16. Nonetheless, in the Roman church during the first three centuries, the term occurs frequently and can signify almost any binding norm of true Christianity, expressed with a variety of technical nuances. For instance, Irenaeus, in the second century, could already speak of various familiar canons: "the canon of truth" (in preaching), "the canon (rule) of faith" (Lat., *regula fidei*, or the essential truth of the gospel), and "the ecclesiastical canon" (Lat., *regula veritatis*, expressing both true confession and correct ritual participation in the church). Likewise, the term could characterize any authorized list or collection of decisions or persons. Thus one could speak of a "canonical" set of laws, a list or collection of "canonized" saints, papal decretals (ninth century), church leaders, monks, nuns, and so on. Hence, early in the history of Christianity, the Greek *kanōn* was carried over as *canon* or *regula* in the Latin used in churches of the East and the West. By the Middle Ages, the whole collection of binding decisions by the Roman church came to be regarded as the *ius canonicum* (canonical laws), either touching on secular matters (Lat., *lex;* or Gr., *nomos*) or belonging to the juridical, religious, and ethical canons of the church. Gratian's *Decretum* (1139–1142 CE) provided the foundation for canon law in Roman Catholicism.

The relationship between "canon" and "scripture" in Christianity is more complicated. The earliest Christian scripture was either the Hebrew Bible of Judaism or the old Greek version of it (the so-called Septuagint). Within Judaism, neither prerabbinic nor rabbinic literature ever chose to refer to this scripture as a "canon." At about the same time as the flowering of rabbinic Judaism in the second century, Irenaeus—probably borrowing the use of the term from Marcion, his gnostic competitor—began to speak of a "New Testament" as a group of "inspired" Christian traditions distinct from the "Old Testament" inherited as scripture from Judaism. The Christian terminology of "inspiration," although grounded in Jewish understanding, occurs first in the later Pauline traditions and undoubtedly reflects influence from related Hellenistic conceptions that had previously been applied to the *Iliad* and the *Odyssey*. However, not until shortly after 450 CE did the term *canon* begin to be used by Christians, apparently first by Athanasius, to designate the biblical books of scripture.

Within rabbinic Judaism, the Hebrew scripture began to be called Miqra' ("that which is read"), and the entire collection came to be referred to as Tanakh, an acronym of the names of the three major divisions of the Hebrew scriptures: Torah (Pentateuch), Nevi'im (Prophets), and Ketuvim (Writings). Instead of speaking about "canonization," as was typical later in Christianity, Jewish sources describe an endeavor to determine which books "defile the hands" and, therefore, constitute sacred scripture, as distinguished from other normative traditions. The extrabiblical traditions in the Mishnah and Talmud were, consequently, authoritative (arguably "canonical" in that sense) but considered to be "oral law," which did not defile the hands, in contrast to the scripture or "written law." Prior to these designations within Judaism and Christianity, the Hebrew Bible (Old Testament) was denoted by a variety of diverse expressions, such as "the law and the prophets and the other books of our fathers" (Prologue to *Ben Sira*); "the law and the prophets" (e.g., *Mt.* 5:17); "the law of Moses, the prophets, and the psalms" (*Lk.* 24:44); the "oracles of God" (*Rom.* 3:2); "the scripture" (e.g., *Mk.* 12:24); "the holy scriptures" (Philo Judaeus, *On Flight and Finding* 1.4); "the book"; "the sacred book"; and others. In view of this evidence scholars continue to disagree whether the weight of the later Christian references to the term *canon* for scripture turns primarily on the term's denotation of either a binding "norm" or an ecclesiastically approved "list" of inspired books.

In Islam, another "religion of the Book" associated with the children of Abraham, the Qur'ān replaces the imperfect rendering of revelation in Judaism and Christianity. While Muslim interpreters never traditionally identified the Qur'ān as a "canon," they did employ the term to designate the law, in a manner reminiscent of some early Christian understandings of the biblical law of God.

Contemporary Usage. Certainly, the use of the term *canon,* despite its association with Christianity, can prove to be an illuminating heuristic device in describing other world religions and their principal texts. The analogies with the formation of Western religious canons provides an attractive, yet to be fully explored, way of thinking about religion in general. For example, such terminology can be helpful in understanding aspects of Eastern religions. Although Confucius (K'ung-tzu), who died in the fifth century BCE, claimed of his teaching, "I have transmitted what was taught to me without making up anything of my own" (*Lun-Yü* 7.1), the "Five Classics" as we now know them only became a scripturelike guide to Confucianism from the first century CE onward. Obviously innovations entered into this work long after the death of Confucius. Moreover, competing views within Confucianism led to some groups' diminishing the importance of this work or adding to it new canons that were viewed as complementary (e.g., Ssu Shu, or "Four Books," and still later in the Ch'ing era, the "Thirteen Classics"), almost in the same manner as Christianity added the New Testament to the "Old."

Just as Christians debated whether the Old Testament "canon" should be the Hebrew version, with Judaism, or the expanded old Greek version, language and culture influenced the formation of "canonical" distinctions in many religions. Centuries after the death of the Buddha, ancient traditions were combined in South Asia to form what is presently called the "Pali canon" (c. 29–17 BCE). A century or so later, a different "canonical" literature developed in India, written in Sanskrit and eventually translated into Chinese and Tibetan, which became foundational for Mahāyāna Buddhism. In contrast to adherents of the Pali canon, these Buddhists regarded the *sūtra*s of the Mahāyāna ("great vehicle") as an alternative canon, the only true authority regarding what the Buddha himself taught. Even within later Zen Buddhism, where the idea of a canon seems antithetical, one may consider the lists of *kōans*, questions and answers developed in regional monasteries for training and testing students, as attaining "canonical" status as a constant feature of the instructions given by particular Zen masters.

Just as some "Christian" gnostics dismissed the Hebrew Bible in favor of a "New Testament," one may find an analogy with the development of Hinduism as a reaction against certain aspects of Vedic religion. Similar to the Jewish distinction between written and oral law was the distinction made by brahmans between two kinds of "canonical" literature. *Śruti* ("heard") generally refers to the ritualistic literature found in the Upaniṣads and is believed to be revealed directly from divinity, while *smṛti* ("remembered") designates the epics, the later Purāṇas and other legal and philosophical writings touching on practical matters of personal, social, and domestic conduct. Even if *śruti* has a higher status, it can be viewed as a lower kind of ritualistic knowledge in comparison with the immediate moral implications of *smṛti*. So, too, even if the oral law does not defile the hands, it may provide a more explicit and pragmatically significant register of the demands of a holy life in Judaism than one can find by simply reading the written law.

Hermeneutical Implications. The above descriptions adumbrate some of the possibilities and problems in the use of *canon* as a technical term in the study of religion. The term inherently vacillates between two distinct poles, in both secular and religious usage. On the one hand, it can be used to refer to a rule, standard, ideal, norm, or authoritative office or literature, whether oral or written. [*See also* Authority.] On the other hand, it can signify a temporary or perpetual fixation, standardization, enumeration, listing, chronology, register, or catalog of exemplary or normative persons, places, or things. [*See* Scripture.] The former dimension emphasizes internal signs of an elevated status. The latter puts stress on the precise boundary, limits, or measure of what, from some preunderstood standard, belongs within or falls outside of a specific "canon." For the purpose of illustrating these significant differences, I shall call the former "canon 1" and the latter "canon 2." This "ideal" distinction only demarcates poles in a continuum of options, since the essential nature and status of a normative tradition or a "scripture" within a religion inevitably emerges through its own unique, dialectical interplay between these polarities. The interplay itself engenders a systemic ambiguity in any discussion of religious canons and helps account for the variety of ways, sometimes conflicting, in which the term *canon* has been employed in recent scholarship.

Canon 1. In its first usage as rule, standard, ideal, or norm, the term *canon* in the secular domain may apply to a wide range of fields in which a standard of excellence or authority governs the proper exercise of a discipline. For example, it can reflect criteria by which one makes decisions within a field of inquiry, whether these choices conform to grammatical and mathematical principles or indices of aesthetic excellence in rhetoric, art, or music. Implicit in such canons is some political and social theory of intellectual consensus about the quality, worth or preservation, and validity of that which is being judged and remembered. Likewise, religious iconography, Buddhist organization of a city, and church architecture reflect implicit canonical assumptions. The success of "pop art" in the 1960s may have resided partly in its ability to make our implicit canons explicit. The Campbell's Soup can we had accepted in some unconsciously canonical sense suddenly appears before us in an explicitly canonical form through the medium of art. The dynamism possible within such canons becomes evident when, for instance, one surveys the changing collections of art museums and contrasts their content with the work being done in artists' studios.

In examining religious scriptures as "canons," one may generalize that the founding leaders of religions almost never compose for their disciples a complete scripture. The one obvious exception is that of the third-century Mani, founder of Manichaeism. There are usually substantial periods after the death of a leader or founder when oral and/or written traditions function authoritatively as canonical, in the sense of representing a scripture without specific dimension. This dynamic process may be influenced greatly by later disciples, and the scriptures may for long periods of time, if not indefinitely, lack the public form of a fixed list of books or a standardized "text." At the same time, canonical criteria, such as "inspiration," incarnation of the Dharma, and so on, are sufficient for them to sustain their scriptural status. The initial recognition of some traditions as being crucially foundational or scriptural sets in motion political and economic pressures within the religion that usually lead to the formation of a scripture in the latter sense of *canon* (canon 2).

From the standpoint of Christian history, one may argue that the term *canon* has been and may continue to be useful in the designation of extrabiblical oral or written decisions that are binding in matters of faith and practice, as part of a church's teaching magisteria. Certainly, prior to the fourth century, some Christian traditions were explicitly canonical (canon 1) in the sense that they provided normative religious guidance outside of the Hebrew Bible. Justin Martyr cites from the "Sayings of the Lord" source as authoritative alongside the Hebrew Bible and arguably refuses to do the same with the Gospel narratives or Paul's letters. It is unlikely that these "sayings" belong to a fixed list. Therefore, one can say that Christian scripture had a canonical status (canon 1) long before the church decisions of the fourth century delimited a fixed list of books (canon 2). More precisely, the canonization (canon 2) is by degree, since even in the fourth and fifth centuries the standardization of the actual text had not taken place.

Despite the silence of the rabbinic tradition on the subject, recent studies of Judaism commonly refer to "canon(s)" and "canonization." In a provocative study, Sid Leiman regards a religious book as "canonical" if it is "accepted by Jews as authoritative for religious practice and/or doctrine . . . binding for all generations . . . and studied and expounded in private and in public" (Leiman, 1976, p. 14). Because this definition conforms to criteria of canon 1, Leiman can claim that the oral law is "canonical," although it both is "uninspired" and does not defile the hands as scripture. Relying on this principle of normativeness, Leiman can distinguish between different kinds of books: "outside" or banned books; secular or "Homeric" books that deserve reading; inspired canonical books (scripture); and uninspired canonical books (oral law, i.e., Mishnah/Talmud). Consequently, the Jewish discussion at the end of the first century CE at Yavneh over the status of the *Book of Ecclesiastes* concerned only its "inspiration," not its canonicity, for it could continue to be cited as normative even if not as "scripture."

Conversely, other scholars, (see, for example, Jacob Neusner, 1983, pp. 11–37) argue that the ritual difference, "defiling the hands," did not produce any clear levels of canonical authority between the Hebrew Bible, the Mishnah/Talmud, other religious books, and the "inspired" commentary of a rabbi. If canonicity (canon 1) is determined by the norm of revelation itself, then distinctions either among levels of canonicity or between canonical and noncanonical literature begin to blur. If, as Neusner suggests, the rabbis themselves embodied the *torah* (law), then for students of religion there is only limited value in a descriptive appeal to certain texts as "canonical." If the meaning of these texts resides in a spiritual or "Midrashic" sense held by consensus among "inspired" rabbis rather than in a "plain" literary, or *peshaṭ*, sense, then the semantic import is not publicly available through a reading of the scripture per se. Similarly, some Catholic scholars currently locate the canonical sense of Christian scripture in the teaching magisterium (canon 1) of the church hierarchy rather than in either a literary or historical-critical assessment of biblical texts themselves. In such an approach, a scripture may be viewed as the deposit of a variety of historical traditions, any of which may or may not be "canonical" (canon 1) according to an "inspired" norm or standard inherent within the leadership of the religion itself. In this case, identifying a scripture may shed only modest light on the beliefs of a religion.

From a historical perspective, the final formation of a scripture (canon 2) usually results from an earlier, often obscured process of redaction, expansion, and selection of texts (canon 1), whether one thinks of the *Tao-te ching* of Taoism, the various Buddhist canons, the extensive collection of Jain "canonical" literature, or the Hindu *Mahābhārata* and the *Bhagavadgītā* along with the older Vedas.

Often some underlying traditions of a scripture were considered normative or "canonical" for the earliest disciples, while other traditions gain an elevated status as scripture not anticipated by their celebrated founders, as, for example, through the posthumous deification of Lao-tzu. Repeatedly one finds evidence of how earlier oral or written traditions or writings, whose normativeness depended originally on more modest criteria, gradually gain greater authority, in terms of a later perception of religious genius, inspiration, revelation of the law (e.g., *dharma*), or the presence of ultimate reality, perfection, or some other transcendent value. This adjustment in the believers' vision of canonical traditions within a religion often entails a radical shift in the perception, understanding, and significance of older traditions when they are caught up into the new context of a scripture.

Most often, canon and community are related dialectically in a process of semantic transformation. The steps taken by editors in this process may go unrecognized by the believers or may be seen as essential elements in the orchestration of the traditions in order to protect them from heretical misinterpretation. In sum, the recognition of canon 1 materials, defined as traditions offering a normative vehicle or an ideal standard, occurs in most world religions and usually contributes momentum to an impulse within the history of a religion to totalize, to circumscribe, and to standardize these same normative traditions into fixed, literary forms typical of canon 2.

Canon 2. The second usage of the term *canon* will be in the sense of a list, chronology, catalog, fixed collection, and/or standardized text. Scholars of comparative religion such as Mircea Eliade and Wilfred Cantwell Smith have placed emphasis on the full appearance of a religion complete with its "scripture," reflecting whatever norms of excellence, truth, goodness, beauty, or revelation may be affirmed by the respective religious adherents. In religious studies, the foundational religious documents are most easily approached at this more developed stage, when they constitute a publicly available, delimited canon (canon 2) in the maturity of particular religious movements. Of course, only the most presumptuous type of "protestant" interpretation of other religions would presume that the ideas and beliefs of a religion can be grasped solely by a literary study of such religious canons. Smith has amply illustrated the problems that arise in the study of Islam because of this naïveté.

As already noted, the normativeness of religious traditions is usually acknowledged long before these same traditions attain a fixed dimension and textual standardization, the elements of canon 2. So, for example, after the death of the Buddha the disciples sought, although not without controversy, to envision the diverse sermons (canon 1) of the Blessed One as part of a larger collection (canon 2), a larger normative and publicly recognized canon.

Conversely, Mani claimed to write by inspiration "my scriptures," which combined the essence of older books or scriptures into one "great wisdom" (*Kephalaia* 154). His work remains exceptional in part because he is perhaps the only founder of a major religion who was self-consciously "inspired" to compose a complete "scripture." His work represents the best-known example of a canon that attained both normative authority and distinct literary boundaries at the same time. Even so, other generations of believers expanded and modified the canon. Mani's use of the Judeo-Christian concept of scripture corresponds to his hope of absorbing these two religions into his own, much as Islam aspired in its early development to bring Jews and Christians into its more universal fold.

Unlike most other religious canons, completed centuries after their founders had died, Islam settled most dimensions of the Qur'ān within only twenty-three years after the death of Muḥammad. One of the significant differences in the comparison of Islam with Judaism, Christianity, and Manichaeism is that the Qur'ān is not a "scripture" in the sense of an inspired, historically accommodated writing. The Qur'ān is the actual word of God, representing an eternal archetype of revelation cast in heavenly language. Unlike Christianity's scripture of "books" *(ta biblia)*, the Qur'ān is more simply "the Book." Nevertheless, during the lifetime of the

Prophet, his disciples did not have the book of the Qur'ān as we now know it. The order of the chapters and other significant editorial influence belongs to the hands of the disciples who succeeded the Prophet. Moreover, the later collections of the *sunnah* (customary practice of the Prophet), now found in the *ḥadīth*, provided a normative and, therefore, "canonical" (canon 1) guide to Muslim exegesis. As with the Jewish Karaites and the Antiochene Christian exegetes, many "spiritualists" within Islam could lay claim to their own direct insight upon scripture in a manner that diminished the significance of the *ḥadīth* and could appear to assign normative, and in that sense, "canonical" status to the Qur'ān alone.

Regarding the final delimitation of the Hebrew scriptures, most scholars agree that the promulgation by Ezra of a five-book Torah in the early postexilic period constituted a decisive moment in the formation of Judaism. Unlike the later case of the Christian Gospels, the Pentateuch comprised a single, allegedly Mosaic "book of the Torah" (*Jos.* 1:7–8). From a traditional-historical standpoint, this Mosaic Torah appears to combine multiple older, normative *torot*, or laws, in the sense of canon 1 and/or canon 2 (e.g., *Proto-Deuteronomy*) into a fixed and integrated collection of books (canon 2). This combination of traditions most likely reflects the legislation preserved and venerated by two different groups from the Babylonian exile—bearers of Jerusalemite priestly tradition (e.g., the laws in *Exodus* 22ff.) and deuteronomistic interpreters (e.g., the Decalogue in *Deuteronomy* 5 and the subsequent laws). The effect would be to make much private tradition public and to set all of the laws forward to be interpreted together as parts of the same revelation of law delivered by God to Moses prior to the conquest of Palestine.

Similar to the codification by the Egyptians of the Fifth Pharaonic Law early in the same period, the promulgation of the Mosaic Torah probably occurred in response to a benevolent policy under Persian sovereignty. As a reward for this codification and public promulgation of the private or secret religious law, the Persians sanctioned the right of Jewish leaders to make juridical decisions according to it in exchange for obedience to Persian civil and international law. In any case, these events undoubtedly helped to accelerate the forces behind the formation of a part of a religious canon.

The compilation of the exact list of books that make up the completed Hebrew Bible could not be completed until late in the first century, perhaps not until the second. Furthermore, the textual standardization of the Bible continued up to the end of the first millennium, culminating in a relatively uniform consensus regarding the orthography, punctuation, and vocalization of the so-called Masoretic text of the Tanakh, the Hebrew scriptures. Here, as in the case of Christianity and many other religions, the process of canonization in the sense of canon 2 entails a resolution of the limits of the collection before a full standardization of the text can take place. Centuries might elapse during this process of full canonization (canon 2), and it may be much easier for believers to debate the authority of the latest stages in the process of the text's stabilization than it is for them to reopen the question of whether a book really belongs in the scripture at all. The length of the process of full canonization may often affect the believer's assessment of what represents the final text.

The semantic import of the formation of a canon 2 should not be underestimated. Christianity and Judaism amply illustrate this feature. Unlike the above-mentioned instance of the Pentateuch, the individual Christian Gospels retained their independence from one another despite the assumption that they collectively convey the same "one" gospel of Jesus Christ. Perhaps the late ending of Mark attests to an effort at bringing that work into greater harmony within the canonical collections of gospels. Paul's letters illustrate a different feature, for they include in a single collection some original letters in edited and unedited form, for example, *Galatians, Romans, 1* and *2 Corinthians*, together with deutero-Pauline traditions reflective of a later generation, for example, *2 Thessalonians*. The original Pauline letters, which were written before the composition of the Gospels, were, through canonization, subordinated to the Gospels as commentary upon them. Similarly, the *Gospel of John* is read contextually within scripture in connection with the so-called Johannine letters *(1, 2,* and *3 Jn.)*, even though the historic evidence of common authorship is extremely weak. Again, this type of canonization alters the religious vision of the preceding authoritative traditions (canon 1) as being part of a larger "inspired" New Testament. The terms *New Testament* and *Old Testament* likewise signal a change in the perceived significance of the Hebrew Bible when read as part of a Christian text in the context of a purportedly new revelation. The difference in religious visions of the "shared" scripture implies profound distinctions between the import of the Tanakh within Judaism and that of an "Old Testament" within Christian interpretation.

Scripture and Canon. These ideal distinctions between canon as a norm and canon as a list or standardization of text usually overlap in the actual assessment of a particular religion. For example, in the Tanakh and the New Testament one can detect evidence of "canon-conscious redactions," whereby assumptions about the normativeness (canon 1) of the traditions and of their being read together in a specific collection (canon 2) coincide.

Historicized titles added to the psalms assigned to David link these prayers contextually to the narrative about David in *1* and *2 Samuel.* The epilogue to *Ecclesiastes* summarizes the essence of the book in a manner that puts the "wisdom," or Solomonic, books in full continuity with the Torah. The addition of titles to some of the Christian Gospels makes their character and common witness together as Gospels more explicit than their original authors could have envisioned. The *Gospel of Luke* in the Western tradition has now been separated from its original sequel, *Acts of the Apostles,* by the *Gospel of John.* In this way, the Gospels were read collectively and *Acts* came to mark a transition from the teachings of Jesus to that of the apostle Paul. This type of organization of highly diverse traditions into partially harmonized canons of literature is also common to the canons of other world religions.

As has already been shown, considerable differences of opinion exist among scholars over the appropriate relationship between the terms *scripture* and *canon.* At a minimum, these terms both gain and lose some of their historical significance when they are taken away from the specific religious vocabulary of Judaism and Christianity for the purpose of an etic assessment of world religions. Frequently scholars have used *scripture* and *canon* synonymously, although ambiguity in both terms, particularly in the latter, suggests the need for more careful definitions and historical finesse. In the application of both terms to a religion, the interpreter stands within a hermeneutical circle. Only by some prior judgment regarding the identity of the believers of a given religion can any description be proffered regarding their "canons" and their modes of interpreting the same. Moreover, this judgment is hindered by the ethnocentrism of the outside observer, as well as by the difficulty in taking a term indigenous to one religion and assigning to it a technical usage appropriate for describing features of other religions.

Nevertheless, contemporary efforts to understand how canons achieve formation and exercise significance within a religion has already proved unusually illuminating as a way to describe and to compare religions generally. The interpretation of religion must inevitably assume some operational certitude regarding the identity, the economic character, and the literary sources of revelation or truth to which religions lay claim in the world. It must be carried out with an acute awareness that the heretics and noncanonical sayings of some will likely be viewed as the saints and scripture of others.

BIBLIOGRAPHY

Beyer, Hermann W. "Kanon." In *Theological Dictionary of the New Testament,* edited by Gerhard Kittel. Grand Rapids, Mich., 1965. An excellent word study of the Greek term in secular and Christian sources.

Bleeker, C. Jouco, ed. *Historia Religionum: Handbook for the History of Religion,* vol. 2, *Religions of the Present.* Leiden, 1971. An excellent overview of religions with careful attention to the historical appearance of normative traditions in each.

Brown, Raymond E. *The Critical Meaning of the Bible.* New York, 1981. A significant Catholic example of the modern attempt to distinguish between the "literal" and the "canonical sense" of the biblical text.

Campenhausen, Hans von. *The Formation of the Christian Bible.* Philadelphia, 1972. A classic study of the canonization of the New Testament.

Childs, Brevard S. *Introduction to the Old Testament as Scripture.* Philadelphia, 1979. An examination of how the canonization of the Hebrew Bible (Old Testament) influenced the "shape" and semantic import of biblical books.

Childs, Brevard S. *The New Testament as Canon: An Introduction.* Philadelphia, 1985. A study of the New Testament from the perspective of the role played by canonization in its formation as scripture.

Eliade, Mircea. *A History of Religious Ideas,* vol. 2, *From Gautama Buddha to the Triumph of Christianity.* Chicago, 1982. A monumental overview in which "canon" and "scripture" are employed as categories to interpret major world religions.

Leiman, Sid Z. *The Canonization of Hebrew Scripture.* Hamden, Conn., 1976. A controversial reexamination of the primary evidence for the canonization of the Hebrew Bible. Leiman helpfully collects and translates relevant texts from the Mishnah, the Talmud(s), and other sources.

Neusner, Jacob. *Midrash in Context.* Philadelphia, 1983. A provocative study of how the oral law came to accompany Jewish scripture in the history of that religion, as well as the implications of "canon" for the same.

Peters, F. E. *Children of Abraham: Judaism, Christianity, Islam.* Princeton, 1982. A comparative investigation into the three "religions of the book," including concern with issues of scripture and tradition.

Sanders, James A. *Canon and Community: A Guide to Canonical Criticism.* Philadelphia, 1984. An attempt to understand the dynamic of religious interpetation in Judaism and Christianity through a hermeneutical theory of canonization.

Sheppard, Gerald T. *Wisdom as a Hermeneutical Construct: A Study in the Sapientializing of the Old Testament.* Berlin and New York, 1980. A monograph that examines the canonical understanding of "wisdom" and "wisdom books" in prerabbinic Judaism and explores similar examples of late "canon conscious redactions" within the Hebrew Bible itself.

Sheppard, Gerald T. "Canonization: Hearing the Voice of the Same God through Historically Dissimilar Traditions." *Interpretation* 36 (January 1982): 21–33. An examination of the semantic import of the selection and editing of traditions in the formation of both the Hebrew Bible and the New Testament.

Smith, Wilfred Cantwell. "The Study of Religion and the Study of the Bible," *Journal of the American Academy of Religion* 39 (June 1971): 131–140. A general theory regarding the proper understanding of "Bible" in the study of comparative religions.

Smith, Wilfred Cantwell. "The True Meaning of Scripture: An Empirical Historian's Nonreductionist Interpretation of the Qur'ān." *International Journal of Middle East Studies* 11 (July 1980): 487–505. A consideration of the problem of understanding what constitutes viable religious interpretation from a history of religions perspective.

Sundberg, Albert C., Jr. *The Old Testament of the Early Church.* Cambridge, 1964. An argument, based on an examination of early Christian appeals to "scripture," that the conception of a "scripture" without specific dimensions preceded the later ecclesiastical decisions regarding a "canonical" Bible conforming to a specific list of books.

GERALD T. SHEPPARD

CANON LAW. The term *canon* is based on the Greek word *kanōn.* Originally signifying a straight rod or bar, especially one used to keep something else straight, *canon* came to mean something that is fixed, a rule or norm. The term has several applications in church usage: the canon of scripture, or that fixed list of books that are determined to belong to sacred scripture; the canon of the Mass, the fixed portion of the eucharistic prayer; the process of declaring a deceased person to be among the fixed list of saints in heaven, or canonization. From the third century, directives for church living and norms for church structures and procedures have been issued as canons.

Canon law refers to the law internal to the church. In the early centuries of Christianity, *canon* was used for internal church norms, to distinguish them from the imperial *nomos* (*leges* in Latin) or laws. Church norms have also been known as sacred or divine, to distinguish them from civil or human laws. At times they are referred to as the "sacred canons" or the "canonical order." The term *ecclesiastical law* is used synonymously with *canon law,* although at times *ecclesiastical law* also refers to the civil law adopted in various nations to regulate church affairs. The term *canon law* is used in the Roman Catholic, Anglican, and Orthodox communions.

Canon law is drawn from sources in scripture, custom, and various decisions of church bodies and individual church authorities. Over the centuries these have been gathered in a variety of collections that serve as the law books for various churches. In the twentieth century the Roman Catholic church adopted a new system of codified canon law whose juridical character is theoretically based on a single legislative act by the pope.

History. Over the centuries three major approaches have characterized the development of canon law. The first corresponds to the more communal structure of Christian churches in the first millennium; the second, a more Western phenomenon, is marked by the *Corpus iuris canonici,* or "body of canon law," developed during the centralization of church authority; the third is the relatively recent development in Roman Catholicism of a code of canon law.

First millennium. The primitive church adopted practical norms in response to specific needs and followed precedents that were thought to have come from the apostles. Some vestiges of this early discipline are evident in Paul's directives in his letters (e.g., *1 Cor.* and *2 Cor.*), Matthew's description of a process for resolving disputes (*Mt.* 18:15–18), and various other pericopes in the synoptic Gospels that show strong influences of early Christian community practices. Collections of these disciplinary norms, frequently attributed to the apostles, were circulated among the various churches from postapostolic times, particularly the *Didache* (second century?), the *Didascalia apostolorum* (third century), and Hippolytus's *Constitutiones apostolicae* (third century). The so-called Apostolic Constitutions and Apostolic Canons were derived from these earlier books and had wide circulation from the fourth century onward.

As local, regional, and eventually ecumenical councils were held, the bishops adopted disciplinary norms they called canons. These were frequently repeated by subsequent councils in the same and other areas. Eventually collections were developed in the East containing conciliar legislation (canons), imperial laws dealing with religious questions *(nomos),* and combinations of the two (nomocanons). These form the body of canon law for Eastern Orthodox churches today, with subsequent modifications enacted for specific autocephalous churches by their respective synods. Eastern churches in communion with Rome are also governed by this traditional body of law, modified through subsequent synods and papal enactments.

The basis for Western canon law can be found in the combination of canons adopted by successive councils in North Africa, Spain, and southern France, the canons of major Eastern regional and ecumenical councils, and decretals of the popes (letters dealing with specific problems). The most influential collections of these laws are the *Dionysiana* (Rome, late fifth century) and the

Hispana (Spain, seventh century). Collections containing both genuine laws and false decretals were circulated in the ninth and tenth centuries to counter efforts of civil authorities in Germanic areas to take over church property and offices. Papal collections were developed as part of reform efforts under Gregory VII (r. 1073–1085). Scholarly efforts to put some order into the growing body of law were attempted by Burchard of Worms (d. 1025), Ivo of Chartres (d. 1116), and Alger of Liège (d. 1132).

Corpus iuris canonici. Around 1140 John Gratian, a monk who had studied at Bologna the rediscovered civil law of the sixth-century Roman emperor Justinian, produced his *Concordia discordantium canonum.* Known popularly as Gratian's *Decretum* ("decree"), this was the most successful attempt to that time to put some sense of order into canon law. With Gratian begins the second major period of history for canon law. His work became the standard textbook and administrative reference manual for Western church law. It contained decrees of councils, decretals of popes, and Gratian's own comments organizing and explaining the interrelationship of his sources.

Gratian's work was later supplemented by official collections of laws either not contained in his *Decretum* or issued since his time: the five books of the *Decretals of Gregory IX* (1234), their supplement published by Boniface VIII as the *Liber sextus* (1298), and the *Clementinae* promulgated by John XXII (1317). Some of these "decretals" were decisions reached at general councils, but all were promulgated on papal authority and hence form a body of papal laws, in contrast to the mixture of conciliar laws, responses of the fathers of the church, and papal decretals that formed the raw material for Gratian.

Commentators on Gratian (decretists) glossed his text in the manner of scripture commentators. Similar studies were developed around the decretals (decretalists), eventually producing the *Glossa ordinaria,* or standard commentaries on the law.

In 1500 the *Corpus iuris canonici* was published at Paris. It contained Gratian's *Decretum,* the three subsequent official collections, and two later private collections of decretals, the *Extravagantes Ioannes XXII* and the *Extravagantes communes,* decretals circulating outside the official collections. This new collection served as the body of canon law for the Roman Catholic church until 1917.

Reformation churches rejected the centralizing papal law and turned to the scriptures, early councils, and decisions of their own synods for their church order. Reliance on civil law in the developing nation-states further reduced the role of canon law within these churches. The Anglican church, however, retained much of the classical canon law but replaced papal centralization with a system of government fashioned on the English civil experience. When the Episcopal church was formed in the United States after the American Revolution, it did much the same, adopting a form of internal government patterned on the new federal constitution.

In Roman Catholicism, the Council of Trent (1545–1563) issued a number of decrees supplementing the canon law on sacraments, clergy discipline, and related issues. The efforts of the Curia Romana to implement Trent and to strengthen church discipline resulted in a growing body of decisions and directives which by the late nineteenth century were viewed as crushing the local bishops. At Vatican I they asked for a simplification of church law similar to the civil law codes being developed in modern European countries at the time.

Codification. Pius X (r. 1903–1914) began the effort of codification, entrusting it to Cardinal Pietro Gasparri. The final product was promulgated by Benedict XV (r. 1914–1922) in 1917. The *Codex iuris canonici* (Code of Canon Law) marks a new stage in the history of canon law. Instead of the previous system, which reported both the law and its historical source, the new code contained canons devoid of historical basis, all having the same authority based on the pope as legislator. Later editions did contain historical notes appended by Gasparri, which were intended to aid in understanding the canons, but the 1917 code represents an entirely new approach to canon law deliberately patterned on civil models.

The code was divided into five books. The first was a set of general norms for interpreting and applying canon law. This was followed by three books patterned on standard Roman law divisions: persons, things, and actions. The book on persons dealt primarily with clergy and religious, and under clergy it provided all the norms for church organization from the pope down to parishes. The book on things encompassed spiritual as well as material "things": sacraments, sacred times and places, teaching authority, benefices, and finances. The book on procedures detailed the functioning of church courts and provided for special processes to be used in marriage cases, in the procedure of declaring canonizations, and in special disciplinary actions. The final book, on crime and punishment, detailed the various penalties under the law and specified a variety of crimes to which they applied either automatically *(latae sententiae)* or after the intervention of a church authority *(ferendae sententiae).*

Subsequent to the code, canon law became a process of interpreting the text of the canons and observing further instructions issued by Roman offices or local bishops. Conciliar activity to produce new canons was restricted to missionary areas, and only rarely did these go beyond the application of the code to local circumstances.

In 1959, when he announced plans to hold the Second Vatican Council, John XXIII also called for a renewal of the code. The work began in earnest in 1965, when the council concluded. Paul VI (r. 1963–1973) directed that the revision not only clear up ambiguities and questions relating to the 1917 code but also implement the new way of thinking characteristic of the council. His desire was for a canon law based on church considerations rather than on imitation of civil legal systems. Two distinct commissions were appointed, one for the Latin church and the other for the Eastern Catholic churches. Canon law experts were named as consultors to each commission to do the actual drafting, although the commissions retained responsibility to propose final texts to the pope for promulgation.

Preliminary efforts were made to develop a common law for Eastern and Western churches, the so-called Fundamental Law of the Church *(lex ecclesiae fundamentalis)*. Serious criticism of the drafts surfaced, both about the concept of developing a legal constitution for the church and about the drafts' fidelity to the positions adopted at Vatican II. The final version of the Fundamental Law was submitted to the pope in 1980 but was never promulgated.

The commission for the Latin code began its work first. Canons for the revised code were circulated in sections (schemata, or drafts) for comments by bishops around the world, revised and reorganized as a new code in 1980, and subjected to further study by an enlarged commission in 1981. The text was then studied by the pope with the aid of six advisers, and a final text of the revised *Codex iuris canonici* was promulgated on 25 January 1983 by John Paul II, twenty-four years after the announcement by John XXIII that the revision would take place. Work on the Eastern code is still in the consulting stage.

1983 Code of Canon Law. Although it continues the system of expressing canons devoid of their historical sources, the new code replaces the organization of the old one with a more theological arrangement of the canons. After an expanded initial book of general norms, there follow three substantive books based on Vatican II categories. The second book of the code, entitled "The People of God," begins with norms that apply to all the Christian faithful. It contains a first effort to provide a common bill of obligations and rights, followed by a set of canons on the obligations and rights of laity. Clergy are treated in combination with laity before the book turns to the hierarchical structures of the church, both at the level of supreme authority and in particular churches (dioceses) and groupings of churches. The final portion of the book considers religious and secular institutes ("consecrated life") and apostolic societies.

Increased importance is given to the word of God in book 3, on the teaching office of the church, and to the sacraments in book 4, on the church's sanctifying office. Canons on temporal goods are grouped into book 5. A revised and considerably reduced section on sanctions is found in book 6, while procedures are detailed in book 7.

The code attempts to provide room for local adaptation and leaves to particular law the regulation of various activities that the former code treated in detail (e.g., the Curia). It is however, a compromise document, reflecting both the compromises struck at Vatican II and the compromises worked out in the code commission itself. Conciliar statements are often repeated only selectively, and the language of the old canons has been retained in many areas. John Paul II has indicated that the 1983 code should be interpreted in light of Vatican II rather than as a repetition of the 1917 code. But commentators have observed that, given its nature as a code and the frequent repetition of canons from the old code, a real effort is needed at times to grasp the new way of thinking that is supposed to underlie the 1983 code.

Current Issues. Several issues mark current canon law discussions in the Roman Catholic church, some of which have significance for other churches that use a system of canon law. There is obviously the debate over the opportuneness of promulgating a code so soon after Vatican II, with many issues still under debate. The consensus articulated in the *Corpus iuris canonici* and later in the 1917 *Codex* is not that evident in Roman Catholicism today.

More fundamentally, the relationship of canon law to theology, to civil law, and even to "law" as such has been questioned. Paul VI sought to find the basis for canon law in the church's own self-understanding, and John Paul II points to scripture as the ultimate source for the new code. Some see in this a genuine effort to provide a more theological basis for canon law, attempting an opening to other churches as well as providing a more ecclesial sense to law within the Roman Catholic church. Others worry that this could be used as an excuse to avoid providing protection for the rights of persons, a characteristic of most modern civil law systems.

Former collections of law were based on civil law systems, whether the Roman law of Emperor Justinian or the civil codes of nineteenth-century Europe. But in a worldwide church, is it possible to have a legal system that does not draw on the insights of other law systems, such as Anglo-American common law or the developing international law? The 1983 code may be only a temporary stage in developing a canon law that is more adaptable to the lived experience of a world church.

Finally, is canon law really "law"? In light of contemporary understanding of religious liberty and the traditional teaching on the freedom of the act of faith, canon law must be seen more as the norm of a voluntary association than as a binding code for a nation or state. Current practice, which relies on administrative action more than on strictly legislative or canonical procedures, may already be a tacit admission of this fact.

Anglican Canon Law. Anglican canon law retains the principles of common ecclesiastical law accepted prior to 1534 as well as decretals and conciliar enactments that had been accepted by English courts, either ecclesiastical or secular. Anglican bishops, however, do not exercise legislative power. The 1919 Enabling Act established a Church Assembly with three houses (bishops, members of the convocations, and laity) that can submit proposals, but they must be enacted by Parliament to become law.

In the Episcopal church, triennial general conventions are held with two houses (bishops, and clerical and lay deputies). These have legislative authority over discipline and worship, issuing canons that form the distinctive canon law of this church. Individual dioceses hold annual conventions that may also issue canons for the local area.

BIBLIOGRAPHY

On the history of canon law, see the detailed synopsis by René Metz in the *New Catholic Encyclopedia* (New York, 1967) and in Amleto Giovanni Cicognani's *Canon Law,* 2d ed. (Philadelphia, 1935). Standard commentaries on the 1917 Code of Canon Law in English are T. Lincoln Bouscaren and Adam C. Ellis's *Canon Law: A Text and Commentary,* 4th ed. (Milwaukee, 1966); John A. Abbo and Jerome D. Hannan's *The Sacred Canons,* 2d ed., 2 vols. (Saint Louis, 1952); and Stanislaus Woywod and Calistus Smith's *A Practical Commentary on the Code of Canon Law,* rev. ed. (New York, 1963). For the 1983 code, see text in *Code of Canon Law, Latin-English Edition* (Washington, D.C., 1983), and the commentary edited by James A. Coriden, Thomas J. Green, and Donald E. Heintschel, *The Code of Canon Law: A Text and Commentary* (New York, 1984). For Anglican canon law, see Eric Kemp's *An Introduction to Canon Law in the Church of England* (London, 1957).

JAMES H. PROVOST

CANTILLATION. *See* Chanting.

CAO DAI is a syncretistic modern Vietnamese religious movement founded in 1926 by Ngo Van Chieu (1878–1932; also known as Ngo Minh Chieu). An official of the French colonial administration, Chieu was widely read in both Eastern and Western religion, and had a particular interest in spiritism. The movement began during séances conducted by Chieu and a group of friends of similar background as Vietnamese intellectuals. An entity called Cao Dai (literally, "high tower," a Taoist epithet for the supreme god) appeared and delivered to the group the fundamental features of the religion: universalism, vegetarianism, the image of an eye in a circle (which became its central symbol), and various details of worship. On 18 November 1926 the movement was inaugurated in a dramatic ceremony that drew some fifty thousand people. Though resisted by Buddhists and French officials, who perceived its nationalistic potential, Cao Dai grew phenomenally. By 1930 it numbered a half million by conservative estimate, and soon had garnered over one million followers, embracing at least one-eighth of the population in what was to become South Vietnam. The remarkable appeal of the eclectic, spiritist faith undoubtedly reflected the yearning of an oppressed Vietnamese population for something new, immediate, indigenous, and idealistic in a situation in which Catholicism was the religion of the alien colonizers, Buddhism was moribund, and Confucianism was linked to a social order clearly passing away.

Cao Dai met those criteria. The substantial Chinese cultural influence in Vietnam is evidenced in the fundamental similarity of Cao Dai to religious Taoist sectarianism in its spiritism, political overtones, and colorful liturgy. Furthermore, like most Chinese religious movements of recent centuries, it also sought to unify the "three faiths," and so it incorporated Confucian morality, Buddhist doctrines such as *karman* and reincarnation, and Taoist occultism. Also like some of its Chinese counterparts, it further sought to unify the religions of the world, enshrining Jesus and Muḥammad in its pantheon as well, and heralding a new age of world harmony. Its elaborate organizational structure, headed by a pope, cardinals, and archbishops, was patently inspired by Roman Catholicism. Besides the supreme god, Cao Dai, the faith also honored a great company of spirits, not only Eastern figures like the Buddha, Lao-tzu, Confucius, and Sun Yat-sen, but also such Westerners as Jesus, Joan of Arc, and Victor Hugo.

Cao Dai worship centers on rituals performed in temples four times daily, and on festivals, celebrated with even greater elaborateness. The rituals consist of prayer, chants, and such simple offerings as incense, tea, and wine presented with highly stylized ceremony.

Séances are held separately and are restricted to set occasions and to mediums appointed by the hierarchy. Despite these rules, Cao Dai has generated a number of subsects, frequently inspired by fresh mediumistic communications.

Cao Dai is headquartered in a sacred city, Tay Ninh, northwest of Saigon. Here it boasts a large main temple and many administrative and ritual offices. Before the unification of Vietnam under the communist Hanoi regime in 1975, the "Holy See" was responsible not only for spiritual and ecclesiastical matters, but also for managing the sect's considerable agricultural and business holdings. During the several decades of strife before 1975, Cao Dai exercised effective control of its headquarters province and, until its forces were disbanded by President Ngo Dinh Diem in 1955, it fielded its own army. Although its alliances shifted among the contending groups, Cao Dai basically labored for an unaligned nationalism.

Reliable information on Cao Dai in Vietnam since 1975 is scanty. Reportedly it has been severely repressed by the government, with a high proportion of its churches confiscated and its clergy arrested or laicized; the Holy See is apparently virtually inactive. On the other hand, by 1985 approximately twenty Cao Dai worship centers had sprung up around the world in Vietnamese refugee communities.

[*See also* Vietnamese Religion.]

BIBLIOGRAPHY

Fall, Bernard. "The Political-Religious Sects of Viet-Nam." *Pacific Affairs* 28 (1955): 235–253.

Oliver, Victor L. *Caodai Spiritism: A Study of Religion in Vietnamese Society.* Leiden, 1976.

Werner, Jayne Susan. *Peasant Politics and Religious Sectarianism: Peasant and Priest in the Cao Dai in Viet Nam.* New Haven, 1981.

ROBERT S. ELLWOOD

CARDS function in the religious context both as instruments for performing divination rituals and as repositories of esoteric sacred teaching. Current historical evidence suggests that cards originated in China and that their sacred usage developed from shamanistic or Taoist divinatory rituals that predated cards themselves. The oldest extant card, found in Chinese Turkistan, dates from no later than the eleventh century. The design of Chinese cards was copied from paper money first used in the T'ang dynasty (618–908 CE). The design of an arrow on the back of the oldest Korean cards suggests that those cards developed from a divination technique for interpreting the pattern of arrows randomly cast onto a circle divided into quadrants.

Number and pattern, and their orderly transformations, are in sacred mathematics symbolic expressions, or hierophanies, of the eternal divine essences and processes that manifest themselves to us in time as the visible cosmos. The pack of divination cards is a homologue of the set of divine mathematical potentialities that can manifest itself in the time and space of the cosmos. The spontaneous play of the cards, like in any other particular act of divination, reveals a meaningful structure homologous to the divine creative process, which manifests itself within worldly events. The interpretation, or reading, of any particular play of cards is essentially a matter of intuiting from the sacred mathematical symbolism of the cards the worldly events whose structure corresponds to that symbolism.

It is not certain when and where cards first appeared in Europe. One hypothesis is that they were brought into southern Europe by the Moors as early as the eighth century. The earliest mention of numbered cards is in Covelluzo's *Istoria della città di Viterbo* (1480). Covelluzo says that they were brought to the city of Viterbo by the Saracens in 1379. In her extensive study *A History of Playing Cards* (New York, 1966), Catherine P. Hargrave says that these early numbered cards were probably European copies of Chinese cards that arrived through Venice. The oldest extant European cards are several tarot cards from a pack designed for Charles VI of France in 1392.

The two most prominent packs of cards used in Europe for divination are the ordinary pack, consisting of fifty-two cards, and the tarot pack, consisting of seventy-eight cards. The ordinary pack is divided into four suits—diamonds, clubs, hearts, and spades. Joseph Campbell (in Campbell and Roberts, 1979) has suggested that the four suits represent the four estates, or classes, of the medieval social order: clergy (hearts), knights (spades), merchants (diamonds), and peasants (clubs). The four suits of the ordinary pack possibly developed under Protestant influence from the earlier tarot suits of chalices, swords, coins, and staves. The fact that the four suits of the ordinary pack culminate in the figures of knave, queen, and king leads Campbell to suppose that the pictorial symbolism of the cards expresses a medieval esoteric initiatory tradition wherein ascent along any of the four lines represented by the suits leads to spiritual realizations of equivalent value and importance.

The tarot pack falls into two sections: the "minor arcana" of fifty-six cards, divided equally into four suits, and the "major arcana" of twenty-one numbered picture cards and one unnumbered card, the Fool. The origin of the tarot deck is not known. The first history of the tarot, *Le jeu des tarots* (Paris, 1781), was written by Court de Gebelin. Gebelin claims that the deck originated in ancient Egypt and represents the esoteric teaching of the god Thoth, recorded and expressed in a hieroglyphic alphabet, in which all the gods are symbolized by pictorial signs and numbers. While Gebelin's theory of Egyptian origins is clearly itself of a mythic nature (the Rosetta Stone, which made translation of hieroglyphics possible, was not discovered until 1790), the evidence of recent research on the history of symbols indicates that the deck is indeed, as Gebelin supposed, a repository of sacred teaching and esoteric knowledge. The pictorial symbolism of the deck is known to have much in common with the symbolism of spiritual initiation rites and instruction in Hellenistic mystery cults, ancient astrology, and medieval alchemy, wherein the processes of manifesting divine energies are represented in the progression of visual and numerical symbols.

BIBLIOGRAPHY

Tarot Revelations by Joseph Campbell and Richard Roberts (San Anselmo, Calif., 1979) is a detailed work summarizing the phenomenological evidence linking the tarot to Hellenistic religion and alchemy as well as the tarot's place in nineteenth-century esoteric societies.

RICHARD W. THURN

CARGO CULTS.

In 1980, a motorcade drove into Madang, a provincial capital in Papua New Guinea (independent since 1975), and stopped outside the local branch of the national bank. The drivers and passengers came from a Catholic village sixty kilometers to the west. Their spokeswoman, Josephine Bahu (about twenty-eight at the time), asked the bank manager, a European, to give her the keys to his vaults, for God had revealed to her the truth about money—its true source and its proper use as a road to economic development.

This incident was a recent example of cargoism, the most common form of millenarianism in Melanesia since the nineteenth century, when colonial rule reduced its inhabitants to the status of cheap labor for European employers. The millennium, as it has inevitably come to be manifested in this context, is the anticipated arrival of bulk supplies of European goods (cargo)—civilian stock, such as tinned meat, cotton cloth, steel tools, and motor vehicles; and military equipment, especially rifles and ammunition—which many of the people believe to be made not by human beings but by a deity or deities aided by the spirits of the dead. This conception of the millennium may give rise to a cargo cult or movement whose devotees perform ritual to induce the cargo god(s) to send the ancestors with supplies of the new wealth (and nowadays, as the initial example suggests, money) for immediate distribution. I begin by describing overt cargo phenomena and then discuss some of the best-known approaches to their study by Western scholars.

Overt Cargo Phenomena. Western scholars first learned about cargo phenomena in 1857 through the publication of the Mansren myth of the Koreri in the Biak-Numfoor area of Irian Jaya, probably the oldest cargo movement in the whole region, although there were manifestations in Samoa in the 1830s and in Fiji in the 1880s. In Papua New Guinea the first known cults were the Baigona, reported in 1912, and the Vailala Madness, reported in 1919, although one movement, centered on Madang, can be dated from 1871 and continues to the present day. Cargoism began to proliferate just before World War II. In Papua New Guinea there has been a plethora of cults; in the Solomon Islands, Marching Rule; and in Vanuatu, the John Frum movement. In recent times the region has seen the rise of various alternatives to cargoism, specifically Pentecostalism and other Christian cults that are independent of the established European missions and that lay stress on healing and salvation. Although it is hard to draw a firm line between cargoism and other modern religious developments in Melanesia, I concentrate on cargo cults as such.

The many forms that cargo cults take depend on a number of variables: (1) a people's socioeconomic structure, basic personality, and traditional religion, which factors together determine the strength of their desire for the new wealth and the extent to which they are prepared to test or reject theological experiments; (2) the nature of the introduced religion, which they may or may not readily interpret as cargo doctrine; and (3) the pattern of initial contact and subsequent relations with Europeans (the actual purveyors of cargo), which underlie the political aspects of the people's responses. Thus, as we learn from the early ethnographic accounts of the Papua New Guinea Highlands—which were brought under administration only after 1933, when Europeans had gained some experience in Melanesian affairs—for some years it seemed likely that strong social structures, hard-headedness, and the predilection for secularism rather than religion, together with good race relations, accounted for the general paucity of cargo cults in the area. On the seaboard, incorporated within colonial administrations soon after 1884, a contrary situation obtained. Relatively weak social structures, an induced inferiority complex, an intellectual system dominated by theology, and often traumatic race relations had created the conditions in which cargoism was bound to flourish. Yet, although differences of this kind do exist, the neat geographical distinction suggested is probably overdrawn. In recent years cargoism, like Pentecostalism, has made inroads into the Highlands, forcing a reappraisal of previous interpretations.

The most obvious signs of a cargo cult's emergence are generally its devotees' preparations for the arrival of the goods they expect. Especially early on, when all cargo came by ship, they built wharves and storehouses in coastal villages. During and after the Pacific war, when the importance of aircraft became apparent, they cleared airstrips. Cargo may also be expected to appear in local cemeteries, which devotees assiduously keep clean and tidy, on alters in churches, which they regard as particularly holy, or at other places the leaders designate. In addition, there have been "flagstaffs," "radio masts," and even "telephones," by means of which the leaders could make contact with the deity and ancestors for news of the goods' arrival. Sometimes both leaders and followers have "demonstrated" the reality of this contact by simulating spirit possession, including shaking fits and other forms of violent seizure.

Yet cargo cannot come by itself: its arrival has to be ensured by means of religious ritual. A cult normally begins when, after a dream, waking vision, or some other extraordinary experience, its leader announces that he has been in touch with the deity, who has revealed to him the source of the desired wealth, the methods by which those who have so far monopolized it (generally Europeans) have defrauded the people of their rights, and the new ritual procedures necessary to redress the balance. Most leaders have been men, but there have been some outstanding women: Josephine Bahu in the 1980s, Philo of Inawai'a village (of the Mekeo language group, Papua) in 1941, and Polelesi of Igurue village (of the Garia language group, New Guinea) in 1947.

In this context, it is essential to distinguish between cults based on paganism, Christianity, and syncretic Christian-pagan doctrine. In a purely pagan cult, the leader has the difficult task of persuading the followers that traditional myths have a meaning which was not mentioned in the past but which has now been revealed to him alone. In quasi-Christian cults the problem is not so great. Christianity is not enshrined in tradition and can be interpreted with greater flexibility. The leader may claim to have visited God in heaven and returned as the Black Jesus. Again, in the course of some such experience, he may have learned that the secret of the cargo is the identification of an indigenous deity with God or Jesus Christ.

These basic differences, which are generally the result of the degree of administrative and more particularly mission influence, determine the nature of the ritual instructions the leader invariably claims to have received from the deity. In a pagan cult, where cultural change is minimal, the leader is likely to do no more than order the performance of mainly traditional rituals in honor of deities and the dead (possibly with a few foreign embellishments), albeit in an intensified form, as happened in the eastern Highlands of Papua New Guinea. But where there has been acculturation, ritual incorporates new forms and becomes more elaborate. Cults based on Christianity may have mass village assemblies with marathon church services and prayers to God, "the Cargo Giver." Disbelievers are threatened with hellfire, and the Second Coming of Our Lord is prophesied as imminent, with all the wealth of Europe going to the faithful. There are mass conversions and baptisms. Polygyny and sexual promiscuity are forbidden, although in some villages in the southern Madang Province in the 1940s cult leaders experimented with wife exchange on the ground that this eliminated the quarrels over adultery that so displeased God. The sanctuaries of traditional deities are often desecrated or destroyed, and all forms of indigenous dancing and exchange outlawed. Christian fervor may go to extremes: in the early 1960s, in a village north of Madang, a man acquiesced in having his throat slit in front of a completely unsuspecting Catholic archbishop. It eventuated that this was a ritual reenactment of the Crucifixion: the victim was the Black Jesus, who was to intercede with God for the economic advantage of his people just as the White Jesus had done for Europeans.

In Christian-pagan syncretic cults, ritual, like doctrine, tends to borrow from both religions. Cults of this degree of sophistication often have two interesting features. First, devotees may root out their crops, cut down their palms and fruit trees, and slaughter their livestock. No ubiquitously satisfactory explanation for this behavior has been found, but in one area, the southern Madang Province, the reason given is that the people want to stress their poverty to the cargo deity and ancestors, thereby hastening the arrival of the new goods. Second, especially in communities which value money as a means of access to cargo, leaders may persuade their followers to place spare cash in a case or chest on the promise that their ritual will increase the sum deposited many times over. Finally, in some areas the people have totally rejected Christianity and its syncretic modifications in favor of paganism for cargoist ends. This heralds the reintroduction of traditional ritual with modern borrowings.

Western Analyses of Cargo Phenomena. The extensive literature on cargoism primarily consists of accounts of single cults, although there are several important comparative analyses. Space precludes detailed consideration of these general works, so I have selected for discussion the approaches of several Western scholars since World War I to indicate the trends in our thinking about the problem.

It took many years to complete detailed studies of cargo cults in which the participants could speak for themselves. Inevitably, therefore, the first European interpretations were ethnocentric. Francis E. Williams, who was from 1922 until 1943 the government anthropologist in Papua, wrote essays in 1922 and 1934 that examined the facts of cargo phenomena in light of the assumptions of his own society. He wrote only about the disturbances in the Gulf Province, the so-called Vailala Madness, a title which, significantly, he never challenged. Although a meticulous field-worker, he never comprehended Melanesian values and epistemology. He made careful notes about the external features of the cult: the people's imitation of European dress, eating habits, and house decoration; their use of Christian beliefs as part of their doctrine; their make-believe Western technology; and their periodic hysteria. But the meaning of it all eluded him: nothing in his personal or academic experience had prepared him for this kind of behavior. He concluded that the people were temporarily insane as a result of misunderstood Christianity and boredom caused by the loss of traditional activities, such as warfare and religious ceremonies. The cure he advocated was the Anglo-Australian boarding-school nostrum: some form of intervillage sport like football.

Peter Worsley, writing in the 1950s, had at his disposal a far larger body of cargoist literature, which he presented with great thoroughness. Yet much of the material was of doubtful value, based as it was on superficial accounts by untrained onlookers during and after World War II. Many of the observations were made when, after a period of optimistic but unproductive cooperation with Europeans (which the authors never appreciated), the people were finally hostile to whites. Hence it was easy for Worsley to offer a Marxist explanation: the cults were an embryonic form of class struggle against economic and political oppression, that is, the people's protest against their colonial overlords.

There are two objections to this kind of analysis. First, although one aspect of cargoism is undeniably its political statement, we have no evidence that cargoism is invariably anti-European. After a bad period, mainly in the nineteenth and early twentieth centuries, colonial rule—certainly as it was known in Papua New Guinea—was relatively benign. Many villagers have adopted cargoism as a means of explaining and manipulating the new order long before unfulfilled hopes have made them antagonistic. As indicated, cargoism can express the desire to fraternize with white men. Second, the Marxist approach to issues raised by cargoism is basically secular and so barely touches on the question of why the people have used religion, virtually on its own, to explain and try to cope with the colonial and postcolonial situations. Many cults are based on intricate philosophies, which cannot legitimately be ignored.

Between 1960 and 1972 three other scholars—Ian Jarvie, Freerk Kamma, and Kenelm Burridge—did much to offset this imbalance. Jarvie, a philosopher with a deep interest in social anthropology and an appreciation of Melanesian religion, approaches cargoism from an uncompromisingly intellectualist point of view. Although he does not deny the importance of the political issues raised by Worsley, he makes it quite plain that his interest lies in the structure of cargo doctrines as means of "teaching" the people the source of European wealth and giving them the prescription for getting it. In the sense that they are based on traditional assumptions and modes of thought, cargo cults are completely logical.

Kamma, a missionary who studied the Koreri movement in the northwestern sector of Irian Jaya, argues that it is a direct continuation of religious traditions aimed at maintaining and improving the people's way of life. With the arrival of European missionaries in the nineteenth century, the people wove Christianity into these traditions and treated cargo as the symbol of the improved way of life. His argument is echoed by John Strelan, another missionary, who reasons that for Melanesians cargo is salvation, an idea akin to Calvin's dictum that worldly success is the basis of *certitudo salutis*.

Burridge, who studied the Tangu in the northern Madang Province, sees cargo cults as the Melanesians' attempt to achieve full human dignity through attainment of economic and sociopolitical equality with Europeans. Their purpose is to create the "new society" and the "new man" able to maintain this principle of equivalence with whites. He stresses the importance of the "myth-dream," in both traditional religions and quasi-Christian cults, as the revelation of the origin of cargo and the secret of the ritual that will make it available.

A Composite Approach to Cargo Phenomena. I have developed a composite approach based on my own research in the southern Madang Province after 1949. I regard it as essential to take all the issues raised by the foregoing scholars and combine them in a way that keeps each one in proper perspective. Broadly, cargoists try to recreate in the modern situation the same kind of predictable cosmic order they knew in the past: an order the gods ordained and human beings maintain by fulfilling social obligations among themselves and ritual obligations toward deities and ancestors. [*See* New Guinea Religions.] This re-creation will give them the key to the new wealth and ensure its fair distribution. In a word, they retain their old cosmic values of anthropocentrism and materialism: man is the center of the cosmos, which exists for his benefit. Cargoism, thus conceived, is a dialogue between the old sociocultural system and the economic, political, and religious policies introduced by colonial administrations. A most important factor is that, although they enabled the people to acquire limited supplies of the new goods, these policies actually achieved few changes in village life. Despite a century of European control, the pattern of economic and sociopolitical life has remained very much intact. The people still have minimal knowledge of the European world, so that their reactions to, and interpretations of, cargo are based primarily on tradition. To this extent, cargoism is conservative.

My "composite approach" to cargoism raises three questions relating to *motivation, conceived means,* and *effects* in cargo cult. Why do the people desire European goods so much that they waste decades in trying to acquire them by obviously futile procedures? Why do they rely on religious ritual rather than secular activity? What have cargo cults done to indigenous society?

Motivation. In absolute terms, Melanesians have never been poor. They have rarely known hunger. Hence cargoism is an expression of relative deprivation. The people want Western goods for two reasons: their obvious utility and technical superiority over indigenous products; and their sociopolitical significance. They quickly saw the practical value of European artifacts, especially steel axes and knives, nails, and cloth. In the nineteenth century European traders took great pains to provide the kinds of goods the people wanted. These traders were always on guard against theft, for the demand for their goods was great, and Melanesians were skillful fighters. By 1900, most Melanesians under colonial administration had adopted steel tools, some Western clothing, and such luxuries as glass beads and mirrors.

This pragmatic incentive has its sociopolitical counterpart, which can be understood only by considering the role of wealth in traditional society. Beyond its usefulness, wealth is a vital content of all social relationships. Bonds between local descent groups, kinsmen, and affines—the prime constituents of social structure—are strengthened by the periodic exchange of goods and services, particularly pigs and valuables. For one party to fail in its commitments is cause for tremendous shame, which nothing can alleviate. The people desire exactly this kind of egalitarian relationship with Europeans, and cargo is the most important part of the goods and services to be exchanged. One cargo leader put it to an Australian officer thus: "We are doing no harm. All we want is to live well—like white men!" Yet the structure of the modern economy necessitates marked inequalities between foreign employers and indigenous employees. European monopoly of the new wealth has become the symbol of this imbalance and hence a primary cause of political unrest.

Although the pragmatic incentive to acquire cargo is a constant, sociopolitical motivation correlates with the climate of race relations, which in its turn determines the kinds of goods the people desire and the political significance of cult activity. This has been documented for one area of Papua New Guinea. In the southern Madang Province, which comprises a large number of separate language groups or virtually autonomous societies, the cargo movement has since 1871 passed through five broad stages that have expressed varying attitudes toward Europeans (ranging from friendship to hostility) and shifting preferences for specific types of goods, civilian or military.

The first stage (1871–c. 1900) began with the arrival of the first European settler, the Russian scientist Baron Miklouho-Maclay, who won the people's friendship by establishing a fair trading partnership with them. He introduced Western civilian goods and new food plants, all of which were enthusiastically received. In 1884 he was followed by German settlers, whose behavior was a complete antithesis: they were arrogant; they alienated a disproportionate amount of coastal land for plantations; and they paid badly for labor. Friendship gave way to hostility, which was the leitmotif also of the second stage (c. 1900–c. 1914). The people now wanted to acquire rifles and ammunition with which to expel the foreigners. In 1904 the administration put down a serious uprising in Madang and in 1912, fearing another emergency, exiled a large part of the local population.

The third stage (c. 1914–c. 1933) saw a *volte-face.* The new Australian administration permitted the exiles to return home, and the people sought an accommodation with the whites, hoping to live in peace with them and acquire civilian goods. Certainly the last expectation was unreal, so that the fourth stage (c. 1933–c. 1945) witnessed a return to enmity toward Europeans and a desire for military equipment. Some cultists collaborated with the Japanese (who occupied the area between 1942 and 1944), armed themselves with discarded Japanese weapons, and set up a quasi-military camp. For a brief time after 1945 the people, under the leadership of Yali Singina, who had served in the Australian army, once again expressed goodwill toward Europeans. Because of a misunderstanding, Yali believed, and so had persuaded his people, that in return for the loyalty of native troops the Europeans would reward the people with bulk cargo. These hopes were dashed in 1947, when it transpired that the "bulk reward" was to be development in the form of hospitals and schools—benefits that ordinary villagers could not then appreciate. This inaugurated the fifth stage (1948–1950), which expressed renewed hostility and, for some of the regional population at least, the hope of getting modern weapons with which to fight the Europeans.

Regrettably, there is no comparable account of this alternating pattern of friendly and hostile race relations elsewhere in Melanesia. Yet the Madang evidence stresses the falsity of the view that cargoism always expresses hostility toward Europeans. Another recent incident supports this argument. In a major cargo cult in the East Sepik Province of Papua New Guinea in 1971, some six thousand people formed a chain gang to remove from the summit of Mount Hurun some military concrete markers, which were believed to be demons impeding the cargo millennium. Before the event local Europeans widely predicted that they would be the target of popular animosity. Yet there was no evidence of this. Cult devotees brought the markers to the station of the local European patrol officer and then peacefully dispersed. Significantly, a year later a similar operation was planned near Madang: the destruction of the monument erected in honor of the German governor von Hagen after his death in 1897 and said to be preventing the arrival of the cargo deity. The sponsors stressed their desire for racial harmony by inviting Europeans and Chinese to take part. They tried to get a message to this effect broadcast over Radio Mandang.

Conceived means. As attacks on trading vessels and uprisings around Madang suggest, Melanesians are prepared to use physical force to gain their economic and political ends. Hence it is perhaps puzzling that at the same time they consistently rely on religious ritual as a means of getting cargo in the face of recurrent failure. It can be said, of course, that once they appreciate the power of colonial administrations they are afraid to take direct action. But this does not explain why they are convinced that religion will provide a solution or why, in some cases, they combine it with secular economic activity. For instance, the people of Karkar Island and Mount Hagen, now rich from cash crops, either believe in or actually practice cargo ritual.

The only possible answer is that Western contact has not destroyed the people's traditional intellectual assumptions: that religion is the source of "true knowledge" and that ritual is a pragmatic technology with no mystical attributes. The forces that governed the old cosmic order should govern the new one. This idea was expressed to me early in my research by a highly intelligent informant: "Everything that we have was invented by a deity: taro, yams, livestock, artifacts. If we want taro to grow, we invoke the taro goddess, and so forth. Well, then, you people come to us with all your goods, and we ask, 'Where is the god of the cargo and how do we contact him?'" The continuing search for the divine source of Western goods after each negative result is consistent with this statement.

Here again the southern Madang Province is illustrative, as the area saw a succession of five cargo beliefs or doctrines that correlated more or less with the sociopolitical stages already summarized. The first of these beliefs (1871–c. 1900) expressed the people's conclusion that the early European visitors were indigenous gods suddenly appearing in their midst. Miklouho-Maclay was either Kilibob or Manup, the two deity brothers who between them were said to have created all the sociocultural systems of the region's seaboard. He had invented the new goods he brought especially for them, and as a measure of their friendship they had to reciprocate with gifts of food. They do not appear to have honored him with ritual while he was living in their midst. Ordinary social behavior sufficed. Although they at first expected to establish comparable exchange ties with the Germans, ultimately they came to regard them, because of their haughtiness, as hostile gods whose purpose was to enslave them with their rifles. But, as the second cargo belief (c. 1900–c. 1914) indicated, they decided that the Germans were human beings who, because of a cosmic accident, had acquired sole access to the cargo deity, Kilibob or Manup, and so misappropriated the wealth properly destined for Madang.

The third cargo belief (c. 1914–c. 1933) expressed the people's renewed goodwill toward Europeans because the missionaries had consistently shown concern during their exile and the new administration had brought them home, which they interpreted as signs that the cargo secret would be revealed to them. To this end, they adopted Christianity and revised it as a cargo religion. God, Jesus Christ, and the ancestors lived in Heaven (a suburb of Sydney, Australia), where they made cargo. Baptism and assiduous worship of the kind already described would induce God to send the ancestors with cargo to the ships (and later aircraft) that would deliver it to the Madangs. But after twenty years the people were no better off. Thus the fourth cargo belief (c. 1933–c. 1945) spelled out their distrust of, and enmity to, Europeans, especially the missionaries, who had hidden the truth from them. The new doctrine and ritual were syncretic. Kilibob and Manup were equated with God and Jesus Christ, the cargo deities kept prisoner by the whites in Australia. The aim was to honor them in such a way as to ensure their return: through church services, dancing, feasting, and food offerings. The Japanese soldiers, of course, were either spirits of the dead or emissaries of the cargo god sent to punish the Europeans for their duplicity. The fifth cargo belief (1948–1950) marked the end of dependence on a foreign religion. All the traditional gods of the southern Madang Province were now proclaimed cargo deities. The missionaries had hidden them in Australia, but Manup (alias Jesus Christ) had found them and taught them to make cargo. It was now the people's duty and interest to get them back to Madang to establish the millennium. To do this, they had to reject all Christian teaching and worship, and return to traditional ritual, especially dancing, feasting, initiatory ceremonies, and food offerings to gods and ancestors set out on specially prepared tables.

Effects. Until recently a main interest of Anglo-Australian social anthropology has been the study of political structure and function, and it is not surprising that the effect of cargoism on traditional society has been evaluated predominantly in that field. Early suggestions were that cargoism might help lay the foundations of future nationalism in two ways: by uniting the populations of whole regions and thereby breaking down sectionalism based on clan, village, and language group; and by preparing the people to accept genuine development when it was presented to them in realistic administrative projects. We should be careful on both these counts.

In the first context, although cargo cults have at times brought together social aggregations far larger than was possible before contact, it is doubtful whether this process has been universal and automatic or whether the leaders have deliberately fostered it. The evidence suggests rather that these aggregations occur only when their members have a single doctrine to unite them. When this is lost, the aggregations disperse. I consider again the southern Madang Province. In the second stage of the cargo movement, although the people of the whole coast under administration may have been hostile to the Germans and may have hoped for a return of Kilibob or Manup, they did not form a grand alliance. The politico-military groups in the revolts of 1904 and 1912 appear to have been based on old rather than new alignments: traditional clan alliances and marriage or kinship ties. In the third stage, widespread conversion to Christianity gave the people of the whole region a sense of common consciousness: together with Europeans, they were all descended from Adam, Eve, and Noah. Yet there was no attempt to create a wide political organization to exploit the new attitude. In the fourth stage, this widespread common consciousness was considerably attenuated because the new syncretic doctrines based on the amalgam of the Kilibob-Manup myth and Christianity were restricted entirely to the littoral. The quasi-Christian cargoists of the inland, who had no rights to the traditional myth, were at once excluded. Nevertheless, the coastal villagers following the new doctrine did evince a degree of solidarity never known in the past. Finally, in the fifth stage, Yali Singina agreed to become the movement's leader only when he was satisfied that Jesus-Manup had transferred the power to make cargo to all the indigenous deities so that he, as an inland dweller, could not be accused of theft for meddling with a coastal myth. The new doctrine had the potential to unite the people of the whole region in a mass anti-European cult. Yet, although antagonism was rife, Yali's organization was too inefficient and parochial to turn it into an effective political force. In short, the process of expanding political cohesion is probably unconscious and haphazard rather than deliberately planned.

In the second context, there appears to be even less evidence to support the view that cargoism arouses among the people such energy and enthusiasm for modernization that it helps facilitate the change to indigenous government and administration. Indeed, the facts suggest that cargoism is—and that its devotees see it as—ontologically quite different from the national structure established and bequeathed by the former colonial power, and that cargoism cannot easily be assimilated to that structure, which, moreover, it may deliberately impede. By presenting itself as a seemingly logical alternative system, the movement offers those unwilling to experiment with new ideas the opportunity to engage in activities which may be consistent with tradition but are bound to be sterile—an argument relevant not only to the political field but to the economic and educational fields as well.

In the field of politics, it is necessary to consider the behavior of cargoists in two situations; in the electorate at large; and within parliament and local government councils. During election campaigns cargoists have indeed made extravagant claims. In 1967–1968 Yali Singina, who now prefixed his name with the title god-king, campaigned for a seat in the national parliament in Port Moresby on the following platform. He would go to the House, where he would discover the indigenous deities, whom the administration had now placed there in a secret room. He would occupy the Speaker's Chair, take control of the Mace, and liberate the gods, with whom he would return to Madang, where he would usher in the cargo millennium and proclaim self-government, administering the country with the aid of those European officers of whom he approved. He was not elected. Again, in 1971, he rejected an offer of an electoral alliance from the Madang representatives of Pangu Pati (the senior government party) on the grounds that as "king" of Papua New Guinea he could not share power. Yet, in 1972, he belatedly but unsuccessfully tried to take up the offer because he believed that Pangu was a cult organization like his own. Matias Yaliwan, the chief cargo prophet in the East Sepik Province, claimed to have been told in a dream that he had been appointed leader of the country. He was elected to parliament in 1972 and subsequently told his followers that it was through his special aura that self-government was achieved. By the same token, in the 1980s Josephine Bahu's senior followers wrote to the prime minister that she should be made head of state.

Apart from Matias Yaliwan, a number of known cargoists have been elected to parliament and local government councils, where their behavior has generally been far more circumspect. Real politics does not provide an arena in which they can operate with success. Matias resigned his seat when he realized that his claim to personal leadership was being quietly ignored. Other cargoists have remained largely quiescent, making few speeches and little contribution to proceedings beyond voting. In the same way, Yali Singina and his "deputy" Dui Yangsai sat for many years on the Rai Coast Council but, despite their flamboyant pronouncements elsewhere, never advocated cargoist policy in the chamber.

A comparable conflict of interest and interpretation obtains in the fields of economic development and education. Although on Karkar and at Mount Hagen the people have succeeded in cash cropping while at the same time engaging in cargoism, there are many other cases in which cargoists and developers are continually at loggerheads. The cargoists assert that the developers prevent the millennium by paying all their attention to their plantations and denying the cargo god the ritual honor due to him. Also, it is questionable how genuine economic success on Karkar and at Mount Hagen can be when many people still appear to regard purely secular activity as a poor second best. Cargoism could well hold them back from innovations that might lead to expansion, so that they may remain always the satellites of European businessmen, who still provide all the initiatives. Finally, many people misunderstand and are disenchanted with modern education. In the past, parents have taken their children away from mission schools when they discovered that the cargo secret was not in the curriculum. Some have even denied the value of mission schools, which are attended by children of both sexes: genuine education—that is, powerful religious secrets—is given only to males during and after initiation. In cargoist areas secular education has been equally badly received. Many children see no point in it, and the dropout rate for secondary schools is very high. Unsuccessful pupils have been drawn into cargo organizations as "secretaries" and "clerks." With their smattering of Western knowledge, these young members give the cults an appearance of increased sophistication and provide explanatory systems so persuasive that the ordinary villager finds it hard to fault them. It is no wonder that both national and provincial politicians and public servants, concerned for the future of their country, view these counterintellectuals with disquiet, as a fifth column that can vitiate genuine achievement.

BIBLIOGRAPHY

Berndt, Ronald M. "A Cargo Movement in the Eastern Central Highlands of New Guinea." *Oceania* 23 (September 1952): 40–65; (December 1952): 137–158; (March 1953): 202–234. An early paper describing what was until recently one of the few cargo cults in the Highlands of Papua New Guinea.

Burridge, Kenelm. *Mambu: A Melanesian Millennium.* London, 1960. A humane and sophisticated analysis of cargo activity in the northern Madang Province of Papua New Guinea. Emphasizes the people's efforts to reestablish their self-respect by achieving socioeconomic and political equality with Europeans. Burridge expands and projects his argument into the field of international millenarianism in his *New Heaven, New Earth* (New York, 1969).

Cochrane, Glynn. *Big Men and Cargo Cults.* Oxford, 1970. An analysis of the role of leaders in cargo cults, with emphasis on Papua and the Solomon Islands.

Guiart, Jean. *Un siècle et demi de contacts culturels à Tanna, Nouvelles-Hebrides.* Paris, 1956. An important historical analysis of administrative and mission influence and popular response (including cargoism) in Vanuatu.

Hanneman, E. F. "Le Culte du Cargo en Nouvelle-Guinée." *Le monde non Chretién,* n.s. 8, (October-December 1948): 937–962. An early demonstration of the possibilities of an intellectualist approach to cargoism. A classic work.

Harding, Thomas G. "A History of Cargoism in Sio, North-east New Guinea." *Oceania* 38 (September 1967): 1–23. A paper important not only for its ethnographic content: here Harding coins the term *cargoism* and establishes the movement as a philosophy in its own right.

Jarvie, Ian C. *The Revolution in Anthropology* (1964). New York,

1967. A prominent work: the first internationally recognized study of cargoism in intellectualist terms and, at the same time, an astute critique of positivist social anthropology.

Kamma, Freerk C. *Koreri.* The Hague, 1972. A detailed history and analysis of cargoism in western Irian Jaya, with a most valuable summary and assessment of other works on the general subject.

Lawrence, Peter. *Road Belong Cargo.* Manchester and Melbourne, 1964. A full history of the cargo movement in the southern Madang Province of Papua New Guinea, with a rounded analysis of the movement in its economic, sociopolitical, and intellectual contexts. The analysis of the people's intellectual interpretation of cargo and the right way to get it, independently parallels and endorses Jarvie's argument in *The Revolution in Anthropology,* mentioned above.

May, Ronald J. "Micronationalism in Perspective" and "Micronationalism: What, When, and Why?" In *Micronationalist Movements in Papua New Guinea,* edited by Ronald J. May. Canberra, 1982. The most recent and precise analysis of the relationship between cargoism and nationalism in Papua New Guinea.

McSwain, Romola. *The Past and Future People.* Oxford, 1977. A thorough examination of a Papua New Guinea society (Karkar Island) undergoing development preparatory to becoming part of a new independent nation-state; discusses the way in which the people have interwoven new economic, political, and educational projects with cargoism.

Ogan, Eugene. *Business and Cargo.* Canberra, 1972. A most valuable account of the relationship between commercial development and cargoism among the Nasioi of Bougainville, Papua New Guinea, a people living in the shadow of a major mining venture to which much of the local economy was tied.

Plutta, Paul, and Wendy Flannery. "'Mama Dokta': A Movement in the Utu Area, Madang Province." In *Religious Movements in Melanesia,* edited by Glen W. Bays. Goroka, Papua New Guinea, 1983. A vivid description of cargoist activity in modern postindependence setting; illustrates the uneasy relationship between cult devotees and the indigenous government.

Schwartz, Theodore. "The Paliau Movement in the Admiralty Islands, 1946–1954." *Anthropological Papers of the American Museum of Natural History* 49 (1962): 211–421. An important work. Describes and analyzes an indigenous, as against a government-sponsored, development movement and its ambivalent relationship with a cargo cult.

Steinbauer, Friedrich. *Melanesian Cargo Cults.* Saint Lucia, Australia, 1979. A most comprehensive survey and discussion of the literature on cargo cults and of European scholars' approaches to them.

Strathern, Andrew. "The Red Box Money-Cult in Mount Hagen 1968–71." *Oceania* 50 (December 1979): 88–102; (March 1980): 161–175. A paper important for dispelling the mistaken notion that Highlands societies in Papua New Guinea are not prone to cargoism; valuable too for showing how the people experiment with cargo activity while engaging in vigorous cash cropping.

Strelan, John G. *Search for Salvation.* Adelaide, Australia, 1977. An enterprising general analysis of cargoism from a Christian missionary's point of view. Strelan suggests that Melanesians are now working out their own distinct theology.

Williams, Francis E. "The Vailala Madness" and "The Vailala Madness in Retrospect." In *Francis Edgar Williams: The Vailala Madness and Other Essays,* edited by Erik Schwimmer, pp. 351–384 and pp. 385–395. London, 1976. Two early accounts of cargo cult, most valuable for their careful description of its external features but lacking insight into its socioeconomic, political, and epistemological bases.

Worsley, Peter. *The Trumpet Shall Sound: A Study of "Cargo" Cults in Melanesia* (1957). New York, 1968. An early general work important because it did much to bring the phenomenon of cargoism to the attention of Western scholars. Describes many of the outbreaks of cargo cult up to the 1950s. The first edition is written from a strictly Marxist perspective, at least part of which the author renounces in the second.

PETER LAWRENCE

CARIBBEAN RELIGIONS. [*This entry consists of two articles.* Pre-Columbian Religions *treats the religious traditions of the aboriginal Carib and Arawak inhabitants of the West Indies.* Afro-Caribbean Religions *discusses the syncretic systems of belief and practice that emerged from the contacts between Christianity, aboriginal island traditions, and the religions brought to this part of the New World by African slaves. For treatment of specifically Christian forms of Caribbean religious life, see* Christianity, *article on* Christianity in the Caribbean Region.]

Pre-Columbian Religions

European explorers noted three major aboriginal groups in the Caribbean at the time of contact (1492 and the years immediately following): Island Arawak, Island Carib, and Ciboney. There is an abundance of information concerning the religious practices of the Island Arawak and Island Carib, but very little is known of Ciboney religion. Our knowledge of the Ciboney has increased somewhat, especially through the work of Cuban archaeologists such as Osvaldo Morales Patiño, but there remain many gaps in the archaeological and ethnohistorical records.

This essay will focus on the Island Arawak and the Island Carib. The Island Arawak were concentrated in the Greater Antilles, a group of large, mainly sedimentary islands. The principal islands of the Greater Antilles are, moving from east to west, Puerto Rico, Hispaniola (now divided between Haiti and the Dominican Republic), Jamaica, and Cuba. The Island Carib inhabited the small, mainly volcanic islands of the Lesser Antilles (Saint Christopher–Nevis, Antigua, Guadeloupe, Dominica, Martinique, Saint Lucia, Barbados, Grenada, Saint Vincent, and Tobago). Trinidad, Margarita, Cubagua, and Coche are usually considered a part of the Caribbean region, but culturally these islands have much in common with the South American mainland (Glazier, 1980b; Figueredo and Glazier, 1982).

Earlier scholars, such as Hartley B. Alexander (1920), emphasized differences between Island Arawak and Island Carib religions. This tradition continues in the work of contemporary scholars such as Fred Olsen (1974) and Charles A. Hoffman (1980), for example, who postulate strong Maya influence on the religious systems of the Greater Antilles. Over the past ten years, however, scholars have paid greater attention to the similarities in Arawak and Carib belief systems—for example, the many parallels in Arawak and Carib shamanism—than to their differences.

Both the Island Arawak and the Island Carib originally migrated from the South American mainland (Rouse, 1964). The Island Arawak settled in the Greater Antilles at about the beginning of the common era and were followed several hundred years later by the Carib, who claimed to have begun their migrations into the Lesser Antilles only a few generations before the arrival of Columbus. The Island Carib asserted that they conquered the Arawak of the Lesser Antilles, killing the men and marrying the women. Douglas M. Taylor (1951) suggests that the women's language prevailed, because the language spoken by the descendants of the Island Carib belongs to the Arawakan family of languages. Of course, another possible explanation is that all the peoples of the Lesser Antilles were of Arawak origin.

It should not be assumed that the Island Arawak of the Greater Antilles and the Arawak of the South American mainland are members of the same ethnic group. The Island Arawak and Arawak proper did not speak the same language. Irving Rouse points out that their two languages were "no more alike than, say, French and English" (Rouse, 1974). Moreover, inhabitants of the Greater Antilles thought of themselves not as "Arawak" but as members of local chiefdoms, each of which had its own name. Since each chiefdom was totally independent of all others, the group we know as the Island Arawak had no need for an overall tribal name.

In 1920, Hartley Alexander suggested that the sea must have been a tremendous barrier to cultural transmission in the Caribbean (Alexander, 1920). Contemporary archaeologists, however, recognize that water did not constitute a barrier for these peoples. Therefore, archaeologists no longer study individual islands in isolation. This has many implications for the study of aboriginal Caribbean religions as it becomes increasingly apparent that religious developments on one island were likely to have affected religious developments elsewhere in the region. Various island groups seem to have been in constant contact with one another.

Over the past sixty years, archaeologists have established a firmer and more comprehensive chronology for the Caribbean region (Rouse and Allaire, 1978). They also have discovered much greater variation in religious artifacts than was previously thought to exist, which in turn hints at a greater variation within the religious traditions of the Island Arawak and the Island Carib than was previously supposed. Arawak and Carib traditions, for example, may have differed from settlement to settlement on the same island.

Deities. Both the Island Arawak and the Island Carib possessed a notion of a high god, though, as the chroniclers' reports make clear, their high god differed conceptually from the God of Christianity. We know, too, that aboriginal high gods were thought to exert very little direct influence on the workings of the universe. Many of the early chroniclers, including Fray Ramón Pané, Gonzalo F. de Oviedo, and Raymond Breton, refer to Arawak and Carib high gods as kinds of *deus otiosus*; that is, they are inactive gods far removed from human affairs and concerns. Neither the Island Arawak nor the Island Carib conceived of their high god as creator of the universe, and it is unclear how powerful the high god was thought to be. Was it that their high god was able to interfere directly in world affairs but chose not to do so, or was he thought to be totally ineffectual? Chroniclers differ somewhat on this. Pané suggests that the high god was a powerful deity who chooses to be inactive. Other chroniclers stress the inactivity of the high god and the lack of attention accorded him. The bulk of the evidence, including what we know of other American Indian religions (Hultkrantz, 1979), supports the latter interpretation.

Island Arawak. The identification of Island Arawak deities is often a problem. Their high god was known by two names: Iocauna and Guamaonocon (spellings differ from chronicler to chronicler). Peter Martyr reports that the Arawak supreme being was not self-created but was himself brought forth by a mother who has five names or identities: Attabeira, Mamona, Guacarapita, Iella, and Guimazoa. He also reports other appellations for the high god, including Jocakuvaque, Yocahu, Vaque, Maorocon, and Macrocoti. Pané provides an equally complex list of male and female deities, and it is apparent that most deities in the Arawak pantheon were recognized by a number of appellations. Henri Pettitjean-Roget (1983) has suggested that the various names be interpreted as different incarnations of the same deity,

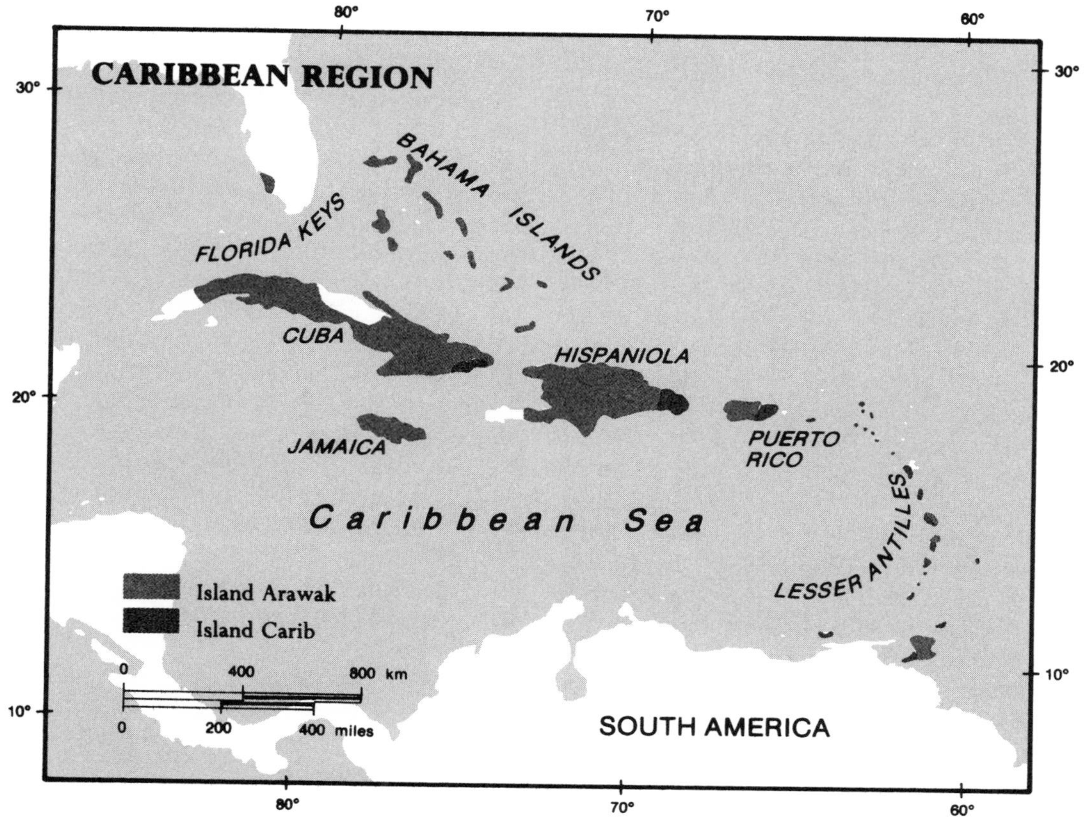

as in the Hindu tradition. Another possible explanation is that different names simply represent local variants.

A number of interpreters (Joyce, 1916; Alexander, 1920) have posited that the Island Arawak possessed a conception of an earth mother and a sky father similar to that of other American Indian groups. This has been called into question. While there are many similarities between the goddess Attabeira and the earth mother of American Indian mythology, there are also many differences. Attabeira does seem to have been associated with fertility, and as Fred Olsen (1974) suggests, her many Arawakan names describe her various functions: mother of moving waters (the sea, the tides, and the springs), goddess of the moon, and goddess of childbirth. Representations of Attabeira frequently show her squatting in the act of parturition, and archaeologists have been greatly impressed with the vividness of these portrayals. Her hands are holding her chin while her legs press into her sides as she struggles in childbirth. In several representations her open mouth and heavy eyebrows ridging over wide-open eyes convey successfully the intensity of her efforts. But there are other characteristics of Attabeira that are not at all like those of an earth mother. Sven Lovén (1935) concludes that Attabeira cannot be identified as a goddess of the earth because she seems to have dwelt permanently in the heavens. He concedes that Attabeira may have been an all-mother, but this does not necessarily imply that she was an earth goddess.

Lovén (1935) also points out that Iocauna was not an all-father. As noted previously, native conceptions of Iocauna would have precluded procreative activities. It is possible that one of Iocauna's names, Yocahu, is related to the yuca (cassava) plant (Fewkes, 1907). Yocahu may have been the giver of yuca or the discoverer of yuca, but he was not believed to be the creator of yuca (Olsen, 1974). It is clear from all accounts that after yuca was given to the Island Arawak, it was cultivated through the cooperation of *zemi* spirits and was not at all dependent on the cooperation of Yocahu.

Other prominent Island Arawak deities include: Guabancex, goddess of wind and water, who had two subordinates: Guatauva, her messenger, and Coatrischio, the tempest-raiser; Yobanua-Borna, a rain deity; Baidrama (or Vaybruma), a twinned deity associated with strength and healing; Opigielguoviran, a doglike being said to have plunged into the morass with the coming of the Spanish; and Faraguvaol, a tree trunk able to wander at will. One difficulty with the various listings provided by the chroniclers is that they do not distinguish mythical beings and deities. This is unfortunate because the Island Arawak themselves seem to have made such a distinction.

As Alexander (1920) has pointed out, there is some evidence that nature worship and/or a vegetation cult existed among the Island Arawak. This remains, however, a much neglected aspect of Island Arawak religion. Pané's elaborate description of the manufacture of wooden religious objects suggests some similarities between the production of these objects and the construction of wooden fetishes in West Africa. While the analogy is not complete, it has been noted that many aspects of Caribbean religions seem to derive from similar attitudes toward material objects (Alexander, 1920).

One of the most important differences between Arawak and Carib religions is that among the Island Arawak nature worship seems to have been closely associated with ancestor worship. The bones of the Island Arawak dead, especially the bones of their leaders and great men, were thought to have power in and of themselves. This notion also existed among the Island Carib, but their ceremonies and representations were not so elaborate. In addition, most chroniclers mention that the Island Arawak painted their bodies and faces, especially in preparation for war. The chroniclers are in agreement that the painted figures were horrible and hideous, but there is little agreement as to what the figures were supposed to represent. Jesse W. Fewkes (1907) has suggested that body paintings had religious importance; most other sources suggest that markings served to distinguish members of the same clan. The practice may have been a form of ancestor worship.

Island Carib. Like the Island Arawak, the Island Carib recognized a multitude of spirit beings as well as a high god whose name varies according to text. Sieur de La Borde (1704) refers to their high god as Akamboüe. According to Raymond Breton (1665), however, Akamboüe means "carrier of the king," and the highest deity in the Island Carib pantheon was the moon, Nonuma. Breton argues that the moon was central in Island Carib religion because the Carib reckoned time according to lunar cycles. The sun, Huoiou, also occupied an important place in the Island Carib pantheon. Although the sun was said to be more powerful than the moon, Huoiou was also said to be more remote from human affairs and therefore less significant.

Of the spirits directly involved in human affairs, Icheiri and Mabouia are the most frequently mentioned. Icheiri, whose name comes from the verb *ichéem*, meaning "what I like" (Breton, 1665, p. 287), has been interpreted as a spirit of good, while Mabouia, from the same root as the word *boyé*, or "sorcerer," has been interpreted as a spirit of evil. The Carib informed Breton that it was Mabouia who brought about eclipses of the sun and caused the stars to disappear suddenly.

The terms *icheiri* and *mabouia* have been widely discussed in the secondary literature. I believe that these were not names of spirits, but were general categories within the spirit world, and that spirits were classified primarily according to their relation to the individual. One man's *icheira* (helper) could be another man's *mabouia* (evil spirit) and vice versa (Glazier, 1980a). The most important consideration, as far as the Carib were concerned, was to get a particular spirit on one's side.

Another major category in the Island Carib spirit world was that of the *zemiis*. *Zemi*, too, appears to have been a very general term; the word is of Arawak origin and indicates the strong influence of Island Arawak language and culture on the Island Carib. Among the Carib, to get drunk, *chemerocae*, literally meant "to see *zemiis*." *Zemiis* were thought to live in a paradise far removed from the world of the living, but every so often, according to La Borde (1704), Coualina, chief of the *zemiis*, would become angry about the wickedness of some *zemiis* and drive them from paradise to earth, where they became animals. This is but one example of the constant transformations from deity to animal in Island Carib mythology.

Zemiis were frequently represented by, and in many cases were identical with, conical objects that have been found at both Island Arawak and Island Carib sites. The most common types are triangular (the so-called three-pointers; see figure 1) and/or humpback (see figure 2) in shape. The figures shown here are elaborately carved, but a majority of *zemiis* are plain. Archaeologists have discovered *zemiis* made of wood, conch shell, and stone, but stone *zemiis* are the most prevalent.

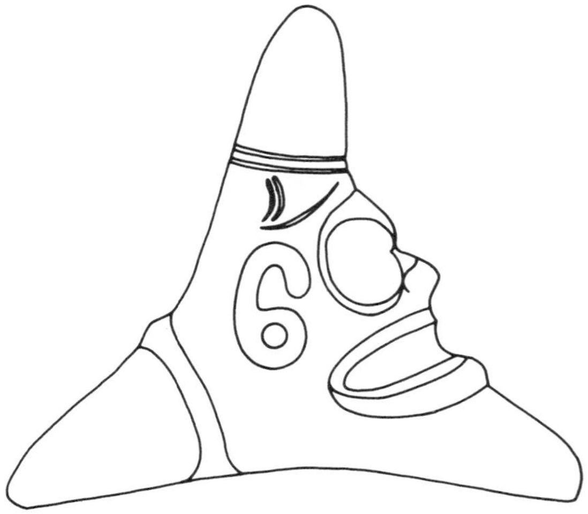

FIGURE 1. *Triangular Zemi*

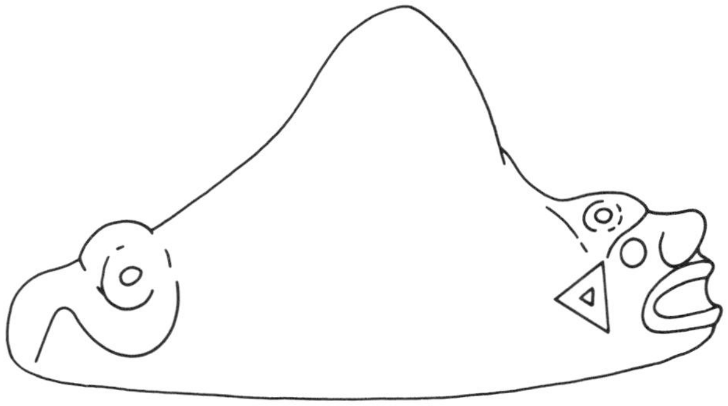

FIGURE 2. *Humpbacked Zemi*

Fewkes (1907) was among the first to suggest the religious import of these objects. He posited that they may have had a magical function, especially in reducing pains associated with childbirth. Olsen (1974) offers a more materialistic explanation. He suggests that the conical shapes of these stones represented the Caribbean islands themselves dramatically rising out of the sea with their pronounced volcanic peaks. Pettitjean-Roget (1983) provides a broader interpretation than Fewkes or Olsen. He postulates that these conical objects were nothing less than an encapsulation of the entire cosmos.

Afterlife. Both the Island Arawak and the Island Carib had a notion of the afterlife. The Island Arawak conceived of spirits of the dead, called *opias* or *hubias*, who were said to wander about the bush after dark. Occasionally *opias* joined the company of the living and were said to be indistinguishable from the living, except for the spirits' lack of navels. In both Arawak and Carib religions, the activities of the dead were thought to resemble the activities of the living. *Opias*, for example, passed their time feasting and dancing in the forest. Their behaviors were similar to native ceremonies.

Pané reports that the Arawak of Haiti believed in a kingdom of death, Coaibai, which was situated on their own island. Every leader of importance had his own kingdom of death, usually located within his own dominion. In addition, there were uninhabited places where the spirits of evil people were said to roam.

The Island Carib, on the other hand, had a much more diffuse notion of the afterlife. All spirits of the body, *omicou*, went to the seashore or became *mabouias* in the forest. There was no concept of an underworld, nor were spirits associated with specific locations, as among the Island Arawak. Each individual was said to possess three souls: one in the heart, one in the head, and one in the shoulders. It is only the heart-soul that ascends to the sky, while the other two souls wander the earth for eternity. The Island Carib asserted that only valiant heart-souls ascended; the implication here is that even the heart-souls of the less valiant sometimes became *mabouias* and roamed the earth.

Elaborate burial ceremonies were noted among both the Island Arawak and the Island Carib. Archaeological evidence indicates that the Island Arawak performed several types of burials: (1) direct interment, with the skeleton in a sitting or flexed position; (2) interment within a raised mound, with the body in a crouched position; (3) interment within a grave covered with an arch of branches topped with earth; and (4) burial in caves, with skeletons in a flexed position. Secondary burials were also prevalent (Lovén, 1935).

Christopher Columbus summarized the different burial customs on Hispaniola as follows: "They open the body and dry it by the fire in order that it may be preserved whole. Often, depending on rank, they take only the head. Others are buried in caves. Others they burn in their houses. Others they drive out of the house; and others they put in a hammock and leave them to rot" (Lovén, 1935). It is apparent that Arawak burial customs differed markedly and that burials for leaders were much more elaborate than burials for the masses. From the archaeological record, it is also apparent that the Island Arawak buried a majority of their dead in crouching or flexed positions. In this they differed from the Ciboney, who buried their dead lying straight (Lovén, 1935).

Burial customs among the Island Carib were not so varied. Breton (1665) noted that the Island Carib dreaded death, and that it was forbidden to utter the name of the deceased. The Island Carib referred to the dead indirectly (e.g., "the husband of so-and-so") because to do otherwise would cause the deceased to come back to earth.

When an Island Carib male died, the women painted his cheeks and lips red and placed him in a hammock. After some time the decomposed body was brought inside a hut, where it was then lowered into a shallow grave. Burial was in the flexed position, with the body sitting on its heels, and with the elbows resting on the knees and hands folded to the breast. Important men were buried with cooking pots and utensils, their dogs, and slaves who were killed so they might continue to serve their masters in the next life. La Borde (1704) notes that the Island Carib frequently burned the bodies of their leaders and mixed the ashes with their drinks. This may not be accurate, for there is little archaeological evidence for cremation among the Island Carib.

Origin Myths. We possess no creation myths for Caribbean peoples. Both Island Arawak and Island Carib seem to have assumed that the universe had always been in existence. They did, however, have many stories concerning the earliest peoples of their respective groups.

Island Arawak. According to the aborigines of Haiti, the earliest people appeared out of two caves. A majority of the people emerged from a cave known as Cicibagiagua, while another, smaller group emerged from the cave Amaiacuva. Alexander (1920) suggests that these two caves represent two different races or tribes. Lovén (1935) argues to the contrary: there is, he says, but one tribal group. Since most of the people emerged from Cicibagiagua, those who emerged from Amaiacuva constituted an elite, the Taino. I find Lovén's interpretation the more plausible. These caves, situated on the mountain of Cauta in the region of Caunana, were believed to actually exist and may have been located in the area of present-day Sierra de Coonao. Where caves did not exist, Island Arawak stress appearance out of the ground.

Island Arawak legends also account for the first appearance of the sun and the moon from a grotto known as Giovaua, and for the origin of fish and the ocean. According to the legend:

> There was a certain man, Giaia, whose son, Giaiael, undertook to kill his father, but was himself slain by the parent, who put the bones into a calabash, which he hung on top of his hut. One day he took the calabash down, looked into it, and an abundance of fishes came forth. The bones had changed into fish. Later, when Giaia the parent was absent, his four sons took the calabash and ate some of the fish. Giaia returned suddenly and in their haste the sons replaced the calabash badly. As a result, so much water ran from it that it overflowed all of the country, and with the water came an abundance of fish.
>
> (Fernández Méndez, 1979; my trans.)

Other stories tell how the four brothers obtained manioc and tobacco from people whom they visited (see Fernández Méndez, 1979). Rouse (1948) suggests that these stories may have been put to song.

The stories of the emergence from caves and the origin of fish are, in Pané's account, followed by stories concerning the adventures of Guaguigiana, a culture hero, and his comrade, Giadruvava. Guaguigiana appears to have been something of a trickster figure, and his adventures resemble those of trickster-fixers associated with other American Indian groups. It is to Pané's credit that he attempted to present stories in the order in which the Island Arawak themselves presented them, even when that order made little intuitive sense to him (Deive, 1976).

Island Carib. Among the Island Carib the first man, Louguo, was said to have descended from the sky. Other men came out of his navel and his thighs. Louguo created fish by throwing cassava scrapings into the sea, and according to La Borde (1704), many of the first men were later transformed into stars.

The constellations were accorded great importance in Island Carib thought: Chiric (the Pleiades) was used to number their years; Sauacou, who changed into a great blue heron, was sent to heaven where he forms a constellation announcing hurricanes; the Great Bear is the heron's canoe; the constellation Achinaou announces gentle rains and high winds; the constellation Caouroumon is associated with heavy waves; the constellation Racumon was changed into a snake; and Baccamon (Scorpio) foretells high winds (Breton, 1665). It is clear that the various constellations were used to divine the future, but it is unclear whether or not the constellations were actually believed to cause earthly events.

Rites and Ceremonies. The most important ceremonies among the Island Arawak pertained to rain and the growth of crops, but there were also important ceremonies for success in war, burial of the dead, curing of the sick, canoe building, cutting hair, the births of children, marriage, and initiation. In most instances these rites took the form of elaborate dances known as *areitos*. Fewkes (1907) notes that dramatization played a part in all ceremonies. For example, in their war dances the entire war sequence was portrayed: the departure of the warriors, surprise of the enemy, combat, celebration of victory, and return of the war party. Singing also played a part in all ceremonies, and some of the early chroniclers incorrectly restricted their use of the term *areitos* to funeral chants or elegies in praise of heroes.

The Island Carib conducted ceremonies on many of the same occasions as did the Island Arawak. According to La Borde, the Island Carib held rites whenever a council was held concerning their wars, when they returned from their expeditions, when a first male child was born, when they cut their children's hair, when their boys became old enough to go to war, when they cut down trees, and when they launched a vessel. Some authorities mention other ritual occasions: when a child reached puberty, when a parent or spouse died, when the Island Carib were made captives, and when they killed one of their enemies.

Island Carib rites met individual as well as societal needs. Each individual had his own personal deity or *zemi*. These personal deities were thought to reveal things to the individual, and it is reported that individuals customarily withdrew from society for six or seven days, without taking any sustenance save tobacco and the juice of herbs. During this period, the individual experienced visions of whatever he or she desired (victory over enemies, wealth, and so on).

Much has been written on alleged cannibalism among

the Island Carib (the word *cannibal* is a corruption of *Caribal*, the Spanish word for "Carib"). The Island Arawak told Columbus that they were subject to raids by man-eating Indians known as Carib, and Columbus directed his second voyage to the Lesser Antilles, where he had been told the Carib lived, in order to confirm Arawak reports. Rouse (1964) credits Columbus with confirming that the Carib practiced ritual cannibalism, that is, they ate captives in order to absorb their fighting ability. Recently the anthropologist William Arens (1979) has suggested that Columbus had no direct evidence for this assertion, and in fact did not really believe that the Carib were cannibals, but he perpetuated the myth of Carib cannibalism for political reasons. The early chroniclers provide some support for this position. In his *Historia general de las Indias, 1527–61*, Bartolomé de Las Casas flatly denies that the Carib were cannibals. Whatever the status of Carib cannibalism, there is agreement that it was not an everyday practice and was largely confined to ritual occasions.

One other Island Carib rite attracted considerable attention in the early literature, and that was the practice of the *couvade*. At the birth of a child, Jean-Baptiste Dutertre reports, Carib fathers would rest as if it were they who were suffering labor pains. For forty days and nights fathers remained isolated from society, fasting or consuming a meager diet. At the end of this period there was a great feast at which the invited guests lacerated the father's skin with their fingernails and washed his wounds with a solution of red pepper. For an additional six months the father was expected to observe special dietary taboos (e.g., it was believed that if the father ate turtle, the child would become deaf). Dutertre records a number of other taboos involving birds and fish. [*See* Couvade.]

Drugs. Tobacco, narcotics, and stimulants played an important part in both Island Arawak and Island Carib rites. Tobacco, called *cohiba*, was used in a number of different forms in all ceremonies. Among the Island Arawak, tobacco smoke was used as an incense to summon the gods. Tobacco was sprinkled on the heads of idols as an offering. Religious leaders among the Island Arawak and Island Carib "stupefied" themselves with tobacco when they consulted their oracles; they also used tobacco in curing rituals.

As Breton (1665) reports, the Island Carib "know tobacco but do not smoke it." They would dry it by a fire, pound it into a powder, add a little seawater to it, and then place a pinch of the snuff between their lips and gums. The Island Arawak, on the other hand, sometimes did inhale tobacco smoke through their nostrils. But its use was limited. Generally there is no evidence that tobacco was burned during ceremonies.

Throwing *aji* (pepper) onto live coals was part of Island Arawak and Island Carib preparations for warfare. Ricardo E. Alegría (1979) contends that the pepper caused irritation of the mucous membrane, a racking cough, and other discomforts that were thought to induce the proper psychological state for war.

Shamanism. The distinction between shamans, who are said to obtain their power directly from the supernatural, and priests, who must learn a body of ritual knowledge from established practitioners, is not useful in distinguishing Island Arawak religious leaders (variously known as *piaies, behutios, buhitihus, behiques*) from Island Carib leaders known as *boyés*. Although the role of the *piaie* appears to have been more priestlike than that of the *boyé*, similarities among *piaies* and *boyés* far exceed their differences.

Island Arawak. Major duties of the Arawak *piaie* were to divine the future by consulting their personal *zemiis* and to direct offering to *zemiis* during public ceremonies. In both of these duties, they served as intermediaries between the Island Arawak and their gods (Deive, 1978).

Accounts of Arawak shamanism provide very little detail concerning the *piaie*'s role in public ceremonies, and it is unclear whether or not all *piaies* were able to conduct public ritual. It is possible that some *piaies* functioned solely as curers or diviners and could not perform other rites.

Pané provides a lengthy account of Arawak healing practices. The curer, he notes, began his treatment of the patient by prescribing a special diet and was himself expected to observe the same diet as his patient. Herrera gives a condensed description of curing procedures:

> When any leading man is sick, he calls a medicine man, who is obliged to observe the same dietary rules as the patient. It is customary for the medicine man to purge himself with an herb that he takes by inhaling until he believes himself inspired. In this condition he says many things, giving the sick to understand that he is talking with an idol. Then the Indians anoint their faces with oil and purge the sick who stand by in silence.
>
> The medicine man first makes two circuits about the patient and, pulling him by the legs, goes to the door of the house, which he shuts, saying: "Return to the mountain or whither you wish; blow and join hands and tremble, and close the mouth." Breathing on his hands, he then sucks the neck, the shoulders, the stomach, and other parts of the body of the sick man, coughing and grimacing; he spits into his hands what he had previously placed in his mouth and tells the sick man that he has taken from the body that which is bad. He also says that the patient's *zemi* had given it to him because he had not obeyed him. The objects that the doctors take from their mouths are for the most part stones, which

> they often use for childbirth or other special purposes, and which they also preserve as relics.
>
> (Herrera, 1937, p. 69; my trans.)

If a patient died, it was thought to be because the *piaie* had not observed the proper diet. The Island Arawak were not very tolerant of unsuccessful healers, and it was not uncommon for a healer to be seized by a deceased person's relatives who would strike him with a stick until his arms and legs were broken, gouge out his eyes, and lacerate his private parts.

Alfred Métraux (1949), in his overview of shamanism in South America, states that in most instances the role of the religious leader was distinct from that of the political leader, but this distinction between political and religious authority does not seem to have been as pronounced among the Island Arawak. For example, Rouse (1948) points out that it is unclear whether the chief and his attendants (the principal men of the village) were also shamans. The attendants, he notes, had a special name, *bohuti*, and were of such high status that they customarily refused to accept commoners as patients.

Island Carib. The Island Carib maintained a rigid distinction between political and religious authority. There are no reports of healers becoming chiefs or chiefs becoming healers. But even in the Lesser Antilles, a certain complicity between religious and political leaders is apparent. For example, a political leader needed a *boyé*'s support in order to wage war, and *boyés* derived direct economic benefits through their association with chiefs.

The Carib never went to war without first consulting the spirit world to find out if conditions were favorable for victory. Since chiefs were unable to make direct contact with spirits, they required the services of a *boyé* whose predictions had tremendous impact on public opinion. It would be difficult for a war chief to override a *boyé*'s predictions and carry out expeditions believed to be inauspicious. Shamans never gained an upper hand, however, for if a chief was dissatisfied with one *boyé*'s prediction, he was free to consult others. Often, several *boyés* were consulted at once, and the old war chief chose the most "correct" prediction. Given the circumstances, it was advantageous for both parties when a chief developed a working relationship with a particular shaman who could be counted on to support his war policies. These relationships often followed kinship lines.

Boyés also needed to develop working relationships with chiefs to defray the high costs of apprenticeship. We have no clear notion of the actual length of apprenticeship for shamans among the Island Carib, though in some tribes of the Guianas apprenticeship is said to have lasted from ten to twenty years (Métraux, 1949). This period of training was probably considerably shorter among the Carib, but we lack details for all but the final months of preparation:

> After a fast of five months, the candidate is brought into the *carbet* (a place in which things have been set aside) before a table on which manioc bread, *ouicou* (sweet potato and manioc beer), and the first fruits of the season are placed. An older shaman chants and blows tobacco smoke to summon his familiar spirit who descends and sits on a hammock to receive offerings (*anaeri*). The elder shaman asks for another spirit to descend and become his apprentice's familiar.
>
> (Dutertre, 1667–1671, vol. 2, pp. 365–366; my trans.)

From this passage, it is clear that five months of training (and possibly more) was required of the would-be shaman. This would constitute a hardship for the apprentice's family, for others had to assume his workload and provide for him while he was in training. Also, they had to provide offerings for sacrifice and make payments to senior *boyés*.

Boyés were a professional class in Island Carib society. They charged for all services, and I contend that they did not train new shamans without demanding something in return. War chiefs and their families, as wealthier members of their society, were in the best position to take on obligations to senior *boyés* (Glazier, 1980).

Island Carib shamanism was not flexible. It was not possible to go off on one's own and become a *boyé*. A would-be shaman had to do an apprenticeship under an established *boyé* and had to undergo formal rites of initiation in order to receive a spirit familiar. Shamans who claimed that their knowledge derived solely from their relationship with spirits probably glossed over their arduous training, wanting instead to stress mystical aspects of their careers. The picture they present of shamanism in the Lesser Antilles is inaccurate.

There is, however, no ambiguity concerning the *boyé*'s authority. While the authority of the war chief may have been that of a charismatic leader, the authority of the *boyé* was clearly that of formal investiture. Breton (1665) put it succinctly: "The *boyés* make other people *boyés*."

Boyés were perhaps the wealthiest members of their society. While war chiefs and families had considerable control over the distribution of some resources and war booty, *boyés* had control over the distribution of goods outside kinship obligations. A *boyé*'s clientele was not restricted to his kin group, and his reputation could well transcend his own island. The *boyé* Iris's reputation, for example, extended beyond his native Dominica (Du Puis, 1972).

The *boyés* had great potential for wealth, for there was always demand for their services. In times of trouble, they were called upon to dispel evil spirits; in times of prosperity, they were called upon to insure its continuance; and when there was doubt, they gave assurances for the future. Major religious activities were sacrifice and offerings, both of which were ultimately appropriated by the *boyés* (Rochefort, 1665). Offerings consisted of foodstuffs and some durable goods, a portion of which went directly to the shaman in return for his services; the remainder, ostensibly for the gods, was appropriated later for the shaman's use. Thus shamans had numerous occasions to accumulate wealth, and in some cases a shaman may have gotten too wealthy and would be forced by public opinion to redistribute part of his property.

Under certain conditions, senior war chiefs were allowed to join with the *boyés* in appropriating offerings intended for the gods. This further differentiates the roles of *boyé* and chief. Only the most senior war chief had the right to do what any *boyé* could do from the moment of his initiation.

BIBLIOGRAPHY

Alegría, Ricardo E. "The Use of Noxious Gas in Warfare by the Taino and Carib Indians of the Antilles." *Revista/Review Interamericana* 8 (1979): 409–415.

Alegría, Ricardo E. *Ball Courts and Ceremonial Plazas in the West Indies.* New Haven, 1983.

Alexander, Hartley Burr. "The Antilles." In *The Mythology of All Races,* edited by Louis Herbert Gray, vol. 11, *Latin-American Mythology,* pp. 15–40. Boston, 1920.

Arens, William. *The Man-Eating Myth: Anthropology and Anthropophagy.* Oxford, 1979.

Benzoni, Girolamo. *History of the New World* (1595). Translated by W. H. Smyth. London, 1857.

Breton, Raymond. *Dictionnaire caraïbe-françois.* Auxerre, 1665.

Charlevoix, Pierre-François de. *Histoire de l'Ile Espagnole ou de Saint-Dominique.* 2 vols. Paris, 1930-1931.

Deive, Carlos Esteban. "Fray Ramón Pané y el nacimiento de la etnografía americana." *Boletín del Museo del Hombre Dominicano* 6 (1976): 136–156.

Deive, Carlos Esteban. "El chamanismo taíno." *Boletín del Museo del Hombre Dominicano* 9 (1978): 189–203.

Du Puis, Mathias. *Relation de l'establissement d'une colonie françoise dans la Gardloupe isle de l'Amérique, et des mœurs des sauvages* (1652). Reprint, Basse-Terre, 1972.

Dutertre, Jean-Baptiste. *Histoire générale des Antilles habitées par les François* (1667–1671). 4 vols. Fort-de-France, Martinique, 1958.

Fernández Méndez, Eugenio. *Art y mitologia de los indios Tainos de las Antillas Mayores.* San Juan, Puerto Rico, 1979.

Fewkes, Jesse Walter. *The Aborigines of Porto Rico and Neighboring Islands.* Annual Report of the Bureau of American Ethnology, no. 25. Washington, D.C., 1907. See especially pages 53–72.

Figueredo, Alfredo E., and Stephen D. Glazier. "Spatial Behavior, Social Organization, and Ethnicity in the Prehistory of Trinidad." *Journal de la Société des Américanistes* 68 (1982): 33–40.

García Valdés, Pedro. "The Ethnography of the Ciboney." In *Handbook of South American Indians,* edited by Julian H. Steward, vol. 4, pp. 503–505. Washington, D.C., 1948.

Glazier, Stephen D. "The Boyé in Island-Carib Culture." In *La antropología americanista en la actualidad: Homenaje a Raphael Girard,* vol. 2, pp. 37–46. Mexico City, 1980. Cited in the text as 1980a.

Glazier, Stephen D. "Aboriginal Trinidad and the Guianas: An Historical Reconstruction." *Archaeology and Anthropology: Journal of the Walter Roth Museum* (Georgetown, Guyana) 3 (1980): 119–124. Cited in the text as 1980b.

Gullick, C. J. M. R. *Exiled from St. Vincent.* Valletta, Malta, 1976.

Herrera y Tordesillas, Antonio de. *Historia general de los hechos de los Castellanos en las islas y Terrafirme del Mar Océano.* 17 vols. Madrid, 1934–1957.

Hoffman, Charles A. "The Outpost Concept and the Mesoamerican Connection." In *Proceedings of the Eighth International Congress for the Study of the Pre-Columbian Cultures of the Lesser Antilles,* pp. 307–316. Tempe, Ariz., 1980.

Hultkrantz, Åke. *Religions of the American Indians.* Los Angeles, 1979.

Joyce, Thomas A. *Central American and West Indian Archaeology.* London, 1916.

La Borde, Sieur de. *Voyage qui contient un relation exacte de l'origine, mœurs, coûtumes, réligion, guerres, et voyages des Caraïbes, sauvages des isles Antilles de l'Amérique.* Amsterdam, 1704.

Las Casas, Bartolomé de. *Historia general de las Indias, 1527–61.* 2 vols. Edited by Juan Perez de Tudela and Emilio Lopez Oto. Madrid, 1957.

Layng, Anthony. *The Carib Reserve: Identity and Security in the West Indies.* Lanham, Md., 1983.

Lovén, Sven. *Origins of the Tainan Culture, West Indies.* Göteborg, 1935.

Métraux, Alfred. "Religion and Shamanism." In *Handbook of South American Indians,* edited by Julian H. Steward, vol. 5., pp. 559–599. Washington, D.C., 1949.

Morales Patiño, Osvaldo. "Arqueología Cubana, resumen de actividades, 1946." *Revista de arqueologia y etnografia* (Havana) 1 (1947): 5–32.

Olsen, Fred. *On the Trail of the Arawaks.* Norman, Okla. 1974.

Oviedo y Valdés, Gonzalo Fernández de. *Historia general y natural de las Indias* (1535). 5 vols. Edited by Juan Perez and Tudela Bueso. Madrid, 1959.

Pané, (Fray) Ramón (Father Ramón). *Relación acerca de las antigüedades de los Indios, 1571.* Edited by José Juan Arrom. Mexico City, 1978.

Pérez de Oliva, Fernán. *Historia de la inuención de las Yndias.* Edited by José Juan Arrom. Publicaciones del Instituto Caro y Cuerva, no. 20. Bogotá, 1965.

Pettitjean-Roget, Henri. "De l'origine de la famille humaine ou contribution à l'étude des Pierres à Trois-Pointes des Antilles." In *Proceedings of the Ninth International Congress for the Study of Pre-Columbian Cultures of the Lesser Antilles*, pp. 511–530. Montreal, 1983.

Rochefort, Charles César de. *Histoire naturelle et morale des îles Antilles de l'Amérique.* 2d ed. Rotterdam, 1665.

Rouse, Irving. "The West Indies." In *Handbook of South American Indians*, edited by Julian H. Steward, vol. 4, pp. 49–565. Washington, D.C., 1948.

Rouse, Irving. "Prehistory of the West Indies." *Science* 144 (1964): 499–513.

Rouse, Irving. "On the Meaning of the Term 'Arawak.'" In *On the Trail of the Arawaks*, by Fred Olsen, pp. xiii–xvi. Norman, Okla., 1974.

Rouse, Irving, and Louis Allaire. "Caribbean." In *Chronologies in New World Archaeology*, edited by R. E. Taylor and C. W. Meighan, pp. 431–481. New York, 1978.

Taylor, Douglas M. *The Black Carib of British Honduras.* New York, 1951.

Wilbert, Johannes. "Magico-Religious Use of Tobacco among South American Indians." In *Spirits, Shamans and Stars: Perspectives from South America*, edited by David L. Browman and Ronald A. Schwarz, pp. 13–38. The Hague, 1979. This article also appears in *Cannabis and Culture*, edited by Vera D. Rubin (The Hague, 1975), pp. 439–461.

STEPHEN D. GLAZIER

Afro-Caribbean Religions

Most West Indians of African descent are affiliated, at least nominally, with a historic Christian denomination or with one of the newer sects. [*See* Christianity, *article on* Christianity in the Caribbean Region.] In many areas of the West Indies, however, a number of hybrid religions have attracted large numbers of followers. In Haiti, virtually the entire population is in some way involved in Voodoo. In Jamaica, the Revivalist, Kumina, and Convince cults continuously attract a small number of adherents. Wherever such cults are found, some persons participate more or less regularly in both a Christian church and a cult, and in times of crisis many who ordinarily ignore the cults become involved in their healing or magical rituals.

I shall concentrate in this essay on four types of syncretic religious cults found in the Caribbean region, which I shall call the *neo-African cults*, the *ancestral cults*, the *revivalist cults*, and the *religio-political cults*. The experience of Caribbean blacks under the political, economic, and domestic conditions of slavery modified character in a stressful direction, and those who were most sensitive to the stress advanced innovative religious and secular systems to deal with their anxiety. The new religious institutions consisted of elements of African and European beliefs and practices, and, in some cases, parts of American Indian and South Asian religious traditions. A number of new religions arose from the interaction of three major variables: socioeconomic, psychological, and cultural. Contingent factors in the development of these hybrid religions include such ecological and demographic variables as the degree to which a group of people had been isolated physically and socially from other segments of the population and the proportion of the total population constituted by various ethnic and racial groups (Simpson, 1978). Successful religions spread, adapt, and persist after the conditions that gave rise to them have changed (or changed to some extent), and individuals are socialized into accepting the revised beliefs and procedures. When this happens, a religion acquires new meanings for its members, and it takes on new functions, the most universal of which is the satisfaction that comes from group activities.

Neo-African Cults. These cults developed during the early stages of cultural contact between persons of European and African origin, because members of the subordinate group could neither acquire the religion of the dominant group nor participate as comembers in the historic Christian denominations. The major cults of this type are Haitian Voodoo, Cuban Santería, and Trinidadian Shango. From the viewpoint of cultural content, these religions represent the most extensive blend of African and European traditions and rituals in the Caribbean region.

Haitian Voodoo. The African dances that were performed in the seventeenth century by slaves in the western part of the island of Hispaniola and the religious beliefs of the Fon, Siniga, Lemba, Yoruba, and other African peoples who had been brought to Hispaniola were combined with certain beliefs of European folk origin about Roman Catholic saints, and, as a result, the neo-African religion of Voodoo developed. As James G. Leyburn (1966) has noted, the period from 1780 to 1790, when the importation of slaves to Hispaniola was increasing, saw the emergence of Voodoo, with a gradual ascendancy of Fon ideas. Finding the rites useful for their cause, revolutionary leaders in the last decades of the eighteenth century and the early years of the nineteenth century brought about further syntheses.

The supernatural phenomena of greatest importance in Voodoo are the *lwa*, also known as *zanj*, *mistè*, and other names. Many of these have names derived from old African gods, but other deities have names derived from African tribal or place names, names of Haitian origin, or names of Catholic saints; others have names of uncertain origin. The confusions and contradictions in the beliefs about these beings are due in part to contradictions in the Fon religious system that the Haitians adopted, and in part to the merging of the Fon system with that of the Yoruba (Courlander, 1960). But the endless variations in these and other beliefs concerning the ultimate reality are also the result of the absence of a hierarchy in the cult and of written documents. Erika Bourgignon (1980) suggests that variety and inconsistency in Haitian Voodoo have developed, and continue to develop, in part through the mechanism of altered states of consciousness, particularly in the forms of possession-trance and dreams. In Haiti, possession-trance is not highly stereotyped and prescribed. During possession-trance, cult leaders and members speak and act in the names of the spirits, behaving in ways that may modify the future performance of the ritual or the adherents' perception of the spirits.

The grand *lwa* comprise both nature spirits and functional spirits that are of African origin. Prominent among the nature spirits are Dambala, the serpent spirit identified with the rainbow and associated with floods; Bade, spirit of the winds; Sogbo, a Fon spirit of thunder; Shango (Yor., Ṣango), the Yoruba spirit of thunder and lightning; and Agwé, spirit of the sea. The functional *lwa* include Legba, the Fon guardian of crossroads and all barriers; the Ogou (Yor., Ogun) family, spirits associated with war; Zaka, associated with crops and agriculture; Ezili, a sea goddess among the Fon, but transformed in Haiti into the personification of feminine grace and beauty; the members of the Gèdè family, the spirits of death; Adja, skilled in the fields of herbs and pharmacy; and Obatala (Yor., Ọbatala), the Yoruba divinity responsible for forming children in the womb (Herskovits, 1937b; Courlander, 1939; Simpson, 1945, 1978; M. Rigaud, 1953; Métraux, 1959).

The *lwa* are also identified with Catholic saints. Thus, Legba is often believed to be the same as Anthony the Hermit, but some say that he is Saint Peter, the keeper of the keys. Dambala is identified with Saint Patrick, on whose image serpents are depicted. Ogou Ferraille is equated with Saint James; while Ogou Balanjo, the healer, is associated with Saint Joseph, who is pictured holding a child whom he blesses with an upraised hand. Obatala becomes Saint Anne; and Ezili, who is believed to be the richest of all the spirits, is identified with Mater Dolorosa and is represented as richly clothed and bejeweled. The *marassa*, spirits of dead twins, are believed to be the twin saints Cosmas and Damian (Price-Mars, 1928; Herskovits, 1937a).

The relationship between Voodoo adherents and the *lwa* is thought to be a contractual one; if one is punctilious about offerings and ceremonies, the *lwa* will be generous with their aid. The *lwa* must be paid once or twice a year with an impressive ceremony, and small gifts must be presented frequently. It is thought that the *lwa* like blood and that animal sacrifices are the means by which favors may be obtained. It is believed also that neglect of one's *lwa* will result in sickness, the death of relatives, crop failure, and other misfortunes (Simpson, 1980).

In West Africa, concepts of the "soul" are highly elaborated. In traditional Fon belief, all persons have at least three souls, and adult males have four (Herskovits, 1938). In Haitian Voodoo, every man has two souls: the *gro bonanj*, which animates the body and is similar to the soul in the Christian sense, and the *ti bonanj*, which protects a person against dangers by day and by night (Métraux, 1946). "Bad" souls are said to become "bad" *lwa* who divide their time between suffering in hell and doing evil deeds on earth (Simpson, 1945).

Adherents fear the power of the dead and observe funerary and postfunerary rites meticulously. A wake is held on the night of death; the funeral itself follows and, if possible, is held in accordance with the rites of the Catholic church. On the ninth night after death is the "last prayer," and on the tenth night a ritual is held in which sacrifices are offered to all the family dead (Métraux, 1959; Herskovits, 1937b). Also, a family must honor its dead by mentioning their names at subsequent ceremonies and, if family finances permit, by holding memorial services for them annually. In Voodoo belief, the dead rank second only to the *lwa*, and to neglect or anger them is to invite disaster. (For accounts of Voodoo cermonies, see Herskovits, 1937b, pp. 155–176; Simpson, 1940; Simpson, 1946; Rigaud, 1946; Métraux, 1959, pp. 157–212; Courlander, 1960, pp. 41–74.)

François Duvalier, the dictatorial president of Haiti from 1957 to 1971, successfully exploited Voodoo for political purposes (Rotberg, 1976). Nevertheless, most observers agree that the cult has been weakened in recent years. An important factor in its decline has been the decay of the large extended family in the rural areas. Many of the large cult centers have split up into minor sects under priests whose training has been inadequate. A deepening economic poverty in the countryside has brought about the impoverishment of ritual there, and with the expansion of urbanization there have emerged innovative cult leaders who deal with the problems of a heterogeneous clientele rather than with the traditional concerns of farming or the demands of ancestral spirits (Bastide, 1971; Métraux, 1959; Bourguignon, 1980). [*See also* Voodoo.]

Cuban Santería. Most of the non-European elements in the Afro-Cuban syncretic religion known as Santería are derived from Yoruba beliefs and rituals. Animals are sacrificed to Yoruba deities, Yoruba music is played on African-type drums, songs with Yoruba words and music are sung, and dancers are possessed by the *orisha* (Yor., *orịṣa*, "spirit"). Yoruba foods are cooked for the gods and for devotees, beads of the proper color are worn, and leaves with Yoruba names are used in preparing medicines and in washing the stones of the *orisha* and the heads of cult members. In Santería, Elegba (Yor., Ẹṣu or Ẹlẹgba) is identified with Saint Peter, and Shango (Yor., Ṣango), god of thunder, is identified with Saint Barbara. Shakpana (also Babaluaiye; Yor., Ṣọpọna) is equated with Saint Lazarus. Oya (Yor., Ọya), one of Shango's wives, is the equivalent of Saint Teresita. Obatala (Yor., Ọbatala) is Our Lady of Mercy, and Yemaja (Yor., Yemọja) is identified with the Virgin of Regla (a suburb of Havana). Osun (Yor., Ọṣun) is associated with the Virgin of Cobre (a town in eastern Cuba), and Osanyin (Yor., Ọsanyin) known for his skill in healing, is identified with Saint Raphael. Ifa, or Orunmila (Yor., Ọrunmila), the god of divination, is linked with Saint Francis of Assisi. The Ibeji (Yor., "twins"), who behave like young children, are the counterparts of the twin saints Cosmas and Damian. Ogun, the Yoruba god of war and iron, is equated with John the Baptist (Bascom, 1951, 1972).

During a Santería ceremony, the blood of animals sacrificed to the gods is allowed to flow onto the sacred stones of the *santero* (Santería priest). Many instances of spirit possession during a given cermony indicate that the *orishas* have been well fed and are satisfied with the ritual offerings. The herbs serve to cleanse, refresh, and prepare the devotees and ritual objects for contact with the *orisha*. The blood is the food of the deities, and the stones are the objects through which they are fed and in which their power resides (Bascom, 1950). The *lucumis* (Afro-Cubans of Yoruba extraction) honor each of the gods with choral dances and pantomime in accordance with authentic Yoruba tradition (see Ortiz, 1951, for a detailed and vivid account of *lucumi* dances; and Simpson, 1978).

The regime of Fidel Castro has not assisted the Afro-Cuban cults and has taken some measures to control their expansion (Barrett, 1982). Although in recent years Santería has declined in Cuba, the presence of Cuban refugees has stimulated the worship of Shango and the other Yoruba *orisha* in the United States. Today many priests and priestesses officiate in Miami, New York City, Newark, Detroit, Chicago, Savannah, Gary, and other cities (Bascom, 1972). [*See also* Santería.]

The Shango cult in Trinidad. In southwestern Nigeria, each Yoruba deity, including Ṣango, god of thunder and lightning, has his or her own priests, followers, and cult centers. In the Shango cult in Trinidad, Shango is only one of several dozen "powers," which include twenty or more Yoruba deities (Lewis, 1978). Several non-Yoruba powers—especially Gabriel and Mama Latay—are popular in Trinidad. Ancient African gods are identified with certain Catholic saints, as occurs in Haiti, Grenada, parts of Brazil, Cuba, and other countries in the New World. Among these pairings in Trinidad are Obatala and Saint Benedict; Shango and Saint John; Shakpana and, variously, Moses or Saint Francis or Saint Jerome; Oshun and Saint Philomena or Saint Anne; Béji (Ibeji) and Saint Peter; Emanja and Saint Catherine or Saint Anne; Oya and Saint Philomena or Saint Catherine. Each god has his or her favorite colors, foods, and drinks; each is thought to have certain physical traits and to possess certain powers. In Shango, as in Voodoo and Santería, participants can recognize the major spirits who are well known throughout the country, or the principal spirits known in a given locality, by the stylized behavior of devotees possessed by them (Bourguignon, 1980). For example, Ogun, the god of iron and war, is believed to prefer the colors red and white (also the favorite colors of Shango), and rams and roosters are his preferred offerings. When possessed by Ogun, a Shangoist brandishes a sword and behaves in a violent way (Simpson, 1978).

Each Shango cult center holds an annual ceremony in honor of the *orisha* known to its worshipers. The four-day ritual begins with the recitation of original prayers, followed by several repetitions of the Lord's Prayer, Hail Mary, and the Apostle's Creed. The leader then recites in succession prayers such as Saint Francis's prayer, Saint George's prayer, and Blessed Martin's prayer; he recites each prayer line-by-line, and the worshipers repeat each line after him. Next, in an act of dismissal, food for the deity Eshu is placed outside the ceremonial area. (The Yoruba deity Ẹṣu is thought both to serve as a messenger among the gods and to be a trickster.) After Eshu's ejection, the worshipers invite other powers to the ceremony by drumming the powers' favorite rhythms. Ogun's rhythm is the first to be played. Drumming, dancing, singing, and spirit possession continue through the night; the climax comes at dawn with the sacrificing of pigeons, doves, chickens, agoutis, land turtles, goats, and sheep. Similar rites are performed on the following three nights, and often a bull is sacrificed. Aspects of Trinidadian cult life that are closely related to African religious behavior include divination, conjuring, and folk medicine, which are often strikingly similar to West African procedures (Simpson, 1978).

In recent decades, traditional religious, magical, and medical beliefs have been undermined to some extent by the expansion of education, the growth of medical and social services, and the influence of mass communication. Trinidadian Shango has also been modified by the intermixture of some of its aspects with the Spiritual Baptist (Shouters) complex (Simpson, 1978). There are many similarities between the Shango cult of Trinidad and that of Grenada (Pollak-Eltz, 1968; Simpson, 1978).

Ancestral Cults. The second type of hybrid religious cult in the Caribbean, what I call the *ancestral cult*, has fewer African and more European components than does the neo-African–type religion. The Kumina and Convince cults and the Kromanti Dance in Jamaica, the Big Drum Dance of Grenada and Carriacou, Kele in Saint Lucia, and the religion of the Black Carib of Belize exemplify this kind of syncretic religion.

Kumina. According to Monica Schuler (1980), Kumina did not originate among plantation slaves of the eighteenth century but was brought to Jamaica by post-emancipation immigrants from central Africa who chiefly settled in the eastern parish of Saint Thomas. Kumina is primarily a family religion, and each group honors a number of family spirits in addition to other divinities. The three ranks of Kumina spirits (known as zombies) are the sky gods, the earthbound gods, and ancestral zombies. Among the thirty-nine sky gods listed by Joseph G. Moore (1953), only one (Shango) clearly has the name of a West African deity, but some Kumina gods appear to serve tribes or "nations" that are African. Of the sixty-two earthbound gods given by Moore, at least seven have biblical names (e.g., Moses, Ezekiel). The twenty-one ancestral zombies are the spirits of men and women who, in their lifetimes, were dancing zombies (persons who experienced possession by a god and who danced while possessed), *obeah* men (sorcerers), and drummers (Moore and Simpson, 1957). Most Kumina dances are memorial services held to pay respects to the dead ancestors of the participants, but ceremonies are performed on other occasions, such as betrothal, marriage, burial, the naming of a baby, the anniversary of emancipation, and Independence Day (Moore, 1953; Schuler, 1980).

All zombies are invoked through drumming and singing. Songs are of two types: *bilah* songs, which are sung in a dialect of English; and country songs, which are sung in a language referred to as *African* (accent on the last syllable). Kumina ritual ends with the sacrifice of a goat and the dance of the Queen of the Kumina and her attendants. In performing ritual, the living members of a family convey their wishes to the ancestors (Moore and Simpson, 1957, 1958).

Convince. The Convince ritual practiced in the Jamaican parishes of Saint Thomas and Portland has a number of Christian elements, but its principal powers are the spirits of persons who belonged to the cult during their lifetime. The most powerful *bongo* ghosts come from Africa, but the spirits of ancient Jamaican slaves and the Maroons (descendants of runaway slaves), who perpetuated the cult until recent times, are also of importance. The spirits of Jamaicans more recently departed are less powerful than the other ghosts, but those who practiced *obeah* ("conjuration") in their lifetime are used by *bongo* men (i.e., Convince devotees) as partners in divination and conjuring. Each *bongo* man operates independently, and each has one or more assistants called apprentices or grooms. In addition, a number of lesser followers are attached to each cult group, including some persons who are devout Christians (Hogg, 1960).

Each *bongo* man holds a sacrificial ceremony annually and conducts Convince rites as the need for them arises. Christian prayers, the reading of Bible passages, and hymn singing precede the main ceremony. Special *bongo* songs, hand clapping, and dances performed by *bongo* men call the spirits to the ceremony. Later, the spirits of the ancestors (that is, devotees possessed by the ghosts) dance.

According to Donald Hogg (1960), such traits as blood sacrifice, vigorous possession-trance behavior, the materialistic purposes of ceremonies, the involvement with divination and conjuring, religious dancing, the worship of ancestral spirits, and the propitiation of potentially malevolent beings almost certainly have African antecedents. In these respects Convince, like Kumina, shows greater African influence than do the Revival Zion, Pocomania, and Rastafarian cults in Jamaica. Once a nativistic movement, Convince has so declined since the 1950s that it now provides mainly jollification and catharsis.

The Kromanti Dance. The traditional religion of the descendants of "Maroons," escaped slaves of the seventeenth and eighteenth centuries in Jamaica, is known as the Kromanti Dance. One supreme deity, Yankipong, is believed to be remote from human affairs. The spirits of the dead, called *duppies*, *jumbies*, or *bigi-man*, have the power to work good or evil in the daily lives of their descendants, and this power is referred to by the term *obeah* or by the more modern term *science*. No Kromanti Dance can be successful without one or more of the participants becoming possessed by the spirit of an ancestor. Most Kromanti Dance ceremonies require the sacrifice of an animal to the *pakit* (ancestral spirit) of the *fete-man* (ritual specialist). Although the Kromanti Dance is a separate tradition, it bears some similarity to both Kumina and Convince (Bilby, 1981, pp. 52-101).

The Big Drum Dance in Grenada and Carriacou. For numerous residents of Grenada and Carriacou, performing the Big Drum Dance (also known as the Nation Dance, or Saraca—"sacrifice") is a show of respect to their ancestors. In Carriacou, many persons can still recount the African "nations," traced patrilineally, to which they belong. Usually this ceremony is a family occasion, but it may be put on by members of an occupational group—for example, fishermen. Various reasons are given for organizing a festival: to counter the ill health or misfortune of a friend or relative, to dedicate a tombstone for a deceased family member, to start a critically important undertaking, or to launch the marriage preparations of a son or daughter. Offerings of food are prepared for the ancestors and the guests, a space is provided where the spirits of the ancestors can dance, the ancestors are summoned, and the "beg pardon" dance is performed, during which family members kneel and sing, asking the ancestors to pardon them for any wrongdoing (Pearse, 1956). In Carriacou, as M. G. Smith (1971) has noted, Christianity and the ancestral cult are complementary, each supplying what the other lacks.

The Kele cult in Saint Lucia. The Kele ceremony in Saint Lucia resembles, in attenuated form, the Shango ritual in Trinidad. The ritual is performed to ask the ancestors of devotees for health, protection against misfortune in agriculture, and success in important undertakings, as well as to thank the forebears for past favors. The paraphernalia essential for the Kele rite consists mainly of Amerindian polished stone axes (which are called *pièrres tonnerres*, "thunderstones," by devotees, who believe them to have fallen from the sky), drums, and agricultural implements such as machetes, axes, hoes, and forks. Several of the stone axes are placed on the ground to form a cross, with additional axes arranged around the central grouping (Simpson, 1973; Simmons, 1963).

The stone axes, addressed as "Shango," symbolize the African ancestors of the Saint Lucians who participate in Kele. Thunderstones constitute one of the principal symbols of Shango in West Africa, Haiti, Cuba, Trinidad, Grenada, and urban areas of the United States that are heavily populated by immigrants from the Caribbean. Present-day devotees in Saint Lucia seem to be unaware that Shango (Ṣango) is the deity of thunder and lightning in traditional West African belief. To these believers, Shango is simply the name of the thunderstones that enable the living to get in touch with their African ancestors.

Following some preliminary drumming, singing, and dancing, the leader of a Kele ceremony asks the ancestors to intercede with God on behalf of the sponsor of the occasion. A ram is then sacrificed to the ancestors. Communication with God is achieved through possession; the ancestors enter the bodies of some of the men participating in the ceremony. After the ram has been cooked, morsels of the meat, as well as portions of yams, rice, and other foods, are thrown on the ground as offerings to Shango—that is, to the African ancestors. Saint Lucia is a predominantly Catholic country, and some devotees of the cult are active Catholics.

Ancestral cult of the Black Carib of Belize. The Black Carib of Belize are descendants of African slaves who escaped from other parts of the West Indies and settled first among the Island Carib in Saint Vincent. At the end of the eighteenth century, they were deported by the English to Roatan, an island in the Gulf of Honduras, and later they spread out along the coast of the mainland. The Black Carib of Belize speak a South American Indian language, and, as Douglas MacRae Taylor has noted, their "outward cultural manifestations differ but little, in the main, from their neighbors" (Taylor, 1951, p. 37; Stone, 1953, pp. 1–3).

The supernatural beliefs, rites, and practices of the Black Carib are a mixture of African and non-African elements. Singing, drumming, and dancing are intended to placate the ancestors of the family giving the ceremony, and some participants become possessed by the spirits of their deceased ancestors, as occurs in Kumina and Convince in Jamaica, the Big Drum in Grenada and Carriacou, and Kele in Saint Lucia. Sacrifices of food and drink are offered periodically to the spirits of the ancestors; some offerings are taken out to sea and thrown into the water.

Most of the Black Carib are professed Christians and, in the main, Catholics. They see no inconsistency between their Christian faith and non-Christian beliefs. The ancestral spirits are regarded as subordinate to the Christian God, and the evil forces of the universe are manifestations of Satan (Taylor, 1951).

Revivalist Cults. The third type of Afro-Caribbean religious syncretism, the *revivalist cult*, descends from the Afro-Protestant cults of the late eighteenth century and, in the case of Jamaica, from the Great Revival of 1861–1862. Revival Zion in Jamaica, the Spiritual Baptists (Shouters) of Trinidad, and the Shakers of Saint Vincent typify this kind of cult.

Revival Zion. For nearly a hundred years after England acquired Jamaica in 1655, no missionary work was carried on on the island. The official missionary movement did not begin until the 1820s. A religious movement known as Myalism emerged in the 1760s to protect slaves against European sorcery. This "native" Baptist movement was without serious competition during the forty-year period (1780–1820) when a reinterpretation of Christianity spread across Jamaica. Rent and wage disputes between planters and workers were common after the abolition of apprenticeship in 1838. In 1841–1842, Myalists preached the millenarian message that they were God's angels, appointed to do the work of the Lord, and their wrath was directed against both planters and missionaries. The authorities took severe measures against the movement. Popular interest in separatist churches, as well as in regular missions, was stimulated by the Great Revival which swept over the island in 1861–1862, but the enthusiasm dwindled within a short time. The hybrid religion of the Myalists, or Black Baptists, which included dancing, drumming, and spirit possession, resurfaced in 1866. Subsequently, the vitality of this movement was seen in the multiplication and flourishing of black revivalist cults (Curtin, 1955; Schuler, 1979).

Adherents of Revival Zion and the related sects of Revival and Pocomania do not identify old African gods with Christian saints as do participants in Voodoo (Haiti), Santería (Cuba), and Shango (Brazil, Trinidad, Grenada). The Holy Spirit possesses followers during revivalist ceremonies, as do the spirits of Old Testament figures such as Jeremiah, Isaiah, Joshua, Moses, Shadrach, Meshach, and Abednego; New Testament apostles and evangelists such as Matthew, Mark, Luke, John, Peter, and James; the archangels Michael, Gabriel and Raphael; Satan and his chief assistant, Rutibel; beings from Hebrew magical tradition, such as Uriel, Ariel, Seraph, Nathaniel, and Tharsis; Constantine, Melshezdek, and the Royal Angel; and the dead, especially prominent revivalist leaders of the past (Moore and Simpson, 1957; Simpson, 1978).

Drumming, hymn singing, hand clapping, praying, Bible reading, spirit possession, and intermittent commentary by the leader are main features of the weekly services, as is "spiritual" dancing, in which leading participants circle the altar counterclockwise, stamping first with their right feet and then with their left, bending their bodies forward and then straightening up, hyperventilating, and groaning rhythmically. Special revivalist rituals include baptismal ceremonies, death rites (wake, funeral, "ninth night," "forty days," and memorial services held after one or more years have passed since the death), and the dedication of a meeting place. "Tables" (feasts) are given to thank the spirits for assistance or to seek deliverance from trouble (Simpson, 1956).

Spiritual Baptists (Shouters) of Trinidad. In many ways, the Spiritual Baptist cult (Shouters) in Trinidad is similar to Revival Zion in Jamaica, but there are several noteworthy differences. Among the Shouters, no drums or rattles accompany hymn singing. Spiritual Baptists do not become possessed by the wide variety of spirits that possess Revivalists in Jamaica; as a rule, devotees are possessed only by the Holy Spirit. Certain groups among the Shouters do, however, make ritual offerings to the spirits "of the sea, the land, and the river," and occasionally a Shango "power" may enter a person who is taking part in a ritual. In Trinidad, important relationships exist between Spiritual Baptists and Shango groups. (The Shango cult is not found in Jamaica). Shangoists as well as Shouters need to be baptized, and only a Shouters pastor of some standing can perform this service. In addition, "mourning" and "building"—optional rites taken by some members of both cults—are conducted by Spiritual Baptist leaders. Many Shouters attend the annual ceremonies staged by different Shango cult groups, and like their counterparts in syncretic cults elsewhere in the Caribbean, some adherents participate at times in the services of more orthodox religions (Simpson, 1978; Glazier, 1983).

Spiritual Baptists are often men and women of the lower classes. Most are of African descent, but a few East Indians do participate in the cult. Throughout the Caribbean in recent decades, most of the neo-African cults, the ancestral cults, and the revivalist cults, as well as many of the historical churches, have lost membership, while the Pentecostal, Holiness, and Adventist sects and the Rastafarian movement have made impressive gains (Simpson, 1978).

The Shakers of Saint Vincent. English rule of the island of Saint Vincent began in 1783, and the first direct religious influence intended for the slave population was brought to the island by a Methodist missionary in 1787. The Shaker cult, which goes back to at least the early part of the twentieth century, has a Methodist base, with an admixture of elements of other Christian denominational traditions (Anglicanism, Roman Catholicism, Pentecostalism), modified African religious traits, and elements developed locally. An important feature of this religion is the mild state of dissociation, attributed to possession by the Holy Ghost, that some of its adherents experience. The range of Shaker services and the rituals themselves are similar to those of the Spiritual Baptists of Trinidad (Henney, 1974).

Religio-Political Cults. The fourth cult type appears when a society is undergoing severe reorganization, as was the case in Jamaica with the unrest that accompanied the Great Depression of the 1930s. The Rastafarian movement, which appeared in the island during this period, is a mixture of social protest and religious doctrine and so may be called a *religio-political cult*.

Rastafarianism. An important factor underlying the rise of Rastafarianism is that, since at least the beginning of the twentieth century, Jamaican blacks have identified with Ethiopia on account of its biblical symbolism. The verse most often cited is *Psalms* 68:31:

"Princes come out of Egypt; Ethiopia shall soon stretch out her hands unto God." Between 1904 and 1927, Ethiopianism came to the attention of Jamaicans through several essays, articles, and books published in Jamaica and in the United States. The early 1930s saw the founding of a number of associations for black people and the emegence of the Rastafarian movement, named after Ras ("prince") Tafari, who was crowned emperor Haile Selassie of Ethiopia (Abyssinia) in November 1930. Marcus Garvey had formed the Universal Negro Improvement Association in Jamaica in 1914, and his doctrine of racial redemption, together with the coronation of Haile Selassie, furthered interest in the Ethiopian tradition (Hill, 1980).

Since emancipation, persons on the lower rungs of Jamaican society have struggled continuously against exploitation. Higher wages, the granting of civil and political rights, and other gains have come slowly, and often against bitter opposition. In the early 1930s, the basic issues for rural Jamaicans were land, rent, and taxation, and their struggles over these questions gave rise to the millenarian visions of the Rastafarian movement. In that period, Rastafarians were subjected to intense police pressure in Saint Thomas and neighboring parishes. It is likely that the Rastafarian millenarianism, with its vision of black domination, served as a catalyst in bringing about the labor uprisings of 1938 (Hill, 1981).

In 1953, Rastafarianism bore stong resemblance to revivalism in organizational and ritual patterns. The small, independent groups of both movements had similar sets of officers, festivals, and ritual procedures, including the reading of passages from the Bible and the singing of hymns (modified in the case of the Rastafarians to fit the doctrines of the cult), but important differences existed. Drumming, dancing, and spirit possession were prominent features of revivalism, but they never occurred in a Rastafarian gathering (Simpson, 1955). Beards and dreadlocks were present among Rastafarians but were not important aspects of the movement in the early fifties, nor was the place given to *ganja* (marijuana). Rastafarianism was, however, antiestablishment and bitter on the racial question (Chevannes, 1977). Revivalism had no political significance in 1953; its adherents were mainly concerned about personal salvation (Simpson, 1956).

According to Rastafarian doctrines in 1953, (1) black people were exiled to the West Indies because of their transgressions; (2) the white man is inferior to the black man; (3) the Jamaican situation is hopeless; (4) Ethiopia is heaven; (5) Haile Selassie is the living God; (6) the emperor of Abyssinia will arrange for expatriated persons of African descent to return to the homeland; and (7) black men will soon get their revenge by compelling white men to serve them (Simpson, 1955). These remain the basic beliefs of the movement, but not all adherents subscribe to all of them, nor do they give them equal emphasis. Rastafarians reinterpret the Old Testament in claiming that they are true present-day prophets, the "reincarnated Moseses, Joshuas, Isaiahs, and Jeremiahs." They also believe that they are "destined to free the scattered Ethiopians who are black men" (Nettleford, 1970, pp. 108–109).

As revivalism began to decline in the mid-1950s, many of its followers were attracted to Rastafarianism and became active participants in the movement, or sympathizers (Smith, Augier, and Nettleford, 1960). Between 1953 and 1960, the Rastafarian movement grew rapidly and became more complex doctrinally. This growth continued through the 1970s and the early 1980s. Membership—both the fully committed and partially committed—came to be drawn from all levels of the society. The more militant Rastafarians insisted that deliverance from poverty, unemployment, and humiliation must come from forces within Jamaica and not from Haile Selassie or Haile Selassie's spirit. Repatriation to Africa received less emphasis as some bands began to stress black power and "the africanization of Jamaica" (employment, education, and use of the country's resources are to benefit persons of African descent; see Nettleford, 1970; Barrett, 1974; Simpson, 1978).

The militancy of present-day Rastafarianism is seen clearly in its concept of a modern Babylon that includes Britain, the former colonial power; the United States, the present major industrial power; the bourgeois state of Jamaica; and the church. Babylon is said to be the source of Jamaica's misfortunes (Chevannes, 1977). A recent theme of the movement has to do with its concept of nature. In Rastafarian thought nature is nonindustrial society; and this underlies certain aspects of Rastafarian lifestyle—for example, dietary rules, uncombed locks and beards, and the importance of *ganja* (Chevannes, 1977).

Since the early 1960s, Rastafarianism has played an important role in the evolution of Jamaican popular music. The rhythm of the Rastafarians' *akete* drums influenced the development of the fast rhythm called *ska*, and the ska form has developed into reggae. Most reggae songs contain caustic social comments, but they also praise Ras Tafari, Jamaican heroes, freedom, and *ganja* (Barrett, 1977; Chevannes, 1977). In the poetry and prose written by contemporary Rastafarians awareness of an African identity and of Africa itself is a main theme (Johnson, 1980).

Rastafarianism is not a unified movement (Campbell, 1980). Many of the brethren gather in small, informal bodies and are not affiliated with organized groups. Many Rastafarians refuse to take part in elections on the grounds that neither of Jamaica's two political parties represents them. In recent times, however, some Rastafarians have played an increasingly active role in politics (Smith, Augier, and Nettleford, 1960; Chevannes, 1977).

Rastafarian culture has spread to other parts of the Caribbean, and Rastafarian art, poetry, music, and philosophy are well known in London, Paris, and other cities in Western Europe and the United States. Rastafarian music has been diffused to a number of African countries (Campbell, 1980).

The dethronement of Haile Selassie in 1974 and his death the following year have not resulted in a decline of the movement. Rastafarianism arose out of certain conditions in Jamaica and in other countries of the Caribbean and has continued because those conditions, as well as the international situation, have not changed appreciably (Barrett, 1977).

[*For West African antecedents of many of the elements in Afro-Caribbean religions, see* Fon and Ewe Religion; Ṣango; West African Religions; *and* Yoruba Religion.]

BIBLIOGRAPHY

Barrett, David B., ed. *World Christian Encyclopedia: A Comparative Study of Churches and Religions in the Modern World, A.D. 1900–2000.* Oxford, 1982.

Barrett, Leonard E. *Soul-Force: African Heritage in Afro-American Religion.* New York, 1974.

Barrett, Leonard E. *The Rastafarians: Sounds of Cultural Dissonance.* Boston, 1977.

Bascom, William R. "The Focus of Cuban Santeria." *Southwestern Journal of Anthropology* 6 (Spring 1950): 64–68.

Bascom, William R. "The Yoruba in Cuba." *Nigeria* 37 (1951): 14–20.

Bascom, William R. *Shango in the New World.* Austin, 1972.

Bastide, Roger. *African Civilisations in the New World.* New York, 1971.

Bilby, Kenneth M. "The Kromanti Dance of the Windward Maroons of Jamaica." *Nieuwe West-Indische Gids* (Utrecht) 55 (August 1981): 52–101.

Bourguignon, Erika. "George E. Simpson's Ideas about Ultimate Reality and Meaning in Haitian Vodun." *Ultimate Reality and Meaning* (Toronto) 3 (1980): 233–238.

Chevannes, Barry. "The Literature of Rastafari." *Social and Economic Studies* 26 (June 1977): 239–262.

Courlander, Harold. *Haiti Singing.* Chapel Hill, N.C., 1939.

Courlander, Harold. *The Drum and the Hoe: Life and Lore of the Haitian People.* Berkeley, 1960.

Curtin, Philip D. *Two Jamaicas: The Role of Ideas in a Tropical Colony, 1830–1865.* Cambridge, Mass., 1955.

Davis, E. Wade. "The Ethnobiology of the Haitian Zombie." *Journal of Ethnopharmacology* 9 (1983): 85–104.

Glazier, Stephen D. *Marchin' the Pilgrims Home: Leadership and Decision-Making in an Afro-Caribbean Faith.* Westport, Conn., 1983.

Henney, Jeannette H. "Spirit-Possession Belief and Trance Behavior in Two Fundamentalist Groups in St. Vincent." In *Trance, Healing, and Hallucination: Three Field Studies in Religious Experience,* by Felicitas D. Goodman, Jeannette H. Henney, and Esther Pressel, pp. 6–111. New York, 1974.

Herskovits, Melville J. "African Gods and Catholic Saints in New World Negro Belief." *American Anthropologist* 39 (1937): 635–643. Cited in text as 1937a.

Herskovits, Melville J. *Life in a Haitian Valley.* New York, 1937. Cited in text as 1937b.

Herskovits, Melville J. *Dahomey: An Ancient West African Kingdom.* 2 vols. New York, 1938.

Hill, Robert A. "Dread History: Leonard Howell and Millenarian Visions in Early Rastafari Religions in Jamaica." *Epochē* 9 (1981): 30–71.

Hogg, Donald. "The Convince Cult in Jamaica." *Yale University Publications in Anthropology* 58 (1960): 3–24.

Johnson, Howard. "Introduction." In *Boy in a Landscape: A Jamaican Picture,* by Trevor Fitz-Henley. Gordon Town, Jamaica, 1980.

Laguerre, Michel S. *Voodoo Heritage.* Beverly Hills, Calif., 1980.

Lewis, Maureen Warner. "Yoruba Religion in Trinidad: Transfer and Reinterpretation." *Caribbean Quarterly* 24 (September–December 1978): 18–32.

Leyburn, James G. *The Haitian People.* Rev. ed. New Haven, 1966.

Métraux, Alfred. "The Concept of Soul in Haitian Vodu." *Southwestern Journal of Anthropology* 2 (Spring 1946): 84–92.

Métraux, Alfred. *Voodoo in Haiti.* New York, 1959.

Moore, Joseph G. "Religion of Jamaican Negroes: A Study of Afro-American Acculturation." Ph.D. diss., Northwestern University, 1953.

Moore, Joseph G., and George E. Simpson. "A Comparative Study of Acculturation in Morant Bay and West Kingston, Jamaica." *Zaire* 11 (November–December 1957): 979–1019, and 12 (January 1958): 65–87.

Nettleford, Rex M. *Mirror, Mirror: Identity, Race and Protest in Jamaica.* Kingston, Jamaica, 1970.

Ortiz Fernández, Fernando. *Los bailes y el teatro de los negros en el folklore de Cuba.* Havana, 1951.

Pearse, Andrew C. *The Big Drum Dance of the Carriacou.* Ethnic Folkways Library P 1011.

Pollak-Eltz, Angelina. "The Shango Cult in Grenada, British Westindies." In *Proceedings of the Eighth International Congress of Anthropological and Ethnological Sciences,* vol. 3, pp. 59–60. N.p., 1968.

Price-Mars, Jean. *So Spoke the Uncle.* Washington, D.C., 1983. A translation, with introduction and notes, by Magdeline W. Shannon of *Ainsi parla l'oncle* (Paris, 1928).

Rigaud, Milo. *La tradicion vaudoo et le vaudoo haitian: Son temple, ses mystères, sa magie.* Paris, 1953.

Rigaud, Odette M. "The Feasting of the Gods in Haitian Vodu." *Primitive Man* 19 (January–April 1946): 1–58.

Rotberg, Robert I. "Vodun and the Politics of Haiti." In *The African Diaspora: Interpretive Essays,* edited by Martin L. Kilson and Robert I. Rotberg, pp. 342–365. Cambridge, Mass., 1976.

Schuler, Monica. "Myalism and the African Religious Tradition in Jamaica." In *Africa and the Caribbean: The Legacies of a Link,* edited by Margaret E. Crahan and Franklin W. Knight, pp. 65–79. Baltimore, 1979.

Schuler, Monica. *"Alas, Alas, Kongo": A Social History of Indentured African Immigration into Jamaica, 1841–1865.* Baltimore, 1980.

Simmons, Harold F. C. "Notes on Folklore in St. Lucia." In *Iouanaloa: Recent Writing from St. Lucia,* edited by Edward Braithwaite, pp. 41–49. Saint Lucia, 1963.

Simpson, George E. "The Vodun Service in Northern Haiti." *American Anthropologist* 42 (April–June 1940): 236–254

Simpson, George E. "The Belief System of Haitian Vodun." *American Anthropologist* 47 (January 1945): 35–59.

Simpson, George E. "Four Vodun Ceremonies." *Journal of American Folklore* 59 (April–June 1946): 154–167.

Simpson, George E. "Political Cultism in West Kingston." *Social and Economic Studies* 4 (June 1955): 133–149.

Simpson, George E. "Jamaican Revivalist Cults." *Social and Economic Studies* 5 (December 1956): 321–442.

Simpson, George E. "The Kele Cult in St. Lucia." *Caribbean Studies* 13 (October 1973): 110–116.

Simpson, George E. *Black Religions in the New World.* New York, 1978.

Simpson, George E. "Ideas about Ultimate Reality and Meaning in Haitian Vodun." *Ultimate Reality and Meaning* (Toronto) 3 (1980): 187–199.

Smith, M. G. "A Note on Truth, Fact, and Tradition in Carriacou." *Caribbean Quarterly* 17 (September–December 1971): 128–138.

Smith, M. G., Roy Augier, and Rex M. Nettleford. *The Ras Tafari Movement in Kingston, Jamaica.* Mona, Jamaica, 1960.

Stone, Doris. *The Black Caribs of Honduras.* Ethnic Folkways Library P 435.

Taylor, Douglas MacRae. *The Black Carib of British Honduras.* New York, 1951.

GEORGE EATON SIMPSON

CARMATHIANS. *See* Qarāmiṭah.

CARNIVAL. The Christian festival called Carnival takes place on Shrove Tuesday, the eve of Ash Wednesday. In its widest sense, however, the Carnival period is of much longer duration, beginning right after Christmas, the New Year, or the Feast of Epiphany, depending on the region.

The etymological roots of the name *Carnival* may be the Latin *caro* ("meat") and *levara* ("to remove, to take away"), which in vulgar Latin became *carne levamen,* and afterward *carne vale.* Some etymologists also link it to *carnis levamen,* "the pleasure of meat," the farewell to which is celebrated in the festivities that come immediately before the prohibitions of Lent. Another hypothesis links it etymologically to the *carrus navalis,* the horse-drawn, boat-shaped carriage that was paraded in Roman festivals in honor of Saturn, carrying men and women who, in fancy dress and wearing masks, sang obscene songs.

If it is problematic to identify the etymological roots of *Carnival,* it becomes even more difficult to determine the historical origins of the celebration itself. However, the Roman feasts of Saturn, the Saturnalias, are generally recognized as the ancient forerunner of Carnival festivities. They embodied the essential carnival spirit, strongly characterized by the transgression of daily conventions and excesses of behavior. In these feasts, which took place in the midst of great licentiousness, slaves banqueted together with their masters, whom they insulted and admonished. From among them was elected a King of Chaos who, for the period of Saturnalia only, enjoyed full rights to his master's concubines, and gave ridiculous orders that had to be obeyed by everyone. At the end of the festivities, however, he was unthroned and, in the earliest form of the rite, sacrificed to signal a return to order.

Although far in meaning from the Christian Carnival, these Roman rituals contained some elements that would come to define the later and more universal concept of the feast. The inversion of prevailing norms—as when servants rule masters—is of particular importance; the burlesque parodies of power and order, as seen in the dramatization of the Jester King, and the element of exaggeration, both in terms of libidinous excesses and in the inordinate consumption of food and drink, have also become prominent characteristics of Carnival. This unruliness that temporarily suspends the recognized world order has the corollary of introducing a contrast to the parameters of daily life. In other words, these cyclical rituals of disorder and rebellion show themselves incapable of administering real life because they foster the confusion of roles, licentiousness, and the mockery of power; they thus serve as a reminder of the necessity for order, which is reestablished at their conclusion.

In *Rabelais and His World* (Cambridge, Mass., 1968) the Russian essayist Mikhail Bakhtin presents an interesting interpretation of the meaning of Carnival in the context of the Middle Ages and the Renaissance. He treats Carnival as the most evident expression of a joking popular culture with its roots in the Roman Saturnalias, which reflected the playful, irreverent side of human nature and the indestructible festive element in all human civilizations. During the whole of the Middle Ages and the Renaissance, this culture of laughter resisted the official, serious culture. In opposition to the mysticism and dogmatism of the ecclesiastical culture and rigidity of the prevailing political structures, the joking popular culture revealed a world in which a playful mutability was possible and provided an experience, at once symbolic and concrete, of the suspension of social barriers. By dramatizing the comic and relative side of absolute truths and supreme authorities, it highlighted the ambivalence of reality, coming to represent the power of both absolute liberty and farce.

Using these distinctions, Bakhtin contrasts the official and ecclesiastical ceremonies of ordered society with the festivities of carnivalesque culture. He characterizes the former as rituals of inequality because they reinforce the dominant order and seek justification of the present in the past. The latter he regards as rituals of equality because they parody the stratification of power and the cult of religion, as well as provide a symbolic suspension of norms and privileges, harboring a seed of social reaction in satire.

Thus, inversion is universally at the root of Carnival symbolism, and explains the presence of such customs as transvestite costume, or clothes worn inside out, the poor playing the role of the rich, and the weak that of the powerful. This interpretive perspective also makes sense of the symbolism of death, common in Carnival celebrations; here it implies revitalization. Similarly, the dethroning and burning in effigy of the Jester King marks the end of a cycle and suggests the commencement of another, and the scatological aggressions with bodily materials like urine are a symbolic component implying fertilization. From this point of view, one can also amplify the concept of "carnivalization" to include all the symbolic processes that bring about transformations in the representation of social reality.

The most notable carnivalization of late medieval European society was to be found in the Feast of Fools, also called the Feast of Innocents. Although it took place in churches between Christmas and Epiphany, this festival was both an extreme satire of the mannerisms and mores of the court and the high church and a radical mockery of ecclesiastical structure and religious doctrine. The low church and the lower orders played an important part in it, while the high church and the nobility were its principle targets.

For the festival, a King of the Fools or a Boy Bishop, chosen from among the local choir boys, was elected to act out a parody of episcopal functions, including the distribution of blessings to the crowd from a balcony. A comic version of the holy mass was enacted, in which obscene parodies such as "The Liturgy of the Drunkards," "The Liturgy of the Gamblers," and "The Will of the Ass" were substituted for the canticles and prayers. Masked and painted, wearing the garb of the high church or dressed up as women, the revelers danced freely in the cathedrals and banqueted on the altars. The burning of old shoes and excrement replaced incense. Meanwhile, riotous processions of other revelers, wearing goat and horse masks, paraded dancing and singing through the streets.

Dances in churches are not totally unheard of in the history of Christianity; so-called shrine dances, for example, were frequent in the first centuries of its development. However, with the consolidation and institutionalization of the church, these dances were gradually abolished. In any case, the Feast of Fools had an entirely different sense. Its most striking characteristic was that of grotesque buffoonery, and in it the carnivalesque inversion was carried to its ultimate extreme. Focusing on the ecclesiastical hierarchy and religious ethics, the Feast of Fools pointed out the critical relations of medieval society and demonstrated that such a society was capable of self-criticism.

The Feast of the Ass, which took place principally in France, was a variation within the same category of rituals of carnivalesque inversion. Also part of the Christmas cycle, it theoretically commemorated Mary's flight to Egypt. The central character was, however, the ass, or rather the Ass Prince, who was richly adorned and brought in procession under a luxurious canopy to the church, where a mass was celebrated in its honor, punctuated with braying noises to which the celebrants responded by also braying.

For almost a millennium, the Roman Catholic church attempted, with perceptible difficulty, to control or ban the Feast of Fools. One of the first recorded proscriptions dates from the seventh century in Toledo, Spain. That this had little success can be measured by the numerous subsequent proscriptive edicts up to the sixteenth century, like that of Dijon, France, in 1552. The Feast of Fools died out only with the advent of the Reformation and Counter-Reformation. Until then, just as it had come under severe attack, it had also produced its enthusiastic apologists, such as those who wrote the circular of the Theology School of Paris in 1444. This circular maintained that just as fermenting barrels of wine sometimes need ventilation to prevent them from exploding, the wine of human madness must have an outlet at least once a year in order to transform itself into the good wine of pious devotion.

The Feast of Fools continued for a long time in France. It was still a solidly institutionalized event in Nice in the seventeenth century, when various secular laws were passed to regulate the structuring of the profane "Abbeys of the Fools" and to formalize the powers of the "Abbots of the Fools." At the same time, ecclesiastical decrees attempted to prevent the previously uncontrolled participation of the low church in the carnivalesque festivities and dances and bind them to their liturgical duties on the relevant days.

As a result of the Nice ordinance in 1539, the carnivalesque balls were subdivided into four categories, namely, those of the nobles, the merchants, the artisans, and the laborers. Each was the responsibility of one Abbot of the Fools, aided by a certain number of "monks," who policed the ball. The "abbots" were responsible for maintaining order, for making sure that only those suitably dressed, unarmed, and wearing masks, entered, and for preventing members of a different category from attending the wrong ball. The ruling of 1612 increased the number of Abbeys of the Fools to ten and gave the Abbots of the Fools the artistic function of directing the musicians as well as the right to dance at the balls.

The Abbots of the Fools also had the right to collect *charavilh,* a tax paid by betrothed widows upon remarriage. *Charavilh* itself sometimes brought about a sort of carnival, whenever the bridegroom was reluctant to pay it. In such an instance, the "abbot" would barricade the entrance to his house and orchestrate a deafening racket with trumpets and various improvised percussion instruments, such as saucepans and frying pans, until the recalcitrant newlyweds agreed to pay. Although *charavilh* was prohibited in Nice in 1721, it was so deeply rooted in the popular customs of the region that there are records of its occurrence until the end of the nineteenth century.

Nevertheless, by the end of the Middle Ages, the trend everywhere was to discipline Carnival, restricting the extremes of its licentiousness and violence, while encouraging its artistic aspects. To control carnivalesque rebelliousness was, however, the work of centuries. The introduction of masked balls in the sixteenth century in Italy was the first step on the festival's path to a predominantly poetic character. Parades of floats began to compete for a place in the disorderly street processions. From the combination of these two new currents flowered the fusion of carnival with art.

The rise of the Italian *commedia dell'arte* played an important role in the consolidation of the use of masks, lending them an artistic character and codifying human types. Previously, a wide variety of masks had already been featured in Carnival, so that they were easily assimilated into the *commedia dell'arte,* a theatrical genre with a close popular affinity to the festival, imbued with a similar spirit of social satire. The *commedia dell'arte* selected several types of masks from the carnivalesque repertory and reduced these to a certain number of character types, translating regional and psychological characteristics which, as they evolved, became more abstract and universal. It drew strongly on regional inspiration and referred to events in the day-to-day Italian life of the time, as is the nature of improvised theater. From these traditions emerged its famous characters, who, in a stylized form, dominated the three subsequent centuries of the carnivalesque scenario in Europe. [*See also* Masks, *article on* Ritual Masks in European Cultures.]

The characters of the *commedia dell'arte* embodied various satirical social types of the Italy of that period: Pantaloon, for example, was the rich, greedy, and libidinous merchant; the Doctor represented the pedantic drunkard and charlatan; and the Captain was boastful and full of bravado, but a complete coward. Harlequin, Colombine, and Pulcinella are the most famous of these figures. With time, all modified their characteristics. Initially, Harlequin represented the ignorant rustic who thought himself intelligent and whose poverty was evident in the patches, later sophisticated into lozenges, on his clothes. Pulcinella belonged to the same category of clowns and buffoons, though he was also crafty, as did Colombine, who evolved from a simple peasant girl to a calculating and extremely cunning maidservant. From the fusion of the *commedia dell'arte* with the masquerades of other cultures came a number of other characters, such as Pierrot, from France, who became an eternally present and central character in Carnival.

The *commedia dell'arte* and the Italian Carnival had much in common, as a result of their shared spirit of buffoonery and improvisation, each making the other more colorful and fertile. In Renaissance Florence, Carnival songs made fun of the private lives of certain social groups, with themes like "the goldsmith's song," "the song of the poor who accept charity," and "the song of the young wives and the old husbands"; by means of their festive ambivalence, they revealed the ridiculous—and usually censored—side of social conventions. Under the patronage of the Medici family, the Florentine Carnival was typified by the singing of these songs on flower-covered, ornamented triumphal carts, which were the models for the later Carnival floats of the Baroque and Romantic periods. In Turin, too, there were parades of flower-covered carts and floats as well as tournaments and cavalcades. In Venice, as throughout the Italian Peninsula, masks were the distinguishing feature of Carnival. Celebrated with the great solemnity afforded by the presence of the doge and Signoria and accompanied by a fireworks display, it contrasted with what happened in the streets, where there were battles between rival groups and a bull was sacrificed. Another element of Venetian Carnival was the flight of a man on ropes to the top of the campanile of Saint Mark's, since Carnival was also a time to challenge and exorcise the forces of nature.

Carnival in Rome was typified by a complex symbolism of violence, death, and resurrection. In Pope Paul II's time, in the fifteenth century, it was transferred to the Via Latta, which became the traditional setting for the carnivalesque parades called Corso. The Roman Carnival was essentially a series of masquerades and horse parades—these abolished only in 1833—culminating on Shrove Tuesday with an impressive candlelight procession, in which the participants, shouting "Death to him who has no candle," tried in whatever ways they could to put out one another's candles. In the carnivalesque revelry, the literal meaning of the threat of death was tempered, blending into the essential ambivalence of Carnival imagery. The procession ended with a Pantagruelian feast in the early morning of Ash Wednesday, during which immense quantities of meat were consumed in anticipation of the Lenten fast to follow.

As a result of the Romantic movement, the following centuries saw a growing beautification of Carnival. Flowered carriages, parades, allegorical floats that grew ever more majestic and complex, and fancy-dress balls became permanent features of the celebration, wherever it still existed. The elements of violence lessened: fighting, verbal abuse, and the various forms of mock aggression—water jets, the hurling of oranges, plaster confetti—gradually gave way to battles of flowers and colored paper confetti that were the new and prominent aspect of nineteenth-century street Carnival. In this way, the masses of revelers were gradually transformed from participants to spectators, to the detriment of the heterogeneous character of the festival, which had been for everyone and everywhere, unfocused and without privileged actors. In proportion as the crowds grew more controlled, the festival became spatially more limited, subordinated to rational organization, diminishing the spirit of carnivalesque improvisation and burlesque satire. In Nice, for example, where Carnival still preserved its rich tradition, a festival committee was set up in 1873. The functions of this committee were to organize the festivities, parades, and flower battles and to award prizes for the allegorical floats, functions that still exist today.

These artistic and commercial innovations passed by the Carnival in Portugal. The typical form of Portuguese Carnival, like that of the whole Iberian Peninsula, was the Entrudo, a rowdy celebration in which flour, eggs, lupines, mud, oranges, and lemons were thrown on passersby. Dirty water, glue, and various other liquids were also poured onto the crowd, and gloves heavy with sand were dropped from windows. Repeating a common New Year custom, pots and pans and all sorts of useless kitchen utensils were also thrown out of the windows, perhaps symbolizing the discarding of the old, or perhaps heralding the Lenten fast. Fierce battles were waged with plaster eggs, wax lemons, corncobs, and beans blown fiercely through glass or cardboard straws. Blows with brooms and wooden spoons were dealt out liberally. Apart from the violence and filth, the Entrudo was also a Carnival of gluttony: in the better stocked houses—from whose windows cakes and pastries were pitched—guests feasted sumptuously. Even in the convents cakes were widely distributed.

The apogee of the Portuguese Entrudo was in the eighteenth century. This coincided with the period of the greatest popularity and prestige of masked balls in the European courts; in 1715, the Royal Music Academy of Paris transformed its opera hall into a ballroom, in use three times a week throughout the year. Masks had been prohibited in Portugal since 1689, exactly when they were at the height of fashion in the rest of Europe. The first masked ball in Lisbon took place only in 1785, offered by the Spanish ambassador in commemoration of the marriage of Princess Carlota Joaquiná with Prince João, but further masques were prohibited again immediately afterward. So the Entrudo continued to reign largely without rivals.

In Galicia, Spain, the Carnival of flour, eggs, and water was similar. It began with a chariot attack by one neighboring village on another and ended with the burial of Señhor Antroido, for whom a eulogy was written, satirizing the most notable local people and the most notorious events of the previous year.

In nineteenth-century Portugal, there were flower battles in Oporto and Lisbon. Nevertheless, the form of Carnival introduced into the American colonies by Portugal and Spain was, in substance, the Entrudo.

In Europe, it was a weakened Carnival that greeted the contemporary age. In the scientific dogmatists of the end of the nineteenth century, Carnival inspired suspicion and contempt and was viewed as an irrational, primitive, and inexplicable rite. Lacking spontaneous popular support in Europe, Carnival has, with rare exceptions, gradually lost its force in the twentieth century, until it has become a subject of interest chiefly for academics and those who have a strong affection for the past.

In Brazil, meanwhile, Carnival assumed the proportions of a national festival. Because of Brazil's multiethnic population and nearly continental proportions, its Carnival drew on many different cultural and folkloric sources, becoming the melting pot of indigenous, African, and European influences. Instead of surviving merely as a curious anachronism, it is today a living, dynamic phenomenon, modifying itself even in conjunction with the modern resources of mass communications. The Brazilian Carnival, like those of all Hispanic America, stems from the Iberian Entrudo. Begun with the Portuguese colonization in the sixteenth century, the Entrudo lasted more than three centuries before collapsing in the first years of the Brazilian republic. Prohibitions against it, however, date from its very introduction. The first recorded one is a decree of 1604, the first of many that produced no result, despite the stipulated punishments. A decree of 1853 imposed fines and detention for free men and caning and prison sentences for slaves participating in the Entrudo; nevertheless, another with identical content had to be issued in 1857.

The Brazilian Entrudo was very close to its Portuguese source: it involved the throwing of a lot of water and various small projectiles, later substituted by wax lemons. During the Entrudo, so much water was used in Rio de Janeiro that the newspapers invariably warned about risks to the city's water supply. The Entrudo was played even in the imperial palace, and whole families with their slaves dedicated weeks on end to the fabrication of wax lemons. Daniel Kidder, an American missionary who visited Brazil in the nineteenth century, advised in his *Sketches of Residence and Travel in Brazil* (Philadelphia, 1845) that people leaving their houses on these days should take their umbrellas with them to protect themselves against missiles and water.

In the mid-nineteenth century, the Brazilian Carnival showed clear signs of transformation. Masked balls were held, though the use of masks had been prohibited during the whole of the colonial period, just as in Portugal. Processions of allegorical carriages made their first appearance in 1855, in a pompous parade sponsored by competing groups known collectively as the Great Carnivalesque Societies, and this contrasted so strongly with the disorder of the Entrudo that from then on the characteristics of the street Carnival began to change. Originally, among these societies there were a considerable number of intellectuals; one of the relevant features of the parade each year was the presence of a "Float of Criticism," satirizing some important recent political event, about which satirical poems were also distributed.

With the abolition of slavery at the end of the nineteenth century, massive rural contingents migrated to the larger urban centers, bringing with them a great variety of regional folkloric contributions. In the first decades of the twentieth century, the activities involved in Carnival expanded, and a multiplicity of organizations, structured to a greater or lesser extent, began to make their presence felt in the street Carnival.

The Congo, a popular festivity with African roots alluding to the coronation of the "Congolese kings," began to make its contribution at this time. It was made up of several elements, among which were processions and warlike dances. From these came the majestic Maracatus, making their appearance in the Carnival of northeastern Brazil; these are choreographed processions derived from the Congo, with king, queen, and a court of princes, ladies, ambassadors, and standard- and sunshade-bearers, along with a percussion section of rhythmic drums and triangles. There was also an increase in the number of *cordões*—loose groupings of people with masks depicting old people, the Devil, kings, queens, clowns, Bahian women, Indians, bats, Death, and so forth, who sang and danced frenetically to the accompaniment of percussion instruments.

An innovation in the Carnival of the south of Brazil were the *ranchos de reis*, which were taken from devotional Christmas dramatizations performed in procession, reproducing the journey of the Three Kings to Bethlehem to visit the infant Jesus. They were, however, stripped of their religious allusions, carnivalized, and took the form of *rancho carnavalesco*—a slow-march procession accompanied by brass and string instruments, during which costumed male and female choruses, carrying small allegorical images, narrate lyrical stories while singing and dancing.

The most complete expression of the contemporary Brazilian Carnival is the samba school. These schools, which are actually associations, present a kind of mobile popular opera, each year worked around a different theme. This theme is narrated through the music and words of the Carnival samba song *(samba-enredo)*, and the characters are represented collectively by groups of dancers and singers in costume, with the scenery mounted on allegorical floats. A samba school is divided into three basic sections: first comes the drum section *(bateria)*, which has between two hundred and four hundred instrumentalists, who play big bass drums *(surdos)*, side drums, tambourines, triangles, *cuícas*, and bells, among other percussive instruments; second is the group *(ala)* of composers; and last is the main body of dancer-singers and other performers of the school. Schools compete with one another during the festival. The increasing complexity of the parade, and its internal regulation, have brought about the creation of a great number of both financial-administrative and technical-artistic posts, organzing the samba schools to meet certain commercial norms. There are more than a hundred samba schools, concentrated principally in Rio de Janeiro, where they originated, each one with between two thousand and four thousand members.

The rapid rise of the samba schools is an interesting sociological phenomenon. They sprang up in Rio de Janeiro in the 1930s, from the lowest social strata. At that time, the Carnival in Rio de Janeiro was visibly stratified: the upper classes amused themselves with costumed saloon-car processions, tossing confetti and paper ribbons; working-class districts celebrated with *ranchos;* while the samba schools, which were still embryonic associations, attracted the remaining peripheral elements.

At first these associations suffered great persecution. Their participants, the *sambistas,* sometimes had to hide themselves in the centers of Afro-Brazilian cults recognized by the police, where they held clandestine samba parties. There was still a lot of violence and disorder in the Brazilian Carnival; on the one hand, fights and shoot-outs and, on the other, strong police repression, particularly against the lowest social elements.

The samba schools came from the carnival blocks *(blocos carnavalescos),* which were conglomerations of barely organized masked dancers, modelled on the *ranchos* but with rather more limited financial resources. From the *ranchos* they adopted the processional form, the thematic structure, the master of ceremonies and flag-bearer, and the allegories, but the brass instruments were eliminated and the rhythm section increased to correspond to the beat of the samba.

The samba schools soon caught the attention of the governing authorities because of their populist potential, and when Carnival was made official in 1935, it became obligatory to enact national and historic themes. In the 1960s, the intellectuals and the urban middle class became involved in the samba schools, recognizing them as a genuine focus of popular national character. Their complete acceptance by the higher social classes coincided with the aspiration of the poorer element to be accepted and, as a result, the samba schools received a fresh and definitive impulse on the road of growth and social valuation.

The samba schools have now developed into extraordinarily complex institutions, in both their actual parades and their daily organization. They continue to function throughout the year as modest community clubs, always, however, with an eye to raising money for their Carnival expenses. As Carnival draws closer, they open up to allow the participation of the upper classes, until the parade at the climax festival, which is itself a rite of total social integration. Afterward, they retract again to their more modest dimensions. The themes of the parade refer to folkloric tales and events from Brazil's history, which, in the language of Carnival, are translated into an idealized vision of Brazil, depicted as a rich and generous mother country in which the contributions of the three races—white, black, and indigenous—join them in harmony, and where there is always room for hope and optimism. In reality, Brazil is a country marked by deep inequalities, still struggling in its uphill battle for development.

In its historical and contemporary manifestations, the common denominator of Carnival is still the process of the inversion of reality. This inversion is of a symbolic and temporary nature, which classifies as a process of ritual transformation. As a ritual, Carnival allows a glimpse of the axiomatic values of a given culture, as well as its underlying contradictions. The language that relates these contradictions to one another is principally that of satire. But the carnivalesque inversion can equally be expressed through violence and exaggeration. In the Carnival context, violence symbolizes an attack on order, classifying the festival, in this case, as a ritual of rebellion, of which the Entrudo is the clearest example. Carnival retains a close correlation with daily life, though during its celebration the normal and quotidian are inverted and lived as a festival. In this way, carnivalesque rebellion and provocation become a parody of true rebellion and provocation. In any case, ambivalence is inherent in Carnival symbolism, since Carnival itself is on the threshold between order and disorder, hierarchy and equality, real and ideal, sacred and profane. Essentially, Carnival represents confrontation of the antistructure with the structure of society, constituting a channel through which utopian ideals of social organization find expression and suppressed forms of human behavior are released from the restrictions of daily life.

The inversion of the social order inherent in Carnival, when amplified to a larger scale, represents the inverted, profane extreme of the sacred religious festival that Carnival immediately precedes. The two are inextricably interwoven and find their opposites in each other.

BIBLIOGRAPHY

One of the most complete interpretations of the meaning of contemporary Carnival in Brazil is Roberto DaMatta's *Carnavais, malandros e heróis* (Rio de Janeiro, 1979). The same author analyzes the costumes and gestures of Brazilian Carnival in *Universo do Carnaval* (Rio de Janeiro, 1981). For a knowledge of samba schools, their internal organization and ideology, see my *O palácio do samba* (Rio de Janeiro, 1975) and José Sávio Leopoldi's *Escola de samba, ritual e sociedade* (Petrópolis, 1978). For the carnivalization of a sacred rite, refer to Isidoro Maria da Silva Alves's *O Carnaval devoto* (Petrópolis, 1980), which deals with the profane aspects of a religious procession.

For a view of contemporary Carnival in Europe, see Annie Sidro's *Le Carnaval de Nice et ses fous* (Nice, 1979). The catalog edited by Samuël Glotz, *Le masque dans la tradition européenne* (Mons, Belgium, 1975), provides important information about the use of masks at Carnival.

A broad definition that allows a vision of Carnival as a ritual phenomenon can be found in the article by Edmund R. Leach, "Ritualization in Man in Relation to Conceptual and Social Development," in *Philosophical Transactions of the Royal Society of London* 251 (December 1966): 403–408. For notions of structure and antistructure and for a discussion of the symbolic properties and transformation processes of ritual phenomena, essential reading is Victor Turner's *The Ritual Process* (Chicago, 1969).

MARIA JULIA GOLDWASSER

CARO, JOSEPH. *See* Karo, Yosef.

CARROLL, JOHN (1735–1815), first Roman Catholic bishop of the United States (1789). Carroll attended Saint Omer College in French Flanders in 1748 and a few years later joined the Jesuits. By 1771 he had been ordained a priest and made his final vows in the order. When Pope Clement XIV suppressed the Jesuits in 1773, Carroll was briefly under arrest. The next year he returned to his family estate in Maryland, ministering as best he could under the uncertain jurisdiction ex-Jesuits then faced. He joined his cousin, Charles Carroll, and Benjamin Franklin in an attempt at winning Canadian support for political independence, which would open the way for an American Catholic church.

Carroll's church leadership emerged in 1782–1783, inspired by concepts of church-state separation drawn from the writings of Roberto Bellarmino, Francisco Suárez, and English Catholic commentators on the subject. Carroll viewed the relationship between the pope and Roman Catholic congregations as principally spiritual rather than administrative; thus his plan for the American Catholic church placed church property in the United States in its own corporations, both clerical and lay, in this way guarding against foreign intrusion. Carroll also emphasized the spiritual nature of the office of bishop, a view he would explain in a disciplinary decree published in 1797.

In order to ensure against a nonresident appointee by Rome, Carroll advocated electing the first American bishop by vote of the clergy. Thereafter, he expected, the American hierarchy could follow more common ecclesial practices. However, the first American see, Baltimore, remained under the administrative control of the Congregation of the Propagation of the Faith, a body administered by Rome, thus weakening American control over episcopal appointees. Later, as first archbishop of Baltimore (1808–1815), Carroll was to acknowledge the lack of suitable American candidates to fill offices created by four new dioceses.

Consistent with Maryland Catholic tradition, Carroll held that no one should be molested in the free exercise of his religion. He believed that the Maryland constitution honored this principle. He wrote against states with laws that favored Protestantism (1789), arguing that such laws went beyond what was just in interpreting the role of religion in the state's promotion of public morality. In *An Address to the Roman Catholics* (1784), Carroll responded to what he considered distortions of Catholic teachings in these and other areas. His arguments were effective in the era before the rise of Nativism—a movement characterized by hostility toward immigrants, particularly Irish Catholics.

John Carroll was also eminent as a builder of the church in visible form. Emerging into the world of public worship after 1776, the Catholic community under his leadership determinedly built parishes and institutions. Among the lasting legacies of his episcopacy were the establishment of Saint Mary's Seminary, the recruitment of priests from Europe, and the founding of Georgetown College for the laity of all faiths. He placed high value on the ministry and education of women, as seen in his sponsorship of Elizabeth Ann Seton's founding of the Daughters of Charity and of parochial schools. He also sponsored establishments of the Carmelite and Visitation orders. Carroll also contributed his services to Saint John's and Washington colleges and to what became the University of Maryland.

BIBLIOGRAPHY

The primary source for Carroll's writings is *The John Carroll Papers*, 3 vols., edited by Thomas O'Brien Hanley (Notre Dame, Ind., 1976). Arranged in chronological order, it has title and date listings for each volume, useful for the references made above. Annabelle M. Melville's *John Carroll of Baltimore* (New York, 1955) to some extent abridges Peter K. Guilday's biography, *The Life and Times of John Carroll*, 2 vols. (1922; reprint, Westminster, Md., 1954). Joseph Agonito has made the most extensive use to date of the Carroll papers in "Ecumenical Stirrings: Catholic-Protestant Relations during the Episcopacy of John Carroll," *Church History* 45 (1976): 358–373.

THOMAS O'BRIEN HANLEY, S.J.

CĀRVĀKA. A school of "materialists" thought to have been contemporary with early Buddhism, the Cārvāka school, or Cārvākas, has only scant evidence to attest to its existence. Writing in Hastings's *Encyclopaedia of Religion and Ethics,* Louis de La Vallée Poussin noted that "a materialistic school, a system in the exact sense of the term" did not exist in India. Such an opinion was based not upon the failure of scholars to recognize such terms as *lokāyata* ("world-extended"?) or *cārvāka,* or the schools known by these names, but upon the ambiguity and obscurity that certainly surround their origin and exact connotation. In earlier literature the term *lokāyata* did not stand for a doctrine that is necessarily materialistic. In the Buddhist collection *Saṃyutta Nikāya,* two brahmans are described as followers of the Lokāyata view, proponents of which are credited with holding one or more of the following four propositions: everything exists; nothing exists; everything is a unity; and everything is a plurality. Buddhaghosa's commentary identifies the first and third propositions as "eternalist views" *(sassata-ditthiyo)* and the second and fourth as "annihilationist views" *(uccheda-ditthiyo).* Later, the Annihilationist views were regarded as consonant with materialism.

The use of the word *cārvāka* was also initially obscure. Some say that *cārvāka* was a name. Others propose a fanciful etymology, joining *caru* ("beautiful") with *vāk* ("speech") to render a compound connoting "attractive discourse"; thus understood, the doctrines of this school, which denounce religion and religiously founded morality as useless, would have been found attractive by the common man, himself a materialist at heart. In later writings, the name *Lokāyata* came to refer to the Cārvāka school, which was traced to a mythical founder Bṛhaspati. In the latter part of the twentieth century, a number of Lokāyata *Bārhaspatya sūtra*s have been collated from various sources, but their authenticity is open to question.

According to the available sources, the Cārvāka taught that the world is as we see it, that is, as perceived by our sensory organs, and is devoid of all but a purely mechanical order or principle that can be confirmed by recourse to sense evidence alone. A moral or ethical order, admitted in one form or another by all other Indian schools (as in, for instance, their use of the paired terms *dharma* and *adharma*), is thus denied as incompatible with empirical evidence. So too, an omniscient being, God, life after death, and ultimate reward or punishment for one's actions are all denied. It is for this reason, and for the fact that it denies the authority of the Vedas, that the school is termed *nāstika,* or negativist.

Cārvāka ethics, as might be expected, do recognize the claims of superior force and authority. Obedience to the king and to the state are recommended as a practical means of self-preservation; otherwise, a life given to the pursuit of pleasure and wealth is considered the ideal. Political power was deemed by the materialists to derive from the approval of the governed *(lokasiddha bhavet rājā)*; as a consequence, the ruler's mandate to govern was regarded as without divine or transcendental sanction. Cārvāka cosmology recognized four elements—earth, water, fire, and air—as fundamental constituents of all things; when called on to explain the appearance of life or consciousness in material things when the elements themselves are devoid of any such powers or properties, the Cārvāka had recourse to a theory whereby the conjunction of certain elements is accidently invested with properties missing in the original constituents. As evidence of this, they pointed to the power in the fermented drink to intoxicate, which is missing in the unfermented constituents. This empirical methodology might have been the precursor of scientific thought in India.

Cārvāka epistemology regards perception as the only valid source of knowledge and explicitly rejects inference. Eventually, the school produced a very sophisticated philosophical critique of the inductive premise in each act of inference. Sometimes the Cārvāka view is represented as a skeptical critique of knowledge, for, according to Jayarāśi, probably a proponent of Cārvāka doctrines, even sense evidence can mislead.

It is doubtful whether there was ever a well-entrenched traditional "school" called Cārvāka or Lokāyata, for we do not have available to us any independent texts of the classical period that are expressly affiliated with this school. The notable exception is the text of Jayarāśi called *Tattvopaplavasiṃha,* discovered and edited in 1940. In it, the author is revealed as a gifted dialectician. The work itself is a highly sophisticated critique of all the *pramāṇa*s, or valid sources of knowledge, criticizing both Vedic and non-Vedic schools. Theories of perception and inference of the Nyāyā, Buddhist, Sāṃkhya, Mīmāṃsā, and Jain traditions are all faulted. If this text belongs to the Cārvāka-Lokāyata school, then we have to admit that this tradition consists not only of materialism, but combines elements of skepticism and agnosticism as well. In this light, it would be incorrect to credit the Cārvākas with advocacy of pure license and hedonism, charges that, after all, are found only in the writings of their opponents (as, for instance, Haribhadra and Mādhava). All told, the Cārvākas probably represent an anti-religious tradition that rejected religious and spiritual pursuits and sought the basis of moral and social order in human rationality.

[*For discussion of Western materialist schools, see* Materialism.]

BIBLIOGRAPHY

Summary accounts of this school can be found in such compendia of Indian philosophy as Haribhadra's *Ṣaḍdarśanasamuccaya* (seventh century) and Mādhava's *Sarvadarśanasaṃgraha* (fourteenth century). Haribhadra was a Jain and hence belonged to a non-Vedic school; Mādhava was a Vaidika, probably a Vedāntin.

Modern studies include Hara Prasad Shastri's *Lokayata* (Oxford, 1925), a pioneering work that is both suggestive and illuminating; Dakshinaranjan Shastri's *A Short History of Indian Materialism, Sensationalism and Hedonism,* 2d ed. (Calcutta, 1957), a tenuous historical reconstruction of the school; and Debiprasad Chattopadhyaya's *Lokāyata: A Study in Ancient Indian Materialism* (New Delhi, 1959), a Marxist analysis of the history of Indian materialism, including useful materials from nonphilosophical literature.

BIMAL KRISHNA MATILAL

CASSIAN, JOHN (c. 365–c. 435), monastic leader, founder of ascetic theology in the Latin church. According to Gennadius of Marseilles, John Cassian came from Scythia Minor (modern-day Dobruja), a province of the early Byzantine empire. Born of a rich Scythian family, Cassian received a good education. After he moved to Palestine, he entered a monastery in Bethlehem, together with his friend Germanos. Receiving permission for a temporary absence, the two men left the monastery for a short visit to the monastic colonies of Egypt. After they met the first prominent elders there, they were so fascinated that they forgot their promise to return to their monastery in Bethlehem. They continued on their travels as far as the region of Scetis, where they settled. From time to time they made visits to other monastic areas, but they do not seem to have realized their original intention of visiting the Pachomian monasteries at Thebais. Cassian and Germanos stayed in Egypt for over thirteen years, with only a short break to settle the matter of their permission to leave Bethlehem.

During the anti-Origenist persecution of 399 the two men were forced to abandon Egypt because of their association with Origenist monks, whose theological exponent was Evagrios of Pontus. They fled to Constantinople, where they were well received by the archbishop John Chrysostom. There Germanos was ordained a priest and Cassian a deacon. At the beginning of 405, they went to Rome on behalf of Chrysostom to deliver a letter to Pope Innocent I.

After 415 Cassian, now a priest, moved to Marseilles, where he established two monasteries, one for men and one for women. The last record of him is Prosper of Acquitaine's theological attack on him, in about 433. A short time after the attack Cassian died; his last words, reported in *Sayings of the Fathers,* were "I have never done my own will, nor taught anyone something which I had not previously carried out."

Cassian came very late to writing, and he wrote only when requested to do so by important persons. Generally he used the same material as did Evagrios, but he gave it his own personal imprint. More synthetical than Evagrios, he arranged his sources in extensive collections. He was a brilliant Latin stylist, distinguished for his clarity and elegance. Three of his works are still read today with great interest.

1. *Institutes of the Cenoby and the Remedies for the Eight Principal Vices,* written around 420 at the request of Castor, bishop of Apt in Provence, consists of two distinct sections. Books 1–4 discuss clothing, prayer, psalmody, and rules of monastic life; books 5–12 are a moral exposition of the eight evil thoughts, or vices—gluttony, luxury, avarice, wrath, sloth, *acedia* (negligence), vainglory, and pride—and their remedies.
2. *Conferences of the Fathers* has three sections. Conferences 1–10, written around 422 and dedicated to Leo, bishop of Fréjus, and the monk Helladius, recount Cassian's conversations with famous elders from Scetis on the fundamental principles of the ascetic and spiritual life. Conferences 11–17, written around 424 at the request of Honoratus, founder of Lérins monastery, and the monk Eucherius, recount Cassian's conversations with elders of the Nile delta on problems of spiritual theology. Conferences 18–24, written around 426 and dedicated to a group of Gallican monks, present conversations with elders of the Nile delta and Scetis on particular problems of the ascetic life.
3. *On the Incarnation against Nestorius,* written in 430 at the request of the future pope Leo, constitutes the single Western refutation of Nestorian teachings, which Cassian considered a result of Pelagian influence.

Cassian is the first monastic leader in the West to have set forth the theological principles of monastic life.

Although his works encompass not only the anchoritic but also the cenobitic form of monasticism, his real interest lay in anchoritism. On questions of monastic organization, his sources are the institutions of the monastic centers in the East, chiefly Egypt and Palestine. In the theoretical area, he has as his guide the great teacher of ascetical theology, Evagrios, although, because Evagrios had been condemned as a heretic, Cassian avoided citing his name.

Cassian's thought revolves around the spiritual perfection of ascetics, following the classical twofold distinction of the stages of the spiritual life, the active and the contemplative way, for which he used the Greek terms *praktikē* and *theoretikē*. Complete renunciation leads to the active way: "We have two fathers, one to abandon, the other to follow" (*Conf.* 3.6). In the preliminary stage a fierce struggle develops against the passions caused in us by demons and evil thoughts. *Praktikē* becomes the way through which the cleansing of the passions and the establishment of the virtues are effected. *Theoretikē* is the higher stage, in which the contemplation of the divine realities and the acknowledgment of the most secret signs are acquired (*Conf.* 14.1).

Like all ascetic writers, Cassian demands from Christians a hard struggle for the attainment of perfection. This struggle, in turn, requires a strong and free will. Cassian rejected two important theories of his day. He regarded the volitionism of Pelagius as heretical, and the absolute predestination of Augustine of Hippo as sacrilegious. According to Cassian, humankind preserved even after the Fall the ability to turn toward the good and to accept or reject the salvation offered by God.

In the West, Cassian's teaching was criticized by Prosper of Acquitaine, a disciple of Augustine, and later it was condemned by the Council of Orange (529). It is still regarded today as semi-Pelagian. Cassian, however, was an Eastern theologian in the Latin West, and his teaching must be judged by Greek theological criteria. From this point of view, he was in agreement with the entire Eastern tradition and especially with the views of John Chrysostom.

In his last years, Cassian was regarded as one of the leading theologians of the West. Even though his opposition to Augustine kept him out of the mainstream of the Western church, his authority was unofficially accepted. Abridged redactions of his writings were made in both Latin and Greek, while eight of his sayings were preserved in *Sayings of the Fathers*. Through Benedict of Nursia his influence was spread throughout the West.

Gennadius of Marseilles calls Cassian a saint, but in the West he is not venerated, except in Marseilles, where his feast is celebrated on 23 July. In the East the feast is generally celebrated on 29 February.

BIBLIOGRAPHY

Works by Cassian

Guy, Jean-Claude, ed. and trans. *De institutis / Institutions cenobitiques.* Vol. 109 of *Sources chrétiennes.* Paris, 1965.

Migne, J.-P., ed. *Opera omnia.* Vols. 49 and 50 of *Patrologia Latina.* Paris, 1874 and 1863.

Petschenig, Michael, ed. *Opera omnia.* Vols. 13 and 17 of *Corpus Scriptorum Ecclesiasticorum Latinorum.* Vienna, 1886 and 1888.

Pichery, Eugène, ed. and trans. *Conlationes Patrum (Conférences).* Vols. 42, 54, and 64 of *Sources chrétiennes.* Paris, 1955–1959.

Works about Cassian. Cassian's doctrines on nature and grace in opposition to Augustine's view of predestination is the central concern of Alexander Hoch's *Lehre des Johannes Cassianus von Natur und Gnade: Ein Beitrag zur Geschichte des Gnadenstreites im fünften Jahrhundert* (Freiburg im Breisgau, 1895), and Joseph Laugier's *S. Jean Cassien et sa doctrine sur la grâce* (Lyons, 1908). A general picture of the personality and the work of Cassian is given under "Cassien" in *Dictionnaire de spiritualité* (Paris, 1937). Owen Chadwick's *John Cassian: A Study in Primitive Monasticism* (1950; 2d ed., London, 1968) is very important. A number of other studies on special aspects of his monastic activities may be mentioned, such as Hans Oskar Weber's *Die Stellung des Johannes Cassianus zur ausserpachomianischen Mönchstradition* (Munich, 1961), Salvatore Pricoco's *L'isola dei santi: Il cenobio di Lerino e il origini del monachesimo gallico* (Rome, 1978), and Philip Rousseau's *Ascetics, Authority and the Church in the Age of Jerome and Cassian* (Oxford, 1978). Some new studies on the theological teachings are Victor Codina's *El aspecto cristológico en la espiritualidad de Juan Casiano,* "Orientalia Christiana Analecta," vol. 175 (Rome, 1966), and Paul Christophe's *Cassien et Césaire: Prédicateurs de la morale monastique* (Gembloux, 1969).

PANAGIOTIS C. CHRISTOU
Translated from Greek by Philip M. McGhee

CASSIRER, ERNST (1874–1945), German philosopher of culture. Cassirer was born in Breslau, Silesia. He studied at the universities of Berlin, Leipzig, Heidelberg, and Marburg and completed his inaugural dissertation under the direction of the Neo-Kantian Hermann Cohen at Marburg in 1899. Between 1903 and 1919 Cassirer taught as privatdocent at the University of Berlin, and in 1919 he assumed the chair of philosophy at the newly founded University of Hamburg. Cassirer left Germany in 1933 with the rise of Nazism; he taught for two years at Oxford before accepting a professorship at the University of Göteborg in Sweden in 1935. Cassirer left Sweden for the United States in the summer of 1941, teaching first at Yale and then at Columbia.

Cassirer's published writings comprise nearly 125 items, ranging from short articles to books of eight hundred pages. They treat a wide range of subjects in history, linguistics, mythology, aesthetics, literary studies, and science. Because he wrote continuously on so many subjects it is difficult to form a sense of Cassirer's thought as a whole. The largest division within his writings is between his works on the history of philosophy and those that state his own philosophical position. In addition to these are subcategories of works on literary figures, especially Goethe, and on the philosophy of science.

The center of Cassirer's work in the history of philosophy is his four-volume study *Das Erkenntnisproblem in der Philosophie und Wissenschaft der neuern Zeit* (The Problem of Knowledge in Philosophy and Science in the Modern Age). The first two volumes (1906–1907) trace the problem of knowledge from Nicholas of Cusa to Kant. The third (1920) and fourth (first published in English translation in 1950) continue the theme through Hegel and into the first decades of the twentieth century. In addition to this large study, Cassirer's works on the Enlightenment, the Renaissance, Descartes, and Leibniz have become classics in their areas. The central work of Cassirer's original philosophy is his three-volume *Philosophie der symbolischen Formen* (The Philosophy of Symbolic Forms; 1923–1929), the groundwork of which was laid in his theory of scientific concept formation in *Substanzbegriff und Funktionsbegriff* (Substance and Function) in 1910. He extended his theory of concept formation to humanistic thought in *Zur Logik der Kulturwissenschaften* (The Logic of the Humanities; 1942). Cassirer recast his conception of symbolic forms in *An Essay on Man* (1944). This was followed by *The Myth of the State* (1946); both works were written in English.

Cassirer regards religion as part of the symbolic form of myth. In *An Essay on Man* he labels this as the symbolic form of "myth and religion" within a series of symbolic forms that includes also language, art, history, and science. Each of these areas of human culture represents a way in which man forms his experience through symbols. Cassirer defines man as an "animal symbolicum." Consciousness forms its object in many different ways. No one mode of formation offers a "literal" presentation of the real; all human activities are equally "symbolic." The symbol is the medium of all man's cultural activity, whether mythic-religious, linguistic, artistic, historical, or scientific. The interrelationships of all these manners of symbolizing form the system of human culture.

Religion arises as a stage within the mythical mode of symbolizing. In the second volume of *Philosophie der symbolischen Formen* (see part 4) Cassirer says that the break between religious consciousness and the mythical symbol occurs when consciousness begins to regard the images and signs of myth as pointing to meanings beyond immediate existence. Like true linguistic signs, Cassirer says, religious signs are understood as referring to an order of reality beyond the plane of immediate sensuous existence. In mythical consciousness the dancer who wears the mask of the god *is* the god; he does not signify the god who exists in another realm of being. Religion introduces a distinction between a finite and an infinite realm, a distinction that is beyond the power of the mythic symbol. For mythical consciousness, symbol and symbolized occupy a single plane of reality. In religious consciousness the sensuous and the spiritual divide, but they remain in this division as continuously pointing to each other in a relationship of analogy.

In *An Essay on Man* Cassirer approaches the relationship between myth and religion less in terms of the epistemology of the symbol and more in sociocultural and moral terms: "In the development of human culture we cannot fix a point where myth ends or religion begins. In the whole course of its history religion remains indissolubly connected and penetrated with mythical elements" (p. 87). Cassirer says that myth and religion originate in the "feeling of the indestructible unity of life" and in the fear of death as a break in this unity. In his phenomenology of the third volume of *Philosophie der symbolischen Formen,* Cassirer connects myth with the *Ausdrucksfunktion* of consciousness, with the primordial phenomenon of "expression." Religion never loses its roots as an expression of the unity of life and the fear of death.

Religion also has roots in the "sympathy of the Whole" that underlies magical practices in primitive societies. But religion arises, Cassirer says in *An Essay on Man,* when the totem and taboo system of society based on magical practices begins to break down. In the taboo system the individual has no responsibility for his own actions. Religion gives scope to a new feeling, that of individuality. Cassirer regards the prophetic books of the Old Testament as an example of the rise of the new ideal of individual moral responsibility that marks the appearance of religious consciousness out of the taboo system. In religion there develops this first sense of the moral self.

BIBLIOGRAPHY

Works by Cassirer. There are two comprehensive bibliographies of Cassirer's writings: a topical arrangement can be found in *Philosophy and History: Essays Presented to Ernst Cassirer*, edited by Raymond Klibansky and H. J. Paton (Oxford, 1936), pp. 338–353, and a chronological listing appears in *The Philosophy of Ernst Cassirer*, edited by Paul A. Schilpp (Evanston, Ill., 1949), pp. 881–910. Of particular interest to the study of Cassirer's conception of myth and religion are the following: *Philosophie der symbolischen Formen*, 3 vols. (Berlin, 1923–1929), translated by Ralph Manheim as *The Philosophy of Symbolic Forms*, 3 vols. (New Haven, 1953–1957), especially volume 2, *Mythical Thought; Sprache und Mythos* (Leipzig, 1925), translated by Suzanne K. Langer as *Language and Myth* (New York, 1946); *Zur Logik der Kulturwissenschaften: Fünf Studien* (Göteborg, 1942), translated by C. S. Howe as *The Logic of the Humanities* (New Haven, 1961); *An Essay on Man: An Introduction to a Philosophy of Human Culture* (New Haven, 1944); and *The Myth of the State* (New Haven, 1946). *Symbol, Myth, and Culture: Essays and Lectures of Ernst Cassirer 1935–45* (New Haven, 1949), edited by Donald Phillip Verene, is a volume of Cassirer's previously unpublished papers. It includes a description of the corpus of Cassirer's manuscripts housed at Yale University.

Works about Cassirer. For bibliographies of critical work on Cassirer, see "Ernst Cassirer: A Bibliography," *Bulletin of Bibliography* 24 (1964): 103–106, and "Ernst Cassirer: Critical Work 1964–1970," *Bulletin of Bibliography* 29 (1972): 21–22, 24, both compiled by Donald Phillip Verene, and "Bibliographie des textes sur Ernst Cassirer," *Revue internationale de philosophie* 28 (1974): 492–510, compiled by Robert Nadeau. These bibliographies list critical works on Cassirer in all languages. The main source for critical views on Cassirer's thought remains *The Philosophy of Ernst Cassirer*, edited by Paul A. Schilpp (Evanston, Ill., 1949). The essays in this volume cover all aspects of Cassirer's thought, but most are expository. Other book-length works are Carl H. Hamburg's *Symbol and Reality: Studies in the Philosophy of Ernst Cassirer* (The Hague, 1956); Seymour W. Itzkoff's *Ernst Cassirer: Scientific Knowledge and the Concept of Man* (Notre Dame, Ind., 1971) and *Ernst Cassirer: Philosopher of Culture* (Boston, 1977); and David R. Lipton's *Ernst Cassirer: The Dilemma of a Liberal Intellectual in Germany, 1914–1933* (Toronto, 1978). There are two biographies of Cassirer in essay form, one by Dimitry Gawronsky in *The Philosophy of Ernst Cassirer*, the other by Cassirer's wife, Toni Cassirer, *Mein Leben mit Ernst Cassirer* (1950; reprint, Hildesheim, 1981).

DONALD PHILLIP VERENE

CASTE SYSTEM. *See* Varṇa and Jāti.

CASTRATION is a custom found both in mythological tales and in ritual practices of peoples of various origins, cultural levels and geographical locations. Because there is a preponderance of documentation of the custom in the ancient Near East and Mediterranean cultures, the origin and propagating center of this custom has often been ascribed to ancient Semitic culture. But evidence of castration has also been found in other, very different cultures that were never influenced by Semitic culture, which fact seems to rule out a hypothesis of diffusion. Besides, the act of castration, both mythological and ritual, is naturally connected with other practices, beliefs, and doctrines that are all related in some way to sex and sexuality. Their connections (with circumcision, bisexuality, virginity, celibacy, etc.) constitute a kind of compact but multivariegated "symbolic universe."

Many of the cosmogonic myths are based on two cosmic entities, Sky and Earth, who are originally united in a sexual embrace from which violent action alone can separate them. A tale of the Maori in New Zealand says that offspring born of the endless mating of Rangi ("sky") and Papa ("earth") are held in darkness and spacelessness. Finally, they decide to separate their parents, cutting the father's "tendons" (probably a euphemism) and pushing him up, to achieve the present separation of sky and earth. The cosmogonic motif of the primordial couple can be found in almost all Oceanic civilizations and widely in Africa and the Americas. But the act of violent separation of the two cosmic entities is seldom clearly described as a real act of castration, even if its symbolic verisimilitude leads us to think of it in this way. An example of castration that is presented in a straightforward manner is in the Greek cosmogonic myth, Hesiod's *Theogony*. The god Ouranos ("sky") and the goddess Gaia ("earth") conceive a breed of divine beings, but the god exhausts his paternal role in procreation and keeps his children from any kind of activity, thrusting them again into their mother's womb. At last, one of them, Kronos, makes an ambush and cuts off his father's sexual organ, throwing it behind his own back. The goddess Gaia is fertilized by the blood of Ouranos, while from his sexual organ, which falls into the sea, is born the goddess of love, Aphrodite. Thus, the only way to eliminate Ouranos, whose existence consisted of mere sexual and procreative activity, was to castrate him: this is the only opportunity to "murder," in some sense, an immortal god. This castration is a positive event because it breaks off the cycle of endless and useless reproduction and gives Ouranos's offspring a living space between sky and earth. It represents, moreover, a fundamental moment in the establishment of the real and ordered world. From the morphological point of view, the myth of Ouranos's castration is typical of the image of the heavenly divine being who, after his initial performance, leaves the stage, becoming a *deus otiosus*.

Comparative analysis has pointed out important resemblances to the myth of the impotence of Varuṇa, an

Indo-Iranian god, and also to the investiture ritual of the king in India (Dumézil, 1948). Historical analysis, on the other hand, has indicated some parallel cases in cosmogonic myths of the ancient Near East. The Mesopotamian creation epic, *Enuma elish*, tells of the god Enki, who defeats and annihilates his enemy Mummu, taking off his crown, smashing his head, and, finally, cutting off his penis. The Hittite myth of Kumarbi contains even more similarities to Ouranos's story. This cosmogony, combining one of the earliest Hurrian stories with some elements of Assyro-Babylonian mythology, deals with a succession of children's rebellions against their fathers. In this myth Kumarbi pursues his father, Anu, who seeks safety by flying toward the sky, but the son grabs his father's feet, dragging him to the ground. Then, seized by excitement, Kumarbi bites his father's penis, tears it off, and swallows it, laughing and boasting of his bravado. But the swallowed sexual organ makes him pregnant with terrifying gods who will soon defeat him in turn.

Scholars are in agreement that the similarity between Greek and Hittite myths can be explained as an indication of direct historical derivation, on the grounds of similar general structure and the common presence of castration. Nevertheless, there are significant differences between these myths, and there remains a notable uncertainty about how the motif spread. A recurrence of Ouranos's castration can be found in the cosmogony of Philo of Byblos, a late Phoenician author who claims a reference to Sanchuniathon, an ancient Phoenician author. Mixing local information with Greek conceptions in a syncretic and euhemeristic way, Philo ascribes to the god El-Kronos an act of castration against his father. The Hellenic pattern is clearly apparent, but archaeological discoveries at Ugarit (Ras Shamra) in Phoenicia, dating from the second millennium BCE, seem to confirm to some extent the authenticity and antiquity of the myth. In a different case, in the *Prose Edda*, an ancient Germanic cosmogony, the "father of everything," a personal entity with creative power, is also called "the castrated," with no further explanation. Scholars agree that many features of this divine being are not original but derived from Christian influences, and they think also that the castration element can be dated back to the earliest Greek tradition of Ouranos.

Besides these cosmogonic myths we must mention other kinds of myths in which castration constitutes a pattern of ritual action. The close connection between myth and rite in these cases arouses the rightful suspicion that the myth may have been constructed in order to provide a motivation for the ritual practice. The most famous myth is the Greco-Roman story of the goddess Cybele and the god Attis. Cybele, venerated in Rome and in the Roman empire under the name of Great Mother (Magna Mater), was an ancient goddess of fertility known in Anatolia since the second millennium BCE under the name of Kubaba. Some iconographic and onomastic evidence suggests an even more remote origin, going back to the Anatolian Neolithic and, perhaps, Mesopotamian civilization. The young servant-lover Attis, on the other hand, seems to have been introduced along with his mate only after the arrival in Anatolia of the Phrygians (c. eighth century BCE). There are several mythical versions of Attis's castration. (All the literary sources can be found in Hugo Hepding's *Attis, seine Mythen und sein Kult*, 1903; reprint, Berlin, 1967.) We can easily find a constant line of development from more ancient tales—much more intricate and grotesque—to the embellished and romantic later versions. The original stories take place in an environment of unnatural primitiveness, monstrous procreations, violent loves, and bloody punishments. All these versions culminate in the story of Attis, who castrates himself in a fit of madness or out of a desire for absolute chastity. Sometimes, Attis's castration is attributed to a wild boar or to a jealous entity who wants to punish him for his amorous exploits.

The documentation related to ritual practices records, first of all, that the act of castration can sometimes be the result of temporary exaltation or religious fanaticism. The religio-historical as well as ethnographic literature cites some examples, but their rarity and especially their complete isolation from myths, doctrines, and institutionalized interpretations make them subjects for studies in psychology (or psychopathology). The history of religions, on the other hand, is concerned with institutionalized acts of castration, for instance, within the so-called pubertal cults. All these practices belong to a broader category of ritual mutilations, like the custom of removal of one testicle, which is practiced almost exclusively among Camitic populations in Africa, where it seems to serve as a substitute for circumcision, a practice completely unknown to them. In the initiation rites of primitive peoples different practices involving male genitalia are very frequent (circumcision, subincision, etc.), as are those involving female genitalia (clitoridectomy, infibulation, etc.), and their origin and significance seem rather difficult to establish. [*See* Clitoridectomy.] According to some scholars, these practices constitute symbolic equivalents of castration.

Another category of castration is the custom, widespread in the ancient Near East and in Semitic cultures, of castrated priests. The *kurgarru*, for instance, is a eunuch priest of Ishtar who officiates at the orgiastical rites in honor of the god Marduk. Many of the clergy of

Hekate in Stratonicea, Caria, and in Laginas and the clergy of Artemis in Ephesus and of Atargatis in Hierapolis, Syria, were castrated. Some sporadic cases of analogous priestly castration have been recently reported in Brahmanic India, particularly in the northern mountains, and also in Nepal and Tibet. Usually, the castrated priests are connected with a powerful and fertile goddess, sometimes with astral characteristics and at other times with the features of a goddess of animals, who is conventionally called Mother Goddess.

Finally, there is a series of examples in which the ritual of castration appears entirely institutionalized, justified according to the myths of foundation or in accordance with precise beliefs and doctrines. Within the Cybele and Attis cult, the mythical castration of Attis is the foundation of the practice of castration of his priests (and, perhaps, of believers too), which is a kind of sacrament of consecration, a sacrifice recalling the god's passion, and sometimes a votive offering. The Galli—as these priests are most commonly called—dedicated themselves to the goddess Cybele after having willingly castrated themselves during ritual performances in which, in a frenzy of dances, obsessive beating of drums, and self-flagellation, they reached paroxysms of exaltation. The Galli wore female clothing and heavy makeup, their hair was long and loose, and they lived in a wandering missionary community, supporting themselves with alms they received for offering predictions and prognostications. At Pessinus in Asia Minor, they ruled sacerdotal city-states in which temple and royal palace were unified. In Greece they were generally despised and driven away because of their mutilation and their appearance: they were never fully assimilated into official religion. In Rome, where the cult of Cybele was introduced in 204 BCE, and in the Roman empire, they were at first strictly regulated and controlled by the state; then they acquired, little by little, more importance and autonomy. The Roman distaste for eunuchism slowly faded away because of the approval of some emperors of the practice and because of a certain lessening of bloodier and crueler aspects of the cult.

Thus, the cult of Cybele and Attis had its temples, its brotherhood, and its feasts included in the sacral calendar. Little by little, under the influence of a certain spiritualism and new symbolic interpretations, the cult assumed a mystic character and became a kind of mystery cult like other cults of Oriental origin. The castration of believers was easily explained as a sign of the search for perfection, a voluntary renunciation of the pleasures of the flesh, and the Attis figure became more and more spiritualized. During the later Roman empire, the self-castration of believers was probably replaced or integrated into the bloody and spectacular rite called the Taurobolium. A bull was slain and castrated, and its blood was shed over the believer as a lavation of intensified achievement, regenerative and purifying. [*See* Cybele.]

Castration, finally, appears sporadically in practices of groups, sects, and isolated thinkers that link it to doctrines preaching asceticism and sexual abstinence and regard it as an escape from the temptations of the flesh. Such doctrines—which have remarkable precedents and parallels within the pagan as well as the Judaic world—developed during the first centuries of the Christian era and were inclined to radicalize the pronouncement by Matthew on eunuchs (*Mt.* 19:12) as well as the orthodox position (of Paul, for instance) on the prestige of virginity. Strongly connected with sexual and marital morality, bound to the theme of ecclesiastical celibacy and intertwined with the rise of monasticism, this topic evinced itself in some authors as a preaching of the *egkrateia* ("continence"), understood as the complete rejection of any kind of sexual intercourse. If within the ecclesiastical and orthodox line virginity and chastity are recommended solely on the basis of motivations such as the imitation of Christ or in anticipation of the kingdom of heaven, according to these doctrines sexual abstinence becomes a necessary condition of salvation and is based on ontological and protological motivations of the dualistic and Platonic mold. According to some writers, the Greek father Origen (third century) and other ecclesiastic authorities castrated themselves in order to extinguish definitively any desire for sexual intercourse. At the same time, in the mysterious sect of the Valesians (from Valesius, the founder), castration was a normal practice. Epiphanius, bishop of Salamis, refuted the sect and accused it of heresy. It also seems that among the Manichaeans the current obligation of chastity was transformed in some cases into the practice of self-castration. The phenomenon must have been rather widespread, since it was addressed by the Council of Nicaea (325) and a bull of Pope Leo I (c. 395). A recent renewal of the practice of castration for the sake of proselytism and asceticism is found among the Skoptsy ("the castrated"), a Russian sect that developed from the complex movement of the Raskol schism during the mid-eighteenth century. The Skoptsy were long persecuted, but they spread throughout Russia during the next century and survived in some Romanian communities until 1950.

From this brief review of facts relative to castration in some myths and ritual practices, it becomes clear that even if the ancient Semitic (and Mediterranean) world offers the majority of documentation and shows some cases of dependence and evolution, it cannot be considered the unique source of the diffusion of this practice. In the same way, it is impossible to decide on a univocal interpretation of the practice of castration that can explain, in all cases, its causes and motivations. Sometimes the connection with themes of fertility and procreation is primary, so that castration constitutes a dramatic event stopping the flow of life or containing it within more orderly boundaries. At other times, on the basis of doctrinary principles, castration is instead related to a search for asexuality understood as a privileged condition. In some cases, this asexuality resolves itself into a kind of symbolic bisexuality that aims to reproduce in the believer the powerful joint presence of both sexes that is found in certain androgynous primordial figures. Interpretations influenced by psychoanalysis have often been offered to explain these themes. Finally, in many cases castration is clearly demanded as an extreme form of mystical practice in currents of thought that celebrate abstention as a choice in life and as a condition of salvation.

[*Similar religious themes are discussed in* Virginity *and* Androgynes.]

BIBLIOGRAPHY

For a discussion of castration as a form of substitution sacrifice, see Henri Graillot's treatment of the myth and the ritual of Cybele and Attis in his now classic *Le culte de Cybèle, mère des dieux, à Rome et dans l'Empire romain* (Paris, 1912). For a more recent treatment, see Maarten J. Vermaseren's *Cybele and Attis: The Myth and the Cult* (London, 1977). Vermaseren compiles archaeological and literary documents concerning the cult in *Corpus cultus Cybelae Attidisque,* 4 vols. to date (Leiden, 1977–). See the volume edited by Hans Gustav Güterbock, *Kumarbi: Mythen vom churritischen Kronos aus den hethitischen Fragmenten* (Zurich, 1946), for a discussion of Ouranos and Kumarbi. A comparative study of Indian and Iranian ritual is *Mitra-Varuṇa,* 4th ed. (Paris, 1948), by Georges Dumézil. The theme of sexual abstinence is the topic of *La tradizione dell'enkrateia: Motivazioni ontologiche e protologiche,* edited by Ugo Bianchi (Rome, 1985).

DARIO M. COSI

CASUISTRY. Moral knowledge comprises general principles and propositions: for example, "Do unto others as you would have them do unto you," "Honest persons do not lie or steal," and so forth. However, moral knowledge also bears on choices to act in specific ways in unique situations. Thus, general principles must be transformed into particular choices: "I should not make this offensive remark about him because I would not want him to say such a thing about me in the hearing of those people," "I could not consider myself honest if I told her she was capable enough to deserve promotion," and so forth. Casuistry is concerned with the transition from general moral knowledge to particular moral choices. It can be defined as "the technique of reasoning whereby expert opinion is formulated concerning the existence and stringency of particular obligations in light of general moral maxims and under typical conditions of the agent and circumstances of the action."

Religious moralities that rest upon strong divine commands and prohibitions are fertile ground for a casuistry. Unless a divine imperative is couched in terms that direct a particular person to perform or refrain from a particular act at a particular time (e.g., "Moses, you must proclaim the Commandments to the people when you descend the mountain"), interpretation of the general statement of a divine command is necessary. Does, for example, the command "Thou shalt not kill" apply to David facing Goliath? However, it is not only divine commands and prohibitions that generate the need for casuistry. All statements of moral principle are expressed in universal terms; thus, any ethical system, if it is to take effect in the lives and actions of its adherents, must have its universal principles fitted to the various situations in which decisions are to be taken.

Casuistry in Non-Christian Contexts. In the three major ethical monotheisms, Judaism, Christianity, and Islam, certain persons have assumed the role of interpreting to the faithful the overarching moral injunctions of the Lord God. In Judaism, the written law, collected in the five books of the Torah, and the oral law, taught by Moses to the Israelites, were expounded by the scribes. These detailed interpretations of the law, collected in the two Talmuds, were themselves commented upon by the learned teachers of the people. This immense body of literature, as well as the intellectual tradition enshrined in it and continued by the rabbis in the life of the people of Israel, is called *halakhah* ("the way"). Concerned with fidelity to the law in every aspect of daily life, it is the casuistry of Judaism. However, within this tradition, a special form of reasoning, employing very sharp distinctions and clever logic, came to be called *pilpul* ("pepper"). Flourishing in the late Middle Ages, it was criticized by the great rabbi Eliyyahu ben Shelomoh Zalman (1720–1797) and others for twisting the plain truth "like shaping a wax nose." In this respect, *pilpul* resembles the Roman Catholic casuistry of the seventeenth century that gave rise to the pejorative connotation of the word.

Sharī'ah (lit., "the path toward water") designates the holy law of Islam revealed in the Qur'ān. More particularly, the word refers to forms of ritual and social behavior to be observed by the faithful. In the eighth and ninth centuries, schools of interpretation coalesced: they attempted to define precisely the exact content and stringency of the law. The teachers of Islam, *muftīs*, issued *fatwās*, considered opinions for the guidance of the faithful, distinguishing moral acts as obligatory, recommended, permitted, reprehensible, or forbidden. Since God's will is inscrutable, it is permitted to find *ḥiyal* ("stratagems") to avoid the letter of the law in favor of the spirit. Again, it is this aspect of Muslim casuistry that recalls the reprehensible approach that gave casuistry its bad name.

In the Western philosophical and theological tradition, two sources of casuistry are manifest. Socrates suggested cases to test whether the general definitions of virtue proposed by his interlocutors were adequate (e.g., in *Euthyphro, Laches*). Aristotle noted, as the premier methodological point of his *Nicomachean Ethics* that, while the nature of the human good and of virtue can be stated in general, "fine and just *actions* exhibit much variety and fluctuation" (*Nicomachean Ethics* 1.3). The Stoics proposed the most general precepts (e.g., "Follow nature"), and their opponents, particularly the Cynics, retorted with cases to show that rules of such generality could lead to no definite conclusions for action, or even to contradictory ones. Certain questions that become perennial first appear in this debate: for example, "Which of two shipwrecked men clinging to a spar has a right to it?" and "Should a merchant reveal defects of his merchandise?" Cicero recalls these questions and employs them to illustrate his theses regarding the priority of virtue over expedience. The third book of his *On Duties* is, in effect, the first book of casuistry in Western moral philosophy, even though it contains much material from authors of the Late Stoa.

Casuistry in the Christian Era. The teachings of Christ contain many "hard and impossible" commands: "If you will follow me, leave father and mother," "Turn the other cheek," "It is as hard for a rich man to enter heaven as for a camel to pass through the eye of a needle." Those dedicated to following his ideals of love and mercy had to discern how these difficult and paradoxical commands were to be carried out in daily life. They also faced the problem of whether they and all converts from Judaism and paganism were bound by the law of the Jews. There is therefore some casuistry in the Gospels, in the *Acts of the Apostles,* and in the epistles of Paul, all of it employing reasoning of the type familiar to the rabbinical schools. In the early centuries of the church, many Christian writers faced the problem of how the Christian should live. In *Can a Rich Man Be Saved?* Clement of Alexandria advises that the severe words of Jesus do not condemn those who, while rich in goods, are poor in spirit. Augustine's *On Lying* is a premier work of casuistry in which appears the question analyzed centuries later by Kant: "Should a person lie to conceal an innocent person from persecutors?"

In the history of Christianity, casuistry was given its greatest impetus by the practice of confession of sins and absolution by a priest. When private confession first appeared, in the sixth to the eighth centuries, books of direction were written for priests advising them what penances to impose. These "penitential books," while lacking precise analysis of moral acts, show an incipient sense of discrimination regarding the moral seriousness of certain acts and the circumstances that modify or excuse. In the twelfth century the canon law of the church, working with the large corpus of ecclesiastical case law, as well as with rediscovered Roman law, provided distinctions and categories for a more refined casuistry, as did the speculative theology of the thirteenth century. The books for confessors published from the late thirteenth through the fifteenth centuries manifest this influence in careful but succinct delineations of the nature of conscience, of law, and of imputability. These later volumes were stimulated by a universal law of the church requiring that all confess at least yearly and that the confessor deal with penitents "as a prudent physician of the spirit" (Fourth Lateran Council, 1215). These books present innumerable cases involving marriage, commerce, feudal obligations, and justice. In each example the purpose is to assist the confessor in judging whether a particular act that appeared to violate a moral commandment of church law did in fact do so in the particular circumstances of its commission. Raymond Pennafort, Peter the Cantor, Alain of Lille, William of Chobham, and Peter of Poitiers were the principal authors of this genre. In the fourteenth and fifteenth centuries, certain *summae* that presented material in alphabetical order (e.g., from *Absolution* to *Uxoricide*) became immensely popular: the *Summa Astesana*, the *Summa Sylvestrina*, and the *Summa Angelica.*

During the Reformation, casuistry was stimulated by several circumstances. The Council of Trent (1551) required Roman Catholics to confess sins by kind and number, a reaction to Protestant rejection of confession to a priest. The Society of Jesus, founded in 1540, dedicated itself to propagating the proper use of the sacrament of penance and to the education of the Catholic laity and clergy. In the religious turmoil of the last half of the sixteenth century, many settled moral positions were upset. Catholics faced novel problems of personal relationship (e.g., how to deal with non-Catholics) and of public moment (e.g., how to continue to observe traditional prohibitions regarding money lending in the new mercantile economy, how to govern newly discovered lands, whether to give allegiance to rulers of newly formed national states). The Jesuits and other theologians undertook to analyze these problems, both in speculative treatises and in more practical case presentation. They produced a vast literature, known collectively as "cases of conscience." In the century between 1565 and 1665, over six hundred titles appeared, many of them in multiple editions.

In 1663 Blaise Pascal, the great mathematician and physicist who had taken the side of the Jansenists (a Catholic sect of extreme piety and rigor) against the Jesuits, published the *Provincial Letters*. In this brilliant satire, he attacked the Jesuit casuists, citing case after case in which ingenious analysis led to outrageous moral conclusions. The casuists, with their clever distinctions, seemed able and willing to dispense with all moral probity, allowing killing, adultery, and lying, if only the circumstances were right. The criticism, justified to some extent, was too far-reaching: it condemned the entire enterprise of casuistry for the faults of some of its authors and the weakness of some aspects of its methodology. From that time onward, casuistry has carried the opprobrious sense of moral sophistry.

Casuistry continued to be an integral part of Catholic moral theology. Alphonsus Liguori (1696–1787), a most revered Catholic moralist, was a master casuist. By the mid-nineteenth century, however, casuistry had become sterile and was much criticized, within and without the church, for its failure to promote moral ideals and its dwelling on minimal obligation. Nevertheless, some fine casuistic analyses continued to appear: about the just war, the just wage, abortion, and so forth.

Protestant theology showed little interest in casuistry—indeed showed early antipathy. (Luther cast the *Summa Angelica* into the flames, calling it the "Summa Diabolica.") Anglican theologians engaged in a vigorous casuistry in the seventeenth century, with Jeremy Taylor and William Perkins being the leading authors. In the twentieth century, *Conscience and Its Problems* (1927), one of the very few modern English works on casuistry, was written by an Anglican theologian, Kenneth E. Kirk.

In the 1970s, interest in medical ethics led to the revival of a sort of casuistry both within and without the theological context. The occurrence of many cases of note, such as that of Karen Ann Quinlan, brought theological and philosophical moralists to analyze the ethical issues. The National Commission for Protection of Human Subjects of Biomedical and Behavioral Research (1974–1978) employed a method of case analysis to develop the ethics of research. In the 1980s, concern about nuclear armaments further stimulated casuistry, and a case analysis of various "scenarios" of defense was developed. *The Church and the Bomb* (1983), a publication of the Church of England, and the pastoral letter on nuclear warfare (1984) of the American Catholic bishops are both examples of sound casuistry.

Methodology of Casuistry. Casuistry differs from moral philosophy in a number of ways. The work of the casuist is discrimination; that of the moral philosopher, generalization. Casuists discuss moral problems; moral philosophers discuss moral reasoning. Casuists analyze the morality of choice in circumstances; moral philosophers analyze the meaning of moral principle in general. While the work of moral philosophers has been richly described and many methodologies have been proposed, the work of casuists—although we are all, in a sense, casuists in our personal moral deliberations—is hardly understood, and it has no accepted methodology. Even the casuists of the seventeenth century developed no overall method of resolution of moral problems. Inspection of their work, however, reveals the outline of their method.

Casuists developed positions by first stating a case in which the moral obligations entailed by a rule were most clear and then moving, step by step, to more complex cases. These steps were taken by adding various circumstances and weighing their relevance to the stringency of the rule. They assessed the degree of credence that various options deserved and the consequent weight of moral obligation. They aimed at resolving the case not by settling theoretical problems but by practical advice concerning how seriously a person involved in certain sorts of circumstances should consider himself bound by or excused from the moral principles generally incumbent. The strength of the casuists' method lay in an appreciation of exceptions and excuses generated by different circumstances; the weakness lay in the absence of any theoretically established boundaries of this appreciation. Casuistry at its best is vigorous moral common sense; at its worst, it is moral sleight of hand.

[*See also* Christian Ethics.]

BIBLIOGRAPHY

Häring, Bernhard. *The Law of Christ*, vol. 1, *General Moral Theology*. Translated by Edwin G. Kaiser. Westminster, Md., 1961. See especially chapter 1.

Jonsen, Albert R., and Stephen Toulmin. *The Abuse of Casuistry*. Berkeley, forthcoming.

Kirk, Kenneth E. *Conscience and Its Problems: An Introduction to Casuistry*. London, 1927.

Long, Edward L. *Conscience and Compromise: An Approach to Protestant Casuistry*. Philadelphia, 1954.

ALBERT R. JONSEN

CATHARI. Catharism (from *cathari,* "the pure") was distinguished from the other heresies of the Middle Ages by its rejection of basic Christian beliefs, although its adherents claimed that in their pursuit of a pure life they were the only true Christians. In contrast to the Waldensians and other gospel-inspired movements of the twelfth century, the basis of Catharism was a non-Christian dualism deriving ultimately from gnosticism. In place of the Christian conception of an inherently good universe that was wholly God's creation and embraced all existence, spiritual and material alike, this dualism posited two principles: one good, governing all that was spiritual, the other evil, responsible for the material world, including man's body. The consequence was the denial of the central Christian doctrines of the incarnation, Christ's two natures and the virgin birth, bodily resurrection, and the sacraments, all of which involve the acceptance of matter as part of God's design, as well as nullifying the doctrine of the Trinity and the very idea of God's omnipotence.

By the time it reached the West from Byzantium, Catharism had taken two forms, a mitigated and a radical dualism. Mitigated dualism originated with the Bogomils in Bulgaria in the tenth century, spreading to the Byzantine empire, whence it was carried to western Europe. It was closer to Christianity in recognizing only one God, the good God who had created everything good, including Satan, who had been his eldest son Lucifer before he had rebelled against his father. Satan had therefore corrupted himself by his own free will, and that freedom was held, somewhat inconsistently, to belong also to the souls that Satan subsequently imprisoned in bodies. Adapting the Old Testament account of creation in *Genesis,* the Bogomils, and later the Cathari, substituted Satan for God as creator of the firmament and the visible world, although Satan made it from preexisting matter created by God from nothing.

The world was therefore Satan's domain, and the Old Testament was the witness to his tyrannical rule. Hence the Cathari rejected the Old Testament as God's word—one of their distinguishing traits. Although they accepted the New Testament, its meaning was transformed as part of a syncretism of Christian and non-Christian beliefs, expressed as allegories and fables that were the preserve of the initiated—the perfect. Catharism thus not only had its own tenets and practices but also its own canonical literature.

The only thing that Satan had been unable to make was the human soul; it came from the angels and was variously described in the different Cathar fables as having been captured or stolen from heaven and then put in a body. The first two imprisoned souls were Adam and Eve, who by succumbing to Satan's temptations, depicted in strongly sexual imagery, became the progenitors of the human race. The penalty for their fall, which for the Cathari was identified particularly with sexuality, was the procreation of individual souls with their bodies, so that all men were born as souls imprisoned in a body. The whole of Cathar religious practice was directed toward releasing the soul from the body, thereby liberating it from Satan's rule and enabling it to return to its place in heaven. That was also the reason why God, taking pity on the fallen angels, represented by mankind suffering for Adam and Eve's sin, had sent not only Christ, his second son, but also the Holy Spirit into the world to help redeem them. Although they, too, according to some mitigated dualists, were part of God's nature, they were inferior to God. Moreover, as a spirit, Christ in his human form did not have a real body: it was either, according to some, a phantom, or, according to others, some kind of angelic covering. Whatever the case, though, the human Christ of the Cathari was not the word made flesh. He had not been born of Mary but had entered through her ear. Nor did he suffer on the cross, another of the material objects, together with images and the material properties of the Christian sacraments, rejected by the Cathari. The true Christ suffered for mankind in heaven. In this world his role was to show the way and reestablish the truth of God's word. In that sense there was, in keeping with their docetic belief, only one Christ, in heaven; he was not to be found in churches, which were not his house: one more Cathar trait, shared with the Waldensians, although by the late twelfth century in Languedoc, the Cathari did use churches as meeting places for their ceremonies. The struggle of the soul with Satan would finally end not as in the orthodox Christian belief, in the body's resurrection with the soul, but in the body's destruction with all of Satan's handiwork and the soul's ascent into heaven.

The main divergence of radical dualism from the mitigated form lay in its making the opposition between the principles of good and evil absolute and eternal. Good and evil and their creations had always coexisted. And as the good God's creation was heaven, so the visible world created by Satan was hell. Hence to live in this world was to be in hell, in man's case through having a body in which, as with the mitigated dualists, Satan had initially imprisoned the souls of angels taken from heaven. Free will thus played no part in Satan's original fall; and the power of God was correspondingly restricted in never having had control over evil, which was completely autonomous. Nor did individuals have the means of directly returning to God. Although Christ taught the way of salvation, individuals had first to undergo a series of reincarnations until they came to recognize evil by becoming perfect, thereby freeing their souls from the devil. Christ himself, and generally Mary, were regarded as angels, neither having a real body. For both absolute and mitigated dualists, as indeed for orthodox Christians, all souls would at the end be saved or damned. But for the absolute dualists free will seems to have played no part in salvation. At the end the visible world would fall into material chaos from which all souls would have departed, whereas for the mitigated dualists Satan would be captured and all things would return to order.

Accordingly the Cathari shunned all contact with the material, beyond that which was unavoidable to their existence as human beings. That meant the rejection of marriage, of all foods that were the product of sexual generation, of all material elements in worship, and of all involvement in things of this world, whether love of material goods or worldly behavior, including any kind of violence or taking of life, the exercise of jurisdiction, or the swearing of oaths. The result was an extreme asceticism and austerity, which in their moral and practical expression had close affinities with the Christian ideal of evangelical perfection. The Cathari exhibited the same sense of material renunciation and spiritual devotion, and that probably more than anything else accounted for the hold that the Cathari were able to gain in southern France and northern Italy in the twelfth and thirteenth centuries.

Because the demands of Catharism were exceptional, strict practice was confined to a small minority of adepts, the perfect. They represented the Cathar hierarchy; unlike the Christian hierarchy, however, they were a very small elite who had to prove themselves all the time. The mass of ordinary Cathar believers were able to live ordinary lives while accepting the spiritual ministrations and authority of the perfect.

The great dividing line between the perfect and the believers was the reception of the *consolamentum:* the initiation rite of spiritual baptism by the laying on of hands that admitted the recipient into the ranks of the perfect. It was usually performed after a year's probation and the full revelation of Cathar teaching, which was not accessible to the ordinary adherents. Once received, the *consolamentum* remitted the consoled's sins and the consequences of the soul's imprisonment in a body, reuniting his soul with his spirit in heaven and releasing him from Satan's rule. It was then that his testing really began. Any lapse into forbidden sins—and for the Cathari they were all equal—meant the loss of the *consolamentum* both for the sinner and for those who had been consoled by him. He could be reconsoled only after severe penance. But so long as he remained firm to his obedience, he was effectively among the saved, one of the perfect, and revered as such by ordinary believers. For the latter a special *consolamentum* was administered before death to remit their sins and bring salvation; should they recover, a further *consolamentum* was needed. The *consolamentum* thus conferred a gnostic-like certainty of salvation which challenged orthodox Christian revelation.

The precise date of the appearance of Catharism in western Europe has been keenly debated; there is no universal agreement even now. The generally accepted view is that the first firm evidence of Cathari appears at Cologne in 1143 or 1144. That opinion could well be modified in the future. What can be said is that by the 1150s they were in southern France and northern Italy; by the 1160s they were firmly established in both regions. These became their two chief areas, especially Languedoc in the lands of the count of Toulouse. In 1176 a great council of Cathari is reported to have been held at Saint-Félix-de-Caraman where, in addition to an already existing Cathar bishopric at Albi, three more bishoprics were established for Cathar territories. It was from Albi that the southern French Cathari received their name of Albigensians (Albigenses). By 1170 they had become the main heresy to be combated. The papacy sent a succession of preaching missions, including Waldensians, Cistercians, and the founder of the Dominican order, Dominic. As early as 1181 Alexander III's cardinal legate, Henry, abbot of Clairvaux (before whom Valdès also appeared), besieged a castle at Lavaux sheltering two heretics. Alexander's successor, Innocent III, intensified the pressure, using both sanctions and persuasion. Matters came to a head in January 1208, when one of Innocent's legates, Peter Castelnau, was assassinated. Innocent, who had already called upon the king of France to make war against the Cathari, then launched his own crusade under the abbot of Cîteaux. That marked the beginning of the Albigensian crusade, in which the lands of the count of Toulouse were overrun. Although the crusade severely weakened the Cathari, they survived and regrouped. It was not until 1243 that they were effectively destroyed as an organized church with the capture of over 200 perfect at Montségur. Their strength had lain in the widespread support they had received in both town and countryside from the nobles as well as from artisans and members of the professions. For a time before the Albigensian crusade they had overshadowed the Roman Catholic church in southern France.

In Italy, the Cathari never enjoyed the same cohesion as those in Languedoc. They were riven by the conflicts that began early in the 1160s between adherents of the two forms of dualism. They were also mainly located in the cities, where they owed their survival to the opposition of the cities to both imperial and papal authority. It was only in the second half of the thirteenth century, after the ending of the wars between the popes and Frederick II, the German emperor, that the way was cleared for papal action against the Cathari. A series of trials in the larger Italian cities had largely extirpated them by the beginning of the fourteenth century, at which time they also disappeared from Languedoc.

[*See also* Waldensians *and the biography of Dominic.*]

BIBLIOGRAPHY

Borst, Arno. *Die Katharer.* Stuttgart, 1953. The standard work on the subject.

Lambert, Malcolm. *Medieval Heresy: Popular Movements from Bogomil to Hus.* London and New York, 1977. The fullest and most up-to-date account of medieval popular heresies. Particularly strong on the Cathari.

Moore, R. I., ed. *The Birth of Popular Heresy.* London, 1975. A representative selection of translated sources, mainly from the twelfth century, with a useful introduction.

Obolensky, Dimitri. *The Bogomils: A Study in Balkan Neo-Manichaeism.* Cambridge, 1948. The standard account in English.

Russell, Jeffrey B. *Dissent and Reform in the Early Middle Ages.* Berkeley, 1965. A useful, wide-ranging survey of early medieval heresies to the end of the twelfth century.

Thouzellier, Christine. *Catharisme et Valdéisme en Languedoc.* Louvain and Paris, 1969. A very full analysis of the sources.

Wakefield, Walter L. *Heresy, Crusade and Inquisition in Southern France, 1100–1250.* Berkeley, 1974. A clear, brief account with a good bibliography.

Wakefield, Walter L., and Austin P. Evans, eds. *Heresies of the High Middle Ages.* New York and London, 1969. The largest collection of translated sources, particularly valuable for their fullness.

GORDON LEFF

CATHARSIS. The Greek *katharsis* is an action noun corresponding to a verb that literally means "to prune, to clean, to remove dirt or a blemish [*katharma*] for the purpose of rendering some thing, place, or animate being pure [*katharos*]." As denoting the general process of purification, *catharsis* could of course be applied to a very broad range of phenomena in the history of religions. [*See* Purification.] In this article, however, the focus will be specifically on the Greek conception. Although the meaning of *catharsis* and the exact techniques or modalities of purification *(katharmoi)* differ according to context, the sense of *catharsis* always remains negative: it refers to separating, evacuating, or releasing. Whether performed in a strictly ritual setting or understood as a spiritual concept, catharsis maintains this negative meaning of ridding either oneself or an object of something impure or unclean.

Catharsis originally appears as a ritualized process of quasi-material purification that makes use of a variety of substances as purifying agents. Chief among these are the elements water, fire, and sulfur, followed by oil, clay, and bran. [*See also* Water *and* Fire.] Certain other vegetable substances, such as laurel, myrtle, and olive are also used, especially as prophylactics (coronets of leaves) or as supports of cleansing waters (aspersions). Since ceremonial purifications are usually conducted out in the open, the element of air also plays a role.

In the selection and use of such purifying agents, the symbolism of numbers sometimes comes into play, especially of the numbers three, seven, and nine. The gestures involved in aspersions, ablutions, fumigations, and the like, may be repeated a set number of times; a definite number of sacrificial victims may be required; and even the source of the water used in the rite may be determined on the basis of numbers (water coming from a river that arises from three springs was preferred).

When a sacrificial victim was required for purification the pig was the most frequently sacrificed animal. However, once a year, the Athenians purified their city with the sacrifice of two human victims, *pharmakoi,* one bearing the guilt of all the Athenian men, the other bearing the guilt of all the Athenian women. As a general rule whatever served for the purification had to be completely destroyed. Human victims were burned.

The idea of defilement is closely linked to the perception of a disturbance of the natural order or a breach of the day-to-day routine. Contacts or experiences that call into question the physical integrity of the individual or of the general environment require a catharsis. Since health is understood to be normal, illness is seen as something abnormal, as a physical or mental stain requiring purification. Madness, too, and breaches of morality are seen as illnesses and therefore as defilements; thus an army in violation of the law or in revolt can be called back to order, cured of its illness, through purifications. Examples of this "psychosomatic" use of purification are numerous. The Proetides were purified of their madness by the magus Melampus. To cure the Lacedaemonian women struck with nymphomania required the intervention of a *kathartēs* Bakis, delegated by Apollo, the god of healing and purification. The women of Samos were liberated from their sexual exaltation thanks to the *katharmos* of Dexikreon.

The Bacchants were liberated from their maladies quite differently, however—in the orgy, which temporarily identified them with Dionysos, the god of *mania.* The Dionysian orgy is cathartic to the extent that it releases the urges repressed by social and moral constraints. The ritual release of the Dionysian rite is a purification: "Blessed are the dancers and those who are purified, who dance on the hill in the holy dance of god" (Euripides, *The Bacchae* 75ff.). Intoxication from wine or from dance purges the individual of irrational impulses which, if repressed, would be noxious. Ritual madness can also cure internal madness. Music, too, can have a cathartic function (Quintilianus Aristides, *Peri mousikēs* 3.23). The Aristotelian theory of tragedy—initially Dionysiac—defined catharsis from this same perspective: The satiation of the passions by the spectacle of the theater is a therapeutic based, like the Bacchic *ekstasis*, on purgative and liberating homeopathy.

Contact with death requires purification, whether it is a death one has caused, the death of a family member, or any other contact with the dead. The murderer, whether the act was voluntary or involuntary, is defiled. Herakles had to be purified of the deaths of Iphitos, the Meropes, the sons of Proteus, and the centaurs; Achilles of the murder of Thersites (according to Arctinos of Miletus); Jason and Medea of the murder of Apsyrtos; and Theseus of the murder of the Pallantides. In certain cases, only the gods can cleanse the criminal of his wrongdoing. Ixion was apparently the first murderer purified by Zeus. Patricide constituted a particularly grave case, whether of Oedipus or Orestes; the latter was purified by Apollo himself. The stain of death may also be collective, as in the case of the Athenians after the deaths of Androgeus or the Cylonians. In this case a collective purification may be necessary. Even the quelling of malefic creatures such as the brigands killed by Theseus, the dragon killed by Cadmus, or the serpent Python killed by Apollo demands purification.

However, Homer presents us with a somewhat different picture. Odysseus, after having executed the suitors of Penelope, asks that sulfur and fire be brought "to disperse the bad air" (*Odyssey*, 22.481). This is meant to purify the house but not particularly those who have been killed or have done the killing. It is as if the cadaver that defiles a house takes precedence over the idea of moral responsibility for homicide.

Throughout antiquity the sentiment prevails that the contact with death, the presence of the dead under the family roof, demands purification. Iamblichus writes around 300 CE: "It is impious to touch human bodies from which the soul has departed," since "the nonliving mark the living with a stain." Thus the domicile of the deceased should be ritually disinfected. In the morning, vases of lustral water that had to be borrowed from another house were placed at the door of the deceased's home. These were then interred with the dead. The funeral and the subsequent rites had the ultimate purpose of purifying the family and consecrating the boundary that would henceforth separate the dead from the living; any dead person deprived of a tomb thus remained a *katharma*.

Certain sacred places prohibit the presence of tombs. Pisistratus, instructed by the oracles, purified the island of Delos by having the dead disinterred "anywhere in the region within visual range of the sanctuary" (Herodotus, 1.64). Later, in 426, all of the dead found on the island were disposed of (Thucydides, 1.8, 3.104, 5.1). The authorities of Eleusis had the body of a dead man found on the plain of Rharos removed and had the entire plain purified by a *kathartēs*. Contact with the world of the dead was not permissible without prior lustrations (Homer, *Odyssey* 11.25ff.; Lucian, *Nekuomanteia* 7). Conversely, one who was resuscitated had to be washed and nursed like a newborn (Plutarch, *Quaestiones Romanae* 5). Even encountering the dead in a dream requires purification (Aristophanes, *Ranae* 1340). Finally, contact with and, particularly, the eating of dead animals were impure in the eyes of the Orphics, the Pythagoreans, the initiates of the cult of Zagreus (Euripides, *The Cretans* 472), as well as for candidates for certain initiations (Porphyry, *De abstinentia* 4.16; Apuleius, *Metamorphoses* 11.23.2). There was also a blood taboo, which legitimated excluding criminals from the Eleusinian mysteries, but the Lesser Mysteries of Agra prepared them for initiation into the Greater.

The blood taboo explains the relationship of menstruation, generation, and parturition to catharsis. [*See also* Blood.] Hippocrates gives the menstrual periods the name *katharsis* because they relieve women of their menstrual blood. The houses of women giving birth also require purification. Miscarriages require forty days of lustrations. When Delos was purified in 426 all lying-in on the island was forbidden. To approach a woman in labor was, for the superstitious character in Theophrastus (*Characteres* 16.9), as serious as walking on a grave or touching the dead (the two injunctions are often in tandem). The initiates of Ida whom Euripides places on stage in *The Cretans* avoid "assisting at birth or approaching a coffin." The newborn, too, must be purified. By means of several lustrations the Amphidromies of the Greeks and the rites of the *dies lustricus* of the Romans integrate the newborn into the community and preserve him from evil spirits attracted by the blood present at birth.

Sexual contacts demand catharsis just as those with death or the dead. Anyone wishing to approach the chapel of Men-Lunus had to be purified if he had eaten pork or garlic or touched a woman or corpses. Matrimonial rites derive from concerns connected with the taboos of blood, sex, or life. They consist of preliminary lustrations (baths, aspersions, circulating fumigations, the wearing of white vestments and of crowns), which were to safeguard the couple (Euripides, *Iphigenia in Aulis* 1111; Valerius Flaccus, *Argonautica* 8.245f.).

More radically, life itself can appear impure, inasmuch as life comes from a mixture of body and soul, Dionysiac and Titanic elements which, according to Orphism, are implicit in the human makeup. Life is also impure when compared to that of the gods. Contact with the gods thus requires certain lustrations. Access to sacred enclosures (and especially to the *aduton*, the inner sanctúm) is forbidden to those who have not undergone the ritual catharsis. Pools of water for this purpose are located at the entrances to sanctuaries, reminiscent of the holy water fonts of Christian churches. The sacrificial ceremony itself includes purifications of the officiates, of the participants, the victim, the liturgical vessel, the instruments of immolations, and the altar near which the animal is to be slaughtered.

The initiations, which permit man to establish a closer bond with the world of the gods, indeed, to be assimilated to the gods in certain cases, impose on the candidate a rigorous catharsis. Examples include the rituals of Andania and Agra, various types of abstinences, baths in the sea with a sacrificial pig for the candidates for the mysteries of Eleusis, and the continences, abstinences, and ablutions for the initiates of Isis, Mithra, and Dionysos. The Bacchic mysteries could even be regarded as being essentially cathartic. These rites suppose that man himself is too unclean to enter into relationship with the gods. Moreover, he cannot himself proceed with his own purification; he needs to have recourse to the techniques of a priest or of a *kathartēs*.

The philosophers, however, shifted emphasis in the understanding of catharsis, viewing it more in terms of spiritual purification. An inscription at Epidaurus recommends that one approach the gods with a pure spirit (Porphyry, *De abstinentia* 2.19; cf. Cicero, *De legibus* 2.24: "The law bids one approach the gods purely, with a spirit that is in which all things are"). The speculations of the Orphics were particularly important to this change of emphasis. Orphic mythology places a hereditary taint on humanity that has been compared to a sort of original sin. It is said that Zeus, hurling a bolt of lightning, reduced the race of Titans to cinders for having eaten Dionysos Zagreus. The human race is then born from these cinders. Consequently, human beings must be delivered from this Titanic contamination in order to recover their true Bacchic essence. Toward this end, Orphic catharsis serves to actually by reinstate the divine life through the practice of continual asceticism. Similarly, Plato (*Phaedo*, 67c) refers to an "ancient tradition" for the purification *par excellence:* the separation of the soul from the body. The *kathartēs* whom Plato ridicules in *The Republic* (364e) and the Orpheotelestes of Theophrastus (*Characteres* 16.11) offer ritual recipes. The "Orphic life" implies a *spiritual* discipline, a kind of personal sacrifice. Similarly, the Platonists and, later, the Neoplatonists, were to preach the liberation of the spirit. This catharsis is reserved, however, for the elite sages, and with the last of the Neoplatonists the techniques of theurgy tended to overshadow intellectual purification.

After physical death (which the philosopher can anticipate while still in the body), the soul must be stripped of the garments that it has donned in its descent through the planetary spheres (Cumont, 1949, pp. 358, 364; Festugière, 1953, pp. 128ff.). Posthumous catharsis, as understood by the Orphics and Neoplatonists, consists in separating the soul from all heterogeneous elements. Vergil's hell (*Aeneid*, 6.740ff.), which tries the souls by wind, water, and fire, reminds us of the *katharmoi* of Empedocles (frag. 115). Seneca (*Ad Marciam de consolatione* 25.1), by contrast, gives a moral explanation for posthumous purification. The funeral pyre is thought by some to purify the soul from the body. Lightning is also thought to confer apotheosis (Cumont, 1949, p. 330). For others, the universe as a whole is subject to periodic purifications, which in Stoic cosmology consist of deluges and conflagrations (Origen, *Against Celsus* 4.12, 4.21, 4.64, 4.69).

From birth to death, through marriage and initiations, catharsis thus sanctioned the major steps of life. From its therapeutic, magic, or prophylactic functions, catharsis tended to shift in time to a moral and mystical exercise, especially in stipulating the conditions for salvation or apotheosis through radical ablation or liberation.

BIBLIOGRAPHY

Bouché-Leclercq, Auguste. "Lustratio." In *Dictionnaire des antiquités grecques et romains* (1904), edited by Charles Daremberg et al., vol. 3. Graz, 1963.

Boyancé, Pierre. *Le culte des muses chez les philosophes grecs.* Paris, 1937.

Boyancé, Pierre. "Platon et les cathartes orphiques." *Revue des études grecques* 55 (1942): 217–235.

Cumont, Franz. *Lux perpetua.* Paris, 1949.

Dodds, E. R. *The Greeks and the Irrational.* Berkeley, 1951.

Fehrle, Eugen. *Die kultische Keuschheit im Altertum.* Giessen, 1910.

Festugière, A.-J. *La révélation d'Hermès Trismégiste,* vol. 3. Paris, 1953.

Festugière, A.-J. *Études de religion grecque et hellénistique.* Paris, 1972.

Jeanmaire, Henri. *Dionysos: Histoire du culte de Bacchus.* Paris, 1951.

Moulinier, Louis. *Le pur et l'impur dans la pensée des Grecs, d'Homère à Aristote.* Paris, 1952.

Nilsson, Martin P. *Geschichte der griechischen Religion,* vol. 2, *Die hellenistische und römische Zeit.* 3d rev. ed. Munich, 1974.

Parker, R. *Miasma: Pollution and Purification in Early Greek Religion.* Oxford, 1983.

Places, Édouard des. *La religion grecque.* Paris, 1969.

Rohde, Edwin. *Psyche: The Cult of Souls and Belief in Immortality among the Greeks* (1925). Translated by W. B. Hillis. London, 1950.

Spiegel, N. "The Nature of Katharsis according to Aristotle: A Reconsideration." *Revue belge de philologie et d'histoire* 43 (1965): 22–39.

Trouillard, Jean. *La purification plotinienne.* Paris, 1955.

Turcan, Robert. "Un rite controuvé de l'initiation dionysiaque." *Revue de l'histoire des religions* 158 (1960): 129–144.

Wächter, Theodor. *Reinheitsvorschriften im griechischen Kult.* Giessen, 1910.

ROBERT TURCAN

Translated from French by Marilyn Gaddis Rose and William H. Snyder

CATHEDRAL. *See* Basilica, Cathedral, and Church.

CATHERINE OF SIENA (1347–1380), Caterina da Siena; Italian mystic and Christian saint. The particular genius of the spirituality of Catherine of Siena had its earliest beginnings in a visionary experience of Christ when she was six years old, and her subsequent childish yet totally serious vow of virginity. She persisted in her purpose in spite of family opposition until she was accepted as one of the Mantellate, a Dominican third-order group comprising, up to then, only widows. For about three years thereafter she gave herself to prayer and asceticism in almost complete seclusion, until her very prayer (which had become deeply mystical) led her out, first to serve the poor and the sick in her own city, and gradually into wider and wider spheres.

She had learned in her solitude to read, and now she became an enthusiastic conversationalist, feeding insatiably on the theological knowledge of friends she attracted among Dominicans, Augustinians, Franciscans, and Jesuits. She began, too, to draw as disciples people from every walk of life, a circle she would call her *famiglia.* She found an ideal mentor in the Dominican friar Raymond of Capua. Raymond was an astute theologian and diplomat, under whose guidance and in whose company Catherine's scope broadened to include the ecclesiastical and the political—in her mind always of one piece with the spiritual, and all ultimately oriented to the same spiritual ends.

Unlike her contemporary Birgitta of Sweden, Catherine was an ardent promoter and recruiter for the crusade projected by Pope Gregory XI and his successor, Urban VI. A holy war seemed to her a perfect means of uniting in a common cause Christians now at odds among themselves and with the papacy. She saw Palestine as a Christian trust, and she believed with many that the advance of the Turks toward Europe must be halted. A main object of the crusade would be the conversion of the Muslims, who would in their new faith be a leaven to reinvigorate a sick church. And it would provide her and others (she apparently intended to go along) the opportunity to pay Christ "blood for blood."

It was the dissension between Florence and Gregory XI that brought Catherine to that city in 1376 to attempt to mediate a reconciliation. On the mandate, probably, of only certain Guelphs she traveled to Avignon (where the popes had resided since 1309) with no official credentials, only to be ignored by Florentine ambassadors who came later. In subsequent efforts, also, she failed to influence the Florentines significantly in this dispute, which was to her essentially religious but was to them a matter of political survival.

Once rebuffed by Florence, Catherine turned her energy toward the two issues she considered the root of the dissension: the continuing absence of the popes from Rome and clerical corruption. If the pope would return to Rome, she reasoned, Christians would have no more cause for rebellion, and reform could begin. Gregory XI had in fact so resolved but had repeatedly, in fear, put off taking action. Catherine can surely be credited with finally moving him. In fact, when dissent deepened after his return to Rome, many including the pope blamed Catherine's advice.

Gregory XI died on 27 March 1378, and within months his successor, Urban VI, was being denounced by a growing number of the cardinals, who in September of that year elected Clement VII as antipope, thus effectively splitting the church. At Urban's invitation Catherine came to Rome to support his cause. Though her health was by this time failing under her fierce asceticism and exertion, she continued to pray and work tirelessly for unity and reform, both of which seemed to her ever more elusive. The weight of this sense of failure surely contributed to her early death on 29 April 1380. She was canonized in 1461 and proclaimed a doctor of the church in 1970; she and Teresa of Ávila were the first women to receive that title.

Catherine used letters prodigiously as a favored vehicle of influence. The nearly four hundred letters that have been collected and edited date mostly from 1375 to 1380. They are addressed to persons as diverse as popes, high-ranking clergy, nobles, relatives, disciples, prisoners, and prostitutes. Unfortunately, the early compilers' purposes of simple edification led them to delete much that was personal from the letters, but still they open a revealing window on Catherine's evolving thought and on her warm and spontaneous personality.

In 1377 and 1378, in addition to all her other activities, Catherine composed the work since known as *The Dialogue* (because she cast it as an exchange between God and herself). Her intent in writing it was to share with her disciples and others the insights she had gained in prayer and in her own experience. In it she approaches the way of holiness from several vantage points, and develops at length the themes of God's providence, the role of Christ as redeemer and mediator, and the church. Finally, during the last three and a half years of Catherine's life, her secretaries sometimes recorded her prayers when she spoke in ecstasy. Twenty-six such prayers have been preserved.

Through her reading and her associations, Catherine gained a knowledge of the Christian tradition remarkable in an otherwise unschooled person. In her works she draws freely not only from scripture but from Augustine, Gregory the Great, Bernard, and Thomas Aquinas (to name only those most frequently reflected), as well as from contemporaries such as Ubertino of Casale, Domenico Cavalca, Iacopo Passavanti, and Giovanni Colombini. Her own writing, however, is not speculative or systematic or analytical. Rather, she synthesizes into an integrated whole all of the various aspects of Christian faith on which she dwells. Her purposes are eminently practical, her tone warm and personal. She resorts for clarification not to conceptual argumentation but to literary images, developing the meaning of each as she goes and interweaving them one with another.

The central principles around which Catherine's teaching revolves are everywhere evident in her writings: God alone is absolute being, and God's being is at once love and truth—love that is truth and truth that is love. When humankind cut itself off from God by sin, God's endlessly creative and re-creative being took flesh in Jesus Christ, who in himself repaired the breach. The foundation of all spiritual life is knowledge of oneself in God and of God in oneself. Human nature is God's creation and as such is essentially good, and Catherine is therefore understanding and compassionate of human weakness even as she denounces sin. Desire for the truth and love that is God puts all in order, and what God asks of the human heart is infinite desire.

BIBLIOGRAPHY

Works by Catherine of Siena. The most complete recent edition of Catherine's letters is *Le lettere di S. Caterina da Siena,* 4 vols., translated and edited by Niccolò Tommaseo, revised by Piero Misciattelli (1860; reprint, Florence, 1940). The first volume of the only truly critical edition was prepared by Eugenio Dupré Theseider, *Epistolario di Santa Caterina da Siena,* vol. 1 (Rome, 1940); the work on this critical edition is being pursued by Antonio Volpato. A complete English translation from the critical edition is in progress under my editorship. I have translated Giuliana Cavallini's critical editions of *Il dialogo* (Rome, 1968) and *Le orazioni* (Rome, 1978) as *The Dialogue* (New York, 1980) and *The Prayers of Catherine of Siena* (New York, 1983), respectively.

Works about Catherine of Siena. A useful primary source for the life of Catherine of Siena is Raymond of Capua's *The Life of Catherine of Siena* (1385–1389), translated by Conleth Kearns (Wilmington, Del., 1980); other biographies in English are *History of St. Catherine of Siena and Her Companions,* by Augusta Theodosia Drane (London, 1899), good for its inclusion of primary source material not otherwise available in English; *Saint Catherine of Siena: A Study in the Religion, Literature and History of the Fourteenth Century in Italy,* by Edmund G. Gardner (New York, 1907), complete on historical contexts and well indexed; and Arrigo Levasti's *My Servant, Catherine,* translated by Dorothy M. White (Westminster, Md., 1954), which concentrates on Catherine's psychology and spirituality and also gives an excellent bibliography. Eugenio Dupré Theseider's entry "Catherine da Siena, Santa," in *Dizionario biografico degli Italiani* (Rome, 1979), covers very well Catherine's life and theology, including debated points, and offers a very comprehensive bibliography.

SUZANNE NOFFKE, O.P.

CATHOLIC CHURCH. *See* Roman Catholicism.

CATS seem to be surrounded by a special power. Their graceful movements, their liveliness at night, and their inaudible steps as well as their independent spirit have enchanted poets and painters and storytellers in many cultures, but these very traits account also for the aversion many people have had to them. Throughout history, cats have rarely been regarded with indifference; they have generally been considered either sacred or demonic. The earliest known center of their veneration, and probably also of their domestication, was ancient Egypt, where they are documented from 1600 BCE onward. Bast, a popular goddess of pleasure, was represented with a cat's head. Numerous sacred cats lived around her sanctuary in Bubastis, and thousands of mummified cats have been found in that area.

Other goddesses with feline attributes have also been

connected with cats. In a Roman myth, Diana assumes the form of a cat, and in Germanic mythology, Freya's carriage is drawn by cats. In Bengali Hinduism, Śaṣṭi rides or stands on a (usually black) cat. Should a mother be disrespectful to the goddess, a cat will kill her children; such revenge can be averted by pouring sour milk over a black cat and licking it off.

Cats are frequently perceived as malevolent creatures. The idea that a cat can "suck the breath" of sleeping children (i.e., suffocate them) is widely prevalent, and in some myths the cat is represented even as a bloodsucking ogre. Some people think that to swallow a cat's hair will result in tuberculosis. But a cat's tooth can serve as a talisman, for cats have not only "nine lives" but supernatural powers. In Ireland, for example, it is thought that the devil can assume the form of a cat; in China, it is believed that cats can see spirits at night and that a dead cat can turn into a demon. In many places it is thought that cats can sense the presence of death, that they can smell the guiding spirit come to conduct away the departing soul. Because of their supernatural abilities, cats are connected with witches and sorcerers; in fact, they are—especially black ones—typical familiars of witches. In medieval Europe, every owner of such an animal was therefore suspect.

As an agent of the supernatural, the cat became a sacrificial animal in some cultures. In medieval Europe, cats were killed as an expiation in times of plague or were thrown into the Saint John's fire at the summer solstice. As late as the mid-seventeenth century, in the ceremony of the Taigheirm in the West Highlands of Scotland, black cats were roasted on spits to raise the infernal spirits. In Japan, however, as in ancient Egypt and other cultures, it has been thought inadvisable to kill a cat, owing to its special power. Such an act would bring misfortune, or would have to be atoned for (in Muslim Bengal, with five pounds of salt).

In European lore, cats can function as house goblins and are also counted among the shapeshifters; they can assume enormous proportions in case of danger or in order to rescue their benefactor from equally enormous rats. Thus their role can be beneficial as well: friendly cat demons can produce gold and treasures for those who have been kind to them, and cats—especially tricolored cats (which are believed to be always female)—can protect a house from fire and guarantee marital happiness.

In many cultures it is considered a bad omen to see a cat, especially a black one, when leaving a house; likewise, to dream of a black cat, or to cross its path, means misfortune. But the black cat's body serves both medical and magical purposes; a meal of cat's brains may arouse love in someone, or strengthen a man's sexual power, or restore sight. Pulverized cat's gall rubbed into the eyes enables one to see at night, or to see *jinn*. Certain parts of a black cat, prepared with other ingredients, can make a person invisible.

The behavior of cats is also often regarded as an omen. In Germany, if a cat washes itself, a guest will come. In China, the arrival of a strange cat in a house portends poverty, because that cat is believed to have a premonition that many mice will come to live in that house. The cat's sensitivity to atmospheric changes has led, in many places, to belief that it can predict—or, indeed, is responsible for—the weather. In Turkey, if a cat purrs loudly, a severe winter is impending; in England, if a cat sits with its back to the fire, there will be frost. In Java and Sumatra, bathing two cats or throwing one into a river can bring rain.

Folklore often talks about the hypocritical cat. "The cat weeps at the mouse's death," according to a Chinese proverb. The story of the "repentant" cat that appears as a pious ascetic in order to cheat the mice has been told from ancient Egypt to modern Mongolia, and it occurs frequently in Persian literature (see 'Ubayd-i Zakānī's little epic *Mouse and Cat* from the fourteenth century). Hence, in Persian and Ottoman Turkish urban poetry, the term *cat* is sometimes used to characterize a sly person of high rank. The friendship of a cat with a mouse or other weaker animal, or with its archenemy the dog, lasts only so long as both are in danger, as *Kalīlah wa-Dimnah* (The Fables of Bidpai) tells us; once safe, the cat usually eats the mouse. This "hypocrisy" has been expressed in many proverbs that warn against trusting the cat, which may first lick one's hand and then scratch it. The motto of the Mackintosh clan of Scotland is "Touch not a cat but [i.e., without] a glove."

Nevertheless, the cat has many positive aspects. In ancient Rome, the cat was a symbol of liberty, for no animal has so independent a spirit or is so resistant to restraint as a cat. In China, the association of the sign for cat, *mao,* with that for the number eighty has made the cat a symbol of long life.

In Islamic tradition, the cat is born in Noah's ark from the lioness's sneeze, or else she is the lion's, or tiger's, aunt who teaches him various tricks but withholds the last one, that is, how to climb a tree. The positive evaluation of cats in the Islamic world is due to the prophet Muḥammad's fondness for cats. Because he stroked the back of a cat that saved him from a snake's wiliness, cats never fall on their backs, and the trace of his fingers is visible in the dark stripes that appear on the foreheads of most cats. The cat is clean and does not spoil man's purity for prayer (as does the dog), and its drinking water can be used for ritual ablutions. Many Ṣūfīs have had cats as companions, animals that have sometimes performed wonderful feats of clairvoyance or self-sacrifice to save others from danger or death. The most remarkable cult of cats is connected with the North African beggars' order of the Heddāwa, in which cats are treated like humans; however, once in a while a cat is ritually killed by the brethren. Cats can assume the shape of saints or helpers, as in pre-Islamic Arabia, where desert demons, *ghūl,* were visualized with cats' heads. Even the Sakīnah, God's presence, appeared to the Prophet in the shape of a white cat.

Caterwauling, not always appreciated by most people, has sometimes been interpreted as mysterious music. An early Arabian musician learned some superb songs from a black cat in his dreams. Nursery rhymes sing of the cat's fiddling, and the cat's purr has sometimes been interpreted as its prayer.

Benevolent cats occur frequently in folk tales. The Dick Whittington motif of the cat that proves useful in a country without cats is known in the East and the West. The friendly, clever tomcat, manifested in *Puss in Boots,* is a common topic of folk tradition. It is always the youngest of three sons who inherits the resourceful cat. Thus, the cat often uses its magic properties for positive ends and appears as a mediator between the hero and the supernatural world. This expresses best the good side of the cat's ambivalent character and of its role as an animal that is powerful in the three realms of activity: demonic, human, and divine.

BIBLIOGRAPHY

Carl Van Vechten's *The Tiger in the House,* 3d ed. (New York, 1936), includes interesting chapters on cats in the occult and in folklore as well as an extensive, classified bibliography. Since publication of this work, the literature about cats has increased enormously and at present is growing almost daily. Excellent surveys can be found in *Nine Lives: The Folklore of Cats,* by Katharine M. Briggs (New York, 1980), and in *Le chat dans la tradition spirituelle,* by Robert de Laroche (Paris, 1984). For Islamic cat lore, see my discussion in *Die orientalische Katze* (Cologne, 1983).

ANNEMARIE SCHIMMEL

CATTLE. By *cattle* is here meant those bovines that have been brought under domestication *(Bos taurus, Bos longifrons, Bos brachyceros, Bos indicus)* and not merely bovines or domesticated livestock in general. The first datum that must thus concern anyone interested in the religio-historic importance of cattle is the very fact of the domestication of wild bovines, which was one of the central cultural accomplishments of the "Neolithic revolution," now dated in the period roughly between the tenth and sixth millennium BCE. Since the nineteenth century, a debate has continued between those who have argued in favor of a religious motivation for the domestication of this species and those who have stressed material and economic factors. The former position, initially formulated by Eduard Hahn, emphasized the common use of cattle as sacrificial victims throughout ancient Mesopotamia, arguing from this datum that cattle were tamed in order to ensure a regular and adequate supply of victims for the sacrificial cult. While some still maintain this theory, more generally accepted is the opposing point of view, which holds that obtaining reliable sources of milk, meat, and traction power for nonreligious purposes was the primary motive for the initial domestication.

Once tamed, cattle quickly came to occupy a highly important place within both the agricultural and the pastoral economies of Neolithic societies. In those areas where sufficient rainfall and a long growing season made the production of crops feasible, cattle were harnessed to the yoke and used for plowing, a process that greatly increased the agricultural yield. This combination of cereal agriculture and cattle-drawn plows was an extremely dynamic one: increased agricultural production made it possible to feed ever larger herds of cattle (as well as ever more people), which in turn made it possible to bring ever larger areas of land under the plow. As irrigation techniques were mastered, still greater production resulted, ultimately making possible the emergence of urban civilization.

Elsewhere, in terrains less conducive to agricultural production, with perhaps an inadequate water supply and/or a short growing season, pastoral economies proper developed. Here, herds of cattle were exploited more as a source of food and raw materials than for their labor. Milk, butter, cheese, and sometimes the blood of cattle served as chief items of diet, although agricultural products might also be obtained by way of trade. Meat, for pastoralists as for those who practiced mixed herding and agriculture, remained always a highly specialized and prestigious item of diet, the consumption of which was surrounded by religious attitudes and ritual procedures.

Beyond food, cattle provided numerous other necessities of life for such pastoral peoples as the Nilotic tribes of East Africa, the Israelites of the patriarchal period, and the early Indo-Europeans. Among the products derived from cattle were leather hides, used for clothing, shelter, defensive armament, thongs, and the like; bone tools; dung, which served as fuel for slow-burning fires in areas where wood was scarce; and urine, often used as an all-purpose disinfectant. It is thus no overstatement to say that for cattle-herding pastoralists, cattle formed the very means of production, being in effect machines for the conversion of grass into multiple usable forms.

Equally important, however, is the fact that cattle served as the standard measure of wealth and means of exchange. Nor is exchange to be understood as simply trade: rather, the transfer of cattle from one person or group to another establishes a continuing relation between them, the exchange having social, ritual, and sentimental dimensions as well as economic. Convenient examples of this are found in the institutions of bridewealth and wergild, whereby one social group that has caused another group to lose a valued member compensates the latter by bestowing a prescribed number of cattle upon them. These cattle not only restore the economically productive value of the lost individual, but also replace him or her in the affections of the group that receives them. As a result of this exchange, the two groups—one of which would otherwise benefit at the expense of the other—remain in balance and harmony.

Cattle are thus a crucially important part of any pastoral society, for in truth they make social life possible. All moments of passage—births, deaths, marriages, initiations—are marked by an exchange of cattle. And, in addition to horizontal exchanges of cattle (i.e., those between humans, all of whom occupy the same level of the cosmos), vertical exchanges are also frequent, sacrifice being in part an exchange between humans and gods—as for instance in sacrifices performed on behalf of those suffering from disease, in which cattle are given to deities, who in return restore the afflicted person to his or her social group.

One can thus readily see that there exists a constant demand for cattle within pastoral societies, given their enormous importance as means of production, means of exchange, measures of wealth, and signs of prestige. New supplies are obtained through normal reproduction and breeding, of course, but also through violence, for the raiding of neighboring people's herds is an extremely common practice among pastoralists. Such raids stand in marked opposition to the types of exchange discussed above. Involving no reciprocity, they create or perpetuate imbalance and disharmony between the raiding and raided groups, reciprocity and balance (but never harmony) appearing only when the tables are turned and the previously raided group turns raider itself. To ensure success in raids, warrior values and patterns of organization—militarized age-sets, *Männerbünde,* and the like—are particularly cultivated. Specialized training, initiatory rituals, and magical apparatuses prepare young men to go forth on raids, these being not simply expeditions born of socioeconomic utility, but also—from the point of veiw of those who participate, at any rate—sacred, ritual ventures.

The chief means whereby raids are elevated to ritual status is through the propagation of myths that offer a divine precedent for the deeds of warriors. Such myths, in which the exploits of a deity, hero, or primordial ancestor are celebrated, serve to charter and legitimate similar raiding activity, as warriors come to identify with, and pattern themselves after, the mythic models. A case in point is a celebrated Nuer myth, which tells of the first cattle raid launched by the first Nuer against the first Dinka, at the command of God himself:

> There were still no cattle on the earth. Then God collared Nuer and gave him a cow and a calf with the instructions to share them with Dinka—to give the cow to Dinka and to keep the calf himself. Then, he secretly gave Nuer the direction to come to him early in the morning in order to receive his calf. But, unobserved, Dinka had overheard this speech.
>
> Very early—still by night—Nuer came to God's dwelling and said, "Gwah, my Father, I have come; give me my calf."
>
> "Who are you?" asked God.
>
> Whereupon the Nuer said, "I am Nuer."
>
> "But now, who was it who came to me a little while ago and said he was Nuer, and to whom I consequently gave the calf?" God now asked.
>
> The astonished Nuer replied, "I did not come. That must have been Dinka. This was Dinka cunning; he has outwitted me."
>
> Then God said to Nuer, "Good, now you take the cow for the present; then follow Dinka. When you have overtaken him, you may kill him and take the calf from him."
>
> Since that time date the struggles of the Nuer against the Dinka to gain possession of their cattle.
>
> (Crazzolara, 1953, pp. 68–69; my trans.)

As the last sentence of this highly significant text indicates, the Nuer—who are militarily superior to their Dinka neighbors—make use of this myth to justify their raiding activity, for the myth permits them to claim that such aggression (1) sets right an ancient wrong, in which Dinka initially cheated Nuer of his calf, and (2) fulfills a commandment spoken by God. Such an ideology permits the Nuer to make use of their superior force with a sense of perfect self-righteousness; it seems probable that the Dinka herds would be thoroughly depleted by Nuer attacks, were it not for the fact that the Dinka tell more or less the same myth, interpreting it, however, as establishing a sacred charter and precedent for their own continuing theft of Nuer cattle through stealth and guile, qualities in which they exceed their Nuer enemy.

Similar stories are found among many other peoples for whom cattle are a mainstay of the society and economy. Sometimes these circulate in secular versions, as in Ireland, where numerous tales, including the great national epic *Táin Bó Cuailnge* (The Cattle Raid of

Cuailnge) celebrate the raiding exploits of human, if prodigious, warriors. Elsewhere, demigods appear as the prototypical heroes of cattle raids, as with the Greek tale of Herakles and Geryon, or its Roman counterpart, in which Hercules vanquishes Cacus. Both of these are quite similar to the pattern of the Nuer myth, telling how a foreigner stole cattle, which the national or ethnic hero then recovered in a fully justified raid. Yet again, the central figure of raiding myths may himself be a deity, as in numerous myths of Vedic India, in which the warrior god Indra recovers stolen cattle from such enemies as the *paṇis*, Vṛtra, and Vala. In these myths, the cattle raid is lifted to cosmogonic significance, for it is regularly told that in recovering lost cattle, Indra also set free imprisoned waters and light, rescuing the cosmos from possible disaster. Here the rains and the sun's rays are homologized to cattle; they are the cows of the atmosphere and of the heavens respectively, these having been penned up by drought and night but set free by the god's successful cattle raid—a raid that makes all life and prosperity possible and on which human raiding is patterned.

A certain moral ambiguity frequently surrounded raiding, however, in myth as in actual practice. Thus, for instance, the Homeric *Hymn to Hermes* tells how the god Hermes, while still an infant, stole cattle from his brother Apollo. Yet for all that the exploit is celebrated and helped Hermes win elevation to full divine stature (the common initiatory value of raiding is here evident), Hermes' action is also called into question. According to the hymn, he was hunted down by Apollo, forced to stand trial, and ultimately had to make restitution to his brother before peace could be established between them.

Part of the problem was that Hermes had killed some of the cattle that he stole, and the unrightful slaughter of cattle is always a most serious crime among cattle-herding peoples. Thus, for instance, Enkidu was condemned to death for his part in slaying the Bull of Heaven, according to the *Epic of Gilgamesh*, and the men of Odysseus's last ship were all destroyed by a thunderbolt for having killed and eaten the cattle of the sun god Helios, which were pastured on the island of Thrinacia. Again, among Nuer and Dinka alike, any cattle killed for food outside of sacrifice are said to be slain "just for nothing" *(bang lora)*, and it is expected that they will return to haunt their slayer.

The same point is made in this Nuer-Dinka belief as in the story of Odysseus's men: however much hunger may drive one to desire meat, lethal violence directed against cattle constitutes a sacrilege unless it is set within a ritual context—that is to say, carried out with a certain etiquette, solemnity, and decorum (often by specialists), and legitimated by reference to some set of sacred precedents, symbolic constructs, or transcendent principles. These conditions being met, the slaughter of cattle and subsequent distribution of meat is considered sacrifice; these lacking, it is wanton butchery.

Cattle sacrifice is ideologically the most prestigious and significant ritual performed among pastoral peoples, although in practice offerings of lesser economic value (sheep, goats, milk products, cakes, etc.) are often substituted. In part, as has been discussed above, sacrifice always includes among its significances and functions the consecration of meat and the legitimation of the violence requisite for the procurement of meat. Sacrifice is no more a straightforwardly utilitarian procedure, however, than it is a simple or univocal one. Rather, complex symbolisms and multiple dimensions are always present, however much these may differ from one culture area, historical period, or sacrificial performance to another.

Cattle sacrifice in ancient Babylon, for example, while clearly part of the general "care and feeding of the gods" enjoined upon mankind, was also in part a remembrance or repetition of the cosmogony. For as tablet 5 of the creation account *Enuma elish* makes clear, the deity Tiamat—whose death marks the beginning of the cosmos as we know it—was understood to take the form of a cow, although other passages of the text present her as a monstrous, chaotic being. (A similar account of a being simultaneously monstrous and bovine, which must be put to death in order for a proper cosmos and society to emerge, is the golden calf of *Exodus* 32.) Moreover, the sacrifice of cattle was cast as a divine act, as is clear in the declaration of the Babylonian priest who offers an ox, the skin of which will be made into the covering for a temple drum: "These acts—it is the totality of the gods who have performed them, it is not really I who performed them."

Again, the cattle sacrifice of the Greek *polis* (city-state) was informed by myths of the first sacrifice, particularly that performed by Prometheus, as described by Hesiod, which—as Marcel Detienne and Jean-Pierre Vernant (1980) have demonstrated—served to define the essential human position in the universe as that intermediate to those of beasts and gods. Of particular interest in myth and practice alike is the precise definition of portions allocated to the gods—the victim's bones, wrapped in a single layer of fat—and those reserved for humans—the rest of the meat, wrapped within the animal's stomach. In this, some scholars have seen a reminiscence of archaic hunters' rites, the bones being preserved so that the dead animal might be resurrected. Detienne and Vernant have argued, however, for a different line of interpretation, in which bones are contrasted to meat as the undecaying (or immortal) portion of the victim to the decaying (or mortal) portion. The contrast of meat and bones thus replicates and comments upon the contrast of gods and men; the inclusion of the stomach in the human portion further stresses man's need to eat, which spurs him on to kill. [*See* Bones.]

Social processes also figure prominently in the logic and structure of cattle sacrifice, for the distribution of meat tends to be differential and hierarchic, either in the nature of the portions assigned to individuals or in the order in which portions are presented, or both. A clear case in point is the Roman Feriae Latinae, an annual ceremonial to which all members of the Latin League sent representatives and contributions. The central act was the sacrifice and dismemberment of a white bull, pieces of meat from which were assigned to the representatives according to the relative importance of their cities. Change over time was also reflected in the proceedings of the Feriae Latinae, for as a city grew or shrank in size and stature, its portion of meat seems to have been adjusted accordingly. Other societies also possessed mechanisms whereby social hierarchy could not only be signified within a sacrificial context, but could also be contested, as seen in the accounts of brawls and duels fought over the "champion's portion" among the Greeks and Celts.

Cattle sacrifice was also a highly important part of Indo-Iranian religion, reflecting the prominent position of cattle within the society and economy of India and Iran alike. Certainly, cattle figure almost obsessively in the earliest religious texts from India and Iran (the *Ṛgveda* and the *Gāthās* of the Avesta respectively), although some scholars have maintained that most references to cattle should be taken metaphorically or allegorically, while granting that the stimulus for bovine imagery would still come from the real possession of cattle. Controversy also exists as to whether Zarathushtra (Zoroaster) condemned cattle sacrifice in Iran—as some of the Gathic texts seem to indicate—or if it remained always a part of the Zoroastrian cultus.

The rejection of cattle sacrifice is attested elsewhere in history, particularly in cases where a previously pastoral population has abandoned its earlier mode of production and consequent way of life. Thus, for instance, within the Athenian *polis*, details of the foremost cattle sacrifice—the Bouphonia ("ox-slaying")—reveal a profound uneasiness over the violence and bloodshed inherent in the rite. Toward the end of each Bouphonia, a trial was thus held to assess the guilt of those responsible for the victim's death, such guilt ultimately being assigned to the sacrificial knife with which it was killed, the knife then being punished (and purified) by being thrown into the sea.

However much the ritual slaughter of cattle prompted a certain moral disquietude, the practice continued unabated throughout the history of ancient Greece, insofar as sacrifice was a central mechanism for the periodic renewal of social hierarchy and integration within the *polis*. The criticism of sacrifice implicit in the Bouphonia, however, was given a more articulate and aggressive formulation by certain philosophers and mystics possessed of a radically different vision of what the *polis* ought to be and of the guilt incurred through sacrificial violence. Chief among these were Pythagoras and Empedocles, the latter of whom condemned sacrifice in the following terms, contrasting it with an imagined paradisal sort of offering that took place in the distant past and—given his theories of cyclical time—would once again replace the bloody rituals:

> Ares was not a god for them, nor was Battle-din,
> Nor was Zeus the king, nor Kronos, nor
> Poseidon,
> But Aphrodite was queen.
> They appeased her with pious gifts:
> With painted animal figurines, with perfumes,
> With sacrifices of unmixed myrrh and fragrant
> frankincense,
> Pouring libations of golden honey to the ground.
> The altar was not smeared with the unmixed
> gore of bulls.
> Rather, that was the greatest defilement for men:
> Taking away the life-force in order to eat the
> noble limbs.

Although these Greek opponents of sacrificial ritual remained always in a minority—often, what is more, a suspect minority—others were more successful in India, where the doctrine of *ahiṃsā*, "noninjury" to all living creatures, gradually displaced older sacrificial ideology, particularly in the wake of Buddhist and Jain challenges to Brahmanic doctrines and practice. Thus, the Sanskrit legal texts—as Ludwig Alsdorf (1962) first demonstrated—show a clear process of development, in which the eating of meat obtained from sacrifices was first freely permitted, but later came to be condemned.

Although the privileged status of the "sacred cow" in India is in some measure related to the emergence of the *ahiṃsā* ethic, its sources are considerably older. For already in the *Ṛgveda* and also in the Avesta, cows are referred to as "beings not to be killed" (Skt., *aghnya;* Av., *agenya*), a correspondence that indicates that this was already an item of Indo-Iranian belief at the beginning of the second millennium BCE. One must stress, however, that it is only cows—that is, female bovines—that are so designated, and not cattle in general, and it appears likely that the symbolic, sentimental, and socioeconomic importance of the cow as the source of both milk and new bovine life led to the formulation of religious principles protecting it against slaughter, even slaughter within the context of sacrifice.

Within modern Hinduism, however, the "sacred cow" has been treated as the foremost example of the more general principle of *ahiṃsā*, as for instance in a celebrated treatise by Mohandas K. Gandhi entitled "How to Serve the Cow." Vast numbers of cattle roam the Indian subcontinent free from any threat to their well-being (urban riots have been provoked by attempts to drive cattle from busy streets or markets), and numerous homes have been founded for the care of old and sick cattle.

Western technocrats, colonial authorities, and others have generally viewed the "sacred cow" of India as a classic example of the ways in which religious principles can lead large populations into modes of habitual behavior and social organization that are irrational and counterproductive in strictly economic terms. Yet this view has been challenged, largely by the research of Marvin Harris, and a lively debate has resulted, which is still to be resolved. For it is Harris's contention that when one considers the full range of ways in which cattle resources are exploited within India (traction, dung for fuel, milk and milk products, etc.) and the ways in which cattle are fed (scavenging, use of stubble from the fields, etc.), as well as other important seasonal and ecological factors, one is forced to conclude that the prohibition on killing cattle is both rational and productive, even in the most narrow economic sense. Debate still rages over many details of Harris's argument, as well as on his general conclusion, but his writings have been a valuable corrective to studies that emphasize the divergence between religious and socioeconomic considerations. Rather than being contradictory, even in the case of the "sacred cow," these matters are intimately correlated, in ways far richer and more complex than is generally understood.

[*See also* Neolithic Religion *and* Sacrifice.]

BIBLIOGRAPHY

On the religious significance of cattle within pastoral cultures, see my *Priests, Warriors, and Cattle: A Study in the Ecology of Religions* (Berkeley, 1981). A good discussion of the domestication of the species is found in Frederick E. Zeuner's *A History of Domesticated Animals* (New York, 1963). Eduard Hahn's theories on the religious origin of domestication were set forth in a number of publications, most important of which was *Die Haustiere und ihre Beziehungen zur Wirtschaft des Menschen* (Leipzig, 1896).

The importance of cattle in the life and religion of the peoples of East Africa has been treated in a number of excellent publications, among which should be noted Melville J. Herskovits's "The Cattle Complex in East Africa," *American Anthropologist* 28 (1926): 230–272, 361–388; E. E. Evans-Pritchard's *Neur Religion* (Oxford, 1956); Godfrey Lienhardt's *Divinity and Experience: The Religion of the Dinka* (Oxford, 1961); Peter Rigby's *Cattle and Kinship among the Gogo* (Ithaca, N.Y., 1969); Pierre Bonte's "Il bestiame produce gli uomini: Sacrificio, valore e feticismo del bestiame nell' Africa orientale," *Studi storici* 25 (1984): 875–896; and J. P. Crazzolara's *Zur Gesellschaft und Religion der Nueer* (Vienna, 1953).

On sacrifice in general, see Walter Burkert's *Homo Necans* (Berkeley, 1983); *La cuisine du sacrifice en pays grec*, edited by Marcel Detienne and Jean-Pierre Vernant (Paris, 1980); and the papers on the theme "Sacrificio, organizzazione del cosmo, dinamica sociale," *Studi storici* 25 (1984): 829–956.

On the use of cattle as metaphor, see Wolfgang E. Schmid's "Die Kuh auf der Weide," *Indogermanische Forschungen* 64 (1958–1959): 1–12; George G. Cameron's "Zoroaster the Herdsman," *Indo-Iranian Journal* 10 (1968): 261–281; and Boris Oguibenine's "Le symbolisme de la razzia d'après les hymnes vediques," *Études indo-européennes* (1984): 1–17.

On cattle raiding, see Peter Walcot's "Cattle Raiding, Heroic Tradition, and Ritual: The Greek Evidence," *History of Religions* 18 (May 1979): 326–351; Françoise Bader's "Rhapsodies homériques et irlandaises," in *Recherches sur les religions de l'antiquité classique*, edited by Raymond Bloch (Paris, 1980); and Doris Srinivasan's *The Concept of Cow in the Rigveda* (Delhi, 1979).

On *ahiṃsā* in India, see Ludwig Alsdorf's *Beiträge zur Geschichte von Vegetarismus und Rinderverehrung in Indien* (Wiesbaden, 1962). The debate on the sacred cow has taken place largely in the pages of *Current Anthropology* (Chicago) from 1966 to the present. Marvin Harris's arguments are conveniently summarized in *Cows, Pigs, Wars and Witches* (New York, 1974). On the Indian homes for indigent cattle, see Deryck O. Lodrick's *Sacred Cows, Sacred Places* (Berkeley, 1981).

Bruce Lincoln

CAUSATION. *See* Free Will and Determinism *and* Occasionalism.

CAVES. In all cultures and in almost all epochs the cave has been the symbol of creation, the place of emergence of celestial bodies, of ethnic groups and individuals. It is the great womb of earth and sky, a symbol of life, but also of death. It is a sacred place that constitutes a break in the homogeneity of space, an opening that is a passage from one cosmic region to another, from heaven to earth or, vice versa, from earth to the underworld (Eliade, 1959, p. 37).

All caves are sacred. Some, like cosmic mountains or important sanctuaries, are considered the center of the universe. Where the sacred manifests itself, the world comes into existence (Eliade, 1959, p. 63). Every religious man places himself at the center of the world, "as close as possible to the opening that ensures him communication with the gods" (ibid., p. 65). Earth gods live in caves, which are often called "the earth's navel." As the world center, the *axis mundi*, the cave at times blends in religious symbolism with the mountain. Of the elements in Asian geomancy that determine the quality of a place for a settlement, a home, or a tomb, mountains are considered the most important. [*See* Mountains.] Their vital energy gives them the name of "dragon." This magical energy flows into a cave, which is not always a real opening but represents an auspicious site. Geomantic caves are those surrounded by mountains, where wind is stored and where water, which maintains the spiritual energy, is close by. The mountains are believed to have been created in order to form geomantic caves (Yoon, 1976, pp. 28–34). This mountain-cave-water-energy tradition is similar to the ancient Mexican belief that water was contained within mountains, the womb of the water goddess Chalchiuhtlicue, whence it flowed in the form of the rivers and lakes necessary to human settlement.

The Cave as Axis Mundi. The cave as a sacred spot that marks the place for a major religious structure and even for a great city, the *axis mundi* of its time, is well illustrated at Teotihuacán, Mexico. The most impressive monument here (built c. 100 BCE, destroyed c. 750 CE) is the Pyramid of the Sun, built shortly before the beginning of the Christian era over a primitive shrine, which was itself built over a subterranean cave. The cave has the form of a four-petaled flower, one of Teotihuacán's most popular art motifs, possibly symbolizing the four world quarters. The great Sun Pyramid was constructed in such a way that the four-petaled cave lies almost directly beneath its center. Although the cave was ransacked in ancient times, the few remains within suggest that it may have been a cult center for water gods. Or, inasmuch as a sixteenth-century document labels the place in front of the pyramid "Moctezuma's oracle," an oracle may well have dwelt here. Whatever the answer, the sacredness of this cave was such that it had to be preserved by building a shrine over it, then by constructing the immense pyramid over this. Sacred space was thus preserved for all time.

Birth and Creation. Because of its volcanic formation, Mesoamerica is honeycombed with caves. Each is revered, and many are associated with the emergence myth. Chicomoztoc ("seven caves") was the place of creation of many ethnic groups, particularly the Aztec. Its seven caves are represented in ancient pictorial manuscripts and in oral tradition. But before the creation of people, the sun and the moon were made in a grotto. In the myth of the creation of the Fifth Sun (the name given the present era by the Aztec), some chronicles state that after one god threw himself into a fire and became transformed into the sun, another god went into a cave and came out of it as the moon. In a legend of Española (Hispaniola), all men were created in one cave, all women in another (Fray Ramon Pané, in Heyden, 1975). Sustenance, also, originated in caves, according to popular belief. Some caves were called *cincalco*, "house of maize"; in them corn was kept by the gods. A sixteenth-century Mexican chronicle, *Historia de México*, relates that Centeotl, a maize god, was born in a cavern; from different parts of his body cotton and many edible plants grew. According to another early chronicler, Fray Geronimo de Mendieta, a flint knife fell from heaven and landed in Chicomoztoc, where it broke into sixteen hundred pieces, from which that number of gods was created. The cave, then, is a symbol of the womb. According to Fray Bernardino de Sahagún's *Historia general de las cosas de la Nueva España* (the so-called Florentine Codex), a saying is ascribed to Aztec women of the sixteenth-century: "Within us is a cave, a gorge . . . whose only function is to receive."

The Emergence Place. The cave as the center of the world and place of emergence is found in many traditions. Hopi mythology tells of three worlds under the earth where the Hopi lived with the Ant People before they found their way up to the fourth, or present, world. The Zuni, with the same traditions, call the place of emergence *hepatina* ("the middle place") and the last world (which they classify as still underground) the "fourth womb." The modern *kiva* of these and other Pueblo Indian groups is an artificial cave, the ceremonial center of the village, in which there is also a small hole in the ground, symbolic of the place of emergence. *Kiva* ritual follows a man from life to death. As soon as he is born a boy is symbolically initiated into the ritual life and pledged to his father's *kiva*. Zuni society has six divisions, associated with the four world directions, the zenith, and the nadir. Each division has its own *kiva*, around which religion revolves (Leighton and Adair, 1966). The *kiva* evidently has been basic to ritual for many centuries. During the Pueblo Classic period (1050–1300) the underground *kivas* were of tremendous size, as can be seen in the ruins of Mesa Verde and Chaco Canyon. They were caves within caves, partially natural grottoes and partially hacked out of the rocks. A maze design carved on rocks in Arizona—much like the Minoan maze—represents the myth of emergence. It is the Mother Earth symbol, according to the modern

Hopi; the maze represents the paths a person will follow on the road of life (Campbell Grant, 1967, p. 65). [*See* Labyrinth.]

Cave Gods and Rites. Since the rites and deities of different parts of the world, many of them associated with caves, are dealt with in numerous articles of this encyclopedia, this brief section is focused on Mesoamerica, which, in general, is less well known than Europe or the Orient.

Tlaloc, the Aztec rain and earth deity, was also called Path under the Earth, or Long Cave, according to the sixteenth-century chronicler Fray Diego Durán. This name refers to the god's character as fertilizer of the earth with gentle rain, and also to rites in caves where water deities were propitiated. Rain, lightning, and thunder were thought to be controlled in caves and on mountain tops. Toribio Motolinía, another colonial chronicler, describes ceremonies to Tlaloc each year during which four children were sacrificed and their bodies placed in a cave; this was then sealed until the following year, when the rite was repeated. Children were considered special messengers to the water gods.

Oztoteotl literally means "god of caves"; this was the name of a god venerated in a sacred cave at Chalma, a site about two days' march from Mexico City that was the scene of important pilgrimages. Oztoteotl has been supplanted by the Christian Lord of Chalma (a representation of Christ), who is no less venerated, both in the cave and in a church erected here. One rite in Chalma is the leaving of umbilical cords in two caves, one at the top of the hill, one at the bottom, in order to ensure the infants of good fortune in life.

Vegetation gods frequently had rites performed in their honor in caves. For example, the skins of flayed victims (symbolizing corn husks or those of other plants) were stored in an artificial cave at the foot of the Yopico pyramid in Tenochtitlán, the Aztec capital, and bodies of young women sacrificed to Xochiquetzal, the vegetation goddess, were placed in a cave called a "mist house." These instances may constitute a ritual metaphor for seed germination, which takes place in a dark area, comparable to the cave-womb.

Regarding ceremonies, the fabulous grotto of Balankanché, immediately southeast of the ancient Maya city of Chichén Itzá in Yucatán, has revealed a wealth of offerings to the rain god Tlaloc (Chac, among the Maya) and chamber after chamber of ceremonial settings for rites. These date mainly from the ninth century CE, when highland Mexican influence was strong (hence the presence of the god Tlaloc rather than Chac), although the grotto was used for ritual purposes mainly by the Maya, through 3,000 years. Six offertory foci are associated with either underground pools or stalagmitic formations, caused by the action of the water (Andrews, 1970, p. 9). These natural formations have the appearance of altars and were used as such. In the major chamber, floor and ceiling are united by a stalactite-stalagmite "tree" that suggests the ceiba (silk-cotton), the sacred Maya tree that unites earth, sky, and underworld. This structure is called by the modern—and undoubtedly by the ancient—Maya the "throne of the *balam*," that is, of the Jaguar Priest. When the inner chambers were discovered in 1959, this altar-throne was found to be covered with effigy censers, most of them in the form of Tlaloc, some wearing flayed skins and some suggestive of the Aztec vegetation deity Xipe Totec. Other offerings here and in various chambers include miniature vessels, grinding stones, and spindle whorls, perhaps symbolic offerings for use in the otherworld. Enigmatic handprints in red ocher (as suggested below, perhaps evidence of a rite of passage) are on the central, treelike column and on the ceiling of low tunnels. Other chambers with stalagmitic altars yielded many more Tlaloc effigy censers, quantities of shells, jade beads, fragments of a wooden drum, and charcoal from burnt offerings. Numerous fire pits and the charcoal in the censers seem to be evidence of both illumination and ritual hearth use. Inasmuch as smoke was one of the messengers to the gods, the fires may have been intended solely for communication. That this was a major ritual center is indicated by the insistence of the *H-men* (the practitioner of native folk religion) from a village near Balankanché that, because of the cave's sacred nature, when the sealed chambers were discovered, it was necessary to propitiate the deities within in order to ward off supernatural retribution for the profanation. Rites were held involving the ritual drinking of honey-based *balché*, the sacrifice of chickens, and, among other things, the imitation of frogs by two small boys: the entrance to the cave home of the rain god was traditionally guarded by a frog (Andrews, 1970, pp. 70–164).

This type of ceremony is not unique to the cenotes of Yucatán. Marion Oettinger (in a personal communication) records a cave rite in the state of Guerrero dedicated to the water god; in it, stalactites and stalagmites are revered as deities. Corn is believed to come from hollows on the cave floor made by dripping water. Rites dedicated to supernatural beings who control water and vegetation are still held within the cave.

Rites of Passage. Since Paleolithic times caves have been preferred places for many rites of passage. Symbols of passage into another world, of a descent to the underworld, they are the scene of initiation rites for shamans—among the Australian medicine men, among the Araucanian of Chile, among the Inuit (Eskimo), and among peoples of North America, to mention but a few (Eliade, 1964, p. 51). The *iruntarinia* ("spirits") of central Australia create a medicine man when an Aranda (Arunta) candidate goes to sleep at the mouth of a cave; he is dragged into it by one of the spirits and dismembered, and his internal organs are exchanged for others. For example, a fragment of rock crystal, important to shamanic power (a detail reported in Oceania and the Americas also), is placed in his body, which is then returned to his village (Eliade, 1964, pp. 46, 139). Eliade tells also of the initiatory dream-journey of a Nenets (Yurak Samoyed) in his transition from candidate to shaman. In one important episode, the initiate was led into a cave covered with mirrors; there he received a hair from each of two women, mothers of reindeer, with which to shamanize for the animal (p. 41).

In British Columbia, as each Salish adolescent concluded a puberty rite, he or she imprinted a red hand on a cave wall. Furthermore, these and other images painted in red on rock walls recorded remarkable dreams. A spirit quest by a Salish boy led him into the hills, usually to a cave, where, through praying and fasting, he would dream of a supernatural being who would be his guardian in later life (Grant, 1967, p. 29). Among the Dogon in Africa, circumcision rites are recorded by ritual signs and paintings on the rocks; these are also related to ceremonies for the renewal of the cosmos every sixty years. In Mexico's Malinalco rock temple, carved altarlike felines and eagles stand against the walls; the military orders of the Jaguar and the Eagle must have held ceremonies here, such as the initiation of new members into their select ranks.

A rite of passage from illness to health is performed at the grotto at Lourdes, France. The healing waters of Lourdes's spring and the story of the apparition of the Virgin Mary to Bernadette have made this an important pilgrimage center since 1858.

In Mexico, until early this century, a boy child born in the vicinity of the Teotihuacán pyramids was placed in a cave. An animal, it was said, came out from the dark interior and licked his face; if the baby did not cry, he automatically acquired the right to be a *granicero*. *Graniceros* perform curing ceremonies and control rain from within caves. Thus the child experienced two rites of passage, a kind of baptism and initiation into this special group. In a part of Chiapas, as soon as a child moves within his mother's womb, he is said to possess a spirit, and this dwells in caves (Esther Hermitte, cited by Heyden, 1976). At times a cave steals this spirit or that of an adult, whereupon a *curandero*, a healer, must perform a rite in the cave. In one case he captures the lost spirit in a piece of the spirit-owner's clothing and manages to pull it out of the cave (Guido Münch, personal communication, referring to Oaxaca). In these cases of soul loss and recuperation, the rite of passage is a hazardous one between life and death. People also become ill from cave "winds," and *graniceros* can cure them by making offerings to the owners of the caves. A rite associated with these ceremonies is that of dying and resuscitating; the usual way to become a *granicero* is to be struck by lightning, be pronounced dead, and then come to life again. In some regions the healer must "die" twice a year; then his spirit goes to a special cave, where he receives instructions (William Madsen, cited by Heyden, 1976). Exorcism is yet another rite practiced in caves, frequently by saying a mass in the interior, in the presence of the affected person.

Religious Cave Art. Paintings on the walls of ancient caves, or sculptures hewn out of rock within caverns, have been called "invisible art" and likened to "silent music" (Carpenter, 1978, pp. 90–99). That is, such art was created for the initiated few and did not need to be public. Esoteric it is, and it has generally been conceived to possess sympathetic magic. For example, depicting a speared deer would ensure success in the hunt. Undoubtedly this is one meaning, but it is not the only one. Some cave images may be a way of keeping a record of rites. They may also relate to the animal double that each person possesses. Among the North American Indians, a young man, as part of a spirit quest, often gave thanks to his spirit guardian by painting or carving figures on cliff walls or in dark caves. These were addressed to his spirit guardian and were not meant to be seen by living humans; exposure would diminish their powers. Carpenter suggests that many anthropomorphic figures, depicted at times in coitus, in caves or in earth sculpture on mountaintops or desert floors, probably represent the original tribal ancestors and, by extension, the beginning of the world.

European cave paintings dating from the Upper Paleolithic period (c. 35,000–19,000 years ago), among them those at Altamira in Spain and at Lascaux, Cap Blanc, Les Trois Frères, Cougnac, and Rouffignac in France, portray mainly animals. Although Henri Breuil had interpreted these as belonging to hunting-gathering magic, recent studies propose that such art is part of Paleolithic cosmology. Leroi-Gourhan (1965) sees this worldview as based on a male-female division, with sections of the caves, as well as the animals and symbols, divided according to gender. Alexander Marshack interprets certain forms in cave art as calendrical and incisions on bones and antlers as notational; he also claims that some representations have seasonal and ecological significance, symbolized, for example, by flora and fauna typical of certain seasons and regions (cited by Conkey, 1981, p. 23). Ritual art, then, is often a key to the daily life and economy of a people, as well as to their religion.

At El Castillo in Cantabrian Spain, about fifty negative handprints were painted on a wall by blowing red ocher around a hand held there. Although this symbol has not been clearly interpreted by students of the period, it is reminiscent of red handprints on walls in the Maya region of Mexico, prints that according to popular tradition were placed there by slaves who were to be sacrificed. This interpretation may be fantasy, however, for in Pueblo belief (where Mexican influence is often found) the handprint is a "signature" that attracts supernatural blessings or marks the completion of a rite. Some animal representations, evidently men dressed in skins and antlers, have been thought to depict sorcerers. Clusters of bison on the ceiling at Altamira could symbolize different human groups that went to the cave for various reasons and rites. Thus the cave could have been a seasonal aggregation site for people who were dispersed throughout the region (Conkey, 1981, p. 24). Could Altamira have been an early Magdalenian pilgrimage center?

René Huyghe, in discussing Paleolithic cave art, points out that the facsimile is effective in the beliefs of the people who create these magic images. He further explores the function of the facsimile, citing paintings on the walls of Egyptian tombs, where representations of foodstuffs and furniture sometimes substituted for the actual articles needed for life after death. Huyghe has stated that the accomplished technique with which the cave paintings were executed indicates probable teaching by sorcerer-priests (1962, pp. 16, 18). With the transition to the Mesolithic and Neolithic periods, cave art became more realistic and depicted human beings in communal activities. Paintings of this sort are found at the entrance to caves, accessible to the larger group, instead of in dark interiors, where formerly esoteric rites must have been held. This different religio-social art is characteristic of the Iberian coast facing Africa, and its tradition has continued to the present time among the African San. The paintings convey great action, expressed by few, almost abstract lines (running warriors at Teruel, for example), side by side with incipient architecture (the menhir, probably intended as a receptacle for the soul of the deceased). Both reflect more settled activities of Neolithic peoples: flock keeping and agriculture, which spurred new ideas and customs (Huyghe, 1962, pp. 21–24). [*See also* Paleolithic Religion *and* Neolithic Religion.]

America holds a wealth of cave and rock art, from Alaska to South America. Most of it dates from about 1000 CE to the late 1800s. Its subjects are animals, humans, supernatural beings, and abstract designs. Although some scenes are historical or narrative (depicting Spanish horsemen, for example), much of this art is religious. Hunting magic is represented by a heart line drawn within an animal and sometimes pierced by an arrow. The mythical Thunderbird, thought to control thunderstorms but also a clan symbol and sacred ancestor guardian among the Hopi, is often represented. The plumed serpent, known as the god Quetzalcoatl in Mexico, was the guardian of springs and streams in the Southwest, and is seen on *kiva* wall paintings or in rock carvings. In the San Francisco Mountains of Baja California a sixteen-foot long plumed serpent is the object of a ceremony involving red and black men and deer. However, Uriarte sees this great figure as a serpent-deer, joining the natural forces of both creatures (1981, p. 151). The men surrounding it wear serpent-deer headdresses and therefore must be members of a cult group. Uriarte suggests also that the two-in-one animal may represent a male-female creation myth. Hundreds of handprints found in Arizona, Utah, and northern California must have had ceremonial significance. The Chumash of California painted supernatural figures, believed to be related to dreams and visions, in remote mountainous areas. A ceremonial liquor used by the Chumash and other groups was made of the hallucinogenic jimsonweed, which could have spurred such ritual art. Rock paintings by the Navajo marked sacred places where mythological events occurred; these paintings often depicted the *yei*, equivalent to the Pueblo *kachina*, a divine creature usually associated with maize agriculture. Campbell Grant (1967) suggests an important reason for some of the rock art symbols: they were mnemonic devices for rites, and records of certain events. Among present-day Ojibwa, tobacco, prayer sticks, and cloth are placed on rocks below paintings as offerings to the supernatural beings depicted there. The Ojibwa believe that a shaman can enter the rock and trade tobacco with the spirit there for special medicine (Grant, 1967, pp. 32, 147).

In central Baja California, Uriarte (1981) records 72 caves painted with 488 figures or sets of figures, many with the bodies adorned in body paint of various colors. Similar colors are also typical of cave paintings in northwestern Australia. Among the Kulin there, Bunjil was the supreme mythological being, who with all his people turned into stars and whose son was the rainbow. Bunjil's favorite place was Angel Cave; he created it when he spoke to rocks, which then opened up (Aldo Massola, 1968, pp. 59, 106).

Artificial Caves. Some of the world's most renowned painted caves are in India. At Ajantā the Gupta style of the fifth and sixth centuries was the peak of a golden age, although the caves themselves existed by the second century BCE, and painting continued through the eighth century CE. Portrayed on the walls are scenes from the lives of Gautama Buddha, the *bodhisattvas*, and other divine beings conceived in the manner of the palace life of the time. The Jātaka tales painted here illustrate the Buddha's previous earthly experiences. That some of the people are engaged in religious conversation is apparent from the occasional mudras (hand positions). But perhaps the most extraordinary thing about these caves, as well as at Ellora and elsewhere, is that they were carved out of sandstone rock. Entire mountains were turned into sanctuaries by devoted and anonymous sculptor-architects to be used as monastic retreats. The thirty Ajantā caves, excavated in the semicircular face of a mountain in the Deccan region near Aurangabad, are either *caityas* (chapels) or *vihāras* (monasteries). The *caityas* consist of an apse, side aisles, and a central nave in the center of which is a stupa, all hewn out of living rock. In the *vihāras* there are a congregation hall and monks' cells. In the early caves, the Buddha was represented not in his bodily form but with symbols, such as the Bodhi Tree or a set of footprints. Sculpture in relief and in the round later filled the caves and covered the doorways with large figures of the Buddha and the *bodhisattvas* as well as an exuberance of elephants, buffalo, men and women in different positions, lotus medallions, and other floral motifs. The happy marriage at Ajantā of architecture, painting, and sculpture produced an insuperable monument to the Buddhist faith.

Also hewn out of a mountain (sometime between the fourth and ninth centuries CE), the caves at Ellora are a miracle of carving. Unlike the Buddhist caves at Ajanta, these are dedicated to three faiths: the early caves, before 800, are Buddhist; the Hindu caves overlap (600–900), and the Jain caves cover the period from 800 to 1000. At Ellora the great Hindu Kailāśa temple dedicated to Śiva represents Mount Kailāśa, where the gods dwell. In the early Buddhist caves, the vast number of Buddhas, *bodhisattvas*, and *śaktis* express the Vajrayāna philosophy, wherein Buddhahood was obtained through self-discipline and meditation. The Hindu caves are dedicated to Śiva, who is worshiped symbolically in the phallic symbol called the lingam, found always in the shrine. Sculptures of Śiva also represent him in many of his manifestations, as the personification of death and time, as Creator, Destroyer, Divine Lover, and Lord of the Dance. Śiva's wife Pārvatī, goddess of love and beauty, accompanies him, as does his son Gaṇeśa, the elephant-headed god of wisdom. Śiva is sometimes represented in his half-male, half-female form. Brahmā and Viṣṇu are also portrayed in various forms. The composition of Ajantā paintings is at times reminiscent of the *maṇḍala* (or cosmic diagram), while Jain sculpture at Ellora borrowed freely from Hinduism and depicts Hindu deities.

Undoubtedly the most spectacular of the many caves carved out of solid rock in China is the complex known as Lung-men Grottoes at Loyang, in Honan Province. Begun in the fifth century CE, the grottoes continued to be carved over a period of four hundred years. Twenty-one hundred caves and niches and more than forty pagodas house more than one hundred thousand sculptures, the largest 17.4 meters, the smallest only 12 centimeters high. Statues in these grottoes mainly portray the Buddha. Also represented are attendant figures, warriors, the Buddha's disciples, *bodhisattvas*, and a giant lotus—symbol of divine birth, purity, creative force, and Buddha's footsteps—on a ceiling. The walls of one cave, that of the Ten Thousand Buddhas, are covered with a myriad of tiny relief-carved figures of the divinity, which envelop the viewer with an awesome sense of the sacred.

Rock Temples and Tombs. The hypogea, rock-cut tombs of Egypt, attest to the use of natural materials available for building. Stone, abundant in Egypt, was used for the great monuments. From the Middle Kingdom on, tombs were hollowed out of cliffs alongside the Nile for high officials of Upper Egypt. By the time of New Kingdom, the Valley of the Kings, on the Nile's west side facing Luxor, had become the necropolis of pharaohs, who lay in rock-cut tombs on both sides of the valley. The funerary temple of Queen Hatshepsut at Deir al-Bahri was carved out of the mountain on different levels. Under Ramses II, in the nineteenth dynasty, the spectacular rock temple at Abu Simbel was hewn out of a mountain in Upper Egypt.

In Persia, royal rock tombs at Naksh-i-Rustam, near Persepolis, date from the sixth to the fourth centuries BCE. Here the king is represented before a fire altar, above which is the god Ahura Mazdā, whose face is surrounded by a circle, symbol of eternity. At Petra, in modern Jordan, the Nabateans more than two thousand years ago carved their capital city out of rock. Along with temples and civil buildings, some of these artificial caves are tombs for the kings.

In Mexico, shaft tombs—the shaft hollowed out of the earth, ending in a side chamber for the cadaver—were definitely cave representations, the deceased returning to the earth that gave him life. The *temazcal*, the purifying sweat bath, used for millennia in this region, was "the house of flowers" in pre-Columbian times, the flower symbolizing both the womb and the cave.

An outstanding example of funerary caves, albeit in

this case artificial, is that of Rome's catacombs. These were Christian cemeteries begun in the first century CE. They were twice confiscated, during the third century and at the beginning of the fourth; after a bloody persecution by Diocletian, peace was finally granted by Constantine in 313. From then on, catacomb excavations were enlarged and embellished with paintings and inscriptions referring to Christian martyrs; they became the goal of pilgrims.

In the sub-Saharan region of Mali, the Tellem people, who flourished from the eleventh to the sixteenth centuries, buried their dead, accompanied by grave furniture and clothing for the otherworld, in special caves. Objects were ritually destroyed, as they are in other parts of the world, in order to release the spirit. One cave contained three thousand skeletons. Among the offerings left in these high cliff caves were skeletal remains of a crowned crane and of a turtle, both figures in the mythology of the Dogon, who came to the region after the Tellem (Bedaux, 1982, pp. 28–34).

In the lowland Maya region of Mexico and Central America, the limestone floor is honeycombed with *cenotes*. Perhaps because these are the main sources of water in the largely riverless Yucatán Peninsula, they were highly venerated as sacred sites; one of their functions was that of funeral chamber. The great *cenote* at Chichén Itzá is well known, as are tales of fair maidens thrown into the water at this cave-well. It actually was a place of sacrifice to aquatic deities, but adolescents of both sexes were the victims. A sixteenth-century account by Fray Diego de Landa tells of young boys whose hearts were extracted before their bodies were deposited in the *cenote;* propitiation of water gods by child sacrifice was a common rite. The victims were accompanied by incense balls, gold jewels, and the even more highly prized jade, symbol of water and of all that is precious. These sacrificial rites were related to maize agriculture, but also had divinatory and prophetic purposes. Before the rainy season, or during times of drought, child sacrifices increased. Some accounts relate that the victims were lowered alive into the cave-well so that they could communicate with the god, then left to drown. A procession went from the main temple to a shrine next to the *cenote;* there the priests instructed the victim as to the message to be given to the gods; then they consummated the sacrifice. The walls of Guatemala's spectacular Naj Tunich cavern are covered with eighth-century paintings of the ritual ball-game (with celestial and life-death significance), ritual bloodletting, dwarfs (associated with both heavens and the underworld), shells (symbols of birth and of death), and long columns of hieroglyphs, mainly calendrical. George Stuart (1981, pp. 220–235) points out that the Classic Maya considered the numbers and days in their calendar as a procession of gods who marched along an eternal and endless trail. The Maya believed that caves, like the roots of the sacred ceiba tree that held earth and sky together, reached far down into the underworld. Caves were the entrance to this place, called Xibalba, where underworld gods dwelt. Stuart suggests that the great cavern of Naj Tunich was the embodiment of Xibalba, place of death.

BIBLIOGRAPHY

Andrews, Edward Wyllys. *Balankanché, Throne of the Tiger Priest.* New Orleans, 1970.

Bedaux, Rogier M. A. "Rediscovering the Tellem of Mali." *Archaeology* 35 (1982): 28–34.

Carpenter, Edmund. "Silent Music and Invisible Art." *Natural History* 87 (1978): 90–99.

Conkey, Margaret W. "A Century of Palaeolithic Cave Art." *Archaeology* 34 (1981): 20–28.

Eliade, Mircea. *The Sacred and the Profane.* New York, 1959.

Eliade, Mircea. *Shamanism: Archaic Techniques of Ecstasy.* Rev. & enl. ed. New York, 1964.

Grant, Campbell. *Rock Art of the American Indian.* New York, 1967.

Heyden, Doris. "An Interpretation of the Cave Underneath the Pyramid of the Sun in Teotihuacán, Mexico." *American Antiquity* 40 (1975): 131–147.

Heyden, Doris. "Los ritos de paso en las cuevas." *Boletín Instituto Nacional de Antropologia e Historia* (Mexico City) 2 (1976): 17–26.

Huyghe, René. "Prehistoric Art: Art Forms and Society" and "Primitive Art: Art Forms and Society." In *Larousse Encyclopedia of Prehistoric and Ancient Art,* edited by René Huyghe, pp. 16–25, 72–77. London, 1962.

Leighton, Dorothea C., and John Adair. *People of the Middle Place: A Study of the Zuni Indians.* New Haven, 1966.

Leroi-Gourhan, André. *Treasures of Prehistoric Art.* New York, 1965.

Massola, Aldo. *Bunjil's Cave: Myths, Legends and Superstitions of the Aborigines of South-East Australia.* Melbourne, 1968.

Stuart, George E. "Maya Art Treasures Discovered in Cave." *National Geographic* 160 (1981): 220–235.

Uriarte, Maria Teresa. *Pintura Rupestre en Baja California.* "Colección Científica," no. 106. Mexico City, 1981.

Yoon, Hong-key. *Geomantic Relationships between Culture and Nature in Korea.* Taipei, 1976.

DORIS HEYDEN

CELESTIAL BUDDHAS AND BODHISATTVAS. The term *bodhisattva* occurs frequently in early Buddhist literature, usually referring to Śākyamuni Buddha prior to the time of his enlightenment, which he achieved as he sat under the famous Bodhi Tree (Skt., *bodhivṛkṣa,* "tree of enlightenment") a few miles south of Gayā in modern Bihar. *Bodhisattva* means literally "enlightenment being," or, according to a theory that *bodhisattva* is a slightly mistaken Sanskrit spelling of the early dialectical form *bodhisatta* (as preserved in Pali), it could have originally meant "intent upon enlightenment." Whatever the literal meaning (and most scholars would favor the first one), a *bodhisattva* is a living being, usually human but not necessarily so, who has set out on the long path toward Buddhahood, which in accordance with the general Buddhist acceptance of the Indian theories concerning continual rebirth (or transmigration) was calculated to lead the aspirant through a very long series of different lives.

Large collections of such legendary life stories *(jātaka)* were made in the early Buddhist period, illustrating the heroic self-sacrifice of the future Buddha Śākyamuni in his progress toward his last life (also told in legendary style), when his purpose was finally revealed to the world. As Śākyamuni was never regarded as the one and only Buddha, but rather as one in a whole series (seven are named in early texts, but the number is gradually much extended), each of whom appears in a separate world age, it was inevitable that his followers should come to expect a future Buddha for the next world age. Thus, a new *bodhisattva*, Maitreya ("loving kindness"), appears as the first of the many other "great beings," who later extend the Buddhist pantheon to infinity. The cult of Maitreya is certainly attested among the followers of the early Buddhist sects, later referred to disparagingly as Hīnayānists, and his appearance seems to mark the beginning of the considerable devotion that came to be directed toward these celestial beings.

It should be borne in mind that the distinctions between the so-called Mahāyānists and Hīnayānists were not so clear-cut in the early centuries CE as they appear to be later. The same mythological concepts concerning the nature of a Buddha and a *bodhisattva* (a future Buddha) remain fundamental to Buddhism in all its forms, and it can easily be shown that all the later extravagant developments of the Mahāyāna are traceable to tendencies inherent in the earliest known forms of Buddhism. The Mahāyānists differed in their philosophical assumptions and the manner in which they applied the *bodhisattva* theory to normal religious life. For them, the *bodhisattva* career was the only genuine path toward enlightenment, which they distinguished from the goal of *nirvāṇa*, interpreted by them as the limited selfish aspiration of the early disciples. At the same time they followed the same forms of monastic discipline (Vinaya) as their Hīnayāna brethren, often living together in the same monastic compound until doctrinal disputes led them to set up separate communities of their own. Thus freed, the Mahāyānists began to go their own way, but there would appear to have been no very noticeable iconographic changes in their monasteries until several centuries later.

The well-known caves of Ajantā were probably occupied by Buddhist communities up to the eighth century CE, and there is scarcely any image or painting there that might displease a determined adherent of the older sects. The only celestial *bodhisattva* apart from Maitreya to be painted at Ajantā is Avalokiteśvara ("the lord who looks down in compassion"), and he may be quite convincingly interpreted as the future Buddha Śākyamuni, who looked down in compassion from the heaven called Tuṣita ("joyful") before finally agreeing to be born in our world for the benefit of its inhabitants. None of the many Buddha and *bodhisattva* images surviving at Ajantā in carved stone can be identified as particular celestial Buddhas and *bodhisattvas*. Numerous *bodhisattvas* are named in Mahāyāna *sūtras* from the first century CE onward, but a rather more limited number achieved generally accepted iconographic forms, namely those who were especially popular as distinct beings and those who were fitted into *maṇḍalas* and related iconographic patterns.

The earliest iconographic pattern, which resulted in the eventual appearance of three leading *bodhisattvas*, is probably the triad of images representing Śākyamuni Buddha flanked by two attendants. According to early accounts, Śākyamuni was attended by Indian divinities at his birth. Originally, these two attendants may have been thought of as Brahmā and Indra, but they came to be accepted as Buddhist divinities by the simple method of giving them new Buddhist names. They thus become identified as Padmapāṇi ("lotus-holder") and Vajrapāṇi ("*vajra*-holder"). Padmapāṇi comes to be identified with Avalokiteśvara, who also holds a lotus flower, and thus becomes a great *bodhisattva* in his own right. Vajrapāṇi's rise to fame is very much slower, since through the earlier Mahāyāna period he continues to be regarded as Śākyamuni's personal attendant, his function and duties merely being extended to protect all other *bodhisattvas*.

It is not until we reach the early Tantric period as represented by the *Mañjuśrīmūlakalpa* that Vajrapāṇi appears as a powerful *bodhisattva* in his own right, but still as a member of a triad. By this time (perhaps the fifth to the sixth century CE) many non-Buddhist divinities were being spontaneously accepted into the Buddhist fold; they were being accepted for the straightforward reason that those who became supporters of the monks or who even became Buddhist monks themselves did not need to renounce their devotion to other divinities, whose existence and capabilities were never denied either by Śākyamuni himself or by his followers. Local divinities decorate Buddhist stupas (Skt., *stūpas*) from at least the second century BCE onward, and as already noted, the great Hindu divinities were soon incorporated as Buddhist "converts." This process continued throughout the whole history of Indian Buddhism and goes far to explain the existence of so many celestial beings in the ever more elaborate Buddhist pantheon.

In the *Manjuśrīmūlakalpa* these divinities are grouped into various "families," of which the three chief ones are those of the Buddha or Tathāgata, the Lotus, and the Vajra. Divinities who were already accepted as fully Buddhist were placed in the Buddha's family, while gentle divinities due for conversion were placed in the Lotus family under the leadership of Avalokiteśvara; fierce divinities, whose conversion was supposed to be troublesome, were placed under the command of Vajrapāṇi, who was able to subdue them with his powerful *vajra* ("thunderbolt"). Since it was suitable that the original Buddha family should be headed by a *bodhisattva* just like the other two, this position was assigned to Mañjuśrī ("gentle and glorious one," also known as Mañjughoṣa, "gentle voice"), who appears in early Mahāyāna *sūtras* as Śākyamuni's chief spokesman. His origin is obscure but it is significant that he is later linked with Sarasvatī, the Hindu goddess of speech, taking her *mantra* ("Oṃ vāgīśvari muṃ") as his own. It must be emphasized that none of these great *bodhisattvas* has a "history" in the modern sense: they are all mythological creations.

Celestial Buddhas. While the cult of a celestial *bodhisattva* as a Great Being of heavenly associations clearly has its roots in the early cult of Śākyamuni, who was appealed to as both Buddha and *bodhisattva*, its full implications were developed from approximately the first century CE onward by those who began to adopt specific Mahāyāna teachings. Śākyamuni was traditionally acclaimed as the one and only Buddha of our present world age, and early legends tell how he made the vow, when he was a brahman boy named Megha or Sumegha, before a previous Buddha, Dīpaṃkara, to follow the self-sacrificing *bodhisattva* path toward Buddhahood. It must be emphasized that the later concepts never had the effect of negating the earlier ones, and despite the change of viewpoint that I am about to explain, the cult of Buddhas of the past, as well as of the future, was never abandoned. The "Buddhas of the three times" (past, present, and future) are frequently mentioned in Mahāyāna literature and their cult has continued in Tibetan Buddhism to this day.

The change that takes place in Mahāyāna theories results from their perhaps more realistic view of the nature of the cosmos. The early Buddhists viewed the world as a closed system, comprising four main island-continents arranged around a central sacred mountain, known as Meru, identified with Mount Kailāśa in western Tibet. Mahāyāna teachings, on the other hand, were greatly affected by views that envisaged the universe as whole galaxies of world systems, extending endlessly throughout all the directions of space. It followed logically from this that there should also be Buddhas operative in all these other world systems. [*See also* Cosmology, *article on* Buddhist Cosmology.] One of the earliest disputes that arose between Mahāyānists and those who held to the earlier views concerns precisely the problem of whether there can be more than one Buddha at a time, and it is clear that they argue against different cosmological backgrounds. Mahāyāna ideas on the nature of such myriads of world systems may be learned from the reading of any of the Mahāyāna *sūtras*, where Buddhas, surrounded by *bodhisattvas*, continue to preach simultaneously in their various "Buddha fields" *(buddhakṣetra)*.

Not all such worlds are fortunate enough to have a Buddha at any particular time. Those that do are divided generally into two classes, known as "pure" or "impure." The pure fields contain only those beings who are on the way to Buddhahood, that is, *bodhisattvas*, while the impure fields contain beings of all kinds at all stages of spiritual advance and decline. The manner in which *bodhisattvas* may travel miraculously from one Buddha field to another is well illustrated in the important Mahāyāna *sūtra*, the *Vimalakīrtinirdeśa* (The Teaching of Vimalakīrti), where the question is understandably raised as to why Śākyamuni should have elected to be born in an impure field rather than a pure one. His superiority is acknowledged by visiting *bodhisattvas* from a pure field, who exclaim: "The greatness of Śākyamuni is established; it is wonderful how he converts the lowly, the wretched and the unruly. Moreover, the Bodhisattvas who are established in this mean Buddha-sphere (i.e., our world) must have inconceivable compassion" (Lamotte, 1976, pp. 204–218). [*See also* Pure and Impure Lands.]

Śākyamuni's essential identity with all other Buddhas is often asserted, sometimes subtly, sometimes quite explicitly, as in chapter 15 of the *Saddharmapuṇḍarīka Sūtra* (Lotus of the True Law Scripture). In another *sūtra*, the *Śūraṃgamasamādhi* (Lamotte, 1965, pp. 267–270), the *bodhisattva* Dṛḍimati asks Śākyamuni how long his life will last. Śākyamuni tells him to go and ask another Buddha named Vairocana ("resplendent one"), who presides over a world system named Well Adorned, which is to be reached in the eastern direction by crossing over thirty-two thousand Buddha fields. Having traveled there he is told by that Buddha: "My length of life is exactly the same as that of the Buddha Śākyamuni, and if you really want to know, the length of my life will be seven hundred incalculable world ages." Returning to Śākyamuni, the inquiring *bodhisattva* says: "In so far as I understand the words of the Lord, I would say that it is you, O Lord, who are in the world-system named Well Adorned, where with another name you work for the happiness of all living beings."

So many different kinds of Buddha manifestations are taken for granted in the Mahāyāna *sūtra*s that scholarly efforts have been made to reduce them to some order. The best account of such attempts will be found in Louis de la Vallée Poussin's translation of the *Ch'eng wei-shih lun*, Hsüan-tsang's compilation of ten major commentaries to Vasubandhu's *Triṃśikā* (La Vallée Poussin, 1929, vol. 2, p. 762).

The simplest scheme, which gradually gained general acceptance, envisages an "Absolute Buddha Body" (the *dharmakāya* of early Buddhist tradition) manifesting itself as various "glorious bodies" (*saṃbhogakāya*, "body of enjoyment") to high-ranking *bodhisattva*s in celestial spheres, and as various "human bodies" (*nirmāṇakāya*, "manifested body"), which need not necessarily be human but are usually conceived as such, in impure Buddha fields like our own world. Later Tantric tradition suggests the existence of a fourth, supreme body, known as *svābhāvikakāya* ("self-existent"), but earlier this is used as an alternative name for the Absolute Body *(dharmakāya)*. We shall note later the tendency to arrive at ever-more-transcendent states of Buddhahood, when a sixth, supreme Buddha is placed above the set of five cosmic Buddhas. To these we must now give attention as the production of later Mahāyāna speculation and as the foundation of the whole class of *tantra*s known as Yoga Tantras.

Just as Buddha manifestations, conceived in a diachronic time sequence in accordance with the earlier conceptions of Buddhahood, came to be represented by a triad of Buddhas, referred to as the Buddhas of the Three Times, namely Dīpaṃkara, Śākyamuni, and Maitreya (in this later context he is referred to as Buddha and no longer as *bodhisattva*), so those other Buddha manifestations, conceived synchronically as existing simultaneously in all directions throughout space in accordance with later Mahāyāna conceptions of the universe, came to be symbolized by the Five Buddhas of the cosmos, representing the center and the four cardinal points. These have been popularly referred to as *dhyāni-buddha*s ("meditational Buddhas"), a term that Brian Hodgson (1800–1894) seems to have heard used locally in Nepal but that appears to have no traditionally established justification. In the few *sūtra*s and the many *tantra*s and their commentaries in which they are referred to, they are known simply as the Five Buddhas *(pañcabuddha)* or the Five Tathāgatas *(pañcatathāgata)* with no other ascription. If such is required, then the term *Cosmic Buddhas* seems appropriate, in that their primary function is to represent Buddhahood in its cosmic dimension, as symbolized in the fivefold *maṇḍala*.

As may be expected, this set of five Buddhas evolved gradually, and we find at first various sets of names, some of which become gradually stabilized. Two fairly constant ones from the start are Amitābha ("boundless light") or Amitāyus ("boundless life") as the Buddha of the West, and Akṣobhya ("the imperturbable") as the Buddha of the East. It has been suggested with great plausibility that the Buddha of the West was first accepted as an object of devotion by the Buddhists of the far northwest of the Indian subcontinent as a result of Persian cultural and religious influence, since light and life are essential characteristics of the chief Zoroastrian divinity, Ahura Mazdā. This hypothesis is borne out by the very special devotion shown to this particular Buddha in Central Asia and especially in China and Japan, where a particular constellation of sects (known generically as Pure Land) is devoted to his cult. There is no indication that any such special cult developed elsewhere in India, where Amitābha/Amitāyus remains simply one of the Five Buddhas. Judging by the very large number of images found, the most popular Buddha, certainly in northeastern India, where Buddhism survived until the early thirteenth century, is Akṣobhya, the Buddha of the East. Iconographically he is identified with Śākyamuni Buddha, who was challenged at the time of his enlightenment by Māra, the Evil One (the Satan of Buddhism), to justify his claim to Buddhahood. Śākyamuni called the earth goddess to witness his claim by tapping the ground with the fingers of his right hand, and she duly appeared to give testimony, to the total discomfiture of Māra. A Buddha image formed in this style became the typical image of Bodh Gayā (south of Gayā) in eastern India, where Śākyamuni showed himself imperturbable *(akṣobhya)* despite the assaults of the Evil One.

The geographical choice of this particular Buddha (Akṣobhya) as the Buddha of the East in the later formulation of the set of five is not difficult to understand, being the obvious one because of his popularity in the eastern region. The central Buddha came to be identified with the Buddha image, which must have been typical of another famous place of pilgrimage, the Deer

Park (now known as Sārnāth, a few miles from Vārāṇasī), where Śākyamuni was believed to have preached his first sermon. The gesture of preaching is symbolized by the two hands linked in front of the chest in order to suggest a turning wheel, the "wheel of the doctrine," which Śākyamuni is said to have turned, just as the chariot wheels of a universal monarch (*cakravartin*, "wheel-turner") turn throughout the world.

A Buddha's supremacy in the religious sphere was equated in very early Buddhist tradition with the supremacy of the quasi-historical but mainly mythological concept of a "universal monarch," with the result that a *bodhisattva* is generally idealized as a kind of crown prince; thus it is in princely garments that he is generally portrayed. In particular, Mañjuśrī, Śākyamuni's spokesman in early Mahāyāna *sūtras*, is referred to specifically as the prince *(kumārabhūta)*. It is not surprising that as central Buddha of the set of five, the preaching Śākyamuni comes to be referred to as Vairocana ("resplendent one"), the very Buddha of vast age with whom he claims identity in the *Śūraṃgamasamādhi Sūtra*. The full name of that particular Buddha is in fact Vairocana-raśmipratimaṇḍita-vikurvanarāja ("resplendent one, adorned with light-rays, transformation-king"). The remaining two Buddhas, placed to the south and to the north, become generally stabilized in this configuration as Ratnasambhava ("jewel-born"), presumably symbolizing Śākyamuni's boundless generosity, and Amoghasiddhi ("infallible success"), symbolizing his miraculous powers.

Summarizing these various kinds of Buddha manifestations, one may make the following observations:

1. The state of Buddhahood is essentially one and only, or, to use a safer term, nondual, and nonmanifest in any way whatsoever: such is the Absolute Body of Buddhahood.
2. The various stages at which this Absolute Body may assume apparently manifested form have been explained as various grades of Buddha bodies, of which the Glorious Body, or Body of Enjoyment, and the Human Body, or Manifested Body, are the other two terms in more general use.
3. According to the earliest Buddhist beliefs, Buddhas manifest themselves in a kind of historical sequence, each one presiding over a different world age.
4. According to the later Mahāyāna theories, Buddhas are manifest all the time in all the directions of space, presiding over their individual Buddha fields.

These various concepts, which may appear to an outsider as in some measure conflicting, are retained by those who were responsible for the later formulations, while in general the "historical" Buddha Śākyamuni continues to hold the center of the stage.

Bodhisattvas and Goddesses. Large numbers of *bodhisattvas* are mentioned in the Mahāyāna *sūtras* as residing in various Buddha fields, but very few of these come to receive a special cult as great individuals. The three primary ones, Mañjuśrī, Avalokiteśvara, and Vajrapāṇi, have already been mentioned. These are later identified as the "spiritual sons" of the three primary Buddhas, Śākyamuni (alias Vairocana), Amitābha, and Akṣobhya. The concept of Five Buddhas causes the number of Buddha "families," previously three, to be extended to five, and thus two more leading *bodhisattvas* are required to complete the set. They are known as Ratnapāṇi ("jewel-holder") for the Jewel family of Ratnasambhava, and as Viśvapāṇi ("universal holder") for the Sword or Action family of Amoghasiddhi. Both these are latecomers and their artificial nature is suggested by their names.

In the early Mahāyāna *sutras* we find various *bodhisattvas* named, such as the student Sadāprarudita ("always weeping"), whose story is told in the Perfection of Wisdom literature, or Dṛḍhamati ("firm-minded"), who is the main spokesman in the *Śūraṃgama Sūtra*, or again the *bodhisattva* Dharmākara ("expression of the *dharma*"), who sets the conditions for his own Buddha field through a long series of vows, the fulfillment of which is a precondition for his becoming the Buddha Amitābha. None of these achieves individual fame except for the last as the Buddha Amitābha, of whom he is little more than a formative shadow, like the brahman boy Megha who eventually became the Buddha Śākyamuni. Vimalakīrti, already mentioned above, gains a popular following in Central Asia and in China. Of others so far not mentioned there is the one-time *bodhisattva* Bhaiṣajyarāja ("king of medicine"), named in *The Lotus of the True Law* (see Kern, 1963, pp. 378ff.), whom we find soon elevated to the rank of Buddha with the name of Bhaiṣajyaguru. In certain sets of divinities, the *bodhisattva* Ākāśagarbha ("womb of space") replaces Ratnapāṇi as chief of the Jewel family; neither of these leading *bodhisattvas* appears to attract any special cult. Paralleling Ākāśagarbha, at least in name, is the *bodhisattva* Kṣitigarbha ("womb of the earth"). Perhaps by the mere chance form of his name, Kṣitigarbha achieved enormous success in Central Asia and China as the one who controls the welfare of the dead. By far the most popular of all the "great gods" of Buddhism is Avalokiteśvara, who also assumes the name of Lokeśvara ("lord of the world"), normally Śiva's title in Hindu tradition. It is possible that his name was a deliberate parody of Śiva's title, with the syllables changed sufficiently to give the new meaning of "lord who looks down (in compassion)." It remains doubtful if any image of him can be identified specifically before the sixth century, unless we include the lotus-holding (Padmapāṇi) attendant by Śākyamuni's side, already referred to above. However, by the sixth century his cult is well established, as attested by an entire *sūtra*, the *Kāraṇḍavyūha*, compiled in his honor. It is here that the well-known *mantra* "Oṃ maṇipadme hūṃ" ("O thou with the jeweled lotus") can be firmly identified for the first time. This *mantra*, like the one of Mañjuśrī, is in the form of a feminine vocative for reasons that should become immediately clear.

Feminine divinities first appear within the Buddhist pantheon as handmaidens of the great *bodhisattvas*, whom they accompany in much the same way that Indian princes were usually depicted with a small circle of lady companions. Thus we may note that in the *Mañjuśrīmūlakalpa* (Macdonald, 1962, pp. 107ff.) Avalokiteśvara is surrounded by Pāṇḍaravāsinī ("white-clad"), Tārā ("savioress"), Bhrukuṭi ("frowning"), Prajñāpāramitā ("perfection of wisdom"), Tathāgata-locanā ("Buddha-eye"), and Uṣṇīṣarājā ("lady of the wisdom-bump"). We shall meet with some of these again within the scheme of the fivefold *maṇḍala*, but already two and possibly three look forward to devotional cults of their own, since they become the great goddesses of Buddhism. The goddess Prajñāpāramitā represents the fundamental wisdom of Mahāyāna philosophy, as a divine concept corresponding in many respects to Sancta Sophia of Christian tradition. Even more popular is Tārā, whose flourishing was assured by the salvific assurance conveyed by her name. She was soon recognized as the feminine counterpart (not a partner in the Tantric sense) of Avalokiteśvara. Tārā is his feminine expression, just as Sarasvatī becomes the feminine expression of Mañjuśrī. Thus we may note that since the *mantra* of a great divinity is also his expression (his *vidyā* or special knowledge, as it is often called), his *mantra* too assumes a feminine form. Tārā became so important that many other feminine divinities came to be regarded as her various forms. Thus she appears as Bhrukuṭi when she wishes to show her displeasure, or in the triumphant form of Uṣṇīśasitātapatrā ("lady of the wisdom-bump with the white parasol") when she becomes manifest with a thousand arms and a thousand heads, arranged in paintings so as to appear as a high, elaborate headdress, so that she is in no way grotesque. Here, she corresponds to the eleven-headed, thousand-armed form of Avalokiteśvara.

These more complex forms may clearly be related to subsequent Tantric developments, where the central divinity of the *maṇḍala* may be conceived of as comprising in his person all his various directional manifestations, from four to a thousand. Fluctuation in sex is not uncommon in the early stages of elaboration of this vast and complex pantheon; as is well known, in later Chinese Buddhist tradition Avalokiteśvara (Kuan-yin) merges with Tārā so as to become a feminine divinity. Returning to the *Mañjuśrīmūlakalpa*, we may note that just as Avalokiteśvara is surrounded by benign goddesses (except possibly for Bhrukuṭi), so Vajrapāṇi is surrounded by fierce ones, named Vajrāṇkuśī ("lady of the *vajra* hook"), Vajraśṛṅkhalā ("lady of the *vajra* fetter"), Subāhu ("strong-armed one"), and Vajrasenā ("lady of the *vajra* army"). It is sometimes difficult to draw a line between *bodhisattvas* and great goddesses, but Tārā in her various manifestations is as great as the greatest of *bodhisattvas*. She is saluted as the mother of all Buddhas, and in time Śākyamuni's human mother was duly seen as one of her manifestations.

The travelogue of the famous Chinese pilgrim Hsüan-tsang, who visited monasteries throughout Central Asia and the Indian subcontinent between 629 and 645, well illustrates the extent of popular devotion accorded the images of certain great *bodhisattva* figures during the seventh century CE. Himself a scholarly Mahāyāna philosopher, Hsüan-tsang was nonetheless pleased to hear of the miraculous powers of such images, mentioning in particular those of Maitreya, Avalokiteśvara, and occasionally Mañjuśrī and the great goddess Tārā; on many occasions he offered devout prayers to them on his own account. One may also mention that Hsüan-tsang was equally interested in the cult of *arhats* ("worthy ones"), those early disciples of Śākyamuni Buddha, who, having achieved *nirvāṇa*, were often believed to continue in some kind of suspended existence in remote mountain places. More wonderful tales of *arhats*, tales certainly learned from his Mahāyānist brethren in India, are retold in his account than stories about *bodhisattvas*. In fact, the continuing cult of *arhats* (Chin., *lo-han*), which spread through Central Asia to China, survives in a set of sixteen or eighteen Great Arhats well known to Tibetan Buddhists. [*See* Arhat.] These earlier traditions provide an interesting link, all too often ignored, between Hīnayānists and Mahāyānists. Thus, the Buddhist world of the early centuries CE was peopled with a large variety of celestial beings, among whom certain favorite *bodhisattvas* were only just beginning to come to the fore.

Tantric Buddhism, at least in its higher aspirations, may be described as a system of practices, either of ritual *yoga* or of physical and mental *yoga*, by means of which the practitioner identifies himself with his tutelary divinity, who is identified both with the practitioner's own teacher and with the goal of final enlightenment. One of the main means toward such an objective is the *maṇḍala* or mystic circle of divinities who symbolize existence at all its various levels, the essential sameness of which the pupil must learn to experience through the guidance of his teacher *(guru)*. *Maṇḍalas* are described in earlier *tantras*, where a "three-family" arrangement predominates, but it is not until the so-called Yoga Tantras, with their fivefold arrangement of *maṇḍalas*, begin to appear that the new symbolism can be worked out effectively.

In the earlier Tantras there is a gradation of importance in the various families: the Buddha or Tathāgata family predominates; the Lotus family with its gentle divinities comes next; the Vajra family of Vajrapāṇi and his fierce children comes last. However, in the Yoga Tantras Vajrapāṇi comes right to the fore as the chief representative of Śākyamuni, alias Vairocana. He is also called Vajradhara ("holder of the *vajra*") and Vajrasattva ("*vajra* being"), names that at a later stage of Tantric development refer exclusively to a sixth, utterly supreme Buddha. The main *tantra* of the Yoga Tantra class is the *Sarvatathāgatatattvasaṃgraha* and here the chief *maṇḍala* is known as the Vajradhātu Maṇḍala, the Maṇḍala of the Adamantine Sphere, where *bodhisattvas* with Vajra names, all essentially manifestations of Vajrapāṇi, form circles around the Five Buddhas and the four Buddha goddesses. (See figure 1.) Although *maṇḍala* means circle, the main divin-

FIGURE 1. *The Vajradhātu Maṇḍala: Alternate Rendering 1*

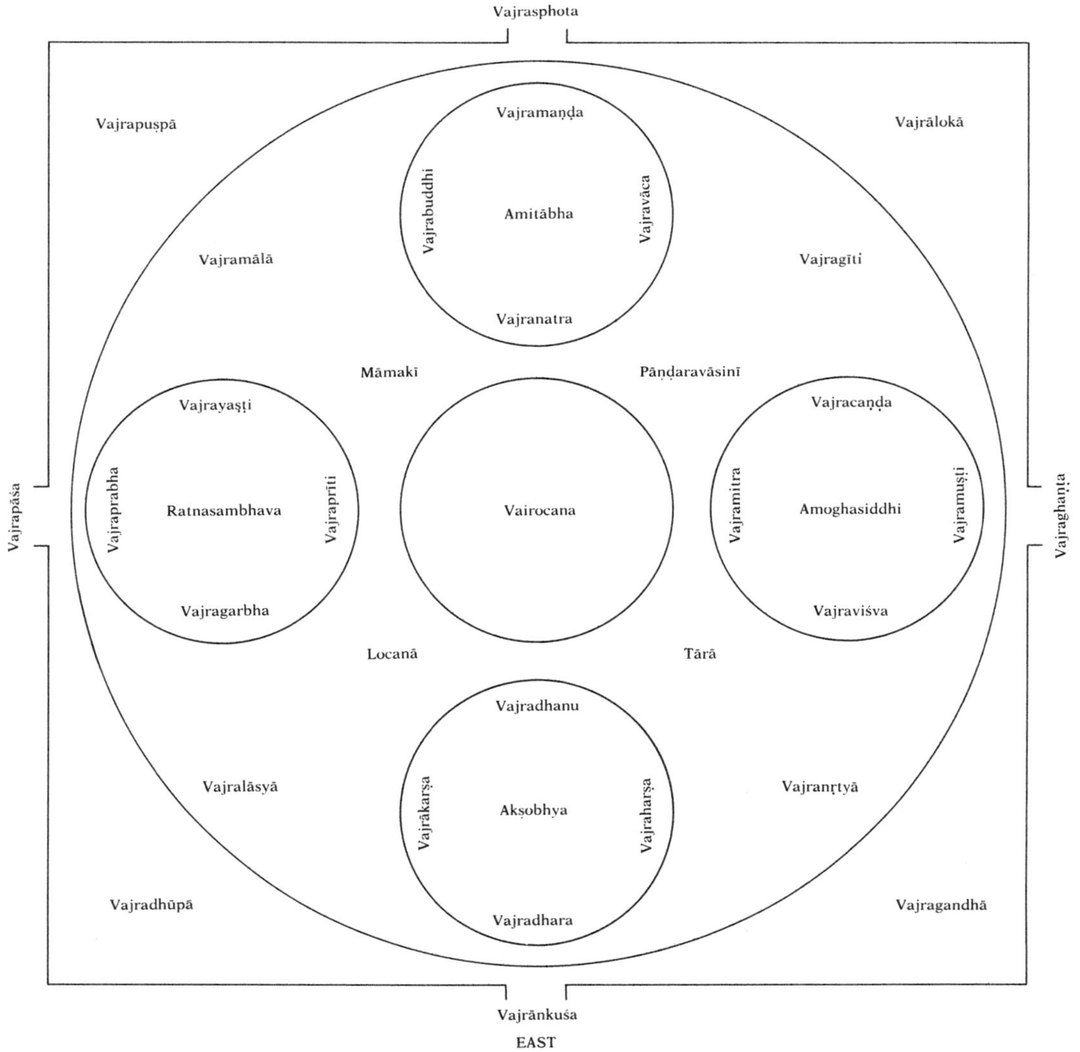

ities may also be arranged around a central square within the main circle, since this square, which is usually provided with four elaborate doorways, represents the sacred palace in which the main divinities dwell. (See figure 2.)

Next in importance after the Five Buddhas are the four Buddha goddesses, who occupy the subsidiary directions of space, namely Locanā, Māmakī ("my very own"), Pāṇḍaravāsinī, and Tārā. They are usually interpreted as symbolizing the four main elements (earth, water, fire, and air), while the fifth (space) coalesces with supreme Buddhahood at the center. In later *tantras* a fifth, central Buddha goddess is named Vajradhātvīśvarī ("lady of the adamantine sphere"), but she does not appear in *maṇḍalas* of the Yoga Tantra class normally, since these coupled male-female divinities (known as *yab-yum,* "father-mother" in Tibetan) do not form part of their symbolism. Apart from the sixteen Great Bodhisattvas, all with Vajra names, we may draw attention to the eight lesser goddesses of the offerings, arranged farther out from the center in the intermediate directions, and the four door guardians at the four main entrances. The eight goddesses of the offerings are mere symbols, as their names indicate at once:

1. Vajralāsyā, or Vajra Frolic
2. Vajradhūpā, or Vajra Incense
3. Vajramālā, or Vajra Garland
4. Vajrapuṣpā, or Vajra Flower
5. Vajragīti, or Vajra Song
6. Vajrālokā, or Vajra Lamp
7. Vajranṛtyā, or Vajra Dance
8. Vajragandhā, or Vajra Scent

The names of the four door guardians, beginning with the eastern one, may be interpreted as Vajra Hook, Vajra Noose, Vajra Fetter, and Vajra Bell.

FIGURE 2. *The Vajradhātu Maṇḍala: Alternate Rendering 2*

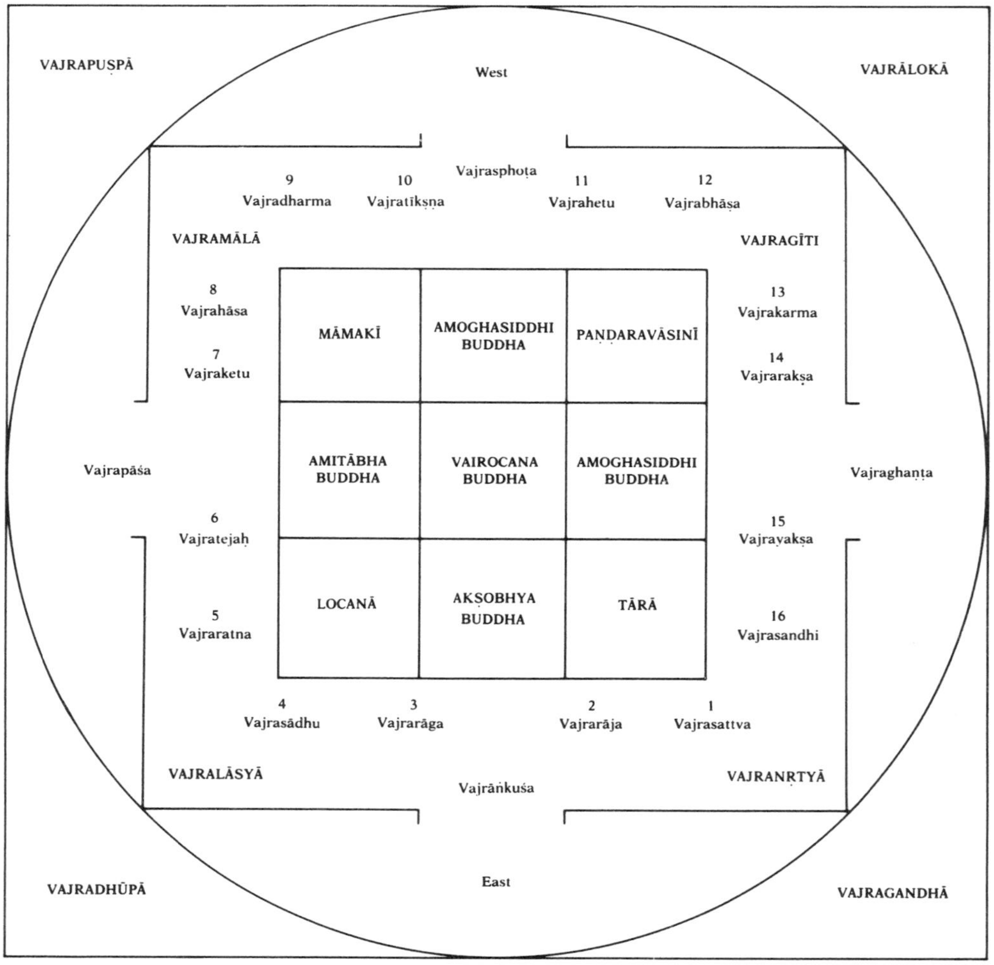

The possible variations within this fundamental pattern are considerable. Thus, the sixteen *bodhisattvas* fall into four groups of four, being allocated in these sets to the four directional Buddhas. The leaders of these four groups are directly identifiable with the chief *bodhisattvas*, already mentioned above, as well as with others who have not yet been mentioned. (See table 1.) Such names are generally interchangeable within the Vajra family, which in the Yoga Tantras is closely associated with the so-called family of All Buddhas. Among the names not met before in this article we draw attention especially to Samantabhadra ("all good"), from whom Vajrapāṇi is said to arise. Since it is also used as a title of Vairocana, the central Buddha, it is not surprising that it is used later as one of the names of a sixth, supreme Buddha.

Other *tantras* of the Yoga Tantra class, while generally retaining all the Buddha goddesses, the sixteen *bodhisattvas*, and lesser divinities, introduce different names and iconographic forms for the Five Buddhas themselves. As devised by Tantric masters in India (presumably from the seventh century onward) from a wide choice of names, to which others could be added as one pleased, the combinations, at least in theory, are infinite. Mañjuśrī in a four-headed and eight-armed manifestation may replace Śākyamuni at the center, and a highly complex *maṇḍala*, which includes the eight Uṣṇīṣa Buddhas as well as the four directional Buddhas together with the sixteen Great Bodhisattvas and a host of lesser divinities, is known as Dharmadhātu Maṇḍala, or the Maṇḍala of the Dharma Sphere, of which a fine example survives in the eleventh-century monastery of Sumda in Zangskar.

Horrific Buddhas. As a result of Śaiva influence transmitted through Tantric yogins of northeast India, celestial Buddhas of horrific appearance become acceptable tutelary divinities in Mahāyāna communities from perhaps the ninth century onward. Most of the *tantras* that describe these divinities provide their own special *maṇḍalas*, with Heruka, Hevajra, Śaṃvara, Caṇḍamahāroṣaṇa, and other such horrific figures clasping their equally horrific feminine partners as they dance on corpses at the center of their circle of *yoginīs*. *Bodhisattvas* are rare in such company. Of the strange Buddha figures just named, only Caṇḍamahāroṣaṇa has male divinities in the four directions, who are all manifestations of Acala ("imperturbable"), a variant of Akṣobhya's name. Claiming superiority over all previous *tantras*, their propagators asserted the existence of a sixth, supreme Buddha, who subsumed the fivefold set, and with whom their particular tutelary divinity is identified. He is usually given the name of Vajrasattva ("*vajra* being") or Vajradhara ("*vajra*-holder"), both of which are titles of Vajrapāṇi in the earlier Yoga Tantras, as has already been noted.

Special mention should be made of the *Guhyasamāja* ("secret union") *Tantra*, for although this *tantra* was later grouped together with the others just mentioned as a so-called Anuttarayoga Tantra ("*tantra* of supreme yoga"), it adheres much more firmly to the fivefold scheme, and although Akṣobhya is made central Buddha of the set of five, the sixth, supreme Buddha is known as Great Vairocana (Mahāvairocana). *Tantras* of the "Old School" (Rñiṅ-ma-pa) of Tibetan Buddhism are to a large extent based on the fivefold scheme of Yoga Tantras with the addition of fierce divinities of the Heruka type. Their supreme Buddha, as in the case of those heterodox Tibetan Buddhists, the Bon-pos, is named Samantabhadra, a title also earlier closely connected with Vajrapāṇi.

Final Survey. While we have pointed out that far too stark a contrast is often drawn between Mahāyāna Buddhism of the early centuries CE with the already developed Buddhism accepted by their Hīnayānist brethren, there is no doubt that the contrast must have been very stark indeed during the last few centuries of Buddhist life in northern India (from the tenth to the twelfth century), concentrated mainly in Kashmir in the far northwest and in Bihar, Bengal, and Orissa in the east. While the monasteries continued to practice the same ancient monastic rules, one of which was adopted by the Tibetans from the eighth century onward (namely that of the order known as Mūlasarvāstivāda, particularly strong in Central Asia and northern India), the cult of Buddhas, *bodhisattvas*, greater and lesser goddesses, and various attendant beings had developed in the manner described above, introducing many new iconographic forms into the temples and covering the walls with murals of the kind that now only survive in the old temples of Ladakh and western Tibet (tenth to thirteenth century). Although no such murals survive in India (those of Ajantā up to the eighth century are the only ones remaining), the close relationship between the early Tibetan paintings and the original Indian ones, now lost, is proved by the many that still can be seen in the form of miniature paintings on manuscripts of the Pāla dynasty, which ruled in eastern India during the last

TABLE 1. *The Four Families of Yoga Tantras*

Family	Associated Deities		
Vajra	Vajrasattva or Vajradhara	Vajrapāṇi	Samantabhadra
Jewel	Vajragarbha	Vajraratna	Ākāśagarbha
Lotus	Vajradharma	Vajranetra	Avalokiteśvara
Karma	Vajraviśva	Vajrakarma	Viśvavajra

Buddhist period. These have survived in Nepal and Tibet, where they were subsequently carried.

It would seem that it was not so much the Mahāyāna that was responsible for the great divergence that develops between the cults of the "early" schools (Hīnayāna) and later Buddhism, despite the very important role that celestial *bodhisattvas* play in Mahāyāna *sūtras*. As noted already, very few of these can be identified iconographically before the sixth or even the seventh century, namely Maitreya, Avalokiteśvara, Mañjuśrī, the great goddess Tārā, and finally Vajrapāṇi, who begins to come to the fore only at the end of this Mahāyāna period. Vajrapāṇi has the best-documented "career" of all Buddhist divinities and it is he (or rather his cult) that results in the Vajrayāna. He appears together with Padmapāṇi ("lotus-holder"), flanking Śākyamuni in several surviving iconographic examples, and the identification of Padmapāṇi with the favorite *bodhisattva* Avalokiteśvara must have suggested a higher status for Vajrapāṇi as well. This he receives in the earliest *tantras*, but he still heads the lowest of the three families, for it is clearly taught that those who receive consecration in his Vajra family cannot perform rites in the two higher families.

It is only in the Yoga Tantras, which become well-known from the eighth century onward, that Vajrapāṇi comes fully to the fore as the leading *bodhisattva*, for all the *maṇḍalas* are based on the Vajradhātu Maṇḍala, even those of the Buddha (or All Buddhas) family. It is thus from this time on that one may correctly speak of a Vajrayāna, as distinct in many ways from the Mahāyāna. All the later *tantras*, which came to be classed as Tantras of Supreme Yoga, belong effectively to the Vajra family. It is even said that Vajrapāṇi himself taught them on the instructions of Śākyamuni Buddha, for although the Yoga Tantras and all earlier ones together with all Mahāyāna *sūtras* are explicitly taught as the word of the Buddha (i.e., Śākyamuni) himself, there was some understandable hesitancy in attributing the Yoginī Tantras, as they were earlier called, directly to him. Moreover, as related above, the sixth, supreme Buddha of these *tantras* is named as Vajrasattva or Vajradhara, titles that are applied exclusively to Vajrapāṇi in the Yoga Tantras. Thus with these exclusive titles and with a slightly developed iconographic form he attains the highest possible rank in the Buddhist pantheon. It has already been pointed out that no later development ever nullifies earlier ones, with the result that Vajrapāṇi continues to fulfill all the roles described above.

Mañjuśrī also becomes the representative of supreme Buddhahood in the Dharmadhātu Maṇḍala; later he receives a form expressing the union of "means" *(upāya)* and wisdom in that he clasps his feminine partner to his breast in the manner of all the great Tantric divinities of this class of *tantra*. Known as Mañjuvajra, he is in essence identical with Vajradhara/Vajrasattva. On the other hand, Avalokiteśvara remains the most popular of the great *bodhisattvas*, especially in his triumphant eleven-headed thousand-armed form. But despite his close relationship with Tārā, his feminine counterpart, neither he nor she is even thought to have lost their virginity. It is interesting to note how all the great *bodhisattvas*, despite iconographic changes, preserve their most essential attributes throughout the whole history of Buddhism. Being a powerful queller of the foe, it is Vajrapāṇi who forcibly converts the great gods of Hinduism, thus becoming their leader and finally the representative of all terrible divinities who are raised to high Buddhist rank. Mañjuśrī remains the representative of pure Buddhist teaching (despite his aberrational form as Mañjuvajra): when the followers of Tsoṅ-kha-pa (1357–1419) look for a suitably holy lineage for the leader of the reformed Tibetan Dge-lugs-pa ("yellow hat") order, they identify him as an incarnation of this particular *bodhisattva*. Avalokiteśvara remains popular for his unbounded compassion for the sufferings of all living beings. In order to save living beings, he is prepared to be born in any of the wretched places of existence, among suffering animals or tormented spirits, and even in the regions of hell. It was thus not difficult to suggest that he might also deliberately appear on earth as a recognizable incarnation. Since the Tibetans, in accordance with their pre-Buddhist beliefs, accepted their early kings (those from the sixth to the ninth century) as divine representatives from the heavens, it is not at all surprising that the king during whose reign Buddhism was first introduced into the country (namely Sroṅ-brstan-sgam-po, d. 650?) should have been retrospectively regarded as an incarnation of the *bodhisattva* Avalokiteśvara.

When the fifth Dalai Lama reunited Tibet under his rule in 1642 this same distinction was claimed for him, and since then all succeeding Dalai Lamas, while being theoretically reincarnations of their predecessors, are at the same time honored as incarnations of Avalokiteśvara. Other interesting high incarnations are those of the Grand Lama of Bkra-śis-lhun-po (Tashilhunpo), who is identified traditionally with the Buddha Amitābha, and the abbess of Bsam-sdings Monastery (now presumably destroyed), near the Yar-'brog (Yamdrok) Lake, who is identified with the boar-headed partner of the horrific Tantric Buddha Cakrasaṃvara, known as Vajravārāhī ("adamantine sow"), a sufficient indication that such "converted" Hindu divinities were in practice accorded *bodhisattva* rank.

From the above comments it should be clear that it is difficult to draw distinctions in late Indian Buddhism and in Tibetan religion, which inherits the greater part of Indian Buddhist traditions, between *bodhisattvas* and other divinities who are effectively raised to *bodhisattva* rank. Thus, to my knowledge the position of the four chief goddesses, Locanā, Māmakī, and so forth, as well as that of the feminine partners of the great Tantric divinities (who are themselves manifestly accorded full Buddha rank) is scarcely definable in traditional Buddhist terms. They are all said to be manifestations of the Perfection of Wisdom, at least according to the later Tantric theories, and thus an associate Buddha rank must be assumed for them. Clearer distinctions, however, continue to remain between Buddhas and *bodhisattvas*, in accordance with the ideas prevalent during the earliest Buddhist period. According to purist theories, once a *bodhisattva* achieves enlightenment and thereby becomes a Buddha ("enlightened") he effectively passes beyond the realm of imperfect living beings. The fact that Śākyamuni Buddha continued to work for the good of others during the forty-five years that elapsed between his enlightenment at the age of thirty-five and his decease *(parinirvāṇa)* at the age of eighty created a philosophical problem for the philosophers of the early schools. Only as *bodhisattva* can there be no doubt of his ability to respond to the needs of lesser beings. It may be for this reason that some early Buddha images are inscribed as *bodhisattva* images, for Śākyamuni in the earliest period could be regarded as both Buddha and *bodhisattva*.

The cult of Maitreya as future Buddha soon supplied the need for a *bodhisattva*, who could still assist living beings so long as he had not entered the impassive state of Buddhahood. His cult was followed by that of Avalokiteśvara, the "lord who looks down (in compassion)," doubtless suggested by Śākyamuni's previous existence in the heavens, when as *bodhisattva* he had looked down on suffering living beings. The whole *bodhisattva* doctrine represents a remarkable aspect of Buddhist religion, expressing a degree of compassionate concern for others that is either far less developed or lacking altogether in other Indian religious traditions. The distinction between a Buddha who represents an ideal state still to be achieved and a *bodhisattva* who assists one on the way there remains fairly clear throughout the whole history of Buddhism. Only rarely can a Buddha become an object of prayer and supplication. One well-known exception is Amitābha, the Buddha of the West. But one may note that his cult, so strong in China and Japan, is based upon the *Sukhāvativyūha Sūtra*, which lists the many aspirations of the monk Dharmākara toward achieving Buddhahood in a Buddha paradise, where he may still be available for the solace of living beings in the most marvelous manner possible. This particular Buddha cult may therefore be regarded as exceptional.

[*For further discussion concerning the nature of the Buddha, see* Buddha *and* Tathāgata. *The career of the* bodhisattva *is treated in* Bodhisattva Path. *The larger cultic and doctrinal contexts of these figures are treated in* Buddhism, Schools of, *articles on* Mahāyāna Buddhism *and* Esoteric Buddhism; Soteriology, *article on* Buddhist Soteriology; *and* Nirvāṇa. *See also* Maṇḍalas, *article on* Buddhist Maṇḍalas. *For discussion of the particular figures referred to here, see especially* Amitābha; Avalokiteśvara; Bhaiṣajyaguru; Kṣitigarbha; Mahāvairocana; Maitreya; Mañjuśrī; *and* Tārā.]

BIBLIOGRAPHY

References

Beal, Samuel, trans. *Si-yu-ki: Buddhist Records of the Western World* (1884). Reprint, Delhi, 1969.

Conze, Edward, trans. and ed. *Buddhist Scriptures*. Harmondsworth, 1959.

Conze, Edward, trans. *The Large Sūtra of Perfect Wisdom*. Berkeley, 1975.

Dayal, Har. *The Bodhisattva Doctrine in Buddhist Sanskrit Literature* (1932). Reprint, New Delhi, 1975.

Hodgson, Brian H. *Essays on the Languages, Literature and Religion of Nepal and Tibet* (1874). Reprint, New Delhi, 1972.

Kern, Hendrik, trans. *Saddharmā-Puṇḍarīka, or The Lotus of the True Law* (1884). Reprint, New York, 1963.

Lamotte, Étienne, trans. and ed. *La concentration de la marche héroïque*. Brussels, 1965. A translation of the *Śūraṃgamasamādhi Sūtra*.

Lamotte, Étienne, trans. *The Teaching of Vimalakīrti*. London, 1976. A translation of the *Vimalakīrtinirdeśa Sūtra*, rendered from Étienne Lamotte's *L'enseignement de Vimalakīrti* (Louvain, 1962).

La Vallée Poussin, Louis de, ed. and trans. *Vijñaptimātratāsiddhi: La Siddhi de Hiuan-tsang*. 2 vols. Paris, 1928–1929.

Macdonald, Ariane, trans. *Le maṇḍala du Mañjuśrīmūlakalpa*. Paris, 1962.

Skorupski, Tadeusz. *The Sarvadurgatipariśodhana Tantra: Elimination of All Evil Destinies*. Delhi, 1983.

Snellgrove, David L. *Indo-Tibetan Buddhism, Indian Buddhists and Their Tibetan Successors*. Boston and London, 1986.

Snellgrove, David L., and Tadeusz Skorupski. *The Cultural Heritage of Ladakh*. 2 vols. Warminster, 1977–1980.

Tucci, Giuseppe. *Indo-Tibetica*. 4 vols. Rome, 1932–1941.

Further Reading

Bhattacharyya, Benoytosh. *The Indian Buddhist Iconography* (1924). 2d. rev. ed., Calcutta, 1958.

Getty, Alice. *The Gods of Northern Buddhism* (1914). Reprint, Oxford, 1963.

Mallmann, Marie-Thérèse de. *Introduction à l'iconographie du tântrisme bouddhique*. Paris, 1975.

Snellgrove, David L., ed. *The Image of the Buddha.* London, 1978.

Tucci, Giuseppe. *Tibetan Painted Scrolls.* 2 vols. Translated by Virginia Vacca. Rome, 1949.

DAVID L. SNELLGROVE

CELIBACY, the deliberate abstinence from sexual activity, derives its religious value from the vital human significance of sex itself. The different roles played by celibacy in the world's religions then reflect different attitudes toward procreation and earthly existence. Thus, traditions oriented toward fecundity and wordly success, like those of most nonliterate peoples, rarely if ever enjoin permanent celibacy for anyone; only periods of temporary celibacy preceding and following childbirth and at crucial communal rituals are prescribed. The great traditions of Hinduism, Buddhism, and Christianity, on the other hand, all oriented toward otherwordly goals, have firmly established roles for celibate monks working out their salvation. And smaller, extreme groups with radically negative views of life in the world may prescribe celibacy as an ideal for all. The reasons offered for celibacy consequently range from concerns for personal physical health to a total rejection of the physical body. Religious institutions, moreover, differ both in the ways of life that they prescribe for the celibate and in the image of the celibate that they present to laypersons.

Traditional Perceptions. The placement of deliberate religious restraints on physical behavior, celibacy is often explained within tradition through physiological as well as metaphysical concepts. Asian esoteric texts, moreover, can be most explicit about the spiritual potentials of reproductive energies. Traditional understandings of celibacy, then, present a continuity that spans ideas about marriage and procreation, spiritual powers, spiritual purity, and chaste marriage to the divine.

Temporary concentration of reproductive energies. The perception that sexual intercourse during pregnancy and lactation will harm an infant is found in many cultures, including some contemporary Western folk traditions. The larger worldviews in which this perception is embedded may thus vary immensely. For the Arapesh of New Guinea, the practice of temporary celibacy has a positive religious significance for procreation. According to Arapesh ideas, the fetus is shaped and nurtured by both parents through several weeks of frequent and purposeful intercourse after the mother's menstruation stops. Yet once the mother's breasts enlarge in the first obvious sign of pregnancy, the child is considered fully formed and all intercourse must cease. After the child is born, the parents are supposed to sleep together with it, devote their energies to it, and give it special attention. If either parent indulges in sexual activity—even with other partners—before the child can walk, they say that it will become weak and perhaps die. With infanticide common among the Arapesh, choosing to keep a child is a deliberate decision, and this extended celibacy surrounding childbirth, once chosen, is normally kept. Celibacy then appears to represent here a conscious channeling and concentration of the reproductive power of both parents for the good of the child, lineage, and community.

The power of holy persons. Adepts in the esoteric traditions of Asia are often aware of transmuting their reproductive power into spiritual power and channeling it within. [*See* Magico-Religious Powers.] This perception lies behind certain occult meditation techniques found in both India and Taoist China that draw on a tension between continence, in a strict sense, and sexual intercourse. Through entering a woman and still remaining continent, the male adept arouses sexual energy in both partners, which can then be absorbed inwardly for spiritual transformation. [*See* Tantrism.] More often, however, adepts practice techniques that entail only physiological imagery: Taoist spiritual alchemy may lead to the generation of an immortal fetus; Hindu yogins speak of channeling the seed upward through higher centers of the body. [*See* Kuṇḍalinī.] For most adepts, then, total celibacy is crucial in order to preserve the spiritual potencies of their own seed, a point also affirmed in popular tradition: Hindu mythological texts are full of stories of ascetics who succumbed to lust and lost their powers.

Thus, the power of holy persons also depends in good part on their self-control. The word *yoga,* in fact, deriving from a root meaning "to yoke," can often be best understood in a very concrete sense: a willful harnessing of the vital energies, which are considered prone to rage like beasts. So even in traditions like Christianity that do not explicitly posit a direct continuity between sexual and spiritual energies, celibacy still appears as a measure of powerful mastery over the senses. Latin Catholicism gives us stories of triumphant (and faltering) ascetics struggling with incubi or succubi, attractive male or female spirits bent on seducing them. Among the American Shakers, a struggle with sexual desire became the distinctive focal point through which an active Protestant sect sought to reform human existence. For the Shakers, the world of sensual experience itself was so overwhelming that a break with it required radical means: absolute abstention. In this instance, perfect celibacy expresses an attempt at total self-mastery.

Separation from the impure. Ascetics who aim to subjugate the flesh usually have no high opinion of the gross physical matter that constitutes it. The eventual aim of controlling the sexual nature for many can then become the achievement of distance from a fundamentally impure, degenerate, and transient world. The perception of the physical body itself as disgusting and ultimately worthless may be actively cultivated in monastic traditions, sometimes through deliberate meditation practice. In the near-canonical *Visuddhimagga,* Theravāda Buddhist monks are enjoined to detach themselves from sensual desire by contemplating the dead body in various stages of decomposition (swollen, bluish, gnawed, worm-eaten) and the live body as filled, among other things, with intestines, excrement, bile, pus, fat, mucus, and urine (chaps. 6, 8). Sexual activity in this context can easily be seen as another disgusting physical function from which all wise people should abstain.

In nonliterate cultures, which usually have fewer qualms about the physical body, the impurity attributed to sex may stem in part from its potential danger to the social fabric. Built up out of kinship bonds, tribal societies may splinter over family tensions and conflicts about women. Temporary celibacy is thus often enjoined at crucial public rituals that highlight communal solidarity—initiations, hunting expeditions, the start of a group journey.

The image of chaste asexuality encompassing the common good is also found in Western religious institutions. Roman state religion, which is often, in fact, understood to derive from the religion of family and clan, exalted the Vestal Virgins. The keepers of Rome's communal hearth, the Vestal Virgins were legally neither men nor women. Buried alive if they violated their chastity, their most crucial obligation was celibacy itself. People in literate as well as nonliterate cultures, then, may believe that sacred institutions maintaining the welfare of humanity as a whole should depend on individuals in an extraordinary state, beyond human sexuality.

Ideas about the impurity of sex known both to the Roman world's ascetics and in its politico-religious institutions were assimilated and transformed by early Christians, who by the fourth century had recognized the source of their own religious institution in the virgin son of a virgin mother. For Christians, then, maintaining virginity can be an imitation of divine models and the purity of permanent celibacy can offer a constant tie to what is realized as primal in religious experience. Appearing as the original state of man born of the spirit, celibacy in Christianity, as in other traditions, promises innocence—eternal childhood in the Lord.

Exclusive attachment to the divine. Being an eternal child in God can free the celibate from many worldly responsibilities. Luke's reference to chaste persons as "equal to angels" (20:35–36) suggests not only the innocence of celibates, but also their roles as agents of God, in no way beholden to man. Certainly, the ability to devote all of one's efforts to spiritual matters without the burden of family obligations is a very frequently voiced justification for celibacy in the East as well as in the West. In India, the practical implications of celibacy for a life devoted to religious pursuits has explicit expression in the semantic range of the Sanskrit word *brahmacarya,* which occurs very frequently in religious writings. Used most often to refer to sexual abstention, *brahmacarya* literally means "walking with *brahman,*" the primal divine essence; at the same time, *brahmacarya* may be used to refer specifically to the first stage in the traditional Hindu life cycle, which is supposed to be devoted to religious study. Thus, a word suggesting adherence to first divine principles explicitly links the concept of celibacy to distinctly religious pursuits and the absence of worldly, adult responsibilities.

In a highly dualistic theology, strict adherence to first principles can demand an absolute withdrawal from involvement in earthly endeavors. Abstinence from sex is required less to follow active religious pursuits freely than to desist from physical procreation. For a gnostic like Marcion (d. 160?), the physical world is the creation of a false god, not the true one; trapped in physical bodies, souls cannot return to their real, original home. From this perspective, making more physical bodies only means making more prisons for human souls, and keeping celibate represents a refusal to further the false, earthly creation.

By inhibiting fruitful physical unions, celibacy may also strengthen the devotee's spiritual union with the Lord. Indeed, in devotional traditions, physical sexual abstinence is often a sign of faithful attachment to the divine beloved. Hindu devotional poetry idealizes the stalwart devotee as the Lord's faithful wife, a concept institutionalized in Catholic orders that identify nuns as brides of Christ. Moreover, Christian as well as Hindu mystics sometimes express themselves in terms of nuptial ecstasy. Though the patriarchal heritages of East and West usually present the aspiring soul in feminine guise, dependent on the will of her Lord, men too can adopt a passionate devotional attitude. In India, both male and female devotees of Kṛṣṇa understand the highest spiritual state in terms of romantic love, and make much of Kṛṣṇa's amorous dalliance with the adoring milkmaids of his pastoral childhood home. Some theologians of Kṛṣṇa worship have further pointed out that the milkmaids were in fact married women, and that the most intense desire between men and women actually takes place outside routinized marriage, between clandestine lovers. So, paradoxically, the milkmaids' passionate attachment to Kṛṣṇa—an important ideal for a large tradition of Indian celibates—is frequently represented as wives' unchaste betrayal of their husbands. Thus, as radical departures from ordinary convention, both celibacy and sexual abandon become religious parallels to one another. [*See* Desire.]

The Place of Celibacy in Society. Like total sexual abandon, moreover, total abstinence is not a generally recommended practice in most traditions, and the social regulation of sexual behavior may entail curbs on celibacy as well as on indulgence. Indeed, traditional cultures often present celibacy and procreation in a complementary relationship, which can be ordered according to the calendrical cycle, the life cycle, or divisions in the society as a whole. At the same time, separate communities of celibates have their own norms of sexual propriety, and the maintenance of these norms is often crucial for the image of the celibate in the eyes of laypersons.

Procreation and abstinence in traditional societies. Clearly, no civilization can survive for long without some provision for procreation, and religious traditions with strong ethnic roots, like Confucianism and Judaism, may have no place at all for the permanent celibate. Although traditional Judaism proscribes sexual relations outside marriage, all Jews are expected to marry and engage regularly in conjugal relations. Indeed, the Sabbath itself is thought of as a bride, and to celebrate its arrival Jewish husbands are enjoined to have intercourse with their wives joyously on Sabbath eve. In Judaism, then, controlled religious pursuits should also embrace sanctified procreation throughout a mature person's life.

The most highly structured relationships between abstinence and procreation are found in traditional India, where classical Hindu tradition sees these relationships ordered not, as in Judaism, in a lifelong weekly cycle, but in the cycle of each individual life. The life stages of classical Hinduism are fourfold: (1) *brahmacarya*, a period of celibate study; (2) *gṛhasta*, the householder stage, in which traditional Hindus were expected to marry and have many children, particularly sons who would perform their death rites; (3) *vanaprastha* ("forest dwelling"), the later stage of marriage, after the children were fully raised and had received most of their inheritance, and when abstinence was prescribed; and finally (4) *saṃnyāsa*, the stage of total renunciation of settled life as well as sex. The classical Hindu life cycle, then, begins and ends in celibacy, but prescribes a sexually fruitful period of life as a householder in between.

Giving celibacy an explicit place in the individual life cycle, Hindu tradition also gives celibate individuals an explicit place in society. [*See* Saṃnyāsa.] Hindus recognize that exceptional individuals will want to live all their lives as celibate ascetics, either prolonging their studies indefinitely as *brahmacārin*s or bypassing the householder stage by making early formal renunciation. Today, Hindus tend to collapse the first and last stages of the cycle and ignore the third, thus resolving the four stages of the life cycle into two social states: householders fruitfully participating in society, nurturing new souls, and supporting ascetics; and solitary celibates outside society, working out their own salvation. In most Indian cosmologies, the participation of householders as well as celibates is required in the proper economy of salvation in the cosmos.

Sexual norms in celibate groups. In Theravāda Buddhism, the complementary roles of the householder and celibate were institutionalized and given a distinctive religious valuation. The community of monks—the *saṃgha*—should be supported by the laity, but the proper ordering of the cosmos (and so the welfare of the laity) depends on the *saṃgha*'s purity, conceived in good part as its sexual purity. Thus, in the Vinaya Piṭaka, the monastic disciplinary code, specific rules governed everyday practices that had even the most subtle sexual implications, from propriety in dress to contact with women. Atonement for even minor sexual infractions required not only confessions but also a formal legal decision handed down in a meeting of the community. Sexual intercourse with a woman was one of the few grounds for immediate expulsion from the *saṃgha*.

Perhaps more crucial than the rules regulating the contact between members of a celibate community and potential sexual partners outside it are those controlling the relationships among the community members themselves. These rules can be especially complex in celibate communities of mixed sex. The Shakers, a mixed celibate community founded by a woman, maintained strict segregation between the sexes; men and women were even to avoid passing each other on stairways. Taking in children and youths to raise, they kept them under tight control. Children were not allowed out at night except for some specific reason (and not for any reason on Saturday evenings); lest they be tempted, children even of the same sex were not to be left unattended at their weekly bath. In whole communities of the same sex, too, provisions are often made to inhibit physical contact among members. Though the *Rule of*

Saint Benedict, which stands behind much of Western monastic life, has little explicit to say about celibacy itself, it does include provisions apparently aimed at the prevention of homosexuality. Monks should sleep in separate beds, clothed and with a light burning; though inmates of monasteries should sleep in groups, young monks should not sleep alone as a group but should be together with older ones (chap. 22). The abbots seemed to recognize that ideals of spiritual love among members of their communities could stand in practical tension with vows of celibacy.

Yet more often than not, the physical chastity of cloistered monks is rarely tested; the crucial spiritual role of sexual restrictions on celibates is less the prevention of sexual activity than of sexual thoughts. For celibates living outside the cloister, continually interacting with laypersons, temptation and desire can become particularly problematic. Necessary celibacy for diocesan priests has been frequently questioned, both inside and outside the Roman Catholic church. In pre-Reformation Europe, many priests openly took concubines, and the last half of the twentieth century has heard continuing discussion of the value of requiring celibacy for all priests. The tensions facing the modern priest are understandable: living in a sexually open society and as a confessor hearing detailed accounts of the intimate lives of individuals, he is nevertheless expected to exercise the same sexual discipline—both mentally and physically—of the cloistered monk.

The image for the layperson. The persistence of sacerdotal celibacy in Roman Catholic tradition may lie, in part, in the image that the priest holds for the laity. As an administrator of divine office, the priest is seen to function within the holy mother church and should reflect her virginal purity. The ideal of virginal purity for its officiants is maintained even in the Eastern Orthodox church: though married men are allowed to become priests, they are not allowed to rise to the highest episcopal office, and once a man has become a priest he may not take a wife. As representatives of a sacred institution regarded as pure, Buddhist monks project a similar image of chaste holiness in Theravāda society. Like priests, monks are formal participants in Theravāda ritual, much of which involves the feeding of monks by laypersons. The religious power of the rite for laypersons depends in part on the monks' perceived purity.

A vow of celibacy, moreover, can make individuals appear remarkable beyond the confines of sanctified ritual. No longer appearing as ordinary mortals, celibates can be relaxed in their socioreligious roles. The Roman Catholic priest can joke and gossip with parishioners and not have to worry too much about a decorous image. A Theravāda monk, even if he is not particularly charismatic, at least withstands the rigors of chastity—an experience familiar to many male Theravādins who have temporarily taken the robe. Among Hindu gurus, the married ones may feel constrained to appear particularly scrupulous in financial matters; celibate gurus, on the other hand, not burdened by family responsibilities, are said to be more easily trusted. And in all traditions, celibate hermits who do not interact readily with laypersons may, through their renunciation of society, seem awesome and powerful.

Conclusion. In setting individuals apart from normal life, deliberate celibacy can render them extraordinary both to themselves and to others. In crucial situations, temporary abstinence is undertaken by members of many cultures, either to achieve distance from impurity during rituals or to channel reproductive energy at the birth of a child. In religions oriented toward salvation, more permanent vows of celibacy affirm the links of individuals to powers higher than this world, often as members of sanctified institutions. In these ways, celibacy makes people seem less grossly, physically human, and thus, sometimes, more divine.

[*See also* Asceticism *and* Virginity.]

BIBLIOGRAPHY

A monograph on celibacy from a cross-cultural perspective has yet to be written, but a number of works offer interesting perspectives on the subject. In *Purity and Danger* (New York, 1966), Mary Douglas gives a valuable anthropological analysis of kinds of sexual abstinence that are derived from ideas of impurity, with a focus on nonliterate cultures. A comparative treatment of Arapesh abstinence at childbirth is found in Margaret Mead's *Sex and Temperament in Three Savage Societies* (London, 1935). In *Taoist Yoga: Alchemy and Immortality* (London, 1970), Charles Luk presents a translation of a turn-of-the-century Chinese text that treats the spiritual transformation of sexual energies. Mircea Eliade's *Yoga: Immortality and Freedom,* 2d ed. (Princeton, 1969), treats this dimension of celibacy along with many others in Hindu religious traditions. Social-scientific insight on the role of celibate monks in Theravāda Buddhist culture is presented in Stanley J. Tambiah's *Buddhism and the Spirit Cults in North-east Thailand* (Cambridge, 1970), and a socioreligious perspective on the Shakers is given in Louis J. Kern's *An Ordered Love* (Chapel Hill, N.C., 1981), which presents the Shakers as a radical Protestant community.

Some of the earliest Christian ideas about chastity are available in Sally Rieger Shore's translations of two of John Chrysostom's tracts, published as *On Virginity; Against Remarriage* (Lewiston, N.Y., 1983). The development of a celibate priesthood in Catholicism is traced in Henry C. Lea's *History of Sacerdotal Celibacy in the Christian Church,* 3d rev. ed., 2 vols. (New York, 1907), which presents a full, but negatively biased, account. *Celibacy in the Church,* edited by William Bassett and Peter Huizing (New York, 1972), presents useful articles reflecting the dialogue on priestly celibacy current in the early 1970s. In the context of that dialogue, the noted Dutch churchman Edward Schillebeekx has written *Celibacy*, translated by C. A. L. Jarrott (New York, 1968), a short but insightful theological monograph with some useful historical background.

DANIEL GOLD

CELTIC RELIGION. Historical references to the Celts begin in the fifth century BCE. Herodotus and Hecataeus of Miletus are the forerunners of a long series of Greek and Latin writers whose reports and comments, both well- and ill-informed, reflect the changing fortunes of the Celtic peoples during the pre-Christian era and their impact on the Greco-Roman world. Herodotus and Hecataeus confirm that by about 500 BCE the Celts were already widely dispersed over central and western Europe, including perhaps Gaul and the Iberian Peninsula, and evidence from the fifth century testifies to further territorial expansion. About 400 BCE this process quickened as tribal bands invaded northern Italy and there established settlements which in due course were to become the Roman province of Gallia Cisalpina. Some Celtic bands raided farther south, as far as Rome and Apulia and even Sicily, and about 387 they captured and sacked the city of Rome, an event of traumatic importance to Roman history. To the east, other Celtic tribes penetrated into the Carpathians and the Balkans during the fourth century BCE. In 279 some of them entered Greece and plundered the shrine at Delphi, and in the following year three Celtic tribes, known collectively to the Greeks as Galatae, crossed into Asia Minor and eventually settled in the region which still bears the name Galatia. In Britain, the final phase of Celtic settlement came with the arrival of the Belgae in the first century BCE, though there is archaeological evidence of earlier immigrations dating back as far as the fifth century BCE. For Ireland, the evidence is complicated, and one cannot confidently infer a Celtic presence before the third century BCE.

By the early third century BCE the Celts extended across the length of Europe from Britain to Asia Minor, and they were considered one of the three or four most important barbarian peoples in the known world. Thereafter, however, their history is one of decline. Harried by Germans in the north, Dacians in the east, and Romans in the south, the continental Celts saw their widespread dominion disintegrate and contract until their realm came to be associated solely with Gaul, where they maintained their independence until their conquest by Caesar (58–51 BCE). In Britain and Ireland the process was longer drawn out, but there too Celtic society was gradually eroded and submerged by foreign domination, and at present Celtic languages are spoken only on the western periphery, in restricted areas of Ireland, Scotland, Wales, and Brittany. The insular languages belong to two distinct branches of Celtic and perhaps reflect an older dialectal division among the Celtic-speaking peoples of Europe: Goidelic, which comprises Irish and Scottish Gaelic (and formerly Manx), and British or Brythonic, which comprises Welsh and Breton (and formerly Cornish). However, Breton, which is largely the product of immigration to Brittany from southwest Britain from around the fourth to the seventh century CE, may also have absorbed surviving elements of Gaulish speech.

The entry of the Celts into the written record coincides with the first evidences of the Second Iron Age, also known as La Tène culture, which refers broadly to those areas of Europe historically associated with the Celts. But the further back we go beyond the fifth century BCE, the more difficult it becomes to use the term *Celts* with reasonable confidence, lacking as we do the correlatives of language and written reference. The cultural phase which preceded La Tène, known as Hallstatt, dates from the ninth century BCE and covers an expanse of territory extending at least from Burgundy to Bohemia. Hallstatt culture is characterized by elaborate chariot burials and by the use of iron rather than bronze for arms and utensils. It is the product of a warrior aristocracy which is generally recognized as Celtic, or at least as the direct ancestor of the Celts of the following period. Obviously, the definition of a Celtic identity must have been the product of a long period of linguistic and cultural evolution, and some archaeologists have ventured to identify as proto-Celtic the peoples of the Urnfield culture and of the Tumulus culture which preceded it in the second millennium BCE, or even the peoples of the Beaker and Battle-Ax cultures of the third millennium BCE. But this is mere speculation; one cannot even say with assurance at what point in the archaeological record the Indo-Europeans made their appearance in central and western Europe. And yet most scholars discern in the culture of the Tumulus peoples features that are echoed in that of La Tène.

Sources. The sources for Celtic religion fall broadly into two categories: the first comprises the various monuments relating to the Celts on the continent, particularly in Gaul, and in Roman Britain; the second comprises the insular Celtic literatures that have been preserved in writing. The two types pose problems that are very different in character. Most dedicatory inscriptions, images of Celtic deities, and commentaries by classical authors belong to the Roman period and probably reflect in varying degrees the effect of Roman influence on Gaulish institutions. For example, since Gaulish sculpture is based for the most part on Greco-Roman models, it is often difficult to assess and interpret its relevance to native belief. Even where motifs and figures seem clearly to derive from pre-Roman religious tradition, as in some of the Celtic coins of the third and second centuries BCE, these are not easily related to what we know of insular Celtic myth and ritual.

The difficulty is that we lack the literature which would provide a context for the iconography as well as a key to its understanding. The druids, as Caesar records, accorded primacy to the spoken word and refused to commit their teaching to writing. Consequently, the whole of the traditional literature, including the mythology which gave the iconography its meaning, was confined to oral transmission and perished with the extinction of the Gaulish language. The total loss of this vernacular literature, which was doubtless comparable in volume and variety with that of early Ireland, renders all the more significant the testimony of those classical authors who recorded their own or others' observations on the Celts. Probably the most important was Posidonius (c. 135–c. 50 BCE), who had firsthand knowledge of diverse cultures, including the Celtic, in southern Gaul, and who devoted the twenty-third chapter of his lost *Histories* to Celtic ethnography. Much of his account of the Celts survives in the work of later writers who borrowed from him, such as the historian Diodorus Siculus, the geographer Strabo, and, most notably of all, Julius Caesar, whose account is crucial for the study of Gaulish religion.

The limitations of the classical sources are obvious. Most of their reports come at second- or third-hand and are subject to the prejudices and preconceptions born of classical civilization—or even, as in the case of Caesar, of internal Roman politics—but that they are not without substance is borne out by the fact that on many points they harmonize remarkably with the later insular sources. For example, classical sources note that in Gaul there were three classes associated with literature and learning: the druids, the bards, and, between them, an order which seems to have been best known by the Gaulish term **vātis* (cognate with Latin *vatis*) and which is not clearly distinguishable from the druids. At a far remove in time and space, the same threefold arrangement occurs in medieval Ireland, comprising here druids *(druïdh)*, *filidh*, and bards *(baird)*. The term *fáith* ("prophet") is the Irish cognate of Gaulish **vātis* and appears frequently as a near synonym of *fili* (pl., *filidh*). [*See also* Druids *and* Filidh.]

Manuscripts. The second main body of evidence, the insular Celtic literatures, is at first glance far removed from the pre-Roman world of the continental Celts. The great historian of Gaul, Camille Jullian, questioned whether it was valid to use Irish and Welsh literary sources to interpret Latin and Greek references to Gaulish institutions and concluded that one could not rely on documents written so long after the Celtic migration to Ireland ("Les choses ont tellement pu changer dans les douze siècles qui ont suivi l'ère chrétienne!"). In fact, the gap is much narrower than the twelve centuries that he supposed, because much of the relevant material is linguistically older than the period of the manuscript collections in which it is now preserved. Further, there is no evidence that Christianity was established in any part of Ireland before the second half of the fourth century or that it impinged much on the traditional culture of the country before the sixth century CE. Moreover, one must consider the highly conservative character of Irish learned tradition which, thanks to the assiduousness of the hereditary *filidh*, survived far into the Christian period and transmitted innumerable elements of form and content, particularly in the area of social institutions, which find their closest detailed analogues in the sacred texts of Vedic and classical Sanskrit.

Written literature in Irish dates from the second half of the sixth century CE, when monastic scholars adapted the Latin alphabet for that purpose, and it gradually increases in volume during the following centuries. In addition to a good deal of typically monastic learning, both religious and secular, the literature comprises a vast amount of varied material recorded or adapted from oral tradition. However, only fragments of this literature survive in contemporary manuscripts, mostly in the form of annals or of notes and glosses accompanying Latin texts; all the vernacular manuscripts written before the end of the eleventh century, some of them known to us by name, have perished through usage or rapine. Then, around 1100, came *Lebhor na hUidhre* (The Book of the Dun Cow), probably written in the monastery of Clonmacnois and the first of a series of great vellum manuscript compilations which are part of a conscious endeavor, in the face of ominous political and social change, to conserve the monuments of native tradition. It was followed around 1130 by an untitled collection now at the Bodleian Library, Oxford (MS Rawlinson B 502), and around 1150–1200 by *Lebhor na Nuachongbhála* (The Book of Leinster), probably compiled in the monasteries of Glendalough and Terryglass respectively. Over the next couple of centuries appeared a number of major manuscripts of which the most important are the Great Book of Lecan, the Yellow Book of Lecan, the Book of Ballymote, the Book of Lismore, and the Book of Fermoy. These are capacious *bibliothecae* which embrace all the various genres of traditional literature: hero and king tales, mythological tales, origin legends, genealogies, onomastic and etymological lore, gnomic texts, legal tracts, eulogy and elegy, battle tales, birth tales, death tales, tales of the otherworld, and so on. It is important to remember that, though the surviving manuscripts date from a relatively late period, the matter they contain has generally been copied more or less faithfully from earlier manuscripts. The result is that the initial redaction of the individual texts can be dated with a fair degree of accuracy on the basis of linguistic criteria. Thus the texts are often demonstrably centuries older than the extant manuscripts.

As well as these manuscript collections there are several specialized compilations, including *Leabhar Gabhála Éireann* (The Book of the Taking of Ireland), commonly known as the *Book of Invasions*, an amalgam of myth and pseudohistory which purports to recount the coming of the Gaels to Ireland and the several immigrations which preceded it; the *Cóir Anmann* (Fitness of Names), a catalog of names of "historical" personages with many imaginative etymologies and references to traditional legends; and the *Dinnshenchas* (Lore of Famous Places), which does in a much fuller and more elaborate fashion for place-names what the *Cóir Anmann* seeks to do for personal names. The features of the Irish landscape and their names, if properly construed, were thought to reveal the history of the country and its peoples from their beginnings. From the first shaping and definition of the land—the clearing of plains, the creation of rivers and lakes, and the assigning of names (as related in *Leabhar Gabhála*), each place was linked indissolubly to momentous events by an association that conferred on it an enduring psychic resonance. The onomastic element is ubiquitous in Irish (and Welsh) literature, and in poetic tracts dating from around the tenth century the history of *dinnshenchas* is included in the course of study prescribed for apprentice *filidh*. During the eleventh and twelfth centuries, a period of intensive compilation, a comprehensive volume of these onomastic legends was assembled. This mythological gazetteer of Irish place-names exists in several recensions, both prose and verse.

Among the many other miscellaneous sources are the lives of the saints, particularly the later ones compiled or redacted from the eleventh century onward. It is often said that they contain more pagan mythology than Christianity.

Evidence indicates that the early oral literature of Wales was comparable in volume and variety with that of Ireland. Unfortunately, because of a weaker scribal tradition, the Welsh literature is poorly documented for the pre-Norman period. This applies particularly to prose, which in the Celtic languages is the standard medium for narrative and hence for most heroic and mythological literature. Of the compositions ascribed to the fathers of Welsh poetry, Taliesin and Aneirin, who belonged to the second half of the sixth century, only a modest proportion is likely to be authentic, and all of that consists of eulogy and heroic elegy. However, from the ninth or tenth century onward Taliesin became the focus of poems and stories (extant only in much later versions) which represent him as a wonder child, seer, and prophet; some of these motifs clearly derive from native mythological tradition. Of written Welsh narrative prose there is little or no evidence before the eleventh century, the period to which most scholars assign the first redaction of the earliest of the group of tales known as the *Mabinogi* or *Mabinogion*. [*See* Mabinogion.] However, the earliest manuscripts containing this prose material date from considerably later: apart from two small manuscript fragments from the mid-thirteenth century, the main texts are the White Book of Rhydderch from the late fourteenth century and the Red Book of Hergest from the late fourteenth or early fifteenth century. Another important source is the *Trioedd Ynys Prydein* (Triads of the Island of Britain), which contains numerous references to mythological as well as historical characters and events; it may have been compiled in the twelfth century, but much of the contents must have been current in oral tradition before then. There is also matter of mythological interest in the poems compiled as part of the Black Book of Carmarthen in the late thirteenth century, some of which may be dated on linguistic grounds to the ninth or tenth century.

Given the diversity of these sources, it would be unrealistic to expect from them a clear image of religious and mythological unity. On the one hand, Gaulish epigraphy and iconography belong preponderantly to the period of Roman domination when native religion was being progressively modified by Roman influence. On the other hand, the insular literatures, though exceedingly conservative in many respects, were recorded and redacted by monastic scribes and scholars who, however well disposed toward their own vernacular tradition, were nonetheless educated Christians and who on matters of crucial importance gave priority to Christian teaching over pagan tradition. In short, nowhere have we the integral tradition as it would have been transmitted and commented on by the druids in an independent Celtic society. Even among the insular Celts history created important disparities. For instance, Ireland escaped the immediate physical presence of Rome which left its imprint so clearly on medieval language and thought in Britain and Wales. One must also acknowledge the imponderable but obviously considerable survival of pre-Celtic religion in Celtic belief and practice in the several areas of Celtic settlement. Yet, despite these sources of dissimilation, the underlying structural and thematic unity of British and Irish ideology is more striking than the superficial differences.

Artifacts. The plastic art of the Celto-Roman period is so evidently based on that of Rome that it might appear at first glance to have been borrowed whole and unchanged, but on closer scrutiny it reveals many elements which derive from the Celtic rather than from the Roman tradition. On the one hand, there are forms quite foreign to classical art, such as the tricephalous god, the god with stag's antlers, and the god depicted in the Buddha-like cross-legged position. On the other hand, there are images more or less in the classical mode but with features not associated with the corresponding deities of Greco-Latin religion: the wheel, for instance, or the mallet. The wheel is seen by some as representing the thunderbolt, by others as representing the sun, and in some cases it may also be the emblem of the god of the underworld. Similarly, the mallet or hammer is thought to have several connotations: it symbolizes thunder and the sky from which it emanates, but it also functions as an apotropaic symbol and as the emblem of an underworld god or a chthonic god of fecundity. The cornucopia, or horn of abundance, is not particularly Celtic, but it appears as a common attribute of the Celtic mother goddess, perhaps the most important divinity of the primitive Celtic pantheon. Animal horns are commonly regarded as signs of fertility, and the antlers which the Celtic deity wears on the Gundestrup Caldron and elsewhere are taken to symbolize his power and fecundity. Another frequent emblem of divinity is the ornamented torque, which, according to Pierre Lambrechts, denotes the "powerful god who affords protection against maleficent spirits"; though it is usually worn around the neck, the torque is sometimes held in the hand, and on the relief of Cernunnos in the Musée de Cluny in Paris the deity carries two torques suspended on his horns.

Probably the most important element in the religious symbolism of the Celts is the number three; the mystic significance of the concept of threeness is attested in most parts of the world, but among the Celts there seems to have been a particularly strong and continuous awareness of it. This is confirmed both by Celto-Roman iconography and by the insular literary tradition. The former has its three-headed and three-faced deities (and even a triphallic Mercury) and its triads of mother goddesses; the latter has an endless variety of ternary groups in which the triad is an expressive restatement of an underlying unity: goddesses like the three Brighids and inseparable brothers like the three companions of the tragic heroine Deirdre. It is commonly accepted that ternary repetition has an intensifying force, expressing totality or omnipotence, though its symbolism may be even more complex and subtle.

Continental Deities and Insular Equivalents. Given that the bulk of the relevant evidence belongs to the Roman period, it follows that our view of Gaulish religion is for the most part through Roman eyes, which means that it is perceived and presented in terms of Roman religion. The *locus classicus* is the passage in Caesar's *Gallic Wars* (6.17) where he lists and defines the principal gods of the Gauls:

> Of the gods they worship Mercury most of all. He has the greatest number of images; they hold that he is the inventor of all the arts and a guide on the roads and on journeys, and they believe him the most influential for money-making and commerce. After him they honor Apollo, Mars, Jupiter, and Minerva. Of these deities they have almost the same idea as other peoples: Apollo drives away diseases, Minerva teaches the first principles of the arts and crafts, Jupiter rules the heavens, and Mars controls the issue of war.

What Caesar offers us here is a thumbnail sketch of the Gaulish pantheon modeled on that of Rome. As part of this *interpretatio Romana* he refers to each deity not by his proper Celtic name but by that of a Roman deity to which it is most easily equated. At the same time he introduces a neat schematism which is quite foreign to all that is otherwise known of Celtic religion. In thus equating gods and divine functions which are not really equal he has posed many problems for modern scholars who seek to identify Caesar's Roman gods in continental Celtic iconography and insular Celtic mythology.

To confound matters further, modern scholars have tended to depreciate Caesar's testimony on the Gauls, first, on the grounds that he distorted the facts in order to enhance his own achievements and, second, on the grounds that he took his information from Posidonius, but used it inaccurately. For example, it has been argued and widely accepted that Caesar, and even Posidonius, exaggerated the social and political importance of the druids, assigning them a dominant role which they never in fact possessed. Yet in this regard, as in others, Caesar's version of things is largely confirmed by the independent evidence of the insular literatures. Once allowance is made for his professional bias and the limitations of his interest in Gaul, there is no reason to assume that his account is not largely authentic. By the time he wrote his account, he had had eight years' experience of the country, and most likely he derived much of his information from personal observation and from the reports of colleagues and acquaintances; certainly there is little basis for the common assumption that he was totally indebted to Posidonius for his knowledge of the land and its people.

The concise precision of Caesar's testimony makes it difficult to correlate with other evidence. Georges Dumézil has remarked that one of the many traits the early Irish shared with the Indians is that they were both fond of classification and careless of order. The result is that Irish literature is often a curious mixture of meticulous detail and incoherence that finds its closest parallel in some of the Indian epics (Dumézil, *Naissance de Rome*, Paris, 1944, p. 26f.). One must therefore adjust one's mental perspective considerably as one moves from Caesar to the vernacular literatures. It may be that something of this prodigal disorder is reflected in the continental Celtic iconography, which may help to explain why identifications with Caesar's deities are often more a matter of speculation than of demonstration. But perhaps a more important consideration is that, as has often been stressed by Françoise Le Roux, Caesar's account and the iconography refer to quite different stages in the history of Gaulish religion. Periods of profound cultural and political change often bring into prominence popular forms of belief and practice which have hitherto been concealed by the dominant orthodoxy. It seems probable that the religion represented in Gallo-Roman plastic art was less clearly structured and delimited than that maintained by the druids in the days of independence before Caesar's conquest.

Modern scholars often have noted, and sometimes have exaggerated, a discrepancy between Caesar's account and the Gallo-Roman evidence, claiming that the evidence does not substantiate Caesar's account of a pantheon of major deities who were worshiped throughout Gaul. In Gallo-Roman dedications, deities may be assigned a Roman name, a native Gaulish name, or a Roman name accompanied by a native epithet. In the last two cases we clearly have to do with indigenous gods, and even with the first group this may be so. For example, the numerous statues and reliefs of Mercury in the guise of the Greco-Roman god might have been intended to honor that god, but equally they might have been intended to honor a native god by borrowing the classical form together with the classical name. Indeed, many of these images have certain features which betray their essential non-Roman character. It has been observed that the great majority of the several hundred names containing a Gaulish element occur only once. Those which occur more frequently tend to do so in regional or tribal groupings, and many of them have a clear local reference (e.g., *Mars Vesontius*, referring to Vesontio, and *Dea Tricoria*, referring to Tricorii). The inference drawn by Joseph Vendryes, Marie-Louise Sjoestedt, and other scholars is that, while the Celts had a multiplicity of gods, their cults were local and tribal rather than national. Scholars also cite Lucan's mention of the deity name *Teutates*, which they interpret as "god of the tribe" based on the etymologies of **teutā* (Celt., "tribe") and an oath formula from Irish hero tales, "Tongu do dia toinges mo thuath" ("I swear to the god to whom my tribe swears").

But this evidence is susceptible of a different interpretation. A large proportion of the Gaulish forms attested in dedications are mere epithets or bynames, and even of those which may be taken to be proper names it would be quite erroneous to suppose that each indicates a separate deity. As Dumézil has remarked in another context (*Dieux des Indo-Européens*, Paris, 1952, p. 5), the names of deities are easily reinvented, and the insular literatures offer examples of major gods known by several different names. As for the form *Teutates*, it may be a title linking the god to the tribe but does not necessarily confine him to it. By the same token, in early Irish law the small tribal kingdom, the *tuath* (from **teutā*), was the unit of jurisdiction, and rules of law were explicitly stated to apply *i tuaith*, "within a *tuath*." Presumably, then, laws originally applied with equal validity only between members of the same tribe; yet substantially the same law, formulated by the same learned class of jurists related to the druids and *filidh*, was common to all the tribal kingdoms (cf. D. A. Binchy, *Celtic and Anglo-Saxon Kingship*, Oxford, 1970, p. 5). Similarly, in primitive Ireland the vital ritual of inauguration was founded in the first place on the small tribal kingdom *(tuath)*, as is enunciated in the law tracts, but it is also replicated at different levels throughout the wider cultural community. And as for the alleged lack of "great divinities common to all the Celtic peoples," this is gainsaid, even in terms of strict nomenclature, by such insular gods as Lugh and Brighid and their continental equivalents. In short, there is at present a growing awareness that, despite its all too obvious complexities, the seeming throng of Celtic gods is both less amorphous and more universal than was formerly believed.

Another criticism leveled at Caesar is that he assigns separate functions to the several Gaulish deities in contradiction of the evidence. Some scholars hold that the deities were polyvalent tribal gods and that to seek to restrict them to distinct spheres of activity is pointless. Others hold that all the various attested gods may be reduced ultimately to a single deity who is both polyvalent and polymorphic. T. F. O'Rahilly, one of the two principal exponents of this view, believed that the core of Irish and Celtic mythology was the conflict in which this universal deity was slain by a youthful hero using the god's own sacred weapon, the thunderbolt. Pierre Lambrechts, the other principal exponent of this view, believed that originally Celtic religion was bound up with one great deity, possibly a ternary deity endowed with multiple and comprehensive attributes, and that during the Roman period this largely undefined and impersonal deity was fragmented into a number of smaller, specialized deities through contact with the Greco-Roman world. This notion of a single all-encompassing god, endlessly varied in form and function, has a certain plausibility (Lambrechts, *Contributions à l'étude des divinités celtiques*, Bruges, 1942, pp. 149, 164ff., 181, 184). Since the Celtic gods were not clearly departmentalized, it was difficult to pair them off neatly with their Roman counterparts, and so one finds such evident anomalies as the occasional use of the same Gaulish byname (e.g., *Iovantucarus* and *Vellaunus*) with different Roman deity names (e.g., *Mars* and *Mercurius*). But, of course, one might agree with Lambrechts and regard this as another argument for simply identifying the two Gaulish deities.

However, although the functional roles of the several deities are not clearly defined and delimited and frequently overlap with one another, this does not imply that they may be reduced to a single, all-purpose divine overlord. It has often been remarked that in polytheistic systems each god tends to move beyond his normal functional field toward a kind of universalism. Yet, despite this tendency toward the assimilation of roles, the insular Celtic gods are far removed from functional indifferentism, and there are some, like Goibhniu, the smith, and Dian Cécht, the leech, whose central responsibilities are defined very precisely. The assumption of undifferentiated polyvalence which underlies the conflicting interpretations of Vendryes and O'Rahilly or Lambrechts, the one tribal and polytheistic, the other vaguely monotheistic, has not been substantiated. In fact, more recent scholars, notably Françoise Le Roux and Anne Ross, have moved in the direction of a typological classification of the gods based on criteria of function. The scheme put forward by Le Roux is in close conformity with the principles established in Dumézil's functional theory of Indo-European mythology. Indeed, it could be argued that this typological approach was anticipated by Caesar in his brief account of the characteristic activities of the major Gaulish deities.

Mercury or Lugh. Caesar's observation that "Mercury" was the deity with the greatest number of images in Gaul is confirmed by the surviving evidence of inscriptions, stone statues and reliefs, bronze statuettes, and terra-cotta figures. His image often appears in the mode of the classical Mercury: youthful, naked, and beardless; equipped with caduceus, petasos, and purse; and accompanied by cock, ram, or tortoise. But his image is also found in Gallo-Roman guise: mature, bearded, and dressed in a heavy cloak. Sometimes, as in the east and the north of Gaul, he is tricephalous. Unlike his Roman counterpart, he has a frequent consort named Maia or Rosmerta, the Provider, and includes the art of war in his range of competence.

One cannot assume that Caesar's "Mercury" coincides with a single native deity throughout the Celtic areas, but there is cogent evidence for identifying him substantially with the Irish god Lugh. First, Lugh's name and cult were pan-Celtic. Further, Caesar speaks of Mercury as *omnium inventorem artium* ("inventor of all the arts"), a close paraphrase of Lugh's sobriquet in Irish, *(sam)ildánach* ("skilled in many arts together"). In fact, an episode in the tale of the Battle of Magh Tuiredh dramatically sets forth Lugh's claim as the only god who was master of all the arts and crafts. At Osma in Spain an inscription was found with a dedication on behalf of a guild of shoemakers to the Lugoves, whose name is the plural of *Lugus*, an older form of *Lugh*. Most likely these divinities, who recur in an inscription from Avenches in Switzerland, are simply the pan-Celtic Lugus in plural, perhaps triple, form. The Middle Welsh tale *Math vab Mathonwy* may well echo this connection with shoemaking, for Lleu, the Welsh cognate of Lugh, operates briefly as a high-class practitioner of the craft.

In Ireland Lugh was the youthful victor over malevolent demonic figures, and his great achievement was to kill the cyclopean Balar with a slingshot. Lughnasadh, his feast, was a harvest festival, and at least two of its principal sites, Carmun and Tailtiu, were the burial places of eponymous goddesses associated with the fertility of the earth (as was, apparently, the Gaulish Mercury's consort Rosmerta). Lugh was the divine exemplar of sacred kingship, and in the tale *Baile in Scáil* (The God's Prophecy) he appears seated in state as king of the otherworld and attended by a woman identified as the sovereign of Ireland, reminiscent of Rosmerta. His usual epithet, *lámhfhada* ("of the long arm"), relates to his divine kingship. In the Christian period Lugh survived in the guise of several saints known by variants of his name—Lughaidh, Molua, and others—and the motif of the arm is reflected in these Christian traditions as well.

Gaulish Mars. A famous passage in Lucan's *Civil War* refers to the bloody sacrifices offered the three Celtic gods Teutates, Esus, and Taranis. A later commentator on Lucan clearly illustrates the difficulty of identifying individual Gaulish and Roman gods, for one of his two main sources equated Teutates with Mercury, the other with Mars. But if, as seems likely, *teutates* is primarily a title ("god of the tribe") rather than a name, then such confusion is explainable: the god of sovereignty and the arts, "Mercurius," will also function as a warrior, while the god of war, "Mars," will often function as the protector of the tribe. Consequently, their functions will sometimes overlap, and it may be a matter of chance or circumstance which is given preeminence in a given time or place. A further complication is that many of the Gallo-Roman dedications to Mars present him not only as a god of war but also as god of healing and guardian of the fields, but this may reflect an extension of his role in the Roman period and does not necessarily discredit Caesar's description of him as god of war. So far as the insular tradition is concerned, a god of war does not come into clear focus, perhaps because fighting is a more or less universal, rather than a differentiating, feature in the heroic context. Thus one cannot easily define the role of Mars, and one cannot so easily assign him a pan-Celtic identity as one can Lugh.

Gaulish Apollo. The classical form of Apollo in Romano-Celtic monuments only partly conceals the several native deities who have been assimilated to him. The use of the plural is probably justifiable, since several of the fifteen or more epithets attached to Apollo's name have a wide distribution, which suggests that they were independent gods. Yet some of these epithets may have referred to a single deity. Belenus was especially honored in the old Celtic kingdom of Noricum in the eastern Alps, as well as in northern Italy, southern Gaul, and Britain. The solar connotations of the stem *bel-* ("shining, brilliant") would have confirmed the identification with the Greco-Roman Apollo. Grannus, whose name is of uncertain etymology, has a widespread cult with one of its principal centers at Aachen. He is sometimes accompanied by a goddess named Sirona. Borvo or Bormo, whose name denotes boiling or seething water, is associated with thermal springs, as at Bourbonne-les-Bains and other sites named after him. His consort is Damona ("divine cow") or Bormana.

This association of healing with springs and wells, which was subsequently taken over into Christian or sub-Christian usage throughout the Celtic countries, tended to encourage localized cults, and it is all the more remarkable that these early names had such an extensive currency. Unlike those already mentioned, *Maponos* ("divine son or youth") occurs mainly in northern Britain, though it is also attested in Gaul near healing springs. Maponos appears in medieval Welsh literature as Mabon, son of Modron, that is, of Matrona ("divine mother"), eponymous goddess of the river Marne in France. A brief but significant episode in the tale of *Culhwch and Olwen* casts him in the role of hunter and alludes to a myth attested elsewhere in insular literature of the youthful god carried off from his mother when three nights old. That his legend was once more extensive in oral tradition than appears from the extant literature is borne out by the survival of his name into Arthurian romance under the forms *Mabon, Mabuz,* and *Mabonagrain*.

His Irish equivalent was Mac ind Óg ("young lad or son"), otherwise known as Oenghus, who was believed to dwell in Bruigh na Bóinne, the great Neolithic, and therefore pre-Celtic, passage grave of Newgrange. He was the son of Daghdha, chief god of the Irish, and of Boann, eponym of the sacred river of Irish tradition. As his name and relationship suggest, he is a youthful god, and, perhaps in keeping with this, he is often treated with a certain affection in the literature, particularly in his familiar roles of trickster and lover. But he is nowhere presented as a god of healing, which merely underlines the impossibility of exactly equating Celtic and Roman gods in terms of their functional range.

Gaulish Minerva or Irish Brighid. The goddesses of insular Celtic tradition are involved in a wide range of activities, only one of which Caesar ascribes to "Minerva," namely arts and crafts. In this respect Caesar gives an inadequate impression of these deities, even though arts and crafts was an important activity in Celtic society. Dedications to Minerva are found throughout the Celtic areas of the continent and in Britain. At Bath she was identified with the goddess Sulis, who was worshiped there in connection with the thermal springs. This healing function, together with her frequent epithet, *belisama* ("very brilliant"), suggests a rapport with the Gallo-Roman Apollo, who was sometimes called Belenus, and confirms the solar character implied by the name *Sulis* ("sun"). Through the plural form *Suleviae,* found at Bath and elsewhere in Britain and on the continent, she is also related to the widespread and important category of mother goddesses.

The nearest equivalent to Minerva in insular tradition is the goddess known in Ireland as Brighid, daughter of the father god, Daghdha. Like Minerva she was concerned with healing and craftsmanship, particularly metalwork, but she was also patron of *filidhecht,* that is, poetry and traditional learning in general. A remarkable continuity stretches from the pagan goddess to her Christian namesake of the early sixth century, the saint Brighid of Kildare, whose monastery of Cell Dara, the "church of the [sacred] oak," was doubtless on the site of a pagan sanctuary. The saint, too, is a patron of poets and men of learning, though her legends place more emphasis than do the learned references to the goddess on her connection with nature, livestock, and the fruits of the earth. Appropriately, her feast day on the first of February coincides with Imbolg, the pagan festival marking the beginning of spring, and is even yet the occasion of popular rituals that are obviously pre-Christian in origin. Giraldus Cambrensis reports that Brighid of Kildare and her nuns guarded a perpetual fire surrounded by a hedge within which no male might enter. This ritual further associates her with the Celtic Minerva at whose shrine in Britain, according to Solinus in the third century, a similar vestal fire was maintained perpetually.

Celtic Vulcan. Though Caesar does not mention a Gaulish Vulcan, his cult was evidently known to all the Celtic peoples; indeed, the evidence suggests that he enjoyed a higher status than his Roman counterpart. Since he functioned as a very specialized deity, there is a strong probability that his native name among the continental Celts made reference to his craft, as it did in Ireland and Wales, where he was known as Goibhniu and Gofannon, both names derived from the word for "smith." The weapons Goibhniu forged with his fellow craft gods, Luchta the wright and Creidhne the metalworker, were unerring in aim and fatal in their effect. Further, those who attended the Feast of Goibhniu and partook of the god's sacred drink were thereby rendered immune to age and decay. He was known for his healing powers and is invoked in an Old Irish charm for the removal of a thorn. Until the nineteenth century, and in some areas even into the twentieth century, the country smith was still believed to retain something of his ancient preternatural faculty, and he was constantly called on for the healing effects of his charms and spells. In the early tradition, Gobbán Saer ("Gobbán the wright"; here *Gobbán* is a hypocoristic form of *Goibhniu*) was renowned as a wondrous builder, and under the modern form *an Gobán Saor* he is the skillful and resourceful mason who outwits his rivals and enemies by his clever stratagems.

Gaulish Hercules or Irish Oghma. Hercules is well represented in Celto-Roman iconography and has a number of regional epithets assigned to him. Doubtless his popularity derives largely from his identification with native Celtic gods who correspond approximately to his classical character. One of these is mentioned in a curious passage by the Greek writer Lucian in the second century CE describing a Gaulish picture of Hercules "whom the Celts call Ogmios." It showed him armed with his familiar club and bow but pictured him uncharacteristically as an old man, bald and gray, with his skin darkened and wrinkled by the sun. He pulled behind him a willing band of men attached by slender chains which linked their ears to the tip of his tongue. The explanation, according to Lucian's Gaulish informant, was that eloquence reaches its apogee in old age: the Celts did not identify eloquence with Hermes, as did the Greeks, but with Hercules, because he was by far the stronger.

A question much debated is whether this hoary champion can be identified with the Irish god Oghma. The functional parallel is adequate: not merely is Oghma known as a *trenfher* ("strong man, champion"), but he is also credited with the invention of the Ogham letters. This system of writing was based on the Latin alphabet and can hardly be older than the fourth century CE, but it almost certainly replaced an older system of magical symbols of the same name.

Gaulish Dis Pater or Irish Donn. Caesar mentions Dis Pater separately from the other gods and states that all the Gauls believed with their druids that they were descended from him. The reference is brief but is sufficient to indicate at least an analogy between the Gaulish god of the dead and his Irish counterpart Donn ("brown or dark one"), whose dwelling place was a small rocky island off the southwest coast of Ireland known as Tech nDuinn ("house of Donn"). Its English name, the Bull, echoes its other name in early Irish, Inis Tarbhnai ("island of Tarbnae"). *Tarbhnae* derives from *tarbh* ("bull"), and thus there are strong grounds for identifying the god Donn with the great bull of Cuailnge which provides the central motivation for the saga *Táin Bó Cuailnge* and which is also called Donn.

In his role as god of death Donn is a rather retiring figure in the early literature. Like Dis Pater, he seems to stand apart from the other deities, but his importance is confirmed by his status in modern folk tradition, where he is represented as the underworld god who creates storms and shipwrecks but also protects cattle and crops. Both early and late sources record the belief that the dead made their way or were ferried to his island after death. As one early text makes clear, these travelers were regarded as Donn's descendants returning to their divine ancestor.

Sucellus and Nantosvelta. Some two hundred monuments, mostly in Gaul, show a deity holding a hammer, and a number name him as Sucellus ("the good striker"?). Besides the characteristic hammer or mallet, he is often depicted with a cask or drinking jar and accompanied by a dog. He is sometimes paired with the goddess Nantosvelta, whose name suggests an association with water (Wel., *nant*, "brook"). Particularly in the Narbonnaise, Sucellus is frequently assimilated to the Roman Silvanus, guardian of forests and patron of agriculture. Because of these associations and attributes he has been seen as controlling fecundity, not an unusual function for a chthonic deity. He has also been equated with the Celtic Cernunnos and the Irish Daghdha, but while there are certain broad similarities between them, the evidence does not suffice to prove a closer connection. [*See* Cernunnos *and* Daghdha.]

Goddesses and divine consorts. The role Caesar assigns to "Minerva," that of teacher or patron of arts and crafts, involves only one of the many interests of the Celtic goddesses in insular tradition. Although Brighid sometimes concerned herself with the domestic arts, she was also the special patron of the free or aristocratic arts of learning, poetry, metalwork, and healing. The activities of other goddesses too went far beyond the liberal or the practical arts to encompass all the functional areas of the male gods. The goddesses were in effect complementary to the male deities in many if not all cases, and this is graphically illustrated in the frequent pairing of god and consort on Celtic monuments. However, the role of the goddesses generally differed from that of the gods, for the goddesses involved themselves through intervention or even manipulation, while the gods participated more directly and continuously.

It is impossible to distinguish clearly between goddesses and the *matres* or *matronae* who appear so frequently in Celtic iconography, often in triadic form like the goddesses of Irish tradition. [*See* Matres.] Both goddesses and *matres* are concerned with fertility and with the seasonal cycle of the earth, and at least the insular goddesses are sometimes identified with the land and cast in the role of its tutelary deities. This intimate connection with the land and with its physical features is reflected in the exceptional importance of the feminine element in the *dinnshenchas*, the vast accumulation of prose and verse which constitutes a virtual mythological topography of Ireland. A goddess's concern for the land in general also becomes a responsibility for the particular region or kingdom with which she is especially associated. Each goddess ensures the material well-being, sovereignty, and physical security of her particular domain, just as Brighid in the guise of her saintly namesake protects Leinster both as goddess of war and as goddess of peace.

Nature associations. Underlying the tradition of *dinnshenchas* is the belief that prominent places and geological features throughout Ireland were the scene of mythic events or the abode, or even the embodiment, of mythic personages. Many of the numerous women who populate this world of onomastic legend are clear reflexes of the multifaceted goddess whose origins are bound up with the physical landscape—figures like Tailtiu and Carmun, whose burial places, named after them, were the sites of great royal assemblies. In the Celto-Roman world the early onomastic lore had disappeared, but something of it remained in the divine nomenclature of these areas.

Apart from the general cult of the earth goddess there exists an extensive repertory of deity names attached to individual places or topographical features. Hilltops and mountaintops are considered particularly appropriate settings for the sacred, as evidenced by dedications to Garra and Baeserta in the Pyrenees and to Vosegus in the Vosges. There was a god of the clearing or cultivated field (Ialonus), of the rock (Alisanos), of the confluence (Condatis), of the ford (Ritena), and of the fortified place (Dunatis). Water, particularly the moving water of rivers and springs, had its special deities, generally female in the case of the rivers. One can perhaps glimpse the lost mythology of such rivers as the Seine (Sequana), the Marne (Matrona), and the Saône (Souconna) through the legends of insular equivalents like the Boyne (Boann). The names of many rivers throughout the Celtic lands, for example, the French Dives or the Welsh Dyfrdwy, are derived from the stem *dēv-* and mean simply "the divine one." Sacred springs are deified, as for example Aventia (Avenches), Vesunna (Périgeux), and Divona (Cahors). Further, there were many divine patrons of thermal waters like the god Borvo, and this particularly widespread cult is reflected in the countless holy and healing wells (some twelve hundred in Wales alone, and no one has thought to reckon the Irish instances) which made the transition from paganism to Christianity with little essential change. However, the abundant material evidence for this pan-Celtic phenomenon is not matched by the early insular literary evidence: many Irish tales mention wells with preternatural powers and associations, but there is hardly anything about healing wells as such. Unless this is due to suppression by the monastic redactors of the literature, the only explanation would seem to be that the frequenting of healing wells had always been regarded, even in pagan times, as a popular practice to be distinguished from the more official tribal cults.

In many instances the holy wells of the Christian period stand close to a specific tree which shares their supernatural aura. Obviously, this is one aspect of the widespread cult of sacred trees. In the Pyrenees there are dedications to the beech (Deo Fago) and to the Six Trees (Sexarbori deo, Sexarboribus) and at Angoulême to the oak (Deo Robori). The Romano-Celtic name of the town of Embrun, *Eburodunum*, contains the name of the deified yew tree. Such continental forms are supplemented by a vast dossier of insular evidence. For example, there were scores of Christian foundations in Ireland evidently located on the sites of pagan cult centers, each with its sacred tree nearby. The literature frequently mentions several great trees which were particularly honored in tradition: the Tree of Tortu (an ash), the Oak of Mughna, the Yew of Ross, the Bough of Dathí (an ash), the Ash of Uisnech, among others. There was even a special term for such trees, *bile,* and this term was sometimes used for the great tree which marked each of the inauguration sites of tribal and provincial kings. Standing theoretically at the center of its kingdom like the *axis mundi* in its greater cosmos, the *bile* symbolized the integrity and independence of the kingdom. When it happened, as it did occasionally, that it was attacked and felled by a hostile neighbor, this must have been a shattering blow to communal pride and self-respect.

Zoomorphic gods. Celto-Roman iconography contains a rich abundance of animal imagery, frequently presenting the deities in combinations of zoomorphic and anthropomorphic forms. Already noted is the probable connection between Donn, the Irish Dis Pater, and the bull of the same name in the epic *Táin Bó Cuailnge.* Neither of the two bulls whose conflict forms the climax of the tale is of natural origin: according to other texts, they had previously undergone many metamorphoses—as ravens, stags, champions, water beasts, demons, and water worms—and in the beginning they had been the swineherds of the lords of the otherworld. This kind of shape shifting, a continuing expression of the unity of the living world of creation, is commonplace in insular Celtic tradition and serves to invest a given deity or heroic demigod with the attributes traditionally ascribed to certain birds and animals. For instance, the bond between animal and human is implicit in the archetype of the divine swineherds, who are doubtless avatars of the great herdsman god. Further, the Brown Bull of Cuailnge cannot be wholly dissociated from the Tarvos Trigaranus ("the bull of the three cranes"), pictured on reliefs from Trèves and Nôtre-Dame-de-Paris and presumably the subject of a lost Gaulish narrative. Among the Celts, as among many other cattle-rearing peoples, the bull was a vivid symbol of power and fertility and appears frequently as a trope in the eulogy of the medieval Irish court poet. It is hardly surprising, therefore, that a god representative of royal and heroic functions should have been represented by this image. Donnotarvos ("brown bull"), the king of the Helvetii mentioned by Caesar, bore a name of great mythic resonance among the Celts, most probably derived from the same deity who appears in the Irish saga as the Brown Bull of Cuailnge.

The animal connections of the Celtic gods are extensive and varied. The iconography shows Cernunnos ("the horned one") associated with the stag, the ram-headed serpent, the bull, and, by implication, with the whole animal world. The iconography also includes boars, horses, dogs, and bears, as well as fish and various kinds of birds, all connected more or less closely with certain deities. This rich diversity is reproduced in even greater abundance in the insular tradition, creating a complex web of connotations and relationships which defy any neat classification. For example, the boar is quite well represented in Celto-Roman sculpture, as in the figure from Euffigneix, Haute-Marne, of a god carrying a boar before him. But in insular literature the boar appears almost ubiquitous. It sometimes leads its pursuers into the otherworld, and often it is in fact a human who was transformed through some mischance or misdeed. Pork was the choice food of the Celts, and, appropriately, in Irish tales the unfailing food of the otherworld is a pig which, though cooked each night, is alive and whole each morning.

The horse, index and instrument of the great Indo-European expansion, has always had a special place in the affections of the Celtic peoples. Sometimes in insular tradition, particularly in folk tales, he is the bearer of the dead to the otherworld, a role probably reflected in some monuments in southern Gaul, such as the frieze of horses' heads on a lintel from the Celto-Ligurian sanctuary of Roquepertuse, Bouches-du-Rhône. Epona (from **epos,* "horse") was an important Celtic deity and was particularly favored as patron of the cavalry of the Roman army. She has insular analogues in the Welsh Rhiannon and in the Irish Édaín Echraidhe (*echraidhe,* "horse riding") and Macha, who outran the fastest steeds. [*See also* Horses.] There was also a Dea Artio (as well as a Mercurius Artaios), whose name connects her with the bear (Ir., *art,* "bear"); a little bronze group from Bern shows her seated before a large bear with a basket of fruit by her side. Dea Arduinna, who appears seated on a wild boar, may be compared with the Irish goddess Flidhais, who ruled over the beasts of the forest and whose cattle were the wild deer.

Gaulish monuments sometimes show a god or goddess with two or more birds seated on the shoulders, birds that may correspond to the supernatural ones familiar from the insular tradition. Some deities assume bird form occasionally; others, like the war goddesses, do so constantly. The catalog of bird imagery is endless. King Conaire's supernatural father came to his mother in bird form, Fann and Lí Ban came to Cú Chulainn as two birds joined by a golden chain, emissaries from the otherworld. Indeed, such wondrous birds are a familiar symbol of the otherworld. Examples include the three birds of the Irish goddess Clíodna with their magic song and the three birds of the Welsh Rhiannon who "wake the dead and lull the living to sleep." They all form part of that rich imaginative intuition which envisaged animals, birds, and the whole domain of nature as a mediating element between gods and men and which underlies Celtic literary tradition as well as the fluid discipline of early Irish art.

Invasions of Gods and Men. When Irish monastic scholars began recording native mytho-historical tradition, probably in the second half of the sixth century, they experienced the same difficulty that Christian historiographers have encountered elsewhere in dealing with traditional sources: how to resolve the conflict between Christian and native versions of cosmic origins. Their solution was the familiar one of substituting the biblical doctrine for the earlier part of the native legend, so that it would seem that the legend derived from the doctrine. The fact that the scholars controlled the art of writing gave their new composite history an authority which it otherwise might not have acquired so quickly. As Christian scholars developed an increasingly close accommodation over the next few centuries with the custodians of native learning, the *filidh*, their revised version gradually won universal acceptance. Although it did not erase all trace of the earlier tradition, it canceled out the substance of the original cosmogonic myth. For instance, although the primary ancestral role of Donn, Nuadhu, and others was not forgotten, Adam was accepted as the progenitor of mankind.

The Book of Invasions. The formulation of this revised teaching is attested in poems of the seventh century or earlier, but it was in the twelfth century that it reached its culmination in the pseudohistory entitled *Leabhar Gabhála Éireann* (The Book of the Taking of Ireland), commonly known as the *Book of Invasions*. The "taking" in question evidently refers to the coming of the Gaels (or Goidels), but in the extant compilation this is preceded by five other immigrations. The first came before the Flood and was led by either Cesair, a daughter of Bith, who was a son of Noah, or by Banbha, one of the eponyms of Ireland. But the only one to survive the Flood was Fintan ("the white ancient one"), who outlived innumerable generations until finally in the Christian period he bore witness to the events of the distant past. The next two settlements were led by Partholón and Nemhedh respectively. During both various crafts and social practices were introduced, many lakes were formed, and plains were cleared. These advances indicate in the familiar manner of myths of beginnings how Ireland attained the reality of permanent morphological definition in those times. Both peoples had to withstand the attacks of the Fomhoire, a race of demonic beings who from their haunts beyond the sea posed a perpetual threat to the existence of ordered society.

The main innovations credited to the fourth settlement, comprising the Fir Bholg, the Gailioin, and the Fir Dhomhnann, were sociopolitical in character. By dividing the country into five they instituted the provinces (literally, "fifths" in Irish), and they introduced the concept of sacred kingship and the relationship between the justice of the king and the fertility of the land. They were followed by the Tuatha Dé Danann ("the tribes or peoples of the goddess Danu"), who came skilled in the arts of druidry and magic. They brought with them four talismans: the stone of Fál which shrieked under the true pretender to kingship, the spear of Lugh which ensured victory, the sword of Nuadhu which none escaped, and the caldron of the Daghdha from which none went unsatisfied. They defeated the Fir Bholg in the First Battle of Magh Tuiredh, but soon they had to take up arms against the Fomhoire. [*See also* Tuatha Dé Danann *and* Fomhoire.]

The Second Battle of Magh Tuiredh. There is also an independent account of the Second Battle of Magh Tuiredh in a text which is perhaps the single most important source for Irish mythology. In it the genesis of the conflict is traced to the First Battle of Magh Tuiredh, in which Nuadhu, king of the Tuatha Dé Danann, lost his arm. Because of his physical defect, he was obliged to abdicate the kingship and was succeeded by Bres ("the beautiful"), who had been fathered by Elatha, a king of the Fomhoire, with a woman of the Tuatha Dé, among whom he was reared. But his rule brought only hardship and oppression for the Tuatha Dé, and there was an end to the generosity and hospitality which characterized a true king. Finally he was lampooned by the poet Coirbre in the first satire composed in Irish, and he was asked to give up the kingship. His response was to go to the Fomhoire to seek their support.

Nuadhu meanwhile was fitted with a silver arm by Dian Cécht the leech and restored to sovereignty, and from that time forth he was known as Nuadhu Airgedlámh ("Nuadhu of the silver arm"). But when Lugh came to the royal court of Tara and gave proof of his mastery of all the arts, Nuadhu immediately gave way so that Lugh might lead the Tuatha Dé to victory. In the battle itself Lugh called upon all the preternatural powers of the craftsmen and magicians of the Tuatha Dé, while Dian Cécht used his own healing magic to revive the slain. The dreaded Balar of the Fomhoire had a "baleful eye" which could destroy armies, but Lugh struck it with his slingstone and killed him. The Fomhoire were then expelled from Ireland forever, and Bres himself was captured, but his life was spared on condition that he divulge to the Tuatha Dé the proper times for plowing, sowing, and reaping.

Gaels and the Tuatha Dé. The primary subject of the *Book of Invasions* was perhaps the final settlement of prehistoric Ireland, that of the Gaels, or Irish Celts. Since its underlying purpose was to "biblicize" the origins of the Gaels, it began, as it were, at the beginning, following them in their long journey from Scythia to Egypt and to Spain, whence they finally came to Ireland under the leadership of Míl Espáine ("Mil of Spain"). The account of this early odyssey is a learned fiction modeled on the story of the wandering of the Israelites given in the biblical book *Exodus*. But as the narrative approaches Ireland, it undergoes a sea change and begins to draw more overtly on native tradition. The crucial role in the landing is assigned to the poet-seer and judge Amhairghin. By virtue of his wisdom and his mantic power he overcomes the opposition of the Tuatha Dé and becomes the first Gael to set foot on Irish soil. As he does so—on the feast of Beltene (May Day)—he sings a song of cosmic affirmation in which he subsumes within himself the various elements of the created universe. Like Kṛṣṇa in the Indian tradition and Taliesin in the Welsh, he embodies the potential of all creation, and the timing of his song is particularly appropriate and decisive. Sung as he arrives at the land's edge from the ocean of nonexistence, his words are the prelude to the creation of a new order of which he is the shaper and the source. Through them and through the judgments he pronounces in the succeeding narrative, the Ireland of history is summoned into being.

Having defeated the Tuatha Dé, the Sons of Míl go to the royal center of Tara and on the way meet the three divine eponyms of Ireland—Banbha, Fódla, and Ériu. At Tara the three kings of the Tuatha Dé—Mac Cuill, Mac Cécht, and Mac Gréine—ask for a respite before surrendering sovereignty. Significantly, they refer its conditions to the judgment of Amhairghin. He decides that the Sons of Míl should reembark and retire beyond the ninth wave, which for the Celts constituted a magic boundary. But when they try to land again, the Tuatha Dé create a magical wind which carries them out to sea. Then Amhairghin invokes the land of Ireland, and immediately the wind abates. The Sons of Míl come ashore and defeat the Tuatha Dé at Tailtiu, site of the annual festival instituted by Lugh.

Though they are defeated, the Tuatha Dé still use their magic powers to extract a reasonable settlement from the Gaels. They agree to divide the country into two parts, the lower half going to the Tuatha Dé and the upper half to the Gaels. Thus is explained the traditional belief that the ancient gods—or the fairies of more modern times—lived underground in *sídhe,* or fairy mounds. That this belief was traditional already in the seventh century is evidenced by a clerical biographer of Patrick who refers to the "*sídh,* or gods who dwell in the earth."

Gods of Britain. Early Welsh literary tradition, like the medieval Welsh language, seems further evolved from its archaic roots than its Irish counterpart. This is probably due partly to the cultural effects of the Roman colonization of Britain from the first to the fifth century and partly to the late redaction of the extant material, particularly the prose. But whatever the causes, the result is that Welsh mythological narrative, while preserving some remarkably archaic elements, nevertheless lacks the extensive context found in Irish narrative and betrays the hand of a later redactor or redactors not wholly familiar with the mythological framework from which their materials derived.

Family of Dôn. The main source for Welsh mythological tradition is the collection of tales known as the *Mabinogi* or *Mabinogion,* especially the group known as the Four Branches. These four tales, which were probably redacted toward the end of the eleventh century, take the gods of Britain as their *dramatis personae.* The last of the four, *Math Son of Mathonwy,* deals in particular with the group of gods sometimes referred to as the family of Dôn. The Math of the title is lord of Gwynedd in north Wales. His peculiarity is that he must keep his feet in a virgin's lap except in time of war. When his virginal foot-holder is violated by his sister's son, Gilfaethwy son of Dôn, with the connivance of his brother Gwydion son of Dôn, Math turns the two brothers into male and female animals—stags, boars, and wolves—for three years, during which time they give birth to three sons.

Subsequently, Math seeks a new foot-holder, and Gwydion suggests his sister, Aranrhod daughter of Dôn. Math asks her to step over his magic wand as a test of her virginity, and as she does so, she drops a yellow-haired boy and something else which Gwydion promptly conceals in a chest. The boy is baptized Dylan and immediately makes for the sea and takes on its nature, for which reason he is henceforth called Dylan Eil Don ("Dylan son of wave"). The object concealed by Gwydion turns out to be another male child, who in due course is given the name Lleu Llaw Gyffes ("Lleu of the skillful hand"). The rest of the tale is taken up with Lleu's relations with his mother, Aranrhod, and with his beautiful but treacherous wife, Blodeuwedd ("flower-aspect"), who had been created for him by Gwydion from the flowers of the oak, the broom, and the meadowsweet. The name *Lleu* is, of course, the cognate of the Irish *Lugh* and the Gaulish **Lugus*.

The same tale refers incidentally to Gofannon son of Dôn, the "divine smith" whose name is cognate with the Irish *Goibhniu*. There is mention elsewhere of Amaethon son of Dôn, the divine plowman, and there are various references in medieval poetry which indicate the existence of extensive oral tradition about the family of Dôn. Their communal association with magic is reminiscent of the Irish Tuatha Dé Danann, and it has been suggested that *Dôn* is the equivalent of Irish *Donu* ("the mother of the gods"), the original form of the name *Danann*.

Family of Llŷr. The three members of the family of Llŷr—Branwen, Bendigeidvran ("Brân the blessed"), and Manawydan—appear in the Second Branch of the *Mabinogi*, though it is only in the Third Branch that Manawydan assumes an independent role. The tale is dominated by the enormous figure of Bendigeidvran. When his sister Branwen is ill treated in Ireland, where she has gone as the wife of Matholwch, king of Ireland, he goes with an army to exact vengeance. The British gain victory in a fierce battle with the Irish, but only seven of them survive beside Bendigeidvran, who is wounded in the foot by a poisonous spear. He commands his companions to cut off his head and to bury it at the White Mount in London as a safeguard against invasions. They set out for London and on the way enjoy two periods of otherworldly peace and joy in the presence of his uncorrupted head, at Harlech and on the isle of Gwales.

Clearly, the children of Llŷr are not comparable with those of Dôn: in no sense do they form a pantheon of deities; indeed, Branwen's antiquity is not beyond question. But the association of Brân (as Bendigeidvran was known earlier) and Manawydan is old, and there is an early verse reference to them presiding together over the otherworld and its feast. Manawydan's Irish counterpart is Manannán mac Lir ("son of the sea"), and it is a curious and perhaps significant coincidence that Manannán figures with an Irish Bran in an early lyric tale which tells of a journey made by Bran to the otherworld. But Manannán is represented as god of the sea, probably replacing the god Nechtan in this role, while Manawydan has no such function in Welsh.

Pwyll, Rhiannon, and Pryderi. In the First Branch of the *Mabinogi*, Pwyll, lord of Dyfed in southwest Wales, comes to the aid of Arawn, king of Annwn, by slaying his otherworld enemy Hafgan in a single combat which is in fact an ordeal by battle of the kind known in early Irish as *fír fer* ("truth of men or heroes"). As a result he is henceforth known as Pwyll the Head of Annwn. The *Mabinogi* represents him here as a mortal, but since his name literally means "wisdom" and since he is designated lord of Annwn, the otherworld, it is probable that he was originally a deity. The latter part of the tale is concerned with the death of the hero Pryderi. Pwyll marries the lady Rhiannon, who first appears to him riding a white horse, and from their union Pryderi is born. But the newborn child is mysteriously abducted, to be discovered later by Teyrnon, lord of Gwent Is-coed, and reared by him and his wife for several years until they realize the child's true origins and restore him to Pwyll and Rhiannon. After Pwyll's death Pryderi succeeds to the lordship of Dyfed. Later, in the Third Branch, Rhiannon becomes the wife of Manawydan.

The above merely sketches a complicated narrative whose reference to the underlying mythology is extremely difficult to decipher with any confidence. Teyrnon's name (from **Tigernonos*, "great/divine lord") implies a more important role than the one he plays in the tale and, in fact, is a more appropriate title for the lord of the otherworld. Rhiannon (whose name derives from **Rīgantona*, "great/divine queen") may be an equivalent of Epona, the Celtic horse goddess, while Rhiannon and Pryderi seem to offer a parallel to the pairing of Modron ("great/divine mother") and Mabon ("great/divine son"). The problem is similar to that posed by much of the Welsh mythological evidence in the medieval poetry and the collections of triads: there are numerous references to mythological persons, objects, and events, but these appear without sufficient accompanying matter to set them in context.

Goddesses of the Insular Celts. J. M. Synge in his *The Aran Islands* (1907) says of the Aran islanders of the beginning of the twentieth century that they were interested in fertility rather than eroticism, and on the evidence of the extant monuments and literature, his observation could apply to those people who created the mythology of the Celtic goddesses. The Celts had no goddess of love, and so far as one can judge from insular tradition, the numerous sexual liaisons of the goddesses generally were motivated by ritual or social causes, not by erotic ones. Their sexuality was merely the instrument of their fertility, whether in terms of progeny or of the fruitfulness of the land with which they were so often identified.

The cult of the mother goddess, attested in Gaul from prehistoric times, underlies a great deal of Irish and Welsh tradition. The Second Branch of the *Mabinogi* describes Branwen daughter of Llŷr as "one of the three great ancestresses of Britain." The other two presumably are Rhiannon and Aranrhod, and it is clear from Irish literature that the typical goddess figure was often esteemed as the genetrix of peoples. Her personification of the earth tended to be defined and delimited by cultural and political boundaries: the eponymous triad of Ériu, Fódla, and Banbha represent both the reality and the concept of Ireland in its totality, but there also exists a multitude of analogous characters connected with lesser areas—a province, a district, or a particular locale. Some of the latter, like Áine, Aoibheall, and Cliodhna, have retained their niche in popular tradition and in toponymy to the present day. In this domain the supernatural female often becomes a dominant figure overshadowing her male counterpart.

One of the most enduring myths of the Celts was that of the solemn union between a ruler and his kingdom, where the kingdom is conceived in the form of a divine woman. It appears, slightly veiled, in the Arthurian romances and may be reflected at times in the frequent pairing of god and goddess in Celto-Roman sculpture, but its influence is most profound in Irish tradition. The normal way of reporting the inauguration of a king was to say that he was married to (literally, "slept with") his kingdom. From the hundreds if not thousands of references to this theme one gains some idea of the ritual union of king and consort as it must have been performed before the effective christianization of the political establishment in the sixth century. The ritual union had two main elements: a libation offered by the bride to her partner and the coition. The divine nature of Queen Medhbh of Connacht is evidenced by her name as well as by her actions: she who was famed for the number of her successive husbands was called Medhbh, "the intoxicating one," and under the slightly variant name *Medhbh Lethdherg* it was said of her that "she would not permit a king in Tara unless he had her for his wife." The central element was the sexual meeting, and its profound significance is brought out in countless poems and narratives in which the woman is transformed from repulsive age and ugliness to radiant youth and beauty by the act of intercourse with her ordained mate.

As leader of the Connacht armies Medhbh is associated with war as well as with sovereignty, but in general the warlike aspect of the goddess is manifested indirectly: she influences the fortunes of war rather than actually participating. Other goddesses teach the art of fighting; examples include Buanann ("the lasting one"); Scáthach ("the shadowy one"), from whom Cú Chulainn acquired his heroic skills; and the formidable trio of Morríghan ("phantom queen"), Bodhbh ("scald-crow"), and Nemhain ("frenzy") or Macha, who haunt the battlefield to incite the fighters or to hinder them by their magic. These had their equivalents throughout the Celtic world: the name *Bodhbh Chatha* ("crow/raven of battle") is the exact cognate of *Cathubodua*, attested in Haute-Savoie, and the trio of war goddesses recurs in Britain in the Benwell inscription "Lamiis tribus" ("to the three Lamiae").

In direct contrast to these ruthless furies are those charming women who inhabit the happy otherworld in such numbers that it came to be called Tír inna mBan, "the land of women." Sometimes they come as emissaries from the land of primeval innocence where the pleasures of love are untainted by guilt and where sickness and disease are unknown. Conla son of Conn is induced to go there by "a young and beautiful woman of noble race whom neither death awaits nor old age," and Bran son of Febhal is similarly persuaded by a woman bearing a silvery branch from the wondrous apple tree which is a characteristic feature of the Celtic otherworld. But the multiforms of the insular Celtic goddesses are endless, and sometimes the named figure changes her role from one context to another. For example, Georges Dumézil has sought to demonstrate from three separate tales that the goddess Macha, eponym of the old pagan center of Emhain Mhacha and of the Christian metropolis of Ard Macha (modern Armagh), reflects in her several roles the Indo-European trifunctional system of religion, warrior prowess, and fertility he defines in his *Mythe et epopée* (Paris, 1968, vol. 1, pp. 602–612).

Mythic Space and Time. In a tradition in which the natural and the supernatural realms frequently converge, it is not surprising that there is a constant awareness of the relativities of time and space. This is particularly true of texts relating explicitly to the otherworld, but it is common throughout Irish and much of Welsh literature. [*See* Sídh.] The land of Ireland itself, with its place-names and physical features, seems to shift with enigmatic ease between the two levels of perception. The early redactors of the written texts were fascinated by the contrasting effects of changing perspective, as when the god Manannán describes the sea as a flowery plain or the monks of Clonmacnois observe a boat sail in the sky over their head and drop its anchor by their church door.

But certain places are permanently set apart from their secular environment: cult sites, the precincts of sacred festivals, and, above all, the notional center of the cultural world of native tradition. This concept of the center is one of the constants of Celtic ideology, and it retained a good deal of its ancient symbolism in Irish learned literature as late as the seventeenth century. Caesar reports that the Gaulish druids assembled each year at a holy place in the lands of the Carnutes which was regarded as the center of Gaul. His term *locus consecratus* may well translate the word *nemeton*, "sacred place," which is found in place-names throughout the

Celtic world. According to Strabo, the Council of the Galatians met at a place known as Drunemeton ("oak sanctuary"). In Ireland the druids were closely associated with Uisnech, the "navel" of Ireland, the location of the primal fire, and reputedly the site of a great festival. The focus of sacral kingship was at Tara in the central province of Midhe ("middle").

The great social assemblies of ancient Ireland were generally held at one or another of the seasonal festivals. The Irish year, like the Indo-European year, was divided into two halves, *samh,* or summer, and *gamh,* or winter. The summer half began at Beltene or Cédshamhain, the first of May, and the winter half at Samhain, the first of November. [*See* Halloween.] These halves were further subdivided by the quarter days of Imbolg, the first of February and the beginning of spring, and Lughnasadh, the first of August and the start of the harvest festival associated with the god Lugh. The old binary division is found also in the famous bronze calendar discovered at Coligny, near Bourg, which probably dates from the early first century CE or late first century BCE. Judging from the calendar, the Gaulish druids divided the year into two halves beginning with the months Samon(i-) and Giamon(i-). Of the two names for the beginning of summer, Beltene may have referred originally to the fire ritual traditionally held at that time: *bel-* probably means "shining or bright," and *tene* looks like the Irish word for "fire." In the course of time, however, *Beltene* displaced the older term *Cédshamhain* or *Cédamhuin* (cf. the Welsh cognate *Cyntefin*) as the name for the festival season itself.

Kings and Heroes. Virtually all early Irish narrative literature is to some degree heroic, but there are differences of emphasis that distinguish the king tales from the more specifically heroic narratives. Though the king tales involve heroic values, these are not their main preoccupation. Rather, they are concerned with the affirmation of political and social realities: the status and functions of the king, the ritual of inauguration and relations with the goddess of sovereignty, the origins of tribes and dynasties, battles of historical moment, the deeds and judgments of famous rulers, and so on. The sacral kingship was both the pivot and the foundation of the social order, and the king was its personification; if his conduct or even his person were blemished in any way, this blemish would be visited on his kingdom, diminishing its integrity and prosperity. As the instrument of justice, the king must be fair and flawless in his decisions. Thus the great Cormac mac Airt is pictured as a paragon of kingship and as an Irish Solomon: his accession came about when he proposed a just judgment after his predecessor Lughaidh mac Con had been deposed for delivering an unjust one. Conaire Mór is likewise an exemplary king whose reign brings peace and well-being to the land until he tempers justice with excessive mercy in the case of his three marauding foster brothers. Immediately a train of events is set in motion which leads inexorably to his death in a welter of violence.

The welfare of the king and his people depended on his justice or *fír flathemon* ("truth or righteousness of a prince"). The literary genre of the *speculum principum* ("mirror of princes"), consisting of advice to a king, is a familiar one in Irish. The earliest written instance, *Audhacht Morainn* (The Testament of Morann), dates from the seventh century CE, but the genre was already long established in oral tradition, and it is widely accepted that the European *speculum principum* derives partly from the Irish model. Every kingdom, however small, had its sacred king and its inauguration site, but the focus of sacral kingship was at Tara, the goal of ambitious kings throughout the early Middle Ages. Situated in the central province, Midhe (lit., "middle"), and surrounded by the other four provinces, Tara is itself the heart of the Irish cosmographic system, and the traditional accounts of the disposition of the court of Tara show that it was conceived as a microcosmic replica of this cosmographic schema. Feis Temhra ("the feast of Tara") was the great festival held in pagan times to confirm a new king and to celebrate his ritual marriage to his kingdom. At Tara stood the Lia Fáil ("stone of Fál"), the "stone penis" which cried out when it came in contact with the man destined to be king.

In primitive Irish and Celtic society the twin guardians of social order were the king and the druid or hieratic poet. One of the clearest expressions of this crucial relationship was the formal eulogy which functioned in part as an exemplary paradigm of kingly conduct. Its ideological importance for Indo-European society and its derivatives have been discussed by Georges Dumézil, among other authors. It is this regulative and conservative role which accounts for the seemingly disproportionate volume of praise-poetry which has survived in Ireland and Wales, particularly from the post-Norman period when traditional society and culture were being increasingly threatened.

Ulster cycle. Like the sacral king of prehistoric tradition, the hero occupied an ambiguous status between god and men: typically he has a divine as well as a human father, and his trials and achievements bring him into contact with supernatural powers more frequently than other mortals. He has many incarnations in insular Celtic literature, but it is above all the Ulster cycle that represents him in the quintessential heroic setting.

The cycle is set in the province of Ulster when it was

dominated by the Ulaidh, the people from whom the province derived its name, at a time somewhere between the coming of the Celts about the third century BCE and the conquest of the Ulaidh, which may have taken place in the early fifth century CE. The cycle portrays an aristocratic warrior society with a La Tène type material culture, and in many respects the society shows striking correspondences with what is reported of independent Gaul. The king of the Ulaidh at this time was Conchobhar mac Nessa, who had his royal court at Emhain Mhacha near the present city of Armagh. He presided over a numerous company which included the youthful Cú Chulainn, the senior heroes Conall Cernach and Ferghus mac Roich, and such others as the druid Cathbhadh, the wise peacemaker Sencha mac Ailella, and the inveterate mischief-maker Bricriu, known as Nemhthenga ("poison-tongue"). These characters constitute the cast of an extensive literature of which the centerpiece is the great saga *Táin Bó Cuailnge* (The Cattle Raid of Cuailnge). It tells of Queen Medhbh of Connacht's incursion into Ulster with the object of seizing the great Brown Bull of Cuailnge, which was of divine origin. As a result of a curse by the goddess Macha, the Ulstermen are unable to resist the attack, and it falls to the young Cú Chulainn to defend the province single-handedly. By engaging in a series of single combats with heroes of the Connacht army, he hinders their advance until the Ulstermen recover their strength and rout their enemies. The climax and finale of the tale is the tremendous encounter in which the bull of Cuailnge slays the Finnbhennach, the "white-horned" bull of Connacht. [*See also* Táin Bó Cuailnge.]

As the heroic milieu *par excellence*, the court of Conchobhar at Emhain became the focus for a wide variety of tales reflecting the different facets of the heroic ethos, and as the quintessential hero Cú Chulainn became the subject of many narratives exploring the nature of the hero's mediating role between gods and men and his singular relationship with his own community. Cú Chulainn experiences the perennial dilemma of the supreme hero caught in the insoluble contradictions of his ambiguous status. Neither divine nor merely human, Cú Chulainn lives within the tribe and yet does not wholly belong; member of a heroic confraternity, he characteristically stands alone. His initiation to the heroic circle is recounted in a section of *The Cattle Raid of Cuailnge* narrating his "boyhood deeds" *(macghnimhartha)*. Linguistically this section is not part of the oldest stratum of the text (it may belong to the ninth century) but its content is part of an archaic tradition. For his first exploit Cú Chulainn slays the three fearsome sons of Nechta Scéne who have been a scourge upon the Ulstermen. The narrative thus reproduces an old Indo-European motif of the hero's victory over a trio of adversaries or a three-headed monster. He also for the first time experiences the *riastradh*, or grotesque distortion, and the phenomenal body-heat which are the external manifestations of his battle fury and which mark him in Irish tradition as a hero above heroes. These traits also have old and widespread analogues.

Cú Chulainn's career is a short one, but since it constitutes a paradigm of the hero, it is natural that mythmakers and storytellers should have taken the critical stages of his life and woven a web of narrative around each: his threefold birth distinguished by incest and divine paternity, familiar marks of the sacred conception of the hero; his martial training with the otherworldly Scáthach; his wooing of Emher and his marriage; and finally his death, which, since he was invincible by merely human means, could only be effected through trickery and sorcery. This framework has also accommodated a number of other more occasional tales, such as those of his adventures in the otherworld or the tragic *Aided Aenfhir Aífe* (The Death of Aífe's Only Son), which brings Cú Chulainn to slay his own son through a combination of moral compulsion and mistaken identity.

But Cú Chulainn and his life cycle are only a part of the larger cycle of the Ulster tales, in many of which he plays a relatively small role or none at all. His singular importance is that he epitomizes the heroic virtues and values. By the seventh century CE he had become a focus for archaic traditions pertaining to what Dumézil defined as the second of the Indo-European social functions, that of the warrior.

Fionn cycle. In early Irish the Fionn cycle was also known as the *Fianaighecht*; the cycle is a group of stories and traditions about the Fian, the band of hunter-warriors led by Fionn mac Cumhaill. Today the cycle is commonly called the Fenian cycle, a modern anglicization, or the Ossianic cycle, after Fionn's son Oisín (or Ossian). Etymologically the term *fian* (pl., *fiana*) embodies the notion of living by the hunt or by force of arms, and this notion corresponds exactly with the role of the Fiana in Irish tradition. Originally there were several groups of *fiana*, but the fame of Fionn's company relegated the others to obscurity. Each *féinnidh*, or individual member of the Fian, was required to undergo initiatory trials of his skill and endurance before admittance, and once accepted he had to sever his legal and social connections with his kin and his tribe and abandon the associated rights and responsibilities. Yet, although he placed himself outside the tribal community, he did not place himself outside the law, for the *fiana* were recognized by law and tradition as fulfilling a legitimate function. Many legends picture the *fiana* as the defenders of Ireland against the incursions of foreign—that is, supernatural—enemies. From the eleventh or twelfth century onward, and perhaps even earlier, these enemies are often identified in an ambiguous, mythopoeic fashion with the Viking raiders of the ninth century.

The Celtic form **vindos* ("white"), from which the Irish *Fionn* and Welsh *Gwynn* derive, occurs on the continent in the deity name *Vindonnus,* and it has been concluded that Fionn himself was originally divine. **Vindos* is related to the Indo-European stem **ui-n-d-* ("finds out, knows"), and it also has been suggested that Fionn's name means "he who finds out, he who knows." This accords with his role in tradition, which represents him as poet and seer as well as warrior-hunter, perhaps like his Welsh counterpart Gwynn ap Nudd, who appears fleetingly in Welsh tradition as a "magic warrior-huntsman." Fionn is sometimes said to have acquired his supernatural knowledge by tasting the otherworldly liquor. His normal means of divination was simply to chew his thumb, with which he had once touched the Salmon of Knowledge, which he was cooking for his master in poetry and magic. Moreover, poetry and preternatural vision have always been characteristic attributes of the Fionn cycle as a whole.

Like Cú Chulainn, Fionn too is the subject of a narrative recounting his boyhood deeds. His birth followed soon after his father's death at the hands of the rival band of the Sons of Morna. He was reared secretly in the forest by two female warriors until he was ready to assert his precocious claim to the leadership of the Fian. He killed a malevolent being called Aillén mac Midhna who came each year to burn down the royal court of Tara. (This is only one of several variants of a myth in which Fionn figured as conqueror of a supernatural one-eyed arsonist.) Even within the Fian his archrival was Goll ("one-eyed") mac Morna, also known as Aodh ("fire"). There is an obvious analogy here with the myth of Lugh's defeat of Balar, and it has in fact been argued that Fionn was simply another name and persona for that deity. However, Lugh is the divine archetype of the sacred king, whereas Fionn's relationship to kingship is ambiguous, to say the least. Fionn and his followers became closely associated with the king of Tara as a kind of standing army, but this seems to be a fairly late development. Earlier their role as mercenaries was much more marginal and ambivalent.

This marginal status may partly explain why the *Fianaighecht* was accorded little space in the written texts before the eleventh and twelfth centuries, though it is attested as early as the Ulster cycle. By and large the literature of prestige, like the Ulster cycle, reinforced the structures and usages of organized aristocratic society within its clearly defined political boundaries. But the Fian's environment was outside and beyond this cultivated domain in the forest and the wilderness. Here they roamed at will, on foot or on horseback, unlike the Ulster heroes, who traveled in chariots. Intimately connected with nature, both animate and inanimate, their world blurred and often dissolved the boundaries of social and natural categories. For example, several of the *féinnidi* were born of mothers in animal form, and the Fian's great hounds Bran and Sgeolang had a human mother. It is hardly surprising that Fian mythology has always had a firm hold on the popular imagination and that it only gained prominence in the written tradition when the learned class began to react to the pressure of sociopolitical change in the eleventh and twelfth centuries.

The liminality of the region inhabited by the Fian emerges clearly in their relations with the otherworld. Whereas in the Ulster tales the association of the two worlds tends to happen at specific times, at the great calendar festivals, for instance, or during initiation rituals, among the Fian these associations are casual and continual. The Fian's liminal status ensures that they can participate freely in both the natural and the supernatural world. In this as in much else they correspond to the heroes of Arthur's court. There can be little doubt that the cycles of Fionn and Arthur, whatever their later vicissitudes, derive from the same sector of insular mythology.

The Elopement of Diarmaid and Gráinne, one of the most popular tales in the *Fianaighecht,* tells how the mature Fionn loses the beautiful Gráinne to Diarmaid ua Duibhne, "the master and charmer of women," just as Arthur loses Gwenhwyfar (Guinevere) to Medrawd (Melwas). The tale is one of several Irish analogues of the romance of Tristan and Iseult, and it also ends in tragedy, when Diarmaid is killed by the magic boar of Beann Ghulban. Gráinne's name, meaning, literally, "ugliness," suggests that she was that same sovereign goddess who appears as a repulsive hag and is transformed in union with her rightful partner. Diarmaid Donn ("brown, dark") may originally have been the god Donn who ruled the otherworld of the dead.

The most comprehensive source for the *Fianaighecht* is a long frame-story entitled *Agallamh na Senórach* (The Converse of the Old Men), which was probably compiled near the end of the twelfth century. The title indicates the convenient device upon which the massive narrative rests: Caoilte mac Rónáin, one of the principal members of the Fian, long outlives his contemporaries and eventually meets with Saint Patrick, who is on his mission of christianization. Caoilte accompanies Patrick on his journey throughout the Irish countryside and tells him the stories associated with its hills, rivers, plains, and other natural features. The result is a vast thesaurus of place-name lore *(dinnshenchas)*, which brings together the several streams of learned and popular tradition that went into the making of the Fionn cycle.

System or Chaos. Matthew Arnold admired the Celts for their lyric gifts but claimed, perhaps not without reason, that they lacked the sense of *architectonicé* in their literary compositions. It is a sentiment that has been echoed by many students of Celtic religion and mythology when confronted with the frustratingly formless and unfinished character of the rich corpus of evidence. This feeling has been aptly expressed by Marie-Louise Sjoestedt in her *Gods and Heroes of the Celts* (London, 1949):

> In travelling through the dense forest of the insular legends, and stirring the ashes of the continental Celtic world, we did not hope to uncover the plan of a vast edifice, a temple of the Celtic gods, partly overrun by the luxuriant wilderness and partly ruined by invaders. The indications are that this edifice never existed. Other people raised temples to their gods, and their very mythologies are temples whose architecture reproduces the symmetry of a cosmic or social order—an order both cosmic and social. It is in the wild solitude of the *nemēton* and sacred woodland, that the Celtic tribe meets its gods, and its mythical world is a sacred forest, pathless and unbounded, which is inhabited by mysterious powers. . . . We seek for a cosmos and find chaos. . . .
>
> The investigation of the insular tradition leaves one with a sense of something missing. One searches in vain for traces of those vast conceptions of the origin and final destiny of the world which dominate other Indo-European mythologies. Was there a Celtic cosmogony or eschatology? Must we suppose from the few allusions, vague and banal as they are, which Caesar or Pomponius Mela have made to the teaching of the druids, that a whole aspect, and an essential aspect, of this mythical world is hidden from us and will remain hidden? Should we explain the silence of our texts by the censorship of Christian monks, who were nevertheless liberal enough to allow the preservation of episodes much stained with paganism, and features most shocking to the Christian mentality? (p. 92)

Sjoestedt's own reply to this last rhetorical question would have been a clear negative, but some more recent studies suggest a qualified affirmative. In fact, there are grounds for believing that the early monastic redactors, for all their undoubted tolerance, did censor pagan learned tradition by omission as well as by emendation and that their omission most seriously affected those areas where conflict of doctrines was least acceptable to Christian orthodoxy: ritual, cosmogony, and eschatology.

In 1918 Joseph Vendryes demonstrated in an important article (*Mémoires de la Société de Linguistique de Paris* 20, 1918, pp. 265–285) that the Celtic languages, and particularly early Irish, preserve the remnants of an old Indo-European religious vocabulary originating with the hieratic ancestors of brahmans, pontifs, and druids. Since then it has become increasingly clear that these particularities of terminology are not to be seen as isolated fossils but rather as reflecting interrelated elements of a system of socioreligious thought and practice which must have persisted substantially unchanged until a relatively late date, perhaps—in Ireland at least—until the establishment of Christianity. The numerous survivals of archaisms from Indo-European ideology, ritual, and liturgy in early Irish recorded tradition strongly support this conclusion. So also does the "deep structure" of early Irish narrative that is gradually being uncovered by the close analysis of individual texts. In the context of such fundamental and constantly recurring themes as the sacral kingship, the king as mediator between the secular and the supernatural world, the antinomy of ideological unity and political fragmentation, and the concept of social or cosmic order, these early texts often reveal a complex weave of structured allusion that presupposes in the not too distant past a coherent and authoritative system of politico-religious and juridico-religious belief and speculation.

But it would be wrong to assume that the texts offer a complete and consistent record of that system, not merely because monastic redactors practiced conscious censorship and selectivity, but also because the texts were recorded long after druidic paganism had ceased to be the official and uncontested religion of the country. By reason of this remove in time and motivation the early Irish documentation belongs largely to the category to which Georges Dumézil has applied the term *mythologie littérarisée*. It is the concern of contemporary scholars to analyze and interpret this rich documentation and to restate it in mythico-religious rather than literary terms.

[*Many of the Celtic deities, kings, and heroes mentioned herein are the subjects of independent entries.*]

BIBLIOGRAPHY

Duval, Paul-Marie. *Les dieux de la Gaule*. Rev. ed. Paris, 1976. An excellent compendium of what is known and surmised about the Gaulish gods. Its exposition of the data is clear, and its commentary balanced and judicious.

Gray, Elizabeth A. *Cath Maige Tuired: The Second Battle of Mag Tuired*. London, 1982. An edition of this important mythological text. Gray's "Cath Maige Tuired: Myth and Structure," *Eigse* 18 (1981): 183–209 and 19 (1982–1983): 1–35, 230–262, is a detailed interpretive analysis of the content of the tale.

Mac Cana, Proinsias. *Celtic Mythology*. Rev. ed. Feltham, Middlesex, 1983. A short survey of the subject with illustrations of sculpture, metalwork, and so on.

MacCulloch, J. A. *The Religion of the Ancient Celts.* Edinburgh, 1911. Reprinted as *Celtic Mythology* (Boston, 1918). Still useful if read in conjunction with more recent accounts.

MacNeill, Máire. *The Festival of Lughnasa.* Oxford, 1962. A comprehensive inventory of all the local festivals in Ireland that can be shown to continue the Celtic feast of Lugh, together with a very helpful commentary and a rich collection of texts, largely from the oral tradition.

Meyer, Kuno, ed. and trans., and Alfred Nutt. *The Voyage of Bran, Son of Febal, to the Land of the Living.* 2 vols. London, 1895–1897. This work includes a long commentary on the Celtic concept of the otherworld and the doctrine of rebirth. Largely superseded by more recent studies, it still contains many useful insights.

Murphy, Gerard, ed. and trans. *The Book of the Lays of Fionn,* vol. 3, *Duanaire Finn.* Dublin, 1953. Includes a long and valuable commentary on the history of the Fionn cycle and on the relationship between medieval manuscript and modern oral versions.

Nagy, Joseph Falaky. *The Wisdom of the Outlaw: The Boyhood Deeds of Finn in Gaelic Narrative Tradition.* Berkeley, 1983. An excellent, comprehensive interpretation of the Irish Fionn Cycle, or Fianaighecht, and the first extended study of the cycle in terms of modern mythological theory. It explores the internal consistency of the cycle as reflected in some of its constituent narratives and brings out the markedly liminal character of Fionn and his followers.

Ó Cathasaigh, Tomás. *The Heroic Biography of Cormac mac Airt.* Dublin, 1977. A perceptive exposition of the status and function of the Irish hero-king as reflected in the legends of Cormac mac Airt.

O'Rahilly, Thomas F. *Early Irish History and Mythology.* Dublin, 1946. Valuable for its coverage of Irish literary resources in all periods, and for its brilliant analyses of medieval texts, but sometimes rather outmoded and idiosyncratic in its treatment of mythological topics by viewing essentially mythological narratives as reflections of historical events.

Rees, Alwyn, and Brinley Rees. *Celtic Heritage.* London, 1961. An important and stimulating work that seeks to structure insular Celtic tradition in terms of a number of ideological concepts and motivations. It is inspired by the Dumézilian system of analysis, applied in a flexible and imaginative fashion.

Ross, Anne. *Pagan Celtic Britain.* London, 1967. Surveys the British repertory of images for the Celtic gods and their attributes. Contains an extensive and detailed discussion of the several main categories of deity which they comprise (horned god, warrior god, divine animals, among others). Valuable also for its rich comparative documentation from insular literary and folklore sources.

Sjoestedt, Marie-Louise. *Dieux et héros des Celtes.* Paris, 1940. Translated by Myles Dillon as *Gods and Heroes of the Celts* (London, 1949). A short but perceptive survey of Celtic, mainly Irish, mythology and hero tales. At the time of its publication it offered fresh insights into the nature of Celtic myth and is still necessary reading.

Vendryes, Joseph. *Les religions des Celtes.* "Mana," Introduction à l'histoire des religions, vol. 1. Paris, 1948. This is largely a *catalogue raisonné* of the varied data, both continental and insular, relating to Celtic religion. More descriptive than theoretical, it is still a useful source of information.

Vries, Jan de. *Keltische Religion.* Stuttgart, 1961. A comprehensive treatment of the whole of Celtic religion. It is well documented and strong on Indo-European and other comparative aspects, less so on the insular tradition, although the latter is still given generous coverage.

Proinsias Mac Cana

CENTER OF THE WORLD. The importance of the symbolism of the center of the world can hardly be overstated, for it establishes the order of the universe, drawing together the spiritual destiny of collective humankind and that of the individual human being. The term *center of the world* refers to that place where all essential modes of being come together; where communication and even passage among them is possible. The center of the world is the heart of reality, where the real is fully manifest. The nature of this manifestation may vary greatly from one culture to another, taking the form of a vague, undefined power or of the direct appearance of a divinity. Since this center stands apart as the extraordinary place where the real is integral, it is always a sacred place, qualitatively different from mundane space. In the religious world view, every ordered and habitable area possesses such a center, a space that is sacred above all others. For this reason, the center of the world should not be portrayed in purely geometric terms or forms. It is because the center of the world is defined by its special relationship to the sacred that there can be multiple centers in any cosmos or microcosm. Cultures in Mesopotamia, India, and China, for example, saw no inconsistency in recognizing a large number of sacred places, each one called "the center of the world." The center of the world is a locus in mythic geography, a symbolic portrayal of the real, known, and essential aspects of the world, rather than a detached and objective reckoning of abstract space.

In cultures that conceive of the universe as multiple realms of heavens, hells, and strata for various kinds of beings, the center of the world is that point where all realms intersect and where the most direct contact with the sacred is obtained. Existence of a sacred center allows for the establishment of a world system, a body of imaged realities that are related to one another: a sacred point that stands apart from the homogeneity of general space; symbolic openings from one level of reality to another; an *axis mundi* (tree, mountain, ladder, vine, or pillar) that symbolizes the communication between cosmic regions; and the extension of an organized and habitable world that exists around the center. This cosmos constructed around a sacred center lies in opposition to the chaotic space beyond it, which has neither been ordered by the gods nor consecrated in rituals imitating the divine creative acts. That indeterminate space beyond the cosmos remains uninhabitable by human beings because it is a place where communication with the supernatural world is impossible. In the "other world" dwell demonic beings, ghosts, monsters, souls of the dead, or foreigners.

Symbolic Forms. In order to illustrate how widespread is the concept of the center of the world and how constant is its basic meaning, some of its most common symbolic forms may be noted. Among these are the sacred mountain; the cosmic tree; the bridge or ladder connecting cosmic realms; sanctuaries, temples, tombs; sacred cities; domestic space; personal space; and sacred sound.

In Asia one finds the elaborate religious symbolism of Mount Meru, the cosmic mountain whose complex symbolic meanings are put forth especially in the post-Vedic literature of India, particularly in the Purāṇas of Hinduism, and in certain Buddhist texts. On its peak lie the cities of the gods. It has existed since the beginning of time. Upon its slopes the waters of immortality are stored in Lake Anavatapta. The sacred river Ganges flows from Mount Meru. It is the fixed point about which revolve the sun and the stars. Around it are gathered other sacred mountains. In ascending the slopes of Mount Meru, one passes through all possible spiritual states of being until, arriving at the summit, one transcends the particularities of any of them. Similarly, in early Taoism, K'un-lun is a cosmic mountain paradise connecting heaven and earth. In some accounts concerning the primordial human being named P'an-ku, K'un-lun makes its appearance from out of the chaotic flood waters that deluged the earth. It was here at the center of the universe that human life was created and the world regenerated.

In the *Chuang-tzu* and *Lieh-tzu*, K'un-lun is the place where the Yellow Emperor "dies" to the mundane world and flies to heaven in the immortal form of a bird-man. Also in the *Lieh-tzu* is a description of the mountain Hu-ling, which forms the center of a paradise whose inhabitants are rejuvenated by the water bubbling forth from the sacred spring on its summit. The spirit is the only vehicle that can transport one on a journey across the slopes of this cosmic mountain. To find one's way to this mountain is to return to the beginning of time, where one's adult body becomes once again virginal, and one's mind attains undifferentiated knowledge, limitless as a bottomless spring. The ascent transcends all particular states and attains the mode of preexistence, the condition of the "spirit man" *(shen-jen),* spoken of as the Taoist ideal of the holy man in the *Lieh-tzu, Huai-nan–tzu,* and the *Chuang-tzu.*

Examples of cosmic mountains that stand at the center of the world make up a very long list. The central mountain of Uralo-Altaic cosmology, Sumbur, Sumur, or Semeru, lay directly under the North Star, which fixed the central point of the heavens. In Norse mythology, Himinbjorg, the "heavenly mountain," lies at the center of the earth, where the rainbow touches the celestial vault. In the Hebrew Bible (*Jgs.* 9:37) Mount Gerizim is referred to as *ṭabur ha-arets,* "the navel of the earth." Indeed, there are traditions that report that the land of Palestine is so high, located as it is near the heights of the cosmic mountain, that it alone remained unflooded during the Deluge. Mount Tabor, in its very name, may share associations with the navel, *ṭabur,* of the earth. A ninth-century Islamic tradition argued by al-Kisā'ī of Kufa holds the sacred Ka'bah to be the highest place on earth, located directly beneath the North Star (i.e., at the center of the world). In a Christian tradition from the Syrian *Book of the Cave of Treasures,* Golgotha was the center of the world, the summit of the cosmic mountain, and the culmination of salvation history. It was there that Adam was created and buried, in the same place in which the blood of Christ was shed to redeem the world. The image of the cosmic mountain immediately introduces us to the concept of *axis mundi,* the "hub of the world," which symbolizes the communication between cosmic realms. It likewise brings up the symbolism of ascension, since one may transcend the planes of existence along a vertical axis. [*See* Mountains.]

Another widely known symbol of the center of the world is the cosmic tree, which transfixes the levels of the world, making communication and passage among them possible. At the center of the world in the Baltic religious traditions stood the Saules Koks, the "tree of the sun." It grew out of the top of the mountain of heaven, the farmland of the heavenly supreme being Dievs. It is the source of life. Although earthly species of tree may represent the tree of the sun, it is unique and inaccessible. It may be described as made of precious metal, gold, or silver. A supernatural orb descends through its branches, perhaps associated with Saule, the sun herself, who is the mother of all life. Likewise, among the Maya of Mesoamerica during the Classic period (300–900 CE) the universe was centered on Yaxche, the "first, or green, tree," extending upward to the zenith (the white interval between east and west) and downward to the nadir (the yellow interval between west and east).

Certain Babylonian inscriptions refer to the black tree named Kiskanu that grows at Eridu, a place at the center of the world. This sacred tree is described in cosmic terms: it shines with the lapis-lazuli radiance of the starry night and spreads its boughs out toward the cosmic ocean that encompasses the world. It is the place where Ea (Enki), the god of fertility and of cultural skills, is present, and the resting place of Bau, Ea's mother, the goddess of abundant flocks and agriculture. The *Vǫluspa*, the Scandinavian creation story, tells of Yggdrasill, the cosmic tree whose roots penetrate the center of the earth. Óðinn (Odin) leaves his eye in the Spring of Mímir ("memory" or "meditation"), located near Yggdrasill, in exchange for the privilege of refreshing his wisdom there whenever he returns. Near the foot of Yggdrasill, at the Spring of Urðr (Urd) located there, the divinities pronounce judgments. Water is drawn from the Spring of Urðr by the three Norns, maidens who govern the fate of humans. In the branches of Yggdrasill, which spread out across heaven and earth, live supernatural animals. At the foot of the tree lies the enormous cosmic serpent, Niðhǫggr (Nidhogg), who threatens the very existence of the tree by gnawing continually upon it. At the very top of the tree perches an eagle who does daily battle with the destructive serpent. The *Vǫluspa* describes not only the creation of the world but its demise when it gives way to a paradisal epoch. Even at that time, Yggdrasill will endure. [*See* Trees.]

The symbolism of the center of the world may be expressed through a range of other symbols—a ladder, a vine, a rope, a bridge—all of which serve as an *axis mundi* connecting heaven and earth or various cosmic realms of being. [*See, for example,* Bridges.] For example, for the Desana, a Tucano-speaking group of the Vaupés River area of southern Colombia, the center of the world is occupied by the Go'a-mëe, which transfixes all zones of the universe through their center. Go'a-mëe is likened to the penis of the creator Sun Father. In the image of a tubular bone *(ve'e go'á)*, it joins all the cosmic levels together in an act of continuous intercourse. This immense phallus at the center of the world is a fundamental part of the creation, since it carries the "yellow intention," the solar semen of the creator, into the cosmic uterus, Ahpikondía ("river of milk"), from which all life comes.

The image of the center as the locus of all powers and passage makes clear the religious significance of a range of holy sites, from informal sanctuaries to temples, cathedrals, or even whole cities. The Mandan, a Plains Indian group now living in North Dakota, placed a circular shrine in the center of each of their villages. It was constructed of wood panels nearly two meters in height. In the center of the shrine stood a cedar post, the image of the supernatural being named One Man, who lived in the times spoken of in myth. One Man was the brother of the first human being. The Achilpa, an Aranda (Arunta) tribe in Australia, install Kauwa-auwa, a sacred pole fashioned from the trunk of a gum tree, in their settlements. It is the pillar that their legendary ancestor Numbakula constructed, anointed with blood, and used to ascend into the sky during the mythic period. It is the means of communication between this world and the world above; between this period of time and the mythical time of the ancestor. Whenever the Achilpa wander as a group, they carry Kauwa-auwa with them and head in the direction toward which the sacred pole inclines. In this way communication with the supernatural will always be possible.

Standing at the center of the world, the temple too spans all levels of reality. The Rock of Jerusalem reaches down into the waters below the earth (Heb., *tehom*). Directly over this watery chaos, the Mishnah locates the Temple. The Rock of the Temple of Jerusalem thus closes "the mouth of the *tehom*." The Babylonian sanctuaries of Nippur and Larsa were given the title *duranki*, "link between heaven and earth." In ancient Babylon the temple also served to connect heaven and earth: it was built upon *babapsu*, "gate of *apsu*," the watery chaos that existed before creation. The stupa of Borobudur in Java was built in the form of a mountain occupying the center of the cosmos. It is here at the center of the universe that one may have the most direct contact with Buddhahood. By ascending the stages of the stupa, the pilgrim passes through all realms of reality. [*See* Temple.]

In some cases, a city becomes the sacred place where heaven and earth come together. Architects designing sacred capitals oriented the sites to the cosmic powers that filled them with their sacred force and rendered them habitable. Ritual actions focused the supernatural power of a kingdom within the city confines. In Thailand a new monarch performed a ceremonial tour *(liap mo'aṅ)* around his capital. In Egypt, a ceremony called the Circuit of the White Wall was celebrated when a new pharaoh came to Memphis. The practice was modeled on the actions of Menes, who had designed the sacred city. When Romulus determined the circumference of Rome, he plowed a furrow in such a way as to form the city on the model of the cosmos as a whole. This line, the *pomerium*, was marked then by stones and considered holy. Not only was the capital city made habitable by its consecration as a sacred place, the capital itself became the center for diffusion of sacred forces throughout the wider kingdom. Through the city gates, sacred power, generated at the center of the capital during its ceremonies, passed out to the extended world. In this way, the city, often built on a heavenly model, becomes a source of resanctification and sacred renewal for a world corrupted over time. Such was the function of the sacred cities of Cuzco, the Inca capital in the Andes of South America, and Tenochtitlán, the Aztec capital and center of life forces throughout Mesoamerica in the early sixteenth centery CE. Tenochtitlán was called "the root," "the navel," and "the heart" of the earthly layer in the cosmos. It was the "supreme" place in which the world of humans was joined with the Giver of Life, for it supported the multiple layers of the celestial realm and communicated with the underworld. As the Aztec adage says: "Who would conquer Tenochtitlán? Who could shake the foundation of heaven?" (cited in Miguel León-Portilla, *Pre-Columbian Literatures of Mexico*, Norman, Okla., 1968, p. 87). [*See* Cities.]

The symbolism of the center of the world is by no means limited to extravagant cases. The house often contains the center of the world. [*See* Home]. The Barasana of the northwest Amazon conceive of their *maloca,* the longhouse in which an extended family lives, in the image of the universe, especially at the time of the Yurupary festival. During the rites known as He, the longhouse becomes the center of the universe, where life began when a mythic ancestor anaconda swam there and disintegrated into the many separate parts which formed the separate lineages of the tribe. From his long bones came the sacred flutes and long trumpets played during the festival. These instruments are laid end to end to reconstruct—literally to re-member—the ancestor as he was, whole and entire, at the beginning of time at the center of the house-universe. In the Barasana tradition the whole house is "cosmicized" for the cermonial occasion. In other cultures, some structure in the house serves as an image of the center of the world; a central beam, center post, or chimney, the smoke hole or hearth, and so on.

The tendency to find the center of the universe in multiple locations may be carried as far as the discovery of it within one's own body. Such is the case in certain Tantric schools that rejected the validity of an external *maṇḍala* but insisted rather on locating the center of the *maṇḍala* within the yogin. The interior *maṇḍala,* an image of the universe, enabled the yogin to identify his "mystical body" as a whole microcosm. As each internal *cakra,* the "wheel" where cosmic life and psychic life intersect, is activated, the practitioner progressively penetrates into the center of an interior *maṇḍala,* an image of the universe.

There is an impulse to replicate the image of the center of the universe in multiple forms. At one stage in the creation of the universe, according to the Dogon of Mali, a supernatural being connected the heavenly and earthly realms with thread fibers into which he wove symbols of the creative word spoken by Amma, the supreme being. The symbolism of fibers passing back and forth from heaven to earth is repeated in the image of a special drum, whose two heads are bound together in an intricate pattern of thread fibers. The same meaning is continued in children's games in which the child's hands are identified with the hands of the supernatural being, and the "cat's cradle" of thread drawn between the child's fingers imitates the creative word-threads communicated between heaven and earth. Weaving itself, and the loom, are invested with the same symbolic value. Rains are imagined to be moist breath-threads rewound into the heavens along the sun's rays by the copper spirals of moisture that entwine the sun. This sort of replication of the image of the *axis mundi* in village sites, house plans, ritual furnishings, personal ornaments, games, and cooking utensils tends to identify the fullness of being characteristic of the center of the world with the universe as a whole.

Although emphasis falls on the center of the world as a point of contact with the heavenly world and, therefore, associated with the symbolism of ascent, it should be made clear that, at the center of the world, one also communicates with underground realms of being. Insofar as these underground realms may be connected with death and the descent of the soul at death, rituals that employ symbolic death (such as initiations) often take place at the center of the world. Death requires passage from one state of being to another. On the Northwest Coast of North America the Kwakiutl candidate, undergoing a symbolic death during his initiation into a dancing society, declares "I am at the center of the world!" He stands at the foot of a cedar "cannibal pole" wrapped in red bark, which imbues it with supernatural power, *nawalak.* On the other hand, the kind of death associated with the center of the world may be more literally conceived. In these cases, the tomb comes to be the center of the world.

Intriguing also is the suggestion that at the center of the world is found a sound or set of sounds, usually sacred music of some sort, which effects the transition between world levels. Already mentioned is the image of the Dogon drum, the percussive instrument that effects transition and embodies the image of the *axis mundi* in its own construction. In the universe of the Warao Indians of the Orinoco Delta of Venezuela, transition from one realm of the cosmos to another is made by crossing a snake-bridge. The snake has musical bells on its horns. The shaman learns how to pass from one cosmic zone to another by singing the sounds he hears (sung by flowers, insects, supernatural beings) when he first makes the journey. The Chiripá shamans of eastern Paraguay sing a sacred song that is said to be "like a bridge" that permits communication between the heavenly and earthly worlds. Especially in religious worldviews wherein every kind of being possesses sounds unique to it, ritually controlled combinations of sound in sacred music "convocalize," or convoke, different realms of being by bringing them together at one time. The spatial images discussed earlier bring multiple realms of being together in the same place; sacred music and sound may bring together multiple realms of being in the same time.

Associated Actions and Attitudes. Even these few illustrations demonstrate a number of actions consistently appropriate to the range of ideas and symbols associated with the center of the world. To begin with, the sacred place, the locus of the center of the world, is set apart, deliberately made sacred; that is, in spite of its ordinary and profane aspects it is a place where communication with extraordinary beings is possible. The place may be made sacred by the arbitrary and unprovoked appearance of a supernatural power (kratophany), or the sacralizing event may be the appearance of a god (theophany). Generally speaking, we may say that a place may be set apart by an appearance of the sacred (hierophany). A second means of setting a place apart from profane space is through acts of deliberate consecration carried on by human beings in ritual. The examples cited show how closely the center of the world is associated with creation. This makes it easier to understand why the ritual construction of sacred spaces repeats, in stylized and symbolic form, the actions of the cosmogony. Just as the primordial moment of creation underlies all creative instances, so too does the place of origin become the point toward which all other life-filled space is oriented.

In the rites of Vedic sacrifice, for example, "the sacrificer makes himself a ladder and a bridge to reach the celestial world" (*Taittirīya Saṃhitā* 6.6.4.2). Before he (sometimes in company with his wife) can ascend to the upper world, the sacrificer must first prepare and consecrate the sacrificial stake, the *yūpa*. This is fashioned from a tree likened to the cosmic tree. After the *yūpa* is made, it is installed as a cosmic pillar, upholding and connecting all realms of being: "Lift thyself up, O Lord of the Forest, unto the summit of the earth!" (*Ṛgveda* 3.8.3). The idea is made explicit in the *Śatapatha Brāhmaṇa* (3.7.1.4): "With thy summit thou dost hold up the heavens, with thy branches thou fillest the air, with thy foot thou steadiest the earth." While ascending the stake, he may extend his arms, just as a bird stretches out its wings, and exclaim, "I have attained to heaven, to the gods: I have become immortal!" (*Taittirīya Saṃhitā* 1.7.9).

The consecration of sacred space undertakes to create the world, in symbolic terms, and thus make it habitable; that is, make communication possible with powerful beings who are the source of creativity. Consecration, then, involves installation of the structures of the cosmos. [*See* Consecration.] The sacred lodge of the Algonquin people of North America embodies the essential structures of the universe. The construction itself is the cosmogony: the doors and windows are the four cardinal directions, each with its own color. The roof is the vault of heaven, the floor the earth. Human beings situate their cultic life at the center of this microcosm. The rites of the center include not only constructions reenacting the cosmogony but also rites of ascent, descent, and transition between states of being. Rites of sacrifice are properly celebrated at this point, where the spirit of the victim may pass from one plane to another. Construction sacrifices consecrate foundations and give life to the forms of buildings and bridges by using the cosmogony as their model. Curing rituals are often performed at the center, where life can be regenerated, powerful and fresh, just as it was once generated for the first time at the moment of creation.

All of these symbolisms of the center reflect the spiritual need for orientation to what is sacred. It is this proximity to the sacred that makes human life possible, for it satisfies the mature spiritual need for what is real and has meaning.

The examples depict an ambivalence inherent in the symbolism of the center. The spatial images themselves suggest two things at the same time: communication and distant separation. The very cosmic tree and mountain that join heaven and earth together also hold them apart from one another. This ambivalence of the center describes well a primary quality of religious experience. On the one hand, the journey to the center may be arduous and dangerous. No one may have access to the center, to different states of being, without careful preparation and spiritual strength. The journey to the center may require a complete transformation of one's spiritual being. On the other hand, the image of the center of the world is replicated in multiple forms. This ensures that communication with the fullness of reality is everywhere possible. Easy access to other modes of being is reminiscent of the paradisiacal state of the universe when it first came into being. The difficulty of passage to the center appears to be founded on the experience that communication with or acquisition of new states of being means a cessation, or "death," of one's profane state of being. Nevertheless, the ease with which one may enter the center of the world draws upon a profound knowledge of the nature of religious symbolism, in this case, the symbolism of the center: its multivalent character makes it capable of extending its significance to multiple levels of meaning and planes of reference. For example, the symbolism of the center, with great consistency of meaning, applies to the center of the universe, the center of the residential unit, the center of the village, the home, the ritual space, the human physiology mystically conceived, and the act of spiritual concentration. On every plane, the significance of the symbolism of the center of the world underlines the fact that at the heart of existence lies an experience and a mode of being entirely different from the ordinary world centered on it. Paradoxically, it is from this conjunction of beings that the reality of this world derives.

[*See also* Axis Mundi *and* Orientation.]

BIBLIOGRAPHY

Extensive bibliography and lucid discussion of the symbolism of the center of the world can be found in Mircea Eliade's *Patterns in Comparative Religion* (New York, 1958), esp. pp. 367–387. See also Eliade's *The Sacred and the Profane: The Nature of Religion* (New York, 1959), pp. 20–67, and his *Images and Symbols: Studies in Religious Symbolism* (New York, 1969), pp. 27–56.

Recent studies, with helpful bibliographies, investigate specific images and instances of the center of the world. On the cosmic mountain, see Joseph W. Bastien's *Mountain of the Condor: Metaphor and Ritual in an Andean Ayllu* (Saint Paul, Minn., 1978), and I. W. Mabbett's "The Symbolism of Mount Meru," *History of Religions* 23 (August 1983): 64–83. On the cosmic tree, see Y. T. Hosoi's "The Sacred Tree in Japanese Prehistory," *History of Religions* 16 (November 1976): 95–119. For a discussion of ways in which the mountain, cosmic tree, city, cave, and temple may be drawn together and overlap in the symbolism of the center, see the essays in *Mesoamerican Sites and World-Views*, edited by Elizabeth P. Benson (Washington, D.C., 1981). Regarding the personalization of cosmic space, see Catherine L. Albanese's "The Multi-Dimensional Mandala: A Study in the Interiorization of Sacred Space," *Numen* 24 (April 1977): 1–25. On the image of a city, see Werner Müller's *Die heilige Stadt: Roma quadrata, himlisches Jerusalem und die Mythe vom Weltnabel* (Stuttgart, 1961); Paul Wheatley's *The Pivot of the Four Quarters: A Preliminary Enquiry into the Origins and Character of the Ancient Chinese City* (Chicago, 1971); and Paul Wheatley and Thomas See's *From Court to Capital: A Tentative Interpretation of the Origins of the Japanese Urban Tradition* (Chicago, 1978). See also Davíd Carrasco's "City as Symbol in Aztec Thought: The Clues from the Codex Mendoza," *History of Religions* 20 (February 1981): 199–223. For a comparative treatment of the role of city as center in religious literature and poetry, see James Dougherty's *The Fivesquare City: The City in the Religious Imagination* (Notre Dame, Ind., 1980). For a discussion of the center of the world as that place where the creative act imposes order on chaos, see N. J. Girardot's *Myth and Meaning in Early Taoism: The Themes of Chaos* (Berkeley, 1983).

For Buddhist cosmographies and descriptions of Mount Meru as the center of all world systems, see George Coedès's *Les trois mondes* (Paris, 1973). For treatment of the cosmic symbolism applied to the residence space, see Werner Müller's *Die blaue Hütte* (Wiesbaden, 1954). Concerning the "paradise" found as a sacred mountain in the center of the universe, see Michel Soymié's "Le Lo-feou chan: Étude de géographie religieuse," *Bulletin de l'École Française d'Extrême-Orient* 48 (1956): 1–139. On the conception of the house as a microcosm, with the hearth or dance plaza as the center for ritual, see Anthony Jackson's *Na-khi Religion: An Analytical Appraisal of Na-khi Ritual Texts* (The Hague, 1979) and Christine Hugh-Jones's *From the Milk River: Spatial and Temporal Processes in Northwest Amazonia* (Cambridge, 1979), pp. 40–49, 235–282. For a discussion of sacred sound as an image of the *axis mundi*, see Lawrence E. Sullivan's "Sacred Music and Sacred Time," *World of Music* (Berlin) 26, no. 3 (1984): 33–52; and Rodney Needham's "Percussion and Transition," *Man* 2 (December 1967): 606–614. For a discussion of how the cosmic winds of the four quarters become centered and "holy" in the sacred sounds of ritual speech, see James K. McNeley's *Holy Wind in Navajo Philosophy* (Tucson, 1982) and Gary Witherspoon's "The Central Concepts of Navajo World View," *Linguistics* 119 (1974): 41–59. On the temple as a locus of the union of beings, see David Dean Shulman's *Tamil Temple Myths: Sacrifice and Divine Marriage in the South Indian Saiva Tradition* (Princeton, 1980).

For a consideration of the way in which the sacredness of the center relates, in a paradoxical way, to the boundaries of space, see Victor Turner's "The Center Out There: Pilgrim's Goal, " *History of Religions* 12 (February 1973): 191–230, and Gerardo Reichel-Dolmatoff's *Amazonian Cosmos: The Sexual and Religious Symbolism of the Tukano Indians* (Chicago, 1971), esp. pp. 47–55, 116–117.

MIRCEA ELIADE and LAWRENCE E. SULLIVAN

CENTRAL ASIAN RELIGIONS. *For a broad overview of the religious systems of the peoples of that part of Asia stretching from the Caucasus to the Great Wall of China and from the Himalayas to Siberia, see* Inner Asian Religions. *For discussion of the religious systems of the peoples of Central Asia, that area that approximates modern-day Turkistan, see* Buddhism, *article on* Buddhism in Central Asia, *and* Islam, *article on* Islam in Central Asia.

CENTRAL BANTU RELIGIONS. The term *central Bantu*, as used here, refers to speakers of languages belonging to the Bantu branch of Niger-Congo who live in the Kongo (Zaire) Basin. They are spread over thousands of square miles stretching from the mouth of the Kongo River on the Atlantic to Lake Malawi and the

Shire Basin in the east, lying between 4° and 17° south latitude. They occupy much of Zaire, Angola, Zambia, and Malawi, spilling over into the Congo Republic, Tanzania, and Zimbabwe. Much of the region is forested savanna interspersed with grasslands, except where the great equatorial forest thrusts southward into Kuba and Lele territory in northern Zaire.

In 1980 the central Bantu peoples were estimated to number around ten million, divided among many groups varying in size from half a million to a few hundred. The best known are the Bakongo, Basuku, Bakuba (including the Bushong), Basilele, Baluba, Basongye, Balunda, Bachokwe, Bandembu, Balubale, Balozi, Baila, Batonga, Balamba, Babemba, Babisa, Bachewa, and Bafipa. The nominal prefix *ba* is frequently dropped and the groups are referred to simply as Kongo, Suku, and so on. Lele and Ndembu religions, through the writings of Mary Douglas and Victor Turner, have done much to shape current thought on religious symbols and the nature of ritual.

The Luba and Lunda stress patrilineal descent. The Lozi have a bilateral system. The other central Bantu are matrilineal, but residence upon marriage varies: in Zaire, Angola, and south and west Zambia, the rule was that a wife moved to her husband's residence, and her sons returned to her brothers at maturity. In northern Zambia and Malawi, on the other hand, men joined their wives, and the long-lasting links were those between women. During the twentieth century, residence became more flexible. Prior to the late nineteenth century (before the colonial period) political organization varied. The Bushong, Luba, Lunda, and Kongo (Zaire), Lozi and Bemba (Zambia), and Chewa (Zambia and Malawi) had created centralized states dominated by royal courts. Others, such as the Tonga of Zambia, lived in small communities whose leaders depended on personal influence. In Zaire, Angola, and western Zambia, religious systems emphasized the central importance of charms in both public and private rituals and made the spiritual realm manifest with carved figurines and masked dances. Elsewhere charms were used primarily in the private search for power, while public rituals centered on prayer and offering. Despite the differences, the social and religious systems of the savanna region had a common base.

Common Base. A comparison of the myths and ritual symbols of the Kuba, Luba, and Lunda of Zaire and the Bemba of Zambia led Luc de Heusch to the conclusion that the savanna peoples share a common symbolic vocabulary. He attributes this to their common ideological heritage from proto-Bantu ancestors. This common heritage was reinforced with the expansion of centralized states, which tended to imitate each other, and the growth of trading networks, which by the seventeenth century linked much of the region into one great system. Myths, he suggests, moved along the trade routes like merchandise (de Heusch, 1982, pp. 245–247). In fact, given the importance of charms or fetishes, which could be bought or sold, much ritual material was merchandise, encouraging the spread of cultic objects and organizations.

These materials could be accepted more easily because before the period of colonial rule the religious systems of the region shared common values and beliefs about the nature of the cosmos and the role of humans, spirits, and impersonal powers in the cosmic order. All were based on the assumption that a good human life is part of the natural order laid down at creation. The supreme being, or creator, was seen as beneficent but remote. Spirits active in relation to human interests, whether ancestral spirits or spirits of nature, were beneficent in principle. Power also existed throughout the cosmos and was inherent in all phenomena—in plants, animals, rocks, streams, and pools. It lay ready to be tapped and used by those who learned the correct techniques, and when it was converted into magic or a charm it could then be used to enhance human felicity or to destroy it.

Another common feature of central Bantu religions was the belief that human disorder disturbed the cosmic order. Drought, other natural disorders, infertility, and illness occurred because of human failure or evil. Malevolent and ambitious men and women who harnessed power for their own ends brought about suffering, death, and social and natural chaos. Evil, then, was due to human intervention and was seen as a perversion of the natural order. This was witchcraft. The natural order could be preserved or restored only by controlling the human disorder. When deaths or illnesses mounted, drought persisted, or general malaise afflicted a community, people first appealed to known spirits in rituals that cast out anger and demonstrated solidarity while in turn, the spirits were asked to cool their wrath. In case of failure, people tried extraordinary measures, replacing charms and rituals that had lost power with new, vigorous ones or summoning those who claimed to be able to identify and strip witches of their magic. As the community was purified and revitalized, the natural order was restored. De Craemer, Vansina, and Fox (1976) believe that the religious history of the Kongo Basin has been marked by a sequence of revitalization cults conforming to the same pattern. [*See* Witchcraft, *article on* African Witchcraft.]

Central Bantu religions were also pragmatic, emphasizing ritual and practice rather than doctrine. Heresy could not exist. Rituals, moreover, were a means to immediate practical ends and were not intended to merge the human with the divine. They were performed to obtain rain, fertility of crops and women, success in hunting, protection from misfortune, recovery from illness, and to regulate the transition of community members from one life phase to another (especially from death to "protecting ancestor" status). Researchers in the region have not reported the existence of highly developed mythologies, and theories about the nature, origin, or history of spiritual beings appear not to have been elaborated. What spirits did—not what they were—was important. Spirits were identified by effect, and when in doubt a diviner was consulted. In the area that has become Zaire, Angola, and western Zambia, Bantu-speaking peoples who used images and masks were concerned with symbolic statement about action rather than with a representation of substance. The majority of peoples who lived in the area that is now Zambia and Malawi made no images. They agreed with the Tonga, who said, "We call all spirits wind. Like wind we cannot see them. We only know what they are by what they do."

A further common characteristic has been isolated by MacGaffey (1980), but he concludes that it was common to all Bantu speakers with the exception of the Nyakyusa. According to MacGaffey, all religions of the Bantu-speaking peoples distinguished between good and evil in terms of effects rather than means, and thus had a similar structure. An act was good or bad depending upon the consequences. Diviners, herbalists, rulers, and great hunters were akin to witches in that they sought and used extraordinary power. If evil resulted, then they were witches. All use of power for purely private ends was assumed to be at the expense of others and therefore evil.

These values and the view of a cosmos pervaded with power continue to hold, although today many central Bantu are Christians and a few are Muslims, and many beliefs and rituals reported in the early ethnographies have disappeared during the radical political and economic changes of the twentieth century. What follows, therefore, is a reconstruction based on what we know of nineteenth-century practices.

Social Setting. By the beginning of the twentieth century, most central Bantu were subsistence cultivators, and their religions echoed their concerns. In general the countryside was well watered, but during the long dry season people depended upon springs and pools, especially in the more arid southeast. Rainfall was problematic, again especially in the southeast where droughts are frequent. It is no accident that so much communal ritual was associated with appeals for rains, while spirits linked to territorial cults were thought to dwell in pools and springs or moist caverns.

Because they are subject to leaching, tropical soils lose fertility rapidly. Most soils of the Kongo Basin, except for river alluvials, are poor in nutrients and require long-term fallow. Tsetse flies inhibited the keeping of cattle and sometimes small stock except in a few grassland areas. The Lozi, Ila, Tonga, and a few others had herds of cattle, but most central Bantu depended on hunting and fishing for animal protein. As a result population densities were low, averaging about 6.9 to the square mile in the 1960s after considerable population increase.

Cultivators lived in small villages, ranging in size from forty to five hundred inhabitants, a size that left them highly vulnerable to natural disasters and demographic failure. High value was placed on fecundity and protection against accidents or epidemics. Villages moved to new sites every few years as soils became exhausted and game depleted. Those individuals dissatisfied with village morale or leadership moved away to join kin elsewhere. Since neither permanent buildings nor ownership of land tied people to a single place, communities were fragile, easily disrupted by quarrels or by events that aroused the fear that witches were at work.

Archaeological evidence for agriculture dates back to the early years of the first millennium. Most crops were annuals, although the Kongo had stands of palm oil and kola nut while the Kuba and Lele grew raffia palm. Staple crops were the millets and sorghums first domesticated in Africa, and many agricultural rituals centered on these. By the end of the nineteenth century they were being displaced by maize and cassava, which were first introduced from America to the Atlantic coast in the sixteenth century.

The village and its associated fields were viewed as domestic space subject to human control under the protection of the spirits of the dead. The surrounding bush was untamed space, controlled by nature spirits with whom humans had to come to an understanding since they depended upon the bush even more than upon their fields. The bush provided fuel, building materials, medicines, materials for crafts, and a substantial amount of food. Until the twentieth century game was usually abundant and hunting important. The contrasts between village and bush, domestic and wild, farming and hunting, and birth and death were common ritual motifs.

Cults and Spirits. Secret cults associated with initiation schools and masked performances existed in the area that has become Zaire and Angola and among Luvale, Chokwe, and Ndembu immigrants near the upper reaches of the Zambezi River. Their theme was access to power. The Chewa near Lake Malawi also used masks in the Nyau cult, which mimed the invasion of domestic space by the spirits of the wild and the reign of disorder. Many central Bantu religions lacked such cults, but there were other cults that existed throughout the region. These have been classified into four cult types: domestic or kinship, territorial, professional, and healing. Each was the expression of a particular community of interest—kinship, residence, occupation, and common suffering—and might have its own set of shrines and mediators. Appeals were addressed to ancestors, dead heroes and rulers, and the spirits of nature through these cults.

Absence of a cult of the creator. The creator—known as Nzambe in much of present-day Zaire, Lesa over much of present-day Zambia, and Mulungu among those in contact with Swahili speakers—was the ultimate source of life and the initiator of universal order. Oaths used the creator's name, and the will of the creator provided the ultimate explanation when other explanations had failed. Rain, thunder, and lightning were manifestations of the creator; the falling rain was greeted with, "The creator falls." But there was no expectation that the creator was concerned with human affairs, and a cult with shrines, priests, and offerings was not provided. J. Matthew Schoffeleers believes that the Mbona cult of the southern Chewa was initially a cult of the creator. If so, this would be a unique instance; by historical times Mbona conformed to the pattern common among central Bantu-speaking peoples of offering devotion to a spirit believed to be a former ruler or spirit medium. [*See* Mbona.]

Because central Bantu peoples did not personify the creative force, they had no need to attribute gender to the creator. Bantu languages, which all lack grammatical gender, do not force the speaker to make such distinctions. When the creator became identified with the Christian God through the teaching of missionaries, many came to think of the creator as male and father, but for the most part, the sex of the creator is seen as a matter unknowable to humans.

Spirits that dealt directly with humans might be given sexual attributes, even if it was never believed that they were once human beings. They could be thought to have a definite form, even if it was invisible, and diviners, mediums, and witches were sometimes said to be able to see them. They were given names and sometimes linked through genealogies or arranged in hierarchical ranks of power.

Ancestral spirits and domestic cults. The Kuba and Lele were unique in having no ancestral cults. According to Vansina, this is a recent development among the Kuba, one that is tied to the disappearance of lineage organization. Their dead were thought to be reincarnated after only a brief existence as ghosts.

Other central African peoples who believed in reincarnation thought of the reincarnated spirits as free to come and go in the homesteads of their kin. These spirits were invoked in domestic rituals of households and lineages and also in the professional cults of specialists. It was believed that such spirits affected the welfare of their descendants and members of their descent groups. Whatever the system of descent, children owed service to the spirits of their dead parents, grandparents, and siblings. These spirits were installed as guardians of their households, and they protected their dependents against intruding spirits and against charms sent by human malice. Periodically they were given offerings to assure them that they were remembered and cared for.

Illness or personal misfortune, while it might be attributed to witchcraft, also signified a breach between the dead and the living caused by a living person's neglect or wrongdoing. Divination discovered which ancestor or ancestors harbored anger and why. The offender then made an offering with a prayer for renewed favor. Divination usually named those who had died recently, but the recent dead were asked to bring with them to share in the offering all those they knew who were no longer known to the living. Beyond that range the dead had lost all community with the living and existed only as malevolent wandering shades who could be enlisted by witches.

Since the spirits had the same tastes as the living, the Kongo offered them palm wine and kola nuts, a common provision for honored guests among the Kongo. Elsewhere the offering was of meal and water or beer or kaolin powder. The Tonga first offered meal and water, and if conditions improved (meaning that the right spirit had been identified), they offered beer. The beer had to be brewed from grain grown by the members of the household for which the appeal was being made. Because it was won with their sweat, it was endowed with their life force. Offering, therefore, had an element of sacrifice.

The common place of offering in domestic cults was the doorway of the dwelling, which was associated with the coming and going of the spirits. Most offerings took place in early morning before spirits and people had dispersed for the day. The dwelling itself was a shrine to domesticity, for those who lived within were continuing the domestic life laid down by the ancestors. The sexual activity of the married couple, which created new life, was therefore made sacred, as was the cooking fire that helped to sustain life.

Lineages, where they existed, were ritual communities focused on common ancestors, led by elders who themselves had known many of those whose spirits they now summoned. The elder's dwelling could serve as a lineage shrine as well as his household shrine, but special shrines also existed. They took the form of a simple post, a tree planted when the homestead was built, a miniature dwelling, or a gateway formed of two posts with a crossbar. Like all central Bantu shrines they were simple, impermanent, and could be built again when need arose. First fruits were laid at the shrine. At harvest or before sowing, lineage members gathered to make offerings. This might include the ritual killing of a chicken, which then provided a communion meal. But residential patterns led to the dispersal of lineage members and only those who lived nearby came to the shrine. As a result, most lineages had few members and a shallow time depth.

Individuals who had special skills bestowed upon them by an ancestor dedicated shrines to their spirit sponsor. Here the spirit was invoked before the person embarked on the hunt or other activity, and it was thanked for success in the enterprise. Such shrines also served as reminders that the living followed a way of life created by those now dead and that they could depend upon the knowledge the dead had acquired.

Territorial cults, heroes, and nature spirits. Because villages had populations of diverse origin owing service to different sets of ancestors, lineage cults based on devotion to common ancestors could not serve village or neighborhood interests. Their common interests were the basis of territorial cults whose rituals dealt with rain, the ensurance of a harvest, the communal hunt, and vulnerability to epidemic.

Some territorial cults had no permanent shrines but rather centered on spirit mediums who spoke under possession as the embodiment of nature spirits, of those who had first settled the land, or of ancient heroes or former rulers who had once had some interest in the territory. Other cults used natural shrines that were seen as places where spirits manifested themselves. These were usually deep pools, waterfalls, caves, and high places. Here offerings of black cloth, black beads, beer, domestic stock, meal, and water were made. Hoes and spears, the essential tools of cultivation and the hunt, were also appropriate offerings. Some communities supplemented the natural shrines with miniature dwellings or shelters, set apart from the village, where they appealed to spirits thought to have once lived as members of their social group. Often these were identified as the first couple who had settled in the area and had first come to terms with the spirits of the land, making them proper intermediaries.

Officiants in the territorial cults were priests, priestesses, and mediums. The former, if representative of first settlement, are usually called "earth priests." They were of particular importance among acephalous peoples, but even in the centralized kingdoms where royal shrines catered to public concerns, earth priests led local communities.

The earth priest was chosen from the lineage associated either with settlement or with some later community leader. He had a ritual wife who represented the first wife, and together they followed the routine believed to have been established with the foundation of the community. They carried out the rites that organized the agricultural year, initiating clearing of fields, planting, weeding, bird scaring, eating of first fruits, and harvest. Often wild spinach and fruits were brought to them as they came into season, as well as the first cut of thatching grass. When the community moved, their house was the first to be built, and it was from their rekindled fire that fire was taken by others. Since they were associated with fertility, their ritual intercourse gave validity to the promise of reward for hard agricultural labor. Seeds placed beneath their bed were imbued with vitality and were distributed for planting.

The permission of the earth priest and his wife might also be sought for the felling of large trees associated with spirits or regarded as the embodiment of power or for any disturbance of the earth. They gave permission to hunters to use the bush. Adherents of the local cult would make the first appeal for rain before their house, asking them in turn to appeal to the spirits of the first couple to intervene with the natural spirits to preserve the community that they had founded. Carrying drums and singing, the petitioners subsequently went to the shrine at the gravesite of the first settler or to one of the natural shrines to renew the appeal.

Priests and priestesses gave continuity, but mediums provided for communication and innovation. At regular offerings, men and women told the spirits what they desired; the spirits, in turn, made their own demands and gave warnings through mediums. The spirits chided earth priests and priestesses for ritual neglect or abandonment of ancestral ways. They called for new shrines to be built, instigated changes in routines, and demanded offerings for themselves and their mediums. Sometimes they announced the arrival of previously unknown spirits or threatened to abandon the community. When rain was at stake, black beads and black cloth were appropriate offerings to the mediums, for black symbolized the rain clouds. White was offered when they were asked to stop overly abundant downpours.

When the spirits demanded sacrifices, black animals were provided.

Although some of the most powerful mediums lived separately and could be approached only through their attendants, the majority lived as ordinary men and women except when they were possessed. During possession, people clapped before them as they did before the shrines or in the presence of a ruler.

Just as first settlers continued to watch over their communities, so dead kings and queens continued to oversee their realms. These royal spirits were often associated with regional shrines. While Bemba kings were buried in one royal cemetery, rulers elsewhere were buried at their capitals. Since each ruler built a new capital, royal shrines were widely scattered. Initially the royal shrine was cared for by retired officers of the dead king and by royal widows; the office then became hereditary to their descent lines. The dead ruler might also speak through a medium attached to the shrine, a medium whose post was not usually hereditary. Periodically the living king or queen sent offerings to all the royal shrines throughout the kingdom to invoke the protection of the new ruler. Their anger at his bodily failure or neglect could bring disaster upon the realm.

Some territorial shrines served only a neighborhood, while others served a large region as places of last appeal. Shrines might be interlinked because they were associated with the same spirit, or because mediums in many places claimed possession by the same spirit. The most famous spirits had many mediums. When nearby shrines and mediums failed to give satisfaction, communities sent delegations to distant shrines and mediums, crossing linguistic and political boundaries. This gave witness that in the last analysis all shared the same human interests. Homogenization of belief and rituals was inevitable.

Professional cults. Many types of professional guilds existed in Zaire, each with its own cult. Elsewhere we have good evidence only for hunting cults and sometimes cults of diviners and smiths. Individual cult members could count upon assistance from a sponsoring ancestor, but the guild also had a variety of guild rituals, including those for the initiation of new members. They were taught medicines and spells needed to handle the power inherent in the earth, water, large trees, and big game. Because they dealt with power, guild members were regarded as dangerously close to the temptation of witchcraft. A breaking of the normal rules was attributed to hunters, who in the reckless search for power engaged in incest and sacrificed kin to obtain spirit companions in the hunt. The very presence of the hunter, linked as he was with blood and death as well as with extraordinary power, was dangerous to small children and pregnant women.

Many central Bantu thought that witches, too, had professional guilds. It was a common belief that witches offered human flesh as a feast and delighted in the evil that they had orchestrated.

Cults of suffering. Cults of suffering, or of affliction as Victor Turner has called them, may have been of minor importance prior to the twentieth century. During this century, however, these cults have proliferated. They are based on the belief that various kinds of spirits seize upon or enter human victims, who then must come to terms with them. Treatment requires identification of the spirit and instruction in how to meet its demands. Thereafter the sufferer becomes an adept able to treat new victims. All adepts in the locality are expected to help their fellow sufferers, and this joins them in a ritual community. As the people of surrounding areas become suspicious that the new spirit has begun work in their community, adepts are summoned to diagnose and treat, and so the cults spread rapidly (Beattie and Middleton, 1969).

In the west, in Zaire, Angola, and western Zambia, cults of suffering are associated with spirits known as *mahamba*. Elsewhere in Zambia and in Malawi they are more likely to be referred to as *masabe*. *Mahamba* and *masabe* spirits may be identified as former members of alien ethnic groups who ask those possessed to speak in their own tongue and don their costume. *Mahamba* cults may also invoke the spirits of the sufferer's own ancestors.

Early cults of affliction were concerned with the incursion of animal spirits and spirits of the bush and may have developed out of hunting cults. More recent ones are linked to the uncertainties of alien modern experiences; cults centered on such things as the airplane, railroad, city life, warfare, angels, and on those people taken away as slaves to Europe and America have appeared in the last few decades. Each spirit is identified with its own drum rhythms, songs, medicines, and sometimes costume. Cults are most elaborate, and seem to have greater permanence, in the area inhabited by the west-central Bantu peoples. Elsewhere they came and went with great rapidity until the 1970s and 1980s, when some of the cults of affliction began to take on the semblance of a church and to make claims about their ability to go beyond the control of invading spirits. Some cult leaders now claim that they have the power to heal, provide protection against witches, and control the rains. They often have many spirits, which are seen as helpers.

Although men and women of all ages may be initiated

into cults of suffering, the majority of initiates are women. Lewis (1971) attributes this to the peripheral role women have in the public sphere. But among the central Bantu peoples, only the Lele barred women from participation in public religious actions. In general, central Bantu religions provided women with important ritual and political roles. Women were sometimes political rulers and held offices in both territorial and kinship cults. On death they became ancestral spirits, and living women could make offerings to the ancestors. Lineage offerings usually required the collaboration of a man and woman elder. Women became diviners and herbalists, and some of the most famous mediums were women. The Luba are reported as saying that no man had a body strong enough to support possession by the greatest spirits—only the women were strong enough to withstand such power.

Central Bantu peoples differed in their judgment concerning the association of women with the possibility of evil. Some are reported to have connected maleness with power and death, femaleness with fertility and life. Yet some attributed witchcraft to women. Among the Luba those accused of witchcraft were usually women. The Lamba thought men and women were equally likely to be witches. The Bemba, Tonga, and Chewa usually accused men because men were thought to compete with one another through ambition, and so it was through them that evil disrupted the world. [*See also* Affliction, *article on* African Cults of Affliction.]

Religious Transformation. De Craemer, Vansina, and Fox (1976) believe the basic elements and symbols of central African religions have been stable over the centuries (perhaps for millennia), although specific religious movements have come and gone. Nevertheless the last four centuries have been marked by religious questioning and transformation, paralleling the turmoil and transformation in political and economic regimes. The Kongo on the Atlantic coast first encountered the Portuguese and Christianity at the end of the fifteenth century. Many Kongo people were baptized, and the cross was adopted as a powerful charm. In the sixteenth century the Portuguese also began pushing up the Zambezi River from the Indian Ocean. By that time central Africa had long had trade links with Islamic settlements on the East African coast. Exchange of ideas was inevitable. By the early nineteenth century trading caravans in search of slaves and ivory were disturbing even the most remote areas.

The slave trade brought about the destruction of many of the ancient kingdoms. The Kongo kingdom disintegrated in the sixteenth century in the turmoil provoked by Portuguese slavers. In the mid-nineteenth century Chokwe slave raiders from Angola overran the Lunda and Luba empires. The weakened Chewa kingdoms had already fallen easily to nineteenth-century Ngoni invaders from the south. Royal cults associated with the old kingdoms either disappeared in the chaos or persisted by transforming themselves into other forms of territorial cults.

The dispersal of fleeing populations and the caravan movements led to a spread of epidemic disease on an unprecedented scale and to a questioning of the efficacy of existing religion. At the end of the nineteenth century central Africa was carved up among European powers, and formerly independent rulers became suspect as ritual leaders when they were transformed into bureaucrats in colonial governments. Between 1950 and 1980, independence movements brought African governments into power, but these were no more willing to accept claims to authority based on religious inspiration or cultic position than were the colonial governments.

In the twentieth century people have come to depend on the cash economy and world trade. Market conditions are now as important as rainfall in determining well-being. New crops and agricultural techniques dominate the scene; consequently, territorial cults associated with agriculture have become less important. Hunting has little importance in the 1980s since game has been largely depleted except in a few refuge areas. Hunting cults, not surprisingly, have largely vanished. And as cheap imported goods have spread and undercut local products, rituals associated with other crafts have also faded.

Many adults have been trained in mission schools or otherwise influenced by Christianity. Their children attend government schools where dependence upon ancestors or territorial cults is derided, although the power of charms and witches continues to be admitted.

Religious life has had to adjust to the fact that the central Bantu-speaking peoples are no longer primarily based in rural areas supported by agriculture and the produce of the bush. Many are now wage earners. Most men and women have spent some years in the cities that grew up around mines and trading and administrative centers. A substantial portion of the population is now permanently urbanized. Cities are becoming arbiters of the good life. The twentieth century has seen a loss of faith, and people no longer even know about many of the beliefs that were an important part of their forebears' lives in 1900. It has also seen the rise and rapid spread of new religious movements that promise to free people from the threat of witchcraft and to provide an understanding of the human experience.

Religious systems are not direct reflections of the social order, nor are they compelled solely by economic considerations. Yet they relate to the concerns of those who live in a given time and place. A viable religion must reflect people's desires, fears, and visions of what life ought to be like; provide rituals that speak to these concerns; and somehow link the transitory human experience with some enduring guarantee of order.

It is not surprising that many new religious movements have arisen among migrants in ethnically diverse cities or that these movements center upon the individual's search for a community of the purified rather than on the community of kinship or the common interests of a rural neighborhood. Many people today find religious community through conversion linked with healing and purification, and it is among those who share this experience that they find help to face illness and death and a shield against fears of loneliness, joblessness, and the envy of others.

Many of the new religions have their roots in Christianity, but their founders adapt Christian elements to what they see as African needs and wisdom. Unlike the mission churches, they accept the efficacy of charms and the power of witches and arm their adherents against these dangers. They recognize the continuing existence of the dead and the possibility of possession. They identify the creator with the Christian God but announce that the creator now cares about humanity and is actively at work in the world. Many of these new religions base themselves upon a visionary experience in which the creator appeared to be the founder and seek to provide either a new explication of the Bible or to replace it with a new message for Africans. Such was the Antonine movement founded in 1704 by Dona Béatrice, a Kongo woman, as a response to the disintegration of the Kongo world (Balandier, 1968, 257ff). The churches of Simon Kimbangu, Alice Lenshina, John Maranke, and John Masowe are comparable responses in the twentieth century. Fernandez (1978, p. 222) describes their theology as "lived, sung, and pictured in images, not formulated." [*See also* African Religions, *article on* Modern Movements, *and the biographies of Kimbangu, Lenshina, and Maranke.*]

Cults of suffering and witch-finding movements have also proliferated in this century as the old religious foundations crumbled, but they are more likely to operate in rural areas. Witch-finding movements aim at purification of existing communities to restore them to working order and usually vanish, to be replaced by a successor, when pain and suffering are again found to be the human portion. The Muchapi movement, which swept Malawi and Zambia in the 1920s, was short-lived (Willis, 1970), as was the Mikom iyool current among Luba, Bushong, and Lele in the 1940s (Douglas, 1963, 245ff). Their successors have also not lasted long. But they attest to a continued belief that the world is basically good and that all will be well if humans can be induced to discard malice and control ambition.

[*For discussion of particular central Bantu religions, see* Bemba Religion; Kongo Religion; Luba Religion; *and* Ndembu Religion.]

BIBLIOGRAPHY

Balandier, Georges. *Daily Life in the Kingdom of the Kongo.* Translated by Helen Weaver. London, 1968.

Beattie, John, and John Middleton, eds. *Spirit Mediumship and Society in Africa.* New York, 1969.

Binsbergen, Wim van. "Explorations in the History and Sociology of Territorial Cults in Zambia." In *Guardians of the Land,* edited by J. Matthew Schoffeleers, pp. 47–88. Gwelo, 1978.

De Craemer, Willy, Jan Vansina, and Renée C. Fox. "Religious Movements in Central Africa: A Theoretical Study." *Comparative Studies in Society and History* 18 (October 1976): 458–475.

Douglas, Mary. *The Lele of the Kasai.* London, 1963.

Fernandez, James W. "African Religious Movements." *Annual Review of Anthropology* 7 (1976): 195–234.

Heusch, Luc de. *The Drunken King, or The Origin of the State.* Translated by Roy G. Willis. Bloomington, Ind., 1982.

Lewis, I. M. *Ecstatic Religion: An Anthropological Study of Spirit Possession and Shamanism.* Harmondsworth, 1971.

MacGaffey, Wyatt. "Comparative Analysis of Central African Religions." *Africa* 42 (1972): 21–31.

MacGaffey, Wyatt. "African Religions: Types and Generalizations." In *Explorations in African Systems of Thought,* edited by Ivan Karp and Charles S. Bird, pp. 301–328. Bloomington, Ind., 1980.

Schoffeleers, J. Matthew. "The Interaction of the M'Bona Cult and Christianity, 1859–1963." In *Themes in the Christian History of Central Africa,* edited by T. O. Ranger and John Weller, pp. 14–29. Berkeley, 1975.

Schoffeleers, J. Matthew, ed. *Guardians of the Land: Essays on Central African Territorial Cults.* Gwelo, 1978.

Turner, Victor. *The Forest of Symbols: Aspects of Ndembu Ritual.* Ithaca, N.Y., 1967.

Turner, Victor. *The Drums of Affliction: A Study of Religious Processes among the Ndembu of Zambia.* London, 1968.

Turner, Victor. *The Ritual Process: Structure and Anti-Structure.* Chicago, 1969.

Werbner, R. P., ed. *Regional Cults.* New York, 1977.

Willis, Roy G. "Instant Millennium: The Sociology of African Witch-Cleansing Cults." In *Witchcraft Confessions and Accusations,* edited by Mary Douglas, pp. 129–140. New York, 1970.

ELIZABETH COLSON

CERAMESE RELIGION. *See* Southeast Asian Religions, *article on* Insular Cultures.

CEREMONY is conventionally defined as a highly formalized observance or practice prescribed by custom and undertaken by a collective, or as customary observances and practices considered as a whole. In conventional usage the term *ceremony* is interchanged indiscriminately with *ritual.* In current theoretical discussion, the terms are increasingly distinguished, as *ceremony* is identified as a genre, or type, of ritual behavior. Ceremony is distinguished in terms of its object—a prevalent trend identifies ceremony with secular, as opposed to religious or sacred, interests (i.e., the symbolic representation of sociocultural arrangements), or it is differentiated in terms of its function, which is seen to be essentially conservative: the maintenance of existing sociocultural arrangements as over against their transformation. Following one or the other trend, current theory distinguishes, for example, presidential inaugurations in the United States, in which power is safely transferred so that the political system remains intact, from a tribal initiation rite, by means of which participants undergo a change in social identity and are prepared to adapt to ever changing sociocultural conditions.

The question has been raised whether it is not more proper and useful to approach ceremony as a ritual attitude as opposed to a distinct ritual type. Ronald L. Grimes argues that standard analytic, or classificatory, distinctions among types of ritual—differentiation between "sacred" and "profane" activity, and so on—are insufficient in the analysis of ritual, since they fail to take into account a variety of "embodied attitudes" that emerge during the course of a ritual: ceremony, decorum, ritualization, etc. Ceremony is not so much an analytic type as it is a layer, attitude, sensibility, or "mode" of ritual, contends Grimes. He suggests that when one or another mode becomes dominant, it is proper to speak of a ritual of ceremony, and so on (Grimes, 1982, pp. 223, 35, 41). Aspects of ceremony (i.e., emphasis on formalization, representation and affirmation of existing sociocultural arrangements, etc.) are found in all of the examples of ritual treated in this article, giving reason to view ceremony as a ritual mode.

This article gives an overview of current theoretical discussion, devoting special attention to the discussion of the relation between ceremony and religion, a central concern in the theories. Over against theorists who identify ceremony as a strictly secular ritual, this article suggests that, inasmuch as sociopolitical, religious, and "sacred" interests overlap and even converge, the relation between ceremony and religion is problematic, making difficult any attempt to delineate the phenomenon as something distinct from religion.

Formalization and stylization (i.e., specification of time and place, formulaic speech and gesture, etc.) are indicative of ceremony's scripted character as "intentional" (Grimes, 1982, p. 41) or self-conscious behavior. Ceremony is fundamentally self-reflective performance. As such, ceremony is essentially "self-symbolizing" (Goffman, 1974, p. 58); it has representational intent. Like all symbolic behavior, ceremony points to a larger framework of action. Ceremony's public character is an indication that its more general context is social and cultural life. As Erving Goffman notes, ceremony provides a symbolic means whereby participants represent themselves in one of their central social roles (ibid.). Through dramatization and other representational means ceremony presents those ideologies, values, the social institutions to which they are bound, and other sociocultural constructs that constitute social and cultural life or, in the case of ceremonies undertaken on a smaller scale, group life.

The underlying motivation in the ceremonial representation of the various social and cultural constructs is the confirmation and reinforcement of those organizing frameworks that order sociocultural life in a normative way. "Ceremony," writes Victor Turner, "constitutes an impressive institutionalized performance of indicative, normatively structured social reality" (Turner, 1982, p. 81). As Steven Lukes explains,

> the symbolism of political ritual *represents* . . . particular models or political paradigms of society and how it functions. In this sense, such ritual plays, as Durkheim argued, a cognitive role, rendering intelligible society and social relationships. . . . In other words, it helps to define as authoritative certain ways of seeing society: it serves to specify what in society is of special significance, it draws people's attention to certain forms of relationships and activity—and at the same time, therefore, it deflects their attention from other forms, since every way of seeing [is] also a way of not seeing.
> (Lukes, 1975, p. 301)

Ceremony's confirmatory function gives it a conservative character. Ceremony "*indicates,*" says Turner; it is expressive of social structure. Ceremony does not transform social structure; this is the function of ritual (actually other forms of ritual), which owes its transformative capacity to its liminal character (Turner, 1982, pp. 80–84). Ritual derives its liminal quality, he explains, from separating participants from their everyday social structural identity and, consequently, from creating ambiguous social status as it prepares them to undergo a transition to new social identity. Turner contends that ritual's "antistructural" character is an expression of its dialectical relation to social structure. By relaxing social structural requirements, ritual liminality makes possible the experimentation with social structure that permits social and cultural innovations. Thus ritual enables sociocultural systems to change and grow as new demands, particularly for egalitarian and direct social interchange, challenge existing social structural configurations. Turner's conceptualization of ritual liminality helps explain why spontaneity and disorder seldom emerge during the course of ceremony, and then only during prescribed times or in established places: the intent to conserve the social structural status quo requires that ceremony's liminal aspects be kept in check or at least circumscribed.

Ceremony's conservative function makes it especially suited to exploitation in times of social conflict or potential crisis, when existing norms are challenged or are under threat. Since formalization conveys legitimacy, ceremony lends itself to portraying as indisputable and fixed those ideologies and social institutions that are most in doubt during times of social crisis. Sally F. Moore and Barbara G. Myerhoff note that ceremony's authoritative presentation of its material as "axiomatic" is "paradoxical," since it is the most obviously contrived and hence arbitrary social interaction. They note that preoccupation with order by implication points to the possibility of disorder, chaos, and most important, open choice of other cultural configurations. While ceremony may be intended to mask contradiction, on a more subtle, less conscious level, it may give it expression (Moore and Myerhoff, 1977, pp. 16, 18; cf. Lukes, 1975, pp. 296–302).

A more fundamental motivation in the ceremonial representation of social and cultural constructs identified by Moore and Myerhoff is the cultural declaration of order over against indeterminacy. Ceremony is intended to proclaim "cultural order as against a cultural void," which exist in dialectical tension. It "banishes from consideration the basic questions raised by the made-upness of culture, its malleability and alterability." As Moore and Myerhoff explain, as formalized behavior ceremony is, then, an attempt to assert order: "Through order, formality, and repetition it seeks to state that the cosmos and social world, or some particular small part of them are orderly and explicable and for the moment fixed" (Moore and Myerhoff, 1977, pp. 16–17). Formality thus allows ceremony to authenticate its message, conferring permanence and legitimacy on what is in fact a social construct. "Its medium is part of its message" (ibid., p. 8).

While ceremony symbolizes or reflects the socially and culturally normative, it is not a mere mirror image. Ceremonies, notes Moore, are not simply dramatizations of social and moral norms: they are "performative acts." Ceremonies do not simply communicate information, nor are they merely analogies; "they *do* something," putting into action what they symbolize (Moore, 1977). By presenting an "ontology," ceremony serves "to make it happen—make it actual," explains Clifford Geertz. He notes that ceremony models sociocultural life in a twofold sense. It not only offers idealized representations of normative social arrangements, but to the extent that it represents a way of life that is ideally and actually adapted to the world as it fundamentally is, ceremony predisposes participants to emulate its models. Hence ceremony is paradigmatic in a dual sense: it is both a "model of" and a "model for" social and cultural life (Geertz, 1980). We might add that participants are also predisposed to emulate ceremony's ideal models because they carry an imperative force or authority invested by powerful social institutions, classes, and groups. The fact that ceremony is imbued with the authority of groups that are already in a position of power or that are emerging as a dominant power in part explains why ceremony is one of the predominant frames (Goffman, 1974, pp. 10–11, 48), or principles of organization, by which social arrangements are ordered.

Inextricably linked to ceremony's corroborative and legitimating functions is the assertion and securing of power. Grimes writes that "ceremony consists of power negotiations in ritual form. . . . Ceremonial gestures are bids for authority, prestige, recognition, and control" (Grimes, 1982, p. 224). Presenting social and cultural constructs as postulates secures power for those who have a vested interest, recognized or not, in a specific ideology or social structure. Furthermore, as Grimes observes, because ceremony implies a distinction between the group that is symbolically asserting its power and "the 'other side,' " it is "manifestly competitive, sometimes conflict-laden." The successful symbolization of power requires that the social contradiction inherent in the arbitrary assertion of power be masked and only righteous or legitimate properties be exposed. The potential for power to be a source of conflict and not solely a means of conflict resolution must also be concealed (ibid., p. 42). An underlying interest in asserting and securing power helps to explain ceremony's serious tone, which remains dominant even when ceremony manifests festive aspects.

The link between the ceremonial confirmation and maintenance of social and cultural norms and the negotiation of power is clearly evident in national or civic ceremonies, a predominant form of ceremony, as well as in mass political rallies. The parades, processions, pageants, theatrical performances, and other ceremonious events associated with Independence Day in the United States (Bellah, 1967), Mexico (Vogt and Abel,

1977), and Indonesia (Peacock, 1968), and those associated with May Day, the anniversary of the October Revolution, and Victory Day in the Soviet Union (Lane, 1981) are illustrative. On a smaller scale, examples are found in such "political ceremonials" as ritualized town or public meetings among the Indians and mestizos of Mexico (Hunt, 1977) and the villagers of Kilimanjaro, Tanzania (Moore, 1977). Court trials, installation to office, and academic exercises, such as commencement, are representative examples of ceremonial reflection and negotiation of power on a still smaller scale.

Ceremony and Religion. Two distinct tendencies in delineating the object of ceremony can be found in the theoretical discussion of these conventionalized observances. Ceremony is either identified with secular interests exclusively, or it is associated with both secular and religious, or "sacred," concerns when these are seen to converge. Representing the first trend, both Jack Goody and Max Gluckman contend that while conventionalized nonreligious and religious activities are the same analytic type of behavior (i.e., formalization that has nonrational ends or is of a nontechnical nature), and while they perform similar functions, they entail disparate beliefs and therefore should be differentiated. Conventional action addressed to spiritual beings or concerning the ultimate is designated "religious." Objecting to the tendency to identify formalized collective activity with religious ritual, established as a precedent by Émile Durkheim, Goody distinguishes activity of an "exclusively secular significance." Conventional activity of a nonreligious nature, such as the anniversary of the October Revolution, is identified as "ceremonial." Like formalized "religious" activity, ceremony is made a subcategory of "ritual," the term by which Goody designates the most general category of conventional behavior (Goody, 1961, p. 159). Gluckman prefers *ceremony* as the inclusive term for conventional and stylized, or "ceremonial," behavior. *Ceremonious* becomes a term distinguishing nonreligious formal activity, while *ritual* is reserved for that subcategory of ceremonial activity referring to "mystical notions" (Gluckman, 1962, pp. 22–23).

Goody avoids the terms *sacred* and *profane* in his distinction between religious and ceremonial rituals. Because the dichotomy they represent is a foreign concept within many cultures, he believes that they have limited application as rubrics for analytic categories. The fact that the sacred-profane polarity is not universally recognized suggests, as Goody notes, that these are external categories, imposed by an outside observer, rather than categories held by participants themselves.

As recognized by the second trend in the delineation of ceremony, a strict distinction between secular and religious activity is problematic. Historical phenomena do not exhibit the discrete boundaries found in precise theoretical categories. Although they are dissociated from institutionalized religion, many secular rituals make reference to religious belief or make use of religious symbols. The invocation of God and the use of the Bible in presidential inaugurations (see Bellah, 1967; Wilson, 1979) and Memorial Day observances in the United States (Warner, 1959) and in coronations in Great Britain (Bocock, 1974) are illustrative. The appeal to religious belief and use of religious symbol is an indication and expression of the interdependence of religious and sociocultural systems. Linking ideology, values, and social structure with the transcendent or ultimate assigns the basic organizing principles and structures of social and cultural life the status of absolutes and at the same time serves the legitimation of power.

This interdependence is most evident in religio-political systems. There ceremony occupies a central role by virtue of its legitimating function. State ceremonies associated with divine kingship, long established as a state cult in Asia, the Near East, Africa, and elsewhere are instructive. The classical "state ceremonials" of nineteenth-century Bali are illustrative. Assuming a cosmic basis for worldly status, the Balinese state cult (divine kingship) gave a central role to ceremonies that appropriated Hindu cosmology in representing and securing state power. Royal dedications of palace temples, royal ordinations, royal cremations, and other "state ritual" made use of theatrical performances to represent the king as an image of the divine. Court ceremonies not only portrayed the king as an analogy of divine power; they transformed the king into a manifestation of divine power, further securing for the state the power necessary to shape the social and political order (see Geertz, 1980). Ceremonies drawing attention to "divine election" and divinization in imperial Rome provide instructive premodern examples of securing state power by ritually cosmologizing a political office (see MacCormack, 1981).

The ceremonies associated with "civil religion" are also noteworthy studies in the appropriation of traditional religious symbols to legitimate dominant ideology and social structure and secure state power by investing them with ultimate value and authority. *Civil religion* is Robert Bellah's term designating a form of religion characteristic of highly secularized and technologically oriented modern nation states that is said to exist independently of institutionalized religion, if dependent on organized religion for many of its symbols. In the United States, for example, the use of Judeo-Christian symbols in presidential inaugurations, State of the Union addresses, Memorial Day celebrations, funerals of national leaders, and the like are intended to secure the continuation of divine blessing on the social and political order (see Bellah, 1967; Cherry, 1970; Warner, 1959; Wilson, 1979).

The blurring of boundaries between religious and secular ritual is found on a smaller scale in numerous civic ceremonies. Fiesta, a citywide celebration of the establishment of Santa Fe, New Mexico, as a Spanish city, is instructive. Religious symbols play a central role in the ceremonial negotiation of power among Native American, Hispanic-American, and other Euro-American members of the community not simply because they help to establish group identity, but because they help to legitimate sociopolitical interests. Links between Roman Catholicism and the historic domination of Native Americans by the Spanish are exploited in the Fiesta mass, the procession of "La Conquistadora" (the Virgin), and other church-sponsored events, for example, as Hispanic-Americans assert their power over Native Americans (see Grimes, 1976).

It has been suggested that, if societies do in fact tend to idealize their social condition as that of the cosmic order, then "secular ritual" would always manifest "sacred aspects." "If this is the case it may not be possible to speak of purely religious ritual or of purely secular ceremonial," notes Eva Hunt. Furthermore, argues Hunt, if the secular and religious orders are interdependent, so that the secular models and shapes the religious, which in turn models secular behavior, then "secular and sacred may not be different behaviors but different analytic aspects of the same behaviors" (Hunt, 1977, p. 143).

The problem of distinguishing between secular and religious ritual is compounded if it is admitted, as Moore and Myerhoff contend, that the sacred is a more general category than the religious, if by the sacred is meant unquestionability and traditionalizing. Moore and Myerhoff argue that secular rituals exhibit a sacred dimension when they present ideology, doctrine, and so on as authoritative and incontrovertible and in so doing serve as a tradition-making force. They nevertheless distinguish ceremony from religious ritual by the absence of otherworldly or ultimate explanations; this is said to be the distinct province and function of religious ritual. Ceremony's scope is restricted to specialized aspects of social and cultural life and to its immediate concerns. Hence, the authors argue, unlike religious ritual, ceremony does not act on the other world in order to influence this world; it acts solely on this world.

In order to take account of secular rituals that manifest a sacred dimension and those that do not, rituals that make use of religious symbols, and other possible combinations, including the presence of secular concerns within religious life, Moore and Myerhoff propose the analytic categories "religious" and "nonreligious," "sacred" and "nonsacred" (Moore and Myerhoff, 1977, pp. 3, 10–15, 20–22).

Ceremony may not consistently ascribe ultimacy to the sociocultural order by equating it with cosmic order, contrary to Hunt. There is sufficient evidence, however, as indicated above, to challenge Moore and Myerhoff's suggestion that ceremony can be distinguished on the basis of its "meaning and effect" (ibid., p. 8). Insofar as religious and sociopolitical interests intersect and even converge and the sacred is a social construct representing the ideal or the inviolable, the delineation of ceremony as something distinct from religion will be problematic.

The problem presented by precise categories and sharp distinctions between secular and religious interests arises in a different form when explicitly religious ritual manifests secular interests. Timely examples are found in the rituals associated with the convergence of theology and political ideology in contemporary fundamentalist Christianity in the United States and fundamentalist Islam in the Middle East and elsewhere. Use of the pulpit by fundamentalist Christians to promote rightist interests during the 1980, 1982, 1984, and 1986 national and state elections has received much attention in religious, political, and scholarly circles. While fundamentalist Islam's role in the revitalization of Muslim and Arab cultures has received equal attention, the role played by religious ritual in this process has received less attention outside scholarly discussion. An instructive example is found in the use of ʿĀshūrāʾ, the ritual dramatization and commemoration of the martyrdom of Muḥammad's grandson, Ḥusayn ibn ʿAlī, to legitimate Shīʿī ideology and rule in Iran. Reinterpreting Ḥusayn's death as the final outcome in the struggle of a righteous man against the corruption of true religion by political rulers, the Shīʿah found in ʿĀshūrāʾ a powerful symbol in the service of the revolution of 1979. By giving the ritual new ideological content, identifying the monarchy and allied power structures as forces hostile to Islam and themselves as preservers of true faith, the Shīʿah made use of ʿĀshūrāʾ in their ascendency to power. They continue to exploit the ritual's new ideological content in their effort to maintain power (see Hegland, 1983). As Grimes observes, rituals that are explicitly religious can demonstrate ceremonious aspects and obviously do so when religious ritual is placed in the service of social and political interests (Grimes, 1982, p. 42).

Conclusion. Any attempt to delineate ceremony must take into account the interpenetration of traditional ritual categories: "religious" and "nonreligious," "sacred" and "profane," and the like. As demonstrated in the examples presented above, historical phenomena cannot be compartmentalized as neatly as a number of current theoretical treatments of ceremony suggest. Any attempt to delimit ceremony must also take note of the formalization, corroborative tendencies, and other aspects of ceremoniousness that are inherent in ritual performance or display. As suggested in the examples offered above, the ceremonious mode can be expected to dominate when ritual has been placed in the service of tradition or the legitimation of power. In this instance ritual's liminal aspects are often circumscribed.

[*See also* Ritual.]

BIBLIOGRAPHY

Bellah, Robert N. "Civil Religion in America." *Daedalus* 96 (Winter 1967): 1–21.

Bocock, Robert. *Ritual in Industrial Society: A Sociological Analysis of Ritualism in Modern England*. London, 1974.

Cherry, Conrad. "American Sacred Ceremonies." In *American Mosaic: Social Patterns of Religion in the United States*, edited by Phillip E. Hammond and Benton Johnson, pp. 303–316. New York, 1970.

Geertz, Clifford. *Negara: The Theatre State in Nineteenth-Century Bali*. Princeton, 1980.

Gluckman, Max. "Les Rites de Passage." In *Essays on the Rituals of Social Relations*, edited by Max Gluckman, pp. 1–52. Manchester, 1962.

Goffman, Erving. *Frame Analysis: An Essay on the Organization of Experience*. New York, 1974. Discusses ceremony on pages 43–44, 48, 58, and 126.

Goody, Jack. "Religion and Ritual: The Definitional Problem." *British Journal of Sociology* 12 (1961): 142–164.

Grimes, Ronald L. *Symbol and Conquest: Public Ritual and Drama in Santa Fe, New Mexico*. Ithaca, N.Y., 1976.

Grimes, Ronald L. "Modes of Ritual Sensibility." In his *Beginnings in Ritual Studies*, pp. 35–51. Lanham, Md., 1982. See also "Two Public Celebrations, pp. 221–231.

Hegland, Mary. "Ritual and Revolution in Iran." In *Political Anthropology*, edited by Myron J. Aronoff, vol. 2, *Culture and Political Change*, pp. 75–100. New Brunswick, N.J., 1983.

Hunt, Eva. "Ceremonies of Confrontation and Submission: The Symbolic Dimension of Indian-Mexican Political Interaction." In *Secular Ritual*, edited by Sally F. Moore and Barbara G. Myerhoff, pp. 124–147. Assen, 1977.

Lane, Christel. *The Rites of Rulers: Ritual in Industrial Society; The Soviet Case*. Cambridge, 1981.

Lukes, Steven. "Political Ritual and Social Integration." *Sociology* 9 (May 1975): 289–308.

MacCormack, Sabine G. *Art and Ceremony in Late Antiquity*. Berkeley, 1981.

Moore, Sally F. "Political Meetings and the Simulation of Unanimity: Kilimanjaro 1973." In *Secular Ritual*, edited by Sally F. Moore and Barbara G. Myerhoff, pp. 151–172. Assen, 1977.

Moore, Sally F., and Barbara G. Myerhoff. "Secular Ritual: Forms and Meanings." In *Secular Ritual*, edited by Sally F. Moore and Barbara G. Myerhoff, pp. 3–24. Assen, 1977.

Peacock, James L. *Rites of Modernization: Symbolic and Social Aspects of Indonesian Proletarian Drama*. Chicago, 1968.

Turner, Victor. *From Ritual to Theatre: The Human Seriousness of Play*. New York, 1982. See pages 80–84.

Vogt, Evon Z., and Suzanne Abel. "On Political Rituals in Contemporary Mexico." In *Secular Ritual*, edited by Sally F. Moore and Barbara G. Myerhoff, pp. 173–188. Assen, 1977.

Warner, William Lloyd. *The Living and the Dead: A Study of the Symbolic Life of Americans*. New Haven, 1959.

Wilson, John F. *Public Religion in American Culture*. Philadelphia, 1979.

Bobby C. Alexander

CERNUNNOS, a Celtic god with the horns of a stag, is attested in Gaul by about ten figurative images and one sole inscription from the Roman era, currently preserved in the Musée de Cluny (*Corpus inscriptionum Latinarum*, Berlin, 1863, vol. 13, no. 3026c). A plaque from the Gundestrup Caldron bears the image of the stag-horned god seated in a Buddha-like posture, holding a torque in one hand and a serpent in the other, and surrounded by animals that include a stag. This image suggests that Cernunnos is the Gaulish Jupiter in the latter's aspect as lord of animals.

But there is no certain correspondence from among the insular Celtic cultures, either in name or in personage, if *Cernunnos* is understood as "horned god" and the classical associations with the "horn of plenty" are adopted. However, given that the Celtic words for "horn" (Welsh, *carn*; Breton, *korn*; Irish, *adharc*) are words with different etymologies, it is not clear that this approach is entirely fitting. It is possible that in this context "horn" means something else. If the suffix is treated abstractly, the Gaulish theonym in fact recalls that the Irish surname for Conall is *Cernach*, which means not "horned one" but "victorious one," and if there is a horn in this case it is a symbol not of plenty but of military victory, a symbol fit for a bold and renowned warrior.

In fact, almost nothing is known about Cernunnos, except that the root of his name, **kern-*, refers specifically in Celtic to the crown of the head. It is on the Indo-European level that it is a cognate to words denoting horned beasts in general and the stag in particular.

In the absence of all discursive commentary by Celts themselves, no conclusion can be drawn based solely on iconography. It is not known what the Cernunnos "provider" seated between Apollo and Mercury on a votive stela from Reims really means; nor is the meaning known of the tricephalic Cernunnos accompanied by two horned serpents on a bronze statuette from Autun. In any case Cernunnos is not exactly a stag god, since he is anthropomorphic.

BIBLIOGRAPHY

Bober, Phyllis P. "Cernunnos: Origin and Transformation of a Celtic Divinity." *American Journal of Archaeology* 55 (1951): 13–51.

Holder, Alfred. *Alt-celtischer Sprachschatz*, vol. 1. Leipzig, 1896.

Le Roux, Françoise. "Cernunnos." *Ogam* 5 (1953): 324–329.

FRANÇOISE LE ROUX AND CHRISTIAN-J. GUYONVARC'H
Translated from French by Erica Meltzer

CERULARIOS, MICHAEL (c. 1000–1058), patriarch of Constantinople. Cerularios typified the Byzantine prelate in that he was characterized by experience in imperial and ecclesiastical matters, intellectual inclinations (which included an interest in occultism), and private monastic devotion. But he had one flaw: he was arrogant and relentless in increasing his see's ecclesiastical prerogatives.

Born in Constantinople of a senatorial family, Cerularios rose to power as a civil servant. His tenure was marked by his direct involvement in the conspiracy to depose Emperor Michael IV (1040) in favor of Constantine IX Monomachus. To avoid political banishment, he became a monk. Elected to the patriarchate in 1043, Cerularios held this position until 1058 through the reigns of four emperors.

The events of 1054 caused Cerularios to be viewed as one of the most controversial of patriarchs. His critics do not agree as to the extent of his responsibility for the schism between Rome and Constantinople. The patriarch's relations with Rome, however, must be seen in the greater context of the growing ideological rift that existed between Eastern and Western Christendom and that was manifest in the political, cultural, and theological misunderstandings of the eleventh century. An assessment of Cerularios solely in the light of this dispute unduly minimizes his role as a patriarch who attempted to extend his powers over the state.

The legacy of Cerularios, then, remains a mixed one. Admired by his flock as a champion of orthodoxy and celebrated as a confessor of the faith, Cerularios's aura reminded the faithful, especially during the Fourth Crusade (1204), that compromise with the West was inadmissible. Yet he is not commemorated as a saint. Moreover, he was able, unlike his predecessors, to elevate himself to a position of supra-imperial authority, as evidenced by his wearing of the purple buckskins reserved for the emperor. Ironically, Cerularios was forced to abdicate in 1058 at the height of his glory by the very Isaac I Commenus whose position as emperor he had secured.

BIBLIOGRAPHY

The published works of Cerularios can be found in *Patrologia Graeca*, edited by J.-P. Migne, vol. 120 (Paris, 1864). For Michael Psellus's denunciatory address against Cerularios, see Louis Bréhier's "Un discours inédit de Psellos," *Revue des études grecques* 16 (1903): 375–416 and 17 (1904): 35–75; for Psellus's funeral oration to Cerularios, see Kōnstantinos N. Sathas's *Mesaiōnikē bibliothēkē ē syllogē anekdotōn mnēmeiōn tēs Hellēnikēs historias*, vol. 4 (Paris, 1874), pp. 303–387.

An older but reliable essay on Cerularios is J. B. Bury's "Roman Emperors from Basil II to Isaac Komnenos," in *Selected Essays of J. B. Bury*, edited by Harold Temperley (1930; reprint, Chicago, 1967), pp. 210–214. The classic narrative of the patriarch's role in the schism remains Steven Runciman's *The Eastern Schism: A Study of the Papacy and the Eastern Churches during the Eleventh and Twelfth Centuries* (1955; reprint, Oxford, 1963). A well-documented account of his role in the azyme controversy with updated bibliography is Mahlon H. Smith III's *And Taking Bread: Cerularius and the Azyme Controversy of 1054*, "Théologie historique," vol. 47 (Paris, 1978).

JOHN TRAVIS

CEYLONESE RELIGION. *See* Sinhala Religion.

CHAITANYA. *See* Caitanya.

CHALCEDON, COUNCIL OF. *See* Councils, *article on* Christian Councils.

CH'AN. [*This entry treats the development of the Ch'an tradition in China. For a discussion of the transmission of Ch'an to Japan and its development there, see* Zen.]

Ch'an Buddhism is a particular form of meditation rooted in Indian Buddhism that originally took shape as a distinct religious tradition in China and later spread into the whole of East Asia. The Ch'an way of meditation leads to Ch'an enlightenment. Although at its inception Ch'an did not establish a particular organizational structure, the school developed into one of the Chinese forms within Buddhism, boasting a tradition that reaches back in a direct line of succession to the founder of the Buddhist religion, Śākyamuni.

The essence of Ch'an is contained in a short stanza of apparently late origin, stemming from the time when Ch'an had become firmly established and was enjoying its first full flowering in China. The famous four lines read:

> A special tradition outside the scriptures;
> No dependence upon words and letters;
> Direct pointing at the human heart;
> Seeing into one's own nature and the attainment of Buddhahood.

The formula expresses the outer and inner traits of the way of Ch'an. Different from both the Theravāda (i.e., Hīnayāna) and Mahāyāna branches of Buddhism, Ch'an does not recognize any scriptural authority. This certainly does not mean, as a widespread misunderstanding would have it, that Ch'an Buddhism is unfamiliar with the *sūtra*s that have been handed down or even rejects them. On the contrary, a glance at Chinese Ch'an literature shows that the *sūtra*s, and in particular the Mahāyāna *sūtra*s (above all, the *Prajñāpāramitā, Avataṃsaka, Laṅkāvatāra,* and *Vimalakīrti Sūtra*s), enjoy a great popularity and are used extensively for guidance in the religious career of the devotee. Further characteristics, also expressed in the verse cited earlier, mark the special quality of the Ch'an experience that breaks in upon one suddenly as a vision into the heart of things, not after the manner of an intuition but as an awakening to self-nature. This "nature," which, according to the verse, is "seen into," is nature proper, open and all-encompassing, identical with the Buddha nature, no different from the nature of all things or from the nature of the cosmos and the self. Ch'an's way of enlightenment is a way to become Buddha; its goal is the achievement of Buddhahood.

Historical Development. Before tracing the development of the Ch'an tradition and the various teachings associated with it, it is necessary to examine the sources of available information on the Ch'an school and its leaders. The state of these sources complicates not a little the description of Ch'an's historical development. Its current historical image is based on the Ch'an chronicles of the Northern Sung period (960–1127), especially on the so-called *Five Chronicles* (Chin., *Wu-teng lu*; Jpn., *Gotōroku*), prominent among which is the thirty-volume work compiled by Tao-yüan, *Ching-te ch'uan-teng lu* (Jpn., *Keitoku dentōroku*, T.D. no. 2076), finished before 1004 and published in 1011. Approximately half a millennium lies between the beginnings of Ch'an and the composition of the chronicles. Given this gap in time, the historical value of chronicles from the Sung period for the early period of Ch'an is exceedingly slight. Their credibility is still further weakened by their tendency to unrestrained praise. Everywhere legend is mixed into the transmission. For all that, the historical picture they present cannot simply be cast aside. Further material, in particular that from sources independent of Ch'an, must be consulted for verification and expansion. The great historical document *Hsü kao-seng chuan* (Jpn., *Zoku kōsōden*, T.D. no. 2060) by Tao-hsüan (d. 667) of the Lü (Vinaya) school offers biographies of Bodhidharma and his disciple Hui-k'o (T.D. 50.551b–552c) as well as important remarks on the milieu of the age. Tao-hsüan's historical work was followed up on only at the start of the Sung period. For the long intervening period of some 320 years there remains little material available except for the chronicles from the Sung period.

The *Chronicle of the Laṅkāvatāra Masters* (Chin., *Leng-ch'ieh shih-tzu chi*; Jpn., *Ryōga shijiki*, T.D. no. 2837), originating between 713 and 741 and compiled by Ching-chüeh (638–750), merits special significance in that it informs us of the situation before the break between the Northern and Southern schools. From the same period comes to us a chronicle stemming from the Northern school, the *Chuan fa-pao chi* (Jpn., *Dembōki*, T.D. no. 2838), which raises some questions concerning the lines of succession during the early period that are difficult to resolve. The *Sutra of the Sixth Patriarch*, Hui-neng (638–713), also known as the *Platform Sutra* (Chin., *Liu-tsu ta-shih fa-pao t'an ching*; Jpn., *Rokusodaishi hōbō dangyō*; T.D. no. 2008) because it was recited from an elevated seat in the temple of Ta-fan, marks the turning point in the history of Chinese Ch'an. It is a source of the first rank, although the question of its authorship remains unresolved. Along with this text should be mentioned the sayings of Shen-hui, indispensable for sorting out the issues of the day. Tomb inscriptions from the early period, moreover, contribute not a little to the clarification of the course that history took.

The merit of having provided a reliable presentation of the involved history of the early period of Chinese Ch'an Buddhism belongs to the Japanese scholar Yanagida Seizan, editor of the standard work, *Shoki zenshū shishō no kenkyū*. The later period of the history of Ch'an in China (after the eighth century) offers fewer difficulties. The chronicles from the Sung period incorporate the collections of sayings of the great masters of the later T'ang period and the age that followed; regardless of their many legendary elements, they are possessed of considerable historical value. In the period between the *Sutra of the Sixth Patriarch* and the classical Sung chronicles several richly informative writings appear, above all the *Pao-lin chuan* (Jpn., *Hōrinden*), compiled around 801 by Chih-chü. During the Sung period the sources flow profusely; we may mention only the general historical work, *Biographies of Famous Monks*

Compiled during the Sung Period (Chin., *Sung kao-seng chuan*; Jpn., *Sō kōsōden*, T.D. no. 2061).

The early period. The history of Ch'an Buddhism begins with the legend of Bodhidharma. The son of a southern Indian brahman family, or perhaps of a royal house—according to other reports, a Persian—Bodhidharma is said to have brought the new and distinct way of meditation to China. According to legend, he stood before Emperor Wu (r. 502–550), founder of the Liang dynasty, and told him forthrightly of the uselessness of the customary Buddhist religious practices, the erection of temples to the Buddha, the reciting of *sūtras*, and all sorts of deeds done to earn merit, and then crossed over the Yangtze River on a reed. [*See the biography of Liang Wu-ti.*] During his stay in northern China, the story continues, he sat squatting before a wall in the cloister of the Shao-lin Temple for nine years—for so long that his legs fell off. There he was joined by his first disciple, Hui-k'o (487–593), who proved the seriousness of his intent by cutting off one of his arms and presenting it to the squatting patriarch. Ch'an tradition has richly embellished the core of the legend, to which belongs the presentation of the robe and begging bowl as insignia of becoming a patriarch. According to Ch'an tradition, there are also writings attributed to Bodhidharma.

The historicity of the person and the work of Bodhidharma remain uncertain. Later generations associated the essence of Ch'an with his coming from the West (India). Talks that he is said to have had with his disciples were practiced as *kung-an* (Jpn., *kōan*). In spite of this historical uncertainty, there is no question of disposing of the person of Bodhidharma. The Bodhidharma legend is indispensable for an understanding of Chinese Ch'an and Japanese Zen. Japanese historians are extremely cautious in their judgment. Yanagida Seizan remarks that he knows of no explanation for the "many riddles in the biography of Bodhidharma" and he considers it impossible, with the sources available today, "to reconstruct a description of his life."

In shedding light on the early history of Ch'an in China, it is worth making note of a remark by the American Buddhist Ruth Fuller Sasaki, who draws attention to two important circumstances. "Today we know quite clearly," this well-informed historian of Zen writes, "that Chinese Ch'an did not originate with an individual Indian teacher and that many of its roots lay deep in native Chinese thought." Around the time that the deeds of Bodhidharma in China are dated, numerous Buddhist meditation masters called *ch'an-shih* wandered throughout the country. Bodhidharma may have been one of these. The Chinese soil was further saturated with an indigenous spirituality kindred to Ch'an. With good reason, the monks Seng-chao (384–414) and Tao-sheng (c. 360–434) stand as forerunners of the Ch'an movement. From early on in the course of its sinicization there flowed into Buddhism a broad stream of Taoistic thought, an influence that is particularly in evidence in the Ch'an movement. [*See the biographies of Seng-chao and Tao-sheng.*]

The all-important question of whether Bodhidharma practiced and taught a special way of meditation remains moot for want of adequate historical proof. The only statement that would suggest any such distinctiveness occurs in a text of Bodhidharma on "Mahāyāna wall-gazing," which contemporary scholarship views as inauthentic. It does, however, fit the traditionally popular way of speaking of Bodhidharma as the "wall-staring brahman." There may be a connection between the style of meditation alluded to here and the disciples of Bodhidharma, whom Tao-hsüan mentions in his biography of Hui-k'o as having cultivated the (practice of the) *Laṅkāvatāra Sūtra* handed down to them from Bodhidharma by way of Hui-k'o. Such a transmission is, however, without historical foundation. Sufficient clarity regarding details of the influence wrought by the *Laṅkāvatāra Sūtra* in the early phase of Ch'an Buddhism in China is lacking. [*See the biography of Bodhidharma.*] Seng-ts'an (d. 606), the third of the Chinese Ch'an patriarchs, numbers among the disciples of Hui-k'o who, according to the historical work of Tao-hsüan, spoke of the profound contents of the *Laṅkāvatāra Sūtra*. Another source informs us that Hui-k'o recommended to Seng-ts'an the study and interpretation of this *sūtra*. He is credited with having authored *Chiseled Words of the Believing Heart* (Chin., *Hsin-hsin-ming*; Jpn., *Shinjinmei*, T.D. no. 2010), a poetic work of strong Taoistic stamp.

During the time of the fourth and fifth patriarchs, Tao-hsin (580–651) and Hung-jen (601–674), there was a change in the social situation of the Ch'an movement. While the earliest Ch'an figures were wandering monks, later Ch'an disciples now lived in monastic communities centered around the patriarchs. Living in cloisters, the Ch'an disciples combined concern with the spiritual appropriation of the way of Ch'an with housework and labor in the fields. The change in Ch'an life brought about an incorporation of the movement into the country's social structure and broadened its base in Chinese society. Tao-hsin lived for ten years in the Tao-lin Ssu on Mount Lu, and then spent thirty years on Mount Shuan-feng. His successor, Hung-jen, moved to Mount P'ing-jung, or as it is known in the chronicles, "Eastern Mountain." During that time the Ch'an movement, called the "Dharma of the Eastern Mountain" after the dwelling place of the fifth patriarch (the designation was used retroactively for the Ch'an of the fourth patriarch also), effected a turn toward the *sūtras* of "perfect wisdom" *(prajñāpāramitā)*. The style of Tao-hsin was characterized as a "*samādhi* of one practice" *(i-hsing san-mei*; Jpn., *ichigyō sammai)*. From Tao-hsin derives the collateral Oxhead (Chin., Niu-t'ou; Jpn., Gozu) school, whose first representative, Fa-jung (594–657), introduced into the sect a preference for the Wisdom *sūtras*. Hung-jen is assured a place in the history of Ch'an for the decisive role that he played in the life of his disciple Hui-neng (638–713), who was to become the sixth patriarch of the Ch'an lineage.

The Northern and Southern schools. It is only relatively late that one can speak of a Northern school and a Southern school. There were, however, different lines of succession for the northern and southern Ch'an disciples before the emergence of two opposing schools. Some of Hung-jen's disciples worked in the northern provinces. Outstanding among these is Fa-ju (638–689), who can with some justification be called the pioneer of the Northern school, although he did not initiate his own line of succession. The father of the Northern school is Hung-jen's disciple Shen-hsiu (605?–706), who at the advanced age of fifty was accepted into the monastic community on Eastern Mountain and quickly came to be regarded as "first disciple." Shen-hsiu's biography does not speak of any special relationship between him and the disciple Hui-neng. Statements to that effect in the *Sutra of the Sixth Patriarch* have no historical grounds for credibility. Endowed with the Dharma seal of the fifth patriarch, Shen-hsiu worked from the Yü-ch'uan Ssu for the dissemination of Ch'an meditation and achieved fame as a meditation master, earning at a ripe old age the favor of the imperial palace. His two disciples P'u-chi (651–739) and I-fu (658–736) likewise enjoyed reputations beyond reproach, only slightly tarnished by their involvement in the struggles surrounding the succession of the sixth patriarch. P'u-chi's disciples Tao-hsüan (702–760) and Nan-yüeh Ming-tsan continued the line. Nonetheless, the school fell into a rapid decline and died out.

The split between the Northern and Southern schools was the outcome of the Great Dharma Assembly called by Hui-neng's disciple Shen-hui (670–762) at the Ta-yün Ssu in Hua-t'ai (Hunan Province) on 15 January 732. The assembly set as its goal the "separation of the true from the false." We are informed of this assembly only through reports from the Southern school. Shen-hui took the initiative, insisting that the Northern school had departed from authentic Ch'an tradition and that Shen-hsiu had improperly laid claim to becoming a patriarch. The sixth patriarch should be Hui-neng, whom Hung-jen had presented with the robe and begging bowl, insignia of the patriarchate. In addition, went Shen-hui's second argument, the Northern school was practicing a false form of meditation. Enlightenment is not achieved gradually, but happens suddenly, as if at a single stroke (Jpn., *tantō chokunyū*). In the history of Zen Buddhism these two opposing standpoints have been condensed efficiently into the formula "suddenness of the South, gradualness of the North" (Jpn., *nanton hokuzen*). From that time on the victorious Southern school was considered the only rightful, authentic bearer of the Ch'an tradition. [*See the biography of Hui-neng.*]

The Sutra of the Sixth Patriarch. The *Sutra of the Sixth Patriarch* is the only Ch'an text to bear the title *sūtra*, which is supposed to endow it with the highest authority. Preserved in several versions, many-layered, and comprised of dissimilar parts, the question of its authorship remains unresolved to this day. Experts date the earliest copy at our disposal, the so-called Tun-huang text discovered in the caves of Tun-huang, between 830 and 860. Yanagida Seizan deals exhaustively with the matter of its historical origin and breaks new ground in suggesting the participation of the Oxhead school in its composition. Among the several sources that apparently flow together in the *sūtra* is the important contribution made by Shen-hui and his circle of disciples.

The *sūtra* consists mainly of two dissimilar parts, the doctrinal instructions of Hui-neng, including his autobiography, and other sundry pieces. The autobiography climaxes with the quarrel between Hung-jen's main disciple, Shen-hsiu, and Hui-neng, who was residing in the cloister of the fifth patriarch and working in the granary. With great care Shen-hsiu arrived at this verse:

> The body is the tree of enlightenment [*bodhi*].
> The mind is like a clear mirror.
> Take care at all times to wipe it clean!
> Allow no speck of dust upon it!

In sharp contrast to this finely honed and logically irrefutable verse stands that of the "illiterate" Hui-neng:

> Originally there is no tree of enlightenment,
> Nor is there a stand with a clear mirror.
> From the beginning no single thing exists.
> Where then is a grain of dust to cling?

In addition to the high level of enlightenment that these lines show, many other traits of Hui-neng are detailed in his biography.

The doctrinal instructions of Hui-neng present the Ch'an program of the Southern school. Enlightenment occurs in a sudden awakening of wisdom (Skt., *prajñā*) to the "seeing of nature" (Jpn., *kenshō*). It requires no washing away of defilements since even a defilement is identical with nature. *Prajñā* sees through emptiness, but it is a seeing of non-seeing. The *Sutra of the Sixth Patriarch* develops the fundamental ideas of the doctrine of *prajñā* in negative formulations that are yet in essence positive. Terms like "no-mind" and "non-thinking" are not to be understood psychologically but taken metaphysically in terms of the doctrine of wisdom. [*See* Prajñā.] From the time of Hui-neng, the *Diamond Sutra*, a short but highly expressive text belonging to the group of Prajñāpāramitā Sūtras, was given a position of first rank in Chinese Ch'an, a position apparently enjoyed during the early period by the *Laṅkāvatāra Sūtra*.

In addition to the ideas of the wisdom *sūtra*s, the doctrine of the Buddha nature of all living things, which is the central message of the *Nirvāṇa Sūtra*, plays an important role in the *Sutra of the Sixth Patriarch*. The "nature" seen in enlightenment—also called proper nature, self-nature, original nature, wisdom nature, or Dharma nature—is the same as the Buddha nature. According to one tradition, the *Nirvāṇa Sūtra* is the first Mahāyāna text that Hui-neng encountered. His practice of Ch'an rests on a foundation of the doctrines of perfect wisdom and the Buddha nature.

The full flowering after Hui-neng. Recognized through the Great Dharma Assembly of 732 as the sixth patriarch, Hui-neng became the symbol of integration of Chinese Ch'an Buddhism. The term *Southern school* came mainly, but not exclusively, to be used in contrast to *Northern school*, a term used by Shen-hui. In the end, the Southern school embraced the whole of Chinese Ch'an that recognized Hui-neng as patriarch. This Ch'an was also known as the "Ch'an of the patriarchs" (Jpn., *soshizen*), in distinction to the "Ch'an of the Tathāgata" whose patriarch was considered to be Bodhidharma. There is no opposition intended in the terms (Bodhidharma was also recognized as a patriarch by the Southern school) and Hui-neng was most certainly not accorded any priority over Bodhidharma but, like him, represented an ideal figure valued as a patriarch *par excellence*.

Chinese Ch'an reached its zenith in the Ch'an of the patriarchs of the Southern school, but only with the third generation after Hui-neng. Of the five main disciples of Hui-neng, only Nan-yang Hui-chung (d. 776), who is known by the title of *kuo-shih* ("national teacher"), stands out as a Ch'an master. The line proceeding from the disputatious Shen-hui, another of the disciples of Hui-neng, leads in the fifth generation to Kuei-feng Tsung-mi (780–841) who combined in his person Ch'an and Hua-yen (Jpn., Kegon). From its inception, scientific interests took precedence over practice in this branch. [*See the biography of Tsung-mi.*]

Two main branches of Ch'an stem from Hui-neng's disciples Ch'ing-yüan Hsing-ssu (660–740) and Nan-yüeh Huai-jang (677–744), led in the third generation by Shih-t'ou Hsi-ch'ien (700–790) and Ma-tsu Tao-i (709–790). Both branches are full of the names of highly reputed masters of whom the chronicles, collections of sayings, and *kung-an* (Jpn., *kōan*; "public announcements") recount "strange words and extraordinary deeds." To be sure, legend has been mixed in as well, but the historicity of the movement is beyond dispute. The creative originality and overpowering earthiness of these masters and disciples is manifest in words and deeds that seem to flow out of them with a facility beyond compare. Thanks to the *kōan*, this fascination has been kept alive up to this day in the Japanese Zen halls.

That the strict monastic form stabilized into rules by Pai-chang Huai-hai (720–814) in no way compromised the sparkling spontaneity of life in the monastery halls bears witness to the pureness of the Ch'an of that day. The rule pervaded by the stern and simple spirit of the primitive Buddhist community gave Ch'an stability. Tried and proven in the Ch'an cloisters of China, this rule remains in force in Japan.

The Five Houses. After the persecution of Buddhism in the year 845, many flourishing schools were unable to recover from the damage they had sustained. Ch'an, however, which had spread throughout the country, demonstrated its vitality and vigor of action. Around the end of the T'ang dynasty and during the Five Dynasties period (907–960), the "five houses" were formed. The term *Five Houses* did not signify organized establishments, but rather, as the name suggests, family groups that cultivated their own particular customs and literary genres.

The House of Kuei-yang (Jpn., Igyō) was the first of the Five Houses. Named after the two mountains, Kuei and Yang, on which stood the cloisters of the founders Kuei-shan Ling-yu (771–853) and Yang-shan Hui-chi (807–883), this house testified to the peculiarly rough and hearty manner in which the two founders lived out the master-disciple relationship. Action and silence were combined true to Ch'an style. To the master's question, the disciple responded with a deed. A unique feature of the house was the technique of the "perfect figure" (Chin., *yüan-hsiang*; Jpn., *ensō*) or "circle." One availed oneself of the image of the circle to express completeness and reality. Tradition speaks of ninety-seven circles.

The House of Lin-chi (Jpn., Rinzai), which would become the leading Ch'an school in the Sung dynasty, took shape under Lin-chi I-hsüan (d. 866), the personality in early Chinese Ch'an of whom we have the most reliable historical evidence. The collection of his sayings bears witness to the sharp mind and pure character of this highly gifted master. Lin-chi's powerful style of leadership is famous for his methods of thundering and thrashing that he in turn had taken over from his master, the no less unusually gifted Huang-po Hsi-yün (d. 850). [*See the biography of Lin-chi.*]

Distinctive of the house are the threefold and fourfold dialectical formulas Lin-chi presented his students for practice, for example the "four alternatives" (Chin., *ssu liao-chien*; Jpn., *shiryōken*):

> Take away the individual [subject] once, without taking away the world [object].
> Then take away the world once, without taking away the individual.
> Then take away both the individual and the world.
> And once take away neither the individual nor the world.

The formula has the ring of Mahāyāna metaphysics to it, yet Lin-chi illustrates his sayings through metaphorical imagery.

The House of Ts'ao-tung (Jpn., Sōtō) owes its name to its two founders, Tung-shan Liang-chieh (807–869) and Ts'ao-shan Pen-chi (840–901). In addition to Ts'ao-shan, Yün-chü Tao-ying (d. 902) also stands out among the circle of Tung-shan's disciples. Ts'ao-shan's name is associated with the well-known special trait of this house, the formula of the "five ranks." This most significant dialectical formula in Ch'an Buddhism originated in the House of Ts'ao-tung, stimulated by Shih-t'ou, a fancier of dialectical thinking who appears in the third generation after Hui-neng. In the "five ranks" the noumenal and the phenomenal are related to one another, culminating in the fifth rank with a total unity of unobstructed interpenetration through a freedom transcending all opposition, depicted in the image of a full black circle. The formula of the "five ranks" did not remain restricted to the House of Ts'ao-tung but became common property in Chinese Ch'an and Japanese Zen Buddhism. The House of Ts'ao-tung continues today in the Japanese Sōtō sect.

The House of Yün-men (Jpn., Ummon) is distinguished by its method of the "pass of a single word" practiced by Yün-men Wen-yen (864–945), an outstanding master from the period of the Five Dynasties. Questioned on the essence of Ch'an or enlightenment, the master makes an extremely brief but pertinent reply, often using no more than a single word. The *kōan* collections of the *Pi-yen lu* (Jpn., *Hekiganroku*) and the *Wu-men kuan* (Jpn., *Mumonkan*) contain numerous examples testifying to the striking answers given by this master. For instance, in reply to the question of a monk, "What is the Buddha?," he says simply, "Three pounds of hemp" (*Wu-men kuan*, case 18). To him is also ascribed the splendid saying that climaxes case 6 of the *Pi-yen lu*: "Every day a good day." Unfortunately, the House of Yün-men was destined to be short-lived, yet the contribution it made to Chinese art and culture is a significant one. Hsüeh-tou Ch'ung-hsien (980–1052), the poet who composed the hundred verses of the *Pi-yen lu*, is one of its luminaries.

The House of Fa-yen (Jpn., Hōgen) is the last of the Five Houses. Its founder, Fa-yen Wen-i (885–958), was highly educated and familiar with both Chinese classics and Buddhist literature. As a Ch'an master he had his own way of directing disciples to spiritual awakening. Over and over he would repeat the same word or phrase, without adding any explanation. He had appropriated completely the Hua-yen (Jpn., Kegon) philosophy and strove to lead his disciples to experience the vision of inner unity of the six marks of being: totality and differentiation, sameness and difference, becoming and disappearing. On one occasion, to illustrate the Hua-yen principle of sameness-in-difference, he ordered the bamboo curtain in front of the hall to be rolled up, and two monks carried out his instructions. The *kōan* closes with the words: "Fa-yen spoke, 'The one has grasped it, the other has missed it' " (*Wu-men kuan*, case 26). The house died out with its founder. Already by the following generation, Fa-yen's Dharma successor T'ien-t'ai Te-shao (891–971) had turned to devote himself to the science of the T'ien-t'ai (Jpn., Tendai) school. His disciple Yung-ming Yen-shou (904–975) is representative of the growing syncretistic mixture of Buddhist doctrines and schools. [*See also* Hua-yen *and* T'ien-t'ai.]

Structures and methods during the Sung period. The houses of Lin-chi and Ts'ao-tung developed into schools representing Chinese Ch'an Buddhism during the Sung period (960–1279), the Lin-chi school acquiring a dominant influence. Two important Lin-chi masters appear at the start of the era, Fen-yang Shan-chao (947–1024) and Shih-shuang Ch'u-yüan (986–1039). Shih-shuang, by force of his personal reputation and connections in high places, secured Ch'an entry into imperial circles and the upper classes. Under his two disciples Yang-ch'i Fang-hui (992–1049) and Huang-lung Hui-nan (1002–1069), the school broke into two branches, although this did not produce any differences of doctrine or practice.

During the Sung period the practice of the *kung-an* was introduced into the Lin-chi school. *Kung-an* have as their content anecdotes from the lives of the Ch'an patriarchs and masters, dialogues between masters and disciples (Jpn., *mondō*), paradoxical sayings, pithy or ambiguous statements, and strange gestures and acts. Once proposed to a disciple by the master, the disciple must become concerned with the solution. In doing so, one runs up against the limits of intellectual thinking, since the paradoxical riddle of the *kung-an* does not admit of a rational solution. As doubt takes hold of the one engaged in the practice rational consciousness is finally broken through in experience.

The practice of the *kung-an* has a psychological and a metaphysical-religious relevance. On the one hand, in striving to resolve the unsolvable, psychic concentration is intensified through steady intent on the task. This is the necessary precondition for the breakthrough to experience. On the other hand, the elimination of all conceptuality, in particular of every duality, points up the metaphysical-religious dimension of the practice, whose goal is an unrestricted experience of everything as one. The master-disciple relationship plays an important role in the practice of the *kung-an*. It is not only a matter of the master presenting a *kung-an* to the disciple, but also one of accompanying the disciple in the advance of the practice, keeping informed of psychic experiences, warning against false paths, and helping in every way to reach the ardently desired goal of the experience of enlightenment.

The earliest *kung-an* collections originated in the Lin-chi school. The most important such work, the *Pi-yen lu* (Jpn., *Hekiganroku*), we owe to Yüan-wu K'o-ch'in (1063–1135), who drew up hints, interim remarks, and commentaries for a hundred examples selected by Hsüeh-tou and furnished with verses. The high literary quality of this work, first published in 1128, was nearly to be its undoing. Yüan-wu's disciple and successor Ta-hui Tsung-kao (1089–1163) had all copies of the *Pi-yen lu* to be found in his domain burned, apparently because many Ch'an disciples were showing all too great a dependency on the beauty of the work's form. It was not until some two hundred years later that a new edition appeared, based on some of the copies that had escaped destruction.

Another collection of *kōan* in the Lin-chi school, the *Wu-men kuan* (Jpn., *Mumonkan*; The Gateless Barrier), prepared in 1228 by Wu-men Hui-k'ai (1183–1260), has enjoyed a lasting affection. The collection begins with the perhaps most famous of all *kung-an*, the example of the *wu* (Jpn., *mu*) or nothingness of the Buddha nature of the dog, originally conceived by Chao-chou. It is followed by a number of other famous examples such as "Hsing-yen's Man up in a Tree" (case 5), "Nan-chuan Cuts the Cat in Two" (case 14), and "Yün-men's Shit-stick" (case 21). Master Wu-men, a striking personality, makes the "non-door" his door and calls his work "The Gateless Barrier."

The Ts'ao-tung school was also interested in the practice of *kung-an* and made use of them. Basing his work on a collection of a hundred cases and verses by the Ts'ao-tung master Hung-chih Cheng-chüeh (1091–1157) and taking as his model the *Pi-yen lu*, Wan-sung Hsing-hsiu (1166–1246) compiled an extensive work on the *kung-an* known as the *Ts'ung-jung lu* (Jpn., *Shōyōroku*). The Ts'ao-tung school in no way rejected the *kung-an*, even though it did not assign them the same significance that the Lin-chi school did. A heated confrontation regarding the correct way of meditation broke out between the two schools, summarized in the catch phrases *k'an-hua ch'an* (Jpn., *kanna-zen*; "Ch'an of reflection on the *kōan*") and *mo-chao ch'an* (Jpn., *mokushō-zen*; "Ch'an of silent illumination").

Ta-hui of the Lin-chi school took the offensive, warning against the false path of sitting in silent passivity. The literarily gifted Ts'ao-tung master Hung-chih mustered eloquent words in its defense: "Anyone who has arrived at silent illumination belongs to the house of our tradition. The silent illumination reaches up to the heights; it presses down to the depths."

The controversy calls to mind the early conflict between the Northern and Southern schools, but there are essential differences. Throughout this debate the Ts'ao-tung school professed its adherence to the line of tradition of the sixth patriarch Hui-neng, according to which experiences of sudden enlightenment are held in high esteem. The controversy was mainly centered on the value given the *kung-an* and the distinct use made of them in the two schools. While there are differences of orientation—and this applies to the Lin-chi (Rinzai) and Ts'ao-tung (Sōtō) schools in their Japanese forms as well—both may rightly be viewed as genuine forms of Ch'an or Zen, which is richly diversified and possesses legitimate plurality.

Cultural and Artistic Impact. During the Sung period, Ch'an Buddhism succeeded in effecting a wide-ranging impact on Chinese society. Previous to that time social and political conditions in the country, as well as the processes of development within Ch'an itself, had inhibited any such impact. During the ninth and tenth centuries, as Ch'an came to take a more definite form, the Chinese empire was plagued by unrest. The Sung period was spiritually one of the strongest eras of Chinese history, however, and Ch'an was able at that time to make a considerable contribution to the cultural development taking place in the Chinese empire.

The Five Mountains and Ten Temples. During the Sung dynasty, Ch'an masters earned a place of high esteem in the imperial palace. The number of temples and monks in the Lin-chi school increased, and magnificent temple buildings arose to which smaller cloisters were attached. Such circumstances made organizational regulations seem desirable. Under the powerful protection of the regime, the privileged system of the Five Mountains and Ten Temples took shape during the southern Sung dynasty. All temples and cloisters covered by this system belonged to the Yang-ch'i branch of the Lin-chi school. The unpleasant reverse side of the picture was that participating Ch'an cloisters were forced into a certain dependency on the apparatus of the regime.

Relations to Neo-Confucianism. True to tradition, Neo-Confucianism, the dominant philosophy of the age, set itself up in opposition to Buddhism insofar as Neo-Confucianism derived from classical Chinese philosophy. At the same time, a lively and amicable interchange between the leading figures of the new philosophy and Ch'an Buddhists emerged. Chou Tun-i (1017–1073), the putative founder of the Neo-Confucian school, was allegedly an ardent admirer of Buddhism. His associations with Ch'an Buddhism arose from his metaphysical tendencies. The shift to metaphysics characteristic of Neo-Confucianism served to nourish its close ties to Ch'an. Chang Tsai (1020–1077), second in the line of great Neo-Confucian philosophers, saw in the attractiveness of Buddhist doctrines a danger for the purity of Chinese thinking.

The Ch'eng brothers present a more complex picture. The elder brother, Ch'eng Hao (1032–1085), whose posthumous title is Ming-tao, was a man endowed with a strong intuition and religious nature. In his youth he let himself be drawn to Ch'an Buddhism. He studied Mahāyāna *sūtra*s and kept personal contacts with Ch'an Buddhism, yet maintained a final reserve. His younger brother, Ch'eng I (1033–1107), also acquired a good knowledge of Buddhism. He is said even to have taken part in Ch'an meditation in a cloister, but like all Neo-Confucians of that time he held fast to Chinese philosophy. Chu Hsi (1130–1200), a systematic thinker of the highest caliber who brought Neo-Confucianism to its perfection, undertook a basic study of Buddhist doctrines as well, without acquiring much of a taste for them, however. In the prime of his life he was to campaign vigorously and effectively against Buddhism. His final renunciation inflicted considerable harm on Ch'an Buddhism. The abiding influence resulting from the encounter between Neo-Confucianism and Ch'an Buddhism lies mainly in the deeper penetration of meditation into the Chinese intellectual and spiritual life.

Art. In the field of art the Ch'an monks produced numerous noteworthy achievements. I have had occasion at several points to mention the literary quality of the Ch'an writings, particularly of verses and works testifying to poetic inspiration. Temple constructions during the Sung period also demonstrate their architectural ability and artistic sense. Above all else attention may be drawn to the ink paintings native to the Ch'an movement, which have graced East Asian art with works of a perfection never again achieved. The crowning accomplishments stand as "documents of a spiritual tradition" and "symbols of an attainment of vision and insight" (Dietrich Seckel, *Buddhistische Kunst Ostasiens*, Stuttgart, 1957, p. 228). Portrait and landscape painting is prominent. The Ox-herding Pictures, extant in several versions, are world-famous. The artistic highpoint was reached with the painter Liang K'ai (at the beginning of the thirteenth century), creator of the masterpieces "Śākyamuni's Return from the Mountains" and "The Sixth Patriarch Rending a Scroll," and (toward the end of the century) Mu-ch'i, whose "Fruit of the Kaki" deserves to be called "perhaps the most mature and radical Zen picture there is" (Seckel, 1957, p. 254).

The Decline of the Ch'an Movement. After the Sung period syncretistic endeavors made ever greater inroads into Chinese Buddhism. The Lin-chi school absorbed all groups of Ch'an Buddhism, including, during the Ming period (1368–1644), the Ts'ao-tung school. The notion of the unity of the three doctrines (*san-chiao i-chih*; Jpn., *sankyō itchi*) permeated intellectual life. A general form of Buddhism came into being, principal to which was the cultivation of the recitation of the name of Buddha Amitābha and Ch'an meditation. [*See* Ching-t'u.] Distinguished individual Ch'an masters were active in later centuries also, but the Bodhidharma tradition as a school of particular spiritual transmission no longer played any role. Popular Buddhist religion embraced Amidism, Kuan-yin veneration, and Ch'an meditation. Classical Ch'an had come to an end in China, but not the history of Ch'an Buddhism altogether, as a glance at Zen Buddhism in Japan will show.

[*See also* Buddhist Philosophy; Nirvāṇa; *and* Buddhism, Schools of, *article on* Chinese Buddhism.]

BIBLIOGRAPHY

D. T. Suzuki's three-volume work, *Essays in Zen Buddhism*, The Ataka Buddhist Library, vols. 1–3 (1927–1934; reprint, 3 vols. in 2: Taipei, 1971), discusses many aspects of Zen Buddhism—including its origins and development in China, the practice of *kōan*, enlightenment, its rooting in Mahāyāna—but does not enter into a critique of the historical sources. Among his numerous publications should be pointed out his *Manual of Zen Buddhism*, The Ataka Buddhist Library, vol. 8 (Kyoto, 1935), with translations of texts by the Chinese masters, including two commentaries on the Ox-herding Pictures; and *The Zen Doctrine of No-Mind* (London, 1949), on Hui-neng. In the reference work *Zen Dust*, edited by Isshū Miura and Ruth Fuller Sasaki (New York, 1966) appear two excellent essays on the *kōan* in Lin-chi (Rinzai) Zen: Sasaki's "The Kōan in Japanese Zen," pp. 17–32, and Miura's "Kōan Study in Rinzai," pp. 33–76. Walter Liebenthal's translation, introduction, and commentary on the work of Seng-chao, *Chao Lun: The Treatises of Seng-chao* (Hong Kong, 1968), provides a good insight into the pre-history of Ch'an, as do a series of articles on Tao-sheng he published in *Monumenta Nipponica*: "Chinese Buddhism During the 4th and 5th Centuries," *Monumenta Nipponica* 11 (April 1955): 44–83; "A Biography of Chu Tao-sheng," *Monumenta Nipponica* 11 (October 1955): 64–96; "The World Conception of Chu Tao-sheng," *Monumenta Nipponica* 12 (April 1956): 65–103; "The World Conception of Chu Tao-sheng: Texts," *Monumenta Nipponica* 12 (October 1956): 241–268.

We have Yanagida Seizan to thank for the standard work in Japanese on the early period of Ch'an, *Shoki zenshū shishō no kenkyū* (Kyoto, 1967), with supplementary appendices on particular subjects and critical texts. Ui Hakuju's three-volume study on the history of the Zen school, *Zenshūshi kenkyū* (Tokyo, 1939–1943), is of continued importance. A recently published symposium on *Early Ch'an in China and Tibet*, edited by Whalen Lai and Lewis R. Lancaster (Berkeley, 1983), contains eighteen studies on the beginnings of Ch'an Buddhism based on the research of recent decades. Included also are two contributions by Yanagida Seizan, offering an English summary of his Japanese studies. On the confrontation between the Northern and Southern schools, see the translation of Jacques Gernet's *Entretiens du Maître de Dhyāna Chen-houei du Ho-tso*, "Publications de l'École Française de l'Extrême Orient," vol. 31 (Hanoi, 1949); and of Walter Liebenthal's "The Sermon of Shen-hui," *Asia Major* n.s. 3, no. 2 (1953): 132–155. The best translations of the *Sutra of the Sixth Patriarch* are *The Platform Sūtra of the Sixth Patriarch: The Text of the Tun-huang Manuscript with Translation, Introduction and Notes*, by Philip Yampolsky (New York, 1967); and *The Platform Scripture*, edited and translated by Wing-tsit Chan (New York, 1963). See also the extensive Japanese source book of texts, introductions, and commentaries, *Enō kenkyū*, edited by the Research Institute for the History of Zen at Tokyo's Komazawa University (Tokyo, 1978). The collection of Lin-chi's sayings have been translated into English several times. See especially *The Recorded Sayings of Ch'an Master Lin-chi Hui-chao of Chen Prefecture*, translated by Ruth Fuller Sasaki (Kyoto, 1975). A French translation by Paul Demiéville, *Entretiens de Lin-tsi* (Paris, 1972), stands out for its superior commentary. On the philosophy of Lin-chi and the "five ranks," see Alfonso Verdú's *The Philosophy of Buddhism: A "Totalistic" Synthesis* (The Hague, 1981); and his treatment of the "five ranks" in *Dialectical Aspects in Buddhist Thought: Studies in Sino-Japanese Mahāyāna Idealism* (Lawrence, Kan., 1974).

The two *kōan* collections *Pi-yen lu* and *Wu-men-kuan* are available in several translations. The two have been brought together in a single volume in *Two Zen Classics: Mumonkan and Hekiganroku*, translated with commentaries by Katsuki Sekida and edited by A. V. Grimstone (New York, 1977); see also Thomas Cleary and J. C. Cleary's three-volume translation of the former, *The Blue Cliff Record* (Boulder, 1977), and Shibayama Zenkei's *Zen Comments on the Mumonkan* (New York, 1974), which also contains explanatory talks by the master. Collections of Ch'an and Zen texts in English translation are presented by Lu K'uan Yü (Charles Luk) in his *Ch'an and Zen Teaching*, 3 vols. (London, 1960–1962), and by Nyogen Senzaki and Paul Reps in *Zen Flesh, Zen Bones* (Rutland, Vt., and Tokyo, 1957). John Blofeld has translated texts of two important Chinese masters in *The Zen Teaching of Huang Po on the Transmission of Mind* (London, 1958), and *The Zen Teaching of Hui Hai on Sudden Illumination* (London, 1962). Of further help are extracts from the chronicle *Ching-te ch'uan-teng lu*, translated with an introduction by Chang Chung-yuan in *Original Teachings of Ch'an Buddhism: Selected from The Transmission of the Lamp* (New York, 1969). See my *Geschichte des Zen-Buddhismus*, vol. 1, *Indien und China* (Munich, 1982), of which an English translation is in preparation.

HEINRICH DUMOULIN
Translated from German by James W. Heisig

CHANCE, in the most general sense of the word, is the negation of necessity and the opposite of determinism. The English word *chance*, derived from the Latin *cadere* ("to fall"), has a wide spectrum of meanings encompassing randomness, probability, coincidence, contingence, accident, incident, fortuity, hazard, risk, opportunity, luck, fortune, and fate. Many words related to chance, such as *coincidence*, *contingence*, or the German *Zufall*, indicate a binary structure, the coming together of two causally independent series of events. Something happens, or a certain situation or person is encountered by chance. (The English word *incident* derives from Latin *incidere*, "to befall, to fall out.") Moreover, as a rare or unusual occurrence, chance approaches the idea of miracle.

Ideas of chance are part of a worldview, whether it be indeterministic or deterministic. It may be apprehended positively, as "an essential aspect of any real process" (Bohm, 1957, p. 141); negatively, as the lack of causality or knowledge of such; or neutrally, as the law of probability.

To some, chance denotes human freedom, but to others, fate. Chance can be haphazard; it can be fortunate or unfortunate. It is a highly equivocal, bifacial term, in that one meaning can easily turn into its opposite. This ambivalence may be traced back to the essential unpredictability and unknowability of any occurrence. The insurance business, for instance, rests on its customers' belief in chance (in the sense of unpredictability) but itself uses the theory of chance—that is, probability—to calculate its risks and price its policies (see Knight, 1921).

Though today the theory of probability predicts the course of class events to a great extent, the ultimate unknowability and uncertainty of individual events have yet to vanish (and likely can never vanish) from the realm of human experience (see Von Mises, 1963). This persistent presence of chance can be argued from the contingent nature of our existence or from free will.

Again, the uncertainty and indeterminateness of reality can be the source of inspiration for art or enterprise. The spirit of gambling, for instance, deliberately creates uncertain situations for the enjoyment of the risks themselves (see Rothbard, 1962, p. 500). [*See* Gambling.]

Chance and Causality. According to Dante, Democritus ascribed the world to chance: "Democrito che il mondo a caso pone" (*Inferno* 4.136; cf. Cioffari, 1935, chap. 1). Aristotle also points out that, for Democritus, the cosmos is ordered by chance *(automaton),* that is, out of itself *(auto)* without any reason or purpose *(maton).* (For the etymology of *automaton,* see *Physics* 197b.) In opposition to this view of chance as a spontaneous event, or as "a cause that is inscrutable to human intelligence, as being a divine thing and full of mystery" (*Physics* 196b), Aristotle takes chance *(tuchē* or *automaton)* as an accidental cause of the "efficient order" and as what happens "by accident" *(kata sumbebēkos).* Chance, therefore, is indeterminate, changeful, and unstable. It is whatever comes about, neither always nor usually, but rarely (*Metaphysics* 1026b–1027a, 1065a; *Physics* 196b–198a).

The Christian stance on chance varies somewhat: whereas Augustine denied any possibility of chance or fortune in view of all-controlling providence (*City of God* 5.1), Thomas Aquinas admitted chance *(contingens)* within the providential scheme. Things "happen necessarily or contingently according to God's will" (*Summa theologiae* 1.19.8).

For Spinoza, chance is spoken of "with reference to a deficiency in our knowledge [of the cause]" (*Ethics* 1.33.1); likewise, Laplace took it as the expression of "our ignorance as to the causes of phenomena." Hume declared that "there is no such thing as *chance,*" but "our ignorance of the real cause of any event begets this sort of belief or opinion" (*Concerning Human Understanding* 6). Chance thus understood has merely a subjective reality. Leibniz, on the other hand, considers the world as "the whole assemblage of contingent things" carried by necessary and eternal God (*Theodicy* 7). Contingency is spoken of in relation to truths of facts, while necessity is correlated with truths of reasoning (*Monadology* 33).

In opposition to the mechanical necessitarianists of the late nineteenth century, C. S. Peirce developed a philosophical position that he called "tychism." It preserves the necessary presence of chance (Gr., *tuchē*), "a spontaneity which is to some degree regular," in the evolutionary process of the world, and this accounts for the individual specification (Peirce, 1923, pp. 200–201). Max Born, from the standpoint of quantum mechanics, likewise takes chance to be mixed with "certain regularities," and nature to be "ruled by laws of cause and laws of chance." Distinguishing causality from determinism, Born incorporates chance into the consideration of causality, and thereby he gives quantum mechanics indeterministic foundations (cf. Heisenberg's "principle of indeterminacy" or Niels Bohr's "principle of complementarity"). This indeterministic position was rejected by Einstein, who was convinced that God was not a "dice-playing God" (Born, 1951, pp. 3, 109, 122–123). A Nobel prize winner, the biologist Jacques Monod, declared that "chance *alone* is at the source of every innovation, of all creation in the biosphere" (Monod, 1971, p. 112). Objectors to this view hold that Monod's equation of "chance and man's freedom to choose his own ethical value" is erroneous (see MacKay, 1978, p. 31), or that "physico-chemical determinism" is not synonymous with the "absence of choice and freedom" (Schoffeniels, 1976, p. xix). Not only the old question of the divine providence, human freedom and chance, but the question of scientific discoveries and their philosophical implications occupy the contemporary mind.

Radical Contingency: A Buddhist View. The Buddhist doctrine of dependent co-origination *(pratītya-samutpāda)* may be interpreted as a theory of radical contingency. It holds that there are "no accidental occurrences" and that everything in the world is produced "causally conditioned." Buddhists deny any theory of creation by a transcendental agent or anything like fate. Moreover, things, causally produced in this fashion, have no "self-nature" *(svabhāva).* This view diametrically opposed the determinism of the Indian materialists, the Ājīvikas, as well as the syncretic view of the theory of inner and outer causation held by Jains (see Kalupahana, 1975).

From a certain perspective, this Buddhist doctrine appears to be a deterministic view in that it asserts that everything is subject to the law of causation. But from a reverse perspective, the convergence of causal factors is thoroughly indeterminate; it rests on a radical contingence of various factors, both of the spatio-temporal and psycho-mental nature. Innumerable conditioning elements come together in the arising of a single event at each moment. [*See also* Pratītya-samutpāda.]

Chance and Fortune. Aristotle distinguished two types of chance events, *tuchē* and *automaton,* which stand for subjective and objective aspects of chance, respectively. Alexander of Aphrodisias, a third-century commentator, illustrates this point with an example of a lost horse recovered by chance by his former master. For the master, the event is fortunate *(tuchē),* but for the horse it is simply fortuitous *(automaton). Automaton* has a broader range of denotative meanings than *tuchē,* as it is applicable both to the natural and human worlds, whereas *tuchē* applies only to the latter. This distinction is useful in throwing light on the subjective factor present in the perception of chance (see Kuki, 1966, pp. 63–67). Regarding luck and chance, Aristotle makes the following observation: "We speak of 'good luck' when luck brings us something good, and 'bad luck' in the opposite event, or, in serious cases, of 'good fortune' [*eutuchia*] or 'misfortune' [*dustuchia*]" (*Physics* 197a). Aristotle means by good fortune or chance such qualities as noble birth, good children, wealth, political power, friends, and beauty (cf. *Rhetoric* 1389a). Fortune or chance is the cause of these external goods (*Politics* 1322b). The ethical virtues of justice, courage, temperance, and wisdom, however, lie outside the realm of chance, that is, within human control (cf. *Politics* 1323a).

The Greek word for chance, *tuchē,* echoes the long history of poets' and writers' reflections on the subjects of luck, fate, the vicissitudes of life, and the gods' share in such human events. For Pindar, Soteira Tyche (Fortune the Savior) is "heaven-sent good fortune," the "kindly power who may crown the efforts of man" (Greene, 1944, pp. 72–73). Plato mentions a *theia tuchē,* a divine chance (*Timaeus* 25e), who comes in to save men's folly. For many Greeks, Tyche was perceived as Agathe Tyche and invoked as the goddess of good fortune (*Timaeus* 26e; Greene, 1944, p. 299). According to Aristotle, chance does not enter into the world of morality, but it has, nonetheless, a religio-ethical significance, because fortune and happiness *(eudaimonia)* are somewhat synonymous, and "happiness is a divine gift" (*Nicomachean Ethics* 1099b; Greene, 1944, p. 325); moreover, "the lucky seem to succeed owing to God" (*Ethica Eudemia* 1248b; Cioffari, 1935, p. 27).

But the figure of Tyche is not always benevolent or dependable. Archilochus (c. 700–650 BCE) had to introduce the idea of *tuchē,* along with the already familiar Homeric notion of *moira* (fate), to account for what controlled human destiny. According to Orphic doctrines, fate was the law that controlled the conditions of man's birth, death, and reincarnation, but by the fifth and fourth centuries BCE, Tyche, as goddess, became increasingly important, as witnessed by an anonymous poet: "Fortune [Tyche], beginning and end of men. Thou sittest in the seats of wisdom, and grantest honor to human deeds . . . thou most excellent of Gods" (Loeb ed., *Lyra Graeca,* vol. 3, p. 477). For Sophocles and Euripides the role of *tuchē* is considerable. In the latter, Ion exclaims, "O Tyche, thou who hast brought change to myriads of men, causing them now to suffer misfortune, and now to fare well, by what a narrow margin have I escaped slaying my mother!" (Euripides, *Ion* 1512–1515). Tyche, as the goddess of chance, was associated with Lachesis, one of the Moirai (Fates) and the "dispenser of human lots" (Hesiod), and took on a fickle, unpredictable character. The cult of the native Italian goddess Fortuna revived when she was identified with Tyche. According to Pliny's account:

> Everywhere in the whole world, at every hour by all men's voices Fortuna alone is invoked and named, alone accused, alone impeached, alone pondered, alone applauded, alone rebuked and visited with reproaches; deemed volatile and indeed by most men blind as well, wayward, inconstant, uncertain, fickle in her favors and favoring the unworthy . . . . We are so much at the mercy of chance that Chance herself takes the place of god. (*Natural History* 2.22)

The belief in Fortuna persisted well into Renaissance Europe; she was often depicted with wings, bearing a rudder and wheel, symbolizing swiftly changing fortune.

Chance and fate—these initially contradictory notions are but two counterinterpretations of the experience of unexpected coincidence or happenings that seem arbitrary but nevertheless have a decisive impact on one's life and in some cases totally change it. From a strictly fatalistic point of view, of course, there is no room for chance, for everything is already predetermined prior to the occurrence of things, and everything is already fated.

Divination. Belief in fortune opens the way for divination. Throughout the history of humankind, appeals to divination have been made in times of great trouble or uncertainty. Divination is a means to obtain answers to questions that are insoluble by rational reasoning. Plutarch records a story in which the successor to the Thessalian kingdom was chosen by the drawing of lots at Delphi. In ancient Japan, shrine virgins known as *saigū,* who served at the most auspicious shrine of all, the Ise Shrine, were chosen from among eligible princesses by divination with a turtle shell. As was the case in Shang China, divination originated in a human attempt to fathom the mind of the high god, Ti. It appears that only later did divination come to be interpreted as dealing with chance or randomness. It is noteworthy in this connection that Apollo, the Greek god of knowledge, despised the uncertainty of the lot and handed over the divination dealing with the chances of the dice to Hermes, who thus became the gambler's god.

Belief in chance has a double role to play in the practice of divination—in the method (as the principle of randomness) and in the interpretation (as the principle of coincidence). A deterministic worldview that negates chance can nevertheless employ divination. For example, an African system of divination, Ifa, stands on the assumption that an individual basically cannot change his own destiny, but just as he can spoil it to a degree, so can the practice of Ifa improve it. Even Stoics, who were thoroughgoing determinists, eagerly sought knowledge of the future that fell outside the prediction of scientists, physicians, and other experts. The harmony between the human soul and the divine soul provided them with the basis for divination as a means of communication with God in order that "men might know the divine will in advance and obey it" (William A. Falconer, introduction to Cicero's *De divinatione,* Loeb ed., 1923, p. 216).

Like the widely practiced throwing of pebbles or stones for divinatory purposes, the method of the Chinese *I ching* consists in casting yarrow stalks (or coins) to yield randomly determined odd or even numbers. The philosophers of the later Sung age maintained that this randomness was essential, for "some truths could only be sought by means of the random cast of the stalks and the evolution of the all informing hexagram; this was achieved by means that were anything but systematic or responsive to reason" (Loewe, in Loewe and Blacker, 1981, p. 52). C. G. Jung noted that the Chinese mind appeared to be "exclusively preoccupied with the chance aspect of events. What we call coincidence seems to be the chief concern of this peculiar mind" (Jung, 1967, p. xxii).

Be it bibliomancy, which consists in a random opening of books such as the Bible, the Qur'ān, or Vergil's *Aeneid;* rhapsodomancy, which consists in writing out passages from books on separate slips and drawing one of them at random; or kledonomancy, the practice of appealing to a chance word overheard—all rest on randomness as the vehicle. (Incidentally, the Latin word for fate, *fatum,* comes from *for,* "to say." *Fatum* is "what is said.") As chance is unknowable in essence, so does randomness, a form of chance, appear as an appropriate means to grasp the unknown. The mathematical doctrine of chance can be applied to calculating the outcome of random throwing, but it does not replace the purpose of divination, which is to provide an answer to a question brought to it. [*See also* Divination.]

A skilled interpretation of such signs as those mentioned above is of central importance for divination and may be said to rely on the principle of coincidence or correspondence, according to which signs are somehow related to the human situation under consultation. It is assumed not only that there is a certain correspondence between the method of divination and the meaning obtained through it but that there is a correspondence between human affairs and the larger cosmic movement (as in, for example, the *I ching*) or the divine will. "The casting of lots is familiar in the Old and New Testaments as a method of ascertaining divine will" (Halliday, [1913] 1967, p. 206; cf. *Jos.* 6:14, *Jon.* 1:17, *Acts* 1:26, *Prv.* 16:33), and a divinatory message was regarded as sacred and mysterious (*Prv.* 16:10).

To designate the phenomenon of the coincidence of events and subjective psychic states, C. G. Jung adopts the term *synchronicity.* "Synchronicity," he explains, "takes the coincidence of events in space and time as meaning something more than mere chance, namely, a peculiar interdependence of objective events among themselves as well as with the subjective (psychic) states of the observer or observers" (1967, p. xxiv). Jung is inclined to value the "practical result of chance" more highly than the "theoretical considerations of cause and effect" (ibid., p. xxiii), and for that matter, he continues, "We must admit that there is something to be said for the immense importance of chance" (ibid., p. xxiv).

Miracle. A chance event may be considered a miracle, and a miracle taken for chance. For Hume, who denied chance, a miracle is "a violation of the laws of nature" supported by human testimony and sustained by belief (*Concerning Human Understanding* 10). A traditional Christian understanding is that represented by Thomas Aquinas: "When anything is done outside the order of created nature by a power unknown to us, it is called a miracle as regards ourselves" (*Summa theologiae* 1.110.4.2). He argues that just as ignorance of the cause is the source of amazement, so when the cause is completely hidden, as God is, a thing is wondrous in an unqualified way, and this is a miracle—"what is of itself filled with admirable wonder" (*Summa contra gentiles* 3.101; cf. Augustine, *City of God* 21.8). Over against the Humean interpretation, C. S. Peirce, from his tychistic standpoint, finds Butler's position of "the order of nature is a law to the doctrine of miracles" to be "in consonance with the higher teachings of modern science" ("Hume on Miracles," *Collected Papers* 6.547). Contemporary theists argue that a "dynamically stable world," which embraces chance, affords the possibility of miracles. [*See also* Miracles.]

Chance and the Unknown. Chance events, beyond human ratiocination and calculations, disclose the radical uncertainty that (at least from the human perspective) is present at the heart of reality. The interpretation of what chance is depends on whether one's worldview is religious or nonreligious. The fundamental unknowability of events—their mystery—can inspire awe. The religious mind has perceived in chance something sacred or a manifestation of the divine will. Some have placed chance within the governance of divine providence. Others reject it in deference to the same divine providence, arguing that what happens has already been determined by the transcendent scheme. Hence a seemingly chance occurrence, either fortunate or unfortunate, takes on the meaning of fate. In contrast, chance seen as pointing out the utter indeterminateness of things would signify the presence of free will.

[*See also* Fate.]

BIBLIOGRAPHY

Comprehensive works on chance in English are few. In other languages, one may profitably consult Kuki Shūzō's *Gūzensei no mondai* (1935; Tokyo, 1976), translated as *Le problème de la contingence* (Tokyo, 1966), and Wilhelm Windelband's *Die Lehren vom Zufall* (Berlin, 1870).

On the economic theory of risk, probability, and uncertainty, see Frank H. Knight's *Risk, Uncertainty and Profit* (New York, 1921). On the distinction between "class probability" and "actual singular events," see Ludwig Von Mises's *Human Action*, 3d rev. ed. (Chicago, 1963), and M. N. Rothbard's *Man, Economy, and State*, 2 vols. (Princeton, 1962). For a popular, readable introduction to the laws of chance and probability, see Darrell Huff's *How to Take a Chance* (New York, 1959). For a philosophical treatment of this subject, see D. H. Mellor's *The Matter of Chance* (Cambridge, 1971).

On the ancient Greek view of chance and fate, see William C. Greene's *Moira: Fate, Good and Evil in Greek Thought* (Cambridge, Mass., 1944). On Aristotle and the Scholastics, see Vincenzo Cioffari's *Fortune and Fate: From Democritus to St. Thomas Aquinas* (New York, 1935). On the Buddhist view of chance and causation, see David J. Kalupahana's *Causality: The Central Philosophy of Buddhism* (Honolulu, 1975). For C. S. Peirce's philosophy of chance, see his *Chance, Love and Logic* (1923; New York, 1949).

For a contemporary view of chance from a scientific perspective, see Max Born's *Natural Philosophy of Cause and Chance* (Oxford, 1951) and David Bohm's *Causality and Chance in Modern Physics* (Princeton, 1957). Jacques Monod's position is stated in his *Chance and Necessity* (New York, 1971), and Ernest Schoffeniels's critique is in his *Anti-Chance* (Oxford, 1976).

For a theistic position on chance, see Donald M. MacKay's *Science, Chance, and Providence* (Oxford, 1978), and William G. Pollard's *Chance and Providence* (New York, 1958).

On divination, see *Greek Divination*, by W. R. Halliday (1913; Chicago, 1967), and *Oracles and Divination*, edited by Michael Loewe and Carmen Blacker (New York, 1981), which contains a wide range of material from many cultures.

On the idea of synchronicity, see C. G. Jung's foreword to *The I Ching, or Book of Changes*, 3d ed., translated by Cary F. Baynes (Princeton, 1967), and his essays "Synchronicity: An Acausal Connecting Principle" and "On Synchronicity," in *The Structure and Dynamics of the Psyche*, 2d ed. (Princeton, 1969), vol. 8 of *The Collected Works of C. G. Jung*.

On miracles, see Antony Flew's "Miracles," in *The Encyclopedia of Philosophy*, edited by Paul Edwards (New York, 1967), vol. 5, and C. S. Peirce's "Hume on Miracles," in the *Collected Papers of Charles Sanders Peirce*, edited by Charles Hartshorne and Paul Weiss (Cambridge, Mass., 1960), vol. 6. Richard Swinburne's *The Concept of Miracle* (London, 1970) deals with the problem from the standpoint of philosophy of religion.

MICHIKO YUSA

CHANG CHI-HSIEN (1092–1126), Taoist master of the Sung period. Chang was the thirtieth head priest of the T'ien-shih Tao, or the Celestial Masters branch of Taoism, which derived its lineage from the Five Pecks of Rice (Wu-tou-mi Tao) Taoist movement begun by Chang Lu in the second century. He was also known as Chia Wen and as Tao Cheng. As a Taoist master, his clerical name was Hsiao-jan–tzu.

At the age of nine Chang became the head priest of the Celestial Masters sect and in 1103 he went to the imperial court of Emperor Hui-tsung, where he was admired for his ability to respond to the emperor's questions. In the twelfth month of 1103 he used a talisman to call down the legendary general Kuan-yü to slay a dragon and bring a flood under control. The following year he again served in the court, and after responding to an imperial question about the teachings of Taoism, he built an initiation platform, lectured on Taoism, and presented scriptures and talismans to the emperor. In addition, he performed Taoist ceremonies at the court. The emperor, pleased with these results, bestowed on him the title Hsü-ching Hsien-sheng ("master of tranquillity and the void"). The emperor refused to allow him to return to his home on Mount Lung-hu, but he eventually received permission after beseeching the emperor endlessly. At that time a Taoist temple was erected in his home province.

In response to an imperial command of 1107, Chang performed a Taoist ritual at Mount Lung-hu and used talismans to dispel evil spirits and cure countless sick people at the imperial court. Because of this skill, he was named to the office of *ta-hsü ta-fu* ("minister of the great void"), but he did not accept the position and returned home in the following year. In 1112 he was again summoned by the emperor, but he had a disciple go in his place. He secretly admonished the emperor that the Northern Sung dynasty would fall, but the emperor paid no attention. When the armies of the Chin advanced upon the capital, the emperor at last came to his senses and, recalling Chang's words, sent a messenger to summon him. At the moment the messenger arrived, however, Chang was writing his deathbed poem, and he died soon after; it is said that the capital of the Northern Sung fell that very day. The Sung emperor Wu-tsung, to succor his spirit, bestowed on Chang the posthumous name Hsü-ching Hsüan-t'ung Hung-wu Chen-chü ("perfected lord of tranquillity and the void, extensive in enlightenment and traversing the mysterious").

[*See also* Taoism, *article on* The Taoist Religious Community.]

BIBLIOGRAPHY

There is no monograph on Chang Chi-hsien readily available in English. Readers of Chinese may consult Chang Cheng-ch'ang's *Han t'ien-shih shih-chia,* fasc. 3 of *Tao-tsang,* no. 1066 (Shanghai, 1926).

KUBO NORITADA
Translated from Japanese by James C. Dobbins

CHANG CHÜEH (d. 184 CE), founder of the Yellow Turban sect. Chang Chüeh was heir to the doctrines of Yü Chi, a sorcerer and healer who preached and practiced in Shantung and who was probably the author of the *T'ai-p'ing ch'ing-ling shu* (Book of Great Peace, or Book of Great Equality), a text now lost. Having received a revelation that the "blue heaven" of the Han dynasty was to be replaced by a "yellow heaven" (yellow is the color of the Center) in the first *(chia-tzu)* year of the next new cycle of sixty years (i.e., 184 CE), around the year 175 Chang Chüeh dispatched eight apostles to convert the people of the central and eastern provinces of China. They preached doctrines closely related to those of the Five Pecks of Rice sect in Szechwan. Like the leader of the latter sect, Chang Lu, Chang Chüeh healed the sick by group confession (sins were believed to be the cause of sickness), organized collective worship under a quasi-military church hierarchy, and used sexual techniques to achieve sanctity. [*See the biography of Chang Lu.*]

Chang Chüeh's followers were called Yellow Turbans (Huang-chin) from the yellow kerchiefs they wore on their heads in token of their expectation of the "yellow heaven." They worshiped Huang-lao and were intent on inaugurating a golden age—the age of Great Peace—and a utopian state based on egalitarian ideas, as opposed to the Confucian ideas of social hierarchy. They regularly retired to oratories ("pure chambers," *ching-shih*) where they healed the sick by confession of sins and recitation of sacred scriptures. The followers of the sect were governed by moral codes and divided into thirty-six *fang* (a word that means both "regions" and "magic recipes"), local communities headed by "generals." The "three Changs," Chang Chüeh and his two brothers, Liang and Pao, were respectively generals of Heaven, Earth, and Man, symbolizing their embodiment of the all-embracing triad.

Over a ten-year period, Chang Chüeh enjoyed great success. He had several hundred thousand followers in eight provinces by the time he initiated the Yellow Turban rebellion in 184. Although Chang Chüeh and his brothers were caught and executed in the same year, they left behind a great number of communities of believers, and as late as 205 the Yellow Turbans still posed a military problem for the government. The Yellow Turban uprisings in eastern and northern China, taken together with Chang Lu's uprisings in the west, weakened the Han dynasty and contributed to its fall.

[*See also* T'ai-p'ing; Huang-lao Chün; Taoism, *overview article and article on* The Taoist Religious Community; *and* Millenarianism, *article on* Chinese Millenarian Movements.]

BIBLIOGRAPHY

Eichhorn, Werner. "Bemerkungen zum Aufstand des Chang Chio und zum Staate des Chang Lu." *Mitteilungen des Instituts für Orientforschung* 3 (1955): 291–327.

Fukui Kōjun. *Dōkyō no kisoteki kenkyū.* Tokyo, 1952. See pages 62–92.

Levy, Howard S. "Yellow Turban Religion and Rebellion at the End of the Han." *Journal of the American Oriental Society* 76 (October–December 1956): 214–227.

Michaud, Paul. "The Yellow Turbans." *Monumenta Serica* 17 (1958): 47–127.

ISABELLE ROBINET

CHANG HSÜEH-CH'ENG (1738–1801), Chinese historian and philosopher. A native of Shao-hsing (K'uai-chi district), Chekiang Province, and son of a district magistrate, Chang went to Peking as a student in 1762, and in the next ten years became acquainted with many of the leading writers of the day. Among his associates and mentors were, notably, Chu Yün (1729–81), whom he acknowledged as his master, and the philosopher and philologue Tai Chen (1724–77), whom Chang admired for his philosophical essays but criticized strongly for his opposition to the ideas of the Sung dynasty Confucian moralist Chu Hsi (1130–1200). As a youth Chang developed a keen interest in the art and theory of historical writing, admiring the T'ang dynasty historiographer Liu Chih-chi (661–721). As early as 1770 he had begun to formulate a theory of the development of civilization based on the Han court librarian Liu Hsin's theories of the history of types of writing. In 1778 he passed the examinations for the highest civil service degree *(chin-shih),* but he never took office, and supported himself usually through teaching appointments in local academies, commissions to compile local and family histories, and research and writing sponsored by patrons (notably Pi Yüan, 1730–97).

Chang articulated his vision of the human past in his local history of Ho-chou (1775; only fragments are extant), his *Chiao-ch'ou t'ung-i* (Philosophy of Bibliography, 1779), and especially in his monograph-length essay *Yüan-tao* (The Analysis of the Way, 1789). He saw all moral conventions, institutions, traditions of learning, and genres of writing as taking form in an early state of the human condition in which there was no distinction between public (official) and private aspects of life, when all kinds of writing were naturally beautiful or useful according to their function, anonymous and unmarred by personal vanity. This ideal state of affairs ended some centuries before Confucius. Thereafter, "officials were no longer teachers," and there was no longer a "unity of government *(chih)* and doctrine *(chiao)*"—Chang's idiom (following the Sung polymath Ou-yang Hsiu, 1007–1072) for saying that the primal unity of the human spirit was sundered forever, in an alienation of intellect from action. Intellectual history since that time has been a dialectical process of always incomplete vision of the truth, ages of philosophy, of scholarship, and of literary art succeeding each other endlessly, each age blind to the values it fails to realize. Chang crystalizes his vision in the famous one-line evaluation of the Confucian Classics, opening his collected essays, *Wen-shih t'ung-i* (General Principles of Literary and Historical Criticism): "The Six Classics are all history." By this he means that they are not authored books that formulate the *tao* of human society, but are exemplifications of this *tao*, being documents, residues of the functioning of the ancient society and state, an age when "the *tao* and its embodiments were one" *(tao ch'i ho-i)*. This *tao* cannot be reduced to "empty words" *(k'ung yen)* and formulas; it must be grasped intuitively through the study of institutions and human acts, which the historian must present just as they were, without bias.

In this aspect of his thought Chang is close to the Ming dynasty Confucian moralist Wang Shou-jen (Wang Yang-ming, 1472–1529); but unlike Wang he never himself had a religious drive toward self-cultivation. [*See the biography of Wang Yang-ming.*] Chang had several Buddhist friends, whom he teased good-naturedly, but he was open-mindedly willing to own that Buddhism might be saying something true and valuable in its own way. He could hardly be called a Taoist, but his vision of intellectual history owes not a little to Chuang-tzu. He had strong conservative prejudices about the status of women, expressed in several vigorous essays attacking the poet Yüan Mei (1716–1798). Chang was impatient with the philological scholarship fashionable in his time, his thinking being more akin to the so-called T'ung-ch'eng circle of literary men. He much admired the early Ch'ing historian Huang Tsung-hsi (1610–1695) and other Chekiang authors, and is sometimes classed as a "member" of an "Eastern Chekiang school" of historical learning.

BIBLIOGRAPHY

Demiéville, Paul. "Chang Hsüeh-ch'eng and His Historiography." In *Historians of China and Japan*, edited by W. G. Beasley and E. G. Pulleyblank, pp. 167–185. Oxford, 1961.

Nivison, David S. *The Life and Thought of Chang Hsüeh-ch'eng, 1738–1801*. Stanford, 1966. Includes an annotated bibliography of important Chinese and Japanese sources.

Yü Ying-shih. *Lun Tai Chen yü Chang Hsüeh-ch'eng*. Hong Kong, 1976. An English edition of this work is forthcoming.

DAVID S. NIVISON

CHANG LU (fl. 184–220), grandson of Chang Tao-ling, founder of the sect of the Celestial Masters, and the sect's third Celestial Master. In 184 CE Chang Lu led the sect in rebellion against the Han dynasty and established an independent state in Han-chung, in the west, which he governed for thirty years. In 215 he surrendered to the Han general Ts'ao Ts'ao and was rewarded with honors that included a fiefdom. After the founding of the Wei dynasty in 220 by Ts'ao Ts'ao's son, Chang Lu lived some years at the Wei court. It may be said that both the existence of the sect as an organized church and its official recognition by the government were due to his efforts. The Celestial Masters sect became the first institutionalized Taoist movement, distinguished on this point from the other popular beliefs and messianic movements of the time, and especially from the Taoist seekers after long life, who were unorganized and scattered. The movement of the Celestial Masters spread to North China by the end of the third century and, by the end of the fourth century, to all of China. It counted among its adherents many powerful families.

The church was divided into twenty-four dioceses (later twenty-eight), corresponding to the twenty-four breaths of the year (one every fifteen days) and, later, to the twenty-eight divisions of the Chinese zodiac. The hierarchy of the church and its way of addressing the powers on high were modeled on imperial and bureaucratic usages. The church set up wayside inns all over the state where food and shelter were available to travelers at no charge. Each household of followers contributed a tax of five pecks of rice, whence the name of the sect, the Way of Five Pecks of Rice (Wu-tou-mi Tao).

The focal center of each diocese was the oratory, presided over by "libationers" *(chi-chiu),* a married hereditary priesthood. These priests mediated between the faithful and the divine and knew as well how to ward off demons. The petitions of the faithful, transmitted by the rising smoke of incense and by the spirits exteriorized from the priest's body, were borne to the Three Heavens. Letters could be sent to the Three Officials of Heaven, Earth, and Water *(san-kuan).* One copy, placed on a mountain, rose to Heaven, another was buried in the ground for the Earth official, and a third was cast into the river for the Official of Water. Other rituals involve talismans drawn by priests; these were burned, their ashes were mixed with water, and the talismanic holy water was then drunk by believers. The sung liturgies were based on religious texts, in particular on the *Tao-te ching.* The *Hsiang-erh,* a commentary on the *Tao-te ching* attributed to Chang Lu, was used as a kind of catechism in the instruction of the faithful. Morals and law were combined: diseases were believed to be caused by evil deeds, and hence the sick were healed by rites of expiation, ceremonials, confessions, and punishment. The misdeeds of the faithful, such as theft and drinking, also fell under the jurisdiction of the sect. Road repair or imprisonment was the usual punishment.

The year was marked by a religious calendar. At the equinoxes, offerings were made to the god of the earth and the god of the soil, and healing talismans were distributed to the sect's followers. At the solstices, sacrifices were made for the salvation of the souls of the dead. Communal feasts *(ch'u)* were offered during the first, seventh, and tenth months, and also on religious occasions such as an initiation or the consecration of an oratory. At each new moon a communal sexual ritual was celebrated, the Union of the Breaths *(ho-ch'i),* which Buddhist sources describe as a licentious orgy, but which some texts still extant show to be a ceremony of highly stylized erotic choreography of religious and cosmic significance.

The sect of the Celestial Masters is still in existence, and its leaders claim direct descent from Chang Tao-ling and Chang Lu. Many of the present rituals, sacrifices, and festivals derive from rituals of the Celestial Masters of the third century.

[*See also* Taoism, *overview article and article on* The Taoist Religious Community.]

BIBLIOGRAPHY

Eichhorn, Werner. "Bemerkungen zum Aufstand des Chang Chio und zum Staate des Chang Lu." *Mitteilungen des Instituts für Orientforschung* 3 (1955): 291–327.

Fukui Kōjun. *Dōkyō no kisoteki kenkyū.* Tokyo, 1952. See pages 62–92.

Hsiung Te-chi. "*T'ai-p'ing ching* ti tsuo-chih he ssu-hsiang chi ch'i yü Huang-chin he T'ien-shih-tao ti kuan-hsi." *Li-shih yen-chiu* 4 (1962): 8–25.

Stein, Rolf A. "Remarques sur les mouvements du taoïsme politico-religieux au deuxième siècle ap. J.C." *T'oung pao* 50 (1963): 1–78.

ISABELLE ROBINET

CHANG TAO-LING, semilegendary figure of the second century CE, depicted in hagiographies as a master of long life *(ch'ang-sheng)* who put his disciples to tests, vanquished demons, and prepared the elixir of immortality. He is said to have received in 142 CE a revelation from T'ai-shang Lao-chün, the deified Lao-tzu, who bestowed on him the title of Celestial Master *(t'ien-shih).* The god gave him the "Doctrine of the Orthodox One [Resting on] the Authority of the Alliance" *(cheng-i meng-wei tao),* revealing that the demoniac Six Heavens had been abolished and their reign replaced by a golden age governed by the Three Heavens. The people were to honor no gods other than those of the Alliance, the masters were to eschew all payment, and blood sacrifices were to be banished.

Subsequently, Chang Tao-ling gathered together many disciples in Szechwan and launched a campaign for the reform of the religious practices of a people described as having lapsed into degeneracy. He started a health cult and wrote several books; however, his works are now lost and consequently nearly nothing is known about his doctrines. He is said to have established the basis of a theocratic state divided into twenty-four parishes corresponding to the twenty-four breaths of the year (one every fifteen days). This was later altered to twenty-eight, to correspond to the divisions of the Chinese zodiac. The followers of the sect were obliged to pay a tax of five pecks of rice, whence came the description of the sect as the Way of Five Pecks of Rice (Wu-tou-mi Tao).

Chang Tao-ling is considered the founder of the Taoist sect of the Celestial Masters (T'ien-shih Tao). His eldest son, Chang Heng, succeeded him, and Chang Heng in turn was succeeded by his son, Chang Lu. Under Chang Lu's leadership the movement rose in rebellion against the Han. The Way of the Celestial Masters was the first organized Taoist movement and has continued down to the present day in Taiwan through a succession of Taoist masters who are allegedly lineal descendants of Chang Tao-ling. Many texts in the *Tao-tsang* (the Taoist canon) derive from this religious movement, whose tendency is liturgical, demonological, and more or less shamanistic.

[*See also* Taoism, *overview article and article on* The Taoist Religious Community, *and the biography of Lao-tzu.*]

BIBLIOGRAPHY

Imbault-Huart, Camille. "La légende du premier pape des taoïstes et l'histoire de la famille pontificale des Tchang." *Journal asiatique* 2 (1844): 389–461.

Welch, Holmes. "The Chang t'ien-shih and Taoism in China." *Journal of Oriental Studies* 4 (1957–1958): 188–212.

ISABELLE ROBINET

CHANG TSAI (1021–1077), also known as Chang Heng-ch'ü, the second major Neo-Confucian thinker in the traditional lineage of Neo-Confucian teachers. Chang Tsai was a native of Ch'ang-an in modern Shensi. His study of what became central Neo-Confucian texts began at the age of twenty-one when he corresponded with and then met Fan Chung-yen (989–1052), a prominent Confucian official. Fan suggested that Chang Tsai begin his study with the *Chung-yung* (Doctrine of the Mean). This advice led Chang Tsai to study Confucianism, but like many Neo-Confucians he also studied Buddhism and Taoism, particularly their religious practices such as meditation. Eventually, however, he rejected their philosophies and returned to Confucian classics. Chang Tsai was appointed to office in 1057 and became widely recognized as one of the major interpreters of Confucian teachings. He eventually resigned from office over disagreement with the reform measures of Wang An-shih (1021–1086), a figure of major political influence during the Sung dynasty. Chang was appointed once again, only to retire and die on the trip home from the capital in 1077.

For Chang Tsai, the focus of his return to Confucian teachings was his interest in two of the classics, the *I ching* (Book of Changes) and the *Chung-yung*, works that served as the foundation of his philosophical and religious thought. Chang Tsai's prominent position in the lineage of Neo-Confucian teachers, a position in part the result of the lineage drawn up by the great synthesizer of Neo-Confucianism, Chu Hsi (1130–1200), derives from the interpretive stance he developed toward these works and from his position as teacher to both Ch'eng Hao (1032–1085) and Ch'eng I (1033–1077), two of the most prominent figures in the development of Neo-Confucian thought.

Like Chou Tun-i (1017–1073), the first major Neo-Confucian teacher, Chang Tsai based much of his philosophy upon the *I ching*. For Chang Tsai, the *t'ai-chi*, or Great Ultimate, refers to the source of all existence, which he takes to be *ch'i*, the material or vital force of existence itself. Thus *t'ai-chi* is identified with *ch'i* and *yin* and *yang*, the symbols of polar opposites in Chinese thought, as well as with the Five Elements *(wu-hsing)*, the basis of an early cosmological theory of the nature of change. Although later modified by other thinkers, this *ch'i*-based monism continued to play an important role in Neo-Confucian metaphysics.

Chang Tsai's thought had far-reaching religious implications as well. While Neo-Confucianism has often been thought to be primarily a rationalistic system whose major influence was intellectual, a more recent reassessment of the tradition suggests that Neo-Confucianism also contains a profound religious dimension. The focus of this religious perspective is the central role assigned to the figure of the sage *(sheng)* and to the goal of sagehood. To become a sage became increasingly important as the goal of Neo-Confucian learning and self-cultivation.

When Neo-Confucianism is considered in this context, Chang Tsai's philosophical system is fully religious. In Chang Tsai's most celebrated work, the *Hsi ming* (Western Inscription), the monistic metaphysical structure of *ch'i* is enlarged to include a poetic vision of the unity and interdependence of the universe and its multifaceted phenomena:

> Heaven is my father and earth is my mother, and even such a small creature as I finds an intimate place in their midst.
>
> Therefore that which extends throughout the universe I regard as my body and that which directs the universe I consider as my nature.
>
> All people are my brothers and sisters, and all things are my companions. (de Bary et al., 1964, p. 469)

Some have called this passage the foundation of Neo-Confucian ethics. Others have expanded its meaning to include not only ethics but a religious dimension that ultimately comprehends the religious goal of sagehood.

Later Neo-Confucians primarily valued Chang Tsai's doctrine of the sage "forming one body with the universe." This doctrine represents both the Neo-Confucian continuity with its classical Confucian heritage and an enlargement of the Neo-Confucian system. At the center of Chang Tsai's teaching is the idea of *jen*, humaneness or human-heartedness, in many ways the salient teaching of the classical Confucian tradition. This basic quality, which was for Confucius and Meng-tzu the bond between human society and the ways of Heaven *(t'ien)* and hence fundamental to the underlying moral structure of the universe, was expanded by Chang Tsai to encompass the universe itself, since for the sage to form "one body with the universe" suggests the complementarity and fundamental identity of microcosm and macrocosm. The doctrine illustrates as well Chang Tsai's belief in the fundamental goodness and purpose of the universe and in the potential of the individual to realize the ideal of the sage.

In the teaching of "forming one body with the universe," Chang Tsai also claimed to distinguish Confucianism clearly from Buddhism and Taoism. For him the universe and its processes have a real existence. In turn, human life is looked upon as intrinsically valuable and ultimately the very foundation for the realization of sagehood. For Chang Tsai, such a view is clearly distinguishable from Taoism and Buddhism, both of which require a radical departure from the universe as it is given in order to fulfill the soteriological quest. In Chang Tsai's terms, Taoism and Buddhism both emphasize escape from the world, while Confucianism finds fulfillment and ultimate identity precisely within the changes found in this world, a world of *ch'i* rather than of emptiness. The sage accepts the ultimate reality of *ch'i* and its inherent goodness, he acknowledges the infusion of *jen* throughout the very structure of the universe itself, and thus he can fulfill the ideal of the sage, "forming one body with the universe."

[*Chang Tsai's thought is discussed further in* Jen and I. *See also* Confucian Thought, *article on* Neo-Confucianism; Ch'i; *and* T'ai-chi.]

BIBLIOGRAPHY

The thought of Chang Tsai is introduced with a translation of the *Western Inscription* as well as of his other major work, *Correcting Youthful Ignorance,* in *A Source Book in Chinese Philosophy,* translated by Wing-tsit Chan (Princeton, 1963), pp. 495–517, and *Sources of Chinese Tradition,* compiled by Wm. Theodore de Bary and others (New York, 1964), vol. 1, pp. 465–470. Selections from Chang Tsai's writings are included in the major anthology of Sung dynasty Neo-Confucianism compiled by Chu Hsi and Lü Tsu-ch'ien, translated into English by Wing-tsit Chan as *Reflections on Things at Hand* (New York, 1967). Discussions of Chang Tsai's thought may be found in Fung Yu-lan's *A History of Chinese Philosophy,* 2d ed., vol. 2, *The Period of Classical Learning,* translated by Derk Bodde (Princeton, 1953), pp. 477–498, and in Carsun Chang's *The Development of Neo-Confucian Thought,* vol. 1 (New York, 1957), pp. 159–183. More detailed discussions of specific problems in the thought of Chang Tsai may be found in Siu-chi Huang's "The Moral Point of View of Chang Tsai," *Philosophy East and West* 21 (April 1971): 141–156, and Chun-i T'ang's "Chang Tsai's Theory of Mind and Its Metaphysical Basis," *Philosophy East and West* 6 (1956): 113–136.

RODNEY L. TAYLOR

CHANNING, WILLIAM ELLERY, American Unitarian minister. Channing was born on 7 April 1780 in Newport, Rhode Island, of a distinguished family. He entered Harvard College in 1794, graduated in 1798, and was elected a regent of Harvard in 1801. He began his lifelong ministry at Boston's Federal Street Congregational Church in 1803. Channing defended the liberal Congregationalist ministers in 1815 against an attack in *The Panoplist* by Jedidiah Morse, who accused them of covertly holding the views of the English Unitarian Thomas Belsham, who held that Christ was strictly human in nature, with human imperfections. Channing replied that the liberals were Arians and hence believed that Christ's character included intellectual, ethical, and emotional perfection. Thrust into prominence by this defense, Channing was asked to prepare a manifesto for the liberals, which he did in "Unitarian Christianity," his 1819 ordination sermon for Jared Sparks in Baltimore. This sermon unified the liberals around Channing's leadership; yet when the American Unitarian Association was organized in 1825, he refused the office of president, because he did not want Unitarianism to become a sect.

Channing was the outstanding representative of early American Unitarian theology in the period prior to the Transcendentalist controversy. He emphasized the authority of reason and revelation, the unique and infallible authority of Jesus, human educability to a Christlike perfection, and human essential similarity to God. His thought includes a modified Lockean philosophy, an Arian Christology, and an optimistic view of human nature.

John Locke's influence is present in Channing's arguments for the rational character of revealed religion and his emphases on miracles and fulfilled prophecies as evidences for the truth of Christianity. In his 1819 sermon "Unitarian Christianity," he called for a careful use of reason in interpreting scripture. Channing held that reason judges even the claim of a revelation to authority. Reason approves the claim of the Christian scriptures to authority. Rationally interpreted, these scriptures yield the doctrines of the unipersonality and moral perfection of God.

Channing modified his Lockean epistemology when he became acquainted with the Scottish common-sense philosophy of Thomas Reid, Adam Ferguson, and Francis Hutcheson. In his opinion, Richard Price corrected Hutcheson's thought in a way that more effectively met the arguments of David Hume, thus making room for new ideas other than those derived from sensation and reflection. Disagreements exist, however, about the extent to which Channing's later thought became more akin to that of the Transcendentalists.

Channing's Arian Christology and his optimistic view of human nature were closely related. He viewed Christ as morally perfect. He based his Christology on scriptural evidences of Christ's perfection and his own belief in the freedom of the will. Christ exemplified the perfection to which others can attain. In order to account for Christ's flawless moral perfection, Channing inferred from it Christ's preexistence; yet he maintained that others should aspire to, and can achieve, a similar perfection.

Channing advocated prison reform and opposed alcoholism and other social evils, but he was reluctant to speak out openly against slavery. He acknowledged the fairness of rebukes for his silence. In 1835 he published *Slavery*, which had a marked effect in arousing public opinion against the slave system; thereafter his outspoken opposition to slavery cost him friends and support. His writings during this period show that his optimism and his rejection of the doctrine of depravity in no way blinded him to the reality of sin.

Channing's essays made him famous on both sides of the Atlantic Ocean. These, along with his sermons, lectures, and *Slavery*, were translated into German, French, Hungarian, and other languages. Channing became ill on a vacation trip and died at Bennington, Vermont, on 2 October 1842.

BIBLIOGRAPHY

Works by Channing. The most accessible editions are *The Works of William Ellery Channing*, 6 vols. (Boston, 1903), and *The Works of William E. Channing, D.D., with an Introduction; New and Complete Edition, rearranged; To which is added, The Perfect Life* (Boston, 1886).

Works about Channing. Conrad Wright has written a balanced introduction to Channing's thought in "The Rediscovery of Channing," chapter 2 of his *The Liberal Christians: Essays on American Unitarian History* (Boston, 1970). The most complete study of Channing's philosophy and theology is Robert L. Patterson's *The Philosophy of William Ellery Channing* (New York, 1952), with detailed, informative footnotes. Channing's concern for social issues is emphasized by Jack Mendelsohn in *Channing: The Reluctant Radical* (Boston, 1971). The most recent study is Andrew Delbanco's *William Ellery Channing: An Essay on the Liberal Spirit in America* (Cambridge, Mass., 1981).

JOHN C. GODBEY

CHANTEPIE DE LA SAUSSAYE, P. D. (1848–1920), Dutch theologian, philosopher, and historian of religions.

Pierre Daniël Chantepie de la Saussaye, who was of Huguenot descent, studied theology at the University of Utrecht, where he obtained his doctorate in 1871. After a short stay in Bonn and Tübingen, where he worked with J. T. Beck, he served as a minister in the Dutch Reformed church (1872–1878). In 1878 he was appointed to the new Chair of the History of Religions in the faculty of theology at the University of Amsterdam. There he stayed until 1899, when he was appointed to the Chair of Theological Encyclopaedia, Doctrine of God, and Ethics in the faculty of theology at the University of Leiden, a post that he held until his retirement in 1916. Chantepie de la Saussaye was one of the representatives of the movement in Dutch Protestantism called "ethical theology," which stressed the value of religion both as a reality of the heart and as an existential datum with ethical implications.

Chantepie de la Saussaye defended the autonomy of the new science of religion, but he was always sensitive to its presuppositions and limitations. He had no knowledge of Asian languages; his own historical research concentrated on Old Germanic religion. After his appointment in Leiden, he practically left the field of history of religions and paid attention thereafter primarily to questions of faith and ethics. Among his students in Leiden, Gerardus van der Leeuw seems to have been the most sensitive to what Chantepie de la Saussaye saw as the direction that science of religion in a theological faculty should take.

Chantepie de la Saussaye's major work, the two-volume *Lehrbuch der Religionsgeschichte* (1887–1889; translated as *Manual of the Science of Religion*, 1891), is a handbook of the science of religion in a broad sense. As one of the first of such works, it is one of the discipline's great historical documents, and it deserves close attention. In its first edition the *Lehrbuch* was divided into four sections: an introduction followed by phenomenological, ethnographical, and historical parts. In the introductory section Chantepie de la Saussaye, distancing himself from the philosophical systems and general reductive theories of religion current at the time, discusses the new science of religion. He ascribes its rise to the discovery of many new source materials for ancient religions; to the fact that world history can now be described as an entity; and in particular to the modern philosophical view of religion as one whole. Over against theological distinctions, he asserts, modern philosophy recognizes "the unity of religion in the variety of its forms" and considers religion as a single phenomenon subject to "philosophical knowledge." Significantly, he pays tribute here to G. W. F. Hegel, who distinguished "the various modes for studying religion (metaphysical, psychological and historical) and made us see the harmony between the idea and the realization of religion." For Chantepie de la Saussaye the empirical science of religion is distilled, so to speak, from philosophy of religion as Hegel conceived it.

Chantepie de la Saussaye distinguishes more sharply than Hegel, however, between philosophy and history of religion, and between the "essence" and "manifestations" of religion: whereas philosophy of religion is concerned with the "essence" of religion, history of religion as an empirical discipline studies its "manifestations." History of religion is subdivided into an ethnographical section treating peoples "without history," and a much larger section treating the religions of peoples with written documents.

As for philosophy of religion, it treats religion in both its subjective and its objective aspects, and consequently consists of what Chantepie de la Saussaye calls a "psychological" and a "metaphysical" part. Metaphysical philosophy of religion stresses God's objective speaking in nature and life, whereas psychological philosophy of religion stresses man's subjective reaching out to God. For Chantepie de la Saussaye, as for C. P. Tiele and van der Leeuw, "psychological" denotes not so much an empirical, verifiable reality as a philosophical category indicating the subjective side of human experience. It is important to see how large Hegel still looms in the background of Chantepie de la Saussaye's thinking on religion and consequently his phenomenology.

The *Lehrbuch* was an important contribution to the new science of religion in another respect, too. The phenomenology of religion contained in its second section was the first of its kind and drew largely on Hegel; it was published in 1887 before the work of Franz Brentano and Edmund Husserl, who were to conceive of phenomenology in a totally different way. Appropriately, given the clear distinction that Chantepie de la Saussaye made between philosophy and history of religion—he viewed the latter as an empirical discipline—he conceived of phenomenology as a discipline mediating between history on one hand and philosophy on the other. Its task was to collect and classify the various religious phenomena, and to establish the meaning of the different classes of phenomena.

At the very beginning of the phenomenological section of the *Lehrbuch*, Chantepie de la Saussaye points out that a phenomenology of religious forms deals with facts of human consciousness; that these outward forms of religion can be understood only on the basis of "inward processes"; and that it is their particular "inward relation" that distinguishes religious from nonreligious acts, ideas, and sentiments. Consequently, phenomenology of religion was in principle closely connected with psychology. This was the line taken by his pupil Gerardus van der Leeuw, who was to develop explicitly this psychological-phenomenological research of religion. [*See* Phenomenology of Religion *and the biography of van der Leeuw*.]

Chantepie de la Saussaye himself does not go so far, treating only the forms and not the contents of religious consciousness. Already in his dissertation of 1871 he had considered religion as a kind of species comprising a number of different forms. To develop a classification of these forms, he distinguishes three sectors in religion—cult, doctrine, and religious feeling, of which the first is the most stable sector and the last is practically limited to the present. The *Lehrbuch*'s phenomenological section describes (1) objects of worship, religious acting, sacred persons, religious communities, and sacred writings and (2) religious thinking (myth and doctrine). Religious feeling does not receive separate treatment.

It has often been noted that this phenomenological section was entirely dropped in the second edition of the *Manual*. Chantepie de la Saussaye explained that in his view this section had to be either considerably enlarged or omitted. He chose to omit it for reasons of space, and also because phenomenology constituted a border discipline between history and philosophy requiring separate treatment in a new book. Unfortunately—and significantly—this book never appeared. It was his pupil van der Leeuw who worked in this direction and developed phenomenology of religion as a special branch of the study of religion.

In point of fact, Chantepie de la Saussaye's wish to develop a phenomenology of religion as a special field between history and philosophy—between empirical facts and systematic thought—did not achieve much more than an outward classification and systematization of religious forms. This he did on the basis of the Hegelian legacy, with its distinction between the essence and the manifestations of religion. His phenomenology—which was quite independent of the phenomenological movement started by Franz Brentano, Edmund Husserl, and others—was a very formal discipline relegating the problem of religious meaning mainly to philosophy or to the scholar's intuition, or, worse, to the scholars' personal religious views and convictions.

BIBLIOGRAPHY

For bibliographic data on Chantepie de la Saussaye's person and work, see my book *Classical Approaches to the Study of Religion*, vol. 2, *Bibliography* (The Hague, 1974), pp. 37–38.

Two books by Chantepie de la Saussaye exist in English translation. *Manual of the Science of Religion* (London, 1891) is the English translation of the first edition of the *Lehrbuch der Religiongeschichte*, 2 vols. (Freiburg im Breslau, 1887–1889). The second and third editions of the *Lehrbuch*, of which Chantepie de la Saussaye was no longer the author but the editor, have not been translated into English. *The Religion of the Teutons* (Boston, 1902) is a considerably expanded translation of a book published in Dutch in 1900.

JACQUES WAARDENBURG

CHANTING. Many scholars trace chanting to the earliest stages of human development, a time when speech was presumably not differentiated from chant. Even today Saami (Lapp) women in Finland, Jewish women in Morocco, and Santali women in Bihar, India, unconsciously replace sobbing with chanting while lamenting their dead. Australian Aborigines, when excited, break into a torrent of words governed by rhythms and cadences resembling chant. Hungarian dirges and some Khanty (Ostiak) and Mansi (Vogul) tribal melodies of Siberia consist of sung declamations, while the Zulu, Yoruba, Igbo, and Bantu-speaking peoples possess real "melody languages." Contemporary shamans and medicine men on several continents are known to chant sacred rites in a secret language, often invented by themselves. Furthermore, not only American Indian Navajos, African Khoi, and Liberian Jabos use tone levels in their speech: contemporary Burmese, Siamese, Annamese (Vietnam), and Chinese recognize two to nine different tone levels in their languages. The ancient Chinese even distinguished whole families and clans by musical signs conferred upon them by tradition.

Close observation of ordinary conversation in any culture shows that musical intervals recur in the simplest of sentences. A middle pitch is usually maintained, and emphatic words, clauses, and conclusions are indicated by change of pitch. When a speaker addresses an audience, the pitches become more pronounced, and a "melody of speech" emerges. It is reported that the Greek orator Demosthenes (fourth to third century BCE) employed an assistant to blow a whistle (*tonorion*) during his speeches to remind him of certain pitch levels. Cicero and Gellius (author of *Noctes Atticae*) wrote that some classical authors memorized and performed their speeches with the aid of a flute player to insure the right intonation of the melodic line. Isocrates (436–338 BCE), the Athenian orator and teacher, insisted that the perfect oration was really a musical composition. It is therefore entirely possible that formalized chanting and cantillation of holy scriptures were derived from "singing to speech".

The modern definitions of chant (from Latin *cantare*, "to sing, to intone") and cantillation (from Latin *cantillare*, "to sing low, to hum") apply to the recitation of sacred writings with musical tones, usually improvised, as in synagogues, churches, mosques, and Asian temples. Chant in all these liturgies is usually monophonic, unaccompanied, and in so-called "free rhythm," which results from the recitation of prose texts. The term *chant* applies in particular to the liturgical melodies of the Jewish and Samaritan synagogues, and to the Byzantine, Russian, Armenian, Syrian, Ambrosian, Gallican, Mozarabic, and Roman churches. The latter is better known as Gregorian chant and plainsong. *Chant* also refers to the traditional method of singing psalms and canticles in the daily offices of the Roman and Anglican churches. Chanted also are the Islamic Qur'ān, the Indian Vedas, and Buddhist scriptures.

Hebrew Chant. The term *cantillation* applies primarily to the recitation of the Hebrew Bible by Jews and Samaritans. Cantillation of the Bible on special occasions is already attested to in *Deuteronomy* 31:12, *2 Kings* 22:1–13, and *Nehemiah* 8:1–8. But regular biblical readings were established only in the fifth century BCE, when Ezra the Scribe chanted from the Law in the Jerusalem Temple twice a week on market days to all the people assembled there. This is the earliest evidence of regular biblical recitation in public. Since the reader had to amplify his voice in order to be heard, his unconscious chanting established the first biblical cantillation.

Cantillation gave particular expression to word meaning (accent) and phrasing (syntax). The importance of melody was prescribed in no uncertain terms by the Talmud (*Meg.* 32a), where Yoḥanan (second century) says, "He who reads [the Bible] without a melody and studies without a tune is referred to by the verse 'Wherefore I gave him statutes that are not good . . . ' (*Ez.* 20:25)." The melody was logogenic, or word-bound; in other words, the interpolation of extraneous syllables or words into the text was forbidden. Cantillation was not a prominent practice in the Jerusalem Temple but in the course of time became the most important part of the synagogue service. The Jews preserved biblical cantillation in oral tradition for at least one thousand years (fifth century BCE to fifth century CE).

Melodic patterns or motifs were indicated by a system of finger and hand movements called cheironomy (from Greek *cheir*, "hand"), a practice depicted by Sumerians and Egyptians on bas-reliefs and in tombs in the fourth and third millenium BCE. These gestures were intended to refresh the memory of those who had previously learned the melodies by ear. Cheironomy remained in use until the seventeenth century in Greek monasteries, although modern musical notation was available. Hindus and Jews employ cheironomic signs even today, and various systems have been developed by different groups.

The first cheironomic signs were simple: the rise of the melody was signaled by an upward stroke of the hand (╱), the fall by a downward stroke of the hand (╲), and the rise and the fall on a single syllable by the junction of the two signs (/\). Various combinations of these basic symbols followed. It was musical notation written on the air.

When Hebrew ceased to be a living language, the Masoretes, transmitters of the biblical tradition, devised written symbols to safeguard the proper pronunciation, phrasing, and melodies of biblical Hebrew. The task took five centuries to complete (fifth to tenth century CE). The Masoretes transferred the cheironomic signs from the air to parchment and paper. It must be noted that other cultures employed similar symbols for similar purposes; indeed, scholars disagree as to which culture was the first to transfer hand movements from the air to parchment. Greece, India, the Middle East, and Europe have all been suggested. But the symbols are so elementary that any culture could have invented them independently without outside influence (see table 1).

These first ekphonetic signs (from Greek *ekphōnēsis*, "pronunciation") were later refined, became more complicated, and gave way to neumes (from Greek *neuma*, "nod, sign"). By combining and recombining ekphonetic signs a variety of melodic motifs were created and became neumes. The major difference between ekphonetic signs and neumes is that ekphonetic signs indicate not a freely invented melody but a succession of fixed melodic formulas. Sometimes ekphonetic signs occurred only in the beginning and end of a phrase, as in Samaritan biblical chanting or psalmtones of Gregorian chant.

The *ṭa'amei ha-miqra'*, the Hebrew accents, were invented by grammarians, and many scholars believed in the past that their sole purpose was grammatical. Jews call the oral renditions, the vocal utterances of the biblical text, "cantillation," while the written symbols are called "accentuation." Three different systems of accentuation were developed by the Masoretes. The Palestinian system consisted almost entirely of dots and numbered only ten basic accents. The Babylonian system consisted predominantly of letters positioned above the word (supralinear). Each letter represented the initial of a musical term, such as *z* for *zarqa'* or *y* for *yetib*. This system became very popular in the Middle East and was employed, for example, by the Yemenite Jews until they emigrated to Israel in 1948. The Tiberian system of twenty-eight accents, universally in use today, consists of a combination of dots and other symbols.

The accents were provided for the books of the Bible that were read in public, namely: the Pentateuch, the Prophets, *Esther*, *Lamentations*, *Ruth*, *Ecclesiastes*, *Song of Songs*, *Psalms*, and in some communities *Job* and *Proverbs*. While the Hebrew accents are identical in all the Jewish Bibles of the world, their musical interpretation differs from place to place. The reason for this phenomenon is the indefinite nature of nondiastematic ekphonetic signs, which do not indicate musical intervals or pitches. Hebrew accents never developed an exact pitch notation, unlike the neumes of medieval European churches, which employed signs for single notes as well as for groups of notes.

Four accents in the oral traditions of Babylonian and Yemenite Jews can be compared (see example 1). Neither interval structures nor directions of the melodies agree. This extreme divergence in cantillation motifs was caused by the total isolation of Yemenite Jews. Whereas written communication with Babylonia or Egypt existed, personal encounters were extremely rare. Thus an exchange or transmission of oral musical tradition was curtailed. By contrast, large areas of North Africa, northern Arabia, Persia, and Central Asia (Bukhara) as well as the Mediterranean show similarities in biblical cantillation (see example 2). Furthermore, these cantillations seem closely related to the Babylonian type discussed previously.

The eastern European types of cantillation practiced by Polish, Lithuanian, Hungarian, and Russian Jews are related. These are, however, unrelated to German, Italian, French, or Sefardic (Spanish-Portuguese) cantillations: the latter four are also not related to one another. How is it, then, that Hebrew cantillation is instantly recognizable anywhere in the world? The reasons are unvarying text (Hebrew) and the ekphonetic symbols that are prescribed for every word of the sentence and have a syntactical as well as a musical function. They provide a solid structural basis for cantillation.

In addition to biblical cantillation, Jews recognize formalized chanting without ekphonetic symbols, namely that employed in blessings, certain prayers in the synagogue and at home, the study of Mishnah, the study of the *gemara'*, and the study of the *Zohar*. In addition, Yemenite Jews recite from the Aramaic translation of the Bible on the Sabbath and on holidays in the synagogue. It is worth noting that the Yemenite Jews

TABLE 1. *The Earliest Ekphonetic Signs (Derived from Cheironomy)*

ISRAEL	SAMARIA	GREECE	ROME	ARMENIA	INDIA
qadma pashta /	arqenu-enged /	oxeia /	acut /	sour /	udātta /
silluq sof pasuq /\ *or* :	afsaq .:\ *or* :	bareia \	gravis \	pouth \	anudātta __
atnah ∧ *or* ⊥	ana(h)u ○ *or* <	periponeme ⌒ *or* ∧	circumflex ⌒ *or* ∧	barouk ⌒	svarita ∪ *or* (

are the only ones to perpetuate this Second Temple tradition and translate every Hebrew sentence into the Aramaic vernacular of the time.

Chanting in all these cases is based on a melody that consists of an opening motif (*initium*), followed by an undifferentiated two-tone motif (*tenor*) and a final cadence (*finalis*). The melody varies in length according to the number of words in the sentence, but the melodic motifs do not vary.

A. Z. Idelsohn (1921–1922) demonstrates the similarity of Yemenite Jewish cantillation and Gregorian chant, showing their common origins, perhaps from Temple times (see example 3). In Eastern melodies the formulas are less rigid than those of Gregorian psalmody. In Byzantine melodies the same formulas can be used at the beginning, the middle, or the end of a chant.

The Samaritans cantillate the Hebrew Bible according to *sidra' miqrata'* (the Aramaic form of the Hebrew *seder ha-miqra'*), nondiastematic ekphonetic symbols. There are ten in number, but only three basic ones are remembered (see Spector, 1965, pp. 146–147): *arkenuenged* (has the function of a colon), *afsaq* (full stop), and *anau* (pause, with the function of a semicolon). The Samaritan high priest Amran ben Ishaq still practiced the dynamic interpretations of *shayala'* (question), *z'iqa* (shouting), and *ba'u* (supplication) and sang them into a tape recorder for posterity (recorded 1951–1953).

Of ten extant cantillation styles, two are most prominent (see example 4). The *logogenic*, or word-bound style, does not permit the inclusion of extraneous syllables or words. It was originally practiced by priests only and forbidden to the laity. It was intervallically stepwise, syllabic, and without ornamentation of the melody. The *pathogenic-melogenic* style, derived from passionate emotion and melody, permits the interpolation of extraneous nonsense syllables into the text if the text is shorter than the melody. It is particularly effective in the public reading of the Decalogue on the Festival of Shavu'ot. In this recitation the melody often overshadows the text. The nonsense syllables are "*ee-no-a*."

Byzantium. Scholars apply the term *Byzantine music* to Eastern ecclesiastical chant sung in Greek. In spite of the language it is maintained that this music was not a continuation of ancient Greek music but contained Near Eastern musical elements. (The hellenized Near East was part of the Byzantine empire.)

Byzantine ecclesiastical music, like Near Eastern music, was entirely vocal, monophonic, unaccompanied, and devoid of meter. The use of organs and other musical instruments was forbidden inside the churches, similar to the prohibition in synagogues and (later) mosques. The liturgical books intended for chanting of lessons were performed in ekphonetic style, midway between recitation and singing. On solemn occasions actual singing replaced the cantillation. For training Christian congregations in singing, Jewish readers and precentors from synagogues were chosen who had previously converted to Christianity. Especially trained for the office, they made it possible to introduce into Christian worship not only chanting but also antiphonal singing, particularly psalms for solo voice with congregational responses. Performances varied from simple recitation to elaborate cantillation. The musical structure of the psalm melody consisted of (1) an initial clausula (*initium*), leading to the note on which the verse is chanted, (2) a repeated or slightly changed note of the recitation (*tenor*), (3) an occasional *mediant*, or half clause, and (4) the *finalis*, a cadence marking the end of the verse. In Eastern melodies the formulas are less rigid than those of Gregorian psalmody. In Byzantine melodies the same formulas can be used at the beginning, the middle, or the end of a chant.

The rise of the Kontakion is closely associated with the name of Romanus, who was a Jew by birth (d. 555 CE). Born in Syria, he became deacon of the Christian church in Phoenicia and went to Constantinople. He was culturally a Near Eastern musician-priest. It is reported that Romanus composed more than one thousand Kontakia. The first part of a monostrophic hymn in his honor has been preserved; it was sung on the first day of October, when the Byzantine church celebrates the Feast of Saint Romanus (see example 5).

Gregorian Chant. Gregorian chant is the traditional music of the Roman Catholic church. Scholars maintain that it is rooted, like the music of the Byzantine church, in the pre-Christian service of the Jews. It acquired distinctive characteristics in the third and fourth centuries and was fully developed by the seventh century. It deteriorated in the sixteenth century and was revived in the nineteenth.

Many Gregorian practices were taken from the synagogue. The hours of the daily office are modeled after the prayers of the Jews, beginning with the evening prayer after sunset. The *Book of Psalms*, already used in the Jerusalem Temple, was made even more prominent by the church. The terms *Alleluya* and *Amen* are Hebrew. The Sanctus of the Mass was derived from the Qiddush of the Jews, as demonstrated by Eric Werner (1946, p. 292). The melodies show stepwise movement. Melodic rises or falls of the intervals of a second and a third are common, but those of a fifth are rare. The melodies can be classified as syllabic (one note to a syllable), neumatic (two to five notes to a syllable), and melismatic (long, highly ornamented phrases). The chant consists of one melodic line with neither harmony nor polyphony to support it.

EXAMPLE 1. *Comparison of Four Accents in Babylonian and Yemenite Cantillation* SOURCE: Spector (1951).

EXAMPLE 2. *Comparison of Accents for Intoning the Pentateuch in Six Traditions of Cantillation*

SOURCE: Idelsohn (1967), p. 44.

EXAMPLE 3. *Similarity of Yemenite Jewish Cantillation and Gregorian Chant.* (1) From Psalm 81. (2) From *Commemoratio brevis,* ascribed to Hucbald (tenth century). SOURCE: Idelsohn (1921–1922), pp. 28–29.

EXAMPLE 4. *Two Styles of Cantillation.* (1) Logogenic style. (2) Pathogenic-melogenic style. SOURCE: Spector (1965), p. 149.

(1)
Bådeš eššēlíši elsíyyat bắni
In the third month, when the children
yišrá'el miyyáres mísrem: beyyom
of Israel were gone out of the land of Egypt: the same
ezze ba'u medbar sini ⁄.·.
day came they into the wilderness of Sinai ⁄.·.
(2)
3
Bådeš eššēlíši elsíyyat bắni ee-no-a
In the third month, when the children
yišrá'el miyyáres mísrem : beyyom
of Israel were gone out of the land of Egypt: the same
ezze ba'u medbar sini ⁄.·. ee-no
day came they into the wilderness of Sinai ⁄.·.

EXAMPLE 5. *Byzantine Hymn Sung on the Feast of Saint Romanus* SOURCE: Wellesz (1961), p. 155.

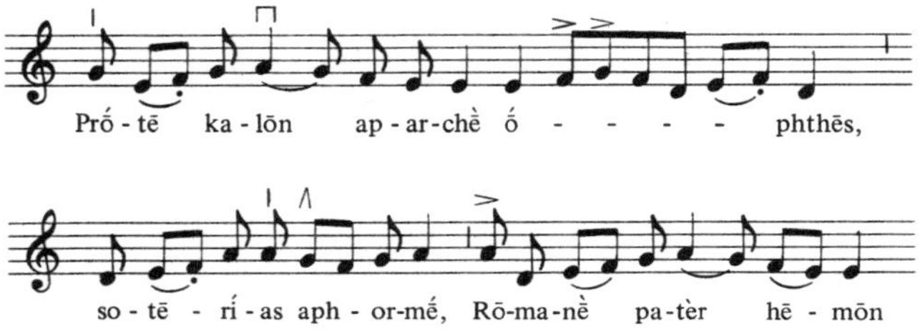
Prṓ - tē ka - lōn ap - ar - chḕ ṓ - - - - - phthēs,
so - tē - rí - as aph - or - mḗ, Rō - ma - nḕ pa - tèr hē - mōn

EXAMPLE 6. *Comparison of (1) Yemenite Jewish Psalmody with (2) Gregorian Psalmtone* SOURCE: Apel (1970), p. 35.

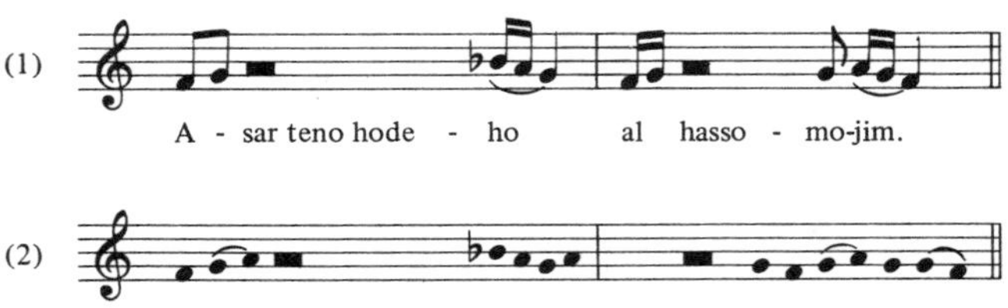
(1)
A - sar teno hode - ho al hasso - mo-jim.
(2)

EXAMPLE 7. *Comparison of (1) Kyrie Eleison with (2) Biblical Chanting (Ex. 12:21) of Babylonian Jews*
SOURCE: Idelsohn (1921–1922), pp. 517–518.

(1)
a b
Ky - ri - e e - le - i - son, Do - mi - ne mi - se - re - re. Chri - stus Do - mi - nus, fac - tus est
c b d b
o - be - di - ens us - que ad mor - tem. Qui pas - su - rus ad - ve - nis - ti prop - ter nos.
(2)
a 3 b
Wa - jiq - ra mo - šę lĕ - ḥol ziq - ne jis - ra - el wa - jo - mẹr ă - le - ḥẹm, mi - šĕ - ḥu
c 3 3 3 b 3
uq - ḥu la - ḥẹm ṣon lĕ - miš - pĕ - ḥo - tẹ - ḥẹm wĕ - ša - ḥă - ṭu hap - pa - saḥ

Example 8. *Qur'anic Call to Prayer.* (1) From Istanbul. (2) From Palestine.

Sources: (1) Lachmann (1929), p. 120; (2) Idelsohn (1967), p. 30.

Example 9. *Recitation of the Ṛgveda*

Source: Fox-Strangways (1967), p. 247.

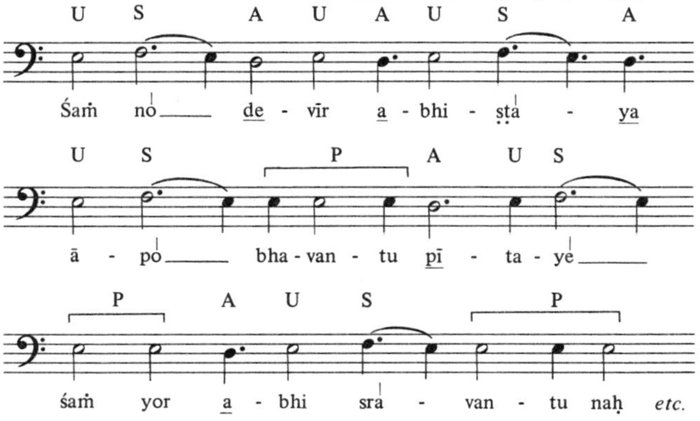

Example 10. *Recitation of the Yajurveda*

Source: Fox-Strangways (1967), p. 248.

EXAMPLE 11. *Recitation of the Sāmaveda* SOURCE: Jairazbhoy (1975), p. 51.

transposed from A♭ to D
♩= 59
Om o - o gnā - i ā yā - ā - hi vo - i - to - yā - ā - ā - i to - yā - ā - ā - i
gṛ - ṇā - no ha - vya - dō - to yā - ā āī to - yā - ā - āī nā - i - ho -
tā tā - ā - ā tā - ā - āī bā - ā - ā - ā - au - ho - va hi - i - i - ṣi

EXAMPLE 12. *Tibetan Recitation Chant of Phyogs Dus Kun Nas* SOURCE: Ellingson (1979), p. 123.

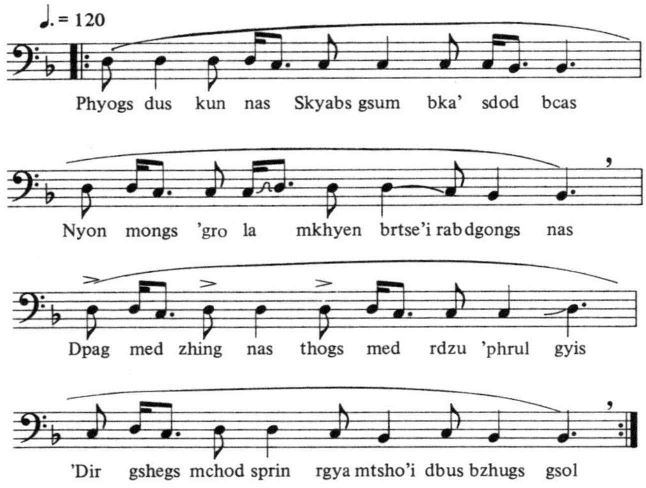
♩. = 120
Phyogs dus kun nas Skyabs gsum bka' sdod bcas
Nyon mongs 'gro la mkhyen brtse'i rabdgongs nas
Dpag med zhing nas thogs med rdzu 'phrul gyis
'Dir gshegs mchod sprin rgya mtsho'i dbus bzhugs gsol

EXAMPLE 13. *Tibetan Melodic Chant of Mgon Po'i 'Debs* SOURCE: Ellingson (1979), p. 127.

♩= 60
(solo)
♩= 48
(chorus)
Voices
Cymbals* and drums
Hūṃ ngön po
Mgon po'i
thugs dam bskang ba dang gzhan gyi
gnod pa bzlog pa dang (etc.)

EXAMPLE 14. *Tone Contour Chant of Khrung Khrung Gi Lam Glu Ring Mo* SOURCE: Ellingson (1979), p. 145.

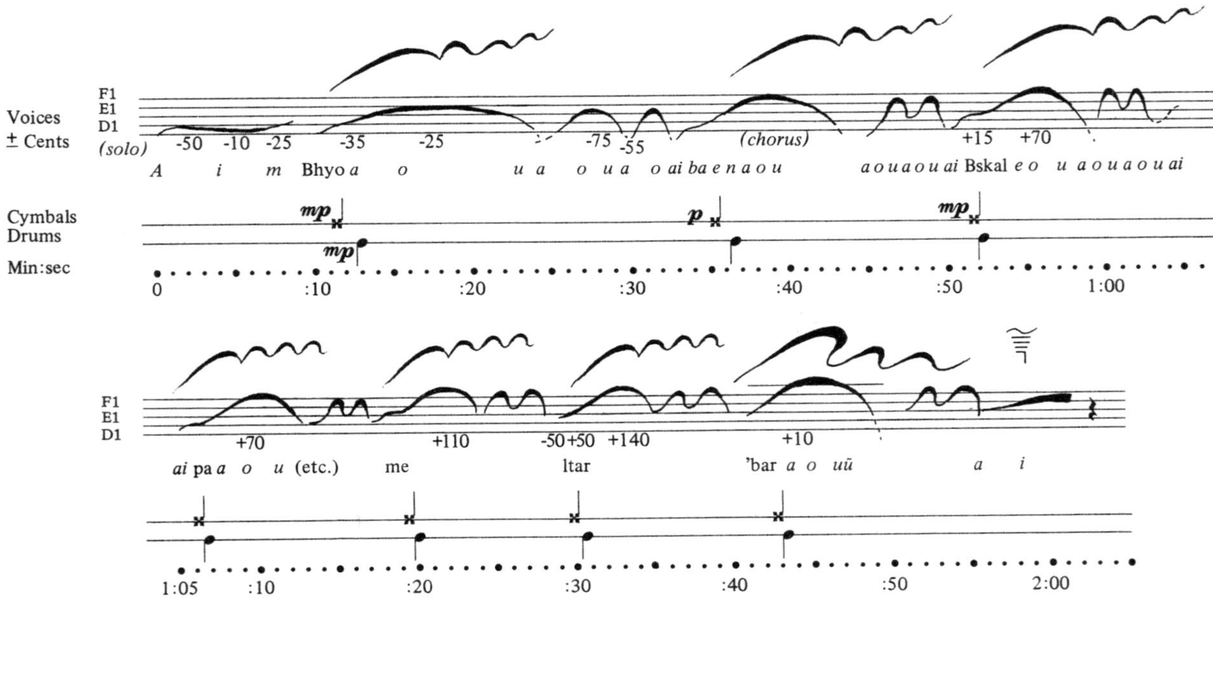
Voices ± Cents
F1
E1
D1
(solo)
-50 -10 -25 -35 -25 -75 -55 (chorus) +15 +70
A i m Bhyo a o u a o u a o ai ba e n a o u a o u a o u ai Bskal e o u a o u a o u ai
Cymbals
Drums
Min:sec
mp
p
0 :10 :20 :30 :40 :50 1:00
+70 +110 -50+50 +140 +10
ai pa a o u (etc.) me ltar 'bar a o uū a i
1:05 :10 :20 :30 :40 :50 2:00

Similarities between Yemenite Jewish psalmody and the first Gregorian psalmtone can be shown (see example 6). A. Z. Idelsohn (1921–1922) shows parallels between Babylonian, Persian, Yemenite, and Oriental Sefardic melodies of the Jews and Gregorian chant. Not only are the same motifs employed but similar modes as well (see example 7). The mode, the Greek Dorian, an E-mode, is the Pentateuch mode of the Jews, and is in widespread use in Middle Eastern and Mediterranean countries.

Armenia. The Armenian ekphonetic signs and neumes called *khaz* have never been deciphered, although rich source materials from the ninth to the twelfth centuries exist in Soviet Armenian, European, and Israeli libraries and museums. Contemporary scholars (e.g., Robert Atajan, 1978) believe in an independent origin of the *khaz* and reject an earlier theory (see, for example, Fleischer, 1895–1904) that the Armenian *khaz* were derived from Greek neumes. The Armenian *khaz* consist of two independent systems, a prosodic system for recitation and a musical system for singing according to *khaz*. The Hebrew and Samaritan ekphonetic signs discussed previously have no such division: one system governs both prosody and melody.

The Armenian *khaz* numbers ten symbols, five prosodic (*thaw*, *sosk*, *aibatatz*, *entamna*, and *storat*) and five musical (*erkar*, *ssuch*, *shesht*, *olorak*, and *buth*). According to Robert Atajan, the prosodic *khaz* relate to the peculiarities of Armenian phonetic pronunciation and have no bearing on the music. Syntactic symbols in the prosodic system, however, are of particular significance in the musical structure of the sentence: *storaket* ("deep point") is a comma, *mitshaket* ("middle point") is a semicolon or colon, and *vertchaket* ("final point") is a period. The musical signs *erkar* and *ssuch* indicate a lengthening or shortening of tone duration. The other three, *shesht*, *olorak*, and *buth*, represent tone pitches or rather melodic formulas based on Armenian folk tunes (see table 2).

Armenian musical notation was already mentioned in the fifth century CE by Kasar Parbezi in his *History of Armenia*, but no musical symbols were preserved. From the tenth to the twelfth centuries art and music flourished, and twenty-five neumes were developed to indicate pitch, volume, duration, tone color, ornamentation, syntax, and prosody. From 1400 to 1600, *khaz* notation went into decline; it was revived only in the nineteenth century by the music theorist Baba ("father") Hamparzum (born Hamparzum Limonjian) in Constantinople. In this new and simplified *khaz* notation a great number of liturgical chants and folksongs were written down by the musicologist Komitas and are thus preserved for future generations.

TABLE 2. *The Ten Basic Symbols of the Armenian Khaz*

MUSICAL	PROSODIC
erkar ~	thaw ⸝ *or* ⸝
ssuch o	sosk ↗
shesht ⁄ *or* /	aibatatz ..?.
olorak ⁄ᴘ *or* ⁄ᴘ	entamna ·◡·
buth — *or* \	storat ·;·

The Qur'ān. The chanting of the Qur'ān is regulated not by ekphonetic signs or neumes but by oral tradition, which varies from place to place. The word is paramount, and no ornamentation is permitted. Sudden stops within the Qur'anic sentence are a special feature. The call to prayer varies from country to country. Syllabic, elaborate melismas are often incorporated (see example 8; both examples are in *maqam* Hijaz, but other *maqamat*, or modes, are used in different Muslim areas). [*For further discussion of Qur'anic recitation, see* Tilāwah.]

India. The Vedas (from Sanskrit *vid*, "to know, to understand"), the sacred texts of the Hindus, were probably composed by Aryan tribes who invaded India from the northwest around 1500 BCE. The sacred texts had been handed down in oral tradition with accents at least since the fourth century BCE, as reported by the grammarian Pāṇini, who presumably knew the living practice. The interpretation of the accents is by no means uniform. Pāṇini wrote: "A vowel pronounced in a high register is called *udātta*, a vowel pronounced in a low register is called *anudātta*, and the connection of both is called *svarita*." Some modern scholars maintain that *udātta* is a middle tone, higher than *anudātta*, and that *svarita* is higher than *udātta*. Only male members of the priestly brahman caste are eligible to recite the Vedas.

The Vedas were for hundreds of years handed down orally and not committed to writing, unlike the sacred books of the Jews, Christians, and Muslims. The Hindus relied on the spoken word for three thousand years, and even today the Vedas are recited from memory; every precaution is observed to avoid the smallest error, which, it is believed, may produce disaster. This belief is similar to the one held by the Jews of Yemen, who maintain that a mistake in the public reading of the Bible in the synagogue can cause the death of little children. To avoid catastrophe the precentor who commits an error has to repeat the entire verse in the synagogue.

As the Vedic language evolved into classical Sanskrit,

the priests feared that the archaic language of the Vedas might become corrupt and the meaning of the texts forgotten. Consequently the Vedas were written down. The earliest surviving manuscripts date from the eleventh century.

Four compilations of the Vedas exist: (1) the *Ṛgveda*, the Veda of verses, contains more than 1,000 hymns; (2) the *Yajurveda*, the Veda of sacrificial sayings (*yajus*), contains verses and formulas dealing with sacrifices; (3) the *Sāmaveda*, the Veda of songs (*sāman*), contains verses of the *Ṛgveda* set to notated melodies for singer-priests; (4) the *Atharvaveda* is a collection of magical formulas and spells, little known today. The Vedas occur in two forms: the form in which they are recited for the purpose of preservation and transmission to students, and the form in which they are recited at sacrifice. Since large-scale sacrifices are infrequent today, little is known about the sacrificial form.

The *Ṛgveda* is recited to three tones: the "raised" (*udātta*), the not raised (*anudātta*), and the "sounded" (*svarita*). The *svarita* is marked with a perpendicular line over the syllable, the *anudātta* with a horizontal line beneath; the *udātta* and *pracaya* ("accumulated tone" following *svarita*) are unmarked (see example 9, where U = *udātta*, A = *anudātta*, S = *svarita*, and P = *pracaya*). The *Yajurveda* is recited on the notes D, E, F or F# (see example 10).

The *Sāmaveda* is the most musical of all (see example 11). It alters and expands the words of the *Ṛgveda* to make them suitable for chanting. The original text was often distorted by the insertion of meaningless words and syllables. The grammatical and prosodic specifications of the *Ṛgveda* have been given a musical meaning. The practitioners of the *Sāmaveda* believe that the *sāman* is a melody to which words were found, not the other way around. The three-tone nucleus (C–E) of the *Ṛgveda* and *Yajurveda* was extended both upward and downward by approximately semitone in each direction B–F). The *Atharvaveda* does not seem to be recited according to set rules.

Tibet. Tibetan Buddhist chants are divided into *'don*, recitation chants; *rta*, melodic chants; and *dbyaṅs*, tone contour chants. The general designation for the monastic chant repertoire is *'don cha*. The recitation chants are stylized recitations that employ reiterating pitch and rhythmic patterns according to the words in the sentences (see example 12).

Rta are melodic chants with distinctly patterned melodies. Unlike *'don*, they are relatively independent of their texts; unlike *'don* they are considered melodic and musical. However, their performance is called "speaking." They are similar to melodies in Western and non-Tibetan performance traditions (see example 13).

Dbyaṅs are tone contour chants and are considered the most beautiful chants used in Tibetan music. They are very slow, low-pitched, and most complex. In contradistinction to *'don* and *rta*, which are "spoken," the *dbyaṅs* are "intoned." They include changes in intonation, pitch, loudness, and (most remarkably) overtone mixtures, which are perceived as two or more pitches produced simultaneously by one singer. Unlike the simpler *'don* and *rta*, they are notated (see example 14). The melodic contour is defined by thickening lines that indicate increasing loudness; rising lines indicate rising pitch, falling lines falling pitch; sharp angles indicate interruptions, breath pauses, and so forth. (All Western notations are by Ter Ellingson.)

Secular Chant. Secular chanting is prominent in the epic poetry of many countries; thus it is used for the most dignified and elaborate form of narrative poetry dealing with heroic, legendary, and historical events as well as with the drama and romance of love. Epics are usually chanted by a single performer, but in some Asian countries contests between two rival performers are customary and may last several days. In ancient times the narrator of epics chanted without instrumental accompaniment. This custom survives in certain areas, for example Tibet and Kurdistan. (The Jews of Kurdistan have epics of their own, such as *David and Goliath* and the *Crossing of the Red Sea*, whose narratives are distinct from the biblical texts.) Contemporary performers, however, accompany themselves on a stringed instrument, preferably a violin (Persian, *kemanje*; Turkmen, *ghyjjak*) or a lute (Kirghiz, *kobuz*; Turkmen, *dutar*; Tajik and Uzbek, *dumbura*). Melodies are word-bound (logogenic), and the musical structure admits of little improvisation. The melodies tend to be predictable and repetitious.

Chant is usually defined as an intermediate stage between speaking and singing. Some writers call chant "elevated speech." Chant, however, can take many forms—from speaking on one tone (*Sprechgesang*) to singing in full voice, as in some churches. The melody is always word-bound and moves usually stepwise within intervals of fourths or fifths. Notation for chant developed from hand movements (cheironomy) to ekphonetic notation and neumes. Today, chant is written in contemporary musical notation.

[*For further discussion of the relation of religion and music, see the various articles under* Music; *for discussion of Japanese Buddhist chant, see especially* Music and Religion in Japan.]

BIBLIOGRAPHY

Apel, Willi. *Gregorian Chant* (1958). Bloomington, Ind., 1970.
Atajan, Robert. "Armenische Chasen." In *Essays on Armenian*

Music, edited by Vrej Nersessian, pp. 131–148. London, 1978.

Belayev, Victor M. *Ocherki po istorii muzyki narodov SSSR*. 2 vols. Moscow, 1962–1963.

Ellingson, Ter. "*Don rta dbyangs gsum*: Tibetan Chant and Melodic Categories." *Asian Music* 10 (1979): 112–156.

Fleischer, Oskar, *Neumen-Studien*. 2 vols. Leipzig, 1895–1904.

Fox–Stragways, A. H. *The Music of Hindostan* (1914). Oxford, 1967.

Høeg, Carsten. *La notation ekphonétique*. Copenhagen, 1935.

Idelsohn, A. Z. "Parallelen zwischen gregorianischen und hebraeisch-orientalischen Gesangsweisen." *Zeitschrift für Musikwissenschaft* 4 (1921–1922): 515–524.

Idelsohn, A. Z. *Jewish Music in Its Historical Development* (1929). New York, 1967.

Jairazbhoy, N. A. "An Interpretation of the Twenty-two Śrutis." *Asian Music* 6 (1975): 38–59.

Lachmann, Robert. *Die Musik des Orients*. Breslau, 1929.

Spector, Johanna. "A Comparative Study of Scriptural Cantillation and Accentuation (Pentateuch)." Ph. D. diss., Hebrew Union College, 1951.

Spector, Johanna. "The Significance of Samaritan Neumes and Contemporary Practice." In *Studia Musicologica*, edited by Zoltan Kodály, vol. 7, pp. 141–153. Budapest, 1965.

Spector, Johanna. "Musical Tradition and Innovation." In *Central Asia: A Century of Russian Rule*, edited by Edward Allworth, pp. 434–484. New York, 1967.

Szabolcsi, Bence. *A History of Melody*. Translated by Cynthia Jolly and Sara Karig. London, 1965.

Wagner, Peter. *Einführung in die gregorianischen Melodien*. 3 vols. Leipzig, 1895–1921. Volume 1 has been translated as *Origin and Development of the Forms of the Liturgical Chant* (London, 1901).

Wellesz, Egon. *A History of Byzantine Music and Hymnography*. 2d ed. Oxford, 1961.

Werner, Eric. "The Doxology in Synagogue and Church, a Liturgico-Musical Study." *Hebrew Union College Annual* 19 (1946): 275–351.

JOHANNA SPECTOR

CHAOS, in the history of religions, refers primarily to the primordial condition, precosmic period, or personified being found in many oral and literary mythologies. It is commonly, although not always legitimately, taken to mean the horribly confused state, muddled matrix, vacuous condition, or monstrous creature preceding the foundation of an organized world system. By extension, the idea of chaos in myth and ritual may also apply to any anomalous condition, event, or entity outside conventionally sanctioned codes of order. The meaning and significance of chaos in world mythology has, moreover, a special thematic relationship with the idea of the beginnings of the world, or of any structured condition. [*See* Cosmogony.] The word *beginning* is, in fact, etymologically connected with the Old English *on-ginnan* and the Old Norse *gina*, in both of which lurks the mythological image of the cosmogonic Ginnungagap, the primordial void that spawned the giant Ymir (the Primordial Man) in ancient Norse tradition. From a cross-cultural perspective, the image of chaos is therefore especially prominent in cosmogonic and anthropogonic myths, as well as in many types of origin myths and passage rituals concerned with some transitional situation in human life or with some significantly altered state of affairs, whether for well or ill. Chaos appears, for example, within the context of the condition of death or the dream time of sleep, flood mythology, apocalyptic imagery in general, or foundational legends and rites pertaining to a new sociopolitical tradition.

The English word *chaos* derives directly from the Greek *chaos*, which in Hesiod's *Theogony* (c. eighth century BCE) denoted a cosmogonic "yawning gap, chasm, or void," from which generated the successive worlds of the gods and mankind. Hesiod, who drew upon earlier mythological sources, rather neutrally depicted the original chaos as merely the empty, dark space that allowed for the penetrating movement of erotic desire and for the appearance of Earth (Gaia) as the secure home for all subsequent created forms and beings. But the *Theogony* also displays the mythological premise for a more negative evaluation of chaos, since the earliest generations of Titanic gods, most closely identified with the untrammeled passion and anarachy of the primitive chaos condition, must be violently defeated by Zeus to insure the permanence and universality of the Olympian order. The primal chaos is itself only the blind abyss necessary for the creation of the physical world, but *chaos* here also refers to the mythic period—and, by implication, to a kind of "chaos-order" or condition—of the pre-Olympian gods who struggle against the imposition of Zeus's all-encompassing rule.

Because of their general impact on the colorations of meaning popularly conjured up by the modern use of the term *chaos*, it is worth citing two other ancient Western documents. In the priestly tale of *Genesis* (c. fourth century BCE) found in the Hebrew scriptures, chaos is reduplicatively called *tohu va-vohu*, a dark, watery, formless waste or "limbo-akimbo" that must be wrested into order by the willful fiat of a god completely separate from the stuff of creation. In a somewhat similiar vein, although more somberly stressing a hostile jumble of primal matter over blank vacuity, Ovid (43 BCE–18 CE), in his poetic compendium of mythology known as the *Metamorphosis*, describes chaos as "all ruse and lumpy matter . . . in whose confusion discordant atoms warred." As in the biblical version, Ovid's creation requires a nameless god, or "Kindlier Nature," who brings order out of the formless chaos.

The above-mentioned accounts serve to exemplify the commonplace tendency to dichotomize the meaning of existence into the negative-positive polarities of chaos and cosmos, confusion and order, death and life, evil and good, or, more theologically, into some dualistic distinction between the absolutely sacred and creative being of a transcendent "kindlier" God, on the one hand, and the utterly profane nothingness and nonbeing of a passively neutral or actively belligerent chaos. Clearly, these distinctions have both ontological and moral implications, so that it may also be said that the polarized evaluation of the mythic chaos is the backdrop for the theological and philosophical elaborations on such problems as *creatio ex nihilo* and theodicy. Indeed, the overall issue here directly affects the modern academic understanding of religion, since a whole tradition of Western scholarship defines religion as the contrast between the sacred and the profane, or, to use Peter Berger's more straightforward sociological formulation, as the "establishment through human activity of . . . a sacred cosmos that will be capable of maintaining itself in the ever-present face of chaos" (*The Sacred Canopy*, New York, 1967, p. 51).

A comparative assessment of world mythology shows, however, that such pat divisions are not always warranted, so that, for instance, the apparently fundamental contrast between chaos and cosmos may reveal more of a dialectical relationship. This ambivalence is at least suggested by the observation that the Greek root of the term *kosmos* does not so much refer to the creation of an absolute, universal, and final world order (although with Pythagoras in the sixth century BCE it will take on this sense as its basic meaning) as to the more relative and transitive idea of the "cosmetic" alteration of some more natural, plain, and primitive condition. *Cosmos* in this sense is the differentiated, deferential, and ornamental order; it is the painted and tattooed body of chaos—pretty and pleasing primarily to the eye of the beholder. One tradition's chaos, in other words, is another's cosmos, and vice versa. It depends on the vantage point, or, at least, on whether the original cosmogonic chaos is conceived advantageously. In the broadest sense, chaos stands for the root "otherness" and "strangeness" of existence and the ironic indeterminacy of all human constructs.

"Creation out of chaos," in like manner, may not just refer to the appearance of order and reality out of the void, but the creative possibility of many different orders and worlds. As the hidden sum of all potential *kosmoi*, chaos is intrinsically linked to the transformative nature of phenomenal and cultural existence. The tensed relationship of "chaos and cosmos," then, usually has sociopolitical as well as metaphysical implications, and this, it would seem, has much to do with the interpretation of chaos seen in particular myths and cultural traditions. This, of course, begs the question as to the ultimate premise of world construction, but it is exactly the fundamental existential puzzles of "something from nothing" and the interrelationship of unity and multiplicity, plenitude and limitation, that give rise to a moot diversity of possible answers and that are always addressed to some extent in chaos mythology.

Images of Chaos. Any excessive or transitional aspect of the natural world (e.g., the untamed vegetation of a jungle, the blurring of light and dark at twilight, the frenzied winds of a storm, and so on) may be taken as a cipher for the mythological chaos; but, as already suggested by the biblical allusions, the most prevalent natural metaphor for chaos is water. [*See* Water.] Given water's infinite fluidity, its protoplasmic vitality, as well as its lethal and regenerative potencies, it is hardly surprising that images of a vast ocean, a turbulent sea, or some other murky, cloudy, frothy, and misty mixture of air and water is used in many myths to depict the original broth of creation.

Common also are references to the moist darkness and foggy gloom of the precosmic condition, along with various depictions of a swirling vortex or whirlpool that links the water imagery with the more abstract ideas of the abysmal void. Other traditions speak of a primal muddle of earth and water, as in the "earth diver" myths that tell of a fragment of muddy soil (often imagined as a central hillock or mountain) rescued from the depths by some animal god or sky deity. Both in tribal cultures and in ancient civilizations there are descriptions of a watery, labyrinthine underworld of the dead, and accounts of limitless seas and rivers surrounding and penetrating the inhabited world; these imply that the dark waters of creation continue to flow around, through, and beneath the hollows of the established cosmos. Finally, there are the worldwide myths of a great flood (or of excessive heat and drought) in the distant past or apocalyptic future that are clearly charged with the cosmogonic idea of a regression to an initial state of total solvency. In these myths, the twin potency of chaos comes to the fore, since the deluge is devastating to the existing world yet simultaneously establishes the necessary precondition for a new creation.

Another important category of chaos symbolism concerns the universal imagery of an embryonic condition or womblike form. This is especially exemplified in the so-called "cosmic egg" myths (along with the analogous myths involving a bloody lump of flesh or a creatively fertile yet "empty" vessel, such as a pot, sack, gourd, cocoon, or drum), that stress the preexistence of some ovarian matrix within which is mysteriously harbored the structured multiplicity of all cosmic forms. [*See* Egg.] While they sometimes involve an external agent of creation responsible for the production and development of the cosmic zygote, these myths often emphasize the organic conjunction of cosmogonic unity and phenomenal duality as well as the spontaneous self-sufficiency of the creation. It is in this way that the undifferentiated unity and implicate order of the cosmic egg can be said to come before any divine chicken, or, in the words of Samuel Butler, "a hen is only an egg's way of making another egg."

Theriomorphic and anthropomorphic personifications of chaos are often imagined as the gigantic and misshapen offspring of the primal waters, embryonic condition, or dark void. Recalling Hesiod's portrait, such creatures represent the individualized embodiments of chaos within the differentiated world. The actions of these creatures, moreover, show that chaos has a "history" that continuously impinges upon human history. The primary denizens of the chaos time can be categorized as: (1) dragon-serpent figures, often having composite avian-aquatic features (e.g., Vṛtra in Vedic mythology); (2) animal or hybrid man-animal trickster figures (e.g., Raven and Crow in North American Indian tradition); (3) a female demoness, a terrible mother, or chaos hag who has associations with the primal waters and "mother earth" imagery (e.g., Tiamat in Babylonian myth); (4) cosmic giant figures who, while theoretically androgynous, are often more male than female (e.g., P'an-ku in Chinese tradition); and (5) an incestuous brother and sister couple or a set of divine twins of ambiguous sexuality (e.g., Izanagi and Izanami in Japanese mythology). All of these chaos creatures are particularly related to cosmogonic and other origin myths, are often combined within a single mythic tradition, and are frequently portrayed in rituals concerned with significant seasonal and social transitions (e.g., worldwide celebrations of the New Year). While they may be suppressed, hidden, and transformed in various ways, all of them have popular folkloric surrogates (e.g., the revenant, demon, witch, and fool) and continue their ambivalent careers at the margins of the human world. [*See especially* Dragon.]

The underlying logic that emerges from this rapid cross-cultural survey suggests that chaos is both prior to the world as its cosmogonic source and existentially interstitial to the world as its transformative ground. Because it lies before and between any single order, or always "in relation" to any explicit world, the religious meaning of chaos remains profoundly ambiguous. By its very nature, then, chaos can be variously imagined as simply before and other than, as negatively destructive of, or as creatively challenging to, some ordered world system. Given this queasy multivalence, it is also possible to see why in cultural history any single cosmological tradition will most often seek to deny the relativity of its own vision of order by officially upholding a predominantly negative image of chaos.

Negative and Positive Evaluations. The negative evaluation of chaos commonly takes the form of a mythic and ritual scenario of combat, which was first delineated in relation to ancient Near Eastern and biblical materials. But this pattern is not restricted to the ancient Near East; it is clearly found in many diverse oral and literate traditions. While the combat pattern of myth displays many permutations depending on the particular cultural context, the basic plot is typified by the Babylonian *Enuma elish* (dating back, in part, to the second millennium BCE), which tells of the struggle between a chaos monster associated with the primal waters (i.e., the demoness Tiamat and her forces) and a triumphant sky deity responsible for some significant cultural innovation (the warrior god Marduk, who slays Tiamat, divides her carcass to form the world, and establishes the central temple and righteous rule of the city-state of Babylon).

In the *Enuma elish,* Tiamat and her monstrous cohorts represent the older, otiose generation of gods that resist the noisy, rambunctious creative activity of the younger gods championed by Marduk. From this perspective—and it is an interpretive judgment found in many other versions of the combat myth—chaos and its first generation of creatures refer to the impotency of a form that, in time, is drained of its initial creative energy. Tiamat, in other words, stands for the dangerous principle of entropy, the negative, polluting force that seeks to dissolve all new life forms back into the silent slumber and amniotic inertia of death.

The law of cosmic life in this sense is the organic rule of chaotic disintegration that is necessary for new life. Such a cyclic return to chaos may be delayed, but even the younger gods, as part of a cosmos connected by origins with the principle of chaos, are still ultimately subject to the cosmic weariness and senility first displayed by Tiamat. One way to resolve this dilemma, which is seen prominently in monotheistic traditions, is to discover the reality of a dualistic separation between chaos and an absolutely transcendent, wholly spiritual or divine order impervious to the inevitable temporal change and collapse of all cosmic forms. Monistic theories asserting the fundamental unreality or illusory nature of chaos/cosmos represent another strategy.

The combat pattern is also witnessed in many tribal traditions, although the intensity of the antagonistic relationship between chaos and the human order (and consequently the dualistic translation of this as the polarity between death and life, evil and good, demon and god) is ordinarily heightened within the context of the classical or historical religions. Thus, such traditions often suggest that ritual remembrances of the mythic skirmish primarily function to celebrate the victory over chaos and the heroic finality of some authoritarian order. There is an emphasis here on the permanent suppression of chaos, or at least a denial that the primordial enemy possesses any positive attributes. The problem, as previously indicated, is that chaos is never completely overcome in ordinary cosmic life, although for some religions a post mortem heavenly existence (as well as a climactic apocalyptic purification of the cosmos) can be interpreted as a final and total victory over chaos.

While it is true that festivals of licensed folly are found in both tribal and classical traditions, the former tend to accept more readily the instrinsic value and positive ambiguity of a periodic ritual return to a chaotic or "liminal" condition. The danger perceived by such peoples is not so much chaos in the sense of the end of order and life but rather the social entropy and tension of too much deadening order. Chaos in this "primitive" sense is the pivot of cosmic and social equilibrium, and refers to the ritual reappearance of unstructured freedom and sheer potentiality. To refresh life, chaos must be disciplined and periodically embraced, not simply defeated.

The contemporary American satirist Peter De Vries has perversely suggested that if "in de beginning was de void, and de void was vit God," then it is probably the case that one "mustn't say de naughty void" (*Blood of the Lamb*, Boston, 1962, p. 181). In like manner, even when an implacably vile and naughty chaos is portrayed—as in some versions of the combat myth—there is often the contradictory implication that the divine champions are finally congenerous with their primordial foes. The forces of chaos and the watery void are always, it seems, the enemies of righteous order yet originally and simultaneously "vit God."

Chaos, it must be said, is both naughty and nice, or to borrow appropriately enough from Rudolf Otto's classic definition of the sacred (*The Idea of the Holy*, [1917] 1958), chaos is both repulsive and attractive in its awful appeal to the religious imagination. Its repugnant apsects are clearly seen in the many worldwide adumbrations of the combat scenario, but it remains to indicate the somewhat more muted allure of chaos as a positive and beneficial religious principle. Thus, there are what might be called "pro-chaos" religious traditions that in different ways espouse chaos as a goal. Of these there are, in general, three—sometimes overlapping—possibilities: (1) chaos may symbolize the final attainment of, and fusion with, some perfectly unconditioned unity and bliss totally beyond cosmic existence—a "nothingness that glistens with plentitude" (E. M. Cioran, *The Temptation to Exist*, Chicago, 1968, p. 155); (2) chaos may be experienced as a stage, threshold, or "dark night of the soul" at the ultimate edge of cosmic reality that leads to a distinct and higher vision of the absolutely transcendent Divine; and (3) chaos may represent the experience of a more paradoxical state, or *coincidentia oppositorum*, merging transcendent unity and cosmic multiplicity and functioning not as an end, but as a healing way station for a more harmonious inner and social life.

Such options obviously relate to "mystical" forms of world religions, but it should be recalled that a positive attitude toward chaos was already forecast by tribal rituals that periodically welcomed a twilight zone back into the human fold. Because of this sympathy, mystical forms of religion (along with other types of shamanistic-ecstatic, individualistic, and revolutionary religious movements) often manifest a kind of "primitive" sentiment toward chaos that contrasts and challenges the more onesidedly negative evaluations seen in institutionalized religion.

One instance of these contrasting interpretations within a single tradition is found in India, where some radical forms of Upaniṣadic, Buddhist, and *bhakti* mysticism seek a supreme integration with the sacred "emptiness" of chaos. These forms can, in turn, be distinguished from the dharmic system of rigidly differentiated castes seen in Vedic and Puranic Hinduism. Within Western tradition—and frequently in tension with mainstream Christian, Jewish, and Islamic institutions—there are also movements that stress the mystical conjugation of the divine and chaos. Conceptions arising from such movements include, in Christianity, the *Ungrund* (the "unground" or abyss that gives rise to God's self-consciousness), described by Jakob Boehme (1575–1624); the qabbalistic idea of *tsimtsum*, the creative "gap" within God, in sixteenth-century Judaism; and the alchemical *massa confusa* (the prime matter, often imagined as an egg or coiled snake) in both Christian and Islamic esoteric circles after the Renaissance. All allude in some degree to the mythological chaos as a strangely positive image.

There are other cases of this pro-chaos persuasion, but one of the more striking examples is found in Chinese tradition. In ancient China during the Eastern Chou period (c. eighth through second centuries BCE) the mythological chaos was called *hun-tun*, which connoted the image of a Humpty-Dumpty-like, closed, embryonic condition or creature. Confucian thought and the ancient classics stressed the role of a succession of semidivine Sage-Kings who disciplined the chaotic forces of the natural world and carved the hierarchical order of the Middle Kingdom out of the carcass of the primitive condition of *hun-tun*. As a counterpoint to this point of view, the early Taoist texts suggest the existence of a veritable cult of chaos, since for these works the attainment of an authentically spontaneous and harmonious life required the rejection of conventional standards of propriety and recommended a return to an experience of primitive unity by means of the mystical "arts of *hun-tun*." Thus, in early Taoist texts (as distinct from the later institutionalized Taoist religion), the mythical *hun-tun* can be identified with the ultimate principle of the Tao as the rhythmic source and ground of life. Because of his periodic journeys in mind and heart back to the time of chaos, the Taoist mimics the seasonal regeneration of nature and the ritual regeneration of primitive cultural life and is able, therefore, to remain fresh and whole in the world.

Affirmations of the saving power of chaos have had a significant, although largely unorthodox, role to play in the history of religions; and, as broadly protesting all conventionalized truth, the cult and cultivation of chaos can be said to have inspired a whole spectrum of countercultural irruptions, "interstitial events," or "liminoid phenomena" throughout history. Because it rubs against the customary order of things, the religious, philosophical, artistic, and political "art of chaos" is always a risky enterprise, as indicated by the checkered careers of assorted Taoist mystics, Zen monks, holy fools, clownish alchemists, utopian Ranters, Romantic poets, Nietzschian nihilists, frenzied surrealists, neo-pagan anarchists, the Maoist "Gang of Four," and deconstructionist critics.

Conclusion. Perhaps the most responsible way to end an investigation of chaos is to refuse the temptation to parse a subject so hopelessly ironic. It is, after all, the principle of chaos that opens the abyss of indeterminacy and undecidability in all interpretive endeavors. Suffice it to say that, despite its decidedly negative public reputation, the image of chaos may be found in fact to have positive religious value. Even more important is the recognition that the idea of chaos represents one of the honored ways religions have tried to imagine the ambiguous origins and equivocal nature of existence. For this very reason the meaning of chaos in the history of religions maintains its imaginative integrity by remaining chaotic. Respecting the root topsy-turviness of chaos should not, however, prevent careful reflection on its imaginative history since, even in its most negative guise, the phantomlike shapes of chaos are directly related to the way particular religions have envisioned reality. The nature and significance of chaos, therefore, touches upon a number of issues that are central to the overall interpretive understanding and definition of religion.

BIBLIOGRAPHY

Concerning the general theoretical background to the religious and philosophical understanding of chaos and order, see *The Concept of Order*, edited by Paul G. Kuntz (Seattle and London, 1968), for an eclectic selection of articles—especially pertinent are James K. Feibleman's "Disorder" (pp. 3–13) and, for the religious context, Charles Hartshorne's "Order and Chaos" (pp. 253–267) and Joseph M. Kitagawa's "Chaos, Order, and Freedom in World Religions" (pp. 268–289). See also David L. Hall's *Eros and Irony* (Albany, 1982), which provocatively analyzes cultural history in relation to varying conceptions of creation, chaos, and cosmology.

Barbara C. Sproul's *Primal Myths: Creating the World* (San Francisco, 1979) is a convenient sourcebook for the more important creation myths and includes some abbreviated, but helpful, commentary on the different religious images of chaos. More valuable for their discussions of the relation between the ideas of "creation" and "chaos" are Mircea Eliade's *Myth and Reality* (New York, 1963), which investigates the mythological and ritual meaning of chaos as correlated with the author's theory concerning the "prestige" of cosmogony, and Charles H. Long's *Alpha: The Myths of Creation* (New York, 1963), which includes some of the important mythological source materials as well as an extensive comparative examination of the structural significance of chaos imagery. For the ritual themes of "liminality" and "pollution" as suggestively analogous to the mythic idea of chaos, especially among tribal traditions, see Victor Turner's *The Ritual Process* (Ithaca, 1977) and Mary Douglas's *Purity and Danger: An Analysis of Concepts of Pollution and Taboo* (New York, 1966).

The myth and ritual theme of combat that promotes a negative and dualistic evaluation of chaos is classically presented for ancient Near Eastern and biblical materials by Hermann Gunkel's *Schöpfung und Chaos in Urzeit und Endzeit* (Göttingen, 1895). But see also the more recent studies by Bernhard W. Anderson, *Creation versus Chaos* (New York, 1967), which emphasizes the biblical context; Mary K. Wakeman, *God's Battle with the Monster* (Leiden, 1973), which comparatively reexamines the ancient Near Eastern documentation; and Joseph Fontenrose, *Python: A Study of Delphic Myth and Its Origins* (Berkeley, 1959), which focuses on Greek tradition but draws upon a broad assortment of cross-cultural materials (i.e., Indo-European, ancient Near Eastern, East Asian, American Indian, etc.).

For studies that examine the more positive and ambiguous dimensions of chaos symbolism, along with related imagery, see, for India, Wendy Doniger O'Flaherty's *Women, Androgynes, and Other Mythical Beasts* (Chicago and London, 1980) and, for the ancient Chinese theme of *hun-tun*, my own *Myth and Meaning in Early Taoism: The Theme of Chaos* (Berkeley and London, 1983). In addition to their primary subject areas, both of these works comparatively cite a broad range of cross-cultural materials. Finally it is worth noting, among other possibilities, William Willeford's *The Fool and His Scepter* (London, 1969) and Mircea Eliade's *Mephistopheles and the Androgyne: Studies in Religious Myth and Symbol* (New York, 1965). The former is a fascinating literary study of the folkloric and popular embodiments of chaos in the Western tradition of the fool or jester, and the latter is a rich comparative study of different symbolic themes touching on the religious ideas of duality and the "coincidence of opposites."

N. J. GIRARDOT

CHARDIN, PIERRE TEILHARD DE. *See* Teilhard de Chardin, Pierre.

CHARISMA. The word *charisma* comes from the Greek *charis,* meaning "grace, kindness, favor." In the Greek Bible it indicated a gift of grace, a spiritual gift with special endowments. [*See also* Grace.] The term was first rendered in English as *charism* or *charisme,* with reference to the charisms of healing, prophecy and other gifts of the Spirit. In nineteenth-century English the form *charisma* appeared to describe such special powers or gifts; this meaning is still to be found, but there has been extension in meaning and application in recent years.

Max Weber stated in his *Theory of Social and Economic Organization:* "The term 'charism' will be applied to a certain quality of an individual personality by virtue of which he is set apart from ordinary men and treated as endowed with supernatural, superhuman, or at least specifically exceptional powers or qualities" (trans. Henderson and Parsons, New York, 1946, p. 358). In this sense charisma is a gift or power of leadership or authority. The charismatic individual may be regarded as having an aura or emanation of supernatural origin. Or charisma may be a human quality, without reference to the supernatural, as when one speaks of "the Kennedy charisma"; but this sense may also imply admiration for, or even identification with, the object of attention.

The adjective *charismatic* has undergone similar extensions of meaning. Formerly it applied to the spiritual gifts *(charismata)* which would come with charistmatic endowment. Now it may be used of persons who are thought to exhibit or possess a charisma or to have charismatic authority. The social or political organization of one-party states may be said to be directed by a "charismatic tribal leader."

More recently, *charismatic* has been used to describe movements of spiritual revival whose members claim to exhibit or possess charisma, who have charismatic powers, or form charismatic communities. [*See* Pentecostal and Charismatic Christianity.] Such charismatic movements resemble traditional Pentecostalism, which claimed to continue or reproduce the spiritual experiences and gifts of the Pentecost (*Acts* 2) which initiated the Christian church. Pentecostalism saw the power of the Spirit as central to its religious life and as the cause of such gifts as speaking in tongues and healing by faith. Neo-Pentecostalism, or the Charismatic Movement, developed in America in the 1950s first among Protestant evangelicals and later among Roman Catholics, and then spread to Europe and other continents. It manifested traditional Pentecostal charismatic elements: glossolalia, prophecy, healing, and deliverance. The adjective became a noun—*charismatics*—denoting persons belonging to communities whose leaders are believed to possess spiritual gifts, and for their followers who may not produce such gifts but who see them to be manifested in others. In this sense, the charismatic, or at least the leader, is held to possess charisma, such as may be observed in many societies, old and new.

The first usage of *charisma,* to mean special graces, can be amply illustrated in the New Testament, where Paul in *1 Corinthians* 12–14 writes of spiritual gifts, or *charismata.* These are said to be manifestations of the spirit of God in different ways: wise words, special knowledge, faith, healings, miracles, prophecy, distinguishing spirits, ecstatic utterances and their interpretation. All such charismata are attributed to the same divine spirit, who distributes them to each person as he sees fit. Paul claims that all charismata have their place, but he exhorts his readers to seek the best of them and goes on to stress that love is the greatest spiritual gift.

Such charismata have parallels in many religions, from the ecstatic possessions of prehistoric or illiterate shamans to the whirling dervishes of Islam. In some new religions in Japan the attributes of breath, food, water, ecstasy, and dancing are considered charismata.

The charisma of a religious leader relates both to his nature and to his powers. Frequently charisma is considered the result of contact with a supernatural being, from which the individual receives revelation and power enabling him to mediate spiritual grace to other people. The experience is intense and immediate, often involving possession or ecstasy. Although the experience must relate to the social environment and bear the stamp of the surrounding culture, it also possesses a superhuman or transsocial dimension that must be considered seriously when examining the nature of charisma. [*See also* Magico-Religious Powers.]

Examples of this sort of contact may be drawn from almost any level of religion, past or present. In Australia religious specialists, medicine men, or shamans are believed to be in close relation with supernatural beings, to talk with them, and to see the spirits of ancestors. While such a person may have a nature that inclines him toward meditation or trance, he is called to spiritual work by special signs or inspiration.

Australian Aborigines, like shamans in Asia and elsewhere, often claim to be able to fly through the air as their mythic ancestors did. They are believed to have the power to rise up to the sky, go down into the depths of the earth, disappear and reappear. By surpassing normal human powers, such specialists behave like spiritual beings and partake of their charisma. They are radically changed beings and become central to the religious life of their tribe. They can heal the sick by seeing what spiritual forces caused the illness. They are rainmakers, like Elijah in ancient Israel. The value of their charisma to society is evident in claims that they defend the tribe against magical attacks, by using a "pointing bone" or by "singing" poisons against enemies. They re-create the myths and rituals of the mythic Dreaming time and help others to reenact their own sacred history.

Although spiritual office may confer charisma on its holder, a distinction may be made between officeholders who perform routine functions and those who are specially inspired—between priests and prophets. Among the Nuer of the Sudan a prophet is a "possessor of a spirit" *(gwan kwoth),* a spirit that gives him powers lacking in other persons. A priest, on the other hand, is a traditional functionary, and his powers are transmitted from another priest. In contrast, a prophet's powers come from individual inspiration and are "charismatic," as E. E. Evans-Pritchard notes in his study *Nuer Religion* (1956). The priest speaks to God standing on the earth and looking to the sky; but the prophet is the mouthpiece of a spirit or of God or of "one of his hypostases" speaking to man. The prophet names his spirit, saying, "I am so-and-so," just as biblical prophets declared "thus saith Yahveh." However, Nuer society respects both priests and prophets and does not set them in opposition to one another, as did some government officials who feared the disruptive influence of wandering prophets.

Similarly, in West Africa charisma may be first demonstrated through ecstatic possession at a ceremony of public dancing. In Benin (formerly called Dahomey) persons who are possessed in public may be taken into the care of established priests in order to develop a new personality. The neophyte may fall down as if dead and be taken away by fellow dancers for a ritual resurrection and training in a "god-house" or "spirit-enclosure," remaining out of public sight for months or years. When the training is finished the novice receives a new name, speaks a ritual language, wears distinctive clothes, and becomes available for messages to the world of spirits. Priests who function at temples and mediums who speak in ecstacy are commonly marked out by special dress, actions, and taboos. Priests are often not subject to possession, but they direct the mediums, and both classes are revered for their work.

In the Bible it is said that Moses spoke to God face to face. When he came down from Mount Sinai, his face shone and he put a veil over it when speaking to the Israelites. Later Jewish legend tells that at Moses' birth the house was filled with the radiance of the sun and moon and that angels sang when his parents were reunited. Like the Buddha, Moses is said to have walked and talked on the day of his birth; and he began to prophesy when he was four months old. Orthodox doctrine maintained his supremacy, and in the twelfth century the Jewish scholar Maimonides (Mosheh ben Maimon) called him "the chief of the prophets"—a statement incorporated in Orthodox prayer books today.

Many other biblical figures had charisma. Saul stood head and shoulders over other men, and when he had been anointed king by Samuel the spirit of the Lord came mightily upon him so that he prophesied. It was said that God gave him another heart and turned him into another man, so that people asked, "Is Saul also among the prophets?" Saul then became a brave military leader.

Whether because of his brooding character or military misfortunes, Saul fell from Samuel's favor and was ousted by David. Like Saul, David was physically outstanding, with a ruddy and beautiful countenance, and "goodly to look upon." After David's anointing, the spirit of God came on him as on Saul, and David was more successful than Saul in battle. Both of these men were charismatic leaders. However, Solomon, who followed, seems to have been a much more ambitious monarch, and he so oppressed the people that the kingdom broke up after his death. Jesus' remark that Solomon "in all his glory" could not compare with a wildflower (*Mt.* 7:29) was a later reflection of the common people's condemnation of a tyrant.

Prophets had charisma, received as a divine vocation and shown in public action. Elijah challenged the power of King Ahab and chose Jehu to replace him. Alone he faced over eight hundred prophets of other gods; he called on the people to choose between him and these prophets, half of whom he finally slaughtered. In fleeing from the fiery queen Jezebel perhaps his power faltered, but it was restored to him at Mount Carmel, where shrines are dedicated to him to this day.

In the New Testament Jesus received power not only

at his baptism but also at his transfiguration. It was said that his face shone as the sun and his clothing was white as light during his talk with the past heroes Moses and Elijah. Earlier, Jesus had healed the sick and astonished the people by teaching "as one that had authority, and not as the scribes" (*Mk.* 1:22). Possessed people perceived his charisma, as did his disciples, who saw him demonstrate his powers over the elements of nature.

Similar power was attributed to the early apostles. It was said that on the day of Pentecost tongues of fire came upon them, and they were so filled with the Spirit that the multitude marveled. Although the apostles were unlearned or ignorant men, it was seen that they acted with great power; Gamaliel the Elder warned that they should be left alone, for if their power came from God it could not be overthrown (*Acts* 5:34ff.). At his trial Stephen's face shone like an angel. When Paul healed a cripple he and Barnabas were regarded as gods come down in the likeness of men. Such charismatic power served not only to astonish unbelievers but also to unite the faithful as a community.

In the Islamic world *barakah* is a common indication of charisma, as Edward Westermarck illustrates at length in *Ritual and Belief in Morocco* (London, 1926). *Barakah,* an Arabic word meaning "blessing," connotes a wonder-working power believed to be a blessing from God; it has also been translated into English as "blessed virtue" and "holiness." A person who possesses exceptional *barakah* is called *sayyid, faqīr, walī Allāh,* or *mrābat* (cf. English *marabout.*).

The prophet Muḥammad is regarded as having possessed more *barakah* than any other man. Although from the Qur'ān onward it was recognized that there were other prophets—notably Abraham, Moses, and Jesus—Muḥammad is called the Seal of the Prophets (i.e., the last and greatest of the prophets). According to his early biographer, Ibn Isḥāq, when Muḥammad's mother was pregnant with him she saw light coming out of her, which shone to castles in distant Syria. When the time of his vocation was at hand Muḥammad retired to Mount Hira to pray, and it was said that every stone and tree that he passed saluted him as the apostle of God. Muḥammad's night journey and ascent to heaven, "whether he was asleep or awake," were interpreted later not only as signs of power but also as models of mystical ascension. More than any other, this brief Qur'anic reference has been the subject of simple devotions as well as of mystical aspirations toward unity.

Traditions and legends developed the charismatic powers attributed to the Prophet, and he became known as the generous one, the all-compelling one, the giver of graces, the queller, the watchful one. In devotion Muḥammad is called other names as well: the hero of the night ascent, the man of power, the intercessor for all creatures, he who traversed the seven spheres, for whom the palm trees wept, to whom the stones did homage, of whom the gazelles sought intercession, for whom the sparkling water burst forth, at whose light the flowers opened and the fruits matured, to whose robes the wild creatures clung, and at whose light all other lights burst forth. These attributes have been listed by C. E. Padwick in *Muslim Devotions* (London, 1961).

Muḥammad is believed to have translated his *barakah* to the *sharīf*s, the male descendants of his daughter Fāṭimah. Every *sharīf* thus possesses inborn *barakah,* although it may be much diluted; and comparatively few *sharīf*s are regarded as saints. Some sultans, however, have special *barakah* by virtue of both their ancestry and their office. *Barakah* may be transferred from one person to another, even against the will of the possessor. For this reason some men will not shake hands for fear of losing their *barakah. Barakah* may be acquired from the tombs of saints or through extraordinary piety, or by praying, fasting, giving alms to the poor or food to scribes. Scribes receive *barakah* from frequent recitations of the Qur'ān, whence they are called "birds of Paradise."

Both childhood and old age confer *barakah.* Children acquire *barakah* because they are too young to sin, old people for the sake of their gray hairs. Children are said to know the language of angels, to hear the crying of the dead, and to know remedies for sickness. The long lives of the old inspire feelings of awe and respect for God and the Prophet. Hence old men may be regarded as saints and old women as possessors of occult powers. Parents have *barakah* toward their children, and a guest possesses it toward his host, so that hospitality is of great importance. Brides and bridegrooms have *barakah* because marriage is "half of religion." A married man who dies goes to Paradise, whereas a bachelor goes to the evil spirits. There is much *barakah* at circumcision ceremonies, even more when a boy is born circumcised, as saints supposedly were. The prayers, blessings, and curses of saints are particularly efficacious; many are credited with prophetic gifts and healing powers.

In India many kinds of holy men have had their own charisma that distinguished them from ordinary beings. In the *Ṛgveda* (10.156), for example, a long-haired ascetic holds the sky and the earth and reveals everything so that men can see the sun. The gods enter into him in ecstasy, and while mortals can see only his body, he sails through the air and is friend of the gods, heavenly nymphs, and wild beasts. This figure may be a prototype of the yogin, but he is more a shaman, an ecstatic who rides on the horse of the wind, abandoning his body and inhabiting the two seas.

Yogic discipline involves the search for supernatural powers and probably has been practiced in India from the time of the Indus Valley culture in the second and third millennia BCE; seals of that culture show a proto-Śiva sitting in a cross-legged posture. The Upaniṣads describe the discipline and its rules for holding the body steady, controlling the breath, and concentrating the mind. Visions of smoke and light, of sun and moon, and flashes of lightning and crystal are only preliminary appearances, and the yogin proceeds to steadiness and the manifestation of *brahman.* In book 6 of the *Bhagavadgītā* the yogin also seeks to discipline himself. He is considered superior to ascetics or men with knowledge of rituals; and his inner self attains that peace that culminates in rest in God.

In the *Yoga Sūtras* of Patañjali (3.16ff.) there are indications of the charismas or miraculous powers (*siddhis*) sought by yogins in countless ways. It is said that the yogin who has reached the stage of contemplation and unity acquires further knowledge and undergoes further. He has knowledge of past and future, understanding of sounds uttered by any being, knowledge of a previous life and of the minds of others, power of disappearance, knowledge of death, knowledge of the obscure and remote, knowledge of the upper and lower regions and of moon and stars, mastery over the elements, supremacy over all states of being, and omniscience. Finally, the seeds of bondage having been destroyed by nonattachment, isolation or absolute independence *(kaivalya)* is attained.

Yogins have claimed the ability to appear and disappear; their bodies were imperceptible to other people because their color was not visible. They were thought to have power not only over their own bodies but also over nature. Down through the ages the great saint *(mahāsiddha)* has been credited with occult powers, levitation, disappearance, and miracles. Indian mythology is full of stories of ascetics who had great powers, acquired through practices of self-control, that gave them authority over other people. Their charisma became so great that the gods themselves and the entire universe were threatened by their asceticism *(tapas).* Sometimes heavenly nymphs were sent to tempt such holy men, to reduce their power and their threat to order. At times the yogins were overcome despite their efforts at detachment. If they yielded to sensual temptations they would fail on the way toward final emancipation. There are still many yogins today who claim to have extraordinary powers, and some undoubtedly are charlatans.

The Indian teacher *(guru)* has charisma because he imparts sacred knowledge. There are tens of thousands of such "god-men" in India with large and small followings. The great esteem accorded the *guru* dates from the time of the Upaniṣads, which declared that the disciple should have the same loving devotion *(bhakti)* for the *guru* as for God. The divinity of the *guru* comes from his followers' belief in his unity or identity with the deity. His followers believe that he has absolute knowledge and truth and that he will lead them to a similar union with the devine.

Men belonging to the highest caste also have charisma, since they are "twice born" by initiation and are at the top of the social order, which they regulate according to their position and activity. The *Laws of Manu* said that the man who obeyed the laws would gain fame in this world and unsurpassable bliss after death, prestige here and hereafter. So it teaches that the brahman's name denotes things auspicious and happy. The brahman eats facing the east, after performing an ablution with concentrated mind. He recites texts and prayers and is friendly to everyone. He must be saluted with the words "Long life, O gentle one," and a pupil must clasp his feet. If a brahman performs the rites correctly, he is called a *guru,* and his pupil shall consider him as father and mother. A disciple must always be respectful toward the teacher, standing when he is seated, bowing toward him in bed, never uttering his name or mimicking his manner behind his back. If he serves the teacher until he dies, the pupil will reach the eternal mansion of *brahman.*

Similar charismatic virtues are honored in other Indian religions. The ten *gurūs* of the Sikhs are credited with supernatural powers. Their names and deeds are constantly recalled and celebrated on anniversaries. It is said that the *gurūs* were perfect; indeed, they were "sinless." When "sins did come to tempt them, they never gave way"; "everybody else is subject to error, only the Gurū and God are without error." Although there were ten historical Sikh *gurūs*, they are all identified with the first, Gurū Nānak, and his successors signed with his name. Although the succession came to an end with the tenth *gurū,* it was perpetuated in the scriptures called the *Gurū Granth Sahib,* "the living teacher and lord." Both teachers and scripture live within the Sikh, who "incorporates the Gurū" so that "the Gurū lives within his Ṣikhs" and "the Gurū is the Word and the Word is the Gurū."

From its beginning Buddhism credited its founder with supernatural graces. In the canonical *Mahāpadāna Sutta* it is said that when the Exalted One was staying in a pavilion his disciples were discussing previous births, and he intuited this "with a clear and heavenly ear, surpassing the hearing of men." Then he told them of previous Buddhas and how in due course he was besought by hundreds of gods to come to earth as a "Buddha supreme." He gave a brief account of his descent from heaven, his birth in a clan of nobles, his renunciation of the world, and his final enlightenment. He could remember the Buddhas of old and knew all the past, present, and future. The Buddha possessed unique and supernatural gifts; his body bore the thirty-two marks of a superman. Devotees attributed to the Buddha an aura extending several feet around his body, bringing submission to all whom he met. He was omniscient, "teacher of gods and men," and "god beyond the gods."

In China, Lao-tzu was said to have spent sixty years in his mother's womb, so that at birth his hair was white; hence his name, which means "old sir." Like the Buddha, this child spoke as soon as he was born and had long ears, a sign of sanctity. In one famous passage from the *Chuang-tzu,* Confucius is said to have confessed that he could liken Lao-tzu only to a dragon, who flies in the sky and rides on the clouds. At the end of his life Lao-tzu set out for the western mountains, but the keeper of the pass prevailed on him to write down what became the Taoist classic *Tao-te ching.* Then he departed for the west, a cloud enveloping him and his black ox. This Ascension of Lao-tzu, as it is often called, has been a favorite subject of Chinese painters.

In China and Japan holy men and women have charisma according to their office, priestly or prophetic. The shamanistic kind, such as the *miko* (female shaman) of Japan, enter states of trance where spirits supposedly possess them. Whether comatose or fully conscious, the medium transmits messages from the unseen world and is much sought after by the populace. Others are healers, trained by ascetic practices to banish evil spirits or transform them into powers for good. The so-called new religions of Japan, founded by charismatic men and women, continue the tradition of inspiration, revelation, and healing. They are notable for the establishment of large communities, in which rituals provide for repetition of divine gifts, healing, and salvation. Such movements, with their special gifts, parallel movements of the charismatics of the West.

BIBLIOGRAPHY

The histories of charismatic and Pentecostal movements are well summarized in *The Westminster Dictionary of Christian Spirituality,* edited by Gordon S. Wakefield (London, 1983). The classic work on the shaman is Mircea Eliade's *Shamanism: Archaic Techniques of Ecstasy,* rev. & enl. ed. (New York, 1964); his study of *Yoga: Immortality and Freedom,* 2d ed. (Princeton, 1969), provides further material. E. E. Evans-Pritchard's *Nuer Religion* (Oxford, 1956) is an outstanding exposition on African thought and practice. *Ritual and Belief in Morocco,* 2 vols., by Edward A. Westermarck (1926; reprint, New Hyde Park, N.Y., 1968), reveals the importance of Muḥammad's role not only in history but also in the practice of prayer. In *Godmen of India* (London, 1972), Peter Brent gives popular accounts of modern Indian gurus. A thorough study of *Gurū Nānak and the Sikh Religion* (Oxford, 1968) is provided by W. H. McLeod. In *The Parting of the Way* (London, 1957), Holmes Welch described Lao-tzu and the Taoist movement, and in *The Catalpa Bow* (London, 1975), Carmen Blacker depicts shamanistic practices in Japan as well as her own experiences of pilgrimage.

GEOFFREY PARRINDER

CHARISMATIC CHRISTIANITY.

See Pentecostal and Charismatic Christianity.

CHARITY.

The word *charity* derives from the Latin *caritas* and can be traced to the Greek *charis.* In the Western religious tradition, *charity* has become synonymous with the Greek terms *agapē, philanthrōpia, eleēmosunē* (or *eleos*), and even *philia* and *eros;* with the Hebrew words *zedakah, gemilut hesed,* and *aheb;* and with the Latin *amor, amicitia, beneficia,* and *caritas* (or *carus*). Thus, as a theoretical conception, charity has meant both possessive and selfless love, as well as favor, grace, mercy, kindness, righteousness, and liberality. In its practical application, charity denotes the distribution of goods to the poor and the establishment and endowment of such social-welfare institutions as hospitals, homes for the aged, orphanages, and reformatory institutions.

Documents of ancient Mesopotamia and Egypt indicate that charity in the sense of social justice was considered a divinely decreed principle. The reforms of King Urukagina (c. 2400 BCE) were praised because "he freed the inhabitants of Lagash from usury . . . hunger. . . . The widow and the orphan were no longer at the mercy of the powerful." But ideals of charity, social justice, and the principle of social consciousness developed not only because the divinity had so ordained but also because social circumstances, human oppression, and suffering demanded them. The goddess Nanshe and later the god Utu (or Shamash), the orphan's mother and father, were the guarantors of justice, cared for the widow, sought out justice for the poorest, and brought the refugees shelter. King Hammurabi (d. circa 1750 BCE) sought through legislation to eliminate the social inequity that had been created by the malpractices of businessmen or other members of the enterprising Babylonian society. In ancient Egypt, charity was perceived as an inner disposition toward fellow human beings and as a means of propitiating the gods for the purpose of achieving immortality, but it also meant, as *The Book of Going Forth by Day* indicates, "giving bread to the hungry, water to the thirsty, clothes to the naked, and even a boat to the one who had none."

There is little doubt that early Hebrew thought was greatly influenced by the Babylonian, Egyptian, and other peoples of the ancient Near East. But the Hebrews molded what they inherited and added their own religious and social thought as set forth in their scriptures, particularly the Hebrew Bible. The Hebrew root *aheb* refers primarily to love between man and woman, but in its theological use it denotes God's love for mankind, mankind's love for God, and love among human beings. God's love for mankind is caused by its need but also by God's innate qualities (*Dt.* 10:17–18, *Ps.* 145:15–16). A person's love for God is a response to God's love, a gratitude that is also expressed through one's love for other people.

As an applied virtue, charity is expected of everyone, for whoever gives charity will be blessed by the Lord (*Dt.* 15:7–10). In medieval Judaism, in Moses Maimonides particularly, the highest form of charity is not to give alms but to help the poor rehabilitate themselves by lending them money, taking them into partnership, or employing them, for in this way the desired end is achieved without any loss of self-respect for the recipient. But notwithstanding occasional references to liberality toward the gentiles, in Jewish tradition "charity begins at home," and for many centuries the object of charity was the fellow Jew—the individual, the family circle, and the community.

In ancient Greek society charity was synonymous with love *(agapē), philanthrōpia, eleos,* and *philoxenia,* and it was manifested through benevolent deeds on behalf of those in need. In a variety of forms, charity is present in the earliest Greek poetry, drama, and philosophy. Compassion for the afflicted and loving hospitality were greatly emphasized in Mycenaean and archaic Greek society (1400–700 BCE). The care of strangers and suppliants was an ethical imperative because such people had been placed under the direct aegis of the divinity. Zeus became known as Xenios, "protector of strangers." This imperative is expressed in Homer's *Odyssey:* "Receive strangers regardless of who they may be"; "That man is sacred who welcomes a wayfaring stranger." [*See* Hospitality.]

It was believed that when a poor person was expelled from the table of the rich or even rudely handled, the vengeance of the Furies would be visited upon the heartless miscreant, for "gods and Furies exist for beggars." To be merciful and to act out of love were common ethical admonitions. Hesiod (c. 700 BCE) was even more pronounced in his concern for the poor, though he lauded hard work and stressed moderation in the practice of charity while advocating philanthropy, righteous deeds, and reverence for the stranger and the poor. Hesiod writes that in offering hospitality one should "be neither too lavish nor too parsimonious" and that one should not "taunt anyone for his poverty which eats out the heart—even cursed poverty is sent by the immortal gods."

The most important characteristic of Greek thought from as early as the Homeric age is ethical in nature. In the classical Greek city-states, whether in Athens, Thebes, or remote Acragas, charity in the sense of selfless love, almsgiving, pity, and concern for the orphan, the widow, and the elderly was widely and generously practiced. The Greek *charis* originally denoted a gift or favor inspired by the Charites (the three Graces), goddesses who personified not only physical attributes such as charm, grace, and beauty but also kindness, goodwill, and gratitude.

Under the influence of the great philosophers Socrates, Plato, and Aristotle and the Stoics, charity was perceived as a duty toward all "broken and destitute humanity wherever found." It was a moral and religious obligation, a social and economic need. The pre-Socratic philosophers had held that justice and equality were principles of divine origin, as had Pythagoras, who stressed equality and harmony in social relationships. "All human laws are nourished by one, which is divine," writes Heraclitus. There are no political or economic laws, only moral laws.

For the great thinkers of the fifth and the fourth century BCE, doing good for the sake of goodness was the only moral ground for charity. A cardinal principle of Greek religion and social thought was that the divinity is good and the cause of good. Plato writes that for "the cause of evil we must look in other things and not in God" (*Republic* 2.18). Neither God nor man can be really good without in some way communicating his goodness to others. Aristotle adds, "If all men vied with each other in moral nobility and strove to perform the noblest deeds, the common welfare would be fully realized, while individuals also could enjoy the greatest of goods, inasmuch as virtue is the greatest good" (*Nicomachean Ethics* 9.8.7). Thus "the conferring of a benefit where a return is not sought is morally acceptable, and the value of the gift is not to be judged by its intrinsic worth but by the spirit of one giver." Aristotle insisted on the idea of "the cheerful giver." Being good meant doing good.

Poverty should not be tolerated, for it leads to the erosion of a democratic state and constitutes the basis of social revolts (Aristotle, *Politics* 6.3.4). Professional beggars were banned by Homeric society and Solon's and

Plato's Athens as well as by Sparta. Nevertheless, poverty was accepted as a fact of life, and charity a means for its relief. The Greeks invoked curses upon men "who failed to provide water for the thirsty, fire for anyone in need of it, burial . . . , [hospitality, or] directions for a lost stranger."

Much of Greek religious and social thought was adopted by such Roman thinkers as Cicero and Seneca, who in their exposition of *caritas* and *beneficia* echo Aristotle's teachings and the Greek understanding of *philanthrōpia*. Whether for the sake of honor or other motives, much charity was practiced in the Roman empire, especially in the *alimenta*, measures introduced to assist orphans and poor children. Initiated by private philanthropists, the system was adopted by the imperial government after the reign of Nerva (96–98).

Charity in Christianity is synonymous with *agapē*, or love. Whether it was a new commandment, as Christ had taught (*Jn.* 13:34), is controversial. One thing is certain: Christianity proved more ecumenical and proclaimed that "there is neither Jew nor Greek, there is neither slave nor free, there is neither male nor female . . . but all [are] one in Christ Jesus" (*Gal.* 3:28). In the practical application of charity it went beyond Jews, Greeks, and Romans. It stressed that "love is of God, and he who loves is born of God and knows God. He who does not love does not know God; for God is love" (*1 Jn.* 4:7–8). God's love requires that men love one another (*1 Jn.* 4:11). There is no better account of the nature and the fruits of Christian charity than the thirteenth chapter of Paul's *First Letter to the Corinthians*. Charity is defined as the love of God expressed through the God-made-man event in Christ and as man's love of neighbor, the solvent of hatred of the enemy.

In postapostolic and medieval Christian thought, charity was the will of God, an act of propitiation to a means of eternal reward, a social obligation, and an act of righteousness. The motives might be selfless altruism, desire for fame, inner satisfaction, or a desire to imitate the divinity. Byzantine society, its government and church, made charity a major concern and established numerous institutions for the sick, orphans, widows, indigent, and others in need of rehabilitation and assistance. Charity was also a cardinal feature of medieval western European society, which was guided by the church.

Charity as a synonym for love, either as God's love for man or man's reciprocal love for God expressed in acts of love for fellow men, a conception so central to the Western tradition, is not explicitly stated in Buddhism, Hinduism, and Islam. Nor do we find definitions of charity similar to the conceptions of *philanthrōpia* (Plato, Plutarch) or *agapē* (New Testament). The Buddha's Four Noble Truths *(catvāri-ārya-satyāni)* inherently include love and compassion toward fellow human beings. Buddhism sees suffering as a universal reality, but a reality with a cause. Suffering may be relieved through the application of three principles: *metta* or *maitri*, loving-kindness actively pursued; *karuṇā*, compassion, mercy, which does not repay evil with evil; and *muditā*, a feeling of approval of other people's good deeds. These principles find their expression in works of social welfare, including public works projects and the maintenance of hospitals and shelters or hospices.

The meaning of charity in Hinduism depends upon the interpretation of *dharma*, "the primary virtue of the active life of the Hindu." *Dharma* is the inner disposition and the conserving idea, while the action by which it is realized is known as *karman*, which is expressed in physical, verbal, and mental forms. The physical forms consist of good deeds such as hospitality, duties to wife and children, and assistance to those in need. Verbal charity is identified with proper or gentle speech and courteous behavior. Mental charity is synonymous with piety.

Hinduism has given a primary position to personal ethics. And the Upaniṣads clearly indicate that each person is responsible for his economic or social condition. If individuals are moral and perfect and economically safe, society will ultimately be perfect. Thus personal charity is enjoined to a degree that makes organized charity unnecessary.

If man is a creature good by nature, then man can develop an ethics of benevolence, justice, or righteousness. Jainism, in particular, which stresses self-cultivation more than social involvement, sees self-perfection as the best means of alleviating social misery. The value of charity as an act of benevolence is judged by the degree of personal cultivation and sacrifice involved. It is a spontaneous and personal virtue, instinctive rather than acquired. "To love your neighbor as yourself" is inherent in the Vedic formula of unity with the absolute self, "That art thou" *(tat tvam asi)*. Because one loves oneself, one is bound to love one's neighbor, who is not different from oneself.

Charity in Islam depends on the belief in an omnipotent God, master of mankind, which not only receives God's mercy but is always in danger of incurring his wrath. Thus mankind needs to serve God by means of good works, including almsgiving, both voluntary offerings *(ṣadaqāt)* and legally proscribed ones *(zakāt)*, kindness, and good treatment of parents, orphans, and the elderly. [*See* Zakāt.] As the author of moral commandments, God commands, and the believer must practice. A summary of Islam's moral code bearing on charity is found in the Qur'ān's seventeenth surah, lines 23–39.

"The Lord has decreed . . . kindness to parents. . . . Give the kinsman his due, and the needy, and the wayfarer. . . . Come not near the wealth of the orphan. . . ." These and other similar admonitions constitute the outward signs of piety, the means of expiating offenses, and the path to ultimate salvation.

[*See also* Love; Almsgiving; *and* Grace.]

BIBLIOGRAPHY

Berry, Thomas, *Buddhism.* New York, 1975.

Berry, Thomas. *Religions of India: Hinduism, Yoga, Buddhism.* New York, 1971.

Chaudhuri, Nirad C. *Hinduism.* London, 1979.

Constantelos, Demetrios J. *Byzantine Philanthropy and Social Welfare.* New Brunswick, N.J., 1968.

Conze, Edward. *Buddhism: Its Essence and Development.* Oxford, 1951.

Hands, A. R. *Charities and Social Aid in Greece and Rome.* Ithaca, N.Y., 1968.

Jeffrey, Arthur, ed. *Islam: Muhammad and His Religion.* New York, 1958.

May, Herbert G., and Bruce M. Metzger, eds. *The New Oxford Annotated Bible with the Apocrypha.* Rev. ed. New York, 1977.

Nikhilananda. *Essence of Hinduism.* Boston, 1948.

Nygren, Anders. *Agape and Eros.* Translated by Philip S. Watson. Rev. ed. Philadelphia, 1953.

Organ, Troy. *The Hindu Quest for the Perfection of Man.* Athens, Ohio, 1970.

Pétré, Hélène. *Caritas: Étude sur le vocabulaire Latin de la charité chrétienne.* Louvain, 1948.

Pickthall, M. M., trans. and ed. *The Meaning of the Glorious Qur'ān.* New York, 1930.

Pritchard, James B., ed. *The Ancient Near East.* 2 vols. Princeton, 1973–1975.

Quell, Gottfried, and Ethelbert Stauffer. "Agapao, agape, agapetos." In *Theological Dictionary of the New Testament,* edited by Gerhard Kittel, vol. 1, pp. 21–55. Grand Rapids, Mich., 1964.

Demetrios J. Constantelos

CHARLEMAGNE (c. 742–814), also known as Charles the Great and Carolus Magnus; king of the Franks (768–800) and first emperor of a revived Empire in the West (800–814). For three years after the death in 768 of Pépin III (the Short), the *regnum Francorum* was divided between his two sons, but in 771 the elder, Charlemagne, became sole ruler, although not without opposition. His unusually long reign was of major importance in the history of western Europe and the Christian church and the Latin culture associated with it. In 773–774, responding to papal appeal, Charlemagne invaded the Lombard kingdom, annexed it to his own and then visited Rome, where he was ceremonially received and given an "authoritative" text of church law. On a second visit (781) his two sons were baptized by the pope and given subordinate kingdoms.

Involuntary conversions and the establishment of an organized church followed Charlemagne's military victories over the Saxons (beginning in 772), but Saxony was for years beset by bloody and destructive rebellions. Nevertheless, the monastery of Fulda, the bishopric of Würzburg, and new settlements such as Paderborn became centers of organized missionary activity. In 785 the leaders of Saxon resistance accepted baptism, although it may be doubted whether many Saxons followed their example until further pressures, including severe punishment for "pagan" practices, had been employed. The conversion of the Frisians was simultaneously being achieved, although with less violence.

A succession of campaigns (led first by the king himself and then by subordinate commanders) against the Asiatic Avars west of the middle Danube and against Slav tribes to their south ended Avar independence and opened up the region to missionary activity from Salzburg and Aquileia. Campaigns were also conducted intermittently against northern Slav peoples, who then received clergy from the new Saxon bishoprics, and late in the reign the Franks were also in both military and peaceful contact with the Danes. In the southwest, a campaign into Muslim Spain in 778 ended disastrously, supposedly at Roncevalles in the Pyrenees. Subsequently, however, local commanders gradually extended Frankish authority over the predominantly Christian lands as far south as the Ebro (the region of Navarre and the later Catalonia).

Charlemagne inherited a concept of kingship that emphasized the obligation and legitimacy of extending the Christian faith by force of arms while also securing it at home. To these ends came also the utilization of the church hierarchy as well as lay officials as a means of social control; both groups were expected to give effect to the legal rules and pious exhortations expressed in capitularies promulgated in Latin by the assemblies that brought together bishops, abbots, and leading laymen in 779, 789, and frequently in later years. The king's personal devotion to *religio Christiana,* with which he is credited by his biographer Einhard (writing c. 829), was essentially expressed in observance of the externals of worship as provided by the court chaplains, with little regard for spirituality or personal morality. Even before 779, however, church authorities were making the king aware that among his responsibilities should be the encouragement of learning *(eruditio)* as a basis for more effective government and the more correct understanding of the texts on which the Christian faith was grounded.

Peter of Pisa, remembered as the person who taught

Charlemagne "Latin grammar," and other learned Italians joined the still-itinerant court. Around 780 Charlemagne seems to have invited churches and monasteries to supply copies of books in their possession; this was the beginning of a court library that by 790 included a range of patristic writings as well as a remarkable collection of pre-Christian classical texts. A small number of manuscripts, mostly liturgical, were decorated in a distinctive and eventually influential style by resident artists. The circle of scholars was notably enlarged by the arrival of Alcuin and other Englishmen and of the Visigothic Theodulf (later bishop of Orléans). Theodulf is generally accepted as the principal author of the remarkable first example of court scholarship, the so-called *Libri Carolini,* composed and revised (792–793) to counter the current Byzantine and papal concept of images and the adoration due them.

The heterodox views of Spanish ecclesiastics on Christ's relationship with God the Father (adoptionism) were condemned in Frankish councils and challenged in detail by Alcuin, apparently with ultimate success. An increasing concern also with unity of practice in the church was expressed in the provision of standard service texts. However, the "Gregorian" sacramentary sent from Rome was in fact ill suited to the needs of churches in Francia and had to be supplemented; in practice, mixed and divergent books were in use for private and public devotion and study for many decades.

In the 790s the court was providing adolescents (including laymen, e.g., Einhard) who had received a basic education elsewhere with more advanced instruction based on the antique tradition of the "liberal arts" and especially the trivium of grammar, rhetoric, and dialectic. The importance to church and kingdom of correct Latin was emphasized in a royal circular letter, but since this Latin was to be pronounced as spelled, a gap was opened between the language of scholarship and worship on the one hand and everyday speech in Romance (as well as Germanic) regions on the other. Serious attempts were nonetheless made to communicate the elements of the faith to the laity in their vernacular.

Charlemagne and his court increasingly remained at Aachen, where an impressive group of palace buildings including an octagonal chapel was built. This was accompanied by speculation on the nature of the Frankish king's authority over an *imperium Christianum.* In 799 Pope Leo III was the victim of a violent attack in Rome, and he appealed to Charlemagne; the latter's representatives cleared the pope of unspecified charges leveled against him, but final judgment on his attackers was reserved for the king. In the summer of 800 Charlemagne visited Saint-Martin's, Tours, and its abbot, Alcuin, and then journeyed via Ravenna to Rome. On 23 December he presided over an assembly at which the participating bishops declared that they could not pass judgment on the pope. The latter took an oath of innocence, and the Roman rebels were dealt with. On 25 December at mass in Saint Peter's the pope crowned Charlemagne, as he prayed and those present acclaimed him, "Augustus, great and powerful emperor of the Romans."

The ceremonies had obviously been carefully planned to recognize Charlemagne's unique authority and achievements, but he may well have been unprepared for the precise way in which he was made "emperor in the West." Even if he was worried about the reactions of the imperial court at Constantinople, however, his new title was very soon used in official documents and was subsequently carried on a distinctive new coin. Moreover, the almost annual promulgation of capitularies after 802 and his complaints that many were regularly ignored suggest that the emperor felt that he had assumed new responsibilities toward his Christian subjects.

The resident scholars and advisers were now predominantly younger men; the older generation had left the court for bishoprics and abbeys, and offered their views on doctrinal matters, in writing or at special assemblies. In 806 Charlemagne planned to divide his territorial empire, probably without passing on the title. The death of two of his sons left him with a single heir, Louis, and in 813 he was personally crowned by his father at Aachen. In the same year councils were held simultaneously in different parts of Francia to make more detailed regulations for church organization and practice. When Charlemagne died on 28 January 814 he was buried at Aachen in a tomb whose form and simple inscription are known only from Einhard. His death did not constitute the sharp break often supposed: some of the old courtiers remained and there was continuity of artistic activity at the new emperor's court. Louis did, however, have a deeper concern for Christian spirituality, and the fullest flowering of Carolingian learning took place when the territorial and political unity of the empire was already past history.

BIBLIOGRAPHY

The major historical, literary, and documentary sources for the reign of Charlemagne have been edited, some of them several times, in the various series of the "Monumenta Germaniae Historica" (1826–). The Council of Europe Exhibition devoted to Charlemagne and his heritage that took place at Aachen in 1965 was the occasion of the publication of the magnificent *Karl der Grosse: Lebenswerk u. Nachleben,* 4 vols. plus index, edited by Wolfgang Braunfels and others (Düsseldorf, 1965–1968), whose 2,400 pages provide authoritative accounts of almost every aspect of the man and the age. The history of the church is dealt with in volume 1 (organization), volume 2 (learning), and volume 3 (art and architecture). A concise semi-popular account is my *The Age of Charlemagne,* 2d ed. (New York, 1973), to be read in conjunction with my " 'Europae Pater': Charlemagne and His Achievement in the Light of Recent Scholarship," *English Historical Review* 85 (1970): 59–105. The most recent English-language account of the reign is Rosamond McKitterick's *The Frankish Kingdoms under the Carolingians, 751–987* (New York, 1983), chaps. 3, 4, and 6.

Donald A. Bullough

CHASTITY. In many religious traditions, the concept of chastity has generally referred to the adoption of ethical and moral norms in order to achieve a higher and purer life. It is believed to entail the purity of words, thoughts, and deeds. Chastity may also involve the practice of celibacy, but not necessarily. Not only the individual's sexual control but also the control and purity of all the senses are involved. Moral goodness and purity have been considered essential qualities for someone seeking a separation from the world, in order to live a blameless and perfect life in accordance with divine dictates.

Buddhism. In Buddhism, chastity takes on different forms in the lives of monks and lay persons. Members of Buddhist monastic orders practice chastity through celibacy. According to certain Buddhist teachings, keeping the vow of chastity provides tremendous benefits for the monks, who gain insight, vast knowledge, and magical powers, among other miraculous advantages. It has thus been asserted that a chaste monk would be able to rise in the air, to make his body first expand and then shrink, to rain down water and then fire from his body, and even to make two celestial trips around the earth. However, a monk who breaks the vow of chastity after taking it, and the person who causes another to fail in his vow, would be severely punished.

For lay people, on the other hand, chastity involves a more general purity. In this context, the maintenance of the respect and dignity of the institution of marriage is of paramount importance. Monogamy for lay people is favored for the sake of chastity of both sexes. In fact, although matrimonial sexual intercourse is required to produce children, abstention is thought to bring great rewards. According to the Buddhist Eightfold Path, purity and chastity in life are required in order to gain *nirvāṇa.*

Judaism. The notion of chastity has been a dominant theological theme in Judaism. In the early period of Israel's history, warriors were consecrated and consequently were required to be chaste (through celibacy) until after the war. In everyday life as well, people were required to be chaste in various ways. According to Jewish tradition, it was an essential requirement that the high priest be chaste. He married, but in order to maintain his chastity he was not allowed to marry a harlot, a profane woman, a divorcée, or even a widow. Moreover, his children's chastity was a reflection of his own. If the daughter of a high priest was found to be unchaste in her actions, she could be punished by burning, having profaned her father.

Chastity and purity formed a vital element of the marriage system. Except in the case of persons especially devoted to celibacy, marriage in Judaism is recognized as a matter of course and canonically as a holy tie between man and woman. The Talmud teaches that it is imperative for a man to have a wife. After marriage, a man "leaves his father and his mother and cleaves to his wife, and they become one flesh" (*Gn.* 2:24). Consequently, the Jewish people generally consider the chaste marriage to have been established by God. The commands of God regarding the ties of marriage are to be complied with.

Christianity. In early Christianity, the practice of chastity through celibacy was a means of future aggrandizement. Most of the early church fathers considered celibacy a superior form of chastity. According to Clement, God will give virgins, together with holy angels, a special place in his kingdom; this is a reward greater than having sons and daughters. It is even a greater reward than the one received by those who have passed a wedded life in sanctity and whose beds have not been defiled in the sense of Paul's statement that marriage does not defile.

For the person who was earnest in his quest for a life that would be chaste and would lead him closer to God, marriage was considered undersirable. In order to encourage such a person to remain chaste and refrain from marriage, the following biblical passage was frequently cited: "The children of this world marry and are given in marriage; but they that shall be accounted worthy to obtain that world and the resurrection from the dead neither marry nor are given in marriage" (*Lk.* 20:34–35).

Moreover, to be chaste in the Christian monastic system is not only to be celibate but also to keep oneself away from every fleshly interest. To avoid lust and keep pure thoughts is stressed as a cardinal element of chastity. The purity of thoughts was required not only of the celibate Christian but also of the married person, for whom chastity involved the adherence to a code of married life as dictated by divine command.

Islam. In Islam, chastity in general is regarded as the state of spiritual and physical cleanliness. Celibacy is not regarded as an essential element of chastity. Islam rejects the monastic life, and even in the Ṣūfī order marriage is recommended. Chastity is considered a necessity on the path to God, and it involves purity of thoughts and actions, resulting in a life spent according to God's commands. Chastity in relation to one's actions involves sexual restraints; physical chastity thus implies that people refrain from sexual activities outside the bonds of marriage. Moreover, the principles of chastity demand that Muslim couples abstain at certain times from sexual intercourse, for example, during the fasting days of Ramaḍān, or during the pilgrimage to Mecca. Some fundamentalist Islamic teachers also enjoin a dress code to demonstrate chastity. Thus a chaste woman is required in some groups to wear a veil that covers most of her face as well as a dress that is long enough to conceal all of her body. In general, Muslims will stress that modesty in dress is basic to maintaining chastity in life.

BIBLIOGRAPHY

Kirsch, Felix M. *Training in Chastity*. New York, 1930.

Main, John [Elsie Worthington Parson]. *Religious Chastity: An Ethnological Study*. New York, 1913.

Thurian, Max. *Marriage and Celibacy*. London, 1959.

Williams, Harry Abbott. *Poverty, Chastity and Obedience: The True Virtues*. London, 1975.

GABRIEL ABDELSAYED

CH'ENG HAO (1032–1085), also known as Master Ming-tao; one of the originators of Sung dynasty Neo-Confucianism. Ch'eng Hao and his brother, the philosopher Ch'eng I, came from a family of government officials. They spent their childhood in Kiangsi, Anhui, and Honan, where their father served in a variety of governmental posts. The brothers had a period of study under Chou Tun-i (1017–1073) before accompanying their father to Kaifeng, the capital, where they entered the national university.

After passing the highest civil service examination and receiving his degree in 1057, Ch'eng Hao embarked on an official career, serving first in local offices and then in the capital, where he was several times received in imperial audience. However, after 1070 he fell from favor for opposing the reform program of Wang An-shih (1021–1086). Although leaders on both sides of the factional struggle that characterized the bureaucracy shared a common vision of the ideal society, the Ch'engs profoundly disagreed with the content and methods of Wang An-shih's reforms. In 1080 Ch'eng Hao was dismissed from office altogether. He spent the remaining five years of his life living in retirement in Lo-yang, which had become a center for Neo-Confucians and other thinkers opposed to the prevailing policies. For the Ch'engs, as for others, conscientious fulfillment of one's social obligations, including engagement in public affairs, remained the hallmark of the Confucian scholar. Ch'eng Hao wrote little but transmitted his teachings through disciples who recorded the conversations of both brothers, frequently without specific attribution to one or the other.

Ch'eng Hao and Ch'eng I had a close personal relationship: they not only saw eye to eye on politics but also shared a commitment to the Confucian tradition as interpreted by Meng-tzu. They agreed on fundamental philosophical issues such as the metaphysics of *li* ("principle") or *t'ien-li*, ("principle of Heaven"). In discussing self-cultivation both brothers emphasized the crucial importance of *ching* ("reverence, seriousness") and *ch'eng* ("sincerity, genuineness"). It was only later that scholars began to focus upon the differences between the two brothers. Such traditional scholarship traced back to Ch'eng Hao the inward-oriented tradition of Hsin-hsüeh (the school of Mind), the development of which they attributed to Lu Chiu-yüan (Lu Hsiang-shan, 1139–1193) and Wang Yang-ming (Wang Shou-jen, 1472–1529). Conventionally, this tradition was contrasted to what scholars saw as the more rationalistic philosophy of Li-hsüeh (the school of Principle), associated with Ch'eng I and Chu Hsi (1130–1200). The disparities between the teachings of the two brothers can be seen in part as reflecting differences in temperament between the mellow and serene Ch'eng Hao and his solemn and stern younger brother.

Basic to Ch'eng Hao's teachings is an intense sense of the unity of the universe. As a result, his philosophy is more richly evocative and less concerned with drawing clear distinctions than that of his brother. For both brothers, the world is structured by principle, but of prime importance for Ch'eng Hao is its dynamic quality as it generates life in a constant process of production and reproduction.

The ultimate goal for the individual is to achieve unity with the universe, to become "a man of *jen*" and "perfectly form one body with all things." Ch'eng Hao views *jen* (humaneness, humanity, benevolence) not only as the supreme, overarching virtue but also as a very feeling for life. He illustrates this by referring to a medical text that terms numbness or paralysis of hands and feet an "absence of *jen*." A paralyzed individual no longer considers his limbs as parts of himself; similarly, an absence of *jen* prevents a person from realizing that, as Meng-tzu taught, "all things are already complete within me." Ch'eng Hao, like Chou Tun-i, refused to have the grass outside his window cut, for he wanted always to see the spirit of creation at work before him.

Ch'eng Hao believed that when we make artificial distinctions between the internal and the external our identification with the universe is obscured and selfishness results. To dispel selfishness requires the preservation of the original "mind-and-heart" (*hsin*, the seat of our affective as well as our rational faculties) that we share with all things and that is identified with principle. This preservation of *hsin* requires reverence and sincerity in all we do. The objective is to recover our innate moral knowledge and to stabilize and calm our human nature.

Since at least the time of Meng-tzu, human nature (*hsing*), particularly its moral quality, was of central concern to Chinese thinkers. According to Ch'eng Hao, our nature is the material force (*ch'i*) that we receive at birth. In its original tranquil state it cannot be characterized as good or evil, but once aroused good and evil result, although in varying measure depending on the individual. In keeping with his holism, Ch'eng Hao, unlike his brother, held that both good and evil are principles of Heaven (*t'ien-li*). Like the two cosmic forces *yin* and *yang*, good and evil alternate with and are dependent upon each other. The goal for humans is to attain the "mean" (*chung*), for to Ch'eng Hao evil is a matter of either going too far, as Mo-tzu did with his doctrine of universal love, or of not going far enough, as in the case of the hedonistic egotism attributed to Yang Chu (c. 350 BCE).

Like other Sung Confucians Ch'eng Hao was influenced by Buddhism as a young man but later came to argue that it was false and anti-social. Ch'eng Hao believed that dispelling selfishness entails neither rejection of the true self nor denial of the senses. It is because the Buddhists think in terms of their narrow selves, he felt, that they wish to rid themselves of sense perception. But, unable to let go of the self, they become like a man holding a stone who sinks ever deeper into a river, all the while resenting the stone's weight. Far from denying his feelings, Ch'eng Hao's sage has attained a state in which his emotions are perfectly attuned to the world. His anger and joy are without the slightest trace of arbitrariness. Devoid of selfishness, they are in perfect accord with the objective moral value of things and events.

Beyond that, the sage possesses an unfathomable, inscrutable psychic quality that emanates from the realm "above form" (*hsing-erh-shang*) and permeates all things. Called *shen*, a term found in the appendices of the *I ching* (Book of Changes), this quality, conventionally translated "spirit," should not be thought of as an entity. In contrast to Ch'eng I, who rarely mentions the term, *shen* figures importantly in Ch'eng Hao's thought as its does in that of several of his older contemporaries. Consistent with his holism, Ch'eng Hao disagrees with Chang Tsai (1020–1077) in holding that *shen* pervades even impure material force (*ch'i*).

[*See also* Confucian Thought, *article on* Neo-Confucianism; Jen; Li; Hsin; *and the biographies of Meng-tzu, Chou Tun-i, Chang Tsai, and Ch'eng I.*]

BIBLIOGRAPHY

The collected writings and conversations of the Ch'eng brothers may best be consulted in a recent punctuated edition entitled *Erh Ch'eng chi*, 4 vols. (Peking, 1981), which indicates variant readings. The best and most widely used earlier edition is the *Erh Ch'eng Ch'üan-shu*, included in the *Ssu-pu pei-yao* series. Portions have been translated in Wing-tsit Chan's *A Source Book in Chinese Philosophy* (Princeton, 1963). Fully 162 of the selections in the *Chin-ssu lu*, a philosophical anthology compiled by Chu Hsi and Lü Tsu-ch'ien, are taken from Ch'eng Hao. The entire text has been translated by Professor Chan as *Reflections on Things at Hand* (New York, 1967). A. C. Graham's *Two Chinese Philosophers: Ch'eng Ming-tao and Ch'eng Yi-ch'uan* (London, 1958) is a major achievement and remains the only monograph in a Western language. It has been reviewed by Wing-tsit Chan in *Journal of the American Oriental Society* 79 (1959):150–155. The Ch'eng brothers are discussed in all the standard accounts of Chu Hsi, Neo-Confucianism, and Chinese philosophy. Further biographical and bibliographical information may be found in *Sung Biographies*, edited by Herbert Franke (Wiesbaden, 1976).

CONRAD SCHIROKAUER

CH'ENG I (1033–1107), also known as Master I-ch'uan; one of the Northern Sung period originators of Neo-Confucianism. Ch'eng I's youth and education were similar to those of his elder brother, Ch'eng Hao. Both brothers studied for a time with Chou Tun-i before entering the national university. In his university paper, "On What Yen-tzu Loved to Learn," Ch'eng I argued that sagehood does not necessarily depend on an innate knowledge of the good present from the time of one's birth but can also be attained by following a program of study and self-cultivation. The essay so impressed the noted Confucian scholar Hu Yüan (993–1059) that he appointed Ch'eng I to an academic post. Ch'eng obtained his civil service examination degree in 1059 but failed the palace examination and never tried again. In 1064 he declined a university position. Although it was not until 1086 that he accepted an official post, Ch'eng I's interest in government affairs was marked by his outspoken opposition to the ambitious policies of Wang An-shih (1021–1086), the dynasty's greatest reformer. While living in Loyang from 1072 to 1083 Ch'eng associated with many government officials and attracted numerous capable disciples.

Ch'eng I entered government service when, after the death of Emperor Shen-tsung (r. 1067–85), the empress dowager, acting as regent for Emperor Che-tsung (1077–1100), reversed the government policies of their predecessor and filled the highest posts with opponents of Wang An-shih's program. For twenty months Ch'eng I served as imperial tutor. While his unyielding integrity won him admiration, his unbending rigor also made him enemies, with the result that he was transferred to a less sensitive post in Loyang. When, in 1093, Che-tsung assumed personal rule, he reversed government policies once more, and purged the government of the faction opposing Wang An-shih's reforms. In 1097 Ch'eng I was banished to Szechwan and his lands were confiscated. His teachings were condemned, and in 1103 his works were ordered destroyed. Although Ch'eng I was pardoned in 1106, his teachings were still under ban when he died the following year. Only four disciples dared to attend his funeral.

Sharing a common Neo-Confucian world view, the Ch'eng brothers were in substantial agreement on a wide range of political, moral, and philosophical issues, but they differed in their cast of mind. Ch'eng I by no means denied the inner and subjective dimensions of metaphysics and self-cultivation usually associated with his brother, but his original contributions lay elsewhere. In particular, by developing the theory of "principle" or "pattern" *(li)* and the "investigation of things" *(ko-wu)* he did much to give Neo-Confucianism intellectual vigor and persuasiveness.

The expression "the investigation of things," which comes from "The Great Learning" *(Ta hsüeh)* chapter of the *Book of Rites (Li chi)*, had up to the time of Ch'eng I been interpreted ethically. Ch'eng reinterpreted it to mean that one must grasp the principles inherent in everything. It is principle that gives everything its inherent, essential character. Ch'eng said, "every blade of grass and every tree possesses *li* and should be examined." At the same time he equated "things" with (human) "affairs," for, like all Confucians, he was greatly concerned with the world of human relations. For him, there was no difference between the principles governing human behavior and those found in nature and no gap between the normative and the descriptive. The principles of morality had the same ontological status as those of physics.

In moral terms, Ch'eng I's dictum "Principle is one but its manifestations are many" affirms both the distinctions demanded by righteousness *(i)* as well as the unifying force of humaneness *(jen)*. Sung dynasty scholars, deriving the meaning of *li* from veins in jade, thought of *li* as a network or pattern that underlies the world. Li is an abstract pattern that belongs to the world "above form" (*hsing-erh-shang*, i.e., the transcendent) and is equivalent to the way of Heaven.

In his commentary on the *I ching* (Book of Changes) Ch'eng I, like his brother, argues that the world is never static. Change and creation go on constantly as *yin* and *yang*, the cosmic forces, interact, expanding and contracting to produce every new *ch'i*, the material force that constitutes the physical world and gives it its energy. Following Chang Tsai (1020–1077), Ch'eng I understood the old term for spiritual beings, *kuei-shen*, in purely naturalistic terms. For him, "the positive and negative forces *(kuei-shen)* are the traces of creation." Principle alone is eternal. Within and beyond the constant flux, principle remains the same and forever.

Most important for human beings is that principle is accessible. People, like everything else, are composed of a combination of principle and material force. Individuals, however, differ in the quality of their physical nature. Those who receive pure and clear *ch'i* at birth have great capacity and are wise, whereas, at the other extreme, the unfortunates endowed with turbid *ch'i* are stupid. However, regardless of physical endowment, all are alike in their basic, original nature, which is *li* and therefore good. It is therefore possible, at least in theory, for even the least promising to learn and change. Following Meng-tzu, Ch'eng I locates the "four beginnings" of virtue (humaneness, righteousness, propriety, and wisdom) in the original nature that all people share.

Ch'eng I was also concerned with the aspect of principle that inhered in the human mind-and-heart *(hsin)*, which controls the body. Once active, the mind is prone to err, apt to go astray and lose its unity. According to Ch'eng I, the individual must guard against depravity but must not discard sensation, consciousness, or thought. Instead, he must hold fast to the mind through the strenuous inner spiritual and moral practice of *ching* ("reverence, seriousness") attained by concentrating on one thing. Through single-minded seriousness, confusion will be avoided, unity preserved, calmness attained. Inner seriousness will, further, result in proper external deportment.

For Ch'eng I, as for his brother, the inner and the outer are a unity. On one occasion he even said that principle could best be sought within one's own mind. However, the emphasis in Ch'eng I's understanding of "the investigation of things" and the closely related "extension of knowledge" is on reading books, discussing events, and handling affairs, on the cognitive knowledge of the principles in the world at large rather than intuitive recovery of the principles within. While he held that extensive study is valuable, Ch'eng I did not propose that one need investigate everything. Rather, from investigating the principle in one case one can understand by inference other principles. Furthermore, one can begin anywhere since all principles form a single system.

[*See also* Confucian Thought, *article on* Neo-Confucianism; Jen; Li; Hsin; *and the biographies of Meng-tzu, Chou Tun-i, Chang Tsai, and Ch'eng Hao.*]

BIBLIOGRAPHY

The collected writings and conversations of the Ch'eng brothers may best be consulted in a recent punctuated edition entitled *Erh Ch'eng chi* (Peking, 1981), 4 vols., which indicates variant readings. The best and most widely used earlier edition is the *Erh Ch'eng ch'üan-shu,* included in the *Ssu-pu pei-yao* series. Portions have been translated in Wing-tsit Chan's *A Source Book in Chinese Philosophy* (Princeton, 1963). Fully 338 of the selections in the *Chin-ssu lu,* a philosophical anthology compiled by Chu Hsi and Lü Tsu-ch'ien, are taken from Ch'eng I. The entire text has been translated by Professor Chan as *Reflections on Things at Hand* (New York, 1967). A. C. Graham's *Two Chinese Philosophers: Ch'êng Ming-tao and Ch'êng Yi-ch'uan* (London, 1958) is a major achievement and remains the only monograph in a Western language. It has been reviewed by Wing-tsit Chan in *Journal of the American Oriental Society,* 79 (1959):150–155. The Ch'eng brothers are discussed in all the standard accounts of Chu Hsi, Neo-Confucianism, and Chinese philosophy. Further biographical and bibliographical information may be found in *Sung Biographies,* edited by Herbert Franke (Wiesbaden, 1976).

CONRAD SCHIROKAUER

CHEN-JEN.

The term *chen-jen* ("real person") is first encountered in parts of the *Chuang-tzu* that are thought to date from the third century BCE. It may also be translated "perfect person" or "true person." Chuang-tzu's real person is one who does not oppose the human and the natural, who knows how to accept both defeat and victory, joy and sorrow, life and death without being affected by them. Ordinary people, according to Chuang-tzu, "wallow in their passions because they are out of touch with the workings of Heaven. The real person of ancient times knew neither to love life nor to hate death. . . . He took pleasure in what he received; he forgot what he gave back. This is what it means not to throw away the Tao with the heart, not to use what is human to help out what is heavenly. This is what is called a 'real person' " (chap. 6). The "real person" is thus one who possesses what is for Chuang-tzu the highest form of knowledge, the knowledge that enables him to "make all things equal" and so renders him invulnerable to the vicissitudes of human life.

Chuang-tzu uses a whole range of terms to refer to this ideal person, among them "divine person" *(shen-jen),* "accomplished person" *(chih-jen),* and "saintly person" *(sheng-jen).* The last term in particular, being the standard term in the *Lao-tzu,* appears much more frequently than "real person." But the term "saintly person" had the disadvantage, at a time when the battle between the different schools of philosophy had reached its pitch, of referring also to the Confucian ideal person. In the *Lao-tzu* itself, in fact, it refers indifferently to the ruler of men and the person who, even if he does not rule, is worthy of ruling. By Chuang-tzu's time the feudal system of the Chou dynasty was in its final agony, and interstate relationships were characterized by ruse and violence. This political context forced philosophers to choose between "man" and "nature," between politics and integrity, and the term "saintly person" came increasingly to serve only as the designation of the Confucian, that is, political, ideal. In its place the Taoists put the "real person." This person does not yet, by definition, refuse all contact with human society and politics, but if he should happen to "get involved," he will not allow himself to "feel involved."

In chapter 21 of the *Chuang-tzu* we thus read of Sun Shu-ao, who had "thrice been named prime minister without considering it glorious and thrice been dismissed without looking distressed." Someone asks Sun Shu-ao whether he has some special way of "using his heart." "Why should I be any better than anyone else?" he responds. "When [the nomination] came, I could not refuse it; when it left, I could not keep it. Neither getting it nor losing it had anything to do with me." Such a man, comments Chuang-tzu through the mouth of none other than Confucius, is a "real person of old."

This phrase, "a real person of old," shows that the concept of the "real person" is associated from the very first with the notion of a golden age in times past, a paradise lost. On the individual level, it is linked with the preservation of one's original purity and integrity: "The way of whiteness and purity consists exclusively in keeping one's spirit. If you keep your spirit and do not lose it, you will become one with your spirit" (*Chuang-tzu,* chap. 15).

Chuang-tzu makes no explicit reference to the techniques that enable one to maintain one's purity and "keep" one's spirit, but they are implicit in the vocabulary used to describe the "real persons of old." The reference to these techniques is even clearer in another third century BCE text, the *Lü-shih ch'un-ch'iu* (Annals of Mr. Lü): "One who daily renews his seminal energy and gets rid entirely of perverse energies, and [so] lives out his heaven [-appointed] years, is called a 'real person.' " The reference is all the more interesting in that the next line reads: "The saint-kings of the past perfected their persons, and the empire then perfected itself. They regulated their bodies, and the empire was regulated." To solve the crisis of the body politic, says this author, we must find individuals who, like the saints of old, concentrate on the vital energies of their own bodies.

A long dissertation on the Taoist ideal in chapter 7 of the *Huai-nan–tzu* by Liu An (180?–122 BCE) adds little of substance to Chuang-tzu's conception of the "real person." Liu An's language, however, is more explicitly physiological and cosmological: the essence of the "saintly person" or "real person"—the terms remain interchangeable—is "one with the root of Great Purity, and he wanders in the realm of no-form. . . . He makes ghosts and gods to do his bidding." In chapter 14 we learn that the "real person" has such cosmic powers because he has "never become distinct from the Great One." By "closing up his four gates"—the eyes, ears, mouth, and heart—and keeping his vital forces from being wasted on the outside, he "regulates what is within and knows nothing of what is without" (chap. 7). [*See the biography of Liu An.*]

The *Huai-nan–tzu* is no more specific about how to become a "real person" than the *Chuang-tzu.* But his "real person" is obviously far less concerned with the world of politics and society than the "real person" of Chuang-tzu, and he is correspondingly more concerned with his interior world of spirits, souls, and oneness. Within the scope of that world, moreover, he has attained to what can only be called superhuman powers. These powers are precisely those later ascribed to exorcists and Taoist priests.

A wide range of techniques leading not just to supernatural powers but to immortality are described in the *Lieh-hsien chuan* (Biographies of the Immortals, second century CE). The "way of the immortals" might involve a diet of pine seeds or sap, of mushrooms, or simply of clouds; it might mean the ingestion of a variety of elixirs or mineral drugs, the "circulation of energy and the transmutation of the body," the elimination of the five cereals from one's diet, or "nourishing one's energy." "Nourishing one's energy" usually refers to an art of intercourse in which the semen, rather than being allowed to flow out of the body, is "returned" by way of the spinal column to "repair the brain." In the *Lieh-hsien chuan* this technique is specifically attributed to Lao-tzu, who is one of only three immortals in this text to be called a "real person."

The second, Master Fu-chü, makes a living as a wandering mirror-polisher in the region of Wu (southeastern China). He also regularly heals sick clients with "purple pills and red drugs," and the local people first recognize in him a "real person" when he saves thousands from an epidemic with his medicine. Later, before leaving for one of the "isles of the immortals" in the Eastern Sea, he creates a stream with miraculous healing powers for the local people, who, after his departure, set up dozens of sanctuaries for his worship. The third "real person," Chu Huang, is himself first cured of an ailment by a "Taoist" *(tao-shih)* living on a mountain and is then given a book called *Lao-chün huang-t'ing ching* (The Yellow Court Classic of Lord Lao). When he finally returns home eighty years later, "his white hair had all turned black." [*See also* Hsien.]

In his *Lun-heng* (Critical Disquisitions), Wang Ch'ung (27–97 CE) refers to the belief that Lao-tzu became a "real person" by "nourishing his spermatic essence and being chary of his energy" (chap. 7). [*See the biography of Wang Ch'ung.*] A commentary from the second century CE on the *Lao-tzu,* the *Ho-shang kung,* confirms that the "real person" is one who "cultivates the Tao within his body by being chary of his energy and by nourishing his spirits" (chap. 54). The first glimpse of what all this means comes from the oldest extant version of *The Yellow Court Classic,* which alludes to the "Real-Person Infant Elixir" inside the body.

The *Lao-chün chung ching* (Classic on the Center of the Person, first–third centuries CE) identifies the "Real-Person Infant Elixir" as the "father and mother of the Tao, [those who] give birth to the infant" (1.6b). He (or she) is also called the "master of the real self, who is constantly instructing me in the techniques of eternal life, the way of gods and immortals" (1.7b). This internal "real person" also appears in the *T'ai-shang ling-pao wu-fu hsü* (Preface to the Five Symbols of the Potent Treasure of the Most High), a work of the fourth century. The main technique for obtaining immortality described in this text involves absorption of the energies of the heavens of the five directions. The energies of the center are used to nourish the "real person" whose name is Infant Elixir, and who dwells in the Yellow Court.

Every adept thus contains within his or her body a "real person" in embryo. It is the adept's "real self," and if it is properly fed and instructed, it will grow up to replace entirely the "old self." For this nourishment and instruction it relies on what Chuang-tzu called "real persons of the past": in the text of *The Five Symbols,* for example, it is the Real Person of Bell Mountain who reveals to the legendary emperor Yü the "oral instructions for the way to eternal life" (1.6a). When a hermit later explores a cave in which Yü had buried a set of the five symbols, called "real writs," he discovers it to be a "residence full of real persons" (1.9a). The most important of the myriads of "real persons" who come thus to people Taoist caves and heavens is Lao-tzu himself, who is in fact already the real self the adept will become.

In general, the religious content of the term "real person," implicit already in the *Chuang-tzu*, becomes entirely explicit by the fourth and fifth centuries: it refers to the Taoist master or mistress, the one who, in the flesh or in the spirit, transmits sacred secrets. The revelations on Mount Mao (Mao-shan), for example, which date to the years 364–370 and which form the scriptural basis for the Mao-shan tradition, are almost all attributed to *chen-jen*, many of whom are female. By the fifth century, in rituals of the Ling-pao (Potent Treasure) school, living Taoist priests themselves are called "real men." This usage remains current to the present day.

[*See also* Taoism; Priesthood, *article on* Taoist Priesthood; Alchemy, *article on* Chinese Alchemy; *and the biographies of Chuang-tzu and Lao-tzu*.]

BIBLIOGRAPHY

Translations

Erkes, Eduard, trans. *Ho-shang kung's Commentary on Lao tse*. Ascona, Switzerland, 1950.

Forke, Alfred, trans. *Lun-hêng* (1907–1911). 2d ed. 2 vols. New York, 1962.

Lau, D. C., trans. *Tao-te ching* (1963). Reprint, New York, 1976.

Morgan, Evan, trans. and ed. *Tao, the Great Luminant: Essays from Huai-nan tzu* (1935). Reprint, New York, 1969.

Ware, James Roland, trans. *Alchemy, Medicine, Religion in the China of A.D. 320: The Nei P'ien of Ko Hung* (1967). Reprint, New York, 1981.

Watson, Burton, trans. *The Complete Works of Chuang Tzu*. New York, 1968.

Wilhelm, Richard, trans. *Frühling und Herbst des Lü Bu We* (1928). Reprint, Düsseldorf, 1971. A translation of the *Lü-shih ch'un-ch'iu*.

Translations with Studies

Kaltenmark, Max, trans. and ed. *Le Lie-sien tchouan, biographies légendaires des immortels taoïstes de l'antiquité*. Peking, 1953. Contains superb notes on each of the seventy biographies of the immortals.

Larre, Claude. *Le traité VII du Houai Nan Tseu*. Paris, 1982. Contains studies of both the "saint" and the "real person" in the *Huai-nan-tzu*.

Schipper, Kristofer. *Le corps taoïste*. Paris, 1982. Contains good introductions to and partial translations of the *Huang-t'ing ching* and the *Lao-chün chung ching*. See chapters 6 and 8, respectively.

JOHN LAGERWEY

CHEN-YEN Buddhism is a form of Vajrayāna Buddhism that flourished in China from the seventh to the twelfth century. The term *chen-yen* is a translation of the Sanskrit word *mantra* and literally means "real word." The school is also called Mi-chiao ("esoteric teaching") to distinguish it both from all other forms of Buddhism, which are regarded as exoteric, and from Indo-Tibetan Vajrayāna. The Chinese translation of *mantra* by the words *chen-yen* underscores the importance of a realized ontology. *Chen* designates the real, apprehended through words, meditation, and action: it is reality realized.

Although the term *chen-yen* is conventionally used to designate sectarian lineages during the T'ang (618–907) and Sung (960–1278) dynasties, it may also indicate Tantric precursors of the organized lineages and the continued presence of Chen-yen elements in other sects and in popular cults.

History. Buddhism spread across Asia on two levels: clerics with a theological bent missionized the literate elite while healers and wonder-workers ministered to the peasants. Early proto-Tantric materials in China appear at both levels, although their application is largely associated with wonder-workers. Chu Lü-yen translated the first text containing *dhāraṇīs*, the *Mo-teng-ch'ieh ching* (T.D. no. 1300), in 230 CE, yet there is little evidence that it aroused interest at the Wu court in the South. Fo-t'u-teng (d. 348) worked among the people and served the rough Latter Chao emperors Shih Lo (r. 330–333) and Shih Hu (r. 333–348) with a repertoire of *mantras* and *dhāraṇīs*. Like later Chen-yen masters, he used ritual to bring rain, to make military prognostications, to heal, and to influence politics.

During the Six Dynasties period (221–584), the magical use of *mantra* and *dhāraṇī* found greater acceptance in North China while other Buddhist traditions dominated the literary culture of the South. The unification of China under the Sui (584–618) and T'ang dynasties wedded the interests, culture, and family lines of the "barbarian" North with those of the Han South. Meanwhile in India, Tantric ritual, spurned earlier as heterodox by the Buddhist establishment, was being codified and blended with Mahāyāna theology, resulting in the formation of the Vajrayāna. During the first century of T'ang rule other Buddhist schools held sway, and Taoists were patronized by emperors who made much of the fact that they bore the surname (Li) of the sage Lao-tzu.

Tantric teachings remained eclipsed until the arrival of Śubhākarasiṃha (Shan-wu-wei) in 716 and his translation of the *Mahāvairocana Sūtra* (T.D. no. 848). Vajrabodhi (Chin-kang-chih) and his disciple Amoghavajra

(Pu-k'ung) arrived in 720 and produced two selective translations of the *Sarvatathāgatatattvasaṃgraha* (T.D. no. 866, 865). For the next fifty years the wonder-working abilities of these *ācāryas* ("teachers") and the prestige of their newly imported teachings bolstered the school until, under Amoghavajra and Emperor Tai-tsung (r. 762–779), Chen-yen replaced Taoism as the dominant religious force among the elite.

During the T'ang there were two closely related Chen-yen lineages. Śubhākarasiṃha and his disciple I-hsing concentrated on the *Mahāvairocana Sūtra* and its *Commentary* (T.D. no. 1796) and on the *Susiddhikāra Sūtra* (T.D. no. 893). Vajrabodhi, Amoghavajra, and Amoghavajra's disciples Han-kuang, Hui-kuo, and others concentrated on the *Sarvatathāgatatattvasaṃgraha* and also incorporated teachings associated with the *Mahāvairocana Sūtra.* Thus, each lineage had a characteristic textual emphasis. Only the best disciples were initiated into both. Amoghavajra's synthesis was the most influential, although the lineage and teachings of Śubhākarasiṃha continued to be transmitted. Both lineages had links to non-Esoteric sects; that of Śubhākarasiṃha has great influence in T'ien-t'ai, while that of Vajrabodhi developed links to Hua-yen. A similar situation developed in Japan as the Shingon and Tendai Esoteric lineages (Tōmitsu and Taimitsu, respectively) interacted with each other and with other sects. Following Amoghavajra's death in 774 his disciples continued to perform rituals in the Imperial Chapel, at the Green Dragon and Ta Hsing-shan temples in Ch'ang-an, and at the Golden Pavilion on Mount Wu-t'ai. At the beginning of the ninth century Japanese clerics such as Saichō (767–822), the founder of Tendai, and Kūkai (774–835), founder of Shingon and disciple of Hui-kuo, studied the teachings in China. Chen-yen continued to be popular at the court and spread among the upper classes in the provinces. It suffered during the Hui-ch'ang persecution of 845 but was not completely extinguished.

Chen-yen showed renewed vitality during the Sung dynasty owing to a final wave of missionaries from India. Shih-hu, Fa-t'ien, and Fa-hsien presided over an Esoteric revival, translating new scriptures and producing complete translations of earlier works, such as Shih-hu's 1002 CE version of the *Sarvatathāgatatattvasaṃgraha* (T.D. no. 882). Chen-yen ritual elements continued to penetrate other Buddhist sects and when its lineages died these elements continued in the other sects and in popular traditions. Esoteric Buddhism had two further revivals. The first was under the impact of Lamaism during the Yüan (1206–1368), the second during the nineteenth century with the reintroduction of the school from Japan.

Texts. Chen-yen teachings are drawn from two major texts, the *Mahāvairocana Sūtra* and the *Sarvatathāgatatattvasaṃgraha.* The *Mahāvairocana Sūtra* was probably written in North India during the seventh century. The text begins with a theological prolegomenon describing Mahāvairocana Buddha's palace at the summit of the cosmos (Akaniṣṭha Heaven). The palace and the cosmos are manifestations of Mahāvairocana's "wondrous transformation power" *(adhiṣṭhāna),* which is based on the realization of ultimate unconditioned reality (*śūnyatā;* "emptiness"). The unconditioned and the cosmos manifested through transformative power are presented as a *maṇḍala,* first as an exterior *maṇḍala,* then as the *maṇḍala* realized ritually in the heart of the practitioner. The massive *Commentary* (T.D. no. 1796), giving Śubhākarasiṃha's oral explanations as recorded by I-hsing, is indispensable. Another arrangement of the *Commentary* by Chih-yen and Wen-ku was influential in T'ien-t'ai circles.

There are three versions of the *Sarvatathāgatatattvasaṃgraha,* those of Vajrabodhi (T.D. no. 866), of Amoghavajra (T.D. no. 865), and the complete version of Shih-hu (T.D. no. 882), which dates from the Sung. Those of Vajrabodhi and Amoghavajra are highly abridged selections from the text. The *Saravatathāgatatattvasaṃgraha,* apparently written in South India, also begins in the Akaniṣṭha Heaven and presents a series of *maṇḍalas* based on a fivefold visionary structure through which the *bodhisattva* Sarvārthasiddha realizes his identity with Mahāvairocana as the unconditioned *dharmakāya.* Thus, he also realizes his identity with all of the Buddha's wondrous transformations, which form the conditioned world. Amoghavajra's *Shih-pa-hui chih-kuei* (T.D. no. 869) is important in understanding the *Tattvasaṃgraha.*

A third text important to the Chen-yen school is the *Susiddhikāra Sūtra* (T.D. no. 893), a ritual compendium translated by Śubhākarasiṃha and closely associated with the *Mahāvairocana Sūtra.* During the ninth century some lineages regarded the *Susiddhikāra Sūtra* as the synthetic conjunction of the *Mahāvairocana Sūtra* and the *Sarvatathāgatatattvasaṃgraha,* calling Chen-yen the "Triple Great Dharma." Some of Amoghavajra's disciples referred to the total Chen-yen teaching as "the Manuals of *Siddhi,* the Eighteen Assemblies [of the *Sarvatathāgatatattvasaṃgraha*], and the Mahākaruṇāgarbha Maṇḍala [of the *Mahāvairocana Sūtra*]" (T.D. 50.294b).

Teachings. The basic teachings of Chen-yen are common to both textual traditions. Chen-yen teaches the ritual realization of the paradoxical identity of *nirvāṇa* and *saṃsāra,* of the unconditioned and the world, of

Buddha and man. This conjunction is a primary organizing motif in the major texts and in Chinese commentary and ritual adaptions.

The Three Mysteries. Chen-yen proclaims the goal of enlightenment in this world, in this body, not in some distant land aeons hence. According to the *Mahāvairocana Sūtra,* "the complete Chen-yen altar is first established in your own body. . . . [Mahāvairocana] is in this body" (T.D. 18.36c). This immanental realization and a closely guarded initiatory structure distinguish Chen-yen from exoteric Buddhism. Enlightment is actualized in ritual through the "three mysteries" (Chin., *san-mi;* Skt., *triguhya*) of body, speech, and mind. The practitioner realizes that his body, speech, and consciousness in meditation are identical with those of Mahāvairocana. The Three Mysteries therefore allow the practitioner to realize that *bodhi,* the "thought of enlightenment," exists within us. Enlightenment is accomplished through a ritual realization of the enlightened state guided by iconographic, mantric, and meditational conventions.

A key to realizing the Three Mysteries is meditation on the Sanskrit "seed syllable" *A.* The *Mahāvairocana Sūtra* says, "What is the Chen-yen Dharma? It is [the teaching of] the letter *A*" (T.D. 18.10a). *A,* the first letter in the Sanskrit alphabet, is also a negative prefix. Thus, it represents the conjunction of the conditioned and the unconditioned, of *saṃsāra* and *nirvāṇa,* and is the symbol of Mahāvairocana and of *bodhi.* Through ritual and meditation this "seed" is nurtured in the heart, and the meditator becomes Mahāvairocana.

Bodhisattva path. In Mahāyāna Buddhism the path toward Buddhahood is the arduous one of the *bodhisattva.* [*See* Bodhisattva Path.] It begins with the arousal of the "thought of enlightenment" *(bodhicitta)* and passes through ten stages over a period of three great *kalpas* (aeons). Chen-yen collapses the path into a ritual process; the three *kalpas* are interpreted not as units of time but as defilements to be eliminated. "If one transcends the three *kalpas* in one's lifetime, then in one life one attains Buddhahood. Why should time be discussed?" (T.D. 39.600c). From the Esoteric perspective, the last stage of the path is contained in the first. Thus, there are two interpretations of the statement in the *Mahāvairocana Sūtra* that "*bodhi* is the cause, compassion *(karuṇā)* the root, skill in means *(upāya)* the outcome" (T.D. 18.1b–1c). The exoteric view indicates the development of the *bodhisattva* through time. From the Esoteric viewpoint, all three—*bodhi,* compassion, and skill in means, the beginning, middle, and end of the path—are accomplished ritually as a piece. They are a whole, as are roots, trunk, and branches of a tree. Chen-yen collapses the beginning and end of the path: the disciple and the Buddha are really identical. [*See also* Prajñā; Upāya; *and* Karuṇā.]

The goal: siddhi. Success in Chen-yen ritual is called *siddhi* ("accomplishment"; Chin., *ch'eng-chiu*). There are two major typologies of *siddhi.* The first is found in the *Mahāvairocana Sūtra* and is associated with the lineage of Amoghavajra; the second is propounded in the *Susiddhikāra Sūtra* and in Śubhākarasiṃha's *Commentary.* According to the *Mahāvairocana Sūtra,* "mundane," or outer *siddhi (laukikasiddhi)* is overtly aimed at the application of wondrous transformative powers (skill in means) to aid in the salvation of beings. "Supermundane," or inner, *siddhi (lokottarasiddhi)* is aimed at the achievement of enlightenment. All Chen-yen ritual has both components. Burnt offerings *(homa),* for example, involve placing things in a fire and might be performed to expel invading armies. The same rite has an "inner" meaning: one's defilements are incinerated and enlightenment attained. Ritual activity in the world, which is performed for the salvation of beings, is paradoxically an exercise in one's own enlightenment. The second typology of *siddhi,* which may reflect T'ien-t'ai or even Taoist influence, posits three levels of *siddhi:* superior, middling, and inferior. Superior *siddhi* is said to lead to transcendence and emptiness. Middling *siddhi* leads to the various heavenly realms, while inferior *siddhi* leads to command of illusion. We are further told that inferior *siddhi* may yield superior attainment and vice versa (T.D. 18.614a–614c).

Buddhology. Chen-yen teaching on the nature and function of the Buddha is similar to that of other Vajrayāna traditions. Chen-yen posits two theories concerning the Buddha's "bodies." The first is the triple-body theory. The *dharmakāya,* or "body of *dharma,*" represents the unconditioned thought of enlightenment in itself; *saṃbhogakāya,* or "body of bliss," represents the wondrous powers achieved through compassionate deeds; *nirmāṇakāya* is the form taken by a Buddha to apply those powers in aid of suffering beings. The three bodies thus parallel the triade *bodhi,* compassion, and skill in means. In Chen-yen ritual, the three bodies are realized simultaneously. Enlightenment and salvific activity form a conjunction in compassion. The consecration ritual *(abhiṣeka)* is therefore the paradigm of all ritual, for in it the disciple is consecrated as *saṃbhogakāya. Bodhi (dharmakāya)* and skill and means *(nirmāṇakāya)* are joined in compassion *(saṃbhogakāya).* The second theory distinguishes three "wheel bodies" *(san lun-shen, tricakrakāya).* The first "wheel," *svabhāvacakrakāya,* is Buddhahood in itself. It manifests itself in beneficent or horrific forms. Beneficent manifestations such as Avalokiteśvara (Kuan-yin) practice compassion and, according to Amoghavajra, are equivalent to the *saṃbhogakāya.* Horrific manifestations such as the *vidyārājas* Trilokyavijaya and Acala, utilize skill in means to chastise and discipline beings. The Three Wheels are ultimately one. Much of Chen-yen ritual is devoted to the third wheel.

The two maṇḍalas. Unlike most Vajrayāna traditions, Chen-yen focuses on a pair of *maṇḍalas,* the "Womb Maṇḍala," drawn primarily from the *Mahāvairocana Sūtra,* and the "Diamond Maṇḍala," drawn from the *Sarvatathāgatatattvasaṃgraha.* The "Womb Maṇḍala of Great Compassion" (Mahākaruṇā-garbhodbhāva Maṇḍala) is a graphic representation of the cosmos as the wondrous transformations, born of compassion and based on *bodhi,* of Mahāvairocana. The term *garbha* has two meanings. It is *bodhi,* the "embryo" of enlightenment present in all beings, as well as the "womb" of compassion and skill in means in which the embryo grows. The *maṇḍala* has three courts. The first is an eight-petaled lotus on which Mahāvairocanais enthroned amid four Buddhas and four *bodhisattvas.* This court represents the seed of *bodhi,* of enlightened wisdom present in the cosmos. An intermediate court is dominated by beneficent manifestations that embody compassion, such as Avalokiteśvara, Mañjuśrī, and Kṣitigarbha. The "Court of the Outer *Vajras*" represents Mahāvairocana's skill in means as manifested through the *vidyārājas* and the Hindu gods in the traditional Buddhist "six destinies" *(gati).* Thus the *maṇḍala* embodies the triade *bodhi,* compassion, and skill in means.

The Diamond Maṇḍala is actually a selection of nine *maṇḍalas* from the many presented in the *Sarvatathāgatatattvasaṃgraha.* The central *maṇḍala,* the Vajradhātu Mahāmaṇḍala, is the most important since the others are derived from it. The Vajradhātu Mahāmaṇḍala represents the fivefold wisdom that is the basis of enlightenment. The *maṇḍala* has three courts. The first is the Akaniṣṭha Palace of Mahāvairocana, who is enthroned on a lunar disk and surrounded by four Buddhas representative of aspects of his wisdom. Surrounding the palace are the Buddhas of the past, present, and future (the *bhadrakalpa*), whose compassion causes the enlightenment of beings. The outer perimeter of the *maṇḍala* is populated by twenty Hindu divinities who act as protectors of the Dharma. Each of the other *maṇḍalas* described in the *Sarvatathāgatatattvasaṃgraha* focuses on a particular aspect of the whole.

Both the Womb Maṇḍala and the Diamond Maṇḍala are external projections of a reality that must be realized internally through the Three Mysteries. Each *maṇḍala* and each of the two texts has a separate initiatory tradition through which the disciple ritually realizes the reality of Mahāvairocana in the center of the cosmos.

Chen-yen as Chinese Vajrayāna. The Chen-yen *ācāryas* lived in a great cosmopolitan city, Ch'ang-an, a milieu in which Confucian, Buddhist, and Taoist, and even Muslim and Nestorian ideas were freely exchanged. Many of Chen-yen's distinctive teachings were articulated for this audience. Chen-yen's preoccupation with two *maṇḍalas* is a distinctively Chinese adaption of Vajrayāna teachings. Since the two textual lineages came to be regarded as a pair, the *maṇḍalas* drawn from them also constitute a pair. Just as each *maṇḍala* expresses the conjunction of conditioned and unconditioned reality, so too, during the late eighth century, did the pair became a graphic shorthand for that conjunction. Through a reinterpretation of Chinese philosophical categories the Womb Maṇḍala was said to represent Mahāvairocana's numinous reality *(li), bodhi* as universally present in the Buddha's compassionate activities. The Diamond Maṇḍala represented the enlightened mind in itself, wisdom *(chih).* There is evidence that this synthesis was taught by Amoghavajra's disciple Hui-kuo, and it may even have been initiated by Amoghavajra.

Another distinctive innovation is the selection of nine *maṇḍalas* from the *Sarvatathāgatatattvasaṃgraha* and their arrangement in a three by three square. The configuration is clearly based on the *Lo-shu,* one of a pair of ancient Chinese cosmograms representing the "earthly" realm. This cosmogram was the basis of an imperially sponsored Taoist cult of T'ai I ("surpassing unity"), in which the sovereign of the universe circulated through a court of nine thrones. Moreover, Amoghavajra changed the *maṇḍala's* traditional Indian attributions. Mahāvairocana, formerly associated with the color blue and the element ether, was now associated with yellow and earth, the traditional attributes of the Chinese sovereign and those chosen by the T'ang rulers. It is even possible that the paired cosmograms, the *Ho-t'u* and the *Lo-shu,* influenced Chen-yen's pair of *maṇḍalas.*

Another Chinese development was Amoghavajra's promotion of Vajrayāna as the best method both for the attainment of enlightenment and for the protection of the state. Such a teaching appealed to the mid-T'ang emperors, for it joined lofty theological pursuits with practical application, and after the An Lu-shan rebellion the emperor needed all the aid he could get. A series of rites was developed for the protection of the state, for the prolongation of the emperor's life, for the salvation of the imperial ancestors, and for the propagation of rain. The emperor was hailed as a *cakravartin*, the universal worldly ruler and counterpart of the Buddha. The state was portrayed as a Buddha land.

The promotion of the state cult focused on deities who were compassionately active in the world. The *vidyārājas*, or "protectors," were important, as were Avalokiteśvara and Kṣitigarbha, both of whom figured prominently in rites for dead imperial ancestors. Mañjuśrī and Samantabhadra, representing wisdom and the fulfillment of vows, were frequently paired, as for instance, at the Golden Pavilion on Mount Wu-t'ai and in T'ai-yüan, the imperial clan seat. [*See also* Avalokiteśvara; Kṣitigarbha; *and* Mañjuśrī.]

The Legacy of Chen-yen. Although sectarian Chen-yen disappeared after the Sung dynasty, it had widespread influence on Chinese Buddhism. The use of *mantra* and *dhāraṇī* permeated other Buddhist groups, including some Pure Land and Ch'an sects. Tales of wonder-working *ācāryas* added to popular lore. Chen-yen and Taoism influenced each other. During the Six Dynasties, Tantric rituals such as "consecration" *(abhiṣeka)* and pseudo-Sanskrit *mantras* were already in use in Taoist circles. Chen-yen ritual structures, used in rites for imperial ancestors, and even some of the divinities, such as Ti-tsang (Kṣitigarbha), were emulated in Taoist Esoteric rites dating from the Sung. These ancestor rites have remained an economic mainstay for both the Taoists and the Buddhists. The tremendous increase in the popularity of Kuan-yin during the T'ang and Sung is also attributable in part to Chen-yen. Kuan-yin, in one form or another, is invoked in many of Chen-yen's "public" rites. Thus, even after its demise as a recognizable sect, Chen-yen continued to shape Chinese tradition. Finally, it transformed Japanese Buddhism through the teachings of such clerics as Saichō and Kūkai, who formally introduced the sect to Japan.

[*For an overview of Vajrayāna see* Buddhism, Schools of, *article on* Esoteric Buddhism. *Vajrayāna Buddhology and the placement of Buddhist divinities in* maṇḍalas *is discussed in* Mahāvairocana; Celestial Buddhas and Bodhisattvas; *and* Maṇḍalas, *article on* Buddhist Maṇḍalas. *Tantric soteriology is treated in* Soteriology, *article on* Buddhist Soteriology, *and in* Nirvāṇa. *For a discussion of the ideal Tantric practitioner, see* Mahāsiddhas *and the biographies of Śubhākarasiṃha, Amoghavajra, and Vajrabodhi. The introduction of Chen-yen to Japan is treated in* Shingonshū *and in the biographies of Saichō and Kūkai.*]

BIBLIOGRAPHY

Works in Western Languages. The only work available in a Western language that is devoted exclusively to Chen-yen is Chou I-liang's monograph-length article "Tantrism in China," *Harvard Journal of Asiatic Studies* 8 (March 1945): 241–332, an annotated translation of the standard biographies of Śubhākarasiṃha, Vajrabodhi, and Amoghavajra. Amoghavajra's role in the court with particular reference to the Golden Pavilion on Mount Wu-t'ai and the cult of Mañjuśrī is discussed in Raoul Birnbaum's *Studies on the Mysteries of Mañjuśrī* (Boulder, 1983). The Japanese monk Ennin gives us an eyewitness account of Chen-yen just before the persecution of 845 in his diary, translated by Edwin O. Reischauer as *Ennin's Diary: The Record of a Pilgrimage to China in Search of the Law* (New York, 1955). Fo-t'u-teng's exploits are recounted by Arthur F. Wright in "Fo-t'u-têng: A Biography," *Harvard Journal of Asiatic Studies* 11 (1948): 321–371. There are several studies of Shingon, the Japanese offspring of Chen-yen, that cover material in Chen-yen history and texts. These studies present valuable material but must be used with caution, as they advance Shingon interpretations of Chen-yen; these interpretations are not always faithful to those of the Chen-yen masters. In English, see Yoshito S. Hakeda's *Kūkai: Major Works* (New York, 1972) and Minoru Kiyota's *Shingon Buddhism* (Los Angeles, 1978).

On the *maṇḍalas*, Beatrice Lane Suzuki's article on the Womb Maṇḍala, "Shingon School of Mahāyāna Buddhism: II, The Mandara," *Eastern Buddhist* 7 (May 1936): 1–38, is helpful. Masaharu Anesaki's "Buddhist Cosmotheism and the Symbolism of its Art," in his *Buddhist Art in Relation to Buddhist Ideals* (1915; reprint, New York, 1978), is brief but insightful. More difficult to find are two works in French by the Shingon priest Tajima Ryūjun: *Les deux grands maṇḍalas et la doctrine de l'ésotérisme Shingon* (Paris, 1959) and *Étude sur le Mahāvairocana-sūtra* (Paris, 1936). The best full-color illustrations appear in Pierre Rambach's *The Sacred Message of Tantric Buddhism*, translated by Barbara Bray (New York, 1979).

Works in Asian Languages. There is as little secondary material on the Chen-yen school in Chinese as there is an overabundance of it in Japanese. Chinese scholarship on Buddhism has suffered through a period of relative decline in interest during the nineteenth and early twentieth century and then through a period of outright supression during the second half of the twentieth century. Scholarship on Buddhism, Taoism, and other religious traditions is beginning to revive, but for the moment one must make do with a few works that present a decidedly Marxist reading of Chen-yen in particular and of Chinese Buddhism in general. The most extensive and informative work is Kuo Ming's treatment of Esoteric Buddhism in his *Sui-T'ang fo-chiao* (Chi-nan, 1980), pp. 573–610. More heavy-handed Marxist interpretations are Kao Kuan-ju's entry on Esoteric Buddhism in *Chung-kuo fo-chiao*, vol. 1 (Peking, 1980), pp. 312–318, and Fan Wen-lan's *T'ang-tai fo-chiao* (Peking, 1979), pp. 36–46.

There is a wide range of secondary works in Japanese, but nearly all treat Chen-yen from the perspective of Shingon. The best of these, however, are distinguished by careful scholarship and sophisticated historical and doctrinal reasoning. Matsunaga Yūkei's *Mikkyō no rekishi* (Kyoto, 1969) is comprehensive, readable, and views Esoteric Buddhism in the context of the

Tantric systems of India and Tibet. Although old, somewhat hard to find, conservative, and written in Classical Chinese, Omura Seigai's *Mikkyō hattatsushi,* 5 vols. (1918; reprint, Tokyo, 1972) is by far the best textual history of Chen-yen. Finally, I would still recommend two old works by Toganoo Shoun. His *Himitsu bukkyōshi* (Kyoto, 1933), which was reprinted as vol. 9 of *Gendai bukkyō meicho zenshū,* edited by Nakamura Hajime, Masutani Fumio, and Joseph M. Kitagawa (Tokyo, 1964), provides excellent historical coverage, and his *Mandara no kenkyū* (Kyoto, 1936), which chronicles the development and use of *maṇḍalas* in Esoteric Buddhism beginning in India, has yet to be surpassed. Most Japanese works still hold that Tantra emerged in Buddhism at the time of its first textual appearance, that is in the seventh century. Alex Wayman has recently put forward persuasive arguments for dating some Buddhist Tantric texts some three to four centuries earlier in "The Early History of the Buddhist Tantras, Especially the Guhyasamāja Tantra," in his *The Buddhist Tantras: Light on Indo-Tibetan Esoterism* (New York, 1973).

Charles D. Orzech

CH'I is one of the most complex and multifaceted terms in all of Chinese philosophy, religion, and science. No single word can translate it adequately. Its root meaning is "moist emanation." Steam, clouds, and mist are *ch'i,* and the word appears frequently in compounds that refer to meteorological phenomena. Another basic meaning is "breath." Later, these meanings were sometimes amalgamated; the Taoist philosopher Chuang-tzu (fourth century BCE) wrote, "When the Great Clod [the Earth] exhales breath, it is called wind."

During the Warring States period (481–221 BCE), the classical age of Chinese philosophy, the word *ch'i* began to be employed in an expanded variety of meanings. The concept of breath gave rise to the meaning "vital spirit," that is, the life force of all creatures. "Nourishing the vital spirit" *(yang ch'i)* by means of diet, yogic exercises, breath control, or sexual yoga became an important part of the Taoist quest for immortality from the late Warring States period onward. A true adept could dispense with food and even with the physical body itself; immortal spirits nourished themselves on *ch'i. Ch'i* could also be thought of as a flow of energy within the body. To control this flow of *ch'i,* traditional Chinese medicine employed acupuncture, therapeutic massage, and other techniques. The East Asian martial arts, which have a strong spiritual component, emphasize the need to regulate one's *ch'i* in order to achieve absolute physical mastery of the body.

Drawing on such earlier concepts as *yin-yang* and the Five Phases (*wu-hsing,* sometimes misleadingly called "five elements"), Tsou Yen (fourth century BCE) and his followers employed the idea of *ch'i* as the key to a systematic organic natural philosophy. For them, *ch'i* had two sets of meanings. First, it was an extension of the idea of "vital spirit," whereby all things, animate or not, are what they are. Things with similar *ch'i,* as determined by such classificatory criteria as *yin-yang* and the Five Phases, were similar in nature and could interact organically without a demonstrable mechanical cause-and-effect relationship. A typical summation is that found in the second-century BCE *Huai-nan–tzu:* "All things are the same as their *ch'i;* all things respond within their own class." Second, *ch'i* was a sort of ethereal resonating medium through which such interactions took place. Both concepts entered the mainstream of Chinese philosophy during the early Han period (206 BCE–7 CE), especially in the work of the Confucian syncretist Tung Chung-shu (179?–104? BCE). During this period *ch'i* also came to mean something like "power"; thus, character traits and psychological states such as vigor, rage, or fortitude could be described with reference to a person's *ch'i.* This sense survives in the modern vernacular Chinese term meaning "to become angry": *sheng-ch'i,* literally, "to engender *ch'i.*"

In the Neo-Confucian revival of the Northern Sung period (960–1127) the term *ch'i* acquired a radically new meaning. Ch'eng I (1033–1108) and especially Chu Hsi (1130–1200) developed a Neo-Confucian metaphysics according to which all phenomena are manifestations of preexisting ideal principles. *Ch'i* was what gave physical substance to metaphysical ideals *(li).* From the time of Chu Hsi, this sense of *ch'i* tended to be dominant in Chinese philosophy and religion, although the earlier senses persisted as well.

Neo-Confucian metaphysics provided indigenous (non-Buddhist) Chinese philosophy and religion with a comprehensive explanation of the phenomenon of evil. Confucianism had always held that the world and everything in it is by nature good; yet evil undeniably exists. For the Neo-Confucians, the resolution of this enigma involved the concept of *ch'i.* All metaphysical principles *(li)* are inherently good, but their physical manifestations may be good or not, according to the quality of *ch'i.* The *ch'i* that gives physical substance to *li* may be pure, clear, and good, or it may be turbid and flawed. A person whose *ch'i* is "muddy" will exhibit a flawed moral nature and will be capable of acting in evil ways, despite the fundamental goodness of man.

Fortunately, such flaws could be overcome; and the quest to do so was what gave Neo-Confucianism some of the qualities of a personal religion as well as a moral and ethical social philosophy. Sagehood—human perfection—was to be sought through the "investigation of things"; one should, through study and self-cultivation, inquire exhaustively into the perfect and enduring principles of things, and, by imitating them, purge oneself of all that is impure and inharmonious.

However, for later generations of Neo-Confucians, the "investigation of things" too often became the investigation of books. Received authority rather than active inquiry guided attempts at self-cultivation. Partly in response to this tendency, the Ming dynasty philosopher Wang Yang-ming (1472–1529) emphasized instead introspection and meditation. Yet in both cases the goal was the same: the purification of *ch'i,* leading to enlightenment and the perfect unity of consciousness and action.

Used continuously and pervasively in a variety of technical and vernacular senses, the term *ch'i* over the centuries has repeatedly acquired new meanings and connotations while retaining older ones. Any occurrence of the term, therefore, will be correctly understood only through careful attention to its context.

[*For further discussion of* ch'i *within the historical context of Chinese thought, see* Confucian Thought, *article on* Neo-Confucianism.]

BIBLIOGRAPHY

A good explanation of the concept of *ch'i* and its role in Chinese natural philosophy can be found in Joseph Needham's *Science and Civilisation in China,* vol. 2, *History of Scientific Thought* (Cambridge, 1956). Fung Yu-lan's standard *A History of Chinese Philosophy,* 2d ed., 2 vols., translated by Derk Bodde (Princeton, 1952–1953), deals extensively with the term in its various religious and philosophical contexts.

JOHN S. MAJOR

CHIAO. The Chinese term *chiao* (sacrifice) in ancient times referred to a pledge in wine at the wedding ceremony or at the coming of age of a son. But the common meaning that we shall consider here is the sacrificial part of major Taoist services. In this connection *chiao* has historically been associated with *chai,* the rites of abstinence and penitence. Under Buddhist influence, *chai* took the form of rituals for the salvation of the individual and ancestors, whereas *chiao* sacrifices were performed by ordained Taoist priests to renew the community's covenant with the highest powers for blessings and protection. As practiced in Taiwan today, both these functions are generally covered by the single term *chiao.*

Although a dozen varieties of *chiao* are differentiated according to their purpose, in effect only four are performed nowadays with any frequency in Taiwan: (1) for peace and safety *(p'ing-an chiao),* (2) for the prevention of epidemics *(wen chiao),* (3) for blessings in general *(ch'ing-ch'eng chiao),* and (4) for protection from fire *(huo chiao).* Services may be held either at fixed intervals or irregularly, but the latter is much more common. However, in this as in the matter of their duration (from one to as many as seven days and nights) there is considerable variation according to custom and circumstance.

The essential difference between the Chiao and other large-scale religious services is that the powers addressed in the Chiao are the Three Pure Ones (San Ch'ing), hypostases of the Tao, rather than the gods of popular religion. These Taoist powers receive only "pure" offerings—wine, tea, cakes, fruit—in contrast to the "blood sacrifices" of the popular cults. The public is allowed to attend and participate in the rituals of popular religion, but it is strictly barred from the sacred arena where the Taoists perform the Chiao. However, the people of the community prepare themselves for the visit of the Three Pure Ones by observing a fast for several days before the Chiao.

The sacred arena *(tao-ch'ang)* of the Chiao is usually the community temple. But as the purpose of the Chiao is communion with the Three Pure Ones rather than with the deities of popular religion, the sacred arena is rearranged so that the main altar is reserved for the San Ch'ing (represented by painted scrolls bearing the images of the deities) while the other deities are relegated to subsidiary or "guest" status at the altar of the three realms (that is, Heaven, earth, and the waters). The services, complex and protracted, consist of the following essential parts: announcement to the divine powers of the celebration of this Chiao, and an invitation for them to attend; feasting them when they have arrived; presenting official petitions seeking forgiveness of sins and expressing penitence; a formal negotiation for the renewal of the covenant between the highest powers and the community; sending off the eminent guests when this pact has been concluded. As part of the Chiao, rites for the salvation of all souls *(p'u-tu)* are invariably included. The officiants include a high priest *(kao-kung),* several assistants, and a small group of musicians, to whose accompaniment most of the actions are performed. Besides the official celebrants, prominent men of the community who have contributed heavily to the expenses of the Chiao are present within the sacred arena. At specified moments in the liturgy they follow the lead of the Taoist priests in making obeisances to the deities. This special privilege adds to the stature of the donors in the community and at the same time makes or generates religious merit for them.

The people of the community also earn merit by observing the preliminary fast, by contributing money, and through many kinds of assistance in preparation for the Chiao. Although they do not participate in the rituals that take place within the *tao-ch'ang,* they do offer their own sacrifices in prepared areas outside the temple, to ancestors, gods, and bereaved spirits. At certain moments in the Chiao the celebrants appear before the public and perform rituals, usually at the several "outer altars" *(wai-t'an)* that have been erected in vacant lots near the sacred arena. These altars, masterpieces of folk art, are dedicated to various important deities of popular religion.

The festivities which accompany the Chiao are many. One high point, so far as the people are concerned, is a colorful procession to the banks of a river (or ocean), where paper and bamboo rafts are launched. Bearing candles, the rafts float away to invite the souls of the drowned to come for their share of the feast provided by the community (this feast is the public part of the *p'u-tu*). While the priests perform their esoteric liturgy within the temple, a great festival is taking place in the community. Mounds of sacrificial offerings, performances of drama, convivial entertainment of friends, relatives, and even strangers, and a general atmosphere of carnival draw huge crowds from near and far. All of this makes the Chiao not just a liturgical service, but a total community event.

For the Taoists, the Chiao is of more profound significance. According to the most ancient and basic theories of Taoism, to call down the highest powers of the macrocosm is in actuality to practice the exercises of "inner alchemy" *(nei-tan)* within the microcosm of the priest's body. While the high priest outwardly performs the liturgy, addressing the highest powers, he inwardly undergoes a regimen designed to produce the "immortal fetus." In the Chiao, then, the ultimate goal of the Taoist religion is still what it has always been: the attainment of immortality.

[*See also* Worship and Cultic Life, *article on* Taoist Cultic Life; Priesthood, *article on* Taoist Priesthood; *and* Alchemy, *article on* Chinese Alchemy.]

BIBLIOGRAPHY

The most detailed analytical description of the *Chiao* is Michael Saso's *Taoism and the Rite of Cosmic Renewal* (Seattle, 1972). A careful study of one of the constituent rites is in Kristofer Schipper's *Le Fen Teng: Ritual taoïste* (Paris, 1975). Édouard Chavannes gives a translation, with a wealth of annotation, of texts used in the *chai,* in his *Le Jet des Dragons* (Paris, 1916). A rare account of the *Chiao* as practiced in imperial times is in J. J. M. de Groot's *Les fêtes annuellemment célébrées à Émoui (Amoy),* 2 vols. (1886; reprint., Taipei, 1977). For a good description written in popular style with color photographs, see Linda Wu's "The Biggest Festival of Them All," *Echo* 4 (January 1974): 28–44. General information on Taoism and specific information about Taoist communal rituals in pre-T'ang times is given in the fundamental work of Henri Maspero, first published posthumously in *Les religions chinoises* (Paris, 1950), later published in expanded form in *Le taoïsme et les religions chinoises* (Paris, 1971). The latter has been translated into English by Frank A. Kierman, Jr., as *Taoism and Chinese Religion* (Amherst, 1981). The most complete and best informed overall treatment of Taoism since Maspero is the book by Kristofer Schipper, *Le corps taoïste* (Paris, 1982); see especially chapter 5, "Le rituel."

LAURENCE G. THOMPSON

CHIBCHA RELIGION. *See* Muisca Religion.

CHIH-I (538–597), third patriarch of the influential T'ien-t'ai school of Chinese Buddhism. This man is often regarded as having united Chinese Buddhism into a coherent whole by resolving doctrinal and practical strains that had plagued Buddhism virtually from the time of its introduction into China. His literary output was prodigious: about one thousand pages of the *Taishō* edition of the Chinese Buddhist canon are devoted to his extant works, a sum that would correspond to about nine thousand pages in unannotated English translation.

More important, however, than the sheer volume of his works is their synthesizing nature. Chih-i was born at a time when Chinese Buddhism was beginning to move from unquestioning fidelity to Indian Mahāyāna doctrines and practices toward a more mature synthesis of Indic and Chinese religious values. Chih-i was not the only man of his era to contribute to this synthesis: it is well known, for instance, that he borrowed heavily from the "three southern and seven northern" teachers in constructing his own system of doctrinal classification *(p'an-chiao)*. However, Chih-i's scheme of doctrinal classification proved to be more comprehensive and influential than those of his predecessors and contemporaries, in part because of his success at incorporating religious practice as well as doctrine into his great synthesis. In short, he is credited with having united practice with doctrine and doctrine with practice, whereas his predecessors had attempted only to arrange the various doctrines in the *sūtras* into an understandable and consistent whole. His role in uniting these two tendencies in Chinese Buddhism has often been compared to the political achievement of his patron Sui Wen-ti, the first emperor of the Sui dynasty, who succeeded in uniting the north and south of China for the first time in some three and a half centuries. The analogy is apt in that Buddhist historiography commonly views the north of China before the Sui as having been oriented toward the practical side of Buddhism, just as its leaders were men of action, often non-Chinese in ancestry, while the South then tended toward the theoretical or doctrinal side, its leaders and upper classes being aristocrats and Chinese scholar-officials. Thus in uniting doctrine and practice, Chih-i united southern and northern religious cultures in a way comparable to the feat of his imperial patron. In his own words, these two aspects of Buddhism must be considered analogous to the "two wings of a bird" or the "two wheels of a cart," each valueless without the other. Chih-i, therefore, was a kind of nodal point in the development of Chinese Buddhism, embracing in his synthesis virtually all that went before, and influencing virtually all that came after.

In terms of formal lineage Chih-i stands third in the line of T'ien-t'ai patriarchs, following the semilegendary Hui-wen and the historically attested Hui-ssu. However, Chih-i is generally regarded as the de facto founder of the T'ien-t'ai school, named for the mountain where Chih-i built his most important monastery. Because it was associated so closely with the rulers of the Sui, T'ien-t'ai suffered an eclipse with the rise of the T'ang dynasty (618–907 CE), whose rulers were eager to dissociate themselves from the ideological underpinnings of Sui rule. The school was revived a century and a half later by the monk Chan-jan (711–782), one of whose disciples transmitted the T'ien-t'ai teachings to the Japanese monk Saichō (767–822). Saichō in turn introduced the lineage to Japan, where it soon became the dominant tradition. Its center, Mount Hiei near Kyoto, became the training ground for most of the key figures in the development of Kamakura Buddhism. The T'ien-t'ai lineage continues to the present day, with active branches in Taiwan and especially Japan, although nothing is known about the situation in China proper.

Among Chih-i's works the two most prominent are the *Fa-hua hsüan-i* (Profound Meaning of the Lotus Sutra) and the *Mo-ho chih-kuan* (The Great Calming and Contemplation, or The Practice of Meditation According to the Mahāyāna). The former is his principal work on doctrine, the latter his principal work on practice, but Chih-i was careful to relate each aspect to the other in both works. He applied a tripartite analysis to both doctrine and practice, which he classified as sudden, gradual, or variable. The "sudden" doctrine (or teaching) refers to the *Avataṃsaka Sūtra,* understood by Chih-i and some of his predecessors as the text expounded by the Buddha to a mostly uncomprehending audience immediately after his enlightenment. It is referred to as "sudden" because it purports to reveal the Buddha's direct experience of enlightenment just as it is, without making any concessions to the need of its audience for a more "gradual" exposition of the nature of the experience. "Gradual" doctrines (or teachings) refer to the succeeding four stages of the Buddha's teaching, during which he was said to have gradually trained his listeners, in *sūtra* after *sūtra* of deepening truth, for the final revelation of the *Lotus* and *Nirvāṇa Sūtra*s, commonly believed to be the last discourses of the Buddha. "Sudden meditation" is the kind of meditation expounded in the *Mo-ho chih-kuan,* in which preliminary practices are dispensed with and "ultimate reality is taken as the object of meditation from the very beginning." Gradual meditation, like the gradual teaching, moves step by step toward the goal. Finally, by "variable" Chih-i meant certain texts and practices that could function as either sudden or gradual, depending upon the level of religious attainment of the practitioner.

The strength of Chih-i's system lies in its comprehensiveness. By showing how a variety of disparate texts and practices, each of which had its own adherents, could be the product of a historically continuous revelation, beginning with the Buddha's preaching of the *Avataṃsaka Sūtra* and culminating in the message of the *Lotus* and *Nirvāṇa Sūtra*s, Chih-i was able successfully to integrate them all into a single, coherent system. His great synthesis made it possible for the many branches of Chinese Buddhism to be regarded by their adherents as aspects of a loosely integrated, self-consistent whole.

A related and highly influential teaching of Chih-i is the doctrine of the Three Truths: Empty, Provisional, and—Chih-i's addition—Middle. This may be regarded as a Chinese emendation, or even improvement, on the pivotal Indian Mahāyāna concept of the Two Truths, first expounded by Nāgārjuna. While the Indians discerned two levels of meaning in the *sūtras* (i.e., in the Buddha's pronouncements) and regarded the Empty *(śūnya)* as superior to the Provisional, Chih-i and the Chinese Buddhist tradition after him were uncomfortable with this Indian equation of ultimate truth and emptiness. To them, such a formulation seemed too nihilistic. Chih-i was able to find passages in Nāgārjuna's works that justified the addition of a third Truth, namely the Middle, which he also styled the Perfect Teaching. This third level of truth became characteristic of the fundamental orientation of Chinese Buddhism, affirming as it does that ultimate reality (or truth) is not to be found apart from mundane reality (or truth), that the world as it is is already identical to the Absolute. The corollary of this doctrine is the assertion that all beings have the Buddha nature, that is, that without exception all beings have the capacity for Buddhahood. Scarcely any school or teacher in East Asian Buddhism has deviated from these two related teachings, and their influence upon Ch'an and Zen was particularly significant. While Chih-i cannot be said to have originated them—he was always careful to provide scriptural citations for his doctrines, and other Chinese monks were exploring similar notions before him—he argued them with greater eloquence and made them an essential part of his incalculably influential summation of Buddhist doctrine and practice.

[*See also* T'ien-t'ai.]

BIBLIOGRAPHY

Ch'en, Kenneth. *Buddhism in China: A Historical Survey.* Princeton, 1964. The most readable and comprehensive survey available on Chinese Buddhism. One chapter is devoted to T'ien-t'ai and discusses Chih-i.

Donner, Neal Arvid. "The Great Calming and Contemplation of Chih-i: Chapter One, the Synopsis." Ph.D. diss., University of British Columbia, 1977. Available from University Microfilms, Ann Arbor. A closely annotated translation, with introduction, of the important first chapter of Chih-i's major work on meditation.

Hurvitz, Leon N. *Chih-i (538–597): An Introduction to the Life and Ideas of a Chinese Buddhist Monk.* Brussels, 1962. A wealth of biographical information. However, the sections on Chih-i's teachings must be used with caution, as the "five periods and eight teachings" delineated here have recently been found to represent not Chih-i's thought, but that of a much later Korean T'ien-t'ai monk.

NEAL DONNER

CHIH-YEN (602–668), second patriarch of the Hua-yen school of Buddhism in China. Born in the town of T'ien-shui near Ch'ang-an, the capital of the T'ang dynasty, Chih-yen was the son of an official in Shen-chou province. When Chih-yen was twelve years old his family was visited by the first patriarch of the Hua-yen school, Tu-shun, who claimed that Chih-yen was his son and should be returned to him. This declaration was taken by Chih-yen's parents to mean that Chih-yen was to become a Buddhist monk, and they thus entrusted him to Tu-shun.

Ordained in 615, Chih-yen studied Buddhism, mainly the thought of the *She ta-sheng lun (Mahāyānasaṃgraha)* and, later, the thought of the *Hua-yen ching (Mahāvaipulyabuddhagaṇḍavyūha Sūtra),* under many famous Buddhists. During this period he also mastered Sanskrit. His reading of the *Hua-yen ching shu* (Commentary on the *Hua-yen ching*) by Hui-kuang, the founder of the Nan-tao branch of the Ti-lun school, greatly contributed to his religious development. Shortly after this he met a monk who taught him to consider the meaning the Hua-yen teaching of *lu-hsiang* ("six aspects" of reality). At the age of twenty-seven, having followed this monk's teaching, he is said to have realized the truth of the "One Vehicle." Thereafter, he wrote his commentary on the *Hua-yen ching,* the *Sou-hsüan chi.* By pursuing this religious path Chih-yen became the leader of the Hua-yen school at the Chih-hsiang Ssu on Mount Chung-nan. Although Chih-yen did not seek social influence, honor, and wealth, he did engage in social activity when, late in his life, he became a private teacher of Hsien, the king of P'ei. This occurred while he was staying at the Yün-hua Ssu in Ch'ang-an.

Chih-yen's greatest influence was in the development and systematization of Hua-yen doctrine. His work was to pave the way for Fa-tsang's subsequent completion of Hua-yen thought. Chih-yen created the method of classifying the Buddhist teachings into five grades, arranged according to the subtlety of the doctrines, and founded the teaching of *fa-chieh yüan-ch'i* ("dependent origination of the True Realm"). These doctrines were given their final form by Fa-tsang, one of his disciples. However, Chih-yen had his own character, one different from both those of his teachers and of his disciples. For example, he placed high emphasis on T'an-ch'ien's *Wang-shih-fei lun,* a work that praised what it termed *wu-hsin* ("the mind beyond functions"), a mental state based upon the thought of Chuang-tzu, and esteemed Hsin-hsing's Sect of the Three Stages, which was generally treated as heretical. Chih-yen's extant works are as follows:

1. *Sou-hsüan chi* (T.D. no. 1732)
2. *I-sheng shih-hsüan men* (T.D. no. 1868)
3. *Wu-shih-yao wen-ta* (T.D. no. 1869)
4. *Hua-yen ching k'ung-mu chang* (T.D. no. 1870)
5. *Chin-kang ching lüeh-shu* (T.D. no. 1704)

Chih-yen had two disciples of special importance for the tradition. The first, Fa-tsang (643–712), went on to become the great systematizer and so-called third "patriarch" of Hua-yen Buddhism in China. Through his efforts, Hua-yen became one of the prestigious and lavishly patronized traditions of the T'ang dynasty (618–907). The other, Ŭisang (625–702), returned to his native Korean state of Silla and was instrumental in establishing Hua-yen as one of the most important Buddhist traditions there.

[*See also* Hua-yen *and the biographies of Fa-tsang and Ŭisang.*]

BIBLIOGRAPHY

Kamata Shigeo. *Chūgoku kengonshisōshi no kenkyū.* Tokyo, 1965. Pages 79–106 discuss Chih-yen's importance to the Hua-yen tradition.

Kimura Kiyotaka. *Shoki chūgoku kegonshisō no kenkyū.* Tokyo, 1977. This work, a comprehensive study of early Hua-yen Buddhism, focuses on Chih-yen's thought.

KIMURA KIYOTAKA

CHILD. The child is a universal symbol of future potentiality as well as the carrier of the heritage of the past. The child is symbolic of the past, coming into being from generative forces that preceded it, yet for it the future is an open possibility. In *Essays on a Science of Mythology* (1949), Károly Kerényi states that the image of the primordial child represents the childhood of the world itself, even the origin of life. There is a mystery about the child, for what it will be as an adult is not yet and cannot be known. The child represents innocence, purity, wonder, receptivity, freshness, noncalculation, the absence of narrow ambition and purpose. As yet innocent of life, the child portrays the beginning, the origin of all. It symbolizes a primordial unity, before differentiation has taken place. Gender differences are mainly in potentiality; consciousness has not been separated out from the unconscious; choice has yet to become a burden and a responsibility.

In the alchemical tradition of medieval Europe, a child wearing a crown or regal garments was a symbol of the philosopher's stone, that is, of a wholeness realizing the mystical union of the inner spirit with the eternal spirit. Something of this feeling may sustain the devotion to the Infant Jesus of Prague, whose statue, preserved since 1628 in the Church of Our Lady of Victory in Prague, portrays the infant Jesus as Christ the King, with his left hand encircling a miniature globe surmounted by a cross and his right hand bestowing a blessing.

Because the child requires care and nurture, it represents the needs and demands of utter dependency. The child's closeness to nature is indicated in numerous stories telling of a special child being cared for by animals. Children are further associated with the Great Mother, and thus with maternal elements such as water; in legend, then, one finds children brought by fishers such as the stork, or by water dwellers such as the frog, or born from Mother Earth under a bush or in a cave. Children are often used to personify the seasons: Spring, amid leaves and flowers; Summer, holding ears of corn; Autumn, with fruit; Winter, wrapped in a cloak. Growth and development are implicit, for childhood is a temporary state. The child represents incredible power, vitality, and persistence toward growth; one grows up physically, whether one wishes to or not. Furthermore, there is rejoicing at growth, no matter how charming a child may be. There is grief at the death of a child but not at the loss of a child to adulthood.

Children and old people have something in common and usually get along well with one another; both must accept dependency. The child also symbolizes that stage of life in which the old person, transformed, acquires a new simplicity. Together, they represent the continuity and flow of life. The child symbolizes a higher transformation of individuality, the self transmuted and reborn into perfection. Thus, not surprisingly, the motif of the child is found in religions and mythologies from earliest times and all around the world. In Christianity, for example, the baby in the crèche and the adult on the cross are the two poles between which the liturgical year moves, each in different ways pointing to the tasks of human life for spiritual development.

The Child in Mythology. The symbolism of the child implies a connection with the mythology of the hero. The potential of the child is indicated in many myths depicting heroic nature as predestined rather than simply achieved. Almost invariably, the hero is described as endowed with extraordinary powers from the moment of birth, if not of conception.

In *The Myth of the Birth of the Hero* (1959), Otto Rank identifies many of the principal motifs associated with the divine child. Typically, the child has parents of royal or noble lineage. In many stories the father is a god and the mother a human, or some other miraculous quality characterizes the birth. Since extraordinary difficulties attend the birth of a hero, the child is endangered. Often the father is the source of danger, or a ruler who has been warned that the child will kill or supplant him. The infant is abandoned, exposed, or sent away. In every myth of sanctified childhood, the world assumes the care of the child. However rejected, the child is rescued by a providential act of nature or by rural people close to nature. Upon maturity the child discovers his or her true identity and sets up a new order, rectifying previous wrongs.

Not all hero myths have birth stories, but most of them do, and the same motifs are found throughout the world, as Joseph Campbell demonstrates in *The Hero with a Thousand Faces* (1968). In a story from the Hindu epic *Mahābhārata,* the hero, Karna, is born of a virgin and the sun god, Sūrya. According to one account, the *bodhisattva* who later became Gautama Buddha entered his mother's womb from the right side, and at the end of ten months left the right side of his mother again in full consciousness. The North American Algonquin tell a story of the miraculous birth of Michabo, who, in one form of the myth, is said to be the grandson of the Moon and the son of the West Wind and a maiden who had been miraculously fecundated by the passing breeze. His mother died in giving him birth, but he did not need the fostering care of a parent, for he was born "mighty of limb and with all the knowledge that it is possible to attain." The mother of the Aztec hero Quetzalcoatl also died at his birth, but the newborn at once possessed speech, reason, and wisdom.

A rather common incident in the stories of American Indian heroes is their immediate growth from early childhood to manhood, as in the case of Young Rabbit of the Sioux, Bloodclot Boy of the Blackfeet, and the Divine Twins of the Pueblo Indians. In Roman mythology, Romulus and Remus were born of a king's daughter and the war god, Mars. In Greek mythology, King Acrisius of Argos, having been warned by an oracle against male descendents, locked his daughter in an iron chamber; but Zeus penetrated the roof in the guise of a golden rain, and Danaë became the mother of Perseus. In Christian tradition, Jesus was born of the Virgin Mary by the power of the Holy Spirit.

The extraordinary difficulties at the hero's birth take a variety of forms. Sometimes the father is the child's enemy, as was Kronos, who devoured his children to prevent his predicted demise by a child of his; or the father may be merely absent, as Zeus was when Dionysos was being torn to pieces by the Titans. Jesus was threatened by the edict of Herod, who, having heard of the birth of a king, ordered all male children under two years of age put to death. The infant Moses, being in similar danger from the Egyptian pharaoh, was placed in a basket to float down the Nile. In the Hindu story, Karna was likewise placed in a basket on a river, while in an Old Norse saga, Siegfried was put in a glass vessel to float down a stream to the sea. Romulus and Remus, when condemned by the king, were set afloat in a tub on the river Tiber. The delivery of the hero from danger is frequently effected by the waters of a river or sea. In Oceanic mythology, the hero Māui was cast into the sea by his mother, because he was so small and scrawny that she thought he was dead. The father of Oedipus ordered him exposed to die, because an oracle had advised him that he would be killed by his own son.

Typically, the rejected child is rescued either by animals or by simple, rural folk. In a Greek story about a hero of the Medes, Cyrus, the baby, upon being ordered exposed by his royal grandfather, was raised by a herder who did not carry out the order but substituted his own still-born child. In another Greek story, Paris, the son of Priam of Troy, was ordered exposed by his father and was left on a mountaintop; a she-bear nursed the child for five days, and when he was found still alive, the servant who had left him there took him home to raise him himself. Kṛṣṇa, an incarnation of the Hindu god Viṣṇu, grew up among cowherders and is famed for his sport with the *gopīs*, or cowherdesses. A child that is abandoned to nature, then saved and brought up by her, no longer shares the common experience of humankind, for as Mircea Eliade points out in *Patterns of Comparative Religion* (1958), the abandoned child has reenacted the cosmological instant of beginning and grows up not in the midst of a family but in the midst of the elements. He is dedicated to a destiny that no ordinary person could attain.

These stories commonly present the exile or the despised one as handicapped, or make the hero an abused son or daughter, orphan or stepchild. The child of destiny has to face a long period of obscurity. This is a time of extreme danger, with many obstacles. The myths agree that an extraordinary capacity is required to face and survive such experience: heroic infancies abound in anecdotes of precocious strength, cleverness, and wisdom.

In time, the hero, now a youth, returns to his proper home, often to overthrow his father and set himself in his place, as did Oedipus and Perseus. Jesus said that he did not come to abolish the Law but rather to fulfill it; however, his followers understood his teaching to be a new covenant as the basis of relationship with God. Gautama Buddha, rejecting the scriptures and the caste system of traditional Hinduism, offered a new way, the Eightfold Path, for dealing with the problems of life.

Psychological Interpretation. Many students of mythology, such as Károly Kerényi and Joseph Campbell, have made use of C. G. Jung's concept of archetypes to interpret the worldwide occurrence of motifs like that of the child. In Jung's view, an archetype is a pattern through which human nature has repeatedly expressed itself, employing different imagery in different cultures but reflecting in each case a recognizable form common to all humankind. In his essay "The Psychology of the Child Archetype" (1949), Jung suggests that one function of the child motif in the adult psyche is to compensate or correct, in a meaningful manner, the one-sidedness and extravagances of the conscious mind, by revealing the possibility for future development.

The symbolism of the child has no one meaning, but on the other hand it is not unlimited. Most personality theories assume that the psyche, like the body, has a built-in mechanism for healing itself. Just as the body produces antibodies to ward off attack from foreign invaders, so the psyche produces images that are suggestive or corrective for its health. The motif of the child, when occurring in the unconscious of an individual (as in a dream, an obsession, or a fascination) or in the mythologies and fables of a culture, may suggest a future potential development for the individual or the culture.

The child symbolizes movement toward maturity. Being itself the product of the union of two opposites, male and female, it is a symbol of wholeness. In the mythologies of the divine child, there is a union of the divine and human; spirit and body have become one, which is the essence of the human experience. The miraculous element in the stories indicates that a special manifestation of the immanent divine principle has become incarnate in the world. The child is a symbol, then, of the wholeness toward which life moves. The mythologies of the child hero or divine child illustrate the problems encountered in psychological growth and development toward wholeness. As a "miraculous" conception the future potential is a given element, yet it is also precarious: the child as future possibility is abandoned daily. Many difficulties and obstacles have to be overcome in any movement of the psyche toward wholeness.

The motif of the child may also occur as a corrective to a conscious attitude that has become too rigid, too fixed, or stagnated. The child suggests something evolving toward independence, which necessitates detachment from its origins. In this sense, abandonment, though painful, is necessary for the future potential.

The child has a naive view of life, is typically interested in learning more about life, and has a lot of energy for that task. It represents one of the strongest urges in every being, namely, the urge to realize itself. There is an invincibility and uncomplicated vitality about the child that the stories describe in various ways. The obscurity in which the child is typically raised points to the psychological state of nonrecognition, the naive condition of the beginning, before consciousness has become differentiated from the unconscious. As such, the child symbolizes the goal of human development, when there has been a reintegration of consciousness with the unconscious or nature. The wisdom of old age is a state in which the opposites and tensions of life and growth have become reconciled and are more or less at peace. "You must become as little children," Jesus taught. Maturity can be seen as the unclouded joy of the child at play who takes it for granted that he or she is at one, not only with playmates, but with all of life.

The symbol of the child is a source of energy for a new development. In "Reveries toward Childhood" in his *Poetics of Reverie* (1969), Gaston Bachelard says, "The great archetype of life beginning brings to every beginning the psychic energy which Jung has recognized in every archetype, . . . for the archetypes are reserves of enthusiasm which help us believe in the world, love the world, create the world" (p. 124).

[*See also* Virgin Birth *and* Heroes; *for examples of the divine child, see* Jesus *and* Kṛṣṇa.]

BIBLIOGRAPHY

The Hungarian classicist Károly Kerényi has published extensively on mythology; his essay "The Primordial Child in Primordial Times," in Kerényi and C. G. Jung's *Essays on a Science of Mythology* (1949; rev. ed., New York, 1963), has explored the theme of the divine child, drawing primarily on Greek, Roman, Finnish, Russian, and Indian mythologies. Daniel G. Brinton's collection of hero myths of American Indians, *American Hero Myths* (Philadelphia, 1882), demonstrates the presence of similar motifs among the indigenous peoples of the Western Hemisphere. Joseph Campbell's classic work *The Hero with a Thousand Faces* (Princeton, 1968) describes the basic pattern of myths of the hero. Otto Rank's *The Myth of the Birth of the Hero* (New York, 1959) outlines the basic motifs of its subject and offers a psychoanalytic interpretation. Joseph Campbell's *The Mythic Image* (Princeton, 1974) reexamines the motifs Rank identified and offers some illustrations and interpretation in a section on "Infant Exile." C. G. Jung's essay "The Psychology of the Child Archetype" can be found in *Essays on a Science of Mythology* (cited above) and in volume 9 of *The Collected Works of C. G. Jung* (New York, 1959); it provides a psychological interpretation of this worldwide motif. Mircea Eliade's *Patterns in Comparative Religion* (New York, 1958) has in section 87, "Man's Descent from the Earth," a brief discussion of the meaning of the motif of the abandoned child. A philosophical reverie on the meaning of childhood can be found in Gaston Bachelard's "Reveries toward Childhood," in *Poetics of Reverie* (New York, 1969). The fourth issue of the journal *Parabola: Myth and the Quest for Meaning* (August 1979) is devoted to the meaning of the child and childhood.

WALLACE B. CLIFT

CHINESE PHILOSOPHY. The major developments in Chinese philosophy during the past three thousand years will be outlined here; ideas that are essentially religious, treated elsewhere, will be noted only as may be necessary to show the religious relevance and historical context of philosophical themes. This overview will be at once chronological and topical, as follows:

1. The pre-Classical background (to the sixth century BCE)
2. Classical philosophy (late sixth to late third century BCE)
3. The first imperial era (to the third century CE)
4. The development of Buddhism in China (to the ninth century)

5. The Confucian revival (T'ang and Sung periods)
6. The later empire (since the fourteenth century)

The Pre-Classical Background. China circa 550 BCE consisted only of what is now North China; even the states of the Yangtze River valley did not speak the language of what was recognized as the civilized heartland to the north. This known "world" had been in anarchy for more than two centuries, since the overthrow of the last Western Chou king (in present-day Sian) in 771 BCE. By about the sixth century BCE there was a nominal quasi-feudal hierarchy under a powerless successor Chou "king" in Lo-yang, but in fact, the political landscape was dotted with a patchwork of small quarreling states under local lordlings who themselves often had no real power. China was still emerging from the Bronze Age (iron casting had begun circa 700 to 600), but its civilization was old, stretching back in time beyond memory or reliable record. The Chou dynasty had begun about five hundred years earlier with a conquest by a western Chinese state. Archaeology has now validated the tradition of a Shang dynasty before that, centered in Honan, which may have lasted another five hundred years. The tradition of a still earlier Hsia dynasty, again of almost five hundred years, continues to be debated; it was supposed to have started with three marvelously wise rulers, Yao, who chose his own successor, Shun, who in turn selected Yü, the first ruler of the Hsia. [*See* Yao and Shun *and* Yü.]

Speculative philosophy was soon to fill the third millennium BCE with still more (timeless) civilization-creating emperors. The Chinese venerated their past, cherished what they had, and invented what they needed. In the sixth century BCE there existed a modest ancient literature, in large part anonymous: the earliest philosophers often quote the "Odes" *(Shih)* or the "Documents" *(Shu)* to make a moral point; some of these still exist. The earliest known writing, discovered on pieces of shell and bone used by Shang royal diviners, dates from about 1200 BCE, and a few traditional texts surviving even now may date to the eleventh century BCE. There was a wealth of learning for learned men to know. Such persons were among the well born, if not so well born that all their time was taken in ruling or fighting. Most people, then as now, were farmers, and it is said that only the aristocrats kept family records and sacrificed to ancestors.

In the Shang, sacrifices to royal ancestors were often of human beings, and in the Chou it still was common to bury a lord with attendant sacrifices and to sacrifice war captives at one's local altar to the soil. The earliest philosophers denounced these practices. A high god, called T'ien (Heaven), or (earlier) Shang-ti, was worshiped by the king who in theory held from T'ien his "mandate" *(ming)* to rule as long as he maintained the "virtue" *(te)* of the founder of the dynastic line. [*See* T'ien *and* Shang-ti.] Increasing population and the growth of urban centers, combined with constant war, eliminated smaller domains, producing a class of unattached petty "gentlemen" *(shih)* who in an earlier age would have been knights or minor hereditary court officers and who had or aspired to some education. The first philosophers and their disciples are from this group. Dissatisfied with present conditions, they looked back to an imagined better past in which they would have had secure roles, and were critical of the higher aristocrats whose power came from their connections rather than from real ability or character.

The Age of Classic Philosophy: The First Phase. The first philosophers were moralists, motivated by perceived political and social ills. For them the basic ill was disorder, brought about by the greed of local lords or heads of powerful families and by their attempts to seek status to which they had no right. These philosophers were not revolutionary; they accepted the existing authorities, and if they looked for remedies they sought positions for themselves or their students as advisers and ministers. We can distinguish three positions. (1) Confucius (K'ung Ch'iu; traditional dates 551?–479 BCE) would have real political power in the hands of men of cultivated moral character and sought to train his students (and himself) in traditional morals and etiquette to make them employable in court positions. (2) Mo-tzu (c. 450–c. 380), in training his students for office, worked out a specific political program with a supporting philosophical argument that ignores the problem of moral character; for him, an official was "worthy" of his job if he discharged his duties effectively. (3) Yang Chu (fl. c. 400–350) concluded that the times could not be remedied. For him, the only reasonable course was withdrawal and the choice of an optimally satisfactory style of personal life.

Confucius. Confucius (the latinized form of K'ung Futzu, or Master K'ung) stressed the importance of developing traditional virtues, such as filial piety *(hsiao)*, courage, honesty, loyalty, kindliness *(jen)*, and familiarity with the rules of traditional polite behavior and ceremonial *(li)*. In politics he was a legitimist, supporting the Chou king and the rightful authority of the duke of Lu (his native state), which had slipped into the hands of three collateral ducal families, and deploring any behavior in powerful persons that implied an improper claim to status. The good society of the past was to be restored by making traditional standards and values real again. This was Confucius's concept of "rectifying names" *(cheng-ming)*, that is, making the referents of such terms as *father* and *ruler* really correspond to their meaning. Accordingly, traditional religious rituals had great value for him and he held *t'ien* (Heaven) in genuine awe; but he usually turned aside substantive religious queries. His moral philosophy is self-cultivationist: a good life, he held, is one of constant self-improvement. And it is deontological: the world would be better if we were good and always did what is right but that is not what determines what is good and right. Confucius had devoted disciples, but how to teach virtue was a problem for him. He admitted that he taught only eager students and evinced exasperation when a student grasped his teaching but remained unmoved. [*See also the biography of Confucius.*]

Mo-tzu. In sharp contrast to Confucius, Mo-tzu (who may have been originally a wheelwright) is utterly "practical." The earliest strata of the *Mo-tzu* text show him unconcerned with the cultivation of character. He wrote, for example, that officials will be loyal if they are well paid; music—prized by the Confucians for its harmonizing effect on the emotions and the self—he dismissed as a useless expense. An idea or policy is approvable, according to Mo-tzu, if it promotes one of three basic social goods: order, wealth, and population growth. He devotes a whole chapter to ghosts and spirits and another to "the will of Heaven." These entities must be obeyed and sacrificed to lest they punish or withhold gifts such as long life—contrast Confucius, who is willing to "die in the evening" if he can "hear the Way" in the morning—but there is no tone of awe in what we read. The fundamental good is order, its antithesis is offensive war (defensive war is approved; the Moists became experts in its techniques). But each man naturally pursues his own interest and takes as "right" *(i)* that which serves it, fighting with his neighbors. It is the function of the state, by meting out rewards and praise or punishments and censure, to impose one standard of right, which is to be the "will of Heaven." And Heaven's will is that men "love one another impartially" *(chien ai)*. If you love your neighbor's family, city, and state as you love your own, then all fighting will cease. Shown the cool advantages of adopting this attitude toward others, it is inconceivable that an intelligent man will not do so; and rulers know well how to get their subjects to comply with their wishes and favor their ends. Condemning fatalism—a doctrine that, he says, deceives men into thinking human effort is useless—Mo-tzu implies that one can adopt an attitude at will. But his stark logic has at least one flaw: although he demanded absolute obedience and dedication from his followers, nothing in Mo-tzu's system shows them why they should make this sacrifice. Nonetheless, there are accounts of followers giving up their lives for his cause. The Moists were tightly organized and were a force in the world of thought for two centuries, before eventually disappearing by the time of the Ch'in unification of 221 BCE. [*See also the biography of Mo-tzu.*]

Yang Chu. Although none of Yang Chu's writings has survived, his views can be gleaned from other books. He was among the many in this period who concluded that nothing could be done to right the world and that no interest of one's own was served by seeking to advance oneself in it. The best course, therefore, was to keep out of harm's way and "nourish one's life," avoiding office. Although some who shared these views with Yang Chu were hedonists, Yang himself probably was not; he believed that a measured asceticism might well be the wisest way to conserve life and optimize satisfactions. In one account of this type of thought the greatest satisfaction to be enjoyed is *i*. It is probably "honor," rather than "righteousness," that is meant here, and to the extent that others' *i* meant social dutifulness, it would have to be deemed by the follower of Yang as incompatible with life or nature. But such persons who withdraw from society can be seen as engaging in a kind of self-cultivation; their stance is not far from that of the Confucian-minded person who judges that the Way *(tao)* does not prevail in his time and so withdraws into private life to cultivate a personal "purity" uncorrupted by the world's temptations. Yang appears in the pages of the *Chuang-tzu*, and there is reason to think that Chuang-tzu may have at first been a follower. It is plausibly argued that recluses of this kind were the first Taoists.

The Age of Classical Philosophy: The Hundred Schools. By 350 BCE no one took the feeble Chou king seriously. Sometimes tentatively, in the wake of a military victory, and sometimes by mutual agreement, the stronger of the local "dukes" declared themselves "kings" *(wang)*, each thus implying an intention to succeed the Chou. By 320 there were at least eight such "kings." One of the most ambitious was the ruler of Ch'i (modern Shantung Province). Of course, such ambition could only be realized in the end by military action. In the meantime, however, a "king" had to build his prestige by a display of his royal "virtue" *(te)*, and the ruler of Ch'i ostentatiously opened his ears to the advice of all the wise men he could entice into his court. Hundreds of wandering philosophers and their disciples were housed in a suburb of Chi-hsia, the Ch'i capital. (An early philosophical encyclopedia, the *Kuan-tzu*, may be a residue of their work.) Other new "kings" and lesser lords, especially the king of Wei in Ta-liang (Kaifeng), tried to keep pace. Philosophy thrived in great variety. By the third century BCE the main body of Moists had split into three sects, each with its own text of the doctrine. One specialized group developed the science of military defense and had its own texts. Others were experts in the theory of argument; their Canons and Explanations are, in effect, treatises on logic and epistemology.

Other philosophers, perhaps following the lead of the Moist logicians, made reputations for their ability to baffle audiences with clever arguments for impossible theses. The most famous are Hui Shih ("The sun at noon is the sun setting" and other paradoxes) and Kung-sun Lung ("A white horse is not a horse"). [*See also* Moism.] Proto-Taoists such as Shen Tao argued that a conceptual knowledge impedes real understanding. The Confucians had their schools, which stressed ritual, filial piety, or moral psychology and derived from one or another prominent disciple of Confucius. A school of social primitivists, led by one Hsü Hsing, held that market prices should be standardized to prevent cheating and that a good ruler must not be supported by his people but should work in the fields with them. Tsou Yen amazed his lavish royal hosts with grand speculations about the patterns of history and the geography of the world, based on the theories of *yin* and *yang* and the "five powers" *(wu te* or *wu hsing). [See the biography of Tsou Yen.]* Perhaps for the first time, an old manual of divination was caught up in philosophy, with a (now lost) commentary based on *yin-yang wu-hsing* theory. This same manual later acquired a moral commentary attributed to Confucius and, as the *I ching,* became the ranking book in the Confucian classics. In this combination of divination and metaphysics we see a perennial Chinese concept of "resonant causality," one thing in the universe causing something else "like" it—a celestial object or an *I ching* hexagram—to be activated in response.

Meng-tzu. This is the setting of the career of Meng-tzu (Mencius), the ancient philosopher with probably the greatest influence on later Chinese philosophical thought. Meng-tzu belongs to the moral-psychological line of philosophical descent from Confucius. The *Meng-tzu* opens with him, an old man, in conversation with the kings of Wei (known also as Liang) in the year 320, and Ch'i in the year 319, urging them to desist from warfare and to lighten the burdens on their people. He boldly argues that a bad ruler may be justly deposed or killed, but he is in no way egalitarian, arguing (against Hsü Hsing's followers) that rulers and educated men deserve their privileged place in society because they "work with their minds," having the duty of caring for the mass of humanity through a government of foreseeing benevolence. Meng-tzu is best known for his theory of the innate goodness of man: we are all born with psychological "sprouts" implanted in us by Heaven, that if encouraged to grow naturally develop into the virtuous dispositions *(hsin)* of benevolence *(jen),* dutifulness *(i),* sense of propriety *(li),* and moral "knowledge" (*chih,* sense of right and wrong). (Thus, Meng-tzu solves the problem of the teachability of virtue.) Human evil results from the stunting of our originally good "nature" *(hsing)* owing to harsh conditions. Thus, a good government would restore humanity to goodness by improving the people's lot and educating them.

Meng-tzu attacked both the Moists—their "universal love," he argued, denies the special duties we have to parents—and the Yangists, whose "egoism" denies our duties to rulers. He nonetheless draws from both. A life of virtue he held, would be in accord with our nature and would be what we would naturally most enjoy. As for the Moists, by Meng-tzu's time they were coming to see that their doctrinaire program of universal love required a concession to self-cultivation ethics. One must first develop a capacity for loving, which has a natural "root" in affection for parents; at the bidding of doctrine, one can then apply it impartially. It is to this that Meng-tzu objects: the "root" of benevolence, he says, is indeed innate, but it has a deep structure and can be developed and "extended" in only one way, diminished in due degree at removes from the self. Against Kao-tzu, he argues that not only our affective nature but also our sense of duty and respect is "internal" (innate). We can encourage our virtues to grow because we enjoy them; they develop and thrive with practice without being forced. [*See also the biography of Meng-tzu.*]

Chuang-tzu. The *Chuang-tzu* is now recognized to be composite, the later syncretic parts perhaps actually dating to early Han, and other parts, such as a primitivist stratum, dating to the end of the third century BCE. It is usually held that the first seven chapters are by a man named Chuang Chou, about whom almost nothing is known. In any case, these chapters seem to be the earliest. It is necessary to date them after Meng-tzu (the opening of chapter 4 contains an obvious parody of the opening of book 2 of *Meng-tzu*); they were probably written in the early third century BCE (chapter 2 satirizes Kung-sun Lung without naming him; he was a client of a prince of Chao active as late as c. 250). The *Chuang-tzu* uses a novel medium in philosophy. Whereas the *Lun-yü* (Analects) and *Meng-tzu* are collections, over time, of conversations and sayings, and the *Mo-tzu* a series of reasoned treatises (a mode shortly to be copied by Hsün-tzu and Han Fei-tzu), the *Chuang-tzu* makes its points through the use of fiction, sometimes fantastic and often quite funny. Confucius himself is often stolen as a fictional character. It is reasonably argued (by A. C. Graham) that Chuang Chou began as a follower of Yang Chu's school of egoist withdrawal but then had a traumatic "conversion experience." This seems to have shown him that literal withdrawal from the world is merely another posture of involvement; genuine withdrawal must have the form of detachment while one plays the game of life, "walking without touching the ground." In this spirit one may even accept political, social, and familial commitments.

Chuang-tzu carries this attitude to the deepest philosophical level. According to him, we must use language, but we must not suppose that our words really fit, for there is nothing absolutely right about them. This is true of all of our evaluative concepts that we articulate in words; the moral concepts of the Confucians are prejudices, time determined. This applies even to such distinctions as dreams versus reality or life versus death (which may be better than life, for all we know). The favorite word of the moral philosophers, *tao*, or "way," becomes for Chuang-tzu the Way of all nature, of which the wise man sees himself a part in both life and death. He accepts both joyfully, using his mind as a mirror to reflect reality just as it is, without any distorting preconceptions or preferences and "without injury to himself." The book has been perennially popular; the most important philosophical commentary (by Kuo Hsiang or Hsiang Hsiu) dates to circa 300 CE. Chuang-tzu's epistemological-metaphysical outlook anticipates that of the Mādhyamika Buddhist philosophy, which was transmitted to China in the early fifth century CE. Later still, Ch'an Buddhism inherited his provocative blend of humor and paradox. [*See also the biography of Chuang-tzu.*]

Hsün-tzu. The active life of Hsün-tzu extends from the early third century BCE to 238, when he was forced to retire from a magistracy in Ch'u. A native of Chao, he twice spent time in the philosophical center of Chi-hsia in Ch'i, where he was recognized as a successor to and rival of Meng-tzu. Explicitly Confucian, Hsün-tzu was actually eclectic. One probably early essay ("Dispelling Obsessions") describes the mind as a mirror, but unlike Chuang-tzu, Hsün-tzu believed that the mind not only reflects but also stores and, if properly used, leads one not to an uncommitted attitude but to the truth, which is the Confucian Way. As in *Meng-tzu* (6A.15), one can be "obsessed" *(pi)* if one does not reflect carefully; but unlike Meng-tzu, Hsün-tzu held that such obsession is likely to be an unwise intellectual commitment rather than an unevaluated sense appetite. Accordingly, Hsün-tzu is authoritarian; he believed that one must be protected from wrong ideas. This, he maintains, is the business of the state. The moral order itself (*li-i*, "rites and right," for Hsün-tzu) was created by the sage-kings, on whose teachings we therefore depend if we are to be moral.

Hsün-tzu directly opposes Meng-tzu not only in this but also in his related view that "human nature is evil": we are composed, according to Hsün-tzu, of an appetitive "nature" *(hsing)* that if uncontrolled causes men to quarrel for satisfactions (as in Mo-tzu), as well as a capacity for intelligent action *(wei)*, which enabled the wisest (the sage-kings) to see that rules must be ordained if a tolerable social life is to be possible for mankind. Meng-tzu has the problem of explaining convincingly how evil is possible given the goodness of human nature; Hsün-tzu has the converse problem of explaining how morality is possible at all. The sages' *li-i* are justified by their utility, but to be moral we, and they, have to accept them as right. Mo-tzu solves this problem (perhaps he did not recognize it) by requiring that the state-imposed *i* shall be what Heaven wills; Hsün-tzu's Heaven, however, is merely the sky above and the order of Nature, and only the uneducated believe it has divine power. What Hsün-tzu says is that men differ from animals in having *i* not, it seems, in the Mencian sense of an innate disposition to particular duties, but in an innate capacity to be socialized. The wise man will calculate, at a metamoral level, that only a life according to the Confucian Way can give him optimum satisfaction; seeing this, he will necessarily choose it, and will choose to be educated so as to become the sort of man who can live it. At the same time, he sees that it really is right that there should be such standards: given the order of all nature, they are the only solution to the human predicament. Thus the "rites" can be seen as the continuation in the human realm of the natural order of the heavens, and Hsün-tzu writes fervent passages to this effect, religious in tone if not in content. In this way the problem implicit in (and ignored by) Mo-tzu—how we can make a calculated choice of our own attitudes—is avoided without recourse to Meng-tzu's solution to the paradox of virtue (that virtue cannot be taught unless one is virtuous already, as Mencian man is).

Hsün-tzu can be called the first Chinese academic philosopher—reviewing his predecessors, criticizing, picking and choosing, solving problems. He was much appreciated in the ensuing Han era, but by the time Han Yü read him and wrote about him in the ninth century, Hsün-tzu had almost become a curiosity. Still, the more authoritarian of the Neo-Confucians in following centuries are often closer to him than they realized. [*See also the biography of Hsün-tzu.*]

Han Fei–tzu. Two of Hsün-tzu's students were Li Ssu, later prime minister to the First Emperor of Ch'in, and Han Fei, a prince of the Han state and last of the major preimperial philosophers. The last two Chou kings had been deposed by Ch'in in 256 and 249, and after three more decades the last of the resisting states were absorbed. The political philosophy that guided the new order was what Chinese bibliographers call Legalism (Fa-chia), the doctrine that the function of the state is to maximize its strength in agricultural production and in military power by eliminating useless classes (including philosophers) and regimenting the population with a rigidly enforced code of law, using rewards for desired behavior and severe punishments (mutilation or worse) for violations. This would benefit the people and give them order: standing in fear of the state they would behave so that its terrors need never be used. The power of the ruler was to be exalted, but at the same time the ruler was advised to avoid action, keeping his officials in doubt about his intentions lest they combine against him. Thus a curious, quasi-Taoist philosophy of inaction, what H. G. Creel, in his *What Is Taoism?* (Chicago, 1970), calls "purposive Taoism," was the basis of a philosophy of power.

Han Fei–tzu and Li Ssu were both Legalists. The one recommended philosophically, and the other eventually carried out, the infamous "burning of the books" of proscribed philosophical schools, including especially Confucian texts, in 213. Legalism strongly influenced the development of Chinese law, but as a philosophy it was usually condemned by the Confucians, who became dominant a century later. Han Fei–tzu continued to be read and was esteemed highly for his literary style. [*See also* Legalism *and the biography of Han Fei–tzu.*]

Lao-tzu. The Taoist bent in Han Fei–tzu is genuine. The book that collects his writings includes a Legalist commentary to selections from a short text that stands first among the Taoist classics: the *Tao-te ching.* It is ascribed to a certain Lao-tzu, alias Li Erh or Li Tan, supposed to have been an elder contemporary of Confucius and an archivist in the royal Chou court. In fact, a myth was invented sometime in the third century BCE that Confucius had made a trip to Lo-yang to consult him. Although these things are still believed by some scholars, many now take the book to be a third-century work, probably later than the earlier parts of the *Chuang-tzu.* The most radical view, that of D. C. Lau (*Tao Te Ching,* Hong Kong, 1982), sees it as a collage of short fragments of Taoist "hymns" and other lore that got assembled in an editorial tradition into the present booklet of brief, sometimes rhymed sections. According to this view, Lao-tzu is a complete fiction, yet he has become the patron saint of Taoism, even a god. The *Tao-te ching* has become incredibly popular in the West—there are more translations of it than of almost any other book in the world—but no two interpretations are alike. Although Han Fei–tzu saw Legalism in it, Arthur Waley (*The Way and Its Power,* London, 1935) sees it as the work of a late Warring States "quietist" who was opposed to Legalism. The dominant view is that it is filled with the profoundest wisdom concerning life and being. It is conventionally ordered in two parts, the first opening with a meditation on *tao,* the second, with one on *te,* hence the title; however, archaeology has now yielded Han texts that reverse the order.

In the *Tao-te ching* we find again Chuang-tzu's conceptual relativism: the Tao itself is nameless; contrasting concepts generate each other. Many of the sections recommend inaction, nonstriving, not reaching for too much (lest from success one fall back to nothing: "reversion is the order of the Tao"), and adopting a "female," seemingly nonresisting, posture in life and in state policy. The desirable society is one in which the people are kept ignorant and simple. Often the book deals explicitly with the way a ruler should govern his state, suggesting that the way to effective power is inaction. A theme echoing Shen Tao condemns cleverness and "knowledge": "He who speaks does not know; he who knows does not speak." The first virtue is simplicity, like that of a newborn baby or of an "uncarved block" of wood. "The highest virtue *(te)* does not 'virtue' [*te*—i.e., display itself as virtue]; therefore it has virtue" (cf. *Chuang-tzu,* chap. 5). The book teems with such simply stated teasing paradoxes. [*See the biography of Lao-tzu.*]

The First Imperial Era. The late Chou era of contending states was terminated by the Ch'in conquest, complete by 221 BCE; Ch'in disintegrated after the death of its first emperor. The succeeding Han dynasty, from 206 BCE to 220 CE (interrupted by Wang Mang, 9–22) but ineffective after about 190, was followed by a division into Three Kingdoms (221–279). An unstable reunification was ended in 317, when defeats by non-Chinese northern "barbarians" drove the Chin court south to the Yangtze River valley, then still a border area with only a tenth of China's people. At the beginning of the Han dynasty, Legalist political ideas were defended, sometimes vigorously, by some court officials into the first century BCE. Taoism as a personal and political philosophy continued in favor and is represented by the *Huainan–tzu* (c. 130 BCE), an encyclopedic book assembled under the support of Liu An, one of the Han princes. [*See the biography of Liu An.*] A syncretic Taoism, drawing from all of late Chou thought, is represented by chapter 33 of the *Chuang-tzu* (second century BCE). Prominent early Han Confucians include Chia I (200–168) and, especially, Tung Chung-shu (179–104). [*See the biography of Tung Chung-shu.*] With the latter, Confucianism gained imperial favor under the emperor Wu-ti. A system of recruiting scholars for official service was decreed, and court scholars on the Confucian classics were established.

The New Text school. The Ch'in burning of the books left Confucians with the task of recovering their revered texts. This produced a rich scholarship of commentary (much of it now gone) on various textual traditions of this or that classic. It also, more significantly, led to a lasting division between the so-called New Text schools, which used texts existing only in the "new" reformed Ch'in-Han script, and the Old Text traditions, which were based on manuscripts in antique script that (allegedly) had survived the Ch'in suppression. The two sides had opposed philosophical orientations, as well as their own favored texts. The New Text partisans favored the *Kung-yang Commentary* on the *Ch'un-ch'iu* (Spring and Autumn Annals of Lu, ascribed to Confucius). They held that Confucius had been a "throneless king," founder of a theoretical "dynasty" intervening between Chou and Han. In his *Ch'un-ch'iu,* New Text thinkers claimed, Confucius had actually used "subtle" language to lay down the moral and ritual rules of an ideal world order and had predicted the rise of Han. This theory was fitted into a speculative philosophy of history in Tung's *Ch'un-ch'iu fan-lu,* further developed by the later Han writer Ho Hsiu (129–182), according to whom history goes through three great stages, culminating in an era of "great peace" *(t'ai-p'ing).* A similar idea occurs in the classic called the *Li chi,* composed of short prose pieces probably by Han court ritualists; as a millenarian concept, it has repeatedly surfaced in philosophy, religion, and popular rebel ideology during the past two thousand years.

The New Text persuasion saw Heaven as a personal deity. Any unusual celestial phenomenon—such as a comet or unpredicted eclipse—was Heaven's sign of displeasure with the behavior of the ruler. Heaven and human affairs were intimately linked by way of Yin-yang and Five Elements *(wu-hsing)* metaphysics, which grouped all aspects of the world in groups of fives (into which fours were forced); thus, water, black, winter, north, anger, and storing are in the same interacting category. The middle and late Han "apocrypha" *(wei shu),* representing Confucius as quasi-divine, are also the result of this type of thought, which was markedly numerological; for example, the Shih-ch'ü and Po-hu imperial conferences on the classics, 51 BCE and 79 CE, were convoked on the five hundredth anniversary of Confucius's supposed birthdate (and probably the one thousandth anniversary of the supposed date of the beginning of the Chou) and on the eight hundreth anniversary of the first year of the *Ch'un-ch'iu* chronicle, respectively. Divination was in great vogue; this was the age when the *I ching* became the foremost classic. In moral philosophy and moral psychology, Tung Chung-shu and his persuasion were more or less in accord with Meng-tzu, holding that we are at least potentially "good" by nature.

The Old Text school. The Old Text faction in scholarship includes Liu Hsin, court librarian in the Wang Mang era, who was later charged with forging some of these texts (notably the *Tso chuan* commentary to the *Ch'un-ch'iu*). A type of philosophy contrasting with the Tung and Ho Hsiu sort is usually typed Old Text. Naturalistic and skeptical, its major writers were Yang Hsiung, who held that human nature is a mixture of good and bad, and, especially, Wang Ch'ung (27–c. 100), who thought that Meng-tzu, Hsün-tzu, and Yang were each right about the natures of some people. [*See the biography of Wang Ch'ung.*] Like Hsün-tzu, these thinkers take Heaven to be a natural entity, not a being with intentions intervening in human affairs. Wang's *Lun heng* admits that portents foretell important historical changes but holds that they are the spontaneous effect of *ch'i* (matter-energy); Heaven's Way is "nonactivity." Wang holds a bleak fatalism: to him, nothing we do can alter what will happen in our individual lives or in history (here he is unlike Hsün-tzu). He does not hesitate to criticize Confucian doctrines and texts, and explicitly approves the naturalism of philosophical Taoism. [*See also* Chinese Religion, *article on* Religious and Philosophical Texts.]

Taoism. Taoism in this age and later was of two sorts. One, which became a religion, shared with New Text Confucianism the correspondence metaphysics of *yin-yang* and *wu-hsing* but was aimed at individual survival. For the person who could afford it, this Taoism meant adopting a regimen of life, breathing exercises, diet, and alchemy designed to make one's physical body immortal. For others, there was the possibility of getting one's life prolonged as a reward for good deeds—an idea found in early Chou bronze inscriptions, in the *Shang shu,* and in Mo-tzu but not in the work of other Chou philosophers—or of getting reborn as an immortal after death. In time, this cult developed a system of gods, rituals, heavens, and hells. [*See also* Afterlife, *article on* Chinese Concepts; Alchemy, *article on* Chinese Alchemy; *and* Taoism.]

A second, quite different type of Taoist thought continues or revives the Taoism as personal philosophy found in early Han texts and in the *Chuang-tzu.* The naturalistic skepticism of Wang Ch'ung moves in this direction, but whereas Wang's thought was a fatalism of despair, the revived interest in Chuang-tzu and Lao-tzu of the end of Han and following centuries was a naturalism of detachment. Wang Pi (226–249) is the author of the standard commentary to *Lao-tzu* and of a commentary to the *I ching (Chou i yüeh-li)*. [*See the biography of* Wang Pi.] An important philosophical commentary to the *Chuang-tzu* is attributed to both Hsiang Hsiu (late third century) and Kuo Hsiang (d. 312). [*See the biography of* Kuo Hsiang.] These and others who applied themselves to "the study of the Mysterious" *(hsüan-hsüeh)* actually continued to take Confucius as the greatest sage, but he became for them a Taoist in fact (in the *Chuang-tzu* he had been a Taoist in humorous fiction). He surpassed even Lao-tzu in his attainment of "nothing" *(wu)*, that is, "nonattachment" and "desirelessness," since he had passed beyond the desire even for these things.

The interest in semantics and metaphysical paradoxes of the early third century BCE was also revived; most of the extant text attributed to Kung-sun Lung was fabricated at this time. These interests were expressed in a fashion of precious philosophical conversation that came to be called "pure talk" *(ch'ing-t'an)*. Other important additions to philosophical literature, probably from the third century CE, are the *Lieh-tzu*, another Taoist classic similar to Chuang-tzu and pretending to be a Chou work, and the forged Old Text chapters of the *Shang shu*. The *Lieh-tzu*, like the Hsiang-Kuo commentary, praises an ethic of following one's nature, which, when practiced among the aristocracy, led from aestheticism to eccentric hedonism. Ko Hung (c. 250–330) criticized this ethic—from a Confucian point of view—as well as the Taoist philosophical anarchism of his contemporary Pao Ching-yen. Ko, however, was eclectic, and his own book *Pao-p'u–tzu* is, among other things, an important work on alchemy as a method of attaining immortality. [*See the biography of* Ko Hung.]

The Development of Buddhism in China. There is evidence of a Buddhist presence in China from as early as the late Western Han dynasty. In the Eastern Han period there were centers of Buddhism in a few cities, including Lo-yang, where a Parthian, An Shih-kao, arrived circa 148 and began translating texts in meditation in the Hīnayāna tradition of escape from psychic causation *(karman)*. More popular among philosophically minded Chinese Buddhists and their Taoist friends were "wisdom" *(prajñā)* treatises, and later texts, in the Mādhyamika tradition of Nāgārjuna (second century CE), which teach that the elements of phenomenal existence and our concepts of them are conditioned, relative, and impermanent and thus "empty" *(śūnya)*. Realization of this concept leads to a saving mental detachment; thus this kind of thought converged with philosophical Taoism. [*See the biography of* Nāgārjuna.] Early Chinese philosophical Buddhists of this kind include Chih Tun (314–366) in the South and Seng-chao (384?–414) in the North.

Six Dynasties period. Seng-chao was a disciple of Kumārajīva (344–413), a Central Asian who was brought to Ch'ang-an in 401 and is famous as a translator, especially of Mādhyamika texts. Another important northerner was Tao-an (312–385), who was learned in all aspects of Buddhism and philosophical Taoism and the author of an early catalog of translations. Among Tao-an's many disciples was Hui-yüan (334–416) in the South, a believer in Amitābha and his Pure Land *(ching-t'u)* paradise and the author of a treatise on immortality.

By the sixth century, cults of salvation by faith came to assume a "three ages" theory of history, in which the present epoch was regarded as a final, degenerate age in which men can no longer save themselves by adhering to the pristine Buddhist message as taught by Śākyamuni Buddha. This idea combined with the Mādhyamika concept of multiple truth (see, for example, Chi-tsang, 549–623), which holds that the mind must move through stages of ordinary thought before it can grasp emptiness, greatly increasing the speculative range of Buddhist philosophy. Hui-yüan's most famous disciple was Tao-sheng (c. 360–434), another southerner, whose theories anticipate important ideas in the T'ien-t'ai and Ch'an schools of the T'ang era and prefigure central issues in Neo-Confucianism. Drawing on the *Mahāparinirvāṇa Sūtra*, Tao-sheng argued that all beings have the "Buddha nature," which he identified with "emptiness" *(śūnyatā)* and with the "true self" *(chen-wo)*. Enlightenment has to be "sudden" (but after gradual training), since ultimate wisdom cannot be analyzed. Another major translator was Paramārtha (499–569, arriving at the southern court of Liang in 548), who rendered important Yogācāra (idealistic) texts of fully developed Mahāyāna Buddhism. [*With the exception of Chih Tun, all of the figures mentioned above are the subjects of independent entries. For a discussion of multiple truths, see* Buddhist Literature, *article on* Exegesis and Hermeneutics. *See also* Mappō.]

Since Buddhist thought in China of this period flows in large part from the introduction and translation of texts, texts themselves rather than great teachers are often the focus of schools. These schools did not endure as distinct ideological traditions but represented a major intellectual development toward the sort of "systematic theology" found in the great schools of the T'ang era. Mādhyamika thought is the focus of the San-lun (Three Treatises) school, based on three treatises translated by

Kumārajīva, and noteworthy for its concept of three levels of truth at successively more complete stages of negation. The Nieh-p'an, or Nirvāṇa, school, based on the *Mahāparinirvāṇa Sūtra,* developed out of the interests of Tao-sheng, until it was absorbed later into T'ien-t'ai. The so-called Ti-lun school was based on the *Shih-ti ching-lun,* a translation, popular in the North, of a treatise by Vasubandhu on a *sūtra* describing the ten stages of a *bodhisattva.* The Ti-lun school merged in the T'ang with Hua-yen. The She-lun school was based on Asaṅga's *Mahāyānasaṃgraha* through Paramārtha's translation in 563, and was later superseded by the Fa-hsiang, or "mere ideation," school. Another well-known philosophical text in this tradition, widely read even by non-Buddhists, is the *Ta-sheng ch'i-hsin lun* (Treatise on Awakening of Faith in the Mahāyāna), which was important both for Fa-hsiang and Hua-yen adherents.

During the long period of North-South division (317–588), Buddhism became the dominant religion in China, but it developed differently in the two areas. In the North, Buddhist institutions were wholly under the control of the state and were even used as a means of control of the populace. In the South, temples were lavishly patronized by emperors (especially Liang Wu-ti), but monks maintained much independence, and there was a more active climate of debate between Confucians and Taoists; of special interest is the debate over the immortality of the soul. A Confucian, one Fan Chen, wrote *Shen-mieh lun* (On the Mortality of the Soul, c. 500), an essay attacking the Buddhist view (for example, that of Hui-yüan) and arguing that the soul is to the body as function *(yung)* is to essence/structure *(t'i)* or as sharpness is to a knife. (Buddhists continued to deny the permanence of the phenomenal self, regarding it as mere appearance or "function" [*yung*], as distinct from the real self which is "essence" [*t'i*], or Buddha nature; popular faith, however, ignored the distinction. Here, Fan provocatively alters the categories *t'i* and *yung.*) Many vigorous replies to Fan are preserved. In the South, critics of the new religion warred with words; in the North, however, there were episodes of state repression, instigated by Confucian and religious Taoist advisers to the emperor, in 446 and between 574 and 577. The most severe of these came later, in 845, under a Taoist T'ang emperor.

Sui-T'ang period. It was under the reunified empire of the Sui (589–618) and T'ang (618–905) that Buddhism reached its greatest strength. The Sui emperors used Buddhism as an official ideology to support the throne, while the T'ang emperors claimed descent from Lao-tzu and favors to Buddhism were made more cautiously. But it is in the philosophical schools that flourished in the T'ang that fully developed Chinese Buddhism is seen best. The San-chiao Chieh, a sect based on the concept of the three ages, started in the Sui by Hsin-hsing (540–594), was suppressed in 713. One of the most important schools of doctrine was T'ien-t'ai, systematized by the monk Chih-i (538–597). T'ien-t'ai synthesizes the great variety of Buddhist *sūtras* and doctrines by holding that there are different levels of truth and that the Buddha went through different stages of teaching offering different means to salvation. For followers of T'ien-t'ai, the *Lotus Sutra (Saddharmapuṇḍarīka Sūtra)* is said to represent the final and most complete teaching of the Buddha. The school is often characterized as holding that the world is universal mind, comprising both a universal, pure (Buddha) nature (compare Tao-sheng) and an impure nature that produces ordinary phenomena, attachment, and evil. Chih-i himself, however, was much more a Mādhyamika than an idealist. He emphasized that mind and object are both "ungraspable" (i.e., empty), and that delusion is not ultimately different from enlightenment; perhaps the most famous metaphysical dictum of T'ien-t'ai is that "all phenomena are (ultimately) real" *(chu fa shih hsiang).* A later master, Chan-jan (711–782) held that even inanimate things have the Buddha nature.

Another master, Hsüan-tsang (596–664), was the most famous of the Chinese who went to India, brought back texts, and recorded their travels (others were Fa-hsien, who left in 399, and I-ching, who traveled in the seventh century). With his translations, Hsüan-tsang and his disciple K'uei-chi (632–682) started the Fa-hsiang ("dharma-appearance"), or Wei-shih ("mere ideation"), school, based on the views of Asaṅga and Vasubandhu that the external world is illusory. There has been a recent revival of this idealist philosophy in China led by Ou-yang Ching-wu (1871–1943) and the monk T'ai-hsü (1889–1947.)

The important masters of another prominent T'ang school, the Hua-yen (Avataṃsaka), were Fa-shun, or Tu-shun (557–640), Chih-yen (602–668), Fa-tsang (643–712), and Ch'eng-kuan (738?–820?). Hua-yen thinkers held all reality to be a blend of a "world of principle *(li)*" and a "world of things *(shih)*," all phenomena being manifestations of one ultimate principle. Even more than the T'ien-t'ai scheme, this suggests the dominant metaphysics of the Neo-Confucianism of the following dynasties. The usually dominant Ch'eng-Chu school of Neo-Confucianism, however, tended toward a metaphysical dualism; monistic varieties of Neo-Confucianism are, perhaps, closer to Hua-yen, which appeals to the fundamental "non-obstruction" of *li* and *shih (li-shih wu-ai).* The last master of Hua-yen was Tsung-mi

(780–841). Another tradition of dualistic monism that leaves its mark on Buddhist art, if not on wider philosophy, is the Chen-yen (Tantric) school, whose *maṇḍalas* and sexual imagery represented wisdom and compassion in a female-male *(yin-yang?)* relation.

The most important schools, after the persecution of 845, were the Pure Land (Ching-t'u) and Ch'an. The former, preaching that one can be reborn in paradise by reciting the name of Amitābha, had as its early master (after Hui-yüan) the northern monk T'an-luan (476–542); important T'ang masters were Tao-ch'o (562–645) and Shan-tao (613–681). The Ch'an school represents itself as deriving from an Indian monk, Bodhidharma, said to have come to China about 520, who was a master of meditation (dhyāna, hence the name Ch'an); the school also sees itself as preserving a "mental transmission" of true insight from the Buddha himself. The school recognized a series of "patriarchs," the sixth, according to some northern texts, being Shen-hsiu (seventh century); his status was challenged by a southern monk, Shen-hui (670–762), who claimed that the actual sixth patriarch was a certain Hui-neng (638–713). The *Platform Sutra* attributed to Hui-neng is one of the most widely read and influential texts in and beyond Buddhism. All of the major Neo-Confucian masters from the Sung dynasty onward were probably familiar with it, and many had experimented with Ch'an early in their careers. The Ch'an religious goal is enlightenment rather than rebirth in a ("Pure Land") paradise, and the Hui-neng episode marks a division between "northern" and "southern" Ch'an, the alternatives being final insight reached gradually through meditation and a direct and sudden insight into the real nature of the self and phenomena in the midst of ordinary activity. Two schools have been prominent since 845, the Ts'ao-tung and the Lin-chi. (Of three others, the Yun-men was active in the Northern Sung dynasty.) Lin-chi makes use of physical shocks and baffling, often humorous puzzles to break the mind loose from ordinary thinking; while iconoclastic, it actually owes much to Mādhyamika and to the Taoism of Chuang-tzu. [*Most of the thinkers and traditions mentioned above are the subjects of individual entries. For an overview of Buddhism in China, see* Buddhism, *article on* Buddhism in China, *and* Buddhism, Schools of, *article on* Chinese Buddhism.]

The Confucian Revival. Han Yü (768–824) strongly criticized Buddhism as socially parasitic, and in eloquent essays and letters regarded as models of style he represented himself as reviving the pre-Buddhist Confucianism of Chou times. Confucians of the Sung dynasty (960–1279) regarded him and Li Ao (d. 844) as their precursors. A revival of Confucian thought, as the primary philosophy of social and political participation, was stimulated by the reconstitution of the imperial state in Sui-T'ang and the development of the modern civil service examination system, which from the Sung onward required a thorough knowledge of the Confucian classics. Other factors contributed: the growth of cities, the invention of printing, and especially the development of the Confucian "academies" (*shu-yüan,* perhaps on the model of Buddhist temple schools), which began to appear in the Five Dynasties period (906–959) and multiplied in Sung and later. Funded both by the state and by private donors, the Confucian academies were the primary forums of philosophical discussion, and in the late Ming (1368–1644) they became partly political, with famous lecturers drawing huge audiences from distant parts. In the Sung the new Confucianism took two forms: One was political, social, and reformist; the other, speculative and metaphysical.

Since the new Confucian thought identified itself as a revival of very ancient ideals, in its reformist aspect it was simultaneously both antiquarian and radical. Fan Chung-yen (989–1052) is known for his adaptation of the *bodhisattva*'s vow—to be the first to suffer hardship and the last to be "saved"—to social service. Ou-yang Hsiu (1007–1072), best known as a historian, criticized Buddhism as a foreign intrusion and a sickness in society that must be cured by the revival, by the state, of ancient customs, communal spirit, and "rites." In this way "government and doctrine" would once again proceed from the same source: state and society would revitalize each other by recombining. This vision of a benevolent and selfless, albeit totalitarian, utopia has bewitched major Confucian philosophers—among them Chu Hsi, Wang Yang-ming, Chang Hsüeh-ch'eng, and K'ang Yu-wei—to the present. Wang An-shih (1021–1086), when directing the government, was the center of a storm of controversy over his reform program. Chu Hsi (1130–1200) too had his reformist side (neglected in later attention to his thought), arguing for a complete revision of the examination and education system.

The other aspect of Sung thought was its speculative metaphysics and moral psychology. The fertile eleventh century has three who can be called cosmologists. Chou Tun-i (1017–1073) offered the *T'ai-chi t'u* (Diagram of the Supreme Ultimate), showing all things as evolved from a first principle that differentiates itself into the *yin* and *yang*, then into the "five elements," and so on. Chang Tsai (1020–1077) saw all things as continually condensing out of and dissolving back into a primordial *ch'i,* and drew the moral conclusion that we and all things are one family. Finally, Shao Yung (1011–1077) tried to explain the universe through *I ching* binary numerology. Moral psychology includes monists Ch'eng

Hao (1032–1085) and Lu Chiu-yüan (Hsiang-shan) and dualists Ch'eng I (Hao's brother, 1033–1108) and Chu Hsi. The latter tried to synthesize the work of his precursors, and his system became orthodox for the imperial civil service examinations in the Yüan and later dynasties.

The preeminence of Chu's thought was confirmed by the imperial publication of the encyclopedia *Hsing-li ta-ch'üan* in 1415. Chu's idea resembles Hua-yen metaphysics: there is a realm of "principle" *(li)* and a realm of "embodiment" *(ch'i,* literally, "vessel," but in effect "matter," as in the homophonous graph *ch'i)*. In the human individual, our moral "nature" *(hsing)* is our principle, identified with *tao,* so that (with Meng-tzu) we are by "nature" good; evil and selfish tendencies in us are the consequence of "impure" *ch'i,* different in different individuals, which must be purified by moral cultivation. Long study, for example, of the classics, increases the sum of principle in the mind until a moment of synthetic moral illumination is attained (here is the Ch'eng-Chu adaptation of the Buddhist "gradual attainment—sudden enlightenment" problem). Later philosophers debated endlessly on the relation between these entities and their relation to the mind, which Lu and later Wang Yang-ming identified with principle. Whatever their metaphysics, such thinkers were moral self-cultivationists who saw the primary moral-religious "task" *(kung-fu)* as the "correcting of the mind," following the *Li chi* chapter *Ta-hsüeh* (Great Learning). This became for them the foremost of the classic texts. The usual program was to "watch oneself" and to scotch each "selfish thought" *(ssu i)* as it arose, recalling the Buddhist anxiety about thoughts of "attachment" being the source of (bad) *karman.* Noteworthy after Chu are his student Chen Te-hsiu (1178–1235) and the Yüan moralist Hsü Heng (1209–1281). This "mind learning" was pursued in some form by all the leading moralists of the ensuing Ming dynasty. [*See the biographies of Chou Tun-i, Chang Tsai, Ch'eng Hao, Ch'eng I, and Chu Hsi.*]

The Later Empire. The most important Ming philosopher was Wang Yang-ming (1472–1529, personal name, Shou-jen). [*See the biography of Wang Yang-ming.*] His most arresting ideas, simple but puzzling enough to provoke a century and a half of controversy, are as follows. (1) We all have, or share, a mental faculty of moral intuition *(liang chih),* and there are no "principles" *(li)* other than the renditions of this faculty, if we only learn to let it operate without "obscuration" *(pi),* which is the source of evil. Thus, "mind" *(hsin)* is "principle" *(li),* and ethics is situational. (2) Complete experience and fully engaged practice involve the operation of this faculty. We do not first apprehend something and then (perhaps consulting a set of rules) decide how to judge it; thus, there is a "unity of knowledge and practice" *(chih hsing ho-i).* (3) A "four-sentence teaching" (based on the *Ta-hsüeh*) explains that the mind in "essence" *(t'i)* is uninvolved in good and evil and that these predicates apply only to its activities of thought and judgment.

Was Wang really a Buddhist? No, but his *liang chih* was the "sun," and "obscuration" was the "clouds" (the images are Hui-neng's). For Wang mind is Mind, universal, as in T'ien-t'ai. And it is in the context of ordinary activity that *liang chih* reveals to itself a "principle" that eludes abstraction; but the context, and the revelation, are moral. Indeed, as Fung Yu-lan suggests, if the Ch'an Buddhist could have accepted family and social relationships as the ordinary activity that is the locus of his *tao,* he would have become a Neo-Confucian. But the problematic of Buddhism continues to be played out within Wang's Confucianism. Moralists after Wang were split, some calling for a moral cultivation of strict discipline and others holding that intuition must be allowed to function without forcing or intervention, "here and now" *(tang-hsia).* Among the latter were Wang Chi (1498–1583), and also Wang Ken (1483–1540) and his followers of the T'ai-chou school, including Ho Hsin-yin (1517–1579) and Li Chih (1527–1602), both of whom were so boldly individualistic that they died in prison.

China concurrently was experiencing one last intellectual revival of Buddhism, prominent teachers being Chu-hung (1535–1615) and Te-ch'ing (1546–1643). [*See the biography of Chu-hung.*] There was a marked syncretist tendency everywhere, and experiments in combining the Three Teachings (Confucianism, Taoism, and Buddhism) were thought interesting. (It was perhaps for this reason that Matteo Ricci, himself a friend of Li Chih, was easily accepted in Chinese intellectual circles.) Some, on the far "left" among post-Wang Confucians, whose *tang-hsia* ethics tended to be antinomian, were known as "mad Chanists." Li himself actually donned monk's garb and played with Legalist ideas. The last decades of the Ming were scarred by factional strife, especially involving the Confucians of the Tung-lin Academy group, many of whom lost their lives in their conflict with court eunuchs.

After the Manchu conquest and establishment of the Ch'ing dynasty in 1644, the freewheeling Ming style of philosophy ceased. The academies were absorbed into the government school structure, and at first the outstanding thinkers were men who avoided government service. Such were Huang Tsung-hsi (1610–1695), noted historian of Sung, Yüan, and Ming philosophy and advocate of limitations on imperial power; Ku Yen-wu (1613–1682), a philologist who accepted Chu Hsi's views but favored "search for evidence" ("the study of *li* is the study of the classics"); Wang Fu-chih (1619–1692), recluse and anti-Manchu philosopher of history; and Yen Yüan (1635–1704), a "pragmatist" who rejected Sung-Ming metaphysics as impractical and meaningless. [*See the biographies of Ku Yen-wu and Wang Fu-chih.*] Ku set the intellectual tone for the next two centuries, which prized philological scholarship (often patronized by the imperial court or by wealthy officials who financed expensive projects of compilation, drawing many scholars together) and tended to disparage mere "empty words," that is, speculative philosophy. But the Ch'ing emperors vigorously promoted Ch'eng-Chu moral philosophy for its disciplinary value, and they were assured by flatterers that at last, as in the golden age of antiquity, "government" *(chih)* and true "doctrine" *(chiao)* were again one.

This echo of Ou-yang Hsiu stirred the imagination of a genuinely independent thinker of the next century, Chang Hsüeh-ch'eng (1738–1801), a local historian whose philosophy of history pictured antiquity as a concrete "unity of knowledge and practice" ("the Six Classics are all history") or of *tao* and *ch'i*. Chang much admired the experiments in Mencian ethics of his contemporary Tai Chen (1724–1777), but he censured Tai for his impatience with Chu Hsi. Intellectualist and not at all self-cultivationist, the famous philological scholar Tai held that principles and human desires are not antithetical and that to become a sage one must feed the mind with knowledge, testing candidate principles by applying the Confucian golden rule *(shu)* until what is only "natural" *(tzu-jan)* is seen to be "necessary" *(pi-jan)*. For Tai, the prime form of evil is to mistake one's own mere "opinions" *(i-chien)* for true principles and to force them on others. [*See the biographies of Chang Hsüeh-ch'eng and Tai Chen.*]

What had happened in the Ch'ing dynasty turn in thought was both a reaction against the speculative and introspective temper of earlier Neo-Confucianism and, at the same time, a further development of its implications. Wang Yang-ming had insisted that principles cannot be grasped abstractly apart from concrete moral experience; the Ch'ing intellectualist translation of this idea was that philosophical insight cannot be separated from historical and philological "solid learning."

Neither Chang nor Tai received philosophical recognition until the twentieth century. Meanwhile, another intellectual movement was gathering force: Ch'ing philology. Leading many to reject "Sung studies" *(Sung-hsüeh)* for "Han studies" *(Han-hsüeh)*, Ch'ing philology in time led to a reassessment of the Han era New Text philosophy of history of Tung Chung-shu and Ho Hsiu. Their ideas were taken up by K'ang Yu-wei (1858–1927) and others among the group of Confucian intellectuals pushing radical political reforms at the end of the nineteenth century. K'ang urged a revisionist view of the classics (in which the Han court librarian Liu Hsin figured as villian, forging half of them) that portrayed Confucius as a reformer, holding a historical, Western-style theory of progress. Confucianism was to be a religion, since the model of the West showed that a lively religious faith was necessary for progress and national strength. This idea lingered into the twentieth century, naturally enough among the Chinese, for whom the West for generations had been represented by missionaries, and who failed to see that the Western faith that sent the missionaries to China was already waning. [*See the biography of K'ang Yu-wei.*]

The Twentieth Century. The 1920s saw the first real impact of American and European contemporary academic philosophy, notably in the lively controversy on "science and philosophy of life" in 1923. A primary problem for twentieth-century thinkers has been how to reconcile their commitments to historical Chinese values with Western intellectual temptations. Thus, Hu Shih (1891–1962), a student of John Dewey, hunted through Chinese philosophy for examples of pragmatism and logical method. Thus also, Marxists of the Liberation period (c. 1949) wrote one another little essays on "how to study" *(hsüeh-hsi)*, and on how to reform "individual nature" *(ko hsing)* into "party nature" *(tang hsing)*, picking into ancient Confucian (and even Buddhist) self-cultivationist literature. Those who see Communism as a new religion, and the hallmark of religion as the desire for self-change, should not be surprised. Twentieth-century thought sometimes continues the past and sometimes merely uses it, but it seldom ignores it. There are the non-Marxists (Hsiung Shih-li, Confucian-Buddhist; Fung Yu-lan and Ho Lin, Neo-Confucian; Hu Shih, pragmatist; Chang Tung-sun, Neo-Kantian), the Marxists (Li Ta-chao, Ch'en Po-ta, Liu Shao-ch'i, Mao Tse-tung himself), both at once (perhaps, Liang Shu-ming), and both by turns (Fung again). Such deeply thoughtful men as Hsü Fu-kuan and Mou Tsung-san (students of Hsiung) and the late T'ang Chün-i can genuinely be called contemporary religious philosophers within the Confucian mold.

[*For an assessment of China's dominant intellectual tradition, see* Confucian Thought. *Many of the issues raised in the above discussion are also treated in* Chinese Religion, *overview article. For further discussion of the principle terms noted above, see* Tao and Te; Jen and I; Li; Yin-yang Wu-hsing; Ch'i; Hsiao; Hsin; T'ai-chi; *and* T'ai-p'ing.]

BIBLIOGRAPHY

Briere, O. *Fifty Years of Chinese Philosophy, 1898–1950*. Translated by Laurence G. Thompson and edited by Dennis J. Doolin. London, 1956.

Chan, Wing-tsit. *An Outline and an Annotated Bibliography of Chinese Philosophy*. New Haven, 1961.

Chan, Wing-tsit, trans. and comp. *A Source Book in Chinese Philosophy*. Princeton, 1963. Includes an especially useful bibliography.

Ch'en, Kenneth. *Buddhism in China: A Historical Survey*. Princeton, 1964. Includes an especially useful bibliography.

de Bary, Wm. Theodore, ed. *Self and Society in Ming Thought*. New York, 1970.

de Bary, Wm. Theodore, ed. *The Unfolding of Neo-Confucianism*. New York, 1975.

de Bary, Wm. Theodore. *Neo-Confucian Orthodoxy and the Learning of the Mind-and-Heart*. New York, 1981.

de Bary, Wm. Theodore, Wing-tsit Chan, and Burton Watson, comps. *Sources of Chinese Tradition*. New York, 1960.

Fung Yu-lan. *A History of Chinese Philosophy*. 2 vols. 2d ed. Translated by Derk Bodde. Princeton, 1952–1953. Includes an especially useful bibliography.

Furth, Charlotte, ed. *The Limits of Change: Essays on Conservative Alternatives in Republican China*. Cambridge, Mass., 1976.

Graham, A. C. *Two Chinese Philosophers: Ch'êng Ming-tao and Ch'êng Yi-ch'uan*. London, 1958.

Hsiao Kung-chuan. *A History of Chinese Political Thought*, vol. 1, *From the Beginnings to the Sixth Century A.D.* Translated by F. W. Mote. Princeton, 1979.

Needham, Joseph. *Science and Civilisation in China*, vol. 2, *History of Scientific Thought*. Cambridge, 1956. Includes an especially useful bibliography.

Nivison, David S., and Arthur F. Wright, eds. *Confucianism in Action*. Stanford, Calif., 1959.

Wright, Arthur F., ed. *Studies in Chinese Thought*. Chicago, 1953.

Wright, Arthur F. *Buddhism in Chinese History*. Stanford, Calif., 1959. Includes an especially useful bibliography.

DAVID S. NIVISON

CHINESE RELIGION. [*This entry consists of five articles on the religious tradition of the Chinese people:*

An Overview
Popular Religion
Mythic Themes
Religious and Philosophical Texts
History of Study

An Overview *surveys the religious history of the Chinese;* Popular Religion *treats those elements of the tradition centered primarily around family, clan, and local observances;* Mythic Themes *attempts to identify the principal structures of the myths known to us from antiquity;* Religious and Philosophical Texts *outlines the contents of various nonsectarian texts and text collections; and* History of Study *surveys the rise of the modern scholarly study of Chinese religion. For further discussion of the major traditions introduced here, see* Confucian Thought; Taoism; Buddhism, *article on* Buddhism in China; Buddhism, Schools of, *article on* Chinese Buddhism; *and* Chinese Philosophy. *For practices and traditions specific to Taiwan, see* Taiwanese Religions.]

An Overview

[*This article provides an introduction to the rise and development of various religious movements, themes, and motifs over time. Its emphasis is on historical continuities and on the interaction of diverse currents of Chinese religious thought from the prehistoric era to the present*].

Traditional Chinese religious institutions and activities flourish today in Taiwan, Hong Kong, Singapore, and in some overseas communities, as well as in parts of China. These activities are the products of continuous historical development from prehistoric times. In that period the area of present-day China was inhabited by a large number of tribal groups. In around 5000 BCE several of these tribes developed agriculture and began to live in small villages surrounded by their fields. Domesticated plants and animals included millet, rice, dogs, pigs, goats, sheep, cattle, and silkworms. The physical characteristics of these early agriculturalists were similar to those of modern Chinese. The archaeological record indicates gradual development toward more complex technology and social stratification. By the late Neolithic period (beginning around 3200 BCE) there were well-developed local cultures in several areas that were to become centers of Chinese civilization later, including the southeast coast, the southwest, the Yangtze River valley, the northeast, and the northern plains. The interaction of these cultures eventually led to the rise of literate, bronze-working civilizations in the north, the Hsia (before 1500 BCE) and Shang (c. 1500–1050 BCE). The existence of the Hsia kingdom is attested in early historical sources that have otherwise been shown to accord with archaeological discoveries. However, archaeologists are still debating which sites can be confidently assigned to the Hsia. The Shang has been archaeologically verified, beginning with the excavation of one of its capitals in 1928.

There is some evidence for prehistoric religious activities, particularly for a cult of the dead, who were often buried in segregated cemeteries, supine, with heads toward a single cardinal direction. In some sites houses and circles of white stones are associated with clusters of graves, while in others wine goblets and pig jaws are scattered on ledges near the top of the pit, perhaps indicating a farewell feast. In the Wei River area, secondary burial was practiced, with bones from single graves collected and reburied with those of from twenty to eighty others. Grave offerings are found in almost all primary burials, with quantity and variety depending on the status of the deceased; tools, pottery vessels, objects of jade and turquoise, dogs, and, in some cases, human beings. Bodies and faces were often painted with red ochre, a symbol of life. All of these practices indicate belief in afterlife and the prehistoric beginnings of ancestor worship. Other evidence for prehistoric religion includes deer buried in fields and divination through reading cracks in the dried shoulder bones of sheep or deer. This form of divination, attested in what is now northeast China by 3560–3240 BCE, is the direct antecedent of similar practices in historical times. Buried deer suggest offerings to the power of the soil, a common practice in later periods.

Early Historical Period

The early historical period (Shang and Chou kingdoms) saw the development of many of the social and religious horizons that continue to this day to be associated with the Chinese. Although obvious links with the earlier period persist, it is with the emergence of these kingdoms that the religious history of the Chinese properly begins.

The Shang. The formation of the Shang kingdom was due to technological innovation such as bronze casting, and to the development of new forms of social and administrative control. Extant evidence provides information about the religion of the Shang aristocracy, characterized in the first place by elaborate graves and ceremonial objects for the dead. Grave offerings include decapitated human beings, horses, dogs, large numbers of bronze vessels, and objects of jade, stone, and shell. Some tombs were equipped with chariots hitched to horses. These tomb offerings indicate a belief that afterlife for members of the royal clan was similar to that of their present existence, but in another realm, perhaps in a heaven presided over by the Shang high god Shang-ti, the "Lord on High."

There are two other material sources for our understanding of Shang religion: inscriptions on oracle bones and in bronze sacrificial vessels. From these we learn that the most common objects of petition and inquiry were the ancestors of aristocratic clans. These deified ancestors were believed to have powers of healing and fertility in their own right, but also could serve as intermediaries between their living descendants and more powerful gods of natural forces and Shang-ti. Ancestors were ranked by title and seniority, with those longest dead having the widest authority. Since they could bring harm as well as aid to their descendants, it was necessary to propitiate the ancestors to ward off their anger as well as to bring their blessing. Nature deities named in the inscriptions personify the powers of rivers, mountains, rain, wind, and other natural phenomena. Shang-ti, whose authority exceeded that of the most exalted royal ancestor, served as a source of unity and order. [*See* Shang-ti.]

To contact these sacred powers the Shang practiced divination and sacrificial rituals, usually closely related to each other. In divination, small pits were bored in the backs of turtle plastrons or the shoulder bones of oxen or sheep. Heated bronze rods or thorns were placed in these impressions, causing the bones to crack with a popping sound. Diviners then interpreted the pattern of the cracks on the face of the bone to determine yes or no answers to petitions. The subjects of divination include weather, warfare, illness, administrative decisions, harvests, and other practical issues. Among the divination questions are those inquiring about sacrifices to ancestors and deities. Sacrifices to spirits residing above consisted essentially of burning flesh and grain on open air altars. Spirits of the earth were offered libations of fermented liquors, and those of bodies of water, precious objects such as jade. Sacrificial animals included cattle, dogs, sheep, and human beings.

One may presume that these sacrifices were accompanied by petitions addressed to the deity specifying what was desired in return. There is an emphasis on precision in sacrifice; the correct objects offered in the right way were believed to obligate the spirits to respond. Thus, in Shang sacrifice we already see the principle of reciprocity, which has remained a fundamental patten of interaction throughout the history of Chinese religions. Shang concerns for divination, hierarchical structure, and balanced polarities also anticipated later developments.

The Chou. There are many references in Shang oracle bone texts to a people called Chou who lived west of the Shang center, in the area of modern Shensi Province. The Chou, who were considered to be an important tributary state, were at first culturally and technologically inferior to the Shang, but learned rapidly and by the eleventh century BCE challenged the Shang for political supremacy. The final Chou conquest took place in about 1050 BCE. Remnants of the Shang royal line were allowed to continue their ancestral practices in the small state of Sung.

The religious activities of the early Chou aristocracy were focused on their ancestors, who were believed to reside in a celestial court presided over by T'ien,

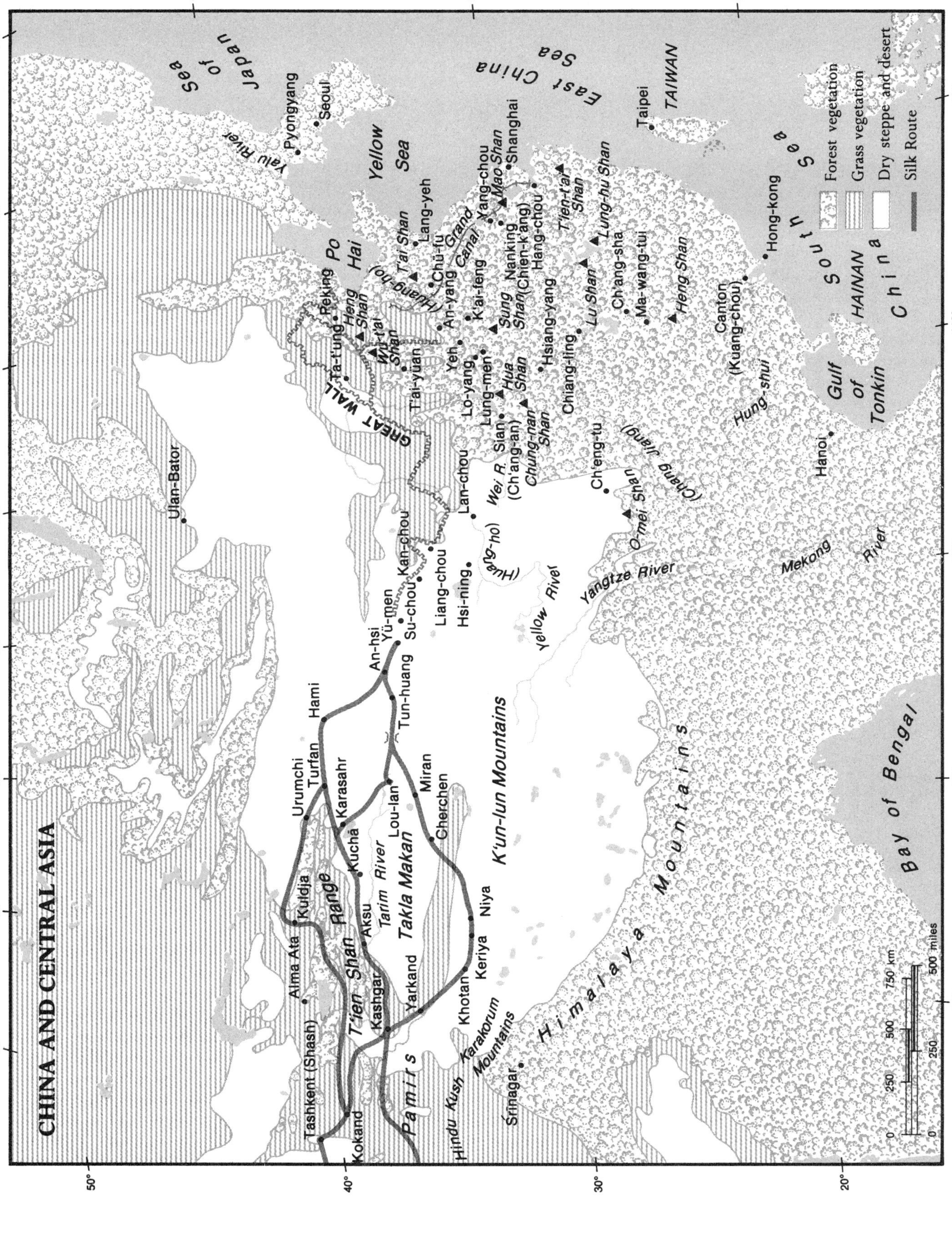
CHINA AND CENTRAL ASIA
Sea of Japan
Yellow Sea
East China Sea
South China Sea
Gulf of Tonkin
Bay of Bengal
Po Hai
TAIWAN
HAINAN
Forest vegetation
Grass vegetation
Dry steppe and desert
Silk Route
0 250 500 750 km
0 250 500 miles
Pyongyang
Seoul
Yalu River
Peking
Ta-t'ung
Heng Shan
Wu-t'ai Shan
T'ai-yuan
T'ai Shan
Lang-yeh
Chü-fu
Grand Canal
Huang-ho
An-yang
K'ai-feng
Yang-chou
Mao Shan
Shanghai
Nanking (Chien-k'ang)
Hang-chou
T'ien-t'ai Shan
Lung-hu Shan
Sung Shan
Yeh
Lo-yang
Lung-men
Hua Shan
Hsiang-yang
Lu Shan
Chiang-ling
Ch'ang-sha
Ma-wang-tui
Heng Shan
Hong-kong
Canton (Kuang-chou)
Hung-shui
Hanoi
Taipei
GREAT WALL
Ulan-Bator
Lan-chou
Sian (Ch'ang-an)
Wei R.
Chung-nan Shan
Ch'eng-tu
O-mei Shan
Chang Jiang
Yangtze River
Mekong River
Yellow River
Huang-ho
Kan-chou
Liang-chou
Hsi-ning
Su-chou
Yü-men
An-hsi
Tun-huang
Hami
Turfan
Urumchi
Karasahr
Lou-lan
Miran
Cherchen
Kuchā
Tarim River
Takla Makan
K'un-lun Mountains
Himalaya Mountains
Niya
Keriya
Khotan
Yarkand
Kashgar
Aksu
Kuldja
Alma Ata
T'ien Shan Range
Tashkent (Shash)
Kokand
Pamirs
Karakorum Mountains
Hindu Kush
Śrinagar
40°
30°
20°
50°
140°
130°
120°
110°
100°
90°
80°
70°

"Heaven," the Chou high god, similar to Shang-ti in scope and function. These ancestors had power to influence the prosperity of their descendants, their fertility, health, and longevity. Through ritual equation with deities of natural forces the ancestors could also influence the productivity of clan lands. In addition, royal ancestors served as intermediaries between their descendants and T'ien. [*See* T'ien.]

Ancestral rituals took the form of great feasts in which the deceased was represented by an impersonator, usually a grandson or nephew. In these feasts the sharing of food and drink confirmed vows of mutual fidelity and aid. The most important ancestor worshiped was Hou Chi, who was both legendary founder of the ruling house and the patron of agriculture. As was true for the Shang, Chou rituals were also directed toward symbols of natural power such as mountains and rivers; most significant natural phenomena were deified and reverenced. The proper time and mode of such rituals were determined in part by divination, which in the Chou involved both cracking bones and turtle shells and the manipulation of dried plant stalks of different lengths. Divination was also employed in military campaigns, the interpretation of dreams, the siting of cities, and in many other situations involving important decisions.

Chou-dynasty diviners eventually produced a text to support and codify their work, the *I ching* (Classic of Change), which classifies human situations by means of sixty-four sets of six horizontal lines (hexagrams), broken and unbroken. The broken line sets represent *k'un*, the female force that completes, while those with solid lines represent *ch'ien*, the male force that initiates; all of experience is a combination of these polarities, in unending cycles of change. Through ritual manipulation, dried plant stalks are arranged in sets with numerical values corresponding to lines in the hexagrams. One thereby obtains a hexagram that reflects one's present situation; additional line changes indicate the structures of the immediate future. Contemplation of these hexagrams clarifies decisions and provides warning or encouragement.

The *I ching* is essentially a book of wisdom for personal and administrative guidance, used since at least the seventh century BCE. However, from the sixth century BCE on commentaries were written to amplify the earliest level of the text and by the first century CE there were ten such levels of exposition, some quite philosophical in tone. The *Classic of Change* was believed to reflect the structure of cosmic movement, and hence became an object of reverent contemplation in itself. Its earliest levels antedated all the philosophical schools, so it belonged to none, though the Confucians later claimed it as a classic. The polarity of *ch'ien* and *k'un* provided a model for that of *yang* and *yin*, first discussed in the fourth century BCE. The *I ching*'s sometimes obscure formulations gave impetus to philosophical speculations throughout the later history of Chinese thought.

A third focus of Chou worship, in addition to ancestors and nature gods, was the *she*, a sacred earth mound located in the capital of each state and in at least some villages. The state *she* represented the sacred powers of the earth available to a particular domain, and so was offered libations upon such important occasions in the life of the state as the birth of a prince, ascension to rule, and military campaigns. Beside the earth mound stood a sacred tree, a symbol of its connection to the powers of the sky.

The early Chou aristocracy carried out sacrificial rituals to mark the seasons of the year and promote the success of farming. These sacrifices, performed in ancestral temples, were offered both to the high god T'ien and to ancestors. These and other Chou rituals were elaborate dramatic performances involving music, dancing, and archery, concluding with feasts in which much wine was consumed.

The most distinctive early Chou contribution to the history of Chinese religions was the theory of *t'ien-ming*, the "mandate of Heaven," first employed to justify the Chou conquest of the Shang. According to this theory, Heaven as a high god wills order and peace for human society. This divine order is to be administered by pious kings who care for their subjects on Heaven's behalf. These kings, called *t'ien-tzu*, "son of Heaven," are granted divine authority to rule, but only so long as they rule well. If they become indolent, corrupt, and cruel, the "mandate of Heaven" can be transferred to another line. This process can take a long time and involve many warnings to the ruler in the form of natural calamities and popular unrest. Those who heed such warnings can repent and rehabilitate their rule; otherwise, the mandate can be claimed by one who promises to restore righteous administration. In practice it is the victors who claim the mandate, as did the founding Chou kings, on the grounds of the alleged indolence and impiety of the last Shang ruler.

The idea of the mandate of Heaven has gripped the Chinese political imagination ever since. It became the basis for the legitimacy of dynasties, the judgment of autocracy, and the moral right of rebellion. This status it owed in part to its support by Confucius and his school, who saw the mandate of Heaven as the foundation of political morality. In sum, early Chou religion was robust and positive in spirit, a spirit that foreshadowed the confident reciprocity of Chinese rituals in later periods, as well as the positive view of human moral potential characteristic of the tradition as a whole.

The early Chou political and social synthesis began to deteriorate in the eighth century as competing local states moved toward political, military, and ritual independence. Within them, rulers from clans originally enfeoffed by Chou kings also lost their power, which reverted to competing local families. This breakdown of hereditary authority led to new social mobility, with status increasingly awarded for military valor and administrative ability, regardless of aristocratic background. There is some evidence that even peasants could move about in search of more just rulers. These political and social changes were accompanied by an increase in the number and size of cities, and in the circulation of goods between states.

Changes in religion accompanied those in economy and society. Although many older rituals were continued, they became more elaborate and were focused on the ancestors of the rulers of the states rather than on those of the Chou kings.

Social change and widespread civil turmoil and suffering led some in this era to question the power of the gods. In theory, the loss of a state was ultimately due to ritual negligence by the ruler, while the victors were supposed to provide for sacrifices to the ancestors of the vanquished. But in practice, many gods charged with protection were deemed to have failed while their desecrators flourished. In the *Shih ching* (Book of Poetry, c. 600 BCE) there are even verses that question the justice of Heaven itself. In any event, by the sixth century a more rationalistic perspective developed in the minds of some, accompanied by a turning away from gods and spirits to the problems of human society and governance.

Confucius. It was in this context that Chinese philosophy was born, in the teachings of Confucius (c. 551–479 BCE). Confucius (the latinate form of K'ung Fu-tzu, or Master K'ung) was the son of an obscure family in the small state of Lu, a state in which the old Chou cultural traditions were strong but that was buffeted both by repeated invasions and by local power struggles. Confucius's goal was the restoration of the ethical standards, just rule, and legitimate government of the early Chou period as he understood them. To this end he sought public office himself and exhorted the rulers of his day. He also gathered a small group of disciples whom he taught to become *chün-tzu* ("superior men"), men of ethical sensitivity and historical wisdom who could administer benevolent government. In the process he initiated a new level of ethical awareness in Chinese culture and a new form of education, education in what he believed were universal principles for mature humanity and civilization. He assumed that the criteria for holding office were intelligence and high moral principles, not hereditary status, and so further undermined the Chou feudal system that was crumbling around him.

Confucius began a long Chinese tradition of ethical reform in the name of apparently reactionary principles. Statements recorded by his disciples show that in crisis situations the master emphasized that he had a mission from Heaven to restore social harmony. His models for such restoration were the founding kings of the Chou dynasty as described in the ancient *Book of Poetry*, kings who ruled with reverence toward their ancestors and kindness toward their people, ever fearful of losing Heaven's approval. These models had mythic force for Confucius, who saw himself as their embodiment in his own age.

All of Confucius's ethical teachings were intended to describe the "way" *(tao)* of the superior man, a way originating in the will of Heaven for its people. At its best, the inner character of such persons was to be formed by *jen* ("perfect co-humanity"), an ultimately transcendental quality that Confucius believed he had never attained. The actions of an ethically aware person were to be carried out in a balanced way in accord with refined social custom *(li)*. [*See* Li.] Confucius's teachings reveal a religious consciousness that was restrained, philosophical, and prophetic; it is thus not surprising to learn that he did not participate in the exorcism and divination common in his day, nor speculate on the nature of lesser deities and spirits, although he did support veneration of ancestors. At this point his attitude is expressed in the statement, "reverence deities and ancestral spirits, but keep them at a distance." So it was that he directed the attention of his disciples away from questions of deities and afterlife toward the situation of human beings in the world. [*See the biography of Confucius.*]

By the fourth and third centuries BCE the end result of Confucius's gentle skepticism was a psychological interpretation of religion in his own school and the absence of any theological discussion by the formative thinkers of other traditions such as the individualists and the theorists of administrative laws and methods (Legalists). But in the culture at large religious beliefs and activities continued unabated; divination and rituals accompanied every significant activity, and a quest for personal immortality was gaining momentum. There was one well-known philosopher who expressed this common concern for religion quite directly, Mo-tzu (fifth century BCE), a thinker from a lower middle-class artisan background.

Mo-tzu. Mo-tzu was a thorough-going utilitarian who taught that the fundamental criterion of value was practical benefit to all. He was from Confucius's home state of Lu, and educated in the emerging Confucian tradition, but turned against what he perceived to be its elitism and wasteful concern with elaborate rituals. In his ethical teaching Mo-tzu reinterpreted along utilitarian lines earlier principles such as righteousness and filial reverence, centered on the theme of universal love without familial and social distinctions. He also attracted a group of disciples whom he sent out to serve in various states in an attempt to implement his teachings.

For the history of Chinese religions the most significant aspect of Mo-tzu's thought is his concern to provide theological sanctions for his views. For Mo-tzu, T'ien, or Heaven, is an active creator god whose will or mandate extends to everyone; what Heaven wills is love, prosperity, and peace for all. Heaven is the ultimate ruler of the whole world; T'ien sees all, rewards the good, and punishes the evil. In this task it is aided by a multitude of lesser spirits who are also intelligent and vital and who serve as messengers between T'ien and human beings. Mo-tzu advocates that since this is the nature of divine reality, religious reverence should be encouraged by the state as a sanction for moral order.

To protect himself from intellectual skeptics Mo-tzu at one point allows that even if deities and spirits do not exist communal worship still has social value. Although his whole attempt to argue for belief in Heaven on utilitarian grounds could be understood as a last stand for traditional religion within a changing philosophical world, there is no reason to doubt that Mo-tzu himself believed in the gods. [*See* Moism *and the biography of Mo-tzu.*]

The fourth century BCE was a period of incessant civil war on the one hand and great philosophical diversity on the other. A variety of thinkers arose, each propounding a cure for the ills of the age, most seeking to establish their views by training disciples and attaining office. Some advocated moral reform through education, others authoritarian government, *laissez faire* administration, rationalized bureaucracy, agricultural communes, rule in accord with the powers of nature, or individual self-fulfillment. Religious concerns were not paramount for these thinkers; indeed, for some they do not appear at all. The two traditions of this period that do warrant discussion here are the Confucian, represented by Meng-tzu (Mencius, c. 371–289 BCE), and that of the mystically inclined individualists, traditionally known as the Taoists.

Meng-tzu. Meng-tzu (or Meng K'e) was a teacher and would-be administrator from the small state of Tsou who amplified Confucius's teachings and placed them on a much firmer philosophical and literary base. Meng-tzu was concerned to prepare his disciples for enlightened and compassionate public service, beginning with provision for the physical needs of the people. He believed that only when their material livelihood is secure can the people be guided to higher moral awareness. This hope for moral transformation is grounded in Meng-tzu's conviction that human nature is potentially good. What is needed are rulers who nourish this potential as "fathers and mothers of the people." These teachings Meng-tzu expounded courageously before despotic kings whose inclinations were otherwise.

Specifically religious concerns are muted in Meng-tzu's teachings, but can be discerned in the deeper assumptions of his work. The first of these is that *t'ien*, or Heaven, is an expression of the underlying moral structure of the world, so that in the long run "those who accord with Heaven are preserved, and those who oppose Heaven are destroyed." Heaven's will is known through the assent or disapproval of the people. The second theme in Meng-tzu's teaching that might be understood as a religious "ultimate concern" is the abovementioned belief that the human mind possesses an innate potential for moral awareness, a potential bestowed by Heaven at birth, so that "to understand human nature is to understand Heaven." Meng-tzu represents a further humanization of the Confucian tradition, and his emphasis on the powers of human nature within did much to shape the religious sensibilities of Chinese philosophy. At this point he is in accord with Chuang-tzu and helped prepare the way for similar emphases in Ch'an (Jpn., Zen) Buddhism and Neo-Confucianism. As had Confucius, Meng-tzu assumed that ancestor veneration was a basic requirement of civilized life, but neither thinker emphasized such veneration as much as did later texts like the *Hsiao ching*, the Classic of Filial Piety (third century BCE). [*See the biography of Meng-tzu.*]

Hsün-tzu. The third most important Confucian philosopher before the Han dynasty (202 BCE–220 CE) was Hsün-tzu (Hsün Ch'ing, d. 215 BCE), a scholar from the state of Chao who held offices for a time in the larger states of Ch'i and Ch'u. Hsün-tzu's thought was influenced by several of the traditions that had developed before his time, including those of the Logicians, Taoists, and Authoritarians (Legalists). Hsün-tzu agreed with the Authoritarian emphasis on the need for strong centralized rule and a strict penal code. He also shared their low estimate of human nature, which in his view tended toward selfishness and competition. Nonetheless, Hsün-tzu believed that human attitudes and behavior are perfectible by dint of much discipline and effort, so his differences with Meng-tzu on this point are those of degree.

Hsün-tzu's chief contribution was his reinterpretation

of *t'ien* as the order of nature, an order that has no consciousness and is not directly related to human concerns. This interpretation is parallel to the views of the *Lao-tzu (Tao-te ching)* and *Chuang-tzu* texts concerning the cosmic "Way" (Tao). Hsün-tzu was concerned to separate the roles of heaven, earth, and man, with human attention directed toward ethics, administration, and culture. In this context rituals such as funeral rites are valuable channels for emotions, but have no objective referent; their role is social, not theological. Ignorant "petty people" who literally believe in the efficacy of rain dances and divination are to be pitied; for the gentleman such activities are "cultural adornment."

Hsün-tzu thus gave impetus to the skeptical tradition in Chinese thought that began before Confucius and was reinforced by later thinkers such as Wang Ch'ung (c. 27–96 CE). Hsün-tzu's teachings at this point provided a theoretical basis for a rough bifurcation between elite and popular attitudes toward religion and for sporadic attempts to suppress "excessive cults." Hsün-tzu's epistemology also set up the intellectual framework for a critique of heresy, conceived of as inventing words and titles beyond those employed by general consensus and sanctioned by the state. These themes had important implications for the remainder of Chinese history, including official attitudes toward religion today. [*See the biography of Hsün-tzu.*]

Early Taoist thought. The earliest writings concerned to direct attention toward the mysterious cosmic "Way" that underlies all things are the first seven chapters of the extant *Chuang-tzu*, a text attributed to a philosopher-poet named Chuang Chou of the fourth century BCE. Chuang Chou was convinced that the world in its natural state is peaceful and harmonious, a state exemplified by the growth of plants and the activities of animals. Disorder is due to human aggression and manipulation, a tendency that finds as much expression in Confucian and Moist moralizing as in cruel punishments and warfare. Such moralizing in turn is rooted in a false confidence in words, words that debators use to express their own limited points of view and thus to dichotomize our understanding of the world. Indeed, all perspectives are limited and relative, conditioned by the interests and anxieties of species, social positions, and individuals. The answer to this problem is to understand and affirm the relativity of views, and thus harmonize them all. This the sage does by perceiving the constant rhythms of change within all life and identifying with them. In his view all dichotomies are unified; hence there is no need for struggle and competition. The sage intuits the Tao within and behind all things, and takes its all-embracing perspective as his own. [*See the biography of Chuang-tzu.*]

The other major early book devoted to discussing the Tao behind all things is the early third-century BCE *Tao-te ching* (The Way and Its Inner Power), also known as the *Lao-tzu*, after its eponymous "author," Lao Tan. The *Tao-te ching* discusses the Way in more direct, metaphysical terms than does the *Chuang-tzu*, all the while protesting that such discussion is ultimately futile. Here we are told that the Tao is the source of all things, "the mother of the universe," the ineffable cosmic womb out of which all emerges. The Tao also "works in the world," guiding all things in harmonious development and interaction. As both source and order of the world the Tao serves as a model for enlightened rulers who gain power by staying in the background and letting their people live spontaneously in response to their own needs. The Tao is the vital force of life perceived at its utmost depth; it works mysteriously and imperceptibly and yet there is nothing it does not accomplish. Its symbols are water rather than rock, valleys rather than hills, the female rather than the male. Although its perspective is profound, its author intended this book to be a handbook of wise and successful living, living characterized by a natural, spontaneous action that does not prematurely wear itself out. [*See* Tao and Te.]

The *Chuang-tzu* and *Lao-tzu* were the sources of a persistent tradition of naturalistic mysticism in the history of Chinese religions. They were the inspiration for much poetry, romantic philosophy, and meditation, all intended as a corrective for the bustle and competition of life, a means to peace of mind, and a clarification and broadening of perspective.

There are several passages in these books that describe the enlightened person as living peacefully and long because he does not waste his vital powers on needless contention and aggression. In the *Tao-te ching*, for example, we are told that "He who knows when to stop is free from danger; therefore he can long endure" (chap. 44), and that one who is "a good preserver of his life" cannot be harmed, "because in him there is no room for death" (chap. 50). Although in some passages of the *Chuang-tzu* an enlightened perspective leads to acceptance of death, a few others provide poetic visions of immortals, those who have transcended death by merging with the Tao. These indications of immortality provided the chief point of contact between these books and those who sought immortality by more direct means, including later practitioners of Taoist religion.

The quest for immortality. An explicit concern for long life *(shou)* had already appeared on early Chou bronzes and in poems in the *Book of Poetry*. Beginning in the eighth century BCE we find terms expressing a hope for immortality, such as "no death," "transcending the world," and "becoming an immortal." By the fourth century BCE there is evidence of an active quest for immortality through a variety of means, including exercises imitating the movements of long-lived animals, diets enforcing abstinence from grains, the use of food vessels inscribed with characters indicating longevity, the ingestion of herbs and chemicals, and petitions for the aid of immortals residing in mountains or distant paradises. It was in this context that Chinese alchemy began. The alchemical quest became the most dramatic form of the struggle against death, growing in popularity during the Ch'in (221–207 BCE) and Western Han (202 BCE–9 CE) dynasties.

The goal of all these practices was to return the body to its original state of purity and power with its *yin* (quiescent, dark, feminine) and *yang* (active, bright, masculine) forces vital and in proper balance. [*See also* Yin-yang Wu-hsing.] The fact that some of the compounds used were poisonous did not deter the experimenters; those who died were believed by devotees to have transferred themselves to another plane of existence, that of the immortals *(hsien)*. [*See* Hsien.] All this effort and expense were considered necessary because in ancient China the person was understood to be a psycho-physical whole, composed throughout of one vital substance, *ch'i*, in different modes and densities. [*See* Ch'i.] The focal points of physical and mental energy were discussed respectively as the *p'o* and *hun*, which are often translated as "souls," but which cannot exist for long separately, or apart from the body. The intelligent mode, *hun*, can exist in an ancestral tablet as long as it is ritually remembered by its descendants, and the *p'o* in some texts is understood to descend to a murky realm underground, the Yellow Springs. These forms of continuation after death were perceived by some to be tenuous and limited, so they attempted to make the entire person/body immortal by transforming its substance. There was no doctrine of an eternal soul to fall back on as in India or the Hellenistic world, so the only alternative was physical immortality. In China this tradition continued to develop through the Eastern (Latter) Han dynasty (25–220 CE) and produced texts of its own full of recipes, techniques, and moral exhortations. As such, it became one of the major sources of the Taoist religion that emerged in the second century CE. [*See also* Alchemy, *article on* Chinese Alchemy, *and* Soul, *article on* Chinese Concepts.]

Spirit mediums. The other important expression of Chinese religious consciousness before the Han dynasty was shamanism, which most commonly took the form of deities and spirits possessing receptive human beings. Spirit mediums both female and male are mentioned in discussions of early Chou religion as participants in court rituals, responsible for invoking the descent of the gods, praying and dancing for rain, and for ceremonial sweeping to exorcise harmful forces. They were a subordinate level of officially accepted ritual performers, mostly women, who spoke on behalf of the gods to arrange for sacrifices. In conditions of extreme drought they could be exposed to the sun as an inducement to rain. Female mediums were called *wu*, a word etymologically related to that for dancing; male mediums were called *hsi*. In the state of Ch'u, south of the center of Chou culture, there were shamans believed able to practice "magic flight," that is, to send their souls on journeys to distant realms of deities and immortals. [*See also* Flight.]

Han historical sources indicate that by the third century BCE there were shamans all over China, many of whom were invited by emperors to set up shrines in the capital. This was done in part to consolidate imperial control, but also to make available fresh sources of sacred power to support the state and heal illness. Sporadic attempts were also made by officials to suppress shamanism. These began as early as 99 BCE and continued in efforts to reform court rituals in 31–30 BCE, and to change local practices involving human sacrifice in 25 CE. However, it is clear that shamanism was well established among the people and continued to have formal influence at court until the fifth century CE. Shamans were occasionally employed by rulers to call up the spirits of royal ancestors and consorts and incidents of court support continued into the eleventh century. Owing in part to the revival of Confucianism in that period, in 1023 a sweeping edict was issued that all shamans be returned to agricultural life and their shrines be destroyed. Thus, the gradual confucianization of the Chinese elite led to the suppression of shamanism at that level, but it continued to flourish among the people, where its activities can still be observed in China, Taiwan, and other Chinese communities. [*See also* Shamanism, *overview article*.]

The Beginnings of Empire

In the fifth century BCE the disintegration of the Chou feudal and social order quickened under the pressure of incessant civil wars. The larger states formed alliances and maneuvered for power, seeking hegemony over the others, aiming to reunify the area of Chou culture by force alone. In 256 BCE the state of Ch'in, under the influence of a ruthlessly applied ideology of laws and punishments suggested in the fourth century BCE by Shang Yang, one of the founders of the Authoritarian school, eliminated the last Chou king and then finished off its remaining rivals. Finally, in 221 the state of Ch'in became the empire of Ch'in (221–207 BCE), and its ruler took a new title, "First Emperor of Ch'in" (Ch'in Shih-huang-ti). With this step China as a semicontinental state was born. There were many periods of division and strife later, but the new level of unification achieved by the Ch'in was never forgotten, and became the goal of all later dynasties.

The Ch'in emperors attempted to rule all of China by the standards long developed in their own area; laws, measurements, written characters, wheel tracks, thought, and so forth were all to be unified. Local traditions and loyalties were still strong, however, and Ch'in rule remained precarious. After the emperor died in 209 he was replaced by a son who proved unequal to the task. Rebellions that broke out in that year severely undermined Ch'in authority and by 206 one of the rebel leaders, a village head named Liu Pang, had assumed *de facto* control of state administration. In 202 Liu Pang was proclaimed emperor of a new dynasty, the Han (202 BCE–220 CE), built upon Ch'in foundations but destined to last, with one interregnum, for over four hundred years.

The Ch'in. The Ch'in was noteworthy both for its suppression of philosophy and its encouragement of religion. The Authoritarian (Legalist) tradition dominant in the state of Ch'in had long been hostile to the Confucians and Moists, with their emphasis on ethical sanctions for rule. For the Authoritarians the only proper standard of conduct was the law, applied by officials concerned with nothing else, whose personal views were irrelevant as long as they performed their task. The only sanctions the state needed were power and effective organization. Not long after Ch'in became an empire it attempted to silence all criticism based on the assumption of inner standards of righteousness that were deemed to transcend political power and circumstance. In 213 BCE the court made it a capital offence to discuss Confucian books and principles and ordered that all books in private collections be burned, save those dealing with medicine, divination, and agriculture, as well as texts of the Authoritarian school. In this campaign, several scores of scholars were executed, and a number of philosophical schools were eliminated as coherent traditions, including the Moists and the Dialecticians. In the early Han dynasty both Taoist philosophy and Confucianism revived, and Authoritarianism continued to be in evidence in practice if not in theory, but the golden age of Chinese philosophy was over. A unified empire demanded unified thought, a dominant orthodoxy enforced by the state. From this perspective variety was a threat, and furthermore, there were no independent states left to serve as sanctuaries for different schools. To be sure, China continued to produce excellent scholars and philosophers, and Buddhism contributed an important body of new material, but most of the issues debated in later Chinese philosophy had already been articulated before the Han. The task of philosophy was now understood to be the refinement and application of old teachings, not the development of new ones. [*See also* Legalism *and the biography of Han Fei-tzu.*]

Ch'in policy toward religion, by contrast, encouraged a variety of practices to support the state. To pay homage to the sacred powers of the realm and to consolidate his control, the First Emperor included worship at local shrines in his extensive tours. Representatives of regional cults, many of them spirit mediums, were brought to the court, there to perform rituals at altars set up for their respective deities. The Ch'in expanded the late Chou tendency to exalt deities of natural forces; over one hundred temples to such nature deities were established in the capital alone, devoted to the sun, moon, planets, several constellations, and stars associated with wind, rain, and long life. The nation was divided into sacred regions presided over by twelve mountains and four major rivers, with many lesser holy places to be worshiped both by the people and the emperor. Elaborate sacrifices of horses, rams, bulls, and a variety of foodstuffs were regularly offered at the major sites, presided over by officials with titles such as Grand Sacrificer and Grand Diviner. Important deities were correlated with the Five Phases *(wu-hsing)*, the modes of interaction of natural forces, the better to personify and control these powers.

A distinctive feature of Ch'in religion was sacrifices to four "Supreme Emperors" responsible for natural powers in each of the four quarters. Only the Emperor could worship these deities, a limitation true as well for two new rites he developed in 219, the *feng* and *shan* sacrifices. These were performed on sacred Mount T'ai to symbolize that the ruler had been invested with power by Heaven itself. Another driving force behind Ch'in encouragement of religious activities was the first Emperor's personal quest for immortality. We are told that in this quest he sent groups of young people across the China Sea to look for such islands of the immortals as P'eng-lai.

The Han. The defeat of Ch'in forces in the civil wars leading up to the founding of the Han dynasty deposed Authoritarian political thought along with the second and last Ch'in emperor. It took several decades for the new Han dynasty to consolidate its power. Since the Authoritarians had developed the most detailed policies for administering an empire, many of these policies were followed in practice in modified form.

Some early Han scholars and emperors attempted to ameliorate royal power with a revival of Confucian concern for the people and Taoist principles of noninterference *(wu-wei)*. For example, a palace counselor named Chia I (200–168 BCE) echoed Meng-tzu in his emphasis that the people are the basis of the state, the purpose of which should be to make them prosperous and happy, so as to gain their approval. A similar point of view is presented in more Taoist form in the *Huai-nan–tzu*, a book presented to the throne in 139 BCE by a prince of the Liu clan who had convened a variety of scholars in his court. This book discusses the world as a fundamentally harmonious system of resonating roles and influences. The ruler's job is to guide it, as an experienced charioteer guides his team. [*See the biography of* Liu An.]

Both Chia I and the *Huai-nan–tzu* assume that the rhythms that order society and government emanate from the cosmic Tao. The ruler's task is to discover and reinforce these rhythms for the benefit of all. This understanding of a Taoist "art of rulership" is rooted in the intuitions of the *Lao-tzu* and *Chuang-tzu*, but in the early Han was expressed in more detail in the writings of the Huang-Lao tradition, the school of the Yellow Emperor and Lao-tzu. Scholars have known of this school for centuries, but its texts had long disappeared, to be rediscovered only in 1973 at Ma-wang-tui, in a tomb sealed in 168 BCE. Four books appended to one of the Ma-wang-tui *Lao-tzu* texts are considered products of the Huang-Lao school, which is here concerned with the Tao as the creative source of both nature and man, their patterns of order, and the ontological basis of law and administration. Here we see an attempt to apply Taoist philosophical principles to the ordering of society by blending them with Legalist ideas. [*See also* Huang-lao Chün.]

However, the oldest and most widely established of the early Han philosophical schools was the Confucian, and the Confucians survived the Ch'in suppression rather well. Numbers of their books escaped the flames of 213 BCE, and those that did not were reconstructed or written anew, with little but the old titles intact. In the third century BCE scholars such as Hsün-tzu had already incorporated the best thought of their day into fundamentally Confucian expositions that advocated a strong centralized state and an ethical teaching enforced by law. This expanded interpretation of Confucius's teachings served his followers well in the early Han. They occupied the middle ground between authoritarianism and Taoist *laissez-faire*. There was room in their perspective for political power, criminal law, advocacy of benevolent rule, moral suasion, religious rituals, and personal ethical development, all supported by a three-century tradition of training disciples to study sacred texts and emulate the models they provided. In addition, by the second century BCE Confucian scholars such as Tung Chung-shu (c. 179–104 BCE) incorporated into their teaching the theories of Tsou Yen and the "Naturalists," who in the fourth century BCE had taught that the world is an interrelated organic whole that operates according to such cosmic principles as *yin* and *yang*. [*See the biography of Tsou Yen.*] The *Huai-nan–tzu* had already given this material a Taoist interpretation, stressing the natural resonance between all aspects of the universe. In the hands of Tung Chung-shu this understanding became an elaborate statement of the relationship of society and nature, with an emphasis on natural justification for hierarchical social roles, focused on that of the ruler. [*See the biography of Tung Chung-shu.*]

Tung Chung-shu provided a more detailed cosmological basis for Confucian ethical and social teachings and made it clear that only a unified state could serve as a channel for cosmic forces and sanctions. Tung was recognized as the leading scholar of the realm, and became spokesman for the official class. At his urging, in 136 BCE the Confucian classics were made the prescribed texts studied at the imperial academy. Texts of other schools including the Taoist theories of administration noted above, were excluded. This meant in effect that Tung Chung-shu's version of Confucianism became the official state teaching, a status it retained throughout the Han dynasty. So it was that the humble scholar of Lu, dead for over three hundred years, was exalted as patron saint of the imperial system, a position he retained until 1911. State-supported temples were established in Confucius's name in cities all over the land, and his home at Ch'ü-fu became a national shrine. In these temples, spirit tablets of the master and his disciples (replaced by images from 720–1530) were venerated in elaborate and formal rituals. As the generations passed, the tablets of the most influential scholars of the age came to be placed in these temples as well, by imperial decree, and so the cult of Confucius became the ritual focus of the scholar-official class. [*See also* Confucian Thought, *article on* The State Cult.]

Han state rituals were based upon those of Ch'in, but were greatly expanded and more elaborate. The first emperor, Kao-tsu, instituted the worship of a star god believed to be associated with Hou Chi, the legendary founder of the Chou royal line. Temples for this deity were built in administrative centers around the realm, where officials were also instructed to worship gods of local mountains and rivers. Kao-tsu brought shamans to the palace and set up shrines for sacrifices to their regional deities. He also promoted the worship of his own ancestors; at his death temples in his honor were built in commanderies throughout the empire.

These efforts to institute an imperial religious system

supported by officials at all levels were energetically continued by Emperor Wu, during whose fifty-four-year reign (140–87 BCE) the foundations of imperial state religion were established for Chinese history into the twentieth century. The emperor's religious activities were in turn supported by the philosophy of Tung Chung-shu, with its emphasis on the central cosmic role of the ruler. Emperor Wu revived the *chiao* or suburban sacrifice at the winter solstice to express imperial support for the revival of life forces. [*See* Chiao.] He also began to worship T'ai I, the "Great Supreme One," a star deity most noble in the heavens, an exalted version of a Chou god. T'ai I was coequal with Heaven and earth, a symbol of both cosmic power and the emperor's status. In the period 112–110 BCE Emperor Wu renewed the *feng* and *shan* sacrifices at Mount T'ai, the sacred mountain of the east, a key place of direct communication with Heaven for the sake of the whole realm. In 109 BCE he ordered that a *ming-t'ang* ("hall of light") be built at the foot of Mount T'ai as a temple where all the major deities of China could assemble and be worshiped. Emperor Wu also toured the realm, sacrificing at important shrines along the way, all to express his religious convictions and assert his authority.

Detailed instructions for these Han rituals were provided by handbooks of ritual and etiquette such as the *Li chi* (Record of Rites), compiled in the second century BCE but including earlier material as well. Here we find descriptions of royal rituals to be performed at the solstices and the onset of the seasons, as well as instructions for such matters as the initiation of young men and the veneration of ancestors. The emphasis throughout is on the intimate correlations of nature and society, so that social custom is given cosmic justification. The *Li chi* complements Tung Chung-shu's philosophy by extending similar understandings to the social life of the literate elite. In this context periodic rituals served as concentrated reminders of the cosmic basis of the whole cultural and political order. Thus did the imperial ruling class express its piety and solidify its position.

It should be noted, however, that the old Chou concept of the "mandate of Heaven" continued to influence Han political thought in a form elaborated and attenuated at the same time. Particularly in the writings of Tung Chung-shu, evidence for divine approval or disapproval of the ruler was discerned in "natural" phenomena interpreted as portents. In accord with this belief, officials were appointed to record and interpret portents and to suggest appropriate responses, such as changes in ritual procedure and the proclamation of amnesties. The developing tradition of political portents recognized the importance of divine sanctions but provided a range of calibrated responses that enabled rulers to adjust their policies rather than face the prospect of rejection by Heaven. The "mandate of Heaven" in its earlier and starker form was evoked chiefly as justification for rebellion in periods of dynastic decay. Nonetheless, portent theory in the hands of a conscientious official could be used in attempts to check or ameliorate royal despotism, and hence was an aspect of the state religious system that could challenge political power as well as support it.

The Han emperor Wu devoted much effort to attaining immortality, as had his Ch'in predecessor. As before, shamans and specialists in immortality potions were brought to court, and expeditions were sent off to look for the dwelling places of those who had defeated death. The search for immortality became quite popular among those who had the money and literacy to engage in it. In part this was due to the transformation of the Yellow Emperor (Huang-ti) into the patron deity of immortality, the earliest popular saving deity of this type in China. This transformation, fostered by "technique specialists" *(fang-shih)* at Emperor Wu's court, included stories that the Yellow Emperor had ascended to Heaven with his whole retinue, including a harem of over seventy. [*See* Fang-shih *and* Huang-ti.]

A more common expression of hope for some sort of continuity after death may be seen in tombs of Han aristocrats and officials, many of which were built as sturdy brick replicas of houses or offices, complete with wooden and ceramic utensils, attendants, and animals, as well as food, drugs, clothing, jade, bamboo books, and other precious objects. To a large extent this may be seen as a modification of Shang and Chou traditions. However, in a few recently excavated Han tombs there were tightly sealed coffins filled with an embalming fluid in which even the skin and flesh of the bodies have been preserved. An elaborate silk banner has been found on top of one of these coffins, painted with a design evidently intended to guide the occupant to a paradise of the immortals, perhaps that of the Queen Mother of the West.

Another destination for the dead was an underworld that was a Han elaboration of the old legend of the Yellow Springs, a shadowy place beneath the earth referred to as early as the eighth century BCE. From the Han period, there are tomb documents by which living officials transferred the dead in their jurisdiction to those of their counterparts in the underworld. There are also references to a realm of the dead inside Mount T'ai. The god of this mountain keeps registers of the lifespans of all, and death may be referred to as "to return to the Eastern Peak." By the third and fourth centuries CE it was believed that there was a subterranean kingdom within Mount T'ai, where judges decided the fate of the dead. These alternative beliefs represent the state of Chinese understandings of afterlife before Buddhist impact. [*See* Afterlife, *article on* Chinese Concepts.]

What came to be called the Former Han dynasty ended in 8 CE when the throne was occupied by a prime minister named Wang Mang (r. 9–23 CE), who established a Hsin ("new") dynasty that was to last for fourteen years. Wang's chief contribution to the history of Chinese religions was his active promotion of prognostication as a way of understanding the intimate relationship between Heaven and the court. In 25 CE Liu Hsiu (r. 25–57), a member of the Han royal line, led a successful attack on Wang Mang and reestablished the (Latter) Han dynasty. Like Wang Mang, he actively supported prognostication at court, despite the criticism of rationalist scholars such as Huan T'an (43 BCE–28 CE), who argued that strange phenomena were a matter of coincidence and natural causes rather than messages from Heaven.

A related development was controversy between two movements within Confucian scholarly circles, the so-called New Text school of the Former Han, and a later rationalistic reaction against it, the Old Text school. The New Text school developed out of Tung Chung-shu's concern with portents. Its followers wrote new commentaries on the classics that praised Confucius as a supernormal being who predicted the future hundreds of years beyond his time. By the end of the first century BCE this interpretation of the sage in mythological terms was vigorously resisted by an Old Text school that advocated a more restrained and historical approach. These two traditions coexisted throughout the remainder of the Han dynasty, with the New Text scholars receiving the most imperial support through the first century CE. After Huan T'an the best known rationalist was Wang Ch'ung, whose *Lun-heng* (Balanced Inquiries) fiercely criticizes religious opinions of his day, including prognostication and belief in spirits of the dead. Although Wang Ch'ung was not well known by his contemporaries, his thought was rediscovered in the third century and established as a key contribution to the skeptical tradition in Chinese philosophy. [*See the biography of Wang Ch'ung*.] An important religious legacy of the New Text school was the exalted interpretation of Confucius as a semidivine being, which was echoed in later popular religion. Its concern with portents and numerology also influenced Taoism.

We have noted the appearance of the Yellow Emperor as a divine patron of immortality, and as a representative of a new type of personified saving deity with power over a whole area of activity. In the latter half of the Han dynasty the number and popularity of such deities increased, beginning with the cult of the Queen Mother of the West (Hsi Wang Mu). She was associated with the K'un-lun mountains in the northwest where she presided over a palace and received a royal visitor, King Mu of the Chou dynasty, whom she predicted would be able to avoid death.

In 3 BCE Hsi Wang Mu's promise of immortality to all became the central belief of an ecstatic popular cult in her name that swept across North China. Although this movement abated in a few months, the Queen Mother herself is commonly portrayed in Latter Han iconography. K'un-lun is described as the center pillar of the world, from where she controls cosmic powers and the gift of immortality. This goddess has continued to have an important role in Chinese religion until the present day. [*See* Hsi Wang Mu.]

Mountain-dwelling immortals constituted another source of personal deities in this period. These beings were believed to descend to aid the ruler in times of crisis, sometimes with instructions from the Celestial Emperor (T'ien-ti), sometimes themselves identified with the "perfect ruler" who would restore peace to the world. By the second century CE the most important of these figures was Lao-tzu, the legendary author of the *Tao-te ching*, who appears as a deity called Huang-lao Chün (Yellow Lord Lao) or T'ai-shang Lao-chün (Most High Lord Lao). [*See* Huang-lao Chün.) By this time Lao-tzu had been portrayed for centuries in popular legend as a mysterious wise man who disappeared without a trace. We have seen that the book in his name contains passages that could be interpreted as support for the immortality cult, and by the first century he was referred to as an immortal himself. In an inscription of 165 CE Lao-tzu is described as a creator deity, equal in status to the sun, moon, and stars. A contemporary text assures his devotees that he has manifested himself many times in order to save mankind, that he will select those who believe in him to escape the troubles of the age, and that he will "shake the Han reign." [*See the biography of Lao-tzu*.] It is this messianic theme that provided the religious impetus for two large popular religious movements in the late second century CE that were important sources of later Taoist religion and the popular sectarian tradition. These movements were the T'ien-shih Tao (Way of the Celestial Master) in the west and the T'ai-p'ing Tao (Way of Great Peace and Prosperity) in the north.

The Way of the Celestial Master established a theocratic state in the area of modern Szechwan Province with an organization modeled in part on Han local administration. Its leader, Chang Lu, ruled through officers, both religious and administrative in function, who presided over a number of distinctive rituals. These included reciting the *Lao-tzu*, penance to heal illness, and the construction of huts in which free food was offered to passers-by. Converts were required to contribute five pecks of rice, from which the movement gained the popular name of "The Way of Five Pecks of Rice" (Wu-tou-mi Tao). In 215 Chang Lu submitted to a Han warlord (Ts'ao Ts'ao) whose son founded the new state of Wei in 220. The sect itself was allowed to continue its activities and taught that Wei had simply inherited divine authority from the Celestial Master Chang and his line. By the fourth century the Celestial Masters developed more elaborate collective rituals of repentance, retrospective salvation of ancestors, and the strengthening of vital forces through sexual intercourse. [*See the biographies of Chang Tao-ling and Chang Lu.*]

We know less about the practices of the Way of Great Peace because it was destroyed as a coherent tradition in the aftermath of a massive uprising in 184 CE. Its leader, also named Chang (Chang Chüeh, d. 184 CE), proclaimed that the divine mandate for the Han rule, here symbolized by the phase wood (green), had expired, to be replaced by the phase earth, for which the color is yellow. Chang Chüeh's forces thus wore yellow cloths as symbols of their destiny, and hence the movement came to be called the Yellow Turbans. The Han court commissioned local governors to put down the uprising, which was soon suppressed with much bloodshed, although remnants of the Yellow Turbans continued to exist until the end of the century. [*See the biography of Chang Chüeh.*]

The Yellow Turbans are better understood as a parallel to the Celestial Master sect rather than as connected to it, although the two movements shared some beliefs and practices, particularly healing through confession of sins. The Way of Great Peace employed a scripture known as the *T'ai-p'ing ching* (Classic of Great Peace), which emphasizes the cyclical renewal of life in the *chia-tzu* year, the beginning of the sixty-year cycle. Both sects were utopian, but the Yellow Turbans represent a more eschatological orientation. In retrospect, both of these groups appear as attempts to reconstruct at a local level the Han cosmic and political synthesis that was collapsing around them, with priests taking the place of imperial officials.

The most important legacy of the late Han popular religious movements was their belief in personified divine beings concerned to aid humankind, a belief supported by new texts, rituals, and forms of leadership and organization. This belief was given impetus by the expectation that a bearer of collective salvation was about to appear in order to initiate a new time of peace, prosperity, and long life. From the third century on this hope was focused on a figure called Li Hung, in whose name several local movements appeared, some involving armed uprisings. This eschatological orientation was an important dimension of early Taoism, which at first understood itself as a new revelation, intended to supplant popular cults with their bloody sacrifices and spirit mediums.

In addition to such organized movements as the Yellow Turbans, Han popular religion included cults of local sacred objects such as trees, rocks, and streams, belief that spirits of the dead have consciousness and can roam about, and a lively sense of the power of omens and fate. By the third century there are references to propitiation of the spirits of persons who died violent deaths, with offerings of animal flesh presided over by spirit mediums.

Feng-shui ("wind and water"), or geomancy, also developed during the Han as a ritual expression of the *yin/yang* and five-phases worldview. It is the art of locating graves, buildings, and cities in auspicious places where there is a concentration of the vital energies *(ch'i)* of earth and sky. It is believed that the dead in graves so located will bless their descendants. The earliest extant *feng-shui* texts are attributed to famous diviners of the third and fourth centuries. Chinese religion was thus developed at a number of levels by the time Buddhism arrived, although Buddhism offered several fresh interpretations of morality, personal destiny, and the fate of the dead.

The Period of Disunion

By the time the first Buddhist monks and texts appeared in China around the first century CE, the Han dynasty was already in decline. At court, rival factions competed for imperial favor, and in the provinces restless governors moved toward independence. Political and military fragmentation was hastened by the campaigns against the Yellow Turban uprising, after which a whole series of adventurers arose to attack each other and take over territory. In the first decade of the third century three major power centers emerged in the north, southeast, and southwest, with that in the north controlling the last Han emperor and ruling in his name. By 222 these three centers each had declared themselves states, and China entered a period of political division that was to last until late in the sixth century. In this time of relatively weak central government control, powerful local clans emerged to claim hereditary power over their areas.

The Beginnings of Buddhism in China. With the gradual expansion of Buddhism, under the patronage of the Kushan rulers, into the oasis states of Central Asia, and with the corresponding expansion of Chinese influence into this same region, it became inevitable that

Buddhism would be introduced into East Asia. Over a thousand-year period from the beginning of the common era until the close of the first millennium the opportunities for cultural exchange with South and West Asia afforded by the so-called Silk Route nourished a vibrant East Asian Buddhist tradition, one that began with earnest imitation of its Indian antecedents and culminated in the great independent systems of thought that characterize the fully developed tradition: Hua-yen, T'ien-t'ai, Ching-t'u, and Ch'an.

From about 100 BCE on it would have been relatively easy for Buddhist ideas and practices to come to China with foreign merchants, but the first reliable notice of it in Chinese sources is dated 65 CE. In a royal edict of that year we are told that a prince administering a city in what is now northern Kiangsu Province "recites the subtle words of Huang-Lao, and respectfully performs the gentle sacrifices to the Buddha." He was encouraged to "entertain *upāsaka*s and *śramaṇa*s," Buddhist lay devotees and initiates. In 148 CE the first of several foreign monks, An Shih-kao, settled in Lo-yang, the capital of the Latter Han. Over the next forty years he and other scholars translated about thirty Buddhist scriptures into Chinese, most of them from pre-Mahāyāna traditions, emphasizing meditation and moral principles. However, by about 185 three Mahāyāna Prajñāpāramitā (Perfect Wisdom) texts were translated as well.

A memorial dated 166, approving Buddhist "purity," "emptiness," nonviolence, and control of sensual desires, further informs us that in that year the emperor performed a joint sacrifice to Lao-tzu and the Buddha. In 193/194 a local warlord in what is now Kiangsu erected a Buddhist temple that could hold more than three thousand people. It contained a bronze Buddha image before which offerings were made and scriptures were read. During ceremonies in honor of the Buddha's birthday thousands came to participate, watch, and enjoy free food and wine. Thus, by the end of the second century there were at least two centers of Buddhist activity, Lo-yang in the north and an area in the southeast. At court Buddhist symbols were used in essentially Taoist rituals, but in the scriptures the novelty and difference of Buddhism were made clear in crude vernacular translations. Such novelty appears in injunctions to eliminate desires, to love all beings equally, without special preference for one's family, and to regard the body as transitory and doomed to decay, rather than an arena for seeking immortality.

Although early sources mention terms for various clerical ranks, rules for monastic life were transmitted in a haphazard and incomplete fashion. Monks and nuns lived in cloisters that cannot properly be called monasteries until a few centuries later. Meanwhile, leadership of the Chinese clergy was provided first by Central Asian monks, then by naturalized Chinese of foreign descent, and by the fourth century, by Chinese themselves. Nuns are first mentioned in that century as well.

The movement of Buddhism to China, one of the great cultural interactions of history, was slow and fortuitous, carried out almost entirely at a private level. The basic reason for its eventual acceptance throughout Chinese society was that it offered several religious and social advantages unavailable to the same extent in China before. These included a full-time religious vocation for both men and women in an organization largely independent of family and state, a clear promise of life after death at various levels, and developed conceptions of paradise and purgatory, connected to life through the results of intentional actions *(karman)*. In addition, Buddhism offered the worship of heroic saviors in image form, supported by scriptures that told of their wisdom and compassion. For ordinary folk there were egalitarian moral principles, promises of healing and protection from harmful forces, and simple means of devotion; for intellectuals there were sophisticated philosophy and the challenge of attaining new states of consciousness in meditation, all of this expounded by a relatively educated clergy who recruited, organized, translated, and preached.

In the early fourth century North China was invaded by the Hsiung-nu, who sacked Lo-yang in 311 and Ch'ang-an in 316. Thousands of elite families fled south below the Yangtze River, where a series of short-lived Chinese dynasties held off further invasions. In the North a succession of kingdoms of Inner Asian background rose and fell, most of which supported Buddhism because of its religious appeal and its non-Chinese origins. The forms of Buddhism that developed here emphasized ritual, ideological support for the state, magic protection, and meditation.

It was in the South, however, that Buddhism first became a part of Chinese intellectual history. The Han imperial Confucian synthesis had collapsed with the dynasty, a collapse that encouraged a quest for new philosophical alternatives. Representatives of these alternatives found support in aristocratic clans, which competed with each other in part through philosophical debates. These debates, called *ch'ing-t'an*, or "pure conversation," revived and refined a tradition that had been widespread hundreds of years before in the period of the so-called One Hundred Schools, a tradition with precise rules of definition and criteria for victory. By the mid-third century these debates revolved around two basic perspectives, that of the "conservative moralists" *(ming-chiao)* and that of those advocating "spontaneous naturalism" *(tzu-jan)*. By the early fourth century Buddhist monks were involved in these debates, supported by sympathetic clans, advocating a middle ground between the conservatives and libertarians, spiritual freedom based on ethical discipline. Although Buddhism was still imperfectly understood, it had gained a vital foothold.

Chinese intellectuals first attempted to understand Buddhism through its apparent similarities to certain beliefs and practices of Taoism and the immortality cult. Thus, *bodhisattvas* and Buddhas were correlated with sages and immortals, meditation with circulation of the vital fluids, and *nirvāṇa* with *wu-wei*, spontaneous and purposeless action. However, Indian Buddhism and traditional Chinese thought have very different understandings of life and the world. Buddhist thought is primarily psychological and epistemological, concerned with liberation from *saṃsāra*, the world perceived as a realm of suffering, impermanence, and death. For the Chinese, on the other hand, nature and society are fundamentally good; our task is to harmonize with the positive forces of nature, and enlightenment consists of identifying with these forces, rather than in being freed from them. The interaction of these worldviews led Chinese Buddhists to interpret psychological concepts in cosmological directions. For example, the key Mahāyāna term "emptiness" *(śūnyatā)* refers primarily to a radically objective and neutral mode of perception, which accepts the impermanence and change of things without trying to control them with human concepts and values. Indeed, the first discussions of this term used it as a logical tool to destroy false confidence in philosophical and religious concepts, particularly earlier Buddhist ones. They are mutually contradictory, refer to nothing substantial, and hence are "empty." In China, however, "emptiness" immediately evoked discussion about the origin and nature of the phenomenal world. "Emptiness" was equated with "non-being," *(pen-wu, wu)*, the fecund source of existence. As their understanding of Buddhism deepened, Chinese thinkers became more aware of the epistemological force of the term "emptiness," but continued to see it primarily as a problem in interpreting the world itself.

Buddhist thought was already well developed and complexly differentiated before it reached China. The Chinese knew of it only through scriptures haphazardly collected, in translations of varying accuracy, for very few Chinese learned Sanskrit. Since all the *sūtras* claimed to be preached by the Buddha himself, they were accepted as such, with discrepancies among them explained as deriving from the different situations and capacities of listeners prevailing when a particular text was preached. In practice, this meant that the Chinese had to select from a vast range of data those themes that made the most sense in their pre-existing worldview. For example, as the tradition develops we find emphases on simplicity and directness, the universal potential for enlightenment, and the Buddha mind as source of the cosmos, all of them prepared for in indigenous thought and practice. The most important early Chinese Buddhist philosophers, organizers, and translators were Tao-an (312–385), Hui-yüan (334–417), and Kumārajīva (334–413), each of whom contributed substantially to the growth of the young church. Tao-an was known principally for his organizational and exegetical skills and for the catalog of Buddhist scriptures he compiled. His disciple Hui-yüan, one of the most learned clerics in South China, gathered a large community of monks around him and inaugurated a cult to Amitābha. Kumārajīva, the most important and prolific of the early translators, was responsible for the transmission of the Mādyamika (San-lun) tradition to China. His lectures on Buddhist scripture in Ch'ang-an established a sound doctrinal basis for Mahāyāna thought in the Middle Kingdom. Another formative early figure was Tao-sheng (d. 434 CE), a student of Kumārajīva. He is known for his emphasis on the positive nature of *nirvāṇa*, his conviction that even non-believers have the potential for salvation, and his teaching of instantaneous enlightenment. These themes helped lay the foundation of Ch'an (Jpn., Zen) later on. [*See the biographies of Tao-an, Hui-yüan, Kumārajīva, and Tao-sheng.*]

The history of monastic Buddhism was closely tied to state attitudes and policies, which ranged from outright suppression to complete support, as in the case of Emperor Wu of the Liang dynasty (r. 502–549), who abolished Taoist temples and built Buddhist ones, and three times entered a monastery himself as a lay servitor. [*See the biography of Liang Wu-ti.*] However, by the fifth century Buddhism was becoming well established among people of all classes, who, to gain karmic merit, donated land and goods, took lay vows, served in monasteries, and established a variety of voluntary associations to copy scriptures, provide vegetarian food for monks and nuns, and carve Buddha images. The most important image-carving projects were at Yün-kang in Shansi and Lung-men in Honan, where huge figures, chiefly those of Śākyamuni and Maitreya, were cut into cliffs and caves. Such major projects of course also involved large-scale official and clerical support.

It was in the fifth century as well that Chinese Buddhist eschatology developed, based in part on predictions attributed to the Buddha that a few hundred years after his entry into *nirvāṇa* the *dharma* would lose its vigor, morals decline, and ignorant, corrupt monks and nuns appear. In addition, from its inception in the second century Taoism had proclaimed itself to be the manifestation of a new age of cosmic vitality, supported by pious devotees, "seed people." A combination of these motifs led to the composition in China of Buddhist scriptures saying that since the end of the age had come, more intense morality and piety were required of those who wished to be saved. These texts also promised aid from saving *bodhisattvas* such as Maitreya, the next Buddha-to-be. In some cases the apocalyptic vision of these texts inspired militant utopian movements, led by monks, but with lay membership. By the early seventh century a few of these groups were involved in armed uprisings in the name of Maitreya, which led eventually to a decline in official support for his cult, although he remained important in popular sectarian eschatology. [*See also* Millenarianism, *article on* Chinese Millenarian Movements, *and* Maitreya.]

The first important school of Buddhist thought developed in China was the T'ien-t'ai, founded by the monk Chih-i (538–597). This school is noted for its synthesis of earlier Buddhist traditions into one system, divided into five periods of development according to stages in the Buddha's teaching. According to T'ien-t'ai, the Buddha's teachings culminated in his exposition of the *Lotus Sutra*, in which all approaches are unified. Chih-i also systematized the theory and practice of Mahāyāna meditation. His most important philosophical contribution was his affirmation of the absolute Buddha mind as the source and substance of all phenomena. In Chih-i's teaching the old Mādhyamika logical destruction of dualities is replaced by a positive emphasis on their identity in a common source. So, in impeccably Buddhist language, he was able to justify the phenomenal world, and thus to provide an intellectual foundation for much of the later development of Buddhism in China. [*See* T'ien-t'ai *and the biography of Chih-i.*]

In 581 China was reunified by the Sui dynasty (581–618) after three and a half centuries of political fragmentation. The Sui founder supported Buddhism, particularly the T'ien-t'ai school, as a unifying ideology shared by many of his subjects in both North and South. After four decades of rule the Sui was overthrown in a series of rebellions, to be replaced by the T'ang (618–907). Although the new dynasty tended to give more official support to Confucianism and Taoism, Buddhism continued to grow at every level of society, and reached the high point of its development in China during the next two centuries.

The Rise of Taoist Religion. Taoism is China's own indigenous higher religion, characterized by the fourth century by a literate and self-perpetuating priesthood, a pantheon of celestial deities, complex rituals, and revealed scriptures in classical Chinese. Although the first elements of this tradition appeared in the second century popular movements discussed above, the tradition underwent futher development at the hands of gentry scholars versed in philosophy, ethical teachings, and alchemy. These scholars saw themselves as formulators of a new, more refined religion superior to the popular cults around them. In retrospect, this movement appears as a reformulation of ideas from the *Lao-tzu* and *Chuang-tzu*, elements of the old state religion, together with those of the immortality cult and some local traditions, combined in a new system led by priests who, though not officials, claimed celestial prerogatives.

Taoism is fundamentally a religion of *ch'i*, the vital breath out of which nature, gods, and humans evolve. The source and order of this vital substance is the Tao, the ultimate power of life in the universe. The gods are personified manifestations of *ch'i*, symbolizing astral powers of the cosmos and organs of the human body with which they are correlated. Under the conditions of existence *ch'i* becomes stale and worn out, so it must be renewed through ritual processes that restore its primal vitality. These rituals consist essentially of visualizing and calling down the cosmic gods to reestablish their contact with their bodily correlates. In this way the adept ingests divine power and so recharges his bodily forces for healing, rejuvenation, and long life. Invocations to the gods are accompanied by exercises, massage, abstinence from grains (expressions of the dark *yin* power of the earth), and taking alchemical elixirs. Accomplished practice can bring about immortality through preparing the embryo of a new self that escapes the body at death. Taoist masters can release their cosmic power through ritual actions that revive the life forces of the community around them.

All branches of Taoism eventually traced their origin to a new revelation from the Most High Lord Lao to Chang Tao-ling, the grandfather of Chang Lu, in 142 CE, establishing him as "Celestial Master." He was empowered to perform rituals and write talismans that distributed this new manifestation of the Tao for the salvation of humankind. Salvation was available to those who repented of their sins, believed in the Tao, and pledged allegiance to their Taoist master. The master in turn established an alliance between the gods and the devotee, who then wore at the waist a list (register) of the names of the gods to be called on for protection. The register also served as a passport to heaven at death. Taoist ritual consists essentially of the periodic renewal of these alliances by confession, visualization, petition, and the offering of incense and sacred documents. Taoist texts are concerned throughout for moral discipline and orderly ritual and organization.

When the Celestial Master sect was officially recognized by the state of Wei (220–266) in the early third century its leadership was established in the capital, Lo-yang, north and east of the old sect base area in modern Szechwan. In the North remnants of the Yellow Turbans still survived, and before long the teachings and rituals of these two similar traditions blended together. A tension remained, however, between those who saw secular authority as a manifestation of the Way and those determined to bring in a new era of peace and prosperity by militant activity. Uprisings led by charismatic figures who claimed long life and healing powers occurred in different areas throughout the fourth century and later.

Meanwhile, in the southeast another tradition emerged that was to contribute to Taoism, a tradition concerned with alchemy, the use of herbs and minerals to attain immortality. Its chief literary expression was the *Pao-p'u-tzu* (The Master Who Preserves Simplicity) written by Ko Hung in about 320. Ko Hung collected a large number of recipes and legends of the immortals, intended to show how the body can be transformed by the ingestion of gold and other chemicals and by the inner circulation of the vital force *(ch'i)*, special diets, and sexual techniques, all reinforced by moral dedication. Ko Hung's concerns were supported by members of the old aristocracy of the state of Wu (222–280) whose families had moved south during the Latter Han period. [*See the biography of Ko Hung*.]

When the northern state of Chin was conquered by the Hsiung-nu in 316, thousands of Chin gentry and officials moved south, bringing the Celestial Master sect with them. The eventual result was a blending of Celestial Master concern for priestly adminstration and collective rituals with the more individualistic and esoteric alchemical traditions of the southeast. Between the years 364 and 370 a young man named Yang Hsi claimed to receive revelations from "perfected ones" (exalted immortals) from the Heaven of Supreme Purity (Shang-ch'ing). These deities directed Yang to make transcripts and deliver them to Hsü Mi (303–373), an official of the Eastern Chin state (317–420) with whom he was associated. Yang Hsi believed his new revelations to be from celestial regions more exalted than those evoked by the Celestial Master sect and Ko Hung. The Perfected Ones rewrote and corrected earlier texts in poetic language, reformulated sexual rites as symbols of spiritual union, and taught new methods of inner cultivation and alchemy. These teachings were all presented in an eschatological context, as the salvation of an elect people in a time of chaos. They prophesied that a "lord of the Way, [a] sage who is to come" would descend in 392. Then the wicked would be eliminated and a purified terrestrial kingdom established, ruled over by such pious devotees as Hsü Mi, now perceived as a priest and future celestial official. It is perhaps not accidental that these promises were made to members of the old southern aristocracy whose status had recently been threatened by the newcomers from the north. [*See* Chen-jen.]

Hsü Mi and one of his sons had retired to Mao Shan, a mountain near the Eastern Chin capital (modern Nanking); hence the texts they received and transcribed came to be called those of a Mao-shan "school." In the next century another southern scholar, T'ao Hung-ching (456–536), collected all the remaining manuscripts from Yang Hsi and the Hsü family and edited them as the *Chen-kao* (Declarations of the Perfected). With this the Mao-shan/Shang-ch'ing scriptures were established as a foundation stone of the emerging Taoist canon. [*See the biography of T'ao Hung-ching*.]

In the meantime another member of Ko Hung's clan had written a scripture in about 397, the *Ling-pao ching* (Classic of the Sacred Jewel), which he claimed had been revealed to him by the spirit of an early third-century ancestor. This text exalted "celestial worthies" *(t'ien-tsun)*, who were worshiped in elaborate collective rituals directed by priests in outdoor arenas. The *Ling-pao ching* established another strand of Taoist mythology and practice that was also codified in the South during the fifth century. Its rituals replaced those of the Celestial Master tradition, while remaining indebted to them. Ling-pao texts were collected and edited by Lu Hsiu-ching (406–477), who wrote on Taoist history and ritual. [*See the biography of Lu Hsiu-ching*.]

Taoism was active in the North as well, in the Northern Wei kingdom (386–534), which established Taoist offices at court in 400. In 415 and 423 a scholar named K'ou Ch'ien-chih (d. 448) claimed to have received direct revelations from Lord Lao while he was living on a sacred mountain. The resulting scriptures directed K'ou to reform the Celestial Master tradition; renounce popular cults, messianic uprisings, and sexual rituals; and support the court as a Taoist kingdom on earth. K'ou was introduced to the Wei ruler by a sympathetic official named Ts'ui Hao (d. 450) in 424 and was promptly appointed to the office of "Erudite of Transcendent Beings." The next year he was proclaimed Celestial Master, and his teachings "promulgated throughout the realm." For the next two decades K'ou and Ts'ui cooperated to promote Taoism at the court. As a result, in 440 the king accepted the title Perfect Ruler of Great Peace, and during the period 444 to 446 proscribed Buddhism and local "excessive cults." Although Ts'ui Hao was eventually discredited and Buddhism established as the state religion by a new ruler in 452, the years of official support for Taoism clarified its legitimacy and political potential as an alternative to Confucianism and Buddhism. Although it continued to develop new schools and scriptural traditions, the basic shape of Taoism for the rest of Chinese history was thus established by the fifth century. [*See the biography of K'ou Ch'ien-chih.*]

The Consolidation of Empire: Seventh to Fourteenth Century

The Chinese religious traditions that were to continue throughout the rest of imperial history all reached maturity during the T'ang (618–907) and Sung (960–1279) periods. These traditions included Buddhism, Taoism, Neo-Confucianism, Islam, and popular religion in both its village and sectarian forms. It was in these centuries as well that other foreign religions were practiced for a time in China, particularly Manichaeism and Nestorian Christianity. Rituals performed by the emperor and his officials continued to be elaborated, with many debates over the proper form and location of altars and types of sacrifices to be offered. During the T'ang dynasty, cults devoted to the spirits of local founders and protectors were established in many cities. These city gods *(ch'eng-huang-shen)* were eventually brought into the ranks of deities to whom official worship was due.

Manichaeism, Nestorian Christianity, and Islam. The area of the T'ang dynasty rivaled that of the Han, with western boundaries extending far into Central Asia. This expansion encouraged a revival of foreign trade and cultural contacts. Among the new foreign influences were not only Buddhist monks and scriptures but also the representatives of other religions. There is evidence for Zoroastrianism in China by the early sixth century, a result of contacts between China and Persia that originated in the second century BCE and were renewed in an exchange of envoys with the Northern Wei court in 455 and around 470. [*See* Zoroastrianism.]

A foreign tradition with more important influence on the history of Chinese religions was Manichaeism, a dynamic missionary religion teaching ultimate cosmic dualism founded by a Persian named Mani (216–277?). The first certain reference to Manichaeism in a Chinese source is dated 694, although it may have been present about two decades earlier. As was true with Zoroastrianism, Manichaeism in its early centuries in China was primarily practiced by foreigners, although its leaders soon composed catechisms and texts in Chinese stressing the congruence of their teachings with Buddhism and Taoism. In 755 a Chinese military commander named An Lu-shan led a powerful rebellion that the T'ang court was able to put down only with the help of foreign support. One of these allies was the Uighur, from a kingdom based in what is now northern Mongolia. In 762 a Uighur army liberated Lo-yang from rebel forces, and there a Uighur kaghan was converted to Manichaeism. The result was new prestige and more temples for the religion in China.

However, in 840 the Uighurs were defeated by the Kirghiz, with the result that the Chinese turned on the religion of their former allies, destroyed its temples, and expelled or executed its priests. Nonetheless, at least one Manichaean leader managed to escape to Ch'üan-chou in Fukien Province on the southeast coast. In Fukien the Manichaeans flourished as a popular sect until the fourteenth century, characterized by their distinctive teachings, communal living, vegetarian diet, and nonviolence. They were called the Ming-chiao ("religion of light"). They disappeared as a coherent tradition as a result of renewed persecutions during the early Ming dynasty (1368–1644). Several Manichaean texts were incorporated into the Taoist and Buddhist canons, and it is likely that Manichaean lay sects provided models for similar organizations that evolved out of Buddhism later. Manichaean dualism and demon exorcism may have reinforced similar themes in Taoism and Buddhism as they were understood at the popular level. [*See* Manichaeism, *overview article.*]

According to a stone inscription erected in Sian (Ch'ang-an) in 781, the first Nestorian missionary reached China in 635 and taught about the creation of the world, the fall of humankind, and the birth and teaching of the Messiah. The ethics and rituals described are recognizably Christian. Chinese edicts of 638 and 745 refer to Nestorianism, which appears to have been confined to foreign communities in large cities on major trade routes. In 845 Nestorianism was proscribed along with Buddhism and other religions of non-Chinese origin, but it revived in China during the period of Mongol rule in the thirteenth and fourteenth centuries. In 1289 the court established an office to supervise Christians, and a 1330 source claims that there were more than thirty thousand Nestorians in China, some of them wealthy and in high positions, no doubt a result of the Mongol policy of ruling China in part with officials of foreign origin. In this period the church was most active in eastern cities such as Hangchow and Yangchow. The Nestorians were expelled from China with the defeat of the Mongols in the mid-fourteenth century, and no active practitioners were found by the Jesuits when they arrived about two hundred years later. So the first Christian contact with China expired, leaving no demonstrable influence on Chinese religion and culture. [*See* Nestorianism.]

The Chinese first learned of Islam in 638 from an emissary of the last Sasanid king of Persia, who was seeking their aid against invading Arab armies. This the Chinese refused, but a number of Persian refugees were admitted a few years later after the Sasanid defeat and allowed to practice their Zoroastrian faith. In the early eighth century Arab armies moved into Central Asia, and in 713 ambassadors of Caliph Walīd were received at court in Ch'ang-an, even though they refused to prostrate themselves before the emperor. However, in 751 a Chinese army far to the west was defeated in the Battle of Talas by a combination of Central Asian states with Arab support. This defeat led to the replacement of Chinese influence in Central Asia with that of the Arabs and the decline of Buddhism in that area in favor of Islam. In 756 another caliph sent Arab mercenaries to aid the Chinese court against An Lu-shan; when the war ended many of these mercenaries remained, forming the beginning of Islamic presence in China, which by the late twentieth century totaled about thirty million people, one of the five basic constituencies of the People's Republic. The eighth-century Arab population was augmented by Muslim merchants who settled in Chinese coastal cities, for a time dominating the sea trade with India and Southeast Asia.

The major influx of Muslim peoples occurred during the Yüan dynasty (1271–1368) when the land routes across Central Asia were secure and the Mongols brought in large numbers of their non-Chinese subjects to help administer China. It was in this period that Islam spread all over China and established major population bases in the western provinces of Yunnan and Kansu. Here their numbers increased through marriage with Chinese women and adoption of non-Muslim children, all converted to Islam. Although the result was a dilution of Arab physical characteristics, the use of the Chinese language, and the adoption of some Chinese social customs, for most the Islamic core remained. Muslims did not accept such dominant Chinese traditions as ancestor worship and pork eating, and kept their own festival calendar. In part this resistance was due to the tenacity of their beliefs, in part to the fact that their numbers, mosques, and essentially lay organization permitted mutual support.

Muslims in China have always been predominantly Sunnī, but in the sixteenth century Sufism reached China through Central Asia. By the late seventeenth century Ṣūfī brotherhoods began a reform movement that advocated increased use of Arabic and a rejection of certain Chinese practices that had infiltrated Islam, such as burning incense at funerals. Sufism also emphasized ecstatic personal experience of Allāh, the veneration of saints, and the imminent return of the Mahdi, who would bring a new age, this last theme due to Shī'ī influence as well.

These reformist beliefs, coupled with increased Chinese pressure on Islam as a whole, led eventually to a powerful uprising in Yunnan between 1855–1873, an uprising allowed to develop momentum because of old ethnic tensions in the area and the distraction of the Chinese court with the contemporary Taiping Rebellion (1851–1864). The Yunnan rebellion was eventually put down by a combination of Chinese and loyalist Muslim forces, and the Muslims resumed their role as a powerful minority in China, called the Hui people.

The chief role of Islam in China was as the religion of this minority group, although in some twentieth-century popular texts it is recognized as one of the "five religions" whose teachings are now blended into a new synthetic revelation, along with Confucianism, Taoism, Buddhism, and Christianity. In historical terms its chief impact was to sharply reduce Chinese contact with India and Central Asia after the eighth century, and thus to cut off the vital flow of new texts and ideas to Chinese Buddhism.

T'ang Buddhism. The first T'ang emperor, Kao-tsu (r. 618–626) approved of a plan to limit both Taoist and Buddhist temples. His son T'ai-tsung (r. 626–649) agreed with the Taoist contention that the imperial family was descended from Lao-tzu, whose legendary surname was also Li; however, T'ai-tsung also erected Buddhist shrines on battlefields and ordered monks to recite scriptures for the stability of the empire. Buddhist philosophical schools in this period were matters of both belief and imperial adornment, so, to replace the T'ien-t'ai school, now discredited on account of its association with the Sui dynasty, the T'ang court turned first to the Fa-hsiang, or Idealist school, the Indian teaching of "consciousness-only." [*See* Yogācāra.] Some texts of this tradition had been translated earlier by Paramārtha (499–569), but it came to be thoroughly understood in China only after the return of the pilgrim Hsüan-tsang in 645. Hsüan-tsang was welcomed at court and provided with twenty-three scholar-monks from all over China to assist in translating the books he had brought back from India. The emperor wrote a preface for the translation of one major Vijñānavāda text, and his policy of imperial support was continued by his son Kao-tsung (r. 649–683). [*See the biography of Hsüan-tsang.*]

However, the complex psychological analysis of the Vijñānavāda school, coupled with its emphasis that some beings are doomed by their nature to eternal rebirth, were not in harmony with the Chinese worldview, which had been better represented by T'ien-t'ai. Hence, when imperial support declined at Kao-tsung's death in 683, the fortunes of the Fa-hsiang school declined as well, despite the excellent scholarship of Hsüan-tsang's disciple K'uei-chi (632–682). [*See the biography of K'uei-chi.*] At the intellectual level it was replaced in popularity by the Hua-yen ("flower garland") school as formulated by the monk Fa-tsang (643–712). This school, based on a *sūtra* of the same name (Skt., *Avataṃsaka*), taught the emptiness and interpenetration of all phenomena in a way consonant with old Chinese assumptions. Furthermore, in Hua-yen teaching the unity and integration of all things is symbolized by a Buddha called Vairocana who presides over his Pure Land in the center of an infinite universe. [*See* Mahāvairocana.] However dialectically such a symbol might be understood by Buddhist scholars, at a political and popular level it was appropriated more literally as a Buddhist creator deity. [*See* Hua-yen *and the biography of Fa-tsang.*]

It is no accident that the Hua-yen school was first actively supported by Empress Wu Chao (Wu Tse-t'ien, r. 690–705) who took over the throne from her sons to set up her own dynasty, the Chou. Since Confucianism did not allow for female rulers, Empress Wu, being a devout Buddhist, sought for supporting ideologies in that tradition, including not only Hua-yen but also predictions in obscure texts that the Buddha had prophesied that several hundred years after his death a woman would rule over a world empire. Monks in Wu-Tse-t'ien's entourage equated her with this empress and further asserted that she was a manifestation of the future Buddha Maitreya.

When Empress Wu abdicated in 705 her son continued to support the Hua-yen school, continuing the tradition of close relationship between the court and Buddhist philosophical schools. However, during this period Buddhism continued to grow in popularity among all classes of people. Thousands of monasteries and shrines were built, supported by donations of land, grain, cloth, and precious metals, and by convict workers, the poor, and serfs bound to donated lands. Tens of thousands of persons became monks or nuns, elaborate rituals were performed, feasts provided, and sermons preached in both monastery and marketplace. Buddhist observances such as the Lantern Festival, the Buddha's birthday, and All Souls Day became universally practiced, while pious lay societies multiplied for carving images and inscriptions and disseminating scriptures. Wealthy monasteries became centers of money lending, milling, and medical care, as well as hostels for travelers and retreats for scholars and officials. In high literature the purity of monks and monasteries was admired, while in popular stories *karman*, rebirth, and purgatory became truths simply assumed. The state made sporadic attempts to control this exuberance through licensing monasteries, instituting examinations for monks, and issuing ordination certificates, but state control was limited and "unofficial" Buddhist practices continued to flourish.

An important factor in this popularity was the rise of two more simple and direct forms of Chinese Buddhism, much less complex than the exegetical and philosophical schools that were dominant earlier. These were the Pure Land (Ching-t'u) school, devoted to rebirth in Amitābha's paradise, and the Ch'an ("meditation") school, which promised enlightenment in this life to those with sufficient dedication. These traditions were universalist and nonhierarchical in principle, yet came to have coherent teachings and organizations of their own appealing to a wide range of people. Both should be understood as products of gradual evolution in the seventh and eighth centuries, as a positive selection from earlier teachings, particularly T'ien-t'ai, and as a reformist reaction against the secularization of the T'ang monastic establishment.

By the third century CE texts describing various "pure realms" or "Buddha lands" had been translated into Chinese, and some monks began to meditate on the best known of these "lands," the Western Paradise of the Buddha Amitābha. [*See* Pure and Impure Lands *and* Amitābha.] In the fourth century Chih Tun (314–366) made an image of Amitābha and vowed to be reborn in his paradise, as did Hui-yüan in 402. [*See the biography of Hui-yüan.*] These early efforts concentrated on visualization of Buddha realms in states of meditative trance. [*See* Nien-fo.] However, in two Pure Land *sūtra*s describing Amitābha and his realm devotees are assured that through a combination of ethical living and concentration on the Buddha they will be reborn at death in his realm, owing to a vow he had made aeons ago to create out of the boundless merit he had accumulated on the long path to Buddhahood a haven for sentient beings. This promise eventually led some monks to preach devotion to Amitābha as an easier way to salvation, available to all, through a combination of sincere thinking on the Buddha and the invocation of his name in faith. To strengthen their proclamation, these monks argued that in fact Amitābha's Pure Land was at a high level, beyond *saṃsāra*, and thus functionally equivalent to *nirvāṇa* for those less philosophically inclined.

Philosophers of the fifth and sixth centuries such as Seng-chao and Chih-i discussed the Pure Land concept as part of larger systems of thought, but the first monk to devote his life to proclaiming devotion to Amitābha as the chief means of salvation for the whole of society was T'an-luan (476–542), a monk from North China where there had long been an emphasis on the practical implementation of Buddhism. T'an-luan organized devotional associations whose members both contemplated the Buddha and orally recited his name. It was in the fifth and sixth centuries as well that many Chinese Buddhist thinkers became convinced that the final period of Buddhist teaching for this world cycle was about to begin, a period (called in Chinese *mo-fa*, the Latter Days of the Law) in which the capacity for understanding Buddhism had so declined that only simple and direct means of communication would suffice. [*See* Mappō *and the biographies of Seng-chao and T'an-luan*.]

The next important preacher to base his teachings solely on Amitābha and his Pure Land was Tao-ch'o (562–645). It was he and his disciple Shan-tao (613–681) who firmly established the Pure Land movement and came to be looked upon as founding patriarchs of the tradition. Although both of these men advocated oral recitation of Amitābha's name as the chief means to deliverance, such recitation was to be done in a concentrated and devout state of mind and was to be accompanied by confession of sins and the chanting of *sūtras*. They and their followers also organized recitation assemblies and composed manuals for congregational worship. Owing to their efforts, Pure Land devotion became the most popular form of Buddhism in China, from whence it was taken to Japan in the ninth century. Pure Land teachings supported the validity of lay piety as no Buddhist school had before, and hence both made possible the spread of Buddhism throughout the population and furthered the development of independent societies and sects outside the monasteries. [*See* Ching-t'u *and the biographies of Tao-ch'o and Shan-tao*.]

The last movement within orthodox Buddhism in China to emerge as an independent tradition was Ch'an (Jpn., Zen), characterized by its concentration on direct means of individual enlightenment, chiefly meditation. Such enlightenment has always been the primary goal of Buddhism, so in a sense Ch'an began as a reform movement seeking to recover the experiential origins of its tradition. Such a reform appeared all the more necessary in the face of the material success of T'ang Buddhism, with its ornate rituals, complex philosophies, and close relationships with the state. Ch'an evolved out of the resonances of Mahāyāna Buddhism with the individualist, mystical, and iconoclastic strand of Chinese culture, represented chiefly by the philosophy of the *Lao-tzu* and *Chuang-tzu*. This philosophy had long advocated individual identification with the ineffable foundations of being, which cannot be grasped in words or limited by the perspectives of traditional practice and morality. Such identification brings a new sense of spiritual freedom, affirmation of life, and acceptance of death.

The importance of meditation had long been emphasized in Chinese Buddhism, beginning with Han translations of *sūtras* describing the process. The T'ien-t'ai master Chih-i discussed the stages and positions of meditation in great detail in the sixth century. Thus, it is not surprising that by the seventh century some monks appeared who advocated meditation above all, a simplification parallel to that of the Pure Land tradition.

The first references to a "Ch'an school" appeared in the late eighth century. By that time several branches of this emerging tradition were constructing genealogies going back to Śākyamuni himself; these were intended to establish the priority and authority of their teachings. The genealogy that came to be accepted later claimed a lineage of twenty-eight Indian and seven Chinese patriarchs, the latter beginning with Bodhidharma (c. 461–534), a Central Asian meditation master active in the Northern Wei kingdom. Legends concerning these patriarchs were increasingly elaborated as time passed, but the details of most cannot be verified. [*See the biography of Bodhidharma*.] The first Chinese monk involved whose teachings have survived is Tao-hsin (580–651), who was later claimed to be the fourth patriarch. Tao-hsin specialized in meditation and monastic discipline, and studied for ten years with a disciple of the T'ien-t'ai founder, Chih-i. He is also noted for his concern with image worship and reciting the Buddha's name to calm the mind.

One of Tao-hsin's disciples was Hung-jen (601–674), who also concentrated on meditation and on maintaining "awareness of the mind." His successor was Fa-ju (d. 689), whose spiritual heir in turn was Shen-hsiu (d. 706), who had also studied with Hung-jen. Shen-hsiu was active in North China, where he was invited to court by the Empress Wu and became a famous teacher. In the earliest and most reliable sources Hung-jen, Fa-ju, and Shen-hsiu are described as the fifth, sixth, and seventh Ch'an patriarchs, with Fa-ju eventually omitted and replaced in sixth position by Shen-hsiu. However, in the early eighth century this succession, based in the capitals of Lo-yang and Ch'ang-an in the North (and hence retrospectively referred to as the "Northern school"), was challenged by a monk named Shen-hui (670–762), who had studied for several years with a teacher named Hui-neng (638–713) in a monastery in Kwangtung Province in the South. Shen-hui labored for years to establish a new form of Ch'an, a "Southern school," centered on recognizing the Buddha nature within the self, and thus less concerned with worship, scripture study, and prescribed forms of meditation.

Shen-hui's most lasting achievement was the elevation of his teacher Hui-neng to the status of "sixth patriarch," displacing Shen-hsiu. This achievement was textually established through the composition of a book entitled *The Platform Sutra of the Sixth Patriarch* (platform here means dais) in about 820 by members of Shen-hui's school. Portions of this book are very similar to the teachings of Shen-hui, who did not cite any writings by Hui-neng although he was no doubt influenced by his study with him. In the *Platform Sutra* Hui-neng is portrayed as a brilliant young monk of rustic background who confounds Shen-hsiu and is secretly given charge of the transmission by the fifth patriarch, Hung-jen (601–674). This book teaches instantaneous enlightenment through realization of inner potential, while criticizing gradualist approaches that rely on outer forms such as images and scriptures. As such it is an important source of the Ch'an individualism and iconoclasm well known in the West. [*See the biography of Hui-neng.*]

The Ch'an tradition as a whole, however, has always been characterized by disciplined communal living in monasteries, centered on group meditation. Although the first extant written codes of monastic conduct are dated 1103 or 1104, they refer back to the teachings of Pai-chang Huai-hai (720–814), a monk in the Hui-neng line of transmission. However, the first monks to establish a new style of monastic life based on communal meditation and manual labor were Tao-hsin and Hung-jen in the seventh century. Other characteristics of early Ch'an monasteries were their independent establishment in remote areas, their rejection of a central hall containing images in favor of "Dharma halls" with meditation platforms along the sides, private consultations with abbots, and frequent group discussions. Frugality and shared responsibility for work were also emphasized in order to reduce dependence on outside donations with the reciprocal obligations they involved. In later centuries agricultural labor was reduced as Ch'an became established and received donations of land and goods from wealthy patrons.

By the ninth century Ch'an was widely supported in Chinese society; during the Northern Sung dynasty (960–1127) it was the major form of monastic Buddhism and hence a focal point of institutionalization. In this context Ch'an produced a new type of literature, the "recorded discussions" *(yü-lu)* of patriarchs and abbots with their disciples as they struggled to attain enlightenment. It is these records, codified as "cases" (Chin., *kung-an*; Jpn., *kōan*), that were meditated upon by novices as they sought to experience reality directly. [*See also* Ch'an.]

Although Buddhism flourished at all levels of Chinese society in the T'ang period, an undercurrent of resentment and hostility toward it by Confucians, Taoists, and the state always remained. This hostility came to a head in the mid-ninth century, strongly reinforced by the fact that Buddhist monasteries had accumulated large amounts of precious metals and tax exempt land. From 843 to 845 Emperor Wu-tsung (r. 840–846), an ardent Taoist, issued decrees that led to the destruction of 4,600 monasteries and 40,000 temples and shrines, and the return of 260,500 monks and nuns to lay life. Although this suppression was ended in 846 by Wu-tsung's successor, monastic Buddhism never fully regained its momentum. Nonetheless, Buddhist ideas, values, and rituals continued to permeate Chinese society through the influence of the Ch'an and Pure Land schools, which survived the 845 persecution because of widespread support throughout the country.

T'ang Taoism. Taoism continued to develop during the T'ang period, in part because it received more support from some emperors than it had under the Sui. As noted earlier, T'ai-tsung claimed Lao-tzu as a royal ancestor, and in 667 the Emperor Kao-tsung (r. 649–683) conferred on Lao-tzu the title of emperor, thus confirming his status. Empress Wu, Kao-tsung's wife, swung the pendulum of support back to Buddhism, but Taoism was favored in later reigns as well and reached the high point of its political influence in the T'ang with great suppression of non-Chinese religions in the 840s.

The most important Taoist order during the T'ang was that based on Mao Shan in Kiangsu, where temples were built and reconstructed, disciples trained, and scriptures edited. Devotees on Mao Shan studied Shang-ch'ing scriptures, meditated, practiced alchemy, and carried out complex rituals of purgation and cosmic renewal, calling down astral spirits and preparing for immortality among the stars. These activities were presided over by a hierarchical priesthood, led by *fa-shih*, "masters of doctrine," the most prominent of whom came to be considered patriarchs of the school.

Taoism in the Sung and Yüan Periods. The destruction of the old T'ang aristocracy in the turmoil of the ninth and tenth centuries helped prepare the way for a more centralized state in the Sung, administered by bureaucrats who were selected through civil service examinations. This in turn contributed to increased social mobility, which was also enhanced by economic growth and diversification, the spread of printing, and a larger number of schools. These factors, combined with innovations in literature, art, philosophy, and religion, have led historians to describe the Sung period as the beginning of early modern China. It was in this period that the basic patterns of life and thought were established for the remainder of imperial history.

During the tenth through thirteenth centuries Taoism developed new schools and texts and became more closely allied with the state. The Sung emperor Chen-tsung (r. 990–1023) bestowed gifts and titles on a number of prominent Taoists, including one named Chang from the old Way of the Celestial Masters, based on Mount Lung-hu in Kiangsi Province. This led to the consolidation of the Cheng-i (Orthodox Unity) sect led by hereditary Celestial Masters. The other official Taoist ordination centers in this period were those at Mao Shan and the Ling-pao center in Kiangsu.

A century later, during the reign of Emperor Hui-tsung (r. 1101–1126), the most famous imperial patron of Taoism, three new Taoist orders appeared, one with a popular base in southeastern Kiangsi, another a revival of Mao-shan teachings, and the third the Shen-hsiao Fa (Rites of the Divine Empyrean), initiated by Lin Ling-su, who was active at court from 1116 to 1119. Lin's teachings were presented in a new, expanded edition of a fourth-century Ling-pao text, the *Tu-jen ching* (Scripture of Salvation). The scripture proclaimed that a new divine emperor would descend to rule in 1112, thus bestowing additional sacred status on Hui-tsung. This liturgical text in sixty-one chapters promises salvation to all in the name of a supreme celestial realm, a theme welcome at a court beset with corruption within and foreign invaders without. The Kiangsi movement, called T'ien-hsin (Heart of Heaven) after a star in Ursa Major, was most concerned with the ritual evocation of astral power to exorcise disease-causing demons, particularly those associated with mental illness. The first edition of its texts was also presented to Hui-tsung in 1116.

In 1126 the Sung capital Kaifeng was captured by the Jurchen, a people from northeastern Manchuria who, with other northern peoples, had long threatened the Sung. As a result the Chinese court moved south across the Yangtze River to establish a new capital in Hang-chou, thus initiating the Southern Sung period (1127–1279). During this period China was once again divided north and south, with the Jurchen ruling the Chin kingdom (1115–1234). It was here in the north that three new Taoist sects appeared, the T'ai-i (Grand Unity), the Ta-tao (Great Way), and the Ch'üan-chen (Total Perfection). The T'ai-i sect gained favor for a time at the Chin court because of its promise of divine healing. Ta-tao disciples worked in the fields, prayed for healing rather than using charms, and did not practice techniques of immortality. Both groups were led by a succession of patriarchs for about two hundred years, but failed to survive the end of the Yüan dynasty. Both included Confucian and Buddhist elements in a Taoist framework.

The Ch'üan-chen sect was founded in similar circumstances by a scholar named Wang Che (1113–1170), but continued to exist into the twentieth century. Wang claimed to have received revelations from two superhuman beings, whereupon he gathered disciples and founded five congregations in northern Shantung. After his death seven of his leading disciples continued to proclaim his teachings across North China. One of them was received at the Chin court in 1187, thus beginning a period of imperial support for the sect that continued into the time of Mongol rule, particularly after another of the founding disciples visited Chinggis Khan at his Central Asian court in 1222. [*See the biography of* Wang Che.]

In its early development the Taoist quest for personal immortality employed a combination of positive ritual techniques: visualization of astral gods and ingestion of their essence, internal circulation and refinement of *ch'i*, massage, eating elixirs of cinnebar and mica, and so forth, all accompanied by taboos and ethical injunctions. By the eleventh century this quest was further internalized, and alchemical potions were reinterpreted as forces within the body, a tendency well expressed in the writings of Chang Po-tuan (983–1082). Under Confucian and Ch'an influence the Ch'üan-chen school "spiritualized" the terminology of these older practices, turning its physiological referents into abstract polarities within the mind, to be unified through meditation. Perhaps in part because of this withdrawal into the mind, Ch'üan-chen was the first Taoist school to base itself in monasteries, although celibacy to maintain and purify one's powers had been practiced by some adepts earlier, and some Taoist monasteries had been established in the sixth century under pressure from the state and the Buddhist example.

The Ch'üan-chen sect reached the height of its influence in the first decades of the thirteenth century, and for a time was favored over Chinese Buddhism by Mongol rulers. Buddhist leaders protested Taoist occupation of their monasteries and eventually regained official support after a series of debates between Taoists and Buddhists at court between 1255 and 1281. After Buddhists were judged the winners, Khubilai Khan ordered that the Taoist canon be burned and Taoist priests returned to lay life or converted to Buddhism. In the fourteenth century the Ch'üan-chen sect merged with a similar tradition from South China, the Chin-tan Tao (Golden Elixer Way) also devoted to attaining immortality through cultivating powers or "elixirs" within the self. The name Ch'üan-chen was retained for the monastic side of this combined tradition, whereas the Chin-tan Tao continued as a popular movement that has produced new scriptures and sects since at least the sixteenth century. The older Taoist schools continued to produce new bodies of texts from the eleventh century on, all claiming divine origin, and powers of healing, exorcism, and support for the state.

The Revival of Confucian Philosophy. Confucianism had remained a powerful tradition of morality, social custom, and hierarchical status since the fall of the Han, but after the third century it no longer generated fresh philosophical perspectives. There were a few Confucian philosophers such as Wang T'ung (584?–617), Han Yü (768–824), and Li Ao (fl. 798), but from the fourth through the tenth century the best philosophical minds in China were devoted to Buddhism. However, in the eleventh century there appeared a series of thinkers determined to revive Confucianism as a philosophical system. In this task they were inevitably influenced by Buddhist theories of mind, enlightenment, and ethics; indeed, most of these men went through Buddhist and Taoist phases in their early years and were converted to Confucianism later. Nonetheless, at a conscious level they rejected Buddhist "emptiness," asceticism, and monastic life in favor of a positive metaphysics, ordered family life, and concern for social reform. With a few exceptions the leaders of this movement, known in the West as Neo-Confucianism, went through the civil service examination system and held civil or military offices.

The key eleventh century founders of this movement were Chou Tun-i (1017–1073), Shao Yung (1011–1077), Chang Tsai (1020–1077), and his nephews Ch'eng Hao (1032–1085) and Ch'eng I (1033–1107), who were brothers. In retrospect we can see that Neo-Confucianism split into two general tendencies, the rationalistic and the idealistic, the first more concerned with the ordering principles *(li)* of life and society, the second with awakening the moral consciousness of the mind *(hsin)*. [*See* Hsin.] These tendencies may be found in eleventh century writings, but did not become explicit until a century later in the work of the "study of principle" *(li-hsüeh)* initiated by Chu Hsi (1130–1200) and the "study of mind" *(hsin-hsüeh)* promoted by Lu Hsiang-shan (1139–1193). Interaction between these poles provided the impetus for new syntheses until the seventeenth century, with the "study of mind" best represented by Wang Yang-ming (1472–1529). The most complete system of thought was produced by Chu Hsi, who sought to enhance the source of moral order within by patient investigation of the patterns of organization in society and nature. Chu Hsi's teachings were made the basis of the civil service examinations in 1313, and hence came to have a powerful influence throughout literate society. [*With the exception of Shao Yung, all of the thinkers mentioned above are the subject of independent entries.*]

In the history of Chinese religions, the impact of Neo-Confucianism is evident at different levels. The intellectual and institutional success of this movement among the Chinese elite led many of them away from Buddhism and Taoism, away from any form of sectarian religion, toward a reaffirmation of the values of family, clan, and state. While the elite were still involved in such popular traditions as annual festivals, geomancy, and funeral rituals, the rational and nontheistic orientation of Neo-Confucianism tended to inhibit their participation in ecstatic processions and shamanism. These tendencies meant that after the eleventh century sectarian and popular forms of religion were increasingly denied high level intellectual stimulation and articulation. Indeed, state support for a new Confucian orthodoxy gave fresh impetus to criticism or suppression of other traditions. Another long term impact of Neo-Confucianism was the confucianization of popular values, supported by schools, examinations, distribution of tracts, and lectures in villages. This meant that from the Sung dynasty on the operative ethical principles in society were a combination of Confucian virtues with Buddhist *karman* and compassion, a tendency that became more widespread as the centuries passed.

All of these developments were rooted in the religious dimensions of the Neo-Confucian tradition, which from the beginning was most concerned with the moral transformation of self and society. This transformation was to be carried out through intensive study and discussion, self-examination, and meditation. In the process one could become aware of the patterns of moral order within the mind, an insight that itself became a means of clarifying and establishing this cosmic order within society. So Confucianism became a more active and self-conscious movement than it ever had been before. [*See* Confucian Thought, *article on* Neo-Confucianism.]

Sung Buddhism. Sung Buddhist activities were based on the twin foundations of Ch'an and Pure Land, with an increasing emphasis on the compatability of the two. Although the joint practice of meditation and invocation of the Buddha's name had been taught by Chih-i and the Ch'an patriarch Tao-hsin in the sixth and seventh centuries, the first Ch'an master to openly advocate it after Ch'an was well established was Yen-shou (904–975). This emphasis was continued in the Yüan (1271–1368) and Ming (1368–1644) dynasties, so that by the late traditional period meditation and recitation were commonly employed together in monasteries as two means to the same end of emptying the mind of self-centered thought.

During the Sung dynasty Buddhism physically recovered from the suppression of the ninth century, with tens of thousands of monasteries, large amounts of land, and active support throughout society. By the tenth century the Ch'an school was divided into two main branches, both of which had first appeared earlier, the Lin-chi (Jpn., Rinzai), emphasizing dramatic and unexpected breakthroughs to enlightenment in the midst of everyday activities, and the Ts'ao-tung (Jpn., Sōtō), known for a more gradual approach through seated meditation. [*See the biography of Lin-chi.*] There was some recovery of philosophical studies in Ch'an monasteries, but it did not recapture the intellectual vitality of the T'ang period. However, for the larger history of Chinese religions the most important development in Sung Buddhism was the spread of lay societies devoted to good works and recitation of the Buddha's name. These groups, usually supported by monks and monasteries, ranged in membership from a few score to several thousands, including both men and women, gentry and commoners. In the twelfth century these societies, with their egalitarian outreach and congregational rituals, provided the immediate context for the rise of independent popular sects, which in turn spread throughout China in succeeding centuries. The Sung associations were an organized and doctrinally aware means of spreading Buddhist ideas of salvation, paradise and purgatory, *karman*, and moral values to the population at large, and so contributed to the integration of Buddhism with Chinese culture.

Popular Religion. The other major tradition that took its early modern shape during the Sung period was popular religion, the religion of the whole population except those who specifically opted out of it, such as orthodox Taoist priests, Buddhist monks, Confucian scholars, and state officials in their public roles. Chou and Han sources note a variety of religious practices current throughout the population, including ancestor worship, sacrifices to spirits of sacred objects and places, belief in ghosts, exorcism, divination, and the activities of spirit mediums. Many of these practices began in prehistoric times and formed the sea out of which more structured and focused traditions gradually emerged, traditions such as the state cult, Confucian philosophy, and Taoist religion. Each of these emerging traditions was associated with social elites who had to define themselves as different from their peasant and artisan surroundings. In the process they came to criticize or even suppress cults active among common folk devoted to local spirits and concerned primarily with efficacious response to immediate needs. Since the Chinese state had always claimed religious prerogatives, the most important factor was official authorization by some level of government. Unauthorized cults were considered "excessive," beyond what elite custom and propriety admitted. Nonetheless, such distinctions were of importance primarily to the more self-conscious supporters of literate alternatives; to their less theologically inclined peers, "popular religion" was a varied set of customs that reflected the way the world was.

Popular religious practices were diffused throughout the social system, based in family, clan, and village, at first devoted only to spirits with limited and local powers. By the Han dynasty personified deities of higher status appeared, along with organized sects such as the Way of the Celestial Masters, with ethical teachings and new myths of creation and world renewal, all reinforced by collective rituals. These developments were produced by literate commoners and minor officials at an intermediate level of education and status, and show remakable resemblance to the first records of such middle-class thought in the writings of Mo-tzu, six hundred years earlier. This level of Chinese religious consciousness was strongly reinforced by Mahāyāna *bodhisattva*s, images, offering rituals, myths of purgatory, and understandings of moral causation. By the fourth century, Taoist writers were developing elaborate mythologies of personified deities and immortals and their roles in a celestial hierarchy.

During the Sung period all these various strands came together to reformulate popular religion as a tradition in its own right, defined by its location in the midst of ordinary social life, its pantheon of personified deities, views of afterlife, demonology, and characteristic specialists and rituals. Its values were still founded on pragmatic reciprocity, but some assurances about life after death were added to promises for aid now.

This popular tradition is based on ancestor veneration and the cult of household gods. [*See also* Ancestors, *article on* Ancestor Cults.] Beyond the household its rituals are performed at shrines for locality gods and at village temples. Temples are residences of the gods, where they are most easily available and ready to accept petitions and offerings of food and incense. Here too, the gods convey messages through simple means of divination, dreams, spirit mediums, and spirit writing. Great bronze incense burners in temple courtyards are the central points of ritual communication, and it is common for local households to fill their own incense burners with ashes from the temple. All families residing in the area of the village are considered members of the temple community.

The deities characteristic of this tradition are human beings deified over time by increasing recognition of their efficacy and status. Having once been human they owe their positions to veneration by the living and hence are constrained by reciprocal relationships with their devotees. They are responsible for specific functions such as providing rain or healing diseases, and under Taoist influence came to be organized in a celestial hierarchy presided over by the Jade Emperor, a deity first officially recognized as such by the Sung emperor Chen-tsung in the beginning of the eleventh century. [*See* Yü-huang.]

Gods are symbols of order, and many of the gods of Taoism and popular religion are equipped with weapons and troops. Such force is necessary because beneath the gods is a vast array of demons, hostile influences that bring disorder, disease, suffering, and death. Although ultimately subject to divine command, and in some cases sent by the gods to punish sinners, these demons are most unruly, and often can be subdued only through repeated invocation and strenuous ritual action. It is in such ritual exorcism that the struggle between gods and demons is most starkly presented. Most demons, or *kuei*, are the spirits of the restless dead who died unjustly, or whose bodies are not properly cared for; they cause disruption to draw attention to their plight. Other demons represent natural forces that can be perceived as hostile, such as mountains and wild animals. Much effort in popular religion is devoted to dealing with these harmful influences.

There are three different types of leadership in this popular tradition—hereditary, selected, and charismatic—although of course in any given situation these types can be mixed. Hereditary leaders include the fathers and mothers of families who carry out ancestor worship in the clan temple and household, and sect leaders who inherit their positions. Hereditary Taoist priests also perform rituals for the community. Village temples, on the other hand, tend to be led by a village elder selected by lot, on a rotating basis. Charismatic leaders include spirit mediums, spirit writers, magicians, and healers, all of whom are defined by the recognition of their ability to bring divine power and wisdom directly to bear on human problems.

Popular religion is also associated with a cycle of annual festivals, funeral rituals, and geomancy *(feng-shui)*. Popular values are sanctioned by revelations from the gods and by belief in purgatory, where one aspect of the soul goes after death, there to be punished for its sins according to the principle of karmic retribution. There are ten courts in purgatory, each presided over by a judge who fits the suffering to the crime. Passage through purgatory can be ameliorated through the transfer of merit money by Buddhist or Taoist rituals. When its guilt has been purged, the soul advances to the tenth court, where the form of its next existence is decided. This mythology is a modification of Buddhist beliefs described in detail in texts first translated in the sixth century.

The Period of Mongol Rule. The Mongols under Chinggis Khan (1167–1227) captured the Chin capital of Yen-ching (modern Peking) in 1215 and established the Yüan dynasty (1271–1368). From China they ruled their vast domain, which extended all the way to central Europe. For the next several decades the "Middle Kingdom" was the eastern end of a world empire, open as never before to foreign influences. In the realm of religion these influences included the Nestorians, papal letters to Khubilai Khan (r. 1260–1298) brought by Nicolo and Marco Polo, a few Franciscan missionaries in the early fourteenth century, and a large number of Tibetan Buddhist monks.

The first Mongol contact with Chinese Buddhism was with Ch'an monks, a few of whom attained influence at court. In the meantime, however, the Mongols were increasingly attracted by the exorcistic and healing rituals of Tantric Buddhism in Tibet, the borders of which they also controlled. In 1260 a Tibetan monk, 'Phags-pa (1235–1280), was named imperial preceptor, and soon after chief of Buddhist affairs. Tibetan monks were appointed as leaders of the *saṃgha* all over China, to some extent reviving the Tantric (Chen-yen) school that flourished briefly in the T'ang. [*See* Chen-yen.]

By the early fourteenth century another form of popular religion appeared, the voluntary association or sect that could be joined by individuals from different families and villages. These sects developed out of lay Buddhist societies in the twelfth century, but their structure owed much to late Han religious associations and their popular Taoist successors, Buddhist eschatological movements from the fifth century on, and Manichaeism. By the Yüan period the sects were characterized by predominantly lay membership and leadership, hierarachical organization, active proselytism, congregational rituals, possession of their own scriptures in the vernacular, and mutual economic support. Their best known antecedent was the White Lotus school, an independent sect founded by a monk named Mao Tzu-yüan (1086–1166). Mao combined simplified T'ien-t'ai teaching with Pure Land practice, invoking Amitābha's saving power with just five recitations of his name. After Mao's death the sect, led by laymen who married, spread across south and east China. In the process it incorporated charms and prognostication texts, and by the fourteenth century branches in Kwangsi and Honan were strongly influenced by Taoist methods of cultivating the internal elixirs. This led to protests from more orthodox leaders of the Pure Land tradition, monks in the east who appealed to the throne that they not be proscribed along with the "heretics." This appeal succeeded, and the monastic branch went on to be considered part of the tradition of the Pure Land school, with Mao Tzu-yüan as a revered patriarch.

The more rustic side of the White Lotus tradition was

prohibited three times in the Yüan, but flourished nonetheless, with its own communal organizations and scriptures and a growing emphasis on the presence within it of the future Buddha Maitreya. During the civil wars of the mid-fourteenth century this belief encouraged full-scale uprisings in the name of the new world Maitreya was expected to bring. The Ming founder Chu Yüan-chang (1328–1398) had for a time been an officer in one of the White Lotus armies, but after his victory tried to suppress the sect. It continued to multiply nonetheless, under a variety of names.

The first extant sectarian scriptures, produced in the early sixteenth century, indicate that by that time there were two streams of mythology and belief, one more influenced by Taoism, the other by Buddhism. The Taoist stream incorporated much terminology from the Golden Elixir school (Chin-tan Tao), and was based on the myth of a saving mother goddess, the Eternal Venerable Mother, who is a modified form of the old Han-dynasty Queen Mother of the West, a figure mentioned in Ch'üan-chen teachings as well. The Buddhist stream was initiated by a sectarian reformer named Lo Ch'ing (1443–1527), whose teachings were based on the Ch'an theme of "attaining Buddhahood through seeing one's own nature." Lo criticized the White Lotus and Maitreya sects as being too concerned with outward ritual forms, but later writers in his school incorporated some themes from the Eternal Mother mythology, while other sectarian founders espousing this mythology imitated Lo Ch'ing's example of writing vernacular scriptures to put forth their own views. These scriptures, together with their successors, the popular spirit-writing texts of the nineteenth and twentieth centuries, constitute a fourth major body of Chinese sacred texts, after those of the Confucians, Buddhists, and Taoists.

The number of popular religious sects increased rapidly during the sixteenth and seventeenth centuries, all part of the same general tradition but with different founders, lines of transmission, texts, and ritual variations. Such groups had been illegal since the Yüan and some resisted prosecution with armed force or attempted to establish their own safe areas. In a few cases sect leaders organized major attempts to overthrow the government and put their own emperor on the throne, to rule over a utopian world in which time and society would be renewed. However, for the most part the sects simply provided a congregational alternative to village popular religion, an alternative that offered mutual support and assurance and promised means of going directly to paradise at death without passing through purgatory.

Popular religious sects were active on the China mainland until the start of the Cultural Revolution in 1966, and they continue to multiply in Taiwan, where they can be legally registered as branches of Taoism. Since the late nineteenth century most sectarian scriptures have been composed by spirit writing, direct revelation from a variety of gods and culture heroes.

Ming and Ch'ing Religion

Mongol rule began to deteriorate in the early fourteenth century, due to struggles between tribal factions at court, the decline of military power, and the devolution of central authority to local warlords, bandit groups, and sectarian movements. After twenty years of civil war Chu Yüan-chang, from a poor peasant family, defeated all his rivals and reestablished a Chinese imperial house, the Ming dynasty (1368–1644). Chu (Ming T'ai-tsu, r. 1368–1398) was an energetic ruler of strong personal religious beliefs who revised imperial rituals, promulgated strict laws against a variety of popular practices and sects, and recruited Taoist priests to direct court ceremonies. For him the mandate of Heaven was a living force that had established him in a long line of sacred emperors; his ancestors were deemed powerful intermediaries with Shang-ti. He elaborated and reinforced the responsibility of government officials to offer regular sacrifices to deities of fertility, natural forces, and cities, and to the spirits of heroes and abandoned ghosts.

Ming Dynasty. Under the Ming, such factors as the diversification of the agricultural base and the monetization of the economy had an impact on religious life; there were more excess funds for building temples and printing scriptures, and more rich peasants, merchants, and artisans with energy to invest in popular religion, both village and sectarian. Sectarian scriptures appeared as part of the same movement that produced new vernacular literature of all types, morality books to inculcate Neo-Confucian values, and new forms and audiences for popular operas. More than ever before the late Ming was a time of economic and cultural initiatives from the population at large, as one might expect in a period of increasing competition for recources by small entrepreneurs. These tendencies continued to gain momentum in the Ch'ing period.

Ming Buddhism showed the impact of these economic and cultural factors, particularly in eastern China where during the sixteenth century reforming monks such as Yün-ch'i Chu-hung (1535–1615) organized lay societies, wrote morality books that quantified the merit points for good deeds, and affirmed Confucian values within a Buddhist framework. Chu-hung combined Pure Land and Ch'an practice and preached spiritual progress through sparing animals from slaughter and captivity. The integration of Buddhism into

Chinese society was furthered as well by government approval of a class of teaching monks, ordained with official certificates, whose role was to perform rituals for the people. [*See the biography of Chu-hung.*]

Buddhism also had a synergetic relationship with the form of Neo-Confucianism dominant in the late Ming, Wang Yang-ming's "study of mind." On the one hand, Ch'an individualism and seeking enlightenment within influenced Wang and his disciples; on the other hand, official acceptance of Wang's school gave indirect support to the forms of Buddhism associated with it, such as the teachings of Chu-hung and Han-shan Te-ch'ing (1546–1623).

Taoism was supported by emperors throughout the Ming, with Taoist priests appointed as officials in charge of rituals and composing hymns and messages to the gods. The Ch'üan-chen sect continued to do well, with its monastic base and emphasis on attaining immortality through developing "internal elixirs." Its meditation methods also influenced those of some of Wang Yang-ming's followers, such as Wang Chi (1497–1582). However, it was the Cheng-i sect led by hereditary Celestial Masters that had the most official support during the Ming and hence was able to consolidate its position as the standard of orthodox Taoism. Cheng-i influence is evident in scriptures composed during this period, many of which trace their lineage back to the first Celestial Master and bear imprimaturs from his successors. The forty-third-generation master was given charge of compiling a new Taoist canon in 1406, a task completed between 1444 and 1445. It is this edition that is still in use today.

By the seventeenth century, Confucian philosophy entered a more nationalistic and materialist phase, but the scholar-official class as a whole remained involved in a variety of private religious practices beyond their official ritual responsibilities. These included not only the study of Taoism and Buddhism but the use of spirit-writing séances and prayers to Wen-ch'ang, the god of scholars and literature, for help in passing examinations. Ming T'ai-tsu had proclaimed that each of the "three teachings" of Confucianism, Buddhism, and Taoism had an important role to play, which encouraged synthetic tendencies present since the beginnings of Buddhism in China. In the sixteenth century a Confucian scholar named Lin Chao-en (1517–1598) from Fukien took these tendencies a step further by building a middle-class religious sect in which Confucian teachings were explicitly supported by those of Buddhism and Taoism. Lin was known as "Master of the Three Teachings," the patron saint of what became a popular movement with temples still extant in Singapore and Malaysia in the mid-twentieth century. This tendency to incorporate Confucianism into a sectarian religion was echoed by Chang Chi-tsung (d. 1866) who established a fortified community in Shantung, and by K'ang Yu-wei (1858–1927) at the end of imperial history. Confucian oriented spirit-writing cults also flourished in the late nineteenth and early twentieth centuries, supported by middle level military and civil officials. These cults produced tracts and scriptures of their own. [*See the biography of K'ang Yu-wei.*]

During the sixteenth century Christian missionaries tried for the third time to establish their faith in China, this time a more successful effort by Italian Jesuits. In 1583 two Italian Jesuits, Michael Ruggerius and Matteo Ricci, were allowed to stay in Chao-ch'ing in Kwangtung Province. By their knowledge of science, mathematics, and geography they impressed some of the local scholars and officials; Ricci eventually became court astronomer in Peking. He also made converts of several high officials, so that by 1605 there were 200 Chinese Christians. For the next several decades the Jesuit mission prospered, led by priests given responsibility for the sensitive task of establishing the imperial calendar. In 1663 the number of converts had grown to about one hundred thousand. The high point of this early Roman Catholic mission effort came during the reign of the K'ang-hsi emperor (r. 1662–1722), who, while not a convert, had a lively curiosity about European knowledge. [*See also* Jesuits *and the biography of Ricci.*]

Nonetheless, Chinese suspicions remained, and the mission was threatened from within by rivalries between orders and European nations. In particular, there was contention over Jesuit acceptance of veneration for ancestors and Confucius. In 1645 a Franciscan obtained a papal prohibition of such practices, and this "rites controversy" intensified in the ensuing decades. The Inquisition forbade the Jesuit approach in 1704, but the Jesuits kept on resisting until papal bulls were issued against them in 1715 and 1742. K'ang-hsi had sided with the Jesuits, but in the end their influence was weakened and their ministry made less adaptable to Chinese traditions. There were anti-Christian persecutions in several places throughout the mid-eighteenth century; however, some Christian communities remained, as did a few European astronomers at court. There were several more attempts at suppression in the early nineteenth century, with the result that by 1810 there were only thirty-one European missionaries left, with eighty Chinese priests, but church membership remained at about two hundred thousand.

The first Protestant missionary to reach China was Robert Morrison, sent by the London Missionary Society to Canton in 1807. He and another missionary made their first Chinese convert in 1814 and completed translating the Bible in 1819. From then on increasing numbers of Protestant missionaries arrived from other European countries and the United States. [*See the biography of Morrison.*]

Christian impact on the wider world of Chinese religions has traditionally been negligible, although there is some indication that scholars such as Fang I-chih (1611–1671) were influenced by European learning and thus helped prepare the way for the practical emphases of Ch'ing Confucianism. Chu-hung and Ricci had engaged in written debate over theories of God and rebirth, and even the K'ang-hsi emperor was involved in such discussions later, but there was no acceptance of Christian ideas and practices by Chinese who did not convert. This is true at the popular level as well, where in some areas Chinese sectarians responded positively to both Roman Catholic and Protestant missionaries. Christians and the sectarians were often persecuted together, and shared concerns for congregational ritual, vernacular scriptures, and a compassionate creator deity. Yet nineteenth century sectarian texts betray few traces of Christian influence, and even when Jesus speaks in later spirit-writing books it is as a supporter of Chinese values.

Ch'ing Dynasty. The Manchus, a tribal confederation related to the Jurchen, had established their own state in the northeast in 1616 and named it Ch'ing in 1636. As their power grew, they sporadically attacked North China and absorbed much Chinese political and cultural influence. In 1644 a Ch'ing army was invited into China by the Ming court to save Peking from Chinese rebels. The Manchus not only conquered Peking but stayed to rule for the next 268 years. In public policy the Manchus were strong supporters of Confucianism, and relied heavily on the support of Chinese officials. Most religious developments during the Ch'ing were continuations of Ming traditions, with the exception of Protestant Christianity and the Taiping movement it helped stimulate.

Before their conquest of China the Manchus had learned of Tibetan or Lamaist Buddhism through the Mongols, and had a special sense of relationship to a *bodhisattva* much venerated in Tibet, Mañjuśrī. [*See* Mañjuśrī.] Nurhachi (1559–1626), the founder of the Manchu kingdom, was considered an incarnation of Mañjuśrī. After 1644 the Manchus continued to patronize Lamaism, which had been supported to some extent in the Ming as well, in part to stay in touch with the dominant religion of Tibet and the Mongols. In 1652 the Dalai Lama was invited to visit Peking, and in the early eighteenth century his successors were put under a Ch'ing protectorate.

Early Ch'ing emperors were interested in Ch'an Buddhism as well. The Yung-cheng emperor (r. 1723–1735) published a book on Ch'an in 1732 and ordered the reprinting of the Buddhist canon, a task completed in 1738. He also supported the printing of a Tibetan edition of the canon, and his successor, Ch'ien-lung (r. 1736–1795) sponsored the translation of this voluminous body of texts into Manchu. The Pure Land tradition continued to be the form of Buddhism most supported by the people. The most active Taoist schools were the monastic Ch'üan-chen and the Cheng-i, more concerned with public rituals of exorcism and renewal, carried on by a married priesthood. However, Taoism no longer received court support. Despite repeated cycles of rebellions and persecutions, popular sects continued to thrive, although after the Eight Trigrams uprising in 1813 repression was so severe that production of sectarian scripture texts declined in favor of oral transmission, a tendency operative among some earlier groups as well.

The most significant innovation in Ch'ing religion was the teachings of the T'ai-p'ing T'ien-kuo (Celestial Kingdom of Great Peace and Prosperity), which combined motifs from Christianity, shamanism, and popular sectarian beliefs. The Taiping movement was begun by Hung Hsiu-ch'üan (1814–1864), a would-be Confucian scholar who first was given Christian tracts in 1836. After failing civil service examinations several times, Hung claimed to have had a vision in which it was revealed that Hung was the younger brother of Jesus Christ, commissioned to be a new messiah. Hung proclaimed a new kingdom upon earth, to be characterized by theocratic rule, enforcement of the ten commandments, the brotherhood of all, equality of the sexes, and redistribution of land. Hung and other Taiping leaders were effective preachers who wrote books, edicts, and tracts proclaiming their teachings and regulations and providing prayers and hymns for congregational worship. They forbade ancestor veneration and the worship of Buddhas and Taoist and popular deities. Wherever the Taipings went they destroyed images and temples. They rejected geomancy and divination and established a new calendar free of the old festivals and concerns for inauspicious days.

In the late 1840s Hung Hsiu-ch'üan organized a group called the God Worshipers Society with many poor and disaffected among its members. They moved to active military rebellion in 1851, with Hung taking the title "Celestial King" of the new utopian regime. Within two years they captured Nanking. Here they established their capital and sent armies north and west, involving all of China in civil war as they went. Although the Ch'ing government was slow to respond, in 1864 Nanking was retaken by imperial forces and the remaining

Taiping forces slaughtered or dispersed. For all of the power of this movement, Taiping teachings and practices had no positive effect on the history of Chinese religions after this time, while all the indigenous traditions resumed and rebuilt. [*See* T'ai-p'ing.]

The End of Empire and Postimperial China

In the late nineteenth century some Chinese intellectuals began to incorporate into their thought new ideas from Western science, philosophy, and literature, but the trend in religion was toward reaffirmation of Chinese values. Even the reforming philosopher K'ang Yu-wei tried to build a new cult of Confucius, while at the popular level spirit-writing sects proliferated. In 1899 a vast antiforeign movement began in North China, loosely called the Boxer Rebellion because of its martial arts practices. The ideology of this movement was based on popular religion and spirit mediumship, and many Boxer groups attacked Christian missions in the name of Chinese gods. This uprising was put down in 1900 by a combination of Chinese and foreign armies, after the latter had captured Peking.

The Ch'ing government attempted a number of belated reforms, but in 1911 it collapsed from internal decay, foreign pressure, and military uprisings. Some Chinese intellectuals, free to invest their energies in new ideas and political forms, avidly studied and translated Western writings, including those of Marxism. One result of this westernization and secularization was attacks on Confucianism and other Chinese traditions, a situation exacerbated by recurrent civil wars that led to the destruction or occupation of thousands of temples. However, these new ideas were most influential in the larger cities; the majority of Chinese continued popular religious practices as before. Many temples and monasteries survived, and there were attempts to revive Buddhist thought and monastic discipline, particularly by the monks Yin-kuang (1861–1940) and T'ai-hsü (1889–1947). [*See the biography of T'ai-hsü.*]

Since 1949 Chinese religions have increasingly prospered in Taiwan, particularly at the popular level, where the people have more surplus funds and freedom of belief than ever before. Many new temples have been built, sects established, and scriptures and periodicals published. The same can be said for Chinese popular religion in Hong Kong and Singapore. The Taoist priesthood is active in Taiwan, supported by the presence of hereditary Celestial Masters from the mainland who provide ordinations and legitimacy. Buddhist monasteries and publishing houses are also doing well in Taiwan and Hong Kong, though lay Buddhist sects have always been more influential among the people in these areas.

The constitution of the People's Republic establishes the freedom both to support and oppose religion, although in practice religious activities of all types declined there after 1949, particularly during the Cultural Revolution of 1966 to 1969. In general religion has been depicted along Marxist lines as "feudal superstition" that must be rejected by those seeking to build a new China. Nonetheless, many religious activities continued until the Cultural Revolution, even those of the long proscribed popular sects. The Cultural Revolution, encouraged by Mao Tse-tung and his teachings, was a massive attack on old traditions, including not only religion, but education, art, and established bureaucracies. In the process thousands of religious images were destroyed, temples and churches confiscated, leaders returned to lay life, and books burned. At the same time a new national cult arose, that of Chairman Mao and his thought, involving ecstatic processions, group recitation from Mao's writings, and a variety of quasi-religious ceremonials. These included confessions of sins against the revolution, vows of obedience before portraits of the Chairman, and meals of wild vegetables to recall the bitter days before liberation. Although the frenzy abated, the impetus of the Cultural Revolution continued until Mao's death in 1976, led by a small group, later called "the Gang of Four," centered around his wife. This group was soon deposed, a move followed by liberalization of policy in several areas, including religion. Since 1980 many churches, monasteries, and mosques have reopened, and religious leaders reinstated, in part to establish better relationships with Buddhist, Christian, and Muslim communities in other countries. There has been a limited revival of popular religion in some areas as well, particularly in Fukien province, which has long had close connections with overseas Chinese. Private enterprise and the leasing of land by individual farmers are practices returning to the countryside; these may encourage ancestor worship and traditional forms of divination and funeral rituals, although it seems unlikely that the pantheon of popular gods will reappear. Nonetheless, one should remember that aspects of the Marxist regime may also be but passing phases in a long history, and may not leave much more impact than did Christianity or the Taipings centuries before.

[*For further discussion of the various traditions treated in this article, see* Buddhism, *article on* Buddhism in China; Buddhism, Schools of, *article on* Chinese Buddhism; Taoism; Confucian Thought; *and* Chinese Philosophy. *For a discussion of the influence of the major monotheistic religions on Chinese religion, see* Islam, *article on* Islam in China; Christianity, *article on* Christianity in Asia; *and* Judaism, *article on* Judaism in Asia and Sub-Saharan Africa. *For the influence of Inner Asian civilizations on Chinese thought, see* Inner Asian Religions, Mongol Religions, *and* Buddhism, *article on* Buddhism in Central Asia. *See also* Domestic Observances, *article on* Chinese Practices, *and* Chinese Religious Year.]

BIBLIOGRAPHY

Berling, Judith. *The Syncretic Religion of Lin Chao-en.* New York, 1980. A detailed study of a Confucian religious teacher in the sixteenth century.

Bilsky, Lester James. *The State Religion of Ancient China.* 2 vols. Taipei, 1975. A detailed discussion of official rituals and deities from the Chou through the early Han dynasties.

Bodde, Derk. *Festivals in Classical China. New Year and Other Annual Observances during the Han Dynasty, 206 B.C.–A.D. 220.* Princeton, 1975. The best study in English of annual festivals in their early development.

Boltz, Judith M. "A Survey of Taoist Literature, Tenth to Seventeenth Centuries." Berkeley, 1985. A very helpful discussion of Taoist texts, schools, and writers.

Chan, Wing-tsit, trans. and comp. *A Sourcebook in Chinese Philosophy.* Princeton, 1963. The standard selection of Chinese philosophical texts in translation. Accurate and comprehensive.

Ch'en, Kenneth K. S. *Buddhism in China, A Historical Survey.* Princeton, 1964. Detailed and comprehensive. The best general view of the topic in English. Good bibliography.

Ch'en, Kenneth K. S. *The Chinese Transformation of Buddhism.* Princeton, 1973. An excellent study of how Buddhist values, rituals, and economic activities adapted to the Chinese environment.

Ch'en Kuo-fu. *Tao-tsang yüan-liu k'ao.* 2 vols. Peking, 1983. Still the standard study of the development of the Taoist canon.

Ch'en Yüan. *Nan Sung ch'u Hopei hsin Tao-chiao k'ao.* Peking, 1941. The first detailed study of the topic; includes a discussion of the Ch'üan-chen school.

Dumoulin, Heinrich. *A History of Zen Buddhism.* New York, 1963. The standard history of Ch'an/Zen in English.

Dunne, George H. *Generation of Giants. The Story of the Jesuits in China in the Last Decades of the Ming Dynasty.* Notre Dame, Ind., 1962. The standard treatment of the topic in English, based primarily on European sources.

Elliott, Allan J. A. *Chinese Spirit Medium Cults in Singapore.* London, 1955. Thorough field-work study of spirit medium initiation and rituals.

Fairbank, John K., ed. *The Missionary Enterprise in China and America.* Cambridge, Mass., 1974. One of several books on American Protestant missions in China produced by Professor Fairbank and his students. Treats missionaries in their political and social contexts.

Fukui Kōjun. *Dōkyō no kisoteki kenkyū.* Tokyo, 1952. Pioneering studies of the beginnings and early development of Taoism, the *T'ai-p'ing ching*, and relationships with Buddhism.

Fukui Kōjun, Yamazaki Hiroshi, Kimura Eiichi, and Sakai Tadao, eds. *Dōkyō.* 3 vols. Tokyo, 1983. The most comprehensive discussion of Taoism available. Includes a lavish bibliography.

Fung Yu-lan. *History of Chinese Philosophy.* 2 vols. Translated by Derk Bodde. Princeton, 1952. The most authoritative and comprehensive study of the topic in English.

Groot, J. J. M. de. *The Religious System of China* (1892–1910). 6 vols. Reprint, Taipei, 1964. Massive study, with translations of Chinese texts provided. Particularly good on funeral rituals, *feng-shui*, demonology, and shamanism.

Hsü, Francis L. K. *Under the Ancestors' Shadow: Chinese Culture and Personality.* New York, 1948. A fine study of ancestor cult in its social context.

Israeli, Raphael. *Muslims in China: A Study in Cultural Confrontation.* London, 1978. The only recent book-length study of the topic in English.

Johnson, David. "The City-God Cults of T'ang and Sung China." *Harvard Journal of Asiatic Studies* 45 (December 1985): 363–457. The most thorough and recent study of the topic.

Jordon, David K. *Gods, Ghosts and Ancestors: Folk Religion in a Taiwanese Village* (1972). Reprint, Taipei, 1986. A good anthropological study of village religion. Sensitive and lively discussion.

Jordan, David K. and Daniel L. Overmyer. *The Flying Phoenix: Aspects of Chinese Sectarianism in Taiwan.* Princeton and Taipei, 1986. The first systematic study of modern Chinese popular religious sects.

Kubo Noritada. *Dōkyōshi.* Tokyo, 1977. Rich material on Taoist history, rituals, beliefs, and relationships with popular religion.

Latourette, Kenneth Scott. *A History of Christian Missions in China.* London, 1929. Long the standard authority on the topic.

Li Shih-yü. *Pao-chüan tsung-lu.* The most comprehensive bibliography of popular religious texts, with good introductory discussions.

Lieu, Samuel N. C. *The Religion of Light: An Introduction to the History of Manichaeism in China.* Hong Kong, 1979. A short introduction to the topic, with an excellent bibliography.

Lieu, Samuel N. C. *Manichaeism in the Later Roman Empire and Medieval China.* Manchester, 1985. The most complete modern study of the topic.

Makita Tairyō. *Gikyō kenkyū.* Koyto, 1976. The best study of Buddhist texts written in China, most of them found at Tunhuang.

Maspero, Henri. *Taoism and Chinese Religion* (1971). Translated by Frank A. Kierman. Amherst, Mass., 1981. Maspero was the pioneering Western scholar of Taoist religion; this is a collection of his essays. Those on immortality cultivation and popular religion remain particularly valuable.

Needham, Joseph. *Science and Civilisation in China.* Cambridge, Mass., 1956–. One of the great scholarly projects of the twentieth century. Rich bibliographies. See particularly vol. 2 (1956) on the history of Chinese thought and the classical worldview, and vol. 5, parts 2–5 (1974–) on Taoist immortality practices and alchemy. Comparative analysis throughout.

Noguchi Tetsurō. *Min-dai Byakuren kyōshi no kenkyū.* Tokyo,

1986. The most comprehensive study of popular religious sects during the Ming period (1368–1644), in their historical, economic, and political contexts.

Obuchi Ninji. *Dōkyōshi no kenkyū*. Okayama, 1964. Authoritative study by a Japanese master of the topic.

Ogasawara Senshū. *Chūgoku jōdokyōka no kenkyū*. Kyoto, 1951. A study of the early Pure Land masters Hui-yüan, T'an-luan, Tao-ch'o, and Shan-tao.

Ogasawara Senshū. *Chūgoku kinsei jōdokyōshi no kenkyū*. Kyoto, 1963. Authoritative study of later Pure Land history and beliefs.

Overmyer, Daniel L. *Folk Buddhist Religion: Dissenting Sects in Late Traditional China*. Cambridge, Mass., 1976. A survey of popular religious sects in the Ming and Ch'ing dynasties.

Reischauer, Edwin O. *Ennin's Travels in T'ang China*. New York, 1955. An excellent account of Buddhism and Chinese life during the ninth century, taken from the travel diary of a Japanese monk.

Sakai Tadao. *Chūgoku zensho no kenkyū*. Tokyo, 1960. A pioneering discussion of the long tradition of books for moral exhortation, written and distributed by both literati and commoners.

Sawada Mizuho. *Zōhō Hōkan no kenkyū*. Tokyo, 1975. Along with the work of Li Shih-yü, the major study of Chinese popular religious scriptures (*pao-chüan*), their types and origins.

Schipper, Kristofer. *Le corps taoïste; corps physique—corps social*. Paris, 1982. A fine survey of Taoist history, ritual, and meditation by the first Western scholar to become an initiated Taoist priest and thus gain access to the oral tradition.

Seidel, Anna. "The Image of the Perfect Ruler in Early Taoist Messianism." *History of Religions* 9 (1969–1970): 216–247. An important study of early Taoist eschatology.

Shih, Vincent Y. C. *The Taiping Ideology*. Seattle, 1967. The most detailed study in English of the religious beliefs of this mid-nineteenth century movement.

Sivin, Nathan. *Chinese Alchemy, Preliminary Studies*. Cambridge, Mass., 1968. A now standard study of the topic.

Strickmann, Michel. "The Mao-shan Revelations: Taoism and the Aristocracy." *T'oung pao* 63 (1977): 1–64. Taoist history, fourth and fifth centuries.

Strickmann, Michel. *Le Taoïsme du Mao-Chan. Chronique d'une révélation*. Paris, 1981. A path-breaking study that reshapes our understanding of Taoist history. Good discussion of important texts.

Strickmann, Michel, ed. *Tantric and Taoist Studies in Honour of R. A. Stein*. 2 vols. Brussels, 1983. Volume two contains several excellent and substantive essays on Taoism.

Suzuki Chūsei. "Sōdai Bukkyō kessha no kenkyū." *Shigaku zasshi* 52 (1941): 65–98, 205–241, 303–333. Important study of the spread of lay Buddhist devotional associations.

T'ang Yung-t'ung. *Han Wei liang Chin Nan-pei-ch'ao fo-chiao shih*. Shanghai, 1938. Long the standard Chinese study of this topic.

Thompson, Laurence G. *Chinese Religion: An Introduction*. 3d ed. Belmont, Calif., 1979. The best one-volume introduction to the topic. Fourth edition in preparation, 1986.

Thompson, Laurence G. *Chinese Religion in Western Languages, A Comprehensive and Classified Bibliography of Publications in English, French and German through 1980*. Tucson, 1985. The only comprehensive bibliography of the subject, organized by topics.

Thompson, Laurence G. *The Chinese Way in Religion*. Belmont, Calif., 1973. A good source book, combining translations of Chinese primary texts with selections from the best scholarly studies.

Tsukamoto Zenryū. *A History of Early Chinese Buddhism: From its Introduction to the Death of Hui-yüan* (1979). 2 vols. Translated by Leon Hurvitz. Tokyo, 1985. By far the most detailed study (1305 pages) of the history of Chinese Buddhism through the early fifth century. Both author and translator are masters of the field.

Ui Hakuju. *Zenshūshi kenkyū*. 3 vols. Tokyo, 1939–1943. The standard Japanese study of the Ch'an school.

Wang Ming. *T'ai-p'ing ching ho-chiao*. Peking, 1960. A work of fundamental importance for the study of the first Taoist scripture produced during the formative period of this tradition in the second century.

Wechsler, Howard J. *Offerings of Jade and Silk: Ritual and Symbol in the Legitimation of the T'ang Dynasty*. New Haven, 1985. The most thorough study in English of medieval Chinese state religion.

Welch, Holmes. *The Practice of Chinese Buddhism, 1900–1950*. Cambridge, Mass., 1967. Thorough study of monastic Buddhism based on interviews with monks.

Welch, Holmes, and Anna Seidel, eds. *Facets of Taoism: Essays in Chinese Religion*. New Haven, 1979. Authoritative essays from the Second International Conference on Taoism, 1972.

Wolf, Arthur P., ed. *Religion and Ritual in Chinese Society*. Stanford, Calif., 1974. An excellent collection of essays by anthropologists, based on fieldwork in Taiwan and Hong Kong on such topics as village temples, shamanism, and the relationship between gods and ghosts. Includes two articles on Taoist ritual.

Yampolsky, Philip B. *The Platform Sutra of the Sixth Patriarch. The Text of the Tun-huang Manuscript, Translated, with Notes*. New York, 1967. The introduction (pp. 1–121) is a reliable guide to modern studies of Ch'an history.

Yanagida Seizan. *Shoki Zenshū shisō no kenkyū*. Kyoto, 1967. Pathbreaking critical study of Ch'an historical legends.

Yang, C. K. *Religion in Chinese Society. A Study of Contemporary Social Functions of Religion and Some of their Historical Factors*. Berkeley, 1961. A classic sociological study, the best and most comprehensive available. Good discussions of relationships between religion and the state, ethical values, diffuse and institutional forms of religious organization.

Yoshioka Yoshitoyo. *Dōkyō to bukkyō*. Tokyo, 1959. Seminal essays on Taoist and Buddhist relations and polemical writings from the Han to the present.

Yoon, Hong-key. *Geomantic Relationships Between Culture and Nature in Korea*. Taipei, 1976. The best study of *feng-shui* in English, based on Chinese texts and fieldwork in Korea.

Zürcher, Erik. *The Buddhist Conquest of China*. 2 vols. Leiden, 1959. Excellent, detailed study of the first Chinese attempts to understand Buddhist philosophy.

Zürcher, Erik. "'Prince Moonlight.' Messianism and Eschatology in Early Medieval Chinese Buddhism." *T'oung pao* 68 (1982): 1–75. A pioneering study of fifth-century eschatology, based on Buddhist scriptures composed in China.

DANIEL L. OVERMYER

Popular Religion

The conglomerate of religious beliefs and practices that pervaded Chinese communities can be referred to as "popular religion." This collection of religious phenomena has no specific name in Chinese—people merely speak of "worshiping the deities" *(pai-shen)* or of worshiping at a specific cult shrine or temple. A loosely structured amalgamation of beliefs, practices, deities, cults, myths, and values, it comprises elements from ancestor worship and the cult of the dead, from nature worship, animism, local cults, popular Taoism, popular Buddhism, and Confucianism. However, the usual Chinese view of the popular religion does not recognize this diversity and simply describes it as a fusion of the Three Doctrines *(san-chiao)*—Confucianism, Taoism, and Buddhism.

By contrast with orthodox Buddhism and Taoism, the popular religion is not highly structured. The most important expression of popular religion is to be seen in local cults, that is, in the sets of beliefs and practices that focus upon the cults of local deities. Even when the same deity is worshiped in several different places each local shrine or temple is autonomous. A temple may be the offshoot of a parent cult, or may even be "friends" with other temples having the same or different primary deity, but the cult it represents is an expression of the sentiment and support of the local community rather than a part of a hierarchy of institutions.

The popular religion pervaded all classes of Chinese people in varying degrees and should not be viewed as exclusively a religion of peasants, the urban poor, or the uneducated. Popular religious practices could be found in the families of even the well educated, either as part of their regular activities or for special purposes (such as the exorcism of evil spirits). This is true even though members of the educated upper class (usually government officials) have traditionally derided such practices and insisted that they believed only in Confucianism or Taoist philosophy. Official hostility to these local cults, and the fragmentary scriptural and historical documentation relating to them, have obscured the history of the popular religion; detailed information mostly dates from no earlier than the nineteenth century.

The various Chinese governments were perennially suspicious of the popular religion as a source of unregulated authority. Consequently, some cults could survive only in secret. The great majority of such secret cults were benign, but during times of very harsh social conditions a few developed extensive organizations and took part in armed insurrection under the banner of messianic deliverance. Such were the Yellow Turbans of the second century and the White Lotus Society of the seventeenth century. Sometimes, secret societies were a source of social disruption and even formed the basis of criminal syndicates, for example, the Triad Society of Hong Kong. [*See* Millenarianism, *article on* Chinese Millenarian Movements.]

Today, the beliefs and practices of popular religion are still part of Chinese life in Taiwan and Hong Kong, and in the overseas Chinese communities of Singapore, Thailand, the Philippines, Indonesia, and even California. The constitution of the People's Republic of China permits the practice of "religion" but not of "superstition." Highly structured religions such as Buddhism, Islam, and Christianity are defined as "religion," while popular religion falls into the category of "superstition." Therefore, popular religious practices are no longer publicly observed and the local temples have all been converted into public buildings such as government offices or markets, or have been demolished. The process of secularizing temple buildings actually began earlier, during the 1920s under the government of the Republic of China, although it was then by no means as thorough or far-reaching. Thus, the present-tense descriptions of popular religion in this essay refer to China before 1949 and to Taiwan, Hong Kong, and the overseas areas up to the mid-1980s.

Beliefs and Values. There is no single sacred text or set of documents that contains all the basic beliefs, doctrines, and values of the popular religion. These basic ideas must be sought instead in many different places and forms: in sacred books, votive art, rites, temple murals, family worship, myths, exemplar tales, and even fiction. That is to say, to a great extent the basic ideas of the popular religion coincide with beliefs and values that pervade Chinese culture as a whole. Such beliefs and values tend to be linked to people's concern with their immediate circumstances, specifically, the survival of the individual, family, and community in a hard and uncertain world. Thus, the object of much religious activity is the prevention or cure of illness, the maintenance of the family and preservation of the family line, the preservation and expansion of the family's resources (such as children, money, and talent), and the well-being of the larger community. Since it is believed that spiritual beings and living people share common needs for sustenance, reciprocity is the basis of the interactions between humans and spirits. Offerings and promises are made to deities with the expectation of tangible help in return—if help is not forthcoming, offerings may be withheld. In turn, ghosts may harass the living in order to obtain sustenance, and will become quiet when propitiated.

Some beliefs are common throughout the popular religion. Heaven *(t'ien),* the divine cosmos, is seen both as a place where the deities and the souls of ancestors reside and as the highest authority controlling the moral direction of the world. In this latter sense, Heaven is often anthropomorphized as the Emperor of Heaven or the Jade Emperor. There are two opposing but interrelated active forces in the world: the *yang* force is positive, light, and dry, and is an attribute of the sun and of males (reflecting the dominant position of males in Chinese society and their importance in the perpetuation of the family line); the *yin* force is negative, dark, and wet, and is an attribute of the moon and of females. The *yin* and *yang* share the same relationship to each other as shade and light do, each being defined in relation to the other, and each contains within itself the generating germ of the other. This is symbolized by a pair of interlocked comma shapes with a dot of the opposite color in the head of each. Most of the phenomena of the physical and social worlds are divided into five categories called the Five Phases (*wu-hsing,* also called Five Elements) and are labeled wood, fire, earth, metal, and water. Colors, seasons, directions, viscera, musical notes, tastes, social virtues, and other phenomena are apportioned among the Five Phases, which are related to each other in dynamic cycles of both generation and decay. Religious symbolism and divination make extensive use of this Five Phases paradigm. [*See* Yin-yang Wu-hsing.]

The span of each human life is decided by the Controller of Fate (Ssu-ming), who records it in a book kept by the rulers of Hell. When one's time has come, bailiffs are sent to bring one to Hell for judgment and punishment for sins. Even though each person's life is governed by fate, fatalism, in the sense of passively allowing the world to work its way, is absent. There is instead a keen interest in fate, because if the course of events can be foreseen, one's life can then be aligned with the direction of fate. It is better to be prepared and go with the current in order to maximize the good of life and minimize the hardship. Consequently, there are numerous forms of divination, from the use of mediums to drawing lots and oracle slips. There are also ways to change or amend one's fate through the selection of an auspicious name, fictive adoption by a deity or a person with great spiritual power, or by seeking the intervention of a powerful deity.

The numerous objectives and values of the popular religion may be divided into six general categories, four concerned with the world of the living and two with the afterlife:

1. Protection of life and property: health and long life, avoidance of accidents, and expulsion of evil spirits
2. Adjustment to the order of nature: favor from the deities controlling rain and drought, careful placement of buildings and graves so as not to disrupt the "energies" believed to be in the earth, and the protection of the guardian deities of the fields and towns
3. Peace and harmony in home life: favor from the deities protecting the hearth and gates, sons to maintain the family line, easy childbirth, protection of children, well-being of the ancestors
4. Success in the struggle for livelihood: favor from the deities of agriculture, fertility, crafts, and wealth
5. Salvation from punishment in Hell: forgiveness of sins, release from suffering
6. Favorable rebirth: reincarnation into a wealthy family, moral perfection in the Buddhist and Taoist heavens

Important beliefs and values are also associated with the cult of ancestors, a significant part of religion since the twelfth century BCE. Preservation of the family line is a crucial objective in all popular religious activities; the family line is regarded as extending back in time to ancestors as well as forward to descendants. Rites to insure the well-being of the earlier members of the family and prayers and rites to beget sons (since the family line is transmitted through the males), are two aspects of the same objective. Great care, and often enormous expense, is devoted to the proper burial of the dead, who must be saved from punishment for sins in Hell, installed among the ancestors, and provided with both immediate and long term sustenance. [*See also* Ancestors, *article on* Ancestor Cults.]

There are many inconsistencies in popular religious belief, but in practice they are of little consequence. What is most important is that rites are carried out sincerely at the proper time and in the proper manner. The family and community must be sustained, the dead must be cared for, and life must go on. Elaborate codification of beliefs and practices are not of great importance, and there is no organization of theologians to debate the details of religious questions.

The beliefs and practices of the popular religion are traditionally divided into those of the "realm of light" *(yang-chieh)*, relating to deities, and those of the "realm of shade" *(yin-chieh)*, relating to the dead. These are not rigidly exclusive categories, however, because there are "bridges" (such as mediums and diviners) through which humans, deities, and the dead can communicate with each other.

The Realm of Light. The Realm of Light includes all beliefs concerning humans and their relations with the deities. There are numerous deities *(shen)* in the popular religion, most of whom are deified humans, although some derive from popular Buddhism, popular Taoism, and nature spirits. Deities are typically depicted in anthropomorphic form, and many cults preserve "biographies" of their deities that clearly reveal their human origins. Popular belief asserts that unusually virtuous humans are rewarded with deification; however, it appears that some deities are humans who died violent deaths or who died without descendants to care for them, and who must therefore serve the public (that is, non-family members) in exchange for sustenance. In this way they are punished for the "sin" of not producing sons who can perpetuate the ancestral sacrifices and the family line.

There is no omnipotent deity, although the Jade Emperor (Yü-huang Shang-ti, also called T'ien-ti or T'ien-kung) is generally acknowledged as chief among the deities. However, his cult is very limited, for he is too distant for a beneficial reciprocal relationship with ordinary people. [*See* Yü-huang.] Beneath the Jade Emperor the ranking of the multitude of other deities is unclear. Varying opinions exist, but the actual hierarchy is not important in practice, since religious activity is focused upon a deity's local cult and the deities are seldom pitted against each other. Generally ghosts of the neglected dead ("homeless ghosts") are regarded as the lowest among the spiritual beings. They are either bought off with minor offerings or exorcised with the aid of a medium and a deity. Even though the rest of the heavenly hierarchy is not clearly delineated, in various ritual practices and myths it is depicted as a bureaucratic organization similar to that of the old Chinese government. The functionaries in Hell form an even more elaborate bureaucratic organization.

Some deities are very powerful, but most function in limited roles. The "gate deities" (*men-shen,* often called "door gods") are depicted as a pair of officials, civil or military, dressed in costumes of about the sixteenth century; they prevent evil spirits from entering the house. An image of the kitchen god, the Lord of the Hearth (Tsao-shen or Tsao-chün), is printed on paper and kept above the kitchen stove. A few days before the New Year, the image's mouth is liberally smeared with honey or sticky candy, then burned; Tsao-chün then ascends to Heaven to report the family's good and bad deeds of that year to the Jade Emperor. Some people say that honey is to insure that the Hearth Deity speaks only sweet words; others say it is to stick his lips together in order to prevent him from speaking altogether.

Some deities specialize in curing illness (such as Hua T'o and Pao-sheng Ta-ti), others control epidemics (such as Tou-shen, who controls smallpox) or locusts. Deities who bring rain in due season and prevent floods are extremely important. They are often "dragon kings" *(lung-wang)*, but can also be powerful local deities. Each craft has its own guardian deity, for example, Lu Pan is the patron of carpentry and Shen-nung that of agriculture. T'ien-shang Sheng-mu (also called Ma-tsu or T'ien-hou) is the protectress of seafarers; her cult is found in all Chinese communities near the oceans. There is even a patron deity of thieves.

Towns and administrative districts each have a patron deity called Deity of Walls and Moats (Ch'eng-huang-shen), also called City God. By the eighth century, the maintenance of this important deity's temple had become a duty of the local government official. Although every City God cult is an independent establishment, they fit into a larger bureaucratic hierarchy parallel to that of the secular authority. The deities are deified humans, and many stories tell of changes made in who should be deified as City God—the previous one was either promoted or demoted and a new person took over. The City God is a divine magistrate who presides over the spiritual affairs of the human magistrate's district. Various subordinate officers and bailiffs, whose images are also in the temple, execute his orders and patrol the district.

An important function of the City God is to represent the bureaucracy of hell in the Realm of Light. When someone is scheduled to die, the City God's bailiff brings the person to the temple, where his or her sins are tallied before he is sent to hell for judgment and punishment. A City God temple can easily be recognized by the giant abacus used to tally sins that hangs on the wall. The City God may help the local official enforce the law; various tales relate how the City God acts as a divine detective to uncover wrongdoers and reveal them to the magistrate.

Well-known subordinates of the City God are the earth deities *(t'u-ti kung* or *fu-te cheng-shen)*, the most humble of all the guardian deities. The earth deities, usually depicted as old men, are the local tutelary deities of the soil. Their tiny shrines guard fields, farms, households, and shops, while their modest-sized temples protect larger neighborhoods or even entire villages.

A few deities are found in nearly all Chinese communities. The most common are Kuan-yin and Kuan-ti. The Kuan-yin (Skt., Avalokiteśvara) of the popular religion is depicted in female form (as opposed to the male *bodhisattva* of the iconographical and scriptural tradition) and was derived from popular Buddhism; she is primarily a deity of mercy who saves people from danger and suffering, but she is also prayed to for other kinds of aid, such as to make a barren woman fruitful. [*See* Avalokiteśvara.] Kuan-ti (also called Kuan-kung) is a deified military hero of the third century. Although he is often called God of War, he is more accurately called Deity of Marital Virtues, since his most important attributes are loyalty and trustworthiness rather than prowess in arms. As a patron of trustworthiness, he is the guardian deity of businessmen and all who deal in contracts. He is the patron deity of law courts, and his portrait often hung behind the judge's chair. During the 1920s and 1930s, the government of the Republic of China promoted his cult to encourage patriotism because he is the patron of patriots and soldiers. He is also the host for certain kinds of divination and spirit-writing séances.

The principle of reciprocity requires deities to be efficacious in responding to the human community. If a deity is perceived as ineffective people will terminate their worship and eventually the cult will fall into oblivion. By contrast, if a local spirit gains a reputation for efficacious response, it may gradually be transformed into a community deity with a temple built to house its cult. Chinese deities have therefore come and gone, a process that continues today.

Shrines and temples. A deity usually presides in a shrine or temple. However, a temple seldom houses only a single deity, for most temples have a primary deity and several secondary deities. Supplicants usually give some kind of recognition to every deity in a temple (at least an obeisance and a stick of incense). A temple is a deity's "home" and therefore is often called a "palace" *(kung);* it can range in size from a tiny roadside shrine to an enormous complex of buildings covering several acres. But a temple is more than a home for a deity. It is also a community center where people meet and rest while their children play in the courtyard. The courtyard, flat and spacious, is used to dry grain during harvest season. The temple is also a repository of the community's values: the elaborate decor in the temple, replete with scenes of heroes and villains illustrating reward and punishment, loyalty, filial piety, and service to the family, is used to teach proper moral and social values to the young. Finally, a temple is a symbol of its community. The largest and most ornate building in a village or neighborhood, it is the center of community activity and its symbol of unity.

Temples of the popular religion do not have resident clergy, in contrast to the temples of Buddhism and Taoism. Daily activities are handled by a caretaker who lives either in the temple or in the immediate vicinity. The caretaker cleans the temple, sells incense and other ritual articles, and occasionally helps supplicants to read the oracle slips. The temple is governed by a committee of local people that raises money for its repair and maintenance, makes policy decisions, and oversees the rites on festival days. Through an elaborate divination process, the temple's deity appoints a "master of the incense brazier" *(lu-chu)* to be the chief celebrant at all ritual activities for the year. A high-ranking priest may be invited to preside over special rites, for example, a Taoist priest for the Rite of Salvation for the dead in the seventh month, or a Buddhist or Taoist priest for a funeral. Low-ranking Taoist priests, who are often illiterate, direct rites for communication with the dead. The Masters of the Incense Brazier, like Taoist and Buddhist priests, do not function outside their roles as ritualists; they do not engage in pastoral work, instruction, or evangelism in the community.

Temples are generally autonomous institutions and are not part of a hierarchical organization. However, when a cult is clearly an offshoot of another cult—when it was established by the ritual transfer of ashes from the deity's sacred incense brazier in the parent temple—a "parent and offspring" relationship between the temples exists. In such cases, the deity's image in the offspring temple is carried back to the parent temple during the major festival of the cult (usually the birthday of the deity) and temporarily installed on the altar, where it is revitalized through contact with the parent image. Temples also establish "friendship" relationships with other temples that may or may not share the same primary cult. Deities and delegations exchange congratulations during festivals, as well as make visits at other times of the year. The Chinese describe these relationships in social terms, "just like a friend coming to visit."

Festivals. Every cult and its associated shrine or temple has at least one major yearly festival focused upon its primary deity. These festivals usually take place on the deity's birthday and are dated in accordance with the Chinese lunar calendar. For a deity's festival day the temple is thoroughly cleaned and the altar elaborately decorated. The deity's image may be given new clothes or a new headdress. The image is often carried throughout the community in an elaborate procession so that the deity can observe its realm and confer blessings upon the inhabitants. Supplicants come in large numbers to pray and offer incense, candles, food, and "spirit money" (paper imitations of gold leaf and money—the deities need money just as humans do). After sufficient time has elapsed for the deity to consume the "essence" of the food, the supplicants take their offerings home to be prepared as a banquet. Food offerings vary according to the occasion and the requirements of the cult—some deities are vegetarians and some are not—but in general consist of staples (rice or steamed bread), fish, meat, fruit, and pastries, some made especially for the occasion. Associated with religious festivals are theatricals and puppet plays put on for the entertainment of the deities and the community. Subjects and styles range from tragedy to comedy but always incorporate the proper moral and social values, so that good deeds are rewarded and evil deeds punished.

Some festivals are common to all communities, most notably the lunar New Year and the Ghost Festival. The New Year festival is one of the most important religious events of the year, although it has become highly secularized in recent times. It is a time for tying up the loose ends of the old year and starting afresh in the new. People clean and repair their houses, buy new clothes, and pay off old debts; everyone takes a vacation from work (from four to fifteen days, depending on one's means) in order to return home to the family. A visit to the local temple is part of the New Year celebration. Prayers for the welfare of the community are offered to the Jade Emperor on the ninth day of the new year, and the festival season concludes with the Lantern Festival on the fifteenth day.

The Ghost Festival (Kuei-chieh) is closely associated with the Realm of Shade. It is believed that during the seventh month the gates of Hell are opened and all the hungry and homeless ghosts are allowed to roam the world. To propitiate these ghosts, whom the Chinese liken to beggars, rites of salvation *(p'u-tu)* are performed at all the temples on the fifteenth day, and large quantities of food are set out to feed the hungry ghosts. The *p'u-tu* rite was originally a Buddhist ritual, but in recent times it is commonly presided over by a high-ranking Taoist priest.

Other major festivals in the lunar calendar are the Dragon Boat (fifth day of the fifth month), the Weaving Girl and Herd Boy (seventh day of the seventh month), Mid-Autumn (fifteenth day of the eighth month), and the Double-Yang (ninth day of the ninth month). The first three were originally joyous religious festivals, but they have become highly secularized during the twentieth century. The Double-Yang festival still retains an undercurrent of dread since it is a day to wear protective amulets and ascend the mountains in order to avoid evil influences in the lowlands.

The only major festival that does not follow the lunar calendar is the day of Clear and Bright (Ch'ing-ming), which follows a traditional solar reckoning and always occurs on April fifth. A festival to commemorate the dead, on this day the family visits the cemetery, where members repair the graves and offer food and incense to the ancestors. This is also called the Grave-sweeping Festival (Sao-mu). [*For further discussion of these festivals, see* Chinese Religious Year.]

A special rite performed when a temple is newly built or renovated—once in twenty or more years—is the Rite of Cosmic and Community Renewal (Chiao) in which the temple and the entire community are renewed, revitalized, and realigned with the forces of the cosmos. The Chiao is an extraordinarily elaborate and expensive activity, but it is also an extremely important event in the community's religious life. [*See* Chiao *and* Priesthood, *article on* Taoist Priesthood.]

Religious instruction. Although many dramatic religious activities take place in the temples, other important aspects of popular religion are carried out at home, usually by the women in the family. The altar in the central room of the house holds images of the family's patron deities as well as the family's ancestral images and tables. Regular offerings to deities are prepared on the second and sixteenth days of each month; offerings are made to the ancestors on their birth and death days as well as on special festival days. Since the women of the family are prominent in the lives of young children, the example and instruction they provide are major influences on the children's later religious attitudes. The women tell stories, take the children to the temples, show them the murals, and explain their moral lessons. Secular education in modern schools often derides popular religion as "superstition," but many of the basic moral, social, and religious conceptions of the young are shaped by the activities of the family. [*See* Domestic Observances, *article on* Chinese Practices.]

More formal sources of religious teaching are the moralistic tracts *(shan-shu)* that are distributed free, as acts of merit, in most temples. The history of these booklets goes back several centuries and their evolution as vehicles of religious doctrine and values is closely related to the spread of literacy and the development of inexpensive printing technology. These tracts, averaging a scant twenty pages in length, are usually associated with a specific deity and contain the appropriate rites and prayers for approaching that deity, a description of the deity's authority, and a revelation from the deity containing injunctions for correct belief, worship, and behavior. Sometimes, testimonials to the efficacy of the deity are also appended. Testimonials to the results of good and evil behavior form the content of other moralistic tracts. The ancient belief that good deeds result in reward while evil brings suffering was developed in China before the arrival of Buddhism. This belief was amplified in the doctrines of popular Buddhism into an elaborate system of retribution *(yin-kuo)* for good and evil deeds. Accounts of such retribution, found in numerous Chinese texts, both religious and secular, also figure prominently in the ubiquitous moralistic tracts. The tracts contain injunctions to respect Heaven and the deities, to obey superiors, be filial toward parents and elders, kind to juniors, strict with children, careful in selecting friends, and polite to neighbors. There are injunctions against killing, stealing, lying, slander, adultery, covetousness, laziness, hypocrisy, insincerity, boasting, complaining, anger, extravagance, waste, drunkenness, gambling, and whoring.

Although the moralistic tracts are good sources of religious knowledge, they were useful only to those who could read, the number of whom until recent decades comprised only a small percentage of the population. Therefore, the teachings and examples of religion at home and in the theatricals at religious festivals constituted the main vehicles of religious instruction for the great majority of people. [*See also* Drama, *article on* East Asian Dance and Theater.]

The Realm of Shade. The dark side of popular religion is concerned with death, for the newly dead, ancestors, and ghosts must all be attended to in proper form. Ideally in Chinese culture, death came only after one has lived a long life, produced many sons and grandsons, and accumulated wealth enough to provide for the family and for one's own funeral. One hoped to die with the body intact and unharmed, a peaceful death at home with all the family in attendance. Elderly people often purchased a coffin and prepared for their own funerals long before they died. Funeral rites varied from place to place in China, but each had specific requirements for the preparation of the corpse, encoffining, burial, and mourning. Buddhist and Taoist priests are engaged to perform the funeral rites, which include rituals to save the dead from harsh judgment and punishment in Hell. The coffin is carried to the cemetery in a procession, the extent and elaborateness of which varies with the economic circumstances of a family. The funeral procession for a wealthy man often stretches out for more than a kilometer, and includes several bands (both traditional and modern brass bands), floats, clowns, bright costumes, and flowers, as well as mourners and the coffin. The noisy pageantry is partly to distract the mourners in their grief and partly to display the dead person's resources to the rest of the community. It is traditional to bury the body and construct a mound over the grave. However, people who have strong orthodox Buddhist beliefs prefer cremation. (In addition, cremation has become the common practice in the People's Republic of China in order to conserve land.) In some parts of South and Southeast China, a family will sometimes exhume the coffin after about seven years, clean the bones, pack them into an urn, and rebury them in a more auspicious place.

Geomancy and Burial. Selecting a burial site is an important and complex procedure. In order to maximize the potential of the earth's "energies" by channeling them through the bones of the deceased, and in order to provide a safe and beautiful home for the new ancestor, a specialist in the geomantic art of siting (*feng-shui*, literally "wind and water") is engaged to locate the most auspicious site for burial. In the best site the mountains, rivers, and wind are related in an especially favorable configuration. *Feng-shui* can be seen as a proto-science that seeks to understand those aspects of the earth's configurations that determine the most appropriate site for a grave or building. Or, since the best grave sites are found in places of the greatest natural beauty, it can also be regarded as an art of natural aesthetics. [*See also* Divination.]

Since the dead are believed to have needs similar to those of the living, during the funeral these needs are supplied in the form of a house, furniture, carriage (nowadays an automobile or airplane), servants, and money, all made of paper and burned at the burial site. Mourning is continuous for a set period after the burial, intermittent for the next period, and then recurs only on the anniversary of the deceased's birth and death and on special festivals that commemorate the dead. A wooden tablet with the deceased's formal name and titles is installed on the family's ancestral altar; part of the dead person's soul (the *yang* aspect, or *hun*) comes to reside in the tablet, and thus the dead person joins the ancestors. [*See also* Soul, *article on* Chinese Concepts.]

Judgment and punishment in Hell. The *yin* aspect (or *p'o*) of the dead person's soul must descend to Hell to be judged and punished for evil deeds committed during life. Hell is better described as purgatory since its purpose is to examine the deeds of life, to set the punishment, and to determine one's level of reincarnation into another life. The Ten Courts of Hell, an adaptation from popular Buddhism, are commonly depicted in a set of paintings displayed at funerals, providing another opportunity for parents to instruct their children on the consequences of evil deeds. Each of the courts, in imitation of earthly bureaucracy, is presided over by a judge, depicted as a sixteenth-century government official, and his subordinates: record keepers, accountants, bailiffs (the two best known are Ox-head and Horse-face), jailors, and torturers. In the First Court is a great mirror in which all the deeds of one's life are displayed. People of perfect virtue are sent directly to the Tenth Court, while the rest are dispatched to other courts that specialize in punishments for specific sins. The punishments are gruesomely physical and last for aeons; the only psychological torture is to ascend the Tower for Gazing at Home where one looks at the loved ones with whom one can never be rejoined.

After the requisite punishments one comes to the Tenth Court, where final judgment on the level of reincarnation is made. The five states of incarnation for all living beings are derived from popular Buddhism: one may be born as a deity, human, animal, demon, or once again among the suffering beings of Hell. Reincarnation is determined by the deeds of the former life—good deeds beget a favorable reincarnation while evil deeds propel one into a suffering life, as a sick or impoverished human or as an animal. After judgment in the Tenth Court, an old woman called Mother Meng gives each person a cup of the "wine of forgetfulness." The punishments are forgotten and, reincarnated with a clean memory, one must choose again whether to do good or evil. [*See also* Afterlife, *article on* Chinese Concepts.]

The restless dead. If the dead are well cared for, that is, if their graves are maintained and they are provided with sustenance through regular offerings, they will rest in peace and may even confer blessings upon their descendants. When they are not properly treated, however, their displeasure will be manifested to their family. Troubles such as family quarrels, crop or business failure, illness, and lack of sons are often attributed to the wrath of the ancestors.

When a spiritual origin for the family troubles is suspected, a medium may be called in to diagnose the situation. There are several kinds of mediums who communicate with the dead by different means. Some go on spiritual journeys during a seance, others go into a trance that allows the dead to speak through their mouths, still others use divination devices (such as a small chair, writing brush, or a stick in a tray of sand) that, when possessed by a deity, relay messages from the dead. Through the medium, the aggrieved ancestor is identified, his or her grievance is explained, and the proper remedy is prescribed. It is believed that if the family accedes to the ancestor's demands and makes the necessary corrections in proper ritual form, the ancestor will be appeased and will cease to cause trouble to the family.

The mediums may be either male or female, young or old. They become mediums after receiving a summons from a particular deity and subsequently undergo training under the guidance of an older medium. A medium is usually attached to a particular deity and can be possessed in the deity's temple or in a temporary shrine set up especially for the occasion. Mediums are not supposed to accept payment for service to their deities, so they earn their livings in other occupations. However, some accept "gifts," and unscrupulous ones will take advantage of the gullible. Most deities have at least one medium in their service, but some deities (such as Tung-yüeh Ta-ti) who specialize in helping people communicate with the dead and whose temples and shrines are devoted to this activity have several mediums.

Sometimes the source of family troubles is a ghost who is not related to the family, or even some sort of demon. In such cases the remedy is exorcism, since there is no need to appease a nonancestral spirit. There are many varieties of exorcism, but they commonly employ strong spells, burning torches, firecrackers, menacing weapons, and threats to the offending spirit. A powerful deity may even be invoked to aid in the exorcism.

Finally, there are the neglected and homeless ghosts. At least for self-protection, if not out of compassion, the living must take care of these homeless ones or they will harass the community in order to satisfy their needs, which are quite meager. Small offerings are placed outside the back door of the house (as the Chinese explain, "You don't invite beggars inside your house"), and larger offerings are provided at the *p'u-tu* rites for the dead in the seventh month. Special shrines are built to house human bones that are unearthed during plowing or construction. They are the bones of homeless ghosts and can be cared for collectively with small offerings.

Humans, ancestors, deities, and ghosts all have their places in the popular religion and all interact with each other. The needs of the living and the dead, the incarnate and the spiritual are reciprocally satisfied that the family and community may survive and perpetuate themselves in an uncertain, and usually difficult, world.

BIBLIOGRAPHY

The most complete bibliography on Chinese popular religion is Laurence G. Thompson's *Chinese Religion in Western Languages: A Comprehensive and Classified Bibliography of Publications in English, French, and German through 1980* (Tucson, 1985). A good survey of religion in China, including popular religion, is Thompson's *Chinese Religion: An Introduction*, 3d ed. (Belmont, Calif., 1979); Thompson's *The Chinese Way in Religion* (Encino, Calif., 1973) is a useful collection of readings covering a wide variety of religious beliefs and practices in China. Popular religion in a village is described by David K. Jordan in his *Gods, Ghosts, and Ancestors: The Folk Religion of a Taiwanese Village* (Berkeley, 1972). A fine study of the complexities of the ancestor cult is Emily M. Ahern's *The Cult of the Dead in a Chinese Village* (Stanford, Calif., 1973). Many useful articles on specific aspects of popular religion are in the volume edited by Arthur P. Wolf, *Religion and Ritual in Chinese Society* (Stanford, Calif., 1974), such as "Gods, Ghosts, and Ancestors" by Wolf, and "When a Ghost Becomes a God" by C. Stevan Harrell; and in the volume edited by Sarah Allan and myself, *Legend, Lore, and Religion in China: Essays in Honor of Wolfram Eberhard on His Seventieth Birthday* (San Francisco, 1979), such as "Chinese Glyphomancy *(ch'ai-tzu)* and Its Uses in Present-Day Taiwan" by Wolfgang Bauer. Wolfram Eberhard uses moralistic tracts to study some basic moral conceptions in *Guilt and Sin in Traditional China* (Berkeley, 1967) and has collected many of his insightful articles exploring beliefs and values in *Moral and Social Values of the Chinese: Collected Essays* (Taipei, 1971).

A large collection of translations from original sources is J. J. M. de Groot's *The Religious System of China: Its Ancient Forms, Evolution, History and Present Aspect, Manners, Customs and Social Institutions Connected Therewith*, 6 vols. (1892–1910; reprint, Taipei, 1967), although de Groot's commentary is rather biased. Henri Maspero's "The Mythology of Modern China," in his *Taoism and Chinese Religion*, translated by Frank A. Kierman, Jr. (Amherst, Mass., 1981), includes a description of many deities in the pantheon, as does Clarence Burton Day's examination of the ubiquitous votive pictures of popular religion, *Chinese Peasant Cults: Being a Study of Chinese Paper Gods* (1940; reprint, Taipei, 1974).

The yearly round of festivals is presented in Wolfram Eberhard's *Chinese Festivals* (1952; rev. ed., Taipei, 1972) and in Juliet Bredon and Igor Mitrophanow's *The Moon Year: A Record of Chinese Customs and Festivals* (1927; reprint, New York, 1966). Michael R. Saso's *Taoism and the Rite of Cosmic Renewal* (Pullman, Wash., 1972) describes the complex *chiao* rite. Ch'ing-k'un Yang's *Religion in Chinese Society: A Study of Contemporary Social Functions of Religion and Some of Their Historical Factors* (Berkeley, 1961), shows the prevalence of popular religion among all social classes. Daniel L. Overmyer's *Folk Buddhist Religion: Dissenting Sects in Late Traditional China* (Cambridge, Mass., 1976) examines messianic religion and its social and political effects. Two other works bear mentioning for the historical and anthropological insights they bring to the study of Chinese religion: Derk Bodde's *Festivals in Classical China* (Princeton, 1975) and Francis L. K. Hsu's *Under the Ancestor's Shadow* (London, 1949).

ALVIN P. COHEN

Mythic Themes

"Who was there to pass down the story of the beginning of things in the remote past? What means are there to examine what it was like before heaven above and earth below had taken shape?" (Hawkes, 1959, p. 46). These cryptic queries, the very first of the "Heavenly Questions" found in the *Ch'u-tz'u* anthology of the early third century BCE, simultaneously suggest the significant presence and problematic nature of ancient Chinese mythology. The fact that myths—stories of the "beginning of things"—were an important subject in the life and literature of ancient China is indicated by the tantalizing diversity of mythic episodes and personnel so familiarly alluded to in the *Ch'u-tz'u* and in other early Chinese literary and artistic works. At the same time, the interrogative format and enigmatic terseness of the "Heavenly Questions" aptly dramatize the overall riddle posed by ancient Chinese mythology.

The Problem of Chinese Myth. There are allusive mythological references in archaic Chinese literature but they are almost always fragmented and disguised in ways that make it very difficult to determine the character and import of specific myths. Moreover, while the rich zoomorphic iconography found on the Shang and Chou dynasty bronze ritual vessels suggests a dualistic system of shamanistic symbolism, the highly stylized and formulaic nature of the evidence (e.g., the bipartite animal mask design known as the *t'ao-t'ieh*) and the lack of any consistent correlation between artistic and literary evidence allow for only very tentative conclusions as to the prevailing mythological universe of meaning. Instead of coherent stories of the gods, animal ancestors, and semi-divine sage-kings of the sacred time of the beginnings, there are only bits and pieces of various myths that pointedly raise the difficult methodological question of knowing "what means there are to examine" such an apparently unmythical deposit of myth.

This situation is compounded by the fact that, while China is not wholly unusual in possessing only fragmented and composite mythological materials from the ancient period, early sinological scholarship tended to portray China as uniquely deficient in mythology. Indeed, assumptions concerning the special "poverty" of Chinese mythology, especially in relation to creation myths, were generally used to support scholarly judgments concerning the essentially "philosophical," "humanistic," or "historical" nature of the ancient tradition. Such opinions about the largely nonmythological and nonreligious character of early China have a long pedigree in the history of scholarship that was reinforced by both orthodox Chinese scholiasts and "enlightened" Western academicians who equated ancient Chinese culture with the "great tradition" of the Confucian classics and agreed on the irrational and degenerate role of religion and myth in human culture.

This discussion will be limited to mythic materials and themes specifically related to the ancient origins, early cultural development, and ultimate political coalescence of Chinese tradition—that is, the formative historical period that extends from the Hsia (tentatively identified with the preliterate Erh-li-t'ou culture) and Shang dynasties of the late third and second millennia, down through the feudal conditions and intellectual ferment in the Chou period (tenth through third centuries), and to the rise of the early Ch'in and Han imperial traditions during the last few centuries before the common era. In contrast to notions of a monolithic classical tradition going back to the prehistoric beginnings of sinitic civilization and as indicated by the "southern" provenance of the *Ch'u-tz'u,* cultural development during the foundational period is best viewed as a dynamic amalgamative process that gradually incorporated various "local" and "barbarian" cultures.

Broken Stories and Thematic Function. It may be possible to find a culture or religion without myths, or with very weakly developed mythological traditions, and it is true that ancient China did have a special preoccupation with ritual behavior. Be this as it may, the pioneering work of Henri Maspero, Marcel Granet, Ku Chieh-kang, Carl Hentze, and Edouard Erkes in the 1920s and 1930s—along with the corroborating efforts of Bernhard Karlgren and Wolfram Eberhard in the 1940s—showed that the supposed absence or special poverty of Chinese mythic fabulation was a view that could not be sustained. As is seen in the clash between Karlgren's historicist perspective and the various comparative methods of some of the other scholars, there was no final agreement as to what could actually be known of the ancient myths, but it is demonstrably certain that mythological traditions played an important role in early Chinese culture.

The increased interdisciplinary study and appreciation of the early Chinese religion and mythology in contemporary scholarship (especially noteworthy is the work of Kwang-chih Chang, Sarah Allan, Rémi Mathieu, Jean Levi, Michael Loewe, and John Major) confirm the conclusions from the first part of this century. This work, together with the unavoidable judgment that recent archaeological discoveries (including epigraphical, textual, and extra-literary evidence) clearly document the centrality of cosmological and religious ideas in ancient China, collectively underscore the vital significance of mythic themes not only for "nonorthodox" materials like the *Ch'u-tz'u, Shan-hai ching,* or *Chuang-tzu,* but also for the classically standardized works espoused by Confucian and imperial tradition. In addition to this, and despite the caution that must be employed when analyzing ancient Chinese documents, there is a growing consensus that Karlgren's strictures against using the "systematized" Han dynasty materials for reconstructing ancient mythology, and his idea that much of Han mythology was an *ad hoc* product of that period, need to be amended. Thus, it is unreasonable to suppose that mythological materials found primarily in Han sources were a fabrication disconnected from earlier traditions. Furthermore, the very fact of a cosmological "system" of thought in the Han dynasty often indicates something important about the nature and function of earlier myths.

Ancient Chinese culture is not an example of an ancient religious or ritual tradition without mythology. The question one must ask is how and why the myths—or the particular recurrent and overlapping constellations of mythic themes, figures, and images from various local cultures—were preserved, combined, and transformed in certain patterned ways within different textual traditions. Given the compelling assumption that there were active oral traditions of myth-telling in both aristocratic and folk circles, it is probably the case that myths in a coherent storied form were present in ancient China. But the more addressable and interesting question is why the broken shards of mythic narratives were so often used in particular thematic ways in different written documents. The very fact that myths were written down in a fractured and composite way most likely indicates that individual mythic traditions were losing some of their original sacred, cultic, or religiously functional character. It still must be asked, however, whether or not the thematic glosses on myth, or the skeletal remains of mythic narratives, found in written sources may still function mythically—even when they appear in the profanized guise of "history" or "philosophy."

In this sense, also, it may be questioned whether the oft-repeated claim that Chinese texts represent a curious instance of the "reverse euhemerization" of earlier mythic stories has any real significance. If "reverse euhemerization" refers to the false historicization of myth, making myths appear real, rather than the making of myths from actual historical events as the standard definition of euhemerization would have it, then it nevertheless seems that the intellectual and imaginative process involved was still primarily mythical in nature. In both cases "history" was fit to the demands of mythic form. Both types of "euhemerization" are made up yet are to some degree historically factual.

Ancient Chinese literature is basically nonnarrative in any extended sense and is not informed by myth in the overarching, dramatic, and epic way of some other ancient literatures. From a structural point of view, however, mythological thought may be seen primarily as an intellectual and imaginative strategy of "bricolage" that constantly juggles, rearranges, and transforms assorted mythological signs—bits and pieces—according to a deeper code of relational contrast and dynamic synthesis. The cultural function and communicative power of myth is to be found at the structural level that perdures beneath the shifting surface dimension of particular mythic images or narrative plot development. What is preserved, and what continues to function mythically in early Chinese literature, therefore, are the thematic structures of different myths that most generally stress formulas of order and disorder, qualities, relations, and states of being as opposed to an interconnected narrative flow of motivations, action, and consequences. It is this basic emphasis on mythic structure over mythic narrative in Chinese literature that may be related, as Andrew Plaks suggests, to the distinctive Chinese concern with ritual issues of correlative spatial relationship.

Thus understood, the bits and pieces of myth found in ancient Chinese texts betray a kind of slated thematic pattern, or repetitive static structure, that functions as an exemplary frame for determining the significance of the past for the present and future. In this way, the constantly changing reality of nature and social life only demonstrated to the ancient Chinese that "history," like the Tao as the first principle of mythic transformation, always stays relatively and structurally the same. Aside from the different manipulations of selected mythical themes seen in particular textual traditions, the underlying abstract logic of mythical thought—stressing binary structural opposition, tertiary synthesis, and numerically coded relational permutation—dwells at the heart of the *yin-yang wu-hsing* cosmological system that became universal in the Han dynasty. [*See* Yin-yang Wu-hsing.]

These considerations concerning the thematic presence and structural function of myth in China are helpful in providing some means of answering the *Ch'u-tz'u*'s "Heavenly Questions," but they do not obviate the fact that formidable problems of content and method still complicate the study of ancient Chinese mythology. Suffice it to say that the basic thematic contours of archaic mythology may be known with reasonable confidence for periods as early as the Western and Eastern Chou dynasties and that it is possible, and desirable, to work with this material inasmuch as it reflects on, and informs, the overall history of archaic Chinese religion; the differing visions of life seen among the various philosophical movements emerging during the Eastern Chou period; the development of a shared tradition of "correlative thought"; and, most generally, the "organismic" Chinese worldview.

Thematic Repertory: Beginnings and Return. Working with the remnants of myths, or more accurately, with composite mythic units found variously in the earliest texts, makes it possible to reconstruct what may be called a typological "sacred history" of the "beginning of things in the remote past." It must be stressed that this typology is only a partial digest of some of the more representative and recurrent mythic themes and that the sequential movement from cosmic to civilizational origins is an artificial construct of a generalized structural logic or mythic grammar inherent in much of early Chinese thought.

By the time of the Han dynasty all of the basic typological themes were shared as a common inheritance of mythic lore, but it is never the case that the different units were fully articulated in the manner presented here—although the eclectically "Taoist" compendium known as the *Huai-nan-tzu* (c. 100 BCE) comes close to being a comprehensive synthetic handbook of Chinese mythic history. [*See the biography of Liu An.*] It is also important to note that the use or exclusion of particular mythic units is a salient factor for distinguishing different textual and ideological traditions. Myth to some extent always refers to the issue of "beginnings" or world foundation. Where the archetypal beginnings are located in the remote past with respect to a particular conception of "world" and "order" will, therefore, have a significant relation to the different understandings of human nature and social life seen in various ideological movements emerging in the Eastern Chou period.

The typology developed here also does not suggest any actual historical priority in the sequential arrangement of thematic units since, for example, it seems from the documentary evidence that full-fledged cosmogonic themes only coincided with the rise of philosophical speculation during the Eastern Chou period, whereas various clan origin myths and cosmic disaster themes can be reliably traced to the much earlier Western Chou dynasty, or perhaps even to the Shang period. In fact, in relation to the datable appearance of individual mythic units and images in extant literary and extra-literary sources, and as a counterpoint to the typological sequence, there was an apparent movement from the earliest myths of clan origin, animal ancestors, and the closeness of heaven and earth to the later myths of the Eastern Chou period, where an antagonistic relationship among men, animals, and the gods was often emphasized. It was in this later period (roughly after the eighth century BCE) that a diminished faith in an active "sky" or "high god" (Shang-ti, T'ien) and the appearance of nontheistic cosmogonic themes, hybrid man-animal mythological imagery, myths of the combat of cultural saviors with chaotic forces, and the accounts of sage-kings and model emperors as "civilizational transformers" came to the fore. [*See* Shang-ti *and* T'ien.] There is an evident relation here with changes in the aristocratic religious tradition, social-political life, and kinship practices that may be linked with the emergence of philosophical and humanistic thought. It is, however, not so much a matter of philosophical or "rational" thought replacing mythic "irrationality" as a question of differing conceptualizations, still modeled on mythic structures and themes, as to what constitutes the fundamental principles of existential "order."

With these various qualifications in mind, it is feasible to consider the overall typological repertory of mythic themes arranged under the four general headings of (1) cosmic and human beginnings, (2) cosmic disasters, beginning again, and cultural saviors, (3) civilizational beginnings, sage-kings, and model emperors, and (4) returning to the beginning as the cultivated renewal of individual and social life. This scheme of four phases of "beginning" has interrelated diachronic and synchronic implications. Diachronically, there is a progressive movement from the cosmic, natural, early cultural, and later civilizational orders or worlds, but structurally each stage represents a new beginning that recapitulates an earlier cosmic situation. The sacred history of the various human worlds as a series of new beginnings presupposes a constant return to some "first" condition of cosmic unity as the precondition for a new creation or renewal of life. In this way there is a kind of cosmogonic intentionality and cosmological methodology that, while not always stated, implicitly informs the ancient Chinese understanding of existence. While the literary use of myths may be broken from specific earlier cultic traditions, there is very much of a religiously "salvational" vision here that is designed to establish and maintain contact between man and the cosmos. The idea of the "sacred," as Mircea Eliade says, "does not necessarily imply belief in God or gods and spirits" (*Ordeal by Labyrinth,* Chicago, 1982, p. 154); rather, it is primarily the experience of existing in a world made meaningful and real by its connections with a greater cosmic order.

Cosmic and human beginnings. There are several clusters of mythic images and themes that are concerned with the question of existential origins and a kind of "fall" from the formative first order of things. From the standpoint of the mythic logic suggested by most of these materials, the primary structural category refers to the primordial, or very first, issue of world creation.

Cosmogonic origins. Contrary to claims that ancient China was devoid of any kind of authentic creation mythology, there was certainly a genre of explicit cosmogonic speculation during the Eastern Chou period that was thematically rooted in the mythic image of a primal chaotic monad or raviolo known as *hun-tun* (variously imagined as a cosmic egg, gourd, rock, sac, dumpling, etc.; also personified as a strangely "faceless" and Humpty-Dumpty-like emperor of the "center" in the *Chuang-tzu* or as a divine bird in the *Shan-hai ching*). *Hun-tun* was that primordial condition or ancestral figure that gave rise to the multiplicity of the phenomenal world through a spontaneous process of separation (i.e., the splitting of the chaotic "one" into the dual cosmic structure of heaven and earth) or transformation (i.e., the metamorphosis of the "one" body of the primal animal ancestor into the multiple parts of the cosmos). The *hun-tun* theme also seems to have incorporated other mythic variants that told of the creative activites of "world parents" or some consanguineous male and female pair of deities (e.g., Fu Hsi and Nu-kua) who generate the world through their incestuous sexual union. These themes, moreover, clearly represent the archaic prototype for the later (c. third to sixth century) depictions of P'an-ku as the primal man or chaos giant who was born from the embryonic *hun-tun.* [*See also* Chaos.]

The theme of the primal unity and precivilizational innocence of the chaotic *hun-tun* is most prominent in the ancient Taoist texts as a metaphor for the "chaotic order," untrammeled freedom, and wholeness of human nature and primitive society, which can be reattained by means of a kind of internalized mystical reversal of the cosmogony. In the guise of P'an-ku, the *hun-tun* theme is associated with the incarnate "cosmic body" of Lao-chün, the revealed savior in later sectarian Taoism. In the classics and other Confucian-inspired texts of the ancient period, on the other hand, the image of *hun-tun* is never presented in a cosmogonic context and is only rarely mentioned as a personified barbarian rebel (Hun-tun) who dangerously challenged the proper ritual order of civilizational life. The underlying structure and logic of the *hun-tun* creation scenario also may be related to the shared cosmological system of *yin-yang* dualism and to the idea of a "third term" or mediating principle (i.e., the cosmological ether known as *ch'i* or the principle of man/shaman/emperor/priest) between the two things of heaven and earth. Most generally, the *hun-tun* theme of a self-generated creational process without a creator is most explicit in the early Taoist texts, but may be said to inform the cosmological metaphysics associated with the ubiquitous ultimate principle of the Tao.

Lay of the land. Themes associated with the creative fashioning, cosmetic arranging, or cartographic determining of the cosmos are found more often than actual cosmogonic accounts; they most often imply that a world inhabited by mankind already existed. Despite this overt fixation on a preexisting human world, it seems that a prior world populated by gods and animal spirits is often intended. Whatever the case may be, the major thematic emphasis is placed on the sacred patterns of space and time that are common to gods or mankind and, in this sense, many different mythic units may be grouped together as cosmographical accounts of the "first" order of material existence.

Throughout most of the earliest texts, and as displayed by iconographical symbolism, there are a number of basic recurrent images that collectively describe the original divine form of things—for example, the image of the heavens as round and the earth as square and the tripartite division of a lower, middle, and upper realm together with the idea of an axis or pillar(s) that connects what is above and below. Various other themes link patterns of space and time so that the solar cycle is said to involve the sequential daily passage of one of ten suns from a sacred mulberry tree in the east to another tree in the extreme west. In general, themes of the sun and moon, as well as those of other celestial bodies, were important in classical sources as indications of the regular cycles of cosmic life as related to the ritual calendar and social order.

Although specific ancient myths of an earth deity are hard to identify (Yü and Huang-ti betray some traces of this kind of figure), the cosmic structure of the natural landscape of the earth is suggested by the prominence given to sacred mountains such as T'ai or K'un-lun (and certain gourd-shaped islands in the eastern sea) that may be taken as the Chinese equivalent to the universal idea of an *axis mundi* connecting the heaven and earth. [*See also* Axis Mundi.] This emphasis on what is "above" and "below" the human landscape and on the sacred lay of the land, especially on those distant and hidden places on the earth that give access to the heavens or otherworld of the ancestors, is also thematically connected with the common motif of a shamanic and initiatory journey between the heaven and earth, or to the mountains, paradise islands, and chaos regions beyond the conventional order of the "middle kingdom." Traveling in space in this way symbolically represents a journey back in time to the pristine conditions of the freshly created cosmos.

Human origins. Aside from a few minor references to Nu-kua, who was said to have created humankind by dragging a string in some mud, most of the accounts that deal with human origins recall clan origin myths that tell of the divine creation of the founding ancestor or "first man" of the ruling families of the early dynasties. Most of this material has been reworked and retrospectively systematized, but a general pattern that has some affinity with a kind of "virgin birth" motif related to the cosmogonic image of a primal egg, rock, or gourd can be detected (e.g., the fragmented origin accounts of the Ssu clan of the Hsia dynasty and the Tzu clan of the Shang dynasty). The most elaborate mythic remnants, as recounted in the *Shih ching,* tell of the descent of the Chou dynasty from the "abandoned one" known as Hou Chi (Lord Millet) whose mother gave birth after she had stepped into the footprint left on earth by the heavenly supreme god (T'ien, Shang-ti?). Fragments of this nature thematically hint at very ancient totemic beliefs. As an assertion of the divine origins and chosen status of a particular ancestral grouping of mankind they were used to support the exclusivist political claims of aristocratic privilege. In this way they represent the contextual mythic prototype for the classical theory of the *t'ien-ming* ("mandate of Heaven") that from the Chou period on was used by the *t'ien-tzu* ("son of Heaven") to sanction the legitimacy of dynastic authority.

Rupture and fall. In Chinese tradition there is no theme of the sinful fall of man or the intrinsic corruption of human nature comparable to what is seen in Western monotheistic traditions, but it is recognized that man somehow does not enjoy the kind of regular harmony and spontaneous virtue that existed in some distantly past period. There is, therefore, a typical Chinese idea of a series of "falls," some of which were not as inevitable, necessary, and permanent as others. Within a cosmic context there was the necessary "separation of Heaven and earth" that created the space that made both natural and human life possible. However, in the course of mythic time there was also a second separation, or rupture, of the ongoing communication between the divine world of the gods and ancestors and the earthly world of mankind. The best known example of this is seen in the two ancient accounts of Chung-li (or Chung and Li as separate figures), who cut the cord binding Heaven and earth after Shang-ti's displeasure over the disruption on earth caused by troublesome barbarian peoples. The issue here seems to be a clash between two rival ritual systems associated with different clan traditions, but the underlying implication is that a "separation" and distinction between two different "orders," divine and human or civilized and barbarian, is inevitable and necessary. Aside from the passing reference to some divine unhappiness over the licentious practice of one rebellious group of mankind, the important point is that the incident was not interpreted as an act of wrathful divine retribution.

Another expression of the idea of a ruptured linkage between heaven and earth concerns the breaking of one of the cosmic pillars (Mount Pu-chou to the northwest) by the "chaos" monster known as Kung-kung (also associated with the deluge theme, and like Hun-tun often identified with rebels and barbarians that threaten the virtuous order of dynastic civilization). This rupture caused the tilt of the ecliptic (i.e., the orbital plane of the moving heavenly bodies—suggesting some affinity with pan-Eurasian astronomical origin myths) and required that rivers flow to the southeast. In one extant account Nu-Kua is presented as a female fashioning deity who repairs the earth (after the disruption caused by Kung-kung?) by smelting together multicolored stones and creating new heavenly props from a turtle's legs. Again, there is an acceptance of the necessarily "flawed" nature of things but no real suggestion that Kung-kung's blundering actions were "sinful" in a way that utterly precludes any human access to the divine. It is always implied that in time there are ways to repair the breach, at least temporarily.

Philosophical expressions of this theme tend to describe humankind's alienation from the Tao as an almost inevitable process of losing an original innocence or faceless spontaneity (as in the face-giving operation on emperor Hun-tun in the *Chuang-tzu* that is equated with death); as a matter of giving up "primitive" social life for the artificial ways of civilization (as in the *Lao-tzu*); or, in contrast to the Taoist position, as a forgetting of the proper rituals and virtue of civilized human intercourse (as in Confucian literature). For both Taoists and Confucians there are different "salvational" methods (ways of mystical, ritual, and moral wisdom that emulate the cosmic knowledge of the mythic ancestors) for returning to the conditions that originally linked man to the Tao.

Cosmic disasters, beginning again, and cultural saviors. Worldwide mythologies concerning some great natural disaster or combat between the forces of chaos and order often allude to a kind of permanent structural tension between the divinely created world of nature that cyclically requires regenerative periods of chaotic regression and the world of human culture that is threatened by the fickleness and chaotic ambiguity of nature and the gods. "Combat mythology" in this sense refers to the theme of the establishment of a human cultural order after the creation of some previous natural and divine world. The secondary creation, or re-creation, of the cultural order, moreover, often implies a challenge to, or usurpation of, the cosmic powers of the chthonic gods and ancestors. The agent responsible for fixing the permanent cultural order is, however, frequently depicted as an ambiguous figure: someone who is partially related to the gods and has beastly characteristics, yet at the same time, a semihuman savior who insures the renewal and continuation of the human order.

In ancient China there are muted indications of this kind of combat mythology seen in the fragmented tales of Yü and I, but they are never accentuated in the epically dramatic, or heroic, fashion seen in Indo-European traditions. As with the Chung-li fragments and the clan origin myths, Yü and I were most commonly associated with the systematized "sage-king and model emperor" lore that recounted the establishment and progressive manifestation of the aristocratic order of dynastic civilization. Regardless of these transformations, the overall thematic pattern of the Yü and I fragments strongly suggest a more universal scenario of creation and cultural genesis that is not necessarily identified with a particular civilizational order.

The deluge and Yü the Great. The references to Yü, his taming of a great flood and the definitive organization of the human world, are attested in the earliest written sources (i.e., in the oldest sections of the classical *Shu ching* and *Shih ching,* as well as in the *Meng-tzu* and numerous other Eastern Chou and Han dynasty documents). In extant sources the deluge is set in the predynastic time of Yao and tells of the diluvian labors of the semi-beastial figures known as Kun and Yü (both names etymologically reveal traces of their totemic status as aquatic, reptilian, or avian animal ancestors). The unexplained occasion of the flood causes the sage emperor Yao (or the sky deity Shang-ti) to charge his minister Kun with the task of controlling the wanton waters that were "swelling up to heaven." After laboring unsuccessfully for nine years, Kun was summarily executed and Shun replaced him with Yü, miraculously born after three years from the split open body of Kun (in some accounts the body had been transformed into a rock). Yü wisely did not try to employ his father's method of damming up the waters, but sought out the hidden channels in the earth and allowed the waters to drain away naturally. Yü then erected mountains, adjusted the flow of the rivers, made the earth suitable for agriculture, conquered various barbarian rebels, and divided up the landscape according to a ninefold plan. In recognition of these accomplishments, Shun established Yü as the founder of the Hsia dynasty, traditionally the first civilized state in ancient China.

There are other random details that can be culled from various sources, but in general terms the story of Yü stresses not the actual flood, or its causes, but the necessary methods of ordering the human world in a way that maintains a harmonious relationship with the secret structure of the cosmos. It is said that Yü assumed the form of an animal, limped from his titanic labors (the so-called "step" or dance of Yü), received the sacred *Lo-shu* (Lo River Writing) and *Ho-t'u* (Yellow River Chart) cosmic diagrams, and cast the nine *ting* cauldrons; these are all symbolic details that suggest Yü's shamanic function and his use of an esoteric methodology. In this way, the theme of Yü's mastery of the techniques of the creative reordering of the world may be associated with the sacred duties of the king and emperor who was responsible for insuring the continuation of the human order. In later liturgical Taoism this same mythic theme, with its emphasis on the hidden methods of re-creating the world, was assimilated into the figure and ritual of the Taoist priest.

The "method" of Yü, his "way" or *tao*, was taken as a model for the fundamental moral principle that "human nature" *(hsing)* can only be effectively cultivated by following the inborn channels of man's natural, or original, dispositions. In fact, the theme of Yü's cosmological methods and cosmogonic power constitutes a paradigmatic reference point for political, religious, and moral techniques designed to renew corporate social life and the human body. From this perspective, then, it may be said that the theme of Yü the Great is not just the classical mythos of the origins of dynastic civilization; rather, it most basically tells of the semidivine technological prowess of human culture. By "reading" the blueprint of the world correctly as a kind of cosmic engineer, and by going with the flow of things, a meaningful cultural and personal order can be created out of the experience of chaos. [*See also* Yao and Shun *and* Yü.]

The ten suns and the archer I. The extremely meager plot of the sun theme tells of the unexplained simultaneous appearance of ten suns during the reign of Yao, and of the resulting conditions of a life-destroying drought. Nine of the suns were shot out of the sky with arrows by the ambivalent salvational figure known as I (or Hou I; there is some confusion between a good and evil I). Further details given in the *Huai-nan–tzu* relate that I, besides shooting the suns, killed and tamed various wild beasts that were disrupting the world. In a manner akin to the labors of Yü, I therefore established the conditions that allowed for the flourishing of human civilization.

The theme of the ten suns and the archer I has, like the deluge theme, many worldwide parallels. In the context of the standarized dynastic tradition, the deluge and sun themes can be linked respectively with the Hsia and Shang cultural orders in a way that suggests a fundamental antagonistic pairing, or cyclic contrast, between the primal forces of water, flood, earth, west, aquatic ancestors (Hsia associations) and the forces of fire, sun, drought, heaven, east, and avian ancestors (Shang associations). There is a hint of the standardized *wu-hsing* cosmological system here (the "five phases" that were aspects of the dual cycle of *yin-yang*), but this kind of emblematic symbolism also points at more archaic traditions of totemic classification related to different clan origin mythologies. Thus, there is some possibility that the ten suns theme represents a dim remnant of early clan mythology connected with the founding ancestors and ritual calendar of the Shang tradition. This kind of analysis is most appealing, but the broader structural implications of the ten suns and deluge theme should not be overlooked: that dynasties, like nature and human nature, follow a dualistic cyclic pattern, and that moments of the overaccentuated presence of any one duality must be combated to ensure the continuation and harmony of the total cycle.

Civilizational beginnings, sage-kings, and model emperors. The sun and flood myths were incorporated into the sequence of civilizational development classically associated with the sage-kings and model emperors of antiquity. There is an important thematic difference, however, between the more demiurgic salvational struggles of I and Yü and the relatively placid unfolding of the civilizational order. Even though they are artificially presented as bureaucrats under Yao and Shun, Yü and I may be said to represent cultural creators. The sage-kings and model emperors, on the other hand (and despite their original mythological identities), are more prosaic examples of what might be called "civilizational transformers" whose accomplishments depend to some degree on the prior establishment of a foundational cosmic landscape and cultural methodology.

In the evolving classical interpretation of the beginnings there is a tendency to incorporate increasingly remote periods of mythical time into a single process of civilizational development. Thus Confucius especially honors the foundational figures of the early Chou period (the kings Wen and Wu, and the sage-minister Chou Kung), but by the Han period the semistandard grouping included three sage-kings (the San Huang) and five model emperors (the Wu Ti) who were held to be the direct predynastic precursors of the founders of the Hsia, Shang, and Chou dynasties. Different figures, all revealing animal traits and other mythic characteristics, were included in these cosmologically coded groupings of three and five, but one fairly typical list would designate Fu Hsi, Sui-jen/Chu-jung, and Shen Nung (the inventor of agriculture) as the San Huang; and Huang-ti (the Yellow Emperor), Chuan-hsü, K'u, Yao, and Shun as the Wu Ti.

These figures were used to trace out a pseudo-historical pattern of cultural development and genealogical inheritance that can be said to have run from the Mesolithic (especially Fu Hsi, Nu-kua, and Sui-jen, who domesticated animals, established marriage ritual, invented fire, and contributed other basic cultural technologies), to the neolithic (Shen Nung, who as the Divine Farmer invented the plow and cleared the land), down to the late Neolithic threshold of city-state civilization (the Wu Ti, who are responsible for creating the ritual principles of state governance). Thus the Yellow Emperor, among his other achievements, is said to have arranged the sixty-year cycle of the calendar and to have instituted the cult of state sacrifice. It should be noted that the Yellow Emperor, as the "first" of the Wu Ti, often assumes a paradigmatic, though ambivalent, role similar to Yü's function as a primordial cultural creator and, like Yü, the Yellow Emperor became a model for "salvational" techniques found in both Taoist and Confucian tradition. [*See* Huang-ti.]

The scheme of the San Huang and Wu Ti is largely the result of the confucianized attempt to charter a particular vision of the cosmic regularity of the dynastic cycle and the sacral implications of aristocratic rule (the "Confucian" implications are especially seen in the role given to "founding ministers"; both Shun and Yü were said to have started their careers as virtuous bureaucrats). One of the basic structural applications of the predynastic cycle (and its dynastic extension to the rise and fall of Hsia, Shang, and Chou) is to mediate the tension surrounding the problem of political succession. The crucial issue, therefore, often concerns the conflict between a hereditary principle of rule (associated with dynastic continuity) and rule by meritorious virtue (associated with dynastic change). This structural pattern and the use of model kings and emperors as a "transformative set" of myths is, however, not limited to Confucian tradition. The fundamental question of the meaning of "virtue" *(te)* as a principle of creativity could, for example, be evaluated in different ways based on which aspects of the mythic cycle were emphasized. In this way, references to the sage-kings and model emperors are found throughout both classical and nonclassical literature of the Eastern Chou and Han dynasties and, depending on how certain figures were treated or ignored, can be used to characterize a particular ideological position. [*See also* Tao and Te.]

Returning to the beginning. The sacred history of the beginnings traced above has already indicated that in ancient China (making some exception for the Fa-chia, or Legalists) the ways of cultivating human life in the present depend on the different "cosmic" methods of remembering and emulating the mythic models from the remote past. This refers especially to the ways or methods of "returning to the Tao" that are modeled on cosmogonic and cosmological notions concerning the *creatio continua* of natural and human life, and the cyclic waxing and waning of dynasties. The inner structure of all forms of existence, it seems, is mythic in nature since change is fundamentally understood as a constant series of new beginnings or sets of structural permutations, that return to the recapitulate the "first" processes of creation. The problem of living after the mythic age is from this perspective primarily a problem of forgetting one's mythical ancestry and continuing linkages with cosmic life. The possibility of living a creatively virtuous life, one that is in tune with the rhythm of regeneration, depends therefore on man's interpretive ability to detect the cosmic signs left in the world by the mythic ancestors. Living a meaningful life, it may be said, hinges on the imaginative perception of the traces of cosmic structure hidden amidst the flux of experience.

Connected with the general principle of return are various golden age or paradise themes that serve as both individual and social ideals. In the Han dynasty utopian visions of the time of the Ta-t'ung ("great unity") and T'ai-p'ing ("great peace") were common phenomena that, upon the collapse of the dynasty, became associated with a messianic and apocalyptic future. In the ancient period, however, such utopian realms were firmly located in the past and early Confucian and Taoist longings can be differentiated in terms of where the golden age is located in mythic time and how it is characterized in relation to the prevailing social order. Thus, in contrast to the Confucian nostalgia for the perfect ritual propriety of the earliest dynastic states, the early Taoists tended to stress the sacredness of an egalitarian rural society. [*See* T'ai-p'ing.]

Another expression of the theme of return is seen in the ancient ideas of the afterlife and the destiny of the dead. By the Han dynasty, one basic aristocratic view imagined death as a kind of journey back into mythic space and time. This is most impressively and graphically illustrated by the Ma-wang-tui funerary banners dating to the second century BCE. The iconography of this silk painting generally shows that death was understood as a kind of voyage of the dead through a mediating cosmic realm shaped like a vase (or, perhaps calabash; a possible allusion to the paradise of K'un-lun Mountain or P'eng-lai Island), accompanied by a host of mythical animal spirits and servants. The dead person's final destination was reached by entering gates that led to the celestial regions associated with the mythical imagery of the ten suns and other mythical creatures and heavenly deities. Death was seen, in other words, as a navigation of a sacred landscape that led back to the heavenly bliss of mythic time when men, animals, and gods lived in total harmony. Finally, it may simply be noted here that the salvational possibility of "no-death" or "long life," as related to the development of "immortality cults" in the Han period (such as those associated with the goddess Hsi Wang Mu) most often implied the use of methods that would allow for this kind of mythic journey before one's natural death. [*See also* Afterlife, *article on* Chinese Concepts, *and* Hsi Wang Mu.]

Myth as the Divination of Structure. To return to the beginning of this essay, it would appear that the *Ch'u-tz'u*'s "Heavenly Questions" can only be answered in the spirit that they were asked: as a puzzling out of an underlying code of meaning known only through the relative shape and fit of individual bits and pieces of myths. Although most of the pieces have been lost, it can still be said that much of the fascination and significance associated with the enigma of Chinese myth is exactly that, as more of the facts of the Chinese past are accumulated and comparatively analyzed, the more it seems that the cultural configuration of those very facts depends on the forms of life imagined mythically and enacted ritually.

At the very outset of Chinese civilization, the Shang dynasty oracle bones suggest that human life was fundamentally perceived as a riddle that could only be deciphered by a method that attended to the pattern of cracks, the divine signs of hidden structure in existence, made manifest on the skeletal remains of animals. In relation to the inscribed form of both the human question and heavenly answer, emphasis was placed on a structural methodology that allowed technically proficient men to divine the holy writ that was secretly traced in the bare bones of animals from the very beginning. In ancient China, it seems, knowing the past or future was not a matter of telling a story; rather, it involved a divination of the mythical structure of meaning. If China does not offer us a heady narrative broth to feast on, it certainly provides us with bones and marrow to gnaw.

[*See also* Structuralism; Myth, *article on* Myth and History; *and* Historiography, *overview article.*]

BIBLIOGRAPHY

General Studies

Allan, Sarah. *The Heir and the Sage: Dynastic Legend in Early China.* San Francisco, 1981.

Bodde, Derk. "Myths of Ancient China." In *Essays on Chinese Civilization,* edited by Charles Le Blanc and Dorothy Borei, pp. 45–84. Princeton, 1981.

Chang, Kwang-chih. *Early Chinese Civilization: Anthropological Perspectives.* Cambridge, Mass., 1976.

Chang, Kwang-chih. *Art, Myth, and Ritual: The Path to Political Authority in Ancient China.* Cambridge, Mass., 1983.

Eberhard, Wolfram. *The Local Cultures of South and East China.* Translated by Alide Eberhard. Leiden, 1968.

Girardot, N. J. "The Problem of Creation Mythology in the Study of Chinese Religion." *History of Religions* 15 (May 1976): 289–318.

Girardot, N. J. "Behaving Cosmologically in Early Taoism." In *Cosmology and Ethical Order,* edited by R. W. Lovin and Frank E. Reynolds. Chicago, 1985.

Henderson, John B. *Development and Decline of Chinese Cosmology.* New York, 1984.

Jacobson, Esther. "The Structure of Narrative in Early Chinese Pictorial Vessels." *Representations* 8 (Fall 1984): 61–83.

Kaltenmark, Max. "La naissance du monde en Chine." In his *La Naissance du monde.* Paris, 1959.

Karlgren, Bernhard. "Legends and Cults in Ancient China." *Bulletin of the Museum of Far Eastern Antiquities* 18 (1946): 199–365.

Major, John S. "Myth, Cosmology, and the Origins of Chinese Science." *Journal of Chinese Philosophy* 5 (1978): 1–20.

Maspero, Henri. "Légendes mythologiques dans le *Chou King.*" *Journal asiatique* 204 (January–March 1924): 1–100.

Mathieu, Rémi. "Introduction à l'étude de la mythologie de la Chine ancienne; Considerations théoriques et historiques." In his *Étude sur la mythologie et l'ethnologie de la Chine ancienne.* Paris, 1983.

Soymié, Michel. "China: The Struggle for Power." Translated by Patricia Beardsworth. In *Larousse World Mythology,* edited by Pierre Grimal, pp. 271–292. New York, 1965.

Studies on Particular Thematic Topics

Allan, Sarah. "Sons of Suns: Myth and Totemism in Early China." *Bulletin of the School of Oriental and African Studies* 44 (1981): 290–326.

Bauer, Wolfgang. *China and the Search for Happiness: Recurring Themes in Four Thousand Years of Chinese Cultural History.* Translated by Michael Shaw. New York, 1976.

Boltz, William G. "Kung-kung and the Flood: Reverse Euhemerism in the *Yao tien.*" *T'oung pao* 67 (1981): 141–153.

Girardot, N. J. *Myth and Meaning in Early Taoism.* Berkeley, 1983.

Graham, A. C. "The *Nung-chia* 'School of the Tillers' and the Origins of Peasant Utopianism in China." *Bulletin of the School of Oriental and African Studies* 42 (1979): 66–100.

Hawkes, David. *Ch'u Tz'u: The Songs of the South.* Oxford, 1959.

Levi, Jean. "Le mythe de l'âge d'or et les théories de l'évolution en Chine ancienne." *L'homme* 17 (January–March 1973): 73–103.

Loewe, Michael. *Ways to Paradise: The Chinese Quest for Immortality.* London, 1979.

Mathieu, Rémi. *Le Mu tianzi zhuan: Traduction annotée, étude critique.* Paris, 1978.

Plaks, Andrew H. *Archetype and Allegory in the Dream of the Red Chamber.* Princeton, 1976.

Schneider, Laurence A. *A Madman of Ch'u: The Chinese Myth of Loyalty and Dissent.* Berkeley, 1980.

N. J. GIRARDOT

Religious and Philosophical Texts

[*This article surveys various of the nonsectarian literatures of China, principally the semicanonical "classics" that have, since the Han period, constituted the core texts of the Confucian tradition. For a survey of the other traditions of religious writing in China, see also* Taoism, *article on* Taoist Literature, *and* Buddhist Literature.]

Confucianism, the dominant force in traditional Chinese society, has produced an extensive body of philosophical and religious literature. For some two thousand years the Five Classics and the Four Books, the basic texts of orthodox Confucianism, were the foundation of education and the main source of guidance, inspiration, and ideas for the educated and uneducated alike. The Confucian classics were the primary medium through which Chinese literate culture was transmitted to Korea, Japan, and other East Asian countries. For the most part, these countries adopted the classics and made them central to their premodern curricula. Although the Confucian classics are no longer the basis of education in East Asia, the ideals they articulate still exert a powerful influence there.

Canonization. Confucius described himself as "a transmitter and not a creator, a believer in and lover of antiquity," as "striving unwearingly [in study] and teaching without flagging" (*Analects* 7.33). The knowledge Confucius transmitted was acquired from various sources, in part from books. The term *books* is used loosely here, for surely books as conventionally understood now were unknown in Confucius's day. There were, however, collections of writings, usually not the creations of private authors but compiled in the bureaus of the royal administration by various officers in the course of their service. For example, it was the responsibility of the Bureau of History to keep daily records of happenings in the kingdom. Such records often provided the basis for the official history of the dynasty. Records kept by the Bureau of Protocol sometimes became standard works on etiquette. As they accumulated age, such records increased in value as repositories of the manners and thought of the increasingly distant past and became an important medium for transmitting tradition. In his educational program Confucius is supposed to have used six such texts known as the *liu shu,* or "six disciplines," later known as the *liu ching* ("six classics"): *I ching* (Book of Changes), *Shih ching* (Book of Odes), *Shu ching* (Book of History), *Ch'un-ch'iu* (Spring and Autumn Annals), *Li chi* (Book of Rites), and *Yüeh ching* (Book of Music). It was the Taoist philosopher Chuang-tzu who first referred to these texts as the Six Classics. Confucius was not the first to promote these texts, but he was the first to use them to educate people both inside and outside the aristocratic pale. His example was followed by later generations of teachers, and by the time of the philosopher Meng-tzu (371–298? BCE) a bewildering variety of teachers had arisen, many with large numbers of followers, to vie with one another for favor at the royal courts.

The first emperor of the Ch'in dynasty (221–206 BCE), seeking to inhibit the influence of the Confucian philosophers, ordered numerous executions and the general burning of Confucian books, sparing only those housed in the imperial archives. Many scholars, therefore, hid their books and themselves. After the Han dynasty (206 BCE–220 CE) overthrew the Ch'in, Confucians were once again permitted to teach and hold government office. In 136 BCE the emperor Wu-ti (r. 140–87), under the influence of the great Confucian scholar Tung Chung-shu, established Confucianism as the state ideology. [*See* Confucian Thought, *article on* The State Cult, *and the biography of Tung Chung-shu.*] In 125 he opened an imperial university with five doctoral chairs *(po-shih)* for the study, interpretation, and dissemination of the Five Classics (five because the sixth, the *Book of Music,* was never fully recovered), an institution that endured until the beginning of the twentieth century. Thus, from the second century on, the Five Classics provided official standards in government, law, education, literature, and religion. In the twelfth century a ritual text, the *Chou Li* (Rites of Chou), replaced the *Book of Music* as the sixth classic.

In the second century alternate versions of the classics from the time prior to the Ch'in book-burning were purportedly found among texts hidden in the walls of certain houses. The Ch'in had standardized the Chinese system of writing characters, giving it the basis of the form that has persisted until modern time, but the newly discovered texts were in the archaic pre-Ch'in script.

Naturally, questions concerning the provenance and authenticity of all the classics arose as a result. The proponents of the newly discovered texts, those written in the "old (i.e., pre-Ch'in) script" *(ku-wen),* came to be known as the Old Script, or Old Text, school. Those who maintained the authenticity of the officially sanctioned recensions, all of which were written in "new (i.e., Han) script" *(chin-wen),* came to be known as the New Script, or New Text, school. But the debate between these two schools concerned more than the issue of the provenance of their respective recensions of the classics, nor was it merely a struggle between the New Text incumbents of the doctoral chairs and the Old Text scholars who coveted the prestige and power of these positions. The rift went much deeper. The Old Text school maintained that Confucius was merely a teacher who transmitted the ancient documents known as the Five Classics but did not himself compose them. The New Text school, citing the historiographer Ssu-ma Ch'ien's assertion that Confucius "abridged" the classics, claimed that he was their author. They also maintained that Confucius was the supreme spiritual and political leader, a figure with special, even divine authority, an "uncrowned king" *(su-wang)* whose great principles are expressed in "subtle words" in the classics. For them, the classics had a supreme social, political, and religious purpose. The New Texts also lent themselves, far more than their Old Text counterparts, to the Yin-yang and Five Elements *(wu-hsing)* cosmological and numerological interpretations that lay at the heart of the Confucian synthesis of Tung Chung-shu and his associates. [*See* Yin-yang Wu-hsing.]

During the last century and a half prior to the beginning of the common era, however, some scholars began to dispute the prevailing orthodoxy. In particular, they rejected the widespread reliance on prognostication and other "superstitions" that they associated with the importation of Yin-yang ideology into the reading of the classics. These men found textual warrant for their opinions in the newly discovered Old Texts. During the final years of the Former Han dynasty Liu Hsin, a cataloger in the Imperial Library, worked to establish the legitimacy of the Old Texts (to the extent that his opponents claimed that they were the products of his hand); Wang Mang's timely patronage of Liu Hsin during the interregnum (the so-called Hsin dynasty, 9–23) also served to consolidate the power of the Old Text scholars, whose interpretations gradually came to dominate the intellectual tenor of Latter Han Confucianism. As late as the twentieth century the debate over the authenticity and appropriateness of these two ideological stances continued to intrigue Confucian thinkers. The scholar K'ang Yu-wei, who engineered the abortive social and political reforms of 1898, was merely the latest to insist that Confucian teachings form the basis of a state religion. [*See the biography of K'ang Yu-wei.*]

During the Han, government officials were recommended and promoted according to their knowledge of the Five Classics. From 606 to 1905 the Five Classics were the basis of the civil service examinations through which the educated could enter the ranks of officialdom. From 175 to 1803 these five and other Confucian classics were repeatedly inscribed on stone to preserve them for posterity. Eight of these inscriptions are still extant in whole or in part.

The Thirteen Classics. In 720 the *Chou Li* (Rites of Chou), the *I li* (Book of Rites), and a collection of three commentaries on the *Spring and Autumn Annals*—the *Kung-yang chuan,* the *Ku-liang chuan,* and the *Tso chuan*—were grouped with the Five Classics to form the Nine Classics. With the inclusion in 837 of the *Lun-yü* (Analects), the *Hsiao ching* (The Classic of Filial Piety), the *Erh-ya,* a dictionary of terms found in the classics, and, in the twelfth century, the *Meng-tzu,* the set became the Thirteen Classics, which remains standard to this day. (See table 1.)

The Book of Odes. The *Shih ching* (literally, "poem classic"), the earliest anthology of Chinese poetry, contains 305 poems that were in circulation during the Western Chou dynasty (1111–770 BCE), five of which may have originated in the Shang dynasty (1751–1112 BCE). According to one tradition, Confucius selected the odes from a collection of three thousand poems. According to another, the Chou kings had the poems collected from among the masses on the supposition that the mood of the kingdom could be surmised by listening to the songs of its people. These two traditions are not mutually exclusive. That Confucius had access to work at least very similar to the *Shih ching* is clear from quotations of verse appearing in the *Analects.* He recommends the work to his disciples by saying, "All three hundred odes can be covered by one sentence, and that is, 'Have no depraved thoughts'" (*Analects,* 2.2).

The work in its present form, the result of Han-dynasty editing, is divided into four sections called *feng* ("winds, airs"), *hsiao ya* ("lesser odes" or "lesser elegants"), *ta ya* ("greater odes" or "greater elegants"), and *sung* ("hymns, eulogies"). The 160 *feng* are folk songs from the fifteen states in northern China under Chou rule. They reflect the occupations, amusements, religion, and emotional life of the common people, often in frankly emotional language. The *hsiao ya* section consists of songs by courtiers and members of the aristocracy. Many of these poems deal with the various pleasures of court life. The *ta ya* differs from the *hsiao ya* in that many of the former concern the founders of the royal house of Chou. The poems are generally of a solemn, eulogistic character. The last forty poems of the *Odes,* known as *sung,* are ceremonial, self-laudatory productions of the Chou court (thirty-one poems), the duchy of Lu (four poems), and the Shang court (five poems). Most scholars agree that the Shang hymns either originated in or were preserved in the state of Sung whose rulers were descendants of the royal house of Shang.

Most of the poems in the *Shih ching* are in rhymed quatrains with four words per line. From the time of its compilation, around 600 BCE, it became the model for all poetic writing. Commenting on the *feng* section Confucius said, "It is expressive of enjoyment without being licentious, and of grief without being hurtfully excessive." This statement sums up the ideal of moderation present throughout the greater portion of the *Shih ching*, a quality that characterizes Chinese poetic writing in general. [*See also* Poetry, *article on* Chinese Religious Poetry.]

The Book of History. Sometimes called the *Shang shu* (Documents of Antiquity), the *Shu ching* (literally, "classic of writing," also translated as the "book of documents") is the earliest Chinese historical work. Tradition has it that Confucius assembled, arranged, and provided introductions to each of the various documents that make up this work. Modern scholars, however, believe that most of the introductions appearing in the standard recensions of the work were written by authors after Confucius. But as Confucius and his disciples often quoted from the documents, Confucius's involvement with the *Shu ching* cannot be entirely discounted. The fifty-eight chapters of this book include six types of documents—canons, counsels, instructions, announcements, oaths, and charges—arranged in chronological order covering about seventeen centuries from the era of legendary sage kings (third millennium BCE) to 630 BCE. Each section consists of a short account of a historical event followed by an essay or dialogue stressing the moral or political import of the event. The work is written in a difficult and often cryptic style and covers a broad range of subjects, including history, government, education, geography, and so forth, from a wide variety of sources.

Because the accounts of its rediscovery and transmission during the Han dynasty abound, scholars have questioned the authenticity of the numerous versions of the *Book of History*. Indeed, this work is perhaps the most intensely debated among the classics. According to one account, during the Ch'in dynasty the scholar Fu Sheng committed a text in thirty-three chapters to memory. When, at the age of ninety, he was unable to respond to the Han emperor Wen-ti's summons to court, he orally transmitted it to a disciple who wrote it in the "modern script" current at that time. Yet another text in fifty-eight chapters (plus a preface) is said to have been found early in the Latter Han dynasty (25–220 CE), when a prince demolished a home belonging to a descendant of Confucius. This work, which quickly went out of circulation, was written in the pre-Ch'in "ancient script." A third text, also written in "ancient script" and composed of the thirty-three chapters of the Fu Sheng version and an additional twenty-five chapters, was presented to Emperor Yüan-ti (r. 317–323) by Mei Tse. For several centuries scholars considered this work the original *Book of History* in fifty-eight chapters. The philosopher Chu Hsi (1130–1200) was among the first to doubt the authenticity of the additional twenty-five chapters. In the seventeenth century Yen Jo-chu assembled 128 pieces of evidence to support the charge that Mei Tse was a forger. Today, the *Book of History* includes fifty-three chapters containing material from all three sources.

TABLE 1. *Four Standard Collections of Chinese Texts*

FIVE CLASSICS	SIX CLASSICS	THIRTEEN CLASSICS		FOUR BOOKS
Shih ching	*Shih ching*	*Shih ching (Mao shih)*		
Shu ching (Shang shu)	*Shu ching*	*Shu ching*		
I ching (Chou i)	*I ching*	*I ching*		
Li chi	*Li chi*	*Li chi*	known collectively as the *san li*	*Ta-hsüeh* } from the *Li chi*
	Chou li (Chou kuan)*	*Chou li*		*Chung-yung*
		I li		
Ch'un-ch'iu	*Ch'un-ch'iu*	*Tso chuan*	commentaries to the *Ch'un-ch'iu*	
		Kung-yang chuan		
		Ku-liang chuan		
	*Yüeh ching**			
		Lun-yü		*Lun-yü*
		Hsiao ching		
		Erh-ya		
		Meng-tzu		*Meng-tzu*

*The *Yüeh ching* was lost during Han times. Since the twelfth century the *Chou li* has served as the "sixth" book.

The Book of Changes. Some scholars believe that the *I ching*, an ancient manual of divination, was already in existence at the time of Confucius. Others believe it is the product of the third century BCE. The probable truth is that it, like many other ancient works, assumed its present form through a long process of evolution. From the earliest times both Confucian and Taoist schools claimed it as their classic. Later, even certain Buddhists consulted, studied, and commented upon it.

The *I ching* consists of sixty-four hexagrams with accompanying explanations and ten "wings" or commentaries. A hexagram is made up of a vertical column of six horizontal lines that are either broken in the middle or whole. The whole lines represent *yang*, the male or active cosmic force. The broken lines represent *yin*, the female or passive cosmic force. A hexagram may be divided into two trigrams, so called because each consists of three lines. Each of the Eight Trigrams (*pa-kua*, the eight permutations of three broken and unbroken lines) making up the sixty-four hexagrams correspond to various natural elements, directions, and moral or mental qualities. A hexagram indicates a situation, and the explanation accompanying it offers a desirable solution or course of action. The twenty-fourth hexagram, *fu* ("to return"), for example, has five *yin* lines on top of one *yang* line. Because the bottom line usually represents how an action is to begin, this hexagram is explained as a return of power or life. Although its structure is obviously conducive to fortune-telling and divination, the *I ching* has also provided some of the most basic concepts of Confucian philosophy and metaphysics. Indeed, the later Taoist and Confucian theories of cosmology were elaborations of the *Book of Changes*'s statement that the *t'ai-chi* ("great ultimate") generates *yin* and *yang*, which in turn interact to produce all things.

It was traditionally believed that the legendary sage-emperor Fu-hsi invented the Eight Trigrams on the basis of signs he found on the back of a "horse-dragon" that emerged from the Yellow River, that King Wen (r. 1171–1122 BCE) then created the sixty-four hexagrams, that he or the Duke of Chou (fl. 1094 BCE) composed explanations of them, and that Confucius wrote the commentaries known as the "ten wings." Modern Chinese scholars have, of course, rejected this tradition. Specialists in the various countries in the Far East nevertheless continue to study the *I ching*. It has been translated into a number of languages and is probably the most popular Chinese classic in Europe and America. [*See also* Divination.]

The Book of Rites. Although the *Li chi* has been variously attributed to the Duke of Chou and Confucius, it was probably written during the fourth century BCE or the early Han dynasty. It is certain that during the second century BCE Prince Hsien (d. 131) circulated a version of the *Li chi*, to which several chapters were later added. In the early part of the first century BCE a certain Tai Te systematized and reduced the 204 chapters to form a single volume in eighty-five chapters. The work (now comprising thirty-eight chapters) came to be known as *Ta Tai chi* (Records of the Elder Tai). His younger cousin Tai Sheng selected what he considered the better portions of the *Ta Tai chi* and compiled a new work in forty-nine chapters that was later called *Hsiao Tai chi* (Records of the Younger Tai), better known as the *Li chi*. The book contains an assortment of texts on such subjects as the regulations of a royal court, the evolution of ritual, ritual articles, guidance for women and the young, education, magic, moral restraint, the meaning of religious sacrifice, funeral attire, and the behavior of a scholar. Many of the texts are cast in the form of anecdotes about, or dialogues between, Confucius and his pupils and contain a wealth of discussion on Confucian ethics. Among the purely philosophical texts in the *Li chi* are two works that became part of the Four Books as defined by Chu Hsi, the *Ta-hsüeh* (Great Learning) and the *Chung-yung* (Doctrine of the Mean).

From the Han dynasty two other texts, the *I li* (Book of Ceremonials) and the *Chou li* (Rites of Chou), coexisted with the *Li chi*. Together, these three works were known as the *san li* ("three books on rites"). The *I li* was probably compiled during the Former Han dynasty (206 BCE–8 CE) and was the only ritual text to be considered a classic during the Han dynasty. It contains detailed, systematic descriptions of how to conduct weddings, banquets, funerals, archery contests, and other ceremonial occasions in the life of the feudal aristocracy. The *Chou li*, ascribed by Liu Ch'in (c. 46 BCE–23 CE) to the Duke of Chou, is held by most scholars to be a forgery of the Warring States period (403–222 BCE). An idealized description of the structure of the government during the Chou dynasty, it contains little reliable historical information. [*See also* Li.]

The Spring and Autumn Annals. The first Confucian chronicle, the *Ch'un-ch'iu* (literally, "spring and autumn," signifying the year), was compiled in Confucius's native state of Lu and covers the reigns of twelve rulers between 722 and 481 BCE. The *Ch'un-ch'iu* describes events in the barest outline, but according to some traditions, the wording of the text indicates the moral judgment of the author, thought by some to be Confucius himself. For example, if a duke is mentioned by name rather than by title, the implication is that he no longer deserved the title. The work expresses the Confucian respect for law and custom and has provided a standard for moral judgment in history and politics.

Of the three commentaries to be included in the Thirteen Classics, the *Tso chuan* (ascribed to Tso Ch'iu-ming, a contemporary of Confucius) fills in the outlines of the chronicle with detailed narrative that is both vivid and dramatic. The other two commentaries, the *Kung-yang chuan* and the *Ku-liang chuan*, were written by pupils of Tzu-hsia, a disciple of Confucius. Their commentaries are founded on the belief that the original chronicle was written by Confucius with "subtle words," or judgment-implying wording. [*See also* Historiography, *overview article.*]

The Analects. The main repository of sayings of Confucius, the *Lun-yü* (literally, "conversations") is a fragmentary collection of dialogues, aphorisms, and records of what Confucius did. Three versions were found in the second century BCE, but only that of the state of Lu has come down to us. It has 492 chapters in twenty books, totaling 12,700 characters. Virtually all the basic Confucian concepts are presented here but never elaborated upon. Confucius taught that one should be a man of *jen* (benevolence, humanity), a quality that includes among other things unselfishness. Such a man was known as a superior man *(chün-tzu)* whose other virtues, such as wisdom, courage, and righteousness, are actuated by moral principles rather than by advantage and profit. Confucius also taught that one should respect Heaven *(t'ien)* and obey its mandates; that one should observe moderation *(chung-yung)* and ritual *(li)*; and that names should be rectified *(cheng-ming)*. This last notion is summed up in such formulas as, "a father should be fatherly" and "the government should govern." [*See the biography of* Confucius.]

The Great Learning. Originally, the short classic the *Ta-hsüeh* (literally, "adult education" or "education of the great"), was chapter 42 of the *Book of Rites*. The authorship of the original text is unclear, but tradition attributes it to Confucius's pupil Tseng Ts'an (also known as Tseng-tzu, 505–436? BCE). Chu Hsi, however, insisted that the opening paragraph of the *Ta-hsüeh* was written by Confucius and that the rest of the work was an elaboration by his pupil Tseng-tzu. Confucians began to pay special attention to this text in the eighth century, and in the eleventh century Ssu-ma Kuang (1019–1086) began the tradition of treating the *Ta-hsüeh* as a separate work by writing a commentary on it. At that time also the text became one of the central objects of study for the Neo-Confucian movement. In the opening paragraph the basic teachings of the *Ta-hsüeh* are presented: the three principles of "manifesting one's clear character *(ming ming-te)*, loving (or renovating) the people *(ch'in-min)*, and abiding in the highest good" *(chih yü chih-shan)*; and the eight steps of investigation of things *(ko-wu)*, extension of knowledge *(chih-chih)*, making the will sincere *(ch'eng-i)*, rectification of the mind *(cheng-hsin)*, cultivation of the person *(hsiu-shen)*, regulation of the family *(ch'i-chia)*, the ordering of the state *(chih-kuo)*, and bringing peace to the world *(p'ing t'ien-hsia)*.

The concepts of the *Ta-hsüeh* have been the object of one of the richest traditions of philosophical debate in the history of Chinese thought. The two main schools of interpretation of the *Ta-hsüeh* were represented by Chu Hsi and Wang Yang-ming. In addition to writing a preface and commentary to this text, Chu Hsi "amended" it by supplying a paragraph on the investigation of things *(ko-wu)*, which became the primary statement of the Neo-Confucian theory of knowledge. Wang Yang-ming wrote *An Inquiry on the Great Learning (Ta-hsüeh huo-wen)*, a profound expression of the theory of the unity of man and Heaven.

The Doctrine of the Mean. Originally chapter 31 of the *Book of Rites*, the *Chung-yung* (literally, "central" and "universal" or "common") presents the strongest tendency toward metaphysical and religious speculation of the ancient Confucian classics. The brief text (it has only 3,567 characters) is composed mainly of putative sayings of Confucius. Tradition has it that Confucius's grandson Tzu-ssu composed it, but many scholars consider it to be a compilation of a much later date. It treats those subjects avoided by Confucius in the *Lun-yü*, topics such as the Way of Heaven, which the *Chung-yung* describes as transcending space, time, substance, and motion, but that at the same time is manifest and evident. In this text we learn that human nature is determined by, and is in harmony with, Heaven, and that spiritual beings are unfathomable but always subtly present during religious sacrifices. Here the word *chung-yung* implies not only moderation, as it did in the *Lun-yü*, but also the harmony of the universe as well as that of human nature and human feelings. The mysticism of the *Chung-yung* began to attract commentaries by Buddhist and Taoist scholars as early as the fifth century. In the twelfth century it became one of the central texts in the Neo-Confucian movement.

The Meng-tzu. *The Book of Mencius* (the latinized form of Meng-tzu) is a compilation of the teachings of the Confucian philosopher Meng-tzu (371–289 BCE), most likely recorded by his disciples. In seven chapters, each in two parts, and divided into a total of 261 sections, the *Meng-tzu* covers most of the same subjects as the *Lun-yü*. It is, however, written in a more elaborate literary style and is more extensive in argument. What distinguishes Meng-tzu from all of his predecessors, however, is his doctrine of the original goodness of human nature, a doctrine that forms the cornerstone of later Confucian concepts of human nature. Meng-tzu also thought that rulers who did not practice "humane government" by sharing their material wealth and happiness no longer enjoyed the "mandate of Heaven" *(t'ien-ming)*, and that this justified rebellion against such rulers. At the same time Meng-tzu stressed the importance of *hsiao* (filial piety) and all of the respect for, and submission to, authority that it implies. [*See the biography of Meng-tzu.*]

The Classic of Filial Piety. The origins of the *Hsiao ching*, the shortest of the Confucian classics (a mere 1,093 characters in length), is the subject of much debate. It is said to have "reappeared" in two versions after the Ch'in-dynasty burning of books in 213 BCE. The text has been variously ascribed to Tseng-tzu, Tzu-ssu, and other of Confucius's disciples, but some scholars have suggested that it is the work of Han-period authors. The work is in the form of dialogues that were supposed to have occurred between Confucius and his disciple Tseng-tzu. Its gist is that filial piety is the root of all virtue and the source of moral education. The *Hsiao ching* is the classic expression of a moral notion that developed into a virtual religion in traditional China. [*See* Hsiao.]

The Four Books. By the twelfth century the *Analects*, the *Meng-tzu*, the *Great Learning*, and the *Doctrine of the Mean* had been incorporated in the Thirteen Classics. In 1190, however, Chu Hsi published them together as the Four Books. The importance of these four texts to the development of Confucian thought had been steadily increasing in previous centuries, but after Chu Hsi made them the special object of study the Four Books promptly replaced the Five Classics as the center of philosophical inquiry. The Four Books are in a simpler idiom than the Five Classics and, more important, they purport to elaborate on or reflect the actual words of Confucius, whereas the Five Classics were compiled mainly from pre-Confucian sources. According to Chu Hsi, "One should first read the *Great Learning* to be sure of the pattern, next the *Analects* to learn the foundation, then the *Meng-tzu* for stimulation, and then the *Doctrine of the Mean* to find the subtlety and profundity." He even said that the purpose of studying the Five Classics is to discover principle *(li)*, and that once principle is discovered the Five Classics may be dispensed with. After the time of Chu Hsi, the Four Books came to be the first texts memorized in elementary school. They became the principle source of topics for the civil service examinations, and Chu Hsi's commentaries came to be considered the orthodox interpretation of the Four Books.

The Apocryphal Texts. In the first century BCE a group of texts appeared called *wei* ("woof of a fabric"), purporting to be supplements to the classics (*ching*, "warp of a fabric"). The *Book of Changes, Book of History, Book of Odes, Book of Rites, Book of Music, Spring and Autumn Annals*, and the *Book of Filial Piety* each had a corresponding *wei* that was supposed to reveal its esoteric meaning. It is clear from the fragments that have survived that the *wei* were in cryptic, archaic language and contained such occult elements from the folk religion as the belief in charms against baleful influences. Some texts theorize on the mystical relation between man and nature.

Along with the *wei* emerged the *ch'an* (prognostication) texts that used such classics as the *Analects* as a point of departure for divinatory or prophetic purposes. These and many of the other apocryphal texts were spuriously ascribed to Confucius, who is presented in them as possessing divine, prophetic powers. Although these texts were in circulation for less than a century, their impact was felt in both popular and elite religious traditions for a long time.

From Philology to Philosophy. The classics were the object of debate for centuries. Not only did commentators argue over the correct interpretation of their philosophical content, they also feuded over the correct construction of the words in the texts. Textual and philological criticism dominated orthodox classical studies from the end of the Han dynasty to the end of the T'ang dynasty (618–907). By the tenth century, however, philology gave way to philosophy. At that time the creative energies of Confucian thinkers once again came to be concentrated on the ideas expressed in the classics. This revival and reinterpretation of the classics during the Sung dynasty (960–1279) is known as *li-hsüeh* in China and as Neo-Confucianism in the West.

The Neo-Confucian interpretation of the *I ching* provides one of the best examples of this new spirit in philosophical discourse. During the early Sung dynasty the *I ching* was still primarily used as it had been for centuries—as a manual of divination. As interpreted by the Neo-Confucians, however, it became a work of profound metaphysical significance. This new interpretation naturally gave rise to contending schools. One school, known as the school of Forms and Numbers, centered around the philosopher Shao Yung (1101–1177). He conceived of the universe as a system of numerical progressions of four. Basically, there are four cosmic forces: the greater *yin*, the greater *yang*, the lesser *yin*, and the lesser *yang*. From the interaction of these four proceed the four seasons, four heavenly bodies, four earthly substances, four kinds of rulers, four ways of transforming the world, and four kinds of mandate of Heaven. Mechanistic and arbitrary as this theory was, it presented reality as dynamic and predictable.

The opposite direction was pursued by the school of Moral Principles, headed by Ch'eng I (1033–1107). It considered the *I ching* primarily a source of moral instruction. According to this school, the hexagram *fu*, for example, is not to be understood in the cosmological sense of cyclic return but as a symbolic rendering of the moral lesson that one can grow only if one is at peace.

The Religious Significance of Confucian Literature. Confucianism is not an organized religion, and its literature is not strictly religious as is the Bible or the Qur'ān. While much of the literature of Confucianism is concerned with political, philosophical, and moral issues, many of the concepts introduced and discussed in the Thirteen Classics betray specifically religious concerns. Certainly, the religious nature of such notions as Heaven, the unity of man and Heaven, the mandate of Heaven, the goodness of human nature as endowed by Heaven, and so forth, cannot be denied. In another sense the influence of the classics on more concrete expressions of a religious sentiment and their promotion of traditional religious institutions such as sacrifices to ancestors, the worship of Heaven, and the various religious rites and ceremonies are noteworthy.

Religious Rites. The verses in the *Book of Odes* were all set to music. Many of them were in fact temple hymns sung in praise of Heaven and royal ancestors, and were accompanied by elaborate ritual and liturgical dances. This is especially true of the *sung* section of the work. Verses from the more popular *feng* and *ya* sections were sometimes sung or quoted on such religious occasions as funerals, the initiation of architectural construction, prayers for rain, harvest festivals, and community banquets. Often, when new ritual texts were composed, the use of quotations and paraphrases from the classics were standard.

Many of the numerous rites and ceremonies that dominate Chinese religious life have existed since very ancient times. The form of the sacrifice to ancestors, for example, is derived from the *Li chi.* The rules governing the forms of many of the other rites and ceremonies still practiced today are fundamentally the same as those set forth in such ancient works as the "Treatise on Rites" chapter in the *Hsün-tzu* and in the *I li.*

Divination. While the *Book of Changes* is generally regarded as a philosophical work, its original use as a manual of divination is still popular among both the educated and uneducated. When a hexagram is chosen by throwing the milfoil stalks or coins, the diviner, be he priest or layman, interprets the position and direction of the lines in the hexagram using the text and its commentaries. In popular religion it is believed that the message is determined by the gods who control man's fortunes and misfortunes. Even among the Confucian scholars who denounced this practice as superstition and chose instead to interpret the text rationally, the use of the *I ching* for divination was never entirely discarded.

Warning to Rulers. The notion that all phenomena arise as a result of the interaction of *yin* and *yang,* and that the human and natural realms correspond to each other and are governed by the same laws has been an important component in Chinese cosmology from the earliest times. The *I ching* is the richest source of ancient thought in this regard. This theory of *yin* and *yang* figured prominently in the teachings of such Chou-dynasty Confucians as Hsün-tzu and was developed into an elaborate system by the Han Confucian Tung Chung-shu in his *Ch'un-ch'iu fan-lu* (Luxuriant Gems of the *Spring and Autumn Annals*). According to Tung, human and natural realms not only correspond to each other but activate each other as well. Catastrophes and anomalies are responses in the natural realm to human behavior that has gone amiss. This is especially true when the human in question is a ruler. Famines, eclipses, and other natural phenomena must therefore be interpreted as direct warnings from Heaven to the ruler and his ministers. The will of Heaven is to love and benefit the people; the ruler can only avert misfortune when the people enjoy prosperity and peace.

Tung held that Confucius wrote the *Ch'un-ch'iu* to set down rules for future dynasties and that the numerous portents recorded there carry an unmistakable message. In this manner the authority of the classics was placed above that of the ruler. Since Confucian scholars were the interpreters of the classics they were in a position to share in that higher authority. Tung's theories were clearly an attempt to place the government in the hands of the Confucians. Although he was influential in establishing the Confucians as the scholar-official class, most of his ideas nevertheless fell out of favor with the fall of the Han dynasty. The theory of portents, however, persisted as a convenient, indirect means to criticize a ruler.

The Confucian classics remained the final authority in society and government throughout most of Chinese history. Their position in China invites comparison with that of the Bible in the West. Twentieth-century revolt against Confucianism has removed from them the status of official authority, but many of the ideals they uphold have withstood the vicissitudes of modernity and still determine the character of many aspects of life in China and other parts of Asia.

[*See also* Confucian Thought.]

BIBLIOGRAPHY

Chiao Hsün (1763–1820). *Meng-tzu cheng-i.*

Ch'ien Mu. *Liang-Han ching-hsüeh ku-chin-wen p'ing-i.* Hong Kong, 1958.

de Bary, Wm. Theodore, Wing-tsit Chan, and Burton Watson, comps. *Sources of Chinese Tradition.* 2 vols. New York, 1964. See especially chapters 1–3 and 8.

Kao Ming. *Li-hsüeh ch'u-t'an.* Hong Kong, 1963.

Karlgren, Bernhard. "The Authenticity of Ancient Chinese Texts." *Bulletin of Museum of Far Eastern Antiquities* 1 (1929): 165–183.

Kono Seiichi. *Chūgoku kotengaku no tenkai.* Tokyo, 1949.

Lau, D. C., trans. *Mencius.* New York, 1970.

Legge, James, trans. *The Chinese Classics* (1893–1895). 5 vols. Reprint, Hong Kong, 1960.

Legge, James, trans. *The Four Books.* Reprint, New York, 1966.

Liu Pao-nan (1791–1855). *Lun-yü cheng-i.*

Marka, Mary Lelia, trans. *The Hsiao Ching.* New York, 1961.

Steele, John, trans. *The I-Li, or Book of Etiquette and Ceremonial.* London, 1917.

Waley, Arthur, trans. *The Book of Songs.* Boston, 1937.

Waley, Arthur, trans. *The Analects of Confucius.* London, 1938.

Wilhelm, Richard, and Cary F. Baynes, trans. *The I Ching or Book of Changes.* Princeton, 1967.

WING-TSIT CHAN

History of Study

The study of Chinese religion is connected intimately with the overall history of Western fascination with Chinese tradition. In the most obvious sense, the important historical role of Christian missionaries in China testifies to a pronounced, and not always strictly apologetic, interest in the subject of non-Christian forms of belief and practice. The question of the nature and significance of Chinese religion has also had a special (and at times contradictory) prominence in the rise of Western secular scholarship. Thus the early awareness of, and debate over, the meaning of Chinese and Asian traditions—especially concerning the comparative "similitude" of "other" cultural manifestations of religion—can be associated with both missionary sentiment and the intellectual revolution in Western thought during the Enlightenment.

In the case of China, these developments took a unique turn. The eighteenth-century skeptical spirit toward "superstitious" and "idolatrous" forms of religion found distinct comfort in the image (conveyed by the Jesuits) of a Confucian China politically ministered by a special class of moral philosophers who condemned the "degeneracy" and "superstition" of Buddhism, Taoism, and popular religion. China was often seen by Voltaire and other Enlightenment thinkers as a special exception to the principle that religious irrationality and priestcraft ruled the history of all major civilizations. This imaginary vision of the classical purity of China is strongly reflected in the history of Sinology and is responsible for traditional difficulties in fully appreciating the rich history of Chinese religious experience.

Although the study of Chinese religion has been broadly intertwined with Western intellectual and cultural history since the seventeenth and eighteenth centuries, this discussion will focus only on the history of certain key figures and movements that have specifically contributed to the scholarly study of Chinese religions. In this regard, Chinese religions will be taken to mean the three literate traditions known as Confucianism, Taoism, and Buddhism (and their interactions); popular folkloric beliefs and sectarian practices: various associated thematic issues such as archaic religion, ancestral belief, ritual, myth, and cosmological symbolilsm: and related topics of comparative method and interpretation. But this straightforward listing of topics must be tempered with the understanding that the history of the study of Chinese religions has always involved the definitional ambiguities associated with the categories of religion, salvation, and the sacred (e.g., the significance of such terms as *tao* and *T'ien,* or *Shang-ti).* Further difficulties concern the porous interrelationships of different literate traditions (thus the problematic nature of the common "three religions" rubric) and the diffuse functional relation between Chinese religions and social and familial life. These considerations have often resulted in overly facile assertions about the syncretic and eclectic nature of Chinese religions or about the fundamental hierarchical dichotomy between "great" (that is, aristocratic, civic, literate, orthodox, and usually equated with state Confucianism) and "little" (folk, popular, oral, nonorthodox, and associated with regional sectarian religions) traditions

The history of the study of Chinese religions is therefore a part of some of the most important developments in Western and East Asian intellectual history, in Christian missionary tradition, and in the emergence of comparative religion and Sinology as distinct academic disciplines. Given this complex historical and intellectual legacy, it will be necessary to condense and organize the following discussion under three general phases of development: (1) seventeenth- and eighteenth-century contributions by Jesuit missionaries and the French Enlightenment roots of academic Sinology; (2) European Orientalism and Protestant missionary scholarship in the nineteenth century; and (3) the emergence of the interdisciplinary study of Chinese religions as an academic area in the twentieth century.

By way of setting the stage for the coming of the Jesuit mission at the end of the sixteenth century, it is sufficient to recognize that the medieval European image of China was mythically associated with legends telling of its fantastic, monstrous, or paradisiacal nature. Such a vision of the "marvels of the east" is most characteristically observed in the semi-fictitious fourteenth-century work known as the *Travels of Sir John Mandeville.* At about this same time, more realistic firsthand accounts of religions in Mongolian-ruled Cathay appeared in the travel reports of early Franciscan missionaries and, most notably, in Marco Polo's *Description of the World.* But it was not until the great Portuguese trade efforts of the sixteenth century that really detailed reports about China and Japan became available in Europe. This new wealth of knowledge is especially exemplified by the widely distributed *Historia . . . del gran Reyno de la China* (1585), written and compiled by the Spanish Augustinian Juan Gonzalez de Mendoza. This work's grudging concern with the hidden similitude of Chinese religion in relation to the "holy, sacred, and Christian religion" typifies a kind of interpretive strategy that was to be reflected in different ways throughout the centuries of Western intercourse with China.

Seventeenth and Eighteenth Centuries. In the same decade that Mendoza's work was published, Matteo Ricci (1553–1610), an Italian Jesuit priest, arrived in the China of the late Ming dynasty and, drawing upon the tradition of Jesuit missions to Asia (already established by Francis Xavier and Alessandro Valignano), inaugurated a new era in the Western understanding of Chinese civilization. Indeed, Ricci may be considered not only the founding father of Sinology as the specialized, linguistically proficient study of China but also the first great interpreter of Chinese religions. The work fostered by Ricci was carried on and enriched by a long line of distinguished Jesuit scholars whose efforts span the early seventeenth century and extend to the second period of the French Jesuit mission at the end of the seventeenth and to the eighteenth century. The pioneering translations of the Chinese classics and the detailed observations of Chinese life and religion produced by these indefatigable missionary-scholars gave rise to the European vogue of *chinoiserie* and, even more profoundly, influenced the intellectual and religious ferment of the Enlightenment, especially in France and Germany.

Ricci's studied openness to Chinese tradition was not as plainly objective as it seemed since the Jesuits tended to adopt the intellectual biases, as well as the dress and etiquette, of China's lettered class, the Confucian scholars and bureaucrats. These men promulgated a canon of classical writings that expressly excluded Buddhist, Taoist, and other heterodox points of view. To study Chinese tradition, therefore, meant first and foremost the perusal of the classics, modeled upon the Neo-Confucian vision of the unity of Chinese civilization and on Chu Hsi's methods of commentarial exegesis. This mandarin perspective meshed with Ricci's own education in a Renaissance and Counter-Reformation tradition of Christian humanism that honored the philosophical and moral worth of classical Greek thought. [*See the biography of Ricci.*]

In the spirit of Mendoza's concern for similitude, Ricci examined the classics and found that ancient China shared a special sympathy with Christianity because of its apparent reverence for the one God, called Shang-ti ("ruler, lord on high, supreme ruler") or T'ien (Heaven). For Ricci these appellations revealed the remnants of an archaic tradition of monotheistic belief and practice that had been lost, it seemed, under the baleful influence of Buddhist and Taoist idolatry. To be successful in China, therefore, Christianity needed only to purify the false pantheistic accretions of latter-day Confucianism and to complete and fulfill the literati's philosophical appreciation of the natural law with the missionaries' gift of divine revelation.

Most of the Jesuit commentators tended to share Ricci's accommodationist methodology, but his sympathetic attitude toward Confucianism, the classics, and ancestral ritual was not universally accepted by all Jesuits (see, for example, Niccolo Longobardo's *Traité sur quelques points de la religion des Chinois,* 1701, which stressed the materialistic atheism of Neo-Confucian thought) or by the other, ecclesiastically contentious orders of Catholic missionaries. In fact, issues of missionary policy toward Chinese religions, including the "term question"—whether Shang-ti (T'ien) could be considered authentically theistic—gave rise to the embittered "rites controversy," which led eventually to the papal suppression of the Jesuit order in 1773. The rites controversy can also be associated in many ways with the growing European debate over the definitional, or "essential," nature of religion as reflected, for example, in the theory of Deism as a "natural religion" of reason. Thus, the whole rites episode, and its related intellectual environment, can be used to understand why the academic discipline of Sinology has often found the Chinese to be less intrinsically religious than other traditions. [*See* Jesuits.]

A second phase in the crystallization of a self-conscious Sinological tradition in the West is seen in the French Jesuit mission sent to China toward the end of the seventeenth century under the royal consent of Louis XIV. This effort continued into the "enlightened" climate of the eighteenth century and was favored by the newly tolerant rule of the Manchu emperor of the K'ang-hsi period during the early Ch'ing dynasty. Like the remarkable clerics of the first part of the seventeenth century, this new wave of missionaries included a roster of truly accomplished scholars who focused on Confucian classical tradition in the broad humanistic spirit of Ricci. These scholar-priests took special care to communicate the fruits of their Sinological labor back to Europe—for example, the impressive translations of the classics by Antoine Glaubil and the still useful compilations of miscellaneous translations and descriptive material about Chinese life and letters known as the *Lettres édifiantes et curieuses* (1703–1776) and the *Mémoires concernant l'histoire, les sciences, les arts, les mœurs, les usages, etc., des chinois* (1776–1814).

The interpretive perspective of the works found in the *Lettres* and *Mémoires* often reflected the old quest for hidden similitude so that, for example, J.-J. Amiot and J.-H. Prémare argued that chapter 14 of the *Lao-tzu* revealed a phonetically encoded reference to Jehovah. More substantial than the occult presence of Jehovah in early Taoist texts, though very much related as an interpretive genre, was the so-called Figurist movement, which was associated with Joachim Bouvet, J.-F. Foucquet, and Prémare. Inspired by the biblical tradition of allegorical interpretation, the Figurist movement basically took Ricci's approach to the Chinese classics to the extreme; it tried to show how the ancient Chinese texts disclosed not only hidden vestiges of monotheism and trinitarian belief but also remnants of ancient Hebrew law and, prefiguring the New Testament, allusions to an incarnate future redeemer.

It was in Paris during this same period that the first steps were taken in the direction of a secular tradition of professional Sinological scholarship. Thus various scholars of the Académie des Inscriptions et Belles-Lettres, such as Nicolas Fréret (1688–1749), the Arabist Étienne Fourmont (1683–1745), and the Syriac specialist Joseph de Guignes (1721–1800), turned their attention from the Near East to the Far East. Making use of the communications coming from the Jesuits—and aided by Arcade Hoang, a native Chinese who had been sent to Paris for training as a priest—these academicians sought to catalog, edit, publish, and sometimes plagiarize the rapidly accumulating materials coming from China. Other, more original efforts concerning religion include, in particular, de Guignes's studies on the Indian origins of Buddhism. Based on his study of Chinese sources. Other works by de Guignes, such as his treatise entitled *Observations sur quelques points concernant la religion et la philosophie des égyptiens et des chinois* (Paris, 1780), represented only a secularized version of the Jesuit fathers' Figurist view and, to some degree, anticipated the nineteenth-century pan-Babylonian diffusionists.

Nineteenth Century. In the face of the West's growing confidence in its imperial destiny, racial superiority, and dynamic progress, the old infatuation with Confucian China gave way to a more negative, and at times contemptuous, conviction that Chinese culture was inherently stagnant. This belief culminates philosophically in the mid- to late nineteenth century with Hegel's idea of the retarded spiritual development of Confucianism in particular and of Chinese civilization in general, as well as with Leopold von Ranke's conclusion that China represented a realm of the "eternal standstill." This more negative evaluation of China, however, was only a special instance of a broader, antipodal Orientalist mode of nineteenth-century scholarship that tended to view all Near and Far Eastern cultures as manifestations of monolithic and backward entity: the Orient, the East, or Asia.

The subject of Oriental religions was particularly important in Western scholarship since it seemed to give access to the underlying, and essentially desiccated "national spirit," or *Volksgeist,* of other cultures. The study of "other" religions, whether Asian or primitive, was central, then, to many new nineteenth-century humanistic sciences, such as folklore studies, comparative philology, sociology, and anthropology—as well as in other comparative historical pursuits, such as *Religionswissenschaft.* But the specific study of Chinese religions was not as relevant to these endeavors as was the study—influenced by pervasive currents of German romanticism—of the Indo-European traditions that seemed to share a common linguistic heritage with the West. In this way the "mystery" and "perennial philosophy" of Indian and "Aryan" religion (and the resultant stereotype of Eastern mysticism, typically identified with Buddhism and Upaniṣadic Hinduism) were often found more stimulating than what Emerson called the arid moralism and "doleful monotony" of Confucian China.

French academic scholarship. The rapid establishment of academic Sinology in France came about as the direct inheritance of the Jesuit tradition and the embryonic eighteenth-century Parisian school of Sinological Orientalism. The fruition of these developments took place in 1814 with the installation of Abel Rémusat (1788–1832) in the first European chair of "langues et littératures chinoises et tartares-mandchoues" at the Collège de France and with the founding in 1822 of the Société Asiatique. An autodidact of the Chinese written language, Rémusat (like almost all of the French Sinologists until Chavannes) was wholly dependent on *livresque* scholarship. Within the sanctuary of his library, however, Rémusat displayed multifaceted interests and can take credit for being the first academic Sinologist to pay some serious, though misguided, attention to the nature and significance of Lao-tzu and early Taoism. In addition to this, Rémusat should be remembered for his translation and study of Chinese sources dealing with Buddhist history outside of China proper.

Rémusat and de Guignes's oblique concern for Chinese sources as they illuminated Buddhist origins became the general approach among French Sinologists and tended to prevent a full analysis of Chinese Buddhism on its own terms. Another factor that contributed to the neglect of East Asian Buddhism was the increasing emphasis, later in the nineteenth century, on the Pali canon. The Pali scriptures were held to be the original expression of authentic Buddhist tradition and were considered moral and philosophical, in contrast to the idolatrous degeneracy of the Sūtra literature and religious practices of Mahāyāna. In like manner, the philosophical mysticism and moral purity of the classical Taoist texts were generally preferred to what were viewed as the corrupt religious superstition and ritual excess of later Taoism. This kind of overemphasis on the earliest Taoist texts, and the almost total neglect of the sectarian religious traditions of later Taoism, typified the field of Taoist scholarship until the late twentieth century.

Several other prominent figures in Paris published on Chinese philosophy and religion during the first part of the century (e.g., Léon de Rosny, the pioneer Japanologist who also wrote on Chinese religions), but Jean-Pierre Guillaume Pauthier (1801–1873) and Stanislas Julien (1797–1873) may be singled out as having been especially influential in the academic discourse of the period. Pauthier, the less substantial scholar of the two, commands notice for his voluminous and popular works. His controversial partial "translation" of the *Lao-tzu (Tao-te ching)* in 1838 led to Julien's more careful translation and commentary in 1841; his publication of *Les livres sacrés de l'orient* (Paris, 1852) anticipates F. Max Müller's monumental series "Sacred Books of the East."

Stanislas Julien, the inheritor of Rémusat's chair at the Collège de France, epitomized the best kind of philologically oriented scholarship of the day. He was, moreover, a tireless and combative promoter of academic Sinology throughout Europe and, through the work of his students, influenced several generations of European scholarship. Much of Julien's work concerned Chinese religion and philosophy. While maintaining the traditional exegetical interest in classical Confucianism, he also produced the first philogically competent translation of the *Lao-tzu* and a detailed study of the Sung dynasty *T'ai-shang kang-ying p'ien* (T'ai-shang's Book of Actions and Response), a sectarian quasi-Taoist tract on popular morality. In keeping with the interests of the French tradition, Julien also published important studies on the celebrated seventh-century Buddhist pilgrim Hsüan-tsang and on the philological principles used in the transcription of Sanskrit Buddhist terms from Chinese texts.

Anglo-American missionary scholarship. In comparison with French and continental scholarhip (in addition to the French scholars, J. H. Plath, August Pfizmaier, Gustave Schlegel, and Charles-Joseph De Harlez should be noted). English tradition generally emphasized the gifted amateur over the professional pedant and tended to display a "singular listlessness" with respect to Sinological scholarship. By the mid-nineteenth century, however, the best and most extensive scholarly work was being done along the coast of China by a sedulous group of British and American Protestant missionaries. As a part of their evangelical faith, and by taking full advantage of their direct exposure to the living Chinese tradition, the missionary scholars made the careful study of Chinese language and culture a significant, and sometimes overriding, aspect of their work. To bring the gospel to China—understood as the "land of Sinim" (*Isaiah* 49:12)—was to them, most of all, a divine calling that had been recorded prophetically in the Old Testament. The diligence of these missionaries cannot be questioned, but it should be noted that the Protestant evangelical theology was most often premised on a Calvinist view of the essentially depraved nature of "pagan" nations and religions. This view differed significantly from the accommodationist perspective and humanistic sympathy of the Jesuits.

The dominant passion of the Anglo-American missionaries, from Robert Morrison in 1807 until those at the end of the century, was to make the one and only true classic, the Bible, available in Chinese translation. To this end an incredible amount of missionary scholarship was devoted to producing a definitive interdenominational edition of the scriptures. These labors had important repercussions because the need to find equivalent Chinese religious terms and concepts for an accurate and intelligible translation of the scriptures led to broad investigations of Chinese religious tradition. In the most pointed sense, such questions led to the heated debate known as the term question.

Like the earlier Jesuit controversy, the term question revolved around the problem of whether the classically sanctioned terms *Shang-ti* and *T'ien* were appropriate for expressing the true meaning of the creator god in the Bible. Despite the rancor, this controversy did have the virtue of forcing the combatants to argue etymology and semantics on the basis of Chinese sources and, in the case of the more liberal faction, to invoke fashionable nineteenth-century philological and comparative theories linking linguistic and cultural development. Thus a series of curious diffusionist works that argued for the Mesopotamian origins of Chinese civilization—a Babylonian variation on de Guignes's old Egyptian theories—appeared during the last part of the nineteenth century.

More important than these quaint examples of early Orientalist license were the general attitude and work of the liberal faction of missionary scholars, a group whose intellectual breadth was especially manifested in such popular China coast periodicals as *The Chinese Respository, The Chinese Recorder,* and *The China Review.* Many of the leading figures in this group (e.g., Walter Medhurst, S. Wells Williams, W. A. P. Martin, John Chalmers, Ernst Eitel, and Joseph Edkins) produced not only responsible scholarship about general aspects of Chinese tradition but also haphazardly objective appraisals of Chinese religions. Especially noteworthy in this regard are Eitel's studies on Buddhism and the popular geomantic art of *feng-shui* and Edkins's influential accounts of the general nature of Chinese religions, his studies on the *I ching,* and his various writings on Chinese Buddhism.

The greatest scholarly figure among the missionaries was the Scottish Congregationalist James Legge (1815–1897). Best known for the *Chinese Classics* (Oxford, 1893–1895), his massive (five volumes) and still standard translations, with copious notes based on traditional Neo-Confucian commentaries, Legge is the Protestant missionary equivalent of Ricci and the scholarly equal of Julien. Starting out as a conventionally pious missionary with a talent for languages and rigorous habits of study, Legge became embroiled in the term question in the 1850s, about the same time he decided to embark on his translation project. It was the combination of these two factors—the bitter recriminations engendered by the term debate and his growing Riccian respect for Confucius and the classics—that progressively alienated Legge from his more parochial colleagues in the mission field and caused him, by the 1860s, to redefine his vocation primarily in scholarly terms.

After assuming the first British chair of Chinese at Oxford University in 1876 and accepting Max Müller's commission to undertake the Chinese volumes for the "Sacred Books of the East" series (Oxford, 1879–1904), Legge produced translations of various Confucian classics, including a controversial rendition of the *I ching.* As a new and surprisingly congenial venture for him, he translated the *Lao-tzu* and *Chuang-tzu,* together with several short sectarian works. Like the extensive prolegomena to his Confucian translations, Legge's long introduction to the Taoist volumes is a valuable overview of classical Taoist studies up to his time (e.g., the work of Julien, John Chalmers, F. H. Balfour, and Herbert Giles). Legge also wrote a rather desultory popular overview of Chinese religions and, in emulation of French scholarship, produced a translation and study bearing on the travels of the Buddhist Fa-hsien. But Buddhist studies were never even a minor vocation for Legge; in this area one must turn to the influential work of Edkins and Eitel, as well as to the relatively more sympathetic studies of Samuel Beal and Timothy Richard.

Jesuit and other amateur scholarship. The nineteenth century is the great age of the Protestant apostolate to China, but after the reconstitution of the Jesuit order in 1814, a renewed Jesuit mission, starting in 1842, again made substantial contributions to the study of Chinese religions. Commendable in this regard are the copious studies found in the *Variétés sinologiques* (established in 1892), which revived the old encyclopedic spirit of the *Mémoires.* Individually important for their emphasis on Chinese philosophy and religion were three outstanding Jesuit scholars: Séraphin Couvreur (1835–1919), Léon Wieger (1856–1933), and Henri Doré (1859–1931). Couvreur and Wieger produced important scholarly translations and studies concerning the classics, Taoism, and Buddhism; Henri Doré is primarily remembered for his eighteen-volume *Recherches sur les superstitions en Chine* (Shanghai, 1911–1938). This was a copious, though not always very representative, descriptive handbook on multifarious popular "superstitions" current at the end of the Ch'ing dynasty. The good father, it should be noted, seems to have partly cribbed his findings from the work of the Chinese Jesuit priest Pierre Hoang (Huang Pai-lu).

Doré's work reflects the fact that, toward the end of the nineteenth century, popular religious tradition was at last receiving some extensive, if often bemused, attention. Representing the earliest ethnographic and folkloric investigation of Ch'ing regional religion, mythology, and ancestral ritual were several outstanding works by Anglo-American and European amateur scholars (Justus Doolittle, N. B. Dennys, J. Dyer Ball, and Arthur H. Smith) who lived in Chinese coastal cities. The most significant figure who can be loosely identified with this scholarly trend is the Dutchman J. J. M. de Groot (1854–1921). After a year in the field preparing for a career as a government interpreter, he published an observant analysis of the seasonal round of popular religious festivals in Amoy (*Les fêtes annuellement célébrées à Emoui: Étude concernant la religion populaire des Chinois,* Paris, 1886). De Groot is most famous, however, for his incomplete, six-volume magisterial synthesis entitled *The Religious System of China* (Leiden, 1892–1910), which moved away from popular religion to a consideration of classical sources and the ancient substratum of all later forms of Chinese religion. This work was intemperate in tone and essentially sought to debunk what de Groot had come to regard as the retarded pretensions of the elite tradition (see also his *Sectarianism and Religious Persecution in China,* 2 vols., Amsterdam, 1903–1904). However, de Groot's idea of the *universismus* (or the underlying archaic unity of elite and popular manifestations of Chinese religion, especially popular Taoism) represented an important, yet mostly ignored, methodological counterpoint to the artificial "three religions" rubric of classically inspired Sinology.

Twentieth Century. The turn of the century saw the passing of the old apologetic missionary movement, which, as a reaction to internal disillusionment and external Chinese antagonism, moved away from an interest in Chinese religion and pure scholarship. Within academic circles, French scholarship continued as the premier Western Sinological tradition, although important work was also done by other European, Russian, and American scholars, as well as by Japanese and Chinese scholars who, in the modernizing spirit of Western critical analysis, had transformed the age-old authoritarian traditions of Confucian classical exegesis.

Early twentieth-century French Sinology. Displaying the technical superiority of French Sinology in the fullest sense was, first of all, Édouard Chavannes (1865–1918), who combined amazingly encyclopedic interests with both philological rigor and humanistic sensitivity. More so than ever before, Chavannes made use of native Chinese textual scholarship and emphasized the importance of linguistic and anthropological field experience in Asia (facilitated by the École Française d'Extrême-Orient, founded in Hanoi at the turn of the century). Chavannes is particularly remembered for *Mémoires historiques de Se Ma Ts'ien* (Paris, 1895–1905), his erudite partial translation of Ssu-ma Ch'ien's *Shih chi.* The elaborate annotations to this five-volume translation often constitute miniature dissertations on multifarious issues concerning ancient Chinese religion and testify to Chavannes's belief in the importance of religion to an understanding of early China. This belief is also seen in his work on the cultic foundations of archaic religion, *Le Dieu du sol dans la Chine antique* (Paris, 1910), and on the popular religious traditions associated with the sacred mountain T'ai. Later works on religion included several studies of Buddhism, Buddhist folklore, and during his last years, Taoist ritual.

The work of Chavannes's colleague and collaborator Sylvain Lévi (1863–1936), along with the even more impressive contributions of the Belgian scholar Louis de La Vallée Poussin (1869–1938), indicates the emergence of a Franco-Belgian school of Buddhology. Concerned with the overall cultural context of Buddhist history, the school demanded philological training in all of the requisite canonical languages (Sanskrit, Pali, Tibetan, and Chinese). Along with its emphasis on the non-Pali Mahāyāna texts and commentaries associated with the East Asian tradition, the Franco-Belgian school distinguished itself from German and English scholarship by characteristically stressing the broad philosophical implications of Buddhist thought.

Cast in the mold of Chavannes but possessing even greater linguistic facility, bibliographical erudition, and breadth of interests was the peripatetic polymath Paul Pelliot (1878–1945). More intently than any of the other scholars of the period, Pelliot took as his mission the social, religious, and intellectual interrelationships of all of the Asian cultures—especially the rich historical interconnections between Central and East Asian traditions. Given this versatility, Pelliot produced a diverse stream of articles and reviews, many of which dealt with aspects of Chinese religious history that often broke with the old classical fixation. One of the most celebrated of Pelliot's accomplishments was his participation in the exploration and appropriation of the Tun-huang manuscripts during the years from 1907 to 1911. In terms of importance for understanding Chinese history and religion, the discovery of a cache of thousands of fragmented Buddhist texts (along with some rare Taoist and Confucian texts) dating from the fifth to the tenth centuries is comparable only to the archaeological recovery of the Shang dynasty in the twenties and thirties and the discovery of the Ma-wamg-tui burial deposit of early Han dynasty texts and artifacts in the seventies.

Following in the grand tradition of Chavannes and Pelliot, but making more significant methodological contributions to the study of Chinese religions, were Marcel Granet (1884–1940) and Henri Maspero (1883–1945). Granet was the more methodologically innovative of the two in that his approach was couched within a broad Durkheimian sociological framework that often lent itself to venturesome speculation. From this perspective, Granet, making use of the broadest assortment of textual materials from differing periods, attempted to reconstruct the social and religious life of ancient feudal China. Religious data of the most diverse sort, especially information relating to the archaic folk tradition, was crucial for Granet's understanding of Chinese civilization and resulted in a series of brilliant, and sometimes overly intuitive, interconnected studies on the cultic and folkloric implications of the *Shih ching* (Book of Poetry), on the mythic and ritual structures at the heart of the feudal tradition of the Chou period, and on the overall religious and intellectual system (*La religion des Chinois*, Paris, 1922; and *La pensée chinois*, Paris, 1934). [*See the biography of Granet.*]

Maspero shared Granet's passion for a synthetic understanding of Chinese history and wrote with great technical mastery about a varied array of topics. Especially noteworthy for its methodological implications is Maspero's long monograph "Légendes mythologiques dans le 'Chou king' " (in *Journal asiatique* 204, 1924, pp. 1–100). By making use of ethnographic data from Tai tribes to reconstruct ancient Chinese mythology and religion only fragmentarily preserved in early Chinese literature, Maspero showed that the classical "history" of the *Shu ching* (Book of History) was fundamentally informed by myth and ritual themes. After 1926, Maspero began to explore the largely unchartered history and meaning of religious Taoism. Anticipating, and to some degree inspiring, the broad interest in the overall Taoist tradition that would emerge in the sixties, Maspero's work surveyed various aspects of sectarian Taoism and generally argued for a continuity between the mysticism of the early Taoist classics and the esoteric practices of the later religious tradition.

Continental and British scholarship before World War II. Besides the French contributions, there were significant works by Scandinavian scholars (e.g., J. G. Andersson, M. W. de Visser, and Bernhard Karlgren) and by German scholars (e.g., Otto Franke, Adolph Forke, Bruno Schindler, August Conrady, Ernst Boerschmann, Eduard Erkes, and Carl Hentze). By far the greatest of these scholars was Karlgren, who is justly renowned for his work on the phonological development of the Chinese language, as well as for his studies of archaic bronze iconography; also important was his long article "Legends and Cults in Ancient China," in the *Bulletin of the Museum of Far Eastern Antiquities* (Stockholm) 18, 1946, pp. 199–365. This article established strict historical criteria for the determination of authentic archaic mythology. In pointed contrast to Karlgren's approach was the work of Erkes and Hentze, which showed the impact of various comparativist schools of German anthropology. The most exaggerated and controversial example of the German influence is found in the work of Hentze. Based on his diffusionist comparisons with primitive cultures and early Mesoamerican civilizations, Hentze found an elaborate religious system of lunar symbolism in the zoomorphic and geometric glyphs on the bronze vessels of the Shang dynasty. Within German circles, special mention must also be made of Max Weber and Richard Wilhelm. As a non-Sinologist, Weber admittedly based his work on China (see his *The Religion of China: Confucianism and Taoism*, translated by Hans H. Gerth, Glencoe, Ill., 1951) on secondhand information and was often ignored by specialists; nevertheless this work demonstrated the relevance of a comparative sociological method for understanding Chinese religions. The Sinologist Richard Wilhelm produced a number of influential studies and translations concerning classical philosophy and religion, but he is best known today for his "scriptural" translation of the divinatory *I ching*. Through the enthusiastic patronage of Carl Jung, this work achieved a broad cultural following in Europe and America during the sixties and seventies.

In England, Legge's classically staid ruminations largely prevailed, although the works of William Soothill, L. C. Hopkins, Perceval Yetts, Herbert A. Giles, and Lionel Giles represent partial exceptions to the rule. It was really not until the maverick genius of Arthur Waley became manifested that British scholarship rose above mere academic competence. Early American scholarship also tended to reflect the amateurish character and methodological narrowness of English Sinology. Outstanding, however, was the pioneering work on Taoist alchemy by the historian of science Tenney L. Davis and the anthropological studies of Chinese local culture and religion by Daniel Kulp and David Crockett Graham. Finally, Friedrich Hirth, Berthold Laufer, and Paul Carus should be mentioned as immigrant scholars whose work frequently dealt with religious topics. The most important of these figures was Laufer, whose erudition and synthetic abililties rivaled those of the French masters. Still valuable are his studies on ancient Chinese religion (e.g., *Jade: A Study in Chinese Archaeology and Religion*, Chicago, 1912), which made brilliant use of comparative linguistics, archaeology, and ethnography. In more of an ephemeral vein was the work of Paul Carus, who, besides bringing the famous Zen Buddhist scholar D. T. Suzuki to the United States, wrote a number of semipopular books on Taoism and Buddhism.

Prewar Japanese scholarship. In Japan the adoption of Western scholarly methods progressed more rapidly than in China. By the early Meiji period at the end of the nineteenth century, the old Kangaku school of Neo-Confucian scholarship had given way to various intellectual movements that emphasized a newly critical approach to classical Chinese civilization and its relation to Japanese tradition. There is often a nationalistic cast to these fledgling adaptations of Western historiography, as well as an element of Eastern Orientalism that typically relegated Chinese and Japanese religions to the margins of the historical process. At the same time, Japanese philological and bibliographical mastery of Chinese sources and the newly engendered passion for a universal understanding of China independent of orthodox dynastic views established the foundations for a truly critical historiographical and social scientific appraisal of Chinese religions.

During the first few decades of the twentieth century Japanese works devoted to religious issues were generally few in number. Blandly bibliographical and descriptive in approach, they were usually confined to compartmentalized studies of textual filiation or to restricted sectarian aspects of Buddhist and Taoist history (particularly valuable were the descriptive surveys of Chinese and aboriginal religions on Taiwan conducted during the Japanese occupation). But by the twenties and thirties, Japanese scholarship, while maintaining its superior talent for critical textual analysis, manifested more of a willingness to study the history of religions as an integral aspect of Chinese sociopolitical history, a development that was partly influenced by the impact of Weberian and Durkheimian methodologies. This new interpretive climate was signaled by the founding in 1936 of the Japanese Society for Historical Research on Chinese Buddhism, which brought together scholars interested in the history of Buddhism and Taoism as related to the larger institutional framework of Chinese tradition.

It was during this period that Japanese scholars, especially in the area of Buddhology, started to engage in cooperative research, as is exemplified by *Hôbôgirin*, 4 vols. (Tokyo, 1929–1931), the joint French-Japanese Buddhist encyclopedia project edited by Paul Demiéville and under the supervision of Sylvain Lévi and Takakusu Junjirō. Another factor, which paralleled related developments in China, was the rise of the Japanese school of folklore studies under the tutelage of Yanagida Kunio. Concerned with anthropological and sociological methods of comparison that in this period often reflected German Kulturkreiselehre diffusionism, it is the Japanese folkloristic tradition of scholarship that constitutes the foundation of the important Japanese participation, after World War II, in the history of religions as an international academic discipline of study.

Prewar Chinese scholarship. Given the greater degree of instability in Chinese political life, it is not surprising that a coherent, Western-style scholarship at first flourished more successfully in Japan than in China. The missionary experience had left many Chinese intellectuals acutely antagonistic toward the relevance of religion, whether Christian or traditional, in Chinese history; this attitude, coupled with the classical Confucian aloofness toward the "spirits" and the more modern secular implications of Western scholarly methods, resulted in a situation that was hardly conducive to the dispassionate study of Chinese religions. The eventual triumph of a new, and officially atheistic, Marxist orthodoxy tended only to reinforce this prejudicial approach to the history of native religions.

In addition to such well-known figures as Liang Ch'i-ch'ao and Hu Shih, who were imbued with Western notions of Social Darwinism, a number of other prominent scholars were influenced by modern methodologies and made lasting, although sometimes rather indirect and polemical, contributions to the academic study of Chinese religions. Perhaps most important in terms of his iconoclastic impact on traditional Chinese historiography was Ku Chieh-kang. Ku was identified with the so-called Doubting Antiquity movement of the twenties and thirties, which produced the seven-volume *Ku-shih pien* (Critiques of Ancient History; Shanghai, 1926–1941). This work signaled the end of the Confucian classical paradigm in historical and textual scholarship and remains to this day a storehouse of miscellaneous materials pertinent to the study of Chinese religion, mythology, and folk tradition. Along with articles and monographs published by the *Yenching Journal of Chinese Studies* and other periodicals influenced by Western social science, the *Ku-shih pien* definitively established the relevance of ancient Chinese mythology and religion to an understanding of the foundations of the very classical tradition that denied them. In addition to his concern with ancient history, Ku also became involved in the analysis of modern popular tradition and religion through his relationship with the Folklore Studies movement, which appeared in South China in the late twenties. Although its motivations were often more political than scholarly in nature, this loose group of scholars produced the first substantial scholarly collections of Chinese folk tales and songs and, drawing upon Arnold van Gennep's Durkheimian *Le Folklore* (Paris, 1924), established the value of a folkloristic theory of culture for Chinese tradition.

Postwar to the present. The postwar years witnessed the growing dominance of social scientific methodologies and the establishment of specialized academic disciplines, departments, and area studies—especially in American universitites. As a result of these developments, the old ideal of Sinology as a holistic pursuit concerned primarily with classical language and literature was abandoned, and the field was splintered into particular subdisciplines that were defined in terms of various discrete historical periods and methodological perspectives. These developments, moreover, tended to reinforce the old devaluation of the history of Chinese religions since, as a part of the growing emphasis on modern and revolutionary China, it seemed self-evident that religion had little importance for understanding communist China. In the study of Chinese tradition, then, the rational and secular presuppositions of Western academic scholarship and social scientific methodology were especially strengthened by a whole set of apparent verifications coming from the conflation of the classical Confucian, turn-of-the-century Chinese modernist, and Chinese communist self-images.

The outcome of these developments was that from the forties to the fifties the focused Sinological study of religion was a low ebb. Yet these relatively quiescent years laid the foundations for the upsurge of interest in Chinese religions seen in the decades that followed. In this transitional sense, it is first worth drawing attention to a loose international group of scholars who often dealt with selected religious topics while maintaining something of the old notion of Sinology as a comprehensive discipline. In this category were, among others, the Americans Derk Bodde, H. G. Creel, Schuyler Cammann, Arthur Wright, Alexander Soper, and Wing-Tsit Chan; those continuing the French tradition, such as Paul Demiéville, Rolf Stein, and Étienne Balasz; and finally other European and Asian scholars, such as Arthur Waley, J. J. L. Duyvendak, Werner Eichhorn, R. H. van Gulik, and Fung Yu-lan.

A second category during this same period more directly forecasts the kind of specialized approach to religion in terms of subject area and methodology that characterizes the seventies and eighties. Thus, in the area of Buddhist and Taoist studies there was the important early work of Max Kaltenmark, Michel Soymié, Erwin Rousselle, and Erik Zürcher in Europe; Yanagida Seizan, Kimura Eiichi, Yoshioka Yoshitoyo, T'ang Yung-t'ung, and Ch'en Kuo-fu in Asia; and Kenneth Ch'en, Richard Robinson, Chang Chung-yuan, Walter Liebenthal, Arthur Link, and Holmes Welch in the United States. Lastly, there were those who studied popular and local tradition from novel social scientific perspectives: Francis L. K. Hsu, who examined village culture and ancestral religion from a social-psychological frame of reference, and Wolfram Eberhard, who studied traditional Chinese religion, mythology, morality, and folklore in relation to the sociocultural history of local cultures.

In the sixties the overall climate concerning the relevance of religion to modern life and the general academic significance of the study of world religions changed in dramatic ways. For the first time the specialized study of Chinese religions became recognizable as a specific professional focus for scholars working in different academic disciplines. This was a gradual, largely unconscious development throughout most of the sixties and early seventies, but by 1974 public acknowledgment came in the form of the founding of the international Society for the Study of Chinese Religions by three American scholars, Holmes Welch, Daniel Overmyer, and Laurence Thompson.

While the overt emergence of the study of Chinese religions as a field of concentration occurred in the seventies, there were several earlier formative developments that should be identified. One of these was the apearance of C. K. Yang's *Religion in Chinese Society* (Berkeley, 1961), which applied a neo-Weberian sociological analysis to Chinese tradition and, arguing against prevailing attitudes, showed the intrinsic significance of religion within even the Confucian milieu of the "great tradition." Even more important for its grand compass, international impact, and interdisciplinary implications was the publication of the first few volumes of Joseph Needham's monumental, and still appearing, *Science and Civilisation in China* (Cambridge, 1954–). Volume 2, which discussed Taoism as a part of the "history of Chinese science," was particularly important. First published in 1956, it did not really capture scholarly attention until the sixties.

The interest in Taoism stimulated by Needham was also complemented by the work that was being done in the sixties on the living liturgical traditions of sectarian Taoism in Taiwan by Kristofer Schipper, a Paris-trained scholar and the first Westerner to be initiated as a Taoist priest. Schipper's revolutionary fieldwork—along with the work of Needham, Nathan Sivin, and others who had been working on Taoist tradition—culminated in the first international conference on Taoist studies, held in Italy in 1969. This event was doubly significant: it not only signaled the rapid development of Taoist studies, which continues to the present, but also—as is shown by the presence of Mircea Eliade at the conference and by the publication of the conference papers in the journal *History of Religions* (1961–)—marked the emergence of a new spirit of cooperation between the study of Chinese religions and the comparative history of world religions, a discipline previously preoccupied with primitive and Indo-European traditions. This kind of collaborative approach was ratified by the establishment of the Society for the Study of Chinese Religions and tends to characterize the interdisciplinary range of articles on Chinese religion found currently in older, established journals in Sinology and in comparative religion, folklore, and philosophy, as well as in several specialized journals that were started in the seventies and eighties (e.g., *Journal of Chinese Religions, Journal of Chinese Philosophy, Early China, Journal of the International Association of Buddhist Studies).*

Given all of these developments in the past few decades, and in sharp contrast with the old legacy of neglect and disparagement, there has been a veritable flood of outstanding scholarship concerning Chinese religions that is in the process of reforming many outdated assumptions about Chinese civilization. Fortunately, this scholarly enterprise is also on the verge of becoming fully international in scope. Besides the continuing contributions of Japanese scholarship and the efforts of Chinese scholars in Taiwan, Singapore, and Hong Kong, the mainland Chinese Academy of Sciences and its affiliated Institute for Research on World Religions have been revitalized.

Current Trends in Sinology. Five areas may be singled out for their prominence in current research. The first of these is the burgeoning field of Taoist studies, which for the first time has attracted a broad, interdisciplinary group of international scholars. Much of their work is concerned with basic—and often revisionary—textual, historical, and interpretive studies of the liturgical tradition. Besides the aforementioned scholars, Max Kaltenmark, Michel Strickman, Michael Saso, Anna Seidel, Isabelle Robinet, John Lagerwey, Manfred Porkert, Ofuchi Ninji, Fukui Kojun, Kubo Noritada, Yoshioka Yoshitoyo, Wang Ming, and Ch'en Kuo-fu may be particularly mentioned. There have also been some important reconsiderations of the ancient texts of the *Lao-tzu* and *Chuang-tzu* (e.g., by D. C. Lau and A. C. Graham) and some preliminary analyses of the Ma-wang-tui materials as related to the Huang-lao, Legalist, and *fang-shih* movements during the Han.

A second important area concerns the study of Buddhism, which has started to break from its old habit of presenting Chinese Buddhism as if it existed in a realm detached from its resident culture. Building on Japanese scholarship, figures such as Demiéville, Stanley Weinstein, Philip Yampolsky, Richard Robinson, Richard Mather, Leon Hurvitz, Jan Yun-hua, and Jen Chi-yu have made significant and technically proficient contributions to the field. Even more promising is the fact that a younger and more hermeneutically inclined group of international scholars has taken up some of the largely unexplored aspects of Chinese Buddhist tradition (e.g., Hua-yen, Pure Land, Ch'an, Chinese Vajrayāna, and the interaction of Buddhism and Taoism).

A third area involves the reappraisal of Confucian tradition, especially Neo-Confucian moral thought and methods of self-cultivation, in relation to new religious and philosophical perspectives. Besides the earlier Hong Kong school of Confucianists (e.g., Mou Tsung-san, Hsü Fu-kuan, T'ang Chun-i), the seventies and eighties have witnessed the emergence, under Wm. Theodore De Bary's leadership, of an influential group of American Neo-Confucian scholars (e.g., Julia Ching, Tu Wei-ming, Antonio Cua). Allowing for several notable exceptions (e.g., the work of Tu, David Nivison, and Donald Munro and the engaging interpretations of the nonspecialist Herbert Fingarette), there has been relatively less progress made in rethinking the import of the classical Confucian texts.

The fourth area that has received considerable innovative attention involves the complex issues of Chinese popular, folk, and heterodox sectarian religion and literature (such as *pao-chuan* scripture). Asian and Western scholars from different disciplines have made valuable descriptive and theoretical contributions (e.g., Li Shih-yu, Suzuki Chusei, Sawada Mizuho, Noguchi Tetsuro, Susan Naquin, Hou Ching-lan, and Daniel Overmyer); also important have been the studies coming from the perspective of social anthropology (e.g., Marjorie Topping, Emily Ahern, David Jordan, Arthur Wolf, Steven Feuchtwang, and Goran Aijmer). As exemplified by the work of Maurice Freedman, this genre of scholarship holds special promise for developing some generalized theories concerning the unity and diversity of Chinese religion.

A final area refers to research on a whole range of topics associated with ancient Chinese tradition and religion. Because of spectacular archaeological discoveries extending from the Neolithic through the Han, there has been an especially heightened appreciation of the roles played by archaic religion, divination, shamanism, cosmological and artistic systems of meaning, and ancestral ritual in the origins and cultural development of Chinese civilization. Mainland Chinese archaeological scholarship has accomplished the basic descriptive work in this area, but more theoretical advances have been made by an international roster of scholars that includes, among others, Chang Kwang-chih, David Keightley, Paul Wheatley, Lester Bilskey, Noel Barnard, Anneliese Bulling, and Michael Loewe. Chang Kwang-chih, and such others as Sarah Allen, Andrew Plaks, and Rémi Mathieu, have also applied new anthropological and comparative methods to the interpretation of ancient Chinese mythology, although there remains further work to be done to understand satisfactorily the relationship between myth and ritual in early China.

Conclusion. Much progress has been made since the sixties in the study of Chinese religions. In a most telling fashion, recent research has demonstrated the dynamic involvement of religion throughout all historical periods and social levels of Chinese cultural life. There are, nevertheless, many fundamental issues that have remained moot, not the least of which is the central definitional and comparative question of religion and religions in China. Given the temporal depth and regional diversity of Chinese religions documented so impressively in current scholarship, there has still been little serious attention given to the question of what—in either a diachronic or synchronic sense—constitutes the common ground of Chinese religiosity.

The integration of historical research and interpretive analysis in the study of Chinese religions is, in other words, still underdeveloped. Scholars such as Joseph Needham and Wolfgang Bauer have written powerfully and synthetically on issues that impinge on broad religious themes, but there have yet to appear any even partly compelling theoretical studies of the overall history of Chinese religions. It is premature to expect such syntheses in the near future. In the meantime, what is needed is more of an approach that always respects the facts of the matter but heuristically experiments with the notion that reading Chinese texts and understanding Chinese religious tradition can only be premised on what is imagined as basic metaphors of comparative similitude. To borrow from Chuang-tzu, it may be said that understanding—whether of butterflies or religions—is always a way of seeing the provisional relation betwen shadow and penumbra.

BIBLIOGRAPHY

Bibliographical Sources. The most important bibliographical compilations relevant to the history of the study of Chinese religions include the following.

Cohen, Alvin P. "A Bibliography of writings Contributory to the Study of Chinese Folk Religions." *Journal of the American Academy of Religion* 43 (1975): 238–265.

Cordier, Henri. *Bibliotheca Sinica.* 5 vols. Paris, 1904–1924.

Marceron, Désiré. *Bibliographie du taoïsme.* Paris, 1898.

Pfister, Louis. *Notices biographiques et bibliographiques sur les jésuites de l'ancienne mission de Chine, 1552–1773.* 2 vols. Shanghai, 1932–1934.

Thompson, Laurence G. *Chinese Religion in Western Languages: A Comprehensive and Classified Bibliography of Publications in English, French, and German through 1980.* Tucson, 1984.

General Historical Studies and Early Period. There are no comprehensive intellectual histories of Sinology or the study of Chinese religions. However, various specialized studies may be consulted, including the following.

Brear, Douglas. "Early Assumptions in Western Buddhist Studies." *Religion* 5 (Autumn 1975): 136–157.

Dehergne, Joseph. "Les historiens jésuites du taoïsme." In *Actes du Colloque International de Sinologie: La mission française de Pékin aux dix-septième et dix-huitème siècles,* pp. 59–67. Paris, 1976.

Demiévile, Paul. "Aperçu historique des études sinologiques en France." *Acta Asiatica* 11 (1966): 56–110.

Girardot, N. J. "Chinese Religion and Western Scholarship." In *China and Christianity,* edited by James D. Whitehead et al., pp. 83–111. Notre Dame, Ind., 1979.

Lach, Donald F. *Asia in the Making of Europe.* 4 vols. Chicago, 1965–1977.

Lancashire, D. "Buddhist Reaction to Christianity in Late Ming China." *Journal of the Oriental Society of Australia* 6 (1968–1969): 82–103.

Maspero, Henri. "La sinologie." In *Société asiatique: Le livre du centenaire, 1822–1922,* pp. 261–283. Paris, 1922

Pinot, Virgile. *La Chine et la formation de l'esprit philosophique en France, 1640–1740.* Paris, 1932.

Rule, Paul A. "Jesuit and Confucian? Chinese Religion in Journals of Matteo Ricci, S.J., 1583–1610." *Journal of Religious History* 5 (December 1968): 105–124.

Soymié, Michel. "Les études chinoises." *Journal asiatique* 261 (1973): 209–246.

Spence, Jonathan D. *The Memory Palace of Matteo Ricci.* New York, 1984.

Sprenkel, Otto Berkelback van der. "Western Sources." In *Essays on the Source for Chinese History,* edited by Donald D. Leslie, Colin Mackerras, and Wang Gungwu, pp. 154–175. Columbia, S.C., 1973.

Thompson, Laurence G. "American Sinology, 1830–1920: A Bibliographical Survey." *Tsing-hua Journal of Chinese Studies* 2, no. 2 (June 1961): 244–290.

Young, John D. *Confucianism and Christianity: The First Encounter.* Hong Kong, 1983.

Modern Period Studies. Again, there are no general surveys of historical and intellectual developments in the twentieth century, but the following are helpful discussions of particular aspects.

Barrett, T. H. "Change and Progress in Understanding Chinese Religion." *Numen* 29 (December 1982): 239–249.

Bodde, Derk. "Myths of Ancient China." In *Essays on Chinese Civilization,* edited by Charles Le Blanc and Dorothy Borei, pp. 45–84. Princeton, 1981.

Ch'en Yao-shen and Paul S. Y. Hsiao. *Sinology in the United Kingdom and Germany.* Translated by William W. G. Wan and T. W. Kwok. Honolulu, 1967.

Demiéville, Paul. "Henri Maspero et l'avenir des études chinoises." *T'oung pao* 38 (1947): 16–42.

Eberhard, Wolfram. *Moral and Social Values of the Chinese: Collected Essays.* Taipei, 1971. See especially the chapter entitled "Studies in Chinese Religions: 1920–1932," pp. 335–399.

Eliasberg, Danielle. "Maspero: L'histoire de la religion populaire chinoise." In *Hommage à Henri Maspero, 1883–1945,* pp. 55–60. Paris, 1983.

Franke, Herbert. *Sinologie An Deutschen Universitäten.* Wiesbaden, 1968.

Freedman, Maurice. "On the Sociological Study of Chinese Religion." In *Religion and Ritual in Chinese Society*, edited by Arthur A. Wolf, pp. 19–41. Stanford, Calif., 1974.

Honey, David B. "The Foundation of Modern German Sinology." *Phi Theta Papers* (Berkeley, 1984): 82–101.

Jong, J. W. de. "A Brief History of Buddhist Studies in Europe and America." *Eastern Buddhist*, n.s. 7, no. 1 (May 1974): 55–106, and no. 2 (October 1974): 49–82.

Kaltenmark, Max. "Henri Maspero et les études taoïstes." In *Hommage à Henri Maspero, 1883–1945*, pp. 45–48. Paris. 1983.

Lalou, Marcelle. "Onze années de travaux européens sur le bouddhisme (mai 1936–mai 1947)." *Museon* 61 (1948): 245–276.

Maspero, Henri. "Édouard Chavannes," *T'oung pao* 21 (1922): 43–56.

Nakamura Hajime. "A Survey of Mahāyāna Buddhism with Bibliographical Notes." *Journal of Intercultural Studies* 3 (1976): 60–145, 4 (1977): 77–135, and 5 (1978): 89–138.

Peiris, William. *The Western Contribution to Buddhism*. Delhi, 1973.

Strickmann, Michel. "History, Anthropology, and Chinese Religion." *Harvard Journal of Asiatic Studies* 40 (June 1980): 201–248.

Wright, Arthur F. "The Study of Chinese Civilization." *Journal of the History of Ideas* 21 (1960): 232–255.

Yu, David C. "Present-Day Taoist Studies." *Religious Studies Review* 3 (October 1977): 220–239.

East Asian Scholarship. Useful studies of East Asian scholarship include the following.

Beasley, W. G., and E. G. Pulleyblank, eds. *Historians of China and Japan*. London, 1961.

Fogel, Joshua A. *Politics and Sinology: The Case of Naito Konan* (1866–1934). Cambridge, Mass., 1984.

Gotō Kimpei. "Studies in Chinese Religion in Postwar Japan." *Monumenta Serica* 15 (1956): 463–511.

Jan Yün-hua. "The Religious Situation and the Studies of Buddhism and Taoism in China: An Incomplete and Imbalanced Picture." *Journal of Chinese Religions* 12 (Fall 1984): 37–64.

Sakai Tadao and Noguchi Tetsuro. "Taoist Studies in Japan." In *Facets of Taoism*, edited by Holmes Welch and Anna Seidel, pp. 269–287. New Haven, 1979.

Schneider, Laurence A. *Ku Chieh-kang and China's New History*. Berkeley, 1971.

N. J. Girardot

CHINESE RELIGIOUS YEAR. The religious year of traditional China may be visualized as a circular base that is the calendar, upon which three overlays are superimposed. The first overlay shows the annual pan-Chinese observances; the second shows the celebrations of local, popular cults centered on the birthdays of particular deities; the third shows the schedule of official state sacrifices. I shall discuss each of these cycles of observances in turn.

The Religious Year and the Calendar. Traditionally, the dates of religious significance in the year were made known through a calendar issued by the Bureau of Astronomy in the Ministry of Rites. This calendar combined lunar and solar calculations, but for the religious year the former were more important. The waxing and waning of the moon was the most conspicuous indicator of change in the heavens, and the new and full moons thus formed focal points in the nexus of natural and human time. Solstices and equinoxes, as determined by the astronomers, were not so obvious, but were nevertheless important moments in the religious year because of their connection with the dominant or recessive phase of *yin* and *yang*.

The official calendar also indicated other kinds of time, of which two were most important in the religious year. The first was the marking of hours, days, months, and years by a cycle of two-character designations formed by sixty combinatory permutations of two series of symbols called the ten "celestial stems" *(t'ien-kan)* and the twelve "terrestrial branches" *(ti-chih)*. The second was the division of the year into twenty-four climatic periods. The pairs serve not simply as a method of marking, but, from the correlations of the stems and branches with other factors in the cosmos, they also hint at the many occult forces affecting the fate of man. The division of the year into fortnightly climatic periods is intimately connected with the timing and meaning of major events in the ritual year. These fortnightly periods are called nodes *(chieh)* or breaths *(ch'i)*. They derive from observations, both celestial (division of the heavens into degrees) and terrestrial (meteorological phenomena), already made in ancient times. Widely applied throughout China, their descriptive names—"clear and bright," "a little warm," "frost descends," "a lot of snow"—show their origination in the northern regions, where four distinct seasons obtain. The term *chieh*, which came to designate the fortnightly periods, has retained its correlative meaning of the celebration of rites at fixed times. Hence, the festivals of the year, particularly those tied to the twenty-four climatic periods, are also called *chieh*.

The calendar was not merely a schedule of times and seasons, but was more in the nature of an almanac, spelling out behaviors suitable, and indeed essential, for every season. Eventually it developed into a handbook containing medical lore, moral guidance, and techniques for prognostication and divination. The issuing of the imperial calendar was an act of religious import in itself, in that it was taken as evidence of the divine mandate possessed by the ruling dynasty. In effect, only such a divinely commissioned ruler could reveal the times and influences according to which all men must govern their lives. The concept of a religious year in the Chinese case must thus be understood as a year-long effort on the part of ruler and people to grasp the complicated processes of the cosmos and make them work for man. In this overall context the observances of the religious year underline the moments of greatest significance to family, community, occupational group, and state.

Pan-Chinese Observances. Rather than present a schematic overview, the following outline focuses on the island province of Taiwan, where the traditions have been fully preserved amidst the changes of modernization. A Chinese summary of the religious year, the section entitled "Sui-shih yü Shen-tan" in Juan Ch'ang-jui's *Chuang-yen-ti shih-chieh* (Taipei, 1982), has been relied upon here.

The twelfth and first months: the New Year. By far the most protracted, the busiest, and the most important of the annual festivals, the New Year begins in the middle of the twelfth month with the Wei-ya ("tail end of the year") observance and continues through to the full moon of the first month. In former times all business came to a virtual standstill during most of this period; nowadays the length of the holiday has been considerably curtailed, but many traditional practices are continued. On "tail end of the year," the twelfth day of the twelfth month, sacrifices are made to T'u-ti-kung (the local earth god), the all-important tutelary deity of household and community. On this evening the proprietors of businesses hold feasts for their employees to thank them for their hard work and to wish for a successful new year.

On the twenty-fourth day of this month, Tsao-chün ("lord of the cooking stove") leads the various deities assigned to terrestrial duties to the court of Yü-huang Shang-ti ("supreme emperor of jadelike augustness"), ruler of the bureaucratic pantheon in Heaven; there he makes the required annual report. [*See also* Yü-huang.] Tsao-chün is in effect the spirit overseer of the household. Presumably because his report will influence the life span recorded in the heavenly registers, he also is considered one of the *ssu-ming fu-chün* ("arbiters of longevity"). On this day, the deity's mouth is smeared with something sweet so that he will have only sweet things to report. The paper icon of Tsao-chün, found above each stove, is then burnt, the smoke conveying the report directly to Heaven. Once the deities have left for the court of Heaven, the house undergoes a thorough cleaning, which also gets rid of any *hui-ch'i* ("inauspicious breaths"). The next day, celestial deities, deputed by the Supreme Emperor of Jadelike Augustness, arrive to make their inspection during the absence of the terrestrial deities. Everyone is on good behavior during this inspection period.

New Year's Eve is called Kuo-nien ("the passing of the old year") or Ch'u-hsi ("the eve of the passing year"). It is observed by seven traditional practices.

1. *Tz'u nien* ("bidding farewell to the old year"). Sacrifices are offered to gods and ancestors, to Tsao-chün, and to Ch'uang-mu, the tutelary "mother of the bed." Propitiary sacrifices are also placed at the gate for *hao-hsiung* ("good elder brothers"), that is, bereaved spirits, souls denied their rightful sacrifices, whose resentment constitutes a menace to the living. On the family altar in the main hall are set offerings of cooked rice, other foods, and strings of money. After the sacrifices have been made, firecrackers are set off to scare off demons.

2. *T'uan-yüan-fan yü wei-lu* ("family reunion meal and surrounding the stove"). The gathering of the family from far and near for the communal meal is also called *shou-sui-chiu* ("wine that safeguards the New Year"). A brazier placed under the round table is festooned with coins and described as "warm as spring, the prospering breath of wealth." The family gathering is thus called "surrounding the stove"; should there be a family member who cannot attend the feast, some of his clothing is draped over an empty chair to indicate his symbolic presence and that the family is thinking of him. At this meal the last course is a fish, which must not be eaten, however, for "fish" is homophonous with "having abundance" *(yü)*

3. *Ya-sui-ch'ien* ("money of the year that is given away"). After the communal feast the elders hand out money to the youngsters. This is also called *fen kuo-nien-ch'ien* ("dividing the money of the passing year"). In the past, one hundred cash were strung together (the old coppers had a square hole in the center), and even though these have now been replaced by paper money, the meaning is still "may you live one hundred years."

4. *Shou-sui* ("safeguarding the year"). After the elders give money to the children, the family sits around the stove, chatting, joking, and playing games to see the old year out. "Safeguarding the year" is said to contribute to the longevity of the parents.

5. *T'iao huo-p'en* ("jumping over the fire pan"). After the feast, all male members of the family take turns jumping over a pan filled with burning rice straw in front of the family gate. They call out certain auspicious phrases as they do so. The passing over fire signifies purification or making a new beginning.

6. *T'ieh ch'un-lien* ("pasting up spring scrolls"). To welcome the new year, "spring scrolls" bearing auspicious words are pasted on the gateposts. Pieces of lucky red paper with the graph for "spring" written on them are pasted on such places as the leaves of the gate and the rice barrels. Other felicitous phrases are pasted elsewhere. The pasting up of spring scrolls derives from the ancient practice of hanging apotropaic peachwood amulets at the gate. There are colored paper scrolls hung over the lintel on blue paper if a male infant has died during the year or on yellow paper if a female infant has died.

7. By ancient custom, on New Year's Eve people attended plays held in front of a temple. If a debtor stayed until dawn of New Year's Day, his creditor would not dare to disturb the gathering by trying to collect the debt. The debt, collectible before the new year, could then be postponed because the new year had arrived. These events were thus called *p'i-tse-hsi* ("fleeing-from-debt plays").

The first five days of the new year are called Hsin-cheng ("correct, or fixed, beginning") or Hsin-ch'un ("beginning of the new spring"). They are greeted with the spring scrolls, firecrackers, and music, while people crowd the streets in a happy bustle. On the first day people eat long noodles symbolic of their hope for longevity. Dressed in new clothes and bearing fruits and other offerings, they go to the temples to burn incense and worship the deities. Then they pay a New Year's call on friends and relatives. On this day everyone takes care to avoid saying or doing things of bad omen. No work is done, and everyone enjoys himself. On the second day newly married girls pay a visit to their natal homes. On the fourth day the deities who had been away at their annual audience at the court of Heaven return to this world and are received with offerings and prayers for good fortune during the new year. With day five life returns temporarily to normal, but the season is not yet over. On the evening of the eighth day everyone takes a bath and observes a fast called Shou-shou ("safeguarding longevity") until midnight. Then, led by the head of the family, all members of the household perform Ta-li, the "great ritual," consisting of "three kneelings and nine knockings" (*k'e-t'ou*, or "kowtow" as it is known in the West) and the presentation of incense. Thus is marked the beginning of the ninth day, the birthday of the Supreme Emperor of Jadelike Augustness, by whose indulgence all beings are born and nurtured.

The fifteenth day marks the close of the New Year festivities. It is called Shang-yüan Chieh ("festival of the First Primordial"). The triad Shang-yüan, Chung-yüan, and Hsia-yüan, of whom the first is recognized here, are otherwise known in Taoism as the San Kuan ("three controllers"), supervisors of the realms of Heaven, earth, and the waters. In popular religion they are also identified with the three sage-kings of legendary antiquity: Yao, who attained perfect goodness, is the Celestial Controller; Shun, who reclaimed the land, is the Terrestrial Controller; and Yü, who tamed the floods, is the Controller of the Waters. The birthday of each controller is widely celebrated. Sacrifices to the Celestial Controller are presented at dawn on the fifteenth.

The major event of the day, however, takes place in the evening and is called Yüan-hsiao Chieh ("festival of the First Primordial night") or Teng-chieh ("lantern festival"). The family again gathers at a communal feast, and special round dumplings of the "First Primordial night" *(yüan-hsiao yüan-tzu)* are eaten. The roundness of the dumplings is like this first full moon of the year and symbolizes the complete family circle as well as completeness or perfection in general. After dark everyone takes to the streets and temples to show and view ingeniously designed lanterns and to enjoy the boisterous dragon and lion dances accompanied by the din of gongs and drums, and the acrobatics of martial arts troupes. With this festival the season comes to an end.

Second month. On the second day of the second month a minor observance balances the "tail end of the year," which, as we saw, falls on the twelfth day of the twelfth month. On the occasion of T'ou-ya ("head of the year"), as on the earlier occasion, the main events are sacrifices to T'u-ti-kung and the giving of a feast by the shopkeeper for his employees.

Third month. The second major festival of the year, Ch'ing-ming Chieh, takes place at the beginning of the climatic period called Ch'ing-ming ("clear and bright") and is dedicated to the ancestors. On the first of the month, families visit the ancestral tombs to tidy them up. A sacrificial meal including auspicious red-colored rice, called *yi-mu kuo* ("saluting-the-tomb rice"), is offered. The family head divides up "longevity noodles" and red-colored rice among all the junior relatives. In general, the services at the tomb, called *p'ei-mu* ("shoring up the tomb"), are quite solemn and impressive. Sacrifices include twelve dishes of edibles in addition to the rice. A peeled egg is left atop the grave to express the idea that "the old gives way to the new" (*hsin ch'en tai hsieh*). The children share some of the "saluting-the-tomb rice" and some money. This is called *yin-mu kuo* ("rice with the seal of the tomb"), and shows the abundant virtue of the ancestors, which in turn abides forever among their descendants. When the visit to the grave is ended, a strip of red paper is left on top in commemoration.

Fourth month. The eighth day is the festival of washing the Buddha, whose birthday it is said to be. The image of the Buddha in every temple is ceremonially washed, incense is burned, and scriptures are chanted.

Fifth month. The fifth of this month is called Tuan-wu ("double *wu*") because both month and day contain the fifth celestial stem (*wu*) in their designations. The great event of the day in the South is the dragon boat races. These are popularly said to be a reenactment of the search for the body of Ch'ü Yüan, a loyal statesman and poet of ancient times who drowned himself when his advice was no longer heeded by his lord. For this day people make a special kind of sweet dumpling wrapped in bamboo leaves that was originally supposed to have been thrown into the water for Ch'ü Yüan's spirit to consume. Nowadays, people exchange such dumplings as presents on Tuan-wu.

Because the fifth month marks the junction of spring and summer and was associated with the onset of epidemic diseases, it has the reputation of being the *tu-yüeh* ("poisonous month"). Precautions are taken against the depredations of disease-causing spirits: strong yellow wine is drunk; a package of calamus, mugwort, and banian branches wrapped in lucky red paper is suspended above the gate; colored threads are tied around the wrists of children and bags of incense are hung by a red string around their necks. The proximity of the "double fifth" to the summer solstice, the moment when the ascendancy of *yang* will begin to give way to *yin*, no doubt has something to do with the prominence of the Tuan-wu festival.

Sixth month. The first and fifteenth of this month are occasions for celebrating the completion of the first half of the year. The deities and ancestors receive sacrifices and thanks for their help, with wishes for their continued support during the remainder of the year. On the sixth day, clothing, books, and paintings are aired to rid them of mildew from the spring rains. Old people also air their *shou-i* ("longevity garments"), the special coats, embroidered with the graph for longevity, that they will wear to the grave. On the nineteenth of the month many women go to the temples to offer sacrifices to Kuan-yin (the *bodhisattva* Avalokiteśvara), their most venerated protectress, who is said to have attained the Way (*te tao*) and to have ascended to Heaven on this day.

Seventh month. On the seventh day of this month the charming legend of the weaving maid and the cowherd (originally simply the names of two stars) comes alive again. This celestial couple can only meet on this one night each year when magpies form a bridge across the Celestial River (Milky Way). On this day, Ch'i Niang-ma ("seventh imperial mother," the deity of the weaving-maid star) receives special sacrifices because she is considered an important protector of children. The fifteenth day is Chung-yüan Chieh ("festival of the Second Primordial"). This day is considered the birthday of the Taoist Controller of Earth, or, in popular view, the ancient sage-king Shun. Sacrifices are offered to deities and ancestors at the family altars.

Despite these festivals, the central concern of the seventh month is the problem of bereaved spirits and damned souls. During this month the gates of the "dark realm" are open, and "hungry ghosts" (from the Indian concept of *preta*) are free to roam about in that invisible but very real dimension that impinges upon the world of the living. Three times during this month religious rituals are performed to counter this danger. On the first day every household sets out generous offerings of food at the entranceway. Incense sticks are placed in bowls, special burial clothes and silver paper spirit-money are burned to send into the invisible dimension. At the gateway is hung a lamp on which are written auspicious words. At the same time that this hospitable attitude is being exhibited, people take good care not to expose themselves to danger.

On the fifteenth, the second and by far the most important of the rituals to cope with the wandering ghosts takes place. The entire community invites these pitiable (and dangerous) visitors to a great feast at which not only will they be able for once to eat their fill, but also will receive the merits that accrue from the religious services held. *P'u-tu*, the ritual that assists all souls to cross over to the other shore of salvation, is performed on a large scale both by households and in temples. Altars are erected, sacrifices are offered to the poor souls, and priests, both Buddhist and Taoist, chant their sacred texts. Tall beacon posts are hung with lanterns and pennants to guide the spirits to the ritual places; paper and bamboo rafts take candles or small lamps out on the waters to attract the attention of the souls of the drowned. Finally, on the last day of the month, the spirits must return to their subterranean prisons and the gates are closed for another eleven months. The beacon lanterns are taken down, final sacrifices are presented, and the worlds of the living and the dead return to their normal condition of separation.

Eighth month. This month sees the minor birthday celebrations of two deities, humble in rank, but intimately involved in the daily life of the people. On the third day sacrifices are offered to Tsao-chün. On the fifteenth day sacrifices are made to T'u-ti-kung and also to the ancestors. The offerings include *yüeh ping* ("moon cakes"), for the fifteenth is also the night of the birthday of Yin Niang-niang (the goddess of the moon). The full moon of this month is one of the most enjoyable festivals of the year, with fine weather contributing to the pleasure of moon-viewing parties. It no doubt originally had specific connections with the harvest, but that connection is no longer apparent.

Ninth month. Despite the promise that the Ch'ung-chiu or Ch'ung-yang ("double-nine") day seems to hold, with its implication of the fullness of *yang* (nine is the number given to *yang* lines in the *I-ching*), nothing seems to remain of any former religious significance of this day. The activities traditionally characterizing "double-nine" are going for a hike in the hills and flying kites.

Tenth month. Like the ninth month, the tenth is not a time of much religious celebration. On the fifteenth day occurs the Hsia-yüan Chieh ("festival of the Third Primordial"), and hence the birthday of the Taoist Controller of the Waters or, in popular understanding, the ancient sage-king Yü.

Eleventh month. The important observance of the eleventh month is the Tung-chieh ("winter festival"), marking the solstice. Just prior to this day there is another gathering of the family to sacrifice to ancestors, called Ch'iu-chi ("autumn sacrifice"). Then, as winter begins, feasts mark the solstice with special foods such as *pu-tung* ("winter supplements"). Soups with dumplings again play on the meaning of the word *yüan* ("round," hence "perfect or complete").

Popular Cults and the Birthdays of Their Deities. Practically every day of the year is designated as the birthday of one or more of the deities. These deities are of varied origins and may be classified in different ways. Aside from those actually deriving from popular, local religions, they include supernaturals originally connected with the traditions of Confucianism, Taoism, and Buddhism. These have largely lost their original significance and are integrated into popular religion where they acquire attributes that suit popular needs. An example of this phenomenon was the identification of the Taoist San Kuan ("three officials") as the ancient sage-kings Yao, Shun, and Yü. The most famous case is the transformation of the *bodhisattva* Avalokiteśvara (Chin., Kuan-shih-yin) into the most popular deity of all, the compassionate mother-figure, Kuan-yin, whose birthday is celebrated on the nineteenth day of the second month.

A few of the deities that originated in popular cults became so important that they were adopted by the state and became objects of official sacrifices as well. The most outstanding example on Taiwan is Ma-tsu ("granny"), who was given the highest imperial rank of T'ien-hou ("consort of Heaven"). Her most important function is to protect all who must venture upon the waters. (Her birthday is celebrated on the twenty-third day of the third month.) Kuan Sheng Ta Ti ("holy great emperor Kuan"), originally a famous general of the Three Kingdoms period (third century CE), became the greatest of the military gods and protector of the empire; his birthday is celebrated on the thirteenth day of the fifth month. While many popular deities are pan-Chinese, their birthdays celebrated everywhere, there are also many others whose cults are only local, or of importance chiefly to certain groups or occupations.

Religious Year of the State. Since ancient times the state has considered the ritual offering of sacrifices to be one of its most basic duties and prerogatives. The calendar issued by the imperial Bureau of Astronomy gave the annual schedule of official sacrifices, which formed a separate system from the universal festivals and from the birthdays of deities celebrated in the popular cults. [*See also* Confucian Thought, *article on* The State Cult.]

In China, as elsewhere, some observances have become more or less drained of religious content and their original significance forgotten by all but scholars or obscured by later rationalizations. In the religious year as a whole a few themes are conspicuous: concern for unity of the family, including filiality to the ancestors and protection of the children; desire for longevity; hopes for blessings in general; and fear of resentful ghosts and attempts to propitiate them. Aside from these hopes and fears, the colorful practices marking the course of the year may be understood as one of the clearest expressions of traditional popular culture. [*See also* Chinese Religion, *article on* Popular Religion.]

BIBLIOGRAPHY

A complete calendar of the religious year can be found in Henri Doré's *Recherches sur les superstitions en Chine*, 18 vols. (Shanghai, 1911–1938). Doré's *opus* has been translated by M. Kennelly as *Researches into Chinese Superstitions*, 13 vols. (1914–1938; reprint, Taipei, 1966); see volume 5, pages 563–656. An abbreviated calendar can be found in Doré's *Manuel des superstitions chinoises*, 2d ed. (Shanghai, 1936), pp. 132–137. The festival year observed in different localities is described in Justus Doolittle's *The Social Life of the Chinese*, vol. 2, edited by Paxton Hood (New York, 1868), chaps. 1–3; J. J. M. de Groot's *Les fêtes annuellement célébrées à Émoui (Amoy)*, 2 vols. (1886; reprint, Taipei, 1977); *Annual Customs and Festivals in Peking*, (1936; reprint, Hong Kong, 1965), an annotated translation by Derk Bodde of a work by the Manchu author Tun Li-ch'en; Lewis Hodous's *Folkways in China* (London, 1929); C. S. Wong's *A Cycle of Chinese Festivities* (Singapore, 1967); and Henry Yi-min Wei and Suzanne Coutanceau's *Wine for the Gods; An Account of the Religious Traditions and Beliefs of Taiwan* (Taipei, 1976). Wolfram Eberhard's *Chinese Festivals* (1952; reprint, Taipei, 1972) discusses the origins and significance of some of the major observances. More specialized treatments include Marcel Granet's *Fêtes et chansons anciennes de la Chine* (Paris, 1919), translated into English by E. D. Edwards as *Festivals and Songs of Ancient China* (New York, 1932), in which see especially part 2; Derk Bodde's *Festivals in Classical China: New Year and Other Annual Observances during the Han Dynasty, 206 B.C.–A.D. 220* (Princeton, 1975); Göran Aijmer's *The Dragon Boat Festival on the Hupeh-Hunan Plains, Central China* (Stockholm, 1964); and Carole Morgan's *Le Tableau du Boeuf du Printemps: Étude d'une page de l'almanach chinois* (Paris, 1980).

LAURENCE G. THOMPSON

CHINGGIS KHAN (1162?–1227), great Mongol leader and founder of a vast empire in Asia. One of the extraordinary personages of world history, Chinggis Khan is a striking example of an emperor who became a god.

Born in Mongolia, northeast of present-day Ulan Bator, and called Temüjin in his youth, he was the eldest son of a chieftain of the Mongol Borjigit clan. Having succeeded in uniting the Mongol and Turkic tribes of the area, he adopted the title of Chinggis Khan and set out to conquer the world. He subdued the Chin empire in North China, the Hsi-hsia kingdom northeast of Tibet, the Turkic states in Turkistan, and the empire of Khorezm, comprising Transoxiana as well as Afghanistan and Eastern Iran. Mongol units even advanced as far as India and the Crimea. When Chinggis Khan died in 1227 near Ning-hsia, capital of Hsi-hsia, he left the broad foundations of an empire that would extend, under his sons and grandsons, from Korea to the Near East and southern Europe and from southern Siberia to Indochina.

The story of Chinggis Khan's life reads like that of an epic hero. Indeed, the thirteenth-century *Secret History of the Mongols*, the first work of Mongolian literature, patterns Chinggis Khan's biography after the model of the hero-king, and thus reflects the indispensable qualities of a ruler and the hopes set upon him. Chinggis Khan possesses the mandate of Heaven and Heaven's support to restore law, order, and peace on earth. He is of noble totemistic descent: his forefather, the ancestor of the Mongol royal family, is a blue-gray wolf whose son is born on the holy mountain Burkhan Qaldun. It is this "good place," the center of the world, where Chinggis Khan's career begins as well. From here he goes forth to conquer nations and peoples in all directions, and to this same place his dead body returns. He has a good wife, a good horse, and good companions, and he finds himself in a situation favorable for his activities.

After Chinggis Khan's death, his character develops in three ways: Chinggis Khan becomes a means of political identification, a figure of political theology, and a deity. Chinggis Khan is used as a means of political identification by the Mongols as well as by the Chinese. To the Mongols, as the founder of their unified state, he is a symbol of Mongol national independence, or at least autonomy. To the Chinese, he is the glorious first emperor of a Chinese dynasty of Mongol nationality, a symbol of the multinational character of Chinese history.

Chinggis Khan's association with political theology is twofold. It was probably during the time of Khubilai, grandson of Chinggis, that the concept of a dual Buddhist world government was introduced: the ruler of the state is the king, as represented by Chinggis Khan and his successors, the Mongolian great khans; the head of the religion is the religious teacher, the lama, as represented by Buddha Śākyamuni and his successors, the Tibetan hierarchs. The two orders of state and religion, based on mutual harmony and distribution of functions, guarantee secular and spiritual well-being. This concept, however, has never been fully realized. Khubilai became not the ruler of a Tibeto-Mongol Buddhist state, but rather the first Mongol emperor of China.

Another notion of Chinggis Khan that links political and religious images proved to be more successful. In this view, Chinggis Khan, protected by Heaven, becomes the son of Heaven (Tengri) or the son of Khormusta, the lord of the gods *(tengri)*, the Indian Indra, whose attribute is the thunderbolt. In Mahāyāna Buddhism, Indra developed into the *bodhisattva* Vajrapāṇi, the "bearer of the thunderbolt," a figure symbolic of power. It is power that is the principal quality of Chinggis Khan and his people, the Mongols. At the same time, however, in ideological or even genealogical terms, Chinggis Khan becomes a successor to the first king of mankind, the Indian Mahāsammata.

There are three aspects to the deification of Chinggis Khan. First, he became the ancestral deity of the ruling Borjigit clan, the state, and the whole Mongol people, guarding them against all evil. Sacrifices to Chinggis Khan, his family, and his war genies *(sülde)* seem to be offered even today in his main sanctuary, the Eight White Yurts, in the Ordos district of Inner Mongolia. He is also still officially venerated by Mongolian refugees in Taiwan. Second, Chinggis was incorporated into the Lamaist-Buddhist pantheon as a local guardian deity of comparatively low rank. In the practice of folk religion he became fused with the ancestral deity. Third, traits of an initiatory god were imputed to Chinggis Khan; as this deity, he introduced marriage customs, seasonal festivals connected with the nomadic economy, and certain ritual practices of daily life.

[*See also* Inner Asian Religions *and* Mongol Religions.]

BIBLIOGRAPHY

Basic observations on the religious role of Chinggis Khan have been made by Walther Heissig in his *Die Religionen der Mongolei* (Stuttgart, 1970), translated by Geoffrey Samuel as *The Religions of Mongolia* (Berkeley, 1980). The ideological development of Chinggis Khan's character is dealt with by Herbert Franke in his excellent study *From Tribal Chieftain to Universal Emperor and God: The Legitimation of the Yüan Dynasty* (Munich, 1978). Indispensable for everyone interested in Chinggis Khan's biography and thirteenth-century Mongol political and religious thought are the anonymous *Secret History of the Mongols* and two Persian chronicles written by al-Juwaynī and Rashīd al-Dīn. The following English translations are available: *The Secret History of the Mongols, for the First Time Done into English out of the Original Tongue and Provided with an Exegetical Commentary,* 2 vols., by Francis Woodman Cleaves (Cambridge, Mass., 1982–); "The Secret History of the Mongols," translated by Igor de Rachewiltz, *Papers on Far Eastern History* 4 (September 1971): 115–163, 5 (March 1972): 149–175, 10 (September 1974): 55–82, 13 (March 1976): 41–75, 16 (September 1977): 27–65, 18 (September 1978): 43–80, 21 (March 1980): 17–57, 23 (March 1981): 111–146, and 26 (September 1982): 39–84 (chaps. 1–10; chaps 11 and 12 are still to be published); *The History of the World-Conqueror, by 'Ala-ad-Din 'Ata-Malik Juvaini,* translated by John Andrew Boyle in two volumes (Cambridge, Mass., 1958); and *The Successors of Gengis Khan,* translated from the Persian of Rashīd al-Dīn Ṭabīb by John Andrew Boyle (New York, 1971). An excellent biography of Chinggis Khan written by a Western historian is René Grousset's *Le conquérant du monde* (Paris, 1944), translated into English by Denis Sinor and Marian MacKellar as *Conqueror of the World* (Edinburgh, 1967). The most recent study on Chinggis Khan's life and activities is Paul Ratchnevsky's *Činggis-Khan: Sein Leben und Wirken* (Wiesbaden, 1983).

KLAUS SAGASTER

CHING-T'U.

The Chinese term *ching-t'u* ("pure land"), pronounced *jōdo* in Japanese, refers to the Chinese Buddhist tradition of devotion to Amitābha Buddha in order to be reborn in his Pure Land as a means of attaining enlightenment. Although an auxiliary spiritual discipline for most Chinese Buddhists, because it guaranteed salvation in the next life through simple practices Pure Land devotionalism was an important refuge for the laity, often becoming a primary and sometimes exclusivistic religious orientation in times of personal or social crises. At the heart of this exclusivistic tendency was despair about achieving enlightenment through traditional practices based on one's own effort, and enthusiasm over the compassionate vow of Amitābha to welcome devotees at death into the blessings of his Pure Land. Beginning in the seventh century CE, this tendency became recognized as a separate religious orientation called the Pure Land teaching *(ching-t'u-tsung).*

Unlike their counterparts in Japan, Pure Land devotees in China never developed into a centrally organized property-holding denomination with formalized methods of succession (except for the White Lotus movement during the twelfth to fourteenth centuries). Instead, the Pure Land devotional movement was a loosely knit association of individuals based on the promises of Indian scriptures interpreted by Chinese thinkers and supported by such practical devices as rosaries, paintings, liturgies, and stories about supernatural visions and deathbed miracles indicating successful rebirth in the Pure Land.

Formation of Chinese Pure Land. The term *ching-t'u* was invented in China to refer to Sukhāvatī, the land of bliss created in the western regions by Amitābha, the Buddha of Infinite Light and Infinite Life, for the purification and enlightenment of beings. Mahāyāna Buddhists believe that all Buddhas have spheres of activity (*kṣetra,* "lands"), but Amitābha's land is the most popular, its popularity based on his vows that ordinary people can be reborn into his land through simple devotion and thereby attain a speedy, painless, and guaranteed enlightenment.

Beginning in 179 CE, when the *Pan-chou san-mei ching* (Skt., *Pratyutpannasamādhi Sūtra*) was translated into Chinese, the visualization of Amitābha was recommended as a meditation practice for bringing a Buddha into one's presence. In the third century more Amitābha scriptures were translated, so that by the fourth century there are reports of the first Chinese Pure Land devotees (Ch'üeh Kung-ts'e and his disciple Wei Shih-tu), the first Pure Land lectures (by Chu Fa-kuang), and the first construction of images and pictures of Amitābha and the Pure Land.

In 402 CE, meditation master Lu-shan Hui-yüan (334–416) formed a devotional group in South China. It consisted of Hui-yüan and 123 lay people and clergy who sought to support one another in visualizing and making offerings to Amitābha to facilitate rebirth in the Pure Land. Centuries later, this group came to be regarded as the original White Lotus Society. After the death of Hui-yüan and his immediate disciples, little is heard of Pure Land practices in the south for the next few centuries. [*See also the biography of Hui-yüan.*]

The Shansi Pure Land movement. In response to the ravages of war, famine, and the uncertainties of the religious life during the sixth century, the monks T'an-luan (c. 488–c. 554) and Tao-ch'o (562–645) pioneered an independent Pure Land movement at the Hsüan-chung Ssu in the remote hills of the Ping-chou area of Shansi Province in North China. By this time, the most important Indian Pure Land scriptures had been translated into Chinese. These included the *Amitābha Sūtra* (Chin., *O-mi-t'o-fo ching*), the "larger" *Sukhāvatīvyūha Sūtra* (Chin., *Wu-liang-shou ching*), the *Kuan wu-liang-shou ching*, and the *Wang-sheng lun*, attributed to Vasubandhu. These texts mention that enlightenment is difficult in our age because of five afflictions *(wu-cho):* war and natural disasters, deluded ideas, greed and hatred, infirmity of body and mind, and shortness of life. According to T'an-luan, the compassionate aid of Amitābha is thus a necessity for salvation.

In his major work, the *Wang-sheng lun-chu* (a commentary to Vasubandhu's treatise), T'an-luan divides Buddhism into two paths, the "difficult" and the "easy." The Difficult Path includes all traditional Buddhist practices based on self-effort. Later, Tao-ch'o referred to this as the Path of the Sages *(sheng-tao)* and proclaimed that such practices were doomed to failure, not only because of the five afflictions but also because our age was the period predicted by the scriptures when true Buddhism would disappear *(mo-fa;* Jpn., *mappō).* Thus it became a key Pure Land idea that salvation through self-effort was impossible. Instead of the Difficult Path, T'an-luan advocated the Easy Path made available through the forty-eight vows of Amitābha recorded in the *Wu-liang-shou ching.* T'an-luan was the first in North China to emphasize how these vows promised rebirth in the Pure Land through the "other power" *(ta-li)* of Amitābha followed by the assurance of nonretrogression and the speedy attainment of enlightenment.

Basing his teachings on the *Wang-sheng lun,* T'an-luan adopted as a curriculum of practice five types of devotion to Amitābha *(nien-fo;* Jn., *nembutsu)* in order to ensure access to Amitābha's power: (1) to make prostrations to Amitābha and wish to be reborn in his land; (2) to sing praises to Amitābha and recite his name; (3) to make vows to be reborn in his Pure Land; (4) to visualize the appearance of Amitābha and the Pure Land; and (5) to transfer these merits to all beings for their salvation. T'an-luan and others emphasized the necessity of seeking the Pure Land not for its own pleasures but to attain enlightenment so as to return to this world to save others. This desire for enlightenment *(bodhicitta)* was held to be a primary condition for rebirth, thus demonstrating a continuity between the values of Pure Land and those of other forms of Buddhism. [*See also the biography of T'an-luan.*]

Vocal recitation. The practice of vocal recitation and singing praises to Amitābha soon became the most striking form of Pure Land devotion in China. For T'an-luan, this involved a mystical union with the name of Amitābha, which he believed had unlimited power, and required an exclusive and total concentration that precluded attention to other Buddhas and subordinated all other practices. Incessant vocal recitation then became a trademark of Tao-ch'o, who made the first rosaries for counting the recitations of Amitābha's name. Since he led laity in this practice, a popular religious movement developed with the slogan "Chant the Buddha's name and be reborn in the Pure Land" ("Nien-fo wang-sheng"). [*See also the biography of Tao-ch'o.*] His disciple Shan-tao (613–681) firmly established scriptural arguments for vocal recitation of Amitābha's name as a minimal but sufficient practice to ensure the rebirth of ordinary people into the Pure Land. Although Shan-tao personally was preoccupied with visualization practices, he is most famous for his list of "five correct practices," in which he substituted chanting the scriptures and reciting Amitābha's name for making a vow and transferring merits. For Shan-tao, the recitation of Amitābha's name was the only "correct and determining action" for salvation. In the next century, Fa-chao furthered this trend by developing a five-tone melodic recitation of Amitābha's name, a practice still popular today. In the Sung dynasty (960–1279), block printing enabled the distribution of devotional pamphlets and recitation cards in which one could record the number of one's recitations as a visible reminder to maintain one's practice.

Consolidation of the Pure Land school. Although Shan-tao studied under Tao-ch'o, he spent his mature years in the capital, Ch'ang-an, where the stature of his achievements in meditation and the comprehensiveness of his writings firmly established the theory and practice of Pure Land devotionalism among Chinese Buddhist leaders. Besides his theoretical and liturgical writings, the *Kuan wu-liang-shou ching shu, Kuan-nien-men, Pan-chou tsan, Wang-sheng li-tsan-chi,* and *Fa-shih tsan,* Shan-tao brought added prestige to the movement by painting more than three hundred images of Pure Land and, at the request of Empress Wu, supervising the construction of the great Vairocana Buddha image at Lung-men between the years 672 and 675. The ascendency of Pure Land devotion as a major force can be seen by the increasing number of sculptures of Amitābha, which in the Lung-men caves came to outnumber those of Śākyamuni by a factor of twelve and those of Maitreya by a factor of ten in the period from 650 to 690. [*See also the biography of Shan-tao.*]

In the generation after Shan-tao, Pure Land writings such as the *Shih ching-t'u ch'un-i lun,* by Shan-tao's disciple Huai-kan, and the *Ching-t'u shih-i lun,* based on the *An-lo-chi* of Tao-ch'o, summarized and applied Pure Land doctrine in the question-and-answer format of a catechism. Studies of Indian Pure Land scriptures and essays on Pure Land subjects faded away in favor of ritual texts and manuals of practice. The *pan-chou san-mei* ritual (based on the practice found in the *Pan-chou san-mei ching*) was propagated by Hui-jih (680–748), Ch'eng-yüan, and Fa-chao, whereas the more exclusive practice of verbal recitation was taught by Ta-hsing and Tao-ching. Thus, by the beginning of the eighth century a cohesive core of Pure Land beliefs, values, and practices had emerged based upon a sense of the inadequacy or inappropriateness of all other Buddhist teachings and the attractiveness of Amitābha and his Pure Land. The Chinese Pure Land movement had reached its full definition and most exclusive form. One could safely live and die within a world of writings and practices devoted only to rebirth in the Pure Land and in which exclusive devotion to Amitābha was trumpeted as the only guaranteed method of salvation for all. For laity and those distressed by their inadequacies, Pure Land offered a simple but potent formula: (1) the miraculous power of *one* practice (*nien-fo* as recitation), (2) directed toward *one* Buddha (Amitābha), (3) to achieve rebirth in *one* place (the Western Pure Land), (4) so that in *one* more rebirth Buddhahood could be achieved. Although other forms of Chinese Buddhist practice had not been abolished, for adherents of Pure Land they had been largely postponed until birth in Sukhāvatī and displaced as a major focus and obligation for the present life.

The spread of Pure Land. As early as T'an-hsien (d. 440), a member of Hui-yüan's community on Lu-shan, advocates of Pure Land devotionalism had collected stories about those who had attained rebirth in the Pure Land. These stories recorded religious practices of devotees and unusual deathbed occurrences that were signs of rebirth in the Pure Land: music emanating from the sky, a sweet fragrance, five-colored clouds, visions of attendants welcoming one to the Pure Land, or pathways of light. The earliest surviving collection of Pure Land biographies is the *Ching-t'u lun,* compiled by Chia-ts'ai in the mid-seventh century. Of the twenty biographies he recorded, six are of monks, four of nuns, five of laymen, and five of laywomen. The enduring prominence of laity and of women in the movement makes it unique among the Buddhist traditions of China.

The Ping-chou area of North China remained the heart of Pure Land practice according to biographical records of eminent monks of the T'ang dynasty (618–906). Among Pure Land collections, the *Wang-sheng hsi-fang ching-t'u jui-ying chuan,* compiled by 805 CE, lists 26 people from North China (Shansi and Shensi provinces) and only 7 from South China (Chekiang and Kiangsu provinces). By contrast, in the treatment of the Pure Land movement in the thirteenth-century *Fo-tsu t'ung-chi,* there are biographies of only 20 people from Shansi, 20 from Shensi, but 129 from Chekiang and 24 from Kiangsu. This marks a definite shift of the locus of Pure Land devotionalism from North to South China. In addition, the sequence of patriarchs offered by the *Fo-tsu t'ung-chi* begins with a Southerner, Lu-shan Hui-yüan, skips T'an-luan and Tao-ch'o, and goes on to Shan-tao, Ch'eng-yüan (713–803), Fa-chao, Shao-k'ang (d. 805), and Yen-shou (904–975). This pattern also appears in the *Lo-pang wen-lei,* compiled by Tsung-hsiao (1151–1214), and it is a standard format in the Ming dynasty (1368–1644) lineages.

Revision and Integration. Pure Land devotionalism did not spread without opposition. In the seventh century, Yogācāra advocates argued against Shan-tao by claiming that the Pure Land was an expedient device for special circumstances that did not ensure final salvation, and that in any event ordinary people were not qualified to be reborn there. More vigorous attacks came in the early eighth century from the Southern Ch'an (Zen) school, which criticized Pure Land as dualistic, encouraging attachment, and promising future enlightenment as a delusive crutch for people of inferior spiritual capacities. Tz'u-min Hui-jih (680–748) criticized Ch'an followers for their arrogant rejection of the many devotional practices recommended throughout Buddhist scriptures and in turn accused them of being ignorant of the higher forms of Indian *ch'an* (Skt., *dhyāna,* "meditation").

Levels of nien-fo. More constructively, the eighth-century *Wu fang-pien nien-fo men* interpreted both Ch'an and Pure Land as having five progressive levels of practice, each of which is regarded as an expedient device (*fang-pien;* Skt., *upāya*). Insofar as practitioners have different spiritual needs and capacities, each level is valid but not exhaustive. The five expedient methods of *nien-fo* are (1) the Buddha's name is called to attain rebirth in the Pure Land; (2) the form of the Buddha is visualized to eradicate sins; (3) all items of perception are seen as mere products of mind; (4) the mind and its objects of perception are both transcended; and (5) the perfect understanding of how true nature arises is gained. This scheme influenced the fourfold *nien-fo* list of Tsung-mi (780–841): (1) vocally calling the Buddha's name; (2) visualizing the Buddha's form as an image or painting to receive the five spiritual powers and see all Buddhas in the ten directions; (3) visualizing the major and minor marks of the Buddha to eradicate all sins; and (4) contemplating the absolute true nature wherein the Buddha has no marks and no name and one uses no-thought *(wu-i)* as the method to contemplate the Buddha *(nien-fo)*. Thus, at the highest level, Pure Land form unites with Ch'an formlessness. This idea of the progressive levels of *nien-fo* culminated in such thinkers as Chih-hsü (1599–1655), who proclaimed Pure Land devotion as supreme because it could include all Ch'an and T'ien-t'ai practices within different levels of *nien-fo*.

Dual cultivation. The Ch'an patriarch Yung-ming Yen-shou (904–975) is famous for advocating the "dual cultivation of Ch'an and Pure Land" *(ch'an-ching shuang-hsiu)* as being doubly effective, like a "tiger wearing horns." His proposal was partially based on Fei-hsi's idea that Ch'an and Pure Land were like the dialectic of emptiness and form, of underlying principle *(li)* and phenomenal events *(shih)*, and each would be incomplete without the other. In his *Wan-shan t'ung-kuei* Yen-shou considered Pure Land and Ch'an to be focused on phenomena and thus to represent only one aspect of the One Mind, namely its external functioning *(yung)*. Basing his teaching on the *Ta-sheng ch'i-hsin lun* (Awakening of Faith in the Mahāyāna), Yen-shou taught that phenomena must be balanced by the other aspect of the One Mind, namely its underlying nature *(t'i)*. The Pure Land, like all phenomena, is mind-only *(wei-hsin)*, and the division between Pure Land and Ch'an is transcended when one is enlightened to the true nature of the One Mind.

Pure Land practices were an important part of the devotional life of many Chinese Buddhists usually identified with other traditions. Monks such as Chih-i, Tao-hsüan, and Chi-tsang, who are normally listed as patriarchs of the T'ien-t'ai, Vinaya, and San-lun schools, respectively, all employed Pure Land regimens in their practice. T'ien-t'ai Chih-i (538–597) had a doctrine of four levels of Buddha lands and advocated a ninety-day practice of chanting Amitābha's name while constantly walking, a practice still undertaken in Japan. T'ien-t'ai became further identified with Pure Land when an eighth-century commentary on the *Kuan ching* was attributed to Chih-i. Later, Ssu-ming Chih-li (960–1028) composed a subcommentary entitled *Miao-tsung ch'ao*, in which he presented his doctrine of "visualizing the Buddha in terms of the [mundane and absolute aspects of] mind" *(yüeh-hsin kuan-fo)*. Basing his doctrine on the *Awakening of Faith*, he argued that all religious practices are the mind's external functioning *(yung)* and are for the sole purpose of revealing the mind's underlying nature *(t'i)*. When our conditioned minds seek enlightenment by visualizing Amitābha, the underlying nature responds with an image in our minds so that there is temporarily a distinction between Buddhas and humans. However, in the act of seeking insight, practitioners are also united with the underlying enlightened nature. These two levels of activity reflect the two aspects of the One Mind; they are Chih-li's interpretation of the *Kuan ching* phrase "This mind is the Buddha, this mind creates the Buddha." This doctrine had enormous influence, since Chih-li's works became authoritative for T'ien-t'ai from the Sung dynasty (960–1279) onward, and most T'ien-t'ai masters came to seek rebirth in the Pure Land.

The revival of Buddhism under the patronage of the Sung dynasty was not marked by the intense textual and doctrinal studies of the T'ang period; rather, they focused on personal cultivation. In spite of Ch'an's initial antagonism to Pure Land, the Ch'an monastic code *Ch'an-lin ch'ing-kuei* (1311) recommended chanting Amitābha's name at funerals. Gradually, Yen-shou's teaching of dual cultivation permeated all aspects of the Ch'an tradition and remains a model up to today. Various masters in the Wen-yen Ch'an lineage taught that the Pure Land is a mental representation only. Tz'u-ch'üeh Tsung-tse formed a *nien-fo* recitation society in 1089, asserting that "one's self-nature is Amitābha." Later teachers who used the practice of meditating on a question *(hua-t'ou)* such as Han-shan Te-ch'ing (1546–1623) urged that disciples ask "Who is it that recites the Buddha's name?" after each recitation of the name of Amitābha in order to achieve Ch'an enlightenment.

White Lotus Society. Lay recitation societies flourished in the Sung dynasty, the most famous being the White Lotus Society, formed by Mao Tzu-yüan (1086–1166) in Kiangsu in 1133. While appealing to Lu-shan Hui-yüan's society as a model, Tzu-yüan added a number of later innovations: vocal recitations; married clergy; strict vegetarianism; the construction of hostels; the active leadership of women; the T'ien-t'ai theories of the four Buddha lands and the inseparability of mind, the Buddha, and living beings; and Chih-li's teaching of visualizing the Buddha in terms of the mundane and absolute aspects of mind. He considered all religious practices to be valid insofar as they all have the same goal, all places are identical to the Pure Land, all phenomena are mind-only, and our own natures are identical to that of Amitābha. For ordinary people, however, Tzu-yüan urged the expedient means *(upāya)* of believing that the Pure Land is to the west and adhering to a gradual religious path based on correct faith, practice, and vows. Correct faith and vows were those that conformed to the teachings of T'an-luan, Tao-ch'o, and Shan-tao. Correct practice could be anything based on a person's abilities, but, like Shan-tao and Yen-shou before him, Tzu-yüan stressed having correct mindfulness at the moment of death to seal rebirth in the Pure Land.

The White Lotus Society had a checkered history of political sponsorship and repression that culminated in its suppression in 1322. By that time it had developed from a centrally organized lay devotional society to a large property-holding movement with White Lotus Halls for charitable activities such as donating cloth to the populace, copying *sūtr*s, and developing bathhouses, waterworks, mills, shops, boats, and land throughout Fukien Province. The reason for its suppression is uncertain, but as a lay society involving women, people from lower levels of society, and working people who met together at night, it probably provoked rumors of rebellion and immorality. The decree of abolishment was prophetic since many later groups with very different beliefs frequently rebelled under the White Lotus name until all White Lotus groups were finally suppressed in 1813. [*See also* Millenarianism, *article on* Chinese Millenarian Movements.]

Modern status. No significant new Pure Land developments occurred after the Sung dynasty, although Pure Land as a supreme path was periodically championed by such figures as Chu-hung (1535–1615), Chih-hsü (1599–1655), the layman P'eng Shao-sheng (1739–1796), his nephew P'eng Hsi-su (who compiled the biographies of approximately five hundred Pure Land devotees), and most recently, Yin-kuang (1861–1940). For the last thousand years Pure Land devotion has been perpetuated in conjunction with T'ien-t'ai and Ch'an, and most contemporary large monasteries include both a Ch'an meditation hall and a Pure Land recitation hall. The most exclusivistic tendencies of Tao-ch'o and Shan-tao have long since been harmonized with the rich symphony of Chinese religious eclecticism, and nowadays the melodic chanting of Amitābha's name drifts above the rooftops of almost every Chinese Buddhist temple.

[*See also* Amitābha; Nien-fo; *and* Pure and Impure Lands.]

BIBLIOGRAPHY

The most comprehensive scholarly study of Ching-t'u is Mochizuki Shinkō's *Chūgoku jōdo kyōri shi* (Kyoto, 1942), which has an unpublished English translation by Leo Pruden (1982). There are no Western monographs dedicated to periods or themes of Chinese Pure Land Buddhism except as contained in *The Pure Land Tradition: History and Development*, edited by James Foard and Michael Solomon (Berkeley, forthcoming), which provides an overview of Pure Land in India and East Asia. Otherwise, for Chinese Pure Land there are studies only of particular leaders and their writings. Besides Fujiwara Ryōsetsu's *The Way to Nirvana: The Concept of the Nembutsu in Shan-tao's Pure Land Buddhism* (Tokyo, 1974) and Daniel Overmyer's *Folk Buddhist Religion: Dissenting Sects in Late Traditional China* (Cambridge, Mass., 1976), all other monographs on Ching-t'u consist of published and unpublished Ph.D. dissertations such as Chun-fang Yü's *The Renewal of Buddhism in China: Chu-hung and the Late Ming Synthesis* (New York, 1981), which is largely focused on the monastic reform efforts of the Pure Land patriarch Chu-hung (1535–1615). Dissertations available through University Microfilms include Roger Corless's "T'an-luan's Commentary on the Pure Land Discourse: An Annotated Translation and Soteriological Analysis of the *Wang-shêng-lun chu* (Ph.D. diss., University of Wisconsin, 1973); my "Tao-ch'o, 562–645: A Pioneer of Chinese Pure Land Buddhism" (Ph.D. diss., Yale University, 1976); and Ingram Samuel Seah's "Shan-tao: His Life and Teachings" (Ph.D. diss., Princeton Theological Seminary, 1975).

David W. Chappell

CHINUL (1158–1210), also known as National Master Puril Pojo; founder of the indigenous Chogye school of Korean Sŏn (Chin., Ch'an; Jpn., Zen). Chinul was born in 1158 to a gentry family in the Koryŏ capital of Kaesŏng. When seven years old, he was ordained into the Sagul-san lineage of the Nine Mountains school of early Sŏn and soon distinguished himself in both meditation and scriptural study. Chinul became dissatisfied with the quality of practice within the degenerate Sŏn schools of his time, however, and increasingly turned for guidance to the sources that he considered to contain authentic information on Buddhist meditative culture: scriptures and commentaries and the records of early Sŏn and Ch'an masters. Prompted by his vision of the basic unity of Sŏn and the scriptural teachings *(kyo;* Chin., *chiao),* Chinul developed an approach to Buddhism that combined the theoretical aids of Hwaŏm (Chin., Hua-yen) doctrine, especially as formulated in works by the Hua-yen commentator Li T'ung-hsüan (635–730), with the practical concerns of Ch'an meditation, as typified in the instructions of Ta-hui Tsung-kao (1089–1163). This unique synthesis is rightly regarded as one of the most distinctively Korean contributions to Buddhist thought and illustrates the syncretic penchant that is so characteristic of the Korean church. Chinul's insights provided a modus operandi for consolidating the divided Koryŏ Buddhist church, which remained bifurcated between the Sŏn and scholastic schools despite Ŭich'ŏn's attempts at unification a century before. More important for the future of the tradition, however, Chinul's thought also served as the inspiration for the development of a truly indigenous Korean school of Sŏn, the

Chogye school, of which he is considered the founder.

Chinul outlined an approach to Buddhist practice that begins with the intuitive grasp of the significance of the scriptural teaching that an ordinary person (i.e., the practitioner himself) is already identical to the Buddhas (enlightened beings). This sudden understanding-awakening *(haeo;* Chin., *chieh-wu)* brings about the provisional entrance into the Buddhist path of practice (Skt., *mārga)* at the first of the ten levels of faith. Awakening was then to be refined continuously in order to remove defilements and develop salutary qualities of mind. This gradual training finally culminates in realization-awakening *(chŭngo;* Chin., *cheng-wu),* the direct experience of the truths that are originally understood intellectually, which takes place at the first of the ten abidings *(daśavihāra),* the formal entrance into the *bodhisattva* path. This approach of sudden awakening/gradual cultivation *(tono chŏmsu;* Chin., *tun-wu chien-hsiu)* was heavily indebted to the insights of the Chinese Ch'an/Hua-yen master Tsung-mi (780–841), another of the main influences on Chinul's thought.

Three principal meditative techniques were used by Chinul to bring about the consummation of this soteriological process: the dual cultivation of concentration and wisdom, as explained in the *Liu-tsu t'an-ching* (Platform Scripture of the Sixth Patriarch); faith and understanding according to the complete and sudden school of Hwaŏm; and the distinctively Sŏn approach of investigating the critical phrase *(hwadu;* Chin., *hua-t'ou).* Chinul was the first Korean master to teach the formal *hwadu* technique developed by Ta-hui Tsung-kao, which is better known by the synonymous term *kongan* (Chin., *kung-an;* Jpn., *kōan*). In several of his writings Chinul provides an exhaustive outline of the correct approach to investigating the *hwadu,* while emphasizing its affinities with more traditional soteriological schemes. The initial investigation of the meaning of the *hwadu (ch'amŭi;* Chin., *tsan-i)* counteracts the discriminative tendencies of thought by focusing the mind on a single insoluble question. This concentration ultimately removes the obstacle of understanding and catalyzes the understanding-awakening. Continuing to investigate only the word itself devoid of any conceptual content *(ch'amgu;* Chin., *tsan-chü)* engenders the state of thoughtlessness *(munyŏm;* Chin., *wu-nien),* which brings about the realization-awakening and the adept's initiation into the formal *mārga.*

[*See also* Buddhism, *article on* Buddhism in Korea; Ch'an; Hua-yen; *and the biography of Tsung-mi.*]

BIBLIOGRAPHY

All of Chinul's major writings are translated and annotated in my *The Korean Approach to Zen: The Collected Works of Chinul* (Honolulu, 1983); a lengthy evaluation of Chinul's place in the Korean Sŏn tradition and his contributions to Buddhist thought may be found in the introduction. Hee-sung Keel has made a valuable survey of Chinul's thought in *Chinul: Founder of the Korean Sŏn Tradition* (Berkeley, 1984). For Chinul's outline of meditation see my article "Chinul's Systematization of Chinese Meditative Techniques in Korean Sŏn Buddhism," in *Chinese Buddhist Traditions of Meditation,* edited by Peter N. Gregory (Honolulu, 1986); for Chinul's contributions to Buddhist hermeneutical theory, see my article "Ch'an Hermeneutics: A Korean View," in *Buddhist Hermeneutics,* edited by Donald S. Lopez, Jr. (Honolulu, forthcoming).

ROBERT EVANS BUSWELL, JR.

CHINVAT BRIDGE, the "crossing" or "bridge of the separator" or of the "decision"—the meaning is not certain—is, in the Zoroastrian tradition, a mythical bridge that souls must cross to go to Paradise. They succeed in crossing it only if they are souls of the *ashavan,* that is, faithful followers of *asha,* truth and order (Vedic, *ṛta*), the fundamental principle of Indo-Iranian religion. If they are souls of the *dregvant,* that is, followers of *druj* (falsehood), they will fall off the bridge, which for them will narrow itself to a razor's edge, and they will forever reside in Hell. Indeed, Chinvat Bridge stretches over the infernal abysses. One of its ends is on the peak of Mount Harā, also known as Alburz or Harā Berez ("high Harā")—a mythical mountain that figures importantly in Indo-Iranian cosmological conceptions; the other end reaches Paradise *(garōdman),* which the soul of the *ashavan* will enter after passing through the "Region of the Mixed" *(hamistagān)* and then through the halls of Good Thought, Good Word, and Good Deed.

Awaiting the soul on Chinvat Bridge is a divine tribunal composed of the deities Mithra, Sraosha ("discipline"), and Rashnu ("the judge"), assisted by Arshtāt ("justice"). It is then that the soul confronts its own inner self, its *daēnā,* the sum of its thoughts, words, and deeds. The *daēnā* can take the form of a magnificent maiden or of a horrible witch, according to the individual case. It serves as psychopomp for the rest of the voyage, accompanying the soul of the *ashavan* to paradise, where it is received by Vohu Manah ("good thought"), one of the Amesha Spentas, or beneficent immortals, and comforted for the difficult and painful test it experienced during its separation from the body.

This scenario is very ancient; Chinvat Bridge and the *daēnā* are both mentioned in the *Gāthās.* Many aspects of this belief—in particular, that of the bridge—are reminiscent of conceptions in other religious traditions, above all those of the shamanistic variety.

A passage to the beyond, Chinvat Bridge can also be considered the path of the soul to heaven during an ecstatic experience (Nyberg, 1938). It thus figures not only in conceptions of the afterlife but also in the religious transports that occur during initiations, which are analogous to death.

BIBLIOGRAPHY

Boyce, Mary. *A History of Zoroastrianism*, vol. 1. Leiden, 1975.

Corbin, Henry. *Terre céleste et corps de résurrection*. Paris, 1961.

Eliade, Mircea. *Shamanism: Archaic Techniques of Ecstasy*. Rev. & enl. ed. New York, 1964.

Gnoli, Gherardo. "Ašavan: Contributo allo studio del libro di Ardā Wirāz." In *Iranica*, edited by Gherardo Gnoli and Adriano V. Rossi, pp. 387–452. Naples, 1979.

Lommel, Herman. *Die Religion Zarathustras nach dem Awesta dargestellt*. Tübingen, 1930.

Molé, Marijan. "Daēnā, le pont Činvat et l'initiation dans le Mazdéisme." *Revue de l'histoire des religions* 158 (1960): 155–185.

Nyberg, H. S. *Die Religionen des alten Iran*. Leipzig, 1938.

Pavry, J. D. C. *The Zoroastrian Doctrine of a Future Life*. New York, 1926.

Widengren, Geo. *Stand und Aufgaben der iranischen Religionsgeschichte*. Leiden, 1955.

Widengren, Geo. *Les religions de l'Iran*. Paris, 1968.

GHERARDO GNOLI
Translated from Italian by Roger DeGaris

CHI-TSANG (549–623), Chinese Buddhist monk of the San-lun (Three-Treatise) tradition. Although half Parthian by birth, Chi-tsang's upbringing and education were entirely Chinese. At the age of ten he became a novice under the San-lun master Fa-lang (508–581) and resided at the Hsing-huang temple in the Southern Dynasties (c. 420–589) capital of Chin-ling (modern Nanking), the center of Buddhist culture in southern China. Until the age of thirty-two, he was under the tutelage of Fa-lang, studying primary San-lun sources as well as the important texts of his age, the Prajñāpāramitā (Perfection of Wisdom) canon, the *Saddharmapuṇḍarīka Sūtra* (Lotus Sūtra), and the Mahāyāna *Mahāparinirvāṇa Sūtra* (Sūtra of the Great Decease). Following Fa-lang's death in 581, Chi-tsang spent some eight years at the Chia-hsiang temple, east of the capital on Mount Ch'in-wang (his posthumous title, Master of Chia-hsiang Temple, is derived from his residence at this temple). In 597 he was invited by the emperor Sui Yang-ti (581–618) to reside at the Hui-jih Tao-ch'ang, one of four monasteries built by that ruler in support of the religion. Chi-tsang spent less than two years at this monastery and, again at the request of Yang-ti, moved in 599 to the new imperial capital of Ch'ang-an. There he resided at the Jih-yen temple, remaining there until his death at the age of seventy-four.

With the reunification of China in 589, Chi-tsang witnessed the controlled revival of Buddhism at a time when the religion was sponsored not only for its own sake but also as a means by which the nation could be consolidated, expanded, and protected. Throughout his life Chi-tsang participated fully in the optimism and luxury of imperial patronage. Under this patronage he produced twenty-six works, collected in some 112 fascicles, a number that makes him one of the most prolific Buddhist writers of his age. Chi-tsang considered himself a specialist on the Perfection of Wisdom literature as well as on the major Mahāyāna *sūtra*s then available to him in Chinese translation. Of his extant works, approximately fifteen are concerned exclusively with the exegesis of *sūtra*s. They cover an extensive range of the topics found in the fertile symbols and ideas of the vast Mahāyāna textual corpus. As an exegete his writings account for some of the major doctrinal trends of Mahāyāna Buddhism and represent one of the earliest Chinese attempts to systematize its canon. Under the influence of the Mahāyāna *Nirvāṇa Sūtra*, the text that dominated Chinese intellectual thought during the fifth and sixth centuries, Chi-tsang wrote extensively on its theme of "Buddha nature" (universal enlightenment). He was the first East Asian Buddhist to argue that even the nonsentient world of wood and stone had the potentiality for enlightenment. As a scholar of the Perfection of Wisdom tradition, he was best known for his essays on the Buddhist concept of the Two Truths, a theory of nonduality achieved through serial negation. These essays established one of the enduring ways by which later East Asian Buddhists came to approach and understand the Buddhist concept of emptiness *(śūnyatā)*.

[*For further elaboration of Chi-tsang's views, see* Śūnyam and Śūnyatā.]

BIBLIOGRAPHY

The most comprehensive work on Chi-tsang and the San-lun tradition is by Hirai Shun'ei, *Chūgoku hannya shisōshi kenkyū* (Tokyo, 1976). A review of this work and the questions it raises regarding the history of San-lun Buddhism may be found in my study " 'Later Mādhyamika' in China: Some Current Perspectives on the History of Chinese *Prajnāpāramitā* Thought," *Journal of the International Association for Buddhist Studies* 5, (1982): 53–62. Critical analyses of the Chinese contributions toward the Two Truths theory may be found in an article by Whalen Lai, "Further Developments of the Two Truths Theory in China: The *Ch'eng-shih-lun* Tradition and Chou Yung's *San-tsung-lun*," *Philosophy East and West* 30 (April 1980): 139–161, and in an article I have written, "The Concept of Practice in San Lun Thought: Chi-tsang and the 'Concurrent Insight' of the Two Truths," *Philosophy East and West* 31 (October 1981): 449–466. Translations of selected portions of Chi-tsang's writings can be found in Wing-tsit Chan's *A Source Book in Chinese Phi-*

losophy (Princeton, 1963), pp. 360–369, and in *The Buddhist Tradition in India, China, and Japan,* edited by Wm. Theodore de Bary, Yoshito S. Hakeda, and Philip B. Yampolsky (New York, 1969).

AARON K. KOSEKI

CH'ŎNDOGYO (Religion of the Heavenly Way) is an indigenous Korean religion influenced by Confucianism and Taoism. It was founded in 1860 by Ch'oe Suun (Che-u; 1824–1864) in reaction to the traditional religions of Korea and in an attempt to offer a new religious dispensation to the masses. Originally known as Tonghak (Eastern Learning), the movement was also a reaction to Christianity, known as Sohak (Western Learning). The name was changed to Ch'ŏndogyo in 1905.

Suun was born in Kyŏngju, the ancient capital of the kingdom of Silla. According to Ch'ŏndogyo tradition, he received from God a revelation of *ch'ŏndo* (the Heavenly Way), a new universal truth. His teaching attracted a large following, but it was regarded as dangerous by the government, and he was martyred. Nevertheless, the movement continued to grow under the leadership of Suun's successor, Ch'oe Haewŏl (Si-hyŏng; 1827–1898), and under the third leader, Sohn Ŭiam (Pyŏng-hŭi; 1861–1922), Ch'ŏndogyo became one of the major religions of Korea. The writings of these first three leaders form the Ch'ŏndogyo scripture *(Ch'ŏndogyo kyŏngjŏn).* The most important part of this canon is Suun's writings, known as Tonghak Scripture or even Ch'ŏndogyo Scripture.

The antigovernmental Tonghak Revolution of 1894, a popular uprising under Tonghak leadership, helped to modernize Korean society. Ch'ŏndogyo also played a leading role among Korean religions in the Samil (1 March) Independence Movement of 1919 against Japanese colonialism. Since the demise of Sohn Ŭiam, Ch'ŏndogyo has remained a religion with a democratic system of ecclesiastical government. Currently, Ch'ŏndogyo membership is approximately one million and its headquarters are in Seoul. The church plays no active role in South Korean politics. In North Korea, Ch'ŏndogyo has been persecuted under Communism since 1945.

Beliefs and Practices. The common term for God in Ch'ŏndogyo is Hanullim, or Heavenly Lord, although scripture also uses the epithet Ch'ŏnju, a Chinese form of Hanullim. (The latter is related to other Korean names for God, Hanŭnim and Hananim.) Ch'ŏndogyo conceives God as the totality of life or the universe, and his immanence is emphasized more than his transcendence.

The Ch'ŏndogyo view of human nature is expressed in two key phrases, "Si Ch'ŏnju" ("Man bears divinity") and "In nae Ch'ŏn" ("Man is God"). Man is one with God in essence and in potentiality, and realizes this oneness in the practice of sincere faith and morality. These ideas reflect a mystical as well as a humanistic tendency. Since man is essentially divine, one must treat others with the utmost concern, respect, sincerity, dignity, equality, and justice. Thus the injunction "Sain yŏch'ŏn" ("Treat man as God") has been the central ethical teaching of Ch'ŏndogyo. This democratic principle was a revolutionary one in nineteenth-century feudalistic Korean society.

The Ch'ŏndogyo concept of human destiny is basically this-worldly, expressed in terms of a divine life or kingdom of heaven on earth. Ch'ŏndogyo emphasizes a cooperative community of mankind.

In Ch'ŏndogyo, the spiritual life is fostered by observance of the Five Practices *(ogwan):*

1. Incantation *(chumun).* Ch'ŏndogyo devotees seek oneness with God by chanting a formula that translates: "Ultimate Energy being here and now, I yearn for its great descent. Bearing God, I become firm and well. Never forgetting, I become aware of all." It is chanted at 9:00 PM every day and also at other times on special occasions. At the Sunday worship service, the second half of the incantation ("Bearing God . . .") is chanted.
2. Pure Water *(ch'ŏngsu).* In all ceremonies and at 9:00 PM daily, a bowl of pure water is placed on a table and the worshipers meditate on the significance of water as a symbol of spiritual purity.
3. Service Day *(siil).* The Sunday worship service includes prayer, hymns, scripture reading, and a sermon.
4. Sincerity Rice *(sŏngmi).* Believers put aside some rice each day and offer it to the church at the end of the month.
5. Prayer *(kido).* Prayer expresses the worshiper's wishes. A silent meditative prayer called *simgo* (heart address) is also practiced at mealtimes, before and after sleeping, and in all ceremonies.

Finally, Ch'ŏndogyo stresses moral discipline. It requires of its followers that they keep a steadfast mind, avoid materialistic desires, and cultivate sincerity, respect for others, and faith.

BIBLIOGRAPHY

My book on Ch'ŏndogyo thought, *The Ch'ŏndogyo Concept of Man: An Essence of Korean Thought* (Seoul, 1978), contains a glossary and an extensive bibliography. Benjamin B. Weems's *Reform, Rebellion, and the Heavenly Way* (Tucson, 1964) deals mainly with the role that Ch'ŏndogyo played in Korean politics, but it also contains much of Ch'ŏndogyo history and cites some Ch'ŏndogyo ideas and practices. It includes a useful glossary, bibliography, and index. These two studies are the only books in English that deal exclusively with Ch'ŏndogyo.

The following books in Korean are good sources for understanding Ch'ŏndogyo: Che-u Ch'oe's *Ch'ŏndogyo Kyŏngjŏn (Tonghak Kyŏngjŏn)* (Seoul, 1961), Paek Se-myŏng's *Tonghak sasang kwa Ch'ŏndogyo* (Seoul, 1956), and Ch'oe Tong-hŭi and Kim Yong-ch'ŏn's *Ch'ŏndogyo* (Iri, 1976).

YONG-CHOON KIM

CHŎNG YAGYONG (1762–1836), foremost representative of Korea's Sirhak (Practical Learning) movement and creator of a theistic Confucian philosophy. He is best known by his honorific name, Tasan. The Sirhak movement was characterized by a spirit of seeking evidence to establish fact, as opposed to more speculative modes of thought, and a spirit of practicality as seen in studies concerned with administrative and economic reform. Contemporary Koreans look to Sirhak as a kind of indigenous proto-modernity within their own tradition, although the movement seems to have largely dissolved by the second half of the nineteenth century. Tasan is especially revered as the preeminent intellectual figure of the movement, a polymath who mastered the principles of Western mechanics to build a town wall, wrote insightful treatises on government and social reform, and in his many works passed in critical review some two thousand years of Confucian learning. He was also one of East Asia's most prolific authors: his collected works, written in literary Chinese, come to more than eighteen thousand pages.

In his youth Tasan was a member of the small group of scholars that became interested in the Chinese writings of the Jesuit missionary Matteo Ricci (1552–1610). In 1784, while on a tribute mission to Peking, one of the members of the group, Yi Sŭnghun, visited a European missionary and was baptized; he returned to Korea and baptized a number of other members in the group, including Tasan's two brothers. The movement spread rapidly, and when the first priest arrived in Korea in 1794 there were already some four thousand Korean Catholics. [*See the biography of Ricci.*]

It is not clear whether Tasan was ever baptized, but his connections to Catholicism were close enough to implicate him in the first large-scale purge of Catholics from government in 1801. The nineteen years of exile that followed these persecutions were a period of enforced seclusion in which Tasan devoted himself completely to study and writing, a style of life he maintained after the ban was lifted. During this long period he occupied himself not only with the practical studies typical of Sirhak but with the whole tradition of Confucian scholarship. In fact more than half of his voluminous collected works is devoted to commentary on the Confucian classics and related matters.

Tasan's reappraisal of the Confucian tradition is unusual, perhaps unique, for he took his viewpoint from the earliest classics, those that preserved an early Chinese theism that was already waning by the time of Confucius. On this basis, he reconstructed not just a primitive theistic Confucianism but a philosophically systematic Confucian theism that matched the sophisticated metaphysical and ascetic systems of the Neo-Confucians. His work in this regard is notable especially for the completeness and maturity with which he grasped the ramifications of a theistic perspective.

Tasan's Confucianism had no intellectual heir. In part this is because he spent his last thirty-five years under a cloud of suspicion and in relative isolation, in part because his accomplishments occurred when Korea was on the threshold of a tumultuous change that dislocated the tradition he had accepted as authoritative.

[*See also* Confucianism in Korea.]

BIBLIOGRAPHY

For general introductions to Sirhak, see *The Traditional Culture and Society of Korea: Thought and Institutions,* edited by Hugh H. W. Kang (Honolulu, 1975), and my article "An Introduction to Silhak," *Korea Journal* 15 (1975): 29–46. A biographical account of Chŏng Yagyong's life can be found in Gregory Henderson's "Chŏng Ta-san: A Study in Korea's Intellectual History," *Journal of Asian Studies* 16 (1957): 377–386. A discussion and analysis of the meeting of theistic and nontheistic worldviews in Chŏng's work is my "Chŏng Tasan's Philosophy of Man: A Radical Critique of the Neo-Confucian World View," *Journal of Korean Studies* 3 (1981): 3–38.

MICHAEL C. KALTON

CHOSEN PEOPLE. *For discussion of various notions of the religious foundations of peoplehood, see* Election.

CHOU TUN-I (1017–1073), also known as Chou Lien-hsi, the first major Neo-Confucian thinker to formulate a Confucian cosmology and metaphysics. Chou Tun-i was a native of Tao-chou in modern Hunan. During the active part of his career he served as tutor to both Ch'eng Hao (1032–1085) and Ch'eng I (1033–1077), the brothers who were to become major exponents of the two principal schools of Neo-Confucianism. For his role in the development of a Neo-Confucian cosmology and metaphysics, Chou Tun-i was considered by Chu Hsi to be the first teacher in the traditional lineage of Neo-

Confucians. Chou Tun-i's major exposition of this cosmology and metaphysics, an interest new to the Confucian school, is found in his two major works, the *T'ai-chi t'u-shuo* (An Explanation of the Diagram of the Great Ultimate) and the *T'ung-shu* (Penetrating the Book of Changes).

At the center of Chou Tun-i's system of thought lies what is called the Diagram of the Great Ultimate (see figure 1), which may have been transmitted to him by a Taoist priest. For Chou, the Great Ultimate *(t'ai-chi)* is seen as the source of all things in the universe, that which lies both within and behind all things. In its capacity for tranquillity it gives rise to *yin,* the symbol of the mysterious and the female in Chinese thought. In its capacity for activity it gives rise to *yang,* the symbol of the rational and the male. It is the source of the basic patterns or phases of change known as the Five Elements *(wu-hsing)* and forms the foundation of the two major symbols of the *I ching* (Book of Changes), *ch'ien,* the heavenly principle, and *k'un,* the earthly principle, themselves again symbols of male and female. Man in Chou Tun-i's system receives the highest, most rarefied form of the Five Elements, and thus is seen as capable of playing a critical role in the life of the universe. On this point the system finds its characteristically Confucian focus, for in man lies the foundation for understanding the universe as a whole. Particularly in his ideal form as a sage, man is the central figure in the universe. In this way, a metaphysical framework is established that incorporates the Confucian emphasis upon the unique relation of mankind and Heaven *(t'ien)* that forms the basic moral structure of the universe.

One of the most frequently debated points of Chou Tun-i's thought is the first sentence of his *Explanation of the Diagram of the Great Ultimate.* The sentence reads "The Non-Ultimate! And also the Great Ultimate" (de Bary, 1964, p. 458). The *wu-chi,* or Non-Ultimate, is often cited as evidence of Taoist influence, for it first occurs in the *Tao-te ching.* To simply identify its source does not, however, explain what particular meaning it has for Chou Tun-i. From Chou's point of view the entire universe, all being itself, is ultimately derived from the Great Ultimate. (See figure 1.) By suggesting that the Great Ultimate is also the Non-Ultimate, Chou affirms the all-inclusive nature of the source of things. The measure of its all-inclusiveness is that even its own opposite is included: there is nothing that is excluded from the Great Ultimate. This interpretation of the Great Ultimate also has a very practical side to it, for by suggesting that the Great Ultimate includes the Non-Ultimate, Chou Tun-i emphasizes the degree to which Confucianism already includes Buddhist and Taoist symbols. Thus what the Buddhists refer to as emptiness

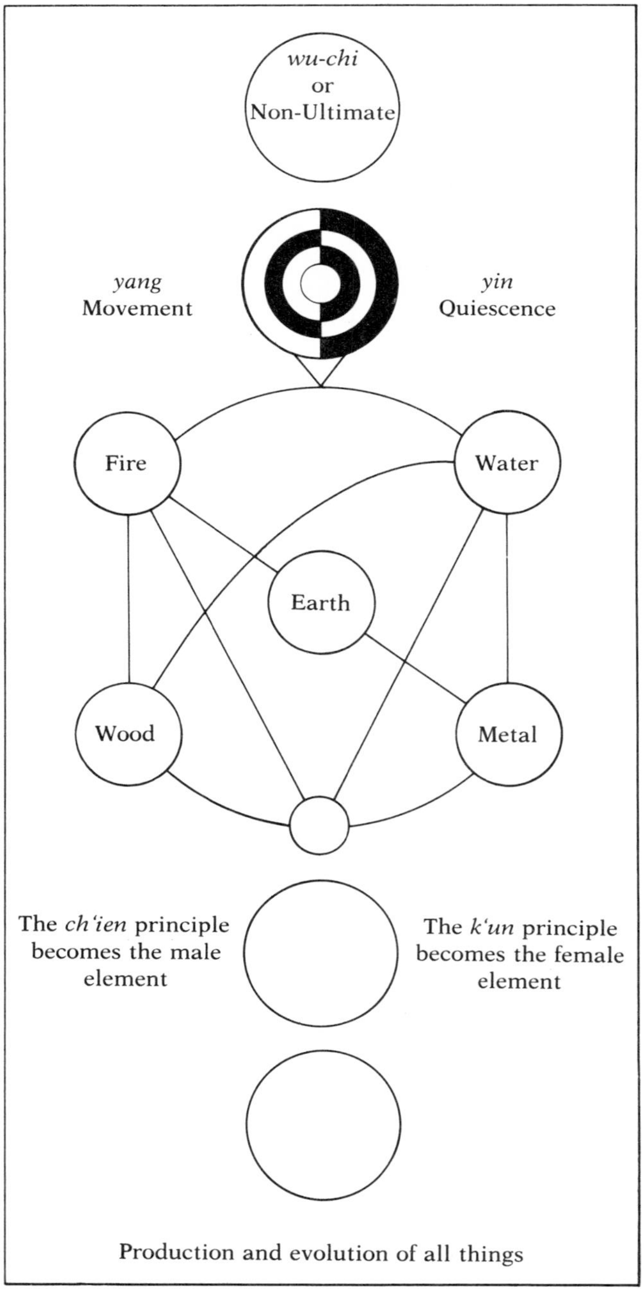

FIGURE 1. *Diagram of the Great Ultimate*

(k'ung) or the Taoists as voidness *(hsü)* is, according to Chou, already subsumed in the Great Ultimate. This is not to be understood as some kind of syncretism, but instead as a reaffirmation of the Confucian claim for the ontological priority of the Great Ultimate and thus of the Confucian affirmation of life itself as the ultimate ground for the achievement of sagehood.

There are other areas of Taoist influence in Chou's

thought beyond that evinced in his interpretation of the Great Ultimate. At the center of his practices and teachings are the ideas of quietude or tranquillity *(ching)* and desirelessness *(wu-yü)*. The sage is defined by Chou Tun-i as one who is able to achieve a state of profound quietude and who is without desires. Chu Hsi felt that such ideas if carried to excess could lead dangerously close to the ways of the Buddhists and the Taoists. It may be because of this reservation that Chu Hsi chose to emphasize the metaphysical structure of Chou Tun-i's thought and qualified Chou's views by insisting upon the need for serious study rather than the cultivation of states of quietude and desirelessness.

The religious significance of Chou Tun-i's thought for the development of Neo-Confucianism is found in part in the degree to which he isolates the Great Ultimate as a symbol of ultimate meaning. The significance of this symbol persists throughout the course of the Neo-Confucian tradition and reaffirms the central Confucian idea of the ultimate importance of life. But Chou Tun-i's own life serves as a Neo-Confucian religious model as well. In Chou Tun-i we have someone who told his disciples that the whole purpose of learning is to achieve the goal of sagehood, someone who in his own life displayed a seriousness and a humility that speak directly to the authenticity of the Neo-Confucian religious perspective. When asked at one point why he refrained from cutting the grass outside his window, Chou said that the grass's feeling and his own were the same. This has suggested to most readers Chou Tun-i's extraordinary respect for and love of all forms of life, not to the detriment of the unique role of man, but rather as the extension and enlargement of man's own focus. It also suggests Chou Tun-i's own religious sense of the continuity of all life and its common root in the Great Ultimate.

[*See also* Confucian Thought, *article on* Neo-Confucianism.]

BIBLIOGRAPHY

Introductory essays on Chou Tun-i with a partial translation of his major writings are found in the two major source books of Chinese thought, *A Source Book in Chinese Philosophy*, translated by Wing-tsit Chan (Princeton, 1963), pp. 460–480, and *Sources of Chinese Tradition*, compiled by Wm. Theodore de Bary and others (New York, 1964), vol. 1, pp. 457–460. Both contain selections from *An Explanation of the Diagram of the Great Ultimate* and *Penetrating the Book of Changes*. Chou Tun-i's writings are included in part in a thirteenth-century anthology of Neo-Confucianism compiled by Chu Hsi and Lü Tsu-ch'ien, translated into English by Wing-tsit Chan as *Reflections on Things at Hand* (New York, 1967). Discussions of specific aspects of Chou Tun-i's thought may be found in Fung Yulan's *A History of Chinese Philosophy*, 2d ed., vol. 2, translated by Derk Bodde (Princeton, 1953), pp. 434–451, and Carsun Chang's *The Development of Neo-Confucian Thought*, 2 vols. (New York, 1957–1962), pp. 137–158.

RODNEY L. TAYLOR

CHRIST. *See* Jesus.

CHRISTENSEN, ARTHUR

CHRISTENSEN, ARTHUR (1875–1945), Danish Orientalist and folklorist. Arthur Emanuel Christensen was born in Copenhagen, where, apart from short periods of study and travel, he spent his life. He studied in Berlin and Göttingen, passing his *Studentereksamen* in 1893 and obtaining his *candidatus magisterii* (master's degree) in French, history, and Latin in 1900. During his university years, Christensen was also a fervent student of Persian, Avestan, Arabic, Sanskrit, and Turkish. He studied under the famous Iranologist F. C. Andreas, and, in 1903, he obtained his Ph.D. He became a teacher and journalist, specializing in foreign politics. In 1919, he was appointed professor extraordinarius of Iranian philology at the University of Copenhagen, an office that he held for the rest of his life.

Christensen was a prolific writer who wrote on many aspects of Iranian cultural history, including language (dialect studies), folklore, general history, history of religions, philosophy, and music. His magnum opus, *L'empire des Sassanides: Le peuple, l'état, la cour* (1907), was written from a religio-historical point of view. Though Christensen elaborated various points in Sasanid history, he was chiefly concerned with chronological and purely historical and legendary elements. Examples of this interest are his *Le règne du roi Kawādh I et le communisme masdakite* (1925), which deals with the fifth-century communalist reformer Mazdak, and "La légende du sage Buzurjmihr" (*Acta Orientalia* 8, 1930), which examines one of the strangest figures of the Sasanid tradition.

Of religious life as such Christensen seems to have had no real sense; in his heart he doubted that it was possible to gain secure knowledge of what had once been a living religion in ancient Iran. His intention was to give a complete representation of the Iranian legendary history, the religious and national heritage that the Sasanids took over and attempted to legitimate as their own. He carried out his plan in a series of works of extraordinary importance for Indo-Iranian research in the areas of legend and religion, and for the understanding of legends and folk tales in general. Through his endeavors to provide a theoretical and practical foundation for the study of tradition, legend, and myth, Christensen encountered the works of folklorists such as Axel Olrik and C. W. von Sydow, which led him into studies of general folklore, folk psychology, and philosophy. Christensen's foremost contribution to the study of folklore is his *Trebrødre- og Tobrødre Stamsagn* (1916), which gives a simple and natural psychological explanation of national ancestral legends.

To Avestan studies Christensen brought new understanding and inspiration. Problems concerning the time and environment of Zarathushtra (Zoroaster) and the chronology of the *Gāthā*s and the *Yasht*s were his main concern. The systematic expression of his thought is given in several works: "Quelques notices sur les plus anciennes périodes du Zoroastrisme" (*Acta Orientalia* 4, 1926, pp. 81–115), *Études sur le Zoroastrisme de la Perse antique* (1928), and *Le premier chapitre du Vendidad et l'histoire primitive des tribus iraniennes* (1943). These works reveal Christensen as a bold interpreter whose theses would both inspire and irritate his contempories and future scholars.

BIBLIOGRAPHY

Christensen's *Recherches sur les Rubā'iyāt de 'Omar Ḫayyām* (Heidelberg, 1905) was written as his doctoral thesis; it was published in Danish in 1903. Later, he returned to this topic with *Critical Studies in the Rubáiyát of Umar-i-Khayyám* (Copenhagen, 1927). His great work, *L'empire des Sassanides: Le peuple, l'état, la cour* (Copenhagen, 1907), was twice revised and expanded under the title *L'Iran sous les Sassanides,* 2d ed. (1944; Osnabrück, 1971); it has also been translated into Persian. An examination of the shortcomings of Christensen's *magnum opus* can be found in Phillipe Gignoux's article "Die religiöse Administration in sasanidischer Zeit: Ein Überblick," *Archäologische Mitteilungen aus Iran* (suppl. 10, 1983): 253ff.

Among Christensen's works on the legendary history of Iran, the following deserve mention: "Reste von Manu-Legenden in der iranischen Sagenwelt," in *Festschrift Friedrich Carl Andreas* (Leipzig, 1916), pp. 63–69; *Les types du premier homme et le premier roi dans l'histoire légendaire des Iraniens,* 2 vols. (Stockholm, 1917–1934); *Les Kayanides* (Copenhagen, 1931); and *Les gestes des rois dans les traditions de l'Iran antique* (Paris, 1936). Notable among Christensen's studies of Iranian folklore are the following: *Contes persans en langue populaire* (Copenhagen, 1918); "Les sots dans la tradition populaire des Persans," *Acta Orientalia* 1 (1922): 43–75; and *Essai sur la démonologie iranienne* (Copenhagen, 1941) in which he shows how ancient Iranian elements of folk belief survive within the framework of present-day Islam. A significant example of Christensen's work of general folklore and folk psychology is his *Politik og massemoral* (Copenhagen, 1911), which was translated by A. Cecil Curtis under the title *Politics and Crowd-Morality* (London, 1915).

A biographical appreciation of Christensen by Kaj Barr and H. Andersen appears in *Oversigt over Det Kongelige Danske Videnskabernes Selskab: Forhandlinger* (Copenhagen, 1945–1946), pp. 65–102; it includes a complete bibliography of 327 items. A biographical note by myself and Frank le Sage de Fontenay appears in *Dansk biografisk leksikon,* 3d ed., vol. 3 (Copenhagen, 1979), pp. 233–236.

JES P. ASMUSSEN

CHRISTIAN ETHICS.

[*This entry provides an overview of the sources, styles, and developments of Christian ethics in Eastern Orthodox, Roman Catholic, and Protestant churches. Approaches to related issues in broader religious perspective are discussed in* Morality and Religion; Cosmic Law; Natural Law; *and* Confession of Sins. *The ethos of various Christian churches is also discussed in* Eastern Christianity; Roman Catholicism; Anglicanism; Protestantism; *and numerous articles on particular churches.*]

The three primary manifestations of Christianity—Eastern Orthodoxy, Roman Catholicism, and Protestantism—have recognized that Christian faith involves a particular way of life. The good news of salvation in Jesus Christ calls for a life of discipleship. The scriptures point out that Christian believers are to live and act in certain ways. Conversion to Jesus Christ and membership in the Christian community involve moral exigencies.

Christian Ethics in General. The Bible is the book of Christianity, but it does not contain Christian ethics as such. The Bible does include moral teachings and descriptions of the moral life of believers in Yahveh and in Jesus. The distinction between morality and ethics is most significant. Morality refers to the actions, dispositions, attitudes, virtues, and ways of life that should characterize the moral person and society, in this case the Christian person and the Christian community. Christian ethics operates on the level of the theoretical and the scientific and tries to explain the Christian moral life in a thematic, systematic, coherent, and consistent manner. It is possible for one to attempt a biblical ethic that makes such an explanation of biblical morality, but that ethic would be based on the moral teaching found in scripture. Biblical ethics and Christian ethics are not coextensive. The subject matter of Christian ethics is the Christian moral life and teaching, which is much broader than biblical moral life and teaching.

The relationship between Christian ethics and philosophical ethics is most important. The significant differences between the two result from the different sources of ethical wisdom and knowledge employed. Philosophical ethics is based on human reason and human experience and does not accept the role of faith and revelation that is central to Christian ethics. However, Christian ethics poses the same basic questions and has the same formal structure as philosophical ethics. All ethics attempts to respond to the same questions: what is the good? what values and goals should be pursued? what attitudes and dispositions should characterize the person? what acts are right? what acts are wrong? how do the individual and society go about making ethical decisions?

Contemporary ethicists speak about three generally accepted formal approaches to ethics. The classical forms are teleology and deontology. The teleological approach determines what is the end or the good at which one should aim and then determines the morality of means in relationship to the end. The deontological model understands morality primarily in terms of duty, law, or obligation. Such an approach is primarily interested in what is right. Recently some contemporary ethicists (e.g., H. Richard Niebuhr) have proposed a third model: the responsibility model, which is primarily interested in what is "fitting." Within Christian ethics all these different models have been employed. Teleology, for example, sees the end of the moral life as union with and participation in God, which becomes the good and the end of the moral life, thus specifying as good those means that attain that end. Deontological Christian ethics has often seen the moral life in terms of the Ten Commandments or the revealed word of God as the law Christians are to follow. God's law determines what is right and wrong. The responsibility model understands the moral life on the basis of the Christian's response to the action and working of God in the world and in history.

The vast majority of Christian ethicists would agree that theological ethics is truly a form of ethics, that it asks the same questions and has the same formal structure as philosophical ethics. However, some Christians working out of a more fundamentalistic approach to the scriptures or out of a Barthian perspective might not agree that Christian ethics is a species of ethics as such.

Sources. What distinguishes Christian ethics from philosophical ethics and other religious ethics are the sources of wisdom and knowledge that contribute to Christian ethics. All Christian ethics recognizes the Christian scriptures, tradition, and church teaching as the revelatory sources of moral wisdom and knowledge. However, there is much discussion as to how these sources relate to one another and to the nonrevelatory sources of Christian ethics. The three major expressions of Christianity—Eastern Orthodoxy, Roman Catholicism, and Protestantism—and their corresponding ethical traditions emphasize different sources of Christian ethics. At least in theory, all these traditions give primary emphasis to sacred scripture, but there is no general agreement about how the scriptures should be used in Christian ethics.

The role accorded scripture in Christian ethics depends heavily on one's understanding of scripture's relationship to other sources of wisdom and knowledge. On such questions as those having to do with conversion or change of heart, the general attitudes a Christian should have, and the goals and dispositions of the Christian life, the scriptures can give much content to Christian ethics. On the question of precise norms and rules of moral action, however, many Christian ethicists are cautious in their attempts to find specific concrete norms that are absolutely binding in all circumstances. Protestantism's emphasis on the primacy of scripture and downplaying of tradition and church teaching distinguishes its ethics from that of the other two major forms of Christianity.

Since the church is a living communion proceeding through different historical and cultural circumstances under the guidance of the continuing presence of the Holy Spirit, God's self-revelation comes also through tradition as the preaching, teaching, celebration, and practice of the Christian faith. Within the general category of tradition, special emphasis is given, especially by the Eastern Orthodox churches, to the teachings of the patristic period and to the councils and legislation of that time. Authoritative or authentic church teaching is a special form of tradition that is found in the councils and synods of the churches, and in Roman Catholicism it is connected with the teaching office of the bishops, especially of the pope as the bishop of Rome and pastor of the universal church.

Christian ethics has always grappled with the question of whether human nature, human reason, and human experience can be sources of ethical wisdom and knowledge. The Roman Catholic tradition has emphasized natural law based on the ability of human reason to arrive at ethical wisdom and knowledge. This emphasis has often been more primary than the influence of revelatory sources. Eastern Orthodox and Protestant ethics have been more suspicious of human reason and experience, although today many ethicists in these traditions give reason an important though still subordinate role.

Early History. In the first one thousand years of Christianity there was no discipline of Christian ethics as such. Moral teaching was primarily pastoral, apologetical, homiletical, and catechetical, although at times there were systematic studies of particular issues. An early problem for the Christian church was the relationship of Christian mores to the culture and mores of the wider society. Pedagogical devices such as "the two ways" (elaborated on in the *Didache* and *Shepherd of Hermas*) and catalogs of virtues and vices were used by the early Christian writers. Often the patristic authors borrowed from Stoic and Neoplatonic philosophies of the times. The apologists of the second century attempted to show that Christian morality was in keeping with the best pagan understandings of morality.

In the third century, Tertullian stressed the differences between pagan and Christian moral teaching and proposed a rigorous and legalistic morality. The early church fathers relied heavily on scriptural teaching and often understood moral life in terms of the imitation of Christ. Exhortation to perseverance in the face of martyrdom, the avoidance of any type of idolatry, and the need for prayer, fasting, almsgiving, chastity, patience, and justice were stressed. Eastern moral thought, as reflected in that of Athanasius and the Alexandrians, stressed the divinization of human beings through the gift of the Holy Spirit. The Antiochian school understood justification in terms of sharing in the suffering, death, and resurrection of Jesus. Throughout the period of persecution great emphasis was put on martyrdom, but afterward substitutions for martyrdom (the word originally meant "witness") were proposed: the monastic life or strict obedience to God's will, sometimes called "the martyrdom of conscience."

In the West after the third century the most significant figures were Ambrose, Augustine, and Gregory I. Ambrose's *De officiis* is perhaps the most systematic, scientific approach to Christian morality, with its basis in the treatise of Cicero. Gregory, in his homilies and his *Moralia in Job*, often relies on the moral teaching of Augustine but emphasizes the practical and pastoral aspects of Christian morality. Augustine defends a Christian moral understanding against the dualism and pessimism of Manichaeans on the one hand and the optimism of Pelagians on the other. Augustine devoted a number of works to specific moral questions, such as lying, continence, marriage, concupiscence. His major works, the *Confessions* and the *City of God*, also contain some methodological and substantive considerations in Christian ethics even though there is no fully systematic treatise on moral theology. Augustine stresses the centrality of the grace of God, which delivers sinners from evil and makes the Christian life possible. The moral life is described in terms of love. The love of God aims at the enjoyment of God for God's own sake and uses everything else for the love of God, whereas desire attempts to enjoy self, neighbor, and earthly things without reference to God. These two different loves are the sources of the good life and the bad life. Augustine's eschatology emphasizes a great difference between the present world and the future reign of God at the end of time, a recognition that grounds his profound realism about life in this world.

In the East, the Fathers showed a great interest in contemplation. Obedience to God's commandments, the practice of asceticism, and contemplation were proposed not only for monks but for all Christians. At the end of the patristic era in the East, John of Damascus (d. 749) summarized patristic teachings on the moral life by using Aristotelian concepts.

Before the end of the first millennium an important development occurred in the practice of the sacrament of penance. In the West, the new form of private penance spread from Ireland to the continent, and with the new repeatable private penance the *libri poenitentiales* came into existence. These books assigned a particular penance for a particular sin and were often used in a very mechanistic way. There were also penitentials in the East, such as the *Penitential of John the Faster* and others, which were borrowed from the West. However, the sacrament of penance in the East always emphasized the spiritual direction aspect of the relationship between penitent and monk-confessor, thereby avoiding at least in theory the dangers of legalism and ritualism. A scientific and systematic Christian ethic developed only in the second millennium.

The Eastern Orthodox Tradition. Eastern Orthodox theology, in both its Greek and Russian approaches, is distinguished from other Christian ethics by its emphasis on tradition, especially the teachings of the church fathers, as important sources of moral wisdom and knowledge. The most distinctive characteristic of Orthodox ethics is its relationship to spirituality. Pastoral practice has emphasized the role of monks and confessors as spiritual directors who help guide the spiritual life of the faithful. The goal or end of the moral life is to become like God. The way to this full deification (*theōsis* in the Greek) is through asceticism and prayer. Contemplation and contemplative prayer as parts of the struggle for deification are stressed. This perfectionist ethic calls for constant deepening of the believer's participation in divine life.

The anthropological basis for this movement toward deification is the creation of human beings in the image and likeness of God. "Image" consists in the human moral capacities of virtue, intellect, ethical judgment, and self-determination. The image of God is darkened and wounded by sin but still remains. "Likeness" refers to the human potential to become like God. In the Orthodox tradition, as in the Roman Catholic tradition, Christian morality is not heteronomous, for Christian morality brings the human to its fullest perfection. In the same way such an ethics stresses both the providence of God and the responsibility of Christians.

Within the Orthodox tradition there is doubt that natural law is a source of ethical wisdom and knowledge. Many affirm such knowledge on the basis of creation and the image of God embodied in human moral capacity, but others strongly deny this knowledge. At times the polemical nature of discussions between the Orthodox and Roman Catholic traditions seems to have influenced the Orthodox denial of natural law.

Law in general has a significant but not exclusive role to play in Orthodox ethics. Law is found in the Ten Commandments, the Beatitudes, the teachings of the New Testament, and the sayings of the church fathers. Although some Orthodox ethicists might have become legalistic or ritualistic, the tradition itself generally guards against legalism, especially by invocation of the principle of "economy." Economy allows exceptions to the law when the law stands in the way of the higher values of human persons and communities.

Orthodox ethics has been accused of lacking a world-transforming aspect and failing to develop an adequate social ethic, but many defenders of the Orthodox tradition deny this charge. In the past, social ethics was colored by recognition of a "symphony" between the church and the state in the single organism of the Christian empire. Today the diverse settings in which the Orthodox church functions have forced it to try to work out a social ethic and the church's relationship to the state. Russian Orthodoxy most often finds itself in relationship to communist governments. In Europe and the United States, Russian and Greek Orthodox churches now also find themselves in a diaspora situation in which they as a minority must develop their own approach to social ethics. Recently the Greek Orthodox church and then the Russian Orthodox church have joined the World Council of Churches, so that Orthodoxy now participates in the current discussions and positions taken on contemporary social questions by the World Council.

Historical Development of Eastern Orthodox Ethics. Christian ethics as a separate discipline emerged comparatively late in the Orthodox tradition. After the Great Schism of the ninth century the penitentials continued to be an important genre of moral teaching in the East. Despite some legalistic and ritualistic tendencies, Orthodoxy's emphasis on spirituality and striving for perfection served as a safeguard against a minimalistic legalism.

In Russian Orthodoxy the seventeenth-century Kiev school attempted to refute Roman Catholicism and its ethics by developing a theology strongly influenced by scholasticism. The *Orthodox Confession* of Petr Moghila (d. 1646), which was approved with slight modifications by the Greek patriarch at the Synod of Jerusalem (1672), explains Christian moral teaching on the basis of the nine precepts of the church, the seven sacraments, the Beatitudes, and the Ten Commandments. However, even the Kiev school stressed more distinctly Russian and patristic theology in its ascetical and spiritual works.

The eighteenth and nineteenth centuries in Russian Orthodox ethics again saw both dialogue and polemics with Roman Catholic and Protestant ethics in the West. Feofan Prokopovich (d. 1736) ignored the Orthodox tradition, rejected Catholic scholasticism, and turned to Protestant authors for his ethical principles. Some subsequent authors followed the same approach, but F. Fiveiskii (d. 1877) returned to more patristic sources and to a more Catholic methodology in his manual of moral theology, the official textbook in all seminaries until 1867.

The years from 1860 to 1863 saw the publication of P. F. Soliarskii's moral theology, which tried to combine patristic, Roman Catholic, and Protestant approaches to ethics. An abridged edition of this influential work was used in the schools for forty years. In the late nineteenth century the influence of modernism and its stress on the role of the natural moral sense influenced some approaches to moral theology. However, in addition to these manuals of moral theology, there was also a spiritual and mystical literature that drew heavily from patristic sources. In the twentieth century, Nikolai Berdiaev and Sergei Bulgakov appealed to the Russian Orthodox tradition in developing what can be called a communitarian personalism with emphasis on subjectivity, freedom, love, and the need to transform the objective world.

According to Stanley S. Harakas, Christian ethics as a separate theological discipline in Greek Orthodoxy developed in the modern period and emerged as a separate, distinct, scientific discipline only in the nineteenth century. Three different schools or approaches characterize Greek Orthodox moral theology from that time. The Athenian school, strongly influenced by philosophical idealism, sees no vital differences between Christian ethics and philosophical ethics. The Constantinopolitan school is Christocentric and depends heavily on scripture and the church fathers. The Thessalonian school is apophatic in character, stresses a personalist perspective, and is heavily dependent on the monastic tradition. In his *Toward Transfigured Life,* Harakas tries to bring these three schools together.

The Roman Catholic Tradition. The characteristics of Roman Catholic "moral theology," as Christian ethics has come to be called in the Catholic tradition, are insistence on mediation, acceptance of natural law, and the role of the church. Mediation is perhaps the most characteristic aspect of Roman Catholic theology in general. There is a distinctive Catholic emphasis on conjunctions—of scripture and tradition, faith and reason, faith and works, grace and nature, the divine and human, Jesus and the church and Mary and the saints, love as well as the virtues and the commandments. This approach is an attempt to be universal and to embrace all elements, but it may fall into dichotomy. For example, rather than seeing tradition as a mediation of revelation whose privileged witness is in sacred scripture, scripture and tradition were seen as two separate fonts of revelation. Further, faith and works, properly understood, mean that the gift of salvation is mediated in and through the human response; a perennial danger is to absolutize works. Likewise, mediation insists on the importance of love, but love mediated through all the other virtues and commandments, which, however, must not be emphasized only in themselves.

In the Roman Catholic tradition, natural law can best be understood as human reason directing human beings to their end in accord with their nature. In the classic tradition based on Thomas Aquinas (d. 1274), human nature has a threefold structure: that which is shared with all substances, that which is common to humans and all the animals, and that which is proper to human beings as such. Human nature has its innate teleology on these three levels, and human reason discovers these ends and directs all human activity to them. In practice, Catholic moral theology often considered life in this world or in the temporal sphere as almost totally governed by natural law and not by the gospel, or by any explicitly Christian considerations. Before Vatican II, Catholic moral theology was dependent on reason and philosophical ethics and downplayed the role of the scriptures and specific theological understandings.

The third characteristic of Roman Catholic moral theology is its insistence on relationship to the church. Catholic ecclesiology recognizes a special teaching office in matters of faith and morals that is given to the church, specifically the pope and the bishops. Since the seventeenth century there has been a growing intervention of authoritative papal teaching in moral matters. Catholic ecclesiology in accord with the teaching of Vatican I (1870) recognizes an infallible teaching function that is exercised through ecumenical councils and the *ex cathedra* teaching of the pope as well as definitive teachings by the pope and the bishops. A noninfallible, authoritative teaching office is also exercised by the councils and especially by the pope through encyclicals, allocutions, and the various offices of the Curia Romana. The vast majority of Catholic moral theologians agree that there has never been an infallible papal teaching on a specific moral matter.

The authoritative church teaching offices have also served to keep the methodology of Catholic ethics somewhat monolithic. In the late nineteenth century and subsequently, the popes have authoritatively directed that Roman Catholic theology and philosophy be taught according to the principles and the approach of Thomas Aquinas. Until comparatively recently, Catholic theology in general and moral theology in particular followed a Thomistic philosophical approach.

Church rites and practice have also influenced Catholic moral theology. Ever since the seventeenth century the primary purpose of moral theology textbooks has been to train confessors for the sacrament of penance, with emphasis on their role as judges. This narrow orientation resulted in an act-centered approach that was casuistic, based primarily on law, and aimed at determining the existence and gravity of sins.

Historical Development of Roman Catholic Ethics. Roman Catholic moral theology or Christian ethics developed into a scientific discipline earlier than in Eastern Orthodoxy. In the thirteenth century, systematic and scientific theology appeared with the work of the great Scholastic theologians, especially Thomas Aquinas. Moral theology in Thomas's thought is an integrated part of his systematic theology, not a separate discipline. The basic structure of Thomas's moral theology is teleological. The ultimate end of human beings is a happiness attained when the intellect knows perfect truth and the will loves the perfect good. For the Christian, the beatific vision fulfills and perfects human nature. The Franciscan school, represented by Alexander of Hales (d. 1245), Bonaventure (d. 1274), and John Duns Scotus (d. 1308), affirmed the primacy of the will and of charity and emphasized moral theology as wisdom.

The fourteenth century saw a criticism of Thomas from a nominalist perspective that grounded the good not in ontological reality but solely in the will of God and employed a more deontological approach to ethics. After the thirteenth century there appeared the penitentials, very practical handbooks without any philosophical basis or analysis, which often arranged in alphabetical order the problems that the confessor would face in practice.

The three-volume *Institutiones theologiae moralis* appeared in the seventeenth century. These manuals, which became the standard textbooks of Catholic moral theology until the Second Vatican Council, began with a brief description of the ultimate end, which was followed by treatises on human acts, law as the objective norm of morality, and conscience as the subjective norm of morality. The virtues are mentioned, but sin remains the central concern. The sacraments are discussed, but almost exclusively from the viewpoint of moral and legal obligations. In the seventeenth and eighteenth centuries a controversy that arose between rigorists and laxists was finally resolved after papal intervention through the moderate approach of Alphonso Liguori (d. 1787), who was later named the patron of Catholic moral theology and of confessors.

Beginning with Leo XIII's encyclical *Rerum novarum* in 1891, a series of official teachings on the social question appeared. Leo and his immediate successors used a natural-law methodology, understood the state as a natural human society, proposed an anthropology that insisted on both the personal and communitarian aspects of human existence (thus avoiding the extremes of capitalism and socialism), recognized the right of workers to organize, and called for the state to intervene when necessary to protect the rights of workers or any particular class that was suffering. The tradition of official social teaching still exists, but now it stresses some of the newer methodological emphases in Catholic theology and deals with contemporary political and economic problems, especially in a global perspective.

There were attempts at renewal in moral theology, especially from the scriptural and Thomistic perspectives, but Bernhard Häring's *The Law of Christ* (1954) was the most significant single work in the renewal of Catholic moral theology in the pre–Vatican II period. Häring proposed a biblically inspired, Christocentric approach to moral theology based on the divine call to be perfect even as the gracious God is perfect.

The Second Vatican Council greatly influenced the renewal of moral theology. Now there was greater dialogue with other Christians, non-Christians, and the modern world in general. Contemporary Catholic moral theology, while upholding the goodness of the natural and of the human, has tried to overcome the dichotomy or dualism between the supernatural and the natural. The gospel, grace, Jesus Christ, and the Holy Spirit are related to what happens in daily life in the world. Contemporary moral theology recognizes the need to consider more than acts and lays more emphasis on the person and the virtues and attitudes of the person. No longer is there a monolithic Catholic moral theology based on a Thomistic natural law; instead, many different philosophical approaches are used. In general there has been a shift from classicism to historical consciousness, from the objective to the subjective, from nature to person, from order to freedom. In addition to developments in methodology, there are also widespread debates in contemporary Catholic moral theology about the existence of intrinsically evil actions, absolute norms, and the possibility of dissent from noninfallible church teaching. As a result of these differences, some contemporary Catholic moral theologians are calling into question some official Catholic teachings in such areas as sexual and medical ethics, but the official teaching office has not changed on these issues.

The Protestant Tradition. Protestant Christian ethics has as its distinctive characteristics an emphasis on freedom, an anticasuistic approach, the primacy of scripture, and an emphasis on the theological nature of the discipline. Martin Luther (d. 1546) and the reformers in general stressed the freedom of the Christian, and freedom has characterized much of Protestant life and ethics. In Protestantism there is no central church teaching authority to propose authoritative teaching on specific issues or to insist upon a particular approach, as in Roman Catholicism. Consequently, in Protestant ethics there is a great pluralism and a diversity of approaches.

The emphasis on freedom colors the Protestant understanding of God and how God acts in human history. God is free to act and to intervene in history. Generally Protestant ethics opposes any attempt to claim that God must always act in a particular way. The stress on God's freedom has also influenced a general Protestant unwillingness to base absolute norms on human reason and nature. The freedom of the believer as well as God is safeguarded in Protestant ethics.

The early reformers objected to the Roman Catholic emphasis on merit. They held that salvation comes from faith, not from human works. Protestantism ultimately rejected the Catholic sacrament of penance and thus never developed the casuistry involved in carrying out the role of the confessor as judge. Protestant ethics has been described as an ethics of inspiration, primarily because it does not usually get into a minute philosophical discussion of the morality of particular acts.

The Reformation insistence on the importance of the scripture characterizes much of Protestant ethics, but scripture has been used in different ways. When God's immanence is stressed, there is a tendency to find in scripture a moral message that can be lived by Christians in this world. When the transcendence of God is stressed, scripture tends to be used more dialectically to include a judging and critical role with regard to every human enterprise. Perhaps the greatest change in Protestantism came to the fore in the nineteenth-century dispute over a critical approach to scripture. Whereas liberal Protestantism and soon most of mainstream Protestantism employed literary and historical criticism to understand the Bible, fundamentalist Protestantism has continued to see the Bible primarily in terms of propositional truths or ethical norms and rules that God has revealed for all time and that Christians are called to obey. Such a deontological approach based on God's absolute laws given in scripture cannot be accepted by Protestants who approach scripture with the hermeneutical tools of biblical scholarship. Many contemporary Protestants see in scripture the description of the mighty acts of God in history to which followers of Jesus must respond, and they consequently adopt a responsibility model of Christian ethics rather than a deontological approach.

Protestantism in general gives more significance to the theological aspects of Christian ethics than did traditional Roman Catholic ethics. Catholic ethics tended to see the moral life of all in this world in the light of natural law, whereas Protestantism has generally understood life in this world in relationship to the Bible and to theological concerns. Soteriology, Christology, and eschatology all have some influence on much of Protestant ethics. For example, Protestant ethics tends to see sin primarily in theological categories as a lack of faith, whereas Roman Catholicism understands sin primarily as actions that are morally wrong.

For some Protestants the primacy of grace and of Christ rules out any significant role for the human and the natural in Christian ethics. For others the effects of sin are so strong that human reason and human nature cannot be valid sources of ethical wisdom and knowledge. Even those Protestant ethicists who would be more open to the human on theological grounds shy away from the ontology and metaphysics that undergird Roman Catholic natural-law thinking. Protestants have also tended to give more significance to history than to nature, because history is more compatible with biblical categories and with the insistence on the freedom of God and of human beings.

Historical Development of Protestant Ethics. The first systematic, scientific, and independent treatment of Protestant ethics separated from dogmatic theology was produced by Georg Calixtus (d. 1656). Although the early reformers did not write scientific Christian ethics as such, they dealt with significant methodological and substantive issues affecting Christian ethics.

Justification by faith active in love stands at the heart of Lutheran theology and is opposed to merit, justification by works, and legalism. The emphasis on scripture, even to the point of accepting the axiom "scripture alone," is another characteristic of the Reformation. Luther stressed freedom above all, but the dialectical aspect of his thought is seen in his famous saying "A Christian is a perfectly free lord of all, subject to none. A Christian is a perfectly dutiful servant of all, subject to all."

Lutheran social ethics is based on the two-realm theory, referring to the realm of creation and the realm of redemption. In the realm of creation, which involves the social life of human beings, there are true vocations for Christians, but the content of these vocations and what one does are not affected by Jesus, faith, or grace. Redemption affects only one's motivations. For this reason Lutheran social ethics has often been accused of passivism and acceptance of the status quo.

John Calvin (d. 1564) shared much of Luther's theological presuppositions but gave greater emphasis to the will both in God and in human beings. God is primarily sovereign will. Justification does not involve a pietistic response in trust; it means that the will of God becomes active in believers. Calvin comes closer to a Roman Catholic understanding, and Calvinists (like Catholics) have tended to become legalists. Calvin is also more open than Luther to a natural-law approach, although not to the Catholic metaphysics of natural law. Like Luther, Calvin stresses the secular vocation of Christians but interprets Christian work in the world in a more active and transforming way. Some later Calvinists see in worldly success a sign of God's predestining will for the individual. In the twentieth century, Max Weber proposed the controversial theory that the spirit of capitalism was compatible with and abetted by Calvinist ethics.

The Anabaptist-Mennonite tradition, or the left wing of the Reformation, from its sixteenth-century origins has stressed the radical call of discipleship, believer's baptism, and a committed, inflexible following of the radical ethical demands of the gospel. The believers form a sect that stands in opposition to the existing culture and society and bears witness to the gospel, especially the call to peace and nonviolence.

There has been no dominant figure in Anglican ethics and thus no established pattern of doing Anglican ethics. However, in the Anglican community there have been important ethical thinkers who have served as a bridge between Roman Catholic ethics and Protestant ethics. Methodism developed a moral theory calling for spiritual growth and moral renewal.

The Enlightenment had a great influence on Protestant theology and ethics. Nineteenth-century Protestantism saw the emergence of liberal theology. Friedrich Schleiermacher (d. 1834), the most outstanding theologian in the nineteenth century, stressed experience and has been called the founder and most famous proponent of Protestant liberalism. Schleiermacher proposed an ethical theory dealing with goods, duties, and virtues, and he saw moral concerns as present and influencing all other areas of life, especially political, intellectual, aesthetic, and religious. Late nineteenth- and early twentieth-century liberal theology stressed the immanence of God working in human experience and history, the possibility of Christians living out the ethics of Jesus, and evolutionary human progress, and downplayed divine transcendence and the power of sin. Within the context of liberal Protestant theology, the Social Gospel movement came to the fore in the first two decades of the twentieth century in the United States, especially under the leadership of Walter Rauschenbusch (d. 1918). In response to the problems created by the industrial revolution and in response to the privatism and individualism of past Christian ethics, the Social Gospel stressed that the kingdom of God should be made more present on earth and that the social order can and should be christianized. In England and in Germany many Christian thinkers embraced a moderate Christian socialism.

The harsh realities of World War I and the Depression occasioned the rise of the neoorthodoxy of Karl Barth in Europe and the Christian realism of Reinhold Niebuhr in the United States. The reaction stressed the transcendence of God, the dialectical relationship between the existing world and the kingdom of God, the power of sin, and the fact that the fullness of God's kingdom lies outside history. In respect to the contemporary international scene, the World Council of Churches has addressed many contemporary social issues with strong support for liberation movements and has called for just, participative, and sustainable societies.

Protestant ethics is still marked by diversity, but there is a growing convergence with Roman Catholic ethics in a number of areas. Protestant ethics has recently paid great attention to specific issues that previously were considered primarily only by Catholics: medical ethics, bioethics, just-war theory, the existence of absolute norms. There is also a growing dialogue with contemporary philosophical ethics. Some Protestant ethicists embrace existentialism and utilitarianism, but others are increasingly interested in avoiding relativity and recognizing the importance of order in the search for justice. Liberation theologians among the poor, blacks, and women exist across denominational lines and bridge differences between Protestants and Catholics. Protestant and Roman Catholic ethicists are addressing the same methodological questions—the use of scripture, the existence of norms, and the role of Christology and eschatology, as well as the substantive questions of personal and social morality facing the contemporary world. Eastern Orthodox ethics, especially in the diaspora situation, is becoming more of a discussion partner in the ecumenical dialogue that characterizes contemporary Christian ethics.

[*For discussion of related issues from a theological point of view, see* Canon Law; Discipleship; Free Will and Predestination, *article on* Christian Concepts; Grace; Justification; Merit, *article on* Christian Concepts; *and* Political Theology. *See also the biographies of church leaders and religious thinkers mentioned herein.*]

BIBLIOGRAPHY

There is no contemporary, satisfactory overview of the history of Christian ethics. The best available work remains Ernst Troeltsch's *The Social Teaching of the Christian Churches,* 2 vols. (1931; Chicago, 1981), which was originally published in 1911 but is still valuable today despite its datedness and somewhat biased perspectives. Troeltsch, like most Westerners writing on the subject, does not discuss Eastern Orthodox ethics. *Christian Ethics: Sources of the Living Tradition,* edited and with introductions by Waldo Beach and H. Richard Niebuhr (New York, 1955), is a textbook comprising selections from the most significant figures in Western Christian ethics. H. Richard Niebuhr's *Christ and Culture* (New York, 1951) is a frequently cited analysis of Western Christian ethics in the light of five possible models for understanding the relationship between Christ and culture.

There are many studies of individual thinkers in the patristic era, but the best history of the period written by a Christian ethicist is George W. Forell's *History of Christian Ethics,* vol. 1, *From the New Testament to Augustine* (Minneapolis, 1979). Forell is planning to write a three-volume history of Christian ethics.

The literature on Eastern Orthodox ethics in modern Western languages is comparatively little. In addition to encyclopedia articles, George A. Maloney's *A History of Orthodox Theology since 1453* (Belmont, Mass., 1976) and *Man: The Divine Icon* (Pecos, N. Mex., 1973) provide both historical details and anthropological considerations for Christian ethics. Georges Florovsky's *Collected Works,* 5 vols. (Belmont, Mass., 1972–1979), and John Meyendorff's *Byzantine Theology,* 2d ed. (New York, 1979), include helpful chapters dealing with Christian ethics. Stanley S. Harakas's *Toward Transfigured Life* (Minneapolis, 1983) provides a systematic Christian ethics from the Greek Orthodox tradition that includes valuable historical data.

For the historical origins of Catholic moral theology, including Thomas Aquinas, see Thomas Deman's *Aux origines de la théologie morale* (Paris, 1951). The most comprehensive study of the Scholastic period is Odon Lottin's *Psychologie et morale aux douzième et treizième siècles,* 6 vols. in 8 (Louvain, 1942–1960). Bernhard Häring's *The Law of Christ,* 3 vols. (Westminster, Md., 1961–1966), contains an often-cited historical survey of moral theology in chapter 1 of volume 1, *General Moral Theology,* and is the most important contribution to moral theology in the twentieth century. Numbers 1–4 of "Readings in Moral Theology," edited by Charles E. Curran and Richard A. McCormick (New York, 1977–1983), indicate the contemporary developments and discussions within moral theology.

Paul Althaus's *The Ethics of Martin Luther* (Philadelphia, 1972) is an authoritative discussion of Luther. For an overview of the historical development of Protestant thought, which includes materials pertinent to Christian ethics, see John Dillenberger and Claude Welch's *Protestant Christianity Interpreted through Its Development* (New York, 1954). James M. Gustafson's *Protestant and Roman Catholic Ethics: Prospects for Rapprochement* (Chicago, 1978) accurately describes the growing ecumenical convergences and differences. Paul Bock's *In Search of a Responsible World Society* (Philadelphia, 1974) summarizes the social teachings of the World Council of Churches, whereas Donal Dorr's *Option for the Poor* (Maryknoll, N.Y., 1983) analyzes from a somewhat liberationist perspective one hundred years of Vatican social teaching.

CHARLES E. CURRAN

CHRISTIANITY. [*This entry consists of an overview of Christian religion and eleven surveys of the regional dispersion of Christianity through time:*

An Overview
Christianity in the Middle East
Christianity in North Africa
Christianity in Eastern Europe
Christianity in Western Europe
Christianity in Latin America
Christianity in the Caribbean Region
Christianity in North America
Christianity in Sub-Saharan Africa
Christianity in Asia
Christianity in Australia and New Zealand
Christianity in the Pacific Islands

In addition to the related articles referred to in this entry, see also biographies of the principal figures mentioned herein.]

An Overview

Christianity is defined by one of its leading modern interpreters, Friedrich Schleiermacher (1768–1834), as "a monotheistic faith . . . essentially distinguished from other such faiths by the fact that in it everything is related to the redemption accomplished by Jesus of Nazareth." While many interpreters of the meaning of Christianity would dispute the content that Schleiermacher gave to each of the crucial terms in that definition, the definition as such would probably stand. It is beyond the scope of this article, or even of this encyclopedia, to present an exhaustive summary of all that Christianity is and has ever been: entire encyclopedias several times the size of this one (some of them listed in the bibliography, below) have been devoted to such a summary, and even they have been far from exhaustive. What this article can do, supported by other articles throughout this work, is to sketch some of the main points in the history of Christianity and then to identify some of the features of Christianity that most students of the movement, whether professing personal allegiance to it or not, would probably recognize as belonging to its "essence." Although both the "history" and the "essence" are, unavoidably, controversial in that not everyone would agree with this (or with any) account of them, such an account as this can claim to represent a majority consensus.

The History of Christianity

Christianity is a historical religion. It locates within the events of human history both the redemption it promises and the revelation to which it lays claim: Jesus was born under Caesar Augustus and "suffered under Pontius Pilate," at particular dates in the chronology of the history of Rome (even though the specific dates of those two events may be impossible to determine with absolute precision). In this respect Christianity shows its continuing affinities with the Judaism out of which it came, for there too the historical process becomes the peculiar arena of divine activity. The primal revelation for Judaism—and for Christianity—is the divine declaration to Moses (*Ex.* 3:6): "I am the God of Abraham, Isaac, and Jacob." To this primal revelation Christianity adds the assertion (*Heb.* 1:1–2) that the God who in past times had spoken through the prophets and acted through the Exodus from Egypt has now spoken definitively and acted decisively in the life, death, and resurrection of Jesus, seen as the "Christ," the anointed and chosen one of God.

Early Christianity. It is, then, with Jesus of Nazareth that the history of Christianity takes its start. [*See* Jesus.] Almost everything we know of him, however, comes from those who responded, in loyalty and obedience, to the events of his life and the content of his teaching. Therefore the history of the earliest Christian communities, to the extent that we are in a position to reconstruct it, is at the same time the history of Jesus as they remembered him. His own immediate followers were all Jews, and it is within that framework that they interpreted the significance of what they had received and perceived: he was the Christ, or Messiah, who had been promised to the patriarchs of Israel. As the record of those promises, the Hebrew scriptures were sacred for early Christians no less than for Jews, enabling them to claim a continuity with the history of the people of God since the creation of the world. The apostle Paul both summarized and reinterpreted the message of the first generation of believers. Together with the written deposit of their memories of Jesus in the Gospels, the writings of Paul and several other documents were circulated widely in Christian communities throughout the Mediterranean world, eventually becoming the

Christian addendum (or "New Testament") to the Hebrew scriptures (or "Old Testament"). [*See also* Biblical Literature; Gospel; *and* Christianity and Judaism.]

Paul was also responsible for the transformation of Christianity from a Jewish sect to a gentile movement by the end of the first century of the common era. The importance of this change for Christian history is impossible to exaggerate. Jesus had been born in an obscure corner of the Roman empire, but now his followers took upon themselves the assignment of challenging that empire and eventually of conquering it in his name. The opposition between empire and church during the second and third centuries sometimes took the form of persecution and martyrdom, but all that was replaced in the fourth century by the creation of a Christian Roman empire, when the emperor Constantine (306–337) first made the new faith legal, then made it his own, then made it the official religion of the realm. [*See also* Persecution, *article on* Christian Experience; *and* Church and State.] As part of their political and philosophical defense against their adversaries, the apologists for Christianity in the second and third centuries had also sought to clarify its relation to Greek and Roman thought, but with its official adoption their successors in the fourth and fifth centuries undertook to interpret Christian theology as the perennial philosophy in which the aspirations of all religions were now corrected and fulfilled. Among these later apologists, Augustine of Hippo (354–430) in his *City of God* articulated the Christian case against those who charged that by undermining the traditional values of Roman religion the church had been responsible for the decline and fall of the Roman empire. On the contrary, he said, Christianity was the support of just rulers and legitimate governments, and by its faith in the God of history, as well as by its moral teachings about work and the family, it promoted the welfare of society; the City of Earth would function best if it acknowledged the transcendent reality of the City of God, which was beyond history but which had made its presence known within this particular history.

The century that began with Constantine and ended with Augustine also saw the stabilization of the internal life and structure of the Christian movement. One by one, alternative ways of thought and belief that were adjudged to be aberrations were sloughed off or excluded as "heresies" or "schisms." Some of these (particularly the various species of apocalyptic or millenarian expectation) were efforts to perpetuate ways of being Christian that no longer suited the needs of the life of the church when the long-expected second coming of Jesus Christ failed to materialize, while others (notably the several gnostic systems) involved the adaptation to the Christian message of schemes of revelation and salvation that were also manifesting themselves in other religions. [*See also* Gnosticism, *articles on* Gnosticism from Its Origins to the Middle Ages *and* Gnosticism as a Christian Heresy.] In opposition to these alternative ways of thought and belief, Christianity, since before the days during which the books of the New Testament were being written, identified the content of orthodox belief and fixed its form in a succession of creedal statements. The earliest of these, including that eventually formulated as the Apostles' Creed, are put into the mouth of one or another or all twelve of the apostles of Jesus, and the most important creedal statement was adopted (under Constantine's patronage) at the Council of Nicaea in 325 (see "The Pattern of Christian Belief," below). [*For further discussion, see* Heresy, *article on* Christian Concepts; Councils, *article on* Christian Councils; *and* Creeds, *article on* Christian Creeds.] ·

During those same early centuries, Christianity was also identifying the structures of authority that were thought to guarantee the preservation of "apostolic" faith and order: the Bible and the bishops. As already noted, the Bible of the Christians consisted of two parts (or "testaments"): the books they had inherited from Judaism, and the combination into a "New Testament" of four gospels about the life and teachings of Jesus, epistles attributed to Paul and other apostolic figures, the *Acts of the Apostles,* and (from among the many extant apocalyptic writings) the *Revelation to John.* The bishops through their uninterrupted succession were believed to certify the continuity of the church with its apostolic foundations. As the church that could claim to have been shepherded by all twelve apostles, Jerusalem held a unique place; but as the church that Peter had governed and to which Paul had written (and where both Peter and Paul had been martyred), and as the congregation at the capital of the civilized world, Rome early acquired a special position as "*the* apostolic see," which it would consolidate by the leadership in faith and life that it exercised during the crises of the fourth and fifth centuries. Actually, the criterion of "apostolicity" was a circular one: apostolic foundation of episcopal sees, apostolic authorship of biblical books, and apostolic orthodoxy of creedal belief supported one another, and no one of them was ever sufficient of itself—even in the case of the see of Rome—to serve as such a criterion in isolation from the others. [*See also* Apostles.]

Official Establishment of Christianity. Constantine's acceptance of Christianity and the eventual establishment of it as the official faith of the Roman empire is rightly seen as the most portentous event—for good or ill or some combination of the two—in all of Christian history; conversely, "the end of the Constantinian era," which is how many thoughtful observers have characterized the twentieth century, has brought about the reshaping and rethinking of all the structures of faith and life that Christianity evolved in the aftermath of its new status from the fourth century on. Both in the Roman West, where Constantine prevailed in 312 "by the power of the cross," as he believed, and in the Byzantine East, where Constantine established the new capital of the Christian Roman empire two decades later, Christianity undertook to create a new civilization that would be a continuation of ancient Greece and Rome and yet would be a transformation of those cultures through the infusion of the spiritual power of Christ as Lord. [*See also* Constantinianism.]

The Christian culture of Byzantium. That pattern of continuation with transformation took a special form in the Christian culture of the Byzantine empire, whose history persisted for more than a thousand years from the creation of Constantinople as "New Rome" in 330 CE to its fall to the armies of the Turkish sultan Mehmed II (and its change of name to Istanbul) in 1453. Constantine and his successors—and, above all, the emperor Justinian (r. 527–565)—saw themselves in their Roman capacity as the legitimate heirs of the ancient pagan caesars, but at the same time in their Christian capacity as "equal to the apostles" *(isapostolos)*. In the exercise of this special authority, they frequently became involved in the administrative, liturgical, and doctrinal affairs of the church, and often without opposition and with great success. Contemporary historians tell us that it was the emperor Constantine who came up with the formula "one in being [*homoousios*] with the Father," which resolved, at the Council of Nicaea in 325, the dispute over the metaphysical relation between Christ and God. Later historians have coined for this special status of the Byzantine emperor the term *Caesaropapism*, implying that what the pope was in the West, the caesar was in the East. While the reign of Constantine, and even more that of Justinian, may have merited such a designation, the patriarch of Constantinople repeatedly asserted the authority of the church to determine its own destiny, above all in the areas of belief and worship. Most notably, in the iconoclastic controversies of the eighth and ninth centuries, which were brought on by the campaign of a series of emperors to remove images from the worship of the church, the defenders of the church's autonomy, who included especially monks and empresses, eventually carried the day, and the authority of the emperor to legislate unilaterally for the church was significantly curtailed. [*See* Icons *and* Iconoclasm.]

One reason for this success in the iconoclastic disputes was the special place of icons in Byzantine (and later in Slavic) Orthodoxy, which one scholar has called its "distinctive identity." As interpreted by its defenders, the cult of the icons was anything but the relapse into idolatrous paganism of which it was accused by the iconoclasts; instead it represented the commitment of Orthodoxy to the reality of the full incarnation of the Son of God in the human figure of Jesus: worship of the image of Jesus Christ was in fact addressed to one who was in his single person completely God and completely man. Thus, to a degree unknown in the West even in the high Middle Ages, Greek Christianity defined itself by its liturgy and devotion, not only (perhaps not primarily) by its dogma and life. The very term *orthodoxia* in Greek, and its Slavic counterpart *pravoslavie*, meant in the first instance "correct worship," which also included "correct doctrine." Embodied as it was in the curriculum of Byzantine educational institutions at all levels, the continuing hold that a christianized Neoplatonism exercised over its expositors enabled them to make use of its metaphysics and epistemology in the service of the church's message. The Byzantine icons were only one part of a total Christian culture, in which architecture, poetry, and music also contributed their special part. One feature of this culture was a commitment to preserving the indigenous culture of each people to which the Christian message came: while the Western missionaries, in introducing the Mass, taught each nation Latin when they taught it the gospel (and thus, even without intending to do so, gave it at least some access to pre-Christian Roman culture), Eastern missionaries translated not only the Bible but also the liturgy into the language of the people. [*See also* Missions, *article on* Christian Missions.] It was, above all, in the Byzantine missions to the Slavs (where the two philosophies about the proper language of the liturgy clashed) that this peculiarity of the Eastern church served to create an integrally Slavic Orthodoxy, through which the Ukraine, Bulgaria, Russia, and Serbia came of age as nations. [*For further discussion, see* Eastern Christianity.]

Christianity in the Middle Ages. In the Latin West, by contrast, the outcome of the Constantinian settlement took a radically divergent form, in which it was not principally the Christian emperor and the Christian empire, but the bishop of Rome and the papacy, that was to set the tone of the historical development of Christianity. [*See* Roman Catholicism *and* Papacy.] With the transfer of the capital to Constantinople, the pope came to symbolize and to embody the continuity with ancient Rome. Within less than a century after that transfer, the bishop of Rome was calling himself "supreme pontiff" *(pontifex maximus)*, a title that had belonged to the pagan caesars. When the various Germanic tribes arrived in western Europe, they found the papacy already present as a political and cultural force. Those tribes that chose to ignore that force by clinging too long to Germanic paganism or to forms of Christianity that had been outlawed as heretical also lost the opportunity to shape the future of European history, but the Franks, by allying themselves with the bishop of Rome, were to determine its subsequent course through much of the Middle Ages. The symbolic high point of the alliance came on Christmas Day in the year 800 with the crowning of the Frankish king Charles, known to history as Charlemagne (c. 742–814), as "emperor" at the hands of Pope Leo III in Rome, even though there was still an emperor in Constantinople. With its own emperor—and, above all, its own bishop and supreme pontiff—the West was free to pursue its own destiny. And although the schism between West and East, in a technical and canonical sense, did not take place until several centuries later, and in a spiritual sense may be said to have happened in 1204, the historical intuition that located it as having originated in the ninth century was in many ways sound. [*For further discussion, see* Schism, *article on* Christian Schism.]

Confrontation with Islam. Each in its own way, both Eastern and Western Christendom were compelled, from the seventh century onward, to come to terms with the reality of Islam. During the one hundred years after the death of the prophet Muḥammad in 632 CE, the geographical spread of Islam was both more rapid and more effective than that of Christianity had been during its first several centuries. Several of the major centers of the Eastern churches—Antioch, Alexandria, Jerusalem itself—became Muslim in government, although a large Christian population was able to practice its faith under varying degrees of pressure. Eventually, in 1453, Constantinople also became a Muslim city. The Muslim conquest of Palestine was likewise responsible for the most historic confrontation ever between Christianity and another faith, in the Crusades, as successive armies of Western Christians sought to reconquer the "holy places" associated with the life of Jesus—an enterprise that eventually failed. [*See* Crusades.]

The monks. Because its administrative structure and intellectual tradition were so different from those of the Byzantine East, the medieval Christianity of the West expressed its relation to society and culture in a distinctive fashion as well. In even greater measure than in the East, the bearers of its civilizing force were monks. [*See also* Monasticism, *article on* Christian Monasticism; *and* Religious Communities, *article on* Christian Religious Orders.] The missionaries who brought the gospel to the barbarians—for example, Boniface (680–754), the "apostle of Germany" sent from Rome, and Cyril (c. 826–869) and Methodius (c. 815–c. 884), the "apostles to the Slavs" sent from Constantinople—were monks. So were the scribes who then brought Classical civilization to the same barbarians; thus the Benedictine monk the Venerable Bede (c. 673–735) laid many of the foundations of scholarship in England. Most of the reformers who throughout the Middle Ages recalled the church to its primitive faith and its ancient loyalties came from monasticism, as was evident above all in the work of Bernard of Clairvaux (1090–1153), "the unmitered pope" of the twelfth century, and then in the program of Francis of Assisi (1181/2–1226). The cloisters likewise supplied most of the theologians who systematized and defended the faith: Anselm of Canterbury (c. 1033–1109) was a Benedictine abbot, Thomas Aquinas (c. 1225–1274) was a Dominican friar, and Bonaventure (c. 1217–1274) and Duns Scotus (c. 1266–1308) were both Franciscans.

Repeatedly, of course, the monastic communities themselves needed to be reformed, and in virtually every century of the Middle Ages there arose movements of renewal dedicated to the purification of the monastic ideal and, through it, renewal of the life of the total church. When the leaders of such movements managed to establish themselves as leaders of the total church, the result was often a great conflict. Thus in the eleventh century the reformer Hildebrand became Pope Gregory VII (in 1073) and set about renewing the administration, the morals, and the faith and life of the church. He sought to enforce the law of clerical celibacy, to root out financial and political corruption, to free bishops and prelates from the dominance of secular princes, and to purge the church of heresy and schism. This brought him into collision both with his own ecclesiastical subordinates and with the empire, but it also gave him the opportunity to formulate for all time the special prerogatives of the church and the bishop of Rome (see "The Community of Christian Worship," below).

Reformation Christianity. Such reform movements, it seemed, could always be counted on to rescue the church in times of crisis—until, through Martin Luther (1483–1546) and the Reformation, a crisis arose in which the primary impetus for reform was to express itself not *through* monasticism or the papacy, but *against* both monasticism and the papacy (although it must be remembered that Luther, too, was originally a monk). Already in various late medieval reformations, such as those of the "Spiritual" Franciscans and the Hussites, there was the sense that (to cite the four standard "marks" of the church enumerated in the Nicene Creed) Christendom could be neither one nor holy nor catholic nor apostolic until it had replaced the secularized and corrupt authority of the bishop of Rome with the authenticity of the word of God, for which some looked to a church council while others put their confidence in the recovery of the message of the Bible. That sense finally found its voice in the program of the Protestant reformers. Beginning with the belief that they were merely the loyal children of Mother Church recalling her to her genuine self, they soon found themselves so alienated from the structures and teachings of the church of their time that they were obliged to look for, and if need be to invent, alternative structures and teachings of their own.

The structures and teachings of the several Protestant groups covered an extremely wide spectrum, such that those at one end of the spectrum (Lutherans and Anglicans) were in many ways closer to Roman Catholicism and even to Eastern Orthodoxy, despite the schisms both of the Middle Ages and of the Reformation, than they were to Socinianism or even to Anabaptism or even perhaps to Calvinism. In their ecclesiastical structures, the churches that came out of the Reformation ranged from a retention of the historic episcopate (e.g., in England and Sweden) to a presbyterian form of church government (e.g., in Scotland and in many, though by no means all, of the Calvinist churches on the European continent) to an insistence on the primacy and autonomy of the local congregation (e.g., in various of the dissenters from Anglicanism in the seventeenth and eighteenth centuries, including the Congregationalists and Baptists, especially in the New World). While the mainstream of Protestantism has in its doctrine maintained a loyalty to the doctrines of the Trinity, of the person of Christ, of original sin, and of salvation through the death of Christ, as these had been developed in the early and medieval church, it has diverged from earlier development (and thus from Roman Catholicism and Eastern Orthodoxy) above all in its understanding of the nature of the church and of the meaning (and hence the number) of the sacraments, with only baptism and the Lord's Supper being regarded as authentic sacraments by most Protestants. (See "The Pattern of Christian Belief," below.) The principal difference, at least as seen both by the Protestant reformers and by their Roman Catholic adversaries, lay in the area of religious authority: not the church or its tradition, not the papacy or a church council, but the Bible alone, was to be the norm that determined what Christians were to believe and how they were to live. [*See also* Reformation.]

The Roman Catholic response to the Protestant Reformation is sometimes called the "Counter-Reformation," although that term has come to be regarded by many scholars as excessively negative in its connotations because it seems to ignore the positive reforms that were not merely a reaction to Protestantism. "The Roman Catholic Reformation" is in many ways a preferable designation. First through a series of responses to the theology and program of the reformers, then above all through the canons and decrees of the Council of Trent (1545–1563), the Catholic Reformation took up the issues addressed by Luther and by his most eminent successor, John Calvin (1509–1564), both in the area of church life and morals and in the area of church teaching and authority. [*For further discussion, see* Trent, Council of.] Many of the corruptions that had acted as tinder for the Reformation received the careful attention of the council fathers, with the result that Roman Catholicism and the papacy emerged from the crisis of the Reformation diminished in size but chastened and strengthened in spirit. The creation of the Society of Jesus by Ignatius Loyola (c. 1491–1556) in 1534 provided the church with a powerful instrument for carrying out the program of reform and renewal, and many of the tools employed by the reformers (e.g., the printing press and the catechism) lent themselves to that program just as effectively. A deepening mystical devotion gave new life to medieval spirituality, particularly in sixteenth-century Spain, and the theology of Thomas Aquinas acquired new authority as the defenders of the faith closed ranks against Protestant thought. The historical coincidence of the discovery of the New World and the Protestant Reformation, which both Protestants and Roman Catholics interpreted as providential, enabled Roman Catholic missionaries to recoup in North and South America the losses in prestige and membership caused by the Reformation. It was above all in Latin America that this recovery became a decisive religious and cultural force. Although divided (by the papal Line of Demarcation of 1493) between Spain and Portugal, Latin America was "united" in the sense that it was colonized and converted by Roman Catholic Christianity; the process of the christianization of native populations was a gradual one, and many beliefs and practices of their pre-Christian history were carried over into their new faith. The effect of these and other missionary campaigns in the sixteenth and seventeenth centuries was to make the term *catholic* in *Roman Catholic* begin to mean in fact what it had always meant in principle: present throughout the known world.

The Christian East. Throughout the Middle Ages and the Reformation there were sporadic efforts in the West to establish (or reestablish) contact with the East; these ranged from the dispatch of various legations, to the translation of various classic works in one direction or the other, to marriages between Western monarchs and Byzantine or Russian princesses. The Crusades, which the East sometimes invited and sometimes dreaded, did at least reacquaint many members of the two traditions with one another, although the most unforgettable instance of such reacquaintance was the catastrophe of the sack of Christian Constantinople by the armies of the Fourth Crusade in 1204. Followed as it was two and a half centuries later by the Muslim capture of Constantinople and the end of the Byzantine empire, the tragedy of 1204 is probably better entitled than any other event to the dubious distinction of being the point at which the Eastern and Western churches came into schism—a schism that, except for repeated but short-lived attempts at reunion (the most notable of which was probably the Union of Florence in 1439), has persisted ever since. Although the loss of Constantinople to the Turks drastically reduced its sphere of influence, the ecumenical patriarchate of Constantinople continued to enjoy a preeminence of honor within Eastern Orthodoxy, as it does to this day. Numerically as well as politically, however, it was Slavic Orthodoxy, above all in Russia, that became the "heir apparent," uniting itself with Russian culture as it had with medieval Greek culture. Plagued though it was by internal schisms, and caught in the political and cultural upheavals of the tsarist empire, the church in Russia went on producing saints and scholars, and through the icons and the liturgy it suffused the faith and life of the common people with the meaning of the Christian faith: the icon painter Andrei Rublev (c. 1360–c. 1430) and, in more modern times, the novelist and spiritual thinker Fedor Dostoevskii (1821–1881) were among the products of this tradition best known in the West. The nineteenth and twentieth centuries witnessed an upsurge of interest in Eastern Orthodoxy throughout Western Christianity, as a consequence partly of the ecumenical movement and partly of the Russian Revolution, as both Protestants and Roman Catholics looked to Orthodoxy for the correction of what had come to be seen as Western deficiencies and overemphases in the aftermath of the Reformation.

Post-Reformation Christianity. The ecclesiastical map of the West after the Reformation shows a Europe divided between an almost solidly Roman Catholic south and a predominantly Protestant north, with the latter in turn divided between Anglican, Lutheran, and Reformed or Calvinist forms of Christianity. [*See* Protestantism; Denominationalism; *and articles on particular denominations.*] The same competition was exported into Christian missions in Africa and Asia and into the Americas. Among the most influential developments of the centuries following the Reformation was the effort, which took a distinct form in each denomination but nevertheless manifested a similarity of spirit, to encourage a deeper seriousness about the claims of the Christian gospel upon personal faith and life: Jansenism within French (and then North American) Roman Catholicism, Puritanism (and later on Methodism) within English Protestantism, and Pietism within the Lutheran and Reformed churches of the continent and of the New World. Especially during the eighteenth century, these movements had it as one of their primary goals to combat and counteract the influence, both in the church and in public life, of the rationalism, freethinking, and "infidelity" associated with the Enlightenment. [*See also* Enlightenment, The.] Combining as it did the application to Christian history and biblical literature of the methods of historical criticism (particularly in German theological scholarship) with the reexamination or even the rejection of the special claims of Christianity to a privileged place in Western society (particularly in the legislation of the French Revolution), the Enlightenment came to represent the campaign for the secularization of culture. An important feature of that combination of emphases in Enlightenment thought was a fundamental reconsideration of the traditional Christian assertions of finality and uniqueness. As the philosophical and historical basis for such assertions was coming under increasing attack from within such traditionally Christian institutions as the theological faculties of universities, the discovery of other religions both in the historical past and in the distant parts of the present world was bringing such concepts as the uniqueness of the Christian message into serious question. The special privileges that Christianity had enjoyed since the Constantinian era were gradually withdrawn. Separation of church and state, as developed especially in the United States, and the growth of religious toleration and religious liberty were the social and political expressions of the new situation that was beginning to become evident at the end of the eighteenth century.

The nineteenth century. Despite the losses in both influence and numbers that it suffered in the period of the Enlightenment, Christianity entered the nineteenth century with a strong sense of its continuing relevance and special mission. The critical reexamination of the Christian toleration of slavery—long overdue, in the opinion of observers inside and outside the church—came to full realization in the nineteenth century, even though a civil war in the United States was necessary to bring this about. It was likewise in the nineteenth century, surnamed "the great century" in the leading history of Christian missions, that most of the major Christian denominations of the West, Protestant as well as Roman Catholic, set out to evangelize the globe. Although the Christian missionary and the colonialist conqueror often marched arm in arm across that globe, the results for native cultures were quite ambiguous: sometimes a loss of national identity and cultural deracination, but on the other hand no less often a deepening sense of historical particularity and the acquisition of scholarly instruments for understanding it and thus of overcoming both the colonialism and the missions. Significantly, it was from the mission schools founded in the nineteenth century that a disproportionately high number of the revolutionary leaders of the twentieth century in developing nations were to emerge. On the home front, the confrontation between traditional Christian beliefs and the discoveries of modern science engaged the attention of the churches. The most violent such confrontation was brought on by the work of Charles Darwin, whose books *The Origin of Species* (1859) and *The Descent of Man* (1871) called into question the traditional Christian belief in a special creation of the human species in the image of God as based on the biblical accounts of creation in the *Book of Genesis*. [*For broader discussion, see* Evolution.] Yet as the nineteenth century ended, there was a widespread expectation that the next would truly be "the Christian century." *Christianizing the Social Order* by Walter Rauschenbusch (1861–1918), first published in 1912, was a representative statement of that expectation.

The twentieth century. As things turned out, the twentieth century proved to be the age of two world wars, of the coming to power of Marxist regimes throughout most of historic Eastern Christendom, and of moral and intellectual crises (including the Nazi Holocaust and the issues raised by modern technology) that would shake the traditional beliefs and historical confidence of Christians with unprecedented force. The reaction was, if not an overt loss of faith, then a growing indifference in many traditionally Christian groups. The most influential Christian theologian of the twentieth century, Karl Barth (1886–1968), protested the synthesis of the gospel with human culture and called for a reassertion of that gospel in its native power and uniqueness. At the same time, however, the most influential Christian event of the twentieth century, the Second Vatican Council of 1962–1965, undertook a reform of Christian faith and life that reached out to other Christians and to other religious traditions with a new openness. The council was the manifestation within Roman Catholicism of a new ecumenical consciousness that had its origins in Protestantism; the divisions that had followed in the wake of the Reformation now came under question in the light of the recognition that what separated Christians from one another was less significant than all the things that still held them together. That ecumenical consciousness throughout the Christian movement found expression in the recovery of historic Christian beliefs, in the creation of contemporary forms of worship, and in the reexamination of patterns of Christian life both individual and corporate. [*For further discussion, see* Ecumenical Movement *and* Vatican Councils, *article on* Vatican II.] It remains to consider these three areas of belief, worship, and life, which, taken together, may be said to constitute the essence of Christianity.

The Essence of Christianity

In these nearly two thousand years of its history, Christianity has manifested an almost infinite variety of expressions as it has spread its presence and influence into all the major cultures of the Western world and into most of those of the East as well. With a billion or more adherents throughout the human race at the end of the twentieth century, it continues to be heterogeneous and pluralistic in its forms of organization and worship, belief, and life—so much so that it appears difficult or foolhardy or impossible to attempt to identify any characteristics as the distinctive genius or continuing essence of Christianity. A well-known criterion was the one proposed by Vincent of Lérins in the fifth century—what has been accepted "everywhere, always, by all" *(ubique, semper, ab omnibus)*—but the welter of detail about the history of Christianity scattered across the hundreds of articles dealing with the subject in the volumes of this encyclopedia should convince even the most casual reader that if there is an "essence of Christianity" it cannot possibly be everything that Christianity has ever been to everyone in every time and every place. Therefore, to quote again from Schleiermacher, "the only pertinent way of discovering the peculiar essence of any particular faith and reducing it as far as possible to a formula is by showing the element which remains constant throughout the most diverse religious affections within this same communion, while it is absent from analogous affections within other communions."

The search for an essence of Christianity is as old as the primary deposits of Christianity themselves. Already in the Hebrew scriptures, which Christianity took over as its Old Testament, the prophet Micah had declared: "God has told you what is good; and what is it that the Lord asks of you? Only to act justly, to love loyalty, to walk wisely before your God" (NEB *Mi.* 6:8). And an unknown first-century Christian writer, author of what came to be called the letter to the Hebrews in the New Testament, stated that "anyone who comes to God must believe that he exists and that he rewards those who search for him" (*Heb.* 11:6). The most successful formula for the essence of Christianity, however, was that of the apostle Paul: "In a word, there are three things that last for ever: faith, hope, and love; but the greatest of them all is love" (*1 Cor.* 13:13). Already in the second century, Irenaeus (c. 130–c. 200), bishop of Lyons, was invoking this formula as a summary of what "endures unchangeably," and in the fifth century it became the basis and the outline for Augustine's *Enchiridion*, to which Augustine himself usually referred as *On Faith, Hope, and Love.* From Augustine, in turn, the formula went on to provide the table of contents for the early catechisms in the age of Charlemagne and then for the rapid expansion in the number and use of catechisms by all parties in the age of the Reformation. Hence it may serve as a device for organizing this description of the essence of Christianity in its historical sweep, its geographical expansion, and its genius. Considered both in its history and in its contemporary expressions, Christianity has been, and is, a system of faith, of hope, and of love, a pattern of belief (and thought), a community of worship (and culture), and a way of life (and society). Paul's triad of faith, hope, and love may thus be used to correspond to the even more universal schema of the true, the beautiful, and the good. [*For further discussion in broad religious perspective, see* Faith; Hope; *and* Love.]

The Pattern of Christian Belief. As a system of faith, Christianity manifests "faith" in all the various meanings that this term has acquired in the history of religion: as loyalty to the divine, based on the prior loyalty of the divine to the world and to humanity; as the confidence that God is trustworthy in truth and love; as dependence on the Father of Jesus Christ, who is the source of all good in this life and in the life to come; as the commitment to direct thought and action in accordance with the divine word and will; and as the affirmation that certain events and declarations, as given by divine revelation, are a reliable index to that will and word. It is the last of those meanings that provides a basis for describing in an epitome what it is that Christianity believes, teaches, and confesses.

"Whoever wishes to be saved must, above all, hold to the catholic faith." These opening words of the so-called Athanasian Creed (not in fact written by Athanasius, but a Latin and Western creed, compiled perhaps in the fifth century) would not, as they stand, automatically elicit the assent and support of all Christians; nor, for that matter, would all Christians who do accept such a statement be agreed on the precise content and extent of that "catholic faith." Differ though they do on these questions, however, Christians throughout history have affirmed the importance of the act of believing, as well as of the content of what is believed, as a mark of identification by which believers would be known.

The person of Jesus Christ. Christian belief began with the need to specify the significance of the person of Jesus, seen as the "Christ." The initial stages of that process are visible already in the pages of the New Testament. Its titles for him—in addition to Christ, such titles as Son of man, Son of God, Word of God (Logos), and Savior—were an effort to account for that significance, for within the events of Jesus' human life the God of Israel and the creator of the world had been disclosed. Before the theologians had invented ways of defining the content of these titles in any satisfying detail, the devotion and worship of the church were already identifying Jesus with God. This is evident, for example, from the earliest non-Christian account of the church that we possess, the letter of Pliny the Younger (62–113), governor of Bithynia, to the Roman emperor Trajan (r. c. 98–117), which describes Christians as gathering for worship and "addressing a song to Christ as to God" *(Christo ut deo).* But this devotional practice had yet to be squared both with the monotheism that the church inherited from and shared with Israel and with the concrete events of the life of Jesus as these were described in the Gospels. During the second and third centuries the reality of his human life needed to be defended; during the fourth century the divine dimension of his being demanded attention; during the fifth and sixth centuries the relation between the divine and the human in him required clarification. What emerged from the process of debate and definition—especially in the creeds formulated at the councils of Nicaea in 325, Constantinople in 381, and Chalcedon in 451—was a picture of Jesus Christ as having two "natures," divine and human: he was simultaneously "one in being" with God and "one in being" with humanity, and therefore able to mediate between them. The full content of the two natures and of the relation between them has continued to engage the speculative talents of Christian theologians ever since. [*See also* God, *articles on* God in the New Testament *and* God in Postbiblical Christianity; Soul, *article on* Christian Concept; Theology, *article on* Christian Theology; *and* Dogma.]

The Trinity. The final creedal statement of the relation between Christ and God was part of a more complete statement of belief, the Christian doctrine of the Trinity, which many theological exponents of Christianity would regard as the central teaching of the Christian faith. Its fundamental outline is already given in the "great commission"—which, according to the Gospels, Jesus entrusted to his disciples before withdrawing his visible presence from them (*Mt.* 28:19)—to baptize "in the name of the Father and of the Son and of the Holy Spirit." Threefold though that single "name" was, it was the relation of the Son to the Father that carried the principal weight in the clarification of the formula. Thus the original creed adopted at Nicaea, after enumerating the various "titles of majesty" belonging to Jesus Christ as the Son of God, simply added "And [we believe] in the Holy Spirit," with no similar elaboration of how and why the Third Person was entitled to stand alongside the Father and the Son. But before the fourth century was over, the status of the Holy Spirit, and thus the complete dogma of God as Trinity, had achieved the form it has held in Christian orthodoxy throughout the history of the church. The dogma presents itself as strictly monotheistic. The opening words of the Nicene Creed are "We believe in one God," and everything that follows about Father, Son, and Holy Spirit is set into that framework. The technical philosophical term for the oneness of God was *ousia* in Greek, *substantia* or *essentia* in Latin. But this single divine *ousia* had its being in three *hupostaseis,* or "persons."

The doctrine of the Trinity has from the beginning been one of the most productive—and one of the most problematic—points of contact between Christian theology and speculative philosophy. Both the Greek Neoplatonist Plotinus (c. 205–270) and the German idealist G. W. F. Hegel (1770–1831), with many others between them, taught a philosophical version of the Trinity with which many theologians felt obliged somehow to come to terms. The metaphysical ingenuity of philosophers and theologians—from the first of Latin theologians, Tertullian (160?–225?), and the boldest of Greek theologians, his contemporary Origen (c. 185–c. 254), to philosophical theologians of the twentieth century, such as the Protestant Paul Tillich (1886–1965) and the Roman Catholic Karl Rahner (1904–1984)—has therefore continually experimented with new ways of accounting for (if not of "explaining") the relation between the One and the Three. Perhaps the most creative of such speculations was that of Augustine's *On the Trinity,* which constructed a series of trinitarian analogies in the universe and in the human mind as "images [or footprints] of the divine Trinity." [*For further discussion, see* Trinity. *Related notions are discussed in broad religious perspective in* Deity; Incarnation; *and* Hypostasis.]

Sin and grace. All the councils that formulated these basic doctrines of the Trinity and of the person of Christ were held in the Greek-speaking eastern part of the Christian Roman empire under the patronage of the Christian emperor, who was from the year 330 onward resident at Constantinople, and the creeds, which are in Greek, bear the marks of that origin. Still it is a mistake to ignore the role of the Latin West in the determination of normative Christian teaching: both at Nicaea and at Chalcedon there were decisive interventions from Western theologians and bishops. Nevertheless, the most distinctive and original Western contributions during the first five centuries came not in the doctrines of God and Christ but in the doctrines of sin and grace. With significant anticipations in various Western thinkers, it was once again Augustine who formulated these latter doctrines in the concepts and terms that were to dominate most of subsequent Christian teaching in the West, that of Roman Catholicism but no less the theology of Protestantism. Many early interpreters of Christian belief—for example, Gregory of Nyssa (c. 335–c. 395) in his treatise *On the Creation of Man*—had articulated the biblical teaching (*Gn.* 1:26–27) that, among all creatures on earth, humans alone possessed the special prerogative of having been created "in the image of God," with the promise of immortal life and of a "participation in the divine nature" (*2 Pt.* 1:4). But in so doing they had often spoken more explicitly about human free will than about human sinfulness. Yet this did not imply, Augustine insisted, that every human being faced the same choice between good and evil that Adam and Eve had faced. On the contrary, humanity had since Adam and Eve been under a curse of what Augustine called "the sin of origin" *(peccatum originis),* which infected every human being except Jesus Christ (and perhaps his mother, the Virgin Mary). Even without committing acts of sin, therefore, each member of the human race was corrupted from birth; the traditional practice of infant baptism (see "The Community of Christian Worship," below) was for Augustine evidence of the universality of this sinful condition. [*See also* Grace *and* Free Will and Predestination, *article on* Christian Concepts. *For discussion of related topics in broad religious perspective, see* Fall, The; Evil; *and* Sin and Guilt.]

Redemption. Neither the belief in God as Trinity nor the dogma of Christ as divine and human in nature nor the doctrine of humanity as created in the image of God but fallen into sin is, however, an end in itself for Christian faith. As a religion of redemption, Christianity presents itself as the message of how, through Christ, reconciliation has been achieved between the holiness of God and the sin of a fallen humanity. But while the Trinity, the person of Christ, and (though less universally or explicitly) the doctrine of original sin all have been subjects of a public and ecumenical confession of the church, the manner of this reconciliation has not received such attention. It has been left more to hymnody and preaching than to dogma and metaphysics to supply the metaphors for describing it. One of the most widely distributed such metaphors in early Christian writers, beginning with the sayings of Jesus himself (*Mt.* 20:28), is the description of redemption as "ransom" (which is, of course, what *redemption* means): the death of Christ was paid (to God or to the devil) as the price for setting humanity free. The difficulties that such a notion entailed for the Christian picture of God made a modification of the ransom theory seem imperative: the death of Christ took place in the course of a battle between God-in-Christ and the devil with his allies, a battle in which death triumphed initially by the nailing of Christ to the cross but in which Christ was victorious in the end through his resurrection. It remained once again for the medieval West to provide the most inventive of these theories. According to Anselm (c. 1033–1109) in his *Why God Became Man,* the reconciliation of the human race with God was fundamentally the reconciliation between the justice of God, which was committed to upholding "the moral order of the universe" *(rectitudo)* and therefore could not ignore human sin or forgive it by a simple fiat, and the mercy of God, which was bent on restoring humanity to the condition for which God had intended it by its creation. God became man in Christ, because as man he would be able, by his death, to produce the satisfaction demanded by divine justice, but as God he would render a satisfaction of infinite worth that could thus be applied to the entire human race. With some modifications and refinements, Anselm's theory has established itself both within Roman Catholicism and within most of classical Protestantism. [*For further discussion, see* Atonement, *article on* Christian Concepts.]

Justification. Classical Protestantism differs from Roman Catholicism in the interpretation of redemption not on the way redemption was achieved by God in Christ, but on the way it is appropriated by the Christian. Luther's doctrine of justification by faith—or, more fully and more precisely, justification by grace through faith—directed itself against what he perceived to be the widespread tendency of medieval Christianity to give human works part of the credit for restoring the right relation between God and man. This he attacked as a denial of the purely gratuitous character of salvation. The role of the human will in salvation was purely passive, accepting the forgiveness of sins as a sheer gift and contributing nothing of its own goodness to the transaction with God. Faith, accordingly, was not (or, at any rate, not primarily) an act of the intellect accepting as true what God has revealed but an act of the will entrusting itself unconditionally to the favor of God as conferred in Christ. Such unconditional trust led to the transformation of human life from the self-centered quest for gratification to the God-centered service of others (see "The Christian Way of Life," below). Partly in response to Luther's doctrine, the Council of Trent at its sixth session affirmed that "faith is the beginning of human salvation, the foundation and the root of all justification," but it condemned anyone who "says that the sinner is justified by faith alone, as though nothing else were required to cooperate." [*For further discussion of Christian views of salvation, see* Justification *and* Merit, *article on* Christian Concepts.]

The Community of Christian Worship. As a system of hope, Christianity holds forth the promise of eternal life through Jesus Christ. In the words of what has been called "the gospel in a nutshell" (*Jn.* 3:16), "God loved the world so much that he gave his only Son, that everyone who has faith in him may not die but have eternal life." But that promise and hope of life for those who have faith does not stand in isolation from the full range of Christian hope, the expectation of all the gifts of God for time and for eternity, and the acceptance of those gifts in thankfulness and praise. Hope, consequently, expresses itself chiefly in prayer and worship, both the personal prayer of the individual Christian believer and the corporate worship of the Christian community.

The holy catholic church. One integral component of Christianity both as " a pattern of belief" and as "a community of worship" is expressed in the words of the Apostles' Creed: "I believe in the holy catholic church, the communion of saints." According to the accounts of the New Testament, it was the intention of Jesus to found a church (*Mt.* 16:18): "I will build my church." Whether one accepts the literal historicity of those accounts or not, Jesus did, in fact, gather a community of disciples and establish a table fellowship. The earliest Christianity we are able to uncover is already a churchly Christianity, to which in fact we owe the Gospels and all the other books of the New Testament. For Christians of every persuasion and denomination, the church is at the same time the primary context of worship.

There is, however, far less unanimity about the nature of the church or about its organization and its authority. The tripartite complex of authority that emerged from the conflicts of early Christianity (see "The History of Christianity," above) vested in the office of the monarchical bishop the visible governance of the church and defined the church accordingly. Two formulas of Cyprian (d. 258), bishop of Carthage, summarize this definition: "Where the bishop is, there the church is" *(Ubi episcopus, ibi ecclesia)* and "There is no salvation apart from the church" *(Extra ecclesiam nulla salus)*. For Cyprian himself, as became evident in his disputes with Stephen I (bishop of Rome from 254 to 257), each bishop carried the authority of the office on his own and was answerable to the authority of Christ and of his brother bishops, but not to any one bishop as monarch of the entire church. But there were already signs of a developing pyramidal structure of authority, with certain centers having clear jurisdiction over others. Among these, the see of Rome had, and has, preeminence. As noted earlier, this understanding of authority led in the Middle Ages to a definition of the church as a visible monarchy, analogous in some ways to other monarchies, of which the pope was the absolute ruler—"judging all, but being judged by none," as the *Dictatus papae* of Gregory VII said. Orthodoxy, by contrast, has resisted the pyramidal model of church authority, preferring to see the entire company of the church's bishops, particularly when they are in council assembled, as a corporate and collegial entity, with the bishop of Rome as "first among equals" *(primus inter pares)* but not as monarch. One of the major accents of the Second Vatican Council was a new emphasis on episcopal collegiality but not at the expense of the primacy of the bishop of Rome within the college. That accent was closely joined in the decrees of the council to a recovery of the definition of the church as principally the community of Christian worship. [*See also* Discipleship *and* Church. *For discussion of community as a sacred phenomenon in broad religious perspective, see* Community.]

Protestant views of the church. The Protestant rejection of the authority of the pope is closely joined to a redefinition of the nature of the church. There had always been the recognition in the medieval doctrine of the church, particularly as this had come down from Augustine, that the organizational, empirical church was not coextensive with the church as it exists in the eyes of God: some who participate in, or even preside over, the church as an institution today will ultimately perish, while others who now persecute the church are destined to become members of the body of Christ. That definition of the true church as "the company of the elect," and hence as invisible in its membership and in its essence, appears in one form or another in the thought of most of the Protestant reformers. It did not imply, except in the polemics of a radical few, that there was no visible church. With differing forms of ecclesiastical administration (see "Reformation Christianity," above), the reformers took over or adapted patterns of organization that would suit the church for its function as the community of Christian worship and the center of Christian instruction. A favorite Protestant term for the church, therefore, is the phrase in the Apostles' Creed, "the communion of saints."

The preaching of the word of God. Although they would agree that the church is the community of Christian worship, the several denominations disagree about the structure of that community—and about the content of that worship. It is characteristic of most Protestant groups that in their liturgies and forms of worship they assign centrality to communication of the Christian message through preaching: "Where the word of God is, there the church is" *(Ubi verbum Dei, ibi ecclesia)* is how they have recast Cyprian's formula. As the leader of the worshiping community, the minister is principally (though never exclusively) the proclaimer of the word of God, a word of God that is found in, or identified and even equated with, the Bible. The emphasis on biblical preaching has sometimes led to a didactic understanding of worship, but this has been counterbalanced in Protestantism by the literally tens of thousands of "psalms and hymns and spiritual songs" (*Col.* 3:16) that the Protestant churches have developed because of their equally great stress on the participation of the congregation and of each individual worshiper in the service. The traditional concern of Protestant Christianity with the authentic faith and experience of the individual—expressed in Luther's axiom "You must do your own believing as you must do your own dying"—is likewise audible in these hymns, many of which, typically, are cast in the language of the first person singular. [*See also* Preaching *for discussion of the role and function of the preacher in various religious traditions.*]

The sacraments. It would, however, be a grave distortion (albeit a distortion to which even sympathetic interpreters of Protestant Christianity have sometimes been subject) to interpret Protestantism as a thoroughgoing individualism in its understanding of worship, for the definition of the church as "the community of Christian worship," in Protestantism as well as in Orthodoxy and in Roman Catholicism, is embodied above all in the celebration of the sacraments. Except for certain details (e.g., whether it is the recitation of the words of institution or the invocation of the Holy Spirit in the epiclesis that effects the transformation of bread and wine into the body and blood of Christ in the Eucharist), Eastern Orthodoxy and Roman Catholicism stand in basic agreement on the nature of sacramental worship and the meaning of the seven sacraments. Among the many definitions of *sacrament* that have appeared in the Christian tradition, two (one from the East and one from the West) may suffice here: "the mystery of faith," since in Christian Greek *mustērion* means both "mystery" and "sacrament"; and, in a formula based on Augustine, "sacred sign," which by a visible means represents (or re-presents) an invisible divine grace. [*See also* Sacrament, *article on* Christian Sacraments.]

The Eucharist. The primary sacrament and the center of Christian worship is, for both the Eastern and the Western tradition, the Eucharist or Lord's Supper, which is, in one form or another, celebrated by all Christian groups. Although the celebration is also a memorial and an expression of community, what sets the Roman Catholic and Orthodox understanding of the Eucharist apart from that of most other groups is their definition of this sacrament as real presence and as sacrifice. In fulfillment of the words and promise of Jesus, "This is my body" and "This is my blood," the bread and wine presented for the sacrament become the very body and blood of Christ, identical in their substance with the body born of Mary, even though the taste, color, and other attributes or "accidents" of bread and wine remain. The Fourth Lateran Council in 1215 defined this doctrine as "transubstantiation," and it was reaffirmed by the Council of Trent in 1551. As the real presence of the body and blood of the one whose death on the cross and resurrection effected the redemption of the world, the Eucharist is as well a sacrifice—not as though the first sacrifice were inadequate and Christ needed to be sacrificed over and over, but "in union with the sacrifice" of Calvary. The daily offering of that sacrifice for the living and the dead is at the center of Roman Catholic worship, devotion, and doctrine; and although Orthodoxy is, characteristically, less explicit in some of its detailed formulations about the metaphysics of the presence and more content to speak of it as a "mystery," its representatives, when pressed, will come up with language not far removed from that of the West—especially of the West as in the twentieth century it has, thanks to a repossession of the tradition of the Greek fathers, come to speak about the mystery of the Eucharist.

Whatever differences of emphasis there may be between Roman Catholicism and Eastern Orthodoxy about the Eucharist, they are much smaller than the differences among the several Protestant groups. Luther objected to transubstantiation as an excessively philosophical formula, and above all to the sacrificial understanding of the Eucharist as a diminution of the redemptive work of Christ, but he vigorously defended the real presence against his fellow Protestants. They in turn laid stress on the "true presence" of Christ in his spirit and power rather than on the "real presence" of the actual body and blood. Within Protestantism, consequently, the memorial aspects of the celebration of the Lord's Supper, which Christ according to the Gospels instituted to be eaten in his remembrance, have been prominent and sometimes even central. The other historic accent of Christian eucharistic worship that has found a new emphasis in Protestant practice and devotion is the understanding of the Lord's Supper as a corporate expression of the "communion" of Christian believers with one another. "Body of Christ" in the New Testament refers sometimes to the Eucharist, sometimes to the church, and sometimes (notably in *1 Corinthians*) to both at the same time. Compared with those two themes of memorial and communion, the specification of just how the body and blood of Christ can be present in the sacrament is of lesser significance. [*For further discussion, see* Eucharist.]

Baptism. The other action of the community of Christian worship on whose "sacramental" character all Christians would agree is baptism. Throughout the *Acts of the Apostles*, baptism functions as the means of initiation into the Christian movement and into the reality of Christ himself, and in the epistles of Paul baptism is the way of appropriating the benefits of the death and resurrection of Christ. Although all the explicit references in the New Testament to the practice of baptism mention only adults as its recipients, and that generally only after a profession of their faith, the custom of administering it also to children began quite early; just how early is a matter of controversy, but by the end of the second century infant baptism was sufficiently widespread to have called forth objections from Tertullian. Except for that difference from subsequent tradition, Tertullian formulated in his treatise *On Baptism* what can be regarded as an all but universal consensus about the effects of baptism: remission of sins, deliverance from death, regeneration, and bestowal of the Holy Spirit. Eastern and Western church fathers, all the medieval scholastics, and many of the Protestant reformers would be able to subscribe to that formulation. Because of their misgivings about any view of any of the sacraments that might appear magical, Protestants have tended to avoid describing the conferral of these effects as something automatic. The Anabaptists of the sixteenth century on the continent, and the several bodies of Baptists in England and especially in the United States since the seventeenth century, have carried that position to the conclusion of repudiating the practice of infant baptism and insisting on "believers' baptism" as the only form of administering the sacrament that is consistent both with the original intention of Jesus and with the true nature of the Christian community. [*For further discussion, including discussion of pre-Christian practices, see* Baptism.]

Other sacraments. Although baptism and the Lord's

Supper are for most Protestants the only two ordinances that qualify as sacraments, the medieval development in the West led to a system of seven sacraments, which Eastern Christianity, when obliged to become specific, has likewise affirmed. The sacrament of penance (together with the reception of absolution) developed as a way of coping with sins committed after the reception of forgiveness in baptism. As the contrition of the heart, the confession of the mouth, and the satisfaction of a work restoring what had been taken away by the sin, penance became, in the Latin Middle Ages, one of the principal means by which the imperatives and the promises of the Christian gospel were applied to individuals and communities. With the universal acceptance of infant baptism, the individual's assumption of the responsibilities of Christian discipleship, originally associated with adult baptism, came to be the central content of the sacrament of confirmation. As infant baptism attended the beginning of life with sacramental grace, so at death, or in a crisis or illness that might portend death, the anointing of the sick (or the sacrament of "extreme unction") brought that grace to the end of life as well. The only one of the seven "sacraments" to which the name was applied in the New Testament (*mustērion* in Greek, *sacramentum* in Latin) was marriage (*Eph.* 5:32); on that authority, it became part of the sacramental system. And as the ordinance by which all the other sacraments were usually made possible, the ordination of priests itself was defined to be a sacrament. Each of the seven, therefore, combines in a special way what is also the special emphasis of Christian hope and of Christian worship: the sacredness of each person, but in the context of the sacred community.

[*For further discussion of Christian worship, see* Worship and Cultic Life, *article on* Christian Worship; Christian Liturgical Year; Priesthood, *article on* Christian Priesthood; *and* Ministry. *Related issues are discussed in broad religious perspective in* Confession of Sins; Prayer; Ordination; Marriage; *and* Repentance. *For discussion of Christian expression in the arts, see* Basilica, Cathedral, and Church; Monastery; Iconography, *article on* Christian Iconography; Music, *article on* Religious Music in the West; Drama, *articles on* European Religious Drama *and* Modern Western Theater; Poetry, *article on* Christian Poetry; *and* Literature, *article on* Religious Dimensions of Modern Literature.]

The Christian Way of Life. As a system of love—and love is, in the formula of Paul, the "greatest" of the three (*1 Cor.* 13:13)—Christianity presented itself to its hearers as a way of life; especially in *Acts*, "the way" became a standard designation for Christianity itself. In its symbiosis with the societies and cultures in which it has taken root, the Christian way of life has been characterized by even greater heterogeneity than Christian belief or Christian worship. That heterogeneity makes generalizations about it in such a summary as this even more hazardous, and the specifics of the forms of Christian ethics in society must be left for treatment elsewhere in this encyclopedia. It is nevertheless possible to single out briefly certain leitmotifs that run across the varieties of Christian morality, both individual and social.

The imitation of Christ. Ever since the New Testament, the human life of Jesus Christ has served as an example set forth for imitation; it has usually been more than an example, but never less. "Bend your necks to my yoke, and learn from me, for I am gentle and humble-hearted; and your souls will find relief" the New Testament (*Mt.* 11:29) represents him as commanding. Just what that imitation implies concretely for the Christian in the world has been, however, a continuing issue and problem, for the Christ whom the believer is invited to imitate was not married, did not hold public office, and was not supported chiefly from a trade or profession. The imitation of his example has come to mean, therefore, the application to one's own situation of the love and faithfulness that Christ brought to his. Repeatedly, when the demands of society or, for that matter, the requirements of the church have proved to be too complex or abstract, "the imitation of Christ" has become a way of reducing them to their essence. Thus, in what has probably been, except for the Bible itself, the most widely circulated book in Christian history, *Imitation of Christ* by Thomas à Kempis (1379/80–1471), the summons of the figure in the Gospels rises above the intervening voices with a clarity and directness that has spoken to followers in every century; and in the twentieth century, *The Cost of Discipleship,* by the young Lutheran theologian and martyr under the Nazis, Dietrich Bonhoeffer (1906–1945), has applied that New Testament summons of "Follow me" to a new generation of disciples.

Obedience. The imitation of Christ has also implied obedience to his will, as this was expressed both in his own teachings and in the Mosaic law. In its treatment of that law, the New Testament manifests an ambivalence: Christ is seen as "the end of the law" (*Rom.* 10:4), and yet he himself is represented as warning in the Sermon on the Mount (*Mt.* 5:17), "Do not suppose that I have come to abolish the law and the prophets." The ambivalence manifests itself likewise in the descriptions of the Christian way of life as obedience. The Christian catechisms that have proliferated especially since the sixteenth century (see "Reformation Christianity," above) have usually incorporated an exposition and application of the Mosaic Decalogue as their description of what it means in practical terms to be a Christian. That has been perhaps even more true of Protestant than of Roman Catholic catechisms, despite the polemic of Protestants against "moralism" and "legalism" in Roman Catholic theology and ethics. But both Roman Catholic and Protestant ethicists and teachers have also repeatedly defined Christian obedience as not the strict observance of a legal code, not even of the legal code in the Ten Commandments, but as the spontaneity of the Spirit. "Love God, and do what you will" was Augustine's characteristically epigrammatic way of describing that spontaneity; but that same Augustine is at the same time one of our earliest authorities for the use of the Ten Commandments in Christian pedagogy. Augustine is as well an early source for the adaptation to Christian purposes of the philosophical consideration of the nature and the number of the "virtues": to the classical (or, as they came to be called in Christian parlance, "cardinal") virtues of prudence, temperance, fortitude, and justice, Christian ethical thought added the three "theological" virtues of faith, hope, and love. Obedience to the will of God and the cultivation of these seven virtues were seen as the content of the Christian way of life. [*See also* Ten Commandments; Christian Ethics; *and* Christian Spirituality.]

The transformation of the social order. Each of the "cardinal" and "theological" virtues makes sense only in a social context, and obedience to the will of God has traditionally been seen as pertaining to society as well as to the individual. The petitions of the Lord's Prayer, "Thy kingdom come, thy will be done, on earth as it is in heaven," have been taken to mean that the reign of God and the will of God have as their object here on earth the creation of a social order that conforms as closely as possible to the reign of God in heaven. That is indeed how both the East (see "The Christian Culture of Byzantium," above) and the West (see "Christianity in the Middle Ages," above) have interpreted their mission through most of Christian history, and that was how they carried out their mission within those societies. Calvinism and Puritanism were especially committed to the creation of social and political institutions that lived up to the will of God, and the pacifism of Anabaptist and Quaker groups during the sixteenth and seventeenth centuries was inspired by a similar commitment. During the nineteenth and twentieth centuries, however, such an interpretation of the Christian mission has taken on new urgency—and has occasioned new controversy—in a society where the institutions of Christianity no longer command attention or widespread obedience. The Social Gospel associated with the name of Walter Rauschenbusch (see "The Nineteenth Century," above) was the most ambitious of modern efforts to rethink the fundamentals of the Christian way of life in relation to the situation of an industrial society and to define the very meaning of salvation (as well as of other themes of Christian teaching and devotion) in social terms. Although the Social Gospel has in greater or lesser measure affected the ethical thought of most Protestant groups, Roman Catholicism has, during most of the twentieth century, been the major center for the development of new social and political theory. In a series of "social encyclicals" beginning with the *Rerum novarum* of Pope Leo XIII (1810–1903) of 15 May 1891, the papacy itself has often taken the lead in stimulating such development. But the application of the theory to twentieth-century society—the phenomenon of "worker priests" in France, and especially the creation of "liberation theology" by Roman Catholic theologians in Latin America—has often produced confusion and provoked controversy. Even those whose political or theological conservatism finds such trends dangerous, however, usually speak in the name of a particular definition of the social order that they regard as conforming, at least in some measure, to the same ideals. [*See also* Political Theology.]

Christian universalism. The Christian way of life as love is conventionally seen as finding its ultimate fulfillment in the church as the loving community of believers set apart from the world. But alongside that strain in the Christian tradition there has always stood a concern and a love for the entire world, a Christian universalism no less pronounced than is Christian particularism. It has sometimes expressed itself in a sense of urgency about Christian missions, to "bring the world to Christ." But a less prominent, yet no less persistent, expression of Christian universalism has sought to probe the implications of the unavoidable statements of the New Testament about the entire world as the object of the love of a God "whose will it is that all men should find salvation and come to know the truth" (*1 Tm.* 2:4). Origen in the third century, Gregory of Nyssa in the fourth century, Nicholas of Cusa in the fifteenth century—these and other theologians, committed though they were to the church and to its orthodoxy, have taken up the exposition of a universal vision in which the love of God revealed in Christ cannot be completely fulfilled until all God's creation has been reconciled.

Faith, Hope, and Love. The complex, sometimes labyrinthine, interactions of faith, hope, and love with one another throughout Christian history and throughout Christianity as a system suggest the absence of a set of universal principles that could, in the fashion of Euclid's geometry, yield *the* Christian worldview. Christianity is, rather, the product of a continuing and organic history. Its principal institutional expression has been the church in its various organizational forms, but Christianity is more than the church. Although its chief intellectual product has been a theological development that spans twenty centuries, the Christian message is not coextensive with its theology. Its most telling effect on history has been in the faith and life of its celebrated saints and seers, but Christianity has consistently declared that its power and spirit can be found as well among the silent in the land, the meek who shall inherit the earth.

BIBLIOGRAPHY

Christianity is fortunate in having had more works of general reference published about it than any other world religion. Probably the most convenient of these is *The Oxford Dictionary of the Christian Church,* 2d ed., rev. (Oxford, 1983). Also in English, and especially helpful for its bibliographies, is *The New Catholic Encyclopedia,* 17 vols. (New York, 1967–1969). With more articles, a good many of which, however, are relatively brief, the *Lexikon für Theologie und Kirche,* 11 vols., 2d ed., edited by Michael Buchberger (Freiburg, 1957–1967), is a masterpiece of condensation. The succeeding editions of the *Realenzyklopädie für protestantische Theologie und Kirche,* 24 vols., 3d ed. (Leipzig, 1896–1913), whose fourth edition is now in preparation, have contained status reports on research into most of the themes treated in this article. And the *Dictionnaire de théologie catholique,* 15 double vols. (Paris, 1909–1950), presents comprehensive articles, some of them entire monographs, on many of the same themes.

The monographic literature on the history and the theology of Christianity is, quite literally, incomprehensible in its scope and cannot engage our attention here. But among more general works, perhaps the best overall treatment of its history is in *Histoire de l'église depuis les origines jusqu'à nos jours,* edited by Augustin Fliche, Victor Martin, and others (Paris, 1934–1964). *The Pelican History of the Church,* 6 vols., edited by Owen Chadwick (Harmondsworth, 1960–1970), is excellent, except for its omission of a volume on the Christian East, and always readable and often incisive. The more ambitious *Oxford History of the Christian Church,* 2 vols. to date, edited by Henry Chadwick and Owen Chadwick (Oxford, 1977–), may well be a collaborative work destined to match Fliche-Martin in comprehensiveness. *Atlas zur Kirchengeschichte,* edited by Hubert Jedin, Kenneth Scott Latourette, and Jochen Martin (Freiburg, 1970), provides a sense of place for ideas and books that in the theological literature sometimes seem to be suspended in midair. The history of those ideas is the concern of my work *The Christian Tradition: A History of the Development of Doctrine,* 5 vols. (Chicago, 1971–), and the books are chronicled with a sureness of touch and with great fairness in Johannes Quasten's *Patrology,* 4 vols. (Utrecht, 1950–1960).

Of the many thousands of attempts at a systematic formulation of Christianity as a religion of faith, hope, and love (and therefore not only of Christian dogmatics, but of the entire Christian message), it may seem presumptuous to select only five: John of Damascus's *On the Orthodox Faith* in the eighth century, which has played a significant part in all three major segments of Christendom, Orthodox, Roman Catholic, and Protestant; Peter Lombard's *Sentences* in the twelfth century, which, with the more than one thousand commentaries that have been written on it, shaped Christian teaching for centuries; Thomas Aquinas's *Summa theologiae* in the thirteenth century, which many students of Christian thought would regard as the climax of its development; John Calvin's *The Institutes of the Christian Religion* in the sixteenth century, which summarized the principal tenets of the Protestant Reformation more masterfully than any other book of theology; and Friedrich Schleiermacher's *The Christian Faith* in the nineteenth century, which, both by its successes and by its failures, is an eloquent statement of the predicament and the promise of the Christian message.

JAROSLAV PELIKAN

Christianity in the Middle East

The *titulus,* or placard, over the cross of Jesus was written in Hebrew and Greek and Latin (*Jn.* 19:20, *Lk.* 23:38). A summary of the early history of Christianity in the Middle East requires a focus on the faith's engagement with the cultures of those three languages. Born in the matrix of Hebrew messianism, Christianity—as its name indicates—had to reckon with the spiritual and social implications of its conviction as to realized messiahship in Jesus, crucified and risen. Given the context of Greek thought and curiosity, its early formulation of belief was in necessary relation to the themes and terms of the Greek intellectual world. Its developing structure of leadership and order, from the pastoral beginnings to the monarchical episcopate and thence to the papacy, owed much to the Latin and Roman ethos, as did also some of the instincts of its theology. It was from the Hebraic, the Greek, and the Latin cultures that the two great tensions in early Christianity grew, leading to the fracturing by which the church was unwillingly "gentilized" by the second century AD and to the Great Schism of the eleventh century that sundered East and West. Each of these extended crises proved decisive in the definition of Christianity. There is much poetic justice in the fact that Pilate should have publicized the crucifixion of Jesus in the languages that shaped the telling and the ordering of the faith it fashioned.

It was to be six centuries before Arabic came upon the Christian scene via Islam, to bring the other great, traumatic conditioning of Christianity in what, to the Arabs,

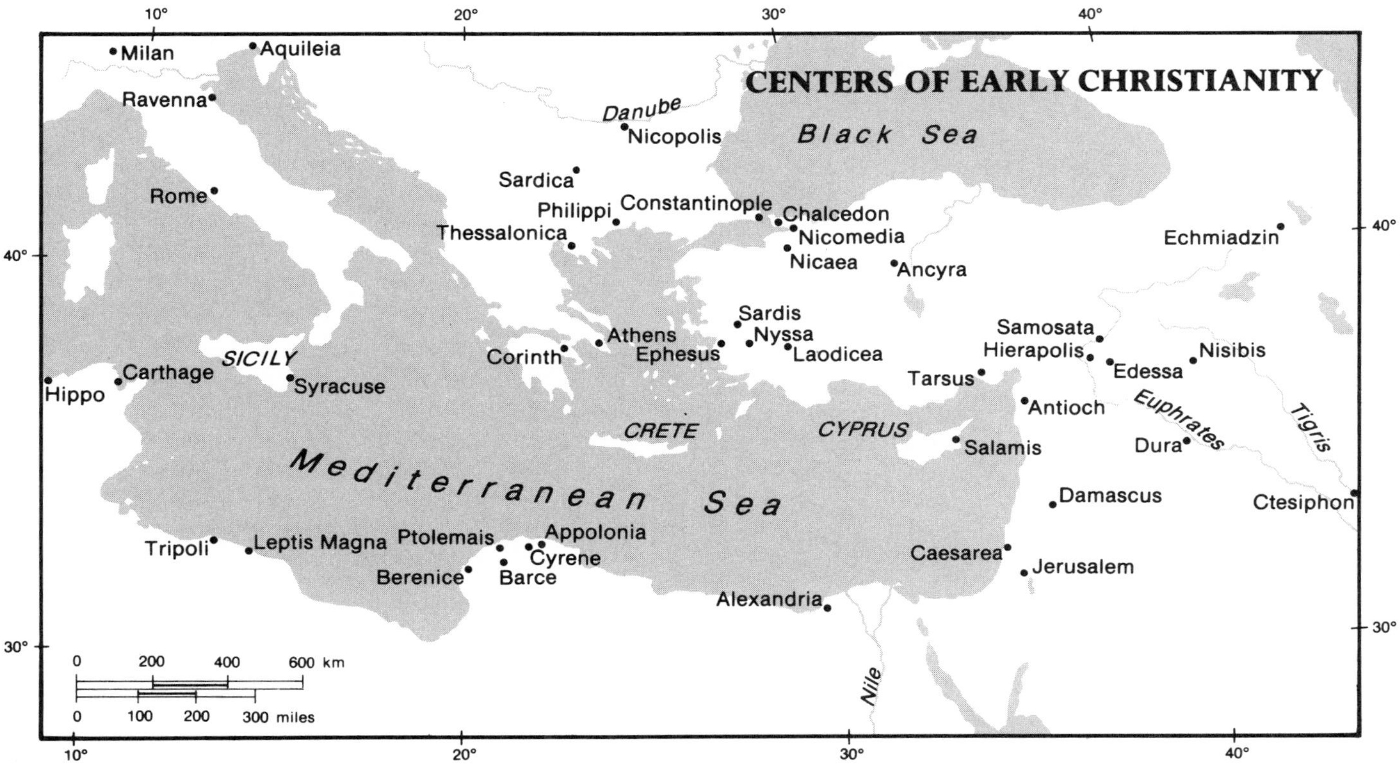

was the near West. By the time of the advent of Islam, though the Great Schism, which culminated in 1054, still lay four centuries ahead, the Hebraic and Greco-Roman factors had written themselves into the constitution of Christianity. Pilate's official languages became the historian's clues.

Jewry, the Christian Messiah, and Peoplehood for God. The central issues in the first decades of the Christian community grew out of the apostolic conviction as to the divine fulfillment of promise in the event of Jesus as the Christ. Such alleged fulfillment, with the Cross at its center, involved a radical crisis for the Judaic heritage. Messianic expectations were various—royal or priestly, political or eschatological, zealot or ethical, central or marginal. But, despite the depth of the sense of pathos in the figure and tradition of "the suffering servant," Jews had not conceived of a crucified messiah. That utter contradiction in terms meant a total scandal for Jewish minds. Yet it was affirmed within the Jewish world and by some Jewish hearts.

With the conception of Jesus as messiah went two further traumas of thought. The new dimension of grace it enshrined seemed to call into question Jewish law as the ground of divine-human (Jewish) relationship. So doing, it also contained a logic of openness to all, which threatened, or seemed to threaten, Jewish exceptionality. On both counts, there developed an inevitable tension between the Jewish seedbed of the new faith and the seed of universality that sprang from it. The gist of the story is evident within the New Testament itself. While there were splendid traditions in the Prophets about "the nations" and "the glory of God," and while what Christianity hailed as their realization was occurring within the world of the Septuagint and Judaic-Greek interculture, the Hebrew spirit instinctively recoiled from the logic of the Christ-event as achieving an open gospel and continued to see its loyal destiny as requiring, even for "the gentiles' sake," its exclusive privacy with God. The growing political struggle and the fall of Jerusalem (AD 70) and of Masada (AD 74) made that tenacity all the more urgent. So there developed (reflected, for example, in the *Gospel of John*) a deep cleavage between being Jewish and being Christian, with bitter contentions over the gray area between. Thus it was that in the second century, the church, despite its deeply Jewish origins, became almost exclusively a "gentile" entity. That consequence, and the emotions and controversies it entailed, have been of continuing significance for religious and social relations, and current developments in the Middle East have left a legacy which further taxes these relations.

But if the growing Christian church had to forego or

forfeit (according to one's reading of the story) its original Hebraic bonds ethnically and institutionally, it clung to them insistently in its choice of scripture (witness the story through three centuries of the canonization of the Bible) and in at least two vital areas of its theology. The theological loyalty to Jewish conceptions of sacrifice and suffering was reflected in the theology of the Cross and forgiveness, and in the sense of organic peoplehood, inherited from Israel but now freed from constrictions of either territory or race and realized as a corporate instrumentality, indifferent to place and birth but "chosen" and "commissioned" nevertheless. It was elsewhere in theology that Christianity found mentors outside Hebraic tradition, but its Judaic ancestry abides unmistakably in its sense of the peoplehood for God, albeit de-ethnicized, and in its vocabulary of redemption drawn from "the blood" and "the lamb" and the "ransom" of the earlier faith. The Judaic legacy can be seen also in the apocalyptic tradition with which the new faith had to reckon, sharpened as it was by the delay in the expected Parousia, or appearing, of Christ. [*See also* Christianity and Judaism.]

Christology in the Greek Idiom. Carrying the basic convictions concerning the Christ as achieved in Jesus into the Greek milieu set a firm intellectualism at the heart of Christian belief, one that could not accept the implication that it would be better to adore than to define. Each was held necessary to the other. A rightly ordered faith was not only its own best security but also a guarantee of its integrity. But, by the same token, formulating the significance of the central messianic fact with relation to God, Jesus, and humanity kindled inevitable tensions over terms and their intention. These tensions were the arena of leadership conflicts and genuine theological controversy, with Antioch, Alexandria, and Rome upholding differing solutions. The concepts of "substance," "person," and "nature" dominated the effort to express the doctrine of God as "Father, Son, and Holy Spirit" and to define a Christology at once divine and human. It was after the conversion of Constantine that the doctrinal work of the earlier mentors, especially Clement of Alexandria, Origen, and Irenaeus, developed into the decisions of the Council of Nicaea (325) holding Jesus to be "of one (not of like) substance with the Father." From that date imperial policy itself abetted the persisting issues as to how a right Christology should understand the divine-human unity-duality in the person of Jesus. The Council of Chalcedon (451) finally laid down the formulas in which the answer should be given. But it could only do so in terms excluding what it did *not* mean and so, in effect (as philosophers often do), leaving the question latent in the form of the answer. The differing positions of Nestorius and the monophysites, albeit condemned at Chalcedon, remained to demonstrate that latency. [*See* Councils, *article on* Christian Councils.]

It is easy to decry the shape of the encounter—cultural, as well as conceptual—of faith in the realized messiahship of Jesus with the Greek demand for its theological expression. But it is unwise to do so, at least in notions of "Christendom divided by a dipthong" (*homo ousios*, or *homoi ousios*). For the alternative notions about Jesus as a "demigod," or simply as a prophet figure, would have imperiled not only the whole structure of his received relevance in salvation but also the entire faith in its conception of God, creation, and history. The "incarnation of the Word" was no idle thesis and certainly of no pagan vintage. It was the direct corollary of the preaching of the Kingdom as Jesus had preached it and lived it and as the disciples received it and carried it into the wider context of the apostolate to which it impelled them. The formulas which housed its transmission—as far as they were able—may be read as the shape in which its significance might be secured in the given context of the time and place.

That it was not a unanimous formulation was due to the complicity of human and political and local factors as well as to the inherent complexity of the meanings themselves. Any appeal to some contrasted simplicity as a criterion of authenticity eludes what it aims to resolve. Muslim theologians, in their defining centuries, found surprisingly parallel issues about the divine and the human, the eternal and the temporal, in their formulations about *tanzīl*, or the "descent" of the Qur'ān, and the "uncreatedness" of that scripture. In the classical period of Christian theology the Christian confidence was that the Holy Trinity, Christology, and the personality of the Holy Spirit were properly to be seen as mutually necessary and mutually explanatory doctrines. The third continued to be the theme of one contentious detail, namely the *filioque* clause, as to the "proceeding" of the Spirit from the Father and (or "through") the Son.

These intricacies of theological statement, occupying both East and West, should not obscure the other legacy of the Greek spirit which characterized what came to be known, indeed, as the Greek Orthodox tradition, namely apophatic theology. Rather they stimulated it by contrast. The will to "love the Lord with a whole mind" need not exclude the love of him "with a whole soul." It was this latter love that contemplative patterns sought, in an instinct to negate the conceptual in the name of the transcendent. The way of knowing finally required the ascetic discipline and the art of prayer. As exemplified in Egypt, notably by Antony (b. 251), this "desert spirituality," whether in actual hermitage or practical austerity, generated an illuminative wisdom and a rigorous discipleship which were powerful elements through a whole millennium and a rich legacy for Europe. [*See* Monasticism, *article on* Christian Monasticism.]

Roman Imperium and Christian Church. For nearly three centuries Christianity suffered under Roman power. Much of Christianity's early story took place within the catacombs. Sporadic persecution, sometimes intense, tested its nerve, burdened it with martyrdoms, and perplexed it over the lapsed. Its will to be innocuous stopped short of loyalty tests which involved pagan sacrifice or emperor worship, while its beliefs and rites were regarded as pestilential by cultured Romans, East and West. The last great imperial effort to crush it came under Diocletian between 303 and 312. In the following year the conversion of Constantine brought imperial policy into its inner debates. The change from persecution to sponsorship was profound. [*See* Persecution, *article on* Christian Experience, *and* Constantinianism.]

Constantine's removal of the capital from Rome to Constantinople may be seen as a major source of the tensions over precedence and primacy which, perpetuated in political theology, reached ultimate schism seven centuries later. That climax only registered into permanence the strains involved in shifting issues of prestige and place born of the power equation among the five great patriarchates of Rome, Constantinople, Antioch, Alexandria, and Jerusalem. [*See* Schism, *article on* Christian Schism.]

But the uneasy marriage with imperium contributed strongly to the concepts and forms of church order. Geographical dispersion from the earliest apostolic times posed the problem of how the many should be one and the one many. The New Testament is clear about apostolate in its accent on "the Twelve," though the exegesis of the famous "on this rock" passage (*Mt.* 16:13–20) and its significance for a Petrine primacy remain controversial. But the nexus of Peter and Rome apart, the circumstances of early Christianity, the travels of Christians and the need to provide travelers with credentials, the pastoral cares and disciplines, all required the emergence of focal persons in the scattered churches. The New Testament presents deacons, elders, and bishops, the latter two sometimes identified. Doctrinal developments around the Eucharist much later helped to turn elders into priests with reserved functions in ritual.

But it was Roman (Latin) instincts, as well as practical considerations with respect to order, which underlay the growth of episcopal leadership and authority toward monarchical forms linked with centers of varying local prestige. That growth was fostered, and sharpened, into power structures that often compromised the original pastoral themes of ministry which, with their Palestinian provenance, married uneasily with Roman pride and system. It was, among other things, the contentions of such pride which paved the way for the expansion of Islam through the whole Middle East in the first decades of the seventh century.

Christianity under Islam. Pilate's trilingual *titulus* and the title deeds of the church now had to submit to a faith with a scripture in its own Arabic, a scripture which firmly de-hellenized the significance of Jesus, named him al-Masīḥ (the Messiah), but disallowed his Christian messiahship. Enclosing the relation of God with mankind in prophethood alone and proclaiming a new, and final, prophetic locus in Muḥammad, Islam radically challenged the entire self-understanding of Christianity and assigned to delusion and obsolescence the christological controversies which had so long and so far engaged the churches.

The physical shock was immediate, but it was not the first generations who bore the total impact of Islam. Arabization and islamization were slow processes, extending over at least a century. The conquest at once detached from Byzantium the whole of the Middle East south of northern Asia Minor. It demolished the old frontier between Persia and Rome and so rearranged the interrelationships of the differing segments of a dislodged Christendom. But the new power, emerging from a relative hinterland of culture, needed to rely strongly on the expertise—administrative, artistic, and political—of the otherwise subjugated faith. Under the Ummayyads at Damascus (661–750) that subjugation, initially modest, sharpened in the eighth century. A freedom to remain Christian under varying disabilities (as distinct from a freedom to propagate that faith) was part of Islamic tolerance, a tolerance that requires a rewriting of the familiar "spread by the sword" summary of Muslim expansion. It is the story of an imperially expressed religion served by power.

Radical as the divergences were over Christology, salvation, and man, there was between the two faiths an evident identity of philosophical universe, as discernible, for example, in the writings of the celebrated John of Damascus (c. 679–749), an early exponent of Muslim-Christian dialogue. The new ingredient of Islam in some ways modified, but in no sense overrode, the continuing controversies among Christian dogmas, seconded as these were by varying fortunes and local vicissitudes under Islam. One tangled aspect of the Islamic impact was the Iconoclastic Controversy of the eighth century, embodied in the decrees of Leo III (the Isaurian) in 726 and 730. The resulting controversies and anathemas embroiled the parties and gave rise to passionate excesses of zeal but did little to resolve perennial themes concerning the arts and worship, symbol and mystery, matter and spirit. [*See* Iconoclasm *and* Icons.]

The tenth century saw something of a Byzantine recovery with the reconquest of Cyprus, Syria, Lebanon, Crete, the Taurus region, and Armenia. The excesses of the caliph al-Ḥākim in the early eleventh century and of the Seljuk Turks kindled the ardor of the Crusades, which through the next two centuries brought the East and West of Christendom into closer contact than at any time since Justinian I (d. 565). Despite their heroism and their few redeeming features, the Crusades did nothing to address, or to heal, the doctrinal and communal tensions between the churches. It is symbolic that the Great Schism of 1054 should have been followed within four decades by the Seljuk devastation of Jerusalem and the egotistical response of the West's First Crusade. Eastern Christendom was the victim of its rescuers. After the Crusaders departed came pagan Mongols, then islamizing Mongols, whose relations with Christians farther east in Asia has to be noted below. The distresses and tribulations of Copts, Orthodox, and monophysites in western Asia under the Mongols and the Mamluks continued to the Ottoman period. [*See also* Crusades.]

The only partial exception was that of the Maronite church in Lebanon, initially founded in the fifth century and brought within papal jurisdiction by Innocent III (1198–1216). Some of the viability it enjoyed by dint of its locale and other features came to be partially ensured to other churches through the *millet* system by which the Ottoman Empire, from the sixteenth to the twentieth century, regulated Christians and others of minority status. The system implemented the Islamic "freedom to remain" concept of toleration by according to Christian minorities the right to their own laws of personal affairs, liberty of education and worship within their families, and, after the fall of Constantinople in 1453, the civil headship of patriarchs within their spirituality. In return the churches were required to submit to fiscal measures, to keep a low profile, and to concede the political and social dominance of Islam. The mentality which the *millet* system developed within the churches, one of introversion and quiescence, has remained a crucial liability for their history. But at least the system ensured their conditional survival. Its legacy determines much in the contemporary situation, most tragically in Lebanon, by perpetuating communalism and inhibiting the growth of sentiments of stable and unitary nationality. In the several nation states of the Middle East which emerged after World War I and the demise of the Ottomans, the power equation within Islam politicized Muslim response to current issues. The strictly religious dimension has rarely been free to bear creatively on the situation in or between communities.

Christianity Eastward of Its Cradle. While the New Testament's record of Christian expansion could well be characterized as "westward ho!" and while Rome's role (in all the meanings of Rome west and Rome east) lay mostly with the Greek and Latin churches, it is important to appreciate the Christianity of Armenia, Persia, and beyond.

Lying between the Black and the Caspian seas, with Georgia to its north, Armenia may claim to have been the first Christian nation. King Tiridates declared the nation's faith in 301, twelve years before Constantine's Edict of Toleration in 313. The declaration was the climax of evangelism and of persecutions going back, at least in tradition, to two of Jesus' disciples—Bartholemew and Thaddeus. Often assumed to be monophysite, the Armenian church in fact recognizes a divine and a human nature in Christ but defines them as one "in the incarnate God." It celebrates the birth and baptism of Jesus on one day, as the single manifestation of his identity. The great Armenian church leader was Gregory the Illuminator, founder in 303 of its abiding center in Echmiadzin. With its tenacious followers, its national script, and its wide contacts with other patriarchates, Armenian Christianity surmounted storm and adversity in its buffer location to withstand Persian Mazdaism, Byzantine enmity, and successive Muslim powers, Abbasid, Seljuk, Mongol, Mamluk, and finally, Ottoman. In the nineteenth century, thanks to Russian incursions into their territory, contention with Persian shahs, and Russian struggles with the Turks, many Armenians scattered both westward into Asia Minor or northward into Russia. Their Christianity was ruggedly maintained despite these desperate hardships, which reached their bitterest in World War I, and the near genocide inflicted by Turkish arms. Tragically dispersed and subject to the vagaries of Soviet policy since 1920, Armenian Christianity has never lost its tenacity and its defiance of adversity. In the 1950s and 1960s, Catholicos Vazgen exemplified these qualities in rallying Soviet Armenians and reorganizing their ecclesiastical structure and spiritual life. [*See* Armenian Church.]

Syriac-speaking Christianity, known as Nestorianism, was the main bearer of the faith of the apostles eastward into Persia and Afghanistan. Antioch, city of Ignatius (martyred c. 107), was the nursery of Nestorius, whose name is associated with the distinctive Christology which developed a remarkable zeal for expansion. It was a Christology loyal to the "two natures" view but divergent in its understanding of the motherhood of Mary within the Incarnation. The great centers of its mission were first Edessa (modern Urfa) and then Nisibis. In the late fifth century its patriarchate was established at Ctesiphon on the Tigris. From these centers its emissaries carried the Christian faith in the Syriac language into Persia, Afghanistan, India, and China. Their script survives, for example, in the Mongol language. They translated widely from the Greek, not only in theology but in secular fields, and thus became the channel by which Greek learning passed into Arabic. Ironically that very service, in the context of the Muslim conquest, brought the steady decay of Syriac literature through the ascendancy of Arabic. [*See* Nestorian Church.]

Nestorians suffered like Armenians from successive powers lording over their lives in comparable sequence from the Persians to the Ottomans. However, lacking the unique cohesion of the Armenians, they were a more ready prey to perils of dispersion, internal disputes, and, in modern times, the secessions into Uniate status with Rome. One feature of all the Eastern churches in the eighteenth and nineteenth centuries was the experience of schisms yielding to Rome. Syriac-speaking Christianity also suffered from its amenability to Western political interests which compromised its local tenure and weakened its identity. Yet in its finest years, as under the great catholicos, Timotheos I (780–823), contemporary of Caliph Hārūn al-Rashīd, it demonstrated with a rare fervor the spiritual and ecclesiastical virtues of a living church. It made notable conversions among Turkish tribes and among the Mongols in their first advances westward. In the late thirteenth century there was a Mongol catholicos. But in 1295 began a sudden islamization of the Mongols and a rapid decline of the Nestorian church. Its fascinating contacts with Buddhists lapsed, and Central or middle Asia came to be completely Muslim. [*See* Uniate Churches.]

Christianity Today. The post–World War II situation is dominated by two factors: (1) the successor states of the Ottoman empire and the position of Christian minority elements within broadly Islamic nationalisms and (2) the implications of the establishment and security demands of the state of Israel. The broadly Christian populace, everywhere a frail minority save in Lebanon, has struggled to reach and to justify a genuine identification with nationhood and to shed the traditions of protégé status vis-à-vis Western powers. The state of Israel generates peculiar strains for Middle Eastern Christianity by reason of its commitment to the politicization of Judaism and Jewry, its close liaison with United States policy and power, and, thereby, its inevitable aggravation of Muslim-Christian relationships through these associations and the suspicions and accusations they arouse.

Because of the tenaciously political nature of Islamic self-expression, the foundation of secular states (as for example in India) has not been available to ease the tensions of religious communalism by comprehending these within a single and juridically neutral statehood. Nor have the tragic struggles of the Palestinians in any way availed to achieve a regional unity of purpose in response to Israel. Rather they have desperately fragmented and destroyed the one country—Lebanon—which, for all its archaic political system, held promise as a viable sanctuary of interreligious sanity and dialogue.

Given this dark and despairing set of circumstances, and other factors originating in the West, there has been a steady attrition of the Christian presence in the Middle East through migration and exile. The steady judaization of Palestine, the hardening of Islamic extremism in some areas and the threat of it in others, have greatly attenuated Christian strength both in numbers and prospects. The lands of the origins of Christian faith will no doubt continue to hold their mystery and meaning. But if they are not to become a museum piece for Christendom, and if such vital Christian communities as do survive are not to atrophy, then solutions must be found to the conflict between Zionism and the Palestinians and to the deep frustrations of the Arab world. With such solutions may be found a new resilience for the heirs of the Christianity which originally "suffered under Pontius Pilate." Maybe that detail, which the creed is careful to state, suggests a paradoxical hint of hope.

But hope must be more than a paradox of adversity. For the problems are not all outward trials. They are also inward symptoms of disunity. Some divisive factors are linguistic, ethnic, and cultural. But others persist too passively from a long history. Diversity is one thing, disunity another. Dogma, tradition, and minority constraints perpetuate the legacy of fragmentation in today's chronic situation. The Great Schism has its entail in Uniate churches. To be Orthodox, monophysite, monothelite, Roman, Protestant, and the rest too far breaches the business of being Christian.

Since 1973 the Middle East Council of Churches has brought together almost all the non-Roman elements and is developing cordial relations with Rome. This group developed out of the earlier Near East Christian Council, a body initially only Protestant and generated by Western mission. It may be that the Council of Churches' internal task of unity will be turned toward the larger tasks of response to interreligious conflict and the desperate search for regional peace. Theological issues which have so long been at stake will then be not so much resolved as outlived.

BIBLIOGRAPHY

Arpee, Leon. *A History of Armenian Christianity.* New York, 1946.

Atiya, A. S. *A History of Eastern Christianity* (1968). Reprint, Millwood, N.Y., 1980.

Attwater, Donald. *The Christian Churches of the East.* 2 vols. Rev. ed. Milwaukee, 1947–1948.

Betts, Robert B. *Christians in the Arab East.* Atlanta, 1978.

Browne, Laurence E. *The Eclipse of Christianity in Asia.* Cambridge, 1933.

French, Reginald M. *The Eastern Orthodox Church.* London, 1951.

Frend, W. H. C. "Christianity in the Middle East: Survey down to A.D. 1800." In *Religion in the Middle East: Three Religions in Concord and Conflict,* edited by A. J. Arberry, vol. 1. Cambridge, 1969.

Frend, W. H. C. *The Rise of Christianity.* Philadelphia, 1984.

Haddad, Robert M. *Syrian Christians in Muslim Society.* Princeton, 1970.

Horner, Norman. *Rediscovering Christianity Where It Began: A Survey of Contemporary Churches in the Middle East and Ethiopia.* Beirut, 1974.

Hourani, Albert. *Minorities in the Arab World.* Oxford, 1947.

Jaeger, David-Maria, ed. *Christianity in the Holy Land.* Tantur, Israel, 1981.

Joseph, John. *The Nestorians and Their Muslim Neighbors: A Study of Western Influence on Their Relations.* Princeton, 1961.

Runciman, Steven. *The Eastern Schism* (1955). Oxford, 1963.

Zernov, Nicolas. *The Church of the Eastern Christians.* London, 1942.

KENNETH CRAGG

Christianity in North Africa

Although we lack written sources, archaeological evidence suggests an early origin for the North African churches. However, we must distinguish between two obvious centers in the first century of the preaching of Christianity on the southern shores of the Mediterranean. One center was in Cyrenaica, within reach of the influence of Alexandria. The other was in Carthage, undoubtedly influenced from neighboring Rome across the sea. [*See map accompanying* Christianity in the Middle East.]

Tradition associates the emergence of Christianity in Cyrenaica with the evangelization of Egypt by the apostle Mark. The existence of a considerable Jewish community in that area even before the birth of Christ surely established continuous communications with Jerusalem during the first century. Participation of Libyans and people from Cyrene in the religious controversies at Jerusalem is confirmed by the *Acts of the Apostles* (2:10, 6:8–9). Moreover, archaeological work has revealed the existence of catacombs in Cyrene that substantiate the development of an organized church with ties to Alexandrian Christianity prior to the third century.

The first mention we have of the church in Carthage came in the year 180, when Tertullian declared that his native Carthage was directly related to Roman apostolic authority. The church that, during the second century, produced so great a giant in the field of Christian theology as Tertullian must have had deep roots in the first century. Carthaginian Christianity was so strong and foundational that it had great influence on the theological controversies of the next several centuries within Western and Eastern Christendom.

Cyrene. Cyrenaica (the easternmost part of Libya) was known as the Pentapolis, or the five towns: Cyrene (modern-day Shaḥḥāt), Apollonia (Marsa Gona), Ptolemaïs (Tolmeta), Berenice (Benghazi), and Barce (Barka). Geographical location and the patterns of caravan trade tied these five towns more closely to Egypt than to Carthage and the rest of the western states of North Africa.

According to tradition, the evangelist Mark was a native Jew of Cyrene, who came to Alexandria by way of the Pentapolis and, after laying the foundations of the new church in Egypt, returned to Cyrene to evangelize. The First Council of Nicaea (325) decreed that Cyrenaica should be considered an obedientiary of the see of Alexandria. To this day the Coptic patriarch carries the five western towns in his title as a province of the see of Mark. We must assume that there was a continuous flow of ecclesiastical and missionary personnel between the two regions, much like the interaction between Carthage and Rome. The overwhelming Greek element in both Cyrene and Alexandria also facilitated communication between them.

Most clerics of Cyrenaica received their education in Alexandria, formerly in the Museion and later in the catechetical school. Alexandrian culture, both philosophically and theologically, had its representative in the Pentapolis in the person of Synesius of Cyrene (c. 370–413), bishop of Ptolemaïs, whose name has come down in history as one of the fathers of the Eastern church.

Synesius was born of wealthy pagan parents in Cyrene around the year 370. After obtaining all the education available in his country he went to Alexandria, where he attended the classes of Hypatia (c. 370–415), the best of the pagan Neoplatonist professors in the Museion. Synesius was captivated by the spell of her teaching and became one of her Neoplatonist disciples. From Alexandria, Synesius went to Athens but was disappointed by the lack of educational opportunities there. On return, his fellow citizens commissioned him to go to Constantinople to plead with the Byzantine emperor for relief from heavy taxation. The success of his mission increased his popularity and paved the way for his leadership of the Libyan people.

At this point Synesius went back to Alexandria, where he was married by Patriarch Theophilus (385–411). This is sufficient proof that he had become a Christian, though there is no evidence of baptism until 410. At that point, in appreciation for his success in Byzantium and for his organization of military defense against the Berbers, his people unanimously elected him to the episcopate. But Synesius was a married man and a staunch Neoplatonist, and he was unwilling to give up either his marriage or his philosophy for the proffered privilege of elevation to bishop. Finally, both the clergy and the people of Ptolemaïs made a strong appeal to the patriarch to consecrate him as their bishop, and their appeal was granted, an exception to Coptic church tradition holding celibacy a requirement for the episcopate.

In the latter decades of his life, Synesius built fortified churches to which his people resorted for prayer and for defensive purposes when harassed by Berber marauders from the south. Remains of these buildings are still standing in the area of the Green Mountains in Cyrenaica. He also composed religious hymns and homilies that inspired his congregations. Yet he retained his sense of humor and found time to write a treatise in praise of baldness. In the realm of literature, however, he is better known for a set of 156 letters, addressed to many people, including Hypatia and the patriarch Theophilus, which he wrote between the years 399 and 413. These letters, which have been translated into English, are a rich source of information about the social life of the period, geography, and the economy of the world he knew. They show elements of syncretism in their considerations of Neoplatonist philosophy and Christian theology. Synesius may have been the greatest personality in the history of the Pentapolis.

On the whole, the Pentapolis followed Alexandria in all phases of its development during the Christian period. It was subjected to the same wave of persecutions under Roman rule. Even in heresy, there arose the same divisions in Cyrenaica as in Alexandria. During the Arian controversy, there were followers of Athanasius and supporters of Arius, including two bishops, Theonas of Marmarica and Secundus of Ptolemaïs. The third-century heresy of Sabellianism, or subordinationism, which made a distinction between the Son and the Father, the Logos and the Creator of the Logos, arose from a discussion by Sabellius, bishop of Ptolemaïs, and was opposed by two other bishops from the Pentapolis, Amon and Euphranor.

Cyrenaican Christianity appears to have been concentrated almost entirely among the Greek population, who fought the Berber natives along the southern frontier of the Sahara. The Berbers were considered a race of marauders whom the Greeks wanted to push into the desert. Thus the Berbers lived as foreigners beyond the border of their homeland. Outside the pale of the church, they retained their old practices. Arab conquest forced Greek emigration, and there was greater rapport between Berbers and Arabs than between Berbers and Greeks. This accounts in part for the sudden disappearance of Christianity from the Pentapolis and the spread of Islam after the advent of the Arabs.

Carthage. Carthage was founded in the eighth century BC by the Phoenicians, accompanied by Jewish traders. After the Roman conquest and the fall of the city in 140 BC, other European settlers came to stay, but the Berber natives remained on the periphery of the agricultural territories. Archaeological work has revealed the extent of Roman culture in North Africa from Leptis Magna (near present-day Tripoli) in the east to Caesarea (northern Algeria) on the Mediterranean shore. The Romans established series of forts along the southern frontier, and these were strengthened by the Byzantines and in particular by the emperor Justinian for defensive purposes. North African agricultural land supplemented Egypt as the granary of the Roman empire. The natives spoke what may be described as Libyan Punic, though the romanized inhabitants and the Roman settlers conversed in Latin, which came to be the official language of the country and the church, in contrast to Greek in Cyrenaica.

Pagan religions of varied character from the Phoenician worship of Baal and Astarte to the animistic beliefs of the natives, later joined by the gods of the Roman pantheon, were in use at the coming of the Christian preachers of the gospel. It is difficult to fix precise dates for the introduction of Christianity into the western section of North Africa, though we may assume that the preaching of the gospel initially came from Rome. This is confirmed by the later demonstrations of close relationship with the see of Rome. The first concrete record of Roman registers revealing the existence of an organized and well-developed church surfaced suddenly just a couple of decades before the end of the second century. Christianity was largely concentrated in Carthage and its adjacent territories. From east to west, these included Tripolitania, Africa Proconsularis, Numidia, Mauretania Caesariensis, and Mauretania Tingitana, covering roughly modern-day Tripolitania, Tunisia, Algeria, and northern Morocco. The spread of Christianity must have taken place rapidly among the Carthaginian population, but it never took root among the Berbers, who remained outside the fold of Roman civilization and were systematically besieged by the church. The position of the church reached a high degree of efflorescence in the following few centuries, thanks to a number of people whose contributions to Christian thought and culture remained a standing monument for Carthaginian Christianity in spite of its sudden disappearance after about five centuries of existence.

In its early days, the church at Carthage was subjected, with the rest of the Roman empire, to persecutions and contributed its full share in martyrdom. Namphamo of Numidia claimed to be the first martyr for his faith, and he could have been of Punic origin. However, the majority of the martyrs of Carthage were either romanized natives or Roman settlers. Despite persecution, the church grew. At the death of Tertullian around 225, Carthage already had more than seventy bishoprics. In the year 250, during Cyprian's episcopate, the number increased to about 150. When the Edict of Milan was issued in 313, the number rose to 250 bishops. The country teemed with new churches. Cyprian mentions eighty-eight in his works, and twenty-nine more were added before the year 325.

In spite of its significant progress, the church began to suffer from internal division with the appearance of the Donatist movement. [*See* Donatism.] Though the source of the division was theological, Donatism began to assume the shape of nationalism, which was concentrated in Numidia against Carthage. The controversy dragged on until the coming of the Vandals in 429. The Vandals were of Arian confession and would have nothing to do with either catholics or Donatists, who were stifled under Vandal rule until the recovery of the country by the Byzantines in 533 on behalf of Emperor Justinian. In keeping with his imperialist policy, Justinian aimed at a unified church and state and discouraged all schismatic tendencies in his provinces, including North African Donatism. Donatism was weakened, but it flickered until the destruction of the church by the Arabs in the seventh and eighth centuries.

Shapers of Christian Thought. The sudden extinction of Carthaginian Christianity could not minimize the glories of the North African church in the first centuries. Foremost among those who gave that church great stature in the annals of Christian civilization are Tertullian, Cyprian, and Augustine of Hippo.

Tertullian (160?–225?) lived in the age of Roman persecutions, and this is reflected in his writings. He was born a pagan in Carthage, but became a Christian in 193. The first church father to write in Latin, Tertullian fought idolatry and heresy in all its forms, whether gnostic, Manichaean, or Marcionite. A prolific theologian, he used his gift of eloquence to defend Christian martyrs. To him we owe the first use of the word *trinity*, a creation of his lucid logic in the definition of the unity of God. He drew the main basic lines of Western theology, parallel to Origen's efforts in the East at the catechetical school of Alexandria. Subsequent generations of theologians continued to build on Tertullian's illuminating trinitarianism and Christology after his death. [*See the biography of Tertullian.*]

Born a pagan and educated in rhetoric, Cyprian (c. 205–258) ultimately became a Christian some decades after the death of Tertullian, whose work he knew. Like Tertullian, Cyprian became an ascetic. He was elected bishop of Carthage shortly after his conversion (c. 248). Cyprian wrote numerous letters, which are among the best sources of the history of the church in the third century, as well as short treatises dealing with practical theological matters, such as the enforcement of rebaptism on heretics. His real strength lay in his pastoral genius as a man of action and a superb organizer. He led a stormy life within the church as well as without, and he was continuously beset with danger. In the year 258, a new wave of persecutions swept the empire by the order of Emperor Valerian, whose agents pursued the bishop. Cyprian did not flee, and he was martyred in 258. [*See the biography of Cyprian.*]

Approximately a century after Cyprian's martyrdom, the genius of the North African church reached its peak in Augustine of Hippo (354–430), whose life and work became one of the greatest landmarks in the development of Christian theology. A native of North Africa and born of a pagan father and a Christian mother, Augustine was bishop of Hippo from 396 until his death in 430. He wrote against many heresies, including Manichaeism, Donatism, and Pelagianism. The two principal works that made Augustine the foremost writer of his age are his spiritual autobiography, the *Confessions*, and the *City of God*, a work seminal for medieval Christian thought. In the *City of God*, Augustine labors to vindicate Christianity against the attribution that the calamitous fall of Rome to the hordes of Alaric in 410 was due to the advent of the new religion. According to Augustine, the kingdom of God, the celestial Jerusalem, was the eternal kingdom that no earthly ravages or philosophical intellectualism could impair, and its only visible form on earth was the catholic church. In this way Augustine was able to substantiate all the elements of patristic thought in the service of catholic Christianity more effectively than any of his predecessors. [*See the biography of Augustine.*]

If the North African church had produced no creative writers beyond Tertullian, Cyprian, and Augustine, it would have more than justified its major importance in Christian antiquity. But North Africa contributed even more in a smaller way through the works of other minor authors. Of these may be cited Arnobius of Sicca (253–327), well-known rhetorician and teacher who was a Christian convert from paganism. Another was Lactantius, also a professor of rhetoric, who lived during the reign of Diocletian (284–304). After Christianity had been declared the state religion, the emperor Constantine in 317 appointed Lactantius to be tutor of his own son Crispus. Lactantius was already advanced in years and died about 320.

Advent of Islam. After the conquest of Egypt in 640–642, a further thrust westward into the Pentapolis and the rest of North Africa by the Arabs became inevitable, initially to safeguard the fairest of their acquisitions, the Nile Valley. Cyrenaica surrendered to the Arab conquerors without difficulty and Carthage fell into their hands in 698. As the Arabs came in, the Greek and Roman populations went out, emigrating en masse to Byzantium, Sicily, Italy, and Spain. With their exit, the churches of North Africa vanished with surprising rapidity.

First among the factors that precipitated the disappearance of Christian foundations in North Africa, despite their remarkable development and past glories, was that the church had remained embedded in urban districts. Its congregations never really cared to undertake missionary work amid the Berber tribes. In contrast, the Arabs, who were nomads like the Berbers, offered the Berbers Islam with equality and full brotherhood. The Berbers accepted the offer and even participated with the Arab armies in further conquests. Second, waves of emigration from Arabia to North Africa came to fill the vacuum created by Christian departure from these regions. Instances of the advent of whole tribes settling in North Africa include the accounts of Banū Hilāl and Banū Sālim, whose adventures in these provinces are still the subject of Arabic folklore. A third factor was that most of the heterodox parties among the Arabs took off to the distant west, where they could pursue their doctrines undisturbed and even launch missionary work for their beliefs. The Khārijī faction inaugurated the movement, and the Shīʿīs followed suit; the latter were eventually able to establish their own caliphate and build an empire of their own. Fourth, the economy of the romanized provinces of North Africa was essentially founded on slavery and slave trade, while Islam offered full enfranchisement to all slaves willing to convert. Finally, there was the burden of Byzantine taxation, which was continually on the ascendance. Though it would be a mistake to contend that total relief accompanied the advent of the Arabs, the Berbers were assured of Arab leniency, and, at any rate, had nothing to lose by the change of masters.

It is therefore no wonder that the Berber population found it more to their advantage to accept the new situation readily and even participate with the conquerors in the extermination of all remaining pockets of Roman settlers, and with them the vestiges of a church that they regarded as the symbol of their past humiliation. These factors account for the precipitous downfall of Carthaginian Christianity and the almost total disappearance of churches from North Africa by the twentieth century. [*See* Berber Religion.]

Even though the door was left ajar for the reappearance of Christian elements from the West during the modern period of European colonization, these do not appear to have had any real impact on the prevalent status of Islam. Although stray Christians mainly of Coptic origin remain, in the present day, all the countries of North Africa, from Libya to Morocco, must be regarded as totally Muslim and without any surviving Christian element.

[*For discussion of particular North African churches, see* Coptic Church *and* Ethiopian Church.]

BIBLIOGRAPHY

Altaner, Berthold. *Patrology*. Translated from the fifth German edition. New York, 1960.

Atiya, A. S. *A History of Eastern Christianity*. Rev. ed. Millwood, N.Y., 1980.

Bardenhewer, Otto. *Patrology: The Lives and Works of the Fathers of the Church*. Saint Louis, 1908.

Buonaiuti, Ernesto. *Il Christianesimo nell'Africa Romana*. Bari, 1928.

Groves, C. P. *The Planting of Christianity in Africa* (1948–1958). 4 vols. Reprint, London, 1964.

Julien, Charles-André. *Histoire de l'Afrique du nord*. 2 vols. Paris, 1956. Translated by John Petrie as *History of North Africa*, 2 vols. (London, 1970).

Leclercq, Henri. *L'Afrique chrétienne*. 2d ed. 2 vols. Paris, 1904.

Quasten, Johannes. *Patrology*. 3 vols. Utrecht and Westminster, Md., 1950–1960.

Synesius. *Letters and Hymns*. Edited by Dionysius Petavius. Paris, 1612. Available also in *Patrologia Graeca*, edited by J.-P. Migne, vol. 66 (Paris, 1859). See also by Synesius: *Hymni*, 2 vols., edited by Nicolas Terzaghi (Rome, 1939–1954), translated by Augustine Fitzgerald as *The Essays and Hymns of Synesius of Cyrene*, 2 vols. (Oxford, 1930); and his letters, in Rudolf Hercher's *Epistolographi Graeci* (Paris, 1873), translated by Augustine Fitzgerald as *The Letters of Synesius of Cyrene* (Oxford, 1926).

A. S. Atiya

Christianity in Eastern Europe

The story of Christianity in eastern Europe and northern Eurasia is complex—a tangled web of changing peoples, nations, and church allegiances, of political, military, and cultural conflicts, and of ideological, social, and spiritual forces, in a seemingly perpetual flux. This article traces the course of twenty centuries of Christian history in this region, which is bounded on the south by the tip of the Greek Peninsula, ringed roughly by the Adriatic, Aegean, Black, and Caspian seas; on the north by the Baltic Sea and the Finnish Peninsula; on the east by the Ural Mountains; and on the west by the eastern slopes of the Alps and the river Elbe.

The history of the Christian church in eastern Europe and northern Eurasia can be understood through the interplay over the centuries of four major factors: Greek/Byzantine, Latin/Roman, and Frankish/German influences and the migrations of peoples who eventually settled in eastern Europe and northern Eurasia, primarily the Slavs. These factors represent distinctive religious, cultural, and ethnic traditions that molded the development of the Christian church over the centuries in this region. There are others, of course, for example the Muslim Ottoman empire in the fifteenth through nineteenth centuries and, in the twentieth century, the U.S.S.R. Nevertheless, the story of how Christianity developed in this area can be told by describing the motives, mentality, interests, and policies, together with the successes and failures, of these four major forces.

Historically, the first actor at work in the molding of Christianity in eastern Europe and northern Eurasia was the Greek/Byzantine tradition. With the apostle Paul's mission to the gentiles and his crossing over into Europe, the Christian church abandoned the exclusivism of its Jewish roots to become a world religion. Although it moved toward Africa, Asia, and the Indian subcontinent, the church's major growth came as it addressed the Greco-Roman world of the Mediterranean basin. As it sought to preach the message of salvation in Jesus Christ, it used not only the lingua franca of its day, the spoken and written Greek of the first century, but also Greek concepts, problematics, and philosophical traditions to communicate, understand, and interpret the faith. Beginning with the New Testament concept of Christ as the Logos (*Jn.* 1), there is an ongoing record of the incarnation of the Christian message in the Greek mind. To be sure, what came out of this process, orthodox Christianity, could not be identified with any specific Greek philosophical system. It was uniquely Christian, but it formulated its faith and practice with the tools of the Greek heritage. Strongly concerned with clear doctrinal formulation of the teachings regarding the Holy Trinity and the person of Jesus Christ, the Greek tradition emphasized the transcendent dimension of faith, the reverence and awe of worship, the conciliar understanding of church life, and the ascetic spirituality of monasticism. This early tradition of Christianity, formulated in the writings of the church fathers primarily within the eastern part of the Roman empire, known as Byzantium, was embodied and essentially preserved in what much later came to be called the Eastern or Greek Orthodox church, with all its various local expressions.

However, while accepting and defending as Christian orthodoxy the formulations of doctrine described above, Christianity in the western part of the Roman empire quickly gave to the Christian message and life nuances and emphases that characterized its Latin heritage. Less theologically speculative, the sober Latin tradition focused on the practical and on the sense of order and pattern required in an increasingly unstable cultural, political, and social milieu produced by the inroads of numerous barbarian tribes beginning in the fourth century. While the Greek mind concerned itself with the subtleties of church doctrine, frequently generating new heresies, Latin Christianity became a stronghold of fundamental Christian orthodoxy, while concurrently remolding this orthodoxy according to its own genius. In practice, that meant an understanding of the Christian faith largely colored by legal concepts. For example, while the Greek East generally tended to understand sin in relational terms (sin as the breaking of the appropriate relationship between the Creator and the creature), the Latin West emphasized its legal dimensions (sin as guilt). This difference, and the exigencies of the breakdown of cultural unity and civil authority in the West between the fourth and eighth centuries, favored the development of a monarchical understanding of the church, leading to the rise of the Roman papacy as the single, supreme ecclesiastical (and frequently, secular) authority in the West. The combination of an early reputation for careful orthodoxy in doctrine, with the centralization of authority in the Roman see, became the source of what eventually would come to be called the Roman Catholic church.

The third group of actors in the drama of Christianity in eastern Europe and northern Eurasia were the Frankish and Germanic kingdoms, which while Roman Catholic in faith, were primarily concerned with their military, economic, and political expansion in the area of eastern Europe. It is not that these concerns were unique to the Frankish and Germanic kingdoms, but that these interests affected the development of Christianity in significantly different ways from that of the see of Rome or of Byzantine Orthodoxy. The reason for this is that Roman Catholicism in the western European region sought actively to differentiate Western Christianity from Eastern Christianity, especially through espousal and promulgation of the *filioque* clause in the creed, which asserts that the Holy Spirit proceeds from the Father and the Son.

In 691 Clovis III became king of all Franks, beginning a process of consolidation of political power in the West. With Charles Martel's victory over Arab forces at the Battle of Tours (732), the integrity of western Europe was assured. A formal political split between the eastern and western parts of the empire, exemplifying the cultural division of Eastern and Western Christianity, occurred with the crowning of Charlemagne by Pope Leo III in the year 800 as the first emperor of the Holy Roman Empire. From that point on, Frankish and Germanic forces perceived the Byzantine empire and its Greek church as rival powers opposed to their interests.

With the inclusion of the doctrinal novelty of the *filioque* in the creed, at the insistence of the Franks (not, originally, by the Roman see) the stage was set for a long drawn-out process of schism between the Western (eventually, Roman Catholic) church and the Eastern (eventually Eastern or Orthodox) church. [*See* Schism, *article on* Christian Schism.] Much of the conflict between East and West played itself out in eastern Europe and northern Eurasia. From the point of view of the history of the church from the ninth through the sixteenth centuries, Frankish, and subsequently Germanic interests in the region translated themselves into efforts to make Roman Catholicism dominant at the expense of Eastern Orthodoxy. In contradistinction, during this and subsequent periods, Eastern Orthodoxy became one of the major forces in the struggle of the peoples in the region to retain their cultural, spiritual, and political identity and autonomy. In the sixteenth century, the Germanic influence in eastern Europe was expanded with the rise of the Reformation. From that time, church history was strongly influenced by Protestant interests in the area.

The final actors in the story of Christianity in eastern Europe and northern Eurasia are the various peoples who historically had lived in the region, or who came from elsewhere to settle there. Southeastern European peoples, primarily in Macedonia, Achaia, Crete, the Aegean Islands, and Byzantium, were able to trace the continuity of their ecclesiastical and cultural roots to early Christianity and beyond. In contrast, central and northern Europe was an area repeatedly overrun by peoples from the Asian steppes. As a result, the continuity of Christian history was repeatedly broken and reestablished, formed and reformed, in eastern Europe.

Primarily, though not exclusively, it was Slavic peoples who began the invasion of Europe, by attacks on Asia Minor and the Balkans around the year 220. Appeased in part by a Byzantine policy that combined military strength, payment of tribute, and settlement, the waves of invaders moved westward in the third to fifth centuries beyond the effective boundaries of the Byzantine empire. In eastern Europe, the newcomers were displaced by new conquerors, and the groups often mingled. Eventually a measure of identity with particular geographic areas was achieved by the settlers.

The history of the Christian church in eastern Europe and northern Eurasia can largely be told in terms of the competition of Greek/Byzantine, Latin/Roman, and Frankish/Germanic efforts to gain the loyalty of these largely Slavic peoples. Or, conversely, the history of the church in this area can be understood as the response of the Slavic and other peoples of the region to what the first three had to offer.

Early Christianity. Christianity entered eastern Europe through the missionary work of the apostle Paul and the subsequent influence of countless Christians who shared the good news of the redemption of humankind by God in Christ through the Holy Spirit. Paul planted the Christian seed primarily in cities. His dramatic entry into Europe, as a result of a dream in which a Macedonian begged him to "Come over to Macedonia and help us," is described in *Acts* 16. The Christian scriptures indicate the first-century establishment of Christianity in cities such as Philippi in Macedonia; Thessalonica, Veroia, and Nicopolis on the western coast of the Greek peninsula; Athens in Attica; Patras, Corinth, and Sparta in the Peloponnese; on the Aegean islands of Chios and Samos; and on the island of Crete.

The northern boundary of the Roman empire in the last decades of the second century extended to the Danube in Illyricum and beyond in the province of Dacia (present-day Romania). On either coast of the Adriatic and the Black Sea there were small enclaves of Christians, but the vast numbers of Thracians, Moesians, Illyrians, and Dacians in the region had not been christianized. Nevertheless, conditions existed favorable to their eventual conversion. For example, the northern branch of the Thracians, the Geto-Dacians (considered to be the ancestors of the Romanian people), although polytheists, believed in a supreme god whom they called Zalmoxis, the god of heaven and light. The Geto-Dacians were known to ancient Greek historians such as Herodotus, who described, in addition to this concept of a supreme god, their strong belief in the immortality of the soul. It is not at all unlikely that during this early period a scattering of Christians existed among the Geto-Dacians as a result of Christian influence in the armies of Trajan (98–117), who had subdued them.

A legend, recorded by Eusebius of Caesarea and attributed to Origen (c. 185–c. 254), holds that the apostle Andrew preached in the land of the Geto-Dacians, then referred to as Scythia. The *Passion of Saint Andrew* included in the Constantinopolitan *Sunaxarion* (lives of saints for liturgical use) claims that Andrew preached in Pontus, Thrace, and Scythia. Although there is a ninth-century legend that Andrew ordained a certain Apion as bishop of Odessus (present-day Varna, Bulgaria), the first historical record of a bishop of the region was made by the historian Socrates regarding Theodore the Thracian at the Synod of Sardica (343–344). A bishop from the area named Terentius participated in the ecumenical council at Constantinople in 381. A Bishop Timothy was recorded in attendance at the ecumenical council held in Ephesus (431).

Under the Roman empire, however, Christians in these, as well as other areas of the empire, were persecuted because of their unwillingness to show loyalty to the emperor through acts of devotion recognizing him as a god. The persecutions were sporadic, but sometimes severe, costing much martyr's blood. Nevertheless, the Christian population continued to expand.

Legitimization and the Barbarian Inroads. When Constantine, together with the co-emperor Licinius, proclaimed Christianity to be a legal religion in 311 with the Edict of Milan, more and more of the population within the boundaries of the empire began to be christianized. But the appearance of the barbarians caused the boundaries of the Roman empire to contract, and with them, whatever earlier Christian presence existed in the area was severely weakened or destroyed. Among the earliest of the barbarian tribes to appear were the Goths.

During the period from 230 to 240 the Goths came out of southern Russia to attack the Roman provinces. A succession of Roman emperors fought against them: Claudius, Aurelian, Diocletian, and Constantine. Christianity in its Arian form seems to have been introduced to the Goths through prisoner exchanges in Cappadocia around the year 264, but it was at least a century before Christians were of any great number among them. By the mid-fourth century there seemed to be an adequate Christian population among the Goths to require a bishop. Thus, in 341 Ulfilas was ordained first bishop of the Goths by the Arian patriarch of Constantinople, Eusebius. His work was primarily in Plevna (in modern-day Bulgaria). Ulfilas translated the scriptures and services into the Gothic tongue. It should be noted here that the orientation of these early efforts at christianization was from the East. Yet, over the next few centuries, the constant incursions and displacement of tribes in a westward direction meant that little permanency of the Christian presence could be expected.

Missions in Conflict. It was not until the ninth century that Christianity began to gain a permanent foothold in the area. By this time, not only had the foundations of Christian doctrinal understanding been formalized through seven ecumenical councils, but the four factors described above had also been clearly defined. As they met on the eastern European stage, they determined the forms that Christianity would take there, and in turn, much of its ethnic and political identity as well. [*See* Greek Orthodox Church.]

The barbarians, although intent on expansion and the acquisition of land, were also attracted by the quality of the Greco-Roman culture of the empire, which they respected. The chief ingredient of this attraction was Christianity. In many cases, these peoples were seized with a strong desire to embrace the faith through what they had seen and heard and through the missionary efforts of the church. Among these in the ninth and tenth centuries were the peoples of Bulgaria to the south, Moravia (present-day Czechoslovakia) to the north, and Russia to the east. The spirit of competitive choice among the recipients of the faith, as well as conflict among the transmitters of the faith, became evident during this period.

In the East, the dominant power was the Byzantine empire, whose fortunes had improved sufficiently in this period to permit consideration of missionary efforts, that is, the spreading of the Greek or Eastern form of orthodox Christianity. In the West, the Frankish empire was divided in 843 at the Treaty of Verdun into three parts, the most eastern of which was to become Germany. Louis I, the German, became the founder of the German Carolingian dynasty, which lasted to 911. This dynasty pursued vigorous missionary efforts in eastern Europe and northern Eurasia.

The first area in which the two missionary efforts came into conflict was Bulgaria. Both German and Byzantine missionaries saw the Bulgarian Slavs as ripe targets for missionizing. The Bulgars, however, in their choice between Western and Eastern forms of Christianity were motivated by their own ethnic, cultural, and political perspectives, with independence as a prime concern. In the year 860 the drama began to unfold. Although at first attracted to the German missionaries, Khan Boris accepted baptism from the Greeks. Feeling that his church was not independent enough, he then turned from Constantinople to the West, admitting German missionaries whose policies even more strongly curtailed the independence of the Bulgarian church. These policies included the imposition of Latin in worship, subjugation of the hierarchy to the pope, celibacy of the clergy, and the *filioque* doctrine, even though it was not current in Rome at the time. By 870 Khan Boris had reacted to these restrictions by expelling the German missionaries and inviting back those from Constantinople. Since then, Eastern Orthodoxy has been the religion of the Bulgarian nation.

During this same period, a somewhat similar drama played itself out to the north, but with opposite results. The major difference here was that Rome and Constantinople supported the same missionary policy in contrast to the rival efforts of the Germans. Around 860 Prince Rostislav of Moravia appealed to Patriarch Photios of Constantinople for missionaries who could preach in the language of the people and conduct worship in Slavonic. Constantine (known later as Cyril) and Methodius, two Greek brothers from Thessalonica, were chosen for the task. [*See* Cyril and Methodius.] Before going to the mission field they created a Slavonic alphabet, into which they translated the Bible and the service books. Their mission policy thus included worship in the language of the people, the preaching of the Eastern form of Christianity (without the *filioque*), and the rapid indigenization of the clergy with its consequent spirit of local autonomy in church government. When they came into inevitable conflict with the German missionaries, Cyril and Methodius appealed to the pope and obtained his approval for their methods in Moravia. The Germans not only ignored this approval but even jailed Methodius for over a year. Following his death in 885, the Germans expelled the Byzantine missionaries and imposed Western Christianity in the region.

During this same period Patriarch Photios also sent missionaries to Russia, and a short-lived mission survived there until 878. As in the past, Christianity nevertheless continued to infiltrate the populace through ordinary contacts from Byzantium in the south, Bulgaria in the west, and Scandinavia in the north. Thus, when Prince Vladimir was baptized in 988, the christianization of the land was readily accomplished, at least in the cities and especially in the region around the capital city, Kiev. As Vladimir had married the sister of the emperor of the Byzantine empire, it was Christianity in its Byzantine form that was adopted. Originally centered in Kiev, Christianity gradually spread north and east, developing deep and strong roots among the people, with social concern, liturgical piety, and monasticism united with the culture and language of the Russian peoples. Nevertheless, Western influences were also present in Russian Christianity, influences that would find resonance many centuries later.

Schism and Imperial Contention. The eleventh and early twelfth centuries were marked by the definitive Great Schism between the Eastern and Western churches. Begun in the ninth century, it is traditionally marked by the mutual excommunications of Patriarch Michael Cerularios and Cardinal Humbert in 1054 and considered completed by the capture of Constantinople in 1204 by the Crusaders. The Venetians, at the head of the Fourth Crusade, established a Latin empire with a Latin patriarch in Constantinople. The Byzantines set up their capital in Nicaea and were unable to return to Constantinople until 1261. The result was that the pattern of conflict in the christianization of the peoples of eastern Europe was intensified over the next few centuries.

On the southwestern shores of the region, in the area roughly marked by modern-day western Yugoslavia, the Croatians had long been subject to efforts at christianization by Latin missionaries in the sixth through eighth centuries, even though the Eastern empire held nominal control over the area. After 800, however, the Franks brought the Croatians fully within the orbit of the West, completing the task by the tenth century. On their eastern border, however, another people—the Serbs—opened themselves up to the disciples of Cyril and Methodius. On the dividing line between Eastern and Western Christendom, their ninth-century Prince Mutimir, after some vacillation, looked toward Constantinople for the form of the faith to be practiced by the Serbs. Slavonic worship and Orthodox practices were accepted and a strong Slavo-Byzantine culture was formed. In 1219 Sava was consecrated in Nicaea, the then Byzantine capital, as archbishop of Serbia. This consecration reflected the strength of the Serbian empire at the time. In 1375, Constantinople recognized the Serbian patriarchate that had been proclaimed three decades earlier.

To the east of Serbia lay Romania, whose early Christian history has been noted. The Romanians are not Slavs, but, as their name indicates, a Latin people. Clearly within the Greek/Byzantine ecclesial tradition, they have maintained much of their orderly Latin heritage. At the same time they have adopted a great deal from their Slavic neighbors, especially in the area of worship. The Romanian church is a fruitful amalgam of these various influences. By the fourteenth century metropolitanates had been set up in various parts of the Romanian region.

At this same time, the Ottoman (Turkish) Muslim forces began to spread into the region from the southeast. They conquered the Bulgarian center of Tŭrnovo in 1393, were able to take control of Serbia in 1441, captured Constantinople and destroyed the last vestige of the Byzantine empire in 1453, subdued Bosnia in 1463, captured the Albanian fortress town of Krüje in 1478, put down the last resistance in Moldavia and Walachia (Romania) by 1490, and conquered Dyrrachium in 1501. The majority of the Christian peoples in this area were Eastern Orthodox in faith. The Muslims governed the conquered peoples in accordance with a system that identified each religion as a "nation." Known as the *millet* system, it required that all Orthodox Christians under Ottoman domination be governed through the patriarchate of Constantinople. This system, over the whole area south of the Danube, was to last for approximately four hundred years, to the mid-nineteenth century.

The major Orthodox nation not to be conquered by the Muslims was Russia. However, the history of the Russians was not without severe disturbances. The establishment of Kievan Orthodox Christianity in the tenth century was followed by a genuine flowering of church life for the next few centuries in Kiev and by active missionary work to the north. Notable were the establishments in Novgorod and Pskov. However, Kievan influence was broken in the thirteenth century with the coming of the Mongols. When in 1240 Kiev fell to them, a century and a quarter of survival efforts aimed at maintaining Russian life were begun by the church. Gradually, power and strength returned to the Russians, but they were now centered in Moscow. The church figured strongly in the rebuilding of the Russian nation, and by the death of Sergii of Radonezh (1392), Moscow was clearly the center of Russian Orthodoxy. In the north, Novgorod and Pskov, while free from the Mongols, were attacked in the mid-thirteenth century by Westerners, the Swedes and the Germanic Teutonic Knights, intent upon imposing Western Christianity in the area. The Russians, under Prince Alexander Nevskii, maintained the relative independence of the area. With the fall of Constantinople, the Russians began to think of Moscow as the "Third Rome" and the metropolitan of Moscow was honored with the rank of patriarch in 1589. The Russians emerged stronger and more united as an Orthodox nation as a result of their response to the Mongol threat. [*See* Russian Orthodox Church.]

To the northwest, the power in the region in the fifteenth century was Hungary, which served to contain the Muslim advance northward. Christianity was introduced into Hungary in the ninth and tenth centuries by Western missionaries; King Stephen I set down a formal constitution for the church in 1001. In 1279, Esztergom (Ger., Gran) was named the see of the primate of the Hungarian church, and until the Reformation, Christianity in the area was Western in form with no real influence from the East.

To the northeast of Hungary were the Poles. The history of the Polish people has been turbulent, and this turbulence has had a great impact on the form of Christianity in that land. Scholars once believed that Christianity had its beginnings in Poland in the tenth century in conjunction with the German see of Magdeburg, but modern scholarship now holds that in all likelihood Christianity came to Poland from Moravia, that is, from the missionary impetus inaugurated by Cyril and Methodius. Situated between northwestern Russia and powerful Roman Catholic neighbors to the west, Poland was subject to influences from both sources. In the eleventh century the civil leaders were allied with the West, although many elements of Eastern Christianity were present in the church. Thus, the Gregorian reforms of the Western church were imposed by civil authorities in the face of stiff episcopal and lower clergy opposition. The influence of Orthodox Russia was also felt and there was a significant Eastern Orthodox population in Poland. Nevertheless, until the Reformation, the church of the Poles was generally under control of the West, while at the same time marked with significant Eastern influence. Its borders often shifting, Poland found itself with sometimes larger, sometimes smaller populations of Orthodox Christians in its eastern regions.

In a similar fashion, the area north of Poland, along the eastern coast of the Baltic Sea, known historically as Lithuania, and more recently as Lithuania, Latvia, and Estonia, was from the beginning of its history caught between the rivalry of Western and Eastern forces, with all its ecclesiastical consequences. Lithuania came into being at the time of the Mongol conquest of Russia, with its first and only king, Trointen (r. 1259-1282) receiving Christianity from the Germans. By 1341 Lithuania had become a large empire as a result of Trointen's expansionist policies. Russian Orthodoxy and Polish Catholicism vied for Lithuania's loyalty, but in 1385 a political union of Lithuania with Poland led to the baptism of the Lithuanians into Roman Catholicism by Polish clergy. This Polish-Lithuanian relationship continued into the sixteenth century. Nevertheless, a significant Orthodox population to the east remained ecclesiastically under the jurisdiction of the metropolitan of Kiev. These Orthodox became the occasion for the inception of a new phenomenon in church history—uniatism.

Conceived as a means of unifying the religion of the populace, uniatism subjected the Orthodox population to the primacy of the pope and Western doctrine while allowing the retention of the liturgical forms and customs of Eastern Orthodoxy. The Council of Brest (1596) split into Eastern and Western factions, with the Western faction opting for the Uniate approach, with many Orthodox bishops accepting it. The Polish king approved the move and initiated a severe persecution of those Orthodox who refused to join. With Jesuit support, the Polish king Sigismund took Moscow in 1607, forcing a short-lived union with Rome on the Russian Orthodox. This effort came to an end in 1613 with Tsar Michael Romanov's restoration of Russian sovereignty. Uniatism, known also as Eastern Rite Roman Catholicism, was henceforth to be a complicating force in the relations of Roman Catholicism and Eastern Orthodoxy. [*See also* Uniate Churches.]

Northernmost of the nations of the region under discussion here is modern-day Finland. Christianity came to this area in the late eleventh and early twelfth centuries concurrently from both the East and the West. Roman Catholicism was introduced by the Crusaders, and Eastern Orthodoxy by Orthodox monks from Novgorod, who established the famous Monastery of Valamo in 1100. The area was subject to the competition of its Roman Catholic Scandinavian neighbors to the west and its Orthodox Russian neighbors to the east.

In the sixteenth century the whole religious map of Europe was changed by the Protestant Reformation. Although the Reformation was primarily a western European phenomenon, it did have significant impact in eastern Europe, in some areas achieving dominance and in others remaining a minority factor. In the north, Finland became largely Lutheran, with only a minority of Orthodox. Lutheranism was introduced into Estonia and Latvia, and soon became dominant, even under Russian control, in the eighteenth century. Protestantism in its Lutheran form entered Poland from Germany, but was nearly erased by the Counter-Reformation. When Poland was partitioned in 1795 with Austria and Prussia assuming control of its western regions, Lutheranism returned to favor. It has remained a "remnant" church in this predominantly Roman Catholic nation.

Protestantism in the geographical area of modern Czechoslovakia has deep roots going back to the fourteenth-century work of Jan Hus and the Brethren of the Common Life. In 1609 the Habsburgs granted the Brethren freedom, but they were soon to be persecuted anew. Protestantism survived among the Brethren, in Reformed and Lutheran forms, albeit among a few, until the establishment of the Czechoslovak state in 1918. Lutheran Protestantism came to Hungary in 1518 but shortly thereafter was supplanted by Reformed Protestantism. Both forms suffered under the Counter-Reformation until their adherents were granted civil rights in 1790 and 1791, and relations with the predominantly Roman Catholic nation were established in 1867.

Protestant churches in small numbers were established in Romania, particularly in Transylvania. It was in this area that Unitarianism began. The Lutheran bodies there have strong German ethnic ties. Although early Reformed Protestantism in Transylvania had Hussite and Lutheran connections, in 1567 it adopted the Second Helvetic Confession of faith. The small number of both Reformed and Lutheran Protestants in modern-day Yugoslavia were incorporated into the nation from border areas, primarily Hungary. The Reformation did not reach Greece, Bulgaria, or Russia until the nineteenth century, and then with only modest results, primarily in evangelical and Baptist forms.

Modern Nation-States. The eighteenth and nineteenth centuries saw the formation of the modern nation-states. The French Revolution set a pattern for self-government along national lines. In Orthodox Russia, tsardom reigned, but the influence of the West, both Protestant and Roman Catholic, was strong. Peter the Great removed the canonical head of the church, the patriarch, through his Ecclesiastical Regulation of 1721, substituting a state church patterned after German Protestant models. Scholastic theology, along with Italian Renaissance music, art, and architecture, was incorporated into Russian church life. This anomalous situation lasted until the revolution of 1917, when the patriarchate was restored.

During the early nineteenth century, as the Ottoman empire began to dissolve, the various Balkan peoples obtained their freedom by revolutions. Each Orthodox Balkan nation as it came into being sought an independent status for the Orthodox church within its boundaries. The nations that had had patriarchates before the Ottoman conquest sought to reinstate them. In 1833 the patriarchate of Constantinople acknowledged the independence of the church of Greece. Following in quick succession, the Bulgarian church received its independence in 1870, the Serbian in 1879, and the Romanian in 1885. In these nations the Orthodox church was recognized as the state church.

Of importance for religious life in Hungary was the creation of an Austro-Hungarian "dual monarchy" in 1867, which allowed a measure of religious freedom for Protestants—a pattern of church-state relations that lasted until World War II. The partition of Poland by Russia, Austria, and Prussia during the second half of the eighteenth century meant that the Orthodox in that country came under the jurisdiction of the Russian church, and the Uniates were compelled to return to Orthodoxy. Although the western part of Poland remained subject to Austria and Prussia, Polish Roman Catholics were severely restricted and Rome was no longer able to exercise control over them. Similarly, Finland was to a large extent occupied by Russia (beginning in 1809), and a strong Russian influence on church life resulted. By the end of the century, however, the Orthodox Finns had asserted their national identity with the institution of services in Finnish.

Eastern Europe and northern Eurasia assumed a definitive national shape in the period just prior to and following World War I. Most notable for church history were the emergence of Finland, Poland, Czechoslovakia, Yugoslavia, and Albania as new nations, primarily as a result of the dissolution of the Austro-Hungarian empire. Finland was over 90 percent Lutheran, with a small Orthodox population that was also recognized as a state church. In 1923 the Finnish Orthodox achieved autonomy under the patriarchate of Constantinople. Similarly, in Poland the Roman Catholic church became totally dominant, but there remained small Lutheran, Old Catholic, Polish Catholic (which came into existence in 1897), and Orthodox churches. The Polish Orthodox church was recognized by the patriarchate of Constantinople as autonomous in 1924. In 1980, 92 percent of the population of Czechoslovakia was Roman Catholic. Small Hussite and Brethren churches exist there, along with a small autonomous Orthodox church recognized by the ecumenical patriarchate in 1922. Albania became an independent nation in 1912 but was always subject to threats of dismemberment by its neighbors. Its population prior to World War II was predominantly Muslim—the only such nation in eastern Europe—with a Roman Catholic minority in the north and an Orthodox minority in the south. The paradigm of the religious situation in eastern Europe is that of Yugoslavia. An amalgam of a number of peoples, it includes Roman Catholics in its western provinces of Slovenia and Croatia, and Orthodox in its eastern provinces of Serbia and Montenegro, thus reflecting the divided status of the church in eastern Europe and northern Eurasia as a whole.

After World War II. Although the redrawing of national boundaries as a result of World War II, primarily at the expense of the U.S.S.R.'s western neighbors, had an impact on church order, the geographical demography of Orthodox, Roman Catholics, and Protestants did not change radically. Affecting all churches, however, were the forces of secularism, communism, and ecumenism. For more than two millennia, the primary struggles of the various churches were among themselves. In the twentieth century, the churches came to share common enemies that discounted the significance of religious faith. Secularism has taken many forms, but the most militant has been Marxism. In the U.S.S.R. and the nations under its influence, Marxism is ideologically antireligion. However, the Communist bloc nations approach the church with varying degrees of opposition. Albania is the first self-declared "atheist state," claiming that all vestiges of religion have been eliminated. The U.S.S.R., while granting freedom of worship, prohibits all other church activity. The rest of the nations in the bloc have made less restrictive accommodations with the church, some out of political reality, such as Poland, and others out of undeniable ethnic and cultural necessity, such as Romania and Serbia. [*See* Marxism.] In these countries the dominant number of believers and the identification of the national culture with religious tradition make a more lenient religious policy by the Marxist governments necessary.

The story of Orthodox, papal, and Franco-German Roman Catholic and Protestant competition in the great expanse of eastern Europe and northern Eurasia may have largely come to an end. The twentieth-century ecumenical movement has brought together in previously unimagined ways the disparate Christian churches. In the post–World War II era Orthodox, Roman Catholics, and Protestants of all kinds have struggled to replace confrontation and conflict with dialogue, understanding, and cooperation. It may be that the return to a pre-Constantinian status vis-à-vis the state may contain within it the seeds of a new unity for Christendom. Whether it does or not remains to be seen. What can be affirmed is that the twentieth century finds the various churches, after twenty centuries of conflict, relating to each other in an unaccustomed and newfound harmony and spirit of cooperation.

[*See also* Ecumenical Movement *and* Eastern Christianity.]

BIBLIOGRAPHY

Dvornik, Francis. *The Slavs: Their Early History and Civilization*. Boston, 1956. A thorough introduction.

Dvornik, Francis. *Byzantine Missions among the Slavs: SS. Constantine-Cyril and Methodius*. New Brunswick, N.J., 1970. The major historical source in English on the topic.

Geanakoplos, Deno John. *Byzantine East and Latin West: Two Worlds of Christendom in Middle Ages and Renaissance*. New York, 1966. Important insights on the cultural sources of ecclesiastical conflicts. Excellent study.

Greinacher, Norbert, and Virgil Elizondo, eds. *Churches in Socialist Societies of Eastern Europe*. Concilium, no. 154. New York, 1982. Centers on Roman Catholic concerns. A collection of articles of varying quality.

Hösch, Edgar. *The Balkans: A Short History from Greek Times to the Present Day*. London, 1972. Readable. A good introduction.

Hussey, Joan M., ed. *The Byzantine Empire*, vol. 4 of *The Cambridge Medieval History*, 2d ed. Cambridge, 1966. A standard reference volume. See parts 1 and 2, "Byzantium and Its Neighbours" and "Government, Church and Civilisation."

Jelavich, Charles, and Barbara Jelavich. *The Balkans*. Englewood Cliffs, N.J., 1965. A clearly narrated introduction with a number of helpful maps.

Lanckoronska, Karolina. *Studies on the Roman-Slavonic Rite in Poland*. Orientalia Christiana Analecta, no. 161. Rome, 1961. Provides evidence of early Eastern influence in Poland.

Latourette, K. S. *The Thousand Years of Uncertainty, A.D. 500–A.D. 1500*, vol. 2 of *A History of the Expansion of Christianity*. New York, 1938. Chapters 3 and 4 cover the early history of the spread of Christianity in eastern Europe from both the West and the East.

Mylonas, George E. *The Balkan States: An Introduction to Their History*. Saint Louis, 1946. A good overview. Argues the Greek position on Macedonia.

Nowak, Frank. *Medieval Slavdom and the Rise of Russia* (1930). Reprint, Westport, Conn., 1970. A readable short history of Russia to Catherine the Great.

Obolensky, Dimitri. *The Byzantine Commonwealth: Eastern Europe, 500–1453*. London, 1974. A history of Byzantium with a focus on the cultural, political, and ecclesiastical cohesion with the peoples of eastern Europe.

Purmonen, Veikko, ed. *Orthodoxy in Finland: Past and Present*. Kuopio, 1981. A collection of essays written by Orthodox Finns regarding their church.

Ware, Timothy. *The Orthodox Church*. Rev. ed. Baltimore, 1964. A clear, detailed introduction to the Orthodox church.

STANLEY SAMUEL HARAKAS

Christianity in Western Europe

Although the history of Christianity in each of the regions to which it has spread manifests certain special characteristics that set it apart, the development of Christianity within the history of western Europe has in many decisive ways shaped its development in all other regions. The English man of letters Hilaire Belloc (1870–1953) formulated the significance of that development—as well as a highly idiosyncratic and debatable philosophy of history—in his epigram of 1912: "Europe will return to the [Christian] faith, or she will perish. The faith is Europe. And Europe is the faith." Belloc's pronouncement is partly historical and partly hortatory, and even those who would vigorously reject the first and hortatory half of his formulation would probably acknowledge the historical force of the second half. Through most of its history, what most people, insiders or outsiders, have identified as the Christian faith has been the particular form that the Christian faith has acquired in its European experience. Asia, Africa, and the Americas have imported most of their Christianity from western Europe or Britain, and while Christianity did indeed begin in Asia Minor, most Christians in Asia Minor now practice and believe versions of Christianity that have come there only after having first been filtered through Europe. The history of Christianity in western continental Europe and the British Isles is, therefore, indispensable to the understanding of Christianity wherever it exists today. It is no less indispensable to the understanding of the history of western Europe itself. And in that sense at least, Belloc was right.

In recounting the history of Christianity in western Europe and the British Isles from the time of the apostle Paul to the present, this article is designed to account for the identification of Christianity with Europe and to describe its later significance. Therefore, various incidents and individual details of persons and places are selected as they illustrate the several stages of the process, and much more must be omitted than can be included.

Beginnings of Christianity in Europe. The coming of Christianity to Europe may in some ways be read as the leitmotif of the *Acts of the Apostles* in the New Testament. The entire life and ministry of Jesus had taken place in Palestine. He did not speak a European language, and except for a few Romans, such as Pontius Pilate, he did not meet any Europeans. *Acts* also begins within Palestine, in Jerusalem, but the story of the second half of the book is set largely in Europe, one of its high points being the confrontation of the apostle Paul with an audience in Athens (*Acts* 17) and its climactic conclusion coming in the final chapter with his arrival at Rome. It was either to Europe or from Europe that Paul addressed the bulk of his letters, including the three longest ones (*Romans* and *1* and *2 Corinthians*), and he wrote all of them in Greek. From the Gospels it would have been difficult to predict that Christianity would become European, much less that Europe would become Christian, but with the career of Paul that direction had begun to become clear.

For the period of two and a half centuries between the career of Paul and the conversion of the emperor Constantine (r. 306–337) there exist many items of information about the appearance of Christianity in one or another part of Europe. One of the most instructive of these is the account, preserved by Eusebius of Caesarea (c. 260/270–c. 339) in book 5 of his *Church History*, of the persecution of a Christian community at Lyons, in Gaul, in 177–178. The church in Gaul is thought by many scholars to have been the source of the earliest Christian missions to the British Isles, which date from the second or third century, when some of the Celtic inhabitants of Britain were converted (hence the usual designation "Celtic church"). The apostle Paul wrote to the church in Rome, "I hope to see you in passing as I go to Spain" (*Rom.* 15:24). Although the evidence for his having ever actually made such a journey to Spain is tenuous, tradition was quick to attribute one to him.

As that reference indicates, however, the most powerful Christian center in Europe was, from the beginning, at the most powerful city in Europe: Rome. One tradition attributes the founding of that community to the apostle Peter around AD 42, but critics of the credibility of that tradition have often pointed to the absence of any reference to Peter in the letter that Paul addressed to Rome fifteen years later (even though the final chapter of that letter is a catalog of proper names). But whoever it was that founded it, the Christian church at Rome was prominent enough both for Paul to send it his most important letter and for the emperor Nero to instigate a persecution of it, during which both Peter and Paul were said to have suffered martyrdom. That persecution did not diminish the power and prestige of the Roman church, which became a significant presence in the city and (especially after the capture of Jerusalem in AD 70 and its consequent decline as the mother city of Christianity) first among the Christian centers of Europe—indeed, of the Mediterranean world.

Although many of the most notable leaders of Christian thought during the second, third, and fourth centuries were not located in Europe but either in Alexandria (Clement, Origen, Alexander, Athanasius, Cyril) or in Roman North Africa (Tertullian, Cyprian, Augustine) or still in Asia Minor (Justin Martyr, Irenaeus, Cyril of Jerusalem, Jerome), most of them had some sort of European connection: Athanasius found asylum in Rome when he was driven out of Alexandria; before Jerome went to Palestine, he had undertaken the translation of the Vulgate at the behest of Pope Damasus, whom he served as secretary; Augustine was brought to Christianity in Europe through the teaching of Ambrose, bishop of Milan. Similarly, although the first seven ecumenical councils of the church were held at such Eastern cities as Nicaea, Constantinople, Ephesus, and Chalcedon, rather than in Rome or any other European city, it was in fact the power and prestige of Christian Europe that often determined their outcome. The Spanish bishop, Hosius of Córdoba, was in many ways the most authoritative of the bishops at Nicaea in 325, and when, according to the contemporary account, the bishops at Chalcedon in 451 declared that "Peter has spoken through the mouth of [Pope] Leo," they were acknowledging once more the special status that European Christianity had achieved as early as the beginning of the fourth century.

The event with the most far-reaching consequences for the history of European Christianity, indeed for the history of Christianity everywhere, was the conversion of the emperor Constantine and the ensuing transformation of the Roman empire into a Christian empire. That change took place on European soil when, in the Battle of the Milvian Bridge on 28 October 312, Constantine defeated the forces of his rival Maxentius, who was emperor for Italy and Africa, and thus became sole emperor. Attributing his victory to the Christian God, Constantine identified the cross of Christ as the "sacred sign" by which the Senate and the Roman people had been restored to their ancient glory. Christianity rapidly moved from being persecuted to being tolerated to being preferred to being established. Constantine in 330 transferred the capital of his newly christianized empire from Rome to Byzantium, renamed Constantinople, or "New Rome." For the history of Christianity in Europe, this move away from Europe served, somewhat ironically, to endow Europe with a position of even greater consequence for the future, for much of the aura that had surrounded Rome and the Roman emperor continued to surround Rome, but now descended instead upon the Roman bishop, who from Europe would declare and enforce his position in the collegial company of bishops as "first among equals" (equals who would become less equal in the process).

Simultaneous with the developing establishment of a Christian empire and of a christianized European society, and in part as a reaction against it, monasticism both Eastern and Western gave institutional form to the ascetic imperatives of primitive Christianity. [*See* Monasticism, *article on* Christian Monasticism.] Now that the sharp line of differentiation between the church and "the world" had been blurred, it was necessary to find a new and more striking way to draw the line by "forsaking the world" and going into a monastery. Above all, it was the work of Benedict of Nursia (c. 480–c. 547), through his *Rule*, that gave European monasticism a settled form. The monks were to become the principal missionaries to the new populations of Europe as well as the principal transmitters of the cultural heritage, classical as well as Christian, and thus the educators of medieval Europe. It was in recognition of this role that Benedict has been designated "patron saint of Europe."

Medieval Europe. In all of these ways European Christianity was developing in the direction of the forms and structures it was to have when it came to deal with the new populations that arrived in Europe. The beginning of the Middle Ages may be defined for our purposes here as the period during which those new populations were becoming Christian.

Some of these, most notably the Goths, had already become Christian before their arrival: Ulfilas, the fourth-century "apostle of the Goths," had worked among them as a missionary, translating the Bible into

Gothic. Paradoxically, however, the christianization of the Goths was to work against them when they came to Europe, because the form of Christianity that Ulfilas had brought them was tainted with the Arian heresy and therefore stood in the way of an immediate political alliance between the Goths and the bishop of Rome. The future of Christian Europe belonged to such an alliance, in which all the Germanic, Celtic, and western Slavic tribes would eventually share. Among these tribes it was the Franks who came to assume a position of leadership when, in a reprise of Constantine's conversion, their king, Clovis, became an orthodox Catholic Christian in 496. With the support of the Catholic episcopate, Clovis set about the task of subduing the "heretical" Visigoths, militarily and then ecclesiastically, in the name of the orthodox faith. As a consequence, in the course of the two centuries after Clovis, the Frankish crown became the principal protector of the Roman see, which reciprocated by supporting Frankish political and territorial ambitions. The coronation as Holy Roman Emperor of the Frankish king Charles, known to history as Charlemagne, by the pope in the year 800 was as much the recognition of an already existing status quo as it was the creation of anything new, but it has served ever since as perhaps the primary symbol of the spiritual unity of "Christian Europe" as a cultural entity.

The christianization of Europe and of the nations that came into Europe was at the same time the conquest of their indigenous religious traditions, sometimes by missionary activity and sometimes by military victory. Formally and externally, the conquest was taken to mean the total obliteration of the old faith. Thus, when in the early 720s Boniface, the Benedictine monk who bears the title "apostle of Germany," chopped down an oak sacred to the worship of the German god Thor at Geismar, this was interpreted to be the replacement of the "false gods" of paganism with the Christian deity. Yet the same Thor or Donar, god of thunder *(Donner)*, was to give his name to the Germanic designations for the sixth day of the Christian week ("Thursday" or "Donnerstag"), the very week that began with a Sunday devoted to the weekly commemoration of the resurrection of Jesus Christ. Similarly, Friday took its name from Frija, Germanic goddess of love and counterpart of Venus, who gave her name to that same day in French. The names of gods were sometimes transformed into the names of saints who often had the same provenance and some of the same functions as the gods. In sending Augustine to Kent, Pope Gregory I (r. 590–604) gave instructions that the new centers of Christian worship should be at the places already revered as holy by the native population; thus, sacred springs and streams became the sites of Christian baptisms. "Conquest," therefore, involved some measure of continuity as well as the more obvious forms of discontinuity.

Conversely, Christianity became European at the cost of increasing discontinuity between itself and Christian churches elsewhere. Such ruptures of continuity took place even within Western Christianity, as the centralized authority of Rome—administrative, liturgical, sometimes also doctrinal—clashed with older regional systems. Much of the *History of the English Church and People* by Bede "the Venerable" (c. 673–735) is devoted to the process by which older "Celtic" practices on such questions as monastic tonsure and the date of Easter had to surrender to customs developed on the continent and enforced by the papacy. Even more dramatic and far-reaching in their implications were the deepening differences between East and West. As "New Rome," Constantinople developed forms of organization and worship that gave to Byzantine Christianity a special character that it was to transmit to its daughter churches in eastern Europe. The dream of a single Christian empire reaching from one end of the Mediterranean to the other, all held together by a Greco-Roman Christian culture, never became a reality for any significant length of time, not even under the emperor Justinian (r. 527–565), who strove to achieve it by every means available, from armies to dogmas to jurisprudence. And as the Christianity of western Europe began to come of age, its family resemblance to Byzantium became less discernible. The rise and rapid expansion of Islam in the seventh and eighth centuries had, among many other consequences, the result of isolating Eastern Christendom and the Christianity of western Europe from each other. Fundamental differences of missionary methodology asserted themselves, most prominently in the christianization of the Slavs during the ninth and tenth centuries. Byzantium sought to make a nation Christian by translating the Bible and the liturgy into that nation's language, Rome sought to do so by teaching it to pray in Latin and to accept Roman primacy. The collision between these two methodologies on the Slavic mission field coincided with increasing tensions over jurisdictional questions (such as the proper titles for the patriarchs of Old and New Rome) and doctrinal disputes (such as that over the procession of the Holy Spirit from the Father and the Son). All of these were symptomatic of the growing alienation—or, to put the matter more positively, of the growing self-awareness of western Europe as a Christian civilization in its own right rather than a Byzantine outpost.

One other difference between Byzantine Christianity and the Christianity of western Europe during the Middle Ages was political. Although the Eastern church was not the servile department of state that Western polemics have often described it to have been, its vision of the Christian empire did view the imperial power as having been transmitted directly from God through Christ to the emperor, without the mediation of church and hierarchy. By contrast, as the symbolism of the coronation of Charlemagne by the pope suggested, the mediation of the church was seen in the West as essential to the legitimacy of political power; it was seen that way by a succession of popes, but also by many emperors and kings, who invoked papal authority to validate their political sovereignty. Claiming the right to "bind" and "loose" (cf. *Mt.* 16:18–19) not only the forgiveness of sins but also political office, the papacy repeatedly came into conflict with the civil power, which often made use of the territorial church in its own land as an instrument of power politics. In the conflict between Pope Gregory VII and Emperor Henry IV, climaxing in their encounter at Canossa in 1077, one of the issues was the tension between the particularistic ambitions both of the German emperor and of the German church and the universal claims of the pope, who, as part of his campaign to purify and reform the church, strove to secure its independence from the economic and political entanglements of the feudal system. A century later, Thomas Becket, archbishop of Canterbury, defended those universal claims against the king of England, Henry II, and was murdered in 1170.

Combining as they did religious zeal, military ambition, national rivalry, and a yearning for the exotic, the Crusades, beginning at the Council of Clermont in 1095 and ending with the Turkish victory over the Christian forces at Nicopolis in 1396, were, on one level, an expression of the medieval ideal of a united Western Christian Europe: England, France, Germany, and Italy joined forces under the cross of Christ and with the inspiration and blessing of the church to rescue the "holy places" in Palestine. On another level, however, the Crusades are frequently interpreted as a disaster both for Christianity and for Europe, for they not only failed to achieve their goal in Palestine but also proved to be divisive within Christendom itself. [*See* Crusades.] The Crusades, as well as the confrontations between "spiritual" and "secular" authority, for which parallels can be found throughout the history of European and British Christianity both in the Middle Ages and since, illustrate the church's paradoxical role as simultaneously the patron of national cultures (whose kings were said to rule "by the grace of God") and the embodiment of a cultural ideal transcending all national boundaries.

That paradox was also at work in other aspects of medieval culture. In the millennium from Boethius (c. 475–c. 525) to Martin Luther (1483–1546), the intellectual history of Europe during the Middle Ages is, to a remarkable extent, the history of Christian thought in its interaction with philosophy, science, and political theory, as these came into medieval Europe both from classical antiquity and from contemporary Islam and Judaism; the Scholasticism of the twelfth and thirteenth centuries, whose most influential spokesman was Thomas Aquinas (c. 1225–1274), was an important chapter in the history of philosophy no less than in that of theology. [*See* Scholasticism.] Much of the architecture of the Middle Ages was made possible by the needs of the church for basilicas, abbeys, and cathedrals, and its art by the themes of Christian worship and devotion. Sacred music and secular music not only coexisted but interacted, both in the monastery and in the community. Early monuments of the literatures of Europe, such as *Beowulf* and the Norse sagas, document the blending of Christian and non-Christian elements in western Europe, and so, under more explicitly Christian inspiration, do late monuments such as *Piers Plowman* and Dante's *Commedia*. Here again, the relation between universal and particular—a Latin literature, which is European, versus the several vernacular literatures, which are national—manifests the ambivalence of the Christian role in what the medieval historian Robert S. Lopez has called "the birth of Europe."

Europe in the Reformation. Thus there were in medieval Europe, and in the Christianity of medieval Europe, centrifugal forces far more powerful than could be acknowledged by the political and ecclesiastical rhetoric of the oneness of the *corpus Christianum*. Such oneness as there was had probably reached its zenith in 1215 at the Fourth Lateran Council, when political and ecclesiastical representatives from all over western Europe had hailed the authority of Pope Innocent III. [*See* Papacy.] But both before and after that council, this authority and the unity it symbolized were in jeopardy. National churches pledged their allegiance to the pope—and went their own way in polity, liturgy, and religious practice. Kings and emperors craved anointing from the church, but often craved its property and power even more. And theologians opened their treatises with affirmations of their creedal orthodoxy, but manipulated the ambiguities of creedal language to ignore or revise or even undermine the dogmatic tradition.

But whatever cleavages of nations, parties, and schools of thought there may have been in medieval Europe, the principle—and the illusion—of unity-within-diversity remained. All of that was shattered by the Reformation of the sixteenth century. [*See* Reformation.] Conditions in the church throughout western Europe during the later Middle Ages had convinced nearly everyone that some sort of reform *in capite et membris* ("in head and members"), as the saying went, was needed; there were widespread complaints about episcopal and clerical negligence, abuses of authority at all levels were perceived to be rampant, ignorance and superstition among the people were being overlooked or even encouraged by the church, and even the most responsible voices in ecclesiastical positions acknowledged that almost every high official (sometimes up to and including the pope) could be suspected of having bought his office and thus of having committed the sin of simony. The spectacle of a schism between two popes, one at Rome and the other at Avignon, seemed to prove that the medieval tradition of reform, as enunciated in the eleventh century by Gregory VII, was inadequate to the crisis of the fifteenth century. During that century, a series of church councils (Pisa, 1409; Constance, 1414–1417; Basel-Ferrara-Florence, 1431–1445) sought to achieve reform by legislating changes in church life, reestablishing (unsuccessfully) ties to the Eastern churches, formulating orthodox doctrine on various issues, such as purgatory, that had not been set down before, and clarifying the relation between the authority of the pope and the authority of the council. This last issue led to new schisms, this time between pope and council. Some advocates of reform, notably Jan Hus in Bohemia, even set into motion forces that would produce separate churches.

In the intellectual and cultural life of Europe, this was at the same time a period of intense activity and of vigorous change. Although it is historically incorrect to interpret the humanism of the Renaissance, whether Italian or Northern, as a rejection of the essential content of Christianity, it did represent an attack on many of its received traditions. Thus the humanists attacked medieval Scholasticism both for its ignorance of classical culture and for its distortion of Christianity. They made the monks the object of ridicule for caricaturing the ethical imperatives of the New Testament, and they pointed to the contradictions between those imperatives and a great deal that was going on in the institutional life of European Christianity. In keeping with the humanistic motto "Back to the sources!" Italian humanists like Lorenzo Valla (1406–1457) and northern humanists like Erasmus (1469?–1536) devoted their scholarly attention to recovering the original text and the authentic message of the New Testament, and in this sense they also belong to the history of late medieval reform. Humanist and churchman at once, Francisco Jiménez de Cisneros (1436–1517) demonstrated the possibility of holding together Roman Catholic orthodoxy and a commitment to educational and ecclesiastical reform. [*See* Humanism.]

What kind of evolution of Christianity all these various reform movements would have brought about on their own is a subject only for speculation. For it was revolution, not evolution, that swept across Christian Europe during the sixteenth century, transforming both the map of Europe itself and the character of European Christianity in the process. The one church of the Middle Ages became the several churches of the Reformation. Each of these reformations was to shape the history of European Christianity in a distinct way.

The Lutheran Reformation carried out into cultural, political, and ecclesiastical structures the impulses set in motion by Martin Luther's struggle for faith. Although Luther began that struggle on the assumption that he could find salvation only within the institutional forms of the Western church, he ended by repudiating many of them, even denouncing the pope as Antichrist. A right relation with God was the consequence not of human moral striving but of the divine gift of forgiving grace. That gift, moreover, was appropriated by faith alone, faith being understood as confidence and trust in the divine promise. And the authority for knowing this promise and being assured of this grace was not the voice of the church, but the word of God in the Bible. To be sure, these three Reformation principles—often cited in their Latin formulations as *sola gratia*, *sola fide*, *sola Scriptura*—became the common property of much of Protestantism, not only of Lutheranism, even though Lutheranism often claimed to be alone in carrying them out consistently. But in the Lutheran churches of Europe, above all in Germany and Scandinavia, these principles, enunciated officially in the Augsburg Confession of 1530, served as the foundation for new developments in many fields of culture. The Lutheran chorale, which began with the hymns of Luther himself, flourished from the sixteenth to the eighteenth century, producing not only hundreds of new liturgies and hymnals but also the sacred music of Johann Sebastian Bach (1685–1750). In formulating the implications of the Reformation principles, the theologians of the Lutheran church constructed systems of Christian doctrine that sometimes rivaled those of the medieval Scholastics for comprehensiveness, if not for philosophical sophistication.

The Calvinist tradition—or, as it has often preferred to identify itself, the Reformed tradition—shared many of the central emphases of the Lutheran Reformation, but sought to carry them out with greater consistency. As worked out in the career and thought of John Calvin (1509–1564), it took *sola Scriptura* to mean an elimination of those features in worship and Christian culture that could not claim explicit biblical warrant. The primacy and sovereignty of divine grace implied that not only salvation, but also damnation, was the consequence of the will of God. Perhaps most important of all was the Reformed belief that the social order, no less than the life of the individual believer, must be brought into conformity with the revealed word of God. In the Calvinist lands of Europe, therefore, far more than in the Lutheran ones, the Reformation brought about a concerted effort to reshape politics and economics in accordance with this standard. Whether or not this helped to create a spiritual climate in which modern European capitalism was able to take seed, as Max Weber and other scholars have contended, is still a matter of controversy, but Calvinism certainly did shape attitudes toward work, property, social justice, and public order not only in the Swiss and other non-Lutheran forms of Protestantism on the continent, but far beyond the borders of western Europe (including North America).

One of the regions in which the Calvinist Reformation became a major cultural force was the British Isles. Through the reformatory work of John Knox (c. 1514–1572), it was the Reformed version of Protestantism that prevailed in Scotland. Doctrinally this meant that the Scots Confession of 1560, which Knox composed together with several colleagues, was to be the first official statement of the teaching of the Reformed Church of Scotland, until it was replaced by the Westminster Confession of 1647. Liturgically, the Reformed character of the Church of Scotland was guaranteed by *The Book of Common Order* (1556–1564), in which Knox and his associates set down forms of worship that in their judgment conformed to the scriptures and affirmed the evangelical commitments of Reformation faith.

The relation of England to the Reformed tradition was considerably more equivocal. Although the earliest influences of the continental Reformation came to England through the writings and the disciples of Luther, the terms of the settlement that emerged from the break with Rome occasioned by the divorce of Henry VIII (1491–1547) avoided putting the Church of England unambiguously into any one confessional camp. *The Book of Common Prayer*, the retention of the apostolic succession of ordaining bishops, and the Thirty-nine Articles, taken together despite their deep differences of approach, defined the settlement. It was only with the rise of Puritanism and its protest against such ambiguity that Reformed patterns of churchmanship and theology began to press for control within Anglicanism. The established church of the sixteenth and seventeenth centuries left a permanent imprint on English culture through such literary monuments as the Authorized Version of the Bible and (despite profound divergences) the works of John Milton (1608–1674).

Unless the term *Reformation* is understood in a polemical and denominational sense as coextensive with the term *Protestantism*, however, it is necessary to include in it the history of the Roman Catholic reformation as well, and not simply to interpret this as a "counterreformation." The Protestant Reformation did not exhaust the imperative sense of reform within the church. In every country of Europe, therefore, Luther's activity evoked not only a defense of Roman Catholic doctrine and order but also a call for greater dedication to the cause of reform. The most abiding expression of that dedication came at the Council of Trent (1545–1563), which reaffirmed the church's teaching by identifying which positions among the many being espoused by churchmen and theologians lay within the bounds of orthodoxy and which did not. No less urgent an item on the council's agenda was the elimination of the abuses to which its fifteenth-century predecessors had already addressed their attention. Bishops were now obliged to be resident in their dioceses, instead of collecting the income and leaving the duties to surrogates. Preaching and teaching were prominent among those duties, and therefore the professional training of future clergy in seminaries was incumbent on the church everywhere. Implementation of the Catholic reformation was entrusted not only to a revitalized episcopate and clergy and a reformed papacy but also to the renewal of the religious orders and to the development of a new religious order, indeed, a new kind of order, in the Society of Jesus, founded by Ignatius Loyola (1491–1556). In part to compensate for the losses of European territory to Protestantism, the Jesuits and other religious orders undertook an intensification of missionary activity in the New World, as well as in Asia.

Also a part of the Reformation in Europe, despite their exclusion from conventional accounts, were the representatives of the several radical reformations. Anabaptism criticized Lutheranism and Calvinism for not having gone far enough in their rejection of traditional Roman Catholic forms, and it pressed for a "believers' church," in which only those who made a public commitment and confession would be members; since that excluded infants, the practice of infant baptism was repudiated. To be consistent, many of the Anabaptists, notably the Mennonites, likewise disavowed the Constantinian union between church and state, and some of them even repudiated the definition of "just war" and hence the theory that Christians could wield the sword. Although such groups as the Mennonites retained the orthodox doctrines of the Trinity and the divinity of Christ, the radical critique of traditional Christianity led others to question these as well. Despite their relatively small numbers, the churches and sects of the radical Reformation were expressing misgivings about the forms of institutional and orthodox Christianity, misgivings that appear to have been widespread, though unacknowledged, throughout Europe, both Roman Catholic and Protestant. Thus the end result of the Reformation was a Europe balkanized into confessions and denominations that continued to divide among themselves, a Europe in which the assumptions of a thousand years about a common Christian worldview were less and less valid.

European Christianity in the Modern Period. If it is correct to characterize the era of the Reformation as a time when revolution began to replace evolution as a means of dealing with the problems of church and state, it is even more appropriate to see the situation of European Christianity in the modern period as one of coping with an age of revolution—or, more accurately, of revolutions in every sphere of human activity. One of the most widely used histories of Christianity in the modern period bears the title *The Church in an Age of Revolution*.

Politically, the Europe that emerged from the conflicts of the Reformation would seem to be the negation of revolution. When history textbooks speak of this as "the age of absolutism," they are referring to the achievement, under such monarchs as Louis XIV of France (r. 1643–1715), of a level of royal authority seldom witnessed before or since, in which the church, though with some reluctance, acted as a buttress of the secular power. Yet before the century that began with Louis XIV on the throne of France had ended, the overthrow of monarchy in France and the proclamation of a new order (even of a new calendar) symbolized the end of secular absolutism, and increasingly the end of Christian hegemony. Many of the leaders of the French Revolution were openly hostile not only to the institutional church but also to the principal teachings of the Christian tradition as a whole; others sought a more positive relation between Christianity and revolution. Both overt opposition and the quest for rapprochement were to play a part in Christian reactions to the successive revolutions of modern Europe, for example in 1848. Christianity was identified, by friend and foe alike, as allied with the ancient regime; and by the time it had come to terms with the revolutionary regime, that was already being overthrown by a new revolution, with which Christianity must once more come to terms. A permanent outcome of those seemingly constant shifts was the creation, in many countries of Europe, of Christian democratic parties, sometimes at the conservative end of the political spectrum but often centrist in their policies, and even of various forms of Christian socialism. The condemnation of socialism and of other modern revolutionary movements in the *Syllabus of Errors* issued by Pope Pius IX in 1864 must be seen in counterpoint with the "social encyclicals," especially those of Pope Leo XIII (r. 1878–1903), which articulated a reconciliation of Christian teachings with the best in the democratic systems; a similar range of political opinion, and thus of response to the revolutions of the time, was present as well in the various branches of European Protestantism during the eighteenth and nineteenth centuries. [*See* Modernism, *article on* Christian Modernism.]

What Christians of all denominations found objectionable in much of revolutionary ideology was not only its attack on political regimes with which the institutional church had made its peace, but also its alliance with intellectual and social movements that seemed bent on undermining the Christian faith itself. Thus the theoretical foundations of both the French and the American revolutions contained many elements of the philosophy of the Enlightenment. Against the traditional Christian insistence on the need for revelation, Enlightenment thought defended the capacity of the natural mind to find the truth about the good life, and against the Christian distinction between the capacities of human nature and the superadded gift of divine grace, it ascribed to human nature the ability to live in accordance with that truth. Enlightenment science, and above all the philosophy that both underlay much of the science and was based upon it, seemed increasingly to make the Christian doctrine of creation irrelevant. [*See* Enlightenment, The.]

Enlightenment thought was the most vigorous expression of the more general attack on traditional European Christianity known as "secularism," which may be defined as the belief that, here in this world (Lat., *saeculum*), religious ideas about revelation and eternal life are not necessary to the development of a good life for the individual or society. Philosophically that belief has expressed itself in the construction of rational systems of thought and of conduct that attacked or simply ignored the claims of supernatural grace and revelation. Politically it took the form of gradually withdrawing from the church the privileged status it had held in the countries of Europe. Public education excluded Christian teaching from its curriculum and Christian ceremonies from its practice. The state would determine the criteria for what made a marriage valid, and the church ritual would at best serve only as a public attestation of a status defined by secular criteria. The clergy, who in medieval Europe had been tried in their own courts even for offenses against the political order (the issue on which Becket had clashed with the English crown) lost their special legal standing. Of the many instances in modern European history when secularism and Christianity clashed, the most renowned was probably the *Kulturkampf* in nineteenth-century Germany, in which the newly united German empire took drastic steps to curb the cultural and political status of the Roman Catholic church. Although most of those steps were in fact eventually reversed, the *Kulturkampf* has come to symbolize a pattern widespread throughout Europe.

The case of the *Kulturkampf* suggests another closely related phenomenon that has also been a major force in redefining the place of Christianity in modern European culture, the dominance of nationalism. The nineteenth century, the "great century" of Christian missions, was as well the century of nationalist expansion into the European colonial empires. As the custodian of nationality and the patron of the national cultures of Christian Europe, Christianity had long maintained a dual role in fostering and yet restraining the devotion to the nation. Now that such devotion was assuming the proportions of a principal rival to the church for the deepest loyalties of European populations, this dual role meant that Christianity sometimes expressed itself in national terms so exclusive as to obscure its universal significance. One of the most frequent arenas for the clash between Christianity and national aspirations has been the effort of national governments to control the governance of the church within their own territories on such questions as episcopal appointments: Gallicanism was the effort by French ecclesiastics and statesmen to assert what were taken to be the historic rights of the church in France against the centralized ultramontane authority of the papacy. The most notorious expression of national religion came in the program of the German Christians in Nazi Germany, who identified the Christian gospel with Germanic ideology and Aryan purity.

As the supreme expression of nationalistic devotion, modern warfare has also been the ultimate test of Christianity's relation to European culture. From Augustine and Thomas Aquinas had come the definition of just war, which Christianity applied, with greater or lesser appropriateness, to modern European wars from the Thirty Years' War to World War II. Church leaders in European nations on both sides during those wars invoked the blessing of the same Christian God not only on the individuals who fought but also on the nationalist cause for which they fought. The same church leaders, however, often reminded their nations of the moral demands of a humanity beyond the nation, and in the efforts for peace and reconstruction after a war Christianity has often played a constructive role. The archbishop of Uppsala, Nathan Söderblom (1866–1931), received the Nobel Peace Prize in 1930 for his work after World War I. In the aftermath of the invention of nuclear weapons, Christianity in Europe—joined then by both Roman Catholicism and Protestantism elsewhere—took the lead in the task of rethinking the very notion of just war. It was also from Christianity in Europe that there came the reminder of what Pope John Paul II called "the common Christian roots of the nations of Europe" and the summons to find in those roots a vision of the continuing relation between Christianity and European culture. Thus, in a sense quite different from Belloc's own, the thesis that "Europe is the faith, and the faith is Europe" has continued to find support.

[*See also* New Religions, *article on* New Religions and Cults in Europe.]

BIBLIOGRAPHY

Bainton, Roland H. *The Reformation of the Sixteenth Century*. New ed. Foreword by Jaroslav Pelikan. Boston, 1985. Deceptively clear yet complex and profound, a splendid introduction to the subject, with bibliographies that carry the reader to the next level.

Cambridge Medieval History. 8 vols. Cambridge, 1911–1936. There is no volume of this comprehensive work without direct relevance to the understanding of the history of Christianity in Europe.

Cambridge Modern History. 13 vols. Cambridge, 1902–1912. Antiquated though it is in both methodology and facts, this remains the most useful account of the entire story. Its very quaintness makes its discussions of Christianity especially helpful.

Chadwick, Owen. *The Reformation*. The Pelican History of the Church, vol. 3. Baltimore, 1964. Together with the other volumes of the series listed below (Cragg, Neill, Southern, and Vidler), the best place for the English reader to begin.

Cragg, Gerald R. *The Church and the Age of Reason, 1648–1789*. Baltimore, 1960. Remarkably free of animus, a thoughtful and provocative reading of the Enlightenment.

Fliche, Augustin, and Victor Martin, eds. *Histoire de l'Église, depuis les origines jusqu'à nos jours*. 21 vols. Paris, 1935–1964. Each volume of this learned set provides information and insight; Émile Amann's *L'époque carolingienne* (Paris, 1937), the sixth volume, stands alone as an account of the Carolingian period and its aftermath.

Latourette, K. S. *A History of the Expansion of Christianity*. 7 vols. New York, 1937–1945. As Stephen Neill (see below) has said, "It is baffling to his successors that, when we think we have made some specially bright discovery of our own, we nearly always find that he has been there before us."

Neill, Stephen C. *A History of Christian Missions*. Baltimore, 1964. European without being Eurocentric, it puts European Christianity into a world context.

Nichols, James. *History of Christianity, 1650–1950*. New York, 1956. As its title suggests, this volume makes "secularization" its central theme.

Pelikan, Jaroslav. *The Christian Tradition: A History of the Development of Doctrine*. 4 vols. Chicago, 1971–1984. Not exclusively, but primarily, European in its focus.

Southern, Richard W. *Western Society and the Church in the*

Middle Ages. Harmondsworth, 1970. Unlike most histories of medieval Christianity, Southern's narrative concentrates on society and culture in the Middle Ages.

Vidler, Alec. *The Church in an Age of Revolution*. Baltimore, 1961. A judicious selection of persons and events to interpret the history of Christianity, especially in Europe, during the past two centuries.

Wand, J. W. C. *A History of the Modern Church from 1500 to the Present Day*. London, 1946. An interesting contrast to the viewpoint set forth by other volumes in this bibliography.

JAROSLAV PELIKAN

Christianity in Latin America

The discovery of Santo Domingo in 1492 marks the beginning of Latin American church history. There were no priests among the one hundred men aboard the *Pinta*, the *Niña*, and the *Santa Maria;* nevertheless, the seamen were Spanish Christians. To be Spanish or Portuguese around the beginning of the sixteenth century meant being impregnated with that particular concept of church and state that had spawned the Crusades, with tragic consequences for the indigenous American peoples. Only ten months before Columbus's landing, Spain had expelled the Moors from Granada and thus concluded its eight-centuries-old war of liberation. Fired by the conviction that the Spanish crown was the divinely chosen instrument for the salvation of the New World, Isabel and Ferdinand, and, later, Philip, promoted the Conquest wholeheartedly. They sent fifteen hundred men in a convoy of seventeen ships on the second expedition in 1493, including civil representatives, an ecclesiastical delegation (headed by the famous Benedictine Bernard Boyl), and a contingent of nobles to garner lands and servants for Christ. The decadent feudal society thus imposed artificially extended Spanish structures and indelibly stamped the organization and future of Latin American society, to the great detriment of both.

The "enemy" to be conquered in the New World bore no resemblance to the evicted Moors. Anthropologists and historians differ widely among themselves as to the nature of the cultural disparity between the Spanish and the higher Indian civilizations. Some estimate that the Indians had reached approximately the level of the first Egyptian dynasty; others reject such cultural comparisons as unilateral. The Aztec, the Maya, and the Inca lived in basically sedentary, agricultural communities, some of which were subject to the higher cultural influence; others were nomadic and tended to be more primitive in culture and religion. The syncretic Indian religions incarnated traditional dualisms: day and night, sun and moon, good and evil, subject to an overarching, implacable fate. The amazing rapidity with which these cultures were destroyed resulted, at least in part, from the superiority of Spanish weaponry, the use of horses (which had disappeared in indigenous prehistory), and the brutal annihilation of ancient beliefs and customs in order to impose a religion and form of life incomprehensible to the Indian peoples.

Agreements between the popes and Iberian Catholic kings go back to the thirteenth century, when Portugal was given ecclesiastical, political, and economic rights over countries discovered and to be discovered. Near the end of the successful reconquest of Granada, two papal bulls were issued, giving the Spanish kings extensive powers over ecclesiastical matters there. In 1493 the Roman pope conceded rights of jurisdiction to the Spanish and Portuguese crowns over discoveries on either side of an imaginary line drawn from north to south 100 leagues (556 km) west of the Azores, moved 370 leagues (2,054 km) farther west in 1494. Although there have been different interpretations as to whether the rights dispensed by the pope were territorial or solely ecclesiastical, the Catholic kings understood both to be included and acted accordingly. The right to the lands was coupled with the duty to evangelize the native peoples. The extension of the kingdom of God was the goal.

The royal rights conferred by the papal concordat included the establishment of bishoprics in the conquered territories, the nomination of bishops, the reception of tithes for the furtherance of evangelical work, the building of convents and churches, the appointment of all clergy, and the sending of missionaries. Thus both civil and ecclesiastical concerns were united under one head, the king, and the pope was effectively excluded from all decision making in the conversion of the Americas. The creation of the Supreme Council of the Indies (1524) facilitated the execution of the king's rights and will through civil authorities: viceroys and their various subordinates were appointed for New Spain (Mexico) in 1535, for Peru (the Andean region) in 1544, for Granada (greater Colombia) in 1717, and for the Plata (River Plate area) in 1776.

Colonial Church (1492–1808). The conquistadors were fired by a medieval devotion to the extension of Christendom. The Catholic monarchs, Ferdinand of Aragon and Isabel of Castile, supported by the staunch integralist Francisco Jiménez de Cisneros and succeeded by Charles I (as Holy Roman Emperor, Charles V) and Philip II, molded Spain into a unified nation that would be capable of what each believed to be a divine mission—the christianization of the Americas. Together they directed the political-ecclesiastical enterprise for 124 years.

Foundations of the colonial church. The first twenty-five years following the discovery of Santo Domingo saw the implantation of Spanish colonies in the Caribbean basin. Few priests accompanied the first voyages. In the ten years following, 125 priests (including 89 Franciscans and 32 Dominicans) went to the West Indies to evangelize an estimated 250,000 natives. Their equipment included materials for the building of churches and monasteries, books, trinkets for opening communication with the Indians, and subsistence items. Of particular significance during this initial period were the prophetic denunciations of the abuse of the Indians made by two Dominicans, Antonio de Montesinos (in 1511) and Bartolomé de Las Casas (from 1514 until 1566). [*See the biography of Las Casas.*] The greatest obstacles to the mission were the use of armed force in the subjection of the natives and the *encomienda* system by which the Indians were assigned to the care of those who received lands for the purposes of work and instruction in the Christian faith.

The conquest and christianization of the mainland began with Hernando Cortés in Mexico (1519) and was extended to Peru by Francisco Pizarro (1531). These men were accompanied by priests, both regular and secular clergy. For the most part the regulars (monastic orders) concentrated on the mission, while the secular clergy served as parish priests of the Spanish, Creole, and, later, much of the mestizo, population.

Church organizations proliferated during the sixteenth century. By the close of the century, some fifteen bishoprics had been established in each of the two then-existing viceroyalties, Mexico and Peru. Soon after the conquest, diocesan and provincial meetings were held to determine polity and practice for institutional and mission work. Of the fifteen provincial councils held during the colonial period, the four of greatest importance were Lima I (1551) and III (1582–1583) and Mexico I (1555) and III (1585).

In Lima I the first forty resolutions established the organization of the Inca Indian Church on the basis of the original tribal and regional divisions of the empire. Also, catechetical instruction in the language of the people was required prior to baptism. The eighty resolutions that followed set forth the colonial ecclesiastical structure, marking clearly the division between Spanish and Indian sectors of society.

The first Mexican council treated with deep concern such matters as the indoctrination of the indigenous peoples, the use of their native languages in evangelization, their need for sacraments, the regulation of their traditional feasts and dances, the establishment of separate villages for them, and their freedom in choosing spouses. The councils of Lima III and Mexico III were influenced by the Council of Trent (1545–1563) and indicated a continuing concern about ecclesiastical and clerical reforms and the welfare of the Indians, whose numbers had dropped substantially during this period.

Civil authorities and churchmen agreed that the separation of the Indians into their own villages was the best policy. For the colonists it assured better control of the native tribes and family groups, and for the missionary priests it made their indoctrination and christianization more effective. As early as 1539 the Franciscan Fray Juan de Almeda established such a village in Huejotzingo, near Puebla in Mexico, for over forty thousand Indians. The Franciscans were soon followed by the Dominicans, Augustinians, and Mercedarians, but many areas in the wide expanses of territory were without spiritual care. Near the end of the sixteenth century, the priest Juan de Mendieta wrote that some priests traveled more than a hundred miles to minister to groups of over one hundred thousand Indians.

Quarrels were frequent between the religious orders over jurisdiction in the villages, but were even more frequent between the orders and the secular priests of the church. Schools, trades, civil government, and hospitals were established in the villages. Early attempts were made to prepare indigenous clergy, but after disheartening experiences, most of the church authorities agreed that the natives were not sufficiently dependable. Several early councils and for a time several monastic orders specifically forbade the ordination of non-Spanish priests.

The church in Brazil developed more slowly than in the Spanish colonies. Although six Jesuits arrived as early as 1549, only seven bishoprics existed at the time of independence. As in Spanish America, the religious orders bravely supported royal edicts commanding decent treatment for the Indians, but the practice of royal governors and landholders, who wanted Indians as slaves, won out over theory. The Jesuits, often criticized for amassing economic power, were expelled from Brazil in 1759.

An explosive situation and a significant number of uprisings both in the black and Indian populations resulted from the large numbers of Africans brought as slaves to Brazil. By 1818 more than half the population (excluding the Indians in the interior) was black; 23 percent were white; 17 percent, mestizo; and 7 percent, Indian.

Missions. Real efforts were made by the kings to christianize the indigenous population, as stipulated in the concordat. After the initial discovery of the Americas, the conquistadors were always well accompanied by priests, chiefly Franciscans, Dominicans, and Augustinians. Within fifty years members of these orders numbered over eight hundred in Mexico alone. Thereafter, the Jesuits and other orders added strength to the missionary effort.

The method of the missionaries, in general, was to uproot old rites and most external manifestations of Indian religion (on the principle of *tabula rasa*) in order to teach the true, Catholic religion. After an initial and not too successful attempt to use translators, many of the priests determined to learn the native languages. Evangelization was carried out in two different ways in the sixteenth century: (1) in the *encomienda* a priest was assigned large numbers of natives for pastoral care, indoctrination, and administration of the sacraments; (2) itinerant priests went from village to village, often suffering great hardships, preaching, baptizing, and defending the Indians against abuse. Although force was still used when necessary, many Indians were converted by peaceful means through the direct approach of the priests. Unfortunately, the good done was often subverted by the subsequent incorporation of the new Christians into the forced labor system.

Historians differ as to the culpability of the Spaniards in their christianization of New Spain (Mexico, which included what is now Texas and the southwest United States) and of Peru (which included parts of Colombia, Ecuador, Bolivia, and Chile). That there was unspeakable cruelty and that large sections of the Indian population were decimated are clear historical facts. It is equally clear that many priests, like Las Casas (e.g., Montolinia, Valdieso, Anchieta, Zumárraga, and Juan del Valle) fought for Indian rights against civil leaders, plantation and mine owners, and even other clerics. A body of ordinances called *New Laws for the Indies* was adopted in 1542, papal encyclicals were issued (e.g., that of Paul III in 1537), and royal edicts were emitted by both Spanish and Portuguese kings, all of which required just treatment of the Indians.

A key point at issue is the number of Indians present in the Americas at the time of the Conquest. Estimates vary from six million to nearly a hundred million. The Brazilian J. V. Cesár, a member of the National Indigenist Council, estimates thirty-five million both at the time of the Conquest and in the late twentieth century (*Atualização* 12, Belo Horizonte, 1981, p. 27). Sherburne F. Cook and Woodrow Borah carefully estimated that the nearly seventeen million Indians in central Mexico in 1532 were reduced to just over one million by 1608 (*The Indian Population of Central Mexico, 1531–1610*, Berkeley, 1960, p. 48). The exaggerated claims for baptisms must be viewed critically: Pedro de Gante claimed fourteen thousand in one day; Bishop Zumárraga of Mexico reported that Franciscans alone had baptized more than one million by 1531. Another chronicler claimed that more than ten million had been baptized solely by Franciscans and Dominicans by the mid-seventeenth century.

The Jesuits, admitted to Brazil in 1549, Peru in 1568, and Mexico in 1572, largely displaced the Mercedarians as a missionary agency. They joined the Franciscans, Augustinians, and Dominicans as the chief executives of mission in the seventeenth and eighteenth centuries. While all the orders served sacrificially and in diverse ways of evangelization, the secular priests tended to the Spanish and mestizo population, and the Jesuits dedicated much of their effort to education and to the establishment of reductions, Indian villages established by the Spanish. They, as well as the other orders, studied the native languages, wrote grammars and dictionaries, and published texts for study. They founded universities to prepare professionals in law and medicine, implant Tridentine theology, and teach arts and languages. The colleges and seminaries founded by the monastic orders paralleled the colonial universities established by royal license, such as the universities of Mexico, Santo Domingo, and Lima. The latter prepared candidates for the secular clergy, while the religious orders each prepared their own candidates. The Jesuits were never really integrated into the episcopal system.

The schools were often developed on land received by royal concession, donated by rich ranchers, given as payment for crimes or as testaments, or contributed by the clergy or members of the order. The efficient operation of these estates covered the cost of the schools and generated capital for further investments and for the respective orders. For example, the landed property of forty-five of the largest Jesuit estates, distributed in diverse regions of Mexico, included a total of 1,100,874 hectares (1 hectare = 2.471 acres) in 1767, less than two centuries after the arrival of the Society of Jesus in Mexico. The greatest concentrations of Indians and mestizo workers were in the smaller plots (500 to 1,000 hectares), while the larger ones (100,000 to 200,000 hectares) were in largely unpopulated areas.

Throughout Latin America the Indian villages organized in the sixteenth century frequently took on the more ordered form called reductions in the seventeenth and eighteenth centuries. In particular, the Franciscans, Dominicans, and the Jesuits established reductions in the areas of California and Mexico, Colombia and Venezuela, Ecuador and Peru, and Brazil and Paraguay. Most noted for their organization and extension were those among the Guaraní people of Brazil, Paraguay, and northern Argentina.

The social organization of the reductions reflected the theocratic character of the Jesuit order: a religious communism strictly ordered and based upon absolute obedience to the Jesuit fathers. The more than thirty reductions of Paraguay, with 3,500 or more Indians in each, occupied a total area of 53,904 square kilometers, with an additional zone of influence comprising over 315,000 square kilometers. The total population reached 150,000 in 1743.

The Indians who entered the reductions were like indentured servants: some entered by personal choice or as a penalty for crimes; as prisoners of war; as purchased property; and some were born in the village. They were bound for life to the mission; their life and work were strictly controlled, and their passive obedience tended to result in an attitude of stoical fatalism. Such was their dependence that after the expulsion of the Jesuit order in 1767 by the Portuguese and Spanish kings, the missions fell into decadence. Natives had not been schooled to provide leadership, to ward off the attacks of the encroaching Spanish or Portuguese seeking lands and slave labor, or to adapt to the new social and political context. Within thirty years half the Indians in Paraguay and Brazil had scattered, many to the nearly inaccessible interior. By the early nineteenth century, no missions remained. By the exclusion of the more than 2,200 Jesuits, the empire lost one of its most cohesive forces.

The success of the missions in colonial times remains a highly controversial issue. The positions taken by various scholars disagree with respect to the relative degree of adaptation or change accomplished by the evangelization. Some basic views are the following:

1. Only an external imposition of liturgy and ecclesiastical forms upon the pagan religion was accomplished. (George Kubler, Julio Jiménez Rueda, J. C. Mariátegui)
2. A kind of syncretism was attained, either by a mixture or a juxtaposition of the Christian and pagan religions. (Pedro Borges Morán)
3. An incomplete evangelization was effected, producing a genuine change through progressive catechesis. (Enrique Dussel)
4. The Indians essentially became Christians; the purity of their faith depended much on the methods of evangelism used. (Constantino Bayle, Fernando de Armas Medina)

The missionary strategy of Catholics and Protestants in the nineteenth and twentieth centuries was profoundly affected by their views on this question.

Later conflicts and crises. The church in the New World faced seemingly insuperable difficulties. The royal claims to the lands in the Americas and to its peoples were contested by many. The Indians and blacks often revolted; the Inquisition was needed to maintain internal order and loyalty; the Protestant nations, through pirates and colonists, contested Iberian exclusiveness; and, finally, local crises shattered the empire.

In the eighteenth century, a major Indian rebellion erupted under the leadership of Túpac Amaru (1742–1781), a lineal descendant of the great Inca chieftain of the same name. Educated by the Jesuits and accorded royal honors and wealth, he was recognized by his people as the heir of the Inca, but he defended them in vain before the Spanish authorities.

Finally, he organized an army of seventy to eighty thousand poorly equipped men. Bolivia, southern Peru, and the north of Argentina soon were under the control of his forces. He hoped that the Spanish could be conciliated and the two peoples could live side by side in peace, but the Spanish authorities called for reinforcements from Buenos Aires and Lima, and within six months Túpac Amaru was captured, horribly tortured, and torn apart by horses tied to his limbs, which were later displayed on poles in rebellious Indian villages. Thousands had joined the revolt, plundering and destroying everything Spanish they could find. Estimates of the total number of victims on both sides reached eighty thousand. The superior arms and power of the Spanish and the Portuguese proved, as always, to be decisive.

The title of apostolic inquisitor was officially given to Zumárraga, bishop of Mexico, in 1535, although Cisneros had conceded the power of inquisitor to all the bishops of the "Indies" in 1517. Other inquisitors were named and exercised their function later in the sixteenth century. The Holy Office of the Inquisition was established by royal decree in 1569 for Mexico and Lima and in 1610 for Cartagena. Its principle objectives were to combat (1) depraved customs (cursing, immorality, witchcraft, lack of respect for civil or ecclesiastical authorities, etc.); (2) heresy (religious or political); and (3) Jewish beliefs and customs. In the sixteenth century 902 cases were processed, 600 were found guilty, and 17 were executed. Estimates place the total number killed at about a hundred. The Inquisition served as a police court for the church in the reforming of wayward clergy, the censure of objectionable literature and plays, the securing of orthodox doctrine, and the punishment of captured sea pirates from Protestant nations. In all this it was largely successful. Some Indians were executed for idolatry before 1575, but thereafter they were judged to be too new in the faith, too weak, and too much like children to be subject to the judgment of the Inquisition.

Between 1529 and 1550 the Protestant Welser Colony settled in northern Venezuela, having received extensive political territory from Charles V. The plan included colonization and trade, especially of black slaves. Three hundred colonists arrived in 1530 and five hundred in 1535, but a lack of workers, anarchy, misery, and bankruptcy practically ended the project, with revocation of the royal concession occurring in 1550.

A French colony of three hundred, mostly Huguenots, with some Catholics, arrived in Brazil in 1555 and 1558, accompanied by pastors from Geneva. The French vice-admiral in charge of the colony broke the agreement of nonintervention in religious matters, and tried and executed three Calvinists. The remaining colonists were totally defeated by the Portuguese in 1567, and the colony came to an end.

Dutch colonists established plantations and factories in northeastern Brazil around 1630. Two "classes" (presbyteries) were founded, and two missionaries, with the help of seven fellow pastors, established mission posts, translated the Bible into Tupí, and took steps for the evangelization of the blacks. The Protestant governor was too tolerant of diverse religious views for some and was recalled. The project came to an official end in 1654. Two chiefs of Indian tribes converted by Dutch missionaries were severely persecuted by the Portuguese authorities.

The church in Latin America faced a growing crisis toward the end of the colonial period. The decadence of the Spanish Bourbon dynasty and its loss of control of the seas contributed to the weakening of the royalist position in the colonies, and Enlightenment thought challenged the existing social structures. Widespread libertinism and immorality, as well as jealous criticism of the church for its extensive possessions (nearly half of the land in Mexico by 1800), aggravated anticlericalism. Finally, the shift from an economy built on trading precious metals to an agriculturally oriented system created serious difficulties for many businessmen and laborers. The church was to struggle for its place in a new world of independent nations.

Church and National States (1808–1960). The liberation of Spanish and Portuguese America from European political control began a radically new period of Latin American church history. No longer did the kings function as the official heads of the church and its mission. The wealthier, educated Creoles (Spanish people born in the Americas) took over the reins of government (both in the church and state) from the Spanish-born elite. The Creoles formed about 20 percent of the population in 1800 and exercised control over the mestizos (mixed Indian and white, 26 percent), Indians (46 percent), and blacks (8 percent).

By the end of the nineteenth century the majority of the population in Guatemala and Bolivia was indigenous; the majority in Mexico, El Salvador, Honduras, Nicaragua, Colombia, Venezuela, Ecuador, Peru, and Paraguay was mestizo; that in Costa Rica, Cuba, Puerto Rico, Chile, Argentina, Uruguay, and Brazil was white; and that in Panama and the Dominican Republic was mulatto.

A different situation existed in the Protestant lands of British Guiana and Dutch Guiana (Surinam). Both had been governed by the Dutch until Britain took the part that was to bear its name during the Napoleonic wars. Blacks and mulattos formed over half of the population in British Guiana, and over 20 percent in Surinam. However, with the abolition of slavery, Hindus, Javanese, Portuguese, and Chinese were brought in as laborers. Indigenes were few. Most of the population became Christian, except for the Hindus. The majority were Protestants; some were Roman Catholics. In Surinam, the Moravians, who had begun work in 1738, were the largest group. In British Honduras and French Guiana the greater part of the population was Roman Catholic, with Protestant minorities.

Identity crisis. It is clear that the emancipation from Spanish rule in Spanish and Portuguese America was a rebellion of the elite. Scarcely 4 percent of the masculine population could vote. The great mass of the population reacted to the change of "lords" with indifference. At times some fought or served as cannon fodder in the cause of emancipation, but socioeconomic structures remained basically unaltered for the great majority. A liberal facade concealed the awful reality of the misery and slavery of the masses.

The rising spirit of nationalism, stimulated and exploited by foreign interference, destroyed hopes for a confederation of Latin American nations, and, consequently, for a united church. Simon Bolívar's plan to unite Colombia, Venezuela, and Ecuador failed, as did the attempted union of Bolivia and Peru in 1838 and the confederation of Central America in 1839.

The majority of the episcopacy, which had been named by the king, initially opposed the independence movement, while many (in some countries, most) of the regular and secular clergy actively participated in it. The patriots wanted to foster a national church but had no patience with those who had militated against the revolution. Many of the new states, such as Argentina (1824), Bolivia (1826), Nicaragua (1830), Colombia (1861), and Mexico (1917), confiscated ecclesiastical properties, especially in rural areas.

The leaders of the new nations believed they inherited the rights of the crown, including its authority over the churches. Religious hospitals passed to state control; the state was the administrator of the tithes (in some cases, they were discontinued); the religious and secular priests were declared responsible to their new "lords" and not to any foreigner; and the Inquisition was suspended. Many national constitutions affirmed that "the Catholic Roman Apostolic religion is the religion of the nation," as it was expressed in Argentina (1813). Nine years later Argentine president Bernardino Rivadavia canceled the right of priests to be tried in eccelesiastical courts, abolished tithes, and closed the smaller monasteries. Such actions eventually took place in most of the republics, but they were considered reforms and not a rejection of the church.

Many bishops, priests, and monks voluntarily left the revolutionary situation for reasons of conscience and loyalty to the previously constituted authorities; others were expelled. In many places this occasioned a severe shortage of priests and a lack of bishops. Pope Pius VII first ordered obedience to the restored Spanish king Ferdinand in 1816. This proved to be an impossibility, creating a crisis for the national churches. The process of official recognition of the new republics began with the naming of bishops by Gregory XVI in 1831.

Thus, during the first part of the nineteenth century, the political tendency of the republics was conservative; the church was recognized, but was subject to state control. The second half of the century and the first decades of the twentieth, however, marked a progressive rupture between church and state. The influx of European liberalism and positivism, the Masonic movement, and the increasing spirit of secularization were decisive factors in promoting the crisis. Such reforms as the official adoption of civil jurisdiction over education, the public use of cemeteries, and freedom of worship became realities in different countries at different times (in Colombia as late as 1930). The struggle of the church in this period was to conserve and restore the church of Christendom, what is often called the *corpus Christianum*, or the integralist vision, akin to the medieval model of the union of the (Catholic) church and state. This, however, proved to be a losing battle.

In the revolutionary period, the crisis between church and state demanded primary attention, and mission played a secondary role. The expulsion of priests and religious orders, repeated across the Americas, caused disruption. In the latter half of the nineteenth century, many religious orders returned to engage in traditional missionary activity. As in previous centuries, however, sickness, wars, and poverty caused the Indian population to decline, from 35 percent of the total inhabitants in 1800 to 8.8 percent in 1950.

The arrival of large contingents of immigrants, mostly Catholics, particularly from Italy, Spain, and Portugal, rapidly increased the relative size of the minority group—the whites. From 19 million in 1800 (fewer than 20 percent of the total population), the white population rose to 63 million in 1900 (over 35 percent) and 163 million in 1950 (44.5 percent). This surge of immigration also promoted the colonization of large untapped areas of Latin America.

The history of the Protestant churches in Latin America took a new turn as a result of the wars of independence. The opposition to the hegemony of Spain and Portugal (and control of the seas by the British and Dutch), which opened doors to commerce with and immigration from northern Europe; the surge of anticlericalism because of the negative attitudes of much of the episcopacy toward the revolution; and the new currents of thought favoring secularization, liberty, and tolerance all prepared the way. Progress, however, was slow; estimates place the number of Protestant missionaries in all Latin America by the end of the nineteenth century at less than nine hundred.

Most of the growth of the Protestant church in the twentieth century occurred because of immigration. Though by far the greatest number of immigrants were Latin and Catholic, the majority of the English and German immigrants were Protestant. The English tended to settle in the cities, while the Germans settled in rural areas. The River Plate region in Argentina and Uruguay early received large numbers of Protestants, and worship services were established, in their respective languages, for Anglicans in 1820, for Scotch Presbyterians in 1825, for German Lutherans in 1843, and for Italian Waldensians in 1859. They were followed by Russian-German contingents, Swiss and Dutch Reformed, Scandinavian Lutherans, Armenian Congregationalists, and Slavic Baptists. In general, these immigrant groups ministered pastorally to their own people without any real interest in the evangelization of others.

The first Protestant missionary to arrive in Spanish America was James Thomson from the British Foreign Bible Society. He came to Argentina in 1818 and, using the English community as a base, promoted the Lancaster system of education, with the Bible as a study text for reading. The new governments were open to this method, as were some Catholic clergy. Thomson and his associates sold thousands of Bibles in Spanish, made visits to at least nine of the Latin American republics, and established centers for Bible distribution in key cities. Throughout the century representatives and missionaries of the Bible societies frequented many cities across the continent. By 1900 they had distributed two million Bibles, testaments, and scripture portions.

In addition to the work of the Bible societies and the impulse given by immigration groups, missionaries from the various denominations overseas constituted a third factor in evangelization. Reports of the work of the Bible societies had aroused much interest in Protestant lands. The earliest mission boards to begin work were English, followed by missionaries from the United States, Canada, and Sweden.

The methods used included public preaching and personal witnessing directed toward a radical conversion from Catholicism. Methodists and Presbyterians in particular established both primary and secondary schools. With the rise in the level of education, religious publications became more important. Only 9 medical institutions were established during the nineteenth century in Latin America, as compared to 94 in Africa and 415 in Asia. Little work was done among the indigenous peoples in this period, except by English Anglicans and, in Argentina, Bolivia, Paraguay, and Chile, by the South American Missionary Society. Especially noteworthy was the conversion of the Miskito Indians of Nicaragua through the work of the Moravians and the formation of a Moravian community of fifteen thousand in that country.

A characteristic inclination of the missions, in addition to their strong anti-Catholicism, was to become replicas of the sending agencies with the missionary as the director and teacher; there was only a partial adaptation to the receiving culture. This marked the Protestant church as foreign and exogenous to Latin society.

Conflict and growth. Several new factors profoundly affected the history of the church near the turn of the twentieth century. First, the center of gravity for commercial and political power shifted from Europe and England to the United States. In 1880 Great Britain had four times more investments in Latin America than the United States; in 1920 they were equal; but by 1950 the United States had four times more investments than Britain. The governments of the Latin American nations were controlled by oligarchies and dictators who frequently maintained close relations with their big northern neighbor.

Second, the twentieth century brought a serious confrontation between the Catholic and the Protestant churches. The Catholics accused the Protestants of introducing liberal individualism that disintegrated the family and community, and of serving as an instrument of North American imperialism. The Protestants denounced Catholicism as pagan and unfit to evangelize the Latin American peoples, as well as being responsible in large part for their poverty.

Third, the rapid population growth of Latin America increased the Catholic church membership to nearly half the worldwide total, while the Protestant churches likewise experienced rapid expansion through immigration and the missions.

Fourth, the character of society was changing rapidly from rural to urban. With the industrialization of the large cities, increasing numbers of people migrated toward metropolitan centers in hopes of improving their marginal social situation. This migration created shanty towns called *villas de miseria* or *favellas*. Church ties and loyalties were much weaker in the city than they were in rural areas (Azevedo, 1980, pp. 121, 122).

Catholicism. The nineteenth century had been marked by hostility to the church in most of the republics; frequently modified concordats were signed beginning in 1852. In the twentieth century new constitutions and/or concordats brought increasing liberty for most religious groups, but Catholicism continued to receive official recognition in countries such as Peru, Argentina, and Paraguay. Many of the national Catholic churches received state subsidies and were subject to varying degrees of state control. Other countries (Chile, Uruguay, Brazil) progressively introduced a separation of church and state that permitted freedom of worship as long as this did not oppose Christian morality and public order. Until Vatican II, however, such permission often remained an empty promise because of strong anti-Protestant popular sentiment and controls exercised by the Roman church. State funds supported missions to the Indians in order better to exercise national control and to use the mission as an instrument of civilization and culture, as in the Concordat of Colombia in 1902. Mexico is an exception to this general trend. The revolution of 1917 resulted in the confiscation of all church properties and the termination of the church's role in education and government. Many priests were deported and church buildings damaged. The relation between the churches and the state remains strained.

The conservatism of Latin American Catholicism at the turn of the century is clearly reflected in the first plenary Latin American Council held in Rome in 1899. The 998 articles produced examine the evils of contemporary society—liberalism, superstition, Masonry, paganism, Protestantism, socialism—and the methods of combating them. No new approaches to these problems were defined by the thirteen archbishops and forty-one bishops from Latin America. The agenda did indicate, however, the revival of Rome's interest in the long-neglected continent.

From this point on, the church began to deepen its intellectual and cultural foundations in the republics. Through new agreements made during the first decades of the century, educational rights were restored to the Catholic church. Many church schools were founded on primary and secondary levels, crowned by the establishment of many church universities, as in Bogotá (1937), Lima (1942), Medellín (1945), Río de Janeiro and São Paulo (1947), Quito (1956), Buenos Aires and Córdoba (1960), and Valparaíso and Guatemala (1961).

One result of this intellectual revival was the study of the neo-Thomism propounded by Jacques Maritain (1882–1973), which provided the foundation for a new social consciousness. A broad movement called Catholic Action, born in Europe and promoted by Pius XI (1922–1939), took root in the Latin American republics after 1929, with strong youth participation. Catholic Action was basically a lay movement under clerical control, directed at the raising of the Christian conscience, particularly that of the upper class with respect to the needs of the common people. It was also aimed at gaining political and civic control for the Catholic church, thus restoring by democratic means the power lost during the tumultuous nineteenth century. The way was prepared for this movement by the organization of Catholic labor unions, agricultural cooperatives, and other groups, stimulated by the papal encyclical *Rerum novarum* (1890). The Christian Democratic political parties that emerged in Latin America after 1930 owe their inspiration to this attempt to reinstate Catholic Christendom by the ballot box. The movement has been basically reformist in character and includes many of the conservative sections of the church. Between 1930 and 1950 the church and state sometimes cooperated for the victory of populist movements (for instance, those of Eduardo Frei in Chile and Juan Domingo Perón in Argentina).

Since 1960 new winds have blown across the continent. The century began with compromises and agreements between church and state; next, Catholicism tried to restore its *corpus Christianum* in conformity to the new situation: and then came the meeting of Vatican II, followed by the meeting of the Latin American Council of Bishops at Medellín (1968), where clear steps were taken toward an identification with the poor.

This last change did not occur all at once. Innovating currents had been present since the fifties, particularly in France and northern Europe, with repercussions in Latin America. The Catholic Action groups shifted from the Italian model to that of the French, from a concentration on doctrinal correctness to existential priorities. Additional contributing factors were the formation of community reflection groups, a new openness to biblical studies, liturgical renewal, and catechetical instruction directed toward responsible living. This marked a significant break from the traditional alignment with the elite and powerful.

Those who favored the new options were of two groups: the progressives, who leaned toward a development model of social reform, and the revolutionaries, who believed that radical structural change, with or without violence, was essential. A third group supported by such organizations as Opus Dei and the Cursillos de Cristiandad, was reactionary, striving to restore Tridentine theology and medieval structures. The majority of Catholics, however, may be considered conservative, being disinclined to identify with any of the other three groups. These four groups—the progressives, the revolutionaries, the traditionalists, and the conservatives—characterize the attitudes of the Catholic church toward society up to the present.

Two types of organization characterize the Catholic churches: the regular dioceses, archdioceses, and congregations, on the one hand, and the mission territories on the other. The number of dioceses and mission territories increased in all of Latin America from about 100 in 1900 (organized during four centuries) to 547 by 1965. In Brazil in particular, the number of ecclesiastical districts increased from 12 in 1889 to 217 in 1975. According to CELAM (Council of Latin American Bishops), the total number of priests in 1967 was 42,589, of whom 15,381, or 36 percent, were foreign, mainly from Spain (54 percent) and the United States (20 percent). The heavy dependence on foreign assistance indicates the more basic problems of the lack of new priests and the abandonment of the office. In 1900 the ratio of priest to population was 1 to 3,829; in 1963 it had dropped to 1 to 4,891. One must remember that only 66.6 percent of the diocesan priests and 31.7 percent of the orders are in congregational service. Thus the number of members under the care of each priest should be doubled to give a true picture.

Since the priests tend to concentrate in the cities, the rural areas feel the shortage more. Prien (1978, p. 1067) gives statistics for Guatemala, from the largest city to the smaller ones: in Guatemala City there is one priest for 5,970 members; in Quetzaltenango, the ratio is 1 to 9,374; in Zacapá, 1 to 16,216; in Jalapa, 1 to 20,556; and in Maturín, 1 to 24,200. The percentages of the monks and nuns working in the capitals of their respective countries in the sixties were as follows: Santiago, 46 percent; Montevideo, 78 percent; San José (Costa Rica), 75 percent; Caracas, 53 percent; and Quito, 45 percent. Estimates vary in placing the number of active Catholics from 10 to 25 percent of the total membership. Papal statistics indicate that in 1970 about 90 percent of the Latin American population was Catholic. David B. Barrett (1982) estimated in mid-1980 over 329 million affiliated Catholics in all Latin America, or 88.6 percent of the population (p. 783).

Some countries, such as Brazil, Peru, Ecuador, and

Colombia, have missionary territories. These function directly under the jurisdiction of the papal Sacred Congregation of the Doctrine of the Faith. Most of the missionaries have come from the monastic orders; some of them were prepared in the Pontifical Seminary for Foreign Missions established in 1920. The number of Christians in areas considered mission districts (largely Indians) has multiplied rapidly: in 1911, there were 472,000; in 1925, 1,675,000; and in 1938, nearly two million.

As of 1980 the vast majority of the total Latin American Indian population was found in five lands: Bolivia (70 percent of its population), Guatemala (60 percent), Peru (55 percent), Mexico (20 percent), and Ecuador. The largest homogeneous language group is the Aymares in Bolivia (one million) and Peru (a half million). Catholic missionary orders have made significant advances among these populations. During World War II the American Catholic Missionary Society shifted much of its efforts to Latin America, bringing in missionaries with previous experience in Asia and Africa. Many entered unchristianized areas in the Amazon and the Andes, regions of difficult access for white civilization. Others worked in Central America, Colombia, Venezuela, Chile, and Bolivia. On occasion they met with opposition from nationalistic governments, though this was more frequent in the case of Protestant missionaries.

Anthropologists and sociologists have criticized the mission effort severely, claiming the unnecessary destruction of Indian cultural and tribal values and accusing the church of collaborating, albeit inadvertently, with the state. Church authorities are sharply divided over the issue, some placing a higher priority on preserving Indian values and others on a vigorous program of evangelization and catechization.

Protestantism. Protestantism in Latin America may be divided into three groups: the historic churches, which arrived through immigration; the mission churches, which were begun by missionaries and foreign resources; and the popular churches or movements that grew spontaneously, without significant outside assistance. Most of the immigrant groups arrived in the nineteenth and early twentieth centuries; in 1914 they constituted about one half of the Protestant community. These groups are strongest in Brazil, Argentina, Chile, Uruguay, and Bolivia, where lands and opportunities for a new life had opened in a temperate zone.

The mission groups represented most of the other half of the total Protestant community in 1914, when their membership was estimated at approximately 470,000. They, more than the historic churches, dedicated their efforts to the Latin population, particularly to the Roman Catholics, but also to the Indians. The increase of Protestant missionaries sent to the southern countries was dramatic: there were 1,438 missionaries in 1903; 2,951 in 1938; 4,488 in 1949; and 11,363 in 1969. This meant an increase of 690 percent, compared with 283 percent for Africa and 39 percent for all of Asia in the same period. What was true for personnel was equally true for the efforts expended in money, religious education, Bible institutes, schools, and seminaries.

The third group of Protestants consists almost exclusively of the Pentecostal churches. Their rise coincides with the growth of popular religiosity in the Catholic church. Those attracted to the Pentecostals tend to be from the lower economic class—the socially segregated, laborers, and the unemployed. There is an emphasis on spontaneous participation in worship, prayers with audible sharing by all, healing, speaking in tongues, opening ministry to everyone qualified by the Holy Spirit, and meetings in homes. The recognition of every member as a bearer of God's Spirit gives a sense of belonging and personal recognition. The growth has been phenomenal. Having begun in 1910, Pentecostalism in 1980 constituted about 70 percent of the estimated eighteen million in the Latin American Protestant community.

The relatively small contingent of evangelicals (the term equivalent to Protestants in Latin America) at the beginning of this century stimulated movements of cooperation among the denominations. The Panama Conference of 1916, with few Latin Americans participating, affirmed what the planners of the 1910 Edinburgh mission conference did not accept, namely, that Latin America was a mission field. The Panama delegates resolved that responsibility for mission in the Latin American countries should be divided among the various mission societies to avoid competition and duplication of efforts. Cooperation was sought in publication of literature, education, regional conferences, missionary meetings, university work, social reform, and preparation of new missionaries. Great efforts were made to approach and convert the elite through education. Three-fourths of the Latin American population could not read in 1900. An effort was made to teach the illiterates in order to give them personal access to the Bible. Other continental meetings were held in Montevideo (1925) and Havana (1929). Later, the Conferencia Evangélica Latinoamericana (CELA) met in Buenos Aires (1949), Lima (1961), and Buenos Aires (1969), with chiefly Latin American participation.

Beginning in 1920, Henry Strachan (later followed by his son, Kenneth) and Juan Varetto launched the mass campaigns that for several decades marked the new approach of the missions. Many of the evangelical churches presented their preaching and teaching in the public arena, some for the first time. This helped to overcome the sense of inferiority and lethargy that had characterized many of the historic churches as well as some of the mission groups.

Reasons given for the increased Protestant activity at this time include the following:

1. the rapid growth of the economic and cultural penetration of the United States into Latin America, which awakened the interest of the churches in mission possibilities there and opened the doors to the coming of the missionaries;
2. the changing social and intellectual situation in Latin America, which made the peoples more accessible to a different presentation of the Christian faith;
3. the active participation of Latin Americans in the promotion and direction of the work, which made Protestantism better adapted to the Latin American situation;
4. the Asian wars, causing large numbers of Asian missionaries from faith missions to come to Latin America and contribute new methods and policies for the work;
5. the growing economic power of the churches in the United States, which made possible the large investments in personnel and funds over a sustained period (Azevedo, 1980, p. 133).

These last factors apply more to the first two Protestant groups than to the Pentecostals, for whom the second and third are most relevant.

Like the Catholics, the Protestant churches in general have been divided on social problems. In most countries during the last few decades positions have had to be taken with reference to military dictatorships and the doctrine of the national security state. Often Protestants and Catholics have suffered persecution, torture, and death for their convictions. Protestant attitudes may be divided into three groups: traditional (obedience to the state in all except false worship); progressive (the right to disobey the state on questions of social justice and the duty to struggle for the establishment of a just society); and radical (a recognition of the need to overthrow unjust social structures by violence, if necessary).

It is impossible to state with accuracy the number of Protestants in Latin America. Barrett (1982, p. 783) affirms that in 1980 they constituted 4.9 percent of the population, or approximately eighteen million in the total community. Dussel (1974, p. 192) gives the following percentages of total population for 1961:

> 10%	Chile, British Guiana, Surinam, French Guiana
5–10%	Brazil
2–5%	Mexico, Guatemala, El Salvador, Nicaragua, Panama
1–2%	Argentina, Uruguay, Paraguay, Bolivia, Honduras
< 1%	Peru, Ecuador, Colombia, Venezuela, Costa Rica

Read, Monterroso, and Johnson estimate the number of Protestant adult communicant members at 4,915,477 in 1967.

Orthodox churches. A variety of Orthodox churches are represented in Latin America. Around 140,000 Arabic-speaking Syrians had come to Argentina and Brazil by 1915. Most were under the spiritual guidance of the patriarch of Antioch, though some priests came from Russia to provide pastoral care. Somewhat less than half a million Orthodox came as refugees in the years following the Russian Revolution and World War II. Many were lost to Orthodoxy, some identifying with spiritism, others with Protestantism. Greek, Russian, and Syrian congregations and dioceses have been organized in Mexico, Brazil, Argentina, Uruguay, Peru, Colombia, Ecuador, and Chile, while the Russian Orthodox also have churches in Venezuela and Paraguay. There is a Russian bishop in São Paulo and an archbishop for Latin America in Buenos Aires. A relatively few number of Uniates, Maronites, and Ruthenians (groups that maintain their national liturgy but acknowledge the supremacy of the pope in Rome) are also present, particularly in Brazil, Argentina, and Chile.

The Church and Signs of New Life. Since the mid-twentieth century, signs of new life have begun to appear both in Roman Catholic and Protestant churches. Efforts to identify with the realities of the Latin American situation do not exclude strong currents of traditional conservatism which, on the Catholic side, continue to support elitist power groups and, on the Protestant side, reject responsibility for societal improvement. But the new movements clearly point to significant changes in church attitudes and programs.

Catholicism. The organization of the Latin American Council of Bishops (CELAM) in 1955 gave to the Roman Catholic churches of the region a formal unity and coherence not found on other continents. This time the unity was not buttressed by civil force or restricted by the *patronato* that had given the national states certain rights over the churches. The chief characteristic of CELAM was its concern for the whole of human life and society.

Evidence of the new weight accorded to the Latin American churches was the large representation at Vatican II (1962–1965). The 601 Latin American bishops (22.33 percent of the total) were second in number only to the Europeans, with 31.6 percent. No Latin American priests had been present at Trent (1545–1563), and only 61 bishops had been at Vatican I (1870).

Catholic scholars judge the second general conference of CELAM at Medellín in 1968 to be a watershed in its history. Before Medellín the pastoral task had been conceived as the dispensation of sacramental grace within the contours of a Christian society. Medellín recognized that society was pluralistic, and that in this society a transformation of traditional values was possible and necessary. The popular manifestations of the faith needed to be impregnated by the word of the gospel. Devotional acts to the saints had to be changed from intercessory devices to models for life in imitation of Christ. The fatalism nurtured by the traditional sacramental view was rejected, and in its place an emphasis was placed on the pastoral task of educating people to become active collaborators with God in the fulfillment of their destiny. A call was made for organizing grass-roots community groups for Bible study and joint action in meeting social needs, especially in marginal economic areas.

In the eleven years between Medellín and CELAM III in Puebla (1979), more than two hundred thousand small ecclesiastical communities began to function effectively, particularly in Brazil, but also in other countries across the continent. Lay groups, sometimes with pastoral presence, were questioning the unchangeableness of their social plight in the light of biblical teaching and were becoming active participants for change. The Puebla Conference took up these concerns by first analyzing the Latin American situation, then making its recommendations. Recognition of the dignity of the human person, and particularly of the rights of the poor and oppressed, was declared to be at the heart of the gospel message.

The Puebla bishops were united in their harsh judgment of capitalism, Marxism, and the national security state: capitalism, for increasing the distance between rich and poor people and nations; Marxism, for sacrificing many Christian values and creating false utopias sustained by force; and the national security state, for supporting dictatorships that abuse police power to deprive human beings of their rights. Differences arise among Christians, however, when basic causes of poverty and oppression are defined and concrete programs for change proposed.

The theology of liberation was formulated after 1960 by theologians and social scientists through reflection on Latin American social and political reality and attempts to transform its oppressive structures. The best-known Catholic exponents include Gustavo Gutierrez (Peru), Juan Luis Segundo (Uruguay), Segundo Galilea (Chile), José Miranda (Mexico), Hugo Assman and Leonardo Boff (Brazil), Jon Sobrino (El Salvador), and Enrique Dussel (Argentina). They affirm the necessity of moving toward a social system characterized by priority for the poor, use of the social sciences in the analysis of reality, recognition of the ideological base from which every person develops religious understanding; and importance given to praxis—active and obedient discipleship, supported by theory, with the eventual goal of the transformation of society. This theology has been variously interpreted in Latin American church hierarchy. The fervor with which it is debated, the mutual concern about the large majority of marginalized peoples, and the evangelical zeal for ministry mark a significant renovation in Catholicism.

Protestantism. Protestantism has likewise developed differently from its mother institutions. The dramatic growth of the Pentecostal church bears a resemblance to other moments in church history when the chief advances were made among the poor. In their search for identity, fulfillment, and meaning there is a strong similarity between the small, spontaneous Pentecostal groups and the Catholic grass-roots communities. The Pentecostals lack the structural cohesiveness and the social commitment of the Catholics, but the inner spiritual vitality, the concern for healing in the church's ministry, and the forthright heralding of the word of the gospel that characterize the Pentecostals have awakened responses from sectors of society largely unresponsive to the historic and mission churches.

In addition to the three Protestant consultations for Latin America (CELA) mentioned earlier, other Protestant ecumenical groups that have arisen since 1960 in response to social and spiritual crises and a felt need for cooperation include a Latin American youth organization (ULAJE, founded in 1941), various university student organizations, an educational commission (CELADEC, 1961), and an association of Protestant churches (UNELAM, 1965). This later group was subsumed into the Latin American Church Council (CLAI), officially organized in 1982, with a broad representation from the three sectors of the Protestant churches. A group of churches with less emphasis on social responsibility formed a parallel organization called the Evangelical Confraternity of Latin America (CONELA) the same year.

Theological education slowly became a priority for Protestantism. The movement called Seminary by Extension was born in Guatemala in an effort to further train a large percentage of pastors and laity who already lead churches. This new educational model has spread rapidly throughout Latin America, Africa, and Asia. Economic problems have made more traditional

Western methods of theological education difficult. Hundreds of Bible institutes and theological seminaries were established to prepare pastoral leadership. A Latin American Committee for Theological Education (CLAET), composed of three regional groupings of institutions, was established in 1979.

Protestant theology has developed slowly. Most of the publications in Latin America have been translations from European and especially United States sources with more local writing in the last two decades. The movement Church and Society in Latin America (ISAL) attempted to provide a theological basis for a Christian attitude toward oppressive social structures. Some of its early efforts formed part of the Protestant contribution to the theology of liberation; among its leading exponents are José Míguez Bonino (Argentina), Rubem Alves (Brazil), and Sergio Arce (Cuba). Publications featuring reflections on this theme have come chiefly from centers of theological education in Buenos Aires, San José, Mexico City, and Puerto Rico. The Latin American Theological Fraternity (FTL) has stimulated writing by theologians across a wide spectrum of positions. These manifestations of the life of the church confirm the increasing integration of Protestantism into Latin America, the identification of its concerns on many pastoral levels with those of the Catholic church (as on human rights issues), and the continuing missionary zeal characteristic of its heritage.

[*See also* Political Theology; Mesoamerican Religions, *article on* Contemporary Cultures; Afro-Surinamese Religions; Afro-Brazilian Cults; *and* Kardecism.]

BIBLIOGRAPHY

General. The best single volume on Roman Catholic church history is Enrique D. Dussel's *Historia de la iglesia en América Latina*, 3d ed. (Barcelona, 1974), translated into English as *History of the Church in Latin America* (Grand Rapids, Mich., 1982). The book has an excellent bibliography according to geographical area but hardly refers to churches other than the Roman Catholic. On both Catholic and Protestant history, the Brazilian Israel Belo de Azevedo gives an excellent recent summary in Portuguese, *As Cruzadas inacabadas* (Rio de Janeiro, 1980). In the preparation of this article I found these two books particularly helpful.

Covering the whole of Latin America will be the series of ten regional volumes published by CEHILA, Comisión de Estudios de Historia de la Iglesia en América Latina, under the general editorship of Enrique D. Dussel, who will write an introductory volume. The goal is to interpret church history from the perspective of the poor and oppressed. Volume 7, *Colombia y Venezuela* (Salamanca, 1981), has appeared in Spanish; volumes 2.1 and 2.2, *Brazil* (Petropolis, Brazil, 1977-1980), have appeared in Portuguese. *Latin American Church Growth* by William R. Read, Victor M. Monterroso, and Harmon A. Johnson (Grand Rapids, Mich., 1969) presents a detailed compilation of statistics from the evangelical Protestant perspective with heavy emphasis on numerical growth. This book also appears in Spanish, *Avance evangélico en la América Latina* (El Paso, Tex., 1970), and in Portuguese, *O crescimiento da igreja no América Latina* (São Paulo, 1969). Prudencio Damboriena does much the same from the Catholic viewpoint in his *El protestantismo en América Latina*, vol. 1, *Etapas y métodos del protestantismo Latino-americano*, and vol. 2, *La situación del protestantismo en los países Latino-americanos* (Bogotá, 1962–1963). These form numbers 12 and 13 of the valuable series FERES (Federación Internacional de los Institutas Católicos de Investigaciónes Sociales y Socio-religiosas), which provides documentation and socioreligious studies about Latin America published in forty-two volumes during the decade of the sixties. See also number 21 of the same series, *La iglesia en América Latina* by Isidoro Alonso (Bogotá, 1964), for a description of recent ecclesiastical structures of the Catholic church. Some of the best general descriptions remain those of the veteran historian K. S. Latourette in his *Christianity in a Revolutionary Age: A History of Christianity in the Nineteenth and Twentieth Centuries*, 5 vols. (1958–1962; reprint, Westport, Conn., 1973); see volume 3, pages 284–352, and volume 5, pages 158–240. See also volumes 5 and 7 of his *A History of the Expansion of Christianity*, 7 vols. (1937–1945; reprint, Grand Rapids, Mich., 1970), pages 68–129 and 164–185, respectively. Two extensive works from the perspective of the United States are Donald M. Dozer's *Latin America: An Interpretative History* (New York, 1962), which has been translated into Portuguese as *América Latina: Una perspectiva histórica* (Porto Alegre, 1966); and Hubert Herring's *A History of Latin America from the Beginnings to the Present* (New York, 1961), which has been translated into Spanish as *Evolución histórica de América Latina* (Buenos Aires, 1972). Herring offers a comprehensive bibliography (pp. 831–845) with emphasis on English titles up to 1960. His history is ably complemented by Germán Arciniegas's *Latin America: A Cultural History* (New York, 1967). After working several years in El Salvador and Brazil, Hans-Jürgen Prien wrote his monumental 1,302-page *Die Geschichte des Christentums in Lateinamerika* (Göttingen, 1978), which has been translated into Spanish as *La historia del cristianismo en América Latina* (Salamanca, 1981). The series "Biblioteca de Autores Cristianos" (Library of Christian Authors) elucidates the Catholic interpretation of the church's history from the Conquest to independence in the two-volume *Historia de la iglesia en la América Española desde el Descubrimiento hasta comienzos del siglo XIX:* no. 248, *México, América Central* by Léon Lopetegui and Félix Zubillaga (Madrid, 1965), and no. 256, *Hemisferio Sur* by Antonio de Egana (Madrid, 1966).

Special Themes. Two brief but excellent analyses of the receiving cultures at the time of the Conquest are Laurette Séjourné's *América Latina: Antiguas culturas precolombinas* (Mexico City, 1971), which has been translated into German as *Altamerikanische Kulturen* (Frankfurt, 1971), and Henri Lehmann's *Les civilisations précolombiennes*, 7th ed. (Paris, 1977), which has been translated into Spanish as *Las culturas precolombinas* (Buenos Aires, 1960). One of the best histories of the relation between the church and state remains J. Lloyd Mecham's *Church and State in Latin America: A History of Politico-Ecclesiastical Relations*, 2d rev. ed. (Chapel Hill, N.C., 1966). The rising phenomenon of Pentecostalism receives careful attention in the studies of Christian Lalive d'Epinay, *El refugio de las masas: Estudio sociológico del protestantismo chileno* (Santiago, 1968), and Emilio Willems, *Followers of the New Faith: Culture Change and the Rise of Protestantism in Brazil and Chile* (Nashville, 1967). For a description of the *encomendero* system and other relevant themes, see Lewis Hanke's *The Spanish Struggle for Justice in the Conquest of America* (Pittsburgh, 1949). Gustavo Gutierrez describes the history of Latin American theology and formulates a new theological perspective in *Teología de la liberación: Historia, política y salvación* (Lima, 1971), which has been translated as *A Theology of Liberation: History, Politics and Salvation* (Maryknoll, N.Y., 1973). For statistics, see the *World Christian Encyclopedia*, edited by David B. Barrett (Oxford, 1982). A complete indexed bibliography of all theological works in Spanish and Portuguese is published annually in the *Bibliografía teológica comentada* (Buenos Aires, 1973–) by the Instituto Superior Evangélico de Estudios Teológicos (ISEDET). Introductions to sections are in Spanish with English summaries. See also *Latin America: A Guide to the Historical Literature*, edited by Charles C. Griffin (Austin, 1971).

SIDNEY H. ROOY

Christianity in the Caribbean Region

One of the distinctive characteristics of Caribbean Christianity is the racial and ethnic diversity of its adherents. A high proportion of the people of the region is either black or Afro-American (mixed African and non-African descent). Although a large proportion of the black population was exposed only superficially to Christian teachings during the period of slavery beginning in the sixteenth century and continuing into the nineteenth, and despite extensive disillusionment with the historical churches in the decades immediately after emancipation, Christianity has continued to spread widely in the region. The long and close relationship between religion and sociopolitical doctrine in the societies from which the dominant class in the colonial period came has persisted in many parts of the Caribbean to the present day.

The Early Years. The sixteenth and seventeenth centuries have been called the missionary centuries in the New World. Priests accompanied the explorers, and Catholic and Protestant missionaries were an important part of pioneer settlements. In 1685 the Code Noir prescribed that all slaves in the French islands were to be instructed and baptized in the Roman Catholic religion. The colonists paid little attention to the code, especially the sections dealing with religious obligations that were opposed to their economic interests. Priests varied greatly during the first half of the eighteenth century; some were zealous about their duties, others attended only to the external aspects of religion. In 1764 the Jesuits in Haiti were accused of stirring up the slaves and were expelled from the colony. With the revolt of the slaves in 1791, the Catholic religion in Haiti almost disappeared.

The first Lutheran congregation was established in Saint Thomas, Danish West Indies, in 1666 and for two and one-half centuries the Lutheran church was the state church. In the late 1750s, a Lutheran mission for the slaves was established in the island. In some parts of the West Indies, in Barbados, for example, the early slaves brought from Africa were not permitted to become Christians. In 1700 the Anglicans organized the Society for the Propagation of the Gospel in foreign parts to preach to the heathen, that is, slaves and free men in North America and the West Indies.

Moravian (United Brethren) missionaries arrived in Saint Thomas in December 1732. Count Nikolaus von Zinzendorf, founder of Moravian missions, opposed the emancipation of the slaves and did not favor teaching them to read and write. In addressing the converts at a mass meeting in 1739, he exhorted them to be obedient to their masters, adding that "your conversion will make you free, not from the control of your masters, but simply from your wicked habits and thoughts, and all that makes you dissatisfied with your lot."

The work of Methodist missionaries in the Caribbean began in 1770, but the Methodist Missionary Society was not founded until 1789. Because it was difficult for missionaries to gain permission from the planters to enter many of the estates in the West Indies, both the Methodists and the Baptists used a system of slave leaders to supervise their followers. The black assistants visited the sick, held prayer meetings, and oversaw the conduct of the members in their charge.

One of the first Baptist missionaries to reach the West Indies was a manumitted slave from Virginia, George Liele (Lisle). Liele organized a church in Jamaica in 1783, and by 1791 had enrolled 450 members, all blacks and most of them slaves. In 1813 the Baptist Missionary Society began to send out missionaries from London. Despite the hostility they encountered, regular services were conducted and schools opened at Kingston, Spanish Town, Falmouth, and other places. Three missionaries were sent to Jamaica in 1800 by the Scottish Missionary Society, a nondenominational body. The established Church of Scotland began its work in Kingston in 1819, a program that was carried on later by the United Presbyterian church.

Social Structure and Caribbean Christianity. Differences in world view that developed in the Caribbean as religions there changed have been related, by Raymond T. Smith, to social structural factors. In one such relation the main characteristics are hierarchial structure of offices and the solemn quality of religious proceedings. The model in this trend has been the Church of England, but the nonconformist churches also became establishment-oriented after the controversy over emancipation had passed. A second trend, ethical and sectarian individualism, is represented in European Protestantism but also in sects originating in the United States, including the Seventh-day Adventists and Jehovah's Witnesses. The third trend involves more demonstrative types of worship and includes such neo-African cults as Shango and such ancestral cults as Kumina; revivalist cults such as the Revival Zionists, the Spiritual Baptists, and the Shakers; and such groups as Pentecostalism, the Salvation Army, and the Nazarenes.

Roman Catholic Church. From the beginning of the Republic of Haiti in 1803 until 1858, a schism existed between the state and the Roman Catholic church. Because the Constitution of 1805 provided for the complete separation of church and state, the Vatican refused to recognize Haiti as a state and forbade priests to enter the country. In 1860 an agreement between the pope and Haitian officials ended the long break. However, Catholicism had not developed deep roots in Haiti, and, during the schism, folk belief was combined with Christianity. Since that time, Voodoo has continued to maintain its hold on the Haitian mass. After President François Duvalier came to power in 1957, the state increasingly exercised control over the Catholic church through intimidation and violence, including the expulsion of the archbishop of Port au Prince and dozens of French and Canadian missionaries, the closing of the major Catholic seminary, the banning of the Catholic daily paper, and the dissolution of the Christian trade union.

The Catholic church has never been as influential in the national life of Cuba as in other Latin American countries. Its decline during the last years of Spanish rule continued after Cuba became independent in 1902. The shortage of priests, the fact that most of the priests and nuns were foreigners, the meager education of the priests, identification of the church with conservatism, its reputation for corruption and antipopular policies alienated it from a large part of the Cuban population.

The situation of the Catholic church in the former British West Indies has been somewhat different. The first Catholic priest to serve in Jamaica came to the island in 1792, but for many years the number of Catholics in the country remained small. Roman Catholics constitute fewer than 10 percent of the population, but the church is influential in Jamaican life. Catholics comprise 36 percent of the population of Trinidad and Tobago, including spiritist Catholics (Catholics who are involved in such cults as Shango).

Anglican Church. Unquestionably the Church of England in Jamaica in the eighteenth century was not a missionary church for the slaves; it was the religion of the white settlers and officials. The twenty Anglican churches in Jamaica in 1800 were small, and probably fewer than three hundred persons attended religious services each Sunday. The Church of England, disestablished in most of the colonies between 1868 and 1870, continues to be an important force in the life of the former British colonies.

Protestant Churches. The United Brethren (Moravian) church in Saint Thomas grew rapidly after 1740, and mission stations established in Saint Johns, Antigua, and in Basseterre, Saint Kitts, became quite successful. Those in Jamaica, Barbados, and Tobago were much less successful. In February 1755 King Frederick V of Denmark ordered that instruction in Christianity be given to the slaves in Saint Thomas, and by 1785 the Lutheran mission in the Virgin Islands was small only by comparison to the Moravian program. Separate services were conducted for the Danish and the black congregations.

In the forty years prior to emancipation, Methodist and Baptist missionaries in the West Indies were harassed for allegedly provoking insubordination among the blacks. Despite this persecution, by the time the Emancipation Act was passed in London in 1833 the Methodist membership in the West Indies had grown to 32,000, two-thirds of whom were slaves. Confusion and suspicion arose in the British West Indies by the time the apprenticeship system came to an end in 1838. Methodism entered a period of decline in membership and enthusiasm when many former slaves became disillusioned by the continuing gulf between whites and blacks. The Methodist church in the West Indies revived somewhat after the excesses of the Great Revival of 1861–1862 had passed. Never among the largest Protestant denominations in the Caribbean, the Methodist church is, nevertheless, an important religion in the region.

The Baptists quickly acquired a following among the slaves, and following emancipation their congregations grew even more rapidly. The Presbyterian church has remained one of the smaller religions in the Caribbean. In the past forty years, Pentecostalism, a part of the fundamentalist movement in American Protestantism, has been the fastest growing religion in the Caribbean. Offering hope of deliverance from unjust social orders, this faith is almost ideally adapted to the needs of the disadvantaged. The Pentecostal style of worship has spread to small supplementary prayer groups within both the Roman Catholic church and a number of the historical Protestant churches.

Demographics. The proportions of adherents to various forms of Christianity differ in each of the Caribbean countries. For example, in Cuba the population of professing Catholics dropped from almost nine-tenths at the beginning of the century to less than three-fourths by the time Fidel Castro came to power in 1959. Two decades later, only one-third of Cubans were professing Catholics; one-fourth of that number were also involved in Santería and other Afro-Cuban cults. Protestants constitute about 1 percent of the Cuban population, the nonreligious and atheists more than half, practicing Christians who keep their religion private approximately one-tenth, and those who are adherents only of Afro-Cuban syncretistic cults less than one-thirtieth.

In Haiti, more than four-fifths of the population is Roman Catholic (nine-tenths of whom are also involved in Voodoo). Approximately one-seventh are Protestants, and less than one-thirtieth belong to indigenous black sects and other religions.

In Jamaica, seven-tenths of the population is Protestant, while Roman Catholics, black indigenous church members, revivalists and other cultists each constitute approximately one-tenth. Finally, in Trinidad and Tobago, Roman Catholics constitute somewhat more than one-third of the population, Protestants three-tenths, and black indigenous sectarians, Shangoists, and other religionists about one-thirtieth.

[*See also* Caribbean Religions, *article on* Afro-Caribbean Religions; Santería; *and* Voodoo.]

BIBLIOGRAPHY

Barrett, David B., ed. *World Christian Encyclopedia: A Comparative Study of Churches and Religions in the Modern World, A.D. 1900-2000.* Oxford, 1982. An excellent reference volume that provides data on religions throughout the world.

Calley, Malcolm J. C. *God's People: West Indian Pentecostal Sects in England.* New York, 1965. A study of West Indian immigrants to England with valuable commentary on Pentecostalism.

Curtin, Philip D. *Two Jamaicas: The Role of Ideas in a Tropical Colony, 1830–1865* (1955). Reprint, New York, 1968. A leading historian's analysis of the roles of Christianity and of Afro-Christian religions in Jamaica in the period before and after emancipation.

Gonzales, Justo L. *The Development of Christianity in the Latin Caribbean.* Grand Rapids, Mich., 1969. A critique of the programs of Christian churches in the French-speaking and Spanish-speaking countries of the Caribbean.

Hollenweger, Walter J. *The Pentecostals: The Charismatic Movement in the Churches.* London, 1972. A lucid account of the Pentecostal movement by a prominent theologian.

Simpson, George Eaton. *Black Religions in the New World.* New York, 1978. A study of religions that have been important to blacks in the New World.

Simpson, George Eaton. *Religious Cults of the Caribbean: Trinidad, Jamaica and Haiti.* 3d ed. Rio Piedras, Puerto Rico, 1980.

Smith, Raymond T. "Religion in the Formation of West Indian Society." In *The African Diaspora: Interpretive Essays,* edited by Martin L. Kilson and Robert I. Rotberg, pp. 312-341. Cambridge, Mass., 1976. This volume includes chapters on slavery and on the religions of blacks in the Caribbean.

GEORGE EATON SIMPSON

Christianity in North America

Christianity came to North America with European explorers, colonizers, and settlers, expressing in a New World version enduring continuity but also substantial change. In what became Canada and the United States (the limits of North America for this article), national and political considerations proved important, but smaller, regional forms of Christianity also flourished. North American Christianity struggled with its plurality, perhaps, ironically, achieving its greatest unity in its large-scale dedication to mission.

Christians Made and Born

Intrinsic to the Christian vision was a commitment to mission—to the task of bringing all peoples to God through the saving power of his son Jesus Christ. So far did the ideology of mission extend in North America that, even in the case of those reared ostensibly as Christians, the mission to convert became in many instances a major concern.

Conversion of Native North Americans. Aims for the conversion of indigenous North American peoples figured large in the rhetoric of the colonizing nations. But the religious impulse was also molded by the political ambitions of European nation-states. Hence, conversion went forward as an arm of the colonial ventures of the Spanish, French, and English governments.

In an often-cited debate between Juan Ginés de Sepúlveda and the Dominican Bartolomé de Las Casas (1550), the Spanish had pondered the question of whether native North Americans were slaves by nature or fit subjects for christianization. The outcome, supporting Sepúlveda and Aristotle's theory of natural slavery, was not surprising, since the Spanish already considered Aztec religion, with its human sacrifice, worship of the devil. Similarly, both English and French called the Indians "savages," wild men without law or religion. Puritans in the Massachusetts Bay Colony saw them as "minions" of the devil, heathen who practiced nefariously in the forests. French Franciscans argued that until Indians were civilized they were not capable of Christianity. And French Jesuits, in the most positive estimate, saw a natural nobility in the "savage" peoples. These early opinions, if expressed more subtly, continued to inform the ideas and work of missionaries who, after Canada and the United States became political realities, carried on their work among the Indians.

Spanish missions. As early as the 1520s, Roman Catholic priests were in Florida and the Chesapeake, and by 1595 there was serious missionary work in Florida. Meanwhile, in New Mexico, Franciscan friars had accompanied the Spanish conquerors, and in 1598 they began an era of forced mission presence among reluctant Pueblo peoples. In California, efforts to convert the Indians proceeded less violently under the missionary leadership of the fabled Franciscan priest Junípero Serra (1713–1784). At its height, the system of missions established by Serra attracted over 21,000 Indians, who settled around the missions, christianized and living according to Spanish order in farm communities.

French missions. If the Spanish arrived in the New World as *conquistadores*, the French came, especially, as fur traders. In this context, both Franciscan Recollets and Jesuits evangelized, the Jesuits particularly among the Hurons, living with them and speaking their language. Although for a time Iroquois hostility effectively ended the work of the Jesuits, by 1668 they were preaching among their former Iroquois persecutors. When the French opened the Mississippi to Europeans, Indians in southern New France heard the gospel, while those at the other end of the French empire also knew the mission presence. Still, by the close of the French era in Canada, the missionaries had been more successful in making the Indians loyal to France than in converting them.

English missions. Evangelization of Indian peoples appears clearly among English intentions in colonizing North America. Yet the English were demonstrably slower and feebler in implementing their aims than either the Spanish or the French. The Mayhew family worked successfully among native North Americans at Martha's Vineyard and Nantucket, and in seventeenth-century New England John Eliot (1604–1690) preached in the Massachuset tongue and translated the Bible and other works for his converts, settling fourteen villages of "praying Indians." Eliot was in at least one sense representative, for Protestant missions in British North America were tied to a deep sense of the importance of the word. Introducing Indians to Christianity meant, above all, introducing them to a sacred book.

Canadian and American (U.S.) missions. After Canadian confederation, Protestant missionary efforts went forward in the West, encouraged in part by the development of the Canadian Pacific Railway. Meanwhile, Roman Catholics had achieved a solid presence among certain groups in the West as well. In the United States, by 1787 the interdenominational Society for Propagating the Gospel among the Indians had been established, to be followed in 1810 by the American Board of Commissioners for Foreign Missions and later, in 1881, by the National Indian Association. As in Canada, Protestants and Roman Catholics alike evangelized, and in both countries the twentieth century saw Christian denominations still at work. Much of the effort continued to be traditional, but there was growing awareness of the problem of cultural imperialism. Christian missionaries learned that cultural contact was a two-way process and that Indians had much to contribute to a renewed Christianity.

Conversion of African North Americans. The christianization of African North Americans largely occurred in the United States. In Canada, economic conditions did not favor slavery, and only a small free black population struggled along. In the United States, the majority of converted slaves embraced some form of Protestantism.

At first, many slaveholders were reluctant to allow proselytizing among their slaves, fearing that Christian baptism might render slaves materially equal or doubting that blacks had souls to save. For their part, blacks did not readily adopt the Anglican Christianity of the early eighteenth century. In time, however, slaveholders became more convinced of the practical value of converting slaves for social control, while by the end of the eighteenth century, Baptist and Methodist missionaries brought a revivalist Christianity that blacks found more attractive.

In the years that followed, two kinds of Christianity evolved. First, there was the official church Christianity that slaveholders fostered and controlled. Second, there was the so-called invisible institution, a form of unchurched Christianity created and controlled by blacks, blending elements of their African past and their lived experience on the plantations with Christian language. An "instant" (conversion-oriented) Christianity, unlike the gradualism of the Anglicans, it was shared in part by European North Americans in the revivals.

Meanwhile, black churches arose not merely at the initiative of white slaveholders. In the northern United States, free blacks had already begun to form their own churches in the late eighteenth century. In the South, prior to the 1830s, Baptist congregations had also enjoyed a measure of independence and control. However, only after the Civil War did black churches, both North and South, proliferate. By the late nineteenth century, the Holiness movement flourished among blacks, and by the early twentieth century, Pentecostalism had become popular. Beyond these, massive immigration to northern cities helped to spawn a series of small but intense religious movements based in Christianity but including new revelation. Yet for the most part, blacks who counted themselves church members in the twentieth century were Baptists or Methodists, usually belonging to separate black congregations of larger white denominations. As a rough estimate, almost two-thirds were Baptists and nearly one-quarter were Methodists.

In Canada, the situation for blacks had been in many ways different. When the imperial parliament abolished slavery in 1833, British North America had already long been free of the institution. But without the long and oppressive incubation period of slavery, Canadian blacks evolved a perhaps less distinctive religious life than American blacks had. Still, by 1840 racial prejudice meant that black congregations were separated from white ones, and blacks willingly fostered distinct institutions within the larger churches. They joined a range of denominations including the Baptist and Methodist as well as the Presbyterian and Anglican. Often, too, blacks in Canada, as in the United States, left the mainstream denominations to form their own sectarian groups. But overall, Baptist fellowships predominated among blacks in Canada as in the United States.

Conversion of European North Americans. Although the American Board of Commissioners for Foreign Missions worked to an extent among native North Americans, it had been founded for work abroad. Other denominational and nondenominational organizations followed, and by late in the nineteenth century the Student Volunteer Movement was aiming at "the evangelization of the world in this generation." Reflective of the tenor of its times, it joined other missionary societies in mingling evangelical zeal with expansionist political ambitions. Similarly, in British North America the Canada Foreign Missionary Society had been established as a nondenominational agency in 1854, and by the beginning of the twentieth century the major Christian groups in Canada were engaged in serious mission work abroad. From 1893, foreign mission boards from the United States and Canada came together in New York, meeting annually until, in 1911, they formed the Foreign Missions Conference of North America.

Despite the clear commitment these nineteenth- and twentieth-century efforts expressed, the more important missionary focus remained the unconverted at home. Typically raised in a Christian milieu and even holding Christian theological beliefs, the unconverted were those who had not experientially encountered the gospel. For a variety of historical and sociological reasons, this mission to the unconverted was most noticeable in the United States. Here the Puritan and revolutionary heritage intensified a religious situation already volatile in all of North America, separated from European culture and institutions and undergoing other forms of change.

Puritanism. The Puritan movement had arisen in England as various separatist and nonseparatist groups sought to purify the Anglican church. Imbued with Calvinism and also with elements from the left wing of the continental Reformation, Puritans sought simplicity in worship and in life, and they preached a free, or gathered, church of the elect. In the English Atlantic colonies, Puritan presence was a major factor, with key colonial governments controlled by different Puritan groups. Moreover, Puritanism in the colonies fostered significant developments in the movement's religious teaching and practice. Increasingly, a doctrine of special chosenness and covenantal relationship with God prevailed. Puritans paid greater and greater attention to inner, emotional states, stressing the necessity for an experience of conversion before one could become a full member of the church. From this perspective, Puritans faced a generation of unbelievers not only among peers who were strangers but even among their children. Puritans could not expend resources converting Indians because, in part, they were already too busy converting their own.

Revivalism. Influenced by this understanding and by frontier conditions and economic forces, in the early middle decades of the eighteenth century the Great Awakening spread in the English Atlantic colonies. Under the preaching, especially, of the itinerant Methodist George Whitefield (1714–1770) and the latter-day Massachusetts Puritan Jonathan Edwards (1703–1758), emotional and physical manifestations became outward signs of God's inward work among thousands. Then, by the turn of the century, the Second Great Awakening brought visible signs of conversion to a new generation. In Kentucky and Ohio, lengthy camp meetings attracted massive crowds who fell under the power of the Spirit, experiencing strong physical and emotional manifestations.

Throughout the nineteenth century and into the twentieth, American revivals followed cyclically. Each regeneration brought converts to the churches, but over time enthusiasm waned and there was need for further missionary effort. With Charles G. Finney (1792–1875) and his deliberate use of "new measures," revivalism became a technique for mass evangelism. Later, as more and more people moved to the cities, urban revivalism found its chief organizer and innovator in the lay preacher Dwight L. Moody (1837–1899). The greatest of the twentieth century's preachers, William A. (Billy) Sunday (1862–1935) and Billy Graham (b. 1918), built on Moody's work and adapted it to new technologies and times. And throughout the century a flourishing Holiness-Pentecostal movement institutionalized physical and emotional religion so that even regular worship services became revivals.

In Canada, revivalism never achieved the spectacular presence that it had in the United States. It is significant that the first notable revival in British North America took place in Nova Scotia, the place to which New Englanders in large numbers immigrated before and during the Revolution. At the opening of the nineteenth century, a great revival spread through Upper Canada (Canada West), with many of the same physical and emotional expressions that characterized the American frontier revival. Itinerating Methodists who crossed the border built a rapidly growing denominational connection, especially among the large numbers of American immigrants to the area. Then, from roughly 1885 to 1900, the Holiness movement and the Salvation Army brought their brand of aggressive revivalism to the disinherited and competed effectively in urban settings. In the twentieth century, emotional religion grew with increasing Pentecostal membership. During the Depression a religious awakening spread in the West, and during the fifteen years after World War II a revival swept through Canada, paralleling one in the United States.

Evangelicalism and moral crusades. Revivalism provided a condensed version of what evangelicalism worked to achieve in North American culture more broadly. The religious imperative of mission meant commitment to transform both individual and society. Canadians and Americans alike responded energetically, and a common moralism pervaded their cultures.

Already in New France, Roman Catholic moral rigorism had blended with harshness of land and climate to produce a quality of asceticism in public life. Later, in the British era, Canadian Protestants displayed even greater rigor. Mid-nineteenth-century ministers denounced alcohol and behavioral impropriety in general, particularly rebuking abuses of the Sabbath. After confederation, the war against alcohol became the great evangelical cause, and sabbatarianism also grew as a public cause.

A more collective social concern was evidenced in the nineteenth-century condemnation of slavery—less of an issue in Canada than in the United States—but it was only in the twentieth century that moralism was effectively transmuted into social witness. The new Social Gospel was more subdued on issues like temperance and sabbatarianism and more emphatic on questions of economic organization and social service. By 1907, Canadian Protestants had established a Social Service Council, while Roman Catholics, in the wake of the social teachings of Pope Leo XIII, inaugurated a visibly successful epoch of Catholic trade unionism.

In the United States, the Puritan legacy of moralism remained, and in the nineteenth-century atmosphere of nonestablishment, the need for public witness to propriety seemed the stronger. From other quarters, the Arminian teachings of religious liberals emphasized personal responsibility in Christian life, while Enlightenment deism, with its stress on the moral life, fostered the moralistic ethos.

Two great public crusades for moral purity, the antislavery and temperance movements, flourished side by side, the former ended by the Civil War, the latter successfully culminating in the Prohibition amendment of 1919. By the second half of the twentieth century, new abolition crusades achieved public prominence, both in conservative struggles to end legal abortion and in liberal challenges to environmental pollution. The Social Gospel, with its calls for the coming of the kingdom of God on earth, was an American movement that spread to Canadian shores. After the Civil War and in the early twentieth century, its concerns were clearly articulated, and in the 1960s it again found a voice in the militant civil rights movement. Meanwhile, from the Roman Catholic side the social teachings of the church had their impact, although in the early century much less prominently than in Canada. Still, the Catholic Worker movement, arising during the Depression, offered a telling witness to social concern within Catholicism. In the post–Vatican II era, that concern became a leading feature of the American church.

Churches, Denominations, and Independent Religious Groups

The Christian genius for organization was nowhere more apparent than in North America. Here the old European church establishments became problematic. In the late eighteenth-century United States, the diversity of colonial establishments made a national church impractical. In New France, military defeat ended official church establishment. And in British Canada, the Anglican establishment found it impossible to become the religion of all or most of the people. Hence, denominationalism became the hallmark of North American Christianity: whatever the claims of an Old World church to universality, now the term *church* became simply a label of convenience. Still, the denominations understood themselves as participating in something larger—a universal church to which all Christian groups belonged.

Beyond the denominations, other forms of Christianity flourished. There were sectarian movements, which maintained strong barriers against the outer world and held to a more intensive religious regimen than the mainstream. There were other religious groups that claimed sources of revelation in addition to Christian scripture or, at least, offered a major reinterpretation of it. The cultural climate of the United States, more than that of Canada, fostered these groups and, likewise, encouraged the multiplication of denominations.

Roman Catholicism. Roman Catholic spirituality stressed tradition as much as the written word of the Bible. Strongly authoritarian, the Roman Catholic church had the most to lose in the evolving denominational situation. Yet in some ways it was more compatible with the North American setting than was Protestantism. With its strong sacramental cast, Roman Catholicism could see nature and the material world as the vehicle for spiritual reality. Hence, in its dealings with Indian peoples, Catholicism perhaps expressed less contempt for native ways and more willingness to incorporate aboriginal forms into a native North American Catholicism. Moreover, among the European immigrants, Catholicism provided the highly tangible institutional and ritual structures that could reassure those who were homesick for cultures and countries left behind.

New France. Catholicism in New Spain had been the religion, mostly, of Spanish conquerors and Indian converts. In New France, however, white settlement meant a transplanted European church that learned quickly to adapt to life on the frontier. Religious orders of men and women had come, the nuns making New France a pioneer in social concern and the French clergy forming a dedicated core. Their flock evidently responded. Although the settlers were remembered for their gaiety and enjoyment of life, European travelers were also impressed by their piety. There were, indeed, tensions between various religious orders and problems arising from the absenteeism of a series of bishops in Quebec, but Catholicism was in northern North America to stay.

British North Atlantic colonies. Roman Catholicism came to the British North Atlantic colonies in a far less privileged position. With a royal charter granted to George Calvert, the first Lord Baltimore (1580?–1632), the Maryland colony was founded as a refuge for Catholics persecuted in England. Laws passed in 1639 and a decade later guaranteed religious liberty, but Puritans quickly took control of the government and in 1654 repealed Maryland's Act of Toleration. Even in the first days of the colony, Catholics had been a minority, and by the early eighteenth century they were denied voting rights although they were paying taxes to support an Anglican establishment. Likewise, New England proved to be hostile ground for Catholic growth.

Growth and change in North American Catholicism. After Quebec fell to the British in 1760, the Church of England was the official established church, but in practice Roman Catholicism enjoyed the privileges of establishment. Closely bound to the culture and ethos of the French Canadians, it became a badge of ethnic identity, the sign of the French nation still flourishing in the heart of British North America. The Quebec Act of 1774 brought a vast territory of British North America into the French Canadian province, retained much of the old French legal and customary structure, conferred citizenship and ability to hold office on Roman Catholics, and permitted their church to maintain its tithing policy. After the Union Act of 1840 made Upper and Lower Canada (Canada West and East) one governmental unit, Catholics in 1845 obtained a return to denominational schools, a pattern that continued—not without challenge—in the Canadian system. By the end of the nineteenth century, French Canadians considered themselves a sacred, if beleaguered, people, with a special destiny to preserve their faith.

Outside French Canada, Roman Catholicism grew apace, brought in part by other immigrants. In the Maritimes, three distinct traditions—Acadian, Irish, and Scottish—flourished despite the tensions between them and despite the largely Protestant environment. To the west, French missions served the settlers, but English-speaking Catholics were not absent. Although their church continued to be dominated by the French, with time the role of the minorities increased. In the last quarter of the twentieth century, Catholicism was Canada's majority religion, and in 1975 some 52 percent of the population counted themselves Roman Catholic.

To the south, the American Revolution had inaugurated an era of religious toleration. To be sure, there was anti-Catholic feeling and, at times, violence against Catholics in the nineteenth and even the twentieth centuries. But the larger saga of Roman Catholicism was one of increasing integration into national life. Indeed, one of the biggest problems Catholics faced was that of becoming too well-integrated, too much like the Protestant majority. Thus, the trusteeship controversy of the early national period centered around the initiatives of Catholic laymen who attempted to follow the Protestant congregational model, calling and dismissing their pastors at will. And later efforts by liberal bishops led in part to Leo XIII's *Testem benevolentiae* (1899), warning against the heresy of "Americanism."

Not only did American Catholicism encounter the Protestant majority with its denominational plurality, but the church also found an abundant ethnic plurality within its own ranks. By the 1840s, a massive Irish immigration was changing the character of American Catholicism, and over time other groups joined the Irish: Germans, Italians, Poles, and Hispanics (the last through territorial acquisition as well as through immigration). There were marked tensions among these groups, but in the end the Irish form of Catholicism won, dominating the hierarchy and imprinting its character on American Catholic life.

Protestantism. Reformation spirituality had been born in protest against sacramentalism and traditionalism in the medieval church. It preached collective return to biblical sources of revelation and individual reliance on the grace of God in winning salvation. In fact, it was only a matter of time before the centrifugal tendencies implicit in the Reformation came to realization. Thus North America, settled largely by dissenting Protestants, proved fertile ground for a series of separate and at times competing denominations. At the same time, with its emphasis on the priestly vocation of all Christians in whatever worldly station, Reformation spirituality encouraged new sources of linkage between religion and culture. If church and state eventually became separated in North America, unofficially they sustained each other.

American denominationalism. The Virginia colony was settled by nondissenting members of the Church of England, but New England and Pennsylvania were colonized by sectarian groups—nonseparatist Puritans, separatist Pilgrims, and separatist Quakers. These "outsider" groups moved from quasi-sectarian status in England to the religious and political center in the New World. But when church nonestablishment was safeguarded by the new constitution, there were officially no religious "insiders" in the nation. Hence, from two directions there was movement toward homogenization. [*See* Denominationalism.]

For the Puritans of New England, however, something of the sectarian character remained. With their emphasis on congregational autonomy, Puritans quickly became Congregationalists. But their moralism and righteousness, their sense of destiny and chosenness, and their millennialism spread throughout religious and political culture. On the one hand, these attitudes engendered in the early republic a public Protestantism with a heavy ideological tinge. On the other hand, these attitudes encouraged, by their clarity, the self-definition of others and the multiplication of religious groups. Moreover, immigrants continued to bring Old World religions to the United States, further increasing the plurality.

After the Revolution, the American Church of England reconstituted itself as the Protestant Episcopal Church (1789). Meanwhile, Presbyterian and Baptist groups continued the Puritan vision, while Methodists, as new arrivals, achieved a separate American organization. The years of the early republic were times of spectacular Methodist development and growth, but Baptist fellowships, Methodism's closest competitors, also flourished, and restorationism (to the primitive New Testament church) grew with the Disciples of Christ, or "Christians" (1832). Thus, the evangelical character of these and other denominations was heavily imprinted on the culture. Nonetheless, a small but important liberal movement in religion had also arisen from Puritanism, assuming institutional form in 1825 as the American Unitarian Association. Liberalism likewise appeared in the popular religion of rural New England as Universalism, so called because of its teaching of universal salvation.

The Civil War brought serious denominational splits, and the post-Civil War epoch yielded new tensions between liberals and conservatives within denominations. With the new science of the era and the growing prestige of Charles Darwin's evolutionary theory, some preached world acceptance, welcoming "higher criticism" of the Bible and propounding a theology of immanence. Others, deeply troubled by these developments, welded millennial and rationalistic themes to shape a fundamentalism stressing biblical literalism and inerrancy. In this milieu, too, a "gospel of wealth," enjoining material prosperity, and a critique of poverty, preaching the Social Gospel, seemed to pull in opposite directions.

The results, for the twentieth century, included a denominationalism that often concealed within the ranks of the same religious organization individuals and groups of quite different theological and ethical bent. After 1925, fundamentalism for a time seemed less important, but the movement enjoyed a widespread resurgence by the last quarter of the century. At the same time, the twentieth century saw the development of a world ecumenical movement in which American denominations participated, especially through the World Council of Churches (1948) and the National Council of Churches of Christ (1950).

Canadian denominationalism. In the territory that became the Dominion of Canada, Protestantism first came with Huguenot traders and settlers. Nearly two centuries later, in 1760, the Church of England officially became the established church. Establishment, however, was mostly a legal fiction. Anglican clergy were insufficient in numbers and enthusiasm, the Anglican relationship to government often proved a liability, and the formal character of worship and gradualist model of Christian life were poorly adapted to life on the frontier.

Protestant groups that reaped benefits from Anglican problems were largely Presbyterians, Methodists, and, to a lesser extent, Baptists. With this denominational spectrum, and with the far greater Roman Catholic population (four times as numerous as Anglicans in 1842), resentment flared periodically over government aid to the Church of England through lands set aside as clergy reserves. When, in 1854, legislation proclaimed the desirability of ending any appearance of connection between church and state and commuted parts of the reserves as a permanent endowment, dissatisfaction remained. But the Church of England, the Church of Scotland, and the Wesleyan Methodist church—along with the Roman Catholic church—all received a share of the commutation. The voluntary principle, in the end, had won.

Generally, if not officially, the Protestant and Roman Catholic churches supported the Confederation of 1867. By 1881, the four major Protestant denominations could count over half the Canadian population as members. Methodists had established themselves as the largest among these churches, while Presbyterians were a close second. Moreover, both denominations, through a series of unions and reorganizations, successfully brought together nearly all groups in their respective denominational families.

These late-century mergers to form national bodies paved the way for the union, in 1925, between the Methodist and Presbyterian churches and the much smaller Congregational Union to form the United Church of Canada. The new church became, in effect, the "national" Protestant church, the body that, of all Protestant bodies, provided a counterweight for Catholicism. A liberal evangelical communion, it supported the Social Gospel. Likewise, when union sentiment arose anew with the ecumenical organization of the Canadian Council of Churches in 1944, the United Church was part of the undertaking. Since close to four out of five Canadian Protestants were United Church members or Anglicans, the denominational center seemed even stronger.

Eastern Orthodoxy. Wherever it existed in North America, Eastern Orthodox spirituality grew in national churches that enjoined continuity with the past. Formality and ritual splendor in the Divine Liturgy mediated a familial closeness, as the mystical Christianity of traditional Orthodoxy blended with the often intense nationalism of its congregations. Although it never became mission-minded, Orthodoxy did adapt to its new setting, introducing English into the Divine Liturgy, erecting pews in churches (unlike the traditional arrangement), and bringing feasts and holy days into conformance with the Western calendar.

The third major branch of Christianity first came to North America in the eighteenth century: Russian Orthodoxy grew in Alaska until, in the beginning of the twentieth century, some one-sixth of its people were Orthodox. Meanwhile, after Alaska became a possession of the United States, Russian Orthodoxy moved to San Francisco (1872) and then, by the end of the century, to New York. In the twentieth century, Greek Orthodoxy—present even before the turn of the century with immigration—grew larger than its Russian cousin, so that by 1975 there were almost two million Greek Orthodox Christians in the United States. Together with one million Russian Orthodox and still another million or so in separate national Orthodox churches, American Orthodoxy had solid grounds for its claim to be the fourth major faith in the nation (after Protestantism, Roman Catholicism, and Judaism).

Early twentieth-century immigration brought Eastern Orthodoxy to Canada as well, when Russians, Greeks, Serbians, and especially Ukrainians came. In 1918, the Ukrainian Greek Orthodox Church of Canada was established, providing a religious center for its adherents in western Canada. Meanwhile, Russian Orthodoxy grew, particularly in Alberta, despite the differences, as in the United States, between various factions. By the late twentieth century, Eastern Orthodox adherents in Canada numbered over 362,000.

Independent Religious Groups. The spirituality of independent religious groups, in general, stressed intensity of commitment and the transforming power of religion in every aspect of life. Frequently millennial in orientation, these groups often expected the dawn of a new age. Moreover, the line between them and the Protestant denominations is difficult to draw. From one point of view, many of the sectarian movements may be considered Protestant, provided that they are not considered closely related to mainstream Reformation churches and, on the other hand, that any roots in Reformation churches are taken into account. Even more, when such sectarian movements lose their exclusiveness and move in a more denominational direction, their inclusion with other Protestant groups becomes virtually automatic. Beyond the sects, religions like Mormonism and Christian Science fall outside the scope of Protestantism, although for practical purposes these religions are also often lumped together with the Protestant churches.

Sectarian movements. Marking their boundaries with the outside world far more strongly than do denominations, sects form tightly knit groups of committed coreligionists. Yet they are often intensely conversionist, with a powerful missionary urge, a sense of impending end to the present era, and an accompanying doctrine and experience of new birth. In short, what the evangelical denominations in North America in many ways adumbrated, its sectarian movements carried to logical and psychological completion. Moreover, in the United States, where sects appeared in far greater number and variety than in Canada, the national ideology of newness helped to foster the experience of new birth.

Some sects in the two countries were simply European imports, attracted by promises of religious freedom and abundance of land. But because of the isolation of such groups (e.g., the Amish, the Mennonites, and the Hutterites) and their relatively smaller numbers, they did not have nearly so much impact on culture as sectarian movements closer in spirit to mainstream Protestantism. Thus, Adventist movements like the Millerites of the early 1840s attracted wide public notice in the United States and Canada—and a following difficult to number, much of it within the Baptist and other evangelical denominations.

In another example, the American Holiness-Pentecostal movement grew from Methodist perfectionism and other sources until, by the late nineteenth century, the expulsion of Holiness associations or their secession from the Methodist churches came about. In congregations like the Church of the Nazarene, Holiness people were, religiously, relatively conservative, but a more radical expression of perfectionism came early in the twentieth century in Pentecostalism. For Pentecostals, the signs of the Holy Spirit—speaking in tongues and added biblical gifts like prayer, prophecy, and healing—descended in an atmosphere of miracle and millennialism. Their movement, interracial at first but then separated along color lines, spread to Canada and throughout the world. In Canada, Holiness had developed indigenously, but it also migrated northward from the United States just at the time that the Canadian West was experiencing a rapid growth of cities. The Nazarenes quickly rose to prominence among the Holiness sects, even as Pentecostalism entered from both the United States and Great Britain, finding a favorable climate for increase.

New religious movements. Like the sects, new religious movements arose far more often and more prominently in the United States than in Canada. In fact, one such movement, the Mormons, by the late twentieth century had established itself as among the largest religious organizations in the United States. In Canada, the Mormons also achieved a presence, appearing in Ontario and Upper Canada and building a temple in Cardston, Alberta. Eventually they could be found throughout Canada. The major development, though, was in the United States, where Mormon founder Joseph Smith (1805–1844) preached a new revelation transmitted to him on golden plates, a salvation history that centered on early America. Smith's written transcription, the *Book of Mormon*, grounded the movement, which evolved a distinctive theology of materialism, supporting the American venture and pronouncing a final goal of deification. [*See* Mormonism.]

Similarly, the founder of Christian Science, Mary Baker Eddy (1821–1910), in *Science and Health* gave her followers a book that they ranked beside the Bible. Built on a Congregational heritage of Puritanism and a resurgence of Platonism in the nineteenth century, Eddy's teaching stressed the illusory nature of the material realm and encouraged followers to look to divine Truth, experiencing physical healings and other material goods as signs of their apprehension of spiritual reality. [*See* Christian Science.]

Eddy's Christian Science church was relatively small in size, but it was the best organized of a series of movements in the United States that preached and practiced mental healing. These metaphysical movements often expressed in more concentrated form a general idealism in American culture, and, in their growing emphasis on themes of prosperity, from their own perspective they too taught a theology of materialism. At the same time, Christian Science and New Thought (the general name for other metaphysical movements such as Unity) traveled across the border into Canada where, in missions and churches, they spread their message.

Numbers of other new religious groups, based at least partially in Christianity, prospered and grew in North America. The typical pattern was foundation in the United States and subsequent migration into Canada, where the movement had a much smaller following. Many of these groups seemed bizarre and exotic to more conventional Christians, but, typically, their members linked themselves to Christianity.

Such disparate groups as the nineteenth-century Oneida community that taught a regulated pluralism of sexual partners in complex marriage, the enduring Spiritualist churches from the second half of the nineteenth century that sought to establish contact with the spirits of the departed, and the apocalyptic Children of God organization from the late 1960s that embraced a totalitarian patriarchalism, all expressed currents in the religious culture of North America. They took religious freedom seemingly as far as it would go—even to a commitment that, paradoxically, sometimes became willing bondage. They announced an alienation from tradition and a yearning for identity and community in a North American society grown perhaps too plural and too large. In short, the spread of new religious movements, from Mormonism to the Unification Church of Sun Myung Moon, must be linked to the history and sociological base of North American Christianity. [*See also* New Religions, *article on* New Religions and Cults in the United States.]

National and Regional Chronicles

By the late twentieth century, the United States and Canada had long since divided sovereignty over North America between them. Christianity was the predominant religion in both countries, and in both it exhibited characteristics suggesting the political and cultural ambience of North America. At the same time, each country showed marked differences from its neighbor in the forms its Christianity assumed.

Canadian Christianity. Because of their special history, Canadians generally thought of themselves as two nations—groups bound by ties of blood, tradition, and ethnic identity—in one political state. The political balance of power between French Canadians and English Canadians had a religious counterpart in the more or less equal division between Roman Catholic and Protestant Christians (although a large proportion of Catholics were English-speaking and not French at all). Protestant Christians comprised fewer denominations than in the United States, historically most belonging to the three or four biggest churches. Hence, it is fair to say that Canadian Christianity was both more and less plural than Christianity in the United States.

Canadian Christianity was more plural because the concentration of Christians into fewer religious groups fostered greater visibility and leverage for denominations with sufficient power and status in the community to count. But Canadian Christianity was also less plural than its American counterpart, for the obvious reason that there were fewer groups in absolute numbers, but also because of an ecumenism especially apparent in Protestant Christianity. It was less plural, too, because of the subtle Erastianism that encouraged all denominations to uphold a central cultural order. Christianity in Canada tended to be "social" Christianity, more conservative than in the United States and less rigid in its boundary between church and state.

Mission-minded and voluntaryistic like the American Christian churches, the Canadian denominations had worked on a huge geographical scale, and so—perhaps more than and ahead of their country's politicians—they thought in terms of the North American continent as a whole. Moreover, with the imposing strength of Roman Catholicism before them, Canadian Protestants were particularly urged in cooperative directions. Thus, in some sense they provided the public unity that the state could not give because of its divisions between English and French. Much more than Christianity in the United States, Canadian Christianity maintained its ties with the past, favoring continuity and tradition over religious change and novelty.

Finally, Canadians overwhelmingly counted themselves denominational Christians, exceeding even the high American church membership (nearly 70 percent of the people) in the late twentieth century. At the turn of the century, 90 percent of Canadians belonged to six major Christian groups (including as the largest the Roman Catholic). By the 1960s, with some substitutions, the figure was higher still, and by the early 1970s over three-quarters of the population were Roman Catholic, United Church, or Anglican church members.

American Christianity. The Puritan ethos left its mark on American religion, and numerical, political, and cultural balance made the United States distinctly Protestant. Although the nation was far more plural than Canada in the number of its Christian groups (a conservative estimate includes more than two hundred), public Protestantism meant that, with less overt cooperation between church and state, the country could become in some ways far more Christian, far less secular, than its northern neighbor.

Thus, while the Canadian system accommodated itself to the support of denominational schools, in the United States the nineteenth-century public schools openly taught Protestant Christianity. Similarly, even as Puritanism faded into other denominational forms, its spirit remained to transform public and political life. Manifest destiny and political imperialism became the harvest of the Puritan past.

Explicitly present in Puritanism, millennialism resurfaced time and again—in liberal expectations of a new era, in sectarian beliefs that the millennium had already come or was just about to break, in fundamentalist announcements of the signs of the swift return of Christ. Nationally, too, political millennialism suffused foreign and domestic policy, so that wars were generally read as epochal events that would determine the future of the nation and even the world.

Tied to this generalized cultural millennialism, ultraism flourished in American social history. The ultraism was evident in the moralistic crusades—which were more strident in the United States than in Canada—over antislavery, temperance, civil rights, and other social issues. Yet for all the mass emotion, the rhetoric of religious individualism became uppermost in the United States. This rhetoric went hand in hand with the ideology of newness and evangelical mission and hand in hand, too, with a pronounced ahistoricism and, in restorationist sentiment, a willingness to skip over long centuries of Christian history. Linked to a search for religious simplicity and sometimes to anti-intellectualism, restorationist movements expressed in institutional form a general spirit in American Christianity.

Certainly, as early as the mid-nineteenth century, Roman Catholicism was the single largest Christian denomination in the United States, and by 1983 it included some 29 percent of the population. But, with a different history and a lesser size, Catholicism never achieved the impact on American culture that had been its birthright in Canada. Simultaneously more and less established than in Canada, public Christianity continued to be Protestant Christianity.

Finally, this public Christianity assumed explicitly political form in what many scholars have called civil religion. While the Enlightenment ideology present at the time of the American Revolution encouraged a form of religious nationalism that was not specifically Christian, later a public alliance between gospel and flag became commonplace. By the 1970s and 1980s, a new Christian Right was working to shape political events. Conservative Christians were probably the fastest-growing Christian groups in Canada as in the United States, but again, because of the different histories of the two countries, they could not capture the public space in Canada in the same way as in the United States. Hence, in American religion, public Protestantism, civil religion, and cultural religion became aspects of the same center. [*See* Civil Religion.]

Regional Christianity. Living together in one area, Christian peoples may share a common history as well as a common religion. Likewise, they sometimes develop ties that, in effect, constitute them as a new "particular people." European sectarian groups that settled in North America offered striking cases of the growth of such religious regionalism. Rural places and urban centers alike often assumed the character of a religious and ethnic group. Meanwhile, more diffused throughout larger areas, identifiable forms of regional Christianity flourished. This was clearly true in the French Canadian Catholicism of the province of Quebec, but it was also true in, for example, the Eastern Cherokee Christianity of western North Carolina after the Indian Removal of 1838. The pattern could be noticed distinctly in the fundamentalist Protestantism of southern Appalachia, and it was strikingly present in black religion as, in sections of the American South, it joined to its Christianity inherited African thought forms and indigenous folk religion.

The Larger North American Landscape. In the end, however, North American Christianity should be seen from a continental perspective. With its voluntaryism, activism, and moralism, it has been generally evangelistic in tone. The call to mission clearly gave it a distinct identity: Roman Catholic and, more, Eastern Orthodox strains of mystical piety never made their mark on Christian culture as a whole. Denominational in organization, the essence of North American Christianity has been at once its plurality and its seeking for a genuine pluralism, a state of pleased acceptance of the plural situation. At the same time, North American Christianity modified the plurality to reflect political and national needs for unity.

With the second half of the twentieth century, religion in North America encountered the increasing secularization of culture. Although in both the United States and Canada Christian church membership included the large majority, it also seemed that, except for the fundamentalist political thrust of the New Right, Christianity had a diminished connection with everyday life. In a certain sense, the mission-minded evangelical ethos seemed more a style or habit than a substantive transformer of the world. On the other hand, North American Christianity has perhaps grown more modest, chastened by a new awareness of the danger of cultural imperialism. Looking ahead to the twenty-first century, it has turned inward to find spiritual roots in its biblical heritage and outward to listen to the words and messages of non-Christian others at home and abroad.

[*For discussion of reactions to Christianity among North American Indians, see* North American Religions, *article on* Modern Movements.]

BIBLIOGRAPHY

The one book that deals with all of North American Christianity as defined in this article is Robert T. Handy's *A History of the Churches in the United States and Canada* (New York, 1977). It is clear and straightforward, written from the perspective of church history and with meticulous attention to detail.

For American (U.S.) Christianity, the most exhaustive source, highlighting the theme of Puritanism, is the monumental work by Sydney E. Ahlstrom, *A Religious History of the American People* (New Haven, 1972). More concise but also informative is Winthrop S. Hudson's *Religion in America*, 3d ed. (New York, 1981). My book *America: Religions and Religion* (Belmont, Calif., 1981) offers a different approach from the previous works, employing the perspectives of history of religions and interdisciplinary history to study the counterpoint between the manyness and oneness of American religion(s).

As a collection of essays that masterfully explores denominationalism and other central themes in American religious history, the classic work by Sidney E. Mead, *The Lively Experiment: The Shaping of Christianity in America* (New York, 1963), is insightful and rewarding. The *Historical Atlas of Religion in America*, rev. ed. (New York, 1976), by Edwin S. Gaustad, is invaluable as a religious atlas. The book is especially useful for its careful charts and graphics. Another invaluable work of historical craftsmanship, edited by Edwin S. Gaustad, is his two-volume documentary collection, *A Documentary History of Religion in America*, vol. 1, *To the Civil War*, and vol. 2, *Since 1865* (Grand Rapids, Mich., 1982–1983). The documents, selected to show a pluralism present in American religious history from the first, contain a wealth of materials for the beginner or the more advanced student. With the possible exception of Mead's essays, all the works above consider American Christianity not exclusively, but as the largest theme in the religious mosaic of the United States, which they seek to describe comprehensively.

Among more specialized studies in American Christianity, *Righteous Empire: The Protestant Experience in America* (New York, 1970) by Martin E. Marty, republished in a second edition as *Protestantism in the United States: Righteous Empire* (New York, 1986), is still the best treatment of Protestantism, reading it in terms of its impact on culture and cultural imperialism. For Roman Catholicism, the account by John Tracy Ellis, *American Catholicism*, 2d ed., rev. (Chicago, 1969), is yet the classic short work. The book by Henry Warner Bowden, *American Indians and Christian Missions: Studies in Cultural Conflict* (Chicago, 1981), is sensitive to the contact situation but suggestive more than comprehensive as a treatment of the christianization of Amerindian peoples in American territory. Still, its account of Huronia provides a highly readable introduction to the work of the Jesuits in New France. The pathbreaking work by Albert J. Raboteau, *Slave Religion: The "Invisible Institution" in the Antebellum South* (Oxford, 1978), considerably advances the study of black Christianity. More comprehensive in scope but written to argue a distinct theological agenda is Gayraud S. Wilmore's *Black Religion and Black Radicalism: An Interpretation of the Religious History of Afro-American People*, 2d ed., rev. and enl. (Maryknoll, N.Y., 1983). Even with the theological *tour de force*, it is the best survey presently available.

Lamentably, Canadian Christianity has not received nearly the scholarly attention that its American counterpart has. The most useful short history, though dated, is H. H. Walsh's *The Christian Church in Canada* (Toronto, 1956). More recent and more expansive is the three-volume work, *A History of the Christian Church in Canada*, produced under the general editorship of John Webster Grant. The first volume of this trilogy, *The Church in the French Era: From Colonization to the British Conquest* (Toronto, 1966), also by H. H. Walsh, intersperses nuanced biographical sketches in its chronicle of events and offers an absorbing, contextualistic account. The second volume, by John S. Moir, *The Church in the British Era: From the British Conquest to Confederation* (Toronto, 1972), continues the chronicle to 1867 within a crisp and comprehensive church historical framework. The third volume, *The Church in the Canadian Era: The First Century of Confederation* (Toronto, 1972), by John Webster Grant, completes the series in somewhat more discursive fashion. For a more popular and colloquial introduction, there is the handsome and illustrated *Religion in Canada: The Spiritual Development of a Nation*, by William Kilbourn, A. C. Forrest, and Patrick Watson (Toronto, 1968). Its impressionistic surveys sweep through Canadian religious history, virtually all of it Christian, to good effect; and its photo essays prove rewarding complements to the text. And for a useful documentary collection, see the volume edited by John S. Moir, *The Cross in Canada* (Toronto, 1966).

More specialized accounts of Canadian Christianity include the important work of John Webster Grant, *Moon of Wintertime* (Toronto, 1984), chronicling the ambiguous encounter between Christian missionaries and Canadian Indians since 1534. More regionally specific, the brief but impressive study by Cornelius J. Jaenen, *The Role of the Church in New France* (Toronto, 1976), supersedes the Walsh volume on New France and argues the role of Catholic Counter-Reformation piety in its cultural formation. Likewise studying Catholicism in Quebec is the work by Nive Voisine with the collaboration of André Beaulieu and Jean Hamelin, *Histoire de l'Église catholique au Québec, 1608–1970* (Montreal, 1971). It is regrettably without notes or index. *L'Église catholique au Canada, 1604–1886* (Trois-Rivières, 1970) by the Abbé Hermann Plante is more widely ranging but unfortunately ends in the late nineteenth century and also contains neither notes nor index.

The short introduction by Douglas J. Wilson, *The Church Grows in Canada* (Toronto, 1966), although it purports to be a general study, almost entirely concerns Protestantism. Its thumbnail sketches of denominations and sectarian movements are useful, but there are inaccuracies. A classic study of evangelism and revivalism in Canada, dated in its interpretive framework but rich in its use of primary source materials and lively, if lengthy, in its account, is *Church and Sect in Canada* (Toronto, 1948) by S. D. Clark. Finally, *Church and State in Canada West: Three Studies in the Relation of Denominationalism and Nationalism, 1841–1867* (1959; reprint, Toronto, 1968) by John S. Moir surveys issues regarding the clergy reserves and education in Canada West (Upper Canada).

CATHERINE L. ALBANESE

Christianity in Sub-Saharan Africa

While it is impossible to obtain precise figures of religious allegiance, it is reasonable to state that the number of Christians in Africa in 1985 was not less than 150 million. Christianity is now either the majority religion, or about to become it, in almost all parts of the African continent south of the equator as well as in important parts north of the equator, notably along much of the west coast. Bantu-speaking Africa, in particular, is becoming overwhelmingly Christian. Some 150 years ago, there were only a handful of Christians, and those were mostly in a few European-controlled coastal settlements. A century ago, the missionary advance into the interior was still only just beginning, while Islam was far better established in both the west and east and set to spread further. The most likely religious future for the continent remained a slow but irresistible islamization like that which had been proceeding for centuries in the West African interior as in eastern areas like Somalia. This did continue in some parts, such as the Tanzanian coast, among the Yao of Malawi and still more widely in much of West Africa.

Elsewhere, however, recent African history has witnessed the most extensive mass movement into Christianity anywhere in the world in modern times. Countries like Zaire, Ghana, Togo, Uganda, Kenya, Rwanda, Burundi, Zambia, Malawi, Zimbabwe, Namibia, Angola, and South Africa have a dominantly Christian sense of identity at the level of culture and popular religion, however mixed this may be with traditional religion—especially in remoter areas. This still inadequately recognized fact has not only profoundly affected the history and future of Africa but also altered the modern worldwide balance of Christianity. Increasingly the Christian churches must appear on the international scene as a racial alliance of white and black to a degree that could hardly have been envisaged in the early decades of the twentieth century.

Beginnings of Christianity in Africa. Before the last decades of the nineteenth century, there was nothing to suggest that Christianity would grow so explosively. Africa had time and again proved to be a continent in which Christianity failed to make a lasting breakthrough. The large and impressive early churches of Egypt and the North African coast were overtaken by Muslim conquest. In Egypt the Christian church survived, at times tenuously, as an underprivileged minority, but to the west it did not. Furthermore, it had failed to penetrate across the Sahara, unlike Islam in subsequent centuries. Certainly, it prospered in Ethiopia and also, for several centuries, in Nubia. [*See* Ethiopian Church.] Nevertheless, any spread southward was limited. Under Muslim pressure Nubian Christianity was extinguished by the fifteenth century while the Ethiopian church only just survived the sixteenth-century *jihād* of Ahmad Grāñ.

From the sixteenth to the eighteenth century, under the patronage of the Portuguese empire, there was a considerable amount of evangelistic work undertaken in several parts of the continent—in some places, notably Warri, the Kongo, and the interior of Angola, with some apparent success. In the seventeenth century especially, the Kongo kingdom seemed deeply christianized in the period of the Capuchin missionaries. However, for a variety of reasons, such as the lack of a steady flow of missionaries, colonial politics and slave-trading, and the failure to establish truly indigenous institutions, almost nothing endured. Little by little, Christian practices were absorbed by the tolerant embrace of African traditional religion, until by the early nineteenth century they had simply faded away.

At this point Catholic missionary efforts were for a while taken over by Protestant efforts in the wake of the evangelical movement, the growth of British imperial power, and the campaign to abolish the slave trade. A small crowd of black people returning to Africa in 1787 under the aegis of a London emancipationist committee may be taken as inaugurating the new era. They were settled in Sierra Leone around what is now Freetown. Reinforced by further settlements, they made of Sierra Leone an Anglican and Methodist powerhouse. Fourah Bay College, founded at Freetown by the Church Missionary Society in 1827, developed into the first institution of higher education for black Africa. Sierra Leone became, for the nineteenth century, the source of a network of West African coastal Christian communities, English in speech and often in nomenclature, confident, and urban-based. Its most outstanding representative was the Yoruba-born Samuel Ajayi Crowther (1809?–1891), Anglican bishop on the Niger. This Krio (creole) Christianity proved highly vocal, the protagonist of a distinct African Christian identity, yet it did not mix easily with the rural multitude, and Sierra Leone as a whole remained one of the least christianized of African countries. A comparable black Christianity—though less elitist and vocal, and more rural—was growing up at much the same time in South Africa, especially among the Xhosa. With Crowther, one can here compare the Presbyterian minister Tiyo Soga (1829–1871), hymn writer and Bible translator.

Elsewhere, the institutional initiative would long remain with the white missionaries. The second half of the nineteenth century was their golden age, presided over by the brilliant, restless, and quite untypical spirit of David Livingstone (1813–1873). Henry Venn, secretary of the Church Missionary Society from 1841 to 1872 and the man responsible for Crowther's appointment, brought a new maturity to Protestant missionary thinking. So too did Cardinal Charles Lavigerie, founder of the White Fathers society for Africa missions (1868), and Bishop Melchior de Marion Brésillac, founder of the Society of Missions of Africa (SMA, 1856), for Roman Catholics.

From the 1870s on there was a marked increase in both the number and the educational level of missionaries. Yet for many years the effect of the new missionary wave may well have appeared to be not much greater than that of its predecessors. The new breed of missionaries on the west coast came into an ill-advised and destructive clash with Bishop Crowther and the Sierra Leoneans. The important legacy of this period was a significant start on translation of the Bible into scores of African languages, that would prove to be the true foundation for African Christianity. Missionaries like Robert Moffat (1795–1883) of Kuruman were often unimaginative, quarrelsome among themselves, and far from strikingly successful in terms of "conversions," but enough of them became remarkable linguists to ensure that the most widely available reading matter for the early generations of literate Africans would be the Christian scriptures. The formal preaching of missionaries seldom proved very convincing or even comprehensible (except to a more-or-less captive audience of house servants and ransomed slaves), but the Bible in its range of historic particularity, legal prescription, and deep mystery provided a compelling vision, and one seemingly more at home in traditional Africa than in nineteenth-century Europe.

By the start of the twentieth century there were several peoples, beyond Sierra Leonean Krios and the Xhosa, among whom a wide movement of Christian conversion was clearly under way: the Yoruba, Igbo, and other West Africa coastal peoples; the Kongo (renewing an old allegiance) and the Ngwato in the south; and the Ganda in the east (following the striking martyrdoms of 1886 under King Mwanga). The Ngwato and the Ganda were exceptional in that they lived in the interior. They remained the exceptions. But the circumstances of the continent as a whole were changing greatly.

The Colonial Period. In the 1890s Africa was parceled out among the European powers, and the fortunes of Christianity would, for a while, depend considerably upon its relationship with the colonial order. The latter undoubtedly helped missionary activity in various important ways, just as missionaries both pressed for, and facilitated, the colonial takeover, so that Christianity and colonial conquest could seem at times like two sides of a single coin. Modern anticolonialism has often branded Christianity in Africa, with some justification, as an accomplice of colonialism. But if the link between the two was often unhealthily close, it is also true that colonial conquest in no way required christianization—indeed, many colonialists would have preferred islamization. The British empire, in particular, had been too profoundly shaped by India to want to christianize its subjects, while the French government at the time was generally anticlerical. Missionaries could occasionally speak out against colonial proceedings on behalf of native rights; they did quite a lot to uncover the atrocities committed in the Congo Free State. They also began quite early in a few places (notably the Free Church of Scotland at Lovedale in South Africa and Livingstonia in Malawi) to provide a level of liberal education for Africans which colonists found both unnecessary and dangerous and which in fact served to cradle modern nationalism. Basically, however, missionaries were seldom a decisively influential part of early colonial society. By 1914, even though Africa was covered by a remarkable network of missions—often in intense rivalry with one another (especially Catholic versus Protestant)—there seemed to have been little decisive impact, except in a few places.

Nevertheless, an enormous religious change had begun to take place in thousands of different places. Three principal instruments were at work: the village school, the catechist, and the vernacular Bible. Colonial requirements, the pressures of modernity, and the deep vitality and adaptiveness of African societies combined to produce a sudden, quick-spreading urge for elementary Western education. No one but the missions tried to meet the demand, which they themselves saw as the hand of God. Everywhere, as a consequence, bush schools were opened and passages from the Bible were read. Baptism followed as a natural sequence. But in the face of the new demand, missionaries were few and none too mobile. The person who could cope with the new situation was the catechist—a poorly trained and more poorly paid village-level representative of both Christianity and modernity.

Besides the catechists, who were officially appointed by the churches, there were thousands of other self-appointed evangelists—miners, shopkeepers, migrant laborers—who spread elements of Christian life with enthusiasm: Bible reading, hymn singing, and even such concomitants as playing football. All this occurred in places well beyond the control of any missionary. The school and the catechist were, in secular terms, the agencies of a new economic and social order, but in religious terms they were the agency of a new biblically fed religious consciousness and sense of community.

The institutional structure and official statistics of the main churches were slow to reflect the deep underlying flow. Many churches imposed long periods of catechumenate before baptism, precisely to avoid the degenerating syncretism of an earlier age. This, together with stern rules of behavior (monogamy, abstinence from alcohol, appropriate dress), ensured that a high proportion of the people who were now coming to regard themselves as Christians were not accepted officially as church members. Training for ordination was far more severely circumscribed. The appointment of Bishop Joseph Kiwanuka as Roman Catholic vicar apostolic of

Masaka, Uganda, in 1939 was absolutely exceptional. The number of the ordained before 1950 was in most countries and churches extremely small, where ordained clergy existed at all. Almost until the coming of political independence to the greater part of black Africa around 1960, official Christianity remained carefully controlled by white missionaries operating from a small number of complex missions—small denominational cities they had built up and ruled. Mission stations were of real importance because of the secondary schools and hospitals they contained, as well as because they provided the administrative and symbolic centers for the vast network of rural Christianity. Their boarding schools ensured that the new elite, as well as the masses, would be christianized in the very process of coming into existence. To a very large extent, Africa's new ruling class sprang from these schools. Even when most critical of missionaries and churches, African politicians seldom fail to express gratitude for their contribution toward secondary education.

But the effective (rather than symbolic) role of the central mission station and the missionaries (increasingly administrators) who staffed it remain secondary in importance for the understanding of the almost ubiquitous, rapid, yet largely uncharted evolution of modern African Christianity. The two levels could easily come into conflict. The character of popular Christianity inevitably left a great deal to be desired from the viewpoint of missionary orthodoxy. Should a zealous but polygamist catechist be retained? Could God be expected to address and instruct new converts through dreams and visions? Could the illnesses of Christians be explained and combated in terms of bewitchment? The missionary answer to such questions was most often a firm no. For their part, Africans frequently remained unconvinced on these matters, and from the end of the nineteenth century a multitude of independent churches began to arise, first in South Africa and Nigeria, then in many other parts of the continent where there was already a significant missionary presence.

Independent Churches. Independent church movements took roughly two chief forms. The first produced what in Nigeria have been called the "African" churches and in South Africa the "Ethiopian" churches. Early examples are the United Native African Church, founded in Lagos in 1891, and the Ethiopian Church, founded in Pretoria in 1892. These are essentially cases of schism, in which full members of an established church, often including some clergy, have divided from the missionary body over issues like the promotion of local leadership, nationalist sympathy and cultural ethos, and acceptance of polygamists in continuing membership. Such new churches sprang mostly from Methodist, Baptist, Presbyterian, or low church Anglican missions, and very seldom from Lutherans, high church Anglicans, or Roman Catholics. They have almost always retained substantial continuity in doctrine, liturgy, and church order with those from which they seceded. They fit closely enough within a pattern of bifurcation characteristic of nineteenth-century Protestantism in both Britain and the United States.

Churches of this sort, of African origin, are found in many parts of the African continent, and new ones have continued to come into existence in almost every decade of the twentieth century. From about the second decade of the century, however, there began the still more widespread development of prophet and healing churches, generally classed as "Zionist" in southern Africa, and in Nigeria called mostly "Aladura," or praying churches. These bodies generally grew out of the career of a prophet, yet they were also influenced by American or European Zionist and Pentecostal groups (e.g., the Christian Catholic Apostolic Church, with its headquarters at Zion City near Chicago, founded in 1896 by John Alexander Dowie). These links, such as they were, were easily left behind. Adoption of the name "Ethiopian" had no administrative or doctrinal significance. It was merely symbolic and persuasive, with its biblical foundation (*Ps.* 68:31, *Acts* 8:27) and reference to the one part of black Africa that had both been Christian for centuries and retained its political and ecclesiastical independence (Ethiopia's military victory over Italian invaders at Adwa in 1896 sent a thrill of excitement across the continent). So too the name "Zion" was appealing as a profound symbol of the immediate renewal of God's holy city as celebrated, for example, in *Psalms* 122–134.

African Zionist and praying churches were much more innovative than Ethiopian ones: their preoccupation was with healing instead of schooling (indeed, they were often opposed to Western education); they grew faster, their membership was poorer. In some places (though this was not true of Nigeria) they could be seen as a fairly typical expression of the religion of the deprived. At the start, they depended mostly upon the personal impact of prophetic founders and often continued to be ruled dynastically by the founders' families, although they were prone to more and more divisions into separate groups. If their prime secular concern was undoubtedly healing, the balance within them between healing, evangelism, and the appeal of a total religious community offering a complex liturgical life centered upon a "sacred city," a Zion of their own, has varied greatly between churches.

The first of the major African prophets of the twentieth century was the native Liberian William Wade

Harris, a Grebo schoolteacher of Methodist and Episcopal background. During a period of imprisonment he experienced visions of the angel Gabriel commanding him to become an evangelist like John the Baptist. His subsequent months of peregrinatory preaching during 1914 in southern Ivory Coast and Ghana produced tens of thousands of baptisms and permanently altered the religious character of the area he traversed. The decisive effect was fully recognized both by missionaries and by colonial officials. Harris had abandoned his European ways, his shoes, and his trousers; he had also abandoned any particular church affiliation. He preached a very simple Christian monotheism, expelled devils, carried the Bible wherever he went, and baptized all who rejected and destroyed their pagan "fetishes." Harris insisted upon the observance of the Sabbath and the Ten Commandments, but not upon monogamy. He established no church of his own, and many thousands of his converts became Roman Catholic or Methodist, but he did leave "twelve apostles" in the villages he converted, and out of these communities the Harrist church subsequently grew. [*See also the biography of Harris*.]

At almost exactly the same time Garrick Braide, an Anglican catechist, carried on a similar mission in the Niger Delta. In the 1920s, the Aladura prophets (Moses Orimolade, Abiodun Akinsowon, Joseph Babalola, and others) were preaching, healing, and destroying "fetishes" up and down Yoruba country in western Nigeria. For a few months in 1921 Simon Kimbangu (1889?–1951), of Baptist background, set an immense prophetic movement afoot in the lower Kongo, west of Kinshasa. At much the same time, Isaiah Shembe was doing the same in Zululand, Ignatius Lekganyane in northern Transvaal, Samuel Mutendi in Rhodesia (present-day Zimbabwe). In the 1930s, John (Johane) Maranke and Johane Masowe were two striking John-the-Baptist figures in Rhodesia (each took the name of John after his vocation experience). In the 1950s it was the turn of Alice Lenshina (Mulenga) in Zambia. And there were many others. [*See the biographies of Kimbangu, Lenshina, Maranke, and Shembe*.]

The major prophets of this sort were frequently surrounded and followed by scores of lesser prophets. No single typology for the prophetic phenomenon in modern Africa can be established, but some general remarks can be made. One should distinguish between the prophet movement itself, especially in its initial outbreak, and the increasingly institutionalized church which usually, though not always, followed it. The latter has a consequential character, deriving from the need for a new community to cater to the prophet's clientele and the inability of existing churches to cope with either the prophet or his clientele, but it does not seem to be a primary intention of the prophet. At least initially, the prophets we have named probably did not see themselves as doing anything very different from many black evangelists working for the mission churches or, indeed, from the early white missionaries themselves. They may have simply taken the Bible more literally than the early white missionaries did, but the prophetic character of many an early missionary, with his long peregrinations, prayers for rain, healing skill, and apparently strange powers of many sorts, should not be overlooked. The prophetic vocation really came from the sheer impact of Bible and missionary upon the more imaginative. For new converts, lacking almost any other literature, the Bible could have an immediacy and an applicability which few of even the most fundamentalist of missionaries could really go along with. Visions, dreams, and miracles of healing seemed to be the staple of this strange book that had been translated into their tongue and presented as having an absolute authority; and these became the staple of early African prophetic Christianity, as they were not of missionary Christianity.

In many places there seemed to be a need for movements of this type regardless of whether any major figure was present or not. Just at the time Harris was making such an impact upon the Ivory Coast, a remarkably similar movement of conversion was developing without any central preacher at all, white or black, in the Usoko district of the Nigerian coast. Such movements, if handled one way, might produce massive new advances for a historic church; if handled another way, they led to an explosion of independency. Significant churches almost always developed from the major prophets: the Harrist church, the Church of Jesus Christ on Earth through the Prophet Simon Kimbangu, the Eternal Sacred Order of the Cherubim and Seraphim of Orimolade, the VaHosanna of Masowe, the Nazareth Baptist Church (Amanazaretha) of Shembe, the Lumpa of Lenshina. Many of these came to be centered upon a holy city—a Zion or New Jerusalem—in which the founder had lived and was eventually buried, to which the sick came for healing, a center for pilgrimage and liturgy. Kimbangu's Nkamba, Shembe's Ekuphakameni, Lenshina's Kasomo are just a few of many examples. With the passing of time, however, in a second and third generation, many churches which were prophetic and Zionist in origin became increasingly administrative and "Ethiopian": spiritual healing was formalized or almost disappeared, schools became a preoccupation. The Kimbanguist church is one clear example. It is also true that some churches which began as "Ethiopian" and were rather Western in form subsequently developed in a more prophetic and healing direction.

African ecclesiastical independency is, then, an immensely varied response both to the scriptures and to the experience of missionary Christianity. It is also, to a greater or lesser extent, in continuity with traditional patterns of African religion and society. Modern African Christianity is heir to African traditional religions as well as to the nineteenth-century missionary movement, but here again the intricacies and varieties of the relationship must not be underestimated. There was a larger measure of harmony between the common pattern of African traditional religion and traditional Christianity (especially in its more Catholic forms) than missionaries recognized. The high god of African religions—Nzambi, Mulungu, Leza, Mwari, Katonda, or whatever name the god took—had attributes extremely similar to the God of the biblical tradition, even if the cult of ancestors often made him seem, especially to the outside observer, unduly remote. Christian theism came to support itself easily upon traditional theism. Nor was the moral law much of a problem area, although missionaries sometimes thought it was (the practice of polygamy provided a special case).

The main point of conflict was, and still largely is, the veneration of ancestral spirits and the many rites—domestic, agricultural, and communal—which involve the invocation of those spirits. Missionaries condemned participation in all such rites, and most churches continue to do so officially, but the majority of Christians probably return to traditionalism for at least some of these occasions. For the most part, independent churches are as opposed to such practices as the mission churches. Indeed, while the latter (especially the Roman Catholic church) have tended to become accommodating with time, the former maintain the inflexibility of opposition of the nineteenth-century missionary.

In regard to some other aspects of traditional culture the case is different. On many points the Old Testament and African traditions appear to be somewhat allied against the New Testament and the missionary church: food taboos are a case in point. When these are recognized in an independent church, it is not clear whether it provides an example of the maintenance of traditional culture or a case of excessive Hebraism. Polygamy is another example. Many an independent church has rejected missionary insistence upon monogamy and appealed to the Old Testament for support, though it must be added that others (like the Kimbanguist and the Lumpa churches) have condemned polygamy without reserve.

Perhaps the most difficult area has been that of witchcraft beliefs. Throughout Africa—among some peoples a great deal more than others—sickness, death, and misfortune were and still are explained in terms of bewitchment. The traditional healer (*nganga* in most Bantu languages) then had to be someone who could both detect and counteract witchcraft. Most missionaries did not believe in the possibility of witchcraft (in this they conformed with colonial law) and countered traditional medicine with Western "scientific" practice. While for the missionaries the difference in kind between Western medicine and the *nganga*'s was clear, for Africans it often was not. Some independent churches have rejected both kinds of medicine in favor of faith healing alone, but others tend to interpret sickness in traditional bewitchment terms and the more concerned they are with healing the more they may be assimilable to a typical antiwitchcraft movement. The prophet can appear to be remarkably like the traditional *nganga*, however much the prophet may denounce the latter. The Holy Spirit to which the prophet appeals in the battle against witchcraft may seem no different from the spirit through which the *nganga* works.

If some independent churches do, then, represent some degree of merging of Christianity and African traditional religion, no generalization may be offered as to which eventually controls the symbiosis. In some of the better-known churches Christian orthodoxy prevails increasingly, but in many smaller groups it is African tradition which prevails. Each has proved naturally inclusive, not only in modern times but also down through the centuries, and it is as possible for elements of Christian thought, vocabulary, and ritual practice to be absorbed into an essentially non-Christian pattern of religion as it is for elements of traditional religion to be carried on, sometimes not incongruously, in the lives of believing and committed Christians. In much of this, the independent churches are no special category. We simply see in them, through the many studies conducted recently, processes which are almost equally at work in all the larger churches of Africa, for we must not forget that more than four-fifths of African Christians belong not to independent churches but to mission-founded churches. If the former may constitute as much as one-third of black Christians in South Africa, and are also very numerous in southern Nigeria, southern Ghana, and central Kenya, they are almost completely absent in some countries, such as Uganda and Tanzania, and in many others they are fewer than 10 percent of the Christian body. [*See also* African Religions, *article on* Modern Movements.]

Traditional Churches. As a whole, African Christianity is denominationally a highly complex reality, the field in which a thousand flowers are free to bloom. Beyond the independent churches, all the main European and American traditions are powerfully represented in one country or another. The Anglican communion is present wherever the British empire used to be present and in Rwanda and Burundi as well, but it is particularly strong in Nigeria, Uganda, Kenya, and South Africa; Methodists are numerous in Nigeria, Ghana, South Africa, Zimbabwe, and Zaire; Presbyterians in Kenya and Malawi; Baptists in Zaire and Liberia; The Dutch Reformed Church in South Africa; Lutherans in Tanzania and Namibia; the Church of the Nazarene in Swaziland. And that is not a complete list. In Zambia the United Church of Zambia was inaugurated in 1965, the year of the country's political independence, with the blessing of President Kenneth Kaunda. It incorporated Presbyterians, Congregationalists, and Methodists, but such unions have not been favored. Ecumenical relations are mostly excellent but the desire to maintain an independent ecclesiastical identity—whether originally the church is mission-founded or independent—is extremely strong.

The nineteenth century was preeminently a period of Protestant mission, and the legacy of a multitude of African churches today reflects that fact. In the twentieth century Roman Catholicism has spread with great effectiveness. The systematic and disciplined efforts of the great Roman Catholic mission societies of priests, monks, and nuns cannot quite be paralleled upon the Protestant side. Today, not only is the Roman Catholic church the church of the majority of all Christians in its older areas of predominance (French- and Portuguese-speaking especially), such as Zaire, Togo, Rwanda, and Burundi, but it has also become the largest single church in almost every country of Africa (Namibia, with its Lutheran predominance, is perhaps—apart from Ethiopia—the most striking exception).

If almost all the main churches have an almost completely black leadership at the level of the episcopate or presiding ministers, it is equally true that almost all are extremely short of ordained men or women (and when they have them, they often find it difficult to pay them). But for the Roman Catholic church, with its rigid pattern of celibate priesthood, this is above all the case. There are now some two hundred black Catholic bishops and half a dozen cardinals (the first being Rugambwa of Bukoba and later of Dar es Salaam, Tanzania). In a few areas, such as the Igbo dioceses of Nigeria, southern Uganda, and parts of Tanzania, there are also hundreds of African priests. Elsewhere the shortage is acute.

While the number of Roman Catholic missionaries in Africa is still remarkably large, it is declining steadily in most countries as a result of political pressures and a decline in the sense of missionary calling in the old sending countries of Europe. Meanwhile, the number of African Christians grows inexorably since political independence, still more than in colonial times. The typical Christian community in rural Africa is a priestless one, led today, as mostly in the past, by a catechist or committee of village elders. Baptism, not the Eucharist, is the sacrament of African Christianity.

African Theology. African theology, of a formal kind, remains a long way from this village reality. Written mostly by professors in university departments, like Kinshasa, Yaoundé, Ibadan, Legon, and Makerere, its principal concern has been with the relationship between traditional religion and Christianity. Harry Sawyerr (Sierra Leone), John Mbiti (Kenya), Bolaji Idowu (Nigeria), John S. Pobee (Ghana), and Ngindu Mushete (Zaire) are among its leading representatives. Their theological or academic contributions have not been of major world significance. In South Africa, African theology has developed less academically as black theology, with a more political and social orientation, a local version of liberation theology. [*See* Political Theology.]

Elsewhere African theology has remained apolitical, despite the often anguished condition of contemporary Africa, a condition which has at times deeply affected the life of the church. The murder of Anglican Archbishop Janani Luwum in Idi Amin's Uganda and that of Cardinal Bayenda in Brazzaville, both in 1977, were symbolic of many other comparable events. In South Africa the long tradition of ecclesiastical criticism of racial discrimination, represented notably by Trevor Huddleston's *Naught for Your Comfort* (1956), is carried on by Bishop Desmond Tutu, formerly secretary of the South African Council of Churches and later the Anglican bishop of Johannesburg.

The strength of the African churches, however, does not lie at this formal and clerical level of written discourse and church organization, useful as it can be to have, for example, international links of the sort represented by the All Africa Conference of Churches (founded in 1963 in Kampala, with a general secretariat based in Nairobi and plenary conferences about every six years). In African Christianity, theologians and bishops are of limited importance. The growth of Christianity in Africa has been a popular and lay phenomenon, a shift in the underlying religious consciousness of half a continent in response to the modern missionary movement, the vernacular Bible, the pressures of colonialism, and the village school. The catechist remains its most characteristic figure, and the hymn, whether a European translation or an indigenous creation, is its most appropriate form of expression and vehicle of its theology. African Christianity is pietistic rather than political.

The future of African Christianity is uncertain, despite its vast vitality. Its northern flanks are being pressed increasingly hard by Islam. Elsewhere it is sure to continue to grow numerically for some time, but its intellectual expression, its ability to cope with secularization and Marxism, the competence of its clerical leadership, and the weight of its influence in future councils of world Christianity are all matters upon which it remains difficult to speak with confidence.

BIBLIOGRAPHY

Charles P. Groves's *The Planting of Christianity in Africa,* 4 vols. (1948–1958; reprint, London, 1964), is in many ways outdated and concentrates too much upon the missionary role, but it is accurate, wide-ranging, and has not been replaced. For recent history, my *A History of African Christianity, 1950–1975* (Cambridge, 1979) is the standard work. The professional rewriting of nineteenth- and early twentieth-century missionary history is represented at its best by J. F. Ade Ajayi's *Christian Missions in Nigeria, 1841–1891* (London, 1965) and John McCracken's *Politics and Christianity in Malawi, 1875–1940* (Cambridge, 1977). Bengt Sundkler's *Bara Bukoba* (London, 1981) is a fine study of the development of a single church—the Lutheran church in Bukoba, Tanzania—by its scholar-bishop. The following four symposia all contain much valuable material: *Christianity in Tropical Africa,* edited by C. G. Baëta (Oxford, 1968); *Christianity in Independent Africa,* edited by E. Fasholé-Luke, R. Gray, A. Hastings, and G. Tasie (London, 1978); *Themes in the Christian History of Central Africa,* edited by T. O. Ranger and John C. Weller (Berkeley, 1975); and *The History of Christianity in West Africa,* edited by O. U. Kalu (London, 1980).

From the very extensive literature on African independent churches, the following may be selected. For South Africa, Bengt Sundkler's early *Bantu Prophets in South Africa* (1948; 2d ed., London, 1961) remains basic, though its approach is significantly modified in the author's much later *Zulu Zion and Some Swazi Zionists* (Oxford, 1976). M. L. Daneel's *Old and New in Southern Shona Independent Churches,* 2 vols. (The Hague, 1971–1974), is the most authoritative and detailed central African study; for West Africa, see Harold W. Turner's *History of an African Independent Church,* 2 vols. (Oxford, 1967), and J. D. Y. Peel's *Aladura* (London, 1968).

David B. Barrett's *Schism and Renewal in Africa* (Nairobi, 1968) attempts an overhasty but not-to-be-ignored continent-wide assessment. John S. Pobee's *Toward an African Theology* (Nashville, 1979) is the most up-to-date guide concerning religious thought, while my *Christian Marriage in Africa* (London, 1973) sums up the issues in one much-contested area. The *Journal of Religion in Africa* (Leiden, 1967–) is indispensable for the study of the whole subject.

Adrian Hastings

Christianity in Asia

This article will focus on three principal areas of Asia: (1) the Far East (the countries bordering the Pacific Ocean), which have been profoundly influenced by the Confucian view of man and of society and by Buddhism; (2) Southeast Asia, where the dominant influence has been Buddhist, though not without Hindu and Islamic factors; (3) the Indian subcontinent, the home of Hindu culture, though with areas in which Hinduism has been almost completely submerged by Islam.

The Far East. The history of Christianity in the Far East is not one story. Introduction and development of the Christian faith have differed considerably in China, Taiwan, Japan, and Korea. In some instances there have been repeated introductions in response to the changing political climate of these lands.

China. By the seventh century CE, Nestorian Christians had made their way from Mesopotamia (Iraq) as far as western China. The discovery, by the Jesuits in 1623, of the famous "Nestorian monument" in the precincts of the old T'ang-dynasty capital, Ch'ang-an, has made available reliable information as to the origins, arrival (AD 635), and fortunes of those engaged in this tremendous adventure. This church survived for about two centuries.

The second Christian incursion came with the Franciscan attempt to establish a mission in Khanbaliq (Peking), with the hope of the conversion of Khubilai Khan, hopes frustrated by the turning of the peoples of Central Asia to Islam and not to Christianity. John of Monte Corvino (d. around 1330) arrived in Peking in 1294, gathered around him Christians of the Uighur race (who had been converted to the Nestorian form of Christianity), and secured consecration as archbishop. Other missionaries had joined him; but distance from the home church made their work difficult, and after about half a century the mission ceased to exist.

The third attempt was made by Jesuits in the sixteenth century. Matteo Ricci (1552–1610) and his colleagues secured the favor of the Chinese by their achievements in astronomy and by introducing striking clocks, learning Chinese, and adopting many Chinese ways. [*See* Jesuits *and the biography of Ricci.*] In the opinion of their critics, Ricci and his colleagues were prepared to go much too far toward adaptation of the Christian gospel to Chinese custom and tradition. In 1744 the pope forbade all such accommodation to non-Roman ways. The mission maintained itself, with varying fortunes, for a century and a half. It never completely died out, but at the end of the eighteenth century it was hardly more than a shadow of what it had been. The discovery of the diary of Andrew Li, a Chinese priest who had been trained in the seminary of Ayudhia (Thailand), in which the students, from many lands, were allowed to talk with one another only in Latin, has shed a great deal of light on this period of decline.

The fourth missionary incursion, Roman Catholic and Protestant, followed the infamous Opium Wars of 1840 to 1842, and the unjust Nanking treaty. Missionaries gradually managed to establish residence in all the provinces of China as far as the borders of Tibet, the Roman Catholics relying on the protection of the emperor Napoleon III and the Protestants for the most part following the advice of Hudson Taylor of the China Inland Mission in making their appeals only to the regularly constituted Chinese authorities. There has never been a mass Christian movement in China; the church grew slowly but steadily through the adhesion of individuals and families. But the Christian mission was always under suspicion as being associated with the hated imperialism of the Western powers.

With the failure of the so-called Boxer Rebellion at the end of the nineteenth century, many Chinese felt driven to seek new moral resources for the restoration of China; they found an answer in the teaching of Jesus Christ, though with more emphasis on the moral and social teaching than on the specifically religious content. An astonishing number of young people accepted baptism; many of them were later to be distinguished in China's national life.

Then, in 1949, the communists overthrew the government of Chiang Kai-shek and took over rule of China. Their attitude was one of hostility to all religions, though some Christians succeeded in making a deal with this hostile government. Churches were closed; the Christians were driven underground. Many observers believed that for the fourth time China had rejected the Christian message and that the church was dead, except perhaps for small house groups. Later, however, when restrictions were withdrawn in favor of greater liberty, Christians came out of hiding. It became clear that the churches were very much alive, and in some areas had even increased their membership.

It is impossible to estimate with any accuracy the number of Christians in China. Guesses vary between three and six million, the former being more probably correct. The Roman Catholics are in a specially ambiguous position, since many Chinese have refused the allegiance to Rome that Rome demands. The Protestants have formed a national council, which has brought them together without eliminating denominational differences, and without allaying the anxieties of those who feel that the council has made too many concessions to the Marxist rulers. [*See also* Chinese Religion, *overview article*.]

Taiwan. The Christian situation on the island is complicated. For a century the main Christian mission on Taiwan was Presbyterian (Canadian in the north, English in the south). When the Presbyterians came to the ninetieth anniversary of the founding of the mission, they asked themselves what they should do to celebrate the centenary and decided that, in the decade leading up to it, they would double their membership and double the number of their places of worship. Strong popular support achieved this goal.

During the period of Japanese colonial occupancy, and in the face of the strongest possible opposition from the Japanese, remarkable Christian movements began to take place among the peoples dwelling in the mountains. These people, who form a comparatively small percentage of the population of the island, seem to be of Polynesian origin, speaking their own languages, and following ancestral traditions entirely different from those of the lowland Taiwanese. In the twentieth century, entire communities have become Christian.

The whole situation in the island changed with the mass emigration from continental China which followed on the collapse of the Kuomintang government. Chiang Kai-shek himself, with many of his leading followers, left their homes to begin a new existence in Taiwan, claiming that they, and not the Marxists, represented the true spirit and succession of China. This was by no means to the liking of the Taiwanese. Under the Japanese they had been compelled to learn the Japanese language; now they were compelled to learn the Mandarin form of Chinese, which is considerably different from the form of the Amoy dialect which the Taiwanese had traditionally spoken. With the continental Chinese came a tremendous proliferation of Christian churches and sects.

Japan. Japan was almost wholly unknown to the West until Francis Xavier, with a small group of Jesuit colleagues, managed to land in the country in 1549 and to remain for the greater part of three years. [*See the biography of Xavier.*] The Jesuit enterprise was crowned with astonishing success. Rulers were converted and were followed into the Christian church by their dependents. At the end of the sixteenth century it was reckoned that there were 300,000 Christians in Japan. Then the climate changed. During a period of terrible persecution, many missionaries died agonizing deaths, though a few recanted and denied their Christian faith. Almost all the faithful reverted to their previous religions; in 1638 it was concluded that "the Christian century in Japan" had come to an end with the elimination of the church. For more than two centuries Christianity was a proscribed religion. However, when at last in 1858 missionaries were able again to enter the closed land, they discovered with astonishment that a remnant of believers had maintained the faith in many of its essentials.

Never, since the sixteenth-century Jesuit success, has

there again been anything like a mass movement of Japanese into the Christian church. Japanese Christians are often marked by three characteristics: intense intellectual activity, with faith depending on thoughtful conviction rather than on emotional decision; a strong spirit of independence, as in the "no-church" movement of Uchimura Kanzō, which refused to be tied to any kind of denominational organization; and a steady determination not to be subject to Western domination. [*See the biography of Uchimura.*]

During World War II, the government decided that only three Christian bodies, the Roman Catholic, the Eastern Orthodox, and a Protestant amalgam called the Kyōdan, should be recognized. Some Anglicans, some Lutherans, and some Holiness churches refused to join the Kyōdan and lost all legal existence, enduring varying degrees of official disapproval and even persecution. When peace came, a good many of the bodies which had accepted the Kyōdan withdrew from it, leaving Methodists, some Presbyterians, and Congregationalists, in what is the largest single Protestant body in the country.

The number of Christians in Japan is small, but Christian influence is strong. The Japanese churches may well have an important role to play as catalyst between the growing churches of Asia and the older churches of the West. [*See also* Japanese Religion, *overview article.*]

Korea. Korea has drawn much from Chinese culture and for a time passed under Japanese rule, but the Korean language and many of the features of Korean life may have originated in Central Asia. After experiencing some rather ineffective attempts at Roman Catholic evangelization, the country remained entirely closed to foreign influences until the second half of the nineteenth century. Christian missionaries during that period were mostly Americans, notably Methodists and Presbyterians. The small Anglican mission distinguished itself by a special concern for the Korean traditions of language and culture.

After initial resistance, many Korean animists, whose adherence to Buddhism was largely formal, responded positively to the Christian message. From the start, the Korean Christians were encouraged to be independent and to serve as evangelists among their own people, the foreigners keeping in the background. In South Korea all churches are independent and self-governing, though many of them are linked to worldwide churches and denominations; since World War II growth among churches there has been exceptionally rapid.

Little information is available regarding the fate of churches and Christians in North Korea. As far as is known, Christian churches have no visible existence under the Marxist regime. From occasional contacts that are possible between Christians in the south and relations and friends in the north, it seems that, as in China, Christians are maintaining their faith under conditions of extreme difficulty. [*See also* Korean Religion.]

Southeast Asia. The countries which stretch in a wide semicircle from the Philippines to Pakistan represent a great variety of races, languages, religions, and forms of culture. It is extremely difficult to reduce them all to any kind of common denominator. It is true that they all have come, at one time or another, under strong Buddhist influence, and that three of these countries have adopted Buddhism as their national religion. With the single exception of Thailand, all have come under colonial domination and have thus been bound to the West in about equal proportions of adaptation and resentment. Beyond that, generalization is difficult, and it will be best to take each country separately, especially as the degree of Christian influence varies greatly from one country to another.

The Philippine Republic. The Philippine Republic is the only Christian nation in Asia. The Spaniards arrived in 1538 and remained in power for three and a half centuries. In the course of those years, almost the entire population was brought within the Roman Catholic church, though a Muslim minority remained in the southern islands.

With the victory of the Americans in the war with Spain (1898), sovereignty passed from the Spaniards to the Americans. To some Filipinos this change seemed like a deliverance, for there had been increasing resentment among Filipinos at the domination of Spaniards in every part of the life of the people, not least in the life of the church.

The majority of the people were Roman Catholics, though at times restless and discontented Roman Catholics. One sign of this was the uprising within the church, which led to the formation of the Philippine Independent Church, often called the Aglipayan Church after its first leader, Gregorio Aglipay (1860–1940). This church came under strong Unitarian influence, but in later times it restored more orthodox Christian tradition and recovered a regular episcopal succession through the American Episcopal church. In the early 1980s the church claimed three million members, though this may be an overestimate.

With the religious freedom brought by the Americans, Protestant missionaries poured in; they converted many discontented Roman Catholics. Almost all the main American Protestant bodies are represented. The first Episcopal bishop, C. H. Brent, well-known for his creative connection with the Faith and Order movement, told his missionaries to go to the mountain peoples, whom the Roman Catholic church had never succeeded in reaching.

It took time for the Roman Catholic church to adapt itself to the new situation. But gradually the lesson was learned, and an indigenous episcopate was brought into being. The church has produced some fine scholars. Ecumenical relations are far better than they were, and, though a number of tensions still exist, cooperation among Christians has been carried further than in many other countries.

Vietnam and Cambodia. Roman Catholic missions had had notable success in Vietnam in the seventeenth and eighteenth centuries. In the twentieth century, the Marxists took over and many Christians fled from the north to the south. With the fall of the South Vietnamese government in 1975, Christians found themselves faced with the alternatives of accepting communist rule or again becoming refugees. Many died in their search for freedom. Because Cambodia was comprehensively neglected by Christian missionaries, Cambodian Christians are very few, and Buddhism has remained the major tradition.

Thailand, Burma, and Sri Lanka. Buddhism, wherever it exists, has proved very resistant to Christian evangelism; Christians who are present in Buddhist countries in many cases have come from non-Buddhist peoples or communities. Thailand, squeezed in the nineteenth century between British and French dominions, has managed to preserve throughout history a somewhat precarious independence: its citizens would probably point to the Buddhist faith as the power that has preserved their country in its integrity. A Buddhist country ruled by a monarchy imbued with Buddhist tradition, Thailand is, however, a tolerant country, and the number of Christian missionaries increased greatly with the advance of the twentieth century. Conversions from Buddhism, however, have not been numerous. The majority of Christians in the country have come from the Chinese minority, not from among the Thais.

Burma, after a century under British rule, obtained its independence in 1947 and declared Buddhism to be the national religion. Actually, large sections of the population are neither Burmese nor Buddhist; it is among these peoples that the Christian churches have made their greatest gains. Baptists are more numerous than any other Christian body in Burma. Their first great missionary, Adoniram Judson (1788–1850), who made himself a Burmese scholar and translated the Bible into that language, was imprisoned by the Burmese authorities and endured terrible sufferings from which he never entirely recovered. It was he who made contact with the Karens, a large non-Burmese group, and discovered among them a tradition concerning a sacred book which they had once possessed, and which one day would be brought back to them by white teachers. This formed a point of entrance for Christianity, and Karens form a large part of the Christian population of Burma. Work has also been carried on successfully among the Chins, Kachins, and other peoples in the areas stretching up to the frontiers with China and India. Roman Catholic activity has also been vigorous. The best-known figure of that church in Burma was Bishop Bigandet (vicar apostolic, 1856–1893), an eminent scholar whose works on Buddhism in its Burmese form are still authoritative.

Restrictions on the residence of foreigners in Burma have led to the withdrawal of all foreign Christian workers. The churches, being thrown back on their own resources, have suffered from a sense of isolation. But the Anglican church, much smaller in number than the Baptists, has reported that its numerical progress is considerably more rapid than in the days when it was under the care and supervision of foreign missionaries.

Sri Lanka is inhabited by adherents of four religions—Buddhism, Hinduism, Islam, and Christianity. But Buddhists prevail. The Buddhist priesthood has been extremely influential in political as well as in religious affairs. Serious attempts have been made to turn Sri Lanka into a Buddhist country and to make Sinhala the only official language. These attempts have led to grave dissensions between those who speak Sinhala and those who speak Tamil, among whom are a good many Christians.

During the Portuguese period, many inhabitants of the island became members of the Roman Catholic church. Under the Dutch a considerable number became Protestants; but, with the religious toleration introduced by the British at the end of the eighteenth century, a large majority of Protestants reverted to the Roman Catholic church, which embraces about four-fifths of all the Christians in the island.

Buddhism in Sri Lanka is marked by the excellence of its scholars and by the powerful influence of its teachings. A few Christians have become Buddhists, among them a former prime minister of the country. Christians in Sri Lanka have become very aware of the vitality of their country's Buddhist tradition. A number of them have studied deeply and have qualified themselves as experts in Buddhism; such inter-religious dialogue is perhaps more active in Sri Lanka than in any other part of the world.

Indonesia. Indonesia, a republic three thousand miles long and including about three thousand islands, stands somewhat apart from the rest of Southeast Asia, showing marks of Hindu, Buddhist, and Islamic religion. It has the largest Muslim population of any country in the world.

The Dutch, when they were dominant, carried on missionary work, with a good deal of success especially in Ambon and northern Sulawesi. But Hendrik Kraemer in his book *From Missionfield to Independent Church* (The Hague, 1958) has drawn a picture of the extent to which state control made impossible the development of any independent indigenous Christianity.

Indonesia is the only country in the world in which there is a steady drift of Muslims into the Christian church. It seems that one cause has been the sharp reaction of many Muslims against the vengeance taken by Muslims against actual or suspected Communists at the time of an attempted Communist coup in 1965.

The most notable success has been obtained among the non-Muslim Batak people of northern Sumatra. Missionary Ingwer Nommensen (1834–1918), when he first saw beautiful Lake Toba in 1885, envisioned a time when the church bell in every village would call the faithful to worship. Since that time millions of Bataks have entered the Christian churches and evangelism continues. The skill and energy with which Indonesian Christians have freed themselves from Dutch and German influences is reflected in the sense of independence which marks Christians of that country, an independence which is being modified by an increasing willingness to enter into the life of the wider Christian world and to accept the help offered by other Christians. [*See also* Southeast Asian Religions, *article on* Modern Movements in Insular Cultures.]

The Indian Subcontinent. In 1757, at the battle of Plassey, the British established themselves as the strongest power in India. British unification of the subcontinent was complete in 1848. This unity lasted for almost a hundred years. In 1947 Muslims asserted their independence through the formation of Pakistan as an independent state (to be followed by the separation of East Pakistan), and the constitution, under the name Bangladesh, of a third independent state in the subcontinent.

The date at which the Christian faith first appeared in India has been the subject of endless debates, and still presents itself as a fascinating historical problem. It is certain that a Christian church has existed in Kerala (in southwestern India) for many centuries. The members of the various churches of the Thomas Christians are at one in their conviction that their church, in its original form, was founded by the apostle Thomas himself.

A number of scholars support the view that churches did exist in India not later than the second century; all but the most skeptical accept a date in the fourth century as almost certain. Through the centuries the church maintained its distinctiveness by retaining Syriac as the language of worship and receiving its bishops from Mesopotamia. Information for the medieval period is very scanty; but when communication with the West was renewed, with the arrival of the Portuguese by the sea route in 1498, the church was found to be in a flourishing state, Christians forming an accepted and respected element in Indian society. This ancient church remained, however, within the narrow compass of the region between the mountains and the sea, and, so far as is known, made no attempts to evangelize other parts of India. In fact, it made rather few attempts to convert local non-Christians.

When the Portuguese occupied Goa (1510) and made it the base for the establishment of their sea-borne empire, the situation was radically changed. The newcomers made no attempts to conquer extensive tracts of land as they had done in the Americas; but they did regard commerce and conversion to Christianity as intimately related to one another. By the end of the sixteenth century, as a result of special privileges for Christians and special hindrances for Hindus, the great majority of the population in the Portuguese possessions had entered the Roman Catholic church. In 1599, at the Synod of Udiyamperur (Diamper), the archbishop of Goa had persuaded the entire body of the Thomas Christians to renounce the patriarch of Baghdad and to accept the authority of the patriarch of Rome. Half a century later a third of the Thomas Christians, in rebellion against the autocracy of the Jesuits, reasserted their independence in the formation of the Malankara Syrian Orthodox Church, in which they still have their home. [*See* Syrian Orthodox Church of Antioch.]

A new complexion was given to missionary work by the great adventure of the Italian aristocrat Robert Nobili (1606–1656 in India) who set to work to turn himself into a brahman in order to win the brahmans. Nobili's considerable knowledge of Sanskrit and extensive literary activity in Tamil left a permanent mark on the Indian church.

With the support of the king of Denmark, the Protestants entered the field in 1706 in the small Danish territory of Tranquebar. Protestant missionary Christian Friedrich Schwartz served in India from 1750 until 1798 and left the indelible impression of a serene and gentle radiance upon Europeans and Indians alike.

In the first half of the nineteenth century, growth both for Roman Catholics and for Protestants was slow. The great period of expansion began in 1858, when the British government took over rule in India from the East

India Company. Christians of many nations entered into the work, which in fifty years spread itself into almost every corner of India except in those areas where independent Indian rulers refused permission for any kind of Christian propaganda in their domains.

Three features of this period deserve special mention. First, the immense educational effort of the missionaries, aided by financial support from the government, produced a large Christian middle class, educated and professional, which prepared the way for the development of independent Indian churches. Second, the underprivileged "outcastes," seeing no hope of a better future under the Hindu system, began to press into the Christian churches. This movement was disapproved of by a great many missionaries and by the majority of educated Indian Christian leaders, but the pressure would not be stayed. Third, many among the aboriginal peoples, having no wish to be incorporated into the Hindu caste system, saw in the Christian way a greater freedom than they could hope to enjoy elsewhere. Some whole peoples have become Christian and others greatly christianized.

In the twentieth century, the great change has been the transfer of power from foreign agents to indigenous leaders. The first Indian Anglican bishop, V. S. Azariah, was consecrated in 1912; the first Indian bishop of the Latin rite, Tiburtius Roche, was consecrated for Tuticorin in 1923. Rome showed its recognition of the maturity of the Indian church by the appointment of the first Indian cardinal, Valarian Gracias of Bombay, in 1953. The four fully united and independent churches of South India, of North India, of Pakistan, and of Bangladesh, have manifested an independent ecumenical spirit.

In the early 1980s, Christians numbered less than three percent of the population in India, much less in Pakistan and Bangladesh. But it may be argued that Christian teaching has had an impact upon contemporary Indian ethical thought. The government of independent India has abolished by law "untouchability." This righteous action owes much to the passionate advocacy by missionaries of the rights of the underprivileged. The Sarda Act, which raised the age of marriage for both boys and girls, was brought forward by Hindu reformers; these reformers were building on the work of Christians whose opposition to child marriage was well known.

British rule came to an end in 1947. When the change took place, both those who welcomed it with enthusiasm and those who viewed it with considerable alarm accepted it without question; not a single missionary left his or her post for reasons of political change. Nevertheless, political change was bound to affect the lives and prospects of Christians in a number of ways. While the Indian constitution contains a statement in favor of religious freedom, Christians often find life more difficult than it was in earlier days.

Pakistan has from the start been riven by dissensions. In any Muslim state Christians face a number of difficulties; Christians in Pakistan may have to face the possibility of increasing difficulties.

Conclusion. In 1948 the World Council of Churches and the International Missionary Council convened in Manila a meeting of leaders in the East Asian churches. The result of the meeting was the formation of the East Asia Secretariat, without any authority but with the expressed aim of promoting fellowship and mutual understanding. This was the beginning of a process which has proved highly productive. The Asian churches have come to feel that they ought to belong to one another. They have, for instance, held a meeting to discuss the problems of Christian faith and order in an Asian setting.

Heroic and largely successful attempts to nurture a specifically Asian Christianity have been made. There has been a good deal of theological writing, mainly in English; but it is perhaps poets, rather than theologians, who have most profoundly and creatively expressed an indigenous Christianity. Of Indian Christian poets, Narayan Vaman Tilok and H. A. Krishna Pillai were both high caste Hindu converts of mature age, who poured into their poems the fullness of their cultural and linguistic experience in both the non-Christian and Christian worlds. The full flowering of Asian theology may be yet to come, just as the full flowering of Christian thought and expression in the Syriac, Greek, and Latin languages did not begin until three centuries after the ministry of Jesus Christ.

BIBLIOGRAPHY

On all the countries dealt with in this survey, there are short summaries in the *World Christian Encyclopedia*, edited by David B. Barrett (Oxford, 1982). For detailed study K. S. Latourette's *A History of the Expansion of Christianity*, 7 vols. (New York, 1937–1945), remains indispensable. Much shorter is my *A History of Christian Missions* (Baltimore, 1964). For recent events in China, the best source is the periodical literature. On Japan, Raymond Hammer's *Japan's Religious Ferment* (London, 1961) is still valuable. For India, my *History of Christianity in India*, 2 vols. (Cambridge, 1984–1985) is complete to 1858. See also M. M. Thomas's *The Acknowledged Christ of the Indian Renaissance* (London, 1969), a very good book by an Indian Christian scholar. On Indian theology, the best authority is R. H. S. Boyd's *An Introduction to Indian Christian Theology* (Madras, 1969). Most of the books recommended here include useful and detailed bibliographies.

STEPHEN C. NEILL

Christianity in Australia and New Zealand

Australia and New Zealand are usually considered to have developed along broadly similar lines. In both, colonization occurred at about the same time largely by British immigrants, major Christian denominations were early on the scene, and some of the same issues have generated sectarian strife. In the case of both countries it has been contended that Christianity and the churches have never played a significant role and are even less important today. Yet there are differences between the two countries, the much greater geographical extent of Australia being only one.

Contact between Christianity and Indigenous Cultures. On 26 January 1788, Captain Arthur Phillip landed at Sydney Cove, Port Jackson, New South Wales, with a party of 1,030 including 736 convicts. In the first part of the nineteenth century free settlers arrived, displacing the Aborigines, who were soon reduced in numbers by disease, loss of traditional hunting grounds, malnutrition, and bloodshed. Provision for religious observances in the settlement took little account of the Aborigines, who were an enigma to officials and missionaries but little more than a nuisance to settlers. The seminomadism of the Aborigines frustrated missionary efforts and made it easy to assume that Aborigines had no real claim to the territory over which they roamed. Missions, schools, and protective measures of various kinds achieved little regarding the Aborigines during the nineteenth century and were often obstructed by settlers.

From the late eighteenth century onward, whalers, sealers, and other traders were attracted to New Zealand. In 1840 New Zealand was annexed as a British colony, and Governor William Hobson signed the Treaty of Waitangi with Maori chiefs. The proceedings generally, especially the part played by missionaries and the meaning of the treaty's terms, remain controversial. Disputes over land erupted into violence, and a tragic period of conflict (1860–1865) was followed by extensive confiscation of land by the British and, among Maoris, deep-seated alienation from the British and the religion they had brought.

Missionary work in New Zealand was begun by the Church Missionary Society partly at the behest of Samuel Marsden (1765–1838), a chaplain to the convict settlement in New South Wales who, perhaps on the basis of experience with the Aborigines, believed that the Maoris should first be taught "the arts of civilization." Marsden preached the first sermon in New Zealand on Christmas Day 1814, but missionary efforts began to be effective only in the 1820s. The general state of Maori society at this time, the nature of the missionaries' impact, and the part played by other factors (e.g., "war-weariness" among the Maoris, the attractions of literacy, improvements in the quality and methods of missionaries, and the role of Maori leadership) are much debated by historians. In time Maori "conversions" to Christianity were numerous, although the Maoris often combined Christian ideas with their own traditional beliefs and practices, at first informally but soon in reactive movements. The Pai Marire and Ringatu movements emerged in the 1860s, the movement associated with Rua Kenana sprang to life in the early years of the twentieth century, and Ratana came into being in the 1920s. [*See also* Australian Religions, *article on* Modern Movements.]

Church Development. An Anglican chaplain was among the first immigrants to Australia in 1788, and convicts were required to attend Anglican services. William Grant Broughton (1788–1853) became the first Anglican bishop of Australia in 1836. His huge diocese was subdivided in 1847, and in 1872 the first general synod was held. Initially no provision was made for the needs of Roman Catholics. Mass was first celebrated on 15 May 1803 by James Dixon, one of three priests deported from Ireland for alleged participation in the Wexford rising of 1798. After disturbances in New South Wales in 1804 in which local Irish were involved, Dixon's ministrations were suspended, and he returned to Ireland in 1808. In 1820 two Irish priests landed in Sydney, but their activities were severely restricted. The Roman Catholic population, however, increased steadily: by 1828, of a total New South Wales population of 36,600, Catholics numbered 11,230. In February 1833, William Ullathorne, an English Benedictine, arrived as vicar-general, and two years later John Bede Polding (1798–1877) arrived as Australia's first Roman Catholic bishop.

By 1803, Presbyterianism was established among free Scottish immigrants in Sydney; by 1850 it was strongly represented, especially in Melbourne. Events in both Scotland and Australia made Presbyterianism prey to controversies and divisions. The first Methodist class meeting was held in Sydney in 1812; the first minister arrived in 1815; the inaugural Australasian conference met in 1855; and in 1902 the Methodist Church of Australasia brought together the diverse branches of Methodism. By the 1830s, some smaller denominations—notably Baptists, Congregationalists, and Lutherans—were represented and, like Methodism, were especially strong in South Australia. By the close of the nineteenth century, Seventh-day Adventists, the Salvation Army, Mormons, and Unitarians added to the denominational variety.

In Australia during the nineteenth century, the overwhelming majority of the population professed nominal adherence to one or another of the major denominations. The Church of England, especially, embraced many nominal adherents and infrequent worshipers. In the course of the move to Australia the Church of England lost status as an established church and became one denomination among others. Methodism, on the other hand, shed any vestiges of a sectarian character to gain denominational status. Roman Catholics and Methodists, especially the former, were initially overrepresented among the lower classes, while Anglicans and Presbyterians were slightly overrepresented in the upper classes.

Systematic colonization of New Zealand began in the 1840s, and two settlements had ecclesiastical associations: Otago (1848) with Presbyterianism, and Canterbury (1850) with the Church of England. George Augustus Selwyn (1809–1878) was consecrated as the first Anglican bishop of New Zealand in 1841 and, until he returned to England in 1867, was a dominant and sometimes dominating figure. By 1869 the original diocese had been subdivided into six dioceses. A constitution of 1857 established the church as an autonomous province and gave synodical representation to clergy and laity while retaining voting by "houses."

Roman Catholic missions began in 1838. John Baptist Francis Pompallier (1801–1871), the first Catholic bishop in New Zealand, was initially concerned with the Maoris (he claimed to have baptized 1,000 Maoris by 1849) but as early as 1848 dioceses of Auckland and Wellington were created. Dunedin followed in 1869 and Christchurch in 1887. The relatively late arrival of Roman Catholics, a lack of financial resources, administrative problems, suspicion aroused by the French nationality of the priests, anti-Catholic sentiment, and later the outbreak of war seriously hindered Catholic missions.

Presbyterianism had beginnings in Auckland in 1840 and in Wellington two years later, and during the 1850s and 1860s it spread into other areas also. Initially, Presbyterianism was organized in two separate bodies, one based on Otago and Southland and the other including areas north of Otago. Reunion moves faltered in the 1860s but succeeded in 1901. Wesleyan Methodists inaugurated missionary efforts in 1822 and, like the Church Missionary Society, began in the northern areas of North Island, later extending farther south. The early presence of Methodist missionaries and an emphasis on lay involvement helped ensure that Methodism was active in the earliest years of the major settlements. The varieties of British Methodism were represented, but they had united by 1913, in which year, also, Methodism in New Zealand became autonomous.

The first Baptist church in New Zealand was formed in Nelson in 1851, and by 1882, when the Baptist Union was formed, there were twenty-five congregations. By 1900, other groups—Congregationalists, Churches of Christ, Quakers, Plymouth Brethren, Seventh-day Adventists, Mormons, Lutherans, and some undenominational societies—were represented in smaller numbers. The social composition of the major churches was broadly similar to that in Australia, but the level of attendance in New Zealand was lower than that in New South Wales, Victoria, and South Australia and, for that matter, in England and Scotland. The difference between Australia and New Zealand may be related to the slightly different denominational composition, since more Anglicans than Methodists and Roman Catholics came to New Zealand. The latter two groups had relatively higher church-attendance figures than did the Anglicans.

Religious Differences. Despite some differences, religious conditions in Australia and New Zealand were not wholly dissimilar. In both countries controversies related to church-state relationships, the control of education, concern for the maintenance of "Christian standards," and sectarian strife marked the years to about 1920.

In nineteenth-century Britain, church-state relations were much debated and this debate extended to Australia and New Zealand. In the case of Australia, the most significant early measure was the New South Wales Church Act of 1836, which effectively broke any Anglican monopoly of financial aid from the government, but still tended to favor larger and wealthier denominations and to fuel sectarian strife. Similar arrangements were made in other Australian colonies. South Australia began with a voluntary system and flirted briefly with state aid, but it set a precedent in 1851 by terminating such aid, which, however, survived in Western Australia until 1895. Hobson, the first governor of New Zealand, was directed to guarantee "the most absolute toleration" to all denominations, but among governors, some officials, and Anglicans in New Zealand there was a hangover effect regarding church-state relations. Once representative government was in place (1854), however, the House of Representatives affirmed "the privilege of a perfect political equality in all religious denominations" and declined to take over responsibility for the stipend of the Anglican bishop.

Like the church-state issue, controversy over the control and funding of education was exported to the colonies. In Australia a pattern of state aid to denominational schools emerged. Erosion of this pattern began in New South Wales in 1866, when separate boards for state and church schools were consolidated, existing denominational schools were regulated, and assistance was withheld from new church schools. All state aid to denominational schools was withdrawn in 1880, and eventually all the states established free, compulsory, and secular education at the primary level and terminated state aid. In New Zealand aid was given to denominational schools during the crown colony period and continued by some provincial governments until 1876 when such governments were abolished. The Education Act of 1877 provided that primary education should be free, compulsory, and secular; state aid was withdrawn. In both Australia and New Zealand some Anglicans, and more especially Roman Catholics, opposed these moves, and the Catholics developed extensive schooling systems at their own expense. Behind the move toward secularization in both countries were a dislike of sectarian squabbling, suspicion of Roman Catholic and Anglican designs, fears of social divisiveness, inefficiencies and inequalities in existing systems, and the growing popularity in government circles of theories of secular education.

The secularizing of primary education may have helped to generate a sense of crisis among Christian leaders in both countries from the 1870s onward. Vigorous moves were made to defend "Christian standards," and some of this sentiment was channeled into agitation against the educational changes, some into evangelistic efforts, and some into securing legislation on a range of issues including Sunday observance, temperance, gambling, prostitution, and book censorship. Protestants and Roman Catholics rarely cooperated. For example, agitation against gambling could not win the support of Catholics, and by no means all Catholics backed the Sabbatarian and temperance causes. To this period belong also the beginnings of social service agencies in the churches; Methodists, with their "city missions," and the Salvation Army were conspicuous. With the exception of a few outstanding individuals, church members seem to have been little concerned with wider issues of social justice.

In both countries, sectarian strife surfaced at intervals. Anti-Catholicism was evident in New South Wales from colonial days. In New Zealand, suspicion of Catholicism first fastened on early missionaries, whose French nationality made them doubly disliked. Disputes over education sustained sectarian conflict in both countries, and the creation of Roman Catholic school systems gave institutional expression to a degree of separatism and reinforced anti-Protestant attitudes. In both countries the two sides to the conflict had their share of public figures with a propensity for inflammatory rhetoric. Among them, Daniel Mannix, archbishop of Melbourne from 1913 to 1963 (coadjutor 1913–1917), personified an increasingly militant Catholicism. During World War I the Irish question and the conscription issue fueled sectarian strife, which continued into the postwar years and was kept alive partly by the emergence of anti-Catholic organizations in both Australia and New Zealand.

From 1920 to 1960. The economic depression of the late 1920s and early 1930s affected the churches in ways that subsequently became important. The churches began by providing measures of relief and continued to do so. As the depression deepened, some in the churches moved to more radical positions critical of government policies. In New Zealand, Methodists and Roman Catholics especially were radicalized, but Anglicans and Presbyterians were also affected. The Labour party capitalized on support from the churches, and that support was a factor in the party's electoral victory in 1935. In Australia the long-term effect of the depression years was more explosive. Some Roman Catholics, who began with a concern to shape a just social order, became anxious about communist influence. Efforts to arrest this influence were one cause of a major split in the Australian Labour party in the 1950s, its political defeat, and its subsequent ineffectiveness until the 1970s. These events further strained a long-standing alliance between the Labour party and Catholicism, which had weakened as Catholics moved up the socioeconomic ladder.

From 1933 to 1971 the proportion of Roman Catholics in Australia rose from 17.5 percent to 27 percent, partly because of extensive postwar immigration, especially from Italy. This wave of immigration diluted the "Irishness" of the Roman Catholic church in Australia, over which there had been tension from around 1914, and added substantially to the Orthodox community as well. In both countries the years from around 1945 to 1965 were in many respects placid and prosperous. In the immediate postwar years there was a strong desire to return to normalcy; rising affluence benefited some, though not all, and suburbs mushroomed. Fund-raising schemes made finances available for building churches and, by Roman Catholics, schools also. Church life was relatively stable: theology, structures, and piety were still largely intact from earlier times.

An Era of Change, 1960–1980. It is difficult to resist the conclusion that the last half of the twentieth century has seen the convergence of some long-term trends with such catalytic events as the Vietnam War. Roman Catholics have also faced the turmoil created by Vatican II and its aftermath, strains on the schooling systems, reaction to the papal encyclical on birth control, and a decline in vocations to the priesthood and the religious life, with a high dropout rate from both. On the more positive side, the grip of a "ghetto mentality" has weakened, and a wider range of social issues now engages Christian attention.

Several trends can be discerned. Church union moves have slowed. In Australia in 1977 the Uniting Church brought together Methodists, about two-thirds of the Presbyterians, and five-sixths of the Congregationalists. In New Zealand, long-standing negotiations between Anglicans, Churches of Christ, Congregationalists, Methodists, and Presbyterians have been stalled, largely by Anglican hesitation. There is now a state of ecclesiastical limbo occupied by local cooperative ventures, unilateral moves often involving Roman Catholics (now much more active on the ecumenical scene in both countries), and a return to denominational "roots." In New Zealand an increasing Polynesian population (89,697 in 1981) is strongly attached to traditional church life.

Maoris and Aborigines, largely as the result of urbanization, are more aware of institutional discrimination and vocal in their protests. Their cause has been taken up by some in the churches, especially through the National Council of Churches (in New Zealand), the Uniting Church in Australia, and the Australian Council of Churches. In recent years all major denominations in New Zealand have, in a variety of ways, given Maoris a larger part in church life: the Maori section of the National Council of Churches became autonomous in 1982. Women, long important in a wide variety of roles and organizations but almost without exception officially subordinate, have become increasingly vocal. Some churchwomen and their organizations uphold traditional views on the roles of women, but there are also relatively small groups of women more attuned to the feminist cause.

Since the 1960s the charismatic movement has been evident in the major denominations but so far predominant in none. Partly coextensive with this movement are a resurgence of fundamentalism and an emphasis on personal evangelism in contrast to social and political action.

In both countries major denominations are experiencing a decline in adherents as a proportion of the total population, and even the number of Roman Catholics, once the sole exception, has recently leveled off and now shows a slight decline. All major denominations, some more than others and with the exception of the Catholics, have an aging population. There is a small but definite increase in those who claim to be atheists or agnostics, or to have "no religion," and growing adherence to smaller denominations, especially Pentecostal. With the exception of funerals, rites of passage are less often observed in Christian settings, and the number who attend church only occasionally is probably falling.

Some scholars relate these statistics to theories of secularization variously interpreted; some seek to relate the decline in church participation to withdrawal from voluntary associations generally; while yet others doubt whether any substantially different patterns of institutional participation have yet emerged. Some scholars stress what they regard as the churches' failure to develop indigenous expressions of Christianity in Australia and New Zealand. The long-term consequences of government aid for church schools (granted from the 1960s onward in increasing measure in both countries) cannot yet be gauged in terms of maintaining participation in church life after schooling.

Both Australia and New Zealand ceased long ago to be colonies; but have the churches yet escaped colonial dependence? Church buildings are one visible reminder of dependence, and recent liturgical revisions are indebted to overseas models. Neither country has produced any new religious movement of the importance of, for example, the Latter-day Saints. The ecumenical and charismatic renewal movements owe a good deal to overseas examples and influences. But this is not the whole story. Especially since around 1950 there has been lessening dependence on imported leadership, and the Uniting Church in Australia is one of very few transdenominational mergers. As early as the nineteenth century, Anglicans in both countries accorded the laity a role in church governance only recently bestowed by their parent body. The total record is one of dependence, independence, and, increasingly, interdependence.

The influence of Christianity on the society and culture of Australia and New Zealand is more difficult to chart; it has been widely discounted, although not always evaluated carefully in all its dimensions. It is difficult to identify any major reform for which the churches have been responsible, but individuals and groups have often been prominent in, and important for, reforming causes. There has been little in the way of theological interpretation of Australian and New Zealand experience by theologians, but some artists, poets, and novelists have achieved something in this regard. If it is true (and it is certainly arguable) that the public role of churches is being diminished and religion is being privatized, Christian influence may be expected to continue through individuals in public roles and associated with single-interest groups. By these means, if not by others, Christianity, the churches, and their members are likely to continue to participate in shaping society and culture in Australia and New Zealand.

BIBLIOGRAPHY

For bibliography, see *Religion in Australian Life: A Bibliography of Social Research*, edited by Michael Mason (Bedford Park, Australia, 1982), and *Religious History of New Zealand: A Bibliography*, edited by Anthony R. Grigg and Peter J. Lineham (Palmerston North, New Zealand, 1984).

For reference purposes, see *The Australian Encyclopaedia*, 10 vols., edited by Alec H. Chisholm (Sydney and East Lansing, Mich., 1958), and *An Encyclopaedia of New Zealand*, 3 vols., edited by A. H. McLintock (Wellington, 1966). For biographical detail, see *Australian Dictionary of Biography*, 9 vols. (Melbourne, 1966–), and *Dictionary of New Zealand Biography*, 2 vols., edited by G. H. Scholefield (Wellington, 1940). A new dictionary of New Zealand biography, edited by W. H. Oliver, is in preparation.

For general background, see *A New History of Australia*, edited by F. K. Crowley (Melbourne, 1974), and the *Oxford History of New Zealand*, edited by W. H. Oliver (Oxford and Wellington, 1981). Both these volumes gather much recent research, but see also, among journals, the *Journal of Religious History* (Sydney, 1960–), *Historical Studies* (Melbourne, 1940–), and the *New Zealand Journal of History* (Auckland, 1967–).

There are no comprehensive histories of religion or of Christianity in either Australia or New Zealand. See, however, John D. Bollen's *Religion in Australian Society: An Historian's View* (Sydney, 1973); *The Shape of Belief: Christianity in Australia Today* (Homebush West, Australia, 1982); *Religion in New Zealand Society*, edited by Brian Colless and Peter Donovan (Palmerston North, 1980; 2d ed., 1985); and *Religion in New Zealand*, edited by Christopher Nichol and James Veitch (Wellington, 1980). The best of the denominational histories in each case are Patrick J. O'Farrell's *The Catholic Church and Community in Australia: A History* (Melbourne, 1977) and W. P. Morrell's *The Anglican Church in New Zealand: A History* (Dunedin, 1973). The latter concentrates more narrowly on institutional history.

COLIN BROWN

Christianity in the Pacific Islands

Christianity has become the religion of almost all the original peoples of the Pacific Islands. The Indo-Fijian population in Fiji and various immigrant groups in Hawaii are the only population groups that remain largely outside any Christian church. The following examples illustrate the fact that the indigenous island peoples hold to Christianity firmly and vigorously. Samoa has more ministers in proportion to its size than does any other country, and it is reported that 80 percent of the people of Vanuatu are in church on Sunday. In Tonga, until recently, the most common occupation after gardening and fishing was the Christian ministry. Both Papua New Guinea and Western Samoa refer to the Christian faith in their constitutions. Finally, in the country of Tuvalu, people not in church are presumed to be sick, and teams from the congregations visit them during the time of the church service.

Introduction and Distribution. The distribution of the various confessional groups in the Pacific reflects the processes by which Christianity was introduced to the region. Almost invariably the predominant church of any island or country is the church of the first missionaries to reach it. The move from the traditional religion to Christianity was normally made by the people as a whole—a whole island group in Polynesia or a whole village in Melanesia—thus preserving the religious unity that had existed previously and making for considerable religious uniformity within each land.

The first missionaries to work in the islands, the Spaniards who came with Sanvitores to the Mariana Islands in 1668, established Roman Catholicism as the religion of the Mariana peoples. That condition continues to the present time. The Catholicism of the Marianas is similar in many ways to that of the Philippine Islands, because the missionaries came from the Philippines and because in the following years there was much immigration from the Philippines. The Catholic missionaries also tried to penetrate the western Caroline Islands, but their work there was subject to many fluctuations, and as a consequence conformity to Roman Catholicism is not so general there.

The Spanish efforts died down, but a new missionary élan in Europe brought fresh Protestant and Catholic workers to the islands in the late eighteenth and early nineteenth centuries. The Protestant pioneer body was the London Missionary Society, and its first emissaries began work in Tahiti in 1797. After many disappointments the missionaries were surprised by a sudden shift to Christianity by the principal ruler, Pomare II, in 1815, and soon thereafter Pomare made himself the undisputed ruler of Tahiti and Christianity the undisputed religion of the island. The Protestant church begun then has continued as the majority religion of Tahiti and of the islands associated with it. The London Missionary Society missionaries then moved on to the Cook Islands and also to Samoa, where they established their largest and most flourishing church. From Samoa they reached out to Tuvalu and the Loyalty Islands, where again they became the church of the majority, and to Kiribati, where they eventually had to share the land equally with the Roman Catholics, who came from France at the end of the century.

Another Congregational body, patterned on the London Missionary Society, began missions in Hawaii. This was the American Board of Commissioners for Foreign Missions. When its first group of missionaries reached Hawaii in 1820, the traditional religion had already been repudiated, the great idols destroyed, and the sacred enclosures desecrated. This resulted from the influence of sailors and merchants from Europe and America who had broken the ancient taboos with impunity and had thus shaken the faith of the people. In the following years, Queen Kaahumanu took the lead in presenting Christianity to the people of Hawaii and gaining their adherence to it.

At about the same time, national movements into Christianity were taking place under the auspices of the English Methodists in Tonga and Fiji. The royal leader who made Methodism the church of Tonga was Taufa'ahau (later known as King George), who was converted in 1831 and thereafter brought the entire kingdom under his control by his military prowess. In Fiji there was a similar pattern. Thakombau, the most rapidly rising chief of the islands, made the decision for Christianity in 1854 and was able to defeat his non-Christian rivals. In both Tonga and Fiji the overwhelming majority of the indigenous people became and remain Methodists.

In the islands north and west of Fiji there are no large political units, so the spread of Christianity was slower—village by village. Vanuatu was the only country where the Presbyterians began the first churches and where they are now the major religious body. The Solomon Islands is the only country in the Pacific Islands where the Anglicans were the first to establish continuing work. Their Melanesian Mission began work not only in the Solomons but also in northern Vanuatu. The Anglican church continues as the largest church in the Solomons, though it divides the country with Methodists in the west, the Seventh-day Adventists in the Morovo Lagoon, the South Sea Evangelical Church on the island of Malaita, and the Roman Catholics on several islands. The South Sea Evangelical Church is unique among the churches thus far considered in that it was begun by a nonchurch mission, inspired and led by an Australian woman, Florence Young, who began her work in the islands in 1904.

After the Spanish decline Roman Catholic missionaries were usually from France. In most lands they came after the Protestants and so had only a minority status. This is true in Tahiti and most of French Polynesia (except the Marquesas), and in the Cook Islands, Samoa, Tonga, Fiji, Vanuatu, and the Solomons. In New Caledonia, however, the Catholics came first. Marist missionaries from France began continuing labors in that island in 1851 and, after many initial difficulties, began what is now the major religious community there. Large French and other Catholic immigrations have swelled this majority, and the church is now fairly evenly divided between the indigenes and the immigrants.

Papua New Guinea does not fit into the usual Pacific pattern of one original and predominant church. It contains as many people as all the other islands put together, and neither its history nor its geography has been conducive to a united Christian development. The London Missionary Society established the first continuing mission in 1871 and soon spread along nearly the whole of the south coast. Methodists, this time from Australia, came in 1875 to the Bismarck Archipelago and later to the islands east of Papua. French Catholics followed shortly in both Papua and the Bismarck Archipelago. After the British and German empires came to rule, the Anglican church established itself on the northeast coast of Papua and strong German-Lutheran and German-Catholic missions developed in German New Guinea. Out of these missions have come the five major church traditions of the country: Congregational, Methodist, Roman Catholic, Anglican, and Lutheran, with the Catholics by far the largest. The number of major religious bodies was reduced by one in 1968, when the Congregationalists and the Methodists combined to form the United Church, but that consolidation did not significantly counterbalance the proliferation of denominations that began in the 1950s, primarily in the New Guinea Highlands. The Highlands had been largely unknown and had been closed to Christian penetration before that time. But in the 1950s and 1960s there came a rush of many church and para-church missions into the area, making it the most variegated part of the Pacific Islands in terms of religion.

Indigenous Missionaries. The missionaries who came to New Guinea and to the other islands of the Pacific were not solely the Europeans who have received most of the attention; there were also Pacific-islanders in abundance. As soon as Tahiti and its neighbors were converted, missionaries radiated out from there to the Cook Islands and Samoa. Usually they were taken to their new posts by European missionaries, but once in place they did the major work of starting the new churches. Tonga sent early missionaries, with royal backing, to start Methodist churches in Samoa and Fiji. The Congregational church in Hawaii in the middle of the nineteenth century launched missions to the Marshall Islands and the eastern Caroline Islands, where they began what are still the principal churches of those islands.

The great challenge and opportunity for islander missionaries came in the late nineteenth and early twentieth centuries when New Guinea and the western Solomons were opening up. The Congregationalists of

Samoa and the Cook Islands and the Methodists of Fiji and Tonga proved to be the great mission-senders for these new lands. Some 650 men, often accompanied by wives who were equally dedicated to missionary labors, went to the new areas. Much of the church life in the lands where they labored bears the imprint of their particular styles of Christianity. Within New Guinea itself the missionary tradition was continued by many hundreds of Christians who went from the coastlands and outer islands into the Highlands when they were opened. Notable are the hundreds of Lutheran pioneers, many of whom went even before the Highlands were officially opened. The Solomon Islands showed a similar activity in the work of the Melanesian Brotherhood, an Anglican order of young men begun in 1926 and numbering over one thousand through subsequent years, who were dedicated to bringing Christianity to the most isolated and resistant areas.

Folk Christianity. Most of the churches of the islands may be described as folk churches; that is, they are deeply intertwined with the societies around them and they are not inclined to distinguish themselves from or to stand out against those societies. Although they were originally the product of alien influences, they now believe themselves to be protectors of the island traditions and opponents of the newer alien influences that are pouring in.

Churches play a large role in village life and are often directly linked to village leadership. The church buildings are usually constructed by the village people and are maintained by them. Protestant pastors are selected, trained, and supported by the churches of which they are a part. Catholic priests are at present primarily expatriates, but the situation is changing steadily, so that the day of the indigenous priesthood is not far off in many countries. By the early 1980s it was already a reality in Samoa, Fiji, Tonga, Wallis-Futuna, and some parts of Papua New Guinea. The Roman Catholic church, of course, maintains its ties to Rome, but it also exercises much independence in national and regional structures. The major Protestant churches have all achieved full independence from the missions and handle their own affairs.

Interchurch Relations. During the nineteenth century the different Protestant missions worked, by design, in different territories and enjoyed fairly cordial relationships. Between Roman Catholics and Protestants, however, there was intense rivalry and much ill feeling. With the coming of the twentieth century the sense of hostility began to subside. After there were no more adherents of traditional religion who might be won by either camp, there was little point in further competition. People who were already Catholics or Protestants seldom changed sides.

New ecumenical attitudes in the wider world have begun to have their effect in the Pacific. Regional conferences of the Protestant churches began to be held in 1926, and eventually, in 1966, these led to the creation of the Pacific Conference of Churches, a body that includes nearly all the major Protestant denominations. The Catholic Bishops' Conference for the Pacific was formed in 1968, and a parallel organization for Papua New Guinea was also created. In 1973 this Conference took the unprecedented step of deciding to join the Pacific Conference of Churches. This was the first time Catholics anywhere determined to join Protestants in a regional church structure. Today all the major churches recognize each other and often engage in cooperative efforts.

New Religious Movements. The unity evidenced by the major churches does not extend to all the minor churches and sects, many of which have entered the islands in more recent years. The newer churches of the New Guinea Highlands have been brought together in a cooperative structure of their own, the Evangelical Alliance, but elsewhere in the Pacific the newer or smaller churches and sects are vigorously competitive and are growing at the expense of the older, established churches, especially in the urban areas. The largest of the smaller churches is that of the Mormons, which is by no means new and may not long be small. It has been growing rapidly and has become one of the larger minority bodies in most Polynesian countries.

In addition to the influx of new religious movements from outside the Pacific, many new movements have been created by the Pacific peoples themselves. These have usually been short-lived, emotionally intense movements that have combined features of traditional island religion and Christianity. The first of these appeared in Tahiti soon after the conversion of that country and was known as the Mamaia cult. Samoa, during the time of its conversion, saw a similiar phenomenon in the cult of Sio Vili. Fiji produced a whole series of such movements that rose and fell in succession. In the years shortly before and after World War II, Papua New Guinea saw a plethora of new movements that drew worldwide attention. They were often called cargo cults, since many of them provided ritual ways of trying to secure the cargo that was seen coming to Europeans. These cults often emerged from the churches and were often led by former church officers. Many tried to enlist entire communities, since the effectiveness of the rituals was believed to require community-wide participation, and thus they damaged and even for a time destroyed church life in certain places. Typically, cult leaders tried to organize and control every aspect of their members' lives in an attempt to establish complete harmony and cooperation. When, however, their own communities developed divisions or the anticipated cargo failed to arrive, members gradually lost interest and the movements died down. In recent years they have largely disappeared, though a few continue in a quieter style and show signs of possible permanence—the Paliau movement in Manus, the Christian Fellowship Church in the western Solomons, the John Frum movement on the island of Tanna in Vanuata, and the Modekgnei movement in Belau. [*See also* Cargo Cults.]

BIBLIOGRAPHY

The history and recent development of Christianity in the Pacific Islands is covered in two books: John Garrett's *To Live among the Stars: Christian Origins in Oceania* (Suva, Fiji, 1982), which concentrates on the nineteenth century, and my *The Island Churches of the South Pacific: Emergence in the Twentieth Century* (Maryknoll, N.Y., 1982), which concentrates on the twentieth. One of the few thorough analyses of Christianity in a Pacific country is Alan R. Tippett's *Solomon Islands Christianity: A Study in Growth and Obstruction* (London, 1967). A fine analysis of the work of an anthropologically sensitive missionary exploring what Christianity might mean to Pacific peoples is James Clifford's *Person and Myth: Maurice Leenhardt in the Melanesian World* (Berkeley, 1982). The basic study of the new religious movements has long been Peter Worsley's *The Trumpet Shall Sound: A Study of "Cargo" Cults in Melanesia* (London, 1957). Many fine studies of particular cults have followed. Of these the best known are Kenelm Burridge's *Mambu, a Melanesian Millenium* (London, 1960) and Peter Lawrence's *Road Belong Cargo: A Study of the Cargo Movement in the Southern Madang District, New Guinea* (Manchester, 1964).

CHARLES W. FORMAN

CHRISTIANITY AND JUDAISM. Christianity began as a movement among the Jewish people in the years prior to the destruction of the Temple in Jerusalem in 70 CE. Jesus of Nazareth (d. around 30 CE) was a Jew who observed Jewish laws and customs, and his first followers were Jews. Jesus' entire life was spent in Palestine, and his message was directed primarily to Jews. At an early stage, however, the new movement spread beyond the Jewish people and outside Palestine. By the beginning of the second century of the common era most Christians were gentiles, not Jews. Nevertheless, Christians continued to use the Hebrew scriptures (the writings that were later to become the Christian Old Testament) as their scriptures; they revered the great figures of Israel's past—for example, Abraham, Moses, Elijah, David, among others—as exemplars of faith and piety (c. f. *Heb.* 11, *1 Clement* 9–12, 17); they saw the history of Israel as part of their history; they appealed to the Hebrew prophets to support their claims about Jesus (see the *Gospel of Matthew* and Justin Martyr's *1 Apology* 30–53); and they, like the Jews, believed in one God, who was the creator of all things and who was known through revelation in historical events. Christians, however, saw in Jesus of Nazareth a more complete revelation of the God of Israel (see *Heb.* 1, *Jn.* 1:1–18), and for this reason they believed that Jewish history had reached its fulfillment in Jesus, whom they called the Messiah (Christ). [*See* Jesus; *see also* History, *especially the article on* Christian Views.]

Christianity's origin shaped the movement's early understanding of itself; it has been a central factor in determining Christian attitudes toward the Jews and in influencing the relations between the two communities. On the one hand, Christians recognized that Judaism was the source and origin of their faith. In the words of Paul of Tarsus, Christianity is a "wild olive shoot" that was grafted onto a domesticated olive tree. It is not "you [the Christians] that support the root, but the root [the Jews] that supports you" (*Rom.* 11:17–18). On the other hand, because few Jews embraced the new movement, even though (according to Christians) Jewish hopes thus had been fulfilled, Jews as a people were viewed as rejecters of Jesus. This gave Christian attitudes and beliefs an enduring anti-Jewish cast. [*See* Anti-Semitism.]

At the time that Christianity began, Jews had been struggling for two hundred years to win and maintain their existence as an independent nation, but they were thwarted first by the power of the Hellenistic monarchies and then by the might of Rome. In 63 BCE, Rome conquered Judaea, and in 69–70 CE, after a protracted war, the Jewish Temple was destroyed and the city of Jerusalem was laid waste. Because these events happened so close to the lifetime of Jesus, it appeared to later Christian observers that the rise of Christianity was coincident with the decline of Jewish institutions and life (Origen, *Against Celsus* 4.22). When this perception was joined with Christian theological ideas about Jesus as the final revelation of God, it seemed to Christians that they had displaced Jews as the inheritors of the tradition of ancient Israel. In most historical accounts of Western history and Byzantium (shaped by the historical conventions of a Christian civilization), the Jews had been almost wholly ignored. But historical studies in the late twentieth century began to alter this view, presenting a new picture of Jewish life and learning in the centuries after the beginning of Christianity through the Middle Ages. In the ancient world, after the war with the Romans in 70 CE, Jewish life continued without interruption in most cities of the Roman empire and in Babylonia, the home of a large Jewish community. Even in Palestine, where the devastation was greatest, Jewish life began to revive by the end of the second century, particularly in Galilee, which became the new center in Palestine (Jerusalem had become a Roman city, Aelia Capitolina). During this period, Judaism as we know it emerged, and the great classical texts—the Mishnah, the Babylonian Talmud, the Palestinian Talmud, and many of the *midrashim* (biblical commentaries)—were written or compiled. [*See* Rabbinic Judaism in Late Antiquity.]

For an understanding of the relation between Christianity and Judaism, the period from the fall of Jerusalem in 70 CE to the Muslim conquest of the eastern Mediterranean in around 640 CE (that is, the era in which both Christianity and Judaism assumed their classical forms) is of capital importance. Christianity defined itself during this period in relation to a living Jewish tradition that was encountered in the cities of the Roman empire (for example, Antioch in Syria, Sardis in western Asia Minor, Alexandria in Egypt, and Caesarea in Palestine), a tradition which claimed to be the authentic inheritor of the scriptures (the Christian Old Testament) and the traditional Jewish way of life. Even gentile observers noted the anomaly that Christians claimed to be the inheritors of the Hebrew scriptures yet did not observe the laws that were prescribed by Moses, the teacher of ancient Israel.

During this early period the line between Christian and Jew was not always clearly defined. Alongside (and sometimes within) the churches and synagogues there were Jews who accepted Jesus as the Messiah yet continued to observe the Jewish laws, to revere the city of Jerusalem, and to retain in other ways their identity as Jews, and there were gentiles who adopted Jewish ways as a result of becoming Christian. Jesus, according to the Gospels, observed the Sabbath and celebrated the Jewish festivals. Why should Christians not do the same? Though Jewish and Christian leaders spoke out against these groups, there is evidence that judaizing Christians and christianizing Jews persisted in their practices even though they were ostracized by both communities. The Christian presbyter Chrysostom, for example, preached a series of sermons against the judaizers among the Christians of Antioch at the end of the fourth century.

The first Christian sources were written by Jews who were seeking to interpret their new way of life in light of their Jewish heritage. The earliest strata of the New Testament portray Jesus and his disciples as Jews who are in conflict with other Jewish teachers, for example, the Pharisees (*Lk.* 11:39–52, 15:15–24), on questions concerning interpretation of Jewish law. The dispute here is within the Jewish community. But as time goes on the cleavage widens, and Christian writings present the Jews as "other." Jewish customs, for instance, have to be explained (*Mk.* 7:3–4). In time the Jews are said to have been rejected by God and the kingdom of God taken from them (*Mt.* 21:43). The Jewish people are blamed for Jesus' death (*Mt.* 27:25). Yet this same writing, the *Gospel of Matthew*, presents the mission of Jesus and his disciples as directed chiefly to the "house of Israel" (*Mt.* 10:6), and Jesus is said to have come not to abolish but to fulfill the law (*Mt.* 5:17–20). And the *Acts of the Apostles*, written toward the end of the first century, depicts the Christian movement as a Jewish sect that respects Jewish law (*Acts* 24:10–15) and whose adherents worshiped in the Temple in Jerusalem while it was standing (*Acts* 3:46, 21:46). On the other hand, the *Gospel of John*, written in a community that had been driven out of the synagogue, reflects sharp animosity toward the Jews (*Jn.* 1.11).

Paul, a Jew from Tarsus in Cilicia who first opposed the Christian movement and then embraced it enthusiastically, displays profound ambivalence toward fellow Jews and the Jewish way of life in his writings. On the one hand, he can boast that he was a faithful and observant Jew (*Phil.* 2) and praise the Jews because to them belong the "sonship, the glory, the covenants, the giving of the law, the worship, and the promises" (*Rom.* 9). Yet he asserts that, in comparison to the splendor that is Christ's, the splendor that was Moses' "has come to have no splendor at all" (*2 Cor.* 3). Paul's new experience "in Christ" led him to devalue and disparage Jewish law. He was convinced that his task was to preach to the gentiles and to join them to the Jewish people without making them submit to the requirements of Jewish law, for example, circumcision, keeping of the Sabbath, eating certain foods, and celebration of Jewish festivals. In one view, Paul is thought to allow the observance of the law by Jews. But he may in fact be rejecting it out of hand because he believed that if one is "in Christ" there is no longer any need for the law's observance; Christianity is a new religion distinct from Judaism. [*See the biography of* Paul.]

However one resolves the ambiguities, even contradictions, in Paul's thinking (a task that has occupied Christian thinkers for centuries), his statements about Jewish law (see *Gal.* 3 and 5), when read by gentiles outside the context of Jewish life, took on a very specific meaning. The ritual requirements of the law had no place in Christian life; only the moral law, the Ten

Commandments, was received and honored (see Augustine, *Letters* 196).

Nevertheless, it was as Jews that the first Christians came to their belief in Jesus as the Messiah and were able to understand themselves as a new people of God. In the hands of Christians, not only Jewish law, but also Jewish beliefs and attitudes toward the land and the city of Jerusalem, toward the history of Israel, and toward the Messiah and expectations for the end of time all had different import. The earliest Christian writings set forth the main lines of the disputes that would mark later relations between Christians and Jews: the messiahship of Jesus, the status of Jewish law, the character of the new community, the significance of Jerusalem, and so on.

By the middle of the second century, Christianity had become a sect independent of the Jews. Just as Christian thinkers began to write works "to the Greeks" to explain and defend their way of life to the Greco-Roman world, they also addressed similar works "to the Jews" *(adversus Iudaeos)*. One of the earliest of these is the *Dialogue with Trypho* by Justin Martyr, in which Justin sets forth in detail arguments from the Old Testament against objections from his Jewish interlocutor. It is interesting to note that in the course of the work Justin acknowledges that he knew some Christians who continued to observe Jewish customs and traditions and that, contrary to the views of most other Christians, he was willing to consider them "kinsmen" as long as they did not impose their ways on others, that is, require that gentile Christians keep the law.

A significant development for relations between Jews and Christians during this period was the rejection of the views of Marcion, an early Christian thinker who refused to acknowledge the authority of the Hebrew scriptures. Marcion was opposed by Christian leaders who insisted that these writings were also the church's Bible. The Hebrew scriptures came to be called the "old covenant [testament]" (the term occurs in Clement of Alexandria's *Stromateis* 5.85.1 and in Tertullian's *Against Marcion* 4.1.1) and were seen to point to the "new covenant [testament]," that is, the writings of the apostles and the evangelists. The Old Testament, particularly the prophetic writings and the narratives of heroic figures of Jewish history, was interpreted in sermons, in commentaries, and in the Christian liturgy as a book that found its fulfillment in Christ, thereby making earlier Jewish history propadeutic to Christianity.

The first five centuries of Christian history are marked by regular and continuous intercourse between Christians and Jews. The Christian side of this commerce is most clearly seen in the works "to the Jews," but it is also evident in biblical commentaries, sermons, historical works, theological writings, and works written in defense of Christianity to pagans (for example, the *Against Celsus* of Origen of Alexandria and the *Against Julian* of Cyril of Alexandria). Jews were part of the foreground of the world that Christians inhabited, and this social fact helps account for the contentious and defensive tone of early Christian comments on the Jews. Christians believed that the church was the new Israel and that the existence of the synagogue and its way of life was an affront. They charged the Jews with misunderstanding the Hebrew scriptures and with continuing to observe ancient practices that had lost their legitimacy. They argued that the prophets had spoken of the coming of Christ and the growth of the church, not of the Jews and a future messianic age.

These early writings were to have a profound effect on Christian attitudes toward the Jews. In the setting in which they were first written, Christians and Jews were rivals, each a minority religion within a pagan culture. However, when these works were copied and translated in other cultural settings (for example, in medieval Europe, Byzantium, and Russia, places where Christians had become the majority), they were to have grave consequences. [*See* Polemics.]

Yet it is insufficient to see the earliest Christian period solely as one of antipathy toward the Jews. Relations were not always hostile, and even when Christians used harsh language to attack the Jews, it is apparent that they sometimes had fruitful exchanges with and learned from them.

Origen of Alexandria spent his most mature years in Caesarea in Roman Palestine (c. 233–253), where he had extensive contacts with Jews. From them he learned Hebrew as well as techniques of exegesis that allowed him to interpret difficult passages from the scriptures. His intention was to free Christians from dependency on the synagogue (which possessed the Hebrew text of the Old Testament), but to do that he had to draw on Jewish learning. Through Origen, Jewish scholarship influenced Christian exegesis in its most formative period. A little over a century later, another Christian biblical scholar, Jerome, learned Hebrew from Jews and sought out Jewish scholars for discussions on points of biblical history and geography. As a result of his studies he realized that the Greek and Latin translations in use by Christians were not always faithful to the original Hebrew text, and he translated the entire Hebrew scriptures into Latin for Christian use. Christians considered the Greek translation (the Septuagint) and the old Latin version (Vetus Latina) inspired texts. Jerome's insistence that Christians base their interpretation of the Old Testament on the Hebrew text set a precedent that has shaped Christian study of the Old Testament ever since. [*See* Biblical Exegesis, *article on* Christian Views.]

In Syriac-speaking lands, Christians had close contact with Jews. They shared a common language, Aramaic (Syriac), and were relatively independent of the conventions of Greek and Latin Christian thought. The Old Testament also played a larger role in Syriac-Christian thinking than it did in the West. Some Christians, for example, Aphraates (early fourth century), had knowledge of Jewish *halakhah* ("law"). Aphraates' biblical commentaries drew on Jewish sources. It appears that in this milieu Christians had adopted certain Jewish practices, and the writings of Aphraates and other Syriac works (e.g., the *Teachings of the Apostles*) deal more concretely with questions concerning Jewish food laws, circumcision, the Sabbath, and Jewish festivals than do most Christian works from the West.

From the earliest period, Christians presented their ideas and beliefs on the basis of the Old Testament, and much of Christian intellectual life in antiquity is devoted to interpreting the Old Testament. The Jews gave Christianity a sacred book and a history, no small factors in helping Christianity gain respect among the Greeks and the Romans. The importance of Judaism for Christian thinking is apparent not only in the work of Origen and Jerome but also in the biblical commentaries of Eusebius of Caesarea, Theodore of Mopsuestia, Diodore of Tarsus, Cyril of Alexandria, Theodoret of Cyrrhus, Augustine of Hippo, and others. In these commentaries, the Hebrew prophets are seen to proclaim a universal message; though this message found its most definitive expression in Christ, its elaboration was possible only through its Jewish sources.

In the early centuries, there is no equivalent response of Jews to the Christians; there was no need for Jews to legitimate their tradition against Christianity. Jewish sources do mention disputes with Christians and other deviants, and it is clear that Jews responded to Christian use of the Hebrew scriptures. But these issues are at the periphery of Jewish concerns. There are no Jewish works from this period that offer a Jewish statement of the issues. It is possible that the existence of Jewish *midrashim* (verse-by-verse commentaries on the scriptures) is evidence of Jewish concern with Christian exegesis, but the *midrashim* include many other topics that cannot derive from Jewish-Christian disputes.

Jesus of Nazareth is mentioned only infrequently in the Palestinian and Babylonian Talmuds; what references there are, are often garbled. Jews of later times (and in some cases Christians) edited out the mention of Jesus. He is pictured as a wayward Jewish teacher who strayed from Jewish practice or as a sorcerer who enticed people to follow him and was put to death. The *Toldot Yeshu* (History of Jesus), an account of Jesus' life, put together by Jews, that was an alternative to that of the Gospels, was not compiled until the Middle Ages. Here Jesus is pictured as a gifted man but disrespectful to his elders and the sages. His mother, Miriam (Mary), is portrayed favorably.

In the medieval period, however, there is a large body of Jewish literature dealing with Christian beliefs and practices. Sa'adyah Gaon (882–942) was the first Jewish thinker to give serious attention to Christianity. In his *Sefer emunot ve-de'ot* (The Book of Beliefs and Opinions; 923 CE), written to establish the claims of rabbinic Judaism against Muslim, Karaite (Jewish sect), Christian, and pagan critics, he discusses the Christian teaching on the Trinity and the abrogation of Jewish law.

Yehudah ha-Levi (1075–1145), a Spanish philosopher and poet, wrote a book called *Kuzari*, which was a dialogue centered on a pagan king's search for true religion. In it he presents Christian views sympathetically, though his purpose was to show the superiority of Judaism. Another Spanish Jew, Avraham ibn 'Ezra' (1092–1167), a biblical scholar, knew Christian exegesis of the scriptures and criticized Christian scholars for ignoring the reasonable meaning of the laws in favor of allegorical interpretations.

The writings of Rashi (Shelomoh ben Yitsḥaq, 1042–1105), a Jewish scholar from Troyes in France, were known to Christian scholars of his day and were studied by Christian biblical commentators later in the Middle Ages. His insistence on the "plain sense" of the scriptures made a deep impression on some Christian thinkers. Another Jewish biblical scholar from this period, David Kimḥi (c. 1160–1235), was familiar with Christian teachings and was able to cite the precise language used by Christians to express their beliefs, arguing, for example, that the plain sense of Psalms 2, 72, and 110 indicated that they referred to David, not Jesus. He also addressed a theme that would mark later Jewish-Christian discussion, namely, whether the Torah was given only for a certain people and for a fixed time, or whether it was given in perpetuity. The Jewish arguments, and the biblical texts cited by Christians to support their teachings, are summarized in several medieval compilations, including the *Sefer Yosef ha-meqanne'* (The Book of Joseph the Zealot) and the *Sefer nitsaḥon yashan* (The Old Book of Polemic).

As these writings indicate, medieval western Europe was not a closed society completely dominated by Christianity. There were other voices, one of which was that of the Jews. Christian attitudes toward the Jews underwent significant alterations during the medieval period, as Christians tried to come to terms with what seemed a foreign body in their midst, one that nevertheless used the same scriptures and claimed that its interpretation of them was more faithful to its sense than Christian interpretation.

Contact with Jewish scholars encouraged Christians to undertake more scholarly and intensive studies of the Old Testament. In the twelfth century, Andrew of Saint Victor in Paris was among a group of scholars familiar with the writings of Rashi and Jewish commentaries. Jewish exegetes had persuaded him that the passage in *Isaiah* 7:14, predicting the virgin birth of Christ, actually referred to events in the time it was written; his acceptance of the Jewish approach validated it. One of Andrew's fellow monks wrote a tract to refute these views. Through disputes of this sort, the idea of a "literal" (as distinct from a spiritual) meaning of the text came to assume a role in Christian biblical interpretation.

From the same period there are a number of Christian writings dealing explicitly with Jewish questions. Whether they arose out of actual discussions with Jews has been a matter of debate. Among these writings are the *Disputatio Iudaei et Christiani* (Disputation of a Jew and a Christian), written by Gilbert Crispin, a close friend of Anselm of Canterbury, at the turn of the eleventh century; the *Dialogus Petri et moysi Iudaei* (Dialogue of Peter and Moses the Jew) of Peter Alfonsi, a convert to Christianity early in the twelfth century; and the *Tractatus adversus Iudaeorum inverteram duritiem* (Tractate against the Long-Standing Intractibility of the Jews) of Peter the Venerable (1092–1156), abbot of Cluny. Though these works are indebted to earlier Christian writings against the Jews, they indicate that contact had led Christian thinkers to less complacent presentations of Christian beliefs; in some cases, for example, the writings of Rupert of Deutz (1070–1129), contact prompted more comprehensive interpretations of the scriptures as a whole.

The promising beginning that took place in relations between Christians and Jews at the end of the eleventh century was frustrated by the intervention of the Crusades (First Crusade, 1096). Although the Crusades were directed against the Muslims in the East, and their goal was to reclaim the Holy Land for Christianity, the zeal of the Crusaders was exercised on the Jews who lived in the lands from which the Crusaders were recruited, that is, in Europe. A popular motif among the Crusaders was vengeance for the death of Jesus, and the Jews became the first victims. Persecution of the Jews occurred in Rouen in 1096, followed quickly by massacres in Worms, Mainz, and Cologne. Christian bishops had preached protection for the Jews, but events overtook them and Jews became more isolated and alienated from medieval Christian society.

Nevertheless there is considerable evidence that contacts between Christians and Jews continued and in some cases intensified. For example, a significant new development was the awareness on the part of Christian thinkers and leaders of the importance of the Talmud in Judaism, reflected in Gregory IX's decree calling for its destruction in 1239. Some Christian leaders, for example, Nicholas Donin, a Jewish convert to Christianity, argued that the Talmud was the basis for Jewish education. It gave Jewish thinkers the resources to respond forcefully and intelligently to Christian critics and hence to resist conversion. "These books cannot be tolerated . . . . without injury to the Christian faith." The most significant Christian figures to urge new ways of dealing with the Jews came from the recently established mendicant orders, the Franciscans and the Dominicans; the Talmud became the object of their attack. The Dominican Raymond of Peñafort (b. around 1185) established schools to study Hebrew in order to convince the Jews on the basis of Jewish sources. This way of responding to the Jews found expression in the debate at Barcelona in 1263 between the Jewish rabbi Moses Nahmanides (Mosheh ben Naḥman, c. 1194–1270) of Gerona and the Dominican convert Pablo Christiani, as well as in Raymond Martini's *Pugio fidei* (Dagger of the Faith; 1278), an immensely learned work with quotations in Hebrew and Aramaic. Like other Christian works against the Jews, Martini's was answered by Jewish scholars.

The disputes over the Talmud convinced Christians that the Jewish laws and traditions were a positive danger to Christianity and had to be banished. That required excluding the Jews from Christian society if they did not convert, as can be seen in the work of Ramón Lull (c. 1232–1316) as well as in the debate at Tortosa, Spain, in 1413–1414. The Jews were expulsed from Spain in 1492.

An important mediating figure in the later Middle Ages is Nicholas of Lyra (1270–1349), the Franciscan biblical scholar. Nicholas stands out because of his knowledge of Hebrew and of Jewish sources. His *Postilla litteralis super Biblia*, the most learned and comprehensive commentary on the Hebrew scriptures from the Middle Ages, drew heavily on Jewish commentators, particularly Rashi. But Nicholas too was influenced by the more aggressive approach to the Jews. In his two smaller works on the Jews, he used his Hebrew learning to establish the deficiencies of the rabbinic interpretation of the Bible.

One of the most fruitful points of contact between Jews and Christians in the Middle Ages was in the field of religious philosophy. Despite sharp polemic, representatives on each side learned ways of responding to common theological and philosophical problems from the other. The rediscovery of the writings of Aristotle, who was held to be the voice of reason, offered a new challenge to Christianity and Judaism, each of which claimed to rest on revelation.

The efforts of the great Jewish philosopher Moses Maimonides (Mosheh ben Maimon, 1135/8–1204) to synthesize revelation and reason met with favor among Christian philosophers. His proofs for the existence of God influenced Thomas Aquinas, as did his position that a temporal creation can only be argued from revelation. Maimonides was also a critic of certain Christian teachings, for example, those on the doctrine of the Trinity, and he defended the validity of the Torah against Christian views. In turn, Thomas's own synthesis of faith and reason proved helpful to Jewish thinkers, and a number of Thomas's writings were translated into Hebrew. Hillel of Verona (1220–1295) translated Thomas's *On the Unity of the Intellect* to answer the arguments of Ibn Rushd (Averroës) against the idea of individual mortality. Another Italian-Jewish philosopher, Yehudah Romano (fourteenth century), also translated works of Thomas as well as Albertus Magnus. In the fifteenth century Yosef Albo, a Spanish-Jewish philosopher who took part in the debates at Tortosa and San Mateo (1413–1414), knew Thomas and used his ideas to offer a reasoned presentation of Judaism.

In the medieval period, contacts between Jews and Christians were not limited to western Europe, as treatises by Eastern Christian writers on the Jews indicate. The issues between Jews and Christians were often the same as in the West, with several notable exceptions. The question of worship of images (icons), a form of devotion that was widespread in the East, became a matter of dispute. Because of their strict monotheism, Jews were thought to be allies of the iconoclasts and were attacked by defenders of icons, as in the work of Nikephoros I (758–829), patriarch of Constantinople. Also, after the year 640, Christians in most parts of the East were under Muslim rule, which altered relations between Christians and Jews. Both were now minorities. Theodore Abū Qurrah (c. 750–825), the first Christian thinker to write in Arabic, defended icons to Jews as well as to Arabs. There is a continuous tradition of works on the Jews in the East in the writings of John of Damascus, Anastasius of Sinai, Theopylactus of Euboea, Nektarios of Casole, Theophanes of Nicaea, and others. An interesting late work from the time of the Turkish conquest of Constantinople in 1453, the *Refutation of the Jewish Error from the Scriptures and from Circumstances and from a Comparison with the Christian Truth*, supposedly by Gennadios Scholarios, is in the form of a dialogue. It draws a parallel between the fall of the Christian capital, Constantinople, in 1453 and the fall of Jerusalem in 70.

In the periods of the Renaissance and the Reformation, Christians took up afresh and with great seriousness the study of the Hebrew language. This was in part due to the new interest in antiquity and in the study of the scriptures. Jews had chided Christians because they lacked the original text of the scriptures. To learn Hebrew, Christians turned, as they had always done, to Jewish scholars. Two key Christian figures in this Hebrew renaissance were Giovanni Pico della Mirandola (1463–1494) and Johannes Reuchlin (1455–1522). Philipp Melanchthon, Martin Luther's colleague in Wittenberg, was a grandnephew of Reuchlin and himself a student of Hebrew. Martin Luther (1483–1546) knew Hebrew, as did many other reformers. Study of the Hebrew language led scholars to consult Jewish commentaries and to become interested in Qabbalah (Jewish mysticism), which was undergoing a renewal in the sixteenth century. Some Christians (for example, Pico) saw Qabbalah as part of a universal religious philosophy; for others it was a kind of ancient wisdom or occult science; still others saw it as a resource, because of veiled hints of Christian teaching, to aid in converting Jews. [*See* Humanism.]

The Reformation, however, did not alter the medieval view of the Jews. Reuchlin combined scholarly respect and hostility in his writings. Erasmus defended Reuchlin in the name of new learning, but he was not sympathetic to the latter's interest in Judaism, which he saw as an occult philosophy. The Old Testament was "a book of shadows, given on loan, until the coming of Christ." Luther shared these attitudes. Even though he wrote a book, *Jesus the Son of a Jewish Mother*, that was warmly received by Jews and translated the entire Hebrew scriptures into German, he shared the same anti-Jewish attitudes as other medievals; his later writings on the Jews are filled with obloquy. He was convinced that, since the appearance of Christ on earth, the Jews as a people had no more future.

Nor did the study of Hebrew and Jewish sources bring a new understanding of Judaism or the Jewish people. The Jews were seen to adhere to a religion of law, of externals, to the regulations of the Old Covenant; this stereotype was passed on by later generations of biblical scholars and students of Hebrew (for example, Johann Buxtorf, 1564–1629) and continued up through the nineteenth and twentieth centuries in the writings of Julius Wellhausen and Wilhelm Bousset, to mention only two representative figures. Even in the Enlightenment, the Jews did not fare well among Christian thinkers. Christians became fascinated with natural and universal religion, and this led them to disparage the particularism of the Jews. An exception was Gotthold Ephraim Lessing (1729–1781), an Enlightenment thinker whose play *Nathan the Wise* presented an appreciative portrait of a Jew as the embodiment of tolerant and enlightened rationalism.

In the eighteenth century, and continuing into the nineteenth and twentieth centuries, there were indications that, for the first time, Jews were making an effort to understand Christianity for its own sake, not simply as a spiritual opponent. Ya'aqov Emden (1697–1776) believed that Jesus did not intend to abrogate the Torah, that his aim was to spread Jewish beliefs to non-Jews. The great Jewish Enlightenment thinker Moses Mendelssohn (1729–1786) was willing to acknowledge Jesus as a prophet. In his view, Judaism was a religion (as was Christianity), not a nation or a people, but it had no binding dogmas (as did Christianity), and it was based on historical events and actions, not on authority. In the nineteenth century, after the "emancipation" of Jews and when Jews were beginning to enter the mainstream of European intellectual life, they contributed to the historical study of Jesus and of Christian origins. Important in this effort were such Jewish thinkers as Joseph Salvador (1796–1873), Solomon Formstecher (1808–1889), and Samuel Hirsch (1815–1889). For some Jews, Christianity was seen as a compelling spiritual option. When Eugene Rosenstock-Huessey converted to Christianity early in the twentieth century, his decision was defended by Franz Rosenzweig (1886–1929), who later (after seriously considering conversion) embraced Judaism enthusiastically, although he came from an assimilated German-Jewish family. Nevertheless, in his later writings, Rosenzweig saw the church as God's agent within history to bring the God of Israel to the other nations. Martin Buber (1878–1965) had a genuine admiration, even affection, for Jesus as a Jew. He called him "Brother" and a "messianic man" though not the Messiah; though he considered the covenant between God and the people of Israel permanent and eternal, he believed that both Christianity and Judaism have a place in God's plan.

In the twentieth century, Christian attitudes toward the Jews underwent a profound transformation as a result of the Holocaust, the destruction of European Jewry by the Nazis during World War II. [*See* Holocaust.] But an equally important factor was the establishment of the state of Israel in 1947 and the new consciousness of Jews and of Judaism that resulted from the political fact of a Jewish state. To Christians, it seemed that the Jewish people had once again entered history, and Christian scholarship began, after centuries of neglect, of polemics, and of caricature, to comprehend Judaism not as the precursor to Christianity but as a religion in its own right. By the second half of the twentieth century, the existence of the Jewish people was seen less as a threat to Christianity and more as a blessing, and contacts with Jews were thought necessary for the spiritual health of the Christian communities.

In the West Christians became aware that traditional Christian attitudes toward the Jews had created a climate of opinion that fostered anti-Semitism. The first efforts to alter these views were made after World War II. At the Seelisberg Conference in 1947, men such as Jules Isaac, a French Catholic historian, and Paul Demann, the theologian and converted Jew, were keenly aware of the depth of Christian anti-Jewish attitudes, and the conference affirmed that the God of Christians and Jews was the same God, that Jesus was born of a Jewish woman, and that the first Christians were Jews. Isaac urged Christians to avoid using the term *Jew* in a derogatory fashion or presenting the death of Christ as something for which the Jews were responsible.

In 1956, the National Council of Churches called for more active effort on the part of the Christian church to correct the misconception about the crucifixion. It affirmed that the Jews did not kill Christ, and it warned against the dangers of anti-Semitism. In 1964, the same body said: "We confess that sometimes as Christians we have given way to anti-Semitism." These opinions are not shared by Christians in the East, particularly in the Arab lands. Changes in attitudes toward the Jews have taken place almost wholly in the United States and in Western Europe. Christians of the East, for example, the Greeks, the Russians, the Copts, and the Armenians, continue to harbor fears and suspicions of the Jews.

At the Second Vatican Council (1962–1965), in a statement on the relation of the church to non-Christian religions, the bishops of the Roman Catholic church included a section on the Jews and affirmed the "bond that spiritually ties the people of the New Covenant to Abraham's stock." The church "feeds upon the root of that cultivated olive tree into which the wild shoots of the Gentiles have been grafted" (*Rom.* 11:17–24). Because Jews and Christians share a "spiritual patrimony," the council encouraged mutual knowledge and respect. It stated that the death of Christ can be attributed neither to all Jews without distinction in Jesus' time nor to the Jews today, and that Jews should not be presented as rejected by God or accursed. The council deplored "hatred, persecutions, displays of anti-Semitism, directed against Jews at any time and by anyone," and it encouraged Roman Catholics to take the initiative in fostering understanding between Christians and Jews.

In turn, some Jews, in spite of the history of prejudice and persecution on the part of Christians, have acknowledged that the modern secular state may prove to be more dangerous to the Jewish people than Christianity has been. The existence of the state of Israel owes much to the support of nations in which many Christians live. To some Christians, particularly American evangelicals, the return of the people of Israel to the land of Israel is seen as the fulfillment of biblical prophecy, and evangelicals have been among the most outspoken supporters of the state of Israel.

[*Aspects of Jewish-Christian interaction are also discussed in* Judaism, *especially articles on* Judaism in Southern Europe, Judaism in Northern and Eastern Europe to 1500, *and* Judaism in Northern and Eastern Europe since 1500. *See also* Christianity, *article on* Christianity in the Middle East, *and the biographies of Christian and Jewish leaders mentioned herein.*]

BIBLIOGRAPHY

Berger, David, ed. and trans. *The Jewish-Christian Debate in the Middle Ages: A Critical Edition of the Nizzaḥon Vetus with an Introduction, Translation and Commentary.* Philadelphia, 1979.

Blumenkranz, Bernhard. *Juifs et chrétiens dans le monde occidental, 430–1096.* Paris, 1960.

Blumenkranz, Bernhard. *Les auteurs chrétiens latins du Moyen-Âge sur les juifs et le judaisme.* Paris, 1963.

Bowman, Steven. "Two Late Byzantine Dialogues with the Jews." *Greek Orthodox Theological Review* 25 (Spring 1980): 83–93.

Cohen, Jeremy. *The Friars and the Jews: The Evolution of Medieval Anti-Judaism.* Ithaca, N.Y., 1982.

De Lange, N. R. M. *Origen and the Jews: Studies in Jewish-Christian Relations in Third-Century Palestine.* Cambridge, 1976.

Dupuy, Bernard. "Le christianisme dans l'œuvre de Martin Buber." *Istina* 25 (1980): 148–160.

Eckardt, A. Roy. *Elder and Younger Brothers: The Encounter of Jews and Christians.* New York, 1967.

Eidelberg, Shlomo, ed. and trans. *The Jews and the Crusaders: The Hebrew Chronicles of the First and Second Crusades.* Madison, Wis., 1977.

Friedman, Jerome. *The Most Ancient Testimony: Sixteenth Century Christian-Hebraica in the Age of Renaissance Nostalgia.* Athens, Ohio, 1983.

Funkenstein, Amos. "Basic Types of Christian Anti-Jewish Polemics in the Later Middle Ages." *Viator* 2 (1971): 373–382.

Gager, John. *The Origins of Anti-Semitism: Attitudes towards Judaism in Pagan and Christian Antiquity.* Oxford, 1983.

Gilbert, Arthur. *The Vatican Council and the Jews.* Cleveland, Ohio, 1968.

Grabois, Aryeh. "The *Hebraica Veritas* and Jewish-Christian Intellectual Relations in the Twelfth Century." *Speculum* 50 (October 1975): 613–634.

Greenberg, Irving. "Cloud of Smoke, Pillar of Fire: Judaism, Christianity, and Modernity after the Holocaust." In *Auschwitz: Beginning of a New Era?,* edited by Eva Fleischner. New York, 1977.

Hailperin, Herman. *Rashi and the Christian Scholars.* Pittsburgh, 1963.

Herford, R. Travers. *Christianity in Talmud and Midrash.* London, 1903.

Jacob, Walter. *Christianity through Jewish Eyes: The Quest for Common Ground.* New York, 1974.

Katz, Jacob. *Exclusiveness and Tolerance: Studies in Jewish-Gentile Relations in Medieval and Modern Times.* Oxford, 1961.

Langmuir, Gavin I. "Majority History and Post-Biblical Jews." *Journal of the History of Ideas* 27 (1966): 343–364.

Lasker, Daniel J. *Jewish Philosophical Polemics against Christianity in the Middle Ages.* New York, 1977.

Lowe, Raphael. "Hebraists, Christian, 1100–1890." In *Encyclopaedia Judaica,* vol. 8. Jerusalem, 1971.

Maccoby, Hyam. *Judaism on Trial: Jewish-Christian Disputations in the Middle Ages.* Rutherford, N.J., 1982.

Oberman, Heiko. *The Roots of Anti-Semitism in the Age of Renaissance and Reformation.* Philadelphia, 1983.

Rengstorf, Karl Heinrich, and Siegfried von Kortzfleisch, eds. *Kirche und Synagoge: Handbuch zur Geschichte von Christen und Juden; Darstellung mit Quellen,* vol. 1. Stuttgart, 1968.

Sanders, E. P. *Paul and Palestinian Judaism.* Philadelphia, 1977.

Schoeps, H. J. *Theologie und Geschichte des Judenchristentums.* Tübingen, 1949.

Schreckenberg, Heinz. *Die christliche Adversus-Judaeos-Texte und Ihr literarisches und historisches Umfeld.* Frankfurt, 1982.

Sermoneta, Giuseppe. "Per una storia del tomismo ebraico." In *Tommaso d'Aquino nel suo settimo centenario: Tommaso d'Aquino nella storia del pensiero,* vol. 2, pp. 354–359. Naples, 1974.

Simon, Marcel. *Verus Israel: Étude sur les relations entre chrétiens et juifs dans l'Empire romain, 135–425.* Paris, 1948.

Smalley, Beryl. *The Study of the Bible in the Middle Ages.* 2d ed. Oxford, 1952.

Stemberger, Bridgette. "Zu den Judenverfolgungen in Deutschland zur Zeit der ersten beiden Kreuzzuege." *Kairos* 20 (1978): 53-72, 151–157.

Thiemann, Ronald F. "Gotthold Ephraim Lessing: An Enlightened View of Judaism." *Journal of Ecumenical Studies* 18 (Summer 1981): 401–422.

Wilken, Robert L. *John Chrysostom and the Jews: Rhetoric and Reality in the Late Fourth Century.* Berkeley, 1983.

Williams, A. Lukyn. *Adversus Judaeos: A Bird's-Eye View of Christian Apologiae until the Renaissance.* Cambridge, 1935.

Robert L. Wilken

CHRISTIAN LITURGICAL YEAR. The Christian liturgical year consists of two cycles, differently defined in Eastern and Western traditions. The Eastern (Byzantine) rite distinguishes between movable and fixed festivals: the former are those whose dates vary each year with the date of Easter but always fall on the same days of the week; the dates of the latter are constant but may fall on any day of the week. Western tradition, on the other hand, includes with the movable festivals certain feasts whose date is fixed (most importantly, Christmas, 25 December) and the seasons dependent on those. This whole cycle is known as the *temporale*, or (as in the present Roman Missal) the Proper of Seasons. The second cycle in Western tradition includes festivals of saints and other anniversaries on fixed dates and is called the *sanctorale*, the Proper of Saints.

Easter, the Christian Passover. The schematizations of the year refer to and are reflected in the organization of liturgical books. The roots of the distinction, however, reach back to the second century, when Easter (Pascha), which had been kept at Jerusalem on the fixed Jewish Passover date, was adjusted to the structure of the week so as to fall always on Sunday, the day of the Resurrection. That adjustment renders Easter's date variable and is, therefore, the basis of the Christian cycle of movable feasts. The precise computation of the date of Easter was fixed at the Council of Nicaea (AD 325) as the Sunday following the full moon after the vernal equinox. Several factors, however, have disturbed that agreement, and the dates set for this major Christian festival differ between East and West in most years, yielding differing dates as well for those seasons and festivals dependent upon the Easter date.

The Paschal Fast. When the observance of Pascha was transferred from the Jewish date to Sunday, the original preceding one-day fast was extended to two days, the Friday on which Jesus was crucified and the Saturday on which he lay in the tomb. By the middle of the third century four more days were added in Syria and Egypt; this six-day total seems universal by the end of that century, yielding the Holy Week still observed by Christians. On Thursday of Holy Week the institution of the Eucharist at the last supper of Jesus with his disciples is celebrated, and the celebration often includes a reenactment of Jesus' washing of the feet of his disciples. In the West an anthem accompanying the ceremony had as its text the verse "A new commandment I give unto you, that you love one another as I have loved you" (*Jn.* 13:34). Its Latin incipit, "Mandatum novum," gave the name *Maundy* to the foot washing and to the Thursday on which it occurred.

A Western pilgrim named Egeria described the services at Jerusalem in 383. She noted that on Friday morning the wood of the cross (discovered in the course of excavating the tomb of Christ) was exposed for the veneration of the people who, one by one, passed by and kissed it. Such veneration attached as well to a major fragment of that wood at Rome in the sixth century, and this led to a similar veneration of a symbolic cross on Good Friday throughout the Western church, still encountered today. Egeria also described a service at Calvary during the hours from noon to three during which the Passion narratives were read from the four Gospels. An extraliturgical service of preaching during these hours was instituted at Lima, Peru, in 1687, and has since achieved wide popularity in both Roman Catholic and Protestant churches, often consisting of seven sermons on Christ's words from the cross, interspersed with hymns.

The Paschal Vigil. Like Passover, the early Christian Pascha was a nocturnal observance, as testified to by the *Epistle of the Apostles*, a work from Asia Minor of the second half of the second century. The earliest detailed account of that vigil's content, the description coming from liturgical directories of the first half of the fifth century, relates activities in Jerusalem. After an initial lamp lighting, the vigil consisted of a series of twelve Old Testament lessons, each followed by prayer. These lessons recalled themes already traditionally associated with Passover: creation, the sacrifice of Isaac, the Exodus from Egypt, and so on. Similar series of twelve lessons are documented later in Spain and Gaul, retaining many of the Jerusalem readings. Such a series became standard in western Europe and was continued in the Roman Missal following the Council of Trent (1545–1563). That series of lessons is found today in the North American *Lutheran Book of Worship*. Similar but shorter series occur in recent revisions of the Roman Missal (1969) and *The Book of Common Prayer* (1979).

A climactic point in the paschal liturgy since the third century has been the conferral of baptism, that rite of initiation by which, as Paul said, we are buried with Christ and risen in him to new life (*Rom.* 6:4). Baptism was performed in a separate chamber during the Old Testament lessons in the fourth and following centuries, but today it is more likely to be performed after them in the presence of the congregation. Following the conferral of baptism, the first Eucharist of Easter is celebrated with exuberant rejoicing over the resurrection of Christ and for the sacramental realization of resurrection in the newly baptized.

In the West today the paschal vigil opens with the lighting of a new fire in the darkness. From this fire the paschal candle, a large candle representing the risen Christ, is lighted and carried into the church in a procession during which a minister proclaims at three points: "The Light of Christ." The same minister then sings over the paschal candle an ancient poem of praise called *Exultet*. The light ritual just described precedes the vigil readings today in Roman Catholic, Anglican, and Lutheran churches. A somewhat simpler light ritual precedes the readings in Orthodox churches now as it did in Jerusalem sixteen centuries earlier. At Jerusalem today, and since the tenth century, the light ceremony has been transferred to a point following the Old Testament readings. There, the Holy Light produced within the tomb of Christ is passed to the ministers and congregation outside the tomb and is carried by them to the other churches of the city in symbolic proclamation of the Resurrection.

Pentecost. Already in the second century the paschal feast initiated a fifty-day period of rejoicing (Pentecost) during which fasting and kneeling were forbidden. But by the final two decades of the fourth century the unified celebration of Christ's resurrection and ascension and the outpouring of the Holy Spirit had given way to distinct festivals: the Pascha of the Resurrection on Easter Sunday, the Ascension on the fortieth day (a Thursday), and the sending of the Holy Spirit upon the church ten days later on Pentecost Sunday. In Gaul not only was fasting resumed after the Ascension, but fasts were ordered on the three days preceding the Ascension on which processions with rogations (litanies) were held to ask protection from natural disaster. Prior to twentieth-century liturgical reforms it was common to extinguish the paschal candle, symbol of the risen Christ's presence with the church, at the conclusion of the gospel reading on Ascension Day. Since Vatican Council II, however, in an effort to recover the integrity of the fifty-day period, the candle burns at all services through the day of Pentecost, and fasting is suspended throughout the period.

The conclusion of the paschal rejoicing at the end of Pentecost Sunday has been marked by a ceremonial return to fasting and kneeling for prayer. The resumption of fasting is noted by Egeria, and in the fifth century, notice is given of devotions performed (while kneeling) at the end of that Sunday on the Mount of Olives. Such a penitential service, called Gonuklisia ("the bending of the knee"), is still observed in the Eastern churches on the evening of Pentecost, marking the end of paschal festivity. The week following Pentecost Sunday is the occasion for one of four seasonal fasts at Rome called, in English, Ember Days, from the German term *Quatember* (Lat., *quatuor tempora,* "the four seasons"). Other Embertides, largely unobserved in Roman Catholic practice today but maintained in Anglican churches, fall in September, in late December, and in the first week of Lent.

Lent and Palm Sunday. Lent is the major fast season of the Christian year, a period of forty days commemorating the fast of Jesus in the wilderness. It is seen by Christians today as preparation for the celebration of Easter. Considerable variety has characterized this fast, stemming from two factors. First, in the West the last of the six weeks is Holy Week, while in the East Lent is the six weeks preceding Holy Week. Second, from the seventh century on there was a general concern that there be forty days of actual fasting. In the Eastern empire Saturday (Sabbath) was not a fast day, with the single exception of the day before Easter, and Sunday was never a fast day. Therefore, a week of fore-fast was added before the beginning of Lent to yield the desired total. In the West, where Lenten Sabbaths were fast days, the original six weeks yielded thirty-six days, and the beginning of the season was set on Wednesday of the preceding week.

Although the Byzantine Lent took on a penitential quality through monastic influence in the eighth century, that quality has never been so pronounced as in the Western church, where Lent was also the time of formal humiliation for those excluded from the community because of grave sins. Admitted to the order of penitents at the beginning of Lent, these separated sinners were solemnly restored to communion in the latter days of Holy Week. One of the ceremonial dimensions of admission to the order of penitents in Gaul was the sprinkling of ashes on their heads. By the eleventh century that penitential discipline had fallen into disuse, but the old ceremonies continued, now for all the faithful. By the end of the eleventh century the imposition of ashes was virtually universal in the West, giving the name *Ash Wednesday* to the first day of Lent. That ceremony continues to mark the beginning of the great fast. This general penitential tone is also manifested in the Western church by the suppression of the joyous acclamation "Alleluia" in all Lenten liturgical services, while "Alleluia" continues to be sung in the Byzantine liturgy during Lent.

The association of Lent with the forty-day fast of Jesus has been taken generally by scholars to be a secondary symbolic interpretation, unrelated to the origins of the great fast, since this time before Easter has no connection in Jesus' life to the temptation that followed immediately upon his baptism in the Jordan. Studies suggest, however, that the forty-day duration of the fast that we encounter after Nicaea may have originated in an earlier Alexandrian "Lent" that followed immediately after the celebration of the baptism of Jesus on 6 January, the Feast of the Epiphany. That six-week period ended with the conferral of baptism in the sixth week and with a "feast of palms" celebrating Christ's triumphal entry into Jerusalem on the following Sunday, all separated from the paschal fast by several weeks. A similar six-week pattern is still visible in the

Byzantine Lent, now prior to Holy Week rather than following Epiphany, hence making Palm Sunday the day before the Holy Week fast.

Egeria describes a procession down the Mount of Olives with palms on the afternoon of this Sunday at Jerusalem in 383, and such a procession was later adopted by other churches, which already called that day the Sunday of the Passion. Palm Sunday is now generally understood to be the beginning of Holy Week. Its focus is a procession with palms or other branches celebrating Christ's entrance into Jerusalem, followed by the Eucharist whose theme is the passion of Christ. In the Byzantine rite, the sixth week of Lent leading into Palm Sunday is called Palm Week, the individual days being similarly characterized, reinforcing the Coptic suggestion that Palm Sunday was originally the conclusion of Lent, rather than the beginning of Holy Week (as it is generally understood in the West today).

Christmas and Epiphany. The principal festivals of fixed date are those associated with the nativity of Jesus. At Rome by 336 such a festival on 25 December marked the beginning of the year. Earlier (perhaps from the beginning of the second century) in the Eastern churches the festival of the nativity known as Epiphania or Theophania, terms associated in classical Greek with the human manifestation of a deity, was set on 6 January. In some churches the themes of Christ's baptism in the Jordan and his first miracle at Cana were celebrated on or near that same day.

The coincidence of the Roman date for the Feast of the Nativity, 25 December, with the date of Natalis Solis Invicti, a winter solstice festival established by the emperor Aurelian in 274 CE, has encouraged the hypothesis that Christmas represents a Christian appropriation of the solstice festival, and similar pagan backgrounds have been proposed for the Epiphany festival on 6 January. Contrary to this prevailing view, Louis Duchesne in his *Christian Worship* (London, 1903) suggests that those dates were computed as nativity dates from the inclusion of the Incarnation (i.e., the conception of Christ) in the themes celebrated at Pascha on known fixed dates, 25 March in Africa and Rome, 6 April in Asia Minor and elsewhere in the East. In modern times, 25 March is celebrated as the Feast of the Annunciation (the conception of Christ) nine months before Christmas, except among the Armenians, who continue to follow the tradition of Jerusalem by observing the Nativity on 6 January and the Annunciation nine months earlier. In the course of the later fourth and fifth centuries other Eastern churches adopted the Roman festival of 25 December, thenceforward devoting 6 January only to the celebration of Christ's baptism. In that same period the January festival was adopted at Rome, and its nativity theme was narrowed to the visit of the Magi, from which it came to be considered the manifestation of Christ to the gentiles.

In most Latin cultures, the Epiphany festival remains the occasion for the exchange of gifts, after the example of the Magi, while in northern Europe and English-speaking countries that custom, continued from pre-Christian year-end festivities, attaches rather to Christmas. In the Byzantine and other Eastern churches where Epiphany celebrates Christ's sanctification of water by his baptism, a major feature of the celebration is a blessing of water that is drawn by the faithful and carried to their homes, a custom for which pre-Christian roots are also claimed in modern scholarship.

Advent. Analogous to the period of preparation for Easter, a fast before the nativity developed in the West into a preparatory season. In addition to the Roman December Embertide, churches in Gaul observed fasts of six weeks or more; a common form was called Saint Martin's Lent, from its beginning on 11 November, the Feast of Saint Martin of Tours. That season, known as Advent, developed themes associated both with the advent of Christ at his nativity and the second advent at the end of this world's history, the two advents having been expressed by the same term *(parousia)* since the Greek theologians of the second century. A forty-day fast is also kept before Christmas in the Eastern churches, but this never received the liturgical articulation of Advent in the West, where Advent today comprises the four weeks (or, in Milan, six weeks) before Christmas.

The Sanctoral Cycle. From the death of Stephen (*Acts* 7), Christianity has honored those whose faith in Christ has brought them to martyrdom. The liturgical expression of this honor is documented as early as the second century, in the case of the martyrdom of Polycarp at Smyrna, and in the following centuries this veneration achieved a high level of local organization as the anniversaries of martyrs' deaths came to be observed by the celebration of the Eucharist at their tombs. A Roman martyrology of 354 includes a few North African martyrs, probably revealing the presence of an African community at Rome. That same document reveals memorial observances of bishops of Rome who were not martyrs. Both the bishops' list (first prepared in 336) and the list of martyrs present the dates of their memorial celebrations in calendrical order (beginning from 25 December) and designate in each case the cemetery where the observance was held. A Syriac martyrology of the following century reveals an increasing unification of these local lists, conflating the martyrs' observances of a great many cities. This tendency to veneration over a wider area and the addition of revered Christians other than martyrs to liturgical calendars led in the Middle Ages to central control over the liturgical veneration of saints; this became in time a complex procedure for beatification and canonization. However, a uniform liturgical calendar of saints was never produced, for local interests continued to be selective. Revision of the Roman calendar in 1969 has given a much larger place to optional observances.

Many feasts represent anniversaries of the dedication of churches, and such a dedication festival at fourth-century Jerusalem is continued in modern calendars as the Feast of the Holy Cross. The dedications of churches also lie behind many other feasts (e.g., of various New Testament figures or angels) where there is no question of a known place of burial. Since the later Middle Ages, still other festivals have been instituted simply as an aid to the promulgation of particular theological or devotional concerns, but this approach to festival is less evident since the Second Vatican Council.

The Liturgical Year since the Reformation. At the Reformation, churches of the reformed tradition placed a renewed emphasis on the weekly observance of Sunday as the primary liturgical articulation of time, while Lutheran and Anglican traditions continued to observe most of the traditional liturgical year but severely restricted the number of feasts of saints, limiting them to New Testament figures for the most part. Since the Second Vatican Council the reform of the Roman calendar has been widely adopted in the United States and Canada, with the general shape of its temporal cycle and accompanying lectionary followed by Roman Catholics, Episcopalians (Anglicans), Lutherans, Presbyterians, Methodists, and other participants in the Consultation on Church Union (COCU). Of these, the Episcopal and Lutheran churches have developed their own calendars of saints, following traditional principles.

Liturgical Colors. In earlier times clergy were garbed in a frequently washed tunic of white linen and an overgarment (worn for warmth) that was usually of a dark colored wool. As these garments became more ceremonial in function, a wider range of colors and materials came to be used. All through the Middle Ages in the West color systems varied from place to place, while reflecting some general principles. The first attempt at standardization of liturgical colors is assigned to Pope Innocent III (d. 1216). He presented a system in which white was assigned to festivals of Christ, the Blessed Virgin, and saints who were not martyrs. Red was for feasts of apostles and martyrs, for feasts of the Cross, and for Pentecost. Black was to be used during Advent and Lent and at masses for the departed, with the option of violet as a substitute for black. For all other occasions, green was the assigned color. While other medieval color systems continue to be followed in some places, the Roman system outlined by Innocent is surely the predominant system in Western churches, except that violet now generally replaces black. The 1969 reform of the Roman Missal, however, assigns red for Palm Sunday and Good Friday, and urges the general principle of the Eastern traditions that on the most festive occasions one should use the richest materials available, without regard to color. While Eastern traditions have never sought to associate feasts and seasons with particular colors, there, too, the natural psychological tendency is to match colors to emotions, to associate, for example, dark with sorrow, bright with joy.

[*See also* Christmas; Easter; *and* Epiphany.]

BIBLIOGRAPHY

A useful but now somewhat dated general historical survey can be had in Allan MacArthur's *The Evolution of the Christian Year* (London, 1953). A more recent presentation of historical development is Adolf Adam's *The Liturgical Year: Its History and Its Meaning after the Reform of the Liturgy* (New York, 1981). Another work arranged not historically but as a commentary through the Christian year is Adrian Nocent's *The Liturgical Year,* 4 vols. (Collegeville, Minn., 1977). For still more current scholarship, see the collection of papers of the 1981 Congress of Societas Liturgica published in *Liturgical Time,* edited by Wiebe Vos and Geoffrey Wainwright (Rotterdam, 1982). For more particular studies of individual festivals, see Patrick Cowley's *Advent: Its Liturgical Significance* (New York, 1960); John Gunstone's *Christmas and Epiphany* (London, 1967); Thomas J. Talley's "The Origin of Lent at Alexandria," *Studia patristica* 17, pt. 2 (Oxford and New York, 1982), pp. 594–612; Roger Greenacre's *The Sacrament of Easter* (New York, 1965); and John Gunstone's *The Feast of Pentecost* (London, 1967).

THOMAS J. TALLEY

CHRISTIAN SCIENCE is a religious movement emphasizing Christian healing as proof of the supremacy of spiritual over physical power. Founded by Mary Baker Eddy, a New Englander of predominantly Calvinistic background, Christian Science emerged as a distinct phenomenon in American religious life during a period of both social and religious crisis. [*See the biography of Eddy.*] The dramatic conflict between science and faith, as witnessed in battles over Darwinism and critical biblical scholarship, was only the most obvious aspect of a developing breakdown in a Christian cosmology that pictured experience as split between a natural and a supernatural order. Christian Science, however, rejected traditional cosmology and was therefore free to address religious issues in a way that was limited neither by creedal formulas nor by assumptions based on nineteenth-century natural science.

Mary Baker Eddy from her earliest years showed a deep-seated longing for the divine that was broadly characteristic of the Christian tradition and especially prominent in Puritanism. She found it impossible, however, to reconcile her deepest religious feelings with the theology of a then decadent Calvinism. Yet while other revolts against Calvinism, such as those of Unitarianism and Transcendentalism, led to an attenuation or even an abandonment of Christian convictions, Eddy's Christianity was so deeply ingrained that she found it impossible to think of any ultimate answer to what she called the "problem of being" outside of a theistic, biblical context. In her own words, "From my very childhood, I was impelled, by a hunger and thirst after divine things—a desire for something higher and better than matter, and apart from it—to seek diligently for the knowledge of God as the one great and ever-present relief from human woe."

Running parallel to this search, and contributing heuristically to it, was Eddy's own long quest for health. She had exhausted the healing methods of the time, including homeopathy, and the techniques of the Maine healer Phineas Quimby, to whom she turned in 1862, and although she found useful hints concerning the mental causes of disease, she never found the permanent health for which she was looking. Her growing disenchantment with all curative methods returned her to her spiritual quest, which led to a radically different perception of God and creation from that held by Quimby, namely, that reality is, in truth, wholly spiritual.

Eddy identified the advent of this conviction with her "instantaneous" recovery in 1866 from the effects of a severe accident while reading an account of one of Jesus' healings. She described the event as follows: "That short experience included a glimpse of the great fact that I have since tried to make plain to others, namely, Life in and of Spirit; this Life being the sole reality of existence." This passage is reminiscent of much mystical writing, but Eddy saw the experience as the point at which she discovered a spiritual truth so concrete that it would be "scientifically" provable in the experience of others.

There can be no doubt that this moment of recovery marked an important turning point in Eddy's life, impelling the development of the theology and metaphysics to which she gave expression in her major book, *Science and Health with Key to the Scriptures,* first published in 1875. The primary purpose of the book was not to set forth a new systematic theology, but rather to serve as a textbook for religious practice. The focus throughout was on awakening the capacity of its readers to experience the presence of God directly; the "honest seekers for Truth," to whom the book was dedicated, were invited to explore the saving and physically healing effects of that experience.

A key point of Christian Science is that the understanding of God must include a changed view of reality itself. In effect, *Science and Health* challenged the traditional Christian view of God as the creator of a material world—not on philosophic grounds, even though Eddy's conclusions are partially articulated in philosophic terms—but on the grounds of a radical reinterpretation of the meaning of the gospel. Christian Science takes the works of Jesus, culminating in his resurrection and final ascension above all things material, as pointing to the essential spiritual nature of being. Accordingly, his life exemplifies the possibility of action outside of and contrary to the limits of a finite, material sense of existence. From the standpoint of traditional Christianity, Jesus' works constituted supernatural interruptions of natural process and law; from the standpoint of Christian Science, they resulted from the operation of divine power comprehended as spiritual law. In biblical terms this meant the breaking through of the kingdom of heaven—of the divine order of things—into ordinary sense-bound experience.

Nineteenth-century Protestant orthodoxy associated the kingdom of heaven with a realm in the beyond and the hereafter; Christian Science, however, views it as the spiritual potential of present experience to be actualized once sinning mortals cease to identify their own limited, erring perceptions as reality. Regeneration or spiritual awakening occurs as one sees through sense appearance to what Eddy called "the spiritual fact of whatever the material senses behold." The spiritual fact for her was not an otherworldly phenomenon, but a transforming power—a reality drastically obscured by the misconceived sense of life, substance, and intelligence, apart from God. So great is this error of misconceiving, or fundamental sin, that a revelatory breakthrough from outside material existence is required in order to manifest the true spiritual nature of creation. The advent of Jesus, according to Christian Science, constitutes the decisive spiritual event that makes possible the salvation of humanity from the flesh.

Christian Science does not deify Jesus, a point that its severest critics have sometimes said separates it conclusively from traditional Christianity. Yet Jesus' actual role in the achievement of humanity's salvation is as important to its theology as for traditional Christianity. His life of obedience and sacrifice is understood as the means through which the reality of being for humankind has broken through in the midst of ordinary human experience. This true spiritual selfhood is identified as the eternal Christ, as distinct from Jesus, although uniquely and fully incarnated in him. His mission is viewed as opening up the possibility for all men and women to make actual their own spiritual union with God. He did this by proving practically that neither sin nor suffering is part of authentic spiritual selfhood, or Christ.

While Christian Science holds that evil has no God-derived existence and therefore can be regarded ontologically as not real, it strongly emphasizes the need for healing rather than ignoring the manifold manifestations of the carnal mind, defined by the apostle Paul as "enmity against God," and as operating with hypnotic intensity in human experience. Such healing is to be accomplished not through personal will or effort but through yielding to the action of the divine Mind. Salvation, while seen as the effect of divine grace, requires prayer, self-renunciation, and radical, unremitting warfare against the evils of the mortal condition.

Salvation includes obedience to Jesus' command to heal the sick. Sickness is one expression of the fundamental error of the mortal mind that accepts existence as something separate from God. Healing, therefore, must be predicated on the action of the divine Mind or power outside of human thought. In Eddy's words, ". . . erring, finite, human mind has an absolute need of something beyond itself for its redemption and healing." Healing is regarded not merely as a bodily change, but as a phase of full salvation from the flesh as well. It is the normalization of bodily function and formation through the divine government of the human mentality and of the bodily system that that mentality governs.

The emphasis in Christian Science upon healing—primarily of sin, secondarily disease—is based on the concrete issues of everyday lived experience. The healing emphasis differentiates Christian Science from philosophies of idealism with which it is often carelessly identified, including the Emersonian transcendentalism that was part of its immediate cultural background. Indeed, departures from Eddy's teaching within the Christian Science movement itself have tended generally toward metaphysical abstraction, wherein her statements almost completely lose their bearings on daily experience.

In the context of Eddy's writings, however, such statements almost always point to the demand and possibility of demonstrating in actual experience what she understood as spiritual fact. Her abstract statement that "God is All," for instance, taken by itself could imply a pantheistic identification of humankind and the universe with God. Taken in the full context of her teachings, it indicates that God's infinitude and omnipotence rule out the legitimacy, permanence, and substantiality of anything contrary to God's nature as Principle, Mind, Spirit, Soul, Life, Truth, and Love, an assertion that is taken to be demonstrably practical in concrete situations, to some degree at least.

The radical claim as to the ultimate unreality of matter is to be assessed in these terms. Christian Science asserts that matter is not the objective substance it appears to be, but is rather a concept of substance shaped by the limitations of the human mind. This assertion no more denies the existence of humankind or natural objects than the challenge posed in physics to conventional views of perception and to the substantiality of matter denies the existence of the universe. But it does point to the necessity of bringing the true spiritual nature of humanity and the universe to light through progressive demonstration.

With this emphasis on practical regeneration and healing, one sees the clearest link between Christian Science and the American Puritan tradition. An undue emphasis on the practical aspect of Christian Science by some followers has sometimes led to a secularization of its teaching, with healing regarded as an end in itself rather than as one element of a full salvation. This tendency clearly characterizes the mind-cure and New Thought movements. These movements, in some respects akin to Christian Science, use similar terms, which, however, bear a notably different meaning.

As with any religious movement, the motives of those who call themselves Christian Scientists vary. Of the 350,000–450,000 who might so identify themselves, it is likely that a majority are not formal members of the Christian Science denomination. While many have made Christian Science a way of life and joined, others have sought it, sometimes intermittently, for comfort and support. There may be limited truth, too, to the hypothesis that activity in the Christian Science movement, in which women have been numerically predominant, has provided an outlet for women in a society that has otherwise restricted their role—particularly in the religious world. On the other hand, such an argument may reflect an unconscious male stereotyping that seeks reductionist explanations when women advance or espouse ideas.

Evidence of the religious experiences of long-term, committed adherents of Christian Science suggests that it may have survived for more than a century because it has met a more basic religious need. Disaffected Protestants, particularly, have seen in it a release not just from bodily suffering but also from spiritual malaise—an alternative to the attitude that accepts with Christian resignation the tragedies of present life in hope of compensation either in a life beyond or according to some transcendent scale of eternal values. Christian Science, however, regards the ultimate spiritual victory over evil prophesied in the Bible as requiring confrontation with all aspects of evil and imperfection in present experience.

Although Christian Science is explicitly committed to universal salvation, it focuses initially and primarily on the potential for transformation and healing within the individual. This focus, deviant as it has often seemed to conservative Christians, tends to associate it with the traditional Protestant concern over individual salvation, giving it a conservative cast in the eyes of more liberal Christians who wish to transform the social order. The identification of Christian Science with a conservative, well-to-do, middle-class ideology may be as misleading in a sociological sense as it is theologically. In fact, a greater segment of the movement comes from rural or lower-middle-class backgrounds than most outside accounts would suggest.

On the whole, the church does not share the social activism of many mainstream denominations, but its purpose in publishing *The Christian Science Monitor*—an international newspaper of recognized excellence—indicates a substantial commitment to an interest in the public good. Eddy founded the *Monitor* in 1908 as the most appropriate vehicle for the political and social expression of the practical idealism of her teaching. In addition, it was intended to educate Christian Scientists about the need for the healing of society at large, not just the individual.

The character of the *Monitor*, to a degree, reflects the educational purpose of the church that publishes it. Eddy, surprisingly sensitive to the dangers of institutionalized religion, conceived of the church in instrumental rather than ecclesiastical terms, shaping it to provide practical means for the study, communication, and teaching of Christian Science as a way of life. It was not part of her original purpose to found a separate denomination; rather, she and a group of her students founded the Church of Christ, Scientist, in 1879, when it became clear that other Christian churches were not disposed to accept her teaching. The overall structure of the church was laid out in a document of skeletal simplicity, the *Manual of The Mother Church*, which Eddy first published in 1895 and continued to develop until her death.

The central administrative functions of this "mother" church, the First Church of Christ, Scientist, in Boston, are presided over by a five-member, self-perpetuating board of directors. The Mother Church, with its branches, including some 3,000 congregations in fifty countries, constitute the Church of Christ, Scientist; the congregations are self-governing within the framework provided by the *Manual*.

Taken as a whole, the church's activities can best be understood as vehicles for disciplined spiritual education. These include the Bible "lesson-sermons" consisting of passages from the Bible and the Christian Science textbook studied by members during the week; the religious periodicals published by the church; and Christian Science lectures, Sunday schools, the intensive two-week course of class instruction, and follow-up refresher meetings attended by those seriously committed to the religion.

The absence of an ordained clergy, ritualistically observed sacraments, and all but the most spare symbols point to the almost Quaker-like simplicity of the Christian Science concept of worship, in which silent prayer has an important role and the sacraments are conceived of as a process of continuing purification and quiet communion with God. Spontaneous sharing of experiences of healing and spiritual guidance marks the Wednesday "testimony meetings."

Christian Science practitioners, listed monthly in *The Christian Science Journal*, are members who devote themselves full time to the ministry of spiritual healing, and a significant body of testimonies of healing—amounting to some 50,000 published accounts—has been amassed in Christian Science periodicals over the years. There is good evidence that this sustained commitment of an entire denomination over more than a century to the practice of spiritual healing has been a significant factor in the reawakening of interest in Christian healing among many denominations in the 1960s and 1970s.

By the 1979 centennial of the founding of the church, the Christian Science movement found itself experiencing greater challenges from the currents of secular materialism than it had encountered since the early days of its founding. The increasing secularization of Western society worked against the kind of radical Christian commitment it required, while at the same time its healing practices encountered new challenges in an increasingly medically oriented society.

The history of the church, however, confirms that it is no exception to the general tendency of religious movements to grow or decline according to inner vitality rather than external pressure. Nor are external signs of growth in themselves altogether valid indicators of spiritual strength; indeed, it was because of this that Mary Baker Eddy forbade the publication of church membership statistics at a time when the movement was growing rapidly. The great numerical growth of the movement in the decades after Eddy's death may well have been attributable more to sociocultural factors unrelated to and, in some respects, opposed to the specific religious and redemptive purposes of the church itself.

It is too soon to assess the long-term significance of some signs of decline of the Christian Science movement. Indeed, these signs must be qualified by other factors, among them the erosion of the insularity and complacency evident to some degree in the church's posture in earlier decades, the maturing of the movement, its willingness to position itself in relation to the rest of the Christian world, and the significant growth it has experienced in some developing nations.

[*For discussion of various religious views of healing in cross-cultural perspective, see* Healing *and* Medicine.]

BIBLIOGRAPHY

The basic document of the Christian Science movement is Mary Baker Eddy's *Science and Health with Key to the Scriptures* (1875; reprint, Boston, 1914), which contains the full statement of its teaching. Extensive historical background on Christian Science can be found in Robert Peel's trilogy, *Mary Baker Eddy: The Years of Discovery, The Years of Trial, The Years of Authority* (New York, 1966–1977). Peel's earlier *Christian Science: Its Encounter with American Culture* (New York, 1958) places Christian Science in its New England cultural context, relating it to both transcendentalism and pragmatism, while my own *The Emergence of Christian Science in American Religious Life* (Berkeley, 1973) gives a full account of Christian Science within the context of American religious development. An early, pathbreaking study of the theology of Christian Science is the essay by Karl Holl, "Szientismus," in *Gesammelte Aufsätze zur Kirchengeschichte*, vol. 3 (Tübingen, 1921–1928). A representative though reductionist treatment of Christian Science from a sociological perspective is the section on Christian Science in Bryan R. Wilson's *Sects and Societies: A Sociological Study of the Elim Tabernacle, Christian Science and Christadelphians* (1961; reprint, Westport, Conn., 1978). Charles S. Braden's *Christian Science Today: Power, Policy, Practice* (Dallas, 1958) attempts an overview of organizational developments, drawing largely on dissident sources. One reason for the paucity of adequate academic accounts of Christian Science is suggested in Thomas C. Johnsen's article "Historical Consensus and Christian Science: The Career of a Manuscript Controversy," *New England Quarterly* 53 (March 1980): 3–22. A popular but slapdash history of the early phases of the movement is Norman Beasley's *The Cross and the Crown* (New York, 1952). Basic documentation on Christian Science healing is given in the church-published *A Century of Christian Science Healing* (Boston, 1966).

STEPHEN GOTTSCHALK

CHRISTIAN SOCIAL MOVEMENTS. The richness of Christianity's particular transcendent vision, the wide constituencies to which it has appealed, and the variety of contexts into which it has moved and to which it has given shape have produced an enormous variety of social movements bearing its name. Yet, certain common features can be found.

Historical Background. In the ancient world, the prevailing religions were linked to specific groups, primarily ethnic or political. Each people and each city had its own gods, and religion secured stability and security for these regimes.

Specific aspects of the Hebraic traditions, however, pressed in different directions. The God of the Hebrew people was understood to be the sovereign and truly universal God, not limited to any people, class, territory, political entity, or particular cultural wisdom. Further, this God was understood especially by the prophets to demand righteousness and change in history. Indeed, the prophets pointed to an expected "messianic age" that would involve radical transformation and full righteousness.

Christianity claimed that it was the true heir of these prophetic directions. In Jesus Christ, the universal and righteous God entered into the concreteness of human history and brought the transcendent vision to an accessible and transforming presence. The announcement and celebration of the divine immediacy of Jesus Christ was the good news that demanded a liberation from inherited patterns of piety based on ethnicity as well as from predominant preoccupations with esoteric wisdom or political wealth and power. Particular population groups seem to have been most attracted to this new vision: the poor; the urban artisans and traders who were "marginalized" by aristocratic elites; those intellectuals who found the old religions, the cults, and metaphysical speculations to be unsatisfying; and, later on, the rulers of the Roman empire. Christianity was, at least in part, a social movement from the start.

It is not that Jesus, Paul, or the early Christian leaders started a social movement with specific social objectives in mind. Nevertheless, wherever Christianity has gone, it has brought with it an impulse to form new patterns of organization distinct from exclusive identification with ethnicity, national culture, political power, and economic class. Whenever Christian congregations have become too closely identified with one or another of these other groupings, "alternative congregations," or "paraecclesial movements," claiming to represent the true, prophetic faith, have challenged that accommodation in the name of the gospel. The relation of these alternative congregations and paraecclesial movements to the majority developments of the church, and their functions in society, are decisive for understanding Christian social movements in the West.

The impulse to organize movements seems always to have pressed in two directions in Christianity. One is toward consolidation of the movement's gains by the establishment of a "church" that would take responsibility for guiding the moral and spiritual life of the people in a territory where the movement has gained influence. The other is sectarian in the sense that it forms congregations that are decidedly distinct from all the established institutions of a society—including the established church. [*See* Sect *and the biography of* Ernst Troeltsch.]

In the medieval period of the West, alternative congregations were, for the most part, channeled into either monastic orders that claimed, with considerable success, to represent the very center of faithfulness or into various "confraternities"—guilds and lay orders. Some orders, such as those founded by Basil and Benedict, were more withdrawing. Orders such as the Dominicans and Franciscans, by contrast, were gently aggressive in their efforts to touch and transform the everyday life of the laity. Others, such as the Templars and Hospitalers, were more aggressive in the conventional sense. In the late Middle Ages and increasingly during the Reformation, sects arose that inspired social movements with more intentionally overt sociopolitical overtones, such as those led by Wyclif, Hus, and Müntzer. Moreover, it is difficult to understand the reformations of Luther and Calvin without seeing their sociopolitical dimensions. [*See* Religious Communities, *article on* Christian Religious Orders, *and* Reformation.]

What Christian churches, orders, and confraternities have in common is not only the confession of Christ, but a social effect that is only partially intended. The formation of new congregations carved out a social space in which Christian social movements based in relatively autonomous institutions could exist. These alternative congregations and paraecclesial movements claimed the God-given right to address sociopolitical matters in terms of the Christian vision of righteousness and change, often without the approval of established political or ecclesiastical bodies.

Modern Movements. Modern Christian social movements are distinguished by their increasing ability to assume the right to organize, by their more overt goals of addressing specific social problems or groups, and by a rebirth of historical consciousness that expects human agency, in the service of God, to establish righteousness and overcome social evil by concerted action. Movements sharing these characteristics have evolved in a variety of directions.

Some organizations have been formed specifically to foster social service objectives. Christian hospitals, orphanages, and homes for mentally and physically handicapped persons can today be found in nearly every sizable community in the Western world as well as, increasingly, in developing countries where mission movements have been active. Until the late nineteenth century, most of the colleges and universities of the West were founded by the churches, orders, or sects, or by authorities wanting to foster a specific religious perspective. Other service organizations, such as the Freemasons, developed altogether outside churches or sects. [*See* Freemasons.]

More radical social action movements are not only found in the Radical Reformation of the sixteenth century, but in subsequent centuries as well. In the course of the Cromwellian Revolution in England, and after the French Revolution, many Christians saw direct political involvement as a duty of faith. Christian political parties were formed in most of the countries of Europe (and, later, in many countries colonized by Europe) in the wake of these democratizing developments. Geared to making the moral and spiritual values of specific Christian groups politically influential, they protected the church groups they represented from domination by other religions or by anti-religious secularization. Paralleling these political developments was the shattering of the traditional patterns of social-economic life by the industrial revolution. Specific churches, sects, and denominations developed special affinities to the new cohorts of the bourgeoisie and proletariat that replaced the older ones of lords, artisans, and peasants, and they geared themselves to become the advocates of their constituency's material interests. While this is increasingly occurring in decolonialized nations, paraecclesial worker or peasant movements, carried out in the name of Christ, respond by protesting the identification of Christianity with elite or middle-class values.

Many argue that it was post-Reformation Christianity that was the key stimulus to modern democratic and technological developments. Others argue that political and technical changes brought about new religious developments. Whatever the case, the religiously legitimated democratizing revolutions of the seventeenth and eighteenth centuries, and the technological revolutions of the nineteenth and twentieth, ushered in a series of new paraecclesial efforts, some of which became movements within established churches, some of which produced new sects, and some of which produced new denominations: that is, disestablished, nonexclusive, pluralistically tolerant religious bodies, essentially reflecting a distinctive understanding of the faith, but also the particular social interests of their constituency. The Lutheranism of the Prussian Junkers, the Catholicism of much continental peasantry, and the Anglicanism of the British agrarian Tories are some groups that became established. More recent movements or denominations include the pietistic circles that developed among the petit bourgeois in the Germanic lands, the early Methodist "classes" among the coal miners of England, and, in the twentieth century, the Innere Mission in Germany, the Salvation Army among the urban poor in England and America, and the (mostly abortive) Christian labor organizations in all the industrializing countries. [*See* Denominationalism; Methodist Churches; Pietism; *and* Salvation Army.]

In America, early pervasive influences from Calvinism and from the aggressive sectarian traditions stamped the structure of religious and civil life in unparalleled ways, especially in its accent on covenant. The notion of "covenant," especially as it is distinguished in Protestant social theology from "contract" and from the "organic orders of nature," suggests that humans can construct or reform their social institutions by voluntary agreement, but that the ethical norms that must govern the agreement and the institutions are established by God. Further, the experience of pilgrimage to a new land reinforced theories of historical change. Immigration and internal religious developments brought a vast pluralization of religions that even theocratic efforts in such states as Massachusetts could not contain. And the fact that American developments took place in an environment that had no established feudal or imperial traditions that had to be overcome produced a widespread process of social experimentation. These factors interacted to produce a variety of alternative congregations and paraecclesial organizations unique in human history. It is in this context that the famous secularized fugitive from Massachusetts, Benjamin Franklin, started some two hundred voluntary associations for social betterment; the dissident Puritan, Roger Williams, who founded Providence on the principle of religious freedom, became the symbolic hero of pluralistic denominationalism; and James Madison argued in *The Federalist* that religious and voluntary-organizational pluralism, supported by checks and balances in government, could preserve a new kind of freedom and prevent tyranny. [*See the biography of* Williams.]

By the time that the last state constitutions in the United States were altered so that all churches were disestablished and legally viewed as voluntary associations (i.e., in the 1830s), even those who had fought the trend became enthusiastic proponents of the idea that Christian social witness was to be carried out by voluntary, paraecclesial social movements. The dominant view became one that held that freedom of religion means not only tolerance but the duty of committed people to organize movements for social service and social change outside government and distinct from the worshiping congregation. It was believed that this was precisely what God had intended from the Exodus, through the prophets, to the Pentecost in the New Testament, though only now was it becoming actualized in human history.

A veritable explosion of social movements took place on these foundations during the nineteenth and twentieth centuries. Nearly all of these claimed to be Christian in root and direction, although they were seldom officially connected to formal church organizations. Mission societies ministering to Native Americans, to the people in the semicivilized Western frontiers, and to the dispossessed inhabitants of the American cities, as well as to the "heathen" abroad, were formed everywhere. Many of the contemporary churches of Asia, Africa, and the Pacific Islands, which today struggle to bring about democratic, pluralistic societies, find their roots in these mission efforts. At home, militant Christian anti-slavery organizations and antisaloon leagues were soon to arise in the wake of revivalisms, themselves paraecclesial movements in many ways, that demanded both the liberation from personal sin by decision for Christ and the mandate to transform toward populism those economic institutions that oppress humans.

After the Civil War, which accelerated the American late entry into the industrial revolution, an enormous number of organizations were formed to evangelize and to build schools and hospitals for and with the newly freed black Americans. Black churches proliferated and became the center of worship and community organization over a wide range of issues.

In many rural areas, Christians organized advocacy and cooperative associations, such as the Farmers' Alliance and the Colored Farmers' National Alliance and Cooperative Union. Less self-consciously rooted in theology is the Patrons of Husbandry (The Grange), which drew some patterns of ritual and belief from the Freemasons. In the northern cities, Christian paraecclesial movements attempted to address the new class conflicts arising with rapid industrialization by using evangelism techniques combined with social service and social action strategies. The immigrants to the cities from the farms and from the underclasses of Europe were met with City Missionary Societies, an expanding Young Men's Christian Association, the newer but also growing Young Women's Christian Association, first efforts at settlement houses, and nascent Christian labor unions.

The methods of raising funds to sustain these organizations, in the late nineteenth and early twentieth centuries, are instructive. The voluntarism of church organization produced a new interpretation of the biblical concept of stewardship, one that called upon church members not only to give sacrificially to sustain the church, but to support mission, outreach, cultural activities, social action, and benevolence agencies by paraecclesial institutions that serve the common good. These exhortations, in a pious country, have surely not been inconsequential. During the 1970s total giving to the some two million nonprofit, voluntary organizations in the United States roughly paralleled the United States defense budget and employed one out of every six professional workers and one out of eleven service workers, providing one of the most striking contrasts between American society and most other societies of the world.

Many of the funds for Christian social movements in the nineteenth century were raised by women's groups in the churches. Victorian women of means and charitable intent, as well as wives of workers and farmers, organized literary societies, bake sales, quilting bees, and knitting parties "for good Christian causes." These informal networks of mutual cooperation issued in such organizations as the Women's Rights Convention (1848), the Women's Christian Temperance Union (1873), and the later Women's Missionary Society, Christian Women's Action Guild, and a host of denominationally connected women's organizations. The full effect of these organizations has yet to be documented; but the existent literature suggests that these efforts provided the skills, opportunities for sisterhood, and organized channels for developing independent perspectives on political and social issues that were to eventuate in the suffrage movement and in later drives advocating other women's rights. Some contemporary women's organizations have been hostile to the churches, but women's organizations in the churches (such as Church Women United and the Women's Division of the United Methodist Church) have been forceful advocates of change in both church and society.

Nearly all the concerns mentioned thus far began to congeal into a full-fledged theological-social realignment in late nineteenth- and early twentieth-century Protestantism under the general rubric, the "Social Gospel." This was less a distinctive social movement per se than a congeries of movements signaled by a common understanding of faith that demanded institutional transformation toward economic and social justice. While Washington Gladden, Richard T. Ely, and Walter Rauschenbusch are among the memorable apologists for the Social Gospel, the enormous variety of social concerns addressed under this mantle are, from the perspective of the meaning of the term for social movements, better cataloged in W. D. F. Bliss's *New Encyclopedia of Social Reform* (1910). [*See the biography of Rauschenbusch.*]

World War I and the Depression shattered this overheated optimism and brought other developments that modified the direction of Christian social movements. First, some advocates of neoorthodoxy in theology argued that all this energetic American activism in the name of Christ had misunderstood both the depth of sin in human history and the message of the gospel. Second, many of the movements generated out of Christian motivations began to lose their distinctive Christian theological bases and became little more than interest groups struggling primarily to get as many material rewards for their own constituents as possible. And third, fundamentalism arose as a new kind of independent social and religious movement specifically critical of Darwinist cosmology, anthropology, and social theories, which fundamentalists felt had displaced the gospel from among these "modernisms." [*See* Evangelical and Fundamental Christianity.]

During the period of the rise of the Social Gospel in American Protestantism, two European movements of considerable consequence were also underway. Socialist proletarians of the left engaged in increasingly sharp criticism of any connection between religion and socially progressive movements, specifically targeting democratic politics and capitalist economics as the enemies of radical social change and the ideological masks of Protestant, bourgeois self-interest. Simultaneously, a series of aristocratic conservatives, from John Ruskin in England, to Bishop Wilhelm Ketteler in Germany, Comte de Mun in France, and Cardinal Mermillod in Switzerland, also undertook the study of emerging social problems and began a series of protests against democracy, which they saw as the conspiracy of Jewish bankers and Protestant industrialists to reduce the worker and farmer to servitude. Both democracy and capitalism, they said, were based on nothing more than individualistic and utilitarian "contracts" without any moral or spiritual foundations.

These Anglo-Catholic and Roman Catholic leaders developed their positive proposals on a view of the duties of the "Christian state," the "Christian family," and the "Christian church" as organic, comprehensive communities based on natural law and revealed dogma by which the lives of all persons were to be sustained and guided. One of the great ironies of the period was that the actual programs of the antireligious, socialist left and the "social Catholic," neofeudal right converged to produce legislation promoting the power of workers' guilds, constraining political and religious pluralism, and limiting the development of economic capitalism. When these themes were propagated by Leo XIII, a new course was set for Catholic engagement with modern social issues, one that is having great consequence today with the rise of (essentially Roman Catholic) "political theology" and "liberation theology."

Several of the American workers' movements in the late nineteenth century were deeply influenced by the root perspectives on which these European developments were based. The flood of Catholic immigrants to the industrializing cities, especially from Ireland and later Italy, brought numerous new voices into the mix of American pluralism as well as sparking fundamentalist anti-Catholic movements. For most of the nineteenth century, Catholic populations were in a defensive and difficult position, and the energy expended and the sacrifices made to find jobs, to build churches, and to establish Catholic schools as an alternative to the largely protestantized public schools are a monument to faith. Catholic lay leaders also formed paraecclesial fraternal orders such as the Knights of Malta and the Knights of Columbus, which echoed ancient motifs already mentioned.

Some Catholics endeavored to form social movements in late nineteenth-century America and adopted motifs from the essentially Protestant Social Gospel. However, when they became too enthusiastic about the virtues of pluralism, democracy, and capitalism as Christian possibilities, their efforts were condemned by Rome as "Americanism" and "modernism." Nevertheless, when Leo XIII's *Rerum novarum* (1891) opened the door to social commentary and action, new patterns of Catholic social thought and activity were stimulated. A new generation of American Catholic scholars and activists fomented social service and social advocacy within a decidedly democratic framework and toward a new form of welfare capitalism. The Bishops' Program of Social Reconstruction (1919) is a landmark of this new direction.

Figures such as T. A. Ryan and John Courtney Murray provided intellectual guidance for Catholic involvement in the democratization of economic opportunities and for Catholic participation in democratic political life. The line from these roots to contemporary Catholic social movements in America is not difficult to draw. Catholic movements against abortion, for peace and justice, and in support of human rights continue to grow, especially since Vatican II spoke of the ministry of the laity. The Roman Catholic Bishops' Pastoral Letter on War and Peace (1982) has been widely adopted as almost a manifesto for numerous Protestant as well as Catholic antinuclear movements. Subsequently, Canadian bishops have issued a major statement on economic life (1984) commending more intense socialization, while the U.S. Catholic bishops have drafted a Letter on the Economy (1986), which both commends the achievements of capitalism and demands active engagement, in the name of Christ, to redress its negative effects. [*See* Modernism, *article on* Christian Modernism, *and the biography of Leo XIII.*]

Internationally, the rise of National Socialism in Germany and Stalinism in the Soviet Union, as well as the painful experience of the Great Depression, caused Christian social movements to become increasingly focused on overtly political strategies to overcome both the threats of political tyranny and the chaos of economic anarchy. On the extreme right, paraecclesial organizations, such as the Ku Klux Klan and the White Citizens Councils, expanded and attributed the ills of the nation to blacks, Catholics, Jews, and communists and attempted to use Christian symbols to legitimate their hate. Nearly all church bodies preached against such organizations and threw their attention instead to a wide variety of theologically based efforts on the other end of the political spectrum such as the Fellowship of Socialist Christians, the Fellowship of Reconciliation, and the Religion and Labor Council. More notable, however, is the successor to the Social Gospel, Christian Realism—a tough-minded theological orientation (often associated with Reinhold Niebuhr) that became the governing form for rearticulation of the Christian vision during the Depression, World War II, and the cold war. [*See the biography of Niebuhr.*] Under this umbrella, many of the social service aspects of previous Christian social movements remained, but government was increasingly pressed to assume responsibility for providing support to those in need. Both the increased involvement of the government in economic matters and the building of vast armies to meet international threats increased the size and scope of political, administrative, and regulative bureaucracies in America. These developments in theology and in government deeply affected Christian social movements: they institutionalized on nonreligious bases many of the programs begun in voluntary, confessional movements; they displaced church and paraecclesial organizations as the agencies most able to provide services in many local communities; and they encouraged many religious social movements to turn their primary attention to political strategies and to become primarily advocates of specific public policy directions for the so-called welfare society.

After World War II, these trends continued, but other trends were also developing. A new generation of leaders arose from the black churches, the most famous of these leaders being Martin Luther King, Jr. [*See the biography of King.*] He organized a new Christian social movement—the Southern Christian Leadership Conference—to confront the "betrayal of the American dream" and the racist organizations that manipulated discriminatory laws. His efforts were soon emulated by others. Women and minorities, such as Hispanic, Native American, and Asian-American groups, developed comparable movements that continue to have significant influence. Awareness of the potential damage done to the ecological environment was also brought to public attention by such authors as Rachel Carson, and soon a variety of Christian efforts to protect God's creation were under way.

The United States involvement in Vietnam also brought about another spate of church and paraecclesial efforts to alter public policy. The organization Clergy and Laity Concerned about Vietnam is perhaps the most important nationally, but local organizations seemed to spring from the chaplain's office on nearly every university campus. Many of the people engaged in the antiwar protests were also those who, after the war, became involved in organizing boycotts against lettuce growers who employed migrant workers at below-standard pay rates, clothing manufacturers who resisted unionization, and infant-formula manufacturers who utilized questionable marketing techniques in very poor countries. Others attempted to mobilize stockholders of corporations doing business in the Republic of South Africa to vote for changes in policies or to divest entirely.

These brief references to international issues from the American perspective should not obscure the fact that one of the most important developments in Christian social movements is now very vital in parts of Africa, Latin America, and Asia—generally under the rubric "liberation theology." Roman Catholic church authorities have been critical of this style of political-theological reflection, suspecting that it is too deeply influenced by Marxist social analysis and too independent of ecclesiastical and doctrinal discipline. Further, scholars disagree on whether the perspectives being developed in these regions of the world can be considered "theology" in any classical sense of the word; but even critics acknowledge liberation theology's social importance and its Christian impulses. [*See* Political Theology.] In Korea, the Philippines, South Africa, and much of Central and South America, these movements may become the most articulate and forceful advocates of human rights, democracy, economic justice, racial equality, and freedom of religion that can be found, or they may become a new form of established folk religiosity legitimating single-party revolutionary governments, as their critics fear.

Returning to the United States, one can see both the effects of these liberation movements and the reactions against them. In North America and in some vigorous new missionary movements spreading throughout the world, one can find reinvigorated conservative and fundamentalist tendencies embodied in such movements as Christian Action Council, World Vision, and the Freedom Foundation that are attempting to redress what they perceive to be the undue balance of ecumenical Christian churches and movements toward left-leaning analyses of political and economic systems. For these movements the crucial issues are what they deem to be the traditional values of evangelization, family life, and personal morality (typically, being opposed to abortion and homosexuality). [*See also* Religious Broadcasting.]

Concluding Observations. The most decisive requirement of a Christian social movement is theology, that is, the systematic and ongoing rearticulation of the core meanings found in the originating vision, constantly recast so as to guide the ethics of public behavior. Wherever this is absent or fails, one may find Christians involved in an interest group centered on ethnic, political, class, or cultural interests but not necessarily a Christian social movement. Where this does obtain, however, the movement must not only provide basic definitions of God's righteousness, justice, and mercy as known in Jesus Christ, but it must identify how, when, and where these are being or could be incarnate in processes of social change.

A Christian social movement must not only be inspired by theology; its members must also understand themselves to be heralds or cooperating agents of God's activity in the process of change. Further, the direction of change desired by God must be understood to be at odds with other possible directions in a society. There must be something to be for and something to be against. On these grounds, every Christian social movement has countercultural elements.

In addition, every social movement requires a leadership and a constituency willing to be led. Founders or early leaders of such movements have often had special charismatic qualities and been persons with a vision of something to be done and the capacity to evoke commitment from others to the cause. Over time, however, leadership needs to have the organizational skills (the capacity to organize decision processes) that will allow the followers to interpret and own the originating vision and to apply it to changing circumstances and in varying contexts.

In order to incarnate organizationally, this originating vision must have at hand, or the capacity to carve out over time, the social space that allows it to operate without undue constriction. Christian social movements are in this respect the natural enemy of totalitarian regimes even if they advocate highly authoritarian policies. Further, every social movement must develop means of communication, financial support, and achievable strategic short-range goals so that supporters see significant gains. Finally, every social movement must have festive celebrations of the vision, theology, leaders, and accomplishments of the movement as well as analyses of the cause of any failures. With these, adherents are convinced to renew their commitments; without these, social movements go dry from within.

BIBLIOGRAPHY

Without question, the most important work on Christian social movements written in the twentieth century remains Ernst Troeltsch's *The Social Teaching of Christian Churches*, 2 vols. (1931; reprint, Chicago, 1981). Key subsequent works interpreting the Western and European traditions are *Puritanism and Liberty*, edited by A. S. P. Woodhouse (London, 1938), which focuses on the Cromwellian period; William O. Shanahan's *German Protestants Face the Social Question* (Notre Dame, Ind., 1954), which documents Lutheran struggles with modernization; and James Hastings Nichols's *Democracy and the Churches* (Philadelphia, 1951), which compares Roman Catholic and Reformed political developments.

Both Arend T. van Leeuwen's *Christianity in World History* (New York, 1964) and *The Protestant Ethic and Modernization*, edited by Shmuel N. Eisenstadt (New York, 1968), trace the impact of Western traditions on developing nations; and my *Creeds, Society, and Human Rights: A Study in Three Cultures* (Grand Rapids, Mich., 1984) compares Western social and religious movements to those of eastern Europe and South Asia.

A formative understanding of Christian social movements in America can be found in H. Richard Niebuhr's *The Social Sources of Denominationalism* (New York, 1929), which stresses the influence of social interests on religious teachings and organizations; while major influences of theological traditions on American social directions are collected in *Voluntary Associations: A Study of Groups in Free Societies*, edited by D. B. Robertson (Richmond, Va., 1966). Timothy Smith's *Revivalism and Social Reform in Mid-Nineteenth Century America* (New York, 1957) and George M. Marsden's *Fundamentalism and American Culture* (New York, 1980) trace the rise and influence of evangelical and fundamentalist movements on American society, while Charles Hopkin's *The Rise of the Social Gospel in American Protestantism, 1865–1915* (New Haven, 1940) and Paul A. Carter's *The Decline and Revival of the Social Gospel* (London, 1956) trace the social teachings and movements of liberal and ecumenical Protestantism. The best new treatment of religious social thought in the United States is A. J. Reichley's *Religion in American Public Life* (Washington, D.C., 1985).

New directions in Roman Catholic social thought, especially as it struggles with pluralistic democracy and the socialism of liberation theology, can be found in David Hollenbach's *Claims in Conflict* (New York, 1979); in the two-volume collection *Human Rights in the Americas*, edited by Alfred Hennelly and John Lagan (Washington, D.C., 1982); and in *Human Rights and Basic Needs in the Americas*, edited by Margaret E. Crahan (Washington, D.C., 1982).

MAX L. STACKHOUSE

CHRISTIAN SPIRITUALITY is an existence before God and amid the created world. It is a praying and living in Jesus Christ. It is the human spirit being grasped, sustained, and transformed by the Holy Spirit. It is the search of believers for a communion that arrives as a gift. It is a present anticipation of the divine kingdom and human salvation awaited in an age to come. Thus Christian spirituality can be described in terms that match the quintuple object of the classic creeds: God the Father, the almighty, universal Creator; Jesus Christ the incarnate Word, the crucified Savior, the risen and expected Lord; the Holy Spirit, the vivifying source of all sanctification; the church, the faithful company sharing in holy things; and the final triumph of eternal life. To that fivefold structure we shall twice return.

Meanwhile, a word about the sources for a description of Christian spirituality. One may appropriately draw on letters, diaries, prayers, and poems in which Christians express their religious and ethical experience. Then there is the testimony borne by others to conspicuous individuals. Counselors give advice. Popular devotions flow from and into the official liturgy of the church. Institutions embody Christian ways of life. Movements well up in the course of history. The scriptures set the norms.

First Impressions

A preliminary general survey will give a few simple impressions of Christian spirituality in the five perspectives indicated above. This will be followed by a more technical theological analysis of the same pattern. Throughout I shall be more interested in constant or recurrent features than in change or development, and a diachronic corrective can be found in several of the studies listed in the bibliography.

Creatures before the Creator. The prime calling and duty of the creatures is to worship their creator (*Rom.* 1:19–25). The first commandment is to acknowledge God's sovereignty (*Ex.* 20:2–6, cf. *Mt.* 4:10). English poetry begins with Cædmon, the cowherd protégé of Abbess Hilda of Whitby in the seventh century:

> It is meet that we worship the Warden of heaven,
> The might of the Maker, His purpose of mind,
> The Glory-Father's work when of all His wonders
> Eternal God made a beginning.
> He earliest stablished for earth's children

Heaven for a roof, the Holy Shaper;
Then mankind's Warden created the world,
Eternal Monarch, making for men
Land to live on, Almighty Lord!

Humankind is to voice the alleluias of the other creatures: Francis of Assisi (1181/2–1226) is painted preaching to the birds, and in his *Cantico delle creature* it is as though, after the example of the "three children" in the Greek *Book of Daniel* (3:52–90), he called for the praise of God not only in but by Brother Sun and Sister Moon, the wind, the water, the fire, and Mother Earth. The ethical counterpart of this doxology is human stewardship of the natural habitat to the glory of God. Christians trust in the providence of the God who feeds the fowl of the air and clothes the grass of the field (*Mt.* 6:25–34). This divine care is evidence of the loving purpose of the creator in creation. Julian of Norwich (1342–1416?) is part of a tradition in which God's love takes on a maternal aspect.

Christ the Mediator. Jesus Christ reveals God to people and reconciles people to God. Christians are devoted to the manger, where the Son of God became human, and to the cross, where he died: the Christmas crèche and the perennial crucifix of the Western church meet in an Eastern iconography in which the swaddling bands and the cave foreshadow the grave cloths and the tomb. A constant theme of spirituality is the *imitatio Christi*, whereby believers not only follow Christ's example in action and suffering (*Mk.* 8:34; *Jn.* 13:14–15, 13:34–35; *Eph.* 5:1–2; *Phil.* 2:1–17; *1 Pt.* 2:21–25) but sacramentally participate in his dying and rising again (*Rom.* 6; *Col.* 2:12–13, 3:1–17; cf. *Jn.* 3:5, 12:24; *Ti.* 3:5). Christians pray for God's kingdom and their salvation in the Lord's Prayer (the Our Father), which Jesus commanded and taught to his disciples. [*See* Lord's Prayer.] In the Jesus Prayer long repeated in the Eastern churches, they also seek refuge in the appointed Savior and Judge: "Lord Jesus Christ, [Son of the Living God,] have mercy on me [a sinner]."

The Sanctifying Spirit. The Holy Spirit, the third person of the Trinity, brings people to confess Jesus as Lord (*1 Cor.* 12:3) and aids them in their prayers for full redemption (*Rom.* 8:18–30, *Eph.* 6:18), which they expect from the God whom the Holy Spirit enables them to address as "Abba, Father" (*Rom.* 8:15–16, *Gal.* 4:6). The Spirit's abiding gifts are faith, hope, and love (*1 Cor.* 13:13). When God's love is poured into believers' hearts by the Holy Spirit (*Rom.* 5:1–5), the fruit of the Spirit is produced in their lives: love, joy, peace, patience, kindness, goodness, faithfulness, gentleness, self-control (*Gal.* 5:16–26). They are thus being changed into the likeness of the Lord Jesus (*2 Cor.* 3:18; cf. *Col.* 3:10). The Holy Spirit inspires "psalms and hymns and spiritual songs," a "melody making unto God" (*Eph.* 5:18–20), and at times in Christian history there have been outbursts of Spirit-given glossolalia, or speaking in tongues (*1 Cor.* 14).

The Communion of the Saints. All Christians have been sanctified unto God (*1 Cor.* 6:11, *1 Pt.* 2:4–10), and the apostle Paul could therefore address the recipients of his letters as "saints" (e.g., *Rom.* 1:7). In this present life, some have so grown in this sanctifying grace that they have become widely revered for their moral and spiritual qualities. Their memories persist after their departure, so that their earthly examples are emulated and their heavenly intercession is sought. A special place in the communion of the saints is occupied by the Virgin Mary, Mother of the Lord. In the Catholic West, the telling of the rosary beads links Mary with her Son in the five joyful mysteries (the annunciation, the visitation, the nativity, the presentation, and the finding of Christ in the Temple), the five sorrowful mysteries (the agony, the scourging, the crowning with thorns, the carrying of the cross, the crucifixion), and the five glorious mysteries (the resurrection, the ascension, Pentecost, and Mary's assumption and coronation). Relics of people in whom the Holy Spirit has conspicuously dwelt are traditionally built into Christian altars. Saints are popularly taken as patrons of particular trades and activities. Protestants have usually rejected a cult of the saints, both for the apparent superstitions that may surround relics and because of the uniqueness of Christ as mediator.

Life in the Divine Kingdom. Christians believe that the present life is surrounded by God's eternal purpose. They live with the prospect of "the four last things": death and judgment, heaven and hell. Their hope lies in the God whose redeeming and saving intent has been embodied in Jesus Christ. They rely on God's mercy, while they are aware that "all must appear before the judgment seat of Christ, to receive good or evil, according to what one has done in the body" (*2 Cor.* 5:10). Sharing in God's final kingdom will mean feasting, worshiping, seeing face-to-face: "man's chief end is to glorify God and to enjoy him for ever" (Westminster Shorter Catechism, 1647–1648). The communal vision of heaven has often brought comfort in earthly distress; it has sometimes encouraged human efforts to bring about its historical approximation. From time to time, expectation of the world's imminent end has given to Christian spirituality an apocalyptic cast like that reflected in much of the New Testament (see Bernard McGinn's *Apocalyptic Spirituality*, New York, 1979). Some respond by what Norman Cohn calls a "pursuit of the millennium"; others adopt a more quietist resignation. In any case, Christians are constantly summoned to a vigilance that includes casting off the works of darkness and putting on the armor of light (*Rom.* 13:11–14).

Theological Analysis

The structure of the classic creeds allows a fivefold theological analysis of Christian spirituality according to the five main areas of doctrine: (1) protology, or the Creator's fundamental purpose for humanity; (2) Christology, or the person, and in this case the work, of Jesus Christ; (3) pneumatology, or the teaching concerning the Holy Spirit; (4) ecclesiology, or the doctrine of the church; (5) eschatology, or the final kingdom of God. In each case, Christian spirituality is stretched between two apparent polar opposites, but there occurs each time enough of a *coincidentia oppositorum* (Nicholas of Cusa) for a third position to stand less as a compromise than as a statement of at least partial mutual inclusion.

Protology. The principal question is that of human knowledge of God. Here, by way of exception, the subject will be treated first at a more ideal or formal level (apophatism, cataphatism, analogy) and then at a more real or material level (fallenness, perfection, discipline).

Apophatism. The transcendent otherness of God may be so stressed that human speech about the divine can, it is held, at most say what God is *not* and is finally renounced altogether *(apo-phēmi)*. This approach is sometimes called the *via negativa*. Its maxim might be the word of John of Damascus in the eighth century, under the influence of the pseudonymous Dionysius the Aeropagite: "Inexpressible is the Deity, and incomprehensible" (*On the Orthodox Faith* 1.1). The experience of this as a fact is one common meaning of *mysticism*, a "knowing by unknowing." Gregory of Nyssa (330–395) traces the progress of Moses from the brightness of the burning bush through the cloud of Mount Sinai to a final vision of God in the darkness (A. J. Malherbe and E. Ferguson, *Gregory of Nyssa: The Life of Moses*, New York and London, 1978, pp. 14–15, 20–21, 148). God will always remain inexhaustible. God as mystery may in this life also be experienced as absence: hence the "dark night of the soul" in Walter Hilton (c. 1340–1396) or John of the Cross (1542–1591). The hidden God, *deus absconditus*, can only be waited for, whether in the Egyptian desert, in Carthusian or Quaker silence, in the quietism of Madame Guyon du Chesnoy and Fénelon, or in the stillness of the Herrnhut Moravians.

Cataphatism. The hidden God graciously becomes the *deus revelatus*. In the first place, the Creator so stamped himself on creation as to be knowable through the natural world (*Rom.* 1:19–20, *Ps.* 19:1). A bold anthropomorphism in conceiving God is encouraged by human theomorphism: humanity was created in the image of God (*Gn.* 1:27). God's self-revelation reached a climax in the incarnation of the Son (*Jn.* 1:14, 1:18). On these bases it is possible to know God directly and to speak of God positively or affirmatively *(kataphasis)*. Powers, qualities, and virtues may be predicated—by the *via causalitatis* and the *via eminentiae*—of the God who is the source and measure of all that is good, true, and beautiful (*Phil.* 4:8, *Rom.* 12:2). God's glory has shone in the face of Christ Jesus (*2 Cor.* 4:6), yet his disciples also know that the light in which God dwells is inaccessible (*1 Tm.* 6:16).

Analogy. The doctrine of analogy follows the potential and limits of the principle enunciated by the Fourth Lateran Council (1215): Between creator and creature, no similarity can be found so great but that the dissimilarity is even greater. Ontologically grounded in the "analogy of being" between creator and creature, language about God may at least point in the right direction; it may express and provoke human experience of God. What is allowed by the ontological and linguistic principle of analogy may take literary and poetic form as metaphor, since metaphor is an imaginative exploitation of similarity and dissimilarity. However, not all metaphors refer to God, and not all language about God need take the literary form of metaphor. Whether it be in propositions, metaphors, or other figures, Christianity requires that language about God be authorized by God's self-revelation, either in the normative events and messages recorded and interpreted in scripture or in the continuing experience of the churchly community. Forms of symbolic communication other than the word alone find their supreme instance in the sacraments, which are held to have been instituted in one way or another by Christ. Icon painters require both tradition and inspiration if their work is to be recognized as an epiphany of the divine. God transcends even authorized and tried words, sacraments, and icons, but these nevertheless provide a "mediated immediacy" of the Godhead, which is the ordinary route of Christian spirituality, in a fashion that respects some impulses of both apophatism and cataphatism. The inadequacy of analogy always leaves room, beyond speech, for a "filled" silence.

Fallenness. Christians recognize that humanity has been dogged by sin since the beginnings of its history (*Gn.* 3). Disobedience has obscured the knowledge of God, although enough remains to render people responsible and "without excuse" (*Rom.* 1:20). "All have sinned and fall short of the glory of God" (*Rom.* 3:23). The seat of sin, which is an attitude before it is an act, is the will. The will needs to be changed before God can be pleased. Christians confess that humans are dependent on the mercy of God, revealed in Jesus Christ, for the forgiveness of their sin and that a rebirth by the Holy Spirit is needed for a continuing life of trust and obedience. Accents have differed concerning the depth of human fallenness, the present and ultimate consequences of failure, the grace needed for retrieval, and the scope of God's will for salvation. The most profound single vision is probably that of Augustine of Hippo (354–430), which has heavily stamped both Catholic and Protestant spirituality: the human race is a *massa damnata,* from which only elect individuals are rescued by the overwhelming grace of God that brings them to faith in Christ. Some have been revolted by the picture conjured up of "sinners in the hands of an angry God" (in a sermon by Jonathan Edwards, 1703–1758). While Calvinists have found in the predestination decrees a "comfortable doctrine" (Edwards's treatise *Religious Affections* suggests signs for detecting the presence of the Spirit in one's life; cf. John Calvin's *Institutes of the Christian Religion* 3.14.18–19), others have seen the implications of a fatalism that could lead to either spiritual despair or moral libertinism. Even the "gracious God" whom Martin Luther eventually found—"Wie kriege ich einen gnädigen Gott?"—may have been bought at too great a price. Under the title "Protestant Piety and Guilt Consciousness," Wolfhart Pannenberg argues the inadequacy of certain brands of penitentialism after Nietzsche and Freud (*Christian Spirituality,* Philadelphia, 1983). Some features of Augustinianism may indeed owe more to Manichaeism and Neoplatonism than to the Bible, yet Augustine's *Confessions* and his *City of God* stand as a permanent challenge to all superficial optimism at the individual or social level.

Perfection. While not ignoring original sin, Eastern Orthodox thought has been inclined to integrate it, in the manner of Irenaeus (c. 130–c. 200), into a pedagogic history of humanity created immature and called to grow into the likeness of God. The work of Christ consists in reopening the gates of paradise (a prominent theme in the fourth-century poetry of Ephraem of Syria), whither all may follow Christ who in him are being daily renewed after the image of their creator (*Col.* 3:10). Eastern writers set their sights high: Christians are to be made "partakers of the divine nature" (*2 Pt.* 1:4). This sharing in the divine life and character is called *theosis* or *theopoiesis,* terms that have been viewed with suspicion in the West as signifying absorption in a pantheistic way.

In the West, perfectionism tends to be treated as a sectarian trait. Perfectionists find themselves exposed to charges of moralism, hypocrisy, and self-righteousness. John Wesley (1703–1791) taught his Methodists to strive for perfection in this earthly life, although by sin he meant only the voluntary transgression of a known law and he did not yet expect them to overcome ignorance and frailty. Wesley's positive definition of perfection, the pure love of God and neighbor (*Mt.* 22:37–40), brings us to the mediating third term.

Discipline. Augustine and the Eastern church emphasized, respectively, the depths of the human condition and the heights of the human vocation. Augustine himself declared of God, "Thou hast made us for Thyself, and our hearts are restless until they find their rest in Thee" (*Confessions* 1.1). The restless heart, *cor inquietum,* is a sign of both the "misery" and the "greatness" of man (Blaise Pascal, 1623–1662). The Christian faith understands itself as a way from sin and death to life and God. Journeying is a theme of its spirituality, whether in the Crusades (problematic to all but the Latins), in visits to sacred shrines, or in the allegory of John Bunyan's popular Puritan classic, *The Pilgrim's Progress* (1678). The journey cannot be undertaken without constant divine aid, yet freely accepted discipline is expected of the travelers. The technical term is *ascesis.* The struggle that this involves, a kind of projection of the apocalyptic battle between good and evil (*Eph.* 6:10–18), has called forth militant imagery, whether in the Jesuit order founded by the Spanish soldier Ignatius of Loyola (c. 1491–1556) or in the Salvation Army of William Booth (1829–1912).

Christology. Sometimes spirituality has focused on the cross of Christ, sometimes on his resurrection. The single paschal mystery of Good Friday and Easter awaits consummation at Christ's Parousia.

The cross. A wall scribbling from the Palatine palace in Rome probably shows how Christians were considered: a man kneels before a crucified figure whose head is the head of an ass, and the legend reads, "Alexamenus worships his god." Gregory of Nazianzus, Martin Luther, and Charles Wesley all spoke of a "crucified God" before Jürgen Moltmann revived the theme in his 1972 book. Tradition has it that the apostle Peter asked to be crucified upside down because the disciple was not fit to be crucified in the same way Jesus was. The letters of Ignatius of Antioch (d. about 107) show him rushing toward martyrdom. Among the martyrs of Gaul in 177, Blandina is said to have been clothed with the Christ she had put on in baptism, and as she was tied to the stake in prayer, her fellow Christians saw in their sister the crucified Lord. Devotion to the crucified Christ has brought Christians to a self-abasement that need not be pathological, an acceptance of suffering that is not necessarily morbid, and a readiness to sacrifice oneself for others that mirrors the active compassion of God.

The later Middle Ages, a time of great pain in the history of Europe, developed a devotion to the suffering

Christ that lasted at least as far as the Pietism of the seventeenth and eighteenth centuries. Francis of Assisi stands at the beginning with his stigmata, the marks of the crucified Jesus borne on his body (see *Gal.* 6:17). Attention focuses on the Sacred Heart of Jesus. Believers tread the *via crucis* as they processionally make the stations of the cross. Protestant hymns sing of the wounds of Christ. To this day, Latin American churches contain gruesome statues of the crucified Jesus, complete with natural hair and the instruments of his torture. Devotion to the suffering Christ produced the magnificent *pietàs* and *Vesperbilder* in wood and stone of the dead Jesus in the arms of his mother; it produced the Isenheim altarpiece of a Matthias Grünewald; and it produced the Passion music of a Bach. Yet the fundamental sensibility here is affective rather than aesthetic.

The resurrection. The East has concentrated on the risen Christ. Icons show the Harrowing of Hell: a characteristic Ethiopian scene depicts Christ raising Adam and Eve from the mire. Great Byzantine cupola mosaics portray Christ the Pantocrator, the human Lord who is divine ruler of all. His vicarious victory over death is sung in the Easter troparia as the restoration of life to those in the tomb. Such a perspective highlights the degree to which salvation is already achieved. The liturgy offers a glimpse of heaven on earth. When Vladimir I, great prince of Kiev (d. 1015), sent his emissaries to investigate the religions of the world, they were overcome by the beauty of worship in the church of Hagia Sophia in Constantinople, and that was the beginning of the conversion of Russia to Christianity. Westerners have sometimes criticized this liturgical vision as escapist.

The Parousia. At the final coming of Christ, the *theologia crucis* and the *theologia gloriae* should be reconciled. The cross will not be forgotten at his glorious advent. Charles Wesley's hymn pictures the return of Christ, when "he comes with clouds descending":

> The dear tokens of his passion
> Still his dazzling body bears . . .
> With what rapture
> Gaze we on those glorious scars.

It is the slain Lamb who wins the day and receives the adoration (*Rv.* 5:6–14, 6:10, 15:3–4), a theme that inspired such an artist as the Flemish Jan van Eyck and percolated to popular culture in the typical English inn sign of "The Lamb and Flag." Meanwhile the life in Christ is lived in the tension of the "already" and the "not yet," the hidden and the to-be-revealed (*Col.* 3:1–4, *1 Jn.* 3:2–3), the fragmentary and the whole (*1 Cor.* 13:12), the interrupted and the lasting, the threatened and the secure.

Pneumatology. The Holy Spirit leads believers into a truth (*Jn.* 16:13–15) that, in biblical terms, is both to be known (*Jn.* 8:31–32) and to be done (*1 Jn.* 1:6). A pendulum swinging between contemplation and action passes through the territory of meditation and prophecy.

Contemplation. John the Divine was "in the Spirit" when he saw his heavenly visions (*Rv.* 1:10, cf. *Rv.* 21:10). The divine Spirit reveals the deep things of God, things the eye has not seen, the ear has not heard, the human heart has not conceived (*1 Cor.* 2). A "man in Christ" may be "caught up" into "the third heaven" (*2 Cor.* 12:1–4). To being "rapt out of the senses" the fourteenth-century Yorkshireman Richard Rolle, in *The Fire of Love,* preferred the rapture of the self-possessed lifting of the mind to God in loving contemplation, which is a "foretaste of everlasting sweetness."

Often the imagery of contemplation is that of upward transcendence, as in *The Ladder of Perfection* of Walter Hilton and *The Ascent of Mount Carmel* of John of the Cross. Sometimes it is the more enveloping imagery of exploring the depths:

> How great a being, Lord, is thine,
> Which doth all beings keep!
> Thy knowledge is the only line
> To sound so vast a deep.
> Thou art a sea without a shore,
> A sun without a sphere;
> Thy time is now and evermore,
> Thy place is everywhere.
> (John Mason, c. 1645–1694)

More immanently, there is the "inscape" of the Jesuit poet Gerard Manley Hopkins (1844–1889), or the "journey inward" made possible by Augustine's "God who is closer to me than myself." For Karl Rahner (1904–1984), God is both the mysterious ultimate "horizon" of human self-transcendence and the "formal cause" of humanity through self-communicating love.

Nuptial themes pervade the language of contemplation. Not only is the church, in the Holy Spirit, the bride of Christ (*Rv.* 22:17; cf. *2 Cor.* 11:2, *Eph.* 5:25–27), but the individual Christian may be wedded to him. Gregory of Nyssa, Bernard of Clairvaux (1090–1153), Hadewijch of Antwerp (mid-thirteenth century), Teresa of Ávila (1515–1582), and English Puritans such as Richard Sibbes and Francis Rous offer spiritual interpretations of the *Song of Songs* or borrow its language to describe the intercourse of the soul with God. In a classic type of mysticism, there is a disciplined route of purgation and illumination before union with the divine.

Contemplation of God is the goal pursued with a "single eye" by enclosed communities of nuns or monks. The sixth beatitude declares without restriction that it is the pure in heart who shall see God (*Mt.* 5:8).

Action. Love, which is the greatest gift of the Spirit (*1 Cor.* 13), is to be directed not only toward God but also toward neighbor. A long tradition, typified by Elizabeth of Thuringia (1207–1231) and Mother Teresa of Calcutta (b. 1910), makes the corporal works of mercy, based on the service to "the least" described in *Matthew* 25:31–46, into the service of God in Christ. Dag Hammarskjöld (1905–1961), the very private Christian who was secretary general of the United Nations, declared in his *Markings* that "in our age, the road to holiness necessarily passes through the world of action." The "dream" (cf. *Acts* 2:17) of the black Baptist preacher Martin Luther King, Jr. (1929–1968) sustained his social and political engagement. King stood for nonviolent action; other, "radical" Christians have committed themselves to revolution (note the jottings of Camilo Torres in his *Revolutionary Priest*, New York, 1971). Although the source and content of their leading idea of justice often remains unclear, many contemporary Latin American liberationists make of orthopraxy at least the test, and in some cases even the foundation, of orthodoxy (whether as right worship or as right doctrine).

Meditation and prophecy. Tension between the contemplatives and the actives has marked even monasticism, as in the East between the traditions of Mount Sinai (where John Climacus, author of *The Ladder of Divine Ascent*, was a seventh-century abbot) and Mount Athos (where Gregory Palamas, the fourteenth-century hesychast, or man of repose, was trained), on the one hand, and the Studite tradition of Constantinople, on the other. Thomas Merton (1915–1968), the traveling Trappist, advocated the combination of contemplation and action for every Christian. A remarkable example is provided by the Little Brothers and the Little Sisters of Jesus, under the inspiration of Charles-Eugènie de Foucauld (1858–1916): exposure to the eucharistic presence of Christ, begun in solitude, is continued in small groups that immerse themselves in the working world.

A more moderate combination of the spiritual impulses that lead to contemplation and/or action is represented by the Benedictine tradition of prayer and work, the alternating rhythm and qualitative fusion of *ora et labora*. The monastic practice is based on *lectio*, *meditatio*, *oratio*, and *intentio:* reading of the inspired scriptures and their spiritual commentators and interpreters is accompanied or followed by individual or communal reflection on them and leads into prayer and resolution. While the daily office is the *opus Dei* par excellence, manual labor is significant and also done within the community.

Although they were developed for his Jesuit "troops," the *Spiritual Exercises* of Ignatius Loyola include forms of meditation that can also be used by laity amid their own secular engagement. Scripturally based meditation, often starting from a scene in the Gospels, is characteristic also of "the French school." According to Francis of Sales (1567–1622), a bishop who counseled his flock in his *Introduction to the Devout Life*, the conclusion of the meditation is a spiritual nosegay to be carried throughout the day. That is not too different from the widespread German evangelical use of the Moravian *Losung*, or "text for the day." A Protestant version of scriptural meditation is "Bible study," whether done individually or in a group. In classic Protestantism, family prayers were part of a pattern that included vigor and integrity in one's occupation, and charitable service to the neighbor.

Familiarity with the scriptures as God's word aims at developing the gift of "discernment" (*Heb.* 4:12–13, 5:12–14). The ability to "distinguish the spirits" (*1 Cor.* 12:10, *1 Jn.* 4:1–6), or, in modern terms, to read the situation for good and evil, is a mark of prophecy. If the Holy Spirit is to speak and work through them in their own times, Christians expect that it will happen only as they follow the mind and example of Christ (*1 Cor.* 2:16, *Phil.* 2:1–12; cf. *Mk.* 13:9–13).

Ecclesiology. Christianity teaches neither an atomistic individualism nor a totalitarian collectivism but rather the integration of members in a body.

The individual Christian. The individual is known and loved by God (*Mt.* 10:29–31), and a personal response is called for (*Mt.* 22:37). Some have felt that this response can only be made alone, hence the anchorites and the hermits. But the fathers of the Egyptian desert led by Antony (251–356), the Syrian stylites perched on platforms above their pillars, and the Russian *startsy*, most notably Serafim of Sarov (1759–1833), all tended to attract people seeking spiritual advice. Even the Danish Protestant recluse Søren Kierkegaard (1813–1855) has helped later generations through his writings. Intentionally or not, these figures prove John Wesley's dictum that there is "no holiness but social holiness."

A strain of elitism marks the Western Catholic distinction in the teachings of the Gospels between evangelical precepts, which are incumbent on all, and counsels of perfection, which are for the chosen few. Even when mitigated by talk of "stages on the way," this double standard has been rejected by Orthodox and Protestants. The help and the challenge, both unlimited, afforded by "the love of the brethren" in both the subjective and the objective sense (*Rom.* 12:10; *Gal.* 5:13; *1 Thes.* 4:9–10; *Heb.* 13:1; *1 Pt.* 1:22, 2:17, 3:8), constitute the context in which each Christian also learns to love God (*1 Jn.* 4:7–21).

The Christian community. The vows of cenobitic monks and nuns bear a communal reference, whether one thinks of the familiar triad of poverty, chastity, and obedience or of the characteristically Benedictine stability of residence. The cenobites sing the daily office "in choir," and the Christian community at large gathers for worship, whether in the morning and evening services of praise and prayer or in the Sunday liturgy. The common life in Christ calls for rejoicing with those who rejoice, weeping with those who weep, and bearing one another's burdens. These daily experiences find their symbolic focus in the worship assembly. At times, among Roman Catholics, Orthodox, and Protestants alike, the church service has degenerated into an occasion for individuals to say their private prayers while the liturgical action is left to the clerics. But the ultimate fruit of the eucharistic communion, according to Thomas Aquinas (c. 1225–1274), is the peace of the heavenly city in God's kingdom. That is a communitarian vision intended to affect both rite and life now.

A sacramental fellowship. By baptism, a sacrament of both grace and faith, people are incorporated into the body of Christ (*1 Cor.* 12:12–13, *Gal.* 3:27–28). They are thereby called to a daily dying unto sin and a continued walking in newness of life, which will be consummated in a final resurrection to eternal life (*Rom.* 6). Eucharistic food, the sacrament of Christ's body and blood, is the viaticum of a pilgrim people, a foretaste of the heavenly banquet. The tangible reality of the sacraments makes clear that what is now done "in the body" is definitive of persons in eternity (*2 Cor.* 5:10). By their behavior, Christians are to "glorify God in their body" (*1 Cor.* 6:12–20; cf. *2 Cor.* 6:14–7:1, *Rom.* 12:1–2). From time to time, a martyrdom, in which rite, reality, and reward are wonderfully concentrated, comes to assure believers that the sacramental game is a serious one: baptism in water is completed by baptism in blood, and the good confessor and faithful servant is at once taken from the Eucharist into the feast of the Master's joy. Those who are spontaneously recognized by the people's love to be "saints" in a special sense are confidently believed to be nearer to God, and the earthly church is joined with them in a fellowship of praise and prayer.

The communion of the saints constitutes a challenge to overcome the scandal of divisions among Christians on earth. The spirituality of the twentieth century has carried a remarkable ecumenical dimension. The French priest Paul Couturier (1881–1953) provides an example of prayer and work for Christian unity, as does the Taizé community—a monastic community in France that includes both Protestants and Roman Catholics—at a somewhat more institutional level.

Eschatology. Attitudes toward the present world in the light of an age to come can conveniently be analyzed according to the five historical and theological types proposed by H. Richard Niebuhr for the relations between Christ and culture (*Christ and Culture*, New York, 1951).

The denial of the world. That "the world lieth in the evil one" (*1 Jn.* 5:19) is a belief understandably adopted when Christians suffer persecution. The world is a place for Christians to be "out of," and persecutors eventually see to their ultimate dispatch. Yet this type of spirituality did not cease with the conversion of Constantine. Bloody martyrdom gave way to the "white martyrdom" of monasticism as a movement of withdrawal that protested, or at least warned, against the dangers of imperial Christianity. "The desert is to the empire as apocalypse is to history" (George Florovsky, *Christianity and Culture*, Belmont, Mass., 1974, p. 128). Another line of world-renouncing Christianity stretches from the ancient Montanists, who attracted Tertullian from the catholic church, to the twentieth-century Pentecostal movement, where glossolalia can be understood as a countercultural protest against the rationalistic and materialistic language of late Western Christendom. Eschatologically, the difficulty with "Christ against culture" in the extreme or simplistic forms of that attitude is that it underestimates the world, either its stubbornness (how much "world" remains unconquered even in the converted) or its destiny as the object of God's love (*Jn.* 3:16).

The more subtle type of world denial, Niebuhr's "dualist," sees Christ and culture in a tense paradox. This attitude combines engagement in the world with an ironic detachment from it. It follows Paul's advice about using worldly institutions "as though not *(hōs mē)* using them" (*1 Cor.* 7). Lutherans are particularly apt to look for things under the opposite or contrary appearance *(sub contraria specie)*. Dietrich Bonhoeffer (1906–1945) was a secular man who maintained the "secret discipline" of prayer. He used his employment in the German secret service to keep up international and ecumenical contacts, and he was executed for his part in the plot to kill Hitler. Bonhoeffer now figures in the sanctorale of the North American Lutheran *Book of Worship*. The Christian lives simultaneously as righteous and as a sinner, *simul iustus et peccator*. When taken as a permanent and unremitting paradox, this understanding leaves little room for growth in grace, although Lutheran practice often happily belies the theory.

A different case of paradox is supplied by the succession of those who, in line with the folly of God that confounds the wisdom of the world (*1 Cor.* 1:18–31), have become "fools for Christ's sake" (*1 Cor.* 4:10, cf. *2 Cor.* 11–12). They have borne witness through their madness, whether real (Jean-Joseph Surin, 1600–1665) or feigned. The story of the holy idiots and spiritual infants, of "Christ's troubadours, jongleurs, and bards," is told in John Saward's *Perfect Fools* (New York, 1980). Popular manifestations figure in Harvey Cox's *Feast of Fools* (Cambridge, Mass., 1969).

The affirmation of the world. Niebuhr found an opposite extreme in "the Christ of culture," where Jesus becomes an adaptable folk hero and Christianity is absorbed by the world. The church was bound to take advantage of the opportunities provided by the Roman emperor's conversion, but the result was a dilution of the faith. The effects of superficial evangelization and cheap christening are part of the burden of Christendom. "Culture-Protestantism" could issue in the "German Christianity" of the Nazi period, where the closeness of culture to (fallen) nature is demonstrated by the slogans "Blood and Soil" and "One Nation, one *Reich*, one *Führer*." Less virulently, modern liberal Christianity has tended to follow the fleeting fashions of a world whose "form is passing" (*1 Cor.* 7:31). In particular, a would-be Christian acquiescence in secularization as the humanly willed "absence of God" has provoked Wolfhart Pannenberg, in his aforementioned book, to recall the disastrous consequences ascribed by the psalmist to the hiding of God's face (*Ps.* 10:1, 44:24, 69:17, 104:29, 143:7; cf. *Rom.* 1:24–32). The "difficulty" of Christian spirituality in modern civilization comes to oblique expression in the poetry of T. S. Eliot (1888–1965). Eschatologically, the problem with the "Christ of culture" type is that it assumes either that the world never needed redemption or that it has been fully redeemed already.

The more subtle type of world affirmation sees Christ and culture in a "synthetic" relation. Niebuhr here invokes Thomas Aquinas: grace comes not to destroy nature (or culture) but to perfect it. The Christian faith brings a critical enhancement of human life. Human efforts are purified and elevated into acceptability before God. The corresponding spirituality sometimes bears an intellectual, and often aesthetic, coloration. The art that serves God can just as well be popular as highbrow. Knowledge, *scientia*, achieves spiritual value only as part of a wisdom, *sapientia*, whose beginning is the fear of the Lord.

The transformation of the world. Niebuhr's fifth and favored type, including impulses of both denial and affirmation, takes Christ as the transformer of culture. The goodness of creation is recognized, but so is its corruption. Transformation implies not replacement but change. The term in spirituality is *conversion*. In the Byzantine rite of baptism, the candidate faces westward to renounce Satan and is turned toward the east to confess allegiance to Christ. The "new creation" (*2 Cor.* 5:17) of the Christian, sacramentally signified in baptism, is an anticipation of the divine act whereby the creation will be set free from its bondage to decay and share in the glorious liberty of the children of God (*Rom.* 8:21). The service of God, says the Anglican collect, is "perfect freedom." Waiting in hope for full redemption (*Rom.* 8:23–25), Christians are summoned to set their hearts on heavenly treasure (*Mt.* 6:19–21, 6:24–34), yet not so as to despise the earthen vessels (*2 Cor.* 4:7). The eucharistic meal is a sacramental sign of the eventual participation of the entire human person and the full range of God's handiwork in the final kingdom of justice, peace, and joy in the Holy Spirit (cf. *Rom.* 14:17). Meanwhile, Christians are to "do everything, in word and deed, in the name of the Lord Jesus, giving thanks to God the Father through him" (*Col.* 3:17).

[*See also the biographies of spiritual leaders mentioned herein.*]

BIBLIOGRAPHY

A wide selection of original Christian texts is included in the multivolume series "Classics of Western Spirituality," published by Paulist Press (New York, 1978–). The best overall introduction, with bibliographies, is provided by an ecumenical work of composite authorship, *The Study of Spirituality*, edited by Cheslyn Jones, myself, and Edward Yarnold (New York and London, 1986). A suitable accompanying work of reference is the similarly oriented *Dictionary of Christian Spirituality*, edited by Gordon S. Wakefield (London, 1983). The most detailed reference work, when complete, will be the *Dictionnaire de spiritualité ascétique et mystique*, begun under the direction of Marcel Viller (Paris, 1932–). A good systematic presentation is made in German by Josef Weismayer in his *Leben in Fülle* (Innsbruck, 1983) Urban T. Holmes III, in his *A History of Christian Spirituality* (New York, 1980), supplies a very schematic sketch, while a fuller historical treatment is found in Louis Bouyer, Jean Leclercq, François Vandenbroucke, and Louis Cognet's *A History of Christian Spirituality*, 3 vols. (New York, 1963–1969). The early history of a theologically controversial phenomenon is traced in Andrew Louth's *The Origins of the Christian Mystical Tradition from Plato to Denys* (Oxford, 1981). Modern use is made of the older spiritual tradition under various angles in a number of books that sometimes almost amount to anthologies: Aelred Squire's *Asking the Fathers*, 2d ed. (Wilton, Conn., 1976); Kenneth Leech's *Soul Friend: The Practice of Christian Spirituality* (San Francisco, 1980), which concentrates on spiritual direction, and *True Prayer* (New York, 1980); Rowan Williams's *The Wound of Knowledge: Christian Spirituality from the New Testament to St. John of the Cross* (London, 1979), also published as *Christian Spirituality: A Theological History from the New Testament to Luther and St. John of the Cross* (Atlanta, 1980); and Simon Tugwell's *Ways of Imperfection: An Exploration of Christian Spirituality* (London, 1984). The changing forms of piety come to expression in Josef A. Jungmann's *Christian Prayer through the Centuries* (New York, 1978). A sympathetic Roman Catholic account of Lutheran and Reformed piety is found in Brunero Gherardini's *La spiritualità protestante* (Rome, 1982). Descriptions from the inside come in *Protestant Spiritual Traditions,* edited by Frank C. Senn (New York, 1986). Raymond E. Brown displays the best modern exegesis of "The Pater Noster as an Eschatological Prayer" in his *New Testament Essays,* 3d ed. (New York, 1982). The Jesus Prayer of the East is treated in Kallistos Ware's *The Power of the Name* (Oxford, 1974). The sacramental perspective is well represented by Alexander Schmemann in his *For the Life of the World: Sacraments and Orthodoxy,* 2d ed. (New York, 1973), also published as *The World as Sacrament* (London, 1966). *The New Oxford Book of Christian Verse* (Oxford, 1982) contains a perceptive introduction and selection by Donald Davie. Fine illustrations accompany Leonid Ouspensky and Vladimir Lossky's *The Meaning of Icons,* rev. ed. (Crestwood, N.Y., 1982). Michael Perham's *The Communion of Saints: An Examination of the Place of the Christian Dead in the Belief, Worship, and Calendars of the Church* (London, 1980) can find sociological complementation in Peter Brown's *The Cult of the Saints: Its Rise and Function in Latin Christianity* (Chicago, 1981) and in Donald Weinstein and Rudolph M. Bell's *Saints and Society: The Two Worlds of Western Christendom, 1000–1700* (Chicago, 1982). An anthropological basis for spirituality in developmental psychology is sought by James W. Fowler in his *Stages of Faith* (San Francisco, 1981).

GEOFFREY WAINWRIGHT

CHRISTMAS is the Christian celebration of the birth of Jesus Christ. The name, English in origin, means "Christ's Mass," that is, the mass celebrating the feast of Christ's nativity. Names for Christmas in Romance languages are derived from the Latin *nativitas.* The French *Noël* comes from either *nativitas* or *nowell,* meaning "news." German employs the term *Weihnachten,* meaning "holy (or blessed) night." Another name for the whole season is *Yule.* Originally this name did not have Christian connotations but derived either from the Germanic *jol* ("turning wheel"), with reference to the gain of sunlight after the winter solstice, or from the Anglo-Saxon *geol* ("feast"). The name of this pre-Christian winter feast of the solstice was eventually applied to the whole of the Christmas season. [*See also* Winter Solstice Songs.]

There is no certain knowledge of the origin of the Christmas feast. It may have been celebrated as early as the beginning of the fourth century in North Africa, but certainly it was observed at Rome by the middle of the same century. Two theories have been advanced for the occurrence of the feast on 25 December. One theory argues that Christmas originated in opposition to or competition with the Roman Feast of the Invincible Sun (Sol Invictus) that had been celebrated on the old date of the winter solstice. [*See* Sol Invictus.] The computation theory, on the other hand, argues that the birth of Christ was calculated on the basis of the idea that the conception of Christ coincided with his death, which supposedly occurred on 25 March.

By the end of the fourth century the observance on 25 December of the feast of Christ's nativity had spread throughout most of the Christian world. At Antioch, Chrysostom regarded it as the actual date of Christ's birth. In the mid-fifth century the Jerusalem church, too, accepted the 25 December date, which then replaced the older celebration of the nativity there on 6 January. The Armenians, however, have never accepted 25 December as the Feast of the Nativity.

The Western Christian observance of Christmas was strongly influenced by the celebration of this feast in the city of Rome. Three masses came to be celebrated by the pope on Christmas Day. The original mass was held at Saint Peter's on Christmas morning. But in the course of the fifth century a second mass was added "in the middle of the night" (first at cockcrow and later at midnight) at the shrine of Christ's crib, which had been erected at the Church of Santa Maria Maggiore as a replica of the crib at Bethlehem. Finally, during the Byzantine period of the sixth century a third mass was added in Rome, this one at dawn at the Church of Sant' Anastasia, a martyr whose feast was celebrated in Constantinople on 25 December. Probably for the sake of convenience, in the course of the eleventh century the original mass celebrated at Saint Peter's was transferred to Santa Maria Maggiore, already the site of the second mass. Since the eighth century the Western Christian celebration of Christmas has been provided with an octave, or eight days of liturgical observance, in imitation of the feasts of Easter and Epiphany.

In the early sixth century the emperor Justinian made Christmas a public holiday. The feast was extremely popular in all European countries during the Middle Ages, inspiring the composition of music and liturgical drama. The observance of Christmas received added impetus in the early thirteenth century when Francis of Assisi originated the devotion of the Christmas crib.

After the sixteenth century most of the Reformation churches retained the Christmas feast. Martin Luther, for example, showed great devotion to Christmas in his preaching. However, the English Puritans tried to do away with the celebration of Christmas altogether in the course of the seventeenth century. The feast was revived with the restoration of the English monarchy in 1660, but on a somewhat more secular basis. Under the Puritan influence in early America, especially in New England, Christmas was a regular workday until the middle of the nineteenth century.

The customs of Christmas in the Northern Hemisphere include, in addition to Christian religious practices and midwinter feasting, various celebrations of the returning light of the sun. In northern European folklore, the twelve days between Christmas and Epiphany are a time when the evil spirits are considered to be especially active, combating the coming of spring and the gradual victory of sunlight over darkness that follows the winter solstice; thus Christmas Eve is called there "the devil's funeral." To celebrate the victory of life over winter's death and to combat evil spirits, homes are decorated in this darkest period of the year with lights and evergreens of all kinds. Similarly, the Yule log was kindled on Christmas Eve in northern countries and kept burning until Epiphany, and remains of the log were kept to kindle the next year's Yule fire. The Christmas tree itself seems to be of rather recent origin: it may be as late as the sixteenth century that Germans first decorated a fir tree with lights, fruits, and tinsel. From Germany the custom spread quickly and became universally popular, even in the Southern Hemisphere.

The custom of sending special greeting cards at Christmas originated in nineteenth-century England. Giving gifts at Christmas probably originated with the pagan Roman custom of exchanging gifts *(strenae)* at the New Year. The popular gift bringer, Santa Claus, is an American invention; he combines features of the traditional children's saint, Nicholas of Myra, with some elements of the Germanic fire god, Thor, who fought the giants of ice and snow from his home in the polar regions. [*See* Gift Giving.]

Other customs of the Christmas season include the baking of special foods, the cooking of poultry dinners on Christmas Day, and the singing of special songs, notably carols, a species of simple song that originally had wider application than as Christmas music. The celebration of Christmas thus includes both Christian observances and wider folkloric customs, the latter relating to general festivity at the time of the winter solstice.

BIBLIOGRAPHY

For a complete bibliography, see Sue Samuelson's *Christmas: An Annotated Bibliography of Analytical Scholarship* (New York, 1982). The most comprehensive treatment of the history of the Christmas celebration is still Hermann Usener's *Das Weihnachtsfest* (Bonn, 1889). For a survey of the liturgical development of the feast, see Ildephonso Schuster's *The Sacramentary* (New York, 1924). A good treatment of the customs associated with Christmas may be found in Francis X. Weiser's *Handbook of Christian Feasts and Customs* (New York, 1958), as well as in the same author's *The Christmas Book* (New York, 1952). For a treatment of the feast from the perspective of the history of religions, see E. O. James's *Seasonal Feasts and Festivals* (New York, 1961).

JOHN F. BALDOVIN, S.J.

CHRISTOLOGY. *See* Jesus.

CHRONOLOGY. The tendency to describe time in human terms inevitably leaves its mark on the various systems used for signifying time in all its widely varying forms and dimensions: from the identification of the period of light and the period of darkness within a day, to the artificial groupings of several days (seven-day week, ten-day week), the month (lunar or solar), the seasons, the year, cycles of many years, and the era. This tendency is found within the most diverse cultures and in everyday life as well as in the world of mythical traditions.

Scholars have long been gathering and analyzing a superabundant documentation relating to the concrete systems (mathematico-astronomical, economic, sacral) that in specific historical situations have been used to signify time. Unfortunately, scholars have not always asked themselves why such an activity should have been necessary. Rather than continuing to collect data of a phenomenological kind on the various methods of describing time, it seems more important to examine closely the ideology underlying them. Very useful for this purpose are historico-religious studies of the calendar, which have now made clear the decisions made in every type of culture to distinguish, within the otherwise vague, indistinct, and insubstantial temporal dimension of reality, that which is elevated to the rank of sacred from that which is deliberately left as profane.

Sacred time is saved from the anonymity of assimilation either to the perpetual self-renewal of nature or to the motionless stability of the mythical world, and is thereby rendered eternal in its periodic ritual scansions. Unlike profane time, sacred time tends to abstract not only from nature's inexorable rhythms (which it seeks in some way to control) but also from the rarefied and static character of the period of origins (which has now been left behind) and from the atmosphere of the festival (which, being out of the ordinary, is not congenial to it). As a result, sacred time always shows a face that is entirely its own, though in forms that vary according to the cultural environment and the historical situation. The phenomenology of sacred time ranges from the relatively simple impositions of taboos at specified times (which are thereby automatically removed from the everyday), to the prudent development of festive parentheses (inserted into profane existence as a means of linking this to the period of origins), and on to the infinitely more complex restructurings of calendrical rhythms. (The motives behind these rhythms—astronomical, economic, political, and/or social—are redeemed at the religious level, while the beginning and end of these rhythms are linked in the celebration of the New Year.)

History, for its part, presents us with well-defined instances of sacral descriptions of the temporal dimension. These include the dedication, in the true and strict sense, of limited periods of time to supreme beings (the "days of the gods" in ancient Egypt and the "week" of the *bolon ti ku* or "lords of the underworld" among the Maya); the indication of such days and months by name (as in the Zoroastrian religion and in the Roman, in which January was named after the god Janus, and March after the god Mars); and finally, the constant tendency to identify the beginning of linear time (time that is supremely profane by reason of the uniqueness of each instant) with events of exceptional religious importance. Such events included, for the Hebrews, creation and, for a more restricted period of time, the destruction of the Jerusalem Temple; for the Romans, the inauguration of the sanctuary of the supreme god, Jupiter Optimus Maximus; for the Western world, the birth of Christ; for Buddhist India and Indochina, the death of the Buddha and his attainment of *nirvāṇa;* and for the Islamic faithful, the emigration of Muḥammad from Mecca to Medina.

On the other hand, the consecration, and therefore surrender, of a period of time (which is thus removed from the crises of everyday life) brings the redemption, for man and for his existential needs and cultural requirements, of the remaining part of the temporal dimension, which is usually the larger part and which he seems anxious to regain possession of as soon as possible. In this context we may think of the care with which, by means of suitable indications on their epigraphical calendars, the Romans set apart the days that were *fasti* (i.e., on which it was permitted to administer justice), to the point of distinguishing within the twenty-four-hour period the time during which such activity was licit between the two phases of sacrifice. The Japanese set apart the *kannazuki* ("months without gods"), during which they, convinced that during these periods the Shintō *kami* neglect their faithful, consider it a duty not to waste time in cultic practices. Similarly, the civil authorities of various countries have brought mounting pressure to bear on the religious authorities to reduce the number of feast days and thus increase the number of workdays. The time that human beings reserve to themselves can—and by reason of existential difficulties must—be henceforth structured in a well-defined functional relation to productive activity.

It seems almost superfluous in our day to call attention to the important influence of various economic motivations on the progressive establishment and stratification of calendrical systems in the most diverse civilizations. Certain widespread phenomena in this area are obvious: the coincidence of the beginning and end of the year with the period when consumer goods are most available; the strategic location of festive periods in relation to essential work periods; and the close relation established between annual and seasonal rhythms and the needs created by human fatigue. I shall therefore only remind the reader of three considerations. First, the specific character of a calendrical structure is often determined by an agrarian economy (e.g., in ancient Egypt, where the New Year coincided with the flooding of the Nile, which was essential to the grain cycle and with which the three seasons of inundation, emersion, and repair of the irrigation system were likewise closely connected). Second, within one and the same civilization there are often several calendrical systems, each of which, with its different set of characteristics, looks to a different economic component of the society in question (e.g., at Rome, where the spelt harvest became fully available only in February, thus determining an agrarian-type New Year in March, whereas 21 April signaled the beginning of the work year for those engaged in pastoral activities). Finally, the names of the months often echo particular rural occupations (e.g., "The Garlic Harvest" in the Iran of the Achaemenids; "The Heaping of the Harvest" in pre-Columbian Peru; "The Sowing of the Rice" in China).

Our consciousness of the influence exercised by the economic factor on the cultural description of time is, moreover, such that we can see it already reflected in the sacral traditions of primitive cultures. In these cultures, myths abound showing that primitive man's anxiety focused not so much on the need of having time as on a concern that the time available be suited ("long enough" or "with daylight enough") for hunting (the Paiute of Nevada; the Caddo of eastern Texas) or for salmon-fishing (the Tlingit of the Northwest Coast).

But whether sacred or profane, time is essentially a reality that is conceived, planned, and activated in service of human beings and therefore must be adapted to their needs. Humans view as habitual and secure the limits represented by the day (among some peoples, only the period of daylight), the month (in some cultures, only the period of the waxing moon), the year (in some societies, only the seasons, which are defined in economic terms), and, sometimes, the century. Beyond these limits, human beings seem to feel displaced, lost, threatened, and crushed by the unnaturally vast dimensions that time appears to take on whenever it is geared no longer to them but to suprahuman beings who live in a "different" time or, more precisely, are thought of as "outside of time." Thus human beings can make nothing of a "day of Brahmā," which in Hinduism is equivalent to an incommensurable *kalpa,* just as they cannot render useful to themselves, except in an ultimately apotropaic way, the vast eras in which, according to certain higher civilizations (Vedic India, the classical world, pre-Columbian America), phases of dissolution usually, and in significant ways, preclude a renewal of cosmic reality or even a termination of human reality. In the final analysis, human beings would even have a struggle appreciating properly the decidedly more restrained yet barely sufficient three millennia that, according to the Zoroastrian religion, the creator Ahura Mazdā needs in order to establish and then annihilate creation, after having imprisoned and destroyed evil within it.

The fact that time should be geared principally to man, tailored to his measure and defined in function of his needs, both existential and cultural, is constantly made clear precisely in those mythical traditions that, from time to time and in one civilization after another, emphasize this point at levels that are diverse but that, in every case, deal with the common necessity of turning absolute time into a human category. To begin with, great importance is attached in myth to the active role played by the human race in the acquisition of time during the period of origins, as compared with the more passive role played by the suprahuman powers. Those who request, take, conquer, or otherwise obtain time may be, according to circumstances, the First Man (natives of Vanuatu; the Sulka of New Britain); the earthly wife of the moon (the Aleut of Alaska); a child (the Micmac of Cape Breton); the carpenter and his sons (the Bambara of the Sudan); the shaman (the Caddo); or mythical kings (Rome and China). Or the social group in its entirety may play this active role by determining to couple peacefully in the dark (the Selk'nam of Tierra del Fuego); by turning in need to Wild Duck against the negative action of Coyote and the ineptitude of Wolf (the Paiute); by paying Bazzagro to keep the sun in the sky, while Coyote appears to play a secondary role in the entire event (the Pomo of California); by crying out their desire for "long days" so that Maikaffo, the master of atmospheric phenomena, cannot but hear and heed (the Hausa of the Sudan); or by claiming and obtaining a certain course of the sun through the sky, while the creator limits himself to granting their desire (the Tsimshian of the Northwest).

In short, individuals or social groups adapt time to their own use, whereas otherwise it would have other proportions, dimensions, and characteristics. There would, for instance, have been as many months of winter as there are hairs in the trickster's fur coat, instead of winters of only seven months (the Assiniboin of Canada); ten cold moons and, for sole nourishment, soup made of refuse, instead of two such moons, with sunflower seeds, roots, and berries to eat (the Atsugewi of California); lunar months of forty days, as Porcupine wanted, instead of months according to rule (the Tsimshian); excessively short days instead of "long days" (the Hausa); periods of either light alone or darkness alone, with either sleeping or fishing excluded, instead of the indispensable alternation of day and night (natives of Mota in Melanesia and the Tlingit).

It is also significant that time is made available in periods that are keyed to specifically human existence. In fact, time alone makes possible the existence of beds and sleep (natives of Mota); fire and the eating of cooked foods (the Sulka of New Britain); the present manner of making love (the Pomo and the Selk'nam); and death (the Luiseño of California and the Bambara). Prior to the acquisition of time, human beings had not yet carved out a special—that is to say, human and cultural—place for themselves that would differentiate them from the suprahuman and subhuman worlds. As long as time did not exist, either absolutely or in its definitive forms and with its definitive characteristics, mythical beings exercised governance (Rome); the gods were not yet born (Egypt); it was possible to marry the moon (the Aleut); men were still like the animals (the Tsimshian); and, finally, it was possible to use the channels of communication between earth and heaven (the Bambara, the Sulka, and natives of Vanuatu).

As for the acquisition or conquest of time as a function of elementary human needs, here, too, there is a widespread and much accentuated mythical motif. Claim was laid to a winter that was not too long and that was mitigated by the summer so that humans might endure the cold (the Assiniboin and the Micmac). There was a desire for daylight in order to obtain food and cook it (the Paiute, Caddo, Tlingit, and Atsugewi), and for the darkness of night in order to safeguard personal privacy (the Selk'nam) and to rest (the Caddo, natives of Mota, and the Sulka). And all manner of efforts were made to divide the year into months in order to have rest from fatigue (the Bambara) and to be able to commemorate the dead (the Luiseño).

Finally, one also finds a marked awareness that the acquisition of this human category of time had immediate and lasting repercussions in relation to the world of nature, which now received its definitive shape. With time, light first appeared (the Tlingit, natives of Vanuatu, Israel), and darkness as well (the Tlingit). With time, the moon rises and begins its successive phases (the Luiseño, Pomo, Aleut, Tlingit, and Bambara), and plants and animals come into existence (the Tlingit and Sulka, natives of Vanuatu, Iran, Israel) and take on their definitive traits (the Paiute, Tsimshian, Tlingit). The gods can now be born and, in turn, generate the world (Egypt), and death comes upon the earth (the Bambara and Luiseño).

Paradoxically, time marks the real beginning of history and opens the way for nature to exist. Nature would otherwise have been different or would not even have existed at all. This enables us to understand how, among the rich and complex systems used for describing time in both primitive cultures and the higher civilizations, those systems that give material embodiment to time by specifically human and cultural means acquire special prominence. One such means in widespread use is the voice. In its most diverse forms, time can be announced in a loud voice to the collectivity by the qualified sacral personnel, or at least by individuals of exalted religious standing. We may think here of the solemn public proclamation of the new moon (on the basis of which the month now beginning acquired its special structure) by a *pontifex minor* (minor pontiff or subpontiff) in Rome; or of Muḥammad's reestablishment in Mecca in 631 of a lunar year uncontaminated by intercalations of any kind. Actions of this type, usually ritualized in various ways according to the particular cultural environment, seem to be found in a significant degree in those cultural traditions in which time has not yet become an integral part of the order of things. Time may make its first appearance as something announced and proclaimed (the Luiseño, Atsugewi, Paiute), but remember also *Genesis* 1:1–5, where God says: "Let there be light!" Or time may be repeated (the Assiniboin and Atsugewi), discussed (the Assiniboin, Paiute, Atsugewi, Nandi of northeastern Africa, and Tsimshian), or even obtained by shouting (the Maidu, Tlingit, and natives of Mota) on the part of suprahuman beings or primitive mankind.

Another system of circumscribing time is that represented by work and, in particular, the manual labor of craftsmen. In archaic societies such work soon acquired a properly creative value in relation to realities that are in themselves abstract and difficult, if not impossible, to regulate, as witnessed by the well-known Roman saying that the individual is the *faber* (creator) of his own destiny. The labor of a handworker and, more specifically, of a weaver, a carpenter, or an engraver—that is, the labor of individuals who are accustomed to using fibers, nails and hammer, or chisel and burin in order to produce something that is new, different, and, above all, irreversible (cloths; various objects; and marble and/or metals that are shaped and moved from one place to another) in relation to the raw material that human labor has now immobilized in a given form and thus rendered usable—is the kind of labor that seems to show through, even if sublimated to a henceforth symbolic level, in conceptions of time as something knotted, nailed, chiseled, or engraved. One can cite the knotted cords used for measuring time among various primitive peoples, as well as the "binding of the sun" into the arc of the seasons or into cycles of many years in pre-Columbian America; or the ritual hammering in of the *clavus annalis* ("nail of the year") at Rome, and the comparable way of marking the passage of the years in Etruria; or various epigraphic calendars.

Given the well-known fact that the specialization of trades appears with the rise of the higher civilizations, conceptions of the kind cited can be found only sporadically in primitive cultures, whereas other cultures give them a privileged place. In the myths of primitive peoples, the kind of toil by which time in its various forms is acquired is far from being the labor of a craftsman; rather, it is related to the habitual activities of the various sectors of these societies. In these stories time is hunted down and captured with bow and arrow (the Caddo); hoisted up by brute strength and ropes (the Aleut and Sudanese); ferried in a canoe (natives of Mota); given new form by means of an obsidian knife (natives of Mota); or even looked upon as something to be traded—for example, "bought" with a basket of pearls or a little necklace or even a pig (the Pomo, Paiute, and natives of Mota, respectively).

A further method of circumscribing or actuating time is even more human and cultural by comparison with the other systems. This is the system that actualizes time, in forms that vary constantly from civilization to civilization, through the more or less massive display of ludic activity. Scholars have long known and studied rituals in both primitive and higher cultures that focus on spectacle. Less well known, on the other hand, is the fact that such rituals (usually celebrated to highlight the salient moments of human, social, and cosmic existence and to create or re-create them from time to time at the sacral level) often specifically signal the passage of time by materially describing, characterizing, influencing, and even "realizing" its several and diverse forms and modalities. Among the Witoto, for example, the ritual game of soccer, in which the ball is identified with the moon, is played in precise relation to the various phases of this heavenly body. In the same context the Shasta of Oregon, try to "strike the moon" by hitting the ball with twelve vertebrae of a salmon, and thus to help the moon increase so that, month by month, it may travel the entire arc of the year; this action, in their view, even accelerates the moon's course in winter. The Pygmies of Africa annually dance around a fire to bring about the succession of the seasons; at the spring feast of Ysiah, the Yakuts of Siberia stage a combat between winter and the salutary season; and the Delaware of Oklahoma assign a clearly solstitial character, value, and purpose to the game of soccer.

Examples of this kind help us to grasp the ultimate function of the countless elements of spectacle (dances and songs, games and contests of every kind, dramatic representations, etc.) that, as is well known, are a constant component of New Year festivals both in the most widely varying primitive cultures and in the archaic higher civilizations. Even in these last, in fact, ludic activity, though tending to become what in the modern world is now simply sport and theatricals, still to a degree seeks to shape the varied and manifold formulations of time by describing its rhythms in the form of spectacles. To multiply examples here would carry us beyond the limits set for this article; we need only think of the Assyrian determination of the years by means of a game of chance, or the Greek custom of dating time in relation to the Olympiads celebrated every fifth year. Reflect, too, on the wealth and complexity of the elements offered by the inevitable projection of motifs of this kind in the mythic traditions of these civilizations. One can cite the Egyptian story told by Plutarch, according to which the five days added annually to the other 360 were made up by the god Thoth out of the fractions of time he had acquired by playing chess with the moon. Thoth's purpose in thus composing these days was to create a specific chronological space that would at last allow the divinities to enter the world, since the sun god Re would not allow them to be conceived and born during the regular year.

Given the limitations of space, I shall restrict myself to a brief consideration of how all this was verified in Roman society, where there were many rituals of a spectacular kind. If we keep in mind that the rotation and revolution of the heavenly bodies, which regulate the course of time, were assimilated in Roman culture to the special movement proper to *ludus* ("play"), we will readily understand the imposition of a complex astronomical symbolism on the space occupied by the circus, where every chariot race was intended to mime the course of the sun through the heavens. We will also see a more specific meaning in the fact that the periodic *ludi* served to mark in a solemn manner the expiration of fixed periods of time. Thus, the *lustrum,* or purificatory sacrifice, defined a regularly recurring cycle of four years; the *ludi saeculares,* or centennial games celebrated the end of a *saeculum;* and the various New Year festivals—the Saturnalia, Feriae Annae Perennae (festival of the goddess of the year), and Palilia (festival of Pales, the tutelary deity of shepherds and cattle)—abounded in spectacle.

When thus reduced to a mere product of a game, time seems to be rendered completely subordinate to a given culture. This does not mean, however, that time is undervalued in the slightest; on the contrary, there is always the greatest esteem for it, independent of cultural contexts and historical situations. The value assigned to time is extremely high in comparison with other categories, as seen in the widespread conviction that time is something "precious" that "must not be lost." This evaluation is independent of oscillations in value when moving from a merely economic level (in myth, time can be "bought," while in the modern world it becomes "money" pure and simple) to a highly ideological level. Thus time is equated with the uniqueness of existence in some myths (the Assiniboin, Luiseño, Bambara) in which the conquest of time has been made possible only by someone's sacrifice, suffering, and death.

[*See also* Sacred Time; History; *and* Calendars.]

BIBLIOGRAPHY

Duval, Paul-Marie. "Observations sur le Calendrier de Coligny." *Études celtiques* 11 (1966–1967): 269–313.

Goudoever, J. M. van. *Fêtes et calendriers bibliques.* Théologie historique, vol. 7. 3d ed. Paris, 1967.

Hallo, William W. "The First Purim." *Biblical Archaeologist* 46 (Winter 1983): 19–26.

Hartner, Willy. "The Young Avestan and Babylonian Calendars and the Antecedents of Precession." *Journal for the History of Astronomy* 10 (1979): 1–22.

Herz, Peter. "Untersuchungen zum Festkalender der römischen Kaiserzeit nach datierten Weih- und Ehreninschriften." Ph.D. diss., University of Mainz, 1975.

Melena, José L. "Reflexiones sobre los Meses del Calendario Micénico de Cnoso y sobra la Fecha de la Caída del Palacio." *Emerita* 42 (1974): 77–102.

Michels, Agnes K. *The Calendar of the Roman Republic.* Princeton, 1967.

Mikalson, Jon D. *The Sacred and Civil Calendar of the Athenian Year.* Princeton, 1975.

Strobel, August. *Ursprung und Geschichte der frühchristlichen Osterkalendars.* Berlin, 1977.

GIULIA PICCALUGA

Translated from Italian by Matthew J. O'Connell

CHRYSOSTOM (c. 354–407), bishop of Constantinople (397–404), father of the Eastern church, biblical commentator, and orator. Born John, the name Chrysostom ("golden mouth") was bestowed in the sixth century. Though probably the most popular of the Eastern church fathers, John Chrysostom is not the most accurately documented, and much remains to be elucidated concerning both his life and the number and authenticity of his works.

John was born at Antioch at an unknown date; 354 is the most likely. The only period of his life for which we have reliable information is that of his tenure as bishop of Constantinople and his trial and exile. The currently accepted version of his story is based on a seventh- or eighth-century biography ascribed to the patriarch George of Alexandria (c. 620–c. 630), which largely draws upon two sources: an apologetic dialogue (c. 408) by Palladius, bishop of Helenopolis in Bithynia and a friend of John, and the church history of Socrates Scholasticus of Constantinople (c. 380–c. 440). According to these sources, John was the son of Secundus, an officer in the Syrian army, and a Greek woman, Theousa, left a widow when John still was a child. The boy was sent to the best schools and was a pupil of the Greek rhetorician and sophist Libanius (314–393). At the age of eighteen he abandoned the pursuit of "vain verbosity" and became a Christian. At this time he was continually in the company of the bishop of Antioch, Meletius (360–381). He was baptized and three years later was advanced to the office of reader. After some time he withdrew from the city to lead an ascetic life, first, for four years, in the company of an old hermit, then, for two years, in solitude. Having ruined his health by immoderate austerities, he returned to Antioch, became a deacon in 381, and in 386 was ordained a priest by Meletius's successor, Flavian I (381–404).

John was a zealous priest and soon achieved a reputation as a pulpit orator. In 397, at the death of Nectarius, bishop of Constantinople, he was forcibly abducted to Constantinople at the emperor's order and elected a bishop. His early popularity as bishop and orator was soon adversely affected by the simplicity of his life, his endeavors to repress abuses in the clergy, his defense of the poor, and his criticisms of injustices and the display of wealth. He finally drew upon himself the hatred of the empress by accusing her openly of avarice and injustice. In 403, John's enemies joined in a mock synod (the Synod of the Oak), presided over by his worst enemy, Theophilus, patriarch of Alexandria, who then initiated a trial against John and declared him deposed. Ordered into exile, he was, however, recalled to Constantinople the following day because of a crisis at the palace, probably a miscarriage by the empress Eudoxia. He is said to have reentered the city immediately and been reconciled with the court. These restored relations were, however, soon impaired once more, after bitter complaints by John that the church offices were being disrupted by public festivities that followed the dedication of a statue of the empress. According to Socrates, the opening words of John's sermon, "Again Herodias raves," were interpreted as an insult to the empress and exploited by his enemies. He was subsequently suspended from his functions and finally banished by order of the emperor. For three years he remained in Cucusus, in Lesser Armenia; then, owing to his continued popularity, chiefly in Constantinople, he was sent to a more remote place near the Black Sea. On the road, he died of exhaustion and maltreatment at Comana on 14 September 407.

Beginning in 404 a bitter conflict arose in Constantinople between John's two successors, Arsacius and Atticus, and his followers, who refused to recognize those who had taken an important part in their bishop's eviction. After the death of Atticus (425) a reconciliation occurred. In 437 Chrysostom's relics were brought back to the capital, and he was venerated as a saint and a martyr.

In recent years, the study of a long unexplored source, the so-called *Life of Chrysostom* (attributed to Martyrius of Antioch), composed by an eyewitness and issued in Constantinople a few weeks after John's death, calls into question the previously unchallenged authority of Palladius and Socrates. Thus the commonly accepted accounts of the Synod of the Oak prove to be unreliable. Many other details of the events of John's life are similarly under reexamination.

John was known chiefly as an orator and composer of homilies, many of which are preserved only in the notes of scribes. Many of his sermons are commentaries on books of the Old and New Testaments: *Genesis*, the *Psalms*, the gospels according to Matthew and John, and the letters of Paul. Other sermons are dogmatical (e.g., baptismal catecheses) or practical and moral (*Against the Circus Games, On Almsgiving*). His eight homilies that bear the common title *Against the Jews* were primarily aimed at Christians who frequented the synagogues or indulged in the superstitious practices in which some Jews seem to have dealt at that time. He wrote occasional orations on liturgical feasts, in praise of saints, and on important political events (*On the Disgrace of Eutropius*). Some speeches relating to his difficulties and banishment, such as the famous sermon against the empress, may have been forged in later years by his enemies or his followers. John also left several treatises, for example, *On the Cohabitation of Clerics and Virgins, On Priesthood, On Vainglory and the*

Education of Children. Dating from the time of his exile are his 236 extant letters, the most important of which are the seventeen addressed to Olympias, a widow, deaconess, and great benefactress of the poor. John's writings have been widely translated.

Though venerated as one of the four fathers of the Eastern church, John was not primarily a theologian. He was a pastor, concerned with the preservation of faith and morals in his flock. His teaching reflects the orthodox doctrine of the church in the period between the crises of Arianism and Nestorianism. He was successful in restoring unity among the divided Christians of Antioch and avoided in his orations and writings any statement that might endanger their mutual understanding. His popularity as a preacher and as a martyr, however, was such that in later times hundreds of works, even those of his opponents and of heretics, were circulated and preserved under his name.

BIBLIOGRAPHY

The most extensive biography of John Chrysostom is Chrysostomus Baur's *Der heilige Johannes Chrysostomus und seine Zeit*, 2 vols. (Munich, 1929–1930), translated as *John Chrysostom and his Time*, 2 vols. (Westminster, Md., 1959–1960). For John Chrysostom as a church father, see volume 3 of Johannes Quasten's *Patrology* (Westminster, Md., 1960), pp. 424–482. An edition of the most ancient source, the text attributed to Martyrius of Antioch, is to be issued in the near future in the series "Subsidia hagiographica" (Brussels). The first detailed studies have been published; see, for example, my "Que vaut le t'émoignage de Pallade sur le procès de saint Jean Chrysostome?," *Analecta Bollandiana* 95 (1977): 389–414.

An exhaustive list of the works of John Chrysostom and their editions can be found in Maurice Geerard's *Clavis Patrum graecorum*, vol. 2 (Turnhout, Belgium, 1974). The first edition of Chrysostom's complete works was made by Henry Savile in 8 volumes (Eton, 1612). The most complete edition was published by Bernard de Montfaucon in 13 volumes (Paris, 1713–1738); it was several times reprinted and finally reproduced in *Patrologia Graeca*, edited by J.-P. Migne, vols. 47–64 (Paris, 1858–1860). In recent times several of his works have been reedited in various collections of patristic literature. For example, *Sources chrétiennes* includes thirteen separate volumes on Chrysostom (Paris, 1947–1983). *Corpus christianorum, series Graeca*, vol. 4 (Turnhout, 1978), reprints a spurious work; four volumes of Chrysostom's works are forthcoming. On spurious works, see J. A. de Aldama's *Repertorium pseudochrysostomicum* (Paris, 1965).

F. van Ommeslaeghe, S.J.

CHUANG-TZU

CHUANG-TZU (369?–286? BCE), the most important exponent of Taoist thought in ancient China. His name was Chuang Chou; *tzu* is a suffix meaning "Master." The brief account of him in chapter 63 of the *Shih chi* or *Records of the Historian* by Ssu-ma Ch'ien (145?–89? BCE) states that he was a native of Meng, served for a time as an official in Ch'i-yüan, and wrote a work in 100,000 words or more that was "mostly in the nature of fable." Scholars disagree as to whether Ch'i-yüan ("lacquer garden") is a place name or simply refers to groves of lacquer trees. The location of Meng is likewise uncertain, though it was probably in present-day Honan.

Early accounts describe Lao-tzu or Lao Tan, the reputed author of the Taoist work known as the *Tao-te ching*, as a contemporary of Confucius, and hence he has traditionally been regarded as the founder of the Taoist school of philosophy and Chuang-tzu's senior. Modern scholarship, however, questions this dating for Lao-tzu, and even his existence as a historical figure, and thus it is impossible at present to say just what relationship exists between Lao-tzu and Chuang-tzu and the texts attributed to them. They may well have been contemporaries who represented two different branches of the Taoist school.

Chuang-tzu's thought, like that of Lao-tzu, is strongly mystical in character. He confronts the same essential problem as that faced by the other early Chinese philosophers: how is one to live in a world beset by disorder, strife, and suffering? But whereas other philosophers customarily proposed some program of political, social, or ethical reform by which such evils might be ameliorated, Chuang-tzu approaches the problem in a radically different fashion. Rather than seeking to remake the world, he would free man from suffering by inducing him to shed the system of values that differentiates pleasure from pain, good from evil, and labels one desirable, the other undesirable. In effect, he would have the individual shuck off all dualistic modes of thinking and learn to achieve a kind of mystical identification with existence as a whole.

This totality of existence, which Chuang-tzu calls the Tao, or the Way, embraces all forms of being, all life, and is in a constant process of change. Once man has learned to accept it as it is and to go along with the process of change without attempting to resist or pass judgment upon it, he can no longer be touched or tormented by conventional ways of thought. He will welcome poverty as he welcomes wealth, rejoice in sickness as he does in health, in death as he does in life, for all are equally part of the eternal Tao.

Chuang-tzu is, of course, fully aware of how difficult it is to pry the mind loose from its habits of dualistic thinking. In his efforts to accomplish this task, he employs all the imagination and literary skill at his command, inventing a wealth of fanciful anecdotes by which to illustrate his ideas. To refute the doctrines of rival thinkers such as the Confucians, for example, he concocts episodes that mischievously satirize their strivings for moral betterment. In other anecdotes he indicates the superiority of his own doctrines by portraying the absolute freedom of the Taoist sage, often in terms of fantastic flights through the air or seemingly miraculous longevity and imperviousness to harm. Such passages were most likely intended to be taken symbolically, but many readers in later ages have interpreted them literally, believing that Chuang-tzu was holding out the possibility of immortality.

In other passages, Chuang-tzu seeks to undermine conventional values by extolling creatures that by ordinary standards are useless, ugly, or deformed, discovering in them qualities of naturalness and spontaneity that the world fails to appreciate. Sometimes he describes the intuitive and unthinking way in which the skilled craftsman or artist pursues his task, employing it as an analogy for the manner in which the Taoist adept moves in instinctive harmony with the Way. In still other passages he parodies the language of philosophical discourse in an effort to destroy the reader's faith in intellection and in the rational nature of language, as in the following well-known passage:

> There is a beginning. There is a not yet beginning to be a beginning. There is a not yet beginning to be a not yet beginning to be a beginning. There is being. There is nonbeing. There is a not yet beginning to be nonbeing. There is a not yet beginning to be a not yet beginning to be nonbeing. Suddenly there is nonbeing. But I do not know, when it comes to nonbeing, which is really being and which is nonbeing. Now I have just said something. But I don't know whether what I have said has really said something or whether it hasn't said something. (Watson, 1968, p. 43)

Needless to say, the person who has attained the level of enlightenment that Chuang-tzu envisions will no longer be able to accept the values of ordinary human society. Its promises of pleasure and material gain will seem empty to him, and he will perceive only the perils that attend one who gains too much worldly prominence. In most cases, therefore, he will in some sense withdraw from society. Sometimes his reclusion will take the form of a retirement to the wilderness, where he will live in amity with the creatures of nature. At other times he will hide in the midst of society, cultivating anonymity and humble station and effacing all outward sign of his superior understanding. In whatever setting, his way of life will embody the Taoist ideal of *wu-wei,* or inaction, by which is meant not a forced quietude, but rather the renunciation of any action that is occasioned by conventional concepts of purpose or achievement, or aimed at the realization of conventional goals.

Such, then, is the vision of spiritual freedom and emancipation from care that Chuang-tzu holds out to the reader. Naturally, it is a vision that can never appeal to more than a small group in society. Indeed, a society made up entirely of Taoists would very quickly degenerate into chaos. But as a kind of antidote to the overwhelmingly political orientation of the other schools of Chinese philosophy and their emphasis upon conformity, the vision of Chuang-tzu and other Taoists has done much to broaden the Chinese character and nourish in it a respect for individualism and the life of the imagination.

The work known as the *Chuang-tzu* consists of thirty-three sections. It seems to have been condensed from a somewhat larger mass of material by Kuo Hsiang (d. 312 CE), a leader of the Neo-Taoist movement, who edited the text and appended a commentary, the oldest now extant. The thirty-three sections are grouped as follows: seven sections called *nei-p'ien* (inner chapters), fifteen sections called *wai-p'ien* (outer chapters), and eleven sections called *tsa-p'ien* (miscellaneous chapters). It is generally agreed that the "inner chapters" are the most brilliant and original in expression and set forth all the important ideas of the work. They are also probably the earliest in date, though so far no method has been found to substantiate this assumption. The remaining chapters, though at times containing passages of almost equal brilliance, are generally less striking in style and content. Some appear to be in the nature of commentaries or explications of the "inner chapters," often wordy and repetitious, while others, such as the last, which contains a survey of the various schools of early Chinese thought, have only a tenuous connection with Chuang-tzu himself. Undoubtedly they are the work of many different hands, and in some cases they may date from as late as the third or fourth century, when Kuo Hsiang edited the text.

As we have seen, Chuang-tzu's thought is highly unconventional in nature, and his method of argumentation is marked by a liberal use of wit, fantasy, and paradox. Sometimes he invents anecdotes featuring historical persons such as Confucius, the logician-philosopher Hui Shih, or the feudal rulers of the period, often attributing to them words and actions that are outrageously at variance with historical fact. At other times he introduces the reader to an antic assortment of gods and mythical heroes, talking birds and beasts, insects and trees, that serve as expositors of his ideas. Seldom does he favor us with a passage of sustained and logical argumentation. Rather, he seems to delight in keeping the reader constantly surprised and off balance, wooing him away from conventional ways of thought by the very strangeness and unpredictability of his discourse.

Because of this disjointed manner of presentation and the combination of whimsy and homey detail that marks the episodes, Chuang-tzu's writings, though of immense literary appeal, are difficult to read, and the difficulties have been greatly compounded by textual corruptions that have crept into the work, presumably as a result of the bafflement of copyists. Countless commentaries have been written in an attempt to elucidate the more obscure passages or suggest possible emendations, though there remain many places where the text is virtually unintelligible.

Despite these difficulties, the *Chuang-tzu* seems never to have lacked for readers. It enjoyed particular popularity at the time of the Neo-Taoist movement in the third and fourth centuries CE, when Confucianism was temporarily in eclipse, and allusions to the text abound in the poetry of the period. When Buddhism began to attract notice in Chinese intellectual circles at about the same time, apparent similarities between Chuang-tzu's thought and that of the Buddhist philosophers were quickly noted, and Taoist terms were frequently borrowed in an attempt to make Buddhism more readily understandable to Chinese minds.

Through the ages, Chuang-tzu's vision of spiritual freedom has done much to shape the Chinese ideal of the carefree recluse who lives in complete harmony with nature, and his descriptions of the process of artistic creation have greatly influenced the development of aesthetic theory. His writings have immeasurably enriched the art and literature of China, and in more recent times, through the medium of translation, have begun to exercise an influence on those of the West as well, an indication that they are coming to be recognized as a classic of world literature. Among the most famous and influential of his anecdotes is the following:

> Once Chuang Chou dreamt he was a butterfly, a butterfly flitting and fluttering around, happy with himself and doing as he pleased. He didn't know he was Chuang Chou. Suddenly he woke up and there he was, solid and unmistakable Chuang Chou. But he didn't know if he was Chuang Chou who had dreamt he was a butterfly, or a butterfly dreaming he was Chuang Chou. (Watson, 1968, p. 49)

[*For further discussion of Chuang-tzu's role in the history of Taoist thought, see* Taoism, *overview article.*]

BIBLIOGRAPHY

Fung Yu-lan. *Chuang Tzu: A New Selected Translation* (1933). 2d ed. New York, 1964. A translation of the "inner chapters," with excerpts from the Kuo Hsiang commentary.

Giles, Herbert A., trans. *Chuang Tzu: Mystic, Moralist, and Social Reformer* (1889). 2d rev. ed. London, 1926. A complete translation into Victorian English.

Graham, A. C. *Chuang-tzu: The Seven Inner Chapters and Other Writings from the Book of Chuang-tzu.* London, 1981. Selected translations by an outstanding Chuang-tzu scholar.

Mair, Victor H., ed. *Experimental Essays on Chuang-tzu.* Honolulu, 1983. Essays by various writers on different aspects of the text.

Waley, Arthur. *Three Ways of Thought in Ancient China* (1939). Garden City, N.Y., 1956. Selected translations from the *Chuang-tzu* with an excellent discussion.

Watson, Burton, trans. *The Complete Works of Chuang Tzu.* New York, 1968. A complete translation into modern colloquial English.

BURTON WATSON

CHU HSI (1130–1200), philosopher, scholar, and formulator of what would for centuries be regarded as mainstream Neo-Confucianism. The son of an official, Chu Hsi passed the highest civil service examination when he was only eighteen. In 1151 he was appointed a district registrar in Fukien Province, where he served until 1158. He did not accept another official post until 1172, when he became prefect of Nan-k'ang in Kiangsi. Except for a month and a half in 1194, when Chu Hsi served at court, his government service was entirely at the local or regional level.

As a local official he built a strong record of conscientious service looking after the economic as well as moral welfare of the people. One notable acccomplishment was the establishment of communal granaries as a measure to combat famine. Less successful was his attempt to conduct a land survey. Most influential in the long run were his activities on behalf of education, especially the rehabilitation of private academies such as the White Deer Grotto Academy in Nan-k'ang. Such academies played a prime role in propagating Neo-Confucianism.

In office or out, Chu Hsi was ever mindful of the plight of the Sung dynasty, which had lost China's northern heartland to the non-Chinese Chin only three years before his own birth. In memorials and personal audiences he urged moral reform of the government beginning with the emperor himself. Both his ideas about moral government and his discussions on specific policy issues, however, had little influence on government. Chu's brief period at court came to an end when a hostile faction came to power. Not content with purging their opponents from government, the men who ousted Chu Hsi went on to denounce him and fifty-eight other philosophers as guilty of "spurious" or "false" learning *(wei-hsüeh)*. Chu Hsi was still in political disgrace at the time of his death.

In his prolific writings and recorded conversations with disciples Chu Hsi ranged over many areas of inquiry encompassing a host of topics and issues. His greatest achievement lay in shaping the varied and diffuse ideas of his eleventh-century predecessors into a coherent, organic philosophy. In the process he not only defined Neo-Confucianism but established the Confucian core curriculum. It was Chu Hsi who joined the *Ta-hsüeh* (Great Learning) and the *Chung-yung* (Doctrine of the Mean), originally two chapters in the *Li chi* (Book of Rites), with the *Lun-yü* (Analects) of Confucius and the *Meng-tzu* to comprise the so-called Four Books, a collection that formed the basis for the education of the Chinese elite until 1905.

Chu Hsi's thought was deeply religious in several senses. On a personal level, his was a creed to guide people's conduct as well as thinking, a quest for wisdom as well as truth, focused on an ideal of self-perfection (sagehood) to be pursued with the most earnest dedication. Part and parcel of this attitude was his reverence for Confucius and other past sages as well as his passionate concern with proper behavior and ritual. Furthermore, his view of the world and man was grounded in a sense of a transcendent reality and a vision of the unity of the cosmos and humanity.

Like Ch'eng I before him, Chu Hsi considered both the physical world of nature and the moral world of human relations as structured by *li* ("principle"), but he went beyond Ch'eng I to identify principle with the "great ultimate" *(t'ai-chi)* discussed by Chou Tun-i (1017–1073) in his *T'ai-chi-t'u shuo* (Explanation of the Diagram of the Great Ultimate). Above and prior to form, the Ultimate is itself without form. It contains all principles even as it is their source. It generates tranquillity and activity, the cosmic forces of *yin* and *yang;* indeed, its activity and tranquillity are *yin* and *yang*. It is transcendent but also immanent, for Chu Hsi stressed the unity of the one and the many. To illustrate this, he used the metaphor of the single moon that shines on and is reflected in rivers and lakes everywhere. Everything has the Great Ultimate within it, yet the Ultimate remains one whole. Chu's contemporary, Lu Chiu-yüan (Lu Hsiang-shan, 1139–1193), objected to Chou Tun-i's formulation, "the Non-Ultimate [*wu-chi*, or Ultimate of Non-being] and yet the Great Ultimate," as constituting the Taoist emphasis on nonbeing. But Chu Hsi insisted on retaining this formula because it makes clear that there is nothing beyond or prior to the Ultimate and that the Ultimate cannot be limited or qualified in any way. As indicated in the diagram, the Non-Ultimate and the Great Ultimate are not two entities. According to Chu Hsi, in some contexts the Great Ultimate need not itself be thought of as an entity at all.

Chu Hsi compared the relationship between The Great Ultimate, which he identified with principle or pattern *(li)*, and the flux of activity and tranquillity, which he identified with material force *(ch'i)*, to that of a man riding a horse, going wherever the horse goes in an inseparable union. In a crucial disagreement with Buddhists, Chu Hsi emphasized that principle is not something empty and detached, insisting instead that principle and concrete things never exist in isolation from one another. Without the material force *(ch'i)*, principle *(li)* would have nothing to attach itself to. Accordingly, *ch'i* plays an important role in Chu Hsi's thought, so much so that an extensive literature has debated whether his thought may be more properly characterized as monism or dualism. Perhaps one may say that he was capable of adopting both perspectives, but that in ultimate metaphysical terms he saw reality as one.

Human beings are, of course, very much part of this reality. Like all Neo-Confucians, Chu Hsi accepted Meng-tzu's teaching that human nature is fundamentally good and that it contains within it the "beginnings" of the virtues. He equates this nature with principle: it belongs to the individual but is also shared with the world. While nature is good in its original quiescent state, once aroused to activity, goodness consists in following it, while evil results from going against it. What makes evil possible is that in man, as in the cosmos, principle needs to attach itself to material force in order to become actualized. Just as water may be clear or turbid, the physical nature people receive at birth may be pure or gross in varying degree. The more turbid the physical nature, the more seriously will principle be obstructed, but human beings, unlike animals, are able to penetrate their turbidity to recover the underlying principles.

Essential to Chu Hsi's view of man and the process of self-perfection is the activity of the "mind-and-heart" (*hsin*, hereafter "mind"). Drawing on Chang Tsai, Chu Hsi held that the mind unites and controls the nature and the feelings. Thus, unlike Lu Chiu-yüan and the "school of Mind" (Hsin-hsüeh), Chu Hsi does not identify the mind with principle. For him, principles are contained in the mind, which, however, is constituted of highly rarefied *ch'i*. While the nature, identified with substance *(t'i)*, is good, the feelings, identified as function *(yung)*, need to be maintained in proper balance. Some, such as the feeling of commiseration, are good, but there is always the danger posed by selfish desires. As a result, the human mind *(jen-hsin)* is in a precarious state, ever subject to errors that prevent it from returning to the original "mind of the Way" (*tao-hsin,* moral mind). The nature, as principle in general, is inert. Consequently, Chu Hsi places special emphasis on the mind as the active master whose role it is to engage in the strenuous effort to discriminate between moral error and the correct way and then to maintain constant correctness. Self-cultivation requires utmost exertion and commitment.

In his methodology of self-development Chu Hsi emphasized intellectual learning, but, in keeping with the general inclusive and synthetic cast of his mind, he by no means rejected meditation, or "quiet sitting" *(ching-tso),* as the Neo-Confucians called it. He once even advised a student to spend half his day in quiet sitting and the other half in reading. As a young man Chu Hsi was greatly influenced by the concept of quietism, but changed his views under the influence of his friend Chang Shih (1133–1180) and the ideas of the philosopher Hu Hung (1106–1162). It was not until 1169 that he worked out a doctrine of self-cultivation that involved watchfulness over one's emotions and feelings both before and after they have been aroused. Central to this doctrine was the cultivation and practice of "seriousness" (*ching,* also rendered as "reverence, mindfulness"). The *locus classicus* for the concept of seriousness, so prominent in the thought of Ch'eng I as well as Chu Hsi, is a passage in the *I ching* (Book of Changes) that couples "seriousness to straighten the internal life" with "righteousness to square the external life."

Chu Hsi is especially noted for stressing "the investigation of things" (*ko-wu,* a term from *The Great Learning*), by which he meant the investigation of the principles of all things and events. It was on this issue that he had his famous debate with Lu Chiu-yüan in 1175 at the Goose Lake Temple in Kiangsi. In contrast to Lu, whose philosophy of inwardness de-emphasized external learning or book knowledge, Chu Hsi maintained that principle was to be investigated in the external world as well as within one's self. According to Chu, the extension of knowledge (*chih-chih,* another term from *The Great Learning*) is a gradual process of investigating the principles of one thing after another until a great breakthrough takes place and the perfection of knowledge is attained. Like other Confucians, he taught that such knowledge must necessarily be manifested in action, but unlike the Ming dynasty philosopher Wang Yang-ming (1472–1529), Chu Hsi taught that knowledge must precede action.

The prime virtue, the source of all other virtues and thus the object of all endeavor is "humaneness" (*jen,* also rendered as "humanity, benevolence"). In keeping with the centrality of this concept in Confucian thought, Chu Hsi gave much attention to working out his own theory of humaneness. Rejecting an interpretation given by one of Ch'eng I's disciples, who defined it as consciousness, as well as that of another disciple, who equated it to unity with all things, Chu Hsi characterized *jen* as the principle of love and the very character of the mind. Vital and creative, *jen* is the spirit of life found in the mind of Heaven and earth. Thus, through humaneness people partake of the creative process of the universe.

This creative process is natural and unending. Because the universe constantly rotates, the heaviest material force concentrates at the center to form the earth while the most rarefied *ch'i* is farthest out, forming the sky, sun, moon, and celestial bodies. When Chu Hsi discussed the "mind of heaven and earth," the word translated as "heaven" is *t'ien,* which, depending on the context, can also be rendered as "sky" or "nature." Asked about its meaning in the classics, Chu Hsi replied that in some cases it meant "the lord" and in some "principle." The question of whether Chu Hsi was a deist was much debated among Jesuit and other Western scholars of Chinese philosophy and forms an important chapter in the history of Western sinology rather than in that of Neo-Confucianism in China or East Asia.

In both his official capacity and in his personal life Chu Hsi participated whole-heartedly in religious ceremonies, including, for instance, prayers for rain in times of drought, sacrifices to former sages, and ancestor worship. As a man of his time, he believed in the existence of ghosts but sought to explain natural phenomena in terms of *li.* He strongly rejected both the Buddhist idea of reincarnation and Taoist beliefs in longevity. Living in disgrace in his old age, he wrote a memorial condemning the men in power, much to the alarm of his disciples, who were concerned for his safety. Finally, they persuaded him to let divination decide whether to risk sending the memorial. Chu Hsi accepted the negative verdict of the milfoil. It was a dramatic and poignant expression of his conviction of the unity of the universe and man.

A brief summary of as subtle and prolific a thinker as Chu Hsi inevitably runs into the danger of oversimplification. It also tends to disguise the extent to which the modern scholar is engaged in a task of interpretation and reconstruction, for Chu Hsi, like other Chinese thinkers, did not set forth his ideas in a systematic *magnum opus.* Although there are some essays on specific subjects, for the most part he developed his ideas in commentaries on the classics, letters to friends, prefaces and the like, as well as in conversations recorded by disciples. His works are a rich source for modern students of many aspects of twelfth-century China and continue to provide scholars within the tradition with numerous issues for cogitation and debate. Recent years have seen major advances in the study of Chu Hsi, but the work continues.

[*See also* Confucian Thought, *article on* Neo-Confucianism; Li; Jen; Ch'i; T'ai-chi; Hsin; *and* T'ien. *Chu Hsi's canonization of the Four Books is discussed in* Chinese Religion, *article on* Religious and Philosophical Texts. *See also the biographies of Meng-tzu, Chou Tun-i, Chang Tsai, Ch'eng I, and Lu Hsiang-shan.*]

BIBLIOGRAPHY

Wing-tsit Chan's "The Study of Chu Hsi in the West," *Journal of Asian Studies* 35 (August 1976): 555–577, is a comprehensive survey and a most useful guide. Professor Chan has included translations from Chu Hsi in his *A Source Book in Chinese Philosophy* (Princeton, 1963) and translated Chu Hsi and Lü Tzu-chi'en's anthology of Northern Sung Neo-Confucianism, the *Chin-ssu lu*, under the title *Reflections on Things at Hand* (New York, 1967). Studies published since the appearance of Professor Chan's article include *Journal of Chinese Philosophy* 5.2 (June 1978), a special issue on Chu Hsi; Hoyt C. Tillman's *Utilitarian Confucianism: Ch'en Liang's Challenge to Chu Hsi* (Cambridge, Mass., 1982); Daniel K. Gardner's *Chu Hsi and the Ta-hsüeh* (Cambridge, Mass., 1986); and *Chu Hsi and Neo-Confucianism*, edited by Wing-tsit Chan (Honolulu, 1986).

Ch'ien Mu's *Chu-tzu hsin hsüeh an* (Taipei, 1971) is an authorative study by an outstanding contemporary scholar. Wing-tsit Chan's *Chu hsüeh lun-chi* (Taipei, 1982) includes an essay on Chu Hsi's religious practice. The best study to appear recently in the Peoples' Republic is Chang Li-wen's *Chu Hsi ssu-hsiang yen-chiu* (Peking, 1981). Japanese scholars have made major contributions to the study of Chu Hsi. The most extensive modern translation of Chu Hsi and others associated with him is the projected fifteen-volume *Shushigaku taikei* (Tokyo, 1974–), of which all but the last volume have been published. For a good introduction to Chu Hsi, see Miura Kunio's *Shushi* (Tokyo, 1979).

CONRAD SCHIROKAUER

CHU-HUNG (1535–1615), also known as Master Yün-ch'i; an important Buddhist leader in the late Ming dynasty (1368–1644). A reformer of monastic Buddhism, a synthesizer of various Buddhist traditions, and a successful promoter of lay Buddhism, Chu-hung was also regarded posthumously as the eighth Pure Land patriarch. However, his influence has never been confined within any sectarian boundary. He has, in fact, been credited with the renewal of Buddhism in Ming China.

Chu-hung was a native of Hangchow. He became a student in the local school at the age of sixteen and quickly achieved a reputation for his knowledge of Confucianism and Taoism. He sat for the higher civil examinations several times but was without success. His interest in Pure Land Buddhism dates from the time when he daily witnessed an old woman calling the name of the Buddha Amitābha (Chin., O-mi-t'o-fo). Thereafter, he kept a vegetarian diet, studied Buddhist scriptures, and practiced *nien-fo* (recitation of Amitābha's name). When Chu-hung was twenty-seven his father died. Shortly afterward his wife and only son also passed away. He then remarried a pious Buddhist laywoman and resolved that if he failed to pass the provincial examinations by the age of thirty and the metropolitan examinations by the age of forty, he would become a monk. Three years later his mother died. When success in the examinations still eluded him he bade farewell to his wife (who later became a nun) and in 1566 entered the monastic order.

After he became a monk, Chu-hung followed the mendicant tradition, spending the next six years traveling throughout the country seeking instruction from prominent teachers. He achieved his first enlightenment on his way to Tung-ch'ang in Shantung. He also took part in five sessions of Ch'an meditation held in different monasteries in the Chekiang area. In 1571 he returned to Mount Yün-ch'i in his native Hangchow. It is said that through the performance of Tantric rituals and the invocation of the Buddha's name, Chu-hung cleared the region of tigers that had been harming men and beasts, and brought rain during a severe drought. In gratitude, villagers rebuilt an abandoned old temple, which he named Yün-ch'i Monastery upon its completion in 1577. Chu-hung stayed there until his death in 1615, making it a model of monastic discipline and a center for the joint practice of Pure Land and Ch'an, a syncretic tradition that was initiated by the Ch'an master Yen-shou (904–975) and that reached its culmination with Chu-hung.

The joint practice of Ch'an and Pure Land rested on the assertion that the two paths were essentially the same insofar as both led to the same goal: the stopping of wrong thoughts and the end of the cycle of *saṃsāra* (Chin., *sheng-ssu*). Chu-hung wrote a four-volume commentary on the smaller *Sukhāvatīvyūha Sūtra* (Chin., *O-mi-t'o-fo ching*) in which he provided a creative interpretation of "one mind" *(i-hsin)*. Using the Hua-yen categories of particularity *(shih)* and universality *(li)*, Chu-hung divided the attainment of *nien-fo* into the "one mind of particularity" and the "one mind of universality." The former is achieved through concentration, which suppresses ignorance, while the latter is achieved through insight, which destroys ignorance. By the "uninterrupted experience and embodiment" of the Buddha's name, he believed, one could attain insight into the true nature of things, the object of Ch'an meditation.

The link between Ch'an meditation and *nien-fo* practice was precisely this one mind. Chu-hung firmly believed that this one mind was nothing other than that to which Bodhidharma was "directly pointing."

Chu-hung was an energetic evangelist of vegetarianism and kindness to animals. Under his advocacy, the practice of "release of life" *(fang-sheng)*, that is, buying fish and other creatures from marketplaces and setting them free, became very popular among lay Buddhists. He wrote the *Tzu-chih lu* (Record of Self-knowledge), which was modeled on the ledgers of merit and demerit long favored by Taoists, to inculcate Buddhist values among the general populace.

Chu-hung was interested in harmonizing Buddhism with Confucianism. He was less impressed by Taoism and clearly hostile toward Catholicism, as can be seen from the four rebuttals supposedly addressed to Matteo Ricci and contained in Chu-hung's collected works, *Yün-ch'i fa-hui*.

[*See also* Ching-t'u.]

BIBLIOGRAPHY

Chu-hung. *Yün-ch'i fa-hui*. 34 vols. Nanking, 1897. The collected works of Chu-hung.

Hurvitz, Leon. "Chu-hung's One Mind of Pure Land and Ch'an Buddhism." In *Self and Society in Ming Thought*, edited by Wm. Theodore de Bary, pp. 451–476. New York, 1970.

Yü, Chun-fang. *The Renewal of Buddhism in China: Chu-hung and the Late Ming Synthesis*. New York, 1981.

CHUN-FANG YÜ

CHURCH. [*This entry includes three articles describing the organization, governance, and theology of Christian churches as well as notions of membership in the Christian communion:*

Church Polity
Ecclesiology
Church Membership

For further discussion of Christian religion, see Christianity, *overview article;* Eastern Christianity; Roman Catholicism; *and* Protestanism. *Particular communions of Christians are the subject of separate entries.*]

Church Polity

The governance of the Christian churches has assumed a variety of forms based on historical factors as well as on theological positions regarding the origin or root of ministerial functions. In a descending degree of local autonomy these forms are broadly classified as congregational, presbyteral, or episcopal, but within each category significant modifications exist. After a historical survey of church governance from its beginnings through the Middle Ages, the organization of the major denominations will be considered individually.

One cannot speak with precision or certitude about ministry in the early church because it is difficult to date and evaluate the documentary evidence, including the New Testament writings, and because of differences of organization in the primitive local communities. At the conclusion of an eighty-year evolutionary process there emerged, apparently first at Antioch around AD 110, a threefold hierarchical leadership that gradually became normative throughout the Christian world. The hierarchy ("sacred rule") consisted of three grades: a single bishop charged with the "supervision or oversight" *(episcopē)* of the community; a group of consultors called presbyters ("elders"); and a subordinate group of deacons, who assisted in the administration of property. Certain functions, such as presiding at the Eucharist, were ordinarily reserved to the bishop. The distinction was thus made between the people and their leaders, soon called "clergy," who were ordained, that is, set apart for the ministry by the imposition of the bishop's hands. The local church presided over by the bishop was in time known as a "diocese" or "eparchy."

Church organization gradually accommodated itself to the political divisions of the Roman empire. The local churches in a Roman province constituted an ecclesiastical province under the presidency of an archbishop or metropolitan who was the bishop of the capital city of the province. By the fourth century the beginnings of a patriarchal system could be detected in the large regional groupings of provinces. Eventually all the dioceses and provinces of the empire were subject to one of five patriarchs ("father-ruler"), namely, the bishops of Rome, Antioch, Alexandria, Jerusalem, and Constantinople. The prominence of these bishoprics may be accounted for on grounds partly theological and partly political.

Among the five patriarchs, the bishop of Rome was accorded a certain primacy that was not clearly defined. The support of the Roman bishop or pope ("father") was particularly crucial in the fifth-century doctrinal disputes over the relation of the divine and human nature of Christ. These controversies were settled at ecumenical ("worldwide") councils or synods of bishops held in Asia Minor. The conciliar condemnation of the Monophysites and Nestorians greatly weakened the patriarchates of Antioch and Alexandria, in which they were largely concentrated. Constantinople emerged from these crises as the bastion of orthodoxy. After the Muslim conquests of the seventh century, only

Rome and Constantinople survived as major churches. The growing estrangement of Eastern and Western Christianity became complete with the sack of Constantinople by the Crusaders in 1204.

In the West the position of the bishop of Rome, the only see (bishopric) to claim apostolic foundation, remained unchallenged for over thirteen hundred years. From the period of the Gregorian Reform (c. 1050), it embarked on a program of centralization, making effective use of councils, papal legates, and revivified canon law. In the wake of the Great Western Schism (1378–1417), during which there were three simultaneous claimants to the papacy, attempts were made to declare the ecumenical council the supreme authority in the church to which even the pope owed obedience. The failure to deal with abuses led in the sixteenth century to the Reformation and the establishment of a number of separate churches with divergent patterns of government. [*See* Papacy; Schism, *article on* Christian Schism; Reformation; *and* Denominationalism.]

Episcopal Form of Government. The Roman Catholic, Orthodox, and Anglican churches, which considered the historical continuity of ministry from the beginning of Christianity to have the highest priority, retained the episcopacy as the key office in the church. The bishops were viewed as the successors of the twelve apostles. [*See* Apostles.] Each of these communions, however, has structured its episcopal commitment in a different way.

Roman Catholic. Echoing the Second Vatican Council, the *Code of Canon Law* promulgated by John Paul II in 1983 affirms: "Just as, in accordance with the Lord's decree, Saint Peter and the other apostles constitute one college, in like fashion the Roman Pontiff, Peter's successor, and the bishops, the successors of the apostles, are united with each other" (canon 330). The special responsibility of Peter continues in the bishop of Rome, the pope, who is head of the college of bishops, the vicar of Christ, and the shepherd of the universal church here on earth. He obtains full and supreme power in the church once he has accepted legitimate election by the cardinals. The college of bishops, whose head is the pope and whose members are sacramentally ordained bishops and officially recognized (i.e., in hierarchical communion), also possesses full and supreme power. The college exercises its power over the universal church in a solemn manner through an ecumenical council that can be convoked only by the pope.

The Second Vatican Council introduced a new structure known as the Synod of Bishops. Since 1965, this representative body of about two hundred bishops chosen from different regions of the world has met, usually every three years, to aid the pope in promoting faith and morals, in strengthening ecclesiastical discipline, and in directing the church's worldwide activity.

The cardinals of the Roman church, who are appointed for life by a reigning pope, constitute a special college whose chief function is to elect the bishop of Rome. In recent years all areas of the world have been represented in the college of cardinals. The number is not fixed, but since Vatican II it has hovered at about 120. The cardinals also act as a body of advisers when summoned to deal with questions of major importance, and they head some of the offices of the Curia Romana.

The pope usually conducts the business of the universal church through the Curia, which acts in his name and by his authority. The Curia consists of the Secretariat of State (which also performs a coordinating function), the Council for Public Affairs, nine congregations (including the Doctrine of the Faith; Sacraments and Divine Worship; the Causes of Saints; and the Evangelization of People), three tribunals, the secretariats (for Promoting Christian Unity, for Non-Christians, and for Nonbelievers), and more than thirty additional offices, including the Pontifical Council for the Laity, the Pontifical Commission for Justice and Peace, the Commission for Latin America, the Pontifical Council of the Family, and the Biblical Commission.

Furthermore, the papacy maintains a corps of representatives throughout the world. When these legates are only to the local churches, they are known as apostolic delegates. If they are accredited to states and governments, they are ranked nuncio, pro-nuncio, or internuncio. (Reciprocally, more than one hundred governments maintain diplomatic relations with the Vatican.) In addition to serving a liaison function, the papal legates, in cooperation with the bishops, clergy, and laity of the country, transmit to Rome lists of potential candidates for the episcopacy.

The Roman Catholic church, over which the pope presides, is made up of particular churches, certain portions of the people of God "in which and from which the one and unique Catholic church exists" (canon 368). A particular church is above all a diocese that is entrusted to a bishop assisted by a presbyterate. As a general rule, a diocese is circumscribed by territorial bounds so as to embrace all the faithful within that area.

It is the prerogative of the pope to appoint bishops to take charge of particular churches or to confirm those who have been legitimately elected. (In a few European dioceses and in the Eastern Uniate churches the right to elect a bishop is recognized.) At least every three years the bishops of an ecclesiastical province are to draw up a list of priests suitable for the episcopacy that is then sent to Rome. A diocesan bishop governs the particular church committed to his care with legislative, executive, and judicial power according to the norms of the law. He exercises legislative power personally, executive power either personally or through vicars, and judicial power either personally or through a judicial vicar. He is aided in his government by the presbyteral council (a body of priests) and by his staff, including vicars, a chancellor, a finance council, a promoter of justice, a defender of the bond (for suits alleging the nullity of marriage or of holy orders). Every five years the bishop is to send to Rome a report on the state of the diocese. Upon reaching the age of seventy-five, he is asked to submit his resignation to the pope.

Every diocese is divided into parishes, which are established by the bishop after consulting the presbyteral council. Parishes are usually territorial, but they may also be determined on a personal basis, for example, all those of Korean nationality or all those belonging to a university community. The parish is to be entrusted to a pastor appointed by the bishop who is considered an extension of the bishop bringing spiritual care to his people. Every parish must have a financial council in which the laity participates. In many dioceses a pastoral council (with only consultative voice) is organized. If the number of parishioners requires it, the bishop may appoint additional priests as parish assistants or curates. Parishes may also be entrusted to religious communities such as the Dominicans or Franciscans.

While the diocese is the basic administrative unit in the Roman Catholic church, there is some provision for supradiocesan structures. These include provinces, a grouping of neighboring dioceses presided over by the metropolitan or archbishop, and the episcopal conference, which includes all the bishops of a given nation or territory. While an archbishop has only a general supervisory role, a conference may make deliberative and binding decisions in particular matters, while in others the diocesan bishop has freedom regarding implementation.

Of the approximately 784 million Catholics in the world, about 12 million belong to the Eastern churches. Except for the Maronites, these churches represent various groups that have reunited with Rome after the sixteenth century. Almost all of them have larger counterparts that are Eastern Orthodox or non-Chalcedonian Orthodox. The Eastern churches, Catholic as well as non-Catholic, follow different "rites," which entail a special liturgy, law, and spiritual tradition. Thus in addition to the Latin rite, to which the vast majority of Catholics belong, there are also seventeen Eastern rites. These rites, with considerable autonomy, especially in the choice of bishops, are headed for the most part by the patriarchs who acknowledge the primacy of the pope. [*See* Uniate Churches.]

Orthodox and other Eastern churches. The Eastern Orthodox and other Eastern churches are firmly committed to apostolic succession and the episcopacy. The Eastern Orthodox churches accept the first seven ecumenical councils (through the Second Council of Nicaea in 787), as do Roman Catholics. The smaller Eastern churches, refusing to recognize the third (Ephesus, 432) and fourth (Chalcedon, 451) ecumenical councils, are divided into two Nestorian churches and four others known collectively as non-Chalcedonian Orthodox. [*See* Nestorian Church; Armenian Church; Coptic Church; Ethiopian Church; *and* Syrian Orthodox Church of Antioch.]

The Eastern Orthodox church is not centrally organized but is a federation composed of fourteen autocephalous, or self-governing, churches and seven others, which are known as autonomous. "Autocephaly" connotes the right possessed by a group of eparchies (dioceses) to settle all internal matters on their own authority and to elect their own bishops, including the head of the church. The boundaries of autocephalies are usually coterminous with those of a state or nation. Four of these autocephalies (Constantinople, Alexandria, Antioch, and Jerusalem) are based upon ancient Christian tradition, as has already been noted. The remaining ten have resulted from modern political developments: Russia, Romania, Serbia, Greece, Bulgaria, Georgia, Cyprus, Czechoslovakia, Poland, and Albania. The autonomous churches, while to a large degree self-governing, have not yet achieved full independence: Finland, China, Japan, Macedonia, and three jurisdictions among Russians outside the Soviet Union. (The head of the monastery of Saint Catherine has the rank of archbishop of Sinai; his jurisdiction over the immediate neighborhood constitutes an autonomous church.) [*See also* Eastern Christianity.]

From antiquity the heads of the churches of Constantinople, Alexandria, and Antioch have been known as patriarchs. That title is also accorded the heads of the Russian, Romanian, Serbian, and Bulgarian churches. The head of the Georgian church is known as catholicos-patriarch; the heads of the others are metropolitans or archbishops. Ecclesiastical provinces in Western Europe, North and South America, and Australia depend upon one of the autocephalous churches or one of the emigrant Russian jurisdictions. There is no bishop among the Orthodox churches who holds a position analogous to that of the pope in the Roman church, but the patriarch of Constantinople is recognized as the ecumenical or universal patriarch. He holds a place of honor and precedence, and his authority over the Orthodox world is a moral one, the first among equals. Supreme authority belongs only to a pan-Orthodox council.

The Greek Orthodox Church in North and South America, the largest body of Orthodox in the Western Hemisphere, with two million communicants, enacted a new constitution, which was ratified by the ecumenical patriarch in 1978. The church consists of the Archdiocese of New York, nine dioceses in the United States, and one each in Canada and South America. The archbishop, who resides in New York, is the primate, the highest authority of the church in the Americas; he is the exarch (viceroy) of the ecumenical patriarchate. The archbishop presides over a Holy Synod of bishops, which makes decisions and regulates ecclesiastical life in accord with the canons or laws of the church. The new constitution frees the archbishop from many of the administrative duties with which he was previously occupied. Instead of being titular or auxiliary bishops, the bishops now have effective power to rule in their respective dioceses. With the archbishop, they have full responsibility for promoting the unity and activity of the entire archdiocese. A clergy-laity conference is held every two years to deal with administrative affairs of the church, but not with questions of faith and doctrine. The archbishop, assisted by an auxiliary bishop, governs directly the parishes of New York State. [*See* Greek Orthodox Church.]

The second largest Orthodox body in the New World is the Orthodox Church in America, with approximately one million members. It received independent status from the Patriarchate of Moscow in 1970 against the will of the ecumenical patriarch, who refused to recognize its autocephaly. It too adopted a new statute, in 1971. The supreme "canonical authority" is the Holy Synod, which includes as voting members all the diocesan bishops under the presidency of the metropolitan (Article 2, *The Statute of the Orthodox Church in America*, Official Text 1974). It meets twice annually and is competent to treat "all matters involving doctrine, canonical order, morals and liturgical practice." The synod regulates the election of bishops and the establishment of new dioceses. [*See* Russian Orthodox Church.]

The All-American Council is "the highest legislative and administrative authority within the Church." It is composed of the metropolitan and all bishops (who must approve all resolutions by a majority), the priests of each parish, and an equal number of lay delegates; priests not having parishes; two delegates from each seminary; and one representative from each organization officially accredited by the Holy Synod. It convenes every two years. The metropolitan is elected by the All-American Council with the approval of the Holy Synod. He is assisted by the Metropolitan Council, the permanent executive body of the church. He is the bishop of one of the dioceses.

The diocese, the basic church body, comprising all the parishes of a determined geographical area, is governed by a diocesan bishop with the advice of an assembly and council. The Diocesan Assembly nominates a candidate for an episcopal vacancy. If the candidate is unacceptable to the Holy Synod, it elects its own candidate. The Diocesan Assembly is made up of all the clergy and an equal number of elected lay delegates. For validity, all resolutions of the assembly must be approved by the diocesan bishop. The Diocesan Council, the permanent body of diocesan administration, meets at least twice a year. Its decisions become effective upon approval by the diocesan bishop. The bishop is "the head of all parishes which constitute his diocese" and appoints the parish clergy. The rector, the head of a parish, is assisted by a parish council elected by a meeting of all the parishioners.

Besides the two main bodies of the Orthodox church, there are a number of smaller national and language jurisdictions, such as an archdiocese dependent upon the Arab-speaking patriarchate of Antioch, and dioceses under the patriarchates of Serbia, Romania, Bulgaria, and Albania. There is also a Standing Conference of Canonical Orthodox Bishops, which seeks to coordinate the activities of the various jurisdictions throughout the Americas.

Anglican and Episcopalian churches. The episcopal constitution of the church and apostolic succession are also fundamental to the Anglican communion, which is made up of about twenty-five autonomous and six nonautonomous churches found mainly in English-speaking countries and former colonies of England. The communion has been described as a federation without a federal government. Usually every ten years, an assemblage of archbishops and bishops of the entire communion, called the Lambeth Conference, convenes in the Lambeth Palace, London, under the presidency of the archbishop of Canterbury. The conference, which does not publish details of its debates, issues resolutions with only moral binding force. At the 1968 conference a body representing the laity and the clergy as well as the bishops was formed. The Anglican Consultative Council, headquartered in London, meets biennially with about fifty delegates.

The parent body, the Church of England, is an established church with the sovereign of the country as its head. Acting upon the advice of the prime minister, the sovereign nominates the archbishops and bishops. In the 1970s, however, procedures that give more weight in the selective process to ecclesiastical authorities have been followed. The church is divided into the province of Canterbury, whose archbishop is styled "Primate of All England and Metropolitan," and the province of York, whose archbishop is called "Primate of England and Metropolitan." The archbishop oversees all the dioceses within the province, confirms the election of every bishop and is his chief consecrator, and hears appeals in his provincial court. The archbishop of Canterbury, with the approval of the crown, may grant licenses and dispensations that are valid throughout the province of York as well. The jurisdiction of the bishop in his diocese is similar to that of a Roman Catholic bishop. He can promulgate binding rules of discipline, but in the matter of parochial appointments he is limited by extensive rights of patronage held by laity and certain corporate bodies. At the parish level, church councils elected by the lay members cooperate with the incumbent in developing church activities.

Each province, not more than three times a year, holds a convocation that, subject to the supreme authority of Parliament, determines policy with regard to doctrine and practice. The convocation, under the presidency of the archbishop of Canterbury, has an upper house of bishops and a lower house made up of senior archdeacons, representatives from each cathedral chapter, and elected representatives from the clergy. Both provinces together form the General Synod or Church Assembly, composed of a third house of laity in addition to the house of bishops and the house of clergy. The Assembly deals with legal and administrative matters but not with doctrine.

In the United States the church affiliated with the Anglican communion is the Protestant Episcopal church. It is governed by a bicameral General Convention meeting triennially or at special call. The House of Bishops consists of all bishops; with the approval of the other house, it elects one of its members as presiding bishop, an office held until retirement. The presiding bishop is entrusted with general executive power over the whole Episcopal church. The House of Deputies comprises not more than four priests and four laypeople elected from each diocese. All legislation must be passed by both houses (Article 1, *Constitution and Canons for the Government of the Protestant Episcopal Church in the United States of America,* 1964). Between sessions of the General Convention the church is governed by the presiding bishop in consultation with the Executive Council, whose members are elected by the General Convention and the Provincial Synods. The council is organized into a number of departments, with staff to coordinate activities at home and abroad.

To establish a diocese there must be at least six parishes and six voting presbyters. The diocese meets in convention annually with all diocesan clergy and representatives from each parish as members. The convention elects clerical and lay delegates to the provincial synod and to the General Convention. Each diocesan convention also elects a standing committee to advise the bishop between sessions. The convention lays down rules and procedures for filling an episcopal vacancy. The person chosen must be confirmed by a majority of the standing committees of all the dioceses as well as of the diocesan bishops in the United States. A bishop must retire at the age of seventy-two.

The diocesan convention is responsible for defining the boundaries of parishes and for establishing new ones. Each parish is governed by a vestry and wardens selected according to diocesan law. The number and qualifications vary from one diocese to another. Similarly, there is no canon specifying their specific duties, term of office, or voting rights. The vestry members are the "agents and legal representatives of the parish." The vestry elects the pastor or rector and notifies the bishop of its choice. Though the bishop may try to dissuade the vestry, he has little option but to accept their choice. The appointment is considered to be for life; the rector cannot be removed against his will except with the consent of the bishop.

Methodist churches. The vast majority of the Methodists in the United States recognize the centrality of the episcopacy in their governing structure, although they do not accept it as an order different from the presbyterate. (Churches deriving from British Methodism do not have bishops.) Apostolic succession in the sense of historic continuity in the ministry is not viewed as necessary. The ordained ministry consists of elders (presbyters) and deacons who are "set apart by the Church for the specialized ministry of Word, Sacrament, and Order" (par. 302, *The Book of Discipline of the United Methodist Church,* 1972). "To be ordained to the ministry of Order is to be authorized to equip the laity for ministry, to exercise pastoral oversight, and to administer the Discipline of the Church" (par. 309.1).

The Annual Conference, "the basic body of the Church," corresponds to a diocese in the Episcopal and Roman Catholic churches. It consists of all the presbyters in a given geographical area plus an equal number of elected lay representatives. A bishop presides over the conference. He is responsible for appointing ministers to parishes after consultation with the district superintendents as well as with representatives of the local congregations. The appointments do not convey tenure but must be renewed annually. Each parish or local congregation has a Charge Conference, which is the "connecting link" with the general church; the Charge Conference elects lay members of the Annual Conference and all local officers.

The Annual Conferences are grouped into Jurisdictional Conferences made up of an equal number of lay and clerical delegates. In the United States there are five regional jurisdictions, which normally meet once every four years. Their chief responsibility is to fill vacancies in the ranks of the bishops, to determine the boundaries of the Annual Conferences, and to provide for the work of the church within the jurisdiction.

The highest legislative authority in the United Methodist church is the General Conference, composed of from six hundred to one thousand delegates, ministers, and lay, chosen by the Annual Conferences based on size of membership. The General Conference also meets quadrennially before the Jurisdictional Conferences. It defines and fixes the powers and duties of all ministers, bishops, and subordinate conferences. It regulates the boundaries of jurisdictional conferences "upon the consent of the Annual Conferences involved." The General Conference initiates and directs all connectional enterprises of the church and provides boards for their implementation.

Presbyteral Form of Government. Presbyterians do not admit as normative a historically validated episcopal succession. They hold that there is no New Testament warrant for a distinct office of bishop; "presbyters" (elders) and "bishops" designate the same leadership body in the church (*Acts* 20:17–28, *1 Tm.* 3:1–13). The polity of presbyterian churches rests on three constitutive principles: (1) "the parity of presbyters" (both clergy and lay); (2) "the right of the people through their representatives or lay elders to take part in the government of the church"; and (3) "the unity of the Church, not simply in faith and order, but in a graduated series of Church Courts [session, presbytery, synod, General Assembly] which express and exercise the common authority of the Church as a divine society" (James Moffatt, *The Presbyterian Churches,* London, 1928).

The basic governing body is the session, which is made up of the minister(s) of the local church and a group of ordained laity ("ruling elders") elected by the congregation. Administrative authority rests with the representative body, not with the whole congregation. The session is charged with the "spiritual oversight of the congregation." While the minister presides, all elders have equal rights of discussion and vote. All congregations in a given geographical area belong to a presbytery, which is composed of all the ordained ministers in the area and elders from each congregation. The presbytery has several key responsibilities similar to those of a diocesan bishop in Roman Catholicism. The presbytery supervises ministerial candidates, ordains ministers, concurs in a "call" to specific pastorates, and in general oversees the discipline of the local congregations. The presbytery elects a moderator and a stated clerk, who may be either clerical or lay. The stated clerk functions as a chief administrator.

The presbyteries of a region are grouped into a synod. A synod must have at least three presbyteries. Elected representatives, both clerical and lay, from each of the presbyteries constitute a synod, which meets once a year. It serves as a court of appeal from actions taken by the presbyteries and stands in an intermediary position between the presbyteries and the General Assembly. The General Assembly, the highest representative body, meets annually for about one week. Its members are elected directly by the presbyteries: one ministerial commissioner and one ruling elder commissioner for a determined number of church members in the presbytery. It is the supreme court of appeal in matters of doctrine and discipline. The General Assembly elects a moderator, a largely honorary official, who acts as titular head of the church for the next year. In fact, however, the stated clerk holds the most powerful leadership position.

In 1983, the two largest Presbyterian bodies in the United States merged to form the Presbyterian Church (U.S.A.). Presbyterians are joined with other churches of the Calvinist tradition in an international confessional group, the World Alliance of Reformed Churches, with headquarters in Geneva.

Congregational Form of Government. Opposed in principle to any form of control above or outside the local church, a third group of Christian denominations is organized along congregational lines so that each community is independent. The defenders of this ecclesial pattern of government maintain that the New Testament does not recognize any higher structure. Paul, for example, sent a general letter to the several churches in Galatia (*Gal.* 1:1–2). The author of *Revelation* was told to write to the seven churches in Asia Minor (*Rv.* 1:4). The *Acts of the Apostles* indicates that each congregation has the right to choose its own leaders (6:3, 13:2). The congregation can also regulate discipline without reference to any bishop, presbytery, or council (*1 Cor.* 5:12, *Mt.* 18:17).

In the United States the Baptists have been the most conspicuous advocates of a democratic polity. Although Baptists do not have an official creed, they generally subscribe to two important confessions of faith, the Philadelphia Confession (1742) and the New Hampshire Confession (1833). Each congregation is self-constituting: the members bind themselves together by covenant, accepting as the sole rule of faith the Bible, which the members interpret according to their own lights. The members choose their own leaders—variously called elders, bishops, pastors—who are set apart for the ministry. The laity retain full control so that all business is determined by majority vote.

Congregational autonomy, however, has had to be accommodated to the needs of fellowship and cooperation with other churches. Historically the chief impetus leading to the formation of "conventions" was the concern for foreign missions that swept the United States at the beginning of the nineteenth century. Baptist churches are grouped into associations at local, state, and national levels. The four largest of the twenty-seven bodies in the United States, embracing about 90 percent of the denomination, are the Southern Baptist Convention; the National Baptist Convention, U.S.A.; the National Baptist Convention of America; and the American Baptist Churches in the U.S.A. In addition there is the Baptist World Alliance, founded in 1905 to discuss matters of common concern; it meets every five years. The delegates, or "messengers," who participate in the meetings of the associations have no power to bind the groups they represent. Even with this understanding there have been protests that the Baptists are drifting toward "denominational centralism" or "presbyterianism." One important function of the associations is to give "counsel" in the selection of ministers. Ministerial standards are set and recommendations are made to the congregations, who proceed to elect and ordain the ministers.

Congregationalism is also espoused by the United Church of Christ, which was formed by the merger of four denominations in 1961: the Congregational Church, the Christian Church, the Evangelical Synods, and the Reformed Church. Each of the uniting churches has maintained its own theological position and form of worship. The constitution of the United Church of Christ states explicitly that "the autonomy of the local church is inherent and modifiable only by its own action" (Douglas Horton, *The United Church of Christ*, New York, 1962). The local congregations, however, are joined together for mutual support. The organization resembles that of the Presbyterian church. The churches of an area are grouped into an association that meets annually and that is made up of all the clergy and elected lay delegates. It accepts new churches into membership and is responsible for licensing, ordaining, and installing ministers. Associations within a region are joined in a conference composed of the ministers and elected lay delegates; meeting annually, it serves as a coordinating body. The "minister" of the conference, also called the superintendent or president, acts as the executive officer. The highest body in the United Church of Christ is the General Synod, which assembles biennially. The conferences elect delegates to the General Synod, which is an equal number of clergy and lay people. The synod chooses a president for a four-year term and a moderator to preside over the synodal sessions. An executive council is elected to transact business between synods.

Not all churches fit neatly into one system or another. The Lutheran church, the third largest body of Christians in the world after the Roman Catholics and the Eastern Orthodox, does not hold that any polity is divinely sanctioned. The sixteenth-century reformers were prepared to continue such existing institutions as the episcopacy, provided that the gospel was preached and the sacraments were administered. Thus there are bishops today in the Scandinavian countries, where Lutheranism is the established church. In general, however, apostolic succession and episcopal ordination are not considered essential to the church.

An early treatise of Martin Luther (1523) suggests that he advocated a congregational type of government *(On the Right and Power of a Christian Congregation or Community to Judge All Doctrine and to Call, Install, and Depose Ministers)*. Although every Christian is a priest (*Rv.* 5:10) and has the "same power in respect to the Word and sacraments," no one may make use of this power except by the consent of the community. Otherwise there would be a "shameful confusion," a kind of "Babylon in the Church, as the Apostle teaches" (Luther, *Concerning the Ministry*, 1523). The congregation retained the right to remove any minister who should preach falsely.

In the United States the three largest denominations, about 95 percent of the nine million Lutherans in the country, acknowledge varying degrees of local autonomy. Parishes are generally grouped into districts, which in turn are organized into territorial synods. The powers exercised by the synod are specified in a constitution. At all levels, pastors and lay representatives participate in the government. Synodal authority is concerned chiefly with the ordination and discipline of the clergy and ownership of property.

Despite the diversity of views about the ministry and government in the church, the ecumenical movement in the twentieth century has uncovered a certain compatibility and explored the possibility of reconciliation. Nine church bodies in the United States—including Methodist, Disciples of Christ, Presbyterian, Episcopal, and United Church of Christ—have committed themselves to an official consultation of church union (COCU). After a number of meetings, *A Plan of Union for the Church of Christ Uniting* was proposed. It was commended to the churches for study and response in March 1970. Since there was a strong negative reaction to immediate organic union, other proposals were prepared and circulated over the next decade. Finally, the 1985 version, *The COCU Consensus: In Quest of a Church of Christ Uniting,* was sent to the member churches urging them to take a series of steps, called "covenanting," through which visible unity would eventually be attained. The three types of polity—episcopal, presbyterian, and congregational—thus appear to be moving toward a mutual recognition of ministries.

BIBLIOGRAPHY

Campenhausen, Hans von. *Kirchliches Amt und geistliche Vollmacht.* Tübingen, 1953. Translated by J. A. Baker as *Ecclesiastical Authority and Spiritual Power in the Church of the First Three Centuries.* Stanford, Calif., 1969. Treats the relationship between ministerial office and charismatic gifts.

Dulles, Avery. *Models of the Church.* New York, 1974. Discusses five major approaches, types, or models through which the character of the church may be grasped.

Empie, Paul C., and T. Austin Murphy. *Papal Primacy and the Universal Church.* Minneapolis, 1974. Lutherans and Catholics in Dialogue V. Scholars from both churches present a historical and theological view of the papacy.

Huizing, Peter, and Knut Walf, eds. *The Roman Curia and the Communion of Churches.* Concilium Series, no. 127. New York, 1980. Analyzes the central government of the Roman Catholic church in the post–Vatican II era.

Kirk, Kenneth E., ed. *The Apostolic Ministry: Essays on the History and the Doctrine of Episcopacy.* London, 1946. A team of writers explores the Christian doctrine of ministry.

Kretschmar, Georg, et al. *The Councils of the Church: History and Analysis.* Edited by Hans J. Margull. Philadelphia, 1966. After a historical treatment of councils, authors from various churches present their respective theologies on the subject.

McNutt, William Roy. *Polity and Practice in Baptist Churches.* Chicago, 1959. An exposition of the congregationalism followed by the Baptist tradition.

Mead, Frank S., ed. *Handbook of Denominations in the United States.* 7th ed. Nashville, 1980. Describes the historical background, main teachings, and governmental organization of more than two hundred and fifty religious bodies.

Meyendorff, John. *The Orthodox Church: Its Past and Its Role in the World Today.* 3d ed. Crestwood, N.Y. 1981. Chapter 8 discusses the autocephalous churches in the post–World War II era.

Neill, Stephen Charles, and Hans-Ruedi Weber, eds. *The Layman in Christian History.* Philadelphia, 1963. Traces the place of laypeople in the church from the beginning up to the present; the Roman Catholic and Protestant traditions are extensively treated.

Niebuhr, H. Richard, and Daniel D. Williams. *The Ministry in Historical Perspectives.* New York, 1956. Nine authors treat the ministry from the primitive church to the twentieth century, with emphasis on Protestantism.

Pelikan, Jaroslav. *Spirit versus Structure: Luther and the Institutions of the Church.* New York, 1968. After sketching Luther's rejection of sacramental ordination, monasticism, and canon law, Pelikan considers the struggles of the reformers to deal with the need for concrete structures.

Portillo, Alvaro del. *Fieles y laicos en la Iglesia.* Pamplona, 1969. Translated by Leo Hickey as *Faithful and Laity in the Church.* Shannon, Ireland, 1972. A Roman Catholic canon lawyer analyzes the rights and duties of the laity that should be recognized in law.

Rudge, Peter F. *Ministry and Management.* London, 1968. An attempt at "managerial theology"; theories of management developed in the lay world of business and public administration are applied to ecclesiastical administration.

Schaver, John Louis. *The Polity of the Churches.* 2 vols. Chicago, 1947. After treating all the Christian churches in the first volume, the author deals in the second volume with the Christian Reformed church.

Stevick, Daniel B. *Canon Law: A Handbook.* New York, 1965. A history of canon law, the constitution of the Protestant Episcopal church in the United States, and the canons of that church. Chapter 3, "Ecclesiastical Polity," provides a good overview of the subject.

John E. Lynch, c.s.p.

Ecclesiology

Every Christian church claims to derive its existence from the unique event that is Jesus Christ and, prior to him, from the events making up the history of Israel. The decisive phases of this history are connected with the names of Abraham, father of believers, and of Moses and David. The factors linked to these phases are election, covenant on the basis of the Law, and divine promises. On these premises the twelve tribes of Israel were formed into a people that was the people of God: "I will be their God, and they shall be my people." This declaration was extended by the prophets to include all nations (*Is.* 45:14; *Is.* 56:7, cf. *Mk.* 11:17). The gathering of the people for the worship of God was designated in Hebrew by the word *qahal,* which the Greek Septuagint translates eighty-one times as *ekklēsia.*

Ekklēsia: The Meaning of the Term. Christians see Jesus as the heir to the promises given to Abraham (*Gal.* 3:16) and David (2 *Sm.* 7; *Is.* 7:13f., cf. *Mt.* 1:23; *Mi.* 5:1f., cf. *Mt.* 2:6). That first self-revelation and self-communication of God becomes, in Jesus, the approach and inauguration of the eschatological reign of God (*Mk.* 1:15; *Mt.* 3:2, 4:17). Jesus not only makes this reign known as a reign of mercy and salvation, but also gives it a certain presence in history by appointing the Twelve, telling them to "do this in memory of me" (*Lk.* 22:19, *1 Cor.* 11:24) and sending them to teach and baptize all nations (*Mt.* 28:19). Not until after the event of

Pentecost and the conversion of Paul did these various provisions become operative. The Holy Spirit is the active principle at work in the spread of the Christian faith, as attested in *Acts*, but the work done is simply that of Christ.

The "spirit of Christ" causes the new Israel to take form as the body of Christ. For "body of Christ" we might well say "church" or "churches." *Ekklēsia*, which had been used to translate *qahal* and which in the Greek world meant the convoked assembly of citizens, occurs sixty-one times in the writings of Paul; in *Acts* the word is used twenty-three times for the local community. The letters of Paul are addressed to various churches, for example, to "the church of God which is sojourning on its pilgrimage" at Corinth. These words make three basic points about the community in question. First, it is a community in a particular place. Second, this community is the church of God, just as other communities in other places are the same church of God. There is only one church, just as there is but one God, one faith, one baptism, one hope. The churches are in communion among themselves because they are in communion with the same spiritual realities. And third, these realities are heavenly. Even though already possessed in part, they are still an object of hope. Christians are journeying toward them; the realities are eschatological. The church with its worship and sacraments thinks of itself as the visible, earthly expression of a people whose true homeland is in heaven. The church is salvation. Such is the overall meaning the early church experienced.

This church also organized its concrete life. The relative diversity of organizational structure in the apostolic period gave way at the beginning of the second century to a distinction between three ordained ministries: deacon, presbyter, and bishop. In the second half of that century local councils met to deal with such movements as Montanism. Christians from the various churches visited one another. A flow of letters and hospitality gave expression to the communion whose supreme form was the communal celebration of the Eucharist. Rome was the principal center of these exchanges.

Historical and Suprahistorical Church. The earthly church is aware of having life because of gifts from God, and it is aware of forming a single society with the citizens of heaven. Two levels of reality are thus united: the church is at once suprahistorical and historical. The same spiritual realities, faith, for example, or the Eucharist, are experienced historically in various forms that depend on two things: (1) cultural contexts: the language, tradition, and special character of each people, its history, and the conflicts it has lived through; and (2) the religious geniuses who have shaped an entire tradition, for example Luther or Wesley. We must therefore distinguish a number of large-scale families that differ in the way they understand and experience the church that had its birth in Jesus Christ and the apostles. In short, the church has a geography and a history, although at the same time it is translocal and transtemporal.

The difference thus introduced into the one and only church is the difference that distinguishes East and West, two terms that must be used broadly here. The West includes the Americas, while the East includes even people who were not part of the Roman or later the Byzantine empire, and who after receiving the Christian faith formed national churches each with its own language, culture, and history. Thus Persia (Iran) formed a national church that extended, as did Persia itself, as far as India, the Caspian Sea, and Mongolia. Armenia, although its population was divided among different overlords, and Ethiopia also formed national churches. [*See* Armenian Church *and* Ethiopian Church.] The Eastern Orthodox church, which comprises twenty-three autocephalous or autonomous churches, is distinct because it has its own genius and tradition. [*See* Eastern Christianity.]

Without repeating what is said elsewhere in articles on the Eastern churches, Roman Catholicism, and Protestantism, this article will indicate how these communions and others of lesser extension understand themselves as churches. Adopting a descriptive standpoint that does not prejudge any dogmatic evaluation, one may take this definition as a starting point: "The Church is the whole body, or congregation, of persons who are called by God the Father to acknowledge the Lordship of Jesus, the Son, in word, in sacrament, in witness and in service, and, through the power of the Holy Spirit, to collaborate with Jesus' historic mission for the sake of the Kingdom of God" (McBrien, 1980, p. 726).

Self-Understanding of the Eastern Church. The above description applies to the Eastern church or, more accurately, the Orthodox church, but the profound genius of this church requires that its originality be recognized. According to Orthodox belief, the church is the mystery of the communication of divine life to created nature. The infinite distance between God and humankind, a gulf made even deeper by sin, is bridged by the incarnation of the Word and the grace of the Holy Spirit. The church is, more specifically, human reality permeated by the divinizing power that flows from the Incarnation and Pentecost. It is the fullness of the communication that restores and transfigures the faithful, or rather reestablishes in them the likeness of God's image that has been disfigured by sin. The emphasis is less on forgiveness of sins than on restoration of the image through participation in the divinizing energies. This participation is achieved in the church, which is the plenitude of God's gifts. By means of relics and holy images (icons), the church has within it the presence of the saints who are already glorified. The term *plenitude* recurs frequently in Orthodox discourse on the church. The church is "heaven on earth," the reality of "the mystery hidden [in God] for ages. . . . Christ in you, the hope of glory" (*Col.* 1:26–27). It is such on the basis of the Incarnation. It is such especially in the sacraments, which are called mysteries. In the final analysis, the church itself is the true sacrament. By participating in the church's life, the believer participates in the energies of grace. The church is all-inclusive for Christian life: to be a Christian and to be sanctified is to share in the church's life. The monks do this in the most perfect way; the monastic ideal is the heart and soul of Orthodox piety. The church also brings the promise of the world's transfiguration, which is the cosmic significance of the church, connected with the events of Easter.

Like its Western counterpart, the Eastern part of the church produced a classic expression of its genius in the fourth and fifth centuries: the age of the Fathers, of the great councils (held in the East), and of the composition of the liturgies, when the foundations of canonical discipline were laid. But there is a difference between East and West. The Western church changed significantly because it experienced "barbarian" invasions that brought in fresh ideas. Consequently, it takes a special effort today to reach back to the classic period of the Western church. The East has remained much closer to its classic sources; it identifies with them and refers to them in a more immediate and ingenuous way. Its liturgy and spirituality are permeated and wholly nourished by the trinitarian and christological dogmas of Nicaea, Constantinople, Ephesus (Mary, Mother of God), and Chalcedon. But it is a Chalcedon accepted in the spirit of Cyril of Alexandria, that is, with an emphasis on the divinity of Christ and with a tinge of what the West perceived as monophysitism. The theologizing of the East is close to that practiced in Western monastic theology. The use of reason as in Latin scholasticism would seem like rationalism to the East.

The church has a canonical organization and rules, but it has not thought of itself as a juridical entity. Rather, it is a spiritual organism animated by faith and love, a communion of life. Only within this communion do individuals reach the fullness of truth. The church is a *sobornost,* a term that Nicholai Berdiaev suggested translating as "togetherness." The entire body of the faithful preserves the faith; they are, as it were, "the sacerdotal pleroma of the bishop" (John Chrysostom). Bishops and priests have the grace of sacramental ordination. Each local church that celebrates the Eucharist embodies fully the mystery of the one, holy, catholic, and apostolic church. But the local church is not isolated. When serious questions, especially in matters of faith, arise to disturb the church, a council must be convoked that is the supreme arbiter. Ordinary life is regulated by the synod of bishops, at the head of which is the patriarch. There is no central or monarchic authority. The patriarch of Constantinople (Istanbul) is only the first among equals.

Self-Understanding of the Western (Catholic) Church. In the West, the church initially spoke and wrote in Greek (Irenaeus, Hippolytus). It was Tertullian (d. 225?) who began to theologize in Latin. This language, along with the culture whose vehicle it was, and buttressed by the prestige of Rome, was to be a powerful instrument of unity. The liturgy was put into Latin. Rome, the only apostolic church in the West (whose apostles were none other than Peter and Paul) had a powerful unifying influence, although Africa retained a certain autonomy in its way of life. While having characteristics of its own that were based in particular on the genius of theologians such as Ambrose, Augustine, and Leo, the Western church of the first eight or nine centuries somewhat resembled the church of the East. It was sacramental and liturgical; the church's life on earth was a translation of the heavenly mystery. It assured salvation.

After the conversion of the "barbarians," Christian kingdoms were established in the West. With Charlemagne, an empire came into being. The church won the support of these temporal powers for achieving its own purposes, for example, by having them use their temporal means, specifically force, in the baptism of the Saxons. In many texts of the Carolingian period, the word *ecclesia* replaces *mundus* in the dualist formula of Pope Gelasius: "Duo sunt quibus hic mundus regitur" (This world is ruled by two powers). The church included temporal society; kings were ministers of the church and, like the church, made the salvation of human beings their goal. Thus the mission of the church was at one with its nature: the church is salvation, and there is no salvation outside of it. [*See* Church and State *and* Christianity, *article on* Christianity in Western Europe.]

Rome, having the chair and presence of Peter, played a decisive role in the West, even in the matter of salvation, since Peter is the gatekeeper of heaven. Those who had the faith of Peter were also obliged to observe the customs and liturgy of Peter, that is, of the Roman church. At the same time, however, the West, and even Rome itself, absorbed many Germanic elements in, among other things, liturgical ceremony, theology (the soteriology of Anselm), and politics (the sacred character of the leader).

The great turning point was the so-called Gregorian reform, beginning in 1059, as a result of which the church emerged from its cohesion with the lay powers and affirmed its own rights, autonomy, and even *de jure* superiority over kings and emperors. Such a development was impossible without the support of a strong pontifical power, so Gregory VII called for a collection of texts to support papal authority. The result was an increased emphasis on papal authority and a development of the church's juridical side. The genius of imperial Rome lent itself to such a program: a genius for transforming the informal and irrational into a structured and regulated society. Juridical science was enriched (the *Decretum* of Gratian, the papal decretals). All this was well and good, but dangerous too. In the name of forming a body of sacred law developed in accordance with abstract logic, thousands of human beings were subsequently tortured, killed, or reduced to slavery, for example, in the Inquisition and the conquests of Latin America. [*See* Inquisition, The, *and* Christianity, *article on* Christianity in Latin America.] As far as the church's conception of itself was concerned, a corporate pattern was superimposed on the ancient sacramental pattern. One sign of this is the way in which, around 1150, the term "mystical body," which had previously referred to the Eucharist, came to mean the church. The church was a social body and therefore had a head: an invisible head, Christ, and a visible head, the pope.

This body-head scheme, in use since the fifth century, henceforth played a very large role. It lent itself to a monarchic, pyramidal vision of the church (the bull *Unam Sanctam* of Boniface VIII, 1302). As a result, privileged attention was given to the universal church, of whose unity the Catholic is keenly aware. The person of the pope is a symbol of this unity, a symbol in which the Catholic invests a great deal of feeling. Such a living icon of unity cannot be created artificially. From a theological standpoint, the symbol involves the idea of personification and representation that makes it possible, in particular, to see the pope as an epitome of the church and to assign to his teaching, under precise and limited conditions, the character of infallibility that the church as a whole enjoys in its faith. [*See* Papacy.]

This kind of development left the Orthodox East untouched. Relations between East and West did not cease, however, nor did attempts at union. Some of these attempts seemed on the verge of success, as, for example, the councils of Lyons (1245) and Florence (1438). But the two churches did not accept each other as variations within a profound oneness of faith, sacramental life, episcopacy, monastic life, and veneration of the saints and above all of the Mother of God, the Most Blessed Virgin Mary. The extensive development of scholastic theology in the West, which finally became part of official teaching, likewise remained foreign to the Orthodox body as a whole. [*See* Scholasticism.]

Catholics feel themselves to be part of the one church and removed from the sectarian attitude described by Max Weber and Ernst Troeltsch. The Mass is both the symbol and the heart of the Catholic's membership in the church. Thanks to the liturgical movement and the reforms outlined by Vatican II, the Mass, which had become overlaid with devotions, recovered its full paschal meaning, which is obviously highly Christocentric. But the church, while believing in contemplation and in consecrating lives for God, also feels it has something to give to the world. First of all, it must proclaim the gospel. This duty expresses itself in various forms. One is the mission of evangelization, with its great historical phases: the saga of the Irish; the sixteenth century, following the geographical discoveries; and the nineteenth century, when dozens of missionary congregations of men and women were founded. Furthermore, the missionary sphere is not purely geographical, but reaches into the personal environments in which people live. Christian action can also be taken in relation to the temporal realities of human life such as human dignity, justice, hunger and poverty, social and international peace. The great papal encyclicals and the pastoral constitution *Gaudium et spes* (Praise and Faith) of Vatican II witness to the church's inner mission. Under Gregory XVI and Pius IX (*Syllabus*, 1864), the church defended itself like a city under siege, and in fact it was being attacked. Vatican II and the popes since John XXIII have opened themselves to ecumenism, a pluralist world, and the questions raised by modernity, obviously not without accepting the risk of being influenced by the world and by Christian currents alien to the Catholic tradition.

The Protestant Reformation. The reformers had no intention of creating a new church, but only of restoring the existing church to its primitive and authentic form, for which the Bible, God's word, provided the norm. The idea of a return to the *ecclesia primitiva* had been advocated since the eleventh century, as for instance by the Waldensians, William of Ockham, Wyclif, and Hus. Many people found it difficult to tolerate the ever expanding role of clerics and monks, the papacy, Scholasticism, devotions, and the temporal and even financial aspects of the church. The reformers criticized and rejected these typically medieval developments and sought to restore a religious relationship or Christian life that depended solely on God and Christ through faith in the word of God and in his grace: *sola fide, sola scriptura, sola gratia.* Ministries were not denied: God had willed that such should exist, but those of the papacy were the result of human presumption. All the baptized are priests and can possess knowledge and even critical judgment through direct access to the word of God, which is the only absolute norm. The Fathers, especially Augustine and, for Calvin, Cyprian, were invoked, but only insofar as they were found to be in conformity with scripture. [*See* Reformation.]

There have always been true believers—the seven thousand who did not bend the knee to Baal (*1 Kgs.* 19:18). It is with this church of believers that continuity exists. In that which appears before the world as "the church" we must distinguish between an *ecclesia ficta,* a church full of hypocrites, and a true church, the church of faith in the word and in grace. It can be said of this true church that it is *abscondita,* or hidden, and even that, as such, it is invisible and known to God alone. This position becomes all the more necessary when Calvin's ideas of election and predestination are introduced. A community of believers can be designated as an evangelical or reformed church by these signs: the preaching of the unaltered word of God and the celebration of the sacraments in conformity with the gospel (which recognizes only two, baptism and the Last Supper, and perhaps, as sometimes in Luther, confession).

Since the older church did not accept this point of view (which denied part of its tradition), the reformers established ("raised up," says Calvin) communities that were in conformity with the gospel. Various professions of faith gave precise statements of doctrine, such as the Augsburg Confession, drawn up by Melanchthon (1530) for the Lutherans. The various Reformed communities also formulated several confessions. Since the bishops refused to ordain ministers for them, the reformers had to appoint them themselves. There now exist Evangelical Lutheran churches that form the Lutheran World Federation on the basis of their confessional documents, and Reformed churches, existing since the time of Zwingli and Calvin, which form the World Evangelical Alliance. These churches have a genuine ecclesial life, as judged by McBrien's definition. Their life is centered around the hearing or reading of the word of God. The pastor is first and foremost a preacher and catechist. The Lord's Supper, which formerly was celebrated only infrequently (four times a year among the Reformed churches), has come to be celebrated monthly and sometimes weekly, with communion in the chalice.

The Protestant churches provide a great deal of room for personal initiative. They are heirs to the respect for the individual that marked the age of the Reformation; their life is based on the universal priesthood, on personal reading of scripture without the mediation of a hierarchy, and on a sense of responsibility in the state of life to which God calls each individual. As a result, in the churches based on justification by faith alone there is an abundance of undertakings and works that are the fruit of faith. There is also a certain individualism; a freedom to be critical, even with regard to the biblical text; and at times the feeling, expressed in many theological texts, that it is the individual believers who constitute the church, which exists through them rather than they through it. Except for the Moravian Brethren, the Protestant churches were rather slow to take an interest in missions; the shift came only at the end of the eighteenth century. Since then, however, they have been very enterprising and creative. As a result, Protestantism has established itself in the world of the "younger churches," those that have emerged alongside the older colonial churches in developing nations.

The Anglican Communion. Anglicanism took form as the result of a series of events: Henry VIII's prohibition of appeals to Rome, and the excommunication of the king (1533, 1534); the declaration by Parliament that the king is "the only supreme head in erthe of the churche of England"; certain Reformation influences under Edward VI (1547–1553) and the Catholic reaction under Mary (1553–1558); and the long and fruitful reign of Elizabeth I (1558–1603). The Anglican church derives its norms from *The Book of Common Prayer* (1549; revised often) and the Thirty-nine Articles of 1562. The genius of this church is that of the *via media* ("middle way"). It has retained the episcopate, traditional ceremonies, and a beautiful liturgy. Possessing a strong sense of Incarnation, it does not talk of an invisible church. It remains faithful to the Fathers and emphasizes the importance of reason, but nonetheless asserts the supremacy of scripture. Its great scholars, heirs to a humanist tradition in the line of Erasmus, have produced now classical biblical studies that avoid the extremes of criticism.

The Anglican church has preserved and developed a tradition of piety that finds expression in the beautiful office of Evensong. It seeks to be in continuity with the older church, of which it has preserved many splendid monuments. One whole sector of Anglicanism has a "catholic" feeling for the church. Another, the "evangelicals," emphasizes conversion and the personal experience of salvation. A spirit of "comprehensiveness" and a pragmatic attitude make it possible to accept opposing currents. But these features did not prevent the Methodists, inspired by the teachings of the Wesley brothers, from moving away from the established church beginning in 1741. The break took place, despite John Wesley's advice against the rupture, in 1795, after Wesley's death. [*See* Anglicanism *and* Methodist Churches.]

The Church of England is only one part of the Anglican communion, which is a federation of independent provinces scattered throughout the world. Except for the Church of England, these several provinces are not "established," not even in the United Kingdom. They all have an episcopal structure. In the United States of America the church belonging to the Anglican communion is called the Protestant Episcopal Church in America. The bishops of the provinces, who number over four hundred, gather in conference every ten years at Lambeth Palace in London, under the presidency of the archbishop of Canterbury. The conference is not a council, having neither jurisdiction nor doctrinal authority, but it strives for agreement on important matters. The unity of the Anglican communion stems from a common ethos and piety that are based on the Bible and *The Book of Common Prayer* (the latter is not everywhere fully identical), on a sacramental tradition, and on the intention of conforming to the church of antiquity, an intention that is qualified by a strong sense of history and a great respect for individual freedom.

Congregationalists and Baptists. One movement that separated itself from "established" Anglicanism in the second half of the sixteenth century has become a sizable entity: congregationalism. It represents an original view of the church whereby the local community possesses complete authority, has no head save Jesus Christ, and therefore acknowledges no bishop or synod over it. A Christian community exists wherever disciples gather in obedience to the word of God and the Holy Spirit. The International Congregational Council (1891) does not have authority but is simply an advisory body.

Another offshoot from the left wing of the Reformation in England, born of the Puritanism of the reign of James I, was to have an important future: the Baptists. The Baptists are baptized adults who live in a direct personal relationship with Jesus Christ and his word, and feel it a duty to communicate the same vital spark. The sense of being a church springs, therefore, not from external structures but from personal conviction. It is in the local community that existence as a church is embodied; more comprehensive structures (a Baptist World Alliance was established only in 1905) are perceived as the inevitable accompaniment of organization. [*See* Denominationalism.]

Ecclesiology in Ecumenical Perspective. Principles comparable to those described are found in many other movements. In the course of history, and as early as the eleventh and twelfth centuries, individuals lived in a direct personal relationship with Christ and the word of God, without the mediation of a clerical hierarchy. At the first assembly of the World Council of Churches in Amsterdam in 1948, a distinction was made between a Catholic and a Protestant, or "evangelical," outlook in regard to unity. The Catholic outlook emphasized the visible continuity of the church and apostolic succession in the episcopal office while the Protestant emphasized the doctrine of justification by faith alone and the initiative of God's word, which evokes a response of faith. The ecumenical movement has shown that this contrast is an oversimplification. The churches taking part in the movement are increasingly in agreement that the church of Christ and of the apostles has an organic and visible unity. Ecumenical agreement does not extend, however, to positions on ministry, which is the means of ensuring this unity. Nor does McBrien's descriptive definition cited earlier make any mention of ministries. In this search for unity the "younger churches" sense themselves strangers to the quarrels that divided the European churches in the sixteenth century. [*See* Ecumenical Movement.]

The questions of orders as a sacrament, of episcopacy, and of the privileges of the pope as bishop of Rome and "successor of Peter" also continue to be divisive issues. Except for the Society of Friends (the Quakers), the churches in the World Council admit that a ministry is needed: there is no church without one. But the nature of this ministry is not a settled question. Neither is there agreement on the meaning of "apostolicity," a central concept in any Christian church. Surely there must be an apostolicity in faith, but is there also one of ministry? Orthodoxy and Catholicism say there must be a sacramental episcopacy and priesthood; both assign a primacy to the bishop of Rome, but understand the primacy differently. At the same time, when Protestants say they want a central ministry of unity, it is a ministry without universal jurisdiction by divine right.

[*See also* Ministry; Priesthood, *article on* Christian Priesthood; *and* Canon Law. *Other dimensions of Christian organizational life are discussed in* Monasticism, *article on* Christian Monasticism; Missions, *article on* Christian Missions; *and* Christian Social Movements.]

BIBLIOGRAPHY

Biblical Studies

Cerfaux, Lucien. *The Church in the Theology of St. Paul.* New York, 1959.

Minear, Paul S. *Images of the Church in the New Testament.* Philadelphia, 1960.

Schnackenburg, Rudolf. *The Church in the New Testament.* New York, 1965.

Torrance, Thomas F. *Kingdom and Church: A Study in the Theology of the Reformation.* Edinburgh, 1956.

General Works

Dulles, Avery. *Models of the Church.* Garden City, N.Y., 1974.

Heiler, Friedrich. *Die katholische Kirche des Ostens und Westens,* vol. 1, *Urkirche und Ostkirche* (1937). Reprint, Munich, 1971. See also Heiler's *Der Katholizismus: Seine Idee und seine Erscheinung* (1923; 2d ed., Munich, 1970), which elicited a response by Karl Adam in *Das Wesen des Katholizismus* (Munich, 1924).

Kirk, Kenneth S., ed. *The Apostolic Ministry: Essays on the History and Doctrine of Episcopacy.* London, 1946.

Küng, Hans. *The Church.* New York, 1967.

Works on Orthodoxy

Bulgakov, Sergei. *L'Orthodoxie.* Paris, 1932. A classic work.

Fedotov, G. P. *The Russian Religious Mind.* 2 vols. Cambridge, Mass., 1946–1966.

Florovsky, Georges. *Bible, Church, Tradition: An Eastern Orthodox View.* Belmont, Mass., 1972.

Works on Roman Catholicism

Ellis, John T. *American Catholicism.* 2d ed. Chicago, 1969. A detailed, descriptive study.

Lubac, Henri de. *Catholicism: A Study of Dogma in Relation to the Corporate Destiny of Mankind.* New York, 1958.

McBrien, Richard P. *Catholicism.* 2 vols. Minneapolis, 1980. A comprehensive account, good for the general reader.

Möhler, Johann Adam. *Die Einheit in der Kirche* (1825). Edited by R. Geiselmann. Cologne, 1957. Like Lubac's work, Möhler's is a classic on the inner meaning of the church.

Works on Reformation Issues

Afanasieff, Nicolas, et al. *La primauté de Pierre dans l'église Orthodoxe.* Neuchâtel, 1960.

Avis, Paul D. L. *The Church in the Theology of the Reformers.* Atlanta, 1981.

Hendrix, Scott H. "In Quest of *Vera Ecclesia:* The Crises of Late Medieval Ecclesiology." *Viator: Medieval and Renaissance Studies* 7 (1976): 347–378.

Jenkins, Daniel T. *Congregationalism: A Re-statement.* London, 1954.

Lund-Quist, Carl E. *Lutheran Churches of the World.* Minneapolis, 1957.

Milner, Benjamin C., Jr. *Calvin's Doctrine of the Church.* Leiden, 1970.

More, P. E., and F. L. Cross. *Anglicanism.* London, 1935.

Neill, Stephen C. *Anglicanism.* 4th ed. London, 1978.

Preus, H. A. *The Communion of Saints: A Study of the Origin and Development of Luther's Doctrine of the Church.* Minneapolis, 1948.

Sykes, Norman. *The Church of England and Non-Episcopal Churches in the Sixteenth and Seventeenth Centuries.* London, 1948.

Tavard, Georges H. *The Quest for Catholicity: A Study in Anglicanism.* London, 1963.

Tillard, Jean-Marie. *L'évêque de Rome.* Paris, 1982.

Vercruysse, Joseph. *Fidelis Populus.* Wiesbaden, 1968.

Wand, J. W. C. *The Anglican Communion: A Survey.* London, 1948.

Woodhouse, H. F. *The Doctrine of the Church in Anglican Theology, 1547–1603.* London, 1954.

YVES CONGAR, O.P.
Translated from French by Matthew J. O'Connell

Church Membership

The question of church membership may be approached from various points of view: the theological, the juridical, and the sociological. The theological approach, which will be emphasized here, grows out of the biblical foundations of the Christian faith.

Old Testament. The "people of God" are identified with Israel as an ethnic group and a nation in various books of the Old Testament (*Dt.* 7:7–8, *Is.* 41:8, 51:2, etc.). By birth the individual received the call to live up to the religious heritage of the people. Especially in the Judaism of the Diaspora, non-Israelites who believed in the God of Israel were admitted to the ranks of the proselytes and could, through circumcision and immersion, become Israelites in the full sense. A person who was once an Israelite could be put under the ban, or could apostatize, but could not cease to be a member of the people of God.

New Testament. There is no discussion of church membership as such in the New Testament, but certain conditions for membership seem to be implied in metaphors such as the net, the flock, the vine and branches, the olive tree, and the New Israel. In *Romans* 12:4–8 and *1 Corinthians* 12:12–31, Paul compares the members of the church to which he is writing to organs or limbs of a body. His letter to the Ephesians speaks of Christians as members of the body of Christ and of one another (*Eph.* 5:30, 4:25). In the New Testament, baptism is seen as the basic sacrament of incorporation, and it is regularly linked with the profession of Christian faith (*Acts* 2:38, 8:37, etc.). According to Paul, baptism makes one a son of God "through faith" (*Gal.* 3:26–27). The Eucharist further unifies the community insofar as all partake of the one bread (*1 Cor.* 10:17). All members of the community are seen as having an active role in keeping with their personal spiritual gifts (*Rom.* 12:6–18, *1 Cor.* 12:7, *1 Pt.* 4:10).

In various ways the New Testament authors indicate that membership or some of its effects may cease. For certain grave offenses, believers are ostracized (*2 Thes.* 3:14), shunned (*Ti.* 3:10), avoided (*1 Cor.* 5:11), treated as heathen (*Mt.* 18:17), and excluded from the homes of the faithful (*2 Jn.* 10). It is even taught that those who quit the Christian fellowship can never have been true Christians (*1 Jn.* 2:19).

Christian Antiquity. As the ancient church wrestled with problems of orthodoxy and discipline, it made provision for the exclusion of heretics, schismatics, and other serious offenders. Once the Roman empire became officially Christian, membership in the church increasingly became a condition for rights of citizenship.

The fathers of the Greek church connected membership with baptism and the Eucharist—sacraments that they viewed as effecting union with Christ and participation in his divine life through faith and charity. These themes continue to be vital, especially in Eastern Christian churches, which emphasize chrismation as a necessary complement to baptism.

Augustine (d. 430) and the later Western fathers, notably Gregory I (d. 604), distinguished two aspects of the church. On the one hand, it is a communion of grace and spiritual gifts; on the other, a visibly organized society with doctrinal, sacramental, and ministerial structures. For the followers of Augustine the visible structures were a sign of, and a means of entry into, the invisible community, which had primary importance. Against the Donatists, Augustine insisted that sinners were still members of the church, though they belonged to it only in an external way. The church in its visible aspect, Augustine recognized, does not perfectly coincide with the communion of the just or of the predestined, who constitute the church in its deeper dimensions.

Middle Ages. Early medieval theologians such as Bede the Venerable (d. 735), following Augustine, spoke of the universal church as having existed from the time of Abel and as including the angels and the souls of the blessed. But they regarded the visible structures of the church as essential to its present historical phase. Before the reforms of Gregory VII (d. 1085), the church was closely identified with the Christian people, who were held to be under two sets of rulers, temporal and spiritual. After Gregory VII a clearer line was drawn between membership in the church and membership in the state.

In the high Middle Ages the great scholastic theologians, including Thomas Aquinas, saw the church primarily as a communion of grace, and consequently they looked on membership principally as a grace-relationship to Christ. Thomas held that all human beings except those already damned are in one way or another united to Christ as head (*Summa theologiae* 3.8.3c). Those gifted with faith and charity are most perfectly members of the church on earth; those who have faith but not charity are imperfectly members; and infidels are members only in potency. Some scholastic theologians, such as Albertus Magnus, held that although sinners are members of the church, they are not members of Christ's mystical body.

In the late Middle Ages some saw membership as a purely individual relationship to God and as being hidden from human eyes. John Wyclif (d. 1348) and Jan Hus (d. 1415) spoke of the church as the "multitude of the predestined" *(numerus praedestinatorum)* known to God alone. For them, reprobates (i.e., those not predestined to glory) were only putative members.

Reformation and Counter-Reformation. The sixteenth-century Protestant reformers Martin Luther, Philipp Melanchthon, and John Calvin held that although the church is visible by reason of its functions of proclaiming the word of God and administering the sacraments, membership in the church is hidden. For practical purposes, they held, we must treat as members those who profess to believe in God and Christ, who partake of the sacraments, and who live as Christians. But God alone knows who belongs to him by sincere faith and election. Reformation theologians often stated that no one could be saved without belonging to the church, but by *church* in this context they meant "communion of saints" rather than a given socially organized institution. Repeating a well-known medieval axiom, they denied that God is bound to the means of grace he has instituted.

In reply to the reformers, Roman Catholics accented the visibility of the church and the guarantees of apostolic succession. For Roberto Bellarmino (d. 1621), church membership required three conditions: external profession of the true faith, sacramental communion, and subjection to the legitimate pastors, especially the pope as vicar of Christ. Whoever is unbaptized or excommunicated or guilty of manifest heresy or schism is not a member of the church of Christ (*De controversiis* 4, *De ecclesia*, bk. 3, chap. 2). Bellarmino, however, recognized that non-Catholics and non-Christians, if they were living in the grace of God, could belong to what he called the "soul" of the church.

For Francisco Suárez (d. 1617), the church had existed in some form since Adam. From the time of Christ, however, it was the "political or moral body of those who profess true faith in Christ" (*De fide*, disp. 4, sec. 1, n. 3). Whereas Bellarmino held that occult infidels were members of the church, Suárez denied this—yet the difference was not sharp, because even for Bellarmino such secret unbelievers were not "true" members (*De controv.* 4.3.10).

Modern Period. Until recently Roman Catholic theologians continued to adhere in substance to the positions of Bellarmino and Suárez. Bellarmino's doctrine was a major influence on Pius XII, who in his encyclical *Mystici corporis Christi* (1943) equated "real" *(reapse)* membership in the mystical body of Christ with being a Roman Catholic. Vatican Council II (1962–1965) modified this stance by avoiding the category of membership and by speaking instead of degrees of relatedness and incorporation. According to the Constitution on the Church *(Lumen gentium)*, non-Christians who live by the grace of God are positively related *(ordinantur)* to the people of God (no. 16). All baptized Christians are joined *(conjunguntur)* with Christ and with Catholics (no. 15), as are also catechumens who explicitly intend to become incorporated into the church (no. 14). To be fully incorporated in the church, however, one must accept the visible structures of Roman Catholicism, be in sacramental communion with the pope, and be gifted with the grace of the Holy Spirit (no. 14). In effect, therefore, Vatican II reserved full membership to Roman Catholics who are living up to their professed faith. The council accepted the Augustinian theme that sinners are in the church in a bodily way but not in their hearts (no. 14). Vatican II's Decree on Ecumenism stressed baptism as the fundamental sacrament of incorporation (nos. 3, 22).

The concept of church membership in Protestantism has undergone notable changes since the Reformation. The "free churches" that arose in the succeeding centuries were often nonaggressive sects or "denominations"—that is to say, voluntary, nonobligatory associations reflecting certain preferences with regard to doctrine, worship, or organization. Membership in a denomination is seen as implying a willingness to abide by the rules of the organization, even though one might wish to change some of those rules. Denominational membership is not equated with belonging to the community of salvation. In some denominations infant baptism is rejected in favor of a "believers' baptism" administered to adolescents. In such denominations small children are not considered church members.

The World Council of Churches in 1961 referred to the mutual recognition of members as an essential of Christian unity. Various ecumenical organizations have taken up this theme. In the United States, the Consultation on Church Union has been pressing since 1974 for a recognition that baptism in any one of the participating churches effects membership in the universal church. A few Christians have practiced or advocated dual or plural church membership as a means of manifesting that the church is one in spite of the multiplicity of the denominations. [*For further discussion, see* Denominationalism.]

Juridical Aspects. The juridical consequences of membership may be inferred by scrutiny of the constitutions of particular ecclesiastical bodies. Some recognize more than one kind of membership, distinguishing, for instance, between communicant and noncommunicant members. To be a communicant (i.e., to be entitled to receive the sacraments), one must have attained a certain minimum age (e.g., thirteen years) and live up to certain requirements, such as church attendance and financial support. Most churches have procedures for excommunication or exclusion from the rights and privileges of membership. [*See* Excommunication.]

Spelled out to some degree in canon law, the juridical consequences of membership are theologically rooted in the status of being reborn in Christ. Among the duties of members the following are commonly mentioned: professing the true faith, participating in the worship of the church, rendering obedience to pastors, maintaining communion with the church, defending the freedom of the church, supporting its ministers, fostering Christian unity, and promoting peace and justice in the world. Among the rights of church members the following are frequently asserted: to hear the word of God, to receive the sacraments, to exercise the apostolate, to inquire freely into theological questions, to have freedom of expression, association, and assembly, to enjoy personal privacy and a good reputation, and to be protected against arbitrary deprivation of office. Some of these "Christian rights" coincide with human rights recognized in secular society.

Sociological Aspects. Sociologists commonly recognize various kinds and degrees of membership depending on the extent to which the individual is identified with, committed to, and active in the church. Joseph H. Fichter, for example, distinguishes four categories: the nuclear member, who is exceptionally active and committed; the modal, who is ordinary; the marginal, who is somewhat alienated or disaffected; and the dormant, who does not believe or practice but has not positively defected. Dormancy, as explained by Fichter, is more a matter of religious ignorance or apathy than of active rejection.

These sociological observations could be applied to non-Christian or nonreligious organizations, such as political parties, and they do not focus on what is specific to the church as a mystery or sacrament of the divine. But sociological analysis raises certain questions of a theological character—for example, whether dormant members should be considered members from a theological point of view.

Present Perspectives. Looking over the history of the theology of membership, one is struck by the correspondence between changes of theory and shifts in the actual situation of the churches. Organic models of membership, developed from such vitalistic metaphors as *body of Christ*, had their strongest appeal when society in general was highly organic and when the individual had little autonomy against the group. Juridical models, which came into vogue in the early modern period, corresponded to the fragmentation of Europe into highly organized competitive groups, such as nation-states and confessional churches, in which the sovereign rulers exercised strong coercive power. Voluntarist theories of membership came to prevail when freedom and individuality were cultivated, especially in the nineteenth century. In a period such as our own, when the social determinants of human existence are keenly felt, such religious individualism may seem inadequate.

Current thinking about membership will presumably be influenced by the contemporary situation of religious pluralism and rapid social change, as well as by the fact that membership in a church and membership in civil society no longer imply each other in most countries. Many Christians, subjected to a variety of influences, seem to be only partially identified with their religious community, yet they are unwilling to leave that community, which they cherish for its positive values. Some suspect that as secularization continues, the church will increasingly consist of a minority who have made an explicit choice, often against the tenor of society.

By forcing new reflection on the idea of membership, the present complex situation makes it evident that the term *membership* does not correspond to any single objective reality. Membership, subjected to analysis, includes various components—for instance, communion with God through grace, faith, hope, and charity; relationship to one's fellow believers; sharing the ideals and doctrines officially professed by the community; eligibility for sacramental life; and active participation. Members who are marginal by some of these criteria may be modal or nuclear by other criteria.

[*For discussion of church membership in a broader context, see* Community, *overview article*.]

BIBLIOGRAPHY

Carrier, Hervé. *The Sociology of Religious Belonging.* Translated by Arthur J. Arrieri. New York, 1965. A valuable, highly objective study of attitudes toward religious groups, conversion, integration, and disaffiliation, from the standpoint of social psychology. Requires some updating.

Congar, Yves. *L'église: De Saint Augustin à l'époque moderne.* Paris, 1970. A history of ecclesiology from a Roman Catholic perspective, with informative comments on changing concepts of church membership.

Les droits fondamentaux du Chrétien dans l'église et dans la société. Acts of the Fourth International Congress on Canon Law. Edited by Eugenio Corecco, Nikolaus Herzog, and Angelo Schola. Fribourg, 1981. A massive collection (1,328 pages) of papers on the rights of Christians, chiefly in connection with the canon law of the Roman Catholic church.

Dulles, Avery. *Church Membership as a Catholic and Ecumenical Problem.* Milwaukee, 1974. A short study that attempts to correlate theological and sociological aspects, taking account of Vatican Council II and the ecumenical movement.

Gassman, Benno. *Ecclesia Reformata: Die Kirche in den Reformierten Bekenntnisschriften.* Freiburg, Basel, and Vienna, 1968. A Tübingen dissertation on the ecclesiology of the Reformed confessional writings, with comparisons between them and Vatican II. The question of church membership is adequately handled.

Internationale katholische Zeitschrift "Communio" 5 (May/June 1976). A theme issue on church membership with articles by Karl Lehmann, Matthäus Kaiser, Yves Congar, Joseph Ratzinger, and Hans Urs von Balthasar.

Moberg, David O. *The Church as a Social Institution.* Englewood Cliffs, N.J., 1962. A standard textbook on the sociology of religion in the American context with several chapters touching on church membership.

Die Zugehörigkeit zur Kirche. Report of the Seventh International Conference on the Sociology of Religion, Königstein im Taunus, 30 June to 2 July 1962. Edited by Walter Menges and Norbert Greinacher. Mainz, 1964. Papers by European scholars on various aspects of membership—historical, sociological, theological, and pastoral.

AVERY DULLES, S.J.

CHURCH AND STATE. This article focuses on the interrelationships of ecclesiastical and civil authorities in certain critical periods in the history of the Roman empire and of Europe. It examines the division of responsibility and jurisdiction between the Christian church and the state, including the kinds of support given by the church to the state and by the state to the church, and the kinds of protection given to the church against the state and to the state against the church. [*For discussion of church-state relations in other periods and places, see regional surveys under* Christianity. *For wider discussion of the relationship of religion and government, see* Law and Religion, *overview article and article on* Law and Religion in the West.]

Roman Empire. In the first three centuries AD the Christian church was largely isolated from official Roman society; it received virtually no support from the Roman political authorities and virtually no protection against oppression by them. Christians refused to acknowledge the divinity of the emperor, as required by Roman law, or to swear the oaths or join the pagan rituals necessary for participation in the government or the army and for litigation in the courts. Imperial edicts proscribed Christian worship as well as all forms of Christian ecclesiastical government and law. Nevertheless, Christian leaders not only urged upon their Roman rulers law reform consonant with scriptural norms but also taught obedience to Roman law and loyalty to the emperor, within the limits set by the Christian faith. Beyond those limits, however, the church in those centuries generally taught civil disobedience and, if necessary, martyrdom. [*See* Persecution, *article on* Christian Experience.]

With the conversion of the emperor Constantine in 312 and the establishment of Christianity as the official religion of the Roman empire in 381, the church was brought under the direct support of the imperial authority. Heretics were barred from government and clerical offices. Orthodox clergy were given special military protection, legal privileges, and financial support to spread the faith, to educate the young, to care for the poor, and to build new churches and monasteries.

The church was also brought within the emperor's direct domain. Though he was no longer worshiped as a god, the emperor remained the supreme ruler of both civil and religious affairs. "I am emperor and I am priest," Constantine declared. He and his successors convoked and presided over ecumenical and local councils, appointed and removed patriarchs, bishops, and other higher clergy, and founded and administered churches and monasteries. Numerous imperial laws regulated the internal activities of the church, the lives of its clerics, and the acquisition and disposition of church property. At a later time this system of imperial dominion within the church was denounced in the West as "caesaropapism." [*See* Constantinianism.]

Neither the Eastern nor the Western emperors, however, ruled the church without restriction. For all their authority, and even sanctity, the emperors were not ordained priests but laymen. During worship they sat in the congregation (though in a place of honor), and they had no authority to administer the sacraments. They had to accept the church's instruction, judgment, and spiritual discipline. They were bound by the laws and teachings of the ecumenical councils, the dictates of scripture, and the traditions of their predecessors. In 390 the bishop of Milan, Ambrose, excommunicated the emperor Theodosius for massacring the people of Thessalonica and readmitted him to Communion only after he had publicly repented his violation of the moral law. In 494 Pope Gelasius wrote to the emperor Anastasius, "This world is chiefly ruled by two: the sacred authority of the priesthood and the royal power." He then added, "The priests will answer for the kings themselves at the divine judgment." Thus while bishops must obey the emperor in the sphere of public order, the emperor "ought to obey [bishops] in matters concerning the reception and right administration of the heavenly sacraments."

In later centuries the action of Ambrose and the admonition of Pope Gelasius were viewed as examples of early "Western" limitations placed on imperial power, but parallel actions and admonitions were sometimes made by leading bishops in the East as well, and Eastern emperors sometimes yielded to them.

Germanic Kingdoms. The system of imperial or royal rule within the church prevailed in the West until the late eleventh century. Before their conversion to Christianity, the Germanic kings, like the pagan Roman emperors, were considered to be divine and were the cult leaders, as well as the military leaders, of their people. Upon conversion, they too lost their divinity yet continued as sacral rulers of the church within their respective territories. They too found in Christianity an important source of authority in their efforts to extend their rule over the diverse peoples that made up their kingdoms and empires. The clergy not only supported the Germanic Christian kings in the suppression of tribal religions but also looked upon figures such as the Frankish emperor Charlemagne (r. 768–814) and the Anglo-Saxon king Alfred (r. 871–899) as their spiritual leaders. The kings in turn supported the clergy in the struggle against Christian heresies and gave them military protection. The interrelationship between imperium and sacerdotium in this period was well expressed in a letter sent by Charlemagne to Pope Leo III, in which the Frankish ruler stated:

> It is our part with the help of Divine Holiness to defend by armed strength the holy Church of Christ everywhere from the armed onslaught of the pagans and the ravages of the infidels, and to strengthen within it the knowledge of the Catholic Faith. It is your part, most holy Father, to help our armies with your arms lifted up to God.
>
> (Ehler and Morrall, 1954, p. 12)

The clergy prior to the late eleventh century did not generally constitute a political threat to the secular authority since the dominant Christian outlook was essentially otherworldly. In Augustine's terms, the Christian believer was one who died to the earthly city and who lived in the eternal city of God. Germanic Christianity, like Eastern Orthodoxy, was not oriented toward a visible ecclesiastical unity or an independent ecclesiastical power. Its main message concerned the life of the world to come, heaven and hell. Its highest ideals were symbolized in monasticism, with its emphasis on spiritual withdrawal from the temporal world. Moreover, the clergy in the West were invested in their spiritual offices by kings and feudal lords, and the church property which they administered was largely held "of" kings and feudal lords. Even the bishop of Rome, who by tradition was the most prestigious and most independent of the higher clergy in the West, and whose consecration was eagerly sought by the Frankish-German kings and emperors of the eighth to early eleventh centuries, was at the same time almost wholly under their political domination.

Papal Revolution. The interrelationship of church and state changed drastically in the century between 1050 and 1150, when a large part of the clergy throughout Western Christendom united under the bishop of Rome to form an independent polity, separate from the secular authority of emperors, kings, and feudal lords. This was the papal revolution, which broke into violence in the Investiture Controversy of 1075–1122. In his famous *Dictates of the Pope* (1075), Gregory VII proclaimed that emperors and kings had no authority over the church; that the bishop of Rome alone had authority to ordain, discipline, depose, and reinstate bishops, to convoke and control councils, and to establish and administer abbeys and bishoprics; that only the pope had authority "to enact new laws according to the needs of the time"; that the papal court was "the court of the whole of Christendom," to which all Christians had a right to resort in matters within the ecclesiastical jurisdiction; and indeed, that the pope "may depose emperors" and that "the pope is the only one whose feet are to be kissed by all princes." [*See* Papacy.]

In the twelfth century the Roman Catholic church established itself as a unified, hierarchical, autonomous, political-legal entity. The Gelasian injunction was transformed into a "two swords" doctrine, with the papacy wielding the "spiritual" sword and emperors, kings, feudal lords, urban rulers, and other political authorities wielding the "temporal" sword. By the Concordat of Worms (1122) the secular arm lost its right to invest priests and bishops with the symbols of their offices. The church also asserted its own independent property rights in the vast ecclesiastical holdings that constituted nearly one-third of the land of western Europe. Thus a dual system of government was introduced: both secular and ecclesiastical authorities ruled in the same territories and over the same people, with overlapping jurisdictions. The secular state raised armies, dealt with violence, taxed, regulated commerce, and governed property relations, and in so doing it inevitably exercised large powers not only over the laity but also over the clergy. The ecclesiastical state not only governed most aspects of the life of the clergy (including their commercial and property relations with each other) but also largely controlled the religious, family, moral, and ideological aspects of the life of the laity. When the Fourth Lateran Council in 1215 forbade priests to participate in ordeals, every secular authority in Europe had to change its system of criminal procedure.

Conflicts between the ecclesiastical and secular authorities had to be resolved at many different levels. For example, when ecclesiastical courts sought to exercise jurisdiction over disputes involving property in which both clerical and lay interests were involved, or over violent crimes committed by clerics, a secular court might issue a writ of prohibition, which the spiritual arm might resist by threatening to excommunicate the secular judges. At a still higher level, popes and kings challenged each other. Thus from 1209 to 1213 the whole of England was under a papal interdiction, and English clergy loyal to Rome refused to perform marriages and other sacraments.

Mostly, however, despite a continual undercurrent of rivalry and tension between them, state and church cooperated with each other. When the church called for crusades against the infidels, the civil authorities generally responded by raising armies; when the church condemned heretics to death, the state generally executed them. [*See* Crusades *and* Inquisition, The.] Similarly, popes, bishops, and priests blessed the armies of kings and lords and generally supported secular law and order. Although there was a certain imbalance between the local temporal arm, centered in a particular kingdom or feudal regime or city, and the universal spiritual arm, centered in Rome, that imbalance was to some extent corrected by the fact that Rome was relatively far away and the local authorities were relatively near at hand.

The dualist character of church-state relationships in the period from Gregory VII to the Protestant Reformation inspired a wide range of theoretical interpretations. In the twelfth and thirteenth centuries the prevailing theory, as set forth by John of Salisbury (c. 1115–1180) and others, taught that Christ as the head of Christendom had appointed the pope as his vicegerent and had vested in him the plenitude of his divine power. As priest, the pope is to intercede for the souls of all persons at the Last Judgment. He is to proclaim the word of God, dispense the mysteries, and provide the spiritual laws and liturgies needed for salvation. He is too pure, however, to wield the unholy temporal sword. Thus God has appointed temporal rulers to whom the pope has delegated the temporal sword. Because he receives authority from the pope, the temporal ruler is the subject of the pope; his laws are bound by spiritual laws; his jurisdiction is defined by spiritual jurisdiction. Nevertheless, within the temporal domain the princes of this world operate independently, so long as they do not offend holy scripture and canon law.

In the fourteenth and fifteenth centuries there were substantial increases in royal power over the church, especially in France, England, Spain, and the various German principalities, and a corresponding decline in papal authority, both in secular affairs and within the church itself. From 1309 to 1376 the popes, seated in Avignon, were increasingly constrained by the kings of France, and in 1415, with rival popes in Avignon and Rome, the German emperor Sigismund convoked at Constance the first of a series of great church councils that declared their authority over church policy and canon law, despite papal disapproval. Secular rulers throughout Europe resisted the heavy taxes imposed by the church to support the Curia Romana. They also gained increased control over the activities of the clergy within their domains and over church property. In England, statutes of 1357 and 1363 limited clerical and lay appeals to Rome. In the Pragmatic Sanction of Bourges (1438) and again in the Concordat of Bologna (1516), French kings banned various papal taxes, limited appeals to Rome, required French bishops to be elected by French church councils called by the king, subjected the clergy in France to royal discipline, and increased royal control over church property. Fifteenth-century Spanish monarchs subordinated the ecclesiastical courts in Spain to the civil courts and assumed exclusive political and legal control, through the Spanish Inquisition, over the prosecution and execution of Christian heretics, Jews, and Muslims. Also in the fourteenth and fifteenth centuries writers emerged who denied the ultimate supremacy of the ecclesiastical arm, arguing that church and state are coordinate powers. One of the most radical royalists, Marsilius of Padua (c. 1275–1342), defended the supremacy of the lay prince even in matters of liturgy, doctrine, and ecclesiastical organization.

Despite such shifts in the theory and practice of church-state relationships, a balance was preserved during this period between the universal jurisdiction of the church of Rome (not only over the clergy, but also over various aspects of the life of the laity) and the plural jurisdictions of the various secular polities of Western Christendom.

Reformation Era. With the Protestant Reformation, however, the very concept of a visible, hierarchical, corporate church, exercising a political and legal jurisdiction, came under attack. Martin Luther (1483–1546) replaced the Gregorian "two swords" theory with a theory of two kingdoms, the earthly and the heavenly. The true church, he declared, is the invisible community of faithful believers established by the gospel as part of the heavenly kingdom. In the earthly kingdom, the church, to be sure, assumes a visible form; nevertheless, it retains its divine government in which all are priests, accountable for the spiritual welfare of each other. Therefore, the church needs no clerical hierarchy to mediate between God and the laity, no canon law to define the various paths for salvation, and no ecclesiastical courts to adjudicate laws and convict criminals. Each individual stands directly before God, is justified by faith alone, and is spared divine sanction only by God's grace. [*See* Reformation.]

Luther's radical separation of the earthly and heavenly kingdoms left all legal and political authority to the civil ruler, the prince. This included legal and political authority over the visible church itself. The Christian prince was called both to establish and to protect the church within his domain, to help define its doctrine and liturgy, to discipline wicked preaching and maladministration of the sacraments, and to aid in the church's care for the poor, in its program of education, and in its efforts to achieve the moral improvement of society.

Lutheranism became the established religion in most of the principalities of Germany and in Scandinavia. Its implications for church-state relations were spelled out most clearly in the Danish Church Ordinance of 1539, which vested in the Christian monarch supreme authority over the church, entitling him to supervise the preaching of the word, the administration of the sacraments, the Christian upbringing of children, and care of the poor. The ordinance ordered all the monarch's subjects to comply with the Augsburg Confession and Luther's catechism. It described in detail proper liturgy, the status of bishops and priests, and the requirements for their education. It empowered mayors and town councils to select local clergy and made the election of bishops subject to royal approval. In passing the ordinance, the king severed all ties with Rome, confiscated land and titles of the Roman Catholic church, closed monasteries and convents, and ordered Catholics to heed his ordinance on pain of banishment. Similar ordinances were passed in Norway at the Diet of Oslo (1539) and the Diet of Bergen (1539) and in Sweden at the Synod of Uppsala (1572). Many of their provisions remained in effect in Scandinavia until the twentieth century.

In Germany, the conflict between the Lutheran and the Roman Catholic parties was resolved in the Peace of Augsburg (1555), which empowered each prince to establish either Catholicism or Lutheranism within his territory, under the principle *cuius regio eius religio* ("The ruler's religion prevails in his territory"). The prince governed the territorial church but had to permit dissenting Christian subjects to emigrate. In the imperial cities, on the other hand, Catholics and Lutherans were to have equal rights. Non-Lutheran Protestants, however, were banned from Germany altogether. Similar territorial religious policies prevailed in Hungary and Austria.

In the English Reformation of the sixteenth century, the Anglican church was established, with the monarch at its head. Through a series of statutes enacted in the 1530s, King Henry VIII severed all ties between the church in England and the pope. The Act of Succession (1534), which annulled Henry's marriage to Catherine of Aragon, denied papal authority over marriage and divorce generally. Succeeding acts effectively divested the Roman church of all its remaining jurisdiction and banned all tithes, annates, and appeals to Rome. The Supremacy Act (1534) declared that "the King's Majesty justly and rightly is . . . the only Supreme Head in Earth of the Church of England called Anglicana Ecclesia." The designation "Erastian" was later given to such complete subordination of church government to the supreme secular ruler. [*See* Anglicanism.]

As spiritual and temporal heads of the new Anglican church, Henry and his successors, through their parliaments, established a uniform liturgy, doctrine, and administration of the sacraments and issued *The Book of Common Prayer* in the vernacular. They also assumed responsibility for poor relief, education, and other activities that had previously been carried on under Roman Catholic auspices. Contraventions of royal religious policy were made punishable as treason. Not only Roman Catholics but also Lutherans, Calvinists, and Anabaptists were subjected to severe repression.

Nevertheless, the monarchs, as laymen, could exercise no sacerdotal functions. They were subject to the instruction and discipline of the clerical hierarchy. Their rule of the church was also limited by parliamentary resistance to excessive royal intervention. Although parliaments could be convened only by royal authority and were subject to royal control, the growing Puritan faction within them sought to prevent the monarch from seizing too much power in the spiritual realm and requiring too narrow a doctrine and liturgy.

In sixteenth-century Switzerland, France, and the Netherlands there emerged a number of Calvinist groups. Although affirming many features of Luther's theology, the Calvinists conceived the visible church not as subordinate to the state in any way but as an equal, independent institution. Calvinist churches emphasized their own internal rules of order and discipline, and their officers were called not only to preach the word and administer the sacraments but also to reform the world.

In France, Calvinists (called Huguenots) denounced both the theology of the Roman Catholic church and the power and greed of the absolute French monarchs. As a result they were outlawed as heretics, their communities were condemned as illegal political associations, their leaders were executed, and their reformist rhetoric and literature were banned. The Calvinists retaliated and the civil wars of religion erupted, ending only with the Edict of Nantes (1598). By this edict, which established Gallican Catholicism, under royal rule, as the official religion of France, those Huguenots who lived elsewhere than in Paris were granted full religious liberty, including the right to hold public office, to receive a university education, and to associate freely; they also received royal financial support to fortify their communities and to build churches and schools. In Paris, public worship by Huguenots continued to be banned, although private worship was permitted in homes and in specified meeting places. At the same time, Jesuits and others who opposed royal domination of the Roman Catholic church were outlawed.

In sixteenth-century Spain, the Habsburg monarchs waged a bloody campaign against Jesuits and other Catholics who opposed their domination of the Roman Catholic church. In the Netherlands the same monarchs persecuted the Calvinists. By the end of the sixteenth century, however, the Spanish monarchy acceded to papal demands for toleration of the Jesuits in Spain and for legal protection of their religious houses and schools, while in the Netherlands it granted Calvinist churches their independence.

Religious Establishment. In the first half of the seventeenth century, Europe experienced bitter wars of religion between and among Roman Catholics and Protestants, which finally ended in the Peace of Westphalia (1648). Confirming the principles of the Peace of Augsburg and the Edict of Nantes, this treaty authorized each ruler to establish either Catholicism, Lutheranism, or Calvinism in his territory. Nonestablished religious groups, though denied the right to worship publicly, were granted special privileges to assemble and to worship privately and to educate their children in their own faith. They were to suffer no further abridgment of political and civil rights. Roman Catholic canon law was barred from all Protestant territories, and Catholic clerics were divested of any remaining privileges and immunities in the civil courts of these territories. Despite severe papal condemnation of the treaty, it remained the fundamental religious law of Europe until the nineteenth century. Its policy of establishment and toleration was gradually accepted by most Protestant and Catholic church leaders.

In France, however, the absolute monarchs gradually abandoned the toleration policy of the Edict of Nantes and the Peace of Westphalia. Supported by the antipapalism of the revived Gallican party and by the theories of absolute monarchy expounded by Jean Bodin and others, the French monarchs organized a national Catholic church, sharply curtailing remaining papal power over church property, ecclesiastical courts, and clerical nomination. Louis XIV passed more than one hundred acts against Huguenots and other dissenters, both Protestant and Catholic, confining their freedoms and imposing crushing taxes upon them. Finally, in the Edict of Fontainebleau (1685), Louis repealed the Edict of Nantes, ordered all Protestant churches and schools destroyed, proscribed all liturgies and theologies that deviated from officially sanctioned Gallicanism, and banished all dissenting clerics from France. [*See* Gallicanism.]

In England, increased royal repression of the growing number of Protestant sects during the early seventeenth century provoked militant Protestant forces to overthrow the monarchy. In 1649 a Puritan commonwealth was created, which suffered no religious establishment and tolerated both Protestants and Anglicans, though not Roman Catholics. This policy was reaffirmed after the reestablishment of Anglicanism in 1660. In the Bill of Rights and the Toleration Act of 1689, Parliament granted freedom of association and worship to all Protestants. Many of the remaining legal restrictions on the civil and political liberties of Protestants were removed in the following decades. Roman Catholicism, however, continued to be proscribed by penal law. Similar policies of toleration of all religious groups except Roman Catholics were adopted by many seventeenth-century English colonies in America. Several colonies had no established church and extended toleration to both Roman Catholics and Jews.

In the eighteenth century the church in many parts of Europe, whether Roman Catholic or Protestant, was increasingly dominated by civil authorities. The most sweeping controls were imposed by the "benevolent despots" of Prussia (especially Frederick II) and Austria (especially Maria Theresa and Joseph II), who placed church property under state administration, appointed Catholic bishops without papal approval and Protestant clergy without synodal approbation, and assumed responsibility for the payment of clerical salaries and for the supervision of clerical teaching and activities. They required that Catholic priests communicate with Rome only through royal chancelleries, and rejected all papal decrees and rescripts of which they disapproved. They freely altered church liturgy, changed diocesan boundaries, taxed convents and religious houses, and closed them if they resisted.

Toleration and Autonomy. The policy of autocratic secular control of the institutional church was generally supported both by antipapal Catholics, including Febronians and Josephinists, and by the Deist and rationalist theories that came to prevail among large sections of the intelligentsia during the eighteenth century. However, these latter theories also led in the direction of religious toleration and radical separation of church and state. Philosophers of the Enlightenment, such as Voltaire, who stressed the autonomy of the individual, the freedom to seek one's own happiness, and a person's right to express his own opinion and will, also advocated the religious neutrality of civil government and civil law. These ideas were eventually embodied in the French Revolution of 1789 and came to vivid practical expression in the disestablishment policies adopted by many countries as they fell under the influence of democratic revolutionary changes in the late eighteenth and early nineteenth centuries. No country of Europe, however, enacted such strong guarantees of religious freedom or such severe restrictions on state support of religion as those provided in the United States Constitution of 1791 and in various American state constitutions of that period. [*See* Law and Religion, *article on* Religion and the Constitution of the United States.]

In France itself the Concordat between Pope Pius VII and the First French Republic (1801) guaranteed the free exercise of religious beliefs and accorded greater papal control over the nomination, appointment, and supervision of Catholic clergy, over the delineation of dioceses, and over church property and religious education. Nevertheless, the French Catholic church remained formally established and under the general supervision of the state throughout the nineteenth century. Its clerics continued to be paid by the government, and its educational programs, religious houses, and parishes still depended on government finances. Only in 1905, under the Law of Separation of Church and State, was the church disestablished and removed from state control and support.

In Belgium the 1831 constitution provided both for freedom and for disestablishment of religion. All religious groups gained the right to worship freely, to define their own theology and doctrine, to build their own schools and churches, and to call their own councils and synods. Catholics also regained the right to communicate freely with Rome. However, the state continued to pay the clergy of the Catholic, Lutheran, and Calvinist churches. The Belgian constitutional provisions served as a model for other countries.

The Prussian constitution of 1850 resulted in the freeing of churches from the pervasive controls that had been introduced a century earlier by Frederick II. Concordats between the papacy and the emperor helped bring about a substantial reduction of state control of churches in the Austro-Hungarian empire.

The Italian Law of Guarantees (1871) provided for religious liberty for all citizens and secured the autonomy of the church in ecclesiastical education, in clerical appointments, and in the publication and execution of disciplinary and spiritual acts and orders. Libelous or physical attacks on the person of the pope and public offenses against the Vatican and Lateran kingdoms were made punishable by state law. These kingdoms were also deemed immune from government searches and seizures, and members of the papal Curia were protected from investigation and prosecution by public authorities.

In England, although the Anglican church remained established and under royal control and support, the Catholic Emancipation Act of 1829 abolished all disabilities preventing Roman Catholics from sitting in Parliament. The Universities Act of 1820 opened public schools and universities to Catholics for the first time. The few remaining legal discriminations against Catholics were removed by the end of the nineteenth century.

Twentieth Century. In the twentieth century most Western governments have adopted policies and laws that insulate the state against ecclesiastical influence and protect a pluralism of religious groups and beliefs. Vestiges of establishment policies still remain in the United Kingdom, France, Scandinavia, and parts of Germany, largely in the form of financial support and special protection of certain churches and religious institutions, and minor regulations of church property, doctrine, and liturgy. Constitutional battles between church and state continue to be waged in some countries over such matters as government taxation of churches, government support of religious schools, and the giving of religious instruction in state-supported schools. Important religious conflicts continue to affect state policies. Church leaders, including new interdenominational councils, often exercise an influence upon public opinion and government policies. Within the churches, a growing academic movement, particularly among neo-Thomists and neo-Calvinists, has brought the issue of church-state relations to the forefront of theological debate. In the United States a growing neofundamentalist movement has sought to bring principles of biblical morality to bear on public issues. In general, however, the great struggles, and the great compromises, between ecclesiastical and civil authorities that dominated Western politics from the eleventh to the nineteenth centuries came, in the twentieth century, to be a kind of ancient history, tremendously significant as a source of understanding and inspiration but no longer a vital factor in the resolution of current tensions between religion and politics.

[*See also* Civil Religion *and the biographies of Constantine, Theodosius, Charlemagne, Augustine, Gregory VII, Marsilius of Padua, and Luther.*]

BIBLIOGRAPHY

Barker, Ernst, ed. and trans. *Social and Political Thought in Byzantium*. Oxford, 1957.

Berman, Harold J. *Law and Revolution: The Formation of the Western Legal Tradition*. Cambridge, Mass., 1983.

Bohatec, Josef. *Calvins Lehre von Staat und Kirche mit besonderer Berücksichtigung des Organismusgedankens* (1937). Reprint, Aalen, 1961.

Carlyle, A. J., and R. W. Carlyle. *A History of Mediaeval Political Theory in the West*. 6 vols. Edinburgh, 1903–1936.

Dawson, Christopher. *Religion and the Modern State*. New York, 1935.

Ehler, Sidney Z, and John B. Morrall, eds. *Church and State through the Centuries: A Collection of Historic Documents with Commentaries*. London, 1954.

Gavin, Frank. *Seven Centuries of the Problem of Church and State*. Oxford, 1938.

Hyma, Albert. *Christianity and Politics: A History of the Principles and Struggles of Church and State*. New York, 1938.

Mueller, William A. *Church and State in Luther and Calvin*. Nashville, 1954.

Southern, Richard W. *Western Society and the Church in the Middle Ages*. Harmondsworth, 1970.

Tellenbach, Gerd. *Church, State and Christian Society at the Time of the Investiture Conflict*. London, 1959.

Tierney, Brian. *The Crisis of Church and State, 1050–1300*. Englewood Cliffs, N.J., 1964.

Tonkin, John. *The Church and the Secular Order in Reformation Thought*. New York, 1971.

Voigt, Karl. *Staat und Kirche von Konstantin dem Grossen bis zum Ende der Karolingerzeit*. Stuttgart, 1936.

Ziegler, Adolf Wilhelm. *Religion, Kirche, und Staat in Geschichte und Gegenwart*. 3 vols. Munich, 1969.

HAROLD J. BERMAN and JOHN WITTE, JR.

CHURCH OF ENGLAND. *See* Anglicanism.

CHURINGA. *See* Tjurunga.

CHUVASH RELIGION. The nearly two million Chuvash-speaking peoples inhabit the Chuvash, the Tatar, and the Bashkir autonomous republics of the Soviet Union. The Chuvash have had a long history of contact with Islam and Christianity that has in varying degrees affected the traditional indigenous religion.

In the first few centuries BCE the Turkic language family separated into two groups: the first now includes the Turkish spoken in Turkey and the Turkic languages spoken in the Soviet Union, Poland, Iran, Afghanistan, and China. The second group, which included Khazar and Bulgar until they became extinct in the Middle Ages, is now made up solely of Chuvash. Thus the Chuvash language and people play a key role in reconstructing most of what is known today of ancient Turkic religion.

In the eighth century the Chuvash moved from the south to the middle Volga region, where they formed the major part of the Volga Bulgar empire, a state that came under Khazar jurisdiction. A gradual islamization from the region of Khorezm, however, led to the Volga Bulgar emperor's acceptance in 922 of the religious authority of the caliph in Baghdad. The empire flourished until the Mongol invasion of 1236, when the Chuvash found shelter and a fair degree of autonomy in the forested regions on the right bank of the middle Volga. The Kipchaks of the Kazan region, however, posed a constant threat and tried to spread Islam. By the middle of the sixteenth century Russian colonization reached the Chuvash territory; after their occupation of Kazan, the Russians began attempts to christianize the Chuvash, who tried to evade conversion by fleeing to the lands between the Volga and the Ural.

The Chuvash joined forces with Muslim Tatars and Bashkirs in several unsuccessful uprisings against the Russians in the eighteenth century. By the 1860s large numbers of Chuvash tried to convert to Islam as a last resort, but these efforts were also thwarted by the Russians, who, in addition to their existing policy of translating the Bible and Russian Orthodox religious books into Chuvash, began to set up schools that featured Chuvash as the medium of instruction and a curriculum that was almost entirely religious. By the end of the nineteenth century more than fifty such schools had been established among the Chuvash. Although many Chuvash finally converted as a result, the indigenous traditions, amalgamated with some Christian and Islamic elements, continued to flourish into the twentieth century.

Chuvash popular religion comprises traditional elements to which have been added significant layers of Islamic influence and a certain, though superficial, stratum of Russian Orthodox Christianity. The core of the traditional religion has preserved elements of the ancient Turkic religion.

The central figure of the Chuvash pantheon is Tură, whose name is a Chuvash derivative of the Old Turkic deity name *Tängri (Tengri)*. The name *Tură* is also used for the Muslim and Christian God and was adopted in the Chuvash translations of the Bible. The Old Turkic name *Tängri* denoted both "God" and "sky." The latter meaning is now absent from Chuvash, but its earlier presence can be inferred, and its disappearance can be attributed to a transformation of beliefs through the influence of Islam and Christianity. The concept is still retained to a certain extent; "to thunder," for example, is expressed in Chuvash by *Tură aśatat*, where *aśa-* carries the original meaning of "father, grandfather, God the father, thunder." Tură, like Tängri prior to contact with Christianity and Islam, is qualified also as the creator, Śuratakan. [*See* Tengri.]

The Chuvash medicine man is called *yumśă* and can be either male or female. The *yumśă*s cure various types of disease, perform particular rituals, trace stolen or lost animals, take part in weddings, and assist at childbirth. Some scholars have identified the *yumśă*s with shamans, but this hypothesis is unacceptable, for the *yumśă*s feature none of the salient characteristics of the shaman, for example, trance, journey to the otherworld, and use of a special garment and a sacred drum. Additionally, it has been recognized that if the *yumśă* were indeed a shaman, the term itself would be etymologically identical to the Turkic *qam*, "shaman." Szalontai-Dimitrieva (1982, pp. 171–178) has pointed out the difficulties of this identification and suggests that the term may be a recent loan from a Tatar term that can be traced to the Old Turkic form, *yumči*, which has a corresponding Mongolian form, *domči* ("sorcerer, medicine man"). Another important Chuvash figure is a different type of sorcerer, the *tuxatmăš*. In this case there is no doubt that the concept and role of the *tuxatmăš* is borrowed. The term can ultimately be traced to the Arabic *du'ā'* ("prayer"). In Chuvash *tuka tu-* or *tuxat-* denotes "to cast a spell or charm," and thus the *tuxatmăš* is the person who casts the spell; the prayer of the Muslim muezzin came to be identified with the sorcerer's incantation. In its present linguistic form, the term appears to have been a recent loan, perhaps from the southern Bashkirs.

Some traits of the Old Chuvash religion can be reconstructed only with the help of other sources. A certain type of sorcerer (Old Turkic, *bögüči*) is no longer extant among the Chuvash but most likely was a part of old Chuvash culture. The evidence for this comes from the Hungarians, who borrowed and preserved the concept and role of the *bögüči* from the Chuvash during their close contact from the sixth to ninth centuries.

Other influences can be found among the Finno-Ugric Mari (Cheremis) people, whose term for sin *(sulak)* is derived from the Chuvash *śilăx*. The Christian Tatars have borrowed their word for prayer, *keläü*, from the Middle Chuvash. Chuvash also borrowed from contacts with other peoples; their word for human being *(śin)* is a loan from the Middle Persian *jān* ("soul"). Later, the same Iranian term came as a New Persian loan into Chuvash a second time through the Tatar in the form of *čun* and retained the meaning of "soul."

Not only comparative linguistics but also contemporary Chuvash folk practices serve as a source for reconstructing traditional Chuvash religion. One of the incantations spelled by a *yumśă* on a sick person refers to a pillar that stands in the middle of the world and supports the sky with the sun and moon on either side. The sky is said to be like the roof of a nomadic tent whose roof cover is closed with a ring. This fits the description of a yurt, although the Chuvash have not lived in yurts for more than seven hundred years. In contrast, the world beneath is not said to be the steppes of the early Chuvash, who were nomads. Rather, this world is said to consist of four types of forest: the "black forest" of leafy trees, the spruce forest, the poplar forest, and the juniper forest. Thus there is a conjunction of the Inner Asian concept of the four cardinal points with the typical "forested" world image of the Finno-Ugric peoples.

The dominant elements of contemporary Chuvash popular religion, however, do not originate from traditional Chuvash religion but from Islam. In some places Chuvash peasants worshiped a god called Xărpan, to whom they sacrificed a white ram. It is thought that the role of this deity, or at least his name, was influenced by Islamic sacrifice, called *qurbān* in Arabic. The lord of the wolves that protect the sheep is venerated as Pixampar, a name derived from the New Persian *payghamber* ("prophet"). The Chuvash recognize an evil spirit, who is called Šuytan, from the Arabic *shayṭān*.

The most respected of all spirits is the *kiremet*. The *kiremet* is the soul of a deceased person. Some Chuvash groups specify that it is the soul of someone who was wicked or evil or who died a violent death. *Kiremet*s dwell beneath the earth, and all localities have their own *kiremet*s. In many regions, forest clearings, meadows, cemeteries, hills, or brooks may be worshiped as *kiremet*s; in this sense the word bears the closest resemblance to its Arabic cognate, *karāmah* ("miracle"). Usually the area is encircled with a fence and cannot be plowed or used for secular purposes. Periodically, sacrifices are offered within this area. In some regions of northern Chuvashia *kiremet*s inhabit trees and have a special guard, the *kiremet ketüśi* ("herdsman of the *kiremet*"). This designation indicates the influence of the nomadic herdsmen on the non-nomadic forest peoples of northern Chuvashia.

The Chuvash also derived their notion of the angel of death from Islam. He is known both as Esrel (cf. Arab. 'Izrā'īl) and Masar Puśĕ ("ruler of the cemetery" cf., Arab. *mazār*). The central orientation in prayer, however, is not toward Mecca, but toward the east, following the Türk tradition. Thus during prayers or sacrifice the Chuvash faces east, and in the grave one's head is positioned on the western side because one must look eastward. The eyes of the dead, and sometimes also the nose, mouth, and ears, are covered with small linen patches. Excavations in the Volga region and in Hungary indicate similar burial customs dating to the ninth century. Until recent times the Chuvash also placed money and food in the grave, and sometimes the saddle, harness, and parts of the horse as well. These practices can be traced to burial customs in southern Russia and Hungary between the eighth and tenth centuries. In some parts of southern Chuvashia the funeral feast is not held until the Friday of the seventh week after death.

In northern Chuvashia the funeral ceremonies include placing a plank between a chair and a table that serves as a "bridge." The soul of the deceased must travel from the chair across the bridge to the table and from there to God. The ceremony is called the Feast of the Gravepost and is derived and transformed from Islam and early Iranian religion. The various elements contributing to Chuvash popular religion are evident in different Chuvash practices; many aspects of this religion, however, remain to be studied systematically by scholars.

[*See also* Turkic Religions *and* Islam, *article on* Islam in Central Asia.]

BIBLIOGRAPHY

Denisov, Petr Vladimirovich. *Religioznye verovaniia chuvash.* Cheboksary, 1959. A historical overview of Chuvash religion with attention to the political history of these peoples.

Magnitskii, Vasilii Konstantinovich. *Materialy k ob"iasneniiu staroi chuvashskoi very.* Kazan, 1881. One of the first descriptions of the "black faith" of the Chuvash, with original texts and Russian translations.

Mészáros, Gyula. *Csuvas népköltési gyüjtemény,* vol. 1, *A csuvas ősvallás emlékei.* Budapest, 1909. Materials collected in 1906 in Chuvashia on religion, customs, and folklore; contains original texts with Hungarian translations.

Nikol'skii, Nikolai Vasil'evich. *Khristianstvo sredi chuvash srednego Povolzh'ia v XVI–XVIII vekakh.* Kazan, 1912. Working with original documents, the author describes not only the christianization of the Chuvash but also their popular beliefs.

Szalontai-Dimitrieva, Judith. "The Etymology of the Chuvash Word *yumśă*, 'Sorcerer.'" In *Chuvash Studies*, edited by András Róna-Tas, pp. 171–178. Budapest and Wiesbaden, 1982. Includes an analysis of the functions of the *yumśă*.

ANDRÁS RÓNA-TAS

CINEMA AND RELIGION. Genuine religious expression in cinema is extremely rare and, significantly, it coincides in large part with the greatest achievements of cinema as an art form. On the other hand, the representation of religious themes has been part of the business of filmmaking since its very beginnings. The French stage magician Georges Méliès has been credited with the invention of the trick film and its repertory of illusions: diaphanous superimpositions; startling metamorphoses (e.g., sudden manifestations and disappearances), which he achieved by stopping and starting the camera without changing the background scene; and grotesque shifts of scale. These allowed him to translate onto film the science fiction fantasies of Jules Verne. As early as 1898, three years after the first film shows, he made a *Temptation of St. Anthony* employing the very same techniques. He was not alone. In the early years of the cinema, companies all over the world imitated the successes of their competitors. By about 1900 the Lumière Brothers company was also distributing a *Temptation of St. Anthony*. Thousands of miracle trick films were made before World War I. Most of them capitalized on popular traditions of the *tableau vivant*, occasionally drawing inspiration from the masterpieces of religious painting. The abiding charm of these films derives from the enthusiasm and inventiveness with which the early filmmakers literalized visionary experiences.

In 1907 the Italian philosopher Giovanni Papini defended this genre of filmmaking in an article entitled "The Philosophy of Cinema." He wrote:

> The world which the cinema presents is filled with a great lesson of humility. It is composed only of tiny images of light in two dimensions which nevertheless give the impression of movement and life. It is a spiritualized world reduced to the minimum, made of the most ethereal and angelic matter, without depth or solidity, rapid, fantastic and as unreal as a dream . . . . Looking at these ephemeral luminous images we feel like gods ourselves, contemplating our creation, in our image and likeness. Involuntarily we are forced to think that *Someone* is looking at us as we are looking upon the cinematographic figures, and that beyond us—concrete, real and eternal as we think we are—we are merely colored images that rush quickly to death to give pleasure to His eyes.
>
> (*La stampa*, Turin, 18 May 1907)

The extravagance of Papini's enthusiasm for the trick film, which he by no means confines to those on religious themes, is unmatched in the subsequent literature. Yet five years later, in his home country, Enrico Guazzoni's *Quo Vadis* (1912), after Henry Sienkiewicz's novel, established the genre of the religious spectacle, which was decisive in the international development of the feature film. Here the representation of miracles was superseded by lavish and elephantine sets, a Coliseum packed with real lions, and melodrama enacted within a pious context. The ultimate monument of this genre was D. W. Griffith's *Intolerance* (1916), an epic montage of the fall of Babylon, the Passion of Christ, the Saint Bartholomew's Day Massacre, and a "modern story" of slum virtue at odds with the hypocrisy of religious reformers.

As a work of ambitious cinema, in both theme and form, *Intolerance* was enormously influential on the history of the art, even though it was a commercial disaster. Goaded by the criticism of his blatantly racist *The Birth of a Nation* (1915), Griffith used a series of religious themes to plead the case, often grossly and hysterically, that jealousy, sexual repression, and economic privilege repeatedly and violently pervert true religion, which he identified with love and tolerance. The inclusion of the Babylonian episode, in which a jealous priest of a minor deity betrays Babylon because the king has instituted a Dionysiac love cult, lifts the theme beyond its otherwise exclusively Christian context. At the same time, the presentation of Catholic slaughter of Protestant Huguenots in sixteenth-century France and Protestant arrogance and oppression of Catholics in the "modern story" was meant to ensure a nonsectarian perspective. The miraculous epilogue in which a superimposed Christ appears, liberating prisoners and ending war, hints that only an apocalypse can terminate the endless cycle of bigotry. In its elaborately intricate manner, Griffith's film seems to be using religious themes to defend the liberated sexual style of the newly established Hollywood industry. He even hammers home the point with ironic intertitles, such as the one following the enactment of the woman taken in adultery: "Now let us see how this Christly example is followed in our story of today. . . ." Later, Christ's words of institution of the Eucharist at the Last Supper give Griffith the occasion to attack the then growing forces of Prohibition.

The repression Griffith opposed became institutionalized in 1922, when the newly formed Motion Picture Producers and Distributors of America hired Will H. Hays to regulate their controversial industry. The following year Cecil B. DeMille, who had previously been the most prominent entrepreneur of the liberated fashion, made *The Ten Commandments.* In the tradition of Griffith and others, he contrasted an extravagant dramatization of the Exodus with a modern story of a freethinking architect who erects a flimsy cathedral only to see it collapse, killing his mother, before he dies of a "disease" contracted from an Oriental woman. Here flamboyant puritanism and melodramatic retribution provide a cover for the director to smuggle erotic vignettes into his portrait of wickedness.

The American biblical spectacular has often been the occasion for technical experimentation or elaboration. *The Ten Commandments* had scenes in two-color Technicolor, as did the 1925 version of *Ben-Hur* by Fred Niblo. Both films were "remade" later in wide-screen formats and became outstanding financial successes, *The Ten Commandments* by DeMille himself in 1956, *Ben-Hur* by William Wyler in 1959. By then the vogue of modern parallel stories was over. The genre itself reflects the contradictions of the American film industry, where seriousness is confused with large budgets.

Charles Chaplin's first feature-length film, *The Kid* (1921), can be viewed as a comic transposition of the modern story of *Intolerance.* In Griffith's film, a young mother is deprived of her child by reformers when her husband goes to jail for a murder he did not commit; only a last-minute confession saves his life. In *The Kid,* the Chaplin tramp adopts and lovingly cares for the child an unwed mother believes she has left in a millionaire's car. In a moment of despair, before the ultimately happy resolution of the drama, the tramp dreams of a paradise in which the villains of the film are angels floating through a redecorated version of the slum where he has raised the boy.

One of the difficulties of locating the religious dimension of the cinematic experience comes to the fore when we consider the work of Chaplin. He was both the most popular figure in the history of the medium and its principal icon of natural piety. Yet only in *The Kid* is there even a tangential association of that natural piety with traditional religion. Before the dream sequence, the outcast mother passes a statue of Christ bearing the cross (apparently in a cemetery). The camera lingers on that image, so that we cannot miss Chaplin's sympathetic association of her burden with his. Yet he is quick to give us a scene of a church wedding in which an unhappy young bride emerges next to a mean-looking and decrepit man; a close-up shows the bridegroom stepping on a flower that has fallen from her bouquet.

The Pilgrim (1923) aroused the hostility of many church groups, for here Chaplin portrayed an escaped convict who is mistaken for a minister. Through comic fate, he saves the church he falsely serves. In the end he must be literally kicked across the Mexican border by a sheriff loath to arrest him. Chaplin's message of the superiority of natural virtue to institutional religion cannot be severed from the intrinsic superiority of the tramp figure to those around him. He invariably compensates for his position as a social and economic pariah with a refinement of imagination, ingenuity, and grace that those who oppress him lack. The poet Hart Crane, writing his *Chaplinesque* after seeing *The Kid,* identifies him as the emblem of all poets, a quester for "a grail of laughter." Yet even in *The Kid* there are traces of Hollywood's special pleading for its lifestyle: the unwed mother goes on to become a wealthy star haunted by the loss of her child, while the caddish artist who got her pregnant degenerates into a second-rate commercial designer. Here Chaplin identifies the triumph of virtue with stardom—at the moment of his own greatest international success.

Although Chaplin's films reveal ambivalence toward religion, many of the best European films of the 1920s were explicitly atheistic and deliberately used blasphemy for shock or for comic effect. The major Soviet filmmakers used cinema to defeat the vestiges of Russian Orthodox "superstition" in the Communist state. Sergei Eisenstein, in his most intellectually ambitious film, *October* (1928), offered a filmic analysis of the phrase "For God and Country," the slogan of the counterrevolutionary General Kornilov during his failed putsch. By rapidly cutting from familiar images of Orthodox ceremonies, icons, and crucifixes to progressively more exotic idols from Asia and Oceania, while at the same time filming them at angles that show up their material construction, he marshaled a perspective from comparative anthropology to undermine the concept of "God." In *The Old and the New* (1929) he contrasted a religious procession that fails to elicit rain during a drought with a cream separator newly acquired by a farming collective. The playful sexual innuendoes of the cream separator scene are picked up by other Dionysiac pagan emblems in the film, including the ceremonial marriage of a stud bull to a cow. The invocation of a more primitive, pagan communality also occurs in the films of the Ukrainian Aleksandr Dovzhenko, who implies that Orthodoxy was a foreign, imperialistic interlude in the history of the fundamentally collectivist Soviet states. His *Zvenigora* (1928), strongly under the influence of *Intolerance,* contrasts the superstition of medieval and seventeenth-century Christianity with modern social reform. In *Earth* (1930) he represents the spontaneous creation of a new, Communist funeral rite (with archaic pagan overtones) for a fallen revolutionary farmer after the services of a reactionary priest are rejected.

The same antireligious themes permeate the finest

Soviet sound films. Eisenstein's anti-Nazi allegory, *Alexander Nevsky* (1938), portrays the enemy as Teutonic knights bringing domination and genocide in the name of Christianity. Dziga Vertov's *Enthusiasm* (1931) intercuts old people praying and making signs of the cross with reeling drunks to couple two forms of "social disease." It also triumphally shows the transformation of a church into a workers' club while icons are burned and artifacts demolished.

While the Soviet filmmakers were using montage as an instrument of reason in their attack on religion, the Surrealists exploited the cinema's ability to represent the irrational. Many of the techniques of the early trick film were revived to represent free association. Antonin Artaud wrote and Germaine Dulac directed (to Artaud's public dissatisfaction) *The Seashell and the Clergyman* (1928). The film evokes the violence and repressed sexual instincts of a priest aroused by a woman in his confessional. In *L'âge d'or* (1930), an early sound film of Salvador Dali and Luis Buñuel, the "rock" of the Roman Catholic church is cemented by a bit of fecal putty, the pope leaves a note pinned to a Vatican window for a relative while he is out of town, and Christ appears as a murderous orgiast staggering out of a party modeled on the Marquis de Sade's *120 Days of Sodom.* Blasphemy became the hallmark of Buñuel's cinema throughout his career. In *Viridiana* (1961) the image of a beggar faking a snapshot of her friends as they parody da Vinci's *Last Supper,* as if her vagina were a camera, has become an icon for Buñuel's irreverence. *El* (1952) bitterly mocks the idea of redemption and the church's forgiveness, representing monasteries as hideouts for criminal degenerates. He even managed to incorporate an atheistic moment in his American film of the same year, *Robinson Crusoe:* a chilling echo of the castaway's supplication of God suggests the absence of a divine auditor. *Nazarín* (1958) describes the misery of a Mexican of Christlike innocence, deliberately reversing the Chaplinesque doctrine of the moral triumph of the oppressed. In this film the hero is merely confused and defeated by his will to do good. Much less ambiguous, however, are *Simon of the Desert* (1965) and *The Milky Way* (1969), which are ruthless parodies of the torments of Saint Simeon Stylites and the pilgrimage to Santiago de Compostela.

Although the cinema has often been more original and energetic in its debunking of religion than in its expression of it, the career of Carl Theodor Dreyer constitutes a remarkable exception. Several of his earliest films hint at the depth of religious feeling and the technical mastery of his mature work: *Leaves from Satan's Book* (1919) compiles a series of episodes of evil from different historical periods in the manner of *Intolerance* without the intercutting or the originality, but *The Parson's Widow* (1920) demonstrates the filmmaker's ability to shift from comedy to an expression of holy awe. It is a lightweight story of a young minister who must marry the aged widow of a succession of pastors in order to secure a position, but the death of the widow at the conclusion of the film suddenly raises the drama to a new plane, which is all the more profound because of the triviality of what preceded it. Dreyer's masterpiece, *Ordet* (1955), employs a similar strategy with more skill and sophistication. *Die Gezeichneten* (1922) was Dreyer's first expression of outrage over anti-Semitism, a lifelong preoccupation. None of these interesting early films, however, quite prepares us for the power of *The Passion of Joan of Arc* (1928), his first major film and the cinema's most convincing expression of hagiography.

Dreyer knew that silent cinema was dying when he undertook the project of filming the recently discovered records of Joan's trial and burning. Since he did not have access to the new sound technology, he deliberately made a monument to the mute style. The mobile camera follows Joan's judges as they whisper questions to each other that will trap her. Then darting camera movements underline the bombastic accusations and sly interrogations as if literalizing the space normally traversed by the human voice. In this swirl of camera pyrotechnics, Joan remains static, pitiful, and inspired, the center of a turbulent circle whose circumference and radii the camera movements trace. In giving his film this circular design, Dreyer invoked a metaphor of divinity that is at least as ancient as Boethius.

Hermann Warm's Expressionistic sets were reduced to an abstract starkness to suggest a medieval book of hours. Meticulous attention was paid to the instruments of torture and the details of the crowd who witness the startlingly realistic burning. The cumulative result is a film in which the gestures, expressions, and words of Joan reflect both her intense fear of torture and execution and her spiritual inspiration.

Ironically, the artistic rigor and originality of *The Passion of Joan of Arc* ruined the director's reputation as a maker of commercially viable films. He had few opportunities to make films in the sound era; nevertheless, *Day of Wrath* (1943) and *Ordet* (The Word, 1955) are among the central achievements of the religious cinema, while *Vampyr* (1932) and *Gertrud* (1964) merit our attention, at least, for the unusual intensity with which they approach the question of death.

Unlike all other vampire films, Dreyer's *Vampyr* gives up suspense and the elaboration of character in order to concentrate, in an oneiric manner, on the representation of the threshold between life and death. The experimental techniques of that early sound film may have been beneficial in the genesis of *Day of Wrath,* which he made after an unwilling hiatus of eleven years. In the latter film, the supernatural overtones of evil only gradually and almost imperceptibly come to replace the historical realism of his representation of witch hunts in the seventeenth-century Danish church. The filmmaker builds his story of the love affair between the young wife of an aged minister and the minister's son by an earlier marriage so skillfully that the viewer's sympathies are recklessly given over early in the film to the adulterous passion and to the rejection of the possibility of witchcraft. Therefore, when the heroine awakens to the destructive power of her will, and accepts the "coincidence" of the old minister's death and her cursing of him as signs of her evil power, we, as viewers, are challenged by the very willfulness with which we have misinterpreted earlier portents in the film because they were associated with characters standing in the way of the romantic liaison. The seductiveness at the core of the motion picture experience and its conventions becomes the focus of Dreyer's severe examination. The film is an allegory of the situation of Nazi-occupied Denmark as well, but one that scrupulously avoids propaganda and smug conclusions; in its evocation of evil, the film acknowledges the deceptiveness of evil.

A parallel change of orientation works in *Ordet.* At first the film seems a provincial comedy about sectarian bigotry. Hollywood had already successfully exploited the charms of religious turmoil foiled, in such films as Leo McCarey's *Going My Way* (1944) and *The Bells of St. Mary's* (1948). Dreyer quickly convinces his viewers that the outdated squabbles between the Borgen family (members of the dominant Grundvigian sect) and the family of the local tailor (a fundamentalist), which stand in the way of a marriage, will be resolved by the wisdom and goodness of Inger, who is married to the eldest Borgen son. But in the middle of the film, Inger's death in childbirth radically shifts the tone of the film, and more and more attention is directed to the tragedy of the Borgen family and their mad son Johannes, who thinks he is Christ. An intense realism, coupled with a unique camera style that perpetually weaves among characters without intercutting their dialogue, marks the entire film until the last minutes; then, the reintroduction of conventional montage, withheld so long, conversely underlines the unequivocal resurrection of Inger by Johannes. The scene is all the more powerful because it is unexpected. As in *Day of Wrath,* the conventions of the genre lead us to misinterpret every hint of Johannes's true link with divinity and to accept the verdict of his madness. The resulting spiritual comedy is one of the most uncompromising expressions of religion in cinema.

In part the unique strength of Dreyer's major films comes from their subtle subversions of the conventions of the genre; liberal skepticism suddenly gives way to an unanticipated depth of conviction. The sensibility behind such films seems displaced from an era before cinema was envisioned. Other films depicting witchcraft or miracles remain within the generic boundaries, which require suspension of disbelief. By far the most successful religious films, aside from Dreyer's, have been those which center on dramas of private redemption. Robert Bresson is a master of this mode, and his films cultivate an intensity of inwardness lacking in the cinema before the 1940s.

Bresson's *Les anges du péché* (1943) and *Les dames du Bois de Boulogne* (1945) indicated a major talent and a fascination with stories of the intricate workings of grace; but his first mature style crystallized with *The Diary of a Country Priest* (from George Bernanos's 1936 novel; 1950). In adapting the fictional journal, Bresson put on the screen images of the priest writing and, more importantly, he reinforced them with voice-over commentary. That stress on the oral and written organization of experience emphasizes both the solitariness and the meaningfulness of the life filmed. The film explores the difference between the public failure and the personal power of the young cleric as he succumbs to cancer of the stomach.

The subtitle of Bresson's subsequent *A Man* [Condemned to Death] *Escaped* (1956), "The wind blows where it will," underlines the role of divine providence in creating the circumstances under which the protagonist, a resistance fighter during the Nazi occupation, manages to escape prison and death. Here, too, Bresson uses a voice-over commentary to turn the otherwise tense drama in the fictional present into a retrospective reflection; but instead of showing the accumulation of a journal, he introduces snatches of Mozart's Mass in C Minor on the sound track, which has the force of suggesting a "classical" design to the events of the film. In *Pickpocket* (1959), loosely adapted from Dostoevsky's *Crime and Punishment,* Bresson uses voice-over, journal, and anachronistic music (Lully) to delineate the hidden order and ineluctable movement toward redemption in the life of a man willfully obsessed with his superiority to moral law.

This period of Bresson's career climaxed with the stark and abstract *Trial of Joan of Arc* (1961), a self-conscious denial of the Expressionism and camera exuberance of Dreyer's classic. Bresson's Joan, like his other protagonists, seems a creature of destiny, a Jansenist saint, ultimately incapable of renouncing her appointed mission. The startling figure of grace in *Au hasard, Balthasar* (1966) is a donkey who suffers a series of masters who embody the weaknesses theologically called "deadly sins." *The Trial of Joan of Arc* also marks the filmmaker's shift of attention away from the solaces of the Roman Catholic church, however peripheral they may have been to the destinies of his protagonists. Three of the later films—*Mouchette* (1966), *A Gentle Creature* (1969), and *The Devil, Probably* (1977)—make the moment of salvation coincide with suicide; another, *Lancelot du lac* (1974), locates grace in a self-destructive rebellion; and *L'argent* (1983) predicts the salvation of an ax-murderer. With the abandoning of the voice-over monologue, Bresson offers progressively more schematic characters who are opaque to us and to themselves. This opacity, shorn of even the most rudimentary psychology we have come to expect from films, along with a directorial style that suppresses the expressiveness of actors (whom Bresson prefers to call "models"), reinforces the determinist dimension of his art.

While the Hollywood cinema flaunted its piety with singing priests and nuns, two prolific directors, Alfred Hitchcock and John Ford, both raised as Catholics, both working for the most part within the conventional genres, often constructed morality plays with specific religious allusions. Ford's most overtly religious films were not among his best: *The Fugitive* (1947) is a timid adaptation of Graham Greene's *The Power and the Glory*, and *Godfathers* (1948), which Ford had earlier filmed (as *Marked Men*) in 1919, magnifies the inherent nobility in escaped convicts who find a dying mother in the desert and take responsibility for her baby. Eventually the one survivor delivers the child to New Jerusalem, under biblical instruction and the supernatural encouragement of his dead comrades. Generally Ford is a stronger director when he looks more skeptically or wryly at religion, as in *Wagonmaster* (1950), where he develops the ironies of the shared needs of puritanical Mormons and "immoral" show people, or *The Quiet Man* (1952), which treats the difference between Catholicism and Protestantism in Ireland lightheartedly. Unlike Bresson or Dreyer, he consistently asserts the moral power of either stoical or iron-willed heroes to catalyze the virtue of weaker men.

In his American films, Hitchcock often subtly acknowledges the superiority of an orthodox Catholic morality while he chooses to dwell on the moral nightmares of those who believe they can master their own destiny. When we think that "Miss Lonelyhearts" in *Rear Window* (1954) is about to kill herself, a quick detail reveals she is actually turning to the Bible. For this she is rewarded with a happy union at the end of the film, although the main attention remains on the unresolved sexual tensions of the protagonists, a photographer of disasters and his affluent girlfriend. Likewise, in *Vertigo* (1958) a nun has the last word—a benediction—for the dead heroine who has been lured into a murder plot and for the obsessed detective whose passion for her is distinctly necrophilic. A cheerful Irish drunk in *The Birds* (1963) tells everyone that the unexplained avian attack is "the end of the world"; but our attention is fixed on the sexual triangle of the rich Melanie, the bachelor Mitch, and his domineering mother.

Hitchcock does not always use religious allusions to indicate the distance of his secular figures from a redeeming faith. In *I Confess* (1952), the privileged secrecy of the confessional keeps a falsely accused priest from revealing that he is not a murderer, until the actual criminal unwittingly gives himself away. More orthodox still is *The Wrong Man* (1957). Here, until he desperately prays for help, an Italian musician seems hopelessly trapped by circumstances into a conviction for a series of armed robberies a look-alike committed. As he focuses on a cheap representation of the Sacred Heart, the image dissolves into the real thief, caught in a final robbery attempt. Eric Rohmer, a longtime admirer of Hitchcock's cinema, made a series of "moral tales" that wittily stress the advantages of resignation and patience for greater goods, in a manner reminiscent of Hitchcock's more covert themes.

At the end of World War II, Italian filmmakers felt the responsibility for forming a new national consciousness through their art. Many of them were committed leftists who derided or ignored the church in their films. Roberto Rossellini was an exception. His *Open City* (1945) portrayed the work and martyrdom of a Resistance priest; more significantly, the film symbolically represents the seven sacraments as transferred from the church to the political arena; a new era is envisioned in which the church will work with the united Left (the heirs of the Resistance) to build a democratic Italy. In his subsequent film, *Paisá* (1946), he treats a group of monks with benign humor as he portrays them incapable of understanding how an American military priest can befriend a Jewish chaplain. That view of monastic naïveté later grew into *The Flowers of St. Francis* (1950), a film version of the *Little Flowers* brilliantly directed with amateur actors (mostly Franciscan monks). Even after the neo-realist period, religion continued to play an important role in his work. At the end of *Viaggio in Italia* (1953), the British couple whose marriage has been dissolving in the film are reunited when they witness a hysterical miracle scene during the festival of San Gennaro in Naples. Late in his career, when the director made historical films for television, he investigated the humanistic dimensions of religious history in *The Acts of the Apostles* (1968), *Augustine of Hippo* (1972), and *Pascal* (1975).

Federico Fellini, initially an assistant of Rossellini's, explored the power and limits of goodness in unlikely beings in his early films of the fifties. In *La strada* (1954) and *Nights of Cabiria* (1956) Giulietta Masina (Fellini's wife) plays, respectively, a mentally impaired clown and a prostitute who is naturally endowed with the ability to rise above the vicious ugliness of her life. Between these two films, Fellini made *The Swindle* (1955), the story of a confidence man whose final scam involves his playing a priest in order to rob the family of a cripple. Yet, in the poetic justice of his fatal beating by his own accomplices (whom he tried to cheat as well), he is absolved by the filmmaker. Conversely, Fellini is harshest on the rich and privileged. His *La dolce vita* (1959) is framed by Dantean allusions: it opens with a medusan effigy, a giant statue of Christ, being towed by helicopter across Rome, and it ends with a parody of Matilda atop the mountain of Purgatory; but in the film the protagonist, a gossip columnist, cannot hear "Matilda's" message and goes off with the worn-out orgiasts with whom he has spent the night. This hell is hard-earned by its inhabitants, who cultivate sensation, suicide, and false miracles, and seem to await the reestablishment of Fascism.

In his early films of the 1960s, the novelist Pier Paolo Pasolini paid homage to his spiritual tutelage under Rossellini and Fellini. In *Accattone* (1961), a brutally naturalistic version of Fellini's *The Swindle*, a pimp seems to find salvation in his last moments. The use of Bach on the sound track is a lesson Pasolini learned from Bresson. But unlike his predecessors, Pasolini purges his religion of God. This fact determines the tone of his *Gospel According to Matthew* (1964), a very original biblical pageant, which is packed with allusions to other movies (e.g., Eisenstein's *Alexander Nevsky* and Dreyer's *Passion of Joan of Arc*), has an extravagantly eclectic choice of music for the sound track, and exploits the antirealistic properties of the zoom lens to concentrate on the parabolic dimensions of Matthew's homely gospel. In contrast to Pasolini, Ermanno Olmi, the most overtly Catholic of the important new generation of Italian filmmakers, tends to pay more attention to the values of work and family life than to church matters, although he did make a biography of Pope John XXIII.

The Marxist filmmakers Jean-Marie Straub and Danièle Huillet, who, like Pasolini, have been tutored by the films of Dreyer and Bresson, among many others, have evoked transcendental experience in a world without God. *The Bridegroom, the Comedienne and the Pimp* (1968) quotes Bach's "Ascension" oratorio at the beginning (as the camera rides past a street of prostitutes in Munich) and the poetry of Saint John of the Cross at the end (concluding an unrealistic drama in which a prostitute shoots her pimp). The most explicit example of the investigation of religion in their films is *Moses and Aaron* (1975), a stark rendition of Schönberg's incomplete opera about the absolute transcendence ("invisible, unimaginable") of the Old Testament God. The scene of Aaron's betrayal of the Mosaic ideal, the erotic dance before the golden calf, has been filmed as an abstraction of Griffith's Babylonian revelers. Straub and Huillet use Schönberg's operatic critique of the banality and sensationalism of grand opera to indict the superficial religiosity of most films.

When we turn from Western cinema to Asian productions, it becomes much more difficult to assess the intensity of religious experience and expression in cinema. Akira Kurosawa's *The Idiot* (1951) is a paradigmatic example. In adapting one of the most important "religious" novels of the European tradition to the screen, he excised the religious dimension entirely. Likewise, when we see *Rashomon* (1950) or *Ikiru* (1952), studies, respectively, of the ambiguity of truth and the encounter with death, the tangential appearance of religious rites does not seem to affect the humanistic current of the films. Western commentators have written of the application of Zen aesthetics to Japanese films, especially to the static and geometrical elements in the work of Yasujiro Ozu. But if religion coincides with a plastic sensibility, it is too intimately enmeshed in the very structure of filmmaking for us to isolate it analytically.

For Western audiences, Ingmar Bergman has been the filmmaker most commonly associated with the religious dimension of cinema. He attained international prominence in the late 1950s with *Smiles of a Summer Night* (1955), *The Seventh Seal* (1957), and *Wild Strawberries* (1957). The first incorporates magical and pagan elements of erotic divinity in a tradition as old as comedy itself, the filmic highlights of which include Chaplin's panic romps and Renoir's *A Day in the Country* (1936). Against the backdrop of the Black Plague, *The Seventh Seal* allegorically represents an encounter between Death and a Crusader agonized over the existence of God. The last of the three films is a psychological drama about an old doctor troubled by the emotional failures of his life. Most of Bergman's cinema has concerned permutations of the elements evidenced in these three films. *The Virgin Spring* (1960) returns to a medieval setting to investigate a miracle: a spring emerges on the site of a young girl's rape and murder after her father has violently avenged her death. The historical distance and the painful skepticism of the dialogue hedge the miracle. Bergman leaves open a naturalistic explanation, such as Dreyer would emphatically have rejected.

Bergman is always more interested in the psychology of religion than in its phenomena. *Through a Glass Darkly* (1961), *Winter Light* (1963), and *The Silence* (1963) constitute a trilogy that moves from the acknowledgment of religion as a hysterical phenomenon (the schizophrenic Karin in the first film imagines that the helicopter coming to take her to a sanatorium is a spider god intent on raping her) that can only be redeemed by an apotheosis of love, to more and more emphatic statements of the absence (or silence) of God. The Lutheran priest of *Winter Light* undergoes a crisis of faith. In *The Silence,* Bergman moved away from his representation of tortured questers after religious conviction, substituting a psychoanalytically informed vision of human interaction. Subsequently, the priests he put on the screen—in *Cries and Whispers* (1973) and *Fanny and Alexander* (1982)—have been monsters of agnosticism or hypocritical sadism.

The preeminence of Bergman as a filmmaker concerned with religious matters is a reflection of the historical situation of the cinema itself. The art emerged in a period of intense skepticism and secularism; it has no artifacts from a period of pious conviction. This may account for the nearly universal recourse to historical representation when cinema encounters religion. The biblical film is merely the most blatantly artificial subgenre of this phenomenon. Kurosawa, Dreyer, Bresson, Rossellini, and Bergman are among many serious directors who have turned to medieval and Renaissance contexts on occasion to open up a zone insulated from modern skepticism in which religion and psychology might coexist. A Dreyer or a Bresson is likely to encounter difficulties with popular audiences and producers when he transports his concerns to a contemporary setting. Bergman, on the other hand, reserves the present for the articulation of severe religious doubt. One indication of the decline, or at least transformation, of the self-assigned permission to evoke the religious experience within the boundaries of the distant past is the recent tendency in the American cinema to displace the religious, in a veiled form, into the future. Stanley Kubrick's *2001: A Space Odyssey* (1968), Steven Spielberg's *E.T.—The Extraterrestrial* (1982), and George Lucas's Tolkien-like *Star Wars* trilogy (1977–1983) project nostalgia for redemptive and transcendentally inspired forces and beings into the realm of science fiction, where currently fashionable notions of human psychology go unchallenged.

In the United States since the end of World War II, a mode of filmmaking has flourished that tends to sustain the Romantic aspiration of securing religious experience without the mediation of religion. Such films eschew psychological drama and depict a world of ritual actions, immanent powers, and magical metamorphoses. Their makers are simultaneously heirs of a tradition of Surrealist and abstract filmmaking in Europe before the war, and of an older strain of native Emersonian Orphism that elevates artistic production to the status of revelation.

Among the major works of this mode are Maya Deren's *Ritual in Transfigured Time* (1946); Kenneth Anger's *Inauguration of the Pleasure Dome* (1954) and *Lucifer Rising* (1974), works inflected by the filmmaker's involvement with the cult of Aleister Crowley; James Broughton's mystical comedies; Harry Smith's qabbalistic cartoon, *No. 12* (about 1960; also called *Heaven and Earth Magic*); the mandalic animations of James Whitney and Jordan Belson; George Landow's *Wide Angle Saxon* (1975); and the prolific work of Stan Brakhage, whose theoretical text, *Metaphors on Vision* (1963), expounds the idea of filmmaking as a visionary experience. There he wrote of filmmaking in terms that complement those of Papini:

> The artist has carried the tradition of vision and visualization down through the ages. In the present time a very few have continued the process of visual perception in its deepest sense and transformed their inspirations into cinematic experiences. They create a new language made possible by the moving picture image. They create where fear before them has created the greatest necessity. They are essentially preoccupied by and deal imagistically with—birth, sex, death, and the search for God. (*Film Culture* 30, 1963)

BIBLIOGRAPHY

The most exhaustive study of the history of the religious cinema, in English, is Ronald Holloway's *Beyond the Image: Approaches to the Religious Dimension in the Cinema* (Geneva, 1977). Like most of the literature, Holloway's book includes films that treat seriously issues of morality, death, and love as works of religion, whether or not they contain explicit religious allusions and regardless of the religious orientation of filmmaker and country of production. There is an extensive bibliography and a section devoted to Dreyer.

The work of Amédée Ayfre remains the most ambitious approach to the subject. His *Dieu au cinéma: Problèmes esthétiques du film religieux* (Paris, 1953) and *Cinéma et mystère* (Paris, 1969) attempt a theological formulation of cinema as a sacred art. The former presents a phenomenology of religious films and their aesthetic problems; the latter, supplemented by a text of Alain Bandelier, proposes a Roman Catholic theology of the image, with emphasis on the "mystery" of the human face, as a mediation of Divine Presence. *Dieu au cinéma* has a bibliography and filmography. Ayfre's books systematize certain dimensions of the critical and theoretical ideas of the influential critic André Bazin, whose essays have been collected and translated in *What Is Cinema?*, 2 vols. (Berkeley, 1967).

Neil P. Hurley, S.J., looks at cinema under the rubric of a series of religious themes (Freedom, Sex, Evil, Death, Grace, Sacrificial Love, and The Future) in *Theology through Film* (New York, 1970).

Thomas M. Martin's *Images and the Imageless* (Lewisberg, Pa., 1981) provides a theoretical context for examining the religious content of films without dwelling on historical or interpretative matters. His book has a unique grasp of the range of film theory and criticism that often falls outside the scope of religious studies.

Movies and Morals, by Anthony Schillaci, O.P. (Notre Dame, 1970), is an introduction to the incorporation of cinema in religious studies and a polemic in favor of films that pose difficult problems (there is a section on Bergman) and against pious commercial films. Several appendixes are written for the directors of workshops. *Film Odyssey: The Art of Film As Search for Meaning*, by Ernest Ferlita and John R. May (New York, 1976), offers analyses of twenty-one films made between 1949 and 1972.

Religion in Film, an anthology edited by John R. May and Michael Bird (Knoxville, 1982), brings together essays by several Americans on genres, theory, and thirteen modern directors from Europe and America, with a bibliography. John C. Cooper and Carl Skrade edited *Celluloid and Symbols* (Philadelphia, 1970), which contains nine essays on major directors (e.g., Ingmar Bergman, Federico Fellini, and Roman Polanski). Two issues (nos. 10 and 11) of *Études cinématographiques* 2 (Autumn 1961), edited by Michel Estève, are devoted to "La passion du Christ comme thème cinématographique," with thirteen essays (including a comprehensive historical survey and studies of Dreyer, Ford, Rossellini, Malaparte, Dassin, Buñuel, Bergman, and Bresson). Less exhaustive is a special issue of *Centrofilm*, no. 34, devoted to "Il sacro e il cinema" (1964), with emphasis on Italian issues.

Paul Schrader's *Transcendental Style in Film* (Berkeley, 1972) attempts to define a comparative typology of Protestant and Catholic Christian and Zen Buddhist representations of transcendence in the films of Dreyer, Bresson, and Ozu, often resorting to a reductive schematicism. Walter Benjamin's justly famous essay "The Work of Art in the Age of Mechanical Reproduction," in *Illuminations* (New York, 1969), remains the most powerful argument against the application of the rhetoric of religion to cinema.

P. ADAMS SITNEY

ČINGGIS KHAN. *See* Chinggis Khan.

CINNABAR. *See* Alchemy, *article on* Chinese Alchemy.

ČINVATŌ PERETU. *See* Chinvat Bridge.

CIRCLE. Awe of the heavens and gratitude that its cycles order and sustain life give the circle special symbolic status. The solar and lunar disks, themselves divinities in many cultures, are the most obvious natural inspirations for circle symbolism. The rotation of the circumpolar stars around the hub of the pole—defining for many peoples the center of heaven and the throne of deity—is a more subtle inspiration for the wheel, the embodiment of circular motion. In earlier times no astronomy was required to arouse immediate feeling for the sacred in these circles in the sky, nor was there any intimation that a future science would someday conceive the sun, moon, and planets actually to move in circular paths.

By historic times, in the third millennium BCE, the potter's wheel was appearing as an instrument of creation, and the wheeled chariot, invented at about the same time as writing (c. 4000 BCE), was becoming a fearful engine of conquest. Built into the languages of our oldest sacred texts is a complex symbolism associating time and the heavens, power, order, insight, and awe with the circle and the wheel. Even today this early synthesis of the sacred and profane strongly resists logical analysis.

Ancient Egyptian Culture. The pictographic nature of Egyptian hieroglyphs lets us observe how imagination turned the solar disk into a pregnant symbol of communication. In the context of a land primarily desert, the perfect circle of the blazing sun, alternating day with night and guaranteeing the harvest on which the agricultural community along the Nile depended, was the most prominent natural object in Egyptian consciousness. By the end of the third millennium BCE, Egyptian polytheism showed a clear tendency to consider the divine spirit permeating the universe "in a more abstract way" (Clark, 1959, p. 74). In a Coffin Text from the Herakleopolitan period, the high god—"spirit of the Primeval Waters," moving across the heavens in his solar bark—describes himself as one "who came into existence as a circle" (ibid.).

The glyph for the sun, as depicted in figure 1, is a circle (1). The range of ideas radiating from the concept of the solar disk can be studied directly in other glyphs containing circles. Such combinations give the additional meanings of "day," "hour," "yesterday," "period," and they designate time generally, including eternity. The sun circle became the body of the uraeus, the sacred asp (2); the asp, placed above the drawing of a seated man, had long been the symbol for the sun god, Re (3). With three pendant rays (4) the circle means

FIGURE 1. *Circle Symbolism in Egyptian Hieroglyphs*

1.	sun	7.	netherworld
2.	uraeus	8.	village
3.	sun god, Re	9.	placenta
4.	sunshine	10.	threshing floor
5.	daytime	11.	realm of the king
6.	eye	12.	New Year's Day

SOURCE: Alan Gardiner, *Egyptian Grammar,* 3d ed. (London, 1957).

"sunshine," "shine," and "rise." A combined form (5) is the abbreviation for "daytime" and for what belongs to the day. Moreover, a circle representing the round pupil is part of the Egyptian ideogram for "eye" (6), which by extension takes on additional meanings for actions of the eye: "see," "look," "weep," "be blind," "be wakeful," thus relating light, sight, and understanding.

The circle surrounding a five-pointed star (7) identifies the netherworld, the land of the dead (originally the circumpolar region) ruled by Osiris. With a cross (8) it means "village or town." With a set of parallel lines (9) it is thought to mean "human placenta." Filled with seeds of grain (10) it signifies the threshing floor, with carryovers in the phonetic script to "time" and "occasion." As a cartouche used to surround an inscription (11), it refers to the region encircled by the sun (i.e., the realm of the king). Set within the horns of an ox (12), it identifies New Year's Day.

These circle variants of the natural solar disk recur in a multitude of other contexts, which extend meanings far beyond those given here. Egyptian usage makes clear the profound complexity of intellectual implication concerning seasonal activities of both *time* and *place,* and both *light* and *insight,* that the circle carried already in ancient times.

Ancient Roman, Greek, Indic, and Hebrew Cultures. The Latin root of *circle* (*circulus,* the diminutive form of *circus,* meaning a "circular figure" or a "ring" but also a "circuit," the most famous of which was the Roman Circus Maximus, is also the term for the orbit of a planet.

The Greek root *kirkos* (related to *krikos,* meaning "ring" or "circle") is the name of a hawk or falcon that flies or wheels in circles. Further relations through *kuklos* extend meanings to anything round, such as a place of assembly, the vault of the sky, the walls surrounding a city, a shield, the eyeballs, a drum, the Cyclops ("round-eye"), the Cyclades (islands surrounding the sacred isle of Delos), and so forth.

The Sanskrit word *maṇḍala* means "circular, round; circle, globe, orb, ring; the path or orbit of the sun, the halo around the sun or moon; multitude, group, band, collection." [*See* Maṇḍalas.] The 1,028 hymns of the *Ṛgveda* associate the sun with Indra; in one classification they are arranged in ten mandalas. *Cakra,* meaning "wheel" (from the Vedic root *car*), is the wheel of the sun's chariot, a potter's wheel, a discus or sharp circular weapon, the circle of the zodiac. In the Tantras it refers to a mystic circle or diagram. The chariot was the instrument of the Aryan conquest of India in the third and second millennia BCE, and the sun's chariot is one of the strongest images of the *Ṛgveda.* In the great creation hymn (1.164) its wheel "formed with twelve spokes [months] . . . joined in pairs together, seven hundred sons and twenty" (i.e., the days and nights in a year). This value agrees with the old Babylonian schematic year of 360 days. The oppressive sense of relentlessly repetitive time cycles that permeates the religions to which India has given birth owes much to a naive view of the heavens, but the explicit numerical content of the *yugas* ("ages of the world"), epochs of fantastic durations, is rooted in primitive number theory, not in astronomy. The most important of these numerical cycles are the *kaliyuga* of 432,000 "years," the *mahayuga* of 4,320,000, the *kalpa* and Brahmā periods of 4,320,000,000 and 8,640,000,000, and the "duration of the universe," or "life of Brahmā," of 155,520,000,000,000, all multiples of 360 (McClain, 1976). Astronomy developed only in the common era, and on a Greek foundation (Neugebauer, 1983). The familiar cosmological myth of the "churning of the sea of milk" (gods and demons grasping opposite ends of the cosmic snake, wound around the drum-shaped holy mountain, Meru, to twirl it like a fire stick), seems likely to have been inspired by the ancient *a priori* commitment to reciprocity and by a Vedic fascination with rotating fire sticks, with their frictional, procreative overtones.

Biblical Hebrew employs a specialized vocabulary for the circle. The verb/noun *ḥug,* referring to the circle of earth or sky, also means "to describe or inscribe a circle" (*Jb.* 22:14, 26:10; *Prv.* 8:27); *savav* means "to complete a circuit" (*1 Sm.* 7:16), *naqaf,* "to move around in circles" (*Is.* 29:1). The word *tequfah* refers specifically to astronomical circles (*Ps.* 19:6), *shanah* (also the Egyptian term for "orb"), to the revolving year (calendrical repetition, or return). *Galgal,* the word for "wheel," may be relevant to Gilgal ("circle of stones,"

Jos. 4:1–9). The four wheels in Ezekiel's vision, each a "wheel within a wheel," are obviously inspired by the chariot, and there are numerous references to the millstone, an application of rotary motion. Neither the Hebrew scriptures nor the New Testament displays much interest in how the heavens move, and both show a distinct preference for rectilinear measures, numerically, not geometrically, inspired. The most significant biblical circle is the "molten sea" in Solomon's Temple; made of brass, thirty cubits in circumference and ten in diameter, it held the water for the priests' ablutions. The capture of Jericho after seven circumambulations suggests the influence of some now-forgotten ancient ritual, still surviving in the Muslim practice of circumambulating the Ka'bah, although both Judaism and Islam are normally proscriptive of such influences. The New Testament bluntly contradicts the ancient cyclic view of time; its eschatology assumes time to be linear, and to be running out.

Ancient Mesopotamian and Chinese Cultures. "Terrifying luminosity" was a primary aspect of deity in Mesopotamia, and luminosity was shared by all things divine (Oppenheim, 1964). In Assyria and Iran, the winged solar disk became the symbol of the highest deity, Ahura Mazdā. By 500 to 400 BCE it appears also on the cylinder seals of Phoenicia.

From Sumerian times (third millennium BCE) a broad belt of twelve constellations had been identified along the ecliptic, the path traveled by sun, moon, and planets, at an angle of about twenty-four degrees from the equator. In the center (occupying approximately the middle third of the band) was the Way of Anu, the highest god, with the Ways of Enlil and Ea, his associated deities, on either side. This conception of a cycle of twelve constellations, each thirty units long—the precursor of our zodiac—gave to the circle a more subtle reference than the solar disk or the revolution about the pole. Circular astronomical tablets have been found dating to about 700 BCE, but the contents of earlier tabulations (c. 1000 BCE) point to even earlier circular prototypes. We do not know what physical concepts accompanied these notions (Neugebauer, 1983).

The zodiac (circle of animals) in its present widely disseminated form is an amalgam of Sumerian, Babylonian, Greek, and Egyptian ideas; its possible relationship with Far Eastern zodiacs is unclear (Gleadow, 1968). Greek astronomical thought transformed a heaven of mere cyclic "appearances" into a heaven that physically moved in circles. Originally conceived as month markers, the zodiacal constellations acquired a new importance with the development of Babylonian horary astrology and Greek homocentric planetary theory, both beginning about 600 BCE. Ptolemy's *Almagest,* about 150 CE, the climax of Greek "cinematic" speculative thought, is a veritable symphony of imagined "epicycles," all set within the grand cycle of a slow "precession" (26,000–36,000 years), discovered by Hipparchus only in the second century BCE. It is uncertain whether the Qur'anic allusions to "seven heavens, one above another" (67:3; 17:44; and 71:15), "seven firmaments" (2:29 and 65:12), and "seven tracts," or "orbits" (23:17) are reflections of Ptolemaic planetary theory (second century CE), perhaps by way of astrology. In general, it was Aristotles' more primitive version (fourth century BCE) of planetary orbits that dominated the thinking of philosophers and theologians into the Middle Ages (Neugebauer, 1983). In popular imagination, however, it is astrology more than mathematical astronomy that is the enduring monument to the ancient cyclic view of time.

In China from the beginning of the second millennium BCE, as earlier in Egypt, attention was centered on the nightly rotation of the circumpolar stars. The emperor represented Heaven by seating himself facing south, so that his subjects were related to him as the other stars to the pole. "Heaven is round, earth square," affirmed in various documents since the second century BCE, presumably owes its meaning to this nightly celestial rotation, coupled with the quartering of the horizon owed jointly to the pole and to the sun. The white marble Altar of Heaven in Peking, built in the fifteenth century CE, 27 feet high, consists of three circular terraces with diameters, respectively, of 210, 150, and 90 feet. A 99-foot-high circular Temple of Heaven, built at the same time, stands on a similar triple circular base.

Neolithic Cultures. Why the Neolithic cultures of western Europe as early as 5000 BCE invested heroic energy in megalithic burial monuments, some of them circular—now documented by studies of hundreds of examples—is hidden from us. The practice seems to have diffused eastward from the Atlantic coast. The great Irish burial mound at Newgrange (c. 4300 BCE) is an artificial mound, 40 feet high and 260 feet in diameter, formed of some two hundred thousand tons of water-rolled stones. The most famous of these circular henges—that at Stonehenge in England, its earliest form predating the pyramids of Egypt—was built originally on an artificial, circular mound nearly 100 meters in diameter and 2 meters high. Cremated human bones were found in most of the fifty-six Aubrey holes, which formed two concentric circles inside this bank. To bring to the site each of its large Sarsen stones, some of them weighing up to fifty tons, and to erect them in an inner circle is estimated to have required the efforts of eleven hundred men for about seven weeks. Viewed from the center, at the summer solstice the sun rises over an enormous heelstone standing just outside the circles, and belonging to the earliest phase of construction. Thus Stonehenge had its origins in sun worship, but the elaborate circular constructions upon which so much labor was expended are not easily explained. A similar circular ditch and bank at Durrington Walls is estimated to have required nine hundred thousand man-hours. A huge earthen cone at Silbury, 40 meters high and dating to 2500 BCE, is estimated to have required eighteen million man-hours (Renfrew, 1973). The interpretation of these monuments of archaeoastronomy is highly controversial; their cost is a measure of their builders' dedication to circles. Some of the alignments suggest the ability to make right angles and perfect ellipses, thus implying a mastery of elementary geometry, and perhaps of an ability to calculate Pythagorean triples (van der Waerden, 1980).

Links between Ancient and Modern Cultures. Circular ground plans employed in the "beehive" homes of early Egypt and in other parts of the world today are as old as Jericho, dating back to the eighth millennium BCE. Plato projected a circular design for his mythical city of Atlantis (in *Critias*) and for an idealized city on Crete (in *Laws*). The ancient Median city of Ecbatana was built for Deioces about 700 BCE in seven concentric circles. The circular villages of the Chavante Indians of Brazil have presumably a ritual origin (Seidenberg, 1981). The radial streets of Paris and Washington, D.C.—capital cities, and as such, spiritual centers—form a wheel. The great circular rose windows of Western cathedrals are a central focus of pride and interest. A circular Aztec calendar stone over 11 feet in diameter, cut in the fifteenth century CE, is a late New World design from a culture that did not know the wheel. But circular design carries more than a symbolic implication; it is also a direct human encounter. As does theater-in-the-round on a more intimate scale, the circular city provides an unusual psychological experience in space. Participation in a round dance—associated the world over with seasonal change—is a special psychic experience. Vision and locomotion apparently conspire to make linear movement more convenient for humans, and thus the intensity of feeling experienced in circular movement is heightened by its infrequency. Circular army camps of the Assyrians, like the defensive circle of an American covered wagon train, are secular examples of a special strength of the circle in minimizing the perimeter of a given area, and of maximizing the equality of distances from the center. The point of interest here is the association of the circle with defensive strategy and thus with power, a primary aspect of deity.

Within the circle of man's horizon, wherever he may be, sun and polestar are now, as in the past, aids to orientation, vital to survival. The "four corners of the earth" are an early and almost universal conception; the infinite symmetries of the circle of the horizon otherwise threaten disorientation. Thus from the beginnings of temple architecture, the square and the circle have been intimately associated "duals" (Seidenberg, 1981). Placing a round dome representing heaven on a square foundation representing earth is itself an interesting problem in technology. (The Dogon of Africa, by contrast, conceive heaven as square, and earth round.) The circular Roman Pantheon, completed in 125 CE, having a diameter of 144 feet and lighted only through a circular opening at the apex of its dome, became Michelangelo's sixteenth-century inspiration for the cupola of Saint Peter's Church, set on four massive pillars. Hindu, Buddhist, and Muslim temples abound in celebratory, virtuoso solutions to the three-dimensional problem of joining the circle to the square.

With the slow rise of a science of astronomy and with the development of other arts and sciences there has come a proliferation of more subtle implications for both the circle and the wheel. The familiar pie-shaped graphs of modern statistics are useful in displaying not only cyclic relations but also the proportional divisions of any horizon of mental discourse. The waterwheel, millstone, and clock, as well as the reciprocating engine (which links linear and circular motion) have transformed life with new notions of power and thus with new implications of deity. In a remarkable chapter titled "The Virgin and the Dynamo," Henry Adams, writing of the Great Exposition of Paris in 1900, likens the forty-foot dynamos displayed there—to him symbols of infinity, of "ultimate energy"—to the power of the Virgin, who hitherto had been "the greatest force the Western world ever felt," and under whose inspiration the towering majesty of the Gothic cathedrals had arisen. In all of these examples of circularity, sacred and profane undertones of implication remain fused.

BIBLIOGRAPHY

An essay by Abraham Seidenberg on "The Ritual Origin of the Circle and Square," *Archive for History of the Exact Sciences* 25 (1981): 1–327, is particularly informative. More specialized is Kapila Vatsyayan's *The Square and the Circle of the Indian Arts* (New Delhi, 1983). For specific accounts of the role of the circle in planetary theory and perceptive examples of the extreme conservatism that has kept religion so out of tune with developments in scientific astronomy, consult Otto Neugebauer's *Astronomy and History: Selected Essays* (New York, 1983). Our foremost historian of science, Neugebauer offers, in succinct fashion and in a way calculated both to restrain undisciplined enthusiasm for any secret ancient science and to make clear the limits of our present knowledge, a wealth of original insights. B. L. van der Waerden's "On Pre-Babylonian

Mathematics," *Archive for History of the Exact Sciences* 23 (1980): 1–46, makes generous concessions to the mathematical knowledge of megalithic builders and to the possible diffusion of a common body of insights by way of Indo-European languages at a very early historical period. The Neolithic story is summarized carefully by Colin Renfrew in *Before Civilization* (New York, 1973). For invaluable introductions, see A. Leo Oppenheim's *Ancient Mesopotamia: Portrait of a Dead Civilization*, 2d rev. ed. (Chicago, 1977), and R. T. Rundle Clark's *Myth and Symbol in Ancient Egypt* (London, 1959). Rupert Gleadow's *The Origin of the Zodiac* (New York, 1968) succeeds in its aim to be "a lively account of the birth and growth of astrology." *The Golden Bough*, 3d ed., rev. & enl., 12 vols. (London, 1911–1915), by James G. Frazer remains a useful source for primitive circle symbolism in the folk rites of many cultures. The specifically "harmonical" inspiration for much of the ancient numerology associated with time cycles is developed in my *The Myth of Invariance* (New York, 1976). Henry Adams's *The Education of Henry Adams* (Boston, 1918) remains a great American classic.

ERNEST G. MCCLAIN

CIRCUMAMBULATION is a ritual term meaning literally "to walk a circle around" a holy place, person, or object. Such rituals are related to the widespread significance of the sacred circle, which is the architectural ground plan and ideational scheme of such monuments as the stupa, such cities as Banaras and Jerusalem, and such ritual constructions as the medicine lodges and Sun Dance lodges of the North American Plains Indians. Thus, our topic is related to that of the sacred circle or the *maṇḍala* and is its ritual extension. [*See also* Circle *and* Maṇḍalas.] One walks around what is set apart, circumscribed as charged or sacred; one might even say that circumambulation sets something apart by circumscribing it with one's own body. It is also to be noted that circumambulation, as a rite of both centering and bonding, is related in some ways to the many types of circle dancing such as the Ghost Dance of the Plains Indians, the maypole dances of the British Isles, and the circular dances and marches of the Shakers; such dance forms, however, will not be discussed here.

Circumambulation is a fundamental rite of orientation, and is often thought of as a human repetition of the apparent movement of the sun. The Lakota would walk "sunwise" around a fire or a ritual arena. The sense of this direction as the natural order also appears in Hindu ritual texts such as the *Śatapatha Brāhmaṇa* and the Gṛhyasūtras, which speak of the sunwise movement of ritual performance in rites meant to secure the blessings of the gods. This sunwise circling is known as *pradakṣiṇa*, "going to the right." *Pradakṣiṇa* around the sacred fire or the teacher, and later around the temple, became an act of centering and honoring in the Hindu tradition.

In Native American and Hindu traditions, as in many others, reversing the direction of circling was considered a reversal of the natural order and was associated with catastrophe or death. This circling to the left, contrary to the apparent course of the sun, was called *prasavya* in the Hindu tradition and was associated with the left hand and with rites for the dead, for the ancestors, and for the *nāgas*, or serpents. Anticipating or recovering from disasters, the Lakota circle counterclockwise after the fashion of the "thunder beings," whose movement, unlike that of the sun, is antinatural. In sixteenth-century England this turning in an unnatural direction came to be called *widdershins* and was associated with danger, magic, and witches.

In the Hindu tradition today, *pradakṣiṇa* is simultaneously an act of taking a place, deity, or person as one's center and of honoring that center, keeping it ever on the side of the auspicious right hand. The most concise *pradakṣiṇa* honoring the sacred place on which one stands, is simply to turn all the way around in place, as pilgrims do at the very southern tip of India at Kanyā Kumārī. The most extensive is the *pradakṣiṇa* of the entire subcontinent of India, from the north at Badrināth, to the east at Purī, to the south at Rāmeśvaram, to the west at Dvārakā (Dwarka), and back to the north again. One of India's great rivers, the Narmadā of central India, has a traditional circumambulation in which pilgrims, beginning wherever they wish, walk its entire length of 801 miles from Amarakaṇṭaka to the Bay of Cambay and back again. Mountains too are circumambulated, as in the well-known routes around Kailāsa in the Himalayan north, Arunācala in the Tamil country of the south, and Kamadgiri and Govardhan in the northern sanctums of Rāma and Kṛṣṇa, respectively. Many of India's sacred cities also have *pradakṣiṇa* routes, the best known being the Pañcakrośī *pradakṣiṇa* of the city of Banaras (modern-day Varanasi). This sacred circuit of the city takes pilgrims five days to perform, passing 108 shrines along the way and circumscribing with their footsteps the perimeter of the sacred zone of the city where simply to die is to attain *mokṣa* ("liberation").

More common, however, is simply the *pradakṣiṇa* of the sanctum sanctorum, the *garbhagṛha*, in a Hindu temple. Depending upon the size of the temple, the pilgrim will circumambulate either the entire complex or merely the inner courts before approaching the deity for *darśana*. There may be several circumambulatories, which usually will include their own circuit of ancillary shrines. In some popular temples, especially in the North, this is a very "close" circumambulation, with the devout running their hands along the temple walls, frequently stopping to touch the place at the back of the temple nearest the image of the divine inside. In the South, however, especially in Kerala and Karnātaka, there are often circumambulatory markers, outside of which the honorific circuit must be made, at a respectful distance of several feet from the temple itself.

The circumambulation of a center also formed a strong part of the early Buddhist tradition of worship, especially the circling of the stupa with its hemispherical dome, originally said to house a relic of the Buddha. The dome of the stupa, called the *aṇḍa* ("egg"), was said to have cosmic significance as the dome of heaven: the smaller superstructure on top was Mount Meru, and the surmounting umbrellas signaled the Buddha's world-kingship. The entire stupa was surrounded by a fence, with gates in the four principal directions. Between the fence and the *aṇḍa* was a *pradakṣiṇapatha,* a circumambulatory path. Very often, as in the case of the stupa of Amaravati in the Andhra area of India, there was an upper circumambulatory of the *aṇḍa* itself, with its own enclosing rail. The famous stupa of Borobudur in Java was built in nine levels, with a circumambulatory around each of the lower six levels that took the pilgrim not only around the stupa but also past bas-reliefs depicting the earthly life, the previous lives, and the instructive deeds of the Buddha.

The circling of the stupa, called the *chedi* in modern Thailand, continues as a common part of festival rituals. In the evening during the Thai celebration of Viśākha Pūjā (the day of the Buddha's birth, enlightenment, and death) monks and laity circle the *chedi* three times, holding lighted candles. Other festival days are marked with a similar threefold circumambulation.

The divine also circumambulates, reaffirming the sacred claim upon the territory circumscribed by the route. In Sri Lanka, for example, the annual procession of the relic from the Temple of the Tooth takes a circumambulatory route through the city of Kandy. In South India, such annual circuits of the gods are common. During the Chittarai festival in Madurai, for example, when the goddess Mīnākṣī moves in her giant chariot through the concentric rectangular circumambulatory streets of the city, she reclaims the four directions as her own.

In the ancient Hebrew tradition, the story of Joshua's siege of Jericho displays the power of the Lord in encircling the city. For six days Joshua's army, led by the Ark of the Covenant and seven priests with seven trumpets of rams' horns, made one circuit a day around the city; on the seventh day they made seven circuits and the city wall fell (*Jos.* 6). In the later tradition, circumambulatory circuits *(haqqafot)* are performed both to mark holy ground and, it would seem, to remember the power of the Lord that was with the children of Israel in the siege of Jericho.

The most festive *haqqafot* take place during the Feast of Booths, Sukkot, when those present make seven ceremonial circuits carrying the festal bouquet of willow branches and lemons around the altar in the synagogue. In the time of Philo Judaeus the procesion, like that of Joshua, took place once a day for six days and seven times on the seventh. At Simḥat Torah, *haqqafot* are performed with the scrolls of the Torah being carried around the synagogue.

Christian worship has tended to focus the attention of the worshiper directionally toward the east or vertically toward the vaulting heavens, rather than inward toward an encompassed center. Even so, Christian architecture displays a tension between the center, which can be circumambulated, and the "transcendent" or the "east," which cannot. In the Middle Ages, churches were built with ambulatories to facilitate the movement of pilgrims through the church and around the altar, beneath which or near which a relic was enshrined. Circumambulation is an important part of pilgrimages, such as that of Saint Patrick's Purgatory on an islet in Lough Derg in Ireland, where pilgrims walk around the basilica four times, saying seven decades of the rosary beads. In the Christian tradition, as in others as well, circumambulation is often part of rites of consecration. For instance, when the new basilica of Our Lady of Guadalupe in Mexico City was consecrated in 1976, the consecrating procession circled the building sprinking it with sanctified water, anointing it with holy oil, and fumigating it with incense.

The Muslim *ḥajj* has the circumambulation *(ṭawāf)* of the Kaʿbah as one of its central rites. [*See* Pilgrimage, *article on* Muslim Pilgrimage.] The original meaning of *ḥajj* is "to describe a circle," and this circling of the Kaʿbah is a pre-Islamic rite, said to have been done naked, a practice that was prohibited by the Prophet. Here the circles are made with the left side, said to be the side of the heart facing toward the sacred Kaʿbah. The *ṭawāf* consists of seven circuits of the Kaʿbah. The full pilgrimage contains three *ṭawāfs:* the initial *ṭawāf* on arrival, which is part of the ordinary *ʿumrah,* or lesser pilgrimages; a *ṭawāf* on return from the journey to Arafat; and a farewell *ṭawāf* before leaving.

The *ṭawāf* is interpreted in a spiritual way by theologians such as al-Ghazālī, who describes *ṭawāf* as a form of prayer. *Ṭawāf* is not merely the circling of the body around the Kaʿbah but the circling of the heart around God. In doing *ṭawāf,* the faithful are like the angels circling the throne of God. Some Sūfīs were believed to have reached such a high peak that the Ka'bah came to circumambulate them, and not they the Ka'bah.

In many traditions, circumambulation is associated not only with places of holiness or of worship, but also with life-cycle rites. Marriage rites often involve circling, since a wedding is preeminently a rite of bonding and union. In some traditional Jewish communities, the bride makes either three or seven *haqqafot* around the groom at the wedding. The circling establishes a common world for the couple. Roman weddings, for instance, called for the circling of the bride and groom around the family altar. In the Agni Pradakṣiṇa rite of the Hindu marriage, the bride follows the groom three times around the sacred fire, her sari tied to his dhoti. The rite immediately precedes the "seven steps," the legal culmination of the marriage ceremony. Interestingly, this rite repeats the groom's three circuits around the sacred fire during his initiation rite, the Upanayana, just before he received the sacred Sāvitrī *mantra* from the guru and thus established the primary bond of his years of education.

In addition to being a rite of honoring, centering, and bonding, circumambulation also can set apart what is circumscribed. This is especially the case for the "dangerous holy," that is, the dead. Both the dead and places associated with the dead are circumambulated, sometimes counterclockwise, as a protective or apotropaic rite to keep the spheres of the living and dead apart.

In the Sefardic and Hasidic traditions of Judaism, seven *haqqafot* are made around a cemetery prior to burial. It has also been the custom in Ireland, Holland, Germany, and elsewhere in northern Europe to carry the casket in procession three times, sunwise, around the cemetery before burial. According to the *Mahāparinirvāṇa Sūtra,* five hundred of the Buddha's disciples circled his body before his cremation pyre was lit. The Hindu cremation rite today begins as the chief mourner, usually the eldest son, circles the pyre four times counterclockwise, carrying the flaming bundle of sacred *kuśa* grass and touching the body symbolically with each round, finally lighting the pyre at the head. In Buddhist Thailand as well the body is circumambulated three times before the cremation. In the case of a king or member of the royal family, a special palace-mountain pavilion called the *phra meru* is built for the cremation. On arrival, the body is borne around the *phra meru* three times, *uttaravatta,* in a "left-hand direction," before being placed upon the elaborate pyre. While the threefold circumambulation in the Buddhist tradition ordinarily marks reverence for the Buddha, the Dharma, and the Saṃgha, here it is said to remind the living of the three wearisome worlds of *saṃsāra*—that of earth, of heaven, and of hell.

BIBLIOGRAPHY

Heiler, Friedrich. *Erscheinungsformen und Wesen der Religion.* Stuttgart, 1961.

Pandey, Raj Bali. *Hindu Saṁskāras.* 2d rev. ed. Delhi, 1969. A description of the major *saṃskāras,* or sacraments from birth to death of the Hindu brahmanical tradition.

Turner, Victor, and Edith Turner. *Image and Pilgrimage in Christian Culture.* New York, 1978. An anthropological study of Christian pilgrimages, looking at both Mexican and Irish pilgrimages as well as Marian pilgrimages in other countries.

Von Grunebaum, G. E. *Muhammadan Festivals.* New York, 1951. A discussion of Muslim worship, including the rites of the pilgrimage to Mecca, the *ḥajj.*

Wells, Kenneth E. *Thai Buddhism: Its Rites and Activities* (1939). Reprint, Bangkok, 1960. A study of daily, weekly, and yearly Buddhist rites and festivals in Thailand, with discussions of major life crisis rites such as ordination to the monastic order and funerals.

DIANA L. ECK

CIRCUMCISION is the surgical removal of the foreskin from the penis; sometimes it also refers to less common practices of uncovering the glans of the penis by removing some of the foreskin and leaving the remainder as a flap, as practiced by the Maasai and Kikuyu of East Africa, or cutting the foreskin away but retaining it as two flaps, as practiced by the Tikopia of Polynesia. Early social theorists speculated about circumcision's origins, suggesting that it may have (1) marked captives, thereby signifying subjection, (2) attracted the opposite sex, (3) been a tribal or ethnic mark, (4) been hygienic, (5) increased sexual pleasure, (6) removed men from maternal bonds, (7) tested bravery, (8) sacrificed part of the self to ensure future rebirth, (9) been a form of symbolic castration to support the domination of youths by their elders, or (10) even simulated menstruation. None of these theories is accepted today, though various combinations of them may be cited by those groups who circumcise.

Geographic Distribution. Circumcision is commonly associated with Semitic religions (Islam, Judaism, and Coptic Christianity), but, in fact, it predates all of these. It was practiced among ancient Egyptians, although not universally. It is widespread among peoples in Africa, western Asia, and the Pacific, including Australia. Early travelers' records and encyclopedias report circumcision among some New World peoples, but these accounts seem dubious, and, at most, the practice there appears to have been rare. Circumcision was not common in Europe or North America (except among Jews) until the 1870s and became widespread only at the turn of the century. Today about 85 percent of newborn American males undergo the operation, but it is far less common elsewhere in the English-speaking world and in Europe. It is our only form of prophylactic surgery, and currently members of the medical profession are in disagreement as to whether it is scientifically justifiable. Some cite its prevalence in America as an indication of a misconceived preoccupation with medicine and hygiene.

Semitic Circumcision. Muslims, Jews, and Coptic Christians usually circumcise during infancy. Ideally Jews circumcise on the eighth day of life. Among Orthodox Jews circumcision is performed by a professional circumciser *(mohel)* rather than a physician, and blood must be drawn from the wound either by mouth or, today, through a suction pump. In America, Jews have figured significantly in developing surgical devices that facilitate the operation. Circumcision is not strictly necessary to make one a Jew: since 1892, for example, Reform Jews have not required it of converts. Before the Hellenistic period circumcision among Jews took a less radical form than it does today. Because some Jews would "blister" the portion of their foreskin that remained in order to appear uncircumcised to the Greeks and Romans, the rabbinate advocated a fuller circumcision. Some hellenized Jews sought to appear uncircumcised because the Greeks and Romans viewed the practice with revulsion and periodically enacted laws to make the custom difficult for Jews and Egyptians under their rule.

Muslim circumcision usually occurs on what is termed the seventh day (in fact it is the eighth day, since the day of birth is not counted). In practice, the time varies widely. Some Muslims perform circumcision within the first five or six years; others delay it until as late as adolescence. While circumcision is not discussed in the Qur'ān, Muslims agree that it must occur before marriage and is required of male converts. In many cases, it is accompanied by lavish feasts and celebrations. A few Arabs combine circumcision with radical flaying and scarification of the lower abdomen.

Coptic Christians (including Ethiopians) circumcise in imitation of Old Testament Jews, but the time at which circumcision is performed varies from the first week of life to the first few years.

Circumcision and Ethnicity. Besides signifying membership in a religion, circumcision may indicate ethnicity or merely a human condition properly marked by the creativity of culture. Thus the Yoruba and Igbo of Nigeria usually circumcise during infancy; for them the operation signifies no religious or moral commitments nor does it distinguish them from their neighbors, who also circumcise. Even in respect to a single society generalizations about circumcision may be formulated with difficulty, as examples from Africa will illustrate. The western Dinka of the Sudan circumcise while the eastern Dinka do not. Their neighbors, the Nuer, do not ordinarily circumcise, but on rare occasions they may, in order to purify someone who has committed incest. Among the Azande of the Sudan and Zaire circumcision was introduced by neighboring peoples, with the result that within even the same village or extended kin group some will be circumcised while others will not. Among the Amba of Uganda circumcision was unknown until an unexplained interest in the custom, learned from neighbors to the west, led to sporadic waves of circumcision among youths and even adults. Among the Sotho of southern Africa circumcision was once universal, but under government and mission influence many have abandoned the practice while others continue to observe it. Among some migratory pygmies in Zaire circumcision has been interpreted as a mark of cultural subjugation to their sedentary African overlords. Even where circumcision is a traditional practice and remains prevalent it now often takes place in hospitals, despite protests from elders, who advocate the old ways.

Circumcision and Rites of Sexual Initiation. Where circumcision is associated with a world religion, it rarely marks sexual maturity. Such an association is common, however, among preliterates, although even among these many peoples circumcise infants or children rather than adolescents. Early circumcision may be a mark of ethnicity, or it may be considered hygienic or aesthetically attractive, but it does not provide a means by which trauma may be harnessed to the inculcation of moral and metaphysical values, as occurs in many rituals of initiation. Nor can infantile circumcision serve as a test of bravery. These aspects of circumcision, however, are of special interest to the anthropologist of religion.

Among the societies that practice circumcision as a rite of passage to adulthood, those of central Australia and East Africa provide the most complex and dramatic examples.

In central Australia circumcision is the primary operation in defining male adulthood, although it is often accompanied by tooth evulsion, bodily scarification, and, a year or two later, subincision. Much pressure is exerted on the initiate to show no fear or pain. Among those Australian Aborigines who practice circumcision (and not all do), the operation marks the beginning of a youth's indoctrination into the men's secret ceremonial life, the preservation of which is believed to be vital for maintaining social and natural harmony. At this time novices witness complex ceremonies in which the mythical origins of the world are enacted and, thereby, the order of the world is reasserted. The initial rites convey only basic features of this information; only after a man has witnessed many such ceremonies over the years, first as a spectator-novice, then as an actor-participant, and finally as an organizer, does he become truly knowledgeable. Circumcision, therefore, is not only the occasion when a youth passes into the circle of informed adults, but it also provides repeated opportunities for him to continue to acquire deeper knowledge of traditions.

Australian circumcision furthers male solidarity by forever separating youths from their mothers. The initiates receive ritual objects that are forbidden to the sight of women. Admitted to frequent and complex secret male ritual activities, they begin to spend longer periods away from camp at ceremonies that exclude women. It is only after these rituals that a youth is likely to have heterosexual relations and marry. Male solidarity sometimes involves a homosexual experience, since a circumciser may be obliged to have sexual relations with a newly recovered novice to whom he will later give a wife.

Aborigines associate circumcision with marriage not simply to prepare a man to take a wife but to reinforce the bonds the man enjoys with the men of his wife's family. Thus a man's potential father-in-law and brothers-in-law, his own father, and his uncles (his father's affinal ties and members of the group that helped to circumcise his father) often figure in his circumcision. Male solidarity and hierarchy are closely associated with the bestowal of and submission to pain, a prevalent theme in Aboriginal belief and ritual. This in turn relates to the fact that periodically in a society circumcision and subincision involve the shedding of male "genital blood," a blessing with deep mystical value for the reestablishment of social and moral order through altruistic, sacrificial suffering.

Circumcision is widespread in East Africa. Among sedentary speakers of Bantu language it is usually performed annually on groups of youths approaching adolescence. These groups are segregated in the bush (the sphere of disorder) apart from villages and women. Novices are stripped, shaved, bathed, and sometimes marked with ashes or white earth, all to denude them of their previous status and to place them in a liminal state, neither minor nor adult. The actual operation is often performed by an expert who is outside or peripheral to the group. Bravery under pain is usually required. The shedding of blood is viewed as polluting, a "hot" procedure that temporarily creates disorder so as to achieve a greater eventual order. Rituals and medicines are therefore applied to "cool" the wound and allow it to heal.

During their weeks of recovery, novices are hazed by older circumcised youths or by elders. They fast and observe numerous prohibitions, as may also their kin, in order to ensure recovery. In their isolated quarters, the novices—vulnerable and impressionable because of the wounds, fasting, and exposure that they have suffered—are subjected to intensive instructions about sexual behavior, moral attitudes, and proper conduct. Toward the end of their confinement, the novices may don strange garb and tour nearby villages representing their status of being nameless, nonsocial creatures. Upon recovery, they return to their homes and enjoy the company of women at dances and feasts that celebrate their new adulthood. Circumcision marks their ritual death as minors and their rebirth as responsible adults.

In other East African societies, especially Para-Nilotes such as the Maasai, rites of circumcision are not held every year. Instead, they are held for several successive years until a sufficient group is recruited; then the rites are not practiced for some time. Through circumcision men enter named tribal age groups whose members provide mutual aid and hospitality and, when young, form fighting units.

In East Africa and Australia circumcision is understood to remove the vestiges of polluting femininity (the foreskin) from a youth, converting him into an adult male. It provides a powerful measure of commitment to group values in the face of considerable suffering, and it represents a permanent moral and physical transformation. Women are afforded no comparable process, and (despite any physical operation) they remain minors subordinate to men, according to the norms that govern social organization. Where such initiation occurs we find the belief that society improves upon nature by transforming the male body into a more proper vehicle for a moral person to inhabit. The social person and the natural body are brought into closer conjunction. The endurance of pain and the observance of ritual restrictions express both a willingness and a capacity to subject personal appetites and feelings to collective ends. At the same time the powers that shape the cultural process assume a physical reality in the experience of bodily suffering.

[*For comparable rites among women, see* Clitoridectomy. *See also* Castration.]

BIBLIOGRAPHY

Beidelman, T. O. "Women and Men in Two East African Societies." In *Explorations in African Systems of Thought,* edited by Ivan Karp and Charles S. Bird, pp. 143–164. Bloomington, Ind., 1980. Contrasts sexual attributes and roles in a Bantu and a para-Nilotic society, including their relation to circumcision, age group, and social life.

Bryk, Felix. *Circumcision in Man and Woman* (1930). Reprint, New York, 1974. Although outdated and not critical of data and theories, Bryk's study is the only anthropological survey of the topic.

Meggitt, M. J. *Desert People: A Study of the Walbiri Aborigines of Central Australia.* Sydney, 1962. Contains the most reliable account of circumcision among a group of Australian Aborigines set within a broader social context.

Morgenstern, Julian. *Rites of Birth, Marriage, Death, and Kindred Occasions among the Semites.* Cincinnati, 1966. Contains a useful survey of Jewish and Muslim circumcision by a distinguished rabbinic scholar. Provides a good bibliography.

Roheim, Geza. *The Eternal Ones of the Dream* (1945). Reprint, New York, 1971. Contains a survey of Australian circumcision and related practices, with a psychoanalytical bias.

Spencer, Paul. *The Samburu: A Study of Gerontocracy in a Nomadic Tribe.* Berkeley, 1965. Contains a useful description of circumcision and related ritual among a para-Nilotic people of East Africa.

Turner, Victor. "Three Symbols of *Passage* in Ndembu Circumcision Ritual: An Interpretation." In *Essays on the Ritual of Social Relations,* edited by Max Gluckman, pp. 124–173. Manchester, England, 1962. Probably the best analysis of the complex symbolism associated with circumcision, in this case that of a Bantu people of central Africa.

Wallerstein, Edward. *Circumcision: An American Health Fallacy.* New York, 1980. A useful general survey by a physician. Deals with the practice cross-culturally, historically, and medically and contains a useful bibliography.

T. O. Beidelman

CIRCUMPOLAR RELIGIONS. *See* Arctic Religions.

CISTERCIANS. The Cistercians are an order of monks and nuns that arose in the twelfth century to foster the integral observance of the rule of Benedict of Nursia (d. 525). [*See the biography of Benedict.*] The order takes its name from the first community to adopt the reform, the Abbey of Cîteaux in Burgundy, France. Benedict's *Rule for Monasteries,* written around the year 500, became virtually the exclusive rule for monasteries in western Europe after the time of Charlemagne (d. 814). With the foundation of Cluny in 909, a reform to bring about a more observant monastic practice was effectively forwarded by a succession of great, holy, and long-lived abbots; however, this was achieved at the cost of local autonomy and the balance of liturgy, sacred reading, personal prayer, and manual work that is so characteristic of Benedict's *Rule.* At Cluny and many of its dependent monasteries, the liturgy was celebrated with great splendor and duration, while manual labor became for the monks a nominal exercise.

In the time of the Gregorian reform, many monastic founders arose who drew their inspiration from the Gospels, monastic traditions, and in some cases Benedict's *Rule.* They laid great stress on poverty, solitude, and simplicity of lifestyle. Most notable among these monks was Robert of Molesme (d. 1110), who, after entering the order at Moutier-la-Celle, near Troyes, attempted reforms in various monasteries and finally succeeded in gathering the hermits of Collan into a notable Benedictine community at Molesme. The community's fervor brought fame and fortune, and then a more relaxed observance of the rule. Again Robert, with the permission of the legate, Hugh of Die, set out to seek the fullness of the Benedictine way of life, establishing the New Monastery at Cîteaux in 1098. He was accompanied by the prior and subprior from Molesme, and nineteen others.

Within two years Robert was required by papal authority to return to Molesme, but the reform was carried forward by Alberic, his prior (d. 1109) and then by Stephen Harding (d. 1135), who had been his subprior. Under the latter, an expansion began which accelerated rapidly with the arrival of Bernard of Clairvaux (d. 1153).

To Stephen is largely attributed the *Charter of Charity,* which bound together Cîteaux and the many monasteries which would spring from it directly or indirectly, forming them into an order. The federated nature of this order respected the autonomy of the local community, while ensuring ongoing regularity of observance by an annual gathering of the college of abbots in a chapter and by a system of annual visitation of all the monasteries. As early as the 1130s these successful elements of the Cistercian reform began to find their way into other Benedictine federations; later, in various forms, chapters and visitation became part of the structure of almost every religious order.

While the concern of the Cistercian reformers to live to the full Benedict's rule too often descended to bickering over observances (see *A Dialogue between a Cluniac and a Cistercian*), its true aim as powerfully expressed by the leading Cistercian fathers—Bernard of Clairvaux, William of Saint-Thierry (d. 1148), Guerric of Igny (d. 1157), and Ælred of Rievaulx (d. 1169)—was to attain to the experience of God through mystical love, the goal pointed to by Benedict in the prologue and epilogue to his *Rule* and in its central chapter, the seventh, "On Humility."

The Cistercian order experienced very rapid expansion with the founding or affiliation of over three hundred monasteries in all parts of western Europe prior to the death of Bernard of Clairvaux. This expansion continued through the following centuries until there were over seven hundred Cistercian abbeys of men, as well as innumerable convents of nuns following their observance. The order was slow to incorporate communities of women; only in the wake of the Second Vatican Council have the abbesses emerged as fully equal members of the college of superiors.

In order that monks might have the opportunity to live the Benedictine rule to the full and strive after a truly contemplative life, the lay-brother vocation was promoted; this system provided larger work forces to build the monasteries and care for the order's ever-growing landholdings. The tensions that inevitably arose between the increasingly clericalized choir monks and the hardworking brothers could even erupt at times into violence.

Through the influence of the schools, scholastic scholarship began to replace a contemplative patristic theology. With the great geographical expansion of the order, the reform structure began to break down, and observance declined. The unlettered who had been attracted to the Cistercian lay brotherhood began, in the thirteenth century, to turn to the new fervent mendicant orders. The Cistercians began to fragment into national or regional congregations. The Protestant Reformation wiped out monastic life in many countries. An attempted reform within the order in the seventeenth century led to a "war of observances" and the emergence of the Strict Observance, prior to further losses through the French Revolution and other secularizing movements. The policies of Emperor Franz Josef forced the monks in the Austrian empire to take up tasks left off by the Jesuits when they were temporarily suppressed.

The Cistercians experienced a renewal in France in the nineteenth century that spilled over to the rest of the world in the next century. In 1892 Leo XIII sought to reunite all the Cistercians, but the pope's efforts resulted instead in the formation of two Cistercian orders, one now known as the Cistercians of the Strict Observance (Trappist), which includes both monks and nuns, and another composed of twelve congregations of monks and over eighty convents of nuns. A number of these congregations have suffered extensively at the hands of the Communists in Eastern Europe and Vietnam and have been largely suppressed or have found refuge in other countries.

The Strict Observance was brought to new prominence by the writings of one of its members, Thomas Merton (Father Louis of Gethsemani Abbey, Trappist, Kentucky). As the largest order of contemplative men in the church today, it has played an increasingly significant role in the contemporary spiritual renewal of the Roman Catholic church.

BIBLIOGRAPHY

The best, most up-to-date, and most complete work on the Cistercians is that of Louis J. Lekai, *The Cistercians: Ideals and Reality* (Kent, Ohio, 1977). For a complementary study from the point of view of the Strict Observance, see Jean de la Croix Bouton's *Histoire de l'Ordre de Cîteaux*, 3 vols. (Westmalle, Belgium, 1959–1968). However, the most extensive study of the origins of the Strict Observance is Lekai's *The Rise of the Cistercian Strict Observance in Seventeenth Century France* (Washington, D.C., 1968). Its later development is found in Anselme Le Bail's *L'Ordre de Cîteaux* (Paris, 1924). Thomas Merton in *Waters of Siloe* (New York, 1949) treats the American segment of Cistercian history most completely. For a deep and authoritative presentation of the spirituality that animates the Cistercian life, see Jean Leclercq's *Bernard of Clairvaux and the Cistercian Spirit* (Kalamazoo, Mich., 1976). Louis Bouyer's *The Cistercian Heritage* (London, 1958) is a more comprehensive and popular presentation of the spirituality of the order. *A Dialogue between a Cluniac and a Cistercian* can be found in *Cistercians and Cluniacs: Documents in the Feud between White Monks and Black Monks*, translated by Jeremiah F. O'Sullivan and Irene Edmonds (Kalamazoo, Mich., 1986).

M. BASIL PENNINGTON, O.C.S.O.

CITIES. A settlement is considered urban with respect to either its size or its density; these are defined differently by authorities. Plato's ideal city (the *Laws*) would have had 5,040 inhabitants; the Hindu *Śilpa Śāstra* treatise by Mānasāra specifies a *nagara*, or planned village, to be between twenty thousand and five million cubits in area and four cubits high, a third of the terrain to be built up and two-thirds to be cultivated. In various conditions, modern planners consider populations of between two and eighty persons per hectare to be urban. Most authorities require evidence of common effort at place-making in their definitions of urban settlement; such effort may include cult centers, ceremonial or trading grounds, or some forms of enclosure or enceinte, either physical or notional.

The Earliest Settlements. There is no necessary relation between intellectual complexity and level of material culture: nothing is known, for example, about the typological or geometric notions of the builders at Arcy-le-Cure in central France, or the similar groupings in Bohemia, Moravia, and southern Russia, all circa 30,000 BCE; although at Arcy the disposition of mammoth tusks around the perimeter dwelling indicates an intention which must be related to a general conception of the dwelling.

In modern structures of a modest technical accomplishment, elaborate formal notions related to visual and kinship patterning may be drawn from very scant physical evidence. In some African and North American circular settlements there seems to be a direct relation between the forms of dwelling and the form of the settlement, as well as a tendency to orient individual dwellings. In some !Kung San villages in southern Africa the entrances to many dwellings are directed to the unmarried men's hut and dancing grounds, the headman's hut, the sacred fire, and rising sun. The round tents, or tipis, of the Cheyenne, Algonquin, and Sioux Indians of North America were formed into circular encampments up to one-half kilometer in diameter, usually opened to the rising sun. Villages of the Trobriand Islanders of New Guinea describe a refined social hierarchy by their concentric planning around a sacred dancing ground and chief's hut.

Small, circular Neolithic foundations, such as Kolomischtschina I of the Tripolje-Ukraine culture, the larger wood and stone henges of the British Isles—cult centers which must have been related to dispersed population—and the much later (tenth century CE) circular forts at Trelleborg and Fyrkat in Danish Jutland, for example, do not show any such relation between form of dwelling and form of settlement. The small, square, earth-embanked village at Polianica, Bulgaria, is neatly quartered by two relatively broad streets forming four square blocks of three or four houses each; at Lepenski Vir, Yugoslavia, on the Danube, is a contemporary unwalled settlement of trapezoidal houses set down to form diagonal paths, including perhaps a public space of the same shape as that of the houses. Nothing is known of the etiology of such forms, but complex metaphoric descriptions are given by the modern makers for much less defined ones.

The houses, as well as the villages, of the Dogon of the south Sahara are described anthropomorphically, as are those of the Trobrianders; such descriptions are also given of various bilaterally symmetrical settlements with a head house, temple, or shrine at the central common ground, such as that of the South Nias Islanders of Indonesia. These descriptions persist through various traditions and reappear as images in classical antiquity (Vitruvius, *De architectura,* late first century BCE), in the fifteenth-century designs of Francesco di Giorgio, and even later. It is not certain that the elaborate stone and earth zoomorphic and geometrical land formations of the Ohio Valley may not have been inhabited; the Andean Nazca lines, and the stone and earth works of the Celts and the Australian Aborigines are analogous forms of figural land constructions without contiguous settlement.

First Urban Structures. Dense and enclosed settlement started, on present archaeological evidence, in southeastern Anatolia, (Haçilar and Çatal Hüyük, Turkey) and in the Jordan Valley (Jericho, Israel). Early Anatolian houses were packed around courtyards and had access over roofs; there may, strictly speaking, have been no streets and no encircling wall other than the backs of houses; Jericho, on the other hand, was heavily fortified. Small, fortified and densely built up settlements with twisted gate paths have persisted in the Mediterranean since the third millennium BCE. These include sites such as the traditional site of Troy (Truva, in Turkey); Byblos (Jubayl, Lebanon); Arad, Lato, Dimini, and Malthi-Dorion in the Aegean; and, over a millennium later, Vilaro d'Olius and La Gessera in the Spanish Baleares.

The Sacred Landscape, Cult Center, and Urban Generation. Fully urban forms of settlement begin in the Old World toward the end of the fourth millennium BCE, on the crop-growing alluvial plains and deltas of the Nile, Euphrates and Tigris, Indus, Yangtze, and Huang. The physical definition of the urban site seems to gel when political authority becomes concentrated in the hands of a single person, group, or class and a clerisy is easily identifiable. Generally, the oldest urban formations seem to have been generated from proto-urban tendencies of early cult centers, where common effort was harnessed for the construction of large ceremonial precincts involving temples, palaces, and assembly buildings whose relation to the habitat follows no fixed rule. Urban forms of settlement may elaborate the basic architectural componenets of the habitat, although their relation to it may be uncertain (Tiryns, An-yang, Chichén Itzá) and thus the palace or cult center may sometimes be identified as the settlement itself (Warka, Luxor, Harappa).

Egypt. In ancient Egypt the Nile was understood as the world axis; the creator was said to have emerged from the waters of chaos on a mound, a primeval hill, rising out of the flood waters; this event was traditionally located at the sun temple at Heliopolis on the lower Nile, even though the site upon which every temple was built was thought to be analogously sacred. The stepped and ramped temple type, as well as the royal or noble tomb, became mythically equivalent to the primeval hill; the solid mass of some temples and of the tombs, rising so distinctly out of the plain, makes such reference explicitly.

At Old Kingdom Medamud, a sacred precinct wall of mud brick enclosed a sacred forest set on a low, isolated hill; other natural features of the landscape were sanctified within Egyptian temples of all periods. Examples of such treatment of the land include the sacred lakes in the temples of Maru-Aten to the south of Amarna, on the right bank, and that of Amenhotep II at Karnak; the sacred island of Philae; and the riverside cliff faces into which temples were built, most often in the New Kingdom.

A journey down the Nile played an important part in the myth of Osiris; it was also the last stage in the life, and the first in the afterlife, of a pharaoh. In causeways and valley temples, both cardinally and diagonally oriented temple and tomb complexes often also addressed the river; Old Kingdom complexes generally faced the rising sun, for example, but at El Kāb, Hierakonpolis, and Abydos diagonal, Mesopotamian-style orientations prevail. The politico-geographic process of unification of the upper and lower Nile was expressed in the structure of Old Kingdom cities by duplicate (perhaps even triplicate) tombs, palaces, and temples. In the first and second dynasties, the locating of the royal palace complex at Thinis and the royal tomb complex (as a permanent royal residence) at adjacent Abydos established a pattern of paired cities of the living and the dead; about the royal mortuary complex, intersecting streets of mastabas belonging to the nobility are grouped according to their rank in life. In about 2650 BCE, the pharaoh Zoser and his minister (and perhaps his architect) Imhotep laid out a mortuary complex at Saqqara and a city, Memphis, probably using comparable principles of arrangement, orientation, and dimension; the step pyramid of Zoser dominated the walled precinct containing numerous courts and temples, chapels and a mock palace, the centerpiece of a vast necropolis, the dimensions of which may have been equivalent to the destroyed monumental and ceremonial core of Memphis. Popular annual pilgrimages to the Thebaic temple complexes on both sides of the river may be the reason for the monumental processional routes leading to the sites, and what seem to be the intertemple orientations which have been identified by some writers; conversely, Amun himself was supposed to visit Luxor and the temples at Deir al-Bahri once a year.

Mesopotamia, Anatolia, and Central Asia. Unlike in Egypt, where the frequent flooding of the Nile Valley facilitated agriculture, the city-states on the plain of the Tigris and Euphrates were the product of a concerted effort at irrigation; the economic and political realities were expressed in the myth of the city god, in whose temple or temple-palace a considerable population worked and lived. The consolidation of a divine society around a single temple site is a mature form; at Eridu (Abu Shahrain, Iraq), for example, thirteen small temples have been identified in the earliest predynastic levels, dating to the first half of the fourth millennium BCE. The formal elaboration of a "holy mountain," or ziggurat, at Kish (al-'Uhaymir, Iraq), is probably derived from constructions such as the White Temple at Sumerian Erech (Warka, Iraq), a thirteen-meter-high platform (circa 2300 BCE) overlaying the remains of earlier sanctuaries. The god was usually understood to be landowner of the temple and its hinterland in perpetuity, the king his bailiff. The earliest ziggurats (Al-'Ubaid, Warka, and Abu Shahrain in the south, and Khafaje to the north) were roughly oval in plan, and priests' dwellings, sacred workshops, granaries, storehouses, and the outer wall of the settlement were gathered concentrically around them. Neo-Sumerian Uruk (Makayyan, Iraq) had two harbor basins connected by a canal within its walls that separated the temple-palace from the residential, or profane, sector of the city. In the late fourth millennium, at the site of what seems to have been a Sumerian trading and administrative colony on the upper Euphrates (at Habuba Kabira South, in northern Syria), a six-hundred-meter-long stretch of city wall was punctuated regularly by gates which gave access to exactly perpendicular straight roads, which were in turn regularly intersected; such orthogonal inclinations may be taken as the regional precedent for the later Mesopotamian cities of Babylon (Babil/El Kasr, Iraq), Tell Barsip (Birs Nimrūd), and Khorsabad (Dur Sharrukin, Iraq), all founded in the ninth and eighth centuries BCE, with diagonally oriented, orthogonally planned roads and walls. Tell Barsip and Babylon, on alternate branches of the Euphrates and within a few kilometers of each other, were planned to straddle the river, dominated by ziggurats, with diverted moat canals surrounding the city walls in the manner of Uruk.

Late third-millennium Guzana (Tell Halaf, also on the Euphrates in Syria) was sited by a natural hill isolated on a wide plain, in analogy not only to Mesopotamian ziggurats but also to later Hittite "holy mountains" (which may have evolved from the Old Kingdom Hittite settlements on natural citadels). The earliest date to the first half of the second millennium BCE, in central Anatolia; later examples are found to the east, in the neo-Hittite and Commagene kingdoms. In the pre-Hittite Hattian phase of the cities which have been discovered at the Turkish sites of Bogazköy, Kultepe, and Acemhüyük, a physical distinction between the citadel hill and the merchant colonies on the lower slopes had already been established; at Bogazköy the acropolis was sited more or less centrally in the irregularly shaped (4.5 square kilometer) city plan, the courtyards leveled from the living rock, the royal palace overlooking five large temple complexes.

The Old Kingdom Hittite city at Alişar Hüyük, near Bogazköy, set around a high, conical hill, seems to have had a roughly circular city wall some 350 meters in diameter; this seems to be an early instance of the unusual circular-plan cities which developed ideas of a sacred landscape, presumably latent in the Mesopotamian-Anatolian tradition. In Soviet and Afghan Turkistan, circular settlements from the third millennium BCE are to be found at Altyn-Dil'jar Tepe, Emschi Tepe, and the Achaemenid site of Kutlug Tepe, which has three concentric sets of city walls; related to these is Dashli Tepe 3, where a circular sanctuary is encircled by a settlement defined by two concentric walls, all set on a square earth platform and defined by a wall and moat.

Aramaic Sam'al (Zinçirli, Syria), in the Commagene, a citadel like that at Bogazköy but built almost a millennium later, was sited on a naturally conical hill, around which a perfectly circular wall with three gates was built; in the mid-eighth century BCE, in neo-Assyrian Khadatu (Turkish Arslan Tash), the strictly oriented summer palace of Teglat Phalsar III stands on a low mound just to the north of a small artificial lake, which is itself at the center of an oval wall probably pierced by three gates.

The formal associations between "holy mountain," sacred citadel, and circular wall persist in accounts of both Herodotus (480–429 BCE) and the *Book of Judith* of the Median city of Ecbatana (Hamadān, Iran), set on a high hill and ringed (c. fifth century BCE) by seven concentric sets of walls, each higher than the last and colored differently to symbolize the planets. The structure of Ecbatana seems not to have been unlike the form of the seven-story ziggurat of Tell Barsip, each level of which was reveted, archaeology has revealed, with a different color of glazed brick; like this ziggurat, the palace-city of Ecbatana was presumably intended to symbolize the cosmos.

The formal and symbolic aspects of circular cities in the Middle East was modified by the second half of the first millennium BCE; some had concentric and radiating structures, while others were gridded orthogonally inside the walls. Parthian Dārāb (Darabgerd in southwestern Iran) may have been modeled on Ecbatana; this site, with its perfectly circular double city wall with eight gates and eight avenues radiating from a high hill at the center of the plan, dates to the first century BCE. The Sasanid king Ardashir I is said to have founded the city of Gūr (Iranian Firuzabad), in the fifth century CE, in the form of the sun; a fire tower stood at the heart of a walled precinct at the center of that city; from it radiated four main avenues in the cardinal directions. The last major foundation of this type was the Abbasid capital, Baghdad (762 CE); here, four main avenues each about two kilometers long, led to the city gates from the diagonally oriented temple–audience hall complex.

The other Parthian cities—the capital Ctesiphon on the Tigris (just to the south of Baghdad, Iraq), Takht-i Sulaymān in the Iranian Zagros foothills (possibly Phraāspa, the legendary birthplace of Zarathushtra), and Hatra (Al-Jasîrah, Iraq)—are formally distinct, their territories organized orthogonally, not radially. At the center of Ctesiphon (which is about three kilometers in diameter) is the parabolic vaulted hall-palace; a sacred lake surrounded by palace buildings and a fire temple are at the center of the plan at Takht-i Sulaymān; a perfectly square palace courtyard was laid down in the geometric center of Hatra. At Sesönk, Karakuş, and Nimrud-Dagh in the Turkish Commagene, circular tumuli, contemporaneous with these cities, seem to be their formal analogues; involved are cardinal orientation and the idea of a "holy mountain" and its ascent (the Indian stupa, Indonesian bayon, and Far Eastern pagoda are comparable forms). [*See also* Mountains.]

Traditions of orthogonal planning in Mesopotamia may date back to the mid-fourth millennium BCE; the most rigorous early example is the ninth-century BCE city revealed at Zernaki Tepe (southeastern Turkey), which belonged to the Urartian kingdom; the reimportation of Greek ideas of orthogonality at the end of the fourth century BCE, reinforced the indigenous tradition, producing a generation of pervasively orthogonal Seleucid cities. The wide, straight avenues and larger *insulae,* or city blocks (75 by 150 meters), in the capital Seleucia-on-the-Tigris (opposite Ctesiphon, founded in 301 BCE on the site of Babylonian Upi) offer a good example of such organization. Another Seleucid city, Dura-Europos (now in Syria) displays a less regular *insula* pattern and city-wall plan; the proportion of streets and squares is, however, distinctly Hellenistic.

Indus Valley. From the mid-third millennium BCE and for eight centuries or so, the main cities of the Indus Valley (Harappa, Mohenjo-Daro, Kalibangan, and Lothal) are urbanizations of cult centers of the pre-Harappan era. At Damb Sadaat, excavations have identified an even earlier large mud-brick platform encircled by massive walls enclosing structures equipped with huge drains; monumental cult platforms in the central western sectors were, in the Harappan period, clearly the focus for extensive lower cities. There is evidence of structures for ritual bathing and sacrifice and for grain storage even for the earliest phases of these buildings; the centerpiece was often a sacred mound or tower symbolizing, perhaps, the world mountain. Since the writing and language of the Harappan peoples are not yet known, it is only by formal association that these cities can be related to the planning tradition of the Indo-European settlers in the subcontinent, who arrived before the second millennium BCE.

The *Śilpaśāstra* of Mānasāra, a building treatise of late Hindu compilation (but possibly as early as the fifth or sixth century CE), specifies many village and town plans; an important feature in many is that they are quartered by two streets, a *rājapatha* ("royal street") and *vanapatha* ("broad street"), and encircled by the *maṅgalavithi,* the auspicious path just inside the walls circumambulated daily by a priest. The orientation of the *rājapatha* would ensure the future of the settlement in the Hindu tradition; in total, these guidelines were part of an all-embracing concept of the *maṇḍala* ("circle"). If the temple complexes of seventeenth-century Madura and eighteenth-century Fatehpur Sikri are compared with the city plans of Srirangam and Jaipur, both of which were developed, extended, and embellished from the sixth to the seventeenth centuries, we can see to what extent those principles of layout that apply to temples were applied to the planning and subsequent development of towns and cities. [*See also* Maṇḍalas.]

The planning of southern Iranian and Afghanistani *qal'āt* (fortified towns and cities) of the tenth to twelfth centuries CE may have also been influenced by the *Śilpaśāstra;* the square, oriented plans of Herāt (Afghanistan) and Bukhara, Khiva, and Shakhrisabz in Uzbekistan (U.S.S.R.) were, it seems, originally quartered by two straight streets intersecting at the center of the plan.

Southeast Asia. Since the seventh century CE, southeast Asia has abounded with cities whose plans synthesize influences from both China and India. About forty-five Khmer towns have been identified, such as Oc-Eo, Sri Deva, and Icanapura. Eighth-century Angkor Thom, capital of Jayavarman II (later rebuilt in the classical period by Jayavarman VII), was a royal, monastic, and pilgrimage city. Laid out in part on the principles of the *Śilpaśastra,* the square central temple built on a naturally oval mound had an oriented long axis; four gates opened to four main cardinally oriented avenues leading to corresponding gates in the city walls and across a city moat one hundred meters wide. The Angkor Wat temple complex occupied the entire southeast quadrant of the city and was itself planned as the city in miniature. Phnom-Bakheng, the central stupa or bayon of Angkor Thom, was considered the gods' abode; the city enceinte corresponded to the world mountain; the moat to the world ocean. These two *ankor*s (cities) were associated with the adjacent Prah Khan monastery and two extensive *bantay*s (reservoir tanks), together making up a built-up region of over eighty square kilometers, as yet without evidence of private dwellings. Hundreds of Khmer *bantay*s, waterways, moats, and carved-rock streambeds seem to confirm Indian ideas (in particular the late Hindu *Garuda Pinara* treatise) associating water with the sanctity of sites. The Sinhala king Parākramabāhu I (1164–1197) repaired and excavated over three thousand watercourses, many in connection with the great ceremonial city of Poḷonnaruva.

In Burma, the eleventh- and twelfth-century city at Arimaddanapura extends for thirty-seven kilometers along the banks of the Irawadi River; successive kings established new palace quarters which became, in the course of their reigns, the central focus of the city. Evidence of an extensive, orthogonally planned network of tanks and channels of the Satingpra culture seems to indicate the intensive habitation of the drained landscape of the Malay Peninsula.

The Thai cities Sukhothai and Satxanlai were carefully oriented and quartered with four main city gates and focused upon a ceremonial precinct; at the center of Sukhothai, the Vat Jai precinct enclosed a myriad of temples organized orthogonally around a large nine-part pagoda.

China and Japan. Cult centers seem to have been created in districts of dispersed villages at Cheng-chou and An-yang in the mid-second-millennium BCE Shang culture in North China. At Cheng-chou, a roughly square wall of heavy tamped-earth construction may be the ancient city of Ngog. Evidence of a ceremonial center set on earth platforms and foundations has been found near Hsiao-t'un in the An-yang district. Here, many human-sacrifice burials and jade finds indicate elite occupation; in fact, the sheep and tortoise divination bones found suggest that this may perhaps have been the cultural center of the Shang era.

A group of sites dating from the end of the second millennium BCE Chou dynasty show the centripetal force of the Shang-type ceremonial center generating dense, walled cities—generally rectangular, but often square and precisely oriented. The walls of the royal Chou city of Wang-ch'eng enclosed about eight square kilometers; an equally early city site at Niu-ts'un is known to have had a ring road inside the walls and a platform at the center, while at P'ing-wang, near Houma Chou, a series of villages with specialized functions were grouped loosely about the city walls.

Perhaps the most fully developed of their type are Han-tan and G'a-to. Its ceremonial structures first mentioned about 500 BCE, Han-tan became the Chou capital in the fourth century BCE. Its 2.1-square-kilometer plan was articulated by an axial arrangement of ceremonial earthwork platforms (three rectangular and one circular, ranging in height from three to thirteen meters) dividing it in half; G'a-to, occupied for about a millennium from around 700 BCE, seems eventually to have extended over some thirty-three square kilometers, including over fifty earthwork platforms, most of them presumably tumuli. Just outside the original city wall of G'a-to, the eight-meter-high Lao-lao platform was articulated with three superimposed square terraces topped by a circular one, a form approximating that of a Chinese diviner's board, or *shih,* in which a discoid plate representing the heavens is imposed on a square earth plate. There are many instances of such imposition of circle upon square, among them the much earlier Bactrian temple-palace town Dashli Tepe 3 in Afghanistan and the Javanese stupa at Borobudur dating from the mid-eighth century CE.

The original magic square, the "nine halls" (three by three squares, each containing a number, each row adding to the same total), dates to the third century BCE, and seems to be of Chinese origin. It is known to have been used for divination in the second century CE and is apparently connected to a long series of square city plans such as the T'ang city of Ch'ang-an, of the early seventh century CE, where a palace occupied the central north square of the three-by-three-part plan, and other monuments were organized symmetrically around the central north-south street. The eighth-century CE foundations of Lo-yang, fourteenth-century Sian-fu, and the twelfth-century Sung city of Hangchow are enormous walled enclosures, quartered by either roads or gates, or as at Hangchow, based explicitly on a nine-part square.

Pei-ching (Peking) was first consolidated by the thirteenth-century Yüan dynasty into a square plan over fifty square kilometers in area, gridded by nine north-south streets and another nine running east-west, creating a one-hundred-block plan. The later Ming inner-city plan was defined by three concentric earth-brick enclosures; axial alignments of gates, courtyards, and platforms have, over centuries of rebuilding, come to represent a richly articulated sacred landscape.

Some Chinese palaces were planned according to the balance and movements of the four seasons and the political geography of the country, so that a monarch could make a symbolic tour of his empire without moving outside his palace. Some temple-palaces or palace-cities seem to reflect Chinese cosmo-magical concepts.

Chinese ideas influenced Japanese layouts as they had Indonesian; residential sectors of Nara, founded around 710 CE on a site that had for over a century been an established religious center with famous temples and monasteries, were explicitly modeled on Ch'ang-an, eventually comprising about twenty square kilometers. In the late eighth and early ninth centuries CE, the Japanese "capital of peace and tranquillity," Heian-kyo, was twenty-seven kilometers square, with a huge ceremonial palace just north of center, the whole plan surrounded by a moat very similar in shape, size, and function to Jayavarman VII's Angkor Wat. The oriented replanning of Heian-kyo into royal Kyoto, in 792, featured a central north-south ceremonial route, along which were placed gates and temples in a slightly asymmetrical fashion; these first indications of picturesque planning developed fully in the thirteenth century, when the all-pervading concentric and axial geometries of the palace were erased, although its "Chinese" position in the city plan was retained.

The Americas. The establishment of temple mounds in the Guatemalan highlands at Kaminaljujú, around 1000 BCE, is the earliest evidence available of focused, if not particularly dense, settlement on the American continents. It became a major cult center, with substantial adobe platforms containing rich burials of chieftains or priests, only in the third century BCE.

In other regions of Mesoamerica, similarly dispersed settlements of up to fifty square kilometers were focused on monumental ensembles, such as the Olmec cult center at La Venta in lowland Tabasco and the Zapotec capital Monte Albán, near Oaxaca (both in Mexico). The Maya built vast monumental building ensembles, some original phases dating before the mid-fifth century CE, and some work went on until the Spanish arrival, at, for example: Copán (Honduras), Chichén Itzá and Uxmal (in Mexico), and Tikal (in Guatemala).

The earliest plaza and mound of Teotihuacán, in the Valley of Mexico, dates from the first centuries CE; subsequently, the site grew across thirty square kilometers, centered upon an intersection of a pair of broad, two-kilometer-long avenues, strictly and cardinally oriented, on which stand the pyramids of the Sun and the Moon; within a few kilometers are what appear to be the remains of communal dwellings with fifty to sixty rooms each, suggesting that the temple precinct itself accommodated only the court and priests. Composed of many dozens of courts, pyramids, platforms, and terraces, interspersed with multichambered buildings, ritual ball-game courts, seminaries, and storehouses, numerous Mesoamerican sites exceed the size of the largest cult centers of the Old World, but very often there is not even the slightest trace of habitation.

The much later Aztec capital Tenochtitlán (present-day Mexico City) was on a square-oriented plan, dominated by a central plaza from which canals ran to the north, south, and west; to the east were placed a great temple and pyramid.

It seems most plausible that the Peruvian sites of Chavín de Huántar, Tiahuanaco, Pacatnamú, and Pachácamac in the central Andes flourished around 1000 CE as pilgrimage centers, even though established much earlier. Twenty-eight square kilometers of fourteenth-century adobe ruins belong to the Chimú city of Chan-chan, the most important of the valley cities in this region; here, many pyramids and cemeteries were incorporated within a dense and strictly orthogonal plan subdivided into ten rectangular clan quarters, each served by its own cult buildings.

Chan-chan's compactness is unusual for this region; more characteristic is the rebuilt fifteenth-century plan of the Inca capital Cuzco. This was in the form of a cult center, separated by open countryside from a circle of residential villages comparable to contemporary settlements of the Yoruba in Nigeria and of prehistoric China.

In North America there is evidence of Pueblo culture between the Colorado River and the Rio Grande at such sites as Betatakin and Canyon de Chelly in Arizona, Mesa Verde in Colorado, and many sites in the Chaco and Frijoles canyons of New Mexico, the best known of which is Pueblo Bonito. Many are theatral valley complexes or are built into large cliffside caves, although there are also rectangularly planned sites, such as walled Aztek. Their precise use is uncertain, however. Here, rectangular rooms have been interpreted as dwellings or stores, and circular rooms, *kiva*s, three to ten meters in diameter, as ceremonial chambers. Mesa Verde is a characteristic cave-sited complex; Pueblo Bonito a classic example of a multilevel, semicircular adobe valley structure organized about a large courtyard.

The Aegean and Europe. Although Minoan valley settlements, many in the shadow of "peak sanctuaries," are to be found in the second half of the third millennium, the monumental palace-cities planned around large courtyards (which may have been used for religious celebrations) at Knossos, Phaistos, Gournia, and Mallia on Crete, appear only at the end of the second millennium BCE. At Knossos, the main courtyard of a multistory building complex of hundreds of rooms was sited at the crest of a hill and at the center of an unwalled city. At Mallia, an adjacent agora, a commercial and social marketplace retained from the proto-palatial phase of settlement, seems to have thrived while the palace did; a duality of palace-city and agora is present in subsequent Greek city forms.

The royal temple-palaces at Tiryns and Mycenae in the Greek Peloponnese and at Gla in Greek Boeotia were administrative and cultic citadels built and used over five centuries or so, until the fourteenth and thirteenth centuries BCE. All are specifically comparable to Hittite citadels. They and many other pre-Hellenic strongholds are part of a long-lived and widespread tradition of settlement in the Mediterranean Basin among peoples such as the Thracians, Lydians, Lycians, Phoenicians, and Dorians. Sometimes, in periods of peace and prosperity, lower cities would develop on the plain below these strongholds, preferably on a littoral or riverbank, leaving the original site as the sacred citadel and, when the community was threatened, a refuge.

Many Archaic Greek sanctuaries of the period 750–480 BCE, such as the Athenian acropolis and the island of Delos, were the location of earlier Mycenaean and Minoan settlements, just as many Mycenaean and Minoan settlements were themselves placed upon older sites. Earlier sacred precincts *(temenoi)*, for example, those at Olympia and Delphi on mainland Greece and Claros and Didyma in Ionian Turkey, became established centers of pilgrimage to consult oracles and hold games. Although removed from cities, they were connected to them by sacred ways and the sites developed into sacred landscapes. The *temenoi* themselves were comprised of sacred lakes, groves, pits, springs, trees, and wells, in addition to temples, votive statues, treasuries, and sometimes an *omphalos* (a marker of the centerpoint of the world); these were developed into ensembles that were added to and revised even into late antiquity. At Olympia, as at Delphi, an extensive stadium for athletic games was associated with the *temenos;* at Athens, festival theaters and processional ways were cut into the flanks of the acropolis.

The nascent polarity of Minoan Mallia matures in the early structure of Athens; the city's acropolis *temenos* is the center of its cultic life and, as in many other Greek city-states, the agora is its sociopolitical focus as well as the marketplace of both the city and its hinterland. There seems, however, to be no prevailing formal association between geometric planning and religious culture. The orthogonally planned cities of Magna Graecia of the late sixth and early fifth centuries BCE, such as Thurii, Paestum (Poseidonia), Agrigentum (Akragas), and Selinus (Selinonte), now all in southern Italy and Sicily; Olynthus and Piraeus in Greece; and the replanned Ionian cities, such as Priene and Miletus, on the west coast of Turkey, involve the principles of social planning more than any expression of religious concepts. This development is generally associated with the city planner Hippodamus of Miletus, probably active in the mid-fifth century BCE.

Once the Greeks became familiar with the idea of the

city as an organic and individual entity, each distinct from all others, it was natural that a single deity should come to be regarded as intimately connected with, even in control of, the fortunes of that city; this idea of city-god or goddess, a *tuchē*, dates from the fourth century BCE; under the empire of Alexander, practically every city had its *tuchē*.

In the north of the Italian peninsula, Etruscan cities such as Tarquinia, Veii, and Vulci, the earliest of which date to the eighth century BCE, and are nearly contemporary with some cities of Magna Graecia, were presumably founded with the recommendation of diviners and according to the best-documented of the many known city foundation rites, the *ritus etruscus*, for which the determinants of topographical features and the solar and stellar movements are crucial.

Rome was founded using this same Etruscan rite. Although a fire maintained by virgin priestesses at the hearth of Vesta was the ceremonial center point of the city, another "center" rite involved the *mundus*, an Etruscan-Latin ritual construction roughly comparable in symbolism to the Greek *omphalos*. The *mundus* was used to mark the place of departure and conclusion of the *ritus Etruscus* on the *via sacra* ("sacred way") with a sacred burial. Corresponding to the plow that was used to cut the sacred boundary furrow was the pomerium itself, the symbolic enclosure describing the extent of the original settlement, identified with the borders of the city's hinterland; according to the second-century writer Aullus Gellius, the borders of Rome were extended only as an honor to those who had extended the boundaries of the empire.

The founding of *coloniae* involved all these ceremonial-monumental concepts, though sometimes their ritual form varied; at Etruscan Marzabotto, probably laid out in the fifth century BCE, a *cippus*, or boundary marker, inscribed with a cross, was buried at the intersection of the two main streets. Similarly, in a crevasse on the rock-cut platform of the *capitolium*, the civic *temenos* of early Roman Cosa, an offering of fruits was buried, apparently as a sacrifice made upon the foundation of the city in 273 BCE; the *mundus* was associated with the god Terminus and the female organ; some writers have seen the Vesta-Terminus coupling as a parallel to the Greek Hermes-Hestia duality.

Whereas the *mundus* of Cosa is on its *capitolium*, its highest point, most Roman *coloniae* were laid down on near ideal topographical conditions—perfectly flat terrain—and their square plans were gridded into square *insulae*, or city blocks, by the *cardines* (the "vertical" streets, often running north and south, which served for ceremonial purposes, and the *decumani*, the cross-axial streets. The location of the forum, made up of the *mundus*, temples, and ceremonial structures, is to the "liturgical north" of the intersection of the *cardo maximus* and the *decumanus maximus*. Examples of such regular city planning are to be found in the first-century BCE plan of Augusta Praetoria (Aosta, in northwestern Italy), the later second-century CE plans of Thamugadi, and the permanent legionary camp Lambaesis (Timgad and Tazoult, Algeria).

The emperor Constantine's edict of 313 CE, officially christianizing the Roman state, acknowledged the emergence of Christianity from among the many eastern mystery cults. Subsequent legislation regarding the fate of pagan *temenoi* was optimistic; some powerful congregations and bishops were able to desecrate and close temples even before the imperial decrees, yet it was not until late in the fifth century that the Parthenon and Theseon in Athens were converted to churches and the Platonic Academy closed.

When he founded the first cathedral in Rome, Constantine chose a villa site on the Lateran hill, just inside the city walls but far from the venerable pagan Forum Romanum and Campus Martius, where very few structures were to be built or converted for Christian use until the sixth century CE. On the other side of the city, over the tomb of Saint Peter in the Vatican cemetery, *extra muros* and around a cemeterial basilica, a Christian city developed and eventually usurped the power of Rome itself. Many other early Christian cities experienced a similar peripheralization of development. The earliest evidence of Christian building is the house-church, *domus ecclesia*, such as that found just inside the city wall of Dura-Europos dated circa 230 CE. Generally, proto-Byzantine cities are the product of unregulated transformation; Apamea ad Orontem (in northwest Syria); Gerasa (Jerash in Transjordanian Israel); Miletus, Sardis, Hierapolis, and Aphrodisias (in Ionian and Carian Turkey); the sites of Stobi and Sirmium (Sremska Mitrovica, both now in Yugoslavia); Carthage (adjacent to Tunis, Tunisia); and Apollonia, Sabrata, and Leptis Magna (in coastal Libya), are cities that experienced much overbuilding of Roman forums, the conversion of temples and baths to churches, theaters to fortresses, and the reconstruction of city walls to enclose a much reduced area. Not only did public institutions fall into disrepair, but the decline in private munificence halted the normal maintenance of street paving and porticoes, while building density increased because of the infilling of streets and courtyards, following a weakening of many traditional social and commercial institutions.

In both urban and suburban settings, Christian sectors developed around the *insula episcopalis*, the ecclesiastical complex attached to the cathedral. Some were intramural developments, such as Hippo Regius (near Annaba, Algeria), Cuicul (Djemila, Algeria), and Side (near Manavgat, Turkey); others were extramural, such as Salona (near Split, Yugoslavia) and Rome; still others grew up beside late-antique cities in western Europe such as Remorium Urbs, or Remi (earlier Durocortorum, now Reims, France), Atrebatum (earlier Nemetacum, now Arras, France), Augustoritum Lemovicensium (Limoges, France), Augusta Treverorum (Trier, Germany) and Colonia Agrippina (Cologne, Germany).

In addition to these centers, it was ideologically important for the early bishops to establish a specifically Christian topography in the face of the well-established and well-known pagan ones; thus the places of notable Christian martyrdoms, miracles, and burials were knit together into a system of holy places that was maintained and greatly enlarged over centuries of worship and pilgrimage by building and rebuilding. Consequently, on or near venerated sites *(marturia, memoria)*, cemeterial basilicas, funerary chapels (all sanctuaries commemorating the dead), and monasteries would develop, often spawning residences and hostels, for which, in turn, auxiliary chapels, baptisteries, and basilicas were built specifically; sometimes these complexes were large enough to be considered urban, such as the town that sprang up beside the Monastery of Saint Simon Stylites (Qal'at Saman, Syria), which developed mainly in the fifth and sixth centuries. Existing towns often prospered by their association with saints, as did the oases that developed into Sergiopolis (Resafah, Syria) and the Marioūt oases in lower Egypt, connected with Sergius and Menas respectively.

Already in the fourth century in the Holy Land, in and around Jerusalem and Bethlehem especially, the grottos, springs, wells, rocks, tombs, and temples referred to in the Bible were developed architecturally into an impressive and sacred Christian landscape. [*See* Pilgrimage, *article on* Eastern Christian Pilgrimage.] Just as there are many copies of the Church of the Holy Sepulcher of Jerusalem across the Christian world, re-creations of the sacred landscape of the Holy Land as a whole have also been constructed. Among these are Patriarch Nikon's Resurrection Monastery at Istra, near Moscow, and Tabachetti's sixteenth-century Sacro Monte, near Varallo, Italy. There, fifty structures, including many mystery chapels, are designed to be visited in a specific order—a real pilgrimage, but in miniature. Not dissimilar to these is the vertical ascent to the twelve stations of the cross built, from the twelfth to fifteenth centuries, into the steep scarp face at Rocamadour in France, one of the many pilgrimage stops on the way to Compostela (now in Spain).

The routes of religious processions in Christian cities differed, even within one town or city, according to the particular purpose of the commemoration. Often they proceeded between an abbey or cathedral *extra muros* and the palace or castle within the original settlement; what was implied was an acknowledgment of secular power such as might be represented by a coronation, expressing a political-theological duality in the urban structure itself.

Some proto-Byzantine and medieval cities were, however, developed *de novo;* in the Byzantine East, the late sixth-century CE extension of the episcopal city at Caričingrad (in east-central Yugoslavia, probably Justiniana Prima), the early sixth-century fortress of Dara in the north Syrian desert, and the minuscule settlement, from perhaps the sixth century, at Arif in Lycian Turkey, all seem to have been orthogonally planned. Much later, in the West (for example, Aigues-Mortes and Montpazier in sourthern France, and León in northern Spain, from the thirteenth and fourteenth centuries), towns were built on a rigorously orthogonal plan, much in the spirit of the Roman surveyors. In all these plans, the orientation of the sanctuaries or churches was maintained as accurately as possible.

Certainly the largest new city building program in this period was the complete reconstruction and enlargement of Roman Byzantium, founded in 330 CE as Constantinople—the new Rome and first Christian capital. Apart from the formal dictates of its triangular site (similar to Babylonian Assur on the Tigris, in Iraqi Mesopotamia), the city was organized in imitation of Rome, divided into fourteen regions on seven hills; vast quantities of classical pagan spoils were brought there to build and decorate its monuments; distinctly pagan foundation rites were practised, and the Roman *tuchē*, Dea Roma (her chief festival being the anniversary of foundation), was christianized.

BIBLIOGRAPHY

The best account of the evidence for the earliest builders is André Leroi-Gourhan's two-volume work, *La geste et la parole* (Paris, 1964–1965), especially chapters 5 and 13; Douglas Fraser's *Village Planning in the Primitive World* (London, 1968) condenses much anthropological research of the last two centuries. For pertinent cross-cultural comparisons with Rome in particular, see the last two sections of Joseph Rykwert's *The Idea of a Town* (Princeton, 1976).

The formal and socioeconomic growth of ancient cities, as they developed from the first urban structures, is best understood from the review provided in a number of separate multivolume surveys; see Mario Coppa's excellently presented two-volume *Storia dell'urbanistica: Dalle origini all'ellenistico* (Turin, 1969) and volume 1 of Pierre Lavedan and Jean Hugueney's three-volume work, *Histoire de l'urbanisme* (Paris, 1926), in combination with Ernst Egli's three-volume *Geschichte des*

Städtebaues (Zurich, 1959–1967), which also takes into consideration evidence from East Asia and the Indus Valley region.

Paul Lampl's *City Planning in the Ancient Near East* (London, 1968) concentrates upon the formal and structural development of some ideas discussed in an excellent collection of essays by Henri Frankfort, Henriette A. Frankfort, John A. Wilson, Thorkild Jacobsen, and William Irwin, *The Intellectual Adventure of Ancient Man* (Chicago, 1957).

Alexander Badawy's three-volume work, *A History of Egyptian Architecture* (vol. 1, Giza, 1954; vols. 2 & 3, Berkeley, 1966–1968), and Henri Frankfort's *The Art and Architecture of the Ancient Orient* (Harmondsworth, 1970) are the best accounts of the role of the cult architecture of these regions. For China in particular, and for all the other regions under consideration as well, Paul Wheatley's *The Pivot of Four Quarters* (Chicago, 1971) is an excellent analysis of the role of cult centers in urban development. Stella Kramrish presents much material pertinent to Indian cities in *The Hindu Temple,* 2 vols. (Calcutta, 1946); Marcel Granet's *Chinese Civilisation* (London, 1930) is still the best account of the cultural background of the later Chinese city.

N. D. Fustel de Coulanges's classic study *The Ancient City* (New York, 1956) remains the finest historical work on the cities of Greece and Rome; Roland Martin's *L'urbanisme dans la Grèce antique,* 2d ed. (Paris, 1974), is a typological study of urban forms.

On the origins of the medieval city, see Edith Ennen's *Frühgeschichte der europäischen Stadt* (Bonn, 1953), which can be used most successfully as a historial source with Pierre Lavedan and Jean Hugueney's *L'urbanisme au Moyen-Âge* (Geneva, 1974). For the earlier urban forms of the Americas, as approached through its architecture, George Kubler's compendium *The Art and Architecture of Ancient America: The Mexican, Maya, and Andean Peoples,* 2d ed. (Harmondsworth, 1975), is excellent.

JOSEPH RYKWERT and MICHAEL MILOJEVIĆ

CIVIL RELIGION is the religious or quasi-religious regard for certain civic values and traditions found recurrently in the history of the political state. Such regard may be marked by special festivals, rituals, creeds, and dogmas that honor great personages and events of the past. The ancient sacred kingships of the Mediterranean world called for worship of the king or emperor as a god, highlighted by rites and ceremonies held at certain times each year. Much the same fusion of the political and the religious is found in Japanese history, at least to World War II, with respect to the emperor. In his classic *The Ancient City* (1864), the nineteenth-century historian Fustel de Coulanges describes the civil religions of the ancient Greek and Roman city-states. Just as the family and its functions, particularly the *rites de passage* of birth, marriage, and death, and the rendering of devotion to ancestors, formed the heart of the Greeks' and Romans' private religion, so the city-state was the heart of the public religion, ornamented by fixed seasonal and other festivals, and by rites and creeds, all honoring the great happenings of the city's past.

Civil religions flourished in the Middle Ages and during the Renaissance in western Europe. The major cities of western Europe, Christian though they were (and thereby under the governance of the papacy), vied with one another in the length, intensity, and sheer color of their civic rites. Cities had their special protective saints. These were often the subjects of the finest artistic efforts of the medieval era; they tended to become submerged in the festivals and ceremonies that took place regularly each year in what was at bottom a worshipful regard for the city itself. The Renaissance did nothing to dilute these expressions of civil commemoration; indeed the fifteenth and sixteenth centuries were marked by a general heightening of celebrations of the city, through the deliberate use of themes and festivals dredged up by the humanists from Greek and Roman antiquities.

Enlightenment and Revolution. Civil religion has been a highly visible aspect of the modern national state in the West. The destructive conflicts between European Protestants and Catholics in the sixteenth and seventeenth centuries, followed by the onslaught against revealed religion of any kind in the Enlightenment, tended to create a vacuum of belief among a substantial number of groups in western Europe. Efforts to make a deistic god, or a god of nature or progress, serve in the place of the traditional Christian conception were not successful. What did prove to be effective, however, was *patrie,* a coinage of the French *philosophes* to refer to a new conception of the political state: a state paternal in its regard for its citizens, something more than the engine of warfare and taxation the state had been, or seemed to be, over so many centuries. It was essentially *patrie* that Rousseau had in mind when he wrote his *Social Contract* (1762) with its glorification of the people and what he called the "general will." At the end of this seminal work in political philosophy Rousseau wrote a chapter titled "The Civil Religion." Believing that a religious need lies in everyone, and believing also that all existing religions, especially Christianity, were inadequate in the ideal state, Rousseau proposed a systematic civil religion "of which the Sovereign would fix the articles." Such articles would be "social sentiments without which a man cannot be a good citizen or a faithful subject." The seriousness of Rousseau's proposed civil religion may be inferred from the sanctions he included—banishment and even death for those who accepted and then flouted these articles of belief.

In a very real sense, the leaders of the French Revolution instituted, at the height of the Revolution in 1793–1794, a civil religion. Robespierre, an almost fanatical adherent of Rousseau's philosophy, led the way in the establishment of what was officially called the Religion of the Supreme Being—the real substance of which was the Revolution itself, which the Jacobin leaders tended to regard as a monumental religious event in human history. With the new religion went on the one hand an effort to "dechristianize" France, to obliterate every evidence of traditional Christianity, and on the other an increasing use of the Terror, including its guillotine, against not just the nobility or wartraitors, but revolutionists themselves—those in whose visible regard for the Revolution there could be detected "hypocrisy," the supreme sin in the final stages of the Revolution. So ardent was the faith of many Jacobins in the new religion that its proclaimed tenets, dogmas, and even rituals, liturgies, hymns, and artworks were rigorously recorded. Almost without exception, these celebrated not only the sacred Revolution but the almost equally sacred events, personages, and acts of the Revolutionary government during its short life. There is nothing astonishing in the fact that most of the rituals had a decidedly Roman Catholic form. What is important is that as a cardinal part of the Revolution—an event that seized the minds of millions in the West—a religion was inaugurated that had the political state, specifically the revolutionary state, as the essence of belief and rite.

Nineteenth-Century Nationalism. The phrase "civil religion" seems to have disappeared from political discourse in the nineteenth century, but what did not disappear, what became indeed one of the two or three most significant phenomena of the age, was what the eminent historian C. J. H. Hayes called "the religion of nationalism." Writing in 1926, Hayes thought "The most impressive fact of the present age is the universality of the religious aspects of nationalism." In a brilliant essay on the subject, Hayes called attention to the vivid parallels between traditional Christianity on the one hand and on the other the new national, or civil, religion, the "God" of which was the national state that had emerged so triumphantly in Europe chiefly as the result of the Napoleonic Wars, more particularly of Napoleon's carrying to every part of the continent the nationalist slogans of the French Revolution.

The fierce flare of nationalism in nineteenth-century Europe, and also in the United States, carried with it an enthusiasm, in the religious sense, that the civil religions of the ancient and medieval worlds generally lacked. Hegel declared the national state (chiefly, his own Prussia) "the march of God on earth," and while many nationalists on both sides of the Atlantic might have rejected Hegel's wording, there is no doubt whatever that the overwhelming majority of nationalists everywhere saw their respective nations, their peoples, as touched by the divine. In France, Germany, Russia, and England the combination of emergent nationalism, militarism, and, not to be overlooked, racialism could and often did lead to mass reactions not seen since the religious wars of the sixteenth and seventeenth centuries. The mention of *la belle France* or of Mother Russia could send essentially religious reverberations through whole populations. Very probably World War I represented the culmination of nationalist religious fervor in Europe. Not since the Crusades of the Middle Ages had so many men gone into battle—into almost certain slaughter, as was evident by 1918—as rapturously and devotedly as did Russians, Germans, English, and French. In poetry, song, pageant, and sermon the divinity of the nation was celebrated, as was the glory of going to one's death for it.

Civil Religion in the United States. The United States is a vivid example of the religion of nationalism and of the degree of intensity possible in creed and ritual in the civil religion. Belief in the divine mission of Americans began with the Puritans in New England. When John Winthrop, taking a phrase from the gospel of Matthew, likened his small band of Puritans in Massachusetts to "a city upon a hill," with the eyes of the world upon it, it was as much in tribute to the New World as to the religious tenets brought by the Puritans from England. There were many, including Cotton Mather, who believed ardently that New England would be the abode of Christ when he returned to govern mankind and thus inaugurate the millennium.

During the eighteenth century we can see the widening of this millennialism from the Puritans alone to all Americans. In sermon, tract, letter, and commentary, the Americans are seen as the unique recipients of God's blessing. It was America and the Americans who shared with God the Great Awakening of the early eighteenth century. In the politically fevered American imagination the history of the new nation could be seen in terms of a new Exodus, a chosen people, a promised land, a covenant, and so on. The nineteenth-century historian George Bancroft, in one of the most widely read books of the century, devoted forty years and ten volumes to demonstrating that America from its colonial beginnings was the divine instrument of Providence, its whole history a fulfillment of "Manifest Destiny" and the nearest approximation in all human history to the ideal state.

Alexis de Tocqueville was struck by the American civil religion when he and his companion Gustave de

Beaumont de la Bonnière visited the United States for nine months in 1830–1831. There was, he observed, a rapt, at times almost mystical, quality in the Americans' regard for themselves and their history. In the American mind, he wrote, the movement westward "has something providential in it; it is like some flood of humanity rising constantly and driven on by the hand of God" (*Democracy in America*, 1835).

The United States is, however, but one instance, albeit a dramatic one, of the religion of nationalism in the West in the nineteenth and early twentieth centuries. In Europe, from France eastward to Holy Mother Russia, the continent was ablaze with newly affirmed or discovered nationalism and with the appointed destiny immanent in its historical development. In countless ways the national state appeared as the new church, recipient of functions and responsibilities historically reserved for family and religion. A political clerisy came into being in every country, one as devoted to the nation as the medieval clerisy had been to the church. Children were now born into, and received their primary identities from, the national state, as they had once been born primarily into the church. Birth, marriage, and death, all became invested with an unwonted civil importance. In such spheres as family, school, and charity the civil government made its way with benign intent as once the church had. Just as the church had long had its saints' days on the calendar, so now did the state. By the end of the nineteenth century the birthdays of great political figures such as Washington, Jefferson, and Lincoln were celebrated as solemnly as had once been the feasts of Christian saints and martyrs. In the same way, great events in the nation's history were given religious regard. In America the Fourth of July took on some of the significance that the Feast of the Nativity had in Christianity—and America was far from being alone in this kind of national celebration. It is no exaggeration to say, in all, that the American civil religion had its widely recognized theology, one complete with creed, catechism, and dogma. A complex ritual surrounded the American flag and other symbols of national civil unity. Protestants who scorned Roman Catholic use of external adornments of faith—statuary, mural, portrait, and the like—saw nothing wrong with such adornments in their national religion. It was a rare public square in America—but also in European countries—that did not have at least one statue of some departed political saint or martyr. There were of course sacred documents and writs—the Declaration of Independence and the Constitution, for example, both on display in a national shrine. Certain addresses such as Washington's Farewell and Lincoln's Second Inaugural came to possess distinctly religious overtones as they were repeatedly invoked in speeches. The Pledge of Allegiance became as standard a rite for school children in America as morning prayers to God had once been.

Civil Religion and Human Community. Although civil religion in the Western nations has not disappeared in the late twentieth century, it is evident that it has lost much of the fervor that characterized it during the nineteenth and early twentieth centuries. During the 1920s, when serious revisionism took place among historians with respect to World War I, and when the mood of disillusionment over the war and its consequences spread widely, much of the religious fervor of nationalism in all Western countries disappeared. World War II did little to rejuvenate it. The paucity of sacred national expressions in song, poem, oration, and public gathering was only too evident when compared with national reactions during World War I. At the present moment, everywhere in the democratic world, patriotism, and with it the civil religion, are at an ebb.

There is nevertheless an eternality to civil religion as to other forms of religion, no matter in what degree these may wane or wax. It was the sociologist Émile Durkheim who, above any other student of religion, discerned the reasons for this eternality. The origin of all religion, Durkheim argued in *The Elementary Forms of the Religious Life* (1912), lies in the ascription of sacredness to the human community—family, clan, tribe, city, and state, in that order. It is the social bond itself that is celebrated in the most primitive religions; external, supernatural deities are not to be found. It is, Durkheim further argued, the social bond, in the form of the cult and the church, that remains the real basis of faith and observance even in the higher, revealed religions such as Christianity, Judaism, and Buddhism. Religions tend to weaken when their visible communal rites begin to wane and when religion itself is declared to be solely a matter of individual faith. There is virtually no limit, Durkheim wrote, to the things that may be regarded by a given cult as sacred, that is, as belonging to a different sphere from the merely utilitarian or secular. Good and evil are alike expressions of the sacred. Hence Durkheim's well-known definition of religion: "A religion is a unified system of beliefs and practices relative to sacred things, that is to say, things set apart and forbidden—beliefs and practices which unite into one single moral community called a Church, all those who adhere to them."

As Durkheim himself noted, cities and nations are as susceptible to the nomenclature of the sacred as are the social bodies we call churches. He cites France during the Revolution at the end of the eighteenth century. Were he alive today, he could point to the Soviet Union where, its official atheism notwithstanding, the clear beginnings of a national religion are evident. Every effort is made by the ruling class to give a sacredness to the Revolution of 1917 and to its principals, especially Lenin, whose tomb has become a national shrine attracting millions every year. In sum, we may say that the centrality of the church or cult—each a form of sacred community—in almost all known religions suggests the susceptibility of any form of community to becoming a sacred bond in human beings' lives, and thus in time to attaining at least quasi-religious status. There are no signs in the world at the present time to suggest that nationalism is becoming a spent force. In human history the nation-state has succeeded household, clan, kindred, and tribe as the dominant political reality in human life. It is only stating the obvious to conclude that at least some of the religious aura of the earlier types of community will attend the nation-state wherever it becomes seriously rooted.

[*For discussion of the ways in which the state has supplanted functions once fulfilled by religious ritual, see* Ceremony. *For further discussion of other themes touched upon in this article, see* Marxism; Politics and Religion; Revolution; Secularization; *and the biographies of Durkheim, Fustel de Coulanges, and Rousseau.*]

BIBLIOGRAPHY

Jean-Jacques Rousseau's *The Social Contract* (1762), book 4, chap. 8, "Civil Religion," is a spirited introduction to the concept of civil religion, although it is written in prescriptive rather than descriptive form. On the French Revolution and its creation of a civil religion, see chapter 13 of Robert R. Palmer's *Twelve Who Ruled* (Princeton, 1941). Still the best treatment of nationalism as a civil religion is Carlton J. H. Hayes's *Essays on Nationalism* (1926; reprint, New York, 1966), pp. 93–125. Robert N. Bellah and Philip E. Hammond's *Varieties of Civil Religion* (San Francisco, 1980) is at once an effort to advance the concept of civil religion for sociological study and a conspectus of scholarly work done thus far in sociology on the subject. Book 3 of Numa Denis Fustel de Coulanges's *The Ancient City* (1864) serves not only as a profound illumination of the civil religions of ancient Athens and Rome but as a valuable model for further work on the subject of civil religion. Émile Durkheim's *The Elementary Forms of the Religious Life* (1912), translated by Joseph Ward Swain (New York, 1915), throws valuable light on the social sources of all religions, including civil or national religion.

ROBERT NISBET

CLASSIFICATION OF RELIGIONS

CLASSIFICATION OF RELIGIONS is necessitated by the diversity, complexity, and greatly increased knowledge of religions and by the development of the scientific study of religion during the past hundred years. The student of religion seeks to find or bring some system of intelligibility to the manifold expressions of religious experience, not only to make the data manageable but to discern common characteristics by which religions and religious phenomena can be grouped together and compared with or distinguished from others. Basically, there are two kinds of classification. One orders historical religions in terms of their similarities and differences; the other orders religious phenomena into categories (e.g., sacrifice, purification, rites of passage).

Early Modern Classification Schemes. The work of F. Max Müller (1823–1900), the father of the comparative study of religions, gave impetus to the classification of religion. Primarily a linguist, Müller used his philological method as a model for the comparative study of religions and the classification of religions along racial-genetic lines. In his view, racial, linguistic, and religious "families" (Aryan, Semitic, and Turanian) coincided. Language provided the primary evidence for this coincidence.

The Dutch scholar C. P. Tiele (1830–1902), one of the founders of the scientific study of religion and a contemporary of Müller, also gave particular attention to the classification of religions. Tiele was impressed by the moral and ethical qualities he found in religions. He saw these qualities as expressions of a "religious idea" that had evolved in the course of history. He distinguished between "nature religions" and "ethical religions." The former were those in which ethical elements were either absent or, at most, minimally present. These religions included polyzoic naturalism (a belief that all nature is endowed with life), polydemonistic-magical religions (animism), therianthropic polytheism (gods in the form of animals), and anthropomorphic polytheism (gods in the form of men). The ethical religions ("spiritualistic ethical religions of revelation") were divided into two categories: natural nomistic (legalistic) religious communions (including Taoism, Confucianism, Brahmanism, and Judaism) and universalistic religious communions (Buddhism, Christianity, and Islam). Of the former category Judaism was considered transitional in the direction of universalistic religions. To the latter category only Buddhism and Christianity fully belong, for Islam is thought to retain some particularistic and nomistic elements.

Tiele's emphasis on the ethical as a new and decisive religious element came to be used frequently in distinguishing the "higher" from the "lower" religions. While it is true that the monotheistic religions emphasize ethics and morality, it is not the case that a concern for morality is absent in so-called primitive religions. The judgment of Tiele and others of his time, and the classifications based on it, reflected prejudices concerning "primitive" peoples.

Types of Classification. Some classifications of religions are extraordinarily broad, the broadest being binary or bipartite. Familiar bipartite classifications give such contrasting pairs as true-false, natural-revealed, literate-preliterate, Eastern-Western, and Christian–non-Christian. The most obvious difficulty with such broad classifications is that they do not distinguish sufficiently to do justice to the diversity and complexity of the religious world.

Normative classification. The most common type of classification, historically, has been normative. Religions have been classified according to the norms or standards of the classifiers. Typically, these norms were religiously, culturally, and historically conditioned, if not derived, and tended to be subjective and arbitrary.

A persistent binary normative classification has been the division of religions in relation to "truth," yielding the two categories: "true religion" and "false religion." This division has appeared frequently among the great monotheistic religions (Judaism, Christianity, and Islam) but has not been limited to them. Normative classifications do not increase understanding.

The use of normative classification by Christians goes back at least to the church fathers. It arose in the context of the religious competition of the early centuries, a time of great religious ferment and rivalry, to meet the needs of Christian apologetics. Thus, for example, other religions were said to exist as the result of divine condescension to the needs and weaknesses of humans and no longer had any validity after the appearance of Christianity. Judaism with its Torah, it was said, had been a "schoolmaster" preparing its adherents for the coming of the Gospel, and the other religions were merely imperfect copies of the true religion, plagiarisms at best.

Other Christian classifications of religions originated in the Middle Ages, and received a status that they retained in large measure through the magisterial authority of Thomas Aquinas (1225–1274). Thomas taught a basic distinction between natural religion and revealed religion, the former based on religious truth that can be known through the use of reason itself and the latter on divinely revealed truth. This distinction coincides in part with the distinction between religions based on "general revelation" and those based on "special revelation."

Protestantism has also provided various binary classifications of religions. Examples from the Reformation include Martin Luther's norm of justification by faith and John Calvin's *sola gratia;* a later instance is the distinction between "heathen religions" and the Christian religion, commonly made at the beginnings of the Protestant missionary movement.

Less obviously normative are classifications of religions that are ostensibly scientific, particularly those classifications based on theories about the origin and development of religion that appeared during the late nineteenth and early twentieth centuries. The theory that enjoyed the greatest vogue, E. B. Tylor's "animism," argued that the earliest form of religion was based on belief in *anima* or souls, spiritual entities capable of separation from the body. Tylor theorized that this primitive belief was based on certain real but misinterpreted universal human experiences (sleep, dreams, trances, hallucinations, and death). He admitted, however, that religion as it is found in the world is more than this, for everywhere it has undergone development. It evolves through various stages, which Tylor tried to sketch out, thereby accounting for the various kinds of theism, including polytheism and monotheism.

The theories of Tylor and others who developed evolutionary schemes typically postulated not neutral stages but scales having normative significance. Evolution was seen as a movement from simple, rudimentary, indeed crude, beginnings, through successive stages, each exhibiting increasing complexity, toward completion and perfection. "Earlier" meant lower and inferior; "later" meant higher and superior. Chronology was given valuative meaning. Not surprisingly, monotheism was seen as the highest religious stage yet attained. Each religion could be distinguished and classified in terms of its place on the scale, the several great monotheisms coming at the top. At the same time, one could reveal the "primitive" foundations and beginnings of all religions, including the highest. The evolutionists, like the later Freudians, believed they could disclose the secret that lay at the beginning. Moreover, they assumed that the nature, the essence of religion, is identical with its origin.

Geographical classification. Geography has been a ready means of classification of religions, especially since many religions and types of religion can be observed to belong exclusively or mainly to certain geographical areas. Again, simple binary classifications have appeared, the most common being "Eastern religions" and "Western religions." Often "Western" means Judaism and Christianity (religions of "Near Eastern" origin, actually), with Islam conveniently forgotten by many classifiers. "Eastern" or "Asian" may mean India and China and the lands under their cultural and religious influence. This simple bipartite division not only groups together religions (especially those of the "East") which differ greatly from one another, but omits important areas of the world and their religions.

The actual geographical distribution of some of the major religions renders problematic classification by geographical distribution. Some, for example Christianity, may be found in most regions of the world, although the proportion of adherents to the general population will vary widely. In this regard Islam is a particularly difficult case. Originating in the Near East, it quickly became a religion of wide geographical distribution, generating the "Islamic world," a great band stretching at least from Morocco in the West to Indonesia in the East, with important communities in the North (the Soviet Union and China) and South (sub-Saharan Africa). The fact that some religions have become virtually extinct in the lands of their origins (e.g., Indian Buddhism) also complicates geographical classification.

Further, it is difficult to stay simply with geographical criteria. Many textbooks on "comparative religion" (under such titles as *Religions of the World* and *Religions of Mankind*) combine the geographical and the historical in their outlines, utilizing such headings as "Religions of Middle Eastern Origin," "Religions of Ancient Rome," and "Religion in the Islamic World" as well as headings of purely geographical designation (e.g., "Religions of the Indian Subcontinent"). Such textbooks tend to leave out some important geographical regions. They may present religions of India, the Near East, the Far East, and perhaps religions of Greece and Rome. They are much less likely to include African religions and the religions of the Amerindians and the Pacific islands peoples.

Geography appears at first to afford the possibility of a convenient, intelligible, neutral classification of religions but turns out not to do so. In any case, its value is doubtful, for the significance of geographical considerations, especially on a large scale, is minimal for the understanding of particular religions and groups of religions, recent studies in the ecology of religion notwithstanding.

Philosophical classification. The philosophical consideration of religions led in the modern period to some attempts in the West to classify religions on a philosophical rather than a theological or geographical basis. Perhaps the most wide-ranging and best-known effort is that of the German philosopher G. W. F. Hegel (1770–1831), especially in his *Lectures on the Philosophy of Religion* (1832). Briefly, Hegel saw religions in relation to the dialectical movement of the whole of human history toward the ultimate realization of freedom. He envisioned a vast scheme of evolution in which Spirit progressively realizes itself through the ongoing dialectical process of thesis, antithesis, and synthesis.

Hegel classified religions in terms of the stages they represent in the progressive self-realization of Spirit. Contrasting self and nature, he considered as the lowest level of religion the religions of nature. In these religions humans are completely immersed in nature and have only such consciousness as derives from sense experience. A higher stage of religion is represented, according to Hegel, by those religions in which humans have begun to emerge from nature and become conscious of their individuality. Specifically, this stage is represented by Greek and Roman religions and Judaism. The highest stage of religion is that in which the opposites of nature and individuality are transcended in the realization of what Hegel called Absolute Spirit. This is the level of Absolute Religion, which he did not hesitate to identify with Christianity.

Hegel's general scheme, as well as his classification of religions, has been criticized for its assumption that human history exhibits continuous progress. Further, Hegel's classification of religions is value-laden, most obviously in its claim that the Christian religion is the absolute religion. One sees again that normativeness is not the sole preserve of theologians.

A somewhat different philosophical approach to classification is found in the work of another nineteenth-century German thinker, Otto Pfleiderer (1839–1908), especially in his *Die Religion, ihr Wesen und ihre Geschichte,* 2 vols. (1869). Pfleiderer's approach focused upon the essence *(Wesen)* of religion. In his view, the essence is found in two elements, freedom and dependence, which are variously interrelated in the religious consciousness generally and in specific historical religions. Some religions (e.g., Egyptian and ancient Semitic religions) emphasize the religious sense of dependence, whereas other religions (e.g., the religions of the Aryans, Greeks, and Romans) stress the opposite pole, freedom. Still other religions clearly contain both elements but in unequal proportion (Brahmanism, Buddhism, Zoroastrianism). In Pfleiderer's view the highest manifestation of religion is one in which the two elements, freedom and dependence, are in equilibrium, reconciled in an ultimate harmony. This possibility he believed is found only in the monotheistic religions, Judaism, Christianity, and Islam. The possibility is fully realized, however, only in Christianity, for Islam is still inclined toward dependence and Judaism toward freedom. Here again a Western Christian thinker's classification of religions is used as a means of affirming the religious superiority of Christianity.

Phenomenology of religion. The term *phenomenology* can mean several things. It can refer to the twentieth-century philosophical school initially associated with the German philosopher Edmund Husserl, and later with Martin Heidegger, Maurice Merleau-Ponty, Paul Ricoeur, and others. In this sense it is phenomenological philosophy devoted to the study of religion. However, the term *phenomenology of religion* refers to the application of phenomenological methods to the study of the history of religions, as, for example, by W. Brede Kristensen, Gerardus van der Leeuw, C. Jouco Bleeker, and Mircea Eliade. In the hands of these scholars phenomenology is less a philosophy than a method for the study of religions.

The interest of phenomenologists of religion is in the classification of religious phenomena that are not limited or specific to a particular historical religion but cross the religious lines. For example, the phenomenologist of religion is interested in such categories as rites of sacrifice, myths of origin, and fertility deities. Further, phenomenologists seek to discern the "meaning" of religious phenomena in a nonreductionistic and nonnormative manner, believing that the phenomena will disclose their meanings to those who approach them "phenomenologically," that is, in a disciplined but open and nonprejudicial way.

W. Brede Kristensen (1867–1953), a Dutch scholar of Norwegian origin and a pioneer of phenomenology of religion, understood phenomenology as a new method of organizing data in the study of religion. One could, of course, organize the data historically or geographically as had been done in the past. But one could also organize data phenomenologically, in which case one would attempt to discern common themes and to describe the meanings of these themes among religions, regardless of their historical tradition or geographical location. Ultimately, one seeks the *essence* of the religious phenomena. In *The Meaning of Religion* (1960), Kristensen described the task of phenomenology of religion as that of classifying and grouping the divergent data of religion in such a way that one may obtain an overall view of their religious content and the religious values therein. The phenomena should be grouped according to characteristics that correspond to the essential and typical elements of religion. Kristensen classified the subjects of the phenomenology of religion into three broad groups: religious cosmology (the world), religious anthropology (humans), and cultus (acts of worship). Within their scope he was able to treat such specific phenomena as the worship of earth gods, conceptions of the soul, and ritual purifications.

Another Dutch phenomenologist of religion was Gerardus van der Leeuw (1890–1950), whose *Religion in Essence and Manifestation* (*Phänomenologie der Religion*, 1933) is considered a classic. His broadest phenomenological categories were the object of religion (which he analyzed in terms of power and the forms of power), the subject of religion (sacred man and community), and object and subject in reciprocal operation. Using these categories, he was able to classify and interpret an impressive number and variety of specific religious phenomena: sacred stones and trees, demons, priests, saints, sects, souls, sacrifices, taboo, sacred times and spaces, festivals, myth, mysticism, faith, and many others.

Unlike Kristensen, van der Leeuw gave some attention to "religions" (i.e., historical religious wholes), quoting Heinrich Frick's assertion that "religion actually exists only in religions." His classification was twelvefold. It was, however, curious and mixed, for it included not only historical religions but types of religion without specific historical form, and forms of religious dynamic. Specifically, van der Leeuw distinguished eight historical forms of religion: (1) religion of remoteness and flight (Confucianism and eighteenth-century Deism); (2) religion of struggle (Zoroastrian dualism); (3) religion of strain and form (Greek religion); (4) religion of infinity and asceticism (Indian religion, especially Hinduism); (5) religion of nothingness and compassion (Buddhism); (6) religion of will and obedience (Jewish religion); (7) religion of majesty and humility (Islam); and (8) religion of love (Christianity). To these forms he added religion of repose and religion of unrest. The former he associated with mysticism and the latter with theism. Both are elements in historical religions but have no proper historical form of their own. Finally, van der Leeuw distinguished two forms of the "dynamic of religions." One manifests itself by syncretism and mission, the other by revivals and reformations.

The usual criticism of phenomenology of religion, including its classifications, whether of phenomena or historical religions, is that it is not sufficiently historical. While phenomenologists of religion often begin with the historical data and seek to understand the data "historically," at least initially, the tendency is often toward abstraction, and then toward reification of these "forms" of religious dynamic, with the result that the phenomenologist's attention is drawn away from the religions in their historical particularity.

Recent Attempts at Classification. The enterprise of classifying religions is no longer in vogue. It is not often that one finds students of religion devoting their energies to this task. While the need to order data continues, other reasons that encouraged classification have diminished. As intimated above, one reason for classification has been to provide a framework for the assertion of the superiority of Christianity. That motive, whether consciously or unconsciously held, has faded. Another reason was directly connected with the vogue of evolutionism, for it encouraged and facilitated classification in terms of religious stages. That, too, has declined.

Nevertheless, there have been some recent attempts

to classify religions. Illustratively, attention may be called to three. The sociologist of religion, Robert N. Bellah, has sought to construct an evolutionary interpretation of religion. In an essay entitled *Religious Evolution* (1964) he proposed a sequence of five ideal typical stages of development: primitive, archaic, historic, early modern, and modern. These stages are examined in terms of their religious symbol systems, religious actions, religious organizations, and social implications. He maintains that the symbol systems have evolved from the simple to the complex. Also, religious collectivities have become progressively differentiated from other social structures. Finally, beginning with the historic stage, the consciousness of the self as a religious subject has increasingly developed. Religious evolution is thus seen as a process of differentiation and development that can best be understood historically and sociologically.

The influential and prolific historian of religions Mircea Eliade has delineated two fundamentally different religious orientations: cosmic and historical. The former is the principal topic of *The Myth of the Eternal Return* (1949). It is the type of orientation characteristic of so-called primitive and archaic religions and, in fact, of all "traditional" religion. Cosmic orientation is distinguished by its experience and conception of time (as cyclical and reversible). Sacred time is mythical, not historical. History is deprecated in favor of transcendental models provided by myth. By means of return to the powerfully creative, mythical time of origins, humans are enabled to overcome the deleterious effects of ordinary, profane time. Moreover, the objects and structures of the world ("nature") are means by which the sacred manifests itself ("hierophanies"). In striking contrast to the cosmic religious orientation, with its distinctive ontology, is the historical religious orientation. It, too, involves a conception of time. Time is linear, chronological, historical. It is irreversible, and historical events are unique (not typical, as in cosmic time). History is affirmed, for it is primarily in and through historical events that the sacred manifests itself. Myth is understood as sacred history. In Eliade's view, this second type of religious orientation is characteristic of the monotheisms—Judaism, Christianity, and Islam—and is largely confined to them. However, even within these religions the contrasting religious orientation makes itself felt, as, for example, in the "cosmic Christianity" of Eastern Europe.

A third recent attempt to classify religions is found in an essay ("Primitive, Classical, and Modern Religions," 1967) by Joseph M. Kitagawa. It relates to both Eliade's and Bellah's classifications. According to Kitagawa, religions can be distinguished by the kinds of religious experience and apprehension characteristic of them. Primitive religion is characterized by an orientation in which the ultimate purpose of life is participation in the creation of "cosmos" out of "chaos" by imitating mythical models. The classical religions, which include the religions of the ancient Near East, Iran, India, the Far East, and the Greco-Roman world, evidence a significant emancipation of *logos* from *muthos*. These religions are further marked by a change in man's view of himself—no longer is he only a part of nature—and by a sophistication and systematization of the theoretical, practical, and sociological expressions of his religious experience.

A completely satisfactory classification of religions continues to elude scholars. Some general requirements for more adequate classification of religions, however, are the following. First, the classification should be comprehensive, that is, inclusive ideally of all religions. Second, the classification should be objective and descriptive, not subjective and normative. Third, the effort should be made to do justice to particular religions and to avoid misrepresenting or caricaturing them because of prejudice or the desire to make them fit a particular scheme of classification. Fourth, judgments should be made in order to distinguish what is essential or fundamental in religions from what is accidental or incidental. Fifth, one should be alert equally to similarities and differences among religions. Finally, it is imperative to recognize that "living religions" are indeed alive and always changing and that "dead religions" have had a history: both, in short, are categories of dynamic entities. This dynamism is one factor that makes the classification of religion an unending task.

BIBLIOGRAPHY

Two studies of the problem of classification have appeared in this century. They are Duren J. H. Ward's *The Classification of Religions: Different Methods, Their Advantages and Disadvantages* (Chicago, 1909) and Fred Louis Parrish's *The Classification of Religions: Its Relation to the History of Religions* (Scottdale, Pa., 1941). The latter is especially complete and contains a useful bibliography for the study of classification. Additional relevant, though less focused works include Morris Jastrow's *The Study of Religion* (1901; reprint, Chino, Calif., 1981), containing chapters on classification; C. P. Tiele's *Elements of the Science of Religion*, 2 vols. (Edinburgh, 1897–1899), especially the first volume; P. D. Chantepie de la Saussaye's *Manual of the Science of Religion* (London, 1891), which is Beatrice S. Colyer Fergusson's translation of volume 1 of his *Lehrbuch der Religionsgeschichte* (1887); Henri Pinard de la Boullaye's *L'étude comparée des religions*, 2 vols. (Paris, 1922–1925), especially volume 2, *Ses méthodes;* F. Max Müller's *Introduction to the Science of Religion* (London, 1873), a clear presentation of his influential views on the comparative method; and, finally, Gustav Mensching's *Die Religion: Erscheinungsformen, Strukturtypen und Lebensgesetze* (Stuttgart, 1959), containing a more recent discussion of the classification of religions.

HARRY B. PARTIN

CLEANLINESS. *See* Purification.

CLEMEN, CARL (1865–1940), Protestant theologian and historian of religions. Carl Christian Clemen was one of the founders of research in the science of religion and of its institutionalization in Germany. After qualifying for a lectureship in New Testament studies in Halle, he taught there from 1892 to 1903 and in Bonn from 1903 to 1908. After visiting the United States as a guest lecturer in 1908 and 1909, he became in 1910 associate professor and in 1920 professor of the history of religions in the philosophy department of the University of Bonn. The breadth of his scholarship is indicated by the fact that his publications number approximately six hundred titles, that he lectured on the Old Testament and on systematic and practical theology, and that he taught Avestan.

His publications first concerned the New Testament and its background in the history of religions. His inaugural lecture at Bonn, published as *Die religionsgeschichtliche Methode in der Theologie* (1904), outlined his program, first, of summarizing the different challenges confronting theology from the religio-historical method, especially that of the Religionsgeschichtliche Schule, and second, of tracing the derivation of religious views in the New Testament. For him the religio-historical method is a principle of research that Christian theology simply must apply if it is to be considered a field of knowledge. In this, however, Clemen believed that the comparison of Christianity with other religions (1) does not hinder the researcher, despite a temporary presumption of the equality of religions, from being convinced of the advantage of a certain religion and church; (2) does not promote the relativization of Christianity or, in its historical observation of Christianity, exclude the confirmation of its absoluteness; and (3) will lead, in fact, in its attempt to explain Christianity by means of other religions, to the verification of Christianity's originality and of its possession of content that was already present and only poured into borrowed forms.

Research is indebted to Clemen, in connection with these arguments, for a more precise definition of the idea of "influence" among religions through his application of three criteria. One can speak of "influence" if any one of the following criteria is met: (1) if a special religious view cannot be explained completely from the original ideas of the religions concerned; (2) if any hypothesized influence of one religion is actually demonstrable in another religion, and the precedence of the former is plausible; and (3) if the manner in which a religious view is transmitted is comprehensible (otherwise a correspondence must be shown to be so far-reaching that the former has to be regarded as the model, even if the way of influence is unknown). A broadly conceived exposition of these ideas appeared in his *Religionsgeschichtliche Erklärung des Neuen Testaments: Die Abhängigkeit des ältesten Christentums von nichtjüdischen Religionen und philosophischen Systemen* (1909; translated as *Primitive Christianity and Its Non-Jewish Sources*, 1912). A German revision of *Religionsgeschichtliche Erklärung* published in 1924 also incorporates his work *Der Einfluss der Mysterienreligionen auf das älteste Christentum* (The Influence of Mystical Religions on Primitive Christianity; 1913), while his book *Die Reste der primitiven Religion im ältesten Christentum* (Traces of Primitive Religion in Primitive Christianity; 1916) adds a portrayal of concepts originating in nature religions. A summary view of the opposite relationships is provided by the late work *Der Einfluss des Christentums auf andere Religionen* (The Influence of Christianity on Other Religions; 1933). Clemen's summary work, *Die Religionen der Erde: Ihr Wesen und ihre Geschichte* (1927), was translated into English as *Religions of the World: Their Nature and Their History* (1931). The broad scope of his approach to method is seen in writings such as *Die Anwendung der Psychoanalyse auf Mythologie und Religionsgeschichte* (The Application of Psychology to Mythology and the History of Religion; 1928) and *Grundriss der Religionsphilosophie* (Outline of the Philosophy of Religion; 1934). Yet his ideal was strongly source-oriented historical research, and his edition of *Fontes historiae religionum ex auctoribus Graecis et Latinis collecti*, beginning with his collection of sources and published as *Die griechischen und lateinischen Nachrichten über die persische Religion* (Greek and Latin Accounts of Persian Religion; 1920), has become an aid of lasting importance to religio-historical research.

BIBLIOGRAPHY

Mensching, Gustav. "Carl Clemen." *Die christliche Welt* 54 (3 August 1940): 353–354.

Rühle, Oskar. "Clemen, Carl." In *Die Religion in Geschichte und Gegenwart*, 2d ed., vol. 1. Tübingen, 1927.

Schrey, Heinz Horst. "Clemen, Carl Christian." In *Neue deutsche Biographie*, edited by Erich Angermann et al., vol. 3. Berlin, 1957.

Waardenburg, Jacques. *Classical Approaches to the Study of Religion*, vol. 2, *Bibliography*. The Hague, 1974. See pages 39–40.

CHRISTOPH ELSAS
Translated from German by Roger Norton

CLEMENT OF ALEXANDRIA (150?–215?), Christian theologian. Little is known about the life of Titus Flavius Clemens. A few details can be gathered from Clement's allusion to his education (*Miscellanies* 1.1, 2.2) and from the report of the fourth-century Christian writer Eusebius of Caesarea (*Church History* 5.10–11, 6.6, 6.11.5–6). Born in the mid-second century to pagan parents, perhaps in Athens, Clement traveled extensively as a young man, seeking an intellectual mentor. This he found in Pantaenus, who, according to Eusebius, served as head of a Christian school in Alexandria. Clement is said to have succeeded Pantaenus as chief of the school in the late second century, probably remaining a layman after his conversion to Christianity. In 202 or 203, when Christians were being persecuted by the Roman emperor Septimius Severus, Clement left Alexandria for Asia Minor. Presumably he died before 215.

The following treatises of Clement are extant: *Exhortation to the Greeks (Protrepticus); The Instructor (Paedagogus); Miscellanies (Stromateis); Who Is the Rich Man That Is Saved? (Quis dives salvetur?);* a collection of excerpts from gnostic teachings, with Clement's comments *(Excerpta ex Theodoto);* and a work of exegetical notes *(Eclogae propheticae)*. Only fragments remain of other treatises. Although scholars disagree on the precise dating of Clement's works, the period 195–210 probably encompasses them all. He wrote the *Protrepticus* first, followed by the *Paedagogus*, the *Stromateis*, and the *Quis dives salvetur?* Clement's influence on later theology was largely channeled through the writings of his brilliant successor, Origen.

Clement's works testify to the diversity of Christians in Alexandria around the year 200. There were "simple believers," wary of speculation, who understood scripture literally and thought ecclesiastical authority enough to direct their lives. Those able to embrace a more advanced theology sought to align the best of classical culture with their faith. (Perhaps this group included those comforted by Clement's assurance that riches did not automatically debar them from salvation if they practiced inward detachment from their wealth and heeded Christianity's call for charity.) In addition to Alexandrians within the catholic fold, there were many gnostics, especially the followers of Valentinus and Basilides, who considered themselves Christians, but whom Clement deemed heretics. Pagan critics who mocked Christianity as a religion for the uneducated were also addressed by Clement in his writings, as they had been by his second-century theological predecessors, the apologists. The pagan writer Celsus's searing attack upon Christianity, *The True Word*, had been composed only fifteen years before Clement began his writing career.

Although Clement did not reject the "simple believers," he advocated higher theological education and an allegorical interpretation of scripture; the Bible, he conceded, was inelegant in style and contained anthropomorphic depictions of God. Responding to more theologically educated Christians and to pagan critics, Clement argued that Christianity was a species of philosophy, far superior to the Greek myths and mystery religions. (Recent scholars have emphasized how indebted Clement was to various philosophical traditions, especially Middle Platonism.) To illustrate how erudite Christian writing could be, Clement quoted several hundred passages from classical authors in his works, although he probably derived many of his citations not from the original sources, but from the handbooks popular in his day. Clement shared a high regard for religious knowledge with the gnostics, but against them he upheld the goodness of God's creation. To this end, he rejected both the libertine and the ascetic sexual teachings of various gnostic sects that derived from their negative assessment of the created world, and he endorsed (albeit lukewarmly) the virtues of Christian marriage. Moreover, since Clement understood gnostic teaching on predestination to mean a fatalistic determinism, he, in contrast, championed the freedom of the will and freely chosen good deeds as necessary components of Christian salvation.

Among the more prominent themes in Clement's works are the following: the progressive activity of God's Word in revealing truth from ancient times to the era of the full disclosure of truth in Christianity; the Greek philosophers' assumed plagiarism from the Old Testament; humans' creation in the "image of God" that forever recalled them to a more godlike life; the understanding of the deity as an incorporeal being not adequately represented by scripture's anthropomorphisms; detailed guidelines for such daily activities as eating and sleeping that the Word gave in his role as instructor; the benefits that philosophy and other secular disciplines, seen as preparatory instruction, might bring to Christians; the possibility of advancement in the Christian life from belief to knowledge and from self-control to impassibility (although good deeds and love were incumbent upon Christians at all stages); and the claiming of the term *gnostic* for the catholic camp rather than conceding it to the heretics, who in Clement's view lacked genuine theological knowledge.

BIBLIOGRAPHY

Bardy, Gustave. *Clément d'Alexandrie.* Paris, 1926. A standard older biography of Clement, with discussion of his writings.

Chadwick, Henry. *Early Christian Thought and the Classical Tradition: Studies in Justin, Clement, and Origen.* New York, 1966. An insightful study of Clement's relation to the classical tradition.

Countryman, L. William. *The Rich Christian in the Church of the Early Empire: Contradictions and Accommodations.* New York, 1980. An examination of Clement's treatise *Who Is the Rich Man That Is Saved?* in relation to early Christian attitudes toward wealth. See especially chapter 1.

Lilla, Salvatore R. C. *Clement of Alexandria: A Study in Christian Platonism and Gnosticism.* Oxford, 1971. A detailed investigation of Clement's philosophical interests and his relation to gnosticism.

Méhat, André. *Étude sur les Stromates de Clément d'Alexandrie.* Paris, 1966. A comprehensive study of the *Miscellanies,* Clement's major work.

Elizabeth A. Clark

CLEMENT OF ROME, supposed author of a letter sent from the church of Rome to the church of Corinth in the last years of the first century CE. The date most commonly given for the letter is 96–97. In the course of the second century the author of this letter came to be identified as Clement and was thought to have been the third bishop of Rome, after Peter and Paul. Although there is no particular reason to doubt that the person who actually penned the letter was so named, there is some doubt as to whether at this time Rome had a bishop in the later sense of the word, that is, a single head of the church.

The letter, known as *1 Clement,* tells us nothing about the person who wrote it. Indeed, the letter is intended to be understood as the expression of a church rather than an individual. In response to disagreements at Corinth, it focuses on the need for harmony and the evils of discord. The author draws upon materials from the Bible (the Hebrew Bible in the Septuagint Greek translation) and from Greco-Roman tradition. He knows several of Paul's letters, perhaps including *Hebrews.* He also uses material similar to what we find in the synoptic Gospels, but it is doubtful whether he knew the Gospels in their present form.

First Clement gives early expression to ideas that would subsequently be very important in the Roman tradition and elsewhere. The leadership of the church is seen as standing in a chain of authority extending from God, through Christ, on through the apostles, and finally to the bishops or presbyters (the terms seem to be used interchangeably), who now stand as a group at the head of the individual churches. To overthrow the established ministers (as apparently had been done at Corinth) when they have been blameless in the performance of their duties is to rebel against God.

Some have interpreted *1 Clement* as the earliest expression of Roman primacy, and Clement of Rome therefore as the first pope on record as having acted papally. This, however, is to exaggerate the authoritarian character of the letter and the individual importance of its author. It is a letter of exhortation from one church to another, both of which shared the tradition of having been evangelized by Peter and Paul.

Clement of Rome was subsequently but erroneously credited with a second "letter" *(2 Clement),* really a sermon, probably written around the middle of the second century, and two third-century letters on virginity. In addition, the fourth-century pseudo-Clementine *Homilies* and *Recognitions* feature Clement as the protagonist of their dramatic narratives. There seems to be no reason to suppose that any historically reliable information about the first-century Clement can be derived from these materials. Subsequent to the time of the pseudo-Clementines, Clement of Rome seems not to have played a large role in Christian tradition. He was remembered as the first pope of whom more than the name alone was known, and as the author of the earliest extant piece of Christian literature outside the New Testament.

BIBLIOGRAPHY

For the English-speaking reader, *1 Clement* is most accessible through the translation and commentary in Robert M. Grant and H. H. Graham's *The Apostolic Fathers,* vol. 2, *First and Second Clement* (New York, 1965). The Greek text is available in Franz X. Funk's *Die apostolischen Väter,* revised by Karl Bihlmeyer (1924), new ed., edited by Wilhelm Schneemelcher (Tübingen, 1970). The scholarly discussion of *1 Clement* is largely a German affair. The most useful monographs are Otto Knoch's *Eigenart und Bedeutung der Eschatologie im theologischen Aufriss des ersten Clemensbriefes* (Bonn, 1964); Karlmann Beyschlag's *Clemens Romanus und der Frühkatholizismus* (Tübingen, 1966); and Gerbert Brunner's *Die theologische Mitte des ersten Klemensbriefs* (Frankfurt, 1972). These books also illustrate the impact of Catholic-Protestant polemics on the study of early Christianity.

James F. McCue

CLITORIDECTOMY. The term *clitoridectomy* covers a range of ritual surgical operations: (1) drawing blood from the clitoral prepuce or removal of the prepuce, (2) excism of the clitoris, (3) excism of the clitoris and labia minora, and (4) infibulation, requiring removal of the clitoris, the labia minora, and the anterior two-thirds of the labia majora, the two sides of which are then joined so that a small posterior opening is left for the passage of urine and menstrual blood. The first type occurs in Islamic countries of the Middle East, Africa, and Asia. The second type occurs in East, West, and central Africa, on the Arabian Peninsula, and in Brazil, eastern Mexico, and Peru. The third type occurs throughout Africa, in Arab countries, and in parts of Aboriginal Australia. Infibulation occurs in Sudan, Ethiopia, Djibouti, Eritrea, southern Egypt, northern Nigeria, Mali, and the Central African Republic.

In countries where clitoridectomy is practiced, the rite may be performed virtually universally or it may have a sparse and patchy distribution. For example, in northern Ghana almost all women in the Kusase ethnic group will have had clitoridectomy, while none in the neighboring Tallensi group will have undergone this ritual. Nor is there a clear relationship between clitoridectomy and religion: in an area of southern Nigeria five contiguous ethnic groups perform the rite, but the Etsako are Muslim, the Esan and Ijan are predominantly Christian, and the Bini and Ukwuani primarily observe their traditional religion.

In Sudan, few women in the south are infibulated, but from 90 to 95 percent of the women in the Arabic north are (Dareer, 1983, p. 41). In neighboring Egypt an estimated 95 percent of women have had some kind of clitoridectomy, but most is of the third type and only relatively few, near the Sudan border, have been infibulated (Aziza, 1983, p. 13). In both countries urban, better-educated women tend to have minimal surgery or no clitoridectomy. Egyptian mummies dated 200 BCE show evidence of clitroidectomy (Dareer, 1983, p. 41), and present-day Coptic Christian as well as Muslim women in Egypt have clitoridectomy, suggesting that it is a pre-Islamic custom. This speculation is further supported by the fact that the Islamic countries of Saudi Arabia, Iraq, Iran, and Afghanistan do not practice clitoridectomy.

There is no mention of clitoridectomy in the Qur'ān, but more or less authentic *ḥadith*s mention its practice in pre-Islamic Arabia. Although texts and dictionaries are not very explicit, evidence suggests minimal excision of the prepuce of the clitoris (Bosworth, 1978, p. 913). In an Islamic tradition preserved by Aḥmad ibn Ḥanbal (d. 855), circumcision is called *sunnah* for males and honorable for females (Wensinck, 1979, p. 20). *Sunnah* means to follow the traditions of the prophet Muḥammad, who according to tradition was circumcised. The commentaries of al-Nawawi, edited in Cairo in 1283, say, however, that circumcision is equally obligatory for males and females, specifying removal of a small part of the skin in the highest part of the genitals (ibid.). Some contemporary Muslim teachers cite the general Islamic rule that forbids cutting parts of the body unless the benefits exceed the pain and injury, and the Sudanese religious and political leader El Sayed Abdel Rahman El Mahadi explicitly forbade infibulation (Dareer, 1983, p. 44). Thus one can understand the confusion revealed in a Sudanese survey where 60 percent of the women said religion and custom demanded infibulation, but of those who disagreed, 50 percent did so on religious grounds (ibid., p. 43).

Clitoridectomy was not practiced in the ancient Jewish religion, and it is not mentioned in either testament of the Bible.

Clitoridectomy is a rite and in its minimal form is performed on girls individually, accompanied by gifts. Or girls may be initiated in a large class with accompanying rites that involve all the women of a village or indeed a whole chiefdom (MacCormack, 1979). The age at which girls experience clitoridectomy varies, but in all cases it should be done by the time of puberty and marriage. Although some Islamic texts prohibit clitoridectomy before the tenth year (Wensinck, 1979, p. 20), in Sudan it is done between two and eleven years, and in Egypt between three and eleven years of age, although there are cases of it being done before the age of one.

Clitoridectomy is usually performed by a traditional midwife. In Egypt the decision is primarily taken by the girl's mother, then in descending order of importance, by both parents together, an aunt, a sister or grandmother, and the father alone (Aziza, 1983, p. 14). However, fathers usually pay for the ceremony, and in the case of infibulation, husbands pay for re-fibulation following each childbirth.

There is no single meaning of clitoridectomy. In all societies that circumcise females, males are also circumcised. The reasons given for both sexes is that it is a ritual of membership into a religious tradition, an ethnic group with the status of adult, or a prerequisite for legitimate and moral marriage, sexuality, and procreation.

In Mediterranean and Islamic countries clitoridectomy is often explained as an aspect of family honor. The phrase "son of an uncircumcised woman" is considered injurious in the sense that it is synonymous with "son of a whore"—that is, a woman of excessive sexual appetite caused by her not being circumcised. In Egypt, for example, clitoridectomy is thought to protect a girl's chastity by reducing her libido, thus maintaining the family's honor and the girl's suitability for a good marriage. In Muslim Java a mild pricking of the prepuce is associated with ritual filing down of teeth, suggesting a symbolic statement about curbing all appetites.

In countries concerned with female modesty as a sign of family honor, public evidence of defloration is often an important rite following marriage. A woman who cannot demonstrate virginity by blood on the marriage bed may be divorced or even put to death at the hands of her own family to preserve their honor. Infibulation may be associated with an extreme expression of that honor.

Nawal El Saadawi (1980) has suggested a Marxist interpretation, following Engels, whereby in societies with patrilineal inheritance an emphasis on female chastity protects inheritance of private property by ensuring that a man's heirs are his own children. Just as ruling classes impose the moral values of renunciation of pleasure on laborers, while they value extravagance themselves, so men constitute a "ruling class" over women and impose the renunciation of sexual pleasure on them while they enjoy sexual freedom and seduction with impunity. This Marxist interpretation cannot be a universal explanation for clitoridectomy because there are societies with patrilineal inheritance of property where women may be punished or even put to death for an infringement of sexual rules, but which lack rites of clitoridectomy.

In a wider comparative framework, the explanation that genital surgery is universally a by-product of male suppression of women is called into question. For example, in coastal West Africa there are groups that practice clitoridectomy but also allow a considerable amount of premarital freedom to women. In the patrilineal Mende area of Sierra Leone, for example, women may even hold overt political office, and the pain of clitoridectomy, experienced in a group, may serve to bond women together into potentially cohesive chapters of a women's secret society, thus enhancing their political power and control of wealth (MacCormack, 1979). Among some Aboriginal Australian and some Melanesian ethnic groups, men undergo much more extreme and painful ritual genital surgery than women, and this usually occurs in societies with patrilineal descent where men are described as being dominant.

Virtually everywhere, clitoridectomy is described as an act of purification, making women clean. On the Sherbro coast of Sierra Leone, women say that without this puberty rite a girl can achieve womanhood biologically but will remain a girl socially. Using a functional model of analysis, we might say that the ritual scar and body modification are the sign of being brought within an adult moral sphere. The man with whom an initiated woman shares an intimate relationship will know that she has been taught the responsible role of potential procreator.

Using a structuralist model of analysis, "making women clean" removes the clitoris, the small male penis, making women fit unambiguously—purely and "cleanly"—within the female category. Furthermore, the pain of clitoridectomy might be seen as a metaphor for childbirth. In Sierra Leone, the position assumed for clitoridectomy is the same as the position assumed in childbirth. The place is the same, since ideally a woman returns to her natal initiation place to give birth, under the hand of the midwife who initiated her. The social group is similarly constituted of local female kin and other townswomen, all being members of the women's secret society. The pain of clitoridectomy, controlled by time, place, and the technical skill of the midwife, is a metaphor for the pain of childbirth. As the midwife controls bleeding and protects against infection in clitoridectomy, so she does in childbirth. Womanhood is symbolically achieved in clitoridectomy and is confirmed, under the midwife's hand, in childbirth. In Sierra Leone the two events are logically related as part of the same message, although they are separated in time (MacCormack, 1979, 1982; see also Griaule, 1965, p. 158).

[*See also* Initiation, *article on* Women's Initiation. *For related discussions, see* Androgynes; Bodily Marks; *and* Circumcision.]

BIBLIOGRAPHY

Aziza, Hussein. *Facts about Female Circumcision.* Cairo, 1983. Issued by the Cairo Family Planning Association.

Bosworth, C. E., et al. "Khafḍ." In *The Encyclopaedia of Islam,* new ed., vol. 4, pp. 913–914. Leiden, 1978.

Dareer, Asma El. "Epidemiology of Female Circumcision in the Sudan." *Tropical Doctor* 13 (1983): 41–45.

Griaule, Marcel. *Conversations with Ogotemmêli: An Introduction to Dogon Religious Ideas.* London, 1965.

MacCormack, Carol P. "Sande: The Public Face of a Secret Society." In *The New Religions of Africa,* edited by Bennetta Jules-Rosette, pp. 27–37. Norwood, N.J., 1979

MacCormack, Carol P. "Health, Fertility and Birth in Moyamba District, Sierra Leone." In *Ethnography of Fertility and Birth,* edited by Carol P. MacCormack, pp. 115–139. London, 1982.

Myers, R. A., et al. "Circumcision: Its Nature and Practice among Some Ethnic Groups in Southern Nigeria." *Social Science and Medicine* 21 (1985): 581–588.

Saadawi, Nawal El. *The Hidden Face of Eve: Women in the Arab World.* Translated and edited by Sherif Hetata. London, 1980.

Wensinck, A. J. "Khitān." In *The Encyclopaedia of Islam,* new ed., vol. 5, pp. 20–22. Leiden, 1979.

CAROL P. MACCORMACK

CLOTHING. [*This entry consists of two articles:* Religious Clothing in the East *and* Religious Clothing in the West. *Together they provide a cross-cultural overview of the symbolic significance of various kinds of religious clothing.*]

Religious Clothing in the East

Eastern religious traditions include sects that place a major emphasis on communal ritual and those for which religious practice is of a more private, individual nature. This division affects the manner in which clothing promotes notions of religious belief.

Ritual Clothing. In those communities where a clergy acts as intermediary between the human and the divine there are often prescribed public rituals or displays. Here special clothes are used to transform the priest into a ritual celebrant. On the other hand, where religious practice is largely self-determined and reclusive, a clergy, if it exists, is less involved with public demonstration; hence clothing plays a less conspicuous role and the notion of vestment is largely absent.

Shamanism. The shamanic practices of the Tunguz-speaking tribal cultures of eastern Siberia provide some of the more dramatic examples of specialized ritual clothing from East Asia. These garments are intended to transform the wearer, often male, into an intermediary capable of bridging the gap between the physical world and the world of the spirits. Masks and garments tend to be highly personal, crafted by the shaman after a vision or intervention of the spirit world. [*See also* Masks.] They often take the form of a bird, bear, or stag. The cut of these garments, whether of animal skin or cloth, is significantly different from normal clothing, in part demonstrating the otherworldliness of shamanic practice. For example, coats may incorporate construction features such as fringes or gussets to simulate the animal they represent. Symbols for the sun, moon, and earth may be painted, appliquéd, or made of iron and attached to the upper body garment. Other decorative devices may evoke the sky gate, the goal of the spirit journey of the shaman. In addition, snakes, birds, horses, and other auspicious beasts are often part of the decorative program. Cross-gender dressing is conspicuous among some groups where male shamans wear feminine garments. [*See* Gender Roles.] A second garment type is decorated with bonelike forms that create an X-ray impression of the wearer's body.

The Cham dances of Tibet arose in pre-Buddhist times and were later incorporated into Tibetan Buddhist ritual. They employ forms of ecstatic dancing that evoke shamanistic practice. Cham costumes include masks, headgear, and garments that evoke birds, stags, horses, and other beasts familiar to the Siberian pantheon. The bone diagram garments were also used in Tibetan Buddhist ceremonial dancing. Although the surviving examples of these costumes are made of imported Chinese and Indian silks, the fluttering scarves and pendant sleeves as well as other construction features differentiate these coats from normal attire. Similar garments were in use among Mongol populations that converted to Tibetan Buddhism in the fourteenth century.

Taoism. Although transformed into a much more sophisticated state religion as a result of the influence of Buddhism, Taoism as practiced in late imperial China used vestments linked to Siberian shamanism. When officiating at public celebrations the highest ranking Taoist priests wear a mantle *(chiang-i)* bearing cosmological symbols similar to those found in Siberian contexts.

This Taoist vestment is a full-length garment, formed of two lengths of cloth seamed up the back and the sides and left open at the front. The back of the garment is decorated with astral symbols, ranked by registers from top to bottom and from center to edge. Symbols for the principle luminaries are arranged across the top of the garment. At the right shoulder, the sun is represented by a red disk with a three-legged cock symbol; the moon at the left shoulder is depicted as a white disk in which a rabbit pounds the elixir of immortality; and a constellation, conventionally depicted as three balls joined by lines, is placed between. Explanation for these astral symbols can be documented to the first century BCE; through these symbols, daily, monthly, and annual time could be calculated, and a calendar—one of the prime requirements for agrarian societies—could be fixed. [*See also* Calendars.]

The decoration of the rest of the garment conveys notions of an unseen heaven. Prominent in this celestial diagram is a central image of paradise, often depicted as a multistoried tower within an ovoid frame of circular discs representing stars. This refers to the Three Isles of the Immortals located in the Eastern Sea. Five abstract forms arranged in a semicircle beneath the tower represent the five mythical peaks of the world. They guard the five principal directions: East, South, West, North, and Center. Below these, four mountain or pavilion structures symbolize the physical directions of the earth gates. Such association with paradise is often enhanced by figural imagery depicting various deities within complex pantheons. The hem may display the universal ocean with dragons, horses, tortoise, and serpent, and other mythical beasts. The front of the coat is generally plain except for a dragon symbolizing the East and a tiger symbolizing the West flanking the front opening and acting as protective devices.

Taoist priests of second rank wear garments with sleeves. The decoration remains largely the same. Unlike shamanic garments, which assist the spirit journey of the individual, Taoist vestments function symbolically, transforming the wearer into an animator of political and religious systems that promoted control and stability.

Among the dance costumes worn at Chinese folk festivals one can also find garments marked with bone diagrams and garments that imitate the animal protectors of shamanist power.

Chinese Religion. The link between religion and politics is particularly evident in the court attire of imperial China and in the Chinese-influenced court attire in Korea, Japan, Vietnam, and various Central Asian kingdoms. Motifs symbolizing water, land, and sky were placed on these garments to represent the physical world over which the ruler held sway. In addition, fabulous mythical beasts, of which the dragon is the most common, represented the supernatural power and moral authority of imperial rule. The arrangement of these motifs conveyed a sense of universal order by reflecting notions of geopolitical control with reference to the points of the compass. Wearing the garment also demonstrated cosmic control and underscored the balance of forces in the universe. The wearer's body symbolized the world axis; the neck of the garment, the gate of heaven, separating the physical world represented by the coat from the spiritual represented by the wearer's head. In effect the garment was only animate when worn, making each courtier an active participant in imperial rule.

The emperor's sacrificial obligations on behalf of the state were confirmed through clothes decorated with a special set of twelve symbols. These included the sun, moon, stars, earth, elements of the natural world, and symbols of political authority. Their use was reserved exclusively for the emperor.

These official garments had impact throughout society. Chinese wedding attire in particular imitated court costume and prerogatives; other types of quasi-official attire were used in conjunction with Buddhist and Taoist festivals and for the special garments made for religious images.

Southeast Asian traditions. Throughout Asia clothing used within religious contexts is among the most primitive garment types preserved by a culture. At one extreme are the palm fiber garments worn by medicine men on the island of Buru in eastern Indonesia. The material is used as it comes from the source without further processing. The capes and mantles of green leaves, or their embroidered imitations worn by images of some of the Taoist immortals, reflect similar primitivism. Although made of luxury silk and greatly embellished, the highest ranking Taoist priests' robes described above are among the most basic East Asian constructions. From the point of view of structure these garments contrast sharply with the more complex constructions having sleeves that are worn by second-ranking priests.

At another level this conservativism is reflected in the preservation of ancient textile forms within religious contexts. The tendency is particularly marked in Southeast Asia. Among the Batak tribes in Sumatra the most prestigious fabrics are those called *ragidup*. These large rectangular cloths are composed of three loom lengths joined along their selvages. Often the center panel is wider and made of lighter colored fiber. The cloth is produced on a simple loom, despite the presence of more sophisticated weaving equipment within the culture. These cloths are used in ritual gift giving and within religious ceremonies. A similar three-panel cloth with a light-colored central panel called a *khamar* is preserved in Bhutan. It is used by Tibetan Buddhists as a mark of esteem. It parallels the use of the *chaksay pankhep* reserved for royalty that is placed over the lap when the owner sits in audience and that is used as a napkin for wiping the hands.

Shintō. Vestments worn by Shintō clergy are linked to the past, but unlike the examples from Sumatra or Bhutan, the forms are neither primitive nor particularly old. The white kimono and white or red trousers *(hakama)* as well as the outer coats *(kariginu)* and black lacquered silk hats are based on tenth-century court attire. Color signifies purity. The style of these garments and their political identification coincides with the period of centralization of priestly power in the hands of clan heads and the more structured form of worship that evolved in reaction to Buddhism and Confucianism from China. Worship began to incorporate public ceremonies in which priests and priestesses conducted ritual observances. Other public gatherings were marked by events such as *kagura* dances that utilized specialized costumes and masks.

Buddhism. Buddhism also appropriated existing costume. Initially it, like Hinduism, from which it developed, was a religion isolated from the population at large. Buddhist devotees lived within monastic communities and adopted clothing that stressed the rejection of worldly society. Over time the three-part costume based on the common attire of the Indian subcontinent became ritual attire. The lower body was covered with a sarong *(antaravasaka)*. A shawl *(uttarasaṅga),* utilizing a length of loom-woven fabric, was draped in various manners around the upper body. A third garment called *saṅghati,* literally "a twelve-fold cloth," was worn over the left shoulder.

The shawl became the most significant garment for Buddhism. It evolved into a rectangle constructed of smaller pieces, thus symbolizing the tattered and patched garments of the mendicant Buddha. The patchwork mantle, also called *kaṣāya,* was formalized to differentiate and identify its wearer as a member of a religious community and became the subject of monastic regulation.

Originally the name *kaṣāya* referred to a color distinction, which set the "impure" colored mantles of monks apart from the normal bleached white clothing of Indian laity. In time the "impure" colored clothing of monks of the Hīnayāna sect was enhanced by yellow dye, which still distinguishes the clothing of the Buddhist monks of Sri Lanka and Southeast Asia.

The specialized patchwork form of the garment spread north and east across Asia accompanying proselytizing Buddhist missionaries. In the less temperate regions of Central Asia, China, Korea, and eventually Japan, the three-part Buddhist costume was abandoned. The mantle was retained as symbolic apparel and worn over the normal dress typical of each region. The monastic clothing used in Tibet among Buddhist communities is a notable exception. Here the sarong and mantle made of red-dyed wool was used. In all the Mahāyāna sects in East Asia a hood offered the tonsured heads of monks protection and conveyed public status. In Tibet the color of the hood distinguished the sect within the larger Buddhist community.

In East Asia, monastic costume continued to be regulated by prescription according to function and rank of the wearer, but the regulations focused on the single garment. In Japan, for example, the meanings of the original names of Buddhist garments were appropriated to describe variations of the pieced mantle. The *antaravasaka* became a five-paneled working outer mantle; the *uttarasaṅga* (the original shawl) defined a seven-paneled mantle worn at assembly. The *saṅghati* was a large mantle used for travel composed of nine panels; two more panels were added for each advance in grade, reserving the twenty-five-panel *kaṣāya* for the highest ranking clergy.

In Central Asia, China, and Japan the patchwork mantle acquired a significant secondary feature. Additional patches at the corners and along the longer side worn closest to the head added symbolic protection. The corner patches, usually in contrasting fabric, were associated with the *deva* kings who serve as guardians of the Buddhist law at each of the cardinal points of the compass. The large patches on the long side and a characteristic of the *uttarasaṅga* type in China and Japan are named after the *boddhisattva*s Samantabhadra and Mañjuśrī, the principal attendants of Śākyamuni, the historical Buddha. These garments, often made of sumptuous secular silks donated to temples by pious devotees, created colorful focus for public ceremonies and demonstrated the power and authority of the Buddhist church.

Islam. In contrast, Islam has produced no vestments. The central religious leaders, whether mullahs, *mujtahid*s, or ayatollahs, are in effect jurists who interpret Islamic law and serve as teachers. Clothing types used by these groups regardless of ethnic origin reflect the basic attire of the Arab founders of the faith: a cotton or wool caftan, a wool mantle *('abā')* and a cotton turban. Worship is an obligation of the faith, and when possible worship is practiced communally, but the prayer leader or imam does not function as intermediary between God and man. His clothing remains undifferentiated from that of the congregation. Individuals are expected to practice their religion while remaining active participants of society. Those who have made the pilgrimage to Mecca are entitled to wear special clothing, although it plays no liturgical role.

Hinduism. Within the Hindu tradition of India, public worship, although extremely complex, also occurs without the intervention of priests. Hinduism is without founder or prophets. It has no ecclesiastical or institutional structures. As a result there are virtually no specialized Hindu religious garments. Traditionally the brahman class was the source of the priesthood; but individual adherents practiced priestly vocation outside society based largely on the study of scriptural sources. For them ritual was largely private, such as the placing of a sacred cord across the shoulder, both binding the devotee to religion and cutting the individual off from society. The central religious figure for Hinduism is the guru, or teacher, who follows a self-determined, often reclusive way of life that aims at purification and extinction from the cycle of rebirth. Clothing worn by brahmans, minimal and very plain, reflects this distancing.

In contrast, the secular Hindu world throughout South Asia provides examples of highly specialized costume that makes links between religion and political culture. The colorful costumes, headdresses, and masks used in Hindu dance drama are the focus of public ceremonies and celebrations associated with religious events, although the dramas themselves are not forms of worship. Court attire within the Hindu-Muslim courts of Java utilized a set of restricted batiked patterns on the sarongs and shawls to distinguish royalty and the higher ranks of the aristocracy. Many of these designs symbolized cosmic principles and underscored the significance of court ceremony and its relationship to religious belief.

Secular clothing. On a more general level secular clothing can convey religious meaning. For some societies specialized clothing marks the community of believers as distinct from society at large: for example, the white clothing of Zoroastrians symbolizes purity. In India a white cotton shirt and white lamb's wool cord form a distinctive costume for the Parsi followers of Zarathushtra (Zoroaster).

Coiffure and headgear are particularly important symbols. [*See* Hair.] In East Asia hair dressed in knots on the top or at the back of the head distinguished populations of the urbanized south from the shaved heads or plaited tresses of northern nomads. The tonsure and queue of Chinese populations enforced by Manchu rulers during the seventeenth through the early twentieth century was an overt symbol of political and cultural domination. Tonsure could also demonstrate commitment to Buddhist monastic practices. In other instances hair styles reflect folk beliefs. Binding hair at the "four corners" of the head into tufts was thought to ward off the danger of Chinese children falling into the hands of demons, as the tufts provided a convenient grip for Buddhist deities or good spirits to retrieve the child.

In western Asia shaving the head or letting certain parts of the hair grow helped distinguish Muslim and Jewish populations. Traditionally, various groups within Islamic societies were distinguished by the color of turbans or special hats to distinguish various groups: white turbans for believers, yellow for Jews, blue for Christians. The skullcap worn by Jewish males, although without religious prescription outside worship, also becomes a religious and political symbol.

BIBLIOGRAPHY

Data about clothing used as vestment or as religious dress within Eastern traditions are scattered and diverse, varying considerably from culture to culture. In those religions with extensive scriptures, such as Islam, Buddhism, Hinduism, or Judaism, descriptions as well as specific proscriptions affect clothing choices.

The best source on shamanic practice is Mircea Eliade's *Shamanism: Archaic Techniques of Ecstasy,* rev. & enl. ed. (New York, 1964), which has exhaustive bibliographic references. Particular reference and illustration of Mongolian shamanic and Lamaist dress can be found in Henny Harald Hansen's *Mongol Costume* (Copenhagen, 1950). Additional information on Tibetan Buddhist practice can be found in Eleanor Olson's *Catalogue of the Tibetan Collections and Other Lamaist Articles in the Newark Museum,* 5 vols. (Newark, N.J., 1950–1971).

One of the most comprehensive references to East Asian religious practices in English is J. J. M. de Groot's *The Religious System of China: Its Ancient Forms, Evolution, History and Present Aspect; Manners, Customs and Social Institutions Connected Therewith,* 6 vols. (Leiden, 1892–1910). This massive study remains one of the best standard references to traditional religious practices in China. Political and religious functions of Chinese court attire are discussed in Schuyler Cammann's *China's Dragon Robes* (New York, 1952) and in my *Decoding Dragons: Status Garments in Ch'ing Dynasty China* (Eugene, Oreg., 1983). A limited discussion of Japanese Shintō practice and vestments can be found in Ono Soykyo's *Shinto, the Kami Way* (Rutland, Vt., and Tokyo, 1962).

Articles by international scholars documenting clothing and textiles throughout the Indonesian archipelago, including descriptions of religious usages can be found in *Indonesian Textiles: Irene Emery Roundtable on Museum Textiles, 1977 Proceedings,* edited by Mattibelle Gittinger (Washington, D.C., 1980). This volume contains a bibliography and extensive citation to a considerable literature in Dutch, German, French, and English. Beyond scriptural sources, references to Hindu and Muslim practice are very scattered.

John E. Vollmer

Religious Clothing in the West

Many factors are responsible for shaping the vestment tradition of a religion. The definition of ministry affects the degree to which ecclesiastical garments differ from secular clothing: the more the clergy is seen in terms of priesthood, the greater will be the visual distinction between the religious leaders and the congregation. Theology, that which a religion teaches as central to its worship, affects vestments. It can decree their use or banish them from the sanctuary, and it provides the interpretation of the external symbols of shape, decoration, and color. Liturgical usage adapts vestments to meet its evolving needs. There is the powerful influence of the cultural context in which the religion develops, with the history, the clothing styles, and the customs it inherits. When the culture changes, the religion will respond with changes of its own in dress as well as in liturgy, language, art, and architecture.

Judaism. Liturgical garments were not worn in the first centuries of Judaism. For nearly 500 years, from the time of Abraham through the Eygptian captivity (which ended in the first half of the thirteenth century BCE), no specialized clothing was required at the simple religious rites, which could be performed by any adult male.

The first mention of clothing within a sacred context was at the dramatic meeting of God and Moses. The awestruck man was commanded to remove his sandals, "for the place whereon thou standest is holy ground." After Moses led the Israelites out of Egypt, religious practice was formalized as part of the development of the law, both moral and religious. This included the simultaneous institution of a place of worship (the Tabernacle), a hereditary priesthood (from the tribe of Levi) to administer the now complex, formal religious ceremonies, and vestments for the priests' use. From its inception, this clothing was intended to express the spiritual dimension contained in God's command to Moses: "And thou shalt make holy garments for Aaron thy brother for glory and for beauty . . . that he may minister unto me in the priest's office" (*Ex.* 28:2–3).

Although the Bible contains many references to laymen offering gifts and sacrifices to the Lord, there were certain formal rituals that were to be performed only by a member of the Levitical priesthood clad in his sacred robes. These vestments were sumptuous in their color and decoration. Linen was dyed in rich hues of blue, purple, and scarlet. Pure gold ornaments embellished the robes. The high priest's gold breastplate *(ḥoshen)* was set with twelve different gemstones, representing the twelve tribes of Israel.

Minutely detailed descriptions from *Exodus* 28 and from the writings of the Jewish historian Josephus Flavius, 37/8–c. 100 CE) enable us to form a fairly complete picture of what was first worn by priests in the Tabernacle, and later in the Temple at Jerusalem. The priests and the high priest wore four articles of linen clothing: 1) drawers or breeches *(mikhnasayim)*; 2) a full-length white tunic *(kuttonet)*; 3) a long, embroidered sash *(avnet)*; and 4) a turban *(migba'at)*.

In addition, the high priest wore four other vestments integral to the administration of his specialized duties as chief religious leader and intercessor. Over the white tunic, he wore a long tunic of blue linen *(me'il)*; its lower border was decorated with scarlet, blue, and purple pomegranates alternating with golden bells. The bells were believed to keep him from incurring instant death when he entered the holy place. Another interpretation of *Exodus* 28:35 is that the tinkling of the bells notified the people that the high priest had not died in the presence of the Lord.

Next the *efod* was put on; it is described by Josephus as a short-sleeved tunic, to which was sewn a belt fashioned of materials more precious than those used for the belts of the common priests. A single onyx stone clasp (*shoham* stone), attaching the front and back halves of the *efod*, was pinned on either shoulder. Each stone was engraved with six of the names of the twelve tribes, symbolizing the high priest's responsibility to carry the needs of the people before the Lord. The breastplate of the *efod*, the most mysterious ornament of his attire, was used in some way to seek the counsel of God and to determine his will.

The miter *(mitsnefet)* completed the high priest's regalia. A gold plate *(tsits)* engraved with the words "Holiness to the Lord" was attached to the front of the miter with blue laces. This plate differentiated the miter from the headdress of the other priests.

On the Day of Atonement (Yom Kippur), the high priest would lay aside his splendid robes and humbly enter the Holy of Holies wearing only a simple white linen tunic, belt, and turban. The tradition of the laity also wearing white on the Day of Atonement as a sign of humility originated among the Ashkenazic Jews of the Middle Ages. White, the color of shrouds, is meant to inspire repentance by its evocation of mortality.

After the destruction of Jerusalem in 70 CE and the subsequent Diaspora of the Jews, Judaism became decentralized and democratic. The Temple was replaced by local synagogues as the symbolic residence of God. Ritual sacrifice performed by the priests became the prayers said by every Jew. The teacher of the law (rabbi) has no sacramental role and therefore has no need of special garments to distinguish him from the laity. Instead, he wears the same ritual attire as the other men of his congregation: prayer shawl *(ṭallit)*, phylacteries *(tefillin)*, and skullcap *(kippah)* or hat.

The prayer shawl evolved from a retangular mantle worn by men in ancient times. Tassels *(tsitsit)* at the four corners were added in obedience to God's decree that the Israelites wear fringes on their clothing. After the Diaspora brought Jews into increased contact with the gentiles, the mantle was discarded as the daily habit and became a religious garment worn at prayer. The phylacteries are two black leather boxes containing scriptural passages. One phylactery is bound to the arm by black leather thongs and the other is placed on the head. Wearing a skullcap or hat is a Jewish tradition. Symbolic of humility and respect before God, all of the ritual garments are visual reminders of God's commandments to Israel, and they also distinguish the Jew from the gentile.

The high priest's regalia has been transformed into the "garments" of the Torah scroll. Under a rich mantle like the priest's tunic *(me'il)*, the Torah is tied with a sash. The staves around which the scroll is rolled are surmounted by crowns (recalling the miter) or by pomegranates and bells (the decorations on the hem of the blue tunic). Suspended from the staves is a large metal breastplate.

Early Christianity and the Development of Roman Catholic Vestments. For 400 years, Christianity made no distinction between the dress of the religious leaders and that of the laity. More than the new religion's poverty and the persecutions it experienced, there was a deliberate policy of the early church hierarchy to preserve a visual equality among all believers. Within the fellowship, no divisions were recognized: Jewish convert from gentile convert, slave from freeborn. The ordained clergy had a specialized role, but they exercised their ministry within a church called by the apostle Peter "a kingdom of priests." At worship services, clergy and congregation wore clean everyday clothing of the Roman world. Over a long linen robe with narrow sleeves (the *tunica alba*, also identified as the *tunica talaris* or the *linea*) was worn a knee-length tunic with short, fitted sleeves (the *tunica*). A knee-length cloak made from a large, circular cloth with a center neck opening (the *paenula*, *planeta*, or *casula*) completed their attire. Clerics were directed by Pope Stephen I (253–257) not to use their "vestments" for daily wear. Some scholars have interpreted this to mean that there were specific liturgical garments by the middle of the third century. However, when the bishops of Gaul (the south of France) introduced the use of new ritual garments, it prompted a stinging rebuke from Pope Celestine I (c. 425): "We bishops must be distinguished from the people by our learning not by our dress, by our life not by our robes, by purity of heart not by elegance . . ."

Inner goodness and outer simplicity were to characterize the dress of the laity as well. In the Sermon on the Mount, Jesus Christ told his listeners not to be preoccupied with what they wore but instead to devote themselves to seeking the kingdom of God and his righteousness (*Mt.* 6:25–34). The apostle Paul exhorted Christians to clothe themselves symbolically with "the armor of God," mentioning the breastplate of righteousness and the shield of faith (*Eph.* 6:11–17).

Women were singled out for special guidance. Their beauty was not to be "that outward adorning of plaiting the hair, and of wearing gold or putting on of apparel," but the ornament of "a meek and a quiet spirit" (*1 Pt.* 3:3–4). (A strict interpretation of these verses has led the Seventh-day Adventists to forbid the wearing of any jewelry, including wedding rings.) The custom of women covering their heads in church, only lately abandoned by the Roman Catholic church, was supported in a letter from Paul to the church at Corinth (*1 Cor.* 11:5-10). The gentile Christians needed to be taught what was unquestioned by the converts from Judaism: that it is shameful for a woman to appear in public bareheaded. Among Orthodox Jews it is not uncommon for a married woman to wear a wig over her own hair. In Western secular culture, for many centuries, veiling a woman's hair denoted modesty and chastity. A woman's "crowning glory" when hidden would not arouse male desire. A wife's headdress proclaimed that her beauty was only for her husband's eyes. When a woman "took the veil" and became a nun, the wimple and the shorn hair beneath it marked her renunciation of the world and the sacrifice of her beauty. Tonsuring monks had its origins in the Jewish custom of shaving the head to signify that a vow had been made (*Acts* 18:18).

Sacred clothing styles began to diverge from the secular in the fifth century with the barbarian invasions and the subsequent fall of Rome (476). New fashions, such as shorter tunics, were adopted by the laity. Clerical dress, however, retained the older forms, whether from conservatism or from a desire to preserve the civilized Roman ways in the face of overwhelming foreign influence. In liturgical vestments the earlier common styles were "frozen"; a similar tendency can occur with liturgical language (e.g., Church Slavonic and Elizabethan English).

The period from the fifth to the ninth century was transitional. The basic ecclesiastical vestments developed and were standardized throughout the West, largely by papal decree. The now-archaic garments took on symbolic meanings, primarily associated with the passion of Christ (reenacted at Mass) and with the spiritual qualities prayed for by the clergy while vesting. Specific vestments became the insignia of an officiant's rank or function.

Between the ninth and the twelfth century theologians were not only interested in the symbolism of the various garments but also in defining a physical correspondence between them and the Levitical vestments of the ancient Jewish priests. Earlier writers, such as Jerome (c. 342–420), had been content to establish a "mystical" equivalence between them. Many vestments that came into use at this time, such as the subcingulum (inner belt), rationale (the counterpart of the high priest's breastplate), miter, tunicle (a revised version of the dalmatic worn by subdeacons), and orale (a short cape worn by the pope at solemn pontifical mass), were probably merely copies or adaptations made to prove the relationship.

No new vestments were introduced after the twelfth century. From the thirteenth to the seventeenth century, however, ecclesiastical garments evolved in form and ornamentation. Magnificent fabrics and embroideries characterize this period. Comparatively minor stylistic refinements were made in the seventeenth and eighteenth centuries. Nineteenth-century vestments sometimes reflect the influence of the Gothic Revival movement in the arts with a return to medieval style, shapes, and symbols.

The traditional ecclesiastical vestments of the Roman Catholic church include the alb, amice, cincture, stole, maniple (now obsolete), dalmatic, chasuble, cope, miter, and pallium. The alb derived from the *tunica alba* (Lat., "white tunic") and is the most unchanged in form of liturgical vestments. It is worn by all orders. Purity is symbolized by the alb's whiteness. Belting the alb with the cincture, made of wool, linen, or silk, indicates alertness and preparation for work. Forming the collar of the alb is the amice, a neckerchief that keeps the skin from chafing against the fabric of the next outer garment and protects the vestments from dirt and perspiration. Next, a long, narrow scarflike vestment, the stole, is put around the neck. The way it is worn indicates the rank of the clergy: the bishop leaves the sides hanging parallel; at one time the priest, who must always wear a stole when celebrating the Eucharist, criss-crossed the stole in front and secured it with the cincture, but now he wears it in the same fashion as a bishop. The deacon wears the stole on a diagonal from the left shoulder to where it is secured at the right hip. The stole evolved from the Roman *orarium* (from Latin *os, or-*, "mouth"), a handkerchief-like cloth used for wiping the mouth or drying the face or hands. Scholars are divided over the reason for the stole's incorporation into Christian liturgical use. As the young boys assisting at pagan Roman sacrifices wore a similar cloth over their shoulders, perhaps the stole had a functional purpose that disappeared when it was made of finer materials. The maniple, a short stole once worn over the left wrist, had a similar evolution from practical cloth to decorative ornament.

Over the alb the deacon wears a dalmatic. This short, T-shaped tunic with wide sleeves was derived from a woolen garment originating in the Greek province of Dalmatia (now part of Yugoslavia). In the fourth century CE, it replaced the awkward Roman toga for general wear and remained a secular garment for emperors, consuls, and the French kings through the seventh century. The English monarch is still invested with a dalmatic at the coronation ceremony.

Of all the liturgical vestments, the chasuble has shown the greatest stylistic modification over the centuries. It was originally the voluminous outdoor cloak (*paenula* or *planeta*) worn by men and women of the later Greco-Roman world. Ancient representations show that it was semicircular in pattern, with the two edges sewn together by a front seam, giving it a conical shape. As early as the sixth century, the chasuble became more stylized. The sides were shortened, and the front cut to a point, probably to increase the celebrant's ease of movement. Eventually, the front and the back were reduced in length also. During the Middle Ages, when the church's hierarchy and ceremony were strongly influenced by the model of king and court, chasubles and other vestments were made out of rich fabrics, heavy with gold and elaborate embroidery. The increased weight necessitated a continued abbreviation of the chasuble's volume. By the eighteenth century, it had become merely two stiff panels joined at the shoulder.

The pallium is an ecclesiastical vestment associated with the pope and papal privilege. It is a circular band worn around the shoulders of the chasuble, with a pendant band in front and in back and is marked with six dark purple crosses. Worn by the pope, it symbolizes the plentitude of the pontifical office, and, when conferred by him on archbishops and bishops, participation in the authority of the pope.

The cope is a semicircular cloak, worn primarily in liturgical processions. It is a refined version of the mantle once worn over the toga by ordinary citizens as a mark of distinction or as a protective garment. The vestigial hood on the cope is a reminder of the latter function.

Part of the insignia of the bishop is the miter, a shield-shaped headdress with two fringed lappets that hang down the back. Before the eleventh century, it was worn only by deaconesses and abbesses. According to liturgical scholar Joseph Braun, the first reliable documentation of an episcopal miter dates from 1049, when Pope Leo IX (1049–1054) bestowed the right to wear the miter on the archbishop of Trier. It became a recognized episcopal insignia conferred only by the pope on bishops or cardinals. The papal tiara is no longer worn, having been abandoned in 1978 by Pope John Paul I (d. 1978).

The major impetus for the modern reform of Roman Catholic ecclesiastical vestments was the Second Vatican Council, which ended in 1965. Pope John XXIII (1958-1963) defined its task as renewing the religious life of the church. Renewal and modernization led to a return to the model of the early church, characterized by simplicity in form and practice, and by a limited visual distinction between clergy and the laity. Vestments that were "obsolete and out of harmony with our age" (in the words of a 1968 church document) were abolished. This included the maniple; its original function as a kind of liturgical hand towel was absent in the impractical strip of silk it had become. In general, the chasuble became ample, with its beauty inherent in its fabric and form rather than its ornamentation. Greater freedom of choice in the selection of material and decoration permitted vestments to be made of local natural materials and appropriate synthetic fibers, allowing for a departure from tradition and enabling each local church to respond to the cultural and aesthetic need and the physical resources of the community.

Modernization also affected the dress of nuns. Their

long, flowing habits and severe wimples were altered to look less medieval and more contemporary. As with clerical vestments, one of the objectives was to make religious appear less remote and more "of the people." Parallel changes were made in the liturgy: translating the Mass from Latin into the vernacular and resuming the westward position for the celebrant (i.e., facing the congregation), which had been customary until the eighth or ninth century. The switch to an eastward position coincided with an era of greater specialization in vestments, each factor contributing to a greater distinction between clergy and laity. The modern church, on the contrary, seeks to minimize the differences. Laypeople who participate in the worship services by reading the Bible or leading the prayers may wear long robes similar to the alb.

Eastern Orthodox Churches. Reform and modernization has not affected vestments of the Eastern Orthodox churches. For centuries, they have remained essentially unchanged. Similar conservatism characterizes both Orthodox liturgy and religious art. Complex symbolism has evolved to explain the mystical significance of the vestments. Church ceremony, interior architecture (particularly the iconostasis screen that separates the altar from the sanctuary), and vestments create an atmosphere of mystery and reverence, and they underscore the division between the clergy and the congregation.

Orthodox vestments can be divided into two categories: (1) those related to Western ecclesiastical garments in appearance and origin, and equivalent in function: the *sticharion, phelonion, orarion, sakkos, zoni, omophorion, epitrachelion,* and miter (or its replacement, the *kamilavchion* and the *epanokamilavchion*); and (2) those unique to Orthodoxy: the *mandyas, epimanikia,* and *epigonation.*

The *sticharion* is a long white tunic similar to the alb; and, like the alb, it is worn by all clerical orders. Its name is taken from the colored bands, or *stichoi,* that once decorated it. These stripes, now restricted to the bishop's garment, symbolize Christ's bonds and the blood that flowed from his side. According to Germanus I, patriarch of Constantinople (c. 715 CE), the whiteness of the *sticharion* "signifies the glory of the Godhead and the bright citizenship of the priests."

The *epimanikia* are cuffs once reserved for bishops but now worn by all clerics to hold back the voluminous sleeves of the *sticharion.* They originated in the gloves that the Byzantine emperor wore when he entered the sanctuary to receive the Eucharist. However, as clerics could touch the bread with their bare hands, those gloves were reduced to cuffs. Different scholars have variously equated the *epimanikia* with Western episcopal gloves and with the maniple. Christ's bonds at the passion are symbolized by the *epimanikia.*

The deacon's *orarion,* like the Western stole, is a long, narrow band of material, often embroidered with the angels' hymn of "Holy, Holy, Holy." Symeon of Thessalonica (d. 1429) believed that the *orarion* gave the deacon the beauty of the angels, whose role he fulfills in assisting at the Divine Liturgy. For Isidore of Pelusium (c. 360–c. 435/449), the *orarion* represents the towel with which Christ dried the feet of the disciples at the Last Supper and so symbolizes humility.

The *epitrachelion* is the equivalent of the Western priest's stole and is worn only by bishops and priests. It is formed by attaching the long sides of an embroidered stole, leaving a keyholelike opening for the head. When the Divine Liturgy is performed the *epitrachelion* must be worn, even if one must be improvised from a belt or a cloth. Various symbolic meanings are given to this garment: the yoke of Christ, the cord put around his neck, the carrying of the cross, the reed scepter put in his hand.

The Roman *paenula* became the *phelonion* worn by priests. In time, it became somewhat shorter in front. It symbolizes humility and the garment worn by Christ at the passion.

The *zoni,* like the Western cincture, is an ecclesiastical belt worn by priests and bishops to keep the *sticharion* and *epitrachelion* in place. Prayers said while vesting refer to its symbolism of innocence and spiritual strength.

The *epigonation* is a lozenge-shaped ornament with a cross or an image embroidered in the center, which is suspended by a ribbon from the *zoni,* and reaches to the right knee. It may have evolved from a ceremonial handkerchief used by bishops. In addition to bishops, other ecclesiastics may wear the *epigonation* as a special privilege. Symbolically, it represents the "sword of the spirit" (*Eph.* 6:17).

The *sakkos* has the same basic T-shape as the dalmatic, but it is not as long and has shorter sleeves. It is a splendid episcopal vestment, richly embroidered, and fastened along the sides with small bells in imitation of the tunic of the Hebrew high priest. Originally the *sakkos* was an imperial, not an ecclesiastical, garment. In both spheres it symbolized humility.

The counterpart of the pallium is the *omophorion,* which is worn by bishops around the shoulders and knotted in front. It may have evolved from the colorful pallium worn under the *paenula* by certain Roman functionaries as a sign of the dignity of their rank. Fourth-century Christian emperors probably conferred it on the bishops. But the church transformed the honorific symbolism to a christological one: the Good Shepherd who carries the lost sheep on his shoulder.

The bishop's miter retains the form of the Byzantine imperial crown, a spherical bonnet decorated with enameled or embroidered medallions. When the miter is not permitted, the bishop wears a black, cylindrical hat called a *kamilavchion* under the *epanokamilavchion*, a lightweight black veil falling to the shoulders and down the back. The *epanokamilavchion* represents modesty and renunciation, fitting symbolism for a garment of monastic origin. Priests, and sometimes deacons, also wear the *kamilavchion*.

Although the *mandyas* and the cope have similar shapes, the two share neither a common origin nor symbolism. One theory suggests that the word *mandyas* derives from a Persian word designating a military mantle. This developed into a precious mantle worn by the emperors of the Eastern Roman empire, and later by the Eastern Orthodox bishops. Another hypothesis is that the *mandyas* evolved from a monastic cloak that was derived from the pagan philosopher's mantle. As bishops are selected from the monastic orders, they introduced this garment into wider ecclesiastical use. Some ornamentation on the *mandyas* is thought to represent the Old and New Testaments, from which flow the streams of doctrines and grace that the bishops should pour out on humanity.

Protestant: Clergy and Laity. The diversity of clerical dress in the Protestant churches reflects the varied concepts regarding the function of the clergy and the role of the liturgy among the different denominations. Generally, the more a church emphasizes the Eucharist as the central act of corporate worship, the more liturgical garments will emphasize the clergy's role as administrator of the sacraments. When a church's emphasis is on preaching and teaching, the religious leader's role is defined as that of pastor (meaning shepherd) or minister (one who serves). Their clothing, therefore, tends to be the same as that of their congregation. Among denominations such as the Baptists, Nazarenes, and Assemblies of God, suits are usually worn: the modern equivalent of the "Sunday best" that was traditional in the early centuries of Christianity. Methodist and Presbyterian churches are more liturgical; their clergy's attire is more formal, modeled on academic robes. Presbyterian ministers, for example, often wear a long, black, full-sleeved robe called a Geneva gown. Another Presbyterian vestment is preaching bands: a pair of short, white, rectangular tabs that are attached to the front neckline. Among the Lutheran clergy, the use and type of ecclesiastical garments varies. Cassock and surplice may be worn, as well as full eucharistic apparel. The clerical or Roman collar of Lutheran, Roman Catholic, and Episcopal clergy is a stylizied version of the neck cloth worn by all gentlemen into the nineteenth century.

Clothing worn by the majority of modern Protestant laymen and laywomen does not have specific religious symbolism. Among certain groups, however, the general style of attire does communicate information about the religiously inspired attitude toward dress. For example, during the 1960s, women of the more conservative Protestant congregations did not wear the popular miniskirts. Their knee-length hemlines, although conservative by their contemporaries' standards, would have scandalized their great-grandmothers. This unfashionable clothing did not have any religious meaning per se, in the sense that a white wedding gown symbolizes purity. It was an expression of the biblical injunction to be dressed modestly in relation to the secular culture.

A stricter interpretation of this concept is followed among the Old Order Amish, a branch of the reform group founded in 1693 under the leadership of the Swiss Mennonite bishop Jacob Amman. Also known as "hooks-and-eyes Mennonites" (because they consider buttons worldly), their distinctively plain, old-fashioned clothing sets them apart from the modern world. This was also true of members of the Church of the Brethren (German Baptists or Dunkers) until the turn of the century.

BIBLIOGRAPHY

Information and bibliography on Jewish ecclesiastical and lay clothing can be found under their Hebrew names in the *Encyclopaedia Judaica* (Jerusalem, 1971). Wharton Booth Marriott's excellent book *Vestiarium Christianum* (London, 1868) includes descriptions of Jewish liturgical dress in translations of Josephus, Jerome, and others, in addition to translations of important primary source documents concerning Christian ecclesiastical vestments. In *Die liturgische Gewändung im Occident und Orient* (Freiburg, 1907), Joseph Braun, S.J., provides a careful interpretation of the above documentation based on a thorough study of the liturgy. Modern scholarship on vestments, liturgy, and priesthood is available in Dom Gregory Dix's book *The Shape of the Liturgy*, 2d ed. (New York, 1982), in the chapter entitled "The Development of Ceremonial." Volumes 7 and 8 of Charles Rohault de Fleury's *La Messe: Études archéologiques sur ses monuments*, 8 vols. (Paris, 1882-1889), deal with the history of ecclesiastical vestments from the view point of prescribed liturgical use.

The exhibition catalog *Raiment for the Lord's Service: A Thousand Years of Western Vestments* by Christa C. Mayer-Thurman (Chicago, 1975) contains essays on the vestments traditions of Roman Catholic, Anglican, and Protestant churches as well as descriptions and explanations of the different vestments, 186 catalog entries and illustrations, and an extensive bibliography. Vestments are arranged chronologically and within an alphabetical list of countries in the *Bibliography of Costume* (New York, 1939) by Hilaire and Meyer Hiler. Mary Symonds and Louise Preece, in *Needlework in Religion* (London, 1924), present clear, well-organized descriptions and good illustrations of vestments, ornamentation, liturgical colors, symbolism, and the liturgical use of vestments in the Roman Catholic, Eastern Orthodox, and Anglican churches. R. A. S. Macalister's book *Ecclesiastical Vestments* (London, 1896) studies the development, usage, and symbolism (including extensive quotes from prayers said while vesting) of liturgical garments in the Western and Eastern churches, as well as the reform denominations. Concise information on these topics is found in the *New Catholic Encyclopedia* (Washington, D.C., 1967) under the headings "Byzantine Rite" and "Liturgical Art." Information specific to Eastern Orthodox church vestments is in *The Byzantine Tradition in Church Embroidery* (London, 1967) by Pauline Johnstone and *Studien zur Geschichte der Messegewänder im byzantinischen Ritus* (Munich, 1965) by Tano Papas.

DEBORAH E. KRAAK

CLOTILDA (c. 470–545), queen consort of Clovis, king of the Franks. Her Christian faith of the Nicene, or catholic, tradition greatly influenced her husband and all of northern Gaul. Clotilda was born a Bergundian, in the Rhone valley in eastern France; her grandfather was Gundioc, king of the Bergundians. Her father, Chilperic, a Christian, was one of four heirs to the king. A violent dispute among the heirs led to Chilperic's death and to Clotilda's having to live with an uncle in Geneva. Commerce between the Bergundians in Geneva and the Salians, a group of Franks living in Paris under King Clovis, led to Clotilda's meeting Clovis and to their eventual marriage.

Clotilda was a Christian devoted to the orthodox faith, as opposed to Arianism. Clovis disdained her faith until the Alemanni, a formidable Germanic people, invaded northern Gaul. He vowed that if he defeated the Alemanni he would accept Clotilda's Christ. His victory in 495 led to his baptism, along with that of three thousand of his warriors, on Christmas Day of 496. The Franks were the first Germanic tribes to convert to the orthodox faith; most of the tribes to the south of them were Arians. With Clotilda's help, Clovis expanded the area of his rule, defended the catholic faith against Arianism, and became an important link in the spread of Christianity in the northwestern part of Europe.

After the death of her husband in 511, Clotilda's four sons engaged in a bitter feud that led to several deaths. Deeply saddened, Clotilda retired to a convent in Tours, a town where the famous Martin had been bishop in the fourth century. She maintained her keen interest in civic matters and became fabled for her piety and her practical deeds of generosity.

BIBLIOGRAPHY

The best biography, and one that is quite readable, is Godefroi Kurth's *Saint Clotilda*, translated by V. M. Crawford (London and New York, 1913).

H. MCKENNIE GOODPASTURE

CLOUDS. Today, clouds are a natural phenomenon to be studied by meteorologists, but in ancient times they were incalculable, awe-inspiring, and profoundly numinous. The *Book of the Month* of the Maya *Chilam Balam* states, "All was created by God our father and by his word. His divinity appeared where there was neither heaven nor earth, and by his power he became a cloud, and created the universe." God is completely identified with a cloud; it is totally numinous. The writers of the Hebrew scriptures claimed that "God made a covenant with man and all living beings" (*Gn.* 9:12) and that "he will set his bow in the cloud as a sign of a covenant between him and the earth" (*Gn.* 9:13). Scripture reports that God's presence was even in the cloud. He spoke to Moses out of the cloud and led the Israelites through the desert in a pillar of cloud for forty years (*Ex.* 13:21). The cloud played the decisive role in the crossing of the Red Sea: "The angel of God which went before the camp of Israel removed and went behind them. And it came between the camp of the Egyptians and the camp of Israel: and it was a cloud and a darkness to them, but it gave light by night to these" (*Ex.* 14:20). At this time, the cloud was almost totally numinous. God was in, and spoke out of, the cloud. The cloud could act as a messenger of God and even create paradoxical effects (e.g., light for the Israelites, darkness for the Egyptians).

The cloud of the psalmists is less numinous. It is neither the divine nor its habitation; rather it is a "chariot" for God as the creator of the universe (*Ps.* 104:3). In some later psalms, the cloud is no more than a part in a gratefully remembered event: "He spread a cloud for the covering; and fire to give light in the night" (*Ps.* 105:39).

The first chapter of *Ezekiel* indicates that the cloud had great numinosity for Ezekiel. "And I looked, and, behold, a whirlwind came out of the north, and a great cloud, and a fire infolding itself, and a brightness was about it, and out of the midst thereof as the color of amber, out of the midst of the fire" (*Ez.* 1:4). At the same time, the cloud is also a natural phenomenon that the writer of *Ezekiel* uses for comparative purposes. "As the appearance of the bow that is in the cloud in the day of rain, so was the appearance of the brightness round about" (*Ez.* 1:28). The cloud is clearly a symbol for the prophet Ezekiel when, in a complex vision of God, he sees the cherubim standing on the right side of the house, "and the cloud filled the inner court" (*Ez.* 10:3).

The use of the cloud as symbol had its most important impact on history when the prophet Daniel proclaimed that the savior will come "with the clouds of heaven: I saw in the visions of the night, and behold one like the son of man come with the clouds of heaven and came to the Ancient of Days" (*Dn.* 7:13). The clouds of heaven have been associated with the savior ever since. Both Matthew and Mark mention clouds in association with the coming of Jesus. When the high priest asked Jesus whether he was the Christ, the Son of God, he answered: "Hereafter shall ye see the Son of man sitting on the right hand of power and coming in the clouds of heaven" (*Mt.* 26:64, *Mk.* 14:62; see also *Mt.* 24:30, *Mk.* 13:26).

In Jesus' own experience, the cloud played a decisive role. The divine spoke to him out of the cloud. Matthew writes: "A bright cloud overshadowed them; and behold a voice out of the cloud which said, 'This is my beloved son in whom I am well pleased: hear ye him' " (*Mt.* 17:5).

During the seventeen centuries in which alchemy accompanied Christianity as a compensatory process, the cloud appeared quite frequently in the fantasies of the "philosophers," as the alchemists called themselves. Like most alchemical terms, the cloud referred to a material, chemical equivalent as well as to a spiritual phenomenon. References to the "cloud rising from the sea" are found in the very ancient treatise of Comarius (first century CE). In some cases, the cloud represented "the comfort of the Holy Ghost and Christ's ascension" (Rabanus Maurus, *Allegoriae in Sacram Scripturam*, cited in C. G. Jung, *Mysterium Coniunctiones*, New York, 1963). Augustine likens the apostles to a cloud that symbolizes the concealment of the creator under the flesh (*Expositions on the Psalms* 7.55). Similarly, Christ was prefigured by the pillar of cloud that guided the Jews through the wilderness (Augustine on Psalm 98; cited in Jung, *Mysterium Coniunctiones*).

In conclusion, it can be said that the image of the cloud appears first as an image of God or one of God's servants (angels). It appears also as an alchemical symbol and hence as something simultaneously concrete and spiritual. In the nineteenth and twentieth centuries, it was considered more and more a true symbol.

BIBLIOGRAPHY

Little has been written on the symbolism of clouds. The *Allegoriae in sacram scripturam* of the first-century Frankish theologian Rabanus Maurua provides several significant associations. My book *The Reluctant Prophet* (Los Angeles, 1973) includes a chapter entitled "The Cloud," in which I discuss a number of nineteenth- and twentieth-century German and French poems that employ cloud imagery. Here the vague and shapeless cloud proves to be a symbol that contains many other symbols within it and finally reveals itself as symbol of the self. Finally, Mai-Mai Sze's *The Tao of Painting* (New York, 1956) is an extensive study of the ritual disposition of Chinese painting. The symbol of the cloud is only one of many touched upon in this work, but it fits very well into the central idea expressed by the title.

JAMES KIRSCH

CLOWNS. The term *clown* is used here as a gloss for a cluster of figures that appear in the religious events of various peoples and that have certain attributes in common. It is, therefore, a term of analysis employed in thinking about the place of such figures in religious performance. This usage is not intended to be homologous with the perceptions of any given people, whose culture is likely to connote more particularistic significance to such characters and their cognates. Instead, I suggest that what ritual-clown figures have in common with one another is a certain logic of composition. Characters of such composition then have crucial functions for the rituals and dramas within which they perform.

The etymology of the word *clown* in the English language suggests the logic of composition for such figures. According to the *Oxford English Dictionary,* the term appeared in English usage in the second half of the sixteenth century: it originally meant "clod," "clot," or "lump." *Clod* and *clot* were long synonymous. *Clod* connotes the coagulation of liquids and a lumpish adhesion of materials. *Clot* connotes a semisolid lump formed by congelation and coagulation. Put together, *clown, clod,* and *clot* connote an entity that is unfinished or incomplete in its internal organization: one that hangs together in a loose and clumsy way. The clown is lumpish in its imperfect—but congealing and adhering—fusion of attributes. It also has a sense of frozen motion, of congealed liquidity, that connotes processuality and dynamism rather than structure and stasis. In the European tradition, the clown had affinities to festival fools, folk fools, and holy fools, all of whom had the tendency to melt the solidity of the world. The word *fool,* according to the *Oxford English Dictionary,* derives from the Latin *follis,* which literally means "bellows" but is also used in the sense of "windbag." The term *buffoon,* with connotations similar to those of *fool,* is cognate with the Italian *buffare,* "to puff." In the derivation of *fool* there is a sense of lightness and motion, and so of processuality. Given the likely affinity between the clown and the fool, there is in the clown a figure that is integrated in a clumsy fashion and that adheres to itself with an incipient sense of internal movement.

Clowns are ambiguous and ambivalent figures. Within their variegated composition they subsume attributes that contradict and invert one another. The clown in ritual is at once a character of solemnity and fun, of gravity and hilarity, of danger and absurdity, of wisdom and idiocy, and of the sacred and the profane. The interior logic of composition of such a figure is not homogeneous. It is neither wholly one attribute of a set nor another. Given this sense of neither/nor, such figures subsume holistically, albeit lumpishly, all of their contradictory sets of attributes.

These contradictions within the ritual clown rarely are resolved. Instead, whichever attribute a clown presents in performance, the projection of its contrary always is imminent. Thus the opposing attributes within the figure continuously oscillate among themselves. Given this attribute of internal oscillation, such clown figures can be said to subsume within themselves a notion of border or boundary that they straddle and across which they move, back and forth, for as long as they remain true to type. The ritual clown is an eminently paradoxical figure: it is neither wise nor foolish, yet it is both without being wholly one or the other. As a paradoxical being, the figure evokes inconsistencies of meaning and referential ambiguities in ritual contexts that otherwise have an appearance of solidity and stability. The clown is a construct with a sense of incompleteness, yet whole (a lump), that is in a condition of transformation (congelation) but that is somehow out of place in context (a clod).

Externally, the ritual clown appears as an ill-formed unity. Pueblo Indian clowns of the American Southwest are lumpish in form or painted in stripes of contrasting colors. Other clowns often are parti-colored or piecemeal beings that hang together loosely. Internally, the ritual clown manifests qualities of multiplicity and fluidity: it is fluctuating and unstable. This interior organization can be summated as a condition of self-transformation: the figure is continually in motion within itself, and so it remains permanently unfinished. It is a powerful figurative rendition of processuality. This makes it a powerful solvent of contexts and structures within which it is located. These attributes are crucial to the roles it performs within ritual and ceremonial occasions.

Clowns seem to have especial affinities to the boundaries of ritualistic occasions. In European folk rites and dramas that were associated with seasonal transitions, especially those from winter to spring, and so with notions of the regeneration of natural and social orders, folk fools at times played the role of master of ceremony. These characters tended to be killed and revived in these events, and so they bridged and mediated cosmic transitions. Among the Tewa, Hopi, and Zuni Pueblo Indians of the American Southwest, ritual clowns were indisputable masters of the boundary. More generally, where such clown figures are common in ceremonials, they either control the overall organization of sequencing of events or they appear during the interludes between phases of rites. In either instance, they are located in transitional zones that connote the sequential movement or transformation of ritual from one context to another. Given that these figures encompass a notion of boundary within the composition of their being—one through which they endlessly oscillate—their affinity to the external boundaries of ritual events, and to those within ritual, should be clear. They are ambulatory manifestations of boundariness, for their composition resonates with, and so is keyed to, borders of ritual in terms of its spatial and sequential ordering.

This delineation of ritual clowns is quite distinct from those modern clowns of the European tradition of the circus and from stock figures of comedy. Circus clown performances usually consist of at least a pair of clowns who are distinguished categorically from one another. The white-faced clown is an epitome of "culture": he is formal, elegant, authoritative, rigid, and overcivilized. By contrast, the "auguste" clown is thoroughly sloppy, ill kempt, amoral, and chaotic: he inverts the attributes of the white-faced clown and is identified with those of "nature." In performance these two clowns are viable in tandem, so that their respective sets of characteristics complement each other.

These clowns also have an intimate relation to boundaries; but theirs is an exterior one, for a sense of boundariness is established by their interplay in performance rather than by their being part of the logic of composition of either or both of them. Thus the boundary between, say, categories of "nature" and "culture" becomes located somewhere between these two figures instead of within one or both of them. Each figure itself has a homogeneous and stable composition, and so the contrast of opposites is evident only when they are together: they manipulate boundaries only as a duo. By way of contrast, the ritual clown dissolves boundaries by itself. Stock comic figures that appear in ritual dramas, and whose ethnographic provenance seems much more extensive than that of ritual clowns, also tend to have homogeneous and internally stable compositions. In general they lack, in and of themselves, the transformative capacities that are integral to clowns in ritual.

Nonetheless, figures that approximate the attributes of ritual clowns, as these are delineated here, do have a fairly widespread distribution among peoples of the world, some of whom are mentioned here, although lack of space prevents adducing these. Clowns in ceremonial and ritual are reported for the Mayo and Yaqui peoples of northern Mexico, for the Pueblo Indian peoples of the American Southwest, and for other native peoples of California, the Great Plains, and the Northwest Coast of North America. In European traditions, festival fools were prominent in various English dramas of springtime and in the Swiss-German *Fastnachtsspiele;* they had affinities to the Italian tradition of *buffo* and perhaps to picaresque literary works. Clownlike figures are reported in the Turkish puppet theater, in some Iranian improvisatory folk theater, and in the traditional Szechwan theater of China. Such figures also are found in modern Javanese *ludruk* performances and in the Javanese puppet theater. They appear quite elaborated in various South Indian traditions: in Carnatic puppet performances, in Kannada *yakṣagaṇa* dance dramas, in the *kūṭiyāṭṭam* dramatic tradition of Kerala, and in Tamil *karakam* dances and *tĕrukkūttu* street dramas as well as in the stories of the sixteenth-century Tamil and Telugu court jester Tĕnāli Rāma. The provenance of such figures extends south to Sri Lanka and north to the tradition of dance dramas in Tibetan monasteries. [*For further discussion of ritual performance, see* Drama.]

There is a multiplicity and duplicity in clowns, a radical emphasis on the disharmonic that at first sight appears out of place in many of the ceremonies and dramas in which they appear. And a sense of unease pervades many of the explanations of why they are there. The commonest, and the least satisfactory, is that clowns provide comic relief, either from the seriousness and tedium of the ritual medium itself or from the everyday suppression of forbidden themes that clowns raise to overt and conscious scrutiny. There are various versions of this thesis. Thus, such figures are said to enable members of audiences to think or to behave in otherwise repressed ways, or it is said that these clowns exist in order to violate taboo, given the need to evoke themes that must be suppressed in the everyday contexts of life. These approaches readily lend themselves to varieties of psychologistic reductionism, such that clowns are said to concretize and to release unconscious psychic tensions by bringing them to conscious thought. An added explanation is that these figures reduce the tension and anxiety that are generated by awesome and mysterious sacrality, since, through harmless burlesque, the frightening is made familiar and known.

Clowns in ritual and drama do indeed invert, mock, and satirize both taken-for-granted conventions of life and those that are sacralized and venerated, whether through gentle irony, through dramatic allegory, or through scatological burlesque. Yet, within the same occasions, they often are the righteous upholders of morality and propriety. Such groups as the Hopi Indians of the American Southwest explicitly recognize that clowns underline moral precepts by their amoral antics. The Hopi state that clowns show life as it should not be. Others, such as the Tewa, Zuni, and Mayo Indians, accord explicit sacred and moral stature to their clowns. Among the Mayo, these are more figures of fright than of amusement. Still other peoples seem to refrain from exegesis and simply summate clowns in ritual as figures of fun.

There are two signal difficulties with discussions of ritual clowning that rely on one or another version of catharsis or of satirical inversion to explain the existence of these contrary characters. In the first instance, either or both of these functions can be and are performed by figures of much simpler composition. Stock comic characters, who appear in ceremonial and dramatic activities, and whose composition is homogeneous and not transformative, often meet such requirements. These are the quintessential butts, bunglers, and schemers, whose rollicking antics and exaggerated amorality serve onlookers with a license to frolic with the unspeakable, and perhaps with the unthinkable, in the security of knowing or feeling that these are unnatural and temporary versions of order that will revert to their moral counterparts and so will reaffirm righteous values and conduct. Why then should clown figures of such complex and inconstant composition be equated in role and function with these facile and straightforward stock comic characters? The likely answer is that they should not be, and that ritual clowns carry out other tasks more in keeping with their own interior organization.

The second difficulty in discussions of ritual clowning is that these clowns are treated as if they reflect, in unmediated ways, themes of more general cultural and psychological significance. In other words, clowns are torn from the contexts of their appearance and performance without any explanation of their presence there. Yet, first and foremost, and prior to a consideration of their significance for more abstract motifs of psychic balance and cultural values, it is in terms of the occasions of their appearance that the presence of clowns should be explicated.

That clowns in ritual are living studies in vivid contrast and in shades of comparison is indicative of their status in performance. As interlocutors and as commentators, their affinities are to boundaries that separate ceremonial or narrative action from the mundane or that distinguish between different phases or contexts within ritual performance itself. In a sense, they keep one foot within an ongoing context of participation and experience, while the other foot is already leading into another. As such, they are agents of change, mediators who dissolve and transform the fixity of categories of performance and narrative that boundaries organize and integrate.

Ritual and ceremonial occasions have programs or texts, prescribed or inscribed, that are their elementary organization. Occasions in which clowns appear are always composed of more than a single adumbrated context of meaning and experience. That is, these occasions are constituted of a number of phases that contrast with one another in their programmatic purpose and that must be shifted, one into another, in sequence. Written or oral texts and programs often suggest that such transitions are accomplished simply because they are inscribed or prescribed. Yet, in the practice of performance, each phase or context of an occasion has the tendency to adumbrate and to reify itself in stable and seamless ways that wholly engross participants in its experience. This lack of discordance works against the necessary decomposition or deconstruction of context, in order to make way for the next, and so to enable the overall occasion to be shifted in sequence through its constituent phases, as specified by program or text.

The design of the clown is precisely that of a whirligig—one that swirls in counterpoint to the adumbration and concordance of any ritual context in which it is located. As it revolves within itself, the clown gathers up the interwoven strands of the coherence of context, mixes them up, and so contradicts their integration and unravels them. Just as the clown upends any configuration of meaning into which it enters, so it takes apart context and opens the way to the cohering of alternative patterns of meaning.

Such occasions often have a sense of climax that arouses within the participants the recognition of some transcendent reality and seamless truth. Then the inherently reflexive properties of the clown must be stilled. Otherwise, true to its own rhythm and logic, it would continue to raise questions and doubts about such contexts, and so it would signify that even the experience of transcendence is artificial and transitory. This likely would destroy the significance of the truths of transcendence for the participants. Therefore, a common fate of clowns in ritual is their demise as contrary, oscillating, reflexive characters. Either they are tamed and brought to heel, or their internal composition is made homogeneous. Then they no longer arouse reflectiveness among participants, for their presence no longer causes the participants to doubt the validity of transcendent experiences. At this point, clowns simply reinforce the values of such truths or revelations in straightforward ways.

This depiction of the clown in ritual recognizes that the especial properties of this figure are a function of its unusual design, and so, too, of its place during religious and dramatic occasions. If the figure of the clown is apprehended as a complex device that unlocks perception to an awareness of the artifice of textual coherence, then it is comprehended also as a dynamic device that enables certain religious occasions to be enacted and accomplished. It is then incumbent upon further thought to search other ceremonial media, in which clowns have no place, for analogous mechanisms that accomplish transformation of context and transitions between contexts and so enable these occasions to progress in sequence through their programs.

[*For discussion of related topics, see* Humor and Satire; Masks; *and* Tricksters.]

BIBLIOGRAPHY

Useful overviews of fools and of clownlike figures in European traditions are found in Enid Welsford's *The Fool: His Social and Literary History* (London, 1935) and in Barbara Swain's *Fools and Folly during the Middle Ages and the Renaissance* (New York, 1932). The complex and contrastive characters of clown figures are discussed evocatively in William Willeford's *The Fool and His Sceptre* (London, 1969). The clown as a solvent of perception and of structure is implied strongly in Wolfgang M. Zucker's "The Clown as the Lord of Disorder," in *Holy Laughter*, edited by M. Conrad Hyers (New York, 1969). The logic of composition of ritual clowns discussed in this entry is expanded and elaborated in my article "The Ritual-Clown: Attributes and Affinities," *Anthropos* 76 (1981): 321–370. Paul Bouissac makes a semiotic analysis of the nature-culture distinction in modern European circus clown performances in "Clown Performances as Metacultural Texts," a chapter in his *Circus and Culture* (Bloomington, Ind., 1976), pp. 151–175. A clear, if simple, example of a cathartic explanation of ritual clowning is John J. Honigmann's "An Interpretation of the Social-Psychological Functions of the Ritual Clown," *Character and Personality* 10 (1941–1942): 220–226. The view that the activity of ritual clowns should be explicated first and foremost with reference to wider themes of culture, outside the contexts of performance, is put ably by Laura Makarius in her article "Ritual Clowns and Symbolical Behavior," *Diogenes* 69 (1970): 44–73. In an ethnographic vein, there are few accessible and complete accounts of ritual clowning in context. One decent description is of a Tewa Pueblo Indian rite, in Vera Laski's *Seeking Life* (Philadelphia, 1958). Louis A. Hieb's "The Ritual

Clown: Humor and Ethics," in *Forms of Play of Native North Americans,* edited by Edward Norbeck and Claire R. Farrer (Saint Paul, Minn., 1979), pp. 171–188, argues against cross-cultural delineations of ritual clowns, since the meanings of such figures are highly specific to particular cultures.

DON HANDELMAN

COATLICUE ("serpent skirt") was one of an array of Aztec earth-mother goddesses, the Teteoinnan, who represented the notion of maternal fertility associated with the earth. Coatlicue's monumental stone image, excavated in 1790 in the heart of Mexico City, is one of the finest and most monstrous achievements of Mesoamerican religious art. It is an eight-foot-tall stone figure consisting of a female form draped with a blouse of severed human hands and hearts, a skirt of intertwined serpents with skull belt buckles in front and back, ferocious rattlesnakes for hands, and a head composed of two giant rattlesnake heads facing one another. According to art historians, these two giant serpent heads emerge from spurts of blood resulting from Coatlicue's decapitation. Her feet are giant jaguar claws. A serpent of blood flows from beneath her skirt of serpents. This masterpiece of Mesoamerican sculpture, located today in the Museo Nacional de Antropología in Mexico City, reflects the combined qualities of terror and destruction associated with some aspects of the goddess cult of the Aztec capital, Tenochtitlán (1325–1521).

Coatlicue's primary creative act, told in book 3 of Fray Bernardino de Sahagún's *Historia general de las cosas de la Nueva España* (compiled 1569–1582; also known as the Florentine Codex), consisted of the dramatic birth of the war god Huitzilopochtli. This *teotuicatl* ("divine song") tells how Coatlicue was sweeping out a temple on Coatepec ("serpent mountain") when a ball of feathers made her pregnant with Huitzilopochtli. Her children, the *centzon huitznahua* ("four hundred southerners"), became outraged at this and prepared for war against their mother. Led by Coatlicue's aggressive daughter, Coyolxauhqui ("she of the golden bells"), the four hundred warriors began their march toward Coatepec. When Coatlicue became frightened, a voice from her womb comforted her, saying, "Do not worry, I know what must be done." When the warriors arrived at Coatepec, Coatlicue gave birth to Huitzilopochtli, fully grown and dressed as a warrior. Using his *xiuhcoatl* ("serpent of lightning"), he dismembered his sister Coyolxauhqui and slaughtered most of the rest of his siblings as well.

Along with the goddess Cihuacoatl ("serpent woman"), Coatlicue represents the aggressive mortuary aspect of Aztec goddesses.

BIBLIOGRAPHY

Brundage, Burr C. *The Fifth Sun: Aztec Gods, Aztec World.* Austin, 1979. See especially Brundage's helpful chapters on "The Quality of the Numinous" (pp. 50–79) and "The Goddesses" (pp. 153–175). Brundage's work takes seriously the religious factor in Aztec society and develops in this book a framework to relate specific aspects of the sacred to a general understanding of the religious system.

Fernandez, Justino. *Coatlicue: Estética del arte indígena antiguo.* 2d ed. Mexico City, 1959. Fernandez's work, with a stimulating prologue by Samuel Ramos, discusses Coatlicue's aesthetic character in relation to a general model of Aztec art.

DAVÍD CARRASCO

COCKS. The cock is preeminently a sun symbol. In western Asia the crowing cock is closely associated with solar rituals; in the ancient Near East it became an integral part of the solar iconography during the second millennium BCE, and the mythology of the "fire cock" has spread widely and survived in the folklore of western Asia. The solar cock is also attested among some of the most primitive peoples of Asia; the Nagas of Assam, for example, believe that the sun is lured out of darkness by the cock's crowing. According to the Miao of southern China, the sun, which hides itself behind the mountain and darkens the whole world, shows itself again with the crowing of a cock. Similarly, Japanese myths tell how Amaterasu, the sun goddess, hides in the heavenly cave but comes out again on hearing the crowing of cocks.

The symbolic importance of the cock is well attested in the Greco-Roman world. There, the motif of the crowing cock, the bird of dawning, was enriched by the motif of the cock as fighter. The fighting cock, although associated with warrior divinities (such as Ares and Athena), was especially connected with Dionysos, in whose theater the official fights occurred. Significantly, the pugnacity of the cock was taken as an aspect of its sexual life; representations of the cock with a human phallus as head and neck are quite numerous. Especially interesting are three associations of the cock with Greco-Roman funerary symbolism: (1) it was one of the animals offered to the deities of the underworld in connection with the cult of the dead; (2) as is suggested by its representation together with Persephone and Hades, the cock was viewed as the herald of the dawn of the new world, the future life; as such, it symbolized hope of life after death; and (3) as the victor of a fight, the cock symbolized the soul of the departed; it was commonly associated, especially on tombstones, with Hermes, the psychopomp who escorted the soul to a blessed life after death. In Mithraism, the cock was frequently used in cult meals, where presumably its connection with the rising sun and immortality or future life was significant.

In Judaism the cock has been used in the Kapparah, a practice designed as a means of ritual atonement for sins. The cock has also been regarded as a charm that could exorcise demons; at the dedication of a new house, Jews used to kill a cock on the spot to purge the house of a demonic presence. Moreover, the crowing cock at dawn was a symbol of the redemption of the messianic age.

Christianity has continued this idea, making the cock a symbol of the risen Lord, Jesus Christ, the new light. In announcing the approach of day, the cock reminds Christians not only of Peter's denial but also of their own resurrection in a future life. Even cockfighting has found its Christian representations, which inspire believers to win the struggle with their own lower nature so that they can inherit eternal life.

In Islam, too, the cock is a benevolent bird. Muslims have believed that a cock would crow when it became aware of the presence of *jinn,* evil spirits. And, as the bird of dawning, the cock still serves to awaken the sleeping faithful for morning prayer.

BIBLIOGRAPHY

The best treatment of the cock in Greek tradition remains Sir D'arcy W. Thompson's *A Glossary of Greek Birds* (1895; reprint, London, 1936), pp. 33–44. See also Erwin R. Goodenough's admirable account of cock symbolism in *Pagan Symbols in Judaism,* volume 8 of his *Jewish Symbols in the Greco-Roman World* (New York, 1958), pp. 59–70.

MANABU WAIDA

CODES AND CODIFICATION. While codes and codification are only rarely discussed in broad studies of religion, there are nevertheless preliminary studies that allow us to outline the subject with some accuracy. Henry Sumner Maine, in his *Ancient Law,* first published in 1861, tried to describe the evolution of human society by comparing all preserved collections of ancient laws. With the discovery and diffusion of the art of writing, laws engraved on tablets took the place of the customary law recollected by privileged aristocracies, and "democratic sentiment" added to their popularity. "Inscribed tablets," Main notes, "were seen to be a better depository of law and a better security for its acccurate preservation than the memory of the aristocracies" (1905, p. 12).

In 1901–1902, when French archaeologists discovered in former Susa the stela with the text of the code of Hummurabi from the eighteenth century BCE, it became clear that Maine's connection of codification with the struggles of plebeians against aristocrats was much too simple. On the other hand, the finding did confirm the existence of the literary genre of the law code. The law code was in widespread use as a means to make legal regulations accessible to the public. We can thus broadly define law codes as collections of laws (in casuistic style) written on stones, papyrus, or parchment and made accessible to the public.

There also existed, however, cultures that did not attach much value to recording their traditions in writing. Among the Celts, for example, the powerful priesthood of the druids considered it fitting that their holy traditions be transmitted only in oral and not in written form, as reported by Caesar in the *Gallic Wars* (4.14). The Zoroastrians handed down their holy texts by word of mouth for centuries until, forced by external circumstances, they wrote them down in the third century CE. In rabbinic Judaism some rabbis advocated that written and oral tradition should be separated. "You are not permitted to recite from writing things that are transmitted orally; those that are written you are not permitted to say orally" (B.T., *Temurah* 14b). And some Islamic *'ulamā'* advanced the view that the *ḥadīth* should not be written down. In these cases oral traditions could become public without being written down.

Means of Codification: Stela, Scroll, and Codex. The oldest texts of law codes of the ancient Near East were written down on stelae, large stones that were inscribed and publicly displayed. In some cases the texts of these stelae were copied on clay tablets by pupil-scribes. By means of these clay tablets Mesopotamian codes were preserved, even though the original stelae had disappeared. In the Hebrew scriptures (Old Testament) two tables *(luḥot)* are mentioned, on both sides of which the text of the Decalogue has been engraved (*Ex.* 32:15–16). The prophet Isaiah received the order to write the word of the Lord on a tablet (made of wood or ivory with a layer of plaster or wax on it), that it might "become an eternal witness for a day to come" (*Is.* 30:8; cf. *Hab.* 2:2). The *Book of Isaiah* (eighth century BCE) also testifies to the transition to writing on papyrus, the pith of an Egyptian water plant. For in *Isaiah* 8:1 the Lord asked the prophet to take a papyrus leaf *(gillayon)* and write on it. The oldest Hebrew papyrus is a palimpsest found in the Wadi Murabba'at that goes back to the eighth century BCE. The sheets of papyrus *(chartēs)* were stuck together to form a scroll with the text on the inside. In the second century BCE parchment came into use. It was prepared from the skin of various animals and turned out to be stronger than papyrus. Pergamon exported parchment of particularly fine quality. Sheets of parchment that could be inscribed on both sides were since the first century BCE put in layers and folded as a codex. Christians promoted the use of the codex, while Jews stuck to the scroll.

Scroll and codex, then, were used in addition to the stela to record collections of laws. The Hebrew Book of the Covenant (*sefer ha-berit; Ex.* 24:7) should be imagined as a scroll; the same holds true for the "book of the *torah*" (*sefer ha-torah; 2 Kgs.* 22:8, 23:2) discovered at the time of the Judahite king Josiah (639–609 BCE), which is partly identical with *Deuteronomy*. The Codex Justinianus, on the contrary, was a manuscript in the form of a codex.

There are some differences between these means of codification. Laws written down as edicts could be sent to bureaus throughout the empire. But there was always the problem of authenticity. "A law that has been sent must be accepted and must undoubtedly be valid, and the power to emend and to revoke shall be reserved to our clemency [i.e., that of the Emperor]" (Codex Theodosianus 1.1.5). The scrolls indeed enabled scribes to make emendations. The scribe could add glosses to the text or introduce new authorized regulations at the end of the transmitted ones. Stelae could scarcely be falsified, but they were not easily used for the dissemination of edicts. It is therefore not surprising that laws sometimes were edited in both fashions. The Jewish law of purification, prohibiting foreigners to enter the Temple, was made public by means of slabs, one of them reading: "No alien [*allogenēs*] shall enter the holy place; if he is caught, he shall die" (Gerhard Pfohl, *Griechische Inschriften*, Munich, 2d ed., 1980, no. 135). In the beginning of the second century BCE, a local official ordered stelae to be set up in his villages recording letters of King Antiochos III that protected these villages from molestation. Stelae inscribed and publicly displayed could make such orders respected.

Custom and Law, Restitution and Punishment. When laws were codified and written down their institutional context was changed. There is a process of assimilation and elimination that is typical of oral transmission in a nonliterate society: what continues to be of social relevance is stored in the memory while the rest is usually forgotten. Literacy puts an end to this process. The tradition becomes a fixed object, and inconsistencies within it become obvious. If systems of writing are complex, as in the ancient civilizations, then a deep gulf may develop between the esoteric literate culture and the popular culture. In the ancient Near East, scribes formed a class of their own, separate from the priesthood and in the service of the king. They became the experts in law and dislodged the elders previously responsible for the transmission of oral tradition (Goody and Watt, 1968).

It is common to discriminate custom from law. We call "custom" any habitual or usual course of action, any established practice. We call "law" a rule of conduct administered by a ruler or his subordinates. Laws are enforced by explicit sanctions while customs are enforced by social control. These are merely logical distinctions. But it is evident that the historical factor of writing worked in favor of laws sanctioned from above. Even if customs remained unchanged, their incorporation in an official code reinforced the power sustaining them. Often the institution of a law code became an opportunity to select from among customary practices. When in 303 BCE Antigonus I granted the citizens of Teos and Lebedos the right to write down their laws, he asked them to draw up only those laws they deemed the best. Sometimes there are clear cases of breaching custom. Solon prohibited in 594–593 loans on the person of the debtor. The regulations concerning debt-slavery in Mesopotamian and Jewish codes show similar attempts to temper severe customs concerning debtors. They reflect efforts to subordinate private power to public control.

We must further discern between two sanctions: restitution and punishment. The law codes are full of examples of this distinction. The codes have the form of a collection of casuistic laws: conditional sentences in the third person. The dependent clause contains the facts supposed and the main clause the sanction. The arrangement of topics conforms to no general logic but seems random and includes homicide, battery, theft, slavery, sexual offenses, property rights, bride-price, inheritance, and so on. The difference between restitution and punishment concerns the sanction. A thief could be forced to restitute what he had stolen. In this case his action was regarded as a civil breach. In other cases theft was regarded as a serious offense, and the thief was made to restitute a multiple value of the thing stolen (as in *Exodus* 21:37–22:3). And finally theft could be judged as a crime to be punished by death or mutilation (as in code of Hammurabi 6f). Stanley Diamond maintains, as previous scholars have, that the customary law followed only the principle of restitution. Only with the rise of the state and legislation did homicide and theft become punishable crimes. The institution of the state was responsible for the severity of sanctions (*In Search of the Primitive*, 1974, chap. 6). Émile Durkheim argued precisely the opposite. He drew a distinction between two types of sanctions: restitutive sanctions and repressive ones. These two types are supposed to correspond to two types of social solidarity: the mechanical and the organic. In societies based on mechanical solidarity there is a predominance of repressive law, whereas restitutive (cooperative) laws prevail in societies based on organic solidarity. Though it holds true that Durkheim vastly overstated the role of repressive law and understated the degree of reciprocity in primitive societies, there remains much testimony that primitive societies are disposed toward penal sanctions. It is therefore improbable that with the creation of the state came repressive sanctions.

On this issue the reflections of Henry Sumner Maine are still valid. He discerned two types of offenses: offenses against one's neighbor and offenses against God (Maine, 1905, pp. 307–309). Offenses against one's neighbor (torts) gave rise to an obligation that was fulfilled by payment. In the Hittite laws, for example, the general sanction for homicide is the handing over of a number of persons. Offenses against God (sins), on the contrary, are punished with severity. Take for example the Jewish laws regarding homicide: "Ye shall take no ransom for the life of a manslayer liable to death, for he shall surely die. . . . So ye shall not pollute the land wherein ye are, for blood polluteth the land and no expiation can be made for the land for the blood which is shed therein but by the blood of him that shed it" (*Nm.* 35:31–33). Durkheim advanced a similar idea: "In primitive societies, criminal law is religious law" (*The Division of Labor in Society*, New York, 1947, p. 92). E. Adamson Hoebel (1954) also subscribed to the view that in primitive society criminal law coincides with certain notions of sin (p. 259).

A. S. Diamond (1935) used this distinction to classify preserved law codes. He arranged them in three groups. In the first group (early codes) the sanctions imposed are only pecuniary, including those for homicide and battery (e.g., the early laws of the peoples of western Europe). The second group ("central" codes) comprises codes in which some civil wrongs are regarded as criminal offenses and others not (e.g., the Hittite laws of the sixteenth century BCE). The last group (late codes) is formed of codes that regard the more serious wrongs—homicide, adultery, rape, and theft—as crimes (e.g., the code of Hammurabi, eighteenth century BCE). Diamond postulated an evolution according to which the field of the law of criminal offenses gradually expanded. Considering the historical dates of the law codes mentioned it seems far more appropriate to speak of logical types of codes. [*See also* Revenge and Retribution.]

Comparison of Law Codes. A review of extant law codes should attempt to address two main scientific problems: Did the codes contribute to public control of private power, as exercised, for example, in the enslavement of others? What are the reasons that law codes differ, principally with regard to sanctions for the same offense?

Mesopotamian codes. The most important Mesopotamian law codes are the following: the laws of the Sumerian king Urnammu (hereafter called LU, 2111–2094 BCE); the laws of King Lipit-Ishtar (LL, 1934–1924 BCE); the code of the city Eshnunna (CE, eighteenth century BCE); the code of the Akkadian king Hammurabi (CH, 1793–1750 BCE); the Hittite laws (HL, c. 1600 BCE); the Assyrian laws (AL, eleventh century BCE). (These texts are collected in Borger, 1982.)

The most famous code is of course the code of Hammurabi. It was written on a diorite stela, topped by a bas-relief showing Hammurabi receiving from Shamash, the sun god and god of justice, the commission to write the law book. The stela was carried off as a trophy of war to the Elamite capital Susa. The code of Hammurabi is particularly valuable because it reveals something of how such a code was intended to function. The epilogue speaks about the motives of the king and the function of the stela. The king set up the stela with the aim of protecting the weak against the strong, procuring justice for the orphan and the widow, and establishing equity in the land (CH 47). The motivations given in the LU (104–116, 162–168) and in the LL (1f., 19.6ff.) are similar. A citizen who has been injured shall read the stela, recognize his legal claims, and thank Hammurabi. If a subsequent king disregards the words of the stela, kingship shall be taken away from him (CH 48f.). The epilogue of LL blesses him who does not damage the stela (19.36–45). It has to be mentioned that among the hundreds of thousands of extant cuneiform tablets the number of copies of these codes is surprisingly small. The codes did not leave clear traces in Mesopotamian jurisdiction. J. J. Finkelstein (1961) concludes that the purpose of these codes was not legislation. Of course a litigant could appeal to the provisions of a code, but such an appeal would have carried moral rather than legal force. The codes must be regarded as political justifications of kingship.

The three codes proclaiming in prologue and epilogue protection of the weak against the strong belong together even in terms of their contents. In the Hittite laws the sanction of killing a free man or woman is the handing over of four persons (HL 1). For theft of cattle the sanction is payment of a stated multiple of the value (HL 45.57ff.). If a man steals from a house, "in former times he restituted for the theft one mine of silver. But now he gives twelve shekels [one-third of a mine] silver" (HL 94). A similar alleviation of punishment is decreed in HL 166–167: here a capital sanction has been replaced by a restitutive one. Only adultery, rape, and sexual offenses are punished with death (HL 187f., 197f.). Herein the code of Hammurabi is in accordance with the Hittite laws (CH 129f; cf. CE 26.28; LU 6f.). But in the other cases the code of Hammurabi inflicts heavy penalties. The following offenses are regarded as crimes punishable by death: an unproved accusation of murder (CH 1), murder (LU 1), false testimony (CH 3), theft of property (CH 6f.; only by night, CE 12f.), kidnapping (CH 14), hiding of a slave (CH 16), burglary (CH 21), robbery (CH 22; LU 2), sorcery (CH 2, AL 47). These severe penalites are imposed only in cases of offenses against citizens. The rape of a female slave, for example, can be requited by a pecuniary payment (LU 8; CE 31, to be compared with 26). The Assyrian laws very often prescribe mutilations—the removal of ears, fingers, eyes, or lips, for example, sanctions quite rare in the code of Hammurabi, which prescribes amputation of a hand only if an overseer steals the seed or fodder of an owner (CH 253).

Did criminal law arise from religion, as Maine, Durkheim, and Hoebel maintain? The codes themselves refer to a more specific concept: The king established justice *(misharum)* on behalf of the gods (LU, prologue; LL, epilogue; CH 5.14ff., 47.84ff.). It is not so much religion in general but the specific idea of a divine, just order that lies behind these codes. We must therefore explain the differences between sanctions (pecuniary versus capital) in terms of different concepts concerning this order. The case of debt slavery can elucidate the essence of these differences. The Hittite laws do not deal at all with enslavement of citizens, though such enslavement did exist. The Assyrian laws, the code of Eshnunna, and the code of Hammurabi, on the other hand, presuppose as a fact that a creditor who has a claim to corn or silver seizes persons of the debtor's family (CH 115; AL 39, 44, 48). This is only illegal if the claim is not substantiated, in which case a fine must be paid (CH 114). The code of Eshnunna gives more details: if the seized person is a female slave, the pledger shall pay silver in full compensation for her; if he doesn't return her and she dies, he shall give two female slaves as replacement; if he distrains the wife or children of a citizen and causes their death, he shall die (CE 22–24). The code of Hammurabi goes beyond these regulations and introduces laws protecting the person legally seized. "If the distress dies in the house of him who has taken him as a distress through blows or ill-treatment, the owner of the distress shall convict his merchant, and if [the distress is] a [free] man's son, his son shall be put to death or, if [he is] a [free] man's slave, he shall pay one-third mine of silver and forfeits anything whatsoever that he has lent" (CH 116). "If a man has become liable to arrest under a bond and has sold his wife, his son or his daughter or gives [them] into servitude, for three years they shall do work in the house of him who has brought them or taken them in servitude; in the fourth year their release shall be granted" (CH 117) These regulations were an effort to establish a public control over the harsh and merciless practice of debt slavery. The customary law of enslaving the debtor's family yields to statute law decreed by the emperor. Some of these emperors ordered at the beginning of their rule a remission of debts. "Whoever has given barley or silver to an Akkadian or an Amorite as an interest-bearing loan . . . because the king has invoked the *misharum* for the land, his document is voided" (Edict of Ammisaduqa 4). "Because the king has instituted *misharum* in the land, he [the enslaved citizen or his wife or his children] is released" (20). The release *(anduraru)* of the debt-slaves is due to justice. As J. J. Finkelstein cogently argued, the *misharum* and the law codes drew from the same concept, a concept of divine, just order that secured the citizen's property (human and otherwise) and reputation from infringement. The code of Hammurabi added to these rights the protection against permanent enslavement.

Jewish codes. The most important Jewish codes were the Book of the Covenant (*sefer ha-berit; Ex.* 24:7) incorporated into *Exodus* (20:22–23:19) and the legal part of *Deuteronomy* (12–26), perhaps identical with the "book of the *torah*" *(sefer ha-torah)*, discovered at the time of Josiah (639–609 BCE) in the Temple (*2 Kgs.* 22:8, 23:2). As compared with the Book of the Covenant, the genre of the law code in *Deuteronomy* has lost its genuine form.

The Book of the Covenant contains casuistic law and apodictic law. Albrecht Alt has argued that the Israelites took over from the Canaanites the secular casuistic law, while the sacral apodictic law belonged to their own heritage. But Alt understated the religious background of the casuistic law in the code of the ancient Near East (see Alt, *Kleine Schriften zur Geschichte des Volkes Israel*, Munich, 1959, pp. 278–332). The Book of the Covenant starts with a prologue. Yahveh commissions Moses to erect an altar and to give the Israelites laws (*mishpatim; Ex.* 21:1) with regard to slaves (21:2–11); the capital offenses, including intentional homicide, abduction, beating and cursing of one's parents (21:12–17); inflicting bodily injuries (21:18–36); and theft, property delicts, and seduction (21:37–22:16). Thereupon follow apodictic laws on different subjects (22:17–23:19).

The Book of the Covenant belongs to the group of codes that regard private wrongs as capital offenses. A comparison with the code of Hammurabi, however, shows similarities and differences. Murder and abduction are in both codes capital crimes. But not all the capital offenses enumerated in the code of Hammurabi are regarded as such in Israel. In Judaism, the thief caught stealing livestock and selling them shall return fivefold (for oxen) or fourfold (for sheep) the number he stole. If the cattle are found in his possession alive he shall pay double. If he has not the means to do so he himself shall be sold. If the owner kills the thief there is no blood revenge, except if it happened in broad daylight (*Ex.* 21:37–22:3). On the other hand, the code of Hammurabi did not regard offenses against parents as crimes deserving death. In Israel offenses against persons and their status seem to weigh more heavily than offenses against property.

The Book of the Covenant acknowledged loans on the person and enslavement of debtors. But it made an attempt to temper the severe customs regarding the Hebrew debtors. The Hebrew slave shall be released after six years. A female slave that doesn't please her master may not be sold to a foreign people (21:7–8). Assault of a debt slave shall be avenged if he dies immediately. Bodily injuries shall lead to his release (21:20–21, 21:26–27). We recognize efforts similar to those in the Mesopotamian codes to alleviate the harsh fate of debt slaves and to institute a public control over it.

Deuteronomy departs from the genuine form of law codes. But Moshe Weinfield (1972) has cogently argued that it still reflects this genre, maintaining that the book marks the transition from a narrow casuistic law corpus to a humanistic law code. Laws concerning property are nearly completely lacking. The Deuteronomic legislator aimed at setting forth a code of laws assuring protection for individuals and particularly persons in need. The debt slave is regarded as a citizen, a brother *(aḥ)*, who only sells his service—but not his person—to his master. He conducts an independent family life. His master is obliged to manumit him after six years (*Dt.* 15:12–18). A slave who seeks refuge shall not be turned over to his master (23:15f.)—an offense punished by death in the code of Hammurabi (CH 16). The code in *Deuteronomy* still follows the casuistic form, but it introduces a new element unparalleled in the codes of ancient Near East: the motive clause. The release of the debt slaves is not only a command of God. The Deuteronomic legislator adds a further reason to follow the law: "Remember that you were a slave in Egypt and your Lord has released you" (15:15). He does not base the political recognizance of his code on the power of kingship but on the personal conviction of citizens.

Greek and Roman codes. The most important codifications are the laws of Solon, the laws of Gortyn, and the Roman Twelve Tables. The legislation of Solon was preceded by that of Draco (seventh century BCE). The *thesmoi* of Draco addresses the prosecution of homicide. Intentional homicide was avenged by the kin of the victim, manslaughter was compensated by payment of a wergeld. The laws of Draco had officially been published on wooden tablets, set up on revolving pillars *(axones)*. The laws of Solon were published in the same way.

The legislation of Solon (594/3 BCE) is only transmitted fragmentarily by Greek historians. The archonship of Solon (594 BCE) was preceded by civil strife in which the enslavement of poor Athenians by wealthy ones seems to have been an important issue. Solon at first ordered a cancellation of debts *(seisachtheia);* afterwards he enacted laws. His laws prohibited loans on the person of the debtor, arranged the population according to property qualifications into four classes, and established rules for electing the magistrates. Solon also made the curious law that whoever in a time of political strife did not take an active part on either side of a conflict should be deprived of his civic rights. He prohibited dowries and changed the rule of inheritance. Citizens without children could convey by testament their property to anyone they wished. Previously the heritage had to remain in the *genos* (kin group) of the deceased. He enacted a law saying that a son who had not been given the chance to learn a craft by his father was not obliged to sustain him later. Another law inhibited the export of agricultural products except olive oil.

Aristotle may have committed a historiographical error when he assigned to Solon the setting up of a constitution *(politeia);* only since the fourth century has Solon been regarded as founder of a constitution. But Aristotle referred rightly to the democratic feature of the laws of Solon (*Athenaiōn Politeia,* 9.1). The law that nobody could contract a loan secured on a person was a breach of the custom of debt slavery. This breach didn't occur all over the Greek world, but the view that law that could breach custom seems fairly common. Law was identified with statute law, and this identification remained characteristic of the whole Greek world. "Unwritten law" *(agraphos nomos)* should not be used by the court. The conflicts that could arise between custom and statute law are illustrated by the *Antigone* of Sophocles. This preference for statute law was a natural corollary of democracy. Justice, to which Solon also had appealed, became subject to the political discourse of citizens.

The most important source of pre-Hellenistic legislation is that found in the city of Gortyn (Crete). An inscription from the fifth century BCE begins with an injunction against taking the law into one's own hands:

"Gods! He who will institute legal proceedings regarding a freeman or a slave shall not take him away before the judgement." But a condemned man or a debtor *(katakeimenon)* can be taken away without punishment. The inscription gives laws concerning rape and adultery (punished with a fine); conveyance of property in case of divorce, adoption, and death; ransom of compatriots; marriage, especially of an heiress; security and liability; and adoption.

There are some texts elucidating the process of codification of Greek law. After the liberation of Chios from the Persians in 333–332 BCE, Alexander ordered that the expelled democrats should return, that Chios should be a democracy, and that scribes should draw up and systematize the laws. I have already suggested that the *sunoikismos* of Teos and Lebedos in Asia Minor should be recognized as an act of common legislation. After his victory over the Egyptian forces in 200 BCE the Seleucid ruler Antiochos III recognized the Jewish customs and laws as *patrioi nomoi.* It was a privilege of political communities to dispose a written law code. The law code—in the ancient Near East a justification of kingship—had in the Hellenic and Hellenistic culture the function of a constitution.

According to Livy, the Roman law of the Twelve Tables was compiled in 450–449 BCE in an attempt to control the struggle between plebeians and patricians and to secure equal liberty for the two groups (Livy, 3.31.7). His account can hardly be considered satisfactory in view of its inconsistencies and improbabilities. The Twelve Tables are known only from later sources. The law code begins with a number of short rules indicating how to start and pursue legal proceedings (cf. the law of Gortyn). They proceed to debt slavery: "Unless they make a settlement, debtors shall be held in bonds for sixty days. On the third market day they shall suffer capital punishment or be delivered up for sale abroad, across the Tiber" (table three). Tables four to six contain fundamental principles of conveyance and of property law. Table eight deals with criminal law. Intentional homicide is a capital offense. For theft the sanctions vary, from paying double the amount of the stolen object's value to a capital sentence.

Some Final Remarks. The later codices of the Roman empire deviated fundamentally from the preceding ones. The Theodosian Code was a compilation of laws issued by the emperors from 313 until 438 CE. In 429 Theodosius ordered such a compilation be made, and nine years later the code was solemnly promulgated. The code contained the legislative enactments issued by the emperors on given dates. These imperial laws (called constitutions) had been *edicta* (official proclamations), *decreta* (decrees in the settlement of lawsuits), *rescripta* (decisions in answer to officials and private persons) and *epistulae* (letters to officials). The emperor was conceived as the sole source of law, and his enactments were considered divine. His orders were called *constitutiones,* since they formed the fundamental law. The contravention of a given statute would be considered a crime, punishable usually be death. The fundamental Greek identification of justice and law was thus fused with monarchy. Again, as in the Mesopotamian codes, there is an emphasis on punishment. And again, not religion in a general sense, but specific notions of justice, had given rise to the code.

Other famous codes are the Syrian lawbooks and the Zoroastrian Madigan-i Hazar Dadastan. In the Islamic community a law code as such did not develop. The Qur'ān was regarded as the supreme source of Islamic law. Besides this source, the *sunnah,* the *ḥadīth,* the consensus of the Islamic community, and the analogical method were used to develop rules.

[*See also* Law and Religion.]

BIBLIOGRAPHY

Borger, Rylke, Heiner Lutzmann, Wilhelm H. P. Römer, and Einar von Schuler. "Rechtsbücher." In *Texte aus der Umwelt des Alten Testaments,* vol. 1, pp. 15-125. Gütersloh, 1982. A fresh translation of Mesopotamian law codes provided with explanations and a list of recent studies.

Diamond, A. S. *Primitive Law, Past and Present* (1935). London, 1971. An attempt to describe the general development of law by studying the offenses regarded as crimes and by arranging the codes in different classes.

Fikentscher, Wolfgang R., Herbert Franke, and Oskar Köhler, eds. *Entstehung und Wandel rechtlicher Traditionen.* Freiburg, 1980. A collection of profound essays dealing with the great cultures and attempting a historical anthropology of law.

Finkelstein, J. J. "Ammiṣaduqa's Edict and the Babylonian 'Law Codes'." *Journal of Cuneiform Studies* 15 (1961): 91–104. Tries to establish the relationship between reform acts and law codes of Mesopotamian kings.

Fried, Morton. *The Evolution of Political Society: An Essay in Political Anthropology.* New York, 1967. A meritorious study that defines the essential notion of social control and sanction, power and authority, custom and law.

Goody, Jack, and Ian Watt. "The Consequences of Literacy." In *Literacy in Traditional Societies,* edited by Jack Goody, pp. 27–68. Cambridge, 1968. A prolific article that sets forth the differences between memorizing in oral cultures and in literate cultures and that evaluates the systems of writing with regard to their spread.

Hoebel, E. Adamson. *The Law of Primitive Man: A Study in Comparative Legal Dynamics.* Cambridge, Mass., 1954. A fundamental study in the anthropology of law.

Kohler, Josef, and Erich Ziebarth. *Das Stadtrecht von Gortyn und seine Beziehungen zum gemeingriechischen Rechte* (1912). Hildesheim, 1972. A valuable study that gives text, translation, and commentary of the inscription of Gortyn and adduces other relevant Greek legal texts.

Maine, Henry Sumner. *Ancient Law: Its Connection with the Early History of Society and Its Relation to Modern Ideas* (1861). London, 1905. Maine's early study, still in print in various editions, recognized the ancient law codes as systems of their own.

Rendtorff, Rolf. *Das Alte Testament: Eine Einführung.* Neukirchen-Vluyn, 1983. A useful overview of the Old Testament, including the legal codes incorporated into it.

Weinfeld, Moshe. *Deuteronomy and the Deuteronomic School.* Oxford, 1972. A comprehensive study comparing the "Book of the Covenant" with *Deuteronomy* and tracing the relation of *Deuteronomy* to Mesopotamian law codes.

H. G. KIPPENBERG

CODRINGTON, R. H. (1830–1922), Christian missionary to Melanesia and scholar of Melanesian languages and cultures. The second son of an Anglican rector, Robert Henry Codrington was educated at Charterhouse and at Wadham College, Oxford, where, as his later high church views suggest, he may have been touched by the Oxford Movement. In 1857, two years after he was ordained, he gave up excellent prospects in England to go to New Zealand with his vicar, Edmund Hobhouse, who had been elevated to the bishopric of Christchurch. In 1863 he accompanied Bishop John Coleridge Patteson on the island voyage of the mission ship *Southern Cross*, and in 1867 he joined the peripatetic Melanesian Mission, which advocated a policy of racial equality and minimal interference in traditional native culture. When Patteson was killed in 1871 by Melanesians previously victimized by Australian "blackbirders" (kidnappers), Codrington declined the bishopric, but he served for some years as acting head of the mission. Despite a propensity to severe seasickness, he did on several occasions make the island voyage; he preferred, however, to direct the mission school on Norfolk Island, to which young Melanesians were brought for training as native teachers. There he also took over the linguistic studies Patteson had begun (in part under the stimulus of the German-born Oxford philologist and comparative religionist F. Max Müller). Through the intermediacy of Lorimer Fison, a Wesleyan missionary-anthropologist with whom he had become acquainted during the public furor surrounding Patteson's death, Codrington established contact with the British social evolutionary anthropologist E. B. Tylor. By 1880 he had begun to send ethnographic material to the *Journal of the Anthropological Institute.*

Returning on leave to England in 1883 to complete the translation of the Bible into Mota (the Melanesian *lingua franca*), Codrington resided for two years in college at Oxford, where he attended lectures by Tylor. While there he published one of his two major works, *The Melanesian Languages* (1885), which long remained a standard reference; the companion study of their culture, *The Melanesians* (1891), was published after a second truncated tour of duty with the mission. After a brief period as rector of a country parish, Codrington served the remainder of his long life as prebendary of the cathedral in Chichester.

As a religious scholar, Codrington is best known for the idea of *mana,* which he saw as the basis of all Melanesian religious belief. Despite his contact with Tylor, Codrington remained closer to the philologically oriented pre-Darwinian "ethnological" tradition to which Müller, too, was tied. Unlike his friend Fison, he was little concerned with evolutionary problems. He remained dubious of the evolutionary socioreligious concept of totemism, and though he did not explicitly reject Tylor's rationalistic doctrine of animism, by implication he called it into question. Suspicious of received anthropological categories, Codrington saw ethnography as a matter of "setting forth what natives say about themselves." It was in this context (as well as in an effort to find a universal substructure for Christian missionizing) that he focused on *mana:* "the persuasion that there is a supernatural power belonging to the region of the unseen"—a power emotionally experienced rather than rationally surmised, which natives could turn to their benefit. Offered originally in a letter to Max Müller, Codrington's definition of *mana* was used by Müller to attack Tylorian intellectualist views in a series of lectures published as *The Origin of Religion* (1878). Subsequently adopted by R. R. Marett as the basis for the concept of "preanimistic" religion, the concept of *mana* played an important role in the critique of social evolution that developed in British anthropology after 1900. It was also manifest in such major critiques of evolutionary rationalism as Durkheim's *Elementary Forms of the Religious Life* (1912) and Freud's *Totem and Taboo* (1912).

BIBLIOGRAPHY

Codrington has not yet found a biographer, and biographical material must be sought in obituaries and standard biographical sources, notably the article by Ernest Beaglehole in the *International Encyclopedia of the Social Sciences* (New York, 1968). A considerable body of his correspondence and relevant printed materials are preserved in Rhodes House, Oxford. A bibliography of his writings is contained in the obituary by Sidney Ray, in *Man* 97 (1922): 169–171.

GEORGE W. STOCKING, JR.

COHEN, HERMANN (1842-1918), Jewish philosopher of religion, founder and exponent of Marburg Neo-Kantian philosophy. Born into a cantor's family in the small-town Jewish community of Coswig/Anhalt, Germany, Cohen received intense religious training from his father, in addition to the general education typical of his time and place. The transition from these beginnings to the modern rabbinical seminary of Breslau was natural. Part of the seminary's curriculum was the requirement of university studies. At the University of Breslau, Cohen decided that philosophy, rather than the rabbinate, was his *métier.*

Transferring to the University of Berlin, Cohen first fell under the influence of the "folk-psychological" epistemologists Heymann Steinthal and Moritz Lazarus, but he quickly progressed to a more Kantian and logicistic outlook. His habilitation thesis on Kant's theory of experience was published in 1871, and in the context of the "back to Kant" movement of the day his ideas had a revolutionary impact. He particularly impressed the radical social reformer and professor of philosophy at Marburg Friedrich Lange (author of the famous idealistic *History of Materialism).* Through Lange, a committed Protestant, the committedly Jewish Cohen received his first appointment at the University of Marburg in 1873. He stayed there until his voluntary, albeit disgruntled, retirement in 1912, thereafter to teach at the Liberal rabbinical seminary in Berlin, the Hochschule für die Wissenschaft des Judentums, where he wrote his last works. Shortly after his arrival in Marburg he married Martha Lewandowski, daughter of the chief cantor of the Berlin Jewish community and liturgical composer, Louis Lewandowski. (She was to die in the concentration camp of Theresienstadt.)

During his long incumbency in Marburg, Cohen not only produced the bulk of his own philosophic oeuvre but also gathered around him a group that came to constitute the Marburg school of Neo-Kantianism. Among the many scholars associated with him in this undertaking were his student and subsequent colleague Paul Natorp and, later, Ernst Cassirer. Cohen attracted many devoted students and disciples, particularly Jews from German-speaking countries, from eastern Europe, and even America. However, his personal, philosophical, and social relations at the university became increasingly strained down through the years, not least because of growing political reaction during that period against the overtly ethical, that is, Kantian, anti-Marxist, and antimaterialist socialism of the Marburg school. (In the politics of the time the names of Cohen's students Kurt Eisner and Eduard Bernstein became quite well known.)

Throughout his life Cohen never ceased to be active in Jewish matters. For example, he published his *The Love of Neighbor in the Talmud: Affidavit before the Royal Court of Marburg* in 1888 (in German) in response to the notorious Rohling/Delagarde anti-Semitic episode in which the old "blood libel" and Jewish xenophobism combined with the then nascent German racism. He wrote voluminously on Jewish subjects; in 1924 his writings were collected in three volumes, edited, and introduced by Franz Rosenzweig, author of *The Star of Redemption.* Just before the outbreak of World War I Cohen made a triumphal tour of the largest Jewish communities in Russia, a trip that the German government supported for political reasons. Cohen hoped also by means of this tour to advance in the East the enlightened Jewish social and educational values of the Jews of the West.

Cohen's Writings. Cohen's work can be divided into three parts: his exegetical readings of Immanual Kant, his "system of philosophy," and his specifically Jewish work.

Exegetical readings of Kant. Several of Cohen's books crystallized and solidified the aprioristic, transcendental, "critical" foundations of the Kantian system: *Kants Theorie der Erfahrung* (1871), *Kants Begründung der Ethik* (1877, 1910), and *Kants Begründung der Ästhetik* (1889). In 1883 he published *Das Prinzip der Infinitesimalmethode und seine Geschichte: Eine Kapital in der Begründung der Erkenntniskritik* (The Principle of the Infinitesimal Method and Its History: A Chapter in the Foundation of the Critique of Cognition), in which he argues that "the (sensuous) given," which Kant treated as the separate, empiricist source of knowledge, is also a rational contruction, and thus that "reality" is totally an aprioristic, regulative product.

The "system of philosophy." Cohen's radicalized, Neo-Kantian understanding of reality and of ethics that developed directly from his critiques of Kant found expression in his *Logik der Reinen Erkentniss* (Logic of Pure Cognition; 1902, 1914), *Ethik der Reinen Vernunft* (Logic of the Pure Will; 1904–1907), and *Ästhetik des Reinen Gefühls* (Aesthetic of Pure Feeling; 1912). Here the universe is determined by the three "interests" of reason (cognition, will, and feeling), which strive for the traditional ideals of truth, goodness, and beauty. All three operate under what Kant had called "the primacy of practical (i.e., ethical) reason." The infinite task of the attainment of practical reason produces the unending history of regulatively progressive science, progress toward the good society (as in ethical socialism), and the synthesis of the two in a world perfectly true and perfectly good, that is, messianically beautiful.

Cohen's specifically Jewish work. His work in this area, intimated in his philosophizing and, increasingly, explicitly identified with it, was systematically elaborated in the final decade of his life and was consummated in the posthumously published *Religion aus den Quellen des Judentums* (Religion of Reason out of the Sources of Judaism; 1919, 1929). Cohen's Jewish philosophical theology (although he did not use this terminology) consists of a translation back into classical Jewish terms of the philosophical position Cohen held he had extracted from Judaism with the help of the progressive line of thought running from Plato through Maimonides to Kant. Thus God is the idea (in the Neo-Kantian, regulative sense) of the normative, infinite realization of the good in the world. This realization is known in religion as the establishment by means of "the imitation of God" of the messianic kingdom on earth. The Law *(halakhah)* is the historical Jewish specifications of the categorical imperative and the foundation of the universal human moral brotherhood of the "Noachide covenant," which is also the religious, "Prophetic," goal of socialism. The last third of *Religion of Reason,* leading up to the religious virtues of truthfulness and peacefulness, is, together with the cited and appended texts, a Jewish restatement of the last third of *Ethics of the Pure Will.* The role of the Jewish people in history is then to represent "ethical monotheism" physically and to disseminate it morally throughout the world. Therefore, Cohen rejected the Zionism that was nascent at the time: the conflict between the two views is well expressed in the classic debate between Cohen and Martin Buber in "Answer to the Open Letter of Dr. M. Buber" (1917) and in the writings of Cohen's former student Jakob Klatzkin, who became the leading theoretician of the radical Zionist "negation of the Diaspora."

Influence of Cohen's Work. Cohen's influence in matters of religion was not limited to Jewry, although here it was magisterial. At the University of Marburg he interacted strongly with the Protestant theology faculty, first with Julius Wellhausen, whose Bible criticism he esteemed highly as a good scholarly undergirding to "Prophetic Judaism," and then especially with the liberal, proto–Social Gospel philosophical theologian Wilhelm Herrmann. Paul Natorp himself became increasingly active in liberal Protestantism. A second generation of Christian thinkers resulted from what might be called this Marburg school of Kantian liberal theology, albeit largely by way of dialectical antitheses: Karl Barth and Rudolf Bultmann deliberately place primary emphasis on the subjectivity of faith in place of Cohen's argument for the objectivity of ethical and social values.

Cohen's philosophical and Jewish influence is scattered in diverse and embattled manifestations. Around the turn of the century a rebellion emerged against what was perceived as the extreme scientific, rationalistic theoreticism of Marburg Neo-Kantianism. In reaction there appeared positions that asserted the ultimate power of "reality" over reason in "life-philosophy," re-hegelianizing historicism, positivism, and nascent existentialist phenomenologism. In German circles the value of historical and even metaphysical "Germanism" *(Deutschtum)* was apostrophized, and in Jewish circles a parallel affirmation of the peoplehood of Israel and the historical or even metaphysical "genius" of the Jewish people was pitted against "bloodless" and "lifeless" assimilationist universalism. The fact that Franz Rosenzweig, a disciple of Friedrich Meinecke and author of important studies on Hegel, became Cohen's last important, brilliant disciple added another complicating element, for Rosenzweig interpreted the "late Cohen" as the precursor of a total break with systematic rationalism in favor of a Schellingian form of metahistoricism.

Politically, religiously, and philosophically very different extrapolations continue to this day to be made from Cohen's fundamental analyses. Leading Jewish Orthodox authorities like Joseph Ber Soloveitchik and Isaac Hutner (d. 1980) never ceased drawing on their Cohenian studies in the 1920s, while rationalistic Reformers like Benzion Kellerman and fully acculturated Westerners like Ernst Cassirer struck out in their own directions from Cohen. These varied approaches demonstrate how decisive the intellectual experience of Cohen has remained for subsequent Jewish thought. Cohen's Jewish writings have been translated into Hebrew, English, and other languages, but the technical philosopher Cohen has remained within the confines of German-language culture. Even there he has suffered many depredations. The Weimar backlash against "cold, brainy" rationalism forced a number of Marburg-influenced figures such as Natorp, Nicolai Hartmann, and Ortega y Gasset, into Husserlian, Heideggerian, and other positions. The Nazi period saw the final destruction of the Neo-Kantianism of Marburg. Since World War II, however, a new, qualified appreciation of "transcendental philosophy" has arisen, through the work of men such as Hans Wagner, Helmut Holzhey, Werner Flach, Wolfgang Marx, and others. But the contributions that Cohen's work can still make toward a fully developed and effective constructionalism in the areas of philosophy of science, ethics, and even of religion, have not yet been fully realized.

BIBLIOGRAPHY

Sponsored by the Hermann-Cohen-Archiv under the direction of Helmut Holzhey, publication of Cohen's *Werke* (Hildesheim and New York, 1978–) is currently under way. Among his works available in English are *Religion and Hope: Selections from the Jewish Writings of Hermann Cohen,* translated by Eva Jospe (New York, 1971), and *Religion of Reason out of the Sources of Judaism,* translated by Simon Kaplan (New York, 1972).

For commentary on Cohen's place in modern Jewish thought, see Julius Guttmann's *Philosophies of Judaism,* translated by David W. Silverman (New York, 1964), pp. 352-367, and Nathan Rotenstreich's *Jewish Philosophy in Modern Times* (New York, 1968), pp. 52-105.

STEVEN S. SCHWARZSCHILD

COKE, THOMAS (1747–1814), chief associate of John Wesley in the organization of worldwide Methodism. Born in Brecon, Wales, Coke attended Jesus College, Oxford, and earned in 1775 the degree of doctor of civil law. Having been ordained a deacon of the Church of England in 1770 and a priest in 1771, he served as curate of South Petherton, Somerset, from 1771 to 1777. In 1776 he fell under the spell of John Wesley and in 1777, largely because of his Methodism, was dismissed from his curacy. Becoming Wesley's colleague, he took over most of the supervision of the Irish societies, served as Wesley's secretary and agent, and employed his legal acumen in 1784 to draw up the deed poll incorporating the British Methodist Conference. In the same year he helped Wesley prepare and publish his revision of *The Book of Common Prayer.*

Wesley conveyed his own ecclesiastical authority to Coke in a form of ordination as "superintendent" for America, and thus transmitted ministerial orders to the Methodists there. Coke ordained Francis Asbury as his episcopal colleague—an act confirmed, at Asbury's insistence, through election by the American preachers—but Coke was the leader in formulating the American preachers' original *Discipline* on the basis of Wesley's "large" *Minutes.* Altogether, Coke spent less than three years in America, so that eventually Asbury took precedence over him, especially after it was discovered that in 1791 Coke had clandestinely sought a union of American Methodism with the Protestant Episcopal Church.

However, Coke had other irons in the fire. Among his many published works were a commentary on the Bible (1801–1807) and a *History of the West Indies* (1808–1811). He formed a tract society in 1782, advocated a missionary society in 1784, began to evangelize the West Indies in 1786, and was traveling to a mission in India at the time of his death. It was he more than any other who kindled Methodism's missionary zeal.

[*See also* Methodist Churches.]

BIBLIOGRAPHY

Easily the best biography is *Thomas Coke, Apostle of Methodism* (Nashville, 1969) by John Ashley Vickers. Additional insights and information can be found in chapter 9 of my book *From Wesley to Asbury: Studies in Early American Methodism* (Durham, 1976) and in *The Encyclopedia of World Methodism,* 2 vols., edited by Nolan B. Harmon (Nashville, 1974).

FRANK BAKER

COLERIDGE, SAMUEL TAYLOR (1772–1834), English Romantic poet, literary critic, journalist, philosopher, and religious thinker. With William Wordsworth, Coleridge helped inaugurate the Romantic era with the publication of *Lyrical Ballads* (1798). A devoted writer, he later worked sporadically as a journalist and lecturer. His life was shadowed by an unhappy marriage, ill health, and a lifelong drug addiction.

Raised in the Church of England by his minister father, Coleridge became a Unitarian during his student years at Cambridge, but he returned definitively to a trinitarian theology in 1805. Although essentially orthodox in his adherence to Church of England doctrine, Coleridge was often daringly innovative in his theological speculations on such concepts as the Logos, the Trinity, original sin, and the church. *Aids to Reflection* (1825) contains profound insights into the nature of faith and the relationship between faith and reason; *On the Constitution of the Church and State* (1830) offers a conservative view of the nature of the church and its "clerisy"; and *Confessions of an Inquiring Spirit* (published 1840) introduces into England the approaches to scripture of the German "higher criticism." His *Notebooks* (published 1957–) and *Marginalia* (published 1980–) also contain perceptive reflections on doctrine, church history, and theological controversy.

Coleridge was one of the most widely read men of his century. Hence, the influences on him were many, including David Hartley, Joseph Priestley, and William Godwin (whose necessitarianism he later rejected); Plato and the seventeenth-century Cambridge Platonists; the medieval Schoolmen; mystics like Jakob Boehme and (to a lesser extent) Emanuel Swedenborg; philosophers in the so-called pantheist tradition like Giordano Bruno and Baruch Spinoza; and the German transcendental philosophers, especially Immanuel Kant and Friedrich Schelling. Each was interpreted, however, according to the needs of Coleridge's own organic philosophy and used to further his own theological speculations.

Coleridge's influence on subsequent religious thought was widespread, both in England and in the United States. He is commonly seen as a forerunner of the

Broad Church movement through such disparate thinkers as Thomas Arnold, Julius Hare, and, especially, F. D. Maurice. There are also strong affinities between Coleridge and John Henry Newman, particularly in the two writers' approaches to religious epistemology. Through the writing of George MacDonald, Coleridge had—especially in his views on symbol, which are deeply grounded in his theology—an indirect influence on the imaginative literature of such writers as G. K. Chesterton, Charles Williams, J. R. R. Tolkien, and C. S. Lewis. Among Coleridge's poems, *The Rime of the Ancient Mariner,* with its anguished spiritual odyssey, became a paradigm for imaginative and spiritual journeying. In the United States, *Aids to Reflection* was particularly influential, made known especially by James Marsh, by W. G. T. Shedd (who published a seven-volume edition of Coleridge in 1853), and by Ralph Waldo Emerson. Through Emerson, Coleridge's influence on American Transcendentalist thought was considerable.

Coleridge struggled against rationalism—both within the Protestant tradition and in the secular world—and against materialism, and he wrote vigorously of the need for a renewal of the spiritual dimensions of society and culture. His most important contribution to the religious thought of his own time may well be his introduction into England of German idealist thought and of higher criticism of scripture, while his most lasting contribution may be his reflections on the nature of religious language, especially on the role of symbol in religious experience.

BIBLIOGRAPHY

The central resource for the study of Coleridge is *The Collected Works of Samuel Taylor Coleridge,* 16 vols., edited by Kathleen Coburn (Princeton, 1970–); the lengthy introductions to these volumes are especially helpful. The most complete studies of Coleridge's religious thought are James D. Boulger's *Coleridge as Religious Thinker* (New Haven, 1961) and my work *Coleridge and Christian Doctrine* (Cambridge, Mass., 1969). Basil Willey's *Samuel Taylor Coleridge* (New York, 1972) is, in the author's own words, an "intellectual and spiritual biography"; it brings both learning and good sense to Coleridge's complex life. Stephen Prickett's *Romanticism and Religion: The Tradition of Coleridge and Wordsworth in the Victorian Church* (Cambridge, 1976) traces skillfully and perceptively the influence of Coleridge, especially his analysis of religious language, in religious writing of the later nineteenth century.

J. Robert Barth, s.j.

COLORS. The religious symbolism of colors is based upon the immediate and universal human experience of color as an essential quality of the objects of ordinary experience. From a strictly scientific point of view, this natural experience of color may seem somewhat naive, since the seemingly simple experience of color is actually the product of many different factors. The subjective sensation of one and the same color can in fact be produced by an almost infinite variety of lighting combinations. But even the naive and immediate experience of color, which knows nothing of spectral analysis and subtle variations in wavelength, can nevertheless give rise to complex speculations. Beginning with a basic distinction of "primary" from "secondary" colors, one is soon led on to such notions as "warm" and "cold" colors or to value systems such as Goethe's scale of brightness, set forth in *Zur Farbenlehre* (1810), by which yellow receives a value of nine (the maximum) and violet the value of three (the minimum).

According to the abstract painter Paul Klee (1879–1940), the primary colors may be associated with different sounds, geometrical forms, and even subjective experiences. Thus for Klee, blue is to be associated with the circle and with the experience of stability, yellow with the triangle and the sensation of speed, and red with the square and the experience of power. Klee's intuitions are well grounded even if they do not represent the only possible schema of this kind.

Wassily Kandinsky (1866–1944), one of the greatest of abstractionist painters, observed that a yellow circle seems to develop outward in an expansive movement, so that it appears to approach the observer, while a blue circle seems to contract and move away. The two examples demonstrate that color gives rise to many more psychological effects than the ones well known to fashion, namely that white "enlarges" and that black "lessens." Besides, according to the available data, the constants of chromatic perceptions seem to have changed historically.

Human sensitivity to color seems to have been greatest initially at the long end of the spectrum, with red, orange, and yellow, at wavelengths between 800 and 550 millimicrons. In prehistoric paintings neither green nor blue appears, even though the preparation of green and blue pigments would probably have presented no difficulty. In the classical world the adjectives *glaucus* and *coerulus* included all shades between green and blue, so that it appears that these colors were not clearly distinguished. In addition, the Greek word *chlōros* ("green") is sometimes used to indicate hues of yellow; the Latin word *viridis* ("green"), connected with fertility, is a coinage of the late first century BCE. The Latin scholar Aulo Gellio *(Noctes Atticae* 2.26), in his attempt to establish a basic list of the colors, uses the Greek *xanthos* ("yellow-gold") and *kirros* ("yellow-orange") as well as the Latin *flavus* ("blond") and *fulvus* ("fawn," said of a lion) to name various hues of red. It seems that in Aulo's enormous work (second century CE) the chromatic variety that is found at the long end of the spectrum is the result of a confused redistribution of perceptual and linguistic values that originally expressed a greater sensitivity to red.

Red is in fact the only color that has had a solid lexical tradition in the sphere of Indo-European languages, in the form of the root **rudhro*. By contrast, the term *hāri* in Vedic Sanskrit could refer to red, yellow-gold, or even yellow-green. In Chinese and Japanese, the same word is used for both green and blue, although in painting (for instance, in the wall paintings at Tun-huang, China) green extracted from malachite and blue extracted from azurite and later from lapis lazuli (as in India and the Occident) were widely used. Malachite green is particularly common in the depictions of the paradises or "pure lands" of Amitābha.

Thus the linguistic expressions of the basic human experience of color are both complex and ambiguous. This same complexity and ambiguity is encountered in the use of colors as symbols. Here colors have taken on a wide range of significations that vary from culture to culture. The Phoenician discovery of purple, for instance, made available a new color that was particularly fit for assuming distinctive and fascinating values because of its rarity and price. In Rome, from the period of the republic, it became a symbol of political power, and senators could be recognized by the broad purple stripe that adorned their togas. Later it became the symbol of divinity and of the emperor's authority (the "imperial purple"). Still later, when associated in Christianity with the preeminent dignity of the priesthood, it became the "cardinal purple" (scarlet). In late Roman and Byzantine times, red porphyry became the symbol of imperial power, perhaps because of its similarity to purple and its hardness as a substance. The Constantinople column (located in the elliptical Forum) is made of porphyry and once supported the image of the emperor Constantine (c. 280–337).

Of particular interest is the use of color in vestments in order to express hierarchical position or to symbolize spiritual attitudes and values. An unusually rich illustration of this is provided by the use of color within the Catholic church. Here the use of color in the vestments of the officiant, on the altar, and in the attire of the altar boys leads to a peculiar symbology that is part of the Christian liturgical year. Related to Hellenistic and above all to Roman traditions, Christian color symbolism was generally based on white, which was the color of joy, innocence, and purity. White was the color of the martyrs, the *candidatus exercitus* ("white-clad army"). Black, by contrast, was considered to be the color of sadness (although it was only later introduced into funeral liturgies). Cobalt blue was the color of darkness and the devil, while red was the color of the empyrean sky and of the angels. Purple, the imperial color, becomes the color of the cardinal's robe, as we saw above.

From the ninth century on, colors were a constant element of Christian ritual. Despite early attempts to standardize church usage, variations persisted. In Greece, for instance, red was the color of mourning (tears of blood?), while in Milan, where the local Ambrosian ritual was in use, red was dedicated to the Holy Sacrament. In France red was the liturgical color on All Saints' Day (1 November)—a clear reference to the blood of the martyrs—while in Rome white, the symbol of triumph, was used for the same feast.

The first real codification of the liturgical colors began under Innocent III (1198–1216) and reached its definitive form under Pius V (1566–1572) after the Council of Trent (1545–1563). According to this final codification, white is used in the sacred vestments for the great festivities of the liturgical year and is regarded according to this final order as a symbol of triumph as well as of innocence and purity. Red is reserved for the feasts of the martyrs, symbolizing the blood of sacrifice and eternal life. On other days green is used, a symbol of hope, and is regarded as midway between white and red. Violet (a kind of "temperate black") is used during the periods of penance (Lent) and in the funeral services. Black has fallen into disuse since it was regarded as the color of the devil by the fathers of the church and again during the late Middle Ages. On occasion silver may replace white, while gold may be used instead of white, green, or red.

The polyvalence of gold is worth noting. It leads us to a consideration of the particular mysticism expressed by the golden backgrounds of Byzantine mosaics and icons and of medieval paintings. The Russian Orthodox philosopher Evgenii Trubetskoi (1863–1920), in his work *Umozrenie v kraskakh* (Speculation in Colors; 1915–1918), noticed the influence of a solar christological mysticism in the golden backgrounds of the icons, since only the color of gold can reflect the supreme sunlight of the heavenly world. Artists devised the "assist"—the insertion of shining golden lines into the dress of divine figures—for this reason. The assist is especially common in depictions of Christ, and above all in depictions of the Transfiguration, the Resurrection, the Ascension, and other post-Resurrection events. It is clearly intended as a symbol of Christ's superhuman glory. Behind it lies the speculative metaphysics of light exemplified in the works of Dionysius the Areopagite (c. 500 CE), who views the words *phōtoeideis* ("of shining appearance") and *chrusoeidēs* ("of golden appearance") as synonyms. The golden backgrounds of the Byzantine mosaics in churches in Ravenna and Byzantium (modern-day Istanbul) aimed at turning the "inner space" of the Roman basilicas into "space-light" and lightening the heaviness of the architectural material. The golden background produces an atmosphere pervaded with "immaterial light" *(phōs to aulon)* and draws the believers toward the contemplation of the divine mysteries.

The golden backgrounds of the mosaics, icons, and paintings on wood were created by applying very thin sheets of gold to a prepared surface. Because this method cannot be used on the larger scale of frescoes, some painters, notably Giotto (1267–1337), filled the backgrounds of murals with a blue pigment made of powdered lapis lazuli, the most precious color of that time. In Giotto's frescoes the blue of lapis lazuli can be compared to the golden backgrounds of the Byzantine Sienese tradition, with the resulting orientation toward a heavenly mysticism and away from the fundamental realism of the paintings. Nevertheless, in the ancient Christian tradition, azure and blue had a negative value, even if azure can be seen shining alongside green in the mosaics of Ravenna and Byzantium.

The blue of lapis lazuli was also widely used in the area of Central Asia that has as its center the caravan town of Kuchā. In many of the Buddhist paintings found in this area, this blue appears alongside green. But here, too, the color appears with an ambiguous value. On the one hand, it was used in Tibetan Buddhist art to depict terrifying gods and evil powers. In the sole surviving wall painting of Tumshuq, and in several others in the area of Kuchā, demonic and inauspicious figures either are completely blue or have blue beards. On the other hand, ascetics and monks are also depicted with blue beards. Remarkably, we meet the same color in a Chinese figure who appears in a Sienese fresco of Oriental inspiration, a work by Ambrogio Lorenzetti (d. 1348) that illustrates the martyrdom of the Franciscans at Tana (India). The presence of this same color in both the East and the West suggests a common source that is most likely Iranian. We may also note that the Indian god Śiva is called "Blue Throat," a title he earned when, after consuming a poison that threatened to destroy the universe, his throat was stained blue.

Compared with blue, gold is free of such ambiguity. As a precious metal, it has a natural and universal symbolic value. [*See* Gold and Silver.] Regarded as a symbol of the Absolute, it can also be a symbol of incorruptibility and royalty (both human and divine). Its use as a symbol for absolute reality is evident in the *Suvarṇaprabhāsottama Sūtra* (Supreme Sutra of the Golden Brillance), in which the Buddha's immaterial body is presented as shining gold and as identical with the *dharmakāya*, the "body of the Law." The essence of the universe is thus compared to a golden light that shines forth like sunlight. In several Gandharan traditions (from the area of present-day Afghanistan and Pakistan, first to fifth century CE) they speak of even the Buddha's shadow as golden and shining, which gives us some idea of the superhuman brightness of the Buddha himself.

Color plays an important role in the Western alchemic tradition. According to this tradition, the alchemic process passes through four stages, each associated with a color: the *nigredo* (black) or initiatory death, the *albedo* (white) or beginning of rebirth, the *rubedo* (red) or sublimation, and the *auredo* (gold), the almost unreachable final stage that represents spiritual perfection. The series seems to coincide with the elementary set of colors that the Greek philosophers Pythagoras (571–497 BCE) and Empedocles (492–432 BCE) regarded as the only ones allowable on a palette, namely black, white, red, and yellow. Here gold might correspond to yellow (it is a gradation of it), but yellow itself is ambiguous.

Color symbolism is also important in Tantric Buddhism. In the *Guhyasamāja Tantra* (Book of the Meeting with the Secret) the universe is said to originate in a motionless (cold?) white light. In time, a vibration develops within this white light, and it comes to be refracted into five centers of color: red, yellow, blue, and green, with white in the middle. Each of these centers corresponds to a "supreme" Buddha. According to the Tibetan arrangements, in the east is Akṣobhya ("unshakable"), who is blue and is the symbol of all the victories of the historical Buddha. In the west is Amitābha ("infinite light"), red like the setting sun. In the north is Amoghasiddhi ("uncorruptible"), who is green, and in the south is Ratnasambhava ("born of the jewel"), who is yellow, probably to be identified with gold. In the middle is Vairocana, white of the dazzling light, who is the essence of the universe and who sums up all the other supreme Buddhas in himself.

Ascribing a color to a divinity means attributing an emanation of the light of that color to it. It is likely that meditation techniques have affected the choice of colors attributed to the different Buddhas, since the color of one and the same Buddha can change from one painting to the next. Nevertheless, certain essential principles do seem to be respected. For instance, a terrifying divinity can never be white or green, but must be either red or, more frequently, black or dark blue. It also seems to be true that here as elsewhere the different colors are in one way or another subordinated to white light, or to the brightness of gold, which alone is truly adequate for symbolizing the highest reality.

BIBLIOGRAPHY

Corbin, Henry. *The Man of Light in Iranian Sufism.* Translated by Nancy Pearson. Boulder, 1978. Discusses color visions.

Fischer, Wolfdietrich. *Farb- und Formbezeichnungen in der Sprache der altarabischen Dichtung.* Wiesbaden, 1965.

Jacobi, Jolande. *Farbgestaltungen der unbewussten Psyche.* Basel, 1963. See pages 15–26.

Portmann, Adolf, and Rudolf Ritsema, eds. *The Realms of Colour.* Leiden, 1974. A special issue of *Eranos Jahrbuch*, vol. 41.

Thorndike, Lynn. "Some Medieval Texts on Colours." *Ambix: The Journal of the Society for the Study of Alchemy and Early Chemistry* (Cambridge) 7 (February 1959): 1–24.

Thorndike, Lynn. "Other Texts on Colours." *Ambix: The Journal of the Society for the Study of Alchemy and Early Chemistry* (Cambridge) 8 (June 1960): 53–70.

Turner, Victor. "Colour Classification in Ndembu Ritual." In *Anthropological Approaches to the Study of Religion*, edited by Michael Banton, pp. 47–84. London, 1966.

Wilson, Michael. *What is Colour?: The Goethean Approach to a Fundamental Problem.* Clent, England, 1949.

MARIO BUSSAGLI

COMENIUS, JOHANNES AMOS (1592–1670), the "grandfather of modern education." Born Jan Amos Komenský in Nivnitz, Moravia, he was orphaned early and did not begin school until the age of sixteen. He died in Amsterdam, a lifelong refugee from religious wars, the last bishop of the Moravian and Bohemian Brethren, formerly known as the Old Church.

Said to be unoriginal in philosophy, Comenius's genius lay in teaching. His philosophy and his teaching were forged from personal experience with both religious intolerance and bad schooling. He was convinced that international tensions were grounded in religious differences, which in turn were grounded in lack of knowledge of the order of nature as well as of others' religions.

His grand strategy was "Pansophia," a philosophy of universal knowledge based on a universal language built on a universal education that included women. Invited to England to develop a system of education, he was prevented from carrying out his program by the Civil War. He visited Sweden and planned the reformation of schools there only to flee the outbreak of war in 1648. He returned to Leszno, Poland, whence he had fled from Nivnitz as a young man, and where he had done most of his writing, but was forced by the war between West Prussia and Poland to escape to Amsterdam in 1655, losing in this final move all his manuscripts.

For Comenius, schools as he found them were "the slaughterhouse of the mind," devoted as they were to the dreary and sometimes desperately enforced study of Latin in a world where that language was no longer used. In his schools there was to be no "stuffing and flogging," but, rather, a reasonable following of "the lead of nature." "A rational creature should be led," he wrote, "not by shouts, imprisonment and blows, but by reason." Nothing was to be learned "for its own sake," but "for its usefulness in life." Everything was to be learned by practice: "Let the students learn to write by writing, to talk by talking, to sing by singing, to reason by reasoning." Comenius likened education to nature, where the existence of objects was prior to the development of language. "The principle of succession," he wrote, in which "nature prepares the material before giving it form, develops everything from within, always ending in particulars, makes no leaps [and] advances only from strength." Knowledge, therefore, comes most naturally through the senses: "The sense of hearing should be conjoined with that of sight, and the tongue should be trained in coordination with the hand." Objects were to be brought into the classroom for use in teaching.

His plans for state schools, radical in his century, are now generally accepted. Schools were to open at a uniform date each year and holidays were to be frequent but short. According to his plans, a definite learning task would be assigned to each hour of the day; after each class there was a recess. The length of the day was longer the higher the grade. Comenius proposed that each teacher have a separate room and all learning be done under the teacher's supervision; there was to be no homework. Comenius hoped for the establishment of a central college which was to be provided with facilities for both advanced learning and teacher preparation. From a generation so trained, he believed, a Christian republic might grow. "There is no more certain way under the sun," he wrote, "to raise a sunken humanity."

Comenius's *Dictionary of Tongues and All Sciences* was translated into Arabic and Russian, as well as into other European languages, and the students of three continents thumbed its pages. *Orbis pictus* (The Visible World), published in 1658, was his most famous text; it was illustrated, featured parallel passages in Latin and in the student's vernacular, and was intended to be employed by students at a rate commensurate with their individual abilities. These texts were based on earlier works: *Gate of Tongues Unlocked* (1631) and *Labyrinth of the World* (c. 1623). His best-known work is *Didactica magna*, written between 1628 and 1632. It has influenced teaching methods in the Western world more, perhaps, than any other book of educational theory.

BIBLIOGRAPHY

A good biography of Comenius is Matthew Spinka's *John Amos Comenius: That Incomparable Moravian* (Chicago, 1943). A good analysis of his contribution to education is John E. Sadler's *J. A. Comenius and the Concept of Universal Education* (London, 1966).

WAYNE R. ROOD

COMMUNION. *See* Eucharist.

COMMUNISM. *For discussion of religion in Marxist societies, see* Marxism *and* Politics and Religion. *For discussion of the life, works, thought, and influence of Marx and the importance of Marxist theory in the study of religion, see the biography of Marx and* Study of Religion, *article on* History of Study. *For discussion of communal life as a religious ideal, see* Utopia.

COMMUNITY. Although groupings or community formations are a regular feature of the phenomenon of religion, it is important to recognize that they are neither necessary nor equally prominent in all religions. There are situations otherwise completely typical of the category "religion" wherein the communal element is lacking, and others wherein it is loosely structured, evanescent, or deemed unimportant. For example, even though monasteries constitute a rigorous and elaborate kind of community, the name for them in Western languages derives from the Greek *monos,* meaning "single, alone." Hermit monks and wandering *saṃnyāsins* take as a major element in their piety and ascetic practice the renunciation of community. Also, many people in modern, industrialized societies consider themselves religious because of certain attitudes, practices, and beliefs but do not take part in a communal structure in which these religious factors are shared or are decisive.

Therefore, in the following paragraphs, as various types of religious communal organization are reviewed and their dynamics analyzed, one must remember that these groups vary in intensity and importance in their respective cultures and traditions, and that they do not exhaust the possibilities for religious life. Nevertheless, it is not too much to say that nearly all religious situations do have a communal dimension and that in many the community is the decisive factor.

It is a prejudice of modern society to speak of "organized religion" as if organization added an extraneous element to what legitimately exists without it. It is possible, of course, to define or to believe in a religion that is a matter of one's aloneness. It should also be recognized, however, that for many other people the social factor—belonging to and having a place in a religious community—may be the dominant aspect of their religious life and that, further, it may be a hidden factor even in the life of the one who rejects its significance.

The following description and typology of religious communities is highly abstract and theoretical. It describes poles, although most groups actually lie somewhere on a continuum between such poles; it speaks of pure types, even though most of life is compromised and blended; it isolates factors and structures that are in actuality mixed with other social patterns as well as influenced and changed by belief, rite, and experience. All this notwithstanding, focusing on these social structures, abstracted from their living contexts, may be helpful in sorting out the communal element from among the many contributing factors in a religious phenomenon and so may lead to a better understanding of the whole.

Characteristics of Religious Community. Some form of initiation usually marks entrance into a religious community. Entrance rituals may also be duplicated, reinforced, or elaborated on subsequent occasions. Later transition ceremonies often mark the beginning of new status within a group (e.g., ordination or monastic profession). There are also rituals and procedures for leaving a group, by incorporation into a higher status beyond the perimeters of the former group, or by censure and repudiation. Even death, which would seem to end an individual's membership in a community, can be understood as an initiation into a yet higher degree of existence in the group. In such cases, certain ceremonies during the ritual year may celebrate the return of the dead to participate in the life of the community.

Communal ritual activities for other purposes or on other occasions than initiation or ordination are also characteristic marks of religious communities. These rituals may be focused on seasonal change, agricultural processes, famous events of history, and doctrines, usually with all these elements blended together. Gathering as a group for such rites is perhaps the most persistent aspect of religious community, and is arguably its reason for being.

Differentiation of function and of merit or value is often recognized in communal structure. In some cases special functions within the group, especially leadership in ritual activities, are assumed by individuals specially selected and consecrated; in other cases leaders emerge from the group charismatically. That is, some religious traditions are highly sensitive to structural arrangements and carefully delineate lines of command and authority, carefully categorizing all functions and degrees. In other traditions the patterns of authority are quite casual, very much dependent on individual initiative and lacking ritual recognition.

Religious communities often validate, or give religious meaning to, natural or social distinctions. Gender, for example, is often a significant determinant of an individual's role in a religious community. One's role in the family (as mother, son, etc.) or one's lineage (e.g., in a caste system) may also determine religious status, and one's political office or status as a leader in the society at large tends to take on religious significance.

Religious communities are different from other social groups in their concept of the community as a sacred phenomenon. Instead of conceiving of the community in practical or casual terms, the distinctly religious group sees itself as part of a larger structure, plan, or purpose, one that transcends the immediate or basic needs of humanity. Conscious correlation of the community with patterns of symbols that are not social in their primary reference is a signal of the presence of religious rather than secular community.

Where nature and its processes are the focal point of religious attention, the community is conceived and structured with reference to the natural world. The subgroups within a tribe, for example, are linked in the mind with animals, stars, and the like. This totemism does not indicate an obliteration of the distinction between nature and culture in such peoples but rather shows an attempt to correlate one with the other or to use the elements of the natural world as a means of labeling and systematizing society.

Among religious groups for whom nature is not the primary concern, the concept of the community as a sacred entity takes a variety of forms. A special relationship with one or more gods or goddesses may be expressed by seeing the group as the servants, the messengers, or perhaps the co-workers of the divine beings. There is a fine line between metaphors and ontological assertions in theological language, so one often does not know how precisely to take images, such as the church as the "body" of Christ, that seem to give a group a kind of organic participation in the sacred.

A concept of the group as sacred can be linked with the merit or attainments of adepts with various degrees of skill. Those who are most advanced in ascetic practice, meditation, or yoga may constitute a sacred core around or below which those of lesser attainments are ranked. This arrangement leads to a pattern illustrated by Buddhism, according to which the term for the community, *saṃgha,* may refer to the inner circle of monks (*bhikkhus*) or to the larger group, the laity, who subscribe to the doctrine but practice it less exclusively.

It is possible, of course, for a religious community to be structured along lines that are not particularly religious from the point of view of believer or observer, as is so, for example, in the military model of the Salvation Army and the constitutional administrative arrangement of some American Protestant denominations. In such cases, concepts of the group as a sacred entity might become almost entirely separate from its actual structural appearance. Tensions can develop in religious groups when the social structure and the theology become too divergent. It is odd, for example, to have a monastic pattern that is almost inevitably based on merit and attainment existing within a tradition that doctrinally asserts equality before God or some alternate kind of sacred hierarchy.

To summarize, we can assume that we are observing a religious community, whether it is so labeled or not, when most or all of the following characteristics are evident in reference to the sacred: rituals of initiation and incorporation (as well as those of rejection); other communal rituals; and status levels and functional distinctions.

"Natural" Religious Groups. One of the clearest distinctions to be made among religious communities is that between groups specifically and self-consciously organized around religious beliefs and activities and those societies or "natural" groups wherein whatever is religious is part of the whole social structure. This distinction may also be made by noting that the specific religious groups are typically or theoretically voluntary, while one is born into the latter type of community, and there is no choice about joining it. A further way of making the distinction is by observing the relationship between the religious dimension and the political or governmental dimension: specific religious groups are not involved per se in governing, whereas the natural religious group is identical with the social group as a whole, including its political functions.

These broad categories have been labeled in many ways; for example, the terms *differentiated* and *undifferentiated* have been used, based on the degree to which the religious group is differentiated from the society as a whole. Sometimes it seems better to designate the natural, or undifferentiated, type of religious community as "folk" religion and, by contrast, to see the specific religious community as "universal" in character. Folk religion is part of the culture of a particular group of people and is not easily distinguished from all the other patterns and practices that define the culture. A universal religious group, however, tries to cross cultural and ethnic boundaries by assuming that all people everywhere can become members of its community.

I use the terms *specific* and *natural* in this article to name these groups, even though the latter term presents a problem of multiple meanings. Many presuppositions lie behind any use of *nature,* and most of these are irrelevant to my present use. I do not assume, for example, that natural religious groups are sociobiologically based in a way that specific groups are not. In fact, nothing that follows need be understood as affecting theories concerning the biological determination of human social behavior. All that is meant by the use of *natural* in this context is the identity of the religious community with those forms of social organization that are mostly inevitable in human life: family, clan, ethnic group, and nation.

Even though one is born into such social structures, initiation into "real" participation in the community is one of the signs that the social unit is also a religious community. At birth or puberty, or at both of these life passages, a ceremony such as circumcision or some act of consecration marks the official (or ontological) entrance into society. In many places such initiation is more marked for boys than for girls, although there may be rituals connected with the onset of menstruation. It is to be expected that gender, lineage, and comparable identifications will be more significant in natural religious groups than in others.

In natural religious groups the religious leaders or functionaries are generally the leaders of the society as a whole. It is rare, however, to find a community that does not also have its religious specialists, perhaps a shaman or medicine man, whose appearance and role depend on a special recognition that is not determined by "nature" in the sense used here.

It should also be noted that specific religious organizations may exist within natural religious groups. The primitive secret society is an example of such a group: it has its own dynamics as a voluntary group with special religious functions and rites apart from the society as a whole. Similarly, groups based on family, gender, ethnic background, and related natural factors may be found within or alongside specific religious communities or may even seem to merge with them. Men's fraternities are a common example of a gender-based grouping, and the practical identity (at least in former years) of Spanish background and Roman Catholicism is an example of the apparent merging of the natural with the specific religious community.

We face a special situation in the phenomenon of the nation as a religious community—special in that the basis of community is not necessarily "natural" in the way that it is for gender, family, or lineage. In a nation, unrelated peoples can be joined together, slaves or slave populations may be incorporated into the political unit, and foreigners may have a place in the society as merchants or mercenaries. When the nation is also a religious community, however, it typically develops a set of stories (a mythology) to make the diverse groups appear to be a family. It is not at all certain, for example, that the ancient Israelites were all descended from Jacob; but new tribes could be included by having their patriarchs included among Jacob's sons. Emphasis on the "natural" in this type of religious nation may also be seen in the Israelites' insistence on the number twelve (the names of the sons of Jacob vary, but they are always twelve in number); this probably reflects a desire to repeat in human society the pattern of the heavens: twelve lunar cycles within a single solar cycle.

To the Israelites and other ancient peoples, political and religious functions were indistinguishable. While in modern times we differentiate between religious and civil law, ancient lawgivers recorded both in the same codes and in the same manner. The king was political, military, and religious functionary in one. Society, nature, and the gods were all seen as part of one interrelated organism. This outlook led to such phenomena as blaming crop failure on the weakness or immorality of the king. The king was characteristically seen as a god, the son of a god, or a representative and link from the heavens to earth and society.

This set of concepts is not entirely limited to the past. Some modern nations take on many of these characteristics (for some of their people) and thus become religious communities of a sort. Nations, both ancient and recent, have been known to cultivate epics of their origin, promote their peculiar concepts of the world, claim special connection with a god or gods, and link their success (or failure) to divine purpose. Not all of these nation-religions are generally recognized as such, but the Shintō tradition of Japan clearly exemplifies this phenomenon.

The religious and political dimensions of human life may be connected in another way as well, one that goes beyond the nation as a political unit. Islam, the most recent of the major religions, exhibits some of the characteristics of the very ancient natural religious community. It is based on the premise that the religious regulation and the civil regulation of life are to be derived from one source and litigated in one way. The international community of Islam thus presumes that a family of nations or peoples can be Muslim in law and belief. Some Muslim nations have begun to reject the notion of a secular government (i.e., one that is determined not by religious belief but by human deliberation) in favor of a religious government based on the Qur'ān. Although Islamic government of this sort does not necessarily have a kinglike figure or a theology of agriculture, in most other ways it is like the ancient nations, a natural religious community.

Specific Religious Communities. Specific religious communities are sometimes called "founded" religions because they have appeared within the scope of recorded history as the result of efforts of a particular person or small group. As noted above, this category could also be termed "universal," "differentiated," or "voluntary." Contemporary pluralistic societies include religious communities of this type, even though some characteristics of natural religious communities can be observed on occasion.

Sociologists of religion, mainly Westerners interested in Christian groups, have put most of their energies into analyzing specific religious groups. As the examination of the social dimensions of religion became a recognized scholarly discipline, the categories "church" and "sect" were developed to distinguish between religious communities. This terminology applied well to sixteenth-century Europe but was insufficient elsewhere. For America it was necessary to add at least the category "denomination." One widely used typology of religious groups that developed out of the earlier distinctions lists six major types of religious community: cult, sect, established sect (or institutionalized sect), denomination, ecclesia, and universal church. These categories were developed particularly with reference to the ways in which the religious community is integrated into the society as a whole and to a lesser degree with reference to the internal dynamics of each group or its theology. Nevertheless, these six types can provide a framework for understanding Christian communities and can be applied with some adjustments to other religions as well.

The kind of group that is least involved in the rest of society is called a "cult." A cult may comprise barely more than the audience for a charismatic leader or healer. It is loosely organized; often it is small and short-lived. Its religious style is personal and emotional.

A "sect" is a religious community that is more clearly organized than a cult, that provides a great amount of religious value to its members (in terms of social relationships, ritual activities, ethical and doctrinal direction, and so forth), but that plays little role in the society at large. Taken to its extreme, a sect can form a completely separate miniature state either mixed into the society geographically or located in its own separate territory.

It is also possible, however, for a sect to move in a different direction and become more stable within the larger society. A sect so changed would be an "established sect," or an "institutionalized sect." In this situation the wider society's acceptance of the sect can be great even though the sect remains exclusive and self-centered. An established sect has lost its appearance of opposition to the rest of the society and other religious groups, but it remains doctrinally or theoretically exclusive. [*See also* Sect.]

At this point the "denomination" assumes its place in the six-type scheme as another type of Western religious community. It is the kind of group that maintains separate and distinct organization despite its acceptance of the legitimacy of other denominations or communities. It may conceive of itself as the best, but hardly the only, community in which adequate religious practice can be found. It is also relatively more involved with and accepted by the larger society.

Students of American religious communities have been struck by the tendency of each Christian sect and denomination to be made up of people from a single socioeconomic class. Furthermore, they note that a sect tends to become an established sect or a denomination and that as it does, the class composition of its members tends to change. Some of the characteristics of the transition from sect to its more established form or to a denomination are an increase in the members' and the institution's wealth; movement toward the center of the surrounding culture and away from criticism of it; less ridicule of other religious communities and more cooperation with them; less exclusion of potential members for being thought potentially unworthy; fewer casually prepared part-time leaders and more professionally trained full-time ministers; more concern for children and education; less emphasis on death and the next world and more attention to life in this world; and less spontaneity and emotion in worship and more use of hymns and texts from the liturgical traditions. The established sect and the denomination might be similar in most of these departures from the patterns of a sect, but the denomination has a different theology, while the established sect, no matter how institutionalized or accepted, retains its exclusive and condemnatory thought and speech.

The next two categories, beyond denomination, represent the most established and, culturally and socially, the most prominent kinds of religious community. One has been called the "ecclesia" and consists of the established national churches, for example, the churches of England and of Sweden. The other is termed "universal church." It is as well established as the ecclesia but exists in many nations and cultures; the classic example is the Roman Catholic church of the thirteenth century.

One of the characteristics of the specific religious community as compared with the natural religious community is its voluntary character. Yet this characteristic is almost completely absent in the ecclesia and universal church and is of little importance in the denomination and the established sect. The sect is noted for its emphasis on conversion, a voluntary, adult decision to join the group. The more established churches, however, incorporate the children of members almost automatically into the community, thus operating somewhat like a natural religious group. Furthermore, kings and other political functionaries tend to become semireligious officials in the ecclesia and the universal church categories.

As noted above, most of the terminology used here has been derived from studies of Western Christian religious communities, but it can be applied to Eastern Christianity and other religions with some limited success. Sunnī Islam can be seen as a universal church; Shīʿī Islam in Iran can be seen as an ecclesia; other Shīʿī groups can be seen as sects or established sects, and so on. Eastern Christian groups are usually of the ecclesia type in their home countries and have had to shift character in order to be denominations in America. In Thailand and Sri Lanka, Buddhism has had ecclesia status; its role in China can be analyzed in various periods as taking the forms of sect, denomination, and so on—all this despite its essentially monastic structure.

It is more important in examining non-Western religious communities to note their patterns of internal relationships and their role in the larger religious tradition than to concentrate on their relationship to the state or society. In non-Western societies, the different mix of natural and specific groups must be considered, as well as the recent and incomplete phenomenon of secularity (the separation of civil from religious jurisdiction). For example, Hinduism is, for the most part, a natural religious community, but some associations within it are of the specific type. These groups (*sampradāyas*) select a certain god or family of gods, a certain style of worship, and certain temples from the whole range of Hinduism, and these elements become the basis for the group's religious life. Thus a community with its own leaders and priests emerges. This phenomenon has many of the characteristics of the denomination in its recognition of other (almost as good) practices and gods in Hinduism, but it is sectarian in its lack of involvement with the society as a whole and in its governmental structures.

The different circumstances of non-Western religious communities can be understood better in terms and categories other than the six reviewed above. The following categories have been developed especially by anthropologists and ethnologists, and they help us understand the subgroups within larger religious communities or traditions.

Communities within Communities. One large distinction that can be made within both natural and specific religious groups is that of "great" and "little" traditions. The professional leadership of a society or a specific religious community promotes a literate, fairly sophisticated, and often transcultural understanding and practice of its religion. The ordinary members of the group, however, may be imperfectly incorporated into this tradition. They may maintain some notions and practices from older religions or participate in the tradition in a way that is based on different media. These two strata do not form clearly separate communities but constitute a pattern in many countries.

On a much smaller scale there are other communal formations that can be found in both natural and specific religious communities. Prominent among these is the master, guru, or teacher with his following. This is the basic format of the cult as defined above, but it is also both a regular phenomenon in almost all religions as well as the point of origin for many new religious communities. The master with his disciples is an evanescent phenomenon. Beyond the first generation it must become something like a sect, pursuing a separate identity; it must institutionalize the master-pupil pattern in a more or less monastic structure; or it may do both (as does, for example, Buddhism). The model of the Hindu ashram or of the Muslim Ṣūfī shaykh with his disciples indicates a recognition of this kind of religious community in their respective traditions but without much regularization or institutionalization.

The monastic community is often to be found within larger religious communities. It may be defined as a group of people drawn from a larger religious community who live together for shorter or longer periods of time in order to cultivate religious techniques and disciplines. This inclusive definition can apply to secret societies or to men's groups within tribal societies as well as to the institutions prominent in Buddhism, Hinduism, and Christianity. Islam displays a variation of this kind of community in the Ṣūfī orders.

Monastic communities may be at the center of their larger traditions, as in Buddhism. Here the monks may be the only leaders of the religious community and thus take on functions characteristic of priests and ministers in other traditions. Within Christianity, however, monasticism has been a supplementary pattern of religious leadership that exists alongside the priestly hierarchy. Often monastic communities as well as other subgroups have originated in a protest against prevailing practices or doctrines in the larger group. When such a protest becomes estranged, a new religion is formed, but often the protest is institutionalized and becomes another option within the larger community.

Certainly the most common subgroup in any large religious community is the worshiping unit. This can be quite an independent group with little involvement in the larger tradition (such as the Christian "congregationalist" polity), or it can be a casual association of people whose primary communal identity is with the larger group (e.g., those Hindus who happen to be at the same temple at any given time). Pilgrimage to a certain shrine can give a very large community the sense of being essentially one worshiping group even when most religious practice actually takes place in various localities. Islam's concept of the *ummah,* with its *ḥajj* and orientation of prayer toward Mecca, is the most prominent example.

[*For a more general discussion of the relationships of social systems and religious systems, see* Society and Religion. *For an overview of communities that have a primarily religious function, see* Religious Communities, *and for treatment of specific, historical communities that have defined themselves in religious terms, see* Church; Saṃgha; Ummah; Jewish People; Monasticism; *and* Secret Societies. *For problems associated with religious community, see* Expulsion; Excommunication; *and* Schism.]

BIBLIOGRAPHY

The most comprehensive typology of religious communities that attempts to cover all religions and cultures is Joachim Wach's *Sociology of Religion* (1944; reprint, Chicago, 1962). There is a shorter typology in Gerardus van der Leeuw's *Religion in Essence and Manifestation,* 2 vols., translated by J. E. Turner from the 2d German ed. (1938; reprint, Gloucester, Mass., 1967). Werner Stark's *The Sociology of Religion: A Study of Christendom,* 5 vols. (New York, 1966–1972) discusses the forms of community extensively, but it ignores non-Christian examples and structures. The distinction between church and sect was formulated by Ernst Troeltsch in *The Social Teaching of the Christian Churches,* 2 vols., translated by Olive Wyon (1911; reprint, New York, 1931). The form of the denomination was added to Troeltsch's pattern by H. Richard Niebuhr in *The Social Sources of Denominationalism* (New York, 1929). The sixfold typology of religious communities was developed by J. Milton Yinger in *Religion, Society, and the Individual* (New York, 1965) and elaborated by him in *The Scientific Study of Religion* (New York, 1970). A survey of the attempts to develop a typology of religious groups is to be found in Roland Robertson's *The Sociological Interpretation of Religion* (New York, 1970) and in Michael Hill's *A Sociology of Religion* (London, 1973). The dichotomy of the great and little traditions was created by Robert Redfield in *The Primitive World and Its Transformations* (Ithaca, N.Y., 1953) and *The Little Community: Viewpoints for the Study of a Human Whole* (Chicago, 1955). Examples of sects, mostly Christian but from many places around the world, are given in Bryan R. Wilson's *Religious Sects: A Sociological Study* (London, 1970).

George Weckman

COMPARATIVE-HISTORICAL METHOD.

A means of studying religion as a whole, as well as the particularities of each tradition or subtradition, the comparative-historical method draws on historical data in comparing religions. As Wilhelm Schmidt (1868–1954) argued, the method aims to show not only the interplay of the general and the particular elements of religion, but also the interplay of influences between religious phenomena and the secular factors in human culture.

General Considerations. The comparative-historical method differs from purely historical approaches because it is cross-cultural. "Pure history" can deal, for example, with the unfolding of European pietism or South Indian *bhakti* without getting involved in comparisons and contrasts between the two phenomena. Obviously the comparative-historical method presupposes "pure history" which, together with ancillary disciplines such as philosophy and archaeology, supplies the facts upon which comparisons depend. It differs from psychology and phenomenology of religion, however, insofar as these disciplines content themselves with exploring timeless patterns or types of religious phenomena. Thus these disciplines may be concerned with patterns of mystical experience, for example, but not with how these patterns arise historically or to what extent they are affected by social and cultural conditions. In the discipline of psychology of religion, religious data are selected in a way that is distinct from the comparative-historical method, but the distinction between phenomenology of religion and the comparative-historical method cannot be put always so clearly. Insofar as phenomenology also deals with various types of changes in religious phenomena over the course of history, the distinctions begin to vanish.

The difference between the comparative-historical method and theology stems less from the selection of data than from the special way that theology approaches data. Theology (a term that usually is shorthand for Christian theology, but that in principle can include other varieties) is essentially the systematic exploration of the truth of a particular religious tradition or subtradition. The comparative-historical method does not begin from the assumption of the truth or falsity of any one religious position. Thus, although the ancillary disciplines of theology (such as church history, the history of ideas, philology, and so on) may overlap with those of the comparative study of religion, their essential aim and ethos are different. The comparative-historical method aims to be as objective as possible about the nature and power of religion; it is not concerned with whether a particular faith is true. Its objective is to relate religion's actual influences and effects within the world of human history.

The comparative study of religion, in the sense indicated, has a forceful rationale: there is an aspect of human culture, namely religion, that calls for interpretation, explanation, and delineation in ways similar to other aspects of human culture, such as politics and economics. This examination is called for whether or not a religion is transcendentally derived—whether, in short, its claims about its origin are true or not. The comparative-historical method considers it important to explore recurrent patterns of religious thought, symbolism, ritual, and experience that can be found cross-culturally. This approach suggests that religions have a relatively independent occurrence—whatever the theory at which we might ultimately arrive regarding their ultimate origin—and so may be used to explain various historical developments. Thus, for example, the occurrence of devotional religion might help to explain certain patterns of social organization.

Problems in Comparative Studies. There are at least two major problems, however, with the comparative study of religion. One has to do with objectivity, and the other with the definition of religion. The first problem has a particular as well as a general form. In particular, there was a reaction in the early twentieth century against the use of the term *comparative,* since Western and colonialist assumptions often entered into the making of comparisons. This criticism contributed to the fashionability of the phrase "phenomenology of religion" as an alternative way of labeling the enterprise. In general, some scholars have doubted whether it is possible to be genuinely objective about religion since religion has necessarily to do with subjectivity, and the study of religion is full of value judgments. In response to this criticism, two considerations are important. On the one hand, objectivity may be better defined as "descriptive success," and so the question is, Can we be descriptively successful in describing different forms of subjectivity? On the other hand, though complete neutrality may not be possible, it is possible to be relatively neutral in regard to value judgments. In a qualified manner, therefore, descriptive success and a kind of detachment are feasible. Here the charge of bias can be turned into an advantage: it stimulates us to examine our assumptions, and thus to generate a new level of self-awareness that is necessary for the practice of *epochē,* or phenomenological detachment.

The other main problem with the comparative-historical method concerns definition. This is a complex problem, for if it is not possible to gain a common definition of religion, can we be sure that we are talking about a "religious factor" in human affairs? Perhaps this factor is merely a chimera based on the conventions of European languages. Further, can we be sure that, given that the religious factor exists, we are not excluding phenomena that are of the same kind, though they may not be conventionally labeled "religious"? The two sides of this problem are interrelated. We might, for instance, define religion as relating to a transcendent being or state (e.g., God or *nirvāṇa*). This definition may adequately group some of the "great" traditions, but it leaves doubt about other religions (Stoicism, some religions of small-scale societies in Africa and elsewhere, etc.), and excludes the symbolic and "religiously functioning" aspects of secular ideologies and ways of life. Pragmatically, it seems best to begin with a religious core and draw into our analysis worldviews and elements of symbolism that exhibit analogies with the religious properties of this core. In this way, we use the comparative method to arrive at a field of inquiry. The field in its widest form is worldview analysis, or the delineation and interpretation of worldviews that are both religious (in the traditional, transcendentally oriented sense) and secular. This approach, however, begins with the kinds of analysis that are specially relevant to the exploration of traditional religious worldviews.

Some scholars, because of the invidious implications of the term *comparative,* prefer *cross-cultural.* This term has some drawbacks, but it also has two considerable merits. First, obviously, it avoids the term *comparative;* and, second, it suggests that analogies are drawn from different cultural traditions, and so may make use of terminology and attitudes that are not Western. As greater numbers of scholars from religious traditions other than those of the West make their contributions to worldview analysis, and as we become in general more globally conscious, a new cross-cultural vocabulary will in all probability emerge. Already there are signs of the appearance of this vocabulary: terms such as *taboo, totem, yoga, bhakti, Tao, nirvana,* and *karma* are in general use in English.

Aims of Comparative-Historical Study. Generally speaking, the comparative-historical method has two preliminary aims: to demonstrate historical connections, and to point out independent occurrences of similar phenomena. The tracing of historical connections indicates the scope of the diffusion of key concepts, rites, institutions, and so on. Often such diffusion is the first hypothesis of many investigators. For example, early investigators who saw the similarities between ideas in the *Bhagavadgītā* and in the New Testament supposed that a single influence, one way or another, informed both. The use of the swastika symbol both in India and among American Indian groups is also suggestive of very ancient diffusion. But the most interesting cases from the theoretical angle are those where a strong degree of independence of cultural origins can be shown and yet the phenomena are similar. It is, for example, striking when the utterances of mystics in apparently independent traditions are similar. Such similarity is suggestive of at least a perennial phenomenology—that is, the existence of certain recurring, characteristic patterns of human experience—if not of a perennial philosophy. It is partly on this basis that scholars build up their phenomenologies of religion.

But the comparative method is also historical. This introduces two complications into any typology of religious factors or themes. The first complication is particularity. Though it may be that a certain recurrent theme occurs in two traditions, it nevertheless has a different contextual meaning in each. For instance, there may appear to be a similar mystical experience described in Sufism and Mahāyāna Buddhism. But the meaning of the two experiences will diverge: the one involves a close unity with God, the other the attainment of ultimate emptiness. The meaning of each experience affects the way each is perceived, both because the Ṣūfī and the Mahāyāna Buddhist have different expectations leading into their experiences and also because, *ex post facto,* the experiences suggest differing accounts of the ultimate. More generally, it may be said that each tradition or subtradition is organic, in that the meaning of each of the particular elements woven together into a whole is affected by the meanings of all the other elements associated with it within the whole. Thus, because the comparative method is historical, it recognizes the importance not only of general similarities but also of the particularity of each historical context. Comparisons are therefore never quite exact but are analogical in character. Although the method upholds the value of comparisons, it nevertheless recognizes the need for contextual modification.

The other complication is that the traditions or elements of traditions under consideration are examined in time; they are the consequences of change, and they themselves give rise to changes. A religious ideology may indeed retain some "original message" or primordial revelation in an unchanged manner. Nevertheless, any such relatively unchanged revelation is still transmitted by a process that can only be described historically. Indeed, it seems as though an element that has been transmitted from an ancient culture down to modern times, in order to have retained its identity through changing contexts, must have had to change its overt message if it has managed to retain the same meaning. Likewise, an overtly unchanged element that has been transmitted "without change" through differing contexts might well have undergone a change in meaning because of the altered context. In either case the historical method involves the exploration of changes.

It follows then that in addition to relatively time-free typological comparisons there are comparisons of kinds of changes. Such a typology, which can be called a "dynamic phenomenology," blurs the distinction between the comparative-historical and phenomenological methods. It also takes us back to some of the early preoccupations of the comparative study of religion, namely, the delineation of the evolution of religion from animism through monotheism. Although the evolutionary model is less fashionable now than in the latter part of the nineteenth century, which saw the emergence of comparative religion as a discipline, there is still an interest in the dynamic patterns of development in society that are generated by religion—an interest stimulated by the work of Max Weber (1864–1920). An example of a recent evolutionary scheme is found in Robert N. Bellah's paper "Religious Evolution" (*American Sociological Review* 29, 1964, pp. 358–374).

Intra- and Extrareligious Explanations. Of greater importance, however, are more detailed studies of the modes under which different religious themes interact both within and outside the bounds of religion, strictly defined. It is, for instance, important to see the ways in which doctrines reflect aspects of experience and myth, or ritual reflects aspects of doctrine and ethics, and so on. These interactions within the boundaries of religion can be called *intrareligious,* and explanations that refer to them might be termed *intrareligious explanations.* It is also important to consider how doctrines, myths, and the rest impinge upon or are affected by social and economic factors in society. Such relations are *extrareligious,* and explanations referring to them are *extrareligious explanations.* The most extreme cases of extrareligious explanations are "projection" theories of religion (an example would be Freud's theory of religion), in which religion is understood to be "caused" by deep structures in nonreligious human nature or human society. Cases of intrareligious explanations include the understanding of "negative" theology as a consequence of mystical experience, worship as a consequence of the numinous experience, priesthood as a consequence of sacramental ritual, and humility as an ethical consequence of worship. Extrareligious interactions can be seen in such phenomena as the erosion of the liturgical year by the new, indifferent rhythms of industrial society; the increase of pilgrimage in South Asia due to the development of buses and railways; and the pressure for gender-related changes in ecclesiastical organization due to women's movements. Cases of the reinforcement of religious symbolism by symbolic factors associated with nonreligious worldviews and ideologies (such as nationalism) can be seen in modern Iranian nationalism, the Buddhist revival in Sri Lanka, and so on.

The recent period, from World War II onward, and especially from the mid-1960s until the mid-1980s, has seen an immense expansion in both historical and comparative studies in the field of religion, notably in the English-speaking world, and particularly in North America. The consequence of this expansion has been a fine array of monographs and studies on varied aspects of religion. But although there has been intensive work in cross-cultural dialogue between religions, there have been few large-scale comparative studies. The times are clearly ripe for such endeavors, which would build upon excellent foundational studies in particular religious traditions. The most flourishing aspect of recent comparative studies has been in the field of mysticism, which has attracted the interest of scholars involved in hermeneutical and philosophical studies as well as historians and others. The interfaces of comparative study in religion with anthropology and sociology as they relate to ritual process has also proved fruitful, as in the influence and work of Victor Turner (1920–1983). The most influential phenomenological synthesis remains Gerardus van der Leeuw's *Religion in Essence and Manifestation* (1938), an indication that the field awaits a new synthetic overview after a period of intense, but on the whole less broad, activity. Already, however, the comparative-historical method is beginning to be seen as a vital tool not only for the framing of new hypotheses about the patterns of religious developments both in the past and today, but also for the testing of older ways of thinking about the nature and provenance of religion.

[*See also* Study of Religion. *For discussion of related topics, see* Comparative Religion; Evolutionism; Hermeneutics; History of Religions; Phenomenology of Religion; Psychology, *article on* Psychology of Religion; Religionsgeschichtliche Schule; Sociology; *and* Women's Studies.]

BIBLIOGRAPHY

The series "Religion and Reason," edited by Jacques Waardenburg (The Hague, 1971–), is an invaluable collection of monographs on the theory of religion; it includes an excellent anthology of classical readings, *Classical Approaches to the Study of Religion*, vol. 1, *Introduction and Anthology* (The Hague, 1973), compiled by Waardenburg. The most up-to-date survey of recent work is Ursula King's monograph-long essay, "Historical and Phenomenological Approaches," in *Contemporary Approaches to the Study of Religion*, vol. 1, edited by Frank Whaling (New York, 1984), pp. 29–164. A complement to the Waardenburg volume is a reader in sociology and anthropology titled *Sociology of Religion*, edited by Roland Robertson (Baltimore, 1969). The most useful history of the field is Eric J. Sharpe's *Comparative Religion: A History* (London, 1975). A discussion of some of the central themes of this article can be found in my book *The Science of Religion and the Sociology of Knowledge* (Princeton, 1973).

NINIAN SMART

COMPARATIVE MYTHOLOGY. An early form of comparative mythology is the so-called *interpretatio Graeca,* that is, the use of Greek names for gods of other peoples. Thus, for instance, Near Eastern storm gods were interpreted by Greek authors as Zeus, who shared essential features with them. Similarly, Roman authors identified Celtic or Germanic gods as Jupiter, Mars, or Mercury. Such identifications, employing *interpretatio Romana,* are readily apparent in the English and French names of the days of the week; the English names are derived from the Germanic gods, the French from the Roman: thus *Tuesday,* Týr's (or Tiu's) day, corresponds to *mardi,* day of Mars; *Wednesday,* Woden's day, corresponds to *mercredi,* day of Mercury; and *Thursday,* Thor's day, corresponds to *jeudi,* day of Jupiter.

As a technical term, *comparative mythology* was introduced in 1856 by the German-born British philologist F. Max Müller. He based his argument on the observation that the Indo-European languages were related to each other and obviously should be derived from one common language. Since, according to Müller, myths originated through literal interpretations of metaphoric expressions leading to a personification of such natural phenomena as the sun and the dawn, it would be useful to compare not only the languages but also the myths of Indo-European peoples. Strangely enough, he made little use of his observation for a comparison of divine names in the various religions; he was more interested in combating evolutionistic interpretations of mythology based on material from "primitive" peoples.

When two or more myths are similar in some respects, there are, roughly speaking, three possible theories. One is that they form part of a common heritage; another is that a myth or mythological motif has spread from one religion to another ("diffusion"); a third is that parallel, independent development has produced similar results in two or more different places. Following the third line of reasoning, we might assume one of two possible explanations: either that similar ecological conditions produce similar myths or that the human mind contains archetypes that are expressed in similar symbols everywhere. However, a combination of these two explanations should not be entirely ruled out.

Indo-European Religions. A common heritage can be assumed in the various Indo-European religions. Linguistic comparison of divine names reveals several interesting facts. For instance, the Vedic *Dyaus* corresponds to the Greek *Zeus*, the Roman *Jupiter* (*Iovpater*, "father Jove"), the Nordic *Týr*, and perhaps also the Latvian *Dievs*. Parjanya is an Indian rain god; the Baltic peoples have a god of the thunderstorm called Perkūnas or Pērkons, while Fjǫrgynn is a somewhat obscure Nordic god. In India, Yama is the first man, in Iran Yima, while Ymir in Nordic mythology is the giant from whose body the world was created. The relationship is especially close between Indian and Iranian religions. The Indian god Mitra corresponds to the Iranian Mithra, with very similar functions: Vedic mythology uses *Vṛtrahan* in the epithet of Indra as the killer of the dragon Vṛtra; in Iran, Verethraghna is a god of war and kingship. The fact that Sanskrit *deva* means "god" but Iranian *daiva* is "demon," while Sanskrit *asura* means "demon" and Iranian *ahura* is the name of the highest god, indicates an early conflict between the two religions. It is worthy of notice that the functions of gods with related names are not always identical.

A different and more promising approach to the comparative mythology of the Indo-European peoples was suggested by the French scholar Georges Dumézil (b. 1898). He started from the observation that most Indo-European religions have a myth about the preparation of a drink of immortality, which was stolen and recovered and then became the object of ritual drinking. Continued researches, however, resulted in the observation that behind the mythology of most of these peoples a tripartite structure could be detected.

As a matter of fact, the gods of the pantheon are organized in such a manner that they reflect the tripartite social structure of Indo-European society. There are the functions of rulership, of warfare, and of fertility and wealth. The first function has two aspects: the mysterious and magical on one side and the orderly and lawful on the other. It is represented by Varuṇa and Mitra in India, by Jupiter and Dius Fidius in Rome, and by Odin and Týr in Scandinavia. The warlike function is represented by Indian Indra, Roman Mars, and Scandinavian Thor. The gods of the third function are admitted to the circle of gods only after a battle, followed by a settlement, which makes the pantheon complete; they are, for instance, the Vedic twin gods Aśvins or Nāsatyas and the Nordic Vanir (Freyr, Freyja, etc.), while in Rome the lesser-known god Quirinus may belong here. Celtic evidence is scanty but can probably be fit into the same pattern. The same structure is reflected in the functions of the Zoroastrian "archangels," the Amesha Spentas, which replace the old gods in Zoroastrian monotheism, and in the characters of the legendary kings of early Rome. Thus Romulus represents the orderly ruler; Numa Pompilius, the priest, is the mysterious one; Tullus Hostilius is the warrior; and Ancus Marcius represents material welfare. It should also be noticed that the Sabinians were admitted into Roman society after a war, just as were the gods of the third function, and only then was the Roman community complete. In other words, mythology has been transformed into legendary history.

An interesting detail is the fact that of two Roman heroes in the wars against the Etruscans, one, Horatius Cocles, is one-eyed, and the other, Mucius Gaius Scaevola, loses his one hand. The Irish war god Nuadha has a silver hand instead of the one he lost in battle, and among the Nordic gods, Odin is one-eyed and Týr has only one arm.

That Greek mythology has only a few traces of this pattern is probably due to influence from pre-Greek Aegean religion. Dumézil's method is not primarily based on philological evidence and is thus not open to criticism based on difficulties in establishing the exact relationship between the Indo-European languages. On the other hand, there is a difficulty in the fact that the names of the gods of one particular function are not always linguistically related, and that related names may appear in different functions.

Near Eastern Mythologies. Comparison of Semitic mythologies can also be based in part on linguistic evidence. *Il* or *el* is in all Semitic languages (except Ethiopic) either the common word for "god" or the name of the highest god. But there are also problems. For instance, in South Arabia, Athtar is a god, perhaps connected with the morning star, but Babylonian and Assyrian Ishtar is a goddess, also connected with the morning star, while the early Canaanite texts from Ugarit know both a god Athtar and a goddess Athtart, the latter identical with the Astarte of the Old Testament. It may be assumed that an originally androgynous deity, perhaps a sky god (like Ethiopian Astar), has been differentiated in two directions as male and female. A similar shift of gender is known also in the case of the sun, sometimes worshiped as a male god (Babylonian Shamash), sometimes as a goddess (South Arabia, Ugarit). The male form in Babylonia may be due to Sumerian influence.

Three themes of ancient Near Eastern mythology are of particular interest here: (1) the dying and reviving god, (2) the killing of the dragon, and (3) death and immortality.

The dying and reviving god. The Sumerian god Dumuzi (Akkadian, Tammuz), the god of flocks and grain, is killed and carried to the netherworld, but it is finally decided that he shall spend part of the year on earth to promote fertility. Baal, the Canaanite god of thunder and fertility, is killed by his enemy Mot, and while he is dead, vegetation withers, but his sister Anat defeats Mot, and Baal is finally restored to life. The story of Aqhat seems to reflect the same pattern: Aqhat is offered immortality by the goddess Anat in exchange for his fine bow but refuses and is killed, which results in the withering of vegetation. His sister seeks him, but here the tablet is broken, and we do not know the outcome. If the point of the story is man's mortality, we should expect him to remain dead; if the vegetation motif is predominant, as in the Baal myth, it is likely that he was revived.

The Egyptian Osiris is somewhat different: he is king and connected with the grain; he is killed by his brother Seth, but his wife Isis finds his dismembered body and restores it to life, and Osiris becomes the ruler of the dead. We know that the god's death and resurrection were celebrated in seasonal festivals. Different again is the Hittite myth of Telepinu: he disappears and vegetation withers and procreation fails; he is found sleeping and brought back, and life returns to normal.

There is a common pattern in these myths, probably reflecting the vicissitudes of vegetation in the seasonal cycle, but the actual form of the myth differs from country to country insofar as the common features have been combined with local elements to form a new unity. The problem is further complicated by the fact that some of the characteristic elements of the pattern reappear in connection with the Nordic god Baldr, who is supposed to be invulnerable but is killed with the only weapon that can hurt him, namely, a twig of mistletoe. Baldr, however, remains dead, though nearly everything weeps for him. Dumézil has found a parallel to this myth among the Ossets, a tribe in the Caucasus, probably descended from the ancient Scythians. Here the willful Syrdon finds out the only way to kill the supposedly invulnerable Soslan (or Sosryko). In both myths Dumézil finds traits that point to some connection with the rites of the summer solstice. It is not clear whether we have here a case of the migration of myths or an example of common Indo-European heritage.

Furthermore, in the Finnish national epic, the *Kalevala,* we are told that the hero Lemminkäinen was killed by means of an inconspicuous plant. His mother found him, reassembled the parts of his body, and brought him back to life. Here is an element that is strongly reminiscent of the Osiris myth. It is also interesting that a bee plays a significant role at the resuscitation of Lemminkäinen, just as a bee wakes up the Hittite Telepinu. It is hard to prove any historical connection among the three myths involved, but it seems that elements from different sources have been combined into a new story. [*See* Dying and Rising Gods.]

The killing of the dragon. In the Babylonian epic of creation the god Marduk kills a monster, Tiamat, representing the primeval ocean, and creates the world out of her body. In Canaanite myth where Baal kills Prince Sea, the result is not creation but the establishment of his rulership and the building of a temple. There are also fragments in Canaanite mythology that tell of the killing of a being called Lotan or *tannin* ("dragon"). Reminiscences of the battle motif are also found in the Old Testament in connection with creation. The defeated party is here called either Leviathan (Lotan) and *tannin* or *tehom* ("the deep"; i.e., Tiamat). The elements of the myth recur, but they are combined differently. Since the motif is absent in the Sumerian myths of creation, it may be of West Semitic origin. The enemy slain is the sea, but the results differ. [*See* Dragons.]

Death and immortality. The hero of the Gilgamesh epic, seeking eternal life, finds the "plant of life," but it is snatched away by a serpent, and he remains mortal. In another Babylonian myth, Adapa is offered the "food of life" but he refuses to eat it and remains mortal. In the Old Testament, Adam and Eve have access to the "tree of life" but are deprived of it through a serpent and are henceforth mortal. The problem is the same: why is man mortal? The symbols of eternal life differ—plant, food, tree—but the result is the same. In other words, the intention of the myth is the same in all three cases, but the concrete expressions differ. [*See* Immortality.]

To sum up: myths intend to answer existential questions; the symbols used are sometimes identical, sometimes differing in details; and mythical motifs can be combined in different ways in different contexts.

Mythologies of Other Cultures. Similar observations can be made in comparative study of mythologies in many other parts of the world. Three mythic themes provide interesting examples: (1) the origin of death, (2) the earth diver, and (3) the flood.

The origin of death. In most parts of Africa there is a myth of the origin of death. Common to most of them is the idea that man was originally intended to live forever. God sent a message to that effect, but the messenger was delayed and overtaken by another messenger, who brought the message of death. Other myths report that the message was distorted so as to imply death instead of life. Other tribes say that man was offered two bundles, one containing life, the other death; by mistake, man chose death. There are also myths that ascribe death to the disobedience of man. In the last case, one might suspect Christian influence, but the other myths, which occur in several versions in several tribes, are certainly indigenous and provide a good example of how the outward form of a myth may vary, though the intention is the same. [*See* Death.]

The earth diver. Creation myths among many North American Indian tribes tell of a primeval sea: a bird or animal dives into the water and brings up some soil from which the earth is created. This myth of the earth diver is known also from several peoples in Northeast Asia. It has the idea of the primeval sea in common with Babylonian, Israelite, and to some extent Egyptian cosmogony; but is any historical relationship possible? Such relationship does exist, however, between North America and Northeast Asia. In some North Asian versions of the earth-diver myth, the motif is combined, rather illogically, with the myth of the great flood. According to one Samoyed myth, seven men who have been saved from the flood send a bird to the bottom of the sea to fetch a turf to form the earth. This is obviously a combination of two elements of different origin. [*See* Cosmogony.]

The flood. The myth of the flood, on the other hand, is a problem in its own right. It is well known from the Bible and from ancient Mesopotamia. A study of the biblical and the three Mesopotamian versions reveals that they have several conspicuous details in common (the god reveals the secret of the coming flood to one righteous man, he builds a ship, he sends out birds to see if the water has receded, and he offers sacrifices after being saved); but it can be shown that the story has been modified in each case to suit the context of a larger narrative complex into which it has been inserted (Gilgamesh epic, Atrahasis epic, the primeval history of *Genesis*). But flood stories are known from many other parts of the world, both in Asia and in North and South America. Have they originated independently in areas where large rivers cause inundations from time to time, or is there any kind of connection? The latter alternative can be proved in the ancient Near East, but the other stories show differences too great to make direct borrowing likely. [*See* Flood, The.]

Conclusion. Thus, comparative study of mythology raises questions that are difficult to answer. Similar myths appearing in different parts of the world seem to have no communication with one another. Neither common heritage nor diffusion seems probable. Myths that are strikingly similar to the Greek myth of Orpheus, who tried to bring his wife, Eurydice, back from the netherworld but failed to do so, appear in several North American Indian tribes, but no historical connection can be shown. Is it possible that such a characteristic myth can develop independently in two distant places? The New Zealand Maori are reported to have a creation myth, according to which there was first darkness and water, but the god Io pronounced a word and there was light, he pronounced a second word and the sky came into being, and a third word and the earth was there. In this case, it seems likely that Christian ideas have influenced either the myth or the one who recorded it. But in other cases we may ask if there is not some truth in Jung's theory of archetypes in the human mind whereby similar existential questions are answered by similar symbols. Or, as Mircea Eliade puts it in a somewhat different terminology, essential aspects of reality appear in the human mind as images and symbols forming certain patterns that meet a need and fulfill a function, that of revealing the hidden modalities of our existence.

A new approach to the study of myth has been suggested by the French structuralist Claude Lévi-Strauss. He breaks down the myth into small units and analyzes their mutual relationships. The units are meaningful only in terms of the positions they occupy in the total structure of the myth and in the context of the culture concerned. Thus there emerges a pattern consisting of thesis, antithesis, and synthesis. In the myth of Oedipus, for instance, there is an overvaluation of kinship (e.g., Oedipus marries his mother), an undervaluation of kinship (e.g., Oedipus kills his father), and a synthesis implying that contradictory kinship relations are contradictory in a similar way. In analyzing a specific myth, Lévi-Strauss often explains the significance of a unit by adducing comparative material from the same culture, but only in the third volume of his *Mythologiques* does he bring in a global perspective.

[*See also* Myth; Indo-European Religion, *article on* History of Study; Grimm Brothers; Comparative Religion; Myth and Ritual School; *and the biography of F. Max Müller.*]

BIBLIOGRAPHY

Max Müller's essay "Comparative Mythology" is found in the second volume of *Chips from a German Workshop* (London, 1868). Together with Åke Ström, I have reviewed the comparative work done in Indo-Iranian and Indo-European studies in *Religions of Mankind Yesterday and Today* (Philadelphia, 1967). In *Arische Religion* (Leipzig, 1914), Leopold von Schroeder deals with the same material.

Georges Dumézil sets forth his theories in many places. Several general introductions are available: *L'idéologie tripartie des Indo-Européens* (Brussels, 1958), *L'héritage indo-européen à Rome* (Paris, 1949), and *Les dieux des Indo-Européens* (Paris, 1952).

My own observations on the comparative mythology of the ancient Near East are published in numerous places: "Remarks on the Method of Comparative Mythology," in *Near Eastern Studies in Honor of William Foxwell Albright,* edited by Hans Goedicke (Baltimore, 1971); "Israel's Place among the Religions of the Ancient Near East," in *Supplements to Vetus Testamentum* 23 (1972): 1–8; and "The Impact of the Ancient Near East on Israelite Tradition," in *Tradition and Theology in the Old Testament,* edited by D. A. Knight (Philadelphia, 1977). For a treatment of Athtar and related deities, consult my *Word and Wisdom* (Lund, 1947), and for a discussion of dying and reviving gods, it is valuable to look at the classic work by James G. Frazer that has been edited by Theodor H. Gaster and published as *The New Golden Bough,* abr. ed. (1959; London, 1980).

African myths about the origins of death are the subject of Hans Abrahamsson's *The Origin of Death* (Uppsala, 1951). Anna Birgitta Rooth has published the article "Creation Myths of North American Indians," *Anthropos* 52 (1957): 497–508, and Åke Hultkrantz sets forth his views on Orpheus traditions among Native Americans in *The North American Indian Orpheus Tradition* (Stockholm, 1957). Flood stories are dealt with by Richard Andree in *Die Flutsagen* (Braunschweig, 1891) and also by Ruth E. Simoons-Vermeer in "The Mesopotamian Flood Stories: A Comparison and Interpretation," *Numen* 21 (1974): 17–34. For an introduction to the theories of Lévi-Strauss and structuralism, see two works by Edmund Leach: *The Structural Study of Myth and Totemism* (London, 1967) and *Lévi-Strauss* (London, 1970).

HELMER RINGGREN

COMPARATIVE RELIGION. The term *comparative religion,* a shortened form of "the comparative study of religion (or religions)," became current in the late nineteenth century as a synonym for "the science of religion" (in German, *Religionswissenschaft;* in French, *la science de religion*). As originally conceived, it centered on the application of the comparative (or scientific) method to the data provided by the religions of the world, past and present. This involved the assignment to each of a place within a scheme of progress, development, or evolution, and the assessment of their value. The function of comparative religion, said an early twentieth-century scholar, "consists in placing the numerous Religions of the world side by side, in order that, deliberately comparing and contrasting them, it may frame a reliable estimate of their respective claims and values" (Louis H. Jordan, *Comparative Religion: Its Genesis and Growth,* Edinburgh, 1905, p. xi). The term *comparative religion* seems not to have been used much before the 1890s; however, in 1873 F. Max Müller had asked: "Why . . . should we hesitate to apply the comparative method . . . to the study of religion?" (*Introduction to the Science of Religion,* London, 1873, p. 15).

Comparative religion could not have developed without an interest in religious traditions other than those dominant in the West. Equally important was a degree of detachment from Western traditions and a desire to discover the laws by which the world of religion operates, usually independent of the notion of revelation. For many centuries there had been curiosity about the world's varied religious beliefs and practices, and much information had been acquired; but only in the late nineteenth century did the Western world find a theory comprehensive enough to cover all the cases. This was the theory of evolution (also called progress or development), as stated in social terms by Comte and Spencer and in biological terms by Darwin, all against a background of geological and paleontological discovery. Comparative religion attempted to apply the universal law of development—which did not always work only in one direction—to the vast amount of material that already existed and that was being augmented daily as new discoveries came to light. Because comparative religion claimed to be a science, and made use of the scientific theories of the time to build up a comprehensive picture of the "natural" history of religion on evolutionary lines, it aroused the suspicion of orthodox Christians, on the grounds that it relativized Christianity and tended to discount revelation altogether. Certainly it did relativize historical Christianity, along with all other historical religions; but in many cases comparative religion was able to make common cause with theological liberalism under the canopy of a theory of "progressive revelation."

Comparative religion never possessed one single method accepted by all. In its early days (1870s–1890s) interest centered mainly on two schools of thought, the philological school of Max Müller and the anthropological school of Adolf Bastian, Theodor Waitz, E. B. Tylor, James G. Frazer, Andrew Lang, and others. Müller established the credentials of comparative study and provided valuable material on which to base it, notably the fifty-volume series "Sacred Books of the East" (1879–1910), but was eccentric in point of method, being interested only in literary evidence and interpreting it too one-sidedly in terms of "solar mythology." He had little feeling for post-Darwinian anthropology, on whose methods the second group relied almost exclusively. "Darwinism makes it possible," wrote R. R. Marett; "reject the Darwinian point of view and you must reject anthropology also" (*Anthropology*, London, 1911, p. 8). Not all anthropologists of the period were equally interested in the evolution of religion; Lewis H. Morgan believed all primitive religions to be "grotesque and to some extent unintelligible" (*Ancient Society*, Chicago, 1877, p. 5) and unsuitable for further examination. Most, however, recognized the need to locate the evolution of religion within the broader categories of the evolution of human society. As with *Homo sapiens*, which had evolved out of something other and lower than itself, so too with religion, which was followed from lowly beginnings to the high point of ethical monotheism (or a no less ethical agnosticism). The beginnings might be seen in experiential terms, as with Tylor's "animism," Marett's "preanimism," and later Otto's "sensus numinis" (a term used much earlier by Andrew Lang); or in social terms, as with the "manism" of Herbert Spencer or the various theories concerning "totemism," magic, and kingship. But none of these questions could have been investigated at all had it not been believed that in religion, as in geology, past beliefs and institutions had laid down layers (strata) and left fossils. It was the theory of "survivals" (beliefs, practices, and institutions that the process of evolution had left behind) that determined the methodology of the early anthropological and sociological comparative religionists. Hence, among other things, the vast amount of attention paid in the early literature to Australian Aborigines, as living examples of "Stone Age man."

Evolutionary presuppositions were less obvious in those studies that were directed toward the world's "higher" civilizations, those of Mesopotamia, Egypt, Greece, Rome, India, China, and Japan, out of which modern Western and Eastern culture had emerged. But they were nonetheless there, for instance in the drawing of distinctions between "higher" and "lower" forms and the assumption that the former had developed out of the latter, the highest point having been reached on the emergence of a consistent ethics. But where these civilizations were concerned (though not only there) an alternative method was much canvassed. Evolutionary theory had to contend with the theory of diffusion, that is, the actual transmission of elements of culture and religion from one part of the world to another by migration, trade, conquest, or mission. Although in the historical records these diffusionary processes were well attested, the primal or prehistoric material was open to either interpretation. Diffusionism was evident in the theories of the neo-Babylonian school of Friedrich Delitzsch and Alfred Jeremias, and it was later carried to extremes by Elliot Smith and William James Perry, who took Egypt as the cradle of both civilization and religion. The "myth and ritual school" of the 1930s received powerful impulses from this type of diffusionism.

Comparative religion at first found it hard to establish its credentials as a scientific discipline. The first chairs were established in Switzerland (Geneva, 1873), Holland (Amsterdam, Groningen, Leiden, and Utrecht, 1877), and France (the Sorbonne, 1886). In Sweden, an older chair of apologetics was turned in the direction of comparative religion in 1901. In England, the Manchester chair was set up in 1904, while the first chairs in Germany, both filled by Scandinavians, were not created until 1910 (Berlin) and 1912 (Leipzig). In Germany, however, *Religionsgeschichte* had already become the catchword of the "history of religion school" of biblical scholars. This school was uninterested in the wider implications of comparative religion, limiting its researches to the background of the Old and New Testaments, and the Berlin and Leipzig chairs were intended in part to correct its one-sidedness. Although Scotland had had the Gifford lectureship in "natural theology" since 1887, and a Scotsman, James Hastings, produced the massive *Encyclopaedia of Religion and Ethics* (1908–1926), there was no chair of comparative religion. In the United States, James Freeman Clarke was appointed professor of natural religion and Christian doctrine at Harvard Divinity School in 1867; similar positions were created at Boston University (1873), Princeton (1881), and Cornell (1891). George Foot Moore became professor of the history of religions at Harvard in 1891, and a department was started at the University of Chicago in 1892. Various journals and encyclopedias furthered the interests of comparative religion. Of the journals, the most outstanding was *Revue d'histoire des religions* (1880–); among the encyclopedias, Hastings's *Encyclopaedia of Religion and Ethics* had no serious competitor except the German *Die Religion in Geschichte und Gegenwart* (1st ed., 1909–1913) representing the history of religion school and therefore basically theological. A sequence of international congresses of the science of religion began in Stockholm in 1897 and Paris in 1900.

After World War I, the evolutionism that had shaped comparative religion fell apart. The name *comparative religion* was retained for many years, but the subject separated into a number of interrelated disciplines, the history, psychology, sociology, and phenomenology of religion among them. Scholars abandoned the vast synthesis for the safer world of the monograph, agreeing on little save the importance of historical technique, supported wherever necessary by firsthand observation. As evolutionism was called in question, so too were the value judgments that had originally shaped comparative religion. Instead, the believing community was left to speak for itself, interpreted more in terms of sociology, ecology, and economics than in developmental categories. Methodological uncertainty and diversity came to be reflected in the wide variety of labels that began to replace the term *comparative religion: history of religions, world religions, religious studies,* and *studies in religion* have all been used. *Comparative religion* as a label survived here and there, though more on the popular than the scholarly level. Today it is seldom used, while the hectic methodological debates of the period since the 1960s show how far the study of religion has moved from the original evolutionary synthesis.

[*For related discussion, see* History of Religions. *See also* Animism and Animatism; Evolutionism; Myth and Ritual School; *and* Preanimism.]

BIBLIOGRAPHY

Jordan, Louis Henry. *Comparative Religion: Its Genesis and Growth.* Edinburgh, 1905.

Jordan, Louis Henry. *Comparative Religion: Its Adjuncts and Allies.* London, 1915.

Pinard de la Boullaye, Henri. *L'étude comparée des religions,* vol. 1. 4th ed. Paris, 1929.

Sharpe, Eric J. *Comparative Religion: A History.* London, 1975.

Smith, Wilfred Cantwell. *The Meaning and End of Religion.* New York, 1963.

Vries, Jan de. *The Study of Religion: A Historical Approach.* New York, 1967.

Eric J. Sharpe

COMPASSION. *See* Love. *For discussion of the Buddhist concept of compassion, see* Karuṇā.

COMTE, AUGUSTE (1798–1857), French philosopher, founder of positivism. Born into a Roman Catholic, royalist family in Montpellier, France, Comte completed his early education by preparing for the École Polytechnique under the direction of Daniel Encontre, from whom Comte learned that philosophy is a complete view of reality. Comte ranked high in the Polytechnique entry competitions, but he studied there only a few years. Republican political opinions, later expressed in his memoirs, moved him to participate in the student rebellions that were instrumental in causing the royalist government to close the school for reorganization.

In 1817 Comte became secretary to Claude-Henri de Rouvroy Saint-Simon, the social philosopher. Comte's writing appeared in numerous publications edited by Saint-Simon. Indeed, Comte's *Sommaire appréciation de l'ensemble du passé moderne* (Summary Evaluation of the Impact of the Recent Past; 1820) came out under Saint-Simon's signature. In this work Comte describes the *ancien régime* as having two poles, or capacities, the theological and the military; these are being superseded by two new poles: the scientific and the industrial.

In *Prospectus des travaux scientifiques nécessaires pour reorganiser la société* (Prospectus of the Scientific Tasks Necessary for the Reorganization of Society; 1822), Comte presented a law of three states through which human history and each of the sciences must pass in their development; he gave one hundred examples. Revised as *Système de politique positive* (System of Positive Polity; 1824), this theory appeared with one thousand examples, unsigned, in a publication of Saint-Simon's. After he left Saint-Simon, Comte gave lessons in mathematics. In 1825 he married Caroline Massin.

Considérations philosophiques sur les sciences et les savants (Philosophical Considerations concerning Sciences and Scientists; 1825) and *Considérations sur le pouvoir spirituel* (Considerations concerning Spiritual Power; 1826) were published while Comte prepared his *Cours de philosophie positive* (Course on Positive Philosophy). He gave the first lesson in this course on 2 April 1826. Among those present were the zoologist Henri-Marie de Blainville, the scientist Louis Poinsot, the economist Charles Barthelemy, and the naturalist Alexander von Humboldt. The course ended with its third meeting because of Comte's mental problems. Melancholic, he attempted to drown himself in the Seine, but was rescued. He took up his work again in the spring of 1828.

The course resumed, and the first volume based on these lectures was published in 1830. In this same year, Comte inaugurated a free public course on astronomy that continued for seventeen years. Beginning in 1832, he served as assistant master at the École Polytechnique, but the minister of instruction offered no reply to Comte's queries about a chair at the Collège de France. In 1842, the sixth and concluding volume of the *Cours* appeared, followed by *Discours sur l'esprit positif,* which appeared as part of his treatise on popular astronomy. Although his request for a chair in the history of positive sciences met with no success, publication of his *Discours sur l'ensemble du positivisme* (Discourse on the Unity of Positivism; 1848), and the creation of a subsidy by Émile Littré through Comte's Société Positiviste (founded 1848), provided financial support for the philosopher.

Comte's four-volume *Système de politique positive* (System of Positive Polity) appeared during 1851–1854. In the preface to his *Catéchisme positiviste* (Positivist Catechism; 1852), Comte presented himself as founder of the religion of humanity. Littré, unable to follow in this new development, broke with him. Also in 1852, the second volume of the *Système* was issued, which contained an important chapter on religion: "General Theory of Religion, or Positive Theory of Human Unity."

The two aims of religion, according to Comte, are regulation of the individual and unification of individuals. For him, the etymology of the Latin *religio* is *religare:* to connect and unite. This unity depends upon both an intellectual and a moral condition; the first determines dogma, the second cult. Beyond individual and social unity lies an external world, here considered as the foundation of faith, as the aim of activity, and as an object of affection. "Faith is but an auxiliary of love" (*Système,* vol. 2, p. 48). Moral unity rests entirely in sociability prevailing over personality (*Catéchisme positiviste,* in the dialogue between the priest and the woman). Positivism is a religion of relation and does not propose a merely individual synthesis. It is rather the great being, or humanity as a whole, that is loved for its perfectibility. Humanity, the positivist God, is behind and before us as the progressive realization of the ideal that reveals itself in realization.

[*See also* Positivism.]

BIBLIOGRAPHY

The writings of Comte can be found in his *Œuvres,* 12 vols. (Paris, 1968–1970). The works available in English translation include *The Positive Philosophy of Auguste Comte,* 2 vols., a condensation of the *Cours* by Harriet Martineau (London, 1853); *The System of Positive Polity,* 4 vols., translated by J. H. Bridges et al. (London, 1875–1877); and *The Catechism of Positive Religion,* translated by Richard Congreve (London, 1858). Henri Gouhier's *La vie d'Auguste Comte,* 2d rev. ed. (Paris, 1965), and Joseph Lonchampt's *Précis de la vie et des écrits d'Auguste Comte* (Paris, 1889) are informative biographies.

ANGÈLE KREMER-MARIETTI

CONALL CERNACH. The father of Conall Cernach was Amhairghin, the famous poet and hero of the Ulstermen, and he himself is represented as the most important of the Ulster heroes save Cú Chulainn. He is also sometimes named as a foster brother of Cú Chulainn, though evidently more mature in years: at the time of Cú Chulainn's birth he was already one of the Ulster warriors, and it was he who guarded the southern border of Ulster when the youthful Cú Chulainn came there to perform his first initiatory exploit in the epic *Táin Bó Cuailnge* (The Cattle Raid of Cuailnge). But whereas Cú Chulainn died without progeny, Conall Cernach appears in the genealogies as the ancestor of the Cruthin or Pictish tribes of Ireland. In *Fledh Bhricrenn* (The Feast of Bricriu) he contests the prize of the "champion's portion" with Cú Chulainn but has to give best to the younger hero. It was Conall Cernach who avenged Cú Chulainn's death, beheading his slayer Lughaidh mac Con Roí. When he himself was slain and beheaded by his lifelong foes the Connachtmen, it is said that his head was so large that it could have held four men playing "chess" *(fidhchell)* or a couple lying together.

He is sometimes described as *cloen* ("crooked") because his inveterate enemy, the Connachtman Cet mac Mághach, to whom he was a nephew, had stamped his heel upon his neck after his birth, for it was prophesied that he would kill half the men of Connacht. The name *Conall* derives from a Celtic form, **cuno-valos* ("strong as a wolf"), and, appropriately, his epithet *cernach* may mean "triumphant" and is so understood in early texts. But there was also an alternative interpretation. According to the *Cóir Anmann* (Fitness of Names), the word *cern* means "bump, protuberance" as well as "victory," and Conall's epithet is said to refer to the fact that he had "a lump on one side of his head as big as the boss of a shield." Because of this and an episode in the tale of *The Cattle Raid of Fróech,* Anne Ross has suggested that there is an affinity between Conall Cernach and the Gaulish horned god Cernunnos (*Pagan Celtic Britain,* London, 1967, pp. 149ff.). Though she does not advert to it, her argument is supported by the fact that Irish *cern* is etymologically related to Irish *corn,* Latin *cornū,* Old High German *horn,* and so on.

BIBLIOGRAPHY

Further information on Conall Cernach can be found in Rudolf Thurneysen's *Die irische Helden- und Königsage bis zum siebzehnten Jahrhundert,* 2 vols. (Halle, 1921), the classic study of *Táin Bó Cuailnge.*

PROINSIAS MAC CANA